E 11/15

HEALTH PSYCHOLOGY

Biopsychosocial Interactions

HEALTH PSYCHOLOGY

Biopsychosocial Interactions

Fifth Edition

Edward P. Sarafino
The College of New Jersey

JOHN WILEY & SONS, INC.

EXECUTIVE EDITOR	Ryan Flahive
ASSISTANT EDITOR	Jessica Bartelt
EXECUTIVE MARKETING MANAGER	Jeff Rucker
PRODUCTION DIRECTOR	Pamela Kennedy
PRODUCTION EDITOR	Sarah Wolfman-Robichaud
PHOTO EDITOR	Ellinor Wagner
SENIOR ILLUSTRATION EDITOR	Sandra Rigby
COVER DESIGNER	Madelyn Lesure
COVER PHOTO	Peter Holms/Age Fotostock America, Inc.
PROJECT MANAGER	Jane Shifflet/GTS Companies: PA/York Campus

This book was set in 9.5/11.5 Noverese Book by GTS Companies: PA/York Campus and printed and bound by R.R. Donnelley-Crawfordsville. The cover was printed by Phoenix Color.

This book is printed on acid free paper. ♾

To order books or for customer service please, call 1-800-CALL WILEY (225 5945).

ISBN 978-0-471-69100-3, 0-471-69100-3

Printed in the United States of America

10 9 8 7 6 5 4 3

To my mother and in memory of my father.
They gave me life, loved, and nurtured me,
and helped me be healthy.

ABOUT THE AUTHOR

Edward P. Sarafino received his Ph.D. from the University of Colorado, and he began his affiliation with the Department of Psychology at The College of New Jersey more than three decades ago. His scholarship has combined areas of health, developmental, and behavioral psychology, particularly with regard to the study of asthma. In addition to having published dozens of research articles and chapters, he is the author of six books. He is a fellow of Division 38 (Health Psychology) of the American Psychological Association, served as an officer (Secretary) of that division, and has been a member of several committees of Division 38 and of the Society of Behavioral Medicine. When he is not working, he enjoys being with friends, traveling, hiking and other outdoor activities, and going to cultural events, especially music and visual arts.

TO CONTACT THE AUTHOR

I would be pleased to receive comments and suggestions about this book from students and instructors so that I may consider those ideas for future editions. You may contact me at sarafino@tcnj.edu. or use my postal address: Department of Psychology, The College of New Jersey, P. O. Box 7718, Ewing, NJ 08628.
Edward P. Sarafino

PREFACE

"The first wealth is health," wrote the poet/philosopher Ralph Waldo Emerson in the 19th century. Although people have probably always valued good health, they are becoming increasingly health conscious. This heightened consciousness generally reflects two beliefs: that we can do things to protect our health and that being sick is unpleasant. As Emerson put it, "Sickness is poor-spirited, and cannot serve anyone." Serious health problems can be quite distressing to a patient and his or her family and friends. These beliefs underlie psychologists' interests in helping people behave in ways that promote wellness, adjust to health problems that develop, and participate effectively in treatment and rehabilitation programs. I wrote this book because I share these interests.

For each edition of this text, my goal has been to create a teaching instrument that draws from the research and theory of many disciplines to describe how psychology and health are interconnected. The resulting book is a comprehensive text that is appropriate for several courses, especially those entitled either Health Psychology or Behavioral Medicine. Two objectives were central regarding the likely audience in these courses. First, although I aimed to make the content appropriate for upper-division students, I wrote in a straightforward style to make the material accessible to most sophomores. The content assumes that the student has already completed an introductory psychology course. Second, I tried to make the material relevant and interesting to students from diverse disciplines—particularly psychology, of course, but also fields such as sociology, medicine, allied health, and health and physical education. Training in health psychology has developed rapidly and can play an important role in helping students from many disciplines understand the interplay of biological, psychological, and social factors in people's health.

The field of health psychology is enormously exciting, partly because of its relevance to the lives of those who study it and to individuals the students know or will work with in the future. The field is also exciting because it is so new, and researchers from many different disciplines are finding fascinating and important relationships between psychology and health every day. Keeping up to date in each area of such a complex field presents quite a challenge. After culling through thousands of abstracts, I examined more than 1,000 new articles and books for the current revision. Most of the more than 2,200 references this edition cites were published within the last 10 years, and hundreds are new, published since the last edition of this book went to press in 2001.

NEW TO THIS EDITION

Although the new edition retains the overall organization and pedagogy that students and instructors have praised in the last edition, two within-chapter organizational changes were made that are particularly important:

- Chapter 2, The Body's Physical Systems, is now structured as six *modules*, one each for the nervous, endocrine, digestive, respiratory, cardiovascular, and immune systems. Instructors can now *choose* to cover *all of the systems at once* (assign the whole chapter) or *distribute* them to other chapters. Appropriate subsequent chapters have salient notices that tell students who are using the distributed approach when to read a specific module that is relevant to the current material. For example, a notice to read Module 4 (The Respiratory System) appears early in Chapter 7 at the start of the discussion of smoking tobacco; a notice with the Key Terms list at the end of that chapter reminds the students to study Module 4.

- Chapter 7, Substance Use and Abuse, is reorganized so that the underlying processes common to using tobacco, alcohol, and drugs are now described together at the start, and the approaches used for preventing use and treating abuse are presented together at the end. This new organization is more efficient and reflects the current view that the underlying processes and the most successful methods for prevention and treatment are very similar across substances.

Every chapter has been updated, and I substantially revised or expanded the coverage of the following topics:

- How stress affects health
- Coping processes and effects on health
- Stages of change and motivational interviewing in health promotion
- Processes in and prevention and treatment of substance use
- Weight control
- Complementary and alternative medicine
- Pain conditions and treatment
- Medical and psychosocial interventions for chronic illnesses
- Age, gender, and sociocultural differences in health and health promotion

Throughout the text, I continued to *internationalize* the content by searching for and citing information about health and health-related behavior of people around the world.

THEMES

A phrase we often hear in psychology is that we need to understand the "whole person." In approaching this goal, this book adopts the *biopsychosocial model* as the basic explanatory theme. I have tried to convey a sense that the components of this model interrelate in a dynamic and continuous fashion, consistent with the concept of *systems*. The psychological research cited reflects an eclectic orientation and supports a variety of behavioral, physiological, cognitive, and social–personality viewpoints. In addition, *gender and sociocultural differences* in health and related behaviors are addressed at many points in the book. In these

ways, this book presents a balanced view of health psychology that is squarely in the mainstream of current thinking in the field.

One additional theme makes this book unique. I have integrated a focus on *life-span development* in health and illness throughout the book, and each chapter contains information dealing with development. For example, the book discusses how health and health-related behavior change with age and describes health care issues and examples that pertain to pediatric and elderly patients. Sometimes this information is organized as a separate unit, as with the sections "Development and Health-Related Behavior," "When the Hospitalized Patient Is a Child," "Assessing Pain in Children," and "Alzheimer's Disease."

ORGANIZATION

This text examines the major topics and problem areas in health psychology by using an overall organization that progresses in main focus across chapters from *primary* to *secondary* to *tertiary* prevention and care. As the table of contents shows, the book is divided into 15 chapters in the following seven parts:

- **Part I.** Chapter 1 presents the history and focus of health psychology and introduces the major concepts and research methods used in the field. Chapter 2 describes the physical systems of the body in an engaging manner a reviewer called "a pleasant surprise." This chapter is now divided into six modules that instructors can assign in two ways—all together or distributed to later chapters—depending on how they like to organize the course. Instructors who cover the modules all together want to present the body systems as an integrated and basic topic that underlies all later topics. They also want students to have a single place to refer back to if needed, such as when reading about the neural transmission of pain signals in Chapter 11. Instructors who distribute the modules want to introduce important physiological principles as they become relevant. Either approach works easily now.
- **Part II.** Chapters 3, 4, and 5 discuss stress, its relation to illness, and methods for coping with

and reducing it. Some modules on body systems in Chapter 2 connect directly to discussions in Chapters 3 and 4, such as the sections entitled "Biological Aspects of Stress," "Physiological Arousal," "Stress, Physiology, and Illness," and "Psychoneuroimmunology." This connection is one reason why stress is covered early in the book. A reviewer recognized a second reason and wrote: "The issue of stress permeates all of the other topics, and it would be useful to have the students read about this first." Chapter 5 includes information on psychosocial methods in helping people cope better.

- **Part III.** The third part of the book examines issues involved in enhancing health and preventing illness. Chapters 6, 7, and 8 discuss how health-related behaviors develop and are maintained, can affect health, and can be changed via psychosocial and public health efforts. Chapter 7 gives special attention to the topics of tobacco, alcohol, and drug use, and Chapter 8 discusses nutrition, weight control, exercise, and safety. The role of stress in health behaviors and decision making is considered in these chapters. The book up to this point focuses mainly on primary prevention.

- **Part IV.** In Chapter 9, the main focus shifts to secondary prevention by describing the kinds of health services that are available and considering why people use, do not use, and delay using these services. This chapter also examines patients' relationships to practitioners and problems in adhering to medical regimens. Chapter 10 discusses the hospital setting and personnel, how people react to being hospitalized and cope with stressful medical procedures, and the role psychologists play in helping patients cope with their illnesses and medical treatments.

- **Part V.** Chapters 11 and 12 explore the physical and psychological nature of pain, ways to assess patients' discomfort, the psychosocial impact pain, and methods for managing and controlling pain.

- **Part VI.** The two chapters in this part of the book emphasize tertiary prevention. They examine different chronic health problems, their impact on patients and their families, and medical and psychosocial treatment approaches. The chapters separate illnesses on the basis of mortality rates.

Chapter 13 focuses on health conditions, such as diabetes and arthritis, that have either very low or moderate rates of mortality and may lead to other health problems or disability. In contrast, Chapter 14 examines four high-mortality illnesses—heart disease, stroke, cancer, and AIDS—and people's experiences with and reactions to terminal illness and loss.

- **Part VII.** Chapter 15 discusses goals and issues for the future of health psychology.

ORGANIZATION

Because some instructors might like some *flexibility in the organization of chapters*, Chapters 10 through 14 were written with this possibility in mind. Chapter 10, Part V, and Part VI were written as three independent units that may be covered in any order. Two examples of alternate sequences that would work nicely after Chapter 9 are: (1) Part V, Part VI, and then Chapter 10; and (2) Part VI, Chapter 10, and then Part V.

LANGUAGE AND STYLE

The field of health psychology involves complex issues and technical information that require extra efforts to make the material readable and clear without sacrificing content. To accomplish this, I have limited the use of jargon in this book and have sought to write in a concrete and engaging fashion. The gradual progression of concepts, choice of words, and structure of each sentence were all designed to help students master and retain the material. When introducing new terms, I define them immediately. Many examples and case studies are included to clarify concepts and to bring them to life.

LEARNING AIDS

This book contains many pedagogical features. Each chapter begins with a *contents* list, giving students an overview of the progression of major topics and concepts. Then a *prologue* introduces the chapter with (1) a lively and engaging vignette that is relevant to the chapter material and (2) an overview of the basic ideas to be covered. The body of each chapter includes many *figures*, *tables*, and *photographs* to clarify concepts or research findings. For example, special figures were created to show how the immune system functions and how gate-control theory explains pain perception. Important terms are **boldfaced,** and *italics* are used liberally for other terms and for emphasis.

Throughout the book, three types of boxed material are presented to fit with the surrounding content. They are identified in the text with the corresponding icons:

Highlight. This type of box focuses on high-interest and in-depth topics. Some of these topics are: careers relating to health and psychology, breast and testicular self- examination, the effects of secondhand smoke, acute pain in burn patients, and the complex medical regimens for diabetes.

Assess Yourself. This boxed feature has students actively examine their own health-related characteristics, such as their lifestyles, typical daily hassles, ways of coping with stress, knowledge about the transmission of HIV, beliefs about alcohol use, and symptoms of health problems.

Clinical Methods and Issues. The third type of boxed material focuses on methods and issues in application efforts in clinical health psychology, medicine, public health, and rehabilitation. We examine, for instance, cognitive and behavioral methods that can help people reduce stress, stop smoking, and eat healthfully; biofeedback and relaxation techniques for treating asthma and some forms of paralysis; and procedures to prepare children for being hospitalized.

Each chapter ends with a substantial *summary* and a list of *key terms*. All these terms are redefined in the *glossary* at the back of the book.

ONLINE SUPPLEMENTS

Instructors who are using this text can access a companion Website at www.wiley.com after registering and obtaining a password. It contains:

- An *instructor's manual* with information to help instructors organize and present the subject matter effectively and enrich the classroom experience through activities and discussion.
- A *test bank*.
- A *computerized test bank*.
- An *image gallery* that contains all of the figures in the text.
- Access to *Psychology Select*, a custom-publishing program that provides a database of materials from which you can create your own custom course-pack of readings, journal articles, and research articles.

The book's companion Website also includes features specifically for students.

ACKNOWLEDGMENTS

Writing this book and revising it have been enormous tasks. I am indebted first of all to the thousands of researchers whose important and creative work I have cited. There would be no health psychology without their work. I also received a great deal of direct help and encouragement from a number of people whose contributions I gratefully acknowledge.

My thanks go to my editor at John Wiley & Sons, Jessica Bartelt, who made valuable suggestions and oversaw and guided the revision process for this edition. I also appreciate the fine work of the Wiley Production Editor, Sarah Wolfman-Robichaud; designer, Madelyn Lesure; illustration editor, Sandra Rigby; and photo editor, Elle Wagner.

The textbook review process generated many helpful suggestions that have made this a better book than it would have been otherwise. Reviewers of the present and past editions of the book deserve my heartfelt thanks for their ideas and favorable comments regarding my plans for the book and the major parts of the manuscript they read. Because the new edition retains many of the features of earlier editions, I continue to be indebted to the following reviewers in my preparation of prior editions: *David Abwender*, State University of New York–Brockport; *Christopher R. Agnew*, Purdue University; *Tony Albiniak*, Coastal Carolina College; *Karen Anderson*, Santa Clara University; *Tom Brozoski*, Grinnell College; *John Carey*,

Sheridan College; *Donald Corriveau*, Southeastern
Massachusetts University; *Candice A. Croft*, Clarke
College; *Alexander Dale*, Allegheny College; *Don Deakins*,
Alfred Adler Institute; *Leonard Doerfler*, Assumption
College; *Dennis Elsenrath*, University of Wisconsin–
Stephens Point; *Robert Emmons*, University of California–
Davis; *Ephrem Frenandez*, Southern Methodist Univer-
sity; *Regan A. R. Gurung*, University of Wisonsin,
Green Bay; *David D. Hanson*, James Madison Univer-
sity; *Robert A. Hayes*, Westfiled State College; *Robert E.
Hersh*, Monroe Community College; *Nicholas Heyne-
man*, Idaho State University; *Craig Holt*, SUNY, Albany;
Joseph Istvan, Oregon Health Sciences University;
Kamau Johnson, Howard University; *Paul Jose*, Loyola
University; *Joanne Joseph*, SUNY Institute of Technol-
ogy; *Lisa Judd*, Winona State University; *Charles Kaiser*,
College of Charleston; *Jacqueline Lederman*, Boston
University; *Wolfgang Linden*, University of British
Columbia; *Brenda Loren*, University of North Carolina–
Wilmington; *Bradley Lown*, Buffalo State College;
Robert MacAleese, Spring Hill College; *Theresa Martin*,
Eastern Washington University; *Joseph Matarazzo*,
Oregon Health Sciences University; *Karen Matthews*,
University of Pittsburgh; *Barbara Melamed*, University
of Florida; *Nancy Norvell*, University of Florida; *Ann
O'Leary*, Rutgers University; *Carrol S. Perrino*, Morgan
State University; *Diane M. Reddy*, University of
Wisconsin, Milwaukee; *Sheila Rood*, University of
North Texas; *Ethel Roskies*, University of Montreal; *John
M. Ruiz*, University of Utah; *Harold Schroeder*, Kent
State University; *Lee Sechrest*, University of Arizona;
Dale Simmons, Oregon State University; *Mareah C.
Sketee*, UNC Chapel Hill; *James Ron Sutterer*, Syracuse
University; *Gerdi Weidner*, State University of New
York–Stonybrook; *David J. Weiss*, California State Uni-
versity; *Josephine Wilson*, Wittenberg University; *Thomas
Wrobel*, University of Michigan, Flint; and *Brian Yates*,
American University. (Affiliations are those when the
reviews were done.)

The new edition has benefited greatly from the
cover-to-cover review process and the excellent per-
spectives of the following colleagues: *Jerry Carden*,
University of Illinois at Urbana-Champaign; *Richard J.
Contrada*, Rutgers, The State University of New Jersey;
Mary Gick, Carlton University; *Douglas M. Gross*, The
College of William and Mary; *Billy R. Hammond, Jr.*,
University of Georgia; *Susan K. Johnson*, University of
North Carolina, Charlotte; *Mark A. Lumley*, Wayne
State University; and *Linda Musante*, University of Tampa.

For the new and past editions of the book, I thank
my very good friend and colleague, Jim Armstrong, for
suggestions on the manuscript and the staff at The
College of New Jersey library for acquiring needed materials. Very personal thanks go to the closest people
in my life—family, friends, and colleagues—for encouraging and supporting my efforts to complete this
book and for tolerating my preoccupation.

Edward P. Sarafino

TO THE STUDENT

"I wish I could help my father stop smoking," a student in my health psychology course said. Maybe she did help—he quit by the end of the semester. This example points out two things that will probably make health psychology interesting to you: (1) the material is *personally relevant*, and (2) many of the things you learn can actually be *applied* in your everyday life. Studying health psychology will also help you answer important questions you may have considered about health and psychology in the past. Does the mind affect our health—and if so, how? What effect does stress have on health and recovery from illness? What can be done to help people lead more healthful lives than they do? Why don't patients follow their doctors' advice, and what can health care workers do to help? What special needs do children have as patients, and how can parents and health care workers address these needs? How can families, friends, and health care workers help patients adjust to disabling or life-threatening health problems?

As these questions indicate, knowledge of health psychology can be relevant both now and later when you enter *your future career*. This is so whether you are studying to be a psychologist, medical social worker, nurse or physician, physical or occupational therapist, public health worker, or health educator. You will learn in this course that the relationship between the person's health and psychology involves a "two-way street"—each affects the other. Psychological factors go hand in hand with medical approaches in preventing and treating illness and in helping patients adjust to the health problems they develop.

THE BOOK AND WEBSITE

This book was designed for you, the reader. First and foremost, it provides a thorough and up-to-date presentation of the major issues, theories, concepts, and research in health psychology. Throughout the book, the major point of view is "biopsychosocial"—that is, that health and illness influence and result from the interplay of biological, psychological, and social aspects of people's lives. Because integrating these aspects involves complex concepts and technical material, I have made special efforts to write in a straightforward, clear, and engaging fashion.

To help you master the material and remember it longer, the book includes the following learning aids:

- **Chapter Contents and Prologue.** Each chapter begins with a contents list that outlines the major topics in the order in which they are covered. The prologue then introduces the chapter with a vignette that is relevant to the material ahead and gives an overview of the basic ideas you will read about.

- **Illustrations.** The many figures, tables, and photographs in each chapter are designed to clarify concepts and research findings and help them stick in your mind.

- **Boxed material.** Three types of boxed material are included in the chapters. Each type of box has a special icon that is used in "Go to . . ." instructions, prompting you to read the appropriate box at the correct point in the text.

- **Summary and Key Terms.** Each chapter closes with two features: (1) the summary, which presents the most important ideas covered, and (2) the key terms—a list of the most important terms in the chapter, arranged in order of their appearance.

- **Glossary.** The glossary at the back of the book gives definitions of important terms and concepts, along with pronunciation keys for the most difficult words. It will be useful when you are studying or reading and are not sure of the exact meaning or pronunciation of a term.

To enhance your learning experience, a *companion Website* for this book can be accessed at www.wiley.com/college/sarafino.

STUDY HINTS

There are many ways you can use the features of this book to learn and study well, and you may want to "experiment" to find the best way for you. I will describe one method that works well for many students.

Survey the chapter first. Read the contents list and browse through the chapter, examining the figures, tables, and photographs. Some students also find it useful to read the summary first, even though it contains terms they may not yet understand. Then read the prologue. As you begin each new section of the chapter, look at its title and turn it into a *question*. Thus, the heading early in Chapter 1, "An Illness/Wellness Continuum," might become "What is an illness/wellness continuum?" Doing this helps you focus on your reading. After reading the section, *reflect* on what you have just read. Can you answer the question you asked when you reworded the title?

When you have finished the body of the chapter, *review* what you have read by reading the summary and trying to define the items in the list of key terms. If there is something you do not understand, look it up in the chapter or glossary. Last, *reread* the chapter at least once, concentrating on the important concepts or ideas. You may find it helpful to underline or highlight selected material now that you have a good idea of what is important. If your exam will consist of "objective" questions, such as multiple choice, using this approach intensively should be effective. If your exam will have essay items, you will probably find it helpful to develop a list of likely questions and write an outline or a complete answer for each one.

I hope that you enjoy this book, that you learn a great deal from it, and that you will share my enthusiasm and fascination for health psychology by the time you finish the course.

Edward P. Sarafino

BRIEF CONTENTS

PART I   An Introduction: Basic Issues and Processes   1

Chapter 1   An Overview of Psychology and Health   1

Chapter 2   The Body's Physical Systems   31

PART II   Stress, Illness, and Coping   61

Chapter 3   Stress—Its Meaning, Impact, and Sources   61

Chapter 4   Stress, Biopsychosocial Factors, and Illness   86

Chapter 5   Coping with and Reducing Stress   116

PART III   Lifestyles to Enhance Health and Prevent Illness   139

Chapter 6   Health-Related Behavior and Health Promotion   139

Chapter 7   Substance Use and Abuse   171

Chapter 8   Nutrition, Weight Control and Diet, Exercise, and Safety   203

PART IV   Becoming Ill and Getting Medical Treatment   236

Chapter 9   Using Health Services   236

Chapter 10   In the Hospital: The Setting, Procedures, and Effects on Patients   266

PART V   Physical Symptoms: Pain and Discomfort   291

Chapter 11   The Nature and Symptoms of Pain   291

Chapter 12   Managing and Controlling Clinical Pain   319

PART VI   Chronic and Life-Threatening Health Problems   343

Chapter 13   Serious and Disabling Chronic Illnesses: Causes, Management, and Coping   343

Chapter 14   Heart Disease, Stroke, Cancer, and AIDS: Causes, Management, and Coping   372

PART VII   Looking to the Future   405

Chapter 15 What's Ahead for Health Psychology?   405

CONTENTS

PART I An Introduction: Basic Issues and Processes 1

Chapter 1 An Overview of Psychology and Health 1

What Is Health? 2
An Illness/Wellness Continuum 2
Illness Today and in the Past 2
Viewpoints from History: Physiology, Disease Processes, and the Mind 5
Early Cultures 5
Ancient Greece and Rome 5
The Middle Ages 6
The Renaissance and After 6
Seeing a Need: Psychology's Role in Health 7
Problems in the Health Care System 8
"The Person" in Health and Illness 8
  Assess Yourself: What's Your Lifestyle Like? 8
How the Role of Psychology Emerged 10
  Clinical Methods and Issues: Behaviorism's Legacy: 12
    Progress in Health Psychology's Goals 12
Health Psychology: The Profession 12
Current Perspectives on Health and Illness 13
The Biopsychosocial Perspective 13
Life-Span and Gender Perspectives 16
Relating Health Psychology to Other Science Fields 17
Related Fields 17
Health and Psychology across Cultures 18
  Highlight: Related Nonpsychology Careers 19
Research Methods 21
Experiments 22
Correlational Studies 24
Quasi-Experimental Studies 25
Genetics Research 27

Chapter 2 The Body's Physical Systems 31

Module 1: The Nervous System 32
How the Nervous System Works 32
The Central Nervous System 34
The Peripheral Nervous System 37
  Clinical Methods and Issues: Biofeedback Treatment for Paralysis 37
Module 2: The Endocrine System 40
The Endocrine and Nervous Systems Working Together 40

Adrenal Glands 41
Other Glands 41
Module 3: The Digestive System 42
Food's Journey Through Digestive Organs 42
  Highlight: Our Physiological Individuality 43
Using Nutrients in Metabolism 46
  Assess Yourself: How Many Calories Do You Burn While Resting? 47
Module 4: The Respiratory System 47
The Respiratory Tract 47
Respiratory Function and Disorders 47
Module 5: The Cardiovascular System 49
The Heart and Blood Vessels 49
Blood Pressure 50
Blood Composition 51
Cardiovascular Disorders 52
Module 6: The Immune System 53
Antigens 53
The Organs of the Immune System 54
  Highlight: When Immune Functions Are Absent 55
Soldiers of the Immune System 55
Defending the Body with an Immune Response 57
Less-Than-Optimal Defenses 58

PART II Stress, Illness, and Coping 61

Chapter 3 Stress—Its Meaning, Impact, and Sources 61

Experiencing Stress in Our Lives 62
What Is Stress? 62
Appraising Events as Stressful 63
  Clinical Methods and Issues Posttraumatic Stress Disorder 66
Dimensions of Stress 66
Biopsychosocial Aspects of Stress 66
Biological Aspects of Stress 66
Psychosocial Aspects of Stress 69
Sources of Stress Throughout Life 72
Sources Within the Person 72
Sources in the Family 72
  Highlight: Gender Differences in Caregiving? 75
Sources in the Community and Society 75
Measuring Stress 77
Physiological Arousal 78
Life Events 79
Daily Hassles 81

Assess Yourself: Hassles in Your Life   82
Can Stress Be Good for You?   83

Chapter 4   Stress, Biopsychosocial Factors,
            and Illness   86

Psychosocial Modifiers of Stress   87
Social Support   87
Assess Yourself: How Much Emotional Support Do
   You Get?   89
A Sense of Personal Control   92
Clinical Methods and Issues: Social Support, Therapy,
   and Cognitive Processes   93
A Hardy Personality   97
Type A and Type B Behavior Patterns   99
How Stress Affects Health   102
Stress, Behavior, and Illness   103
Stress, Physiology, and Illness   103
Highlight: Sudden "Voodoo" Death   104
Psychoneuroimmunology   105
Psychophysiological Disorders   108
Digestive System Diseases   108
Asthma   108
Recurrent Headache   109
Other Disorders   110
Stress and Cardiovascular Disorders   110
Hypertension   110
Coronary Heart Disease   112
Stress and Cancer   113

Chapter 5   Coping with and Reducing Stress   116

Coping with Stress   117
What Is Coping?   117
Functions and Methods of Coping   118
Assess Yourself: Your Focuses in Coping   118
Reducing the Potential for Stress   123
Enhancing Social Support   123
Improving One's Personal Control   124
Organizing One's World Better   124
Highlight: The Amish Way of Social Support
   in Bereavement   125
Exercising: Links to Stress and Health   125
Preparing for Stressful Events   126
Reducing Stress Reactions: Stress Management   127
Medication   127
Behavioral and Cognitive Methods   128
Clinical Methods and Issues: The Case of "Bear"   132
Massage, Meditation, and Hypnosis   134
**Using Stress Management to Reduce
Coronary Risk   135**
Modifying Type A Behavior   135
Treating Hypertension   137

**PART III   Lifestyles to Enhance Health
           and Prevent Illness   139**

Chapter 6   Health-Related Behavior and Health
            Promotion   139

Health and Behavior   140
Lifestyles, Risk Factors, and Health   140
Highlight: Two Health Behaviors: Breast
   and Testicular Examinations   142
Interdisciplinary Perspectives on Preventing Illness   143
Problems in Promoting Wellness   145
**What Determines People's Health-Related
Behavior   146**
General Factors in Health-Related Behavior   146
The Role of Beliefs and Intentions   149
The Role of Less Rational Processes   153
**Developmental, Gender, and Sociocultural Factors
in Health   155**
Development and Health   156
Gender and Health   157
Sociocultural Factors and Health   158
Programs for Health Promotion   160
Methods for Promoting Health   160
Clinical Methods and Issues: Dialogues to Help
   People Stop Smoking   161
Promoting Health in the Schools   164
Worksite Wellness Programs   164
Community-Based Wellness Programs   165
Assess Yourself: Your Knowledge about AIDS   166
Prevention with Specific Targets: Focusing on AIDS   166

Chapter 7   Substance Use and Abuse   171

Substance Abuse   172
Addiction and Dependence   172
Processes Leading to Dependence   173
Smoking Tobacco   174
Who Smokes, and How Much?   175
Why People Smoke   176
Smoking and Health   178
Highlight: Does Someone Else's Smoking Affect
   Your Health?   180
Alcohol Use and Abuse   181
Who Drinks, and How Much?   182
Assess Yourself: What's True About Drinking?   183
Why People Use and Abuse Alcohol   185
Assess Yourself: Do You Abuse Alcohol?   185
Drinking and Health   186
Drug Use and Abuse   187
Highlight: Types and Effects of Drugs   188
Who Uses Drugs, and Why?   188
Drug Use and Health   189

Reducing Substance Use and Abuse 190
Preventing Substance Use 190
Quitting a Substance without Therapy 192
Treatment Methods to Stop Substance Use
and Abuse 194

 Highlight: Where Should Alcohol and Drug Abuse
   Treatment Occur, and What Should Be the Goals
   and Criteria for Success? 195

 Clinical Methods and Issues: Behavioral Methods
   for Treating Substance Abuse 198
Dealing with the Relapse Problem 199

Chapter 8   Nutrition, Weight Control and Diet, Exercise,
              and Safety 203

Nutrition 204
Components of Food 204
What People Eat 205
Nutrition and Health 206
Weight Control and Diet 210
Desirable and Undesirable Weights 210
Becoming Overly Fat 212
Dieting and Treatments to Lose Weight 216

 Highlight: Which "Carbs" to Avoid 217

 Clinical Methods and Issues: Problem-Solving
   Training to Control Weight 219
Anorexia and Bulimia 221

 Assess Yourself: Your Weight Control Patterns 222
Exercise 224

 Highlight: Types and Amounts of Healthful
   Exercise 225
The Health Effects of Exercise 226
Who Gets Enough Exercise, Who Does Not—
   and Why? 228
Promoting Exercise Behavior 229
Safety 231
Accidents 231
Environmental Hazards 232

**PART IV   Becoming Ill and Getting Medical
            Treatment** 236

Chapter 9   Using Health Services 236

Types of Health Services 237
Specialized Functions of Practitioners 237
Office-Based and Inpatient Treatment 237
The American Health Care System 238
Health Care Systems in Other Countries 239
Perceiving and Interpreting Symptoms 240
Perceiving Symptoms 240
Interpreting and Responding to Symptoms 242

Using and Misusing Health Services 244
Who Uses Health Services? 244
Why People Use, Don't Use, and Delay Using Health
   Services 246
Using Complementary and Alternative Medicine 249
Misusing Health Services 250
The Patient–Practitioner Relationship 250
Patient Preferences for Participation in Medical
   Care 251

 Highlight: Fighting for Your Life 252
The Practitioner's Behavior and Style 252
The Patient's Behavior and Style 254

 Assess Yourself: Do You Know Medical Terms'
   Meanings? 255
Compliance: Adhering to Medical Advice 256
Extent of the Nonadherence Problem 256
Why Patients Do and Do Not Adhere to Medical
   Advice 257
Patient–Practitioner Interactions 260
Increasing Patient Adherence 261

 Clinical Methods and Issues: How to Present Medical
   Information 263
Focusing on Prevention 264

Chapter 10   In the Hospital: The Setting, Procedures,
               and Effects on Patients 266

**The Hospital—Its History, Setting, and
Procedures** 267
How the Hospital Evolved 267
The Organization and Functioning of Hospitals 268
Roles, Goals, and Communication 269

 Assess Yourself: Who's Who in Physician Care 269
The Impact of the "Bottom line" 271
Being Hospitalized 272
Relations with the Hospital Staff 272
Sick-Role Behavior in the Hospital 274
Emotional Adjustment in the Hospital 276
Coping Processes in Hospital Patients 276
Preparing Patients for Stressful Medical Procedures 278

 Highlight: Lamaze Training as a Method
   of Psychological Preparation for a Medical
   Procedure 281
When the Hospitalized Patient Is a Child 282

 Clinical Methods and Issues: Preparing Children
   for Impending Hospitalization 285
**How Health Psychologists Assist Hospitalized
Patients** 286
Initial Steps in Helping 287
Tests for Psychological Assessment of Medical
Patients 287
Promoting Patients' Health and Adjustment 289

PART V Physical Symptoms: Pain and Discomfort 291

Chapter 11   The Nature and Symptoms of Pain   291

What Is Pain?   292
The Qualities and Dimensions of Pain   292
Perceiving Pain   294
💡   *Highlight*: Acute Pain in Burn Patients   295
Theories of Pain   298
Early Theories of Pain   298
💡   *Highlight*: Inducing Pain in Laboratory
      Research   299
The Gate-Control Theory of Pain   301
Biopsychosocial Aspects of Pain   303
Neurochemical Transmission and Inhibition of Pain   303
Personal and Social Experiences and Pain   304
💡   *Highlight*: Placebos and Pain   305
Emotions, Coping Processes, and Pain   307
🐾   *Clinical Methods and Issues*: Assessing Difficulty
      Coping with Pain   308
Assessing People's Pain   309
Self-Report Methods   310
Pain Questionaires   311
🐾   *Assess Yourself*: Describing Your Pain   312
Behavioral Assessment Approaches   313
Psychophysiological Measures   315
Pain in Children   315
Pain and Children's Sensory and Cognitive
      Development   315
Assessing Pain in Children   316

Chapter 12   Managing and Controlling Clinical Pain   319

Clinical Pain   320
Acute Clinical Pain   320
Chronic Clinical pain   320
Medical Treatments for Pain   321
Surgical Methods for Treating Pain   322
Chemical Methods for Treating Pain   322
💡   *Highlight*: Types of Pain-Relieving Chemicals   323
**Behavioral and Cognitive Methods for Treating
Pain   326**
The Operant Approach   326
Relaxation and Biofeedback   327
Cognitive Methods   329
🐾   *Clinical Methods and Issues*: Guiding a Client to Pain
      Redefinition   333
Hypnosis and Interpersonal Therapy   333
🐾   *Assess Yourself*: Would Behavioral or Cognitive
      Methods Help Your Pain?   334
Hypnosis as a Treatment for Pain   334
Interpersonal Therapy for Pain   335

Physical and Stimulation Therapies for Pain   336
Stimulation Therapies   336
Physical Therapy   338
💡   *Highlight*: Physical Activity and Back Pain   339
Pain Clinics   340
Multidisciplinary Programs   340
Evaluating the Success of Pain Clinics   341

PART VI Chronic and Life-Threatening Health Problems 343

Chapter 13   Serious and Disabling Chronic Illnesses:
               Causes, Management, and Coping   343

Adjusting to a Chronic Illness   344
Initial Reactions to Having a Chronic Condition   344
Influences on Coping with a Health Crisis   344
The Coping Process   347
Impacts of Different Chronic Conditions   349
Asthma   349
Epilepsy   351
💡   *Highlight*: What to Do for a Seizure   352
Nervous System Injuries   353
Diabetes   355
🐾   *Assess Yourself*: Do You Have Diabetes?   357
💡   *Highlight*: Self-Managing Diabetes   359
Arthritis   360
Alzheimer's Disease   363
**Psychosocial Interventions for People with Chronic
Conditions   366**
Educational, Social Support, and Behavioral
      Methods   366
Relaxation and Biofeedback   368
Cognitive Methods   368
🐾   *Clinical Methods and Issues*: Treating Asthma
      with Biofeedback and Relaxation   368
Interpersonal and Family Therapy   369

Chapter 14   Heart Disease, Stroke, Cancer, and AIDS:
               Causes, Management, and Coping   372

**Coping with and Adapting to High-Mortality
Illness   373**
Adapting While the Prospects Seem Good   373
Adapting in a Recurrence or Relapse   374
Heart Disease   375
Who Is at Risk of Heart Disease, and Why?   375
Medical Treatment and Rehabilitation of Cardiac
      Patients   376
The Psychosocial Impact of Heart Disease   378
Psychosocial Interventions for Heart Disease   380
Stroke   380
Causes, Effects, and Rehabilitation of Stroke   381

Psychosocial Aspects of Stroke   383
  Clinical Methods and Issues: Stroke Rehabilitation
  for Visual Neglect   383
Cancer   384
The Prevalence and Types of Cancer   384
The Sites, Effects, and Causes of Cancer   386
Diagnosing and Treating Cancer   387
The Psychosocial Impact of Cancer   389
Psychosocial Interventions for Cancer   391
Childhood Cancer   392
  Highlight: Can Psychosocial Interventions Improve
  Cancer Survival?   392
AIDS   393
Risk Factors, Effects, and Treatment of AIDS   393
From HIV Infection to AIDS   393
The Psychosocial Impact of AIDS   394
Psychosocial Interventions for AIDS   396
Adapting to a Terminal Illness   396
The Patient's Age   396
Psychosocial Adjustments to Terminal Illness   397
The Quality of Life in Death   399
Medical and Psychological Care of Dying Patients   399
  Assess Yourself: Your Living Will Choices   400
A Place to Die—Hospital, Home, or Hospice?   401
The Survivors: And Life Goes On   402

PART VII   Looking to the Future   405

Chapter 15   What's Ahead for Health Psychology?   405

Goals for Health Psychology   406
Enhancing Illness Prevention and Treatment   406
Improving Efforts for Helping Patients Cope   407

Documenting the Efficacy and Cost-Benefit Ratio
  of Care   407
Enhancing Psychologists' Acceptance in Medical
  Settings   408
  Clinical Methods and Issues: Psychologists
  in the Primary Care Team   409
Careers and Training in Health Psychology   409
Career Opportunities   409
Training Programs   409
Issues and Controversies for the Future   410
Environment, Health, and Psychology   410
Quality of Life   410
Ethical Decisions in Medical Care   411
Future Focuses in Health Psychology   412
  Assess Yourself: Some Ethical Dilemmas: What Do
  You Think?   413
Life-Span Health and Illness   413
Sociocultural Factors in Health   414
Gender Differences and Women's Health Issues   414
Factors Affecting Health Psychology's Future   415

Glossary   417

References   425

Credits   506

Subject Index   507

Author Index   520

1

AN OVERVIEW OF PSYCHOLOGY AND HEALTH

What Is Health?
An Illness/Wellness Continuum
Illness Today and in the Past

Viewpoints from History: Physiology, Disease Processes, and the Mind
Early Cultures
Ancient Greece and Rome
The Middle Ages
The Renaissance and After

Seeing a Need: Psychology's Role in Health
Problems in the Health Care System
"The Person" in Health and Illness
How the Role of Psychology Emerged
Health Psychology: The Profession

Current Perspectives on Health and Illness
The Biopsychosocial Perspective
Life-Span and Gender Perspectives

Relating Health Psychology to Other Science Fields
Related Fields
Health and Psychology across Cultures

Research Methods
Experiments
Correlational Studies
Quasi-Experimental Studies
Genetics Research

PROLOGUE

"Wide load!" the boys shouted as they pressed themselves against the walls of the hallway at school. They were "making room" for a very overweight girl named Ana to pass through. Lunch time in the cafeteria was even more degrading for Ana because when she sat down to eat, her schoolmates would stop eating, stare at her every move, and make pig noises. "Kids can be cruel," her parents would say to console her. One of Ana's aunts told her that she "inherited a glandular problem, and you can't do anything about it," and another aunt said, "You'll lose weight easily in a couple of years when you start getting interested in boys." Is either aunt right?

Ana's parents are concerned about her weight because they know that overweight people often have social problems and face special health risks, particularly for high blood pressure and heart disease. But her parents are not sure why she's so heavy or how to help her. Although her father is a bit overweight, her mother is very heavy and was as a child, which could support the idea of an inherited cause of her being overweight. On the other hand, they know Ana eats a lot of fattening foods and gets very little exercise, a combination that often causes weight gain. As part of their effort to change these two behaviors, they encouraged her to join a recreation program, where she will be involved in many physical activities.

This story about Ana illustrates important issues related to health. For instance, being overweight is associated with the development of specific health problems and may affect the individual's social relations. Also, weight problems can result from a person's inheritance and behavior. In this book, we will examine the relationships between health and a wide variety of biological, psychological, and social factors in people's lives.

This chapter introduces a relatively new and very exciting field of study called *health psychology*. We look at its scope, its history, its research methods, and how it draws on and supports other sciences. As we study these topics, you will begin to see how health psychologists would answer such questions as: Does the mind affect our health? What role does the cultural background of individuals play in their health? Does the age of a person affect how he or she deals with issues of health and illness? But first let's begin with a definition of health.

WHAT IS HEALTH?

You know what health is, don't you? How would you define it? You would probably mention something about health being a state of feeling well and not being sick. We commonly think about health in terms of an absence of (1) objective *signs* that the body is not functioning properly, such as measured high blood pressure, or (2) subjective *symptoms* of disease or injury, such as pain or nausea (Kazarian & Evans, 2001; Thoresen, 1984). Dictionaries define health in this way, too. But there is a problem with this definition of health. Let's see why.

AN ILLNESS/WELLNESS CONTINUUM

Consider Ana, the overweight girl in the opening story. You've surely heard people say, "It's not healthy

to be overweight." Is Ana healthy? What about someone who feels fine but whose lungs are being damaged from smoking cigarettes or whose arteries are becoming clogged from eating foods that are high in saturated fats? These are all signs of improper body functioning. Are people with these signs healthy? We probably would say they are not "sick"—they are just *less* healthy than they would be without the unhealthful conditions.

This means health and sickness are not entirely separate concepts—they overlap. There are degrees of wellness and of illness. Medical sociologist Aaron Antonovsky (1979, 1987) has suggested that we consider these concepts as ends of a continuum, noting that "We are all terminal cases. And we all are, so long as there is a breath of life in us, in some measure healthy" (1987, p. 3). He also proposed that we revise our focus, giving more attention to what enables people to stay well than to what causes people to become ill. Figure 1–1 presents a diagram of an **illness/wellness continuum,** with *death* at one end and *optimal wellness* at the other.

We will use the term **health** to mean a positive state of physical, mental, and social well-being—not simply the absence of injury or disease—that varies over time along a continuum. At the wellness end of the continuum, health is the dominant state. At the other end of the continuum, the dominant state is illness or injury, in which destructive processes produce characteristic signs, symptoms, or disabilities.

ILLNESS TODAY AND IN THE PAST

People in the United States and other developed, industrialized nations live longer, on the average, than they did in the past, and they suffer from a different pattern of illnesses. During the 17th, 18th, and 19th centuries, people in North America suffered and died chiefly from two types of illness: dietary and infectious (Grob, 1983). *Dietary diseases* result from malnutrition—for example, beriberi is caused by a lack of vitamin B_1 and is characterized by anemia, paralysis, and wasting away. **Infectious diseases** are acute illnesses caused by harmful matter or microorganisms, such as bacteria or viruses, in the body. In most of the world today, infectious diseases continue to be the main causes of death (WHO, 2004).

A good example of the way illness patterns have changed in developed nations comes from the history of diseases in the United States. From the early

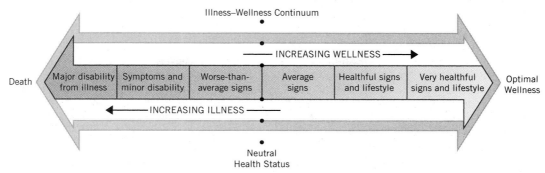

Illness–Wellness Continuum

INCREASING WELLNESS ⟶

| Major disability from illness | Symptoms and minor disability | Worse-than-average signs | Average signs | Healthful signs and lifestyle | Very healthful signs and lifestyle |

Death

Optimal Wellness

⟵ INCREASING ILLNESS

Neutral Health Status

Figure 1–1 An illness/wellness continuum to represent people's differing health statuses. Starting at the center (neutral level) of the diagram, a person's health status is shown as progressively worse to the left and progressively healthful as it moves to the right. The segments in the central band describe dominant features that usually characterize different health statuses, based on the person's *physical condition*—that is, his or her signs (such as blood pressure), symptoms, and disability—and *lifestyle*, such as his or her amount of regular exercise, cholesterol consumption, and cigarette smoking. Medical treatment typically begins at a health status to the left of the neutral level and intensifies as the physical condition worsens. Medical treatment can bring the person's health status back to the midrange of the continuum, but healthful lifestyles can help, too. Increasing wellness beyond the midrange can be achieved through lifestyle improvements. (Based on information in Antonovsky, 1987; Bradley, 1993; Ryan & Travis, 1981.)

colonial days in America through the 18th century, colonists experienced periodic epidemics of many infectious diseases, especially smallpox, diphtheria, yellow fever, measles, and influenza. It was not unusual for hundreds, and sometimes thousands, of people to die in a single epidemic. Children were particularly hard hit. Two other infectious diseases, malaria and dysentery, were widespread and presented an even greater threat. Although these two diseases generally did not kill people directly, they

Epidemics of deadly infectious diseases have occurred throughout the world. Before the 20th century, there were no effective methods for prevention or treatment of the plague, for instance, which is the disease illustrated in this engraving.

weakened their victims and reduced the ability to resist other fatal diseases. Most, if not all, of these diseases did not exist in North America before the European settlers arrived—the settlers brought the infections with them—and the death toll among Native Americans was extremely high. This high death rate occurred for two reasons. First, the native population had never been exposed to these new microorganisms and thus lacked the natural immunity that our bodies develop after lengthy exposure to most diseases (Grob, 1983). Second, Native Americans' immune functions were probably limited by a low degree of genetic variation among these people (Black, 1992).

In the 19th century, infectious diseases were still the greatest threat to the health of Americans. The illnesses of the colonial era continued to claim many lives, but new diseases began to appear. The most significant of these diseases was tuberculosis, or "consumption," as it was often called. In 1842, for example, consumption was listed as the cause for 22% of all deaths in the state of Massachusetts (Grob, 1983). But by the end of the 19th century, deaths from infectious diseases had decreased sharply. For instance, the death rate from tuberculosis declined by about 60% in a 25-year period around the turn of the century.

Did this decrease result mostly from advances in medical treatment? Although medical advances helped to some degree, the decrease occurred long before effective vaccines and medications were introduced. This was the case for most of the major diseases we've discussed, including tuberculosis, diphtheria, measles, and influenza (Grob, 1983; Leventhal, Prohaska, & Hirschman, 1985). It appears that the decline resulted chiefly from *preventive* measures such as improved personal hygiene, greater resistance to diseases (owing to better nutrition), and public health innovations, such as building water purification and sewage treatment facilities. Many people had become concerned about their health and began to heed the advice of health reformers like William Alcott, an advocate of moderation in diet and sexual behavior (Leventhal, Prohaska, & Hirschman, 1985). Fewer deaths occurred from diseases because fewer people contracted them.

The 20th century witnessed great changes in the patterns of illness afflicting people, particularly in developed nations where advances in preventive measures and medical care reduced the death rate from life-threatening infectious diseases (WHO, 2004). At the same time, people's average life expectancy in-

Figure 1–2 Expected total life span for people in the United States at various years since 1900 who were born in the specified year or had reached 1 year, 20 years, or 65 years of age. (Data from USDHHS, 1987, p. 2, for years 1900–1902, 1959–1961, and 1984; USBC, 2003, for 2000.)

creased dramatically. At the turn of the 20th century in the United States, the life expectancy of babies at birth was about 48 years (USDHHS, 1987); today it is 76 years (USBC, 2003). Figure 1–2 shows this change and an important reason for it; the death rate among children was very high many years ago. Babies who survived their first year in 1900 could be expected to live to about 56 years of age, adding 7 years to their expected total life span. Moreover, people in 1900 who had reached the age of 20 years could expect to live to almost 63 years of age. Today the death rate for American children is much lower, and only a small difference exists in the expected total life span for newborns and 20-year-olds.

Death is still inevitable, of course, but people die at later ages now and from different causes. The main health problems and causes of death in developed countries today are **chronic diseases**—that is, degenerative illnesses that develop or persist over a long period of time. More than half of all adult deaths in developed nations are caused by three chronic diseases: heart disease, cancer, and stroke (WHO, 2004). These diseases are not new, but they were responsible for a much smaller proportion of deaths before the 20th century. Why? One reason is that people's lives are different today. For example, the growth of industrialization increased people's stress and exposure to harmful chemicals. In addition, more people today survive to old age, and chronic diseases are more likely to afflict the elderly than younger individuals. Thus, another reason for the current prominence of chronic diseases is that more people are living to the age when they are at high risk for contracting them (USDHHS, 1982).

Are the main causes of death in childhood and adolescence different from those in adulthood? Yes. In the United States, for example, the leading cause of death in children and adolescents, by far, is not an illness, but accidental injury (USBC, 2003). Over 40% of child and adolescent deaths result from accidents, frequently involving automobiles. In childhood, the next two most frequent causes of death are cancer and congenital abnormalities; in adolescence, they are homicide and suicide (USBC, 2003). Clearly, the role of disease in death differs greatly at different points in the life span.

VIEWPOINTS FROM HISTORY: PHYSIOLOGY, DISEASE PROCESSES, AND THE MIND

Is illness a purely physical condition? Does a person's mind play a role in becoming ill and getting well? People have wondered about these questions for thousands of years, and the answers they have arrived at have changed over time.

EARLY CULTURES

Although we do not know for certain, it appears that the best educated people thousands of years ago believed physical and mental illness were caused by mystical forces, such as evil spirits (Stone, 1979). Why do we think this? Researchers found ancient skulls in several areas of the world with coin-size circular holes in them that could not have been battle wounds. These holes were probably made with sharp stone tools in a procedure called *trephination*. This procedure was done presumably for superstitious reasons—for instance, to allow illness-causing demons to leave the head. Unfortunately, we can only speculate about the reasons for these holes because there are no written records from those times.

A skull with holes probably produced by trephination. This person probably survived several of these procedures.

ANCIENT GREECE AND ROME

The philosophers of ancient Greece produced the earliest written ideas about physiology, disease processes, and the mind between 500 and 300 B.C. Hippocrates, often called "the Father of Medicine," proposed a *humoral theory* of illness. According to this theory, the body contains four fluids called *humors* (in biology, the term *humor* refers to any plant or animal fluid). When the mixture of these humors is harmonious or balanced, we are in a state of health. Disease occurs when the mixture is faulty (Stone, 1979). Hippocrates recommended eating a good diet and avoiding excesses to help achieve humoral balance.

Greek philosophers, especially Plato, were among the first to propose that the mind and the body are separate entities (Marx & Hillix, 1963; Schneider & Tarshis, 1975). The mind was considered to have little or no relationship to the body and its state of health. This remained the dominant view of writers and philosophers for more than a thousand years. Many people today still speak about the body and the mind as if they were separate. The *body* refers to our physical being, including our skin, muscles, bones, heart, and brain. The *mind* refers to an abstract process that includes our thoughts, perceptions, and feelings. Although we can distinguish between the mind and the body conceptually, an important issue is whether they also function independently. The question of their relationship is called the **mind/body problem.**

Galen was a famous and highly–respected physician and writer of the 2nd century A.D. who was born in Greece and practiced in Rome. Although he believed generally in the humoral theory and the mind/body split, he made many innovations. For example, he "dissected animals of many species (but probably never a human), and made important discoveries about the brain, circulatory system, and kidneys" (Stone, 1979, p. 4). From this work, he became aware that illnesses can be localized, with pathology in specific parts of the body, and that different diseases have different effects. Galen's ideas became widely accepted.

THE MIDDLE AGES

After the collapse of the Roman Empire in the 5th century A.D., much of the Western world was in disarray. The advancement of knowledge and culture slowed sharply in Europe and remained stunted during the Middle Ages, which lasted almost a thousand years. Galen's views dominated ideas about physiology and disease processes for most of this time.

The influence of the Church in slowing the development of medical knowledge during the Middle Ages was enormous. According to historians, in the eyes of the Church the human being

> was regarded as a creature with a soul, possessed of a free will which set him apart from ordinary natural laws, subject only to his own willfulness and perhaps the will of God. Such a creature, being free-willed, could not be an object of scientific investigation. Even the body of man was regarded as sacrosanct, and dissection was dangerous for the dissector. These strictures against observation hindered the development of anatomy and medicine for centuries. (Marx & Hillix, 1963, p. 24)

The prohibition against dissection extended to animals as well, since they were thought to have souls, too.

People's ideas about the cause of illness took on pronounced religious overtones, and the belief in demons became strong again (Sarason & Sarason, 1984). Sickness was seen as God's punishment for doing evil things. As a result, the Church came to control the practice of medicine, and priests became increasingly involved in treating the ill, often by torturing the body to drive out evil spirits.

It was not until the 13th century that new ideas about the mind/body problem began to emerge. The Italian philosopher St. Thomas Aquinas rejected the view that the mind and body are separate. He saw them as an interrelated unit that forms the whole person (Leahey, 1987). Although his position did not have as great an impact as others had had, it renewed interest in the issue and influenced later philosophers.

THE RENAISSANCE AND AFTER

The word *renaissance* means rebirth—a fitting name for the 14th and 15th centuries. During this period in history, Europe saw a rebirth of inquiry, culture, and politics. Scholars became more "human-centered" than "God-centered" in their search for truth and "believed that truth can be seen in many ways, from many individual perspectives" (Leahey, 1987, p. 80). These ideas set the stage for important changes in philosophy once the scientific revolution began after 1600.

The 17th-century French philosopher and mathematician Rene Descartes probably had the greatest influence on scientific thought of any philosopher in history (Schneider & Tarshis, 1975). Like the Greeks, he regarded the mind and body as separate entities, but he introduced three important innovations. First, he conceived of the body as a machine and described the mechanics of how action and sensation occurred. For example, Figure 1–3 shows his concept of how we experience pain. Second, he proposed that the mind and body, though separate, could *communicate* through the pineal gland, an organ in the brain (Leahey, 1987). Third, he believed that animals have no soul and that the soul in humans leaves the body at death (Marx & Hillix, 1963). This belief meant that dissection could be an acceptable method of study—a point the Church was then ready to concede (Engel, 1977).

In the 18th and 19th centuries, knowledge in science and medicine grew quickly, helped greatly by

Figure 1–3 Descartes' concept of the pain pathway. Descartes used this drawing to illustrate the mechanisms by which people experience and respond to pain: The heat of the fire (at A) sends tiny particles to the foot (B) that pull on a thread that courses from the foot to the head. This action opens a pore (*de*), releasing spirits from a cavity (F) that travel to the parts of the body that respond (e.g., the leg moves away). (From Descartes, 1664, Figure 7.)

improvements in the microscope and the use of dissection in autopsies. Once scientists learned the basics of how the body functioned and discovered that microorganisms cause certain diseases, they were able to reject the humoral theory of illness and propose new theories. The field of surgery flourished after antiseptic techniques and anesthesia were introduced in the mid-19th century (Stone, 1979). Before that time, hospitals were "notorious places, more likely to spread diseases than cure them" (Easterbrook, 1987, p. 42). Over time, the reputation of physicians and hospitals began to improve and people's trust in the ability of doctors to heal increased.

These advances, coupled with the continuing belief that the mind and body are separate, laid the foundation for a new approach, or model, for conceptualizing health and illness. This approach—called the **biomedical model**—proposes that all diseases or physical disorders can be explained by disturbances in physiological processes, which result from injury, biochemical imbalances, bacterial or viral infection, and the like (Engel, 1977; Leventhal, Prohaska, & Hirschman, 1985). The biomedical model assumes that disease is an affliction of the body and is separate from the psychological and social processes of the mind. This viewpoint became widely accepted during the 19th and 20th centuries and still represents the dominant view in medicine today.

SEEING A NEED: PSYCHOLOGY'S ROLE IN HEALTH

The biomedical model has been very useful. Using it as a guide, researchers have made enormous achievements. They conquered many infectious diseases, such as polio and measles, through the development of vaccines. They also developed antibiotics, which made it possible to cure illnesses caused by bacterial infection. Despite these great advances, the biomedical model needs improvement. Let's see why.

PROBLEMS IN THE HEALTH CARE SYSTEM

Scarcely a week goes by that we don't hear through the mass media that health care costs are rising rapidly, particularly for prescription drugs and for hospital and nursing home care. Countries worldwide have been facing escalating costs in health care (WHO, 2003). For example, between 1960 and today the United States saw a 33-fold increase to nearly $4,700 in the amount of money spent per capita on health care, and the economic burden of health costs increased from 5.3 to 13.3% of the gross domestic product (NCHS, 2003). Because medical costs continue to rise rapidly, we need to consider new approaches for improving people's health.

We saw earlier that the patterns of illness affecting people have changed, particularly in developed nations where the main health problems now are chronic diseases. Although a great deal of progress is being made in understanding the causes of chronic diseases, improvements in techniques for treating them have been modest. From the 1950s to the 1980s, for example, gains in cancer survival rates resulted more from earlier detection of the disease than from improved treatments (Boffey, 1987). Although detection occurs earlier today partly because diagnostic methods and technology have improved, another part of the reason is that *people* have changed. Many individuals are more aware of signs and symptoms of illness, more motivated to take care of their health, and better able to afford visits to physicians than they were in the past. These factors are clearly important and relate to psychological and social aspects of the person. However, *the person* as a unique individual is not included in the biomedical model (Engel, 1977, 1980).

"THE PERSON" IN HEALTH AND ILLNESS

Have you ever noticed how some people are "always sick"—they get illnesses more frequently than most people do and get well more slowly? These differences between people can result from biomedical sources, such as variations in physiological processes and exposure to harmful microorganisms. But psychological and social factors also play a role. Let's look briefly at two of these factors: the lifestyle and personality of the person. (Go to 🍎—as described in the Preface, this instruction prompts you to read the nearby boxed material that has the same icon.)

Lifestyle and Illness

Earlier we saw that the occurrence of infectious diseases declined sharply in the late 19th century chiefly because of preventive measures, such as improving

---

ASSESS YOURSELF

What's Your Lifestyle Like?

At various points in this book, you'll find brief self-assessment surveys like this one that you should try to fill out as accurately as you can. These surveys relate to the nearby content of the chapter, and most of them can be completed in less than a minute or two.

This survey assesses seven aspects of your *usual* lifestyle. For each of the listed practices, put a check mark in the preceding space if it describes your usual situation.

_____ I sleep 7 or 8 hours a day.

_____ I eat breakfast almost every day.

_____ I rarely eat between meals.

_____ I am at or near the appropriate weight (see Table 8.2 on page 211)

_____ I never smoke cigarettes.

_____ I drink alcohol rarely or moderately.

_____ I regularly get vigorous physical activity.

Count the check marks—six or seven is quite good. The more of these situations that describe your lifestyle now and in the future, the better your health is likely to be, particularly after the age of 50.

nutrition and personal hygiene. These measures involved changes in people's *lifestyles*—their everyday patterns of behavior, such as in preparing and eating better balanced meals. The chief health problems in technological societies today are chronic diseases. People can reduce these, too, by making changes in their lives. Let's see how.

Characteristics or conditions that are associated with the development of a disease or injury are called **risk factors** for that health problem. Although some risk factors are *biological*, such as having inherited certain genes, others are *behavioral*. For example, it is well known that people who smoke cigarettes face a much higher risk of developing cancer and other illnesses than nonsmokers do. Other risk factors for cancer include eating diets high in saturated fat and having a family history of the disease. People who "do more" or "have more" of these characteristics or conditions are more likely to contract cancer than people who "do less" or "have less" of these factors. Keep in mind that a risk factor is *associated* with a health problem—it does not necessarily *cause* the problem. For example, being an African American man is a risk factor for prostate cancer (ACS, 2004), but that status does not cause the disease—at least, not directly.

Many risk factors result from the way people live or behave, such as smoking cigarettes and eating unhealthful diets. Some behavioral risk factors associated with the five leading causes of death are:

1. *Heart disease*—smoking, high dietary cholesterol, obesity, and lack of exercise.

2. *Cancer*—smoking, high alcohol use, and diet.

3. *Stroke*—smoking, high dietary cholesterol, and lack of exercise.

4. COPD (chronic lung diseases, e.g., emphysema)—smoking.

5. *Accidents* (including motor vehicle)—alcohol/drug use, driving vehicles too fast, and not using seat belts. (*Sources:* McGinnis, 1994; USBC, 2003)

Many of the people who are the victims of these illnesses and accidents live for at least a short while and either recover or eventually succumb. Part of today's high medical costs result from people's lifestyles that contribute to their health problems, and society, not the individual, often bears the burden of medical costs through public and private health insurance programs.

How influential are lifestyle factors on health? Researchers studied this question by surveying nearly 7,000 adults who ranged in age from about 20 to over 75, asking them two sets of questions. One set asked about the health of these people over the previous 12 months—for instance, whether illness had prevented them from working for a long time, forced them to cut down on other activities, or reduced their energy level. The second set of questions asked about seven aspects of their lifestyles: sleeping, eating breakfast, eating between meals, maintaining an appropriate weight, smoking cigarettes, drinking alcohol, and getting physical activity. The questions you answered above are similar to those in this research. When the researchers compared the data for people in different age groups, they found that at each age, health was typically better as the number of healthful practices increased. In fact, the health of those who "reported following all seven good health practices was consistently about the same as those 30 years younger who followed few or none of these practices" (Belloc & Breslow, 1972, p. 419). These health practices were also important in the future health of these people. Breslow (1983) has described later studies of the same people, such as to find out which of them had died in the 9½ years after the original survey. The data revealed that the percentage dying generally decreased with increases in the number of healthful behaviors practiced, and this impact was greater for older than younger people, especially among males. These findings suggest that practicing healthful behaviors can reduce the risk of illness and early death substantially.

You've surely heard someone ask, "Why don't people do what's good for them?" There's no simple answer to that question—there are many reasons. One reason is that less healthful behaviors often bring immediate pleasure, as when the person has a "good-tasting" cigarette or ice cream. Long-range negative consequences seem remote, both in time and in likelihood. Another reason is that people sometimes feel social pressures to engage in unhealthful behavior, as when an adolescent begins to use cigarettes, alcohol, or drugs. Also, some behaviors can become very strong habits, perhaps involving a physical addiction or psychological dependency, as happens with drugs and cigarettes. Quitting them becomes very difficult. Lastly, sometimes people are simply not aware of the dangers involved or how to change their behavior. These people need information about ways to protect their health.

Personality and Illness

Do you believe, as many do, that people who suffer from ulcers tend to be worriers or "workaholics"? Or that people who have migraine headaches are highly anxious? If you do, then you believe there is a link between personality and illness. The term **personality** refers to a person's cognitive, affective, or behavioral tendencies that are fairly stable across time and situations.

Researchers have found evidence linking personality traits and health. For example, low levels of *conscientiousness* in childhood and *poor mental health* in adulthood are associated with dying at earlier ages from diseases such as heart disease and cancer (Friedman, Tucker et al., 1995). In addition, people whose personalities include high levels of *anxiety, depression, anger/hostility,* or *pessimism* seem to be at risk for developing a variety of illnesses, particularly heart disease (Contrada & Guyll, 2001; Smith & Gallo, 2001). These four emotions are reactions that often occur when people experience stress, such as when they have more work to do than they think they can finish or when a tragedy happens. Many people approach these situations with relatively positive emotions. Their outlook is more optimistic than pessimistic, more hopeful than desperate. These people are not only less likely to become ill than are people with less positive personalities, but when they do, they tend to recover more quickly (Scheier & Carver, 2001; Smith & Gallo, 2001).

The link between personality and illness is not a one-way street; illness can affect one's personality, too (Cohen & Rodriguez, 1995). People who suffer from serious illness and disability often experience feelings of anxiety, depression, anger, and hopelessness. But as psychologists Irwin and Barbara Sarason (1984) have pointed out, even minor health problems, such as the flu or a toothache, produce temporary negative thoughts and feelings. People who are ill and overcome their negative thoughts and feelings can speed their recovery. We will examine this relationship in more detail later in this book.

Our glimpse at the relationships of the person's lifestyle and personality in illness demonstrates why it is important to consider psychological and social factors in health and illness. Next we will see how this recognition came about.

HOW THE ROLE OF PSYCHOLOGY EMERGED

The idea that medicine and psychology are somehow connected has a long history, dating back at least to ancient Greece. It became somewhat more formalized early in the 20th century in the work of Sigmund Freud, who was trained as a physician. He noticed that some patients showed symptoms of physical illness without any organic disorder. Using principles from his *psychoanalytic theory*, Freud proposed that these symptoms were "converted" from unconscious emotional conflicts (Alexander, 1950). He called this condition *conversion hysteria*; one form it can take is called *glove anesthesia* because only the hand has no feeling. Symptoms like these occur less often in urban than in backwoods areas, perhaps because urbanites realize that medical tests can generally determine if an organic disorder exists (Rosenhan & Seligman, 1984). The need to understand conditions such as conversion hysteria led professionals to develop the first field dedicated to studying the interplay between emotional life and bodily processes.

Psychosomatic Medicine

The field called **psychosomatic medicine** was formed in the 1930s and began publishing the journal *Psychosomatic Medicine* (Alexander, 1950). Its founders were mainly trained in medicine, and their leaders included psychoanalysts and psychiatrists. The field was soon organized as a society now called the American Psychosomatic Society.

The term *psychosomatic* does not mean a person's symptoms are "imaginary"; it means that the mind and body are both involved. Early research in psychosomatic medicine focused on psychoanalytic interpretations for specific, real health problems, including ulcers, high blood pressure, asthma, migraine headaches, and rheumatoid arthritis. For example, Alexander (1950) described the case of a 23-year-old man with a bleeding ulcer and proposed that the man's relationship with his mother created feelings of insecurity and dependence that caused the ulcer. The man's stomach problems later decreased, presumably because he overcame these feelings through therapy. In the 1960s, psychosomatic medicine began to focus on new approaches and theories (Totman, 1982). It is currently a broader field concerned with the interrelationships among psychological and social factors, biological and physiological functions, and the development and course of illness (Lipowski, 1986).

Behavioral Medicine and Health Psychology

Two new fields emerged in the 1970s to study the role of psychology in illness: one is called behavioral medicine, and the other is called health psychology.

The field of **behavioral medicine** formed an organization called the Society of Behavioral Medicine, which publishes the *Journal of Behavioral Medicine*. This field has two defining characteristics (Gentry, 1984). First, its membership is *interdisciplinary*, coming from a wide variety of fields, including psychology, sociology, and various areas of medicine. Second, it grew out of the perspective in psychology called *behaviorism*, which proposed that people's behavior results from two types of learning:

- *Classical (or respondent) conditioning*, in which a stimulus (the conditioned stimulus) gains the ability to elicit a response through association with a stimulus (the unconditioned stimulus) that already elicits that response.

- *Operant conditioning*, in which behavior is changed because of its consequences: *reinforcement* (reward) strengthens the behavior, *punishment* suppresses it.

Conditioning methods had shown a good deal of success as therapeutic approaches in helping people modify problem *behaviors*, such as overeating, and *emotions*, such as anxiety and fear (Sarafino, 2001). By the 1970s, physiological psychologists had clearly shown that psychological events—particularly emotions—influence bodily functions, such as blood pressure. And researchers had demonstrated that people can learn to control various physiological systems if they are given *feedback* as to what the systems are doing (Miller, 1978).

Why were these findings important? They revealed that the link between the mind and the body is more direct and pervasive than was previously thought. Soon they led to an important therapeutic technique called *biofeedback*, whereby a person's physiological processes, such as blood pressure, are monitored by the person so that he or she can gain voluntary control over them. This process involves operant conditioning—the feedback serves as reinforcement.

As we shall see in later chapters, biofeedback has proven to be useful in treating a variety of health problems, such as headaches.

Behaviorism also served as an important foundation for **health psychology,** a field that is principally within the discipline of psychology. The American Psychological Association has many divisions, or subfields; the Division of Health Psychology was introduced in 1978 (Wallston, 1993) and soon began publishing the journal *Health Psychology.* Joseph Matarazzo (1982), the first president of the Division, outlined four goals of health psychology. Let's look at these goals and some ways psychologists can contribute to them.

- *To promote and maintain health*. Health psychologists study such topics as why people do and do not smoke cigarettes, use safety belts in cars, drink alcohol, and eat particular diets. As a result, they can help in the design of school health-education programs and media campaigns to encourage healthful lifestyles and behaviors.

- *To prevent and treat illness*. Psychological principles have been applied effectively in preventing illness, such as in reducing high blood pressure and, therefore, the risk of heart disease and stroke. For those people who become seriously ill, psychologists with clinical training can help them adjust to their current condition, rehabilitation program, and future prospects, such as reduced work or sexual activity.

- *To identify the causes and diagnostic correlates of health, illness, and related dysfunction*. Health psychologists study the causes of disease; the research we saw earlier showing the importance of personality factors in the development of illness is an example of the work toward this goal. Psychologists also study physiological and perceptual processes, which affect people's experience of physical symptoms.

- *To analyze and improve health care systems and health policy*. Health psychologists contribute toward this goal by studying how characteristics or functions of hospitals, nursing homes, medical personnel, and medical costs affect patients. The resulting knowledge enables them to make recommendations for improvement, suggesting ways to help physicians and nurses become more sensitive and responsive to the needs of patients and to make the system more accessible to individuals who fail to seek treatment.

CLINICAL METHODS AND ISSUES

Behaviorism's Legacy: Progress in Health Psychology's Goals

The perspective of behaviorism led to the development of *behavior modification* techniques, which use principles of learning and cognition to understand and change people's behavior (Sarafino, 2001). These techniques can be grouped into two categories: **Behavioral methods** apply mainly principles of operant and classical conditioning to change behavior. **Cognitive methods** are geared toward changing people's feelings and thought processes, such as by helping individuals identify and alter problematic beliefs; most cognitive methods were developed after the mid-1960s.

How can professionals use behavioral and cognitive methods to promote and maintain people's health and to prevent and treat illness? Let's consider two examples. Using behavioral methods, psychologists reduced work-related injuries at worksites with high accident rates by applying a program of reinforcement for safety behaviors (Fox, Hopkins, & Anger, 1987). In an example that used cognitive methods with patients suffering from chronic back pain, a psychologist reduced their degree of pain, depression, and disability by providing training in ways to relax and think differently about the pain (Turner, 1982).

Psychologists work to achieve these goals in a variety of ways, some of which involve applying techniques that were derived from behaviorism. (Go to .)

An Integration

By now you may be wondering, "Aren't psychosomatic medicine, behavioral medicine, and health psychology basically the same?" In a sense they are. In large measure, the three fields are separate mainly in an organizational sense; they have very similar goals, study similar topics, and share the same knowledge. Many professionals are members of all three organizations. The main distinction among the fields is the degree of focus they give to specific topics and viewpoints. Psychosomatic medicine continues to be closely tied to medical disciplines, especially in the application of psychiatry to understanding and treating physical illness. Behavioral medicine tends to focus on interventions that do not use drugs or surgery. And health psychology draws heavily on other psychology subfields—clinical, social, developmental, experimental, and physiological—to identify and alter lifestyle and emotional processes that lead to illness. Although this book focuses mainly on health psychology, we should keep in mind the overlap with and contributions of the fields of psychosomatic medicine and behavioral medicine. These fields have slightly different perspectives, but they share the view that

health and illness result from the interplay of biological, psychological, and social forces.

HEALTH PSYCHOLOGY: THE PROFESSION

Because the field of health psychology is so new, the profession is developing. Most health psychologists work in hospitals, clinics, and academic departments of colleges and universities. In these positions, they either provide direct help to patients or give indirect help through research, teaching, and consulting activities.

The direct help health psychologists provide generally relates to the patient's psychological adjustment to and management of health problems. Health psychologists with clinical training can provide therapy for emotional and social adjustment problems that being ill or disabled can produce—for example, in reducing the patient's feelings of depression. They can also help patients manage the health problem by, for instance, teaching them psychological methods, such as biofeedback, to control pain.

Health psychologists provide indirect help, too. Their research provides information about lifestyle and personality factors in illness and injury. They can apply this and other knowledge to design programs that help people lead more healthful lifestyles, such as by preventing or quitting cigarette smoking. They can also educate physicians and the other health care workers toward a fuller understanding of the psychosocial needs of patients.

The qualifications for becoming a health psychologist include completion of the doctoral degree in psychology (Belar, 1997). Additional study may be needed if the doctoral program contained little training in health psychology. *Clinical health psychology* is an accredited specialty of the American Psychological Association. State licensing is required to practice clinical techniques, and board certification is available (Deardorff, 1996).

CURRENT PERSPECTIVES ON HEALTH AND ILLNESS

Once we add the person to the biomedical model, we have a different and broader picture of how health and illness come about. This new perspective, called the **biopsychosocial model,** expands the biomedical view by adding to *biological* factors the influence of *psychological* and *social* factors (Engel, 1977, 1980; Kazarian & Evans, 2001). This new model proposes that all three factors *affect* and *are affected by* the person's health.

THE BIOPSYCHOSOCIAL PERSPECTIVE

We can see elements of the biopsychosocial perspective in the story about Ana at the beginning of the chapter. A possible biological contribution to her becoming overweight might be her inheritance, since her mother is overweight and was heavy as a child. Psychological factors are probably important, as shown in Ana's behavior—she eats too much fattening food and gets little exercise. And, although the story did not describe how social factors play a role in her weight problem, they are probably there—for example, if she imitates her mother's dietary and exercise habits. But we *did* see social factors relating to Ana's condition when her schoolmates taunted her and her parents expressed concern and urged her to join a recreation program. Let's look at the elements of the biopsychosocial model in more detail.

The Role of Biological Factors

What is included in the term *biological factors*? This term includes the genetic materials and processes by

which we inherit characteristics from our parents. It also includes the function and structure of the person's physiology. For example, does the body contain structural defects, such as a malformed heart valve or damage in the brain that impair the operation of these organs? Does the body respond effectively in protecting itself, such as by fighting infection? Does the body overreact sometimes in the protective function, as happens in many allergic reactions to harmless substances such as pollen or dust?

The body is made up of enormously complex physical systems. For instance, it has organs, bones, and nerves, and these are composed of tissues, which in turn consist of cells, molecules, and atoms. The efficient, effective, and healthful functioning of these systems depends on the way these components operate and interact with each other.

The Role of Psychological Factors

When we discussed the role of lifestyle and personality in health and illness earlier, we were describing behavior and mental processes, in other words, psychological factors. Behavior and mental processes are the focus of psychology, and they involve cognition, emotion, and motivation.

Cognition is a mental activity that encompasses perceiving, learning, remembering, thinking, interpreting, believing, and problem solving. How do these cognitive factors affect health and illness? Suppose, for instance, you strongly believe, "Life is not worth living without the things I enjoy." If you enjoy smoking cigarettes, would you quit to reduce your risk of getting cancer or heart disease? Probably not. Or suppose you develop a pain in your abdomen and you remember having had a similar symptom in the past that disappeared in a couple of days. Would you seek treatment? Again, probably not. These examples are just two of the countless ways cognition plays a role in health and illness.

Emotion is a subjective feeling that affects and is affected by our thoughts, behavior, and physiology. Some emotions are positive or pleasant, such as joy and affection, and others are negative, such as anger, fear, and sadness. Emotions relate to health and illness in many ways. For instance, people whose emotions are relatively positive are less disease-prone and more likely to take good care of their health and to recover quickly from an illness than are people whose emotions are relatively negative. We considered these relationships when we discussed the role of personality in illness. Emotions can also be important in people's decisions about seeking treatment. People who are frightened of doctors and dentists may avoid getting the health care they need.

Motivation is a term applied to explanations of why people behave the way they do—why they start some activity, choose its direction, and persist in it. A person who is motivated to feel and look better might begin an exercise program, choose the goals to be reached, and stick with it. Many people are motivated to do what important people in their lives want them to do. Parents who quit smoking because their child pleads with them to protect their health are an example.

The Role of Social Factors

People live in a social world. We have relationships with individual people—a family member, a friend, or an acquaintance—and with groups. As we interact with people, we affect them and they affect us. For example, adolescents often start smoking cigarettes and drinking alcohol as a result of peer pressure (Jessor, 1984). They want very much to be popular and to look "cool" or "tough" to others in their community. These clear and powerful motivational elements are social in nature. But our social world is larger than just the people we know or meet.

On a fairly broad level, our *society* affects the health of individuals by promoting certain values of our culture. One of these values is that being fit and healthy is good. The mass media—television, newspapers, and so on—often reflect these values by setting good examples and urging us to eat well, not to use drugs, and not to drink and drive. The media can do much to promote health, but sometimes they encourage unhealthful behavior, such as when we observe celebrities on television smoking cigarettes or drinking excessively. Can individuals affect society's values? Yes. As part of the society, we can affect its values by writing our opinions to the mass media, selecting which television shows and movies to watch, and buying healthful products, for example.

Our *community* consists of individuals who live fairly near one another, such as in the same town or county, and the local government. The influence of communities is suggested in the research finding that they differ in the extent to which their members practice certain health-related behaviors, such as smoking cigarettes or consuming fatty diets (Diehr et al., 1993). There are many reasons for these differences. For instance, a community's environmental characteristics seem to influence residents' walking and other physical activity (Saelens, Sallis, & Frank, 2003). Residents tend to be more active in communities that have parks and are densely populated rather than sprawling, as in suburbs.

The closest and most continuous social relationships for most people occur within the *family*, which

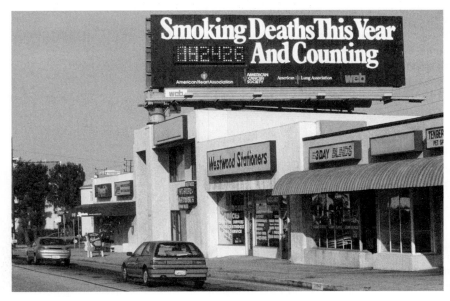

Society can help prevent disease or injury in many ways, such as through advertisements against smoking.

"LORETTA'S DRIVING BECAUSE I'M DRINKING, AND I'M DRINKING BECAUSE SHE'S DRIVING."

Reprinted courtesy of Bunny Hoest.

The role of biological, psychological, and social factors in health and illness is not hard to see. What is more difficult to understand is how health is affected by the *interplay* of these components, as the biopsychosocial model proposes. The next section deals with this interplay.

The Concept of "Systems"

The whole person—as in the sentence, "We need to understand the whole person"—is a phrase we often hear. It reflects our recognition that people and the reasons for their behavior are very complex. Many health professionals strive to consider the impact of all aspects of a person's life as a total entity in understanding health and illness. This approach uses the biopsychosocial model and is sometimes called holistic. This term is derived from the Greek word *holos*, which means "whole" (Lipowski, 1986). But many people today use the term *holistic* to include a broad range of "alternative" approaches to promote health, such as treatments that use aromas and herbs to heal.

George Engel (1980) has proposed that we can conceptualize the whole person by applying the biological concept of "systems." A **system** is a dynamic entity with components that are continuously interrelated. By this definition, your body qualifies as a system, and it includes the immune and nervous systems, which consist of tissues and cells. Your family is a system, too, and so are your community and society. There are levels of systems, as Figure 1–4 depicts. If

can include nonrelatives who live together and share a strong emotional bond. As individuals grow and develop in early childhood, the family has an especially strong influence (Sarafino & Armstrong, 1986). Children learn many health-related behaviors, attitudes, and beliefs from their parents, brothers, and sisters. For instance, parents can set good examples for healthful behavior by using seat belts, serving and eating nutritious meals, exercising, not smoking, and so on. Families can also encourage children to perform healthful behaviors and praise them when they do. Moreover, as we have said, an individual can influence the larger social unit. A family may stop eating certain nutritious foods, such as broccoli or fish, because one member has a tantrum when these foods are served.

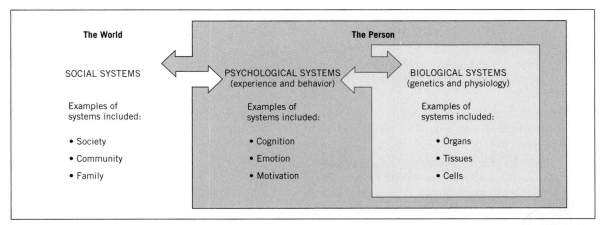

Figure 1–4 A diagram of the interplay of systems in the biopsychosocial model. The person consists of biological and psychological systems, which interrelate; and each of the systems includes component systems. The person interrelates with the social systems of his or her world. Each system can affect and be affected by any of the other systems.

we look at levels within the person, illness in one part of the body can have far-reaching effects: if you fell and seriously injured your leg, your internal systems would be automatically mobilized to help protect the body from further damage. In addition, the discomfort and disability you might experience for days or weeks might affect your social relations with your family and community. As systems, they are entities that are dynamic—or constantly changing—and they have components that interrelate, such as by exchanging energy, substances, and information.

To illustrate how the systems concept can be useful, let's use it to speculate how Ana's weight problem might have come about. Let's assume that she did inherit some factor that affects her weight, such as a liking for sweet foods. When she was a toddler, Ana's parents were not concerned that she was getting heavy because they believed a popular misconception—"A chubby baby is a healthy baby." The meals the family ate usually contained lots of high-fat, high-calorie foods and a sweet dessert. Because Ana was heavy, she was less agile, tired more easily than children who were not overweight, and preferred to engage in sedentary activities, such as playing with dolls or watching television, rather than sports. She and her friends snacked on cookies while watching television commercials that promoted high-fat, sweet breakfast and snack foods, which she got her parents to buy. Thus, interacting biopsychosocial systems can contribute to a person's weight problem.

Using the biopsychosocial model as a guide, researchers have discovered new and important findings and ways to promote people's health and recovery from illness. Here is a sample of discoveries that we will discuss in later chapters:

- Using psychological methods to reduce the anxiety of patients who are awaiting surgery enables them to recover more quickly and leave the hospital sooner.
- Programs that teach safer sex practices have dramatically reduced risky sexual behavior and the spread of HIV infection.
- People who have a high degree of social support from family and friends are healthier and live longer than people who do not.
- Stress impairs the functioning of the immune system.
- Applying psychological and educational programs for cancer patients reduces their feelings of de-

pression and improves their immune system functioning.
- Biofeedback and other psychological techniques can reduce the pain of people who suffer from chronic, severe headaches.

LIFE-SPAN AND GENDER PERSPECTIVES

People change over time through the process called development, and each portion of the life span is affected by happenings in earlier years and affects the happenings in years that will come. Throughout people's lives, health, illness, and the role of different biopsychosocial systems change. Gender also plays a role, such as in the health-related behaviors people perform and the illnesses they develop. This is why it's important to keep the life–span and gender perspectives in mind when we examine health psychology.

In the *life-span perspective*, characteristics of a person are considered with respect to their prior development, current level, and likely development in the future. Health and illness characteristics vary with development. For instance, the kinds of illnesses people have tend to change with age. Compared with older individuals, children suffer from relatively few chronic diseases (USBC, 2003). Illnesses that keep children out of school tend to be short-term infectious diseases, such as colds or the flu. In contrast, many people in late adulthood and old age suffer from heart disease, cancer, and stroke, which often result in disability and death. *Pediatrics* and *geriatrics* are branches of medicine that deal with the health and illness of children and the elderly, respectively.

How do the roles of different biopsychosocial systems change as we develop? Biological systems change in many ways. Virtually all systems of the body grow in size, strength, and efficiency during childhood and decline in old age. The decline can be seen in the slowing down that older people notice in their physical abilities. They have less stamina because the heart and lungs function less efficiently and the muscles are weaker (Tortora & Grabowski, 2003). They also recover from illness and injury more slowly.

Changes occur in psychological systems, too—for example, in cognitive processes. Children's knowledge and ability to think are limited during the preschool years but grow rapidly during later childhood. Before children can assume responsibility for their health, they need to understand how their behavior can affect it. As children get older and their cognitive skills improve, they are more likely to engage in behaviors that promote their health and safety (Maddux et al., 1986). They also become better able to understand the implications of their own illness when they are sick.

How do people's social relationships and systems change with development? For one thing, there are some usual progressions: children usually progress through levels of education, enter a career in adulthood, become parents and grandparents, and retire in old age. Changes in social relationships also relate to health and illness. Children's health is largely the responsibility of adult caregivers—parents and teachers. During the teenage years, adolescents take on more and more of these responsibilities. But age-mates in the community have a powerful influence, and the need to be accepted by peers sometimes leads teens toward unhealthful or unsafe behavior. For example, an adolescent who has a chronic illness that can be controlled—as diabetes can—may neglect his or her medical care to avoid looking and feeling different from other adolescents (La Greca & Stone, 1985).

The *gender perspective* also adds an important dimension to the biopsychosocial perspective in our effort to understand how people deal with issues of health and illness. Males and females differ in their biological functioning; their health-related behaviors and social relationships, such as drinking, dieting, and using safer-sex practices; and the risk of specific illnesses, such as breast cancer.

RELATING HEALTH PSYCHOLOGY TO OTHER SCIENCE FIELDS

Knowledge in health psychology is greatly enriched by information from many other disciplines, including some disciplines within *psychology*, such as the clinical and social areas; *medicine*, including psychiatry and pediatrics; and *allied fields*, such as nursing, nutrition, pharmacology, biology, and social work. We will look at four fields that are very important because they provide information and a context for health psychology.

RELATED FIELDS

To understand health psychology fully, we need to know the context in which health and illness exist.

The field of *epidemiology*—the scientific study of the distribution and frequency of disease and injury—provides part of this context. Researchers in this field determine the occurrence of illness in a given population and organize these data in terms of when the disease or injury occurred, where, and to which age, gender, and racial or cultural groups. Then they attempt to discover why specific illnesses are distributed as they are. You have probably seen the results of epidemiologists' work in the mass media. For example, news reports have described areas of the United States where Lyme disease, a tick-borne illness, occurs at high levels and where certain forms of cancer are linked to high levels of toxic substances in the environment.

Epidemiologists use several terms in describing aspects of their findings (Gerace & Vorp, 1985; Runyan, 1985). We will define five of these terms:

- **Mortality** means death, generally on a large scale. An epidemiologist might report a decrease in mortality from heart disease among women, for instance.

- **Morbidity** means illness, injury, or disability—basically any detectable departure from wellness.

- **Prevalence** refers to the number of cases, such as of a disease or of persons infected or at risk. It includes both continuing (previously reported) and new cases at a given moment in time—for example, the number of cases of asthma as of the first day of the current year.

- **Incidence** refers to the number of *new* cases, such as of illness, infection, or disability, reported during a period of time. An example is the number of tuberculosis cases in the previous year.

- **Epidemic** usually refers to the situation in which the incidence, generally of an infectious disease, has increased rapidly.

Some of these terms are used with the word *rate*, which adds relativity to the meaning. For instance, the mortality rate gives the number of deaths per number of people in a given population during a specified period of time. An example might be a mortality rate of 6 babies per 1,000 births dying in their first year of life in the current year in Canada.

Another discipline of importance to health psychology is *public health*, the field concerned with protecting, maintaining, and improving health through organized effort in the community. People who work in public health do research and set up programs to promote or provide immunizations, sanitation, health education and awareness, and community health services (Runyan, 1985). This field studies health and illness in the context of the community as a social system. The success of public health programs and the way individual people react to them are of interest to health psychologists.

Two other related fields are sociology and anthropology (Adler & Stone, 1979). *Sociology* focuses on human social life; it examines groups or communities of people and evaluates the impact of various social factors, such as the mass media, population growth, epidemics, and institutions. *Medical sociology* is a subfield that studies a wide range of issues related to health, including the impact of social relationships on the distribution of illness, social reactions to illness, socioeconomic factors of health care use, and the way hospital services and medical practices are organized. *Anthropology* includes the study of human cultures. Its subfield, *medical anthropology*, examines differences in health and health care across cultures: How do the nature and definition of illness vary across different cultures? How do people in these cultures react to illness, and what methods do they use to treat disease or injury? How do they structure health care systems? Without the knowledge from sociology and anthropology, health psychologists would have a very narrow view. Knowledge from sociology and anthropology gives us a broad social and cultural view of medical issues and allows us to consider different ways to interpret and treat illness.

The combined information health psychologists obtain from epidemiology, public health, sociology, and anthropology paints a broad picture for us. It describes the social systems in which health, illness, and the person exist and develop. (Go to 💡.)

HEALTH AND PSYCHOLOGY ACROSS CULTURES

Health and illness have changed across the history and cultures of the world, as the following excerpt shows:

> Less than a hundred years ago the infant mortality rate in Europe and North America was as high as it is in the developing world now. In New York City in the year 1900, for example, the IMR [infant mortality rate] was approximately 140 per 1,000— about the same as in Bangladesh today. In the city

of Birmingham, England a survey taken in 1906 revealed an IMR of almost 200 per 1,000—higher than almost any country in the world in the 1980s. A look behind these statistics also shows that the main causes of infant death in New York and Birmingham *then* were much the same as in the developing world *now*—diarrheal disease and malnutrition, respiratory infections, and whooping cough. (UNICEF, cited in Skolnick, 1986, p. 20)

The world-view we get from historical-cultural comparisons can be quite dramatic. Each country's present culture is different from every other's and from the culture it had 200 years ago. Lifestyles have changed in each culture, and so has the pattern of illnesses that afflict its citizens.

Sociocultural Differences in Health

The term **sociocultural** means involving or relating to social and cultural factors, such as ethnic and income variations within and across nations. Epidemiologists have examined sociocultural differences in health and found, for instance, that certain forms of cancer, particularly stomach cancer, have far higher prevalence rates in Japan than in the United States today, but the reverse is true for breast (in females) and prostate (in males) cancers (Williams, 1990). Furthermore, large sociocultural differences exist in rates of specific cancers within the same country, too (Williams & Rucker, 1996). In the United States, for example, Chinese-Americans have far higher rates of liver cancer than Caucasians do. The differences we see in illness patterns between countries, regions, or ethnic groups result from many factors, including heredity, environmental pollution, economic barriers to health care, and cultural differences in people's diets, health-related beliefs, and values (Flack et al., 1995; Whitfield et al., 2002). Although people around the world value good health, some people feel that maintaining health is more important than others do. It seems reasonable that the more people value their health, the more likely they are to take care of it.

Sociocultural Differences in Health Beliefs and Behavior

Differences across history and culture can also be seen in the ideas people have about the *causes* of

Related Nonpsychology Careers

The process of providing care for a patient who is suffering from a chronic illness, serious injury, or disability involves a variety of professionals working together with physicians as a team. Each professional has specific training for a special role in the treatment or rehabilitation process. Most of them have some education in psychology. We've already seen how health psychologists can play a role. Let's look at some careers outside of psychology and the training they require, as described in the *Occupational Outlook Handbook* (USDL, 2004).

Nurses and Physician Assistants

There are two overall categories of nurses: *registered nurses* (RNs) and *licensed practical nurses* (LPNs). RNs work in hospitals, community health clinics, physicians' offices, and industrial settings. They assess and record patients' symptoms and progress, conduct tests, administer medications, assist in rehabilitation, provide instructions for self-treatment, and instruct patients and their families in ways to improve or maintain their health. RNs often deal with mental and emotional aspects of the patient as well. All RNs throughout the United States must be licensed to practice, have graduated from an approved training program in nursing, and have passed a national examination. RN training programs vary in structure and length; college and university programs take 4 or 5 years and lead to a baccalaureate degree.

LPNs work in hospitals, clinics, physicians' offices, and patients' homes. They perform nursing activities that require less training than those performed by RNs. For example, they take and record temperatures and blood pressures, administer certain medications, change dressings, assist physicians or RNs, and help patients with personal hygiene. Like RNs, all LPNs in the United States must be licensed to practice and have graduated from an approved practical nursing program. Training programs for LPNs take about a year to complete and are offered through various types of institutions, such as trade and vocational schools, community and junior colleges, and hospitals.

Physician assistants and *nurse practitioners* usually work closely with medical doctors, performing routine tasks that physicians ordinarily did in the past, such as examining patients with symptoms that do not appear serious and explaining treatment details. Training involves a program of about 2 years of study; admission often requires that applicants have a relevant bachelor's degree, such as in nursing, and prior health care experience.

Dietitians

Dietitians study and apply knowledge about food and its effect on the body. They do this in a variety of settings, such as hospitals, clinics, nursing homes, colleges, and schools. Some dietitians are administrators; others work directly with patients in assessing nutritional needs, implementing and evaluating dietary plans, and instructing patients and their families on ways to adhere to needed diets after discharge from the hospital. Some dietitians work for social service agencies in the community, where they counsel people on nutritional practices to help maintain health and speed recovery when they are ill.

Becoming a dietitian requires a bachelor's or master's degree specializing in nutrition sciences or institutional management. To become a Registered Dietitian, the individual must complete a supervised internship and pass an exam.

Physical Therapists

Many patients need help in restoring functional movement to parts of their body and relieving pain. If they have suffered a disabling injury or disease, treatment may be needed to prevent or limit permanent disability. *Physical therapists* plan and apply treatment for these goals in rehabilitation.

To plan the treatment, physical therapists review the patient's records and perform tests or measurements of muscle strength, motor coordination, endurance, and range of motion of the injured body part. Treatment is designed to increase the strength and function of the injured part and aid in the patient's adaptation to having reduced physical abilities, which may be quite drastic. People who have suffered severe strokes are sometimes left partially paralyzed, for instance. The most universal technique used in

Related Nonpsychology Careers

physical therapy involves exercise, generally requiring little effort initially and becoming more and more challenging. Another technique involves electrical stimulation to move paralyzed muscles or reduce pain. Physical therapists also give instructions for carrying out everyday tasks, such as tying shoelaces or cooking meals. If the patient needs to use adaptive devices, such as crutches or a prosthesis (replacement limb), the therapist provides training.

All physical therapists throughout the United States must have a degree or certificate from an approved training program and be licensed by passing an exam. A bachelor's degree can provide acceptable training to enter the profession, but a master's degree in physical therapy is becoming the minimum educational requirement.

Occupational Therapists

Occupational therapists help physically, mentally, and emotionally disabled individuals gain skills needed for daily activities in a work setting, at school, in the community, and at home. Their patients are often people who had these skills at one time, but lost them because of an injury or disease, such as muscular dystrophy. These professionals usually specialize in working with a particular age group, such as the elderly, and a type of disability—physical, for example. They design and implement educational, vocational, and recreational activities based on the patient's age and the type and degree of disability. The program for a child, for instance, might involve academic tasks and crafts; for an adult, it might involve typing, driving a vehicle, and using hand and power tools.

Occupational therapists in the United States must have a degree or certificate from an approved training program and be licensed by passing an exam. Training requires completing a baccalaureate program as well as either a certificate program or a master's degree in occupational therapy.

Social Workers

The field of *social work* is quite broad. Probably most social workers are employed in mental health programs, but many others work in hospitals, nursing homes, rehabilitation centers, and public health programs. When working with people who are physically ill or disabled, social workers help patients and their families make psychological and social adjustments to the illness and obtain needed community services, including income maintenance. Thus, social workers may arrange for needed nursing care at home after a patient leaves the hospital or refer a patient for vocational counseling and occupational therapy if the illness or disability requires a career change.

Training requires a bachelor's degree in a social science field, usually social work, but often a degree in psychology or sociology is sufficient. Most states mandate some form of licensing or certification. Many positions require an advanced degree, typically a master's in social work, the MSW degree.

---

illness. Recall our discussion of the widespread beliefs in the Middle Ages that evil spirits caused illness. Today, educated people in technological societies generally reject such ideas. But less sophisticated people often do not, as the following excerpt shows:

I've heard of people with snakes in their body, how they got in there I don't know. And they take 'em someplace to a witch doctor and snakes come out. My sister, she had somethin', a snake that was in her arm. She was a young woman. I can remember her bein' sick, very sick, and someone told her about this healer in another little town. And I do know they taken her there. This thing was just runnin' up her arm, whatever it was, just runnin' up her arm. You could actually *see* it. (Snow, 1981, p. 86)

A disadvantaged person in the United States gave this account, which is typical of the level of knowledge generally found in people in underdeveloped regions or countries. This is important to recognize because the large majority of people in the world live in underdeveloped societies.

The United States has been described as a melting pot for immigrants from every corner of the world. Immigrants carry with them health ideas and customs from their former countries. For example, many Chinese immigrants have entered their new country with the belief that illness results from an imbalance of two opposing forces, *yin* and *yang*, within the body (Campbell & Chang, 1981). According to this view, too much *yin* causes colds and gastric disorders, for instance, and too much *yang* causes fever and dehydration. Practitioners of traditional Chinese medicine treat illnesses by prescribing special herbs and foods or by using *acupuncture*, in which fine needles are inserted under the skin at special locations of the body. These methods are intended to correct the balance of *yin* and *yang*. Immigrants and others with these beliefs who are sick will often use these methods instead of or as a supplement to treatment by an American physician. They may also pressure their children and grandchildren to do this, too. As an example, a pregnant Chinese woman who was a registered nurse "followed her obstetrician's orders, but at the same time, under pressure from her mother and mother-in-law, ate special herbs and foods to insure birth of a healthy baby" (Campbell & Chang, 1981, p. 164).

Religion is an aspect of culture. Many religions include beliefs that relate to health and illness. For instance, Jehovah's Witnesses reject the use of blood and blood products in medical treatment (Sacks & Koppes, 1986). Christian Scientists reject the use of medicine totally, believing that only mental processes in the sick person can cure the illness. As a result, sick persons need prayer and counsel as treatment to help these processes along (Henderson & Primeaux, 1981). These beliefs are controversial and have led to legal conflicts between members of these religions and health authorities in the United States, particularly when parents reject medical treatments for life-threatening illnesses for their children. In such cases, the physician and hospital can move quickly to seek an immediate judicial decision (Sacks & Koppes, 1986).

Some religions include specific beliefs that promote healthful lifestyles. Seventh-day Adventists, for example, believe that the body is the "temple of the Holy Spirit" and cite this belief as the reason people should take care of their bodies. Adventists abstain from using tobacco, alcohol, and nonmedically pre-scribed drugs. In addition, they promote in fellow members a concern for exercise and eating a healthful diet (Henderson & Primeaux, 1981). Although it is clear that cultural factors play a role in health, our knowledge about this role is meager and needs to be expanded through more research.

RESEARCH METHODS

Contemporary mass media present lots of scientific findings. Diets high in fiber and low in saturated fats are good for your health. Smoking is not. Dozens of toxic, or poisonous, chemicals can cause cancer. How do scientists discover these relationships? What methods do they use?

Scientists do research. Often their research is planned and conducted to test a **theory**—a *tentative explanation* of why and under what circumstances certain phenomena occur. For example, a leading theory of the cause of heart disease is that excess *cholesterol*, a fatty substance in the blood, is deposited on artery walls. Because this substance, like other saturated fats, is not water soluble, it builds up on the walls over time. This buildup hardens and narrows the diameter of the artery, thereby reducing the flow of blood and nutrients and causing tissue damage to the heart or arteries. Cholesterol comes from two sources. Most cholesterol in the blood is manufactured by the body; the rest of it comes from the foods we eat—especially red meats, egg yolks, butter, and most cheeses.

The cholesterol theory is one of several useful theories of heart disease. By useful we don't necessarily mean that it is correct. We mean that it:

- Is clearly stated.
- Brings together or organizes known facts.
- Relates information that previously seemed unrelated.
- Enables us to make predictions, such as what would happen if cholesterol levels were reduced.

Useful theories play an important role in all sciences. Because theories offer predictions, they guide research programs by suggesting a "road map" of relationships to study.

As you think about the causes of heart disease, you'll realize that both the illness and the theoretical cause—in this case, high levels of cholesterol—can change or vary from one time to another and from one individual to another. That is, the condition of the heart and arteries and the amount of cholesterol in the blood are not constant. Because these things *vary*, they are called *variables*. A **variable** is any measurable characteristic of people, objects, or events that may change. The variables studied in research are of two types: an *independent variable* is studied for its potential or expected influence, as in the case of cholesterol levels; a *dependent variable* is assessed because its value, such as the condition of the heart, is expected to "depend" on the independent variable.

Researchers use a variety of *experimental* and *non-experimental* methods to study health-related variables like the ones we've discussed (Sarafino, 2005).

EXPERIMENTS

An **experiment** is a controlled study in which researchers manipulate an independent variable to study its effect on a dependent variable. In a well-designed experiment—which is often called a *trial* in health research—all other variables are controlled or held constant. The term *manipulate* means that the researchers produce or introduce the levels of the independent variable they are studying.

The Experimental Method: A Hypothetical Example

To illustrate the experimental method, let's see how researchers might test the cholesterol theory of heart disease. One prediction, or *hypothesis*, from the theory is that people's incidence of heart disease should decrease if they reduce their cholesterol levels. We could test this hypothesis by lowering some people's cholesterol levels and seeing if these people develop fewer heart attacks over a suitable period of time than they otherwise would. How can we lower their cholesterol levels? There are two ways to manipulate this independent variable, both of which would require including medical professionals in the research team. One way is to alter the people's diets, and the other is to have them take an anticholesterol drug regularly. We will use the latter approach and assume, for our example, that the drug is new and the only one available.

The first thing we need to do is to select a sample of people—preferably middle-aged, because they have a relatively high risk of having a heart attack in the near future. Then we assign them *randomly* to the conditions or groups in the experiment. One way to assign them randomly is to put their names on cards in a bowl, mix up the cards, and draw the cards out one at a time. The first name drawn would be assigned to one group, the second name to another group, and so on. By doing this, we distribute other characteristics, such as their personality traits and genetic factors, fairly equally across the groups. As a result, the groups will be equivalent: the characteristics will have about the same impact on the dependent variable (heart attacks) for each of the groups.

To test the hypothesis, we will need two groups of people. One group receives the experimental treatment, the anticholesterol pills, and is called the *experimental group*. The other group receives their usual care without the drug, and is called the *control group* (or *comparison* group). By administering the drug to and lowering the cholesterol level of one group, but not the other, we are manipulating the independent variable. We then observe over several years the incidence of heart attacks. If the experimental group has fewer heart attacks than the control group, the hypothesis is supported.

You may be wondering, "Isn't it possible that a decrease in heart attacks for the experimental group could result *not* from the drug per se, but simply from taking *any* substance a medical person prescribes?" Sometimes people's beliefs or expectations can affect their health (Ader, 1997; Sobel, 1990). To control for this possibility, we would have a third group, which would receive an inert, or inactive, substance or procedure—called a **placebo**—in the form of pills that look like medicine. The placebo group would be given the same instructions as the experimental group, and both would have equal expectations about the effectiveness of the pills. Any influence the placebo has on the dependent variable is called a *placebo effect*.

One other control procedure is needed: the person who distributes the pills should not know which pills contain the active drug. Why? This person could inadvertently bias the outcome of the experiment, such as by giving instructions offhandedly to the placebo group and emphatically and precisely to the experimental group. Being unaware of which individuals are getting the experimental treatment is called being *blind* as to the treatment. Since both the individuals receiving and distributing the pills are unaware,

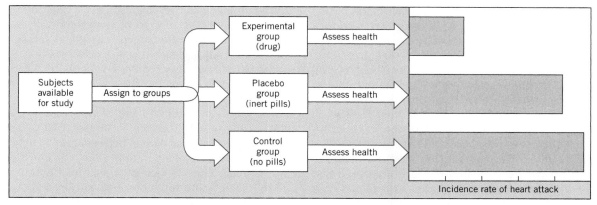

Figure 1–5 The left-hand portion of this diagram shows how the study would be carried out. Subjects are assigned to groups, and, after a suitable period of time, the researcher checks whether they have had heart attacks. The right-hand portion illustrates how the results might appear on a graph: subjects who received the anticholesterol drug had far fewer heart attacks than subjects in the placebo group, who had somewhat fewer attacks than those in the control group.

the method we are using is called the **double-blind** procedure.

Now that we have included these control procedures, let's look at the outcome of our hypothetical experiment. As Figure 1–5 shows, the people in the experimental group had far fewer heart attacks than those in the other groups. Thus we can conclude that lowering cholesterol levels in the blood causes a decrease in heart disease, as the theory predicts. Notice also in the graph that the people in the placebo group had somewhat fewer heart attacks than the controls. This suggests a placebo effect, with expectancy having some effect on heart disease, but not nearly as much as the active ingredient in the anticholesterol drug.

You may have noticed that our conclusion used the word *causes*: lowering cholesterol "causes" a decrease in heart disease. To make a *cause-effect* conclusion, we must be able to see that three criteria have been met:

- The levels of the independent and dependent variables corresponded or varied together.
- The cause preceded the effect.
- All other plausible causes have been ruled out.

Well-designed experiments meet these requirements because the researchers equate the groups in advance, manipulate the independent variable, and control variables that are not being studied. Other

research approaches do not use experimental methods and do not provide the ability to determine what causes what.

Comparing Experimental and Nonexperimental Methods

Research always involves the study of variables, but in *nonexperimental methods*, the researchers *do not manipulate an independent variable*. In addition, there is frequently less opportunity for precise measurement and for control of variables not being studied. As a result, although nonexperimental methods may be used to point out relationships between variables, they do *not* provide direct and unambiguous tests of cause-effect relationships.

Nonexperimental methods are nevertheless very valuable and have some important advantages. Sometimes it is simply not possible or feasible to assign subjects randomly and manipulate the variable of interest. We cannot manipulate the past lifestyles of people, for instance; the past has already happened. Nor can we have individuals in one group of a study do harmful things they would ordinarily not do simply to test an important theory. For instance, it would be unethical to assign people of a sample to a group in which they must smoke cigarettes for the next 5 years if some of these people do not smoke or want to quit. Even if it were ethical, nonsmokers might refuse to do it. What if we didn't randomly assign individuals to groups? If we do not randomly assign them, the groups are not likely to be equal at the start of the study with respect to characteristics, such as genetics or past lifestyle, that could affect the outcome of the research. In situations like this in which ethical considerations prevent the study of humans in research, animals are sometimes used.

In many cases, the aim of a research project requires only that an association between variables be demonstrated. We may want to know, for instance, which people are at greatest risk for a disease so that we may help them avert it. Studies to determine risk factors are examples, which have revealed that people who are among the most likely to develop heart disease are male and/or over 50 years old (AHA, 2004). Researchers can determine this relationship without manipulating gender or age, and a nonexperimental method is, in fact, the most appropriate technique.

The rest of our examination of research methods will focus on nonexperimental approaches in research relating to health psychology and continue to use the cholesterol theory of heart disease as the basis for research examples. Let's turn to correlational studies as the first of these methods.

CORRELATIONAL STUDIES

The term *correlation* refers to the *co* or joint relation that exists between variables—changes in one variable correspond with changes in another variable. Suppose, for example, we did a study of two variables: heart function and people's diets, particularly the amount of cholesterol they consume. A measure of heart function is *cardiac output*, the amount of blood the heart pumps per minute. Working with a physician, we recruit a sample of, say, 200 middle-aged adults and have them keep detailed records of their diets for the 2 weeks prior to the visit when the physician measures their cardiac output. We then calculate the amount of cholesterol consumed on the basis of their records.

Once we know the cardiac output and cholesterol intake of each of the subjects, we can assess the degree to which these variables are related. This is expressed statistically as a **correlation coefficient,** which can range from +1.00 through 0.00 to −1.00. The sign (+ or −) of the coefficient indicates the *direction* of the relationship. A plus sign means that the

association is "positive": high scores on one variable, say, cardiac output, tend to be associated with high scores on another variable, such as blood pressure. Conversely, a minus sign means that the association is "negative": *high* scores on one variable tend to be associated with *low* scores on another variable. For example, high cardiac output is correlated with low concentrations of cells in the blood because cells thicken the blood (Rhoades & Pflanzer, 1996). Thus, there is a negative correlation between cardiac output and concentration of blood cells.

Disregarding the sign of the correlation coefficient, the absolute value of the coefficient indicates the *strength* of association between variables. The higher the absolute value (that is, the closer to either +1.0 or −1.0), the stronger the correlation. As the absolute value decreases, the strength of the relationship declines. A coefficient approximating 0.00 means that the variables are not related. From the information we have just covered, we can now state a definition: **correlational studies** are nonexperimental investigations of the degree and direction of statistical association between two variables.

Let's suppose that our study revealed a strong negative correlation—a coefficient of −.72—between cardiac output and cholesterol intake. This would support the cholesterol theory, because low cholesterol intake should produce less fatty buildup to clog the arteries, thereby allowing the heart to pump more blood per minute. But we cannot say on the basis of our study that these events occurred, and we cannot conclude that low cholesterol intake *causes* high cardiac output. Why? Because we did not manipulate any variable—we simply measured what was there. It may be that some variable we did not measure was responsible for the correlation. For example, the people with low cholesterol intake may also have had low concentrations of blood cells, and it may have been this latter factor that was responsible for their high cardiac output. We don't know. We would only know for sure that the two variables have a strong negative relationship.

Although correlational studies typically cannot determine cause-effect relations, they are useful for examining existing relationships and variables that cannot be manipulated, developing hypotheses that may be tested experimentally, and generating predictive information, such as risk factors for health problems.

QUASI-EXPERIMENTAL STUDIES

Sometimes researchers conduct nonexperimental studies by selecting for or assessing an existing variable and then using it to categorize subjects into one of two or more groups, such as male or female, for example, or high, moderate, or low blood cholesterol levels. Investigations of this type are examples of **quasi-experimental studies**—they *look* like experiments because they have separate groups of subjects, but they are not. The variable—gender or cholesterol level—that defines the groups was *not manipulated*, and the subjects *cannot be randomly assigned* to the groups.

We could do a quasi-experimental study relating to the cholesterol theory of heart disease in the following way. Suppose we wanted to see if people's cholesterol level at the time of a heart attack is associated with the severity of the attack. For this study, we could just consult the medical records of heart disease patients, since it is standard practice to assess both variables. We could categorize the patients as having a high- or low-cholesterol level at the time they were admitted to the hospital. Then we would determine whether the attacks were more severe for one group than for the other.

If we found that the high-cholesterol patients had the more severe heart attacks, could we conclude that higher levels of cholesterol in the blood cause more severe attacks? No—for the same reasons we've discussed before. We cannot tell what caused what. In fact, this particular study could have been turned around. We could have categorized the patients on the basis of the severity of their attacks and then compared these groups for cholesterol levels. We would have found the same relationship: severe heart attacks are associated with a high level of cholesterol in the blood.

In general, the conclusions from quasi-experimental studies are basically correlational. The relationships they reveal do not become causal simply because we categorize subjects. There are many variations to the quasi-experimental method. We will look at a few of the more important ones, beginning with retrospective and prospective approaches.

Retrospective and Prospective Approaches

The prefix *retro* means "back" or "backward," and *spective* comes from the Latin word meaning "to look." Thus, the **retrospective approach** uses procedures that look back at the histories of subjects, such as individuals who do or do not have a particular disease. The purpose of this approach is to find commonalities in the people's histories that may suggest why they developed the disease.

How is the retrospective approach used in a quasi-experimental study? We might identify two groups of individuals. One group would consist of people who have already developed a particular illness, such as heart disease. They would be compared against a control group, consisting of similar people without the disease. We would then examine the two groups for characteristics of their histories that are common to one group, but not the other. We might find, for example, that the heart disease victims reported having eaten higher-cholesterol diets during the preceding 10 years than the controls did. Although the retrospective approach is relatively easy to implement, it has a potential shortcoming: when the procedures rely on people's memories, especially of long-past happenings, the likelihood of inaccurate reports increases.

The **prospective approach** uses procedures that look *forward* in the lives of individuals, by studying whether differences in a variable at one point in time are related to differences in another variable at a later time. We could do this to see whether certain characteristics or events in people's lives are associated with their eventual development of one or more diseases. In using the prospective approach, we would start by recruiting a large group of people—say, 2,000—who did not yet have the illness in question, heart disease. Periodically over several years we would interview them, have a physician examine them, and check their medical records. The interviews would inquire about various events and characteristics, such as cholesterol intake. Then we would categorize the people—for instance, as having or not having had a heart attack—and determine whether these groups differed in some earlier aspects of their lives.

What might our study show? We might find that, compared with people who did not have heart attacks, those who did had eaten diets that were much higher in cholesterol. We might also find that changes in people's diets, becoming higher or lower in cholesterol content over the years, corresponded with their suffering an attack. That is, those who consumed increasing amounts of cholesterol had more heart attacks than those whose cholesterol intake decreased. Because this is a quasi-experimental study, we cannot be certain that high-cholesterol diets caused the heart disease. But the prospective approach gives greater plausibility to a causal link than the retrospective approach would. This is because the diets, and changes in them, clearly preceded the heart attacks.

Retrospective and prospective approaches to study health were developed by epidemiologists. These approaches have been useful in identifying risk factors for specific illnesses.

Developmental Approaches

We saw earlier that the life-span perspective adds an important dimension to the study of health and illness. An essential research approach in studying life-span development is to examine and compare subjects at different ages. Of course, the age of the subjects cannot be manipulated; we can assign individuals to groups based on their age, but this assignment is not random. This approach is quasi-experimental, and, therefore, *age* itself cannot be viewed as a cause of health or behavior.

Two basic approaches are used for studying the age variable. In the **cross-sectional approach,** different individuals of different ages are observed at about the same time. The **longitudinal approach** involves the repeated observation of the *same* individuals over a long period of time. The longitudinal approach is like the prospective method, but it focuses specifically on age as a variable. Let's see how the cross-sectional and longitudinal approaches are used.

Suppose we were interested in examining age-related changes in dietary intake of cholesterol among middle-aged adults. If we use a *cross-sectional* approach, we might evaluate the diets of, say, 50 adults at each of three approximate ages—for example, 35, 45, and 55 years—during the current month. On the other hand, if we use a *longitudinal* approach to examine the same age range, we would evaluate the diets of 50 35-year-olds during the current month and again when they are 45 and 55 years of age. This longitudinal study would take 20 years to complete.

Not all longitudinal studies take so long to do. Often a shorter span of ages—sometimes only a few months—is appropriate, depending on the question or issue the researcher wants to resolve. But the longitudinal approach, and the prospective approach in general, is typically more costly in time and money than the cross-sectional approach. Also, the longer a

study lasts, the greater the likelihood that subjects in the sample will be lost. Some will move away, others will lose interest in participating, and still others may die. Despite these difficulties, it is a valuable research approach that is unique in its ability to examine *change and stability in the lives of individuals* across time. For example, our longitudinal study could tell us whether individuals who eat a high-cholesterol diet at age 35 will generally continue to do so many years later. In contrast, a cross-sectional approach loses sight of stability and individual changes.

Now, let's suppose we did our cross-sectional study and found that the cholesterol content of adults' diets decreased with age. We would then like to know why this is so. One possible answer is that people change their diets as they get older because they feel more vulnerable to heart disease. So we asked the oldest group, using the retrospective approach, if they feel more vulnerable and eat less high-cholesterol food today than they used to. Sure enough, they said yes. But another reason for the current age differences in diet could be that the older adults never ate diets as high in cholesterol as those of the younger adults. So we asked the oldest group to describe the diets they ate 10 or 20 years ago. The diets they described contained less cholesterol than their current diets (which we already knew) *and* the current diets of the 35- and 45-year-olds in our study! This finding reflects the fact that the older subjects grew up at a different time, when food preferences or availability may have been different.

The influence of having been born and raised at a different time is called a **cohort effect.** The term *cohort* refers to a group of individuals who have a demographic factor, such as age or social class, in common. As a result, they share a set of experiences that are distinct from those of adjacent cohorts. In developmental approaches, the meaning of "cohort" is similar to "generation," but the amount of time separating adjacent cohorts can be much shorter than the time separating a generation. For example, suppose researchers at a high school planned to present a drug prevention program to all tenth-graders in a particular year. They might compare attitudes about drug use among the tenth-graders at the end of that year with those of two cohorts: tenth-graders 2 years before and 2 years after the program.

How can research methods take cohort effects into account? One way would be to combine the two developmental approaches. Looking back at our study with middle-aged adults, the combined approach could be carried out by selecting and testing 35-, 45-, and 55-year-olds initially. So far the study is cross-sectional, but we would follow most of these same adults longitudinally and add younger subjects along the way. By doing this in a planned and systematic way, we'll have information on cross-sectional differences, changes within each cohort, and differences between cohorts.

Single-Subject Approaches

Sometimes studies are done with just one subject. One type of research that uses this approach is the *case study*, in which a trained researcher constructs a systematic biography from records of the person's history, interviews, and current observation. This kind of research is useful in describing, in depth, the development and treatment of an unusual medical or psychological problem. Other types of research that use one subject are called *single-subject designs*. This approach is often used for demonstrating the usefulness of a new treatment method for a specific medical or psychological problem. In the simplest of these designs, the statuses of the patient's condition at the beginning and end of therapy are compared. Often, followup assessments are made weeks or months later to see if the patient's condition has regressed. Some single-subject designs have additional phases or features that enable them to provide strong evidence for cause-effect relationships.

The principal disadvantage of single-subject approaches is that information on only one subject, no matter how detailed it is, may not describe what would be found with other individuals. A major purpose of psychological research is to collect information that can be applied or generalized to other people. Nevertheless, studies using one subject stimulate the development of new treatment procedures and suggest topics for further research.

GENETICS RESEARCH

In the 19th century, Charles Darwin speculated that unseen particles called *gemmules* were present in the sperm and ovum. Darwin's concept of gemmules formed the basis for the search for genetic materials. What did this search yield?

Genetic Materials and Transmission

Researchers discovered threadlike structures called *chromosomes* and proposed that these structures contained units called *genes*. Soon they determined the basic substance in all genetic material—*deoxyribonucleic acid*, or DNA for short—and described its structure. Today we know that DNA determines our growth patterns and physical structures (Tortora & Grabowski, 2003). We also know that genes are discrete particles of DNA that are strung together in chromosomes and transmitted from parent to child. Each parent contributes half of the genetic information we inherit.

Chromosomes have identifying features. Photographs taken through a microscope can be arranged according to the size and shape of chromosome pairs. One pair is called the *sex chromosomes* because they carry the genes that will determine whether an individual will be female or male. The normal sex chromosomes for males consist of one large chromosome (called an X chromosome) and one small chromosome (called a Y chromosome); females have two X chromosomes. As with chromosomes, genes come in pairs. Although a single pair of genes may determine some traits a person inherits, others require many genes. And some traits occur in the presence of a single gene, with the paired gene making little or no contribution. Such genes are said to be *dominant*. On the other hand, when a trait occurs only if two identical genes make up the pair, these genes are called *recessive*.

Twin and Adoption Studies

How do psychologists and other scientists determine whether hereditary factors influence people's health and illness? The methods are based on a distinction between two types of twins. *Monozygotic* (MZ), or identical, twins are conceived together and have exactly the same genetic inheritance; *dizygotic* (DZ), or fraternal, twins are conceived separately and are no more genetically similar than singly-born siblings and may, of course, be of different sex.

Much of the research on hereditary factors has focused on the differences in characteristics shown in MZ twins as compared with DZ twins. Investigations using this approach are called **twin studies.** The rationale for making these comparisons, though statistically complex, is logically simple. Because the two individuals in an MZ pair are genetically identical, we can assume that differences between them are environmentally determined. Conversely, the greater the similarity between MZ twins, the more likely it is that the characteristic is genetically influenced. Differences between DZ twins, on the other hand, are due to both genetic and environmental factors, even when they are the same sex. If we could assume that both members of each MZ and same-sex DZ pair that we study have had equal environmental experiences, we could measure genetic influence simply by subtracting the differences for MZ from the differences for DZ twins. Even though both members of each MZ and DZ pair may not have had equal environmental experiences, researchers can take the differences into account—and when they do, important genetic forces are still found (Scarr & Kidd, 1983).

Another way to examine hereditary influences is to study children adopted at very early ages. **Adoption studies** compare traits of adopted children with those of their natural parents and their adoptive parents. Why? Adoptive parents contribute greatly to the rearing environment but are genetically unrelated to the children; the natural parents are genetically related to the children but play little or no role in rearing them. So, if adopted children are more similar to their natural parents than to their adoptive parents, we then have evidence for heredity's influence.

Let's look at a few conclusions relevant to health psychology that have come from twin and adoption studies. First, heredity affects not only physical characteristics, such as height and weight, but also physiological functions, including heart rate and blood pressure (Ditto, 1993). Second, genetic disorders can produce very high levels of cholesterol in the blood, making their victims susceptible to heart disease at very early ages (AMA, 2003). Third, some evidence indicates that heredity has its greatest impact on people's health early in life, and by old age the role of habits and lifestyle become increasingly important (Harris et al., 1992). Fourth, although genetic factors affect people's risk of developing cancer, environmental factors appear to play a stronger role for most people (Lichtenstein et al., 2000).

Linking Specific Genes with Diseases

After having identified which disorders have a genetic basis, researchers began looking for links to specific genes. We now know that every human cell contains 30,000 to 40,000 genes, and almost all of the human system of genes have been identified and mapped

(IHGSC, 2001). Genes control a vast number of traits, including more than 3,000 diseases. For some diseases, researchers have even pinpointed the exact gene locations. We will look at a few of these traits and diseases.

Sickle-cell anemia is a hereditary disease whose victims are usually Black people. In the United States, nearly 10% of the Black population carry a recessive gene for this disease and do not have the disorder (Raphael, 1999). But when a person has two of these genes, the body manufactures large quantities of sickle-shaped red blood cells. Compared with normal blood cells, these defective cells carry little oxygen and tend to clump together in the bloodstream—often they cannot pass through capillaries. As a result, the oxygen supply to vital organs becomes inadequate, and tissue damage often occurs. The condition, which usually develops in childhood, produces painful episodes, progressive organ failure, and brain damage.

Another recessive disease is *phenylketonuria* (PKU). In this disease, which occurs more frequently among Whites than other racial groups, the baby's body fails to produce a necessary enzyme for metabolizing phenylalanine, a toxic amino acid present in many common foods (AMA, 2003). If the disease is not treated, the amino acid builds up and causes brain damage. Placing PKU babies on special diets as soon as possible after birth can prevent this. When the brain is more fully developed after about 5 years of age, many PKU children can switch to normal diets. PKU provides a good example of an inherited disease that can be controlled by modifying the victim's behavior.

Researchers are also closing in on certain *oncogenes*, which are genes that can cause cancer. Researchers have, for example, found oncogenes for certain types of cancers of the colon (Bodmer et al., 1987), breast (Chen et al., 1995; Wooster et al., 1995), skin (Hussussian et al., 1994), lung (Rodenhuis et al., 1987), and prostate (Lee et al., 1994). Oncogenes can be normal genes or mutations that may result from exposure to harmful environmental agents, such as tobacco smoke. Although we don't know fully what causes genes to mutate into oncogenes, assume for a moment that this mutation can result from engaging in certain behaviors, such as smoking cigarettes and eating diets that are high in fats and low in fiber. If this were true, as many researchers believe, we would have additional evidence that behavioral risk factors for cancer constitute major causal links in its development and support for biopsychosocial determinants of this disease.

Which Research Method Is Best?

We have discussed a variety of research methods that are useful in health psychology. Which one is best? Some scientists might say that the experiment is best because it can uncover cause-effect relationships. But precise control and manipulation do not always yield results that help us understand real-life behavior. For example, studying behavior in experimental settings sometimes involves artificial conditions, such as precisely occurring events and special equipment. To the extent that these conditions are unlike the subjects' real world, their behavior may be influenced. As a result, when reading about an experiment, it is useful to keep two questions in mind: Does the experimental situation approximate anything the subjects might experience in real life? If the experimental situation is highly artificial, what specific effect might this have on the outcome of the experiment? A new method called *ecological momentary assessment* may avoid these and other problems in health psychology research by using devices, such as pagers, to cue and collect data on individuals periodically in their day-to-day living (Shiffman & Stone, 1998).

In a sense, all the research methods we discussed are "best," since the investigator must select the most suitable method(s) to answer the specific question(s) under study. This leads us to a final point: it is possible and desirable to use experimental and nonexperimental methods *simultaneously* in one study. Suppose, for instance, we wanted to find out whether people's reading information about the health effects of excessive cholesterol would induce them to modify their diets. Using experimental methods, we would manipulate the independent variable in the following way: the experimental group would read the cholesterol information and a control group might read some unrelated material. But isn't it possible that the success of this experiment might depend on a variable that cannot be manipulated, such as the subjects' age or gender? People who are 50 years of age might be more inclined to follow recommendations to lower their cholesterol levels than people who are 20, for example. We could examine both variables by testing experimental and control groups for each of the two ages. Note, however, that the kinds of conclusions yielded by each variable will differ; only the manipulated variable can yield unambiguous causal statements.

SUMMARY

Health and illness are overlapping concepts that exist along a continuum. One end of the illness/wellness continuum is dominated by health—a positive state of physical, mental, and social well-being that varies over time; the other end is dominated by illness, which produces signs, symptoms, and disabilities. The patterns of illness affecting people have changed across history, especially in the 20th century. Compared with earlier times, today people die at later ages and from different causes. Infectious diseases are no longer the principal cause of death in technological societies around the world. Chronic illnesses now constitute the main health problem in developed nations.

Ideas about physiology, disease processes, and the mind have changed since the early cultures thousands of years ago, when people apparently believed that illness was caused by evil spirits and the like. Greek philosophers produced the earliest written ideas about health and illness, considering how sickness happens and the mind/body problem. During the Middle Ages, the Church had an enormous influence on ideas about illness, and the belief in mystical causes of disease became strong again. Philosophers and scientists from the 17th to the 20th centuries provided the foundation for the biomedical model as a way to conceptualize health and illness.

The biomedical model has been extremely useful, enabling researchers to make great advances in conquering many infectious diseases through the development of vaccines and treatments. But many researchers today have come to recognize that aspects of individual patients—their histories, social relationships, lifestyles, personalities, mental processes, and biological processes—must be included in a full conceptualization of risk factors for illness. As a result, the biopsychosocial model has emerged as an alternative to the biomedical approach and proposed a constant interplay of biological, psychological, and social systems—each interrelated with and producing changes in the others. Psychosomatic medicine, behavioral medicine, and health psychology have introduced new techniques, such as behavioral and cognitive methods, to promote health. Life-span, gender, and sociocultural perspectives add important dimensions to this model by considering the role of people's development, sex, and culture in health and illness. Health psychology draws on knowledge from a variety of other psychology fields and non-psychology fields, such as medicine, biology, social work, epidemiology, public health, sociology, and anthropology. Epidemiology examines the mortality, morbidity, prevalence, incidence, and epidemic status of illnesses.

The study of important variables in health psychology involves the use of experimental and nonexperimental research methods, often testing a theory. A well-designed experiment can lead to cause-effect conclusions because it involves rigorous control, such as with placebo and double-blind methods, and manipulation of variables. Correlational studies test relationships between variables; a correlation coefficient describes an association between variables but does not indicate whether it is a causal relation. Quasi-experimental studies are useful in testing variables that cannot be manipulated, such as the subjects' history, age, and gender; they often use retrospective and prospective approaches. To study people at different ages, researchers use cross-sectional and longitudinal approaches, being watchful of cohort effects. The role of heredity in health and illness can be examined through twin and adoption studies.

KEY TERMS

illness/wellness continuum	health psychology	theory	cross-sectional approach
health	behavioral methods	variable	longitudinal approach
infectious diseases	cognitive methods	experiment	cohort effect
chronic diseases	biopsychosocial model	placebo	twin studies
mind/body problem	system	double blind	adoption studies
biomedical model	mortality	correlation coefficient	
risk factors	morbidity	correlational studies	
personality	prevalence	quasi-experimental studies	
psychosomatic medicine	incidence	retrospective approach	
behavioral medicine	epidemic	prospective approach	
	sociocultural		

2

THE BODY'S PHYSICAL SYSTEMS

Module 1: The Nervous System
How the Nervous System Works
The Central Nervous System
The Peripheral Nervous System

Module 2: The Endocrine System
The Endocrine and Nervous Systems Working
    Together
Adrenal Glands
Other Glands

Module 3: The Digestive System
Food's Journey through Digestive Organs
Using Nutrients in Metabolism

Module 4: The Respiratory System
The Respiratory Tract
Respiratory Function and Disorders

Module 5: The Cardiovascular System
The Heart and Blood Vessels
Blood Pressure
Blood Composition
Cardiovascular Disorders

Module 6: The Immune System
Antigens

The Organs of the Immune System
Soldiers of the Immune System
Defending the Body with an Immune Response
Less-Than-Optimal Defenses

PROLOGUE

When Tom was born 20 years ago, his parents were thrilled. Here was their first child—a delightful baby with such promise for the future. He looked healthy, and his parents were pleased that he was consuming large amounts of milk, often without becoming satiated. They took this as a good sign. But, in this case, it wasn't.

As the weeks went by, Tom's parents noticed that he wasn't gaining as much weight as he should, especially since he was still consuming lots of milk. He started to cough and wheeze often and developed one respiratory infection after another. They became concerned, and so did his pediatrician. After a series of tests, the devastating diagnosis was clear: Tom had *cystic fibrosis*, a chronic, progressive, and eventually fatal disease. Cystic fibrosis is an inherited disease of the respiratory system for which there is no cure and no effective treatment.

Tom has had a difficult life, and so has his family. The respiratory infections he had in infancy were just the beginning. His disease causes thick, sticky secretions that constantly block airways, trap air in the lungs, and help bacteria to thrive. Other body systems also become affected, causing additional problems, such as insufficient absorption of food and vitamins. As a result, he was sick often and remained short, underweight, and weak compared with other children. His social relationships have always been limited and strained, and the burden of his illness has taken its toll on his parents.

When Tom was younger and people asked him, "What do you want to be when you grow up?" he would answer, "I'm going to be an angel when I grow up." What other plans could he have had, realisti-cally? At 20, he has reached the age by which half of the victims of cystic fibrosis die. Physical complications, such as heart damage, that generally afflict several body systems in the last stages of this disease have begun to appear.

We can see in Tom's story that biological factors, such as heredity, can impact health; illness can alter social relationships; and all interrelated physiological systems of the body can be affected. In this chapter we outline the major physical systems of the body. Our discussion focuses on the normal functions of these systems, but we consider some important problems, too. What determines the degree of paralysis a person suffers after injury to the spine? How does stress affect our body systems? What is a heart attack, and what causes it?

This chapter is organized into six *modules* that can be covered *all at once* or *distributed* to other chapters, depending on the approach the instructor prefers. You will find notices at appropriate points in later chapters, each telling students using the distributed ap-proach who've not yet read a specific module to "read it now." As an example, the notice for **Module 4** on the respiratory system appears in Chapter 7, as the students prepare to read the material on cigarette smoking.

MODULE 1: THE NERVOUS SYSTEM

We all know that the nervous system, particularly the brain, in human beings and other animals controls the way we initiate behavior and respond to events in our world. The nervous system receives information about changes in the environment from sensory organs, including the eyes, ears, and nose, and it transmits directions that tell our muscles and other internal organs how to react. The brain—being a repository for our memory of past events—also stores information and provides our capability for thinking, reasoning, and creating.

HOW THE NERVOUS SYSTEM WORKS

The nervous system constantly integrates the actions of our internal organs, although we are not generally aware of it. Many of these organs, such as the heart and digestive tract, are made of muscle tissues that respond to commands. The nervous system provides these commands through an intricate network of billions of specialized nerve cells called *neurons*.

Although neurons in different parts of the nervous system have a variety of shapes and sizes, the diagram in Figure 2–1 shows their general features. Projecting from the *cell body* are clusters of branches called *dendrites*, which generally function as receivers for messages from adjacent neurons. These messages then travel through the *axon*, which splits into branches at the far end. The tips of these branches have small swellings called *synaptic knobs* that connect to the dendrites of other neurons, usually through a fluid-filled gap. This junction is called a *synapse*. Messages from the knobs cross the gap to adjacent neurons and in this way eventually reach their destination. These messages consist of *electrochemical* activity. If the chemical activity at a dendrite produces a sufficient concentration of electrically charged particles, called *ions*, an impulse of electrical potential is triggered. That impulse travels through the axon and stimulates the synaptic knobs to release a chemical called a **neurotransmitter,** which travels to the dendrites of an adjacent neuron. There are dozens of different neurotransmitters. Some tend to *excite* the receiving neuron, increasing the likelihood that an electrical impulse will be generated; others tend to *inhibit* the neuron,

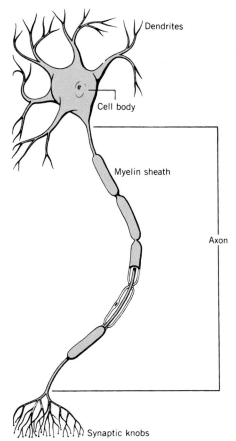

Figure 2–1 An idealized diagram of a neuron and some of its major parts. Electrochemical messages received by the dendrites are transmitted to the synaptic knobs. The myelin sheath covers the axon of most neurons.

making an impulse less likely; and others can have either effect, depending on characteristics of the receiving neuron.

What changes occur in the nervous system as a person develops? By the time the typical baby is born, a basic structure has been formed for almost all the neurons this person will have. But the nervous system is still quite immature. For instance, the brain weighs only about 25% of the weight it will have when the child reaches adulthood (Sarafino & Armstrong, 1986). Most of the growth in brain size after birth results from an increase in the number of *glial cells* and the presence of a white fatty substance called *myelin*. The glial cells are thought to service and maintain the

neurons. A myelin sheath surrounds the axons of most, but not all, neurons. This sheath is responsible for increasing the speed of nerve impulses and preventing them from being interfered with by adjacent nerve impulses, much the way insulation is used on electrical wiring. The importance of myelin can be seen in the disease called *multiple sclerosis*, which results when the myelin sheath degenerates and nerves become severed (Trapp, 1998). People afflicted with this disease have weak muscles that lack coordination and move spastically (AMA, 2003).

As the infant grows, the network of dendrites and synaptic knobs that carry messages to and from other neurons expands dramatically, as Figure 2–2 shows. Initially, the myelin sheath covering the neurons is better developed in the upper regions of the body than in the lower regions. During the first years of life, the progress in myelin growth spreads down the body—from the head to shoulders, to the arms and hands, to the upper chest and abdomen, and then to the legs and feet. This sequence is reflected in the individual's motor development: the upper parts of the body are brought under control at earlier ages than the lower parts. Studies with animals have found that chronic poor nutrition early in life impairs brain growth by retarding the development of myelin, glial cells, and dendrites. Such impairment can produce long-lasting deficits in a child's motor and intellectual performance (Reinis & Goldman, 1980). The brain appears to form few, if any, new neurons after birth, and their development is limited to certain areas of the brain (Kornack & Rakic, 2001).

Beginning in early adulthood, the brain slowly loses weight with age (Tortora & Grabowski, 2003). Although the number of brain cells does not change very much, the synapses do, leading to a decline in ability to send nerve impulses. These alterations in the brain are associated with the declines people often notice in their mental and physical functions after they reach 50 or 60 years of age.

The nervous system is enormously complex and has two major divisions—the central nervous system and the peripheral nervous system—that connect to each other. The **central nervous system** consists of the brain and spinal cord. The *peripheral nervous system* is composed of the remaining network of neurons throughout the body. Each of these divisions consists of interconnected lower-order divisions or structures. We will examine the nervous system, beginning at the top and working our way down.

At birth   At 1 month   At 6 months   At 2 years

Figure 2–2 Drawings showing the neural structure of a section of the human cortex at four different ages. Notice that the number of cell bodies (dark spots) does not change much, while the network of dendrites expands with age. (Drawings from Lenneberg, 1967, Figure 4.6, based on photographs from Conel, 1939–1963.)

THE CENTRAL NERVOUS SYSTEM

Our brains and spinal cords race toward maturity early in life. For example, the brain weighs 75% of its adult weight at about 2 years of age, 90% at 5 years, and 95% at 10 years (Tanner, 1970, 1978). The brain may be divided into three parts: the *forebrain*, the *cerebellum*, and the *brainstem*. Each of these parts has special functions.

The Forebrain

The forebrain is the uppermost part of the brain. As Figure 2–3 shows, the forebrain has two main subdivisions: the *telencephalon*, which consists of the cerebrum and the limbic system, and the *diencephalon*, which includes the thalamus and hypothalamus. As a general rule, areas toward the top and outer regions of the brain are involved in our perceptual, motor, learning, and conceptual activities. Regions toward the center and bottom of the brain are involved mainly in controlling internal and automatic body functions and in transmitting information to and from the telencephalon.

The **cerebrum** is the largest portion of the human brain and includes the *cerebral cortex*, its outermost layer. It controls complex motor and mental activity. The cerebrum has two halves—the *left hemisphere* and the *right hemisphere*—each of which looks like the drawing in Figure 2–4. Although the left and right hemispheres are physically alike, they control different types of processes. For one thing, the motor cortex (shown in the figure) of each hemisphere controls

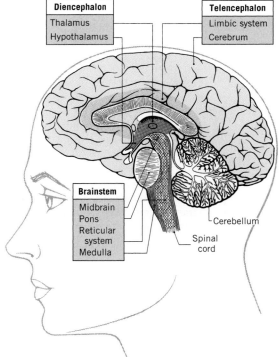

Figure 2–3 A side view of the human brain in cross section, sliced through the middle from front to back. The forebrain, shown shaded in color, consists of the telencephalon (cerebrum and limbic system) and the diencephalon (thalamus and hypothalamus). The remaining divisions of the central nervous system—the cerebellum, the brainstem (shaded gray), and the spinal cord—are also labeled.

Figure 2–4 The surface of the left hemisphere of the cerebrum. The shaded sections show the four parts of the hemisphere, and the areas associated with specific functions are identified. The right hemisphere has the same four parts and functional areas.

motor movements on the opposite side of the body. This is why damage to the motor cortex on, say, the right side of the brain may leave part of the left side of the body paralyzed. The two hemispheres also control different aspects of cognitive and language processes. In most people, the left hemisphere contains the areas that handle language processes, including speech and writing. The right hemisphere usually processes such things as visual imagery, emotions, and the perception of patterns, such as melodies (Tortora & Grabowski, 2003).

Figure 2–4 also shows that each hemisphere is divided into a front part, called the frontal lobe, and three back parts: the temporal, occipital, and parietal lobes. The *frontal lobe* is involved in many functions—for instance, the back region of the frontal lobe contains the motor cortex, which controls the skeletal muscles of the body. If a patient who is undergoing brain surgery receives stimulation to the motor cortex, some part of the body will move. The frontal lobe is also involved in important mental activities, such as the association of ideas, planning, self-awareness, and emotion. As a result, injury to areas of this lobe can produce personality and emotional reactions, like those described by the physician of Phineas P. Gage:

> He is fitful, irreverent, indulging in the grossest profanity (which was not previously his custom),

manifesting but little deference to his fellows, impatient of restraint or advice when it conflicts with his desires, at times . . . obstinate, capricious, and vacillating. . . . His mind was radically changed, so that his friends said he was no longer Gage. (Cited in McClintic, 1985, p. 93)

Phineas had survived a workplace accident in which a tamping iron was blown through the front of his head.

The *temporal lobe* is chiefly involved in hearing but plays a part in vision and memory. Damage to this region can impair the person's comprehension of speech and ability to determine the direction from which a sound is coming. Because the *occipital lobe* houses the principal visual area of the brain, damage there can produce blindness or the inability to recognize an object by sight. The *parietal lobe* is involved mainly in body sensations, such as those of pain, cold, heat, touch, and body movement.

The second part of the telencephalon—called the **limbic system**—lies along the innermost edge of the cerebrum and adjacent to the diencephalon (refer back to Figure 2–3). The limbic system is not well understood yet. It consists of several structures that seem to be important in the expression of emotions, such as fear, anger, and excitement. To the extent that heredity affects a person's emotions, it may do so by determining the structure and function of the limbic system (McClintic, 1985).

The diencephalon includes two structures—the thalamus and hypothalamus—that lie below and are partially encircled by the limbic system. The **thalamus** is a truly pivotal structure in the flow of information in the nervous system. It functions as the chief relay station for directing sensory messages, such as those of pain or visual images, to appropriate points in the cerebrum, including the occipital or parietal lobe. The thalamus also relays commands going out to the skeletal muscles from the motor cortex of the cerebrum.

The **hypothalamus,** a small structure just below the thalamus, plays an important role in people's emotions and motivation. Its function affects, among other things, eating, drinking, and sexual activity (Tortora & Grabowski, 2003). For example, when the body lacks water or nutrients, the hypothalamus detects this deficiency and arouses the sensation of thirst or hunger, which is relieved when we consume water or food. Research with animals has shown that stimulation of specific areas of this structure can cause them to eat when they are full and stop eating when they are hungry. A rare disease that affects this structure can cause people to become overweight. Another important function of the hypothalamus is to maintain *homeostasis*—a state of balance or normal function among our body systems. Our normal body temperature and heart rate, which are characteristic of healthy individuals, are examples of homeostasis. When our bodies are cold, for instance, we shiver, thus producing heat. When we are very warm, we perspire, thus cooling the body. The hypothalamus controls these adjustments (AMA, 2003). Later we will see that the hypothalamus also plays an important role in our reaction to stress.

The Cerebellum

The **cerebellum** lies at the back of the brain, below the cerebrum. The main function of the cerebellum is in maintaining body balance and coordinating movement. This structure has nerve connections to the motor cortex of the cerebrum and most sense organs of the body. When areas of the cerebrum initiate specific movements, the cerebellum makes our actions precise and well coordinated.

How does the cerebellum do this? There are at least two ways. First, it continuously compares our intent with our performance, ensuring that a movement goes in the right direction, at the proper rate, and with appropriate force. Second, it smoothes our movements. Because of the forces involved in movement, there is an underlying tendency for our motions to go quickly back and forth, like a tremor. The cerebellum damps this tendency (McClintic, 1985). When injury occurs to the cerebellum, the person's actions become jerky and uncoordinated—a condition called *ataxia*. Simple movements, such as walking or touching an object, become difficult and unsteady.

Look back to Figure 2–3 to locate the cerebellum relative to the brainstem, which is the next section of the brain we will discuss.

The Brainstem

The lowest portion of the brain—called the **brainstem**—has the form of an oddly-shaped knob at the top of the spinal cord. The brainstem consists of four parts: midbrain, pons, reticular system, and medulla.

The *midbrain* lies at the top of the brainstem. It connects directly to the thalamus above it, which relays messages to various parts of the forebrain. The midbrain receives information from the visual and auditory systems and is especially important in muscle movement. The disorder called *Parkinson's disease* results from degeneration of an area of the midbrain (Tortora & Grabowski, 2003). People severely afflicted with this disease have noticeable motor tremors, and their neck and trunk postures become rigid, so that they walk in a crouch. Sometimes the tremors are so continuous and vigorous that the victim becomes crippled.

The *reticular system* is a network of neurons that extends from the bottom to the top of the brainstem and into the thalamus. The reticular system plays an important role in controlling our states of sleep, arousal, and attention. When people suffer a coma, often it is this system that is injured or disordered (McClintic, 1985). E*pilepsy*, a condition in which a victim may become unconscious and begin to convulse, seems to involve an abnormality in the reticular system. One type of epileptic seizure, called *grand mal*, may result from "reverberating cycles" in the reticular system:

> That is, one portion of the system stimulates another portion, which stimulates a third portion, and this in turn restimulates the first portion, causing a cycle that continues for 2 to 3 minutes, until the neurons of the system fatigue so greatly that the reverberation ceases. (Guyton, 1985, p. 356)

Following a grand mal seizure, the person often sleeps at least a few minutes and sometimes for hours.

The *pons* forms a large bulge at the front of the brainstem and is involved in eye movements, facial expressions, and chewing. The *medulla* contains vital centers that control breathing, heartbeat rate, and the diameter of blood vessels (which affects blood pressure). Because of the many vital functions it controls, damage to the medulla can be life threatening. *Polio*, a crippling disease that was once epidemic, sometimes damaged the center that controls breathing. Patients suffering such damage needed constant artificial respiration to breathe (McClintic, 1985).

The Spinal Cord

Extending down the spine from the brainstem is the **spinal cord,** a major neural pathway that transmits messages between the brain and various parts of the body. It contains neurons that carry impulses away from (the *efferent* direction) and toward (*afferent*) the brain. Efferent commands travel down the cord on their way to produce muscle action; afferent impulses come to the spinal cord from sense organs in all parts of the body.

The organization of the spinal cord parallels that of the body—that is, the higher region of the cord, the higher the parts of the body to which it connects. Damage to the spinal cord results in impaired motor function or paralysis; the duration and extent of the impairment depends on the amount and location of damage. If the damage does not sever the cord, the impairment is less severe and may be temporary. If the lower portion of the cord is severed, the lower areas of the body are paralyzed—a condition called *paraplegia*. If the upper portion of the spinal cord is severed, paralysis is more extensive. Paralysis of the legs and arms is called *quadriplegia*.

Figure 2–5 depicts the spinal cord and its relation to the brain and the branching network of afferent and efferent neurons throughout the body—the peripheral nervous system. (Go to 🧠 .)

THE PERIPHERAL NERVOUS SYSTEM

The **peripheral nervous system** has two parts: the somatic nervous system and the autonomic nervous system. The **somatic nervous system** is involved in both sensory and motor functions, serving mainly the skin and skeletal muscles. The **autonomic nervous system** activates internal organs, such as the lungs

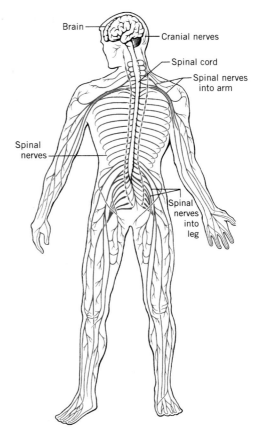

Figure 2–5 Diagram showing the branching network between the spinal cord and the peripheral nervous system.

Biofeedback Treatment for Paralysis

Neuromuscular disorders, which impair the muscles and nerves that control movement, often involve paralysis resulting from a spinal cord injury or a stroke that damages the brain. Biofeedback, the operant conditioning method we described in Chapter 1, is a treatment that psychologists and physical therapists can apply successfully to improve muscle control if the spinal cord is not completely severed (Fogel, 1987). The procedure involves attaching sensors to the skin to detect tiny changes in the activity of an affected muscle, immediately reporting back to the person when the muscle has tensed a bit, and encouraging him or her to tense it more and more. One study found that two biofeedback sessions a week for 6 weeks improved muscle function substantially in patients who had suffered strokes years earlier (Burnside, Tobias, & Bursill, 1982). Biofeedback can also help people gain control over other body processes, enabling them to reduce their blood pressure, for example (Sarafino, 2001).

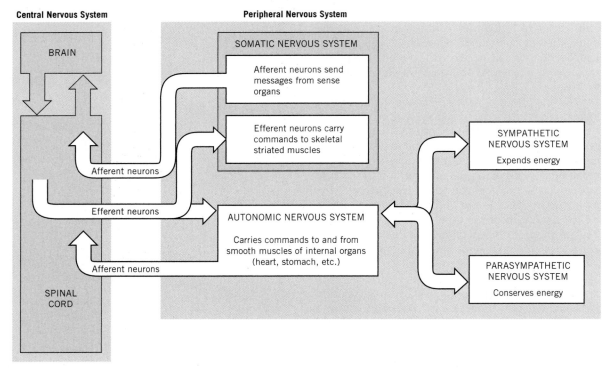

Figure 2–6 Illustration of the flow and function of nerve impulses among the major parts of the nervous system.

and intestines, and reports to the brain the current state of activity of these organs.

In the somatic nervous system, afferent neurons carry messages from sense organs to the spinal cord, as Figure 2–6 diagrams. Efferent neurons carry messages to, and activate, *striated* (grooved) skeletal muscles, such as those in the face, arms, and legs, that we can move voluntarily. A disorder called *myasthenia gravis* can develop at the junction of these muscles and neurons, weakening muscle function of the head and neck. This produces characteristic symptoms—such as drooping eyelids, blurred vision, and difficulty swallowing and breathing—and can lead to paralysis. Medical treatment can improve muscle function, and reducing stress can alleviate symptoms (AMA, 2003).

Figure 2–7 diagrams two other features of the autonomic nervous system. First, neurons carry messages between the spinal cord and the *smooth* muscles of the internal organs, such as the heart, stomach, lungs, blood vessels, and glands. Second, this system itself has two divisions, the sympathetic and parasympathetic, which often act in opposite

ways. The **sympathetic nervous system** helps us mobilize and expend energy in responding to emergencies, expressing strong emotions, and performing strenuous activity. For instance, suppose you are crossing a street, notice a speeding car barreling toward you, and hear its brakes start to squeal. The sympathetic nervous system instantly moves into action, producing several simultaneous changes. For example, it speeds up the heart, dilates certain arteries to increase blood flow to the heart and skeletal muscles, constricts other arteries to decrease blood flow to the skin and digestive organs, decreases salivation, and increases perspiration. These changes, in general, enable you to mobilize energy, and you leap to safety out of the car's path. This system is called "sympathetic" because it acts in agreement with your current emotional state.

What does the parasympathetic division do? The prefix *para* means "alongside of"—this division acts alongside of, and often in opposition to, the sympathetic division. The **parasympathetic nervous system** regulates "quiet" or calming processes, helping our individual organ systems conserve and store energy. One example of parasympathetic

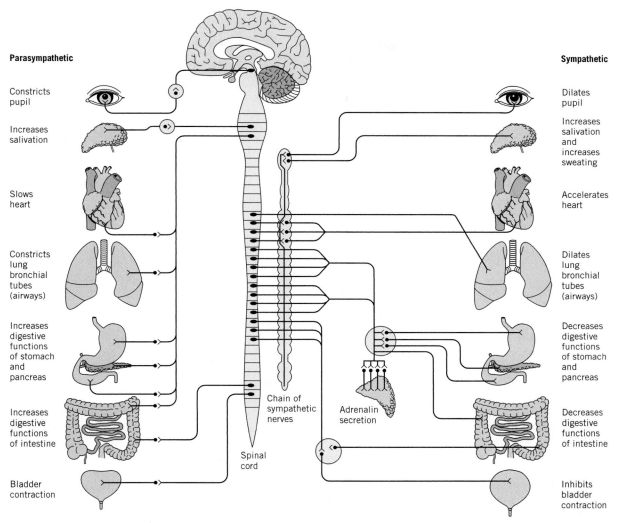

Parasympathetic

Constricts
pupil

Increases
salivation

Slows
heart

Constricts
lung
bronchial
tubes
(airways)

Increases
digestive
functions
of stomach
and
pancreas

Increases
digestive
functions
of intestine

Bladder
contraction

Sympathetic

Dilates
pupil

Increases
salivation
and
increases
sweating

Accelerates
heart

Dilates
lung
bronchial
tubes
(airways)

Decreases
digestive
functions
of stomach
and
pancreas

Decreases
digestive
functions
of intestine

Inhibits
bladder
contraction

Chain of
sympathetic
nerves

Adrenalin
secretion

Spinal
cord

Figure 2–7 The autonomic nervous system and its interconnections between the spinal cord and various organs of the body. The function of the parasympathetic division in conserving energy is shown on the left side of the diagram. The function of the sympathetic division in expending energy is shown on the right side. Notice that each organ connects to both divisions.

activity can be seen in the digestion of food. When you eat a meal, the parasympathetic nervous system carries messages to regulate each step in the digestive process, such as by increasing salivation and stomach contractions. Another example can be seen in the course of emotional or emergency reactions—when an emergency has passed, the parasympathetic division helps restore your normal body state.

Communication within the peripheral nervous system is handled by 12 sets of *cranial nerves*, most of which originate in the brainstem. The *vagus nerve* extends from there to muscles of most major body organs, such as the airways, lungs, heart, and intestines, and is directly involved in the regulation of sympathetic and parasympathetic activity (Porges, 1995; Tortora & Grabowski, 2003). Efferent messages from the brain can target specific organs to increase or decrease their function.

SUMMARY

The central nervous system consists of the brain and spinal cord and is the control center, sending and receiving electrochemical messages, such as with neurotransmitters, through neurons throughout the body. The brain is divided into the forebrain (which includes the cerebrum, limbic system, thalamus, and hypothalamus), the cerebellum, and the brainstem. The uppermost regions of the brain are involved in perceptual, motor, learning, and conceptual activities. Areas toward the center and bottom of the brain are important in controlling internal and automatic body functions and the flow of information to and from the brain. The spinal cord is the major neural pathway that connects the brain to the peripheral nervous system.

The peripheral nervous system is a branching network of afferent and efferent neurons throughout the body. It has two divisions: (1) the somatic nervous system is involved in sensory and motor functions; (2) the autonomic nervous system carries messages between the spinal cord and various internal organs. The autonomic nervous system has two parts, sympathetic and parasympathetic. The sympathetic nervous system acts in agreement with our current emotional state and helps us mobilize and expend energy. The parasympathetic nervous system is involved in processes to conserve and store energy and in calming the body following sympathetic arousal. The nervous system is connected to and regulates all of our other body systems, and the brain is the control center.

MODULE 2: THE ENDOCRINE SYSTEM

The **endocrine system** consists of a set of glands that often work in close association with the autonomic nervous system. These systems share an important function: they communicate with various parts of the body. But they do this in somewhat different ways. Whereas the nervous system uses both electrical and chemical messages, the endocrine system communicates only with chemical substances, which are called **hormones.** Each endocrine gland secretes specific hormones directly into the bloodstream, which carries these chemicals to various parts of the body. Figure 2–8 shows where several important endocrine glands are located. Certain chemicals are produced by both the endocrine and nervous systems and function as both hormones and neurotransmitters.

THE ENDOCRINE AND NERVOUS SYSTEMS WORKING TOGETHER

How are the endocrine and nervous systems associated? The nervous system is linked to the endocrine system by connections between the hypothalamus (in the forebrain) and a gland that lies just below it—the **pituitary gland.** The hypothalamus sends chemical messages directly to the pituitary gland, causing it to release pituitary hormones into the blood. In turn, most of these hormones selectively stimulate the other endocrine glands to secrete chemicals. Because the pituitary gland controls the secretion of other endocrine glands, it is called the "master gland."

Researchers have identified dozens of different hormones that course through our veins and arteries. Each hormone has its own specific effects on cells and organs of the body, thereby directly or indirectly affecting psychological and physical functions. Some hormones, such as estrogens and testosterone, are produced mainly in females' *ovaries* (where egg cells develop) and males' *testes* (where sperm develop). These hormones are especially important in the development and functioning of female and male reproductive systems. Other hormones affect blood pressure, general body growth, and the balance of various chemicals, such as calcium, in the body. Still other hormones help us react to specific situations we encounter in our lives.

We saw earlier that the autonomic nervous system plays an important role in our reaction to an emergency. So does the endocrine system through a process called the *hypothalamus–pituitary–adrenal axis* (Sternberg & Gold, 1997). Let's see how by returning to the incident in which you leaped out of the path of a speeding car. When the sympathetic nervous system reacts to your emergency, the hypothalamus immediately sends a hormone called corticotropin-releasing factor to the pituitary gland. This causes the pituitary

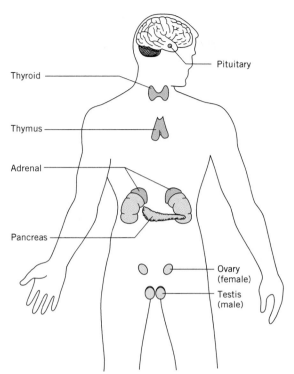

Figure 2–8 Some of the endocrine glands and their locations in the body.

to release ACTH (adrenocorticotropic hormone) into the blood. The ACTH then travels throughout the body and stimulates the release of a variety of hormones—especially those of the adrenal glands—that affect your reaction to the emergency.

ADRENAL GLANDS

The **adrenal glands** are located on top of the kidneys (see Figure 2–8). These glands release several important hormones in response to emergencies and stress (AMA, 2003). One of these hormones, *cortisol*, helps control swelling when we are injured. If when you leaped to avoid being hit by the car you sprained your ankle, this hormone would help reduce swelling. But continued high levels of cortisol and similar hormones over a long time can be harmful to the body. They can lead to high blood pressure and the formation of ulcers, for example.

Two other important adrenal hormones are *epinephrine* and *norepinephrine* (also called adrenalin and

noradrenalin, respectively). These hormones work in conjunction with the sympathetic nervous system to produce such bodily reactions as speeding up heart and respiration rates and increasing the liver's sugar output for quick energy. After the emergency has passed and sympathetic activity has subsided, some impact of the hormones may continue for a while because they are still in the bloodstream.

The impact of the nervous and endocrine systems' activities in emergency situations differs in the speed and persistence of their effect. The nervous system responds by sending messages that move instantly to specific locations; once they reach their destination, they become deactivated or dissipated. For example, the nervous system also produces and uses epinephrine and norepinephrine, but these chemicals function as neurotransmitters, relaying their commands from neuron to neuron and having a localized effect. The impact of the message stops quickly and persists only if additional messages are sent. Hormones from the endocrine system move more slowly and broadly through the bloodstream, and their effects can be delayed and long-lasting.

OTHER GLANDS

Several other endocrine glands are also important. The *thymus gland*, which is located in the chest, is quite large in infancy and childhood but diminishes in size and efficiency after puberty (AMA, 2003). The thymus plays an important role early in life in the development of antibodies and immunities against diseases.

The *thyroid gland*, located in the neck, produces hormones, such as thyroxine, that regulate the body's general activity level and growth. Disorders in thyroid production are of two types: *hypothyroidism*, or insufficient secretion of thyroid hormones, and *hyperthyroidism*, or excessive thyroid secretion (AMA, 2003). Hypothyroidism leads to low activity levels and to weight gain. If the condition is congenital and untreated, dwarfism and mental retardation often result. The condition can be treated medically by having the person take hormone supplements orally. Hyperthyroidism leads to high activity levels, short attention span, tremors, insomnia, and weight loss. Untreated people with a common form of this condition, called *Graves' disease*, act in a highly restless, irritable, and confused manner.

Another endocrine gland is the *pancreas*, which is located below the stomach. Its main function is to regulate the level of blood sugar, or glucose. The pancreas does this by producing two hormones, *glucagon* and *insulin*, that act in opposition. Glucagon raises the concentration of glucose in the blood, and insulin lowers it (AMA, 2003). The disorder called *diabetes mellitus* results when the pancreas does not produce sufficient insulin to balance the action of glucagon. This imbalance produces excess blood sugar levels—a condition called *hyperglycemia*. If this condition persists and is untreated, it may cause coma and death. Diabetes can be medically controlled, generally through diet and either medication or daily insulin injections (AMA, 2003; Kilo & Williamson, 1987) (Go to 💡.)

SUMMARY

The endocrine system also communicates with various parts of the body, but does so by sending chemical messages through the bloodstream. This system consists of several glands that secrete hormones. As the "master gland" in this system, the pituitary gland releases hormones that stimulate other glands to secrete. The adrenal glands secrete hormones such as cortisol and epinephrine (adrenaline), which are important in our response to emergencies and stress. Other glands are important in regulating such factors as general body growth and the level of blood sugar.

MODULE 3: THE DIGESTIVE SYSTEM

Whether we eat an apple, drink some milk, or swallow a pill, our bodies respond in the same general way. The **digestive system** breaks down what we have ingested, converts much of it to chemicals the body can use, and excretes the rest. The chemicals the body uses are absorbed into the bloodstream, which transports them to all of our body cells. Chemical nutrients in the foods we eat provide energy to fuel our activity, body growth, and repair.

FOOD'S JOURNEY THROUGH DIGESTIVE ORGANS

Think of the digestive system as a long hose—about 20 feet long—with stations along the way. The journey of food through this hose begins in the *mouth* and ends at the *rectum*. The digestive organs and major organs in between are shown in Figure 2–9.

Digesting Food

How does this system break down food? One way is mechanical: for example, we grind food up when we chew it. Another way is chemical: through the action of **enzymes,** substances that act as catalysts in speeding up chemical reactions in cells. How do enzymes work? You can see the effect of an enzyme by doing the following experiment (Holum, 1994). Place a bit of liver in some hydrogen peroxide and watch what happens: An enzyme in liver called *catalase* causes the peroxide to decompose, frothing as oxygen is given off as a gas. This is the same reaction you see when you use peroxide to disinfect a wound.

In most cases, the names for enzymes end in the letters *-ase*, and the remainder of each name reflects the substance on which it acts. The following list gives some examples:

- *Carbohydrase* acts on carbohydrates.
- *Lactase* acts on lactose (milk).
- *Phosphatase* acts on phosphate compounds.
- *Sucrase* acts on sucrose (sugar).

As food is broken down into smaller and smaller units in the digestive tract, water molecules become attached to these units (Rhoades & Pflanzer, 1996).

When food is in the mouth, there is more digestive action going on than just chewing. Saliva moistens food and contains an enzyme that starts the process of breaking down starches. The salivary glands release saliva in response to commands from the brainstem, which responds primarily to sensory information from

HIGHLIGHT

Our Physiological Individuality

Think about some differences between two people you know. Probably the first things that come to mind are their physical and behavioral characteristics. One person is tall and has blond hair, blue eyes, and an outgoing personality; the other is short and has dark hair, dark eyes, and is shy. But what about their internal physiological structure and functions?

We don't usually think about internal physiological differences between people. This is partly because the pictures of internal organs we see in books are always the same. As a result, we get the impression that if you've seen one heart or stomach, you've seen them all. This impression is wrong. Our individuality exists not only in our external features, but in our internal organs and bodily chemistry as well. The aorta is a major blood vessel that arches, or curves, over and attaches to the heart. Examples of some of its structural variations are given in Figure 2H–1. The drawing on the left depicts the usual branching that forms at the arch of the aorta, and the other drawings show variations that occur, sometimes quite frequently. Major differences like these occur in virtually all organs (Skolnick, 1986).

Our physiological individuality can have major implications for health and behavior. How? One way is that people's reactions to medicines differ, sometimes quite substantially. Some people may require many times the normal dose of certain drugs before the desired effect occurs. A person's age, weight, and heredity contribute to this variability (Bennett, 1987; USDHHS, 1981). Heavy people usually require larger doses of a drug than other people do. Infants and the elderly seem to be particularly sensitive to the effects of drugs, and overdoses are a danger for them. Blood pressure medication in the elderly may overshoot and lower the pressure too far, for example.

There are gender differences in many organ systems, too. Males generally have larger hearts and lungs, and higher blood pressure, than females do. Their body systems also react to stress differently. We saw earlier that the adrenal glands respond to stress by secreting hormones—two of which are epinephrine and cortisol. When under stress, males secrete more of these hormones than females do (Collins & Frankenhaeuser, 1978).

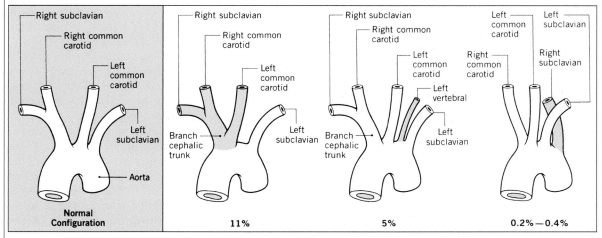

Figure 2H-1 Variations in arterial branching of the aortic arch and the approximate percentages of their occurrence. (Drawings of variations are from Grant, 1972, plate 446.4.)

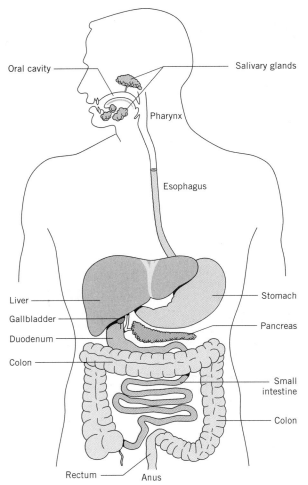

Figure 2–9   Major parts of the digestive system.

taste buds. Simply seeing, smelling, or even thinking about food can produce neural impulses that cause the mouth to water (Rhoades & Pflanzer, 1996).

The journey of food advances to the *esophagus*, a tube that is normally flattened when food is not passing through it. The esophagus pushes the food down to the stomach by wavelike muscle contractions called *peristalsis*. By the time food enters the esophagus, the stomach has already begun digestive activities by releasing small amounts of gastric juice even before food reaches it. Tasting, smelling, seeing, or thinking about food can initiate this process (Feldman & Richardson, 1986). Once food reaches the stomach,

this organ amasses large amounts of gastric juices, including *hydrochloric acid* and *pepsin*, an enzyme that breaks down proteins. (This enzyme name is one of the few that does not end in *-ase*.) The stomach also produces a sticky mucus substance to protect its lining from the highly acidic gastric juices. The muscular stomach walls produce a churning motion—that we are generally not aware of—which mixes the food particles with the gastric juices. This mixing continues for 3 or 4 hours, producing a semiliquid mixture.

Peristalsis in the stomach then moves this mixture on, a little at a time, to the initial section of the small intestine called the *duodenum*. Important digestive processes occur in the small intestine (Rhoades & Pflanzer, 1996; Tortora & Grabowski, 2003). First, the highly acidic food mixture becomes chemically alkaline from substances added from various organs—an important process because the linings of the small intestine and remainder of the digestive tract are not protected from high acidity, as the stomach is. Second, enzymes secreted by the pancreas into the duodenum break down carbohydrates, proteins, and fats further. Third, *absorption* increases. Because the stomach lining can absorb only a few substances, such as alcohol and aspirin, most materials we ingest are absorbed into the bloodstream through the lining of the small intestine (Tortora & Grabowski, 2003). If alcohol is consumed along with fatty foods, very little alcohol is absorbed until it reaches the small intestine. When food is ready to be absorbed through the intestine wall, nutrients have been broken down into molecules—carbohydrates are broken down into *simple sugars*, fats into *glycerol* and *fatty acids*, and proteins into *amino acids*.

How does absorption occur? The inside of the small intestine is made of a membrane that will allow molecules to pass through. To increase the absorbing surface, the intestine wall has many folds that contain projections, as pictured in Figure 2–10. Each of the many thousands of projections contains a network of structures that will accept the molecules and transport them away to other parts of the body. These structures include tiny blood vessels called *capillaries* and a tube called a *lacteal*. Capillaries absorb amino acids, simple sugars, and water; they also absorb some fatty acids, vitamins, and minerals. Lacteals accept glycerol and the remaining fatty acids and vitamins.

The remaining food material continues its journey to the large intestine, most of which is called the

(a)

(b)

Figure 2–10 The interior wall of the small intestine. (*a*) The wall has many tiny projections, shown greatly magnified in the photograph. (*b*) The cross-sectional drawing shows the capillaries and lacteal of each projection.

colon. Absorption, mainly of water, continues in the first half of the colon, and the remaining material is transported on. Bacterial action converts the material into feces, which eventually reach the rectum, where they are stored until defecation occurs.

Disorders of the Digestive System

Judging from the many media advertisements for stomach and "irregularity" remedies, it seems that people have a good deal of trouble with their digestive processes. We will consider a few digestive problems.

One disorder of the digestive system is *peptic ulcers*, which are open sores in the lining of the stomach or intestine, usually in the duodenum. These sores appear to result from excess gastric juices chronically eroding the lining when there is little or no food in the stomach, but bacterial infection plays a primary role (AMA, 2003). Abdominal pain is the chief symptom of the disorder. Victims of ulcers are mostly adults. People seem to be more susceptible to ulcers if they experience high rather than low levels of stress.

Hepatitis is a class of several viral diseases in which the liver becomes inflamed and unable to function well. The first symptoms often are like those of flu. But the symptoms persist, and jaundice, a yellowing of the skin, generally follows. *Hepatitis* A appears to be transmitted through contaminated food, water, and utensils. *Hepatitis* B and C infections occur through sexual contact, transfusion of infected blood, and sharing of contaminated needles by drug addicts, but the modes of transmission may be broader. Some forms of hepatitis can lead to permanent liver damage (AMA, 2003).

Another disease of the liver is called *cirrhosis*. In this disease, liver cells die off and are replaced by nonfunctional fibrous scar tissue. The scar tissue is permanent, and when it becomes extensive, the liver's normal functions are greatly impaired. The liver is not important just in the digestive process; it also cleanses and regulates the composition of the blood. Cirrhosis can result from several causes, including hepatitis infection and, particularly, alcohol abuse (AMA, 2003).

Cancer may occur in any part of the digestive tract, especially in the colon and rectum (ACS, 2004; AMA, 2003). People over 40 years of age have a higher prevalence of cancers of the digestive tract than do younger individuals. Early detection for many of these cancers is possible and greatly improves the person's chances of recovery.

USING NUTRIENTS IN METABOLISM

The term **metabolism** refers to all chemical reactions that occur in the body's cells (Holum, 1994). Three principal outcomes of metabolism are:

- *Synthesis* of new cell material from proteins and minerals to build and repair the body.
- *Regulation* of body processes—by producing enzymes and hormones, for example—through the use of proteins, minerals, and vitamins.
- *Energy* to heat the body and fuel its activities.

We will focus here on the third outcome, energy production.

Metabolism takes place constantly in the cells of all living organisms. Without the energy it produces, all of our body systems would cease to function. The energy to fuel our internal functions and our physical actions comes mainly from the metabolism of carbohydrates and fats (Tortora & Grabowski, 2003). The amount of energy a food contains is measured in *calories*. One calorie is the amount of heat needed to raise one gram of water one degree Celsius. Nutrition researchers measure the calories contained in a given quantity of a food by burning it in a special apparatus.

How much energy do we use to support our basic bodily functions? The number of calories we burn up when our bodies are at rest—an index called the *basal metabolic rate*—depends on the size of the body (Tortora & Grabowski, 2003). For this reason, the basal metabolic rate is expressed in terms of calories per area of body surface (in square meters) per hour. A person who is 67 inches tall and weighs 132 pounds has a body surface area of about 1.7 square meters, for example. The basal metabolic rate also varies with the person's age and gender: the average rate is higher in males than in females and higher in younger people than in older people, as Figure 2–11 indicates.

Figure 2–11   Normal basal metabolic rate for males and females at different ages in the life span. The dashed vertical and horizontal lines give an illustration: an average 24-year-old male's basic metabolism is 38.7 calories per square meter per hour. (Data from Hafen, 1981, Table 16.6.)

What other factors affect the basal metabolic rate? People who are under stress, who live in cold climates, or whose hormone secretion by the thyroid gland is greater than normal tend to have high basal metabolic rates (McClintic, 1985; Tortora & Grabowski, 2003). Factors such as these account for the fact that different people of the same size, age, and gender may have different metabolic rates.

Activity raises metabolism above the basal rate. Food materials that are not used up by metabolic processes are stored as body fat. This means that people become overweight generally because they regularly consume more calories than their body uses to fuel their internal functions and physical actions. To maintain normal body weight, people who do not metabolize all the calories they consume need to eat less, exercise more, or both. (Go to 🍎.)

SUMMARY

The digestive system provides the body with essential nutrients and other substances for energy, body growth, and repair. It also removes wastes from the body. Enzymes break down foods by speeding up chemical reactions in the body's cells. The outcomes of chemical reactions called metabolism that occur in our body cells include the synthesis of new cells, the regulation of body processes, and the production of energy to heat the body and fuel its activity.

How Many Calories Do You Burn While Resting?

To figure out the number of calories your body probably burns while you are just resting, we need to estimate two factors:

1. *Your basal metabolic rate* (BMR). Although we cannot assess your BMR directly, we can use Figure 2–11 to estimate it by finding the average BMR for people of your age and gender. Do this by: (a) finding on the horizontal axis where your age would be, (b) drawing a vertical line from that point to the graph for your gender, and (c) drawing a horizontal line to the vertical axis. The value at this intersect is our estimate of your BMR, which you should enter in the formula (below, right).

2. *Your body surface area* (BSA). Estimates of BSA in square meters are usually made by plotting the person's height and weight on complex graphs. I have used one of these graphs (Hafen, 1981, Figure 16–5) to develop an alternative two-step method. First, start with a BSA score of 1.540 and adjust it based on your height by adding (or subtracting) 0.035 for *each inch* by which you are taller (or shorter)

than 60 inches. Thus, if you are 66 inches tall, your score at this point would be 1.750. Second, take your weight into account by adjusting your score in *one* of four ways: (a) If your body has a small frame and you are very slim, subtract 0.08 to get your BSA. (b) If you have a medium frame and an average weight, do nothing; your current score is your BSA. (c) If your frame is large and/or you are moderately heavy, add 0.08 to get your BSA. (d) If you are overweight by 20 pounds or more, add 0.15 to get your BSA.

Enter your BSA in the formula below and multiply it by your BMR to estimate the number of calories you burn per hour while sleeping or lying down.

_____ BMR × _____ BSA = _____ cal/hr

When engaged in light activities, such as shopping or golfing, you burn 2 to 4 times that much, and when doing moderate or heavy activities, such as scrubbing floors or jogging, you burn 4 to 10 times that much.

MODULE 4: THE RESPIRATORY SYSTEM

Breathing supplies the body with oxygen—but why do we need oxygen? The chemical reactions in metabolism require oxygen, some of which joins with carbon atoms from food to form *carbon dioxide* (CO_2) as a waste product. So breathing has another function—it lets us get rid of this waste product. We will begin our examination of the **respiratory system** by looking at its structures.

THE RESPIRATORY TRACT

After air enters the body through the nose or mouth, it travels past the *larynx*, down the *trachea* and *bronchial tubes*, and into the *lungs*. These organs are depicted in Figure 2–12. The bronchial tubes divide into smaller and smaller branches called *bronchioles* inside the lungs. These branches finally end in millions of tiny air sacs called *alveoli*. Each alveolus looks like a

minute bubble made of a membrane that is thin enough to allow oxygen, CO_2, and other gases to pass through. Alveoli are enmeshed in beds of capillaries so that gases can be transferred to and from the bloodstream quickly and efficiently.

When we breathe, what makes the air go in and out? When we inhale, the rib muscles draw the ribs up and outward and the diaphragm—a horizontal sheet of muscle below the lungs (see Figure 2–12)—contracts, pulling downward on the bottom of the lungs. These actions pull air in and enlarge the lung chambers (Rhoades & Pflanzer, 1996). When we exhale, these muscles relax, and the elasticity of the lungs forces the air out, like a balloon.

RESPIRATORY FUNCTION AND DISORDERS

How do the muscles "know" when it's time to inhale and exhale? Our blood vessels contain sensors that monitor blood gases and send this information to the medulla of the brain, which directs actions of the

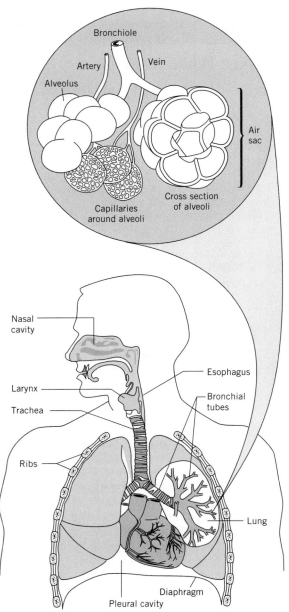

Figure 2–12 Major organs of the respiratory (also called pulmonary) system and closeup of alveoli. The organ shown between the lungs and the pleural cavity is the heart.

muscles to cause us to inhale and exhale. When the CO_2 level is high, the medulla increases the breathing rate; when the level is low, breathing rate is decreased (Rhoades & Pflanzer, 1996).

Foreign matter, such as airborne particles and microorganisms, can readily enter the respiratory tract. The respiratory system therefore needs protective mechanisms to prevent foreign matter from reaching the lungs and entering the bloodstream. Two protective mechanisms are *reflexes*: (1) sneezing in response to irritation in nasal passages and (2) coughing in response to irritation in lower portions of the system. Another protective mechanism is the *mucociliary escalator*. How does this mechanism work? Most of the lining of the respiratory system is coated with a sticky mucus that traps foreign matter. Furthermore, the air passages leading from the mouth to the lungs are lined with tiny hairlike structures called *cilia* that move in such a way as to force the mucus coating up toward the mouth—hence the name "mucociliary escalator." When the mucus reaches the back of the mouth, it is usually swallowed (McClintic, 1985). In this way, the respiratory system cleanses itself and protects the body from harmful matter that we inhale.

The opening story of this chapter is about a young man named Tom who is a victim of cystic fibrosis, a fatal disease of the respiratory system. We will look at several of the many other disorders that attack this system. Some of these disorders mainly affect the alveoli of the lungs, thereby impairing the normal exchange of CO_2 and oxygen. For instance, there are several types of *pneumonia*, which can be caused by either bacterial or viral infection (AMA, 2003). Although this disease often affects the bronchial tubes, the most serious types of pneumonia cause the alveoli to become inflamed and filled with fluid. In another respiratory disease called *emphysema* the walls between alveoli are destroyed. This decreases the lungs' surface area for exchanging gases and their elasticity for exhaling CO_2 (Haas & Haas, 1990; Tortora & Grabowski, 2003). *Pneumoconiosis* is a disease that afflicts people who chronically inhale air containing high concentrations of dust—generally at their workplaces. The black lung disease of coal miners provides an example. Dust that is not removed by protective mechanisms accumulates as thick sheets around the alveoli and bronchioles, damaging these structures and blocking air exchange.

Other disorders of the respiratory system primarily affect the bronchial tubes, usually by narrowing the tubes and reducing airflow. *Asthma* is a disorder in which the bronchial airways narrow because they become inflamed, develop spasms, and secrete too much mucus (ALA, 2003; AAFA, 2004). Attacks usually are temporary and occur in response to an irritant, such as an infection or something to which the victim is allergic. Breathing becomes difficult, and, in very serious attacks, portions of the lungs may collapse temporarily. In *chronic bronchitis*, inflammation and excess mucus occur in the bronchial tubes for an extended period. This condition may be permanent or occur several times a year, lasting 2 weeks or more each episode (Haas & Hass, 1990).

Lung cancer involves an unrestrained growth of cells that crowd out cells that aid respiration. This process usually begins in the bronchial tubes and spreads to the lungs (Tortora & Grabowski, 2003). In its final stages, the diseased cells enter the bloodstream through the capillaries and spread throughout the body. At this point death is almost always near. Many of the respiratory diseases we have discussed can be caused or worsened by smoking cigarettes. This risk factor is also important in diseases of the cardiovascular system.

SUMMARY

The respiratory system provides the body cells with oxygen for energy in metabolism, body growth, and repair. Air enters the body through the nose or mouth and travels to the lungs via bronchial tubes. Oxygen is transferred through alveoli to the bloodstream. The respiratory system also removes carbon dioxide wastes from the body.

MODULE 5: THE CARDIOVASCULAR SYSTEM

The physical design of every complex organism has to deal with a basic problem: How can the body service its cells—supplying the substances they need to function properly and removing the wastes that metabolism produces? In humans and many other animals, this problem is solved by having a **cardiovascular system** to transport these materials. The blood circulates through blood vessels—capillaries, arteries, and veins—within a closed system, one in which the blood does not directly contact the cells and tissues it services. All transfers of oxygen, nutrients, waste products, and other substances occur through membranes that are separated by fluid-filled spaces. The heart is the center of the cardiovascular system.

THE HEART AND BLOOD VESSELS

The *heart* is a fist-sized pump made of muscle that circulates the blood throughout the body. It "beats," or pumps, about 100,000 times a day. The muscular portion of the heart wall is called the *myocardium*. The interior of the heart has four chambers, as the drawing in Figure 2–13 illustrates. The two upper chambers are called atriums, and the two lower ones are called ventricles; the left and right sides are labeled from the body's perspective, not from ours.

Looking at the drawing, we see several blood vessels that connect to the heart. How are arteries and veins different? *Arteries* carry blood *from* the heart, and *veins* carry blood *to* it. You will also notice in the drawing that the shading of some blood vessels is gray, and in others the shading is in color. The vessels with gray shading carry blood that is laden with CO_2 toward the lungs; the vessels with color shading carry blood away from the lungs after it has expelled CO_2 and received oxygen.

Now, let's follow the route of blood through the body. The blood that enters the *right atrium* of the heart is laden with waste products, such as CO_2, from our cells and is deficient in oxygen, which makes the blood bluish in color. After the atrium is filled, the blood passes through a valve to the *right ventricle*. The ventricles provide the main pumping force for circulation as the heart muscle contracts, and their valves prevent the blood from going back up to the atriums. From the right ventricle, the blood enters pulmonary circulation to the lungs, where it becomes oxygenated and, consequently, red in color. The oxygenated blood travels to the *left atrium* of the heart and is passed to the *left ventricle*, which pumps it out through the *aorta* into systemic circulation. It then goes to various parts of the body before returning to the heart and beginning the cycle again. The complete cycle takes about 1 minute in a resting person.

Portions of each quantity of blood pumped by the heart travel through the liver and kidneys, where important functions take place. Figure 2–13 shows

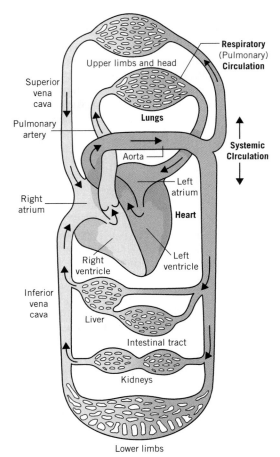

Figure 2–13 Blood circulation in the cardiovascular system. The heart pumps blood through two loops: *respiratory* (pulmonary) circulation and *systemic* (general) circulation. The respiratory loop allows blood to exchange CO_2 for oxygen; the systemic loop transports the blood to and from the rest of the body.

that the *kidneys* receive blood from the general circulatory system, cleanse it of waste products, and pass these wastes on to be eliminated in the urine. The *liver* receives blood from two sources: most of the blood comes from the intestinal tract, and the remainder comes from systemic circulation. What does the liver do to the blood? First, it cleanses the blood of harmful debris, such as bacteria. It is "so effective in removing bacteria that probably not one in a thousand escapes through the liver into the general circulation" (Guyton, 1985, p. 467). Second, the liver removes nutrients and stores them. The blood that comes from the intestinal

tract after we consume a meal is rich in nutrients, such as simple sugars and amino acids. Large portions of these nutrients are retained in the liver until the body needs them. In this way, the ebbs and flows of nutrients in the blood are kept relatively even over time.

BLOOD PRESSURE

Imagine you are holding a long balloon that is filled with air. Its end is tied off. If you squeeze it in the middle, the rest of it expands. This is what happens when pressure is applied to a closed system. The cardiovascular system is also closed, and the myocardium does the squeezing when it pumps blood from the heart. Like the inflated balloon, the cardiovascular system always has some pressure in it. The squeezing increases the pressure.

Our arteries are elastic—they expand when pressure is applied. **Blood pressure** is the force exerted by blood on the artery walls. The heart is at rest between myocardial contractions, while it fills with blood. The resting force in the arteries that occurs at this time is called *diastolic pressure*. When the heart pumps, each contraction produces a maximum force in the arteries, which is called *systolic pressure*. A person's blood pressure is expressed with two numbers: a larger number, representing systolic pressure, followed by a smaller number, representing diastolic pressure. Your physician might tell you that your blood pressure is "120 over 80," for example. Blood pressure readings are standardized in units of *mm Hg* to reflect the number of millimeters (mm) the pressure can raise a column of mercury (Hg).

Blood pressure varies. It changes from one moment to the next, it is higher in one part of the body than in another, and different people have different blood pressures. What determines blood pressure? We can answer this question in two ways; one involves the laws of fluid dynamics, and the other involves factors in people's lives that affect these dynamics. We will start with the first approach and examine five aspects of fluid dynamics that affect blood pressure (McClintic, 1985).

1. *Cardiac output* is the volume of fluid being pumped per minute. Blood pressure increases as cardiac output rises.

2. *Blood volume* refers to the total amount of blood circulating in the system. The greater the volume, the higher the blood pressure needed to move it.

3. *Peripheral resistance* refers to the difficulty fluid encounters in passing through narrow tubes or openings. When you put a nozzle on a hose and turn on the water, the pressure is greater at the nozzle than in the hose. Arteries vary in diameter; resistance is generally greater in small-diameter arteries than in larger ones.

4. *Elasticity*, as we have seen, describes the ease in expanding and contracting. When blood vessels become less elastic, blood pressure—especially systolic pressure—rises.

5. *Viscosity* refers to the thickness of the fluid. The viscosity of blood depends on its composition, such as whether it contains high levels of red blood cells. Thicker blood flows less easily than thinner blood and requires more blood pressure for it to circulate through the cardiovascular system.

What factors in people's lives affect these dynamics? In our everyday lives we experience a variety of states that affect blood pressure. The *temperature* of our environment defines one of these states. When the temperature is high, the blood vessels in our skin enlarge and our cardiac output and diastolic pressure fall, which makes us feel drowsy. Low temperatures have the opposite effect. Another factor is *activity*. For example, exercise increases blood pressure during and after the activity. Simply changing posture can also affect blood pressure. When we go from a lying position to standing, blood flow in the veins that feed the heart slows down because of gravity. This causes a drop in cardiac output and blood pressure. As a result, blood flow to the brain drops and can make us feel dizzy (McClintic, 1985). A third factor is *emotional experience*. When we experience stress, anger, or anxiety, the sympathetic nervous system is activated. This causes cardiovascular reactions, such as increased cardiac output. Both systolic and diastolic pressures increase when people are emotionally aroused (James et al., 1986).

High blood pressure strains and damages the heart and arteries. Some people have high blood pressure consistently over a period of several weeks or more. This condition is called *hypertension*. How high is "high" blood pressure? People whose pressure is at or above 140 (systolic) over 90 (diastolic) are classified as hypertensive, and those at or above 120/80 are "prehypertensive" (AHA, 2004). Optimal blood pressure levels are below 120/80. High blood pressure is a major risk factor for heart disease and

stroke. For instance, when the pressure is very high—such as exceeding 200—the danger is high that a rupture may occur in a blood vessel, particularly in the brain. This is one way by which strokes occur.

There are several known risk factors for hypertension. One risk factor is being overweight (AHA, 2004). Heavy people have more body mass to move when they are active than lighter people do, and they have a larger volume of blood for the heart to pump. Another factor is age—blood pressure generally rises with age. The percentage of individuals who are hypertensive is several times higher among the elderly than among young adults (NCHS, 2003). But aging per se may not be the reason for this relationship. Why? As adults get older, for instance, they tend to get heavier, at least in industrialized countries. In primitive societies where adults do not show an increase in body weight as they get older, blood pressure does not seem to increase with age (Herd & Weiss, 1984).

Other risk factors for hypertension among Americans relate to gender, race, and family history (AHA, 2004; NCHS, 2003; USBC, 2003). The prevalence rate for hypertension is higher for males than for females in adulthood, particularly before about 50 years of age. Thereafter, this gender difference disappears. Black adults develop hypertension at a much higher rate than Whites do. This is so for both sexes and at virtually every age in adulthood. Family history is important, too. People are more likely to become hypertensive if their parents had high blood pressure.

The reasons for these gender, race, and family history differences in hypertension are not fully clear. Evidence from twin studies suggests that genetics plays a role in blood pressure (Rose, 1986; Smith et al., 1987). Perhaps hereditary factors are responsible for these differences. Body weight may also be important: a larger percentage of male than female adults are overweight, and Blacks are more likely than Whites to be overweight; this racial difference is quite pronounced among adult females at all ages (NCHS, 2003). Still other factors, such as stress, may play a role—and so may diet, as we will see in the next section.

BLOOD COMPOSITION

Blood is sometimes thought of as a "liquid tissue" because it consists of cells that are suspended in a liquid. The average adult's body contains about 10 pints of blood (AMA, 2003). Because our bodies can replace blood quickly, we can donate a pint of blood with no ill effects. Blood composition can affect blood pressure. As we saw earlier, the thicker the blood, the more pressure is needed to circulate it. What is blood made of, and how does its composition change its thickness? Blood has two components: formed elements and plasma (Holum, 1994; Tortora & Grabowski, 2003). We'll look at formed elements first.

Formed Elements

Formed elements are the cells and cell-like structures in the blood that constitute about 45% of our blood volume. There are three types of formed elements:

1. *Red blood cells* are the most abundant cells in the blood—there are about 5 million of them per cubic millimeter of blood. They are formed in the bone marrow and have a lifetime of about 3 months. Red blood cells are important mainly because they contain *hemoglobin*, a protein substance that attaches to oxygen and transports this element to body cells and tissues. A*nemia* is a condition in which the level of red blood cells or hemoglobin is below normal (AMA, 2003).

2. *Leukocytes* are white blood cells. Each of several types of leukocytes serves a special protective function—for example, some engulf or destroy bacteria. White blood cells are produced in the bone marrow and various organs in the body. Although there normally are several thousand leukocytes per cubic millimeter of an adult's blood, they are the least abundant type of formed element. *Leukemia* is a malignant disease in which abnormal white blood cells are produced in extremely high quantities, crowding out normal leukocytes, which fight infection, and red blood cells, which prevent anemia (ACS, 2004; AMA, 2003).

3. *Platelets* are granular fragments, produced by the bone marrow, that enable the body to prevent blood loss. They do this by plugging tiny wounds or helping the blood to clot when the wound is larger. H*emophilia* is a disease in which the platelets do not function properly, thereby impairing clotting, because the blood lacks a critical protein (AMA, 2003).

How do formed elements affect the viscosity of blood? The higher the concentration of formed elements suspended in the plasma, the thicker the blood.

Plasma

Plasma is a liquid substance that comprises about 55% of our blood. About 90% of plasma is water, and the remainder consists of proteins and other organic and inorganic elements (Holum, 1994; Tortora & Grabowski, 2003). Plasma proteins increase blood thickness. Although the remaining elements in plasma constitute only a small percentage of its volume, they are very important substances. They include hormones, enzymes, and waste products. They also include the nutrients we derive from digestion—vitamins, minerals, simple sugars, amino acids, and fatty materials.

Fatty materials make up the broad class of substances in the blood called **lipids.** Two of these fatty materials are triglycerides and cholesterol (Holum, 1994; Rhoades & Pflanzer, 1996). *Triglycerides* are the material we commonly think of as fat. Made of glycerol and fatty acids, they are the most abundant lipid in the body. Some of the fatty acids in triglycerides are fully hydrogenated—they cannot take up any more hydrogen—and are called *saturated* for that reason. They are usually solid at room temperature and are mostly derived from animal fat. Other fatty acids are *unsaturated* or *polyunsaturated.* They can take up more hydrogen, are usually liquid at room temperature, and are derived from plants.

Cholesterol is a fatty substance that builds up in patches on artery walls over time and narrows the artery (AMA, 2003). Although the body manufactures most of the cholesterol in the blood, the rest comes from the foods we eat. Eating fats that are highly saturated tends to increase blood cholesterol levels. Let's see why is this a problem.

CARDIOVASCULAR DISORDERS

The accumulation of fatty patches, or plaques, on artery walls is called **atherosclerosis.** These plaques tend to harden. This is a common process by which the diameter and elasticity of arteries is reduced—a condition called **arteriosclerosis** (AMA, 2003). The narrowing and hardening of arteries increase blood pressure. Although arteriosclerosis becomes an increasing problem as adults get older, plaque begins to form early in life. Autopsies on thousands of 15- to 34-year-old American males and females who died of other causes showed that atherosclerosis had begun in all subjects and worsened with age (Strong et al., 1999).

Of the many diseases of the heart and blood vessels, we will describe just a few. One of them is *myocardial infarction*, or "heart attack." Infarction refers to the death of tissue caused by an obstruction in the supply of blood to it. Thus, a myocardial infarction is the death of heart muscle (myocardium) tissue as a result of arterial blockage, usually resulting from a clot in an artery with atherosclerosis (AMA, 2003). Another form of heart disease is *congestive heart failure*, a condition in which an underlying problem, such as severe arteriosclerosis, has reduced the heart's pumping capacity permanently. This condition occurs most frequently in old age. Although its victims can live for years, they are quite disabled. A third form of heart disorder is *angina pectoris*, in which the victim feels strong pain and tightness in the chest because of a brief obstruction in an artery, but little or no damage occurs. Physical exertion or stress often brings on an episode of angina.

One disorder of the blood vessels is an *aneurysm*, a bulge in a weakened section of an artery or vein. If the bulge is in a major blood vessel and it ruptures, the person may die (AMA, 2003). Another disorder of the blood vessels—a *stroke*—occurs when the blood supply to a portion of the brain is disrupted. This can be caused by a rupture in a cerebral artery, causing a hemorrhage in the brain, or by a blood clot, called a *thrombosis*, in a cerebral blood vessel. In either case, damage occurs to the brain. The effects of this damage depend on where it occurs and how extensive it is. It may cause paralysis or sensory impairments, for instance, or even death (AHA, 2004). Aneurysms and strokes can result from atherosclerosis and hypertension.

SUMMARY

The cardiovascular system uses the heart to pump blood through an intricate network of blood vessels. The blood's circulation takes it to body cells, where it supplies oxygen and nutrients for metabolism and takes CO_2 and other waste materials away. Cardiac output, blood volume, peripheral resistance, elasticity, and viscosity affect systolic and diastolic blood pressure. Blood consists of plasma and formed elements. Lipids in the blood can lead to atherosclerosis, the deposit of fatty plaque in arteries, and arteriosclerosis, the thickening and hardening of artery walls.

MODULE 6: THE IMMUNE SYSTEM

You may not realize it, but wars are raging inside your body. They happen continuously, every day. Most of the time they are minor skirmishes, and you are unaware of them. When they become major battles, however, you are usually aware something's going on. The "good guys" are the organs and cells that make up your **immune system.** This system fights to defend the body against "foreign" invaders, such as bacteria and viruses.

The immune system is quite remarkable. Scientists knew little about this intricate and enormously important system until the 1970s. But it is now the subject of major research efforts, and new information about how the immune system functions is emerging rapidly. We know, for instance, that this system is highly sensitive to invasions by foreign matter and is able to distinguish between "self," or normal body constituents, and "not self"—friend and foe.

ANTIGENS

When the body recognizes something as a "not self" invader, the immune system mobilizes body resources and attacks. Any substance that can trigger an immune response is called an **antigen.** Bacteria and viruses are recognized as invaders by telltale aspects of their protein coats and DNA (Krieg et al., 1995).

What triggers an immune response? Some of the first antigens that come to mind are bacteria, fungi, protozoa, and viruses. *Bacteria* are microorganisms that exist in vast numbers throughout the environment—in rivers and oceans, in the air, on and in plants and animals, and in decaying organic matter. Billions of them may populate just one pound of rotting garbage. Because they help in breaking down organic matter into simpler units, their activities are essential to the life and growth of all living things. Some bacteria cause illnesses, such as tuberculosis, scarlet fever, and food poisoning. They do this by growing rapidly and competing with our cells for nutrients and by excreting *toxic*, or poisonous, substances that destroy our cells or impair their metabolic processes (AMA, 2003; Jaret, 1986). Although treatment with antibiotics kills bacteria, these drugs are becoming less effective because they have been overused and bacteria are developing drug-resistant strains (Stolberg, 1998).

*F*ungi are organisms, such as molds and yeasts, that attach to an organic host and absorb nutrients from it. Some of them can cause skin diseases through direct contact, as occurs in ringworm and athlete's foot, and internal diseases by inhaling contaminated air. Other fungi are very beneficial—for example, penicillin is derived from molds. *Protozoa* are one-celled animals that live primarily in water and insects. Drinking water contaminated with protozoa can cause amoebic dysentery, an intestinal illness, and being bitten by an infected mosquito can cause malaria (AMA, 2003; Jaret, 1986).

The tiniest antigens are *viruses*, particles of protein and nucleic acid that are smaller than cells and, strictly speaking, may not even be alive. They consist of genetic information that allows them to reproduce. A virus functions by attaching to a cell, slipping inside, and taking over by issuing its own genetic instructions. The invaded cell abandons its own metabolic activities and becomes a "factory" for making viruses. In short order, enough viruses can be produced to rupture the cell and spread to infect other cells. Viruses can be quite devious, too, developing new strains and lying dormant in the body for periods of time before becoming infectious. They are responsible for a variety of diseases, including flu, herpes, measles, and polio (AMA, 2003).

The immune system also tends to recognize the tissue of an organ transplant as "not self" and treat it as an antigen. This is what physicians mean when they say that the body "rejected" a transplant. There are two basic ways to encourage transplant acceptance. The first is to select the transplant carefully so that the tissues of the donor and the recipient are closely matched. The closer the genetic relationship between the two people, the better the match is likely to be. Identical twins provide the best match, of course. The second approach uses drugs to suppress the immune system so it won't mobilize and reject the organ. A drawback to this approach is that long-term suppression of immune function leaves the patient susceptible to disease.

For many people, the immune system mounts an attack against normally harmless substances, such as pollen, tree molds, poison ivy, animal dander, and particular foods. These people suffer from *allergies*; the specific substances that trigger their allergic reactions, such as sneezing and skin rashes, are called *allergens*. Most allergic people react to some, but not all, of the known allergens—someone with hay fever may not be allergic to poison ivy, for instance. Being allergic is partly determined by heredity (Hershey et al., 1997; Sarafino, 2000). Some allergies can be reduced by administering regular, small doses of the allergen, usually by injection (Coico, Sunshine, & Benjamini, 2003).

THE ORGANS OF THE IMMUNE SYSTEM

The organs of the immune system are located throughout the body (Coico, Sunshine, & Benjamini, 2003; Tortora & Grabowski, 2003). These organs are generally referred to as *lymphatic* or *lymphoid* organs because they have a primary role in the development and deployment of **lymphocytes,** specific white blood cells that are the key functionaries or "soldiers" in our body's defense against invasion by foreign matter. The main lymphatic organs include the bone marrow, thymus, lymph nodes and vessels, and spleen.

Lymphocytes originate in *bone marrow*, the soft tissue in the core of all bones in the body. Some of these cells migrate to one of two organs where they mature. One of these organs is the *thymus*, which is an endocrine gland that lies in the chest. The other organ is not known for certain, but it is thought to have the same function in maturing human lymphocytes that a structure called the "bursa" has in birds (Coico, Sunshine, & Benjamini, 2003). Most of this processing of lymphocytes occurs before birth and in infancy.

The *lymph nodes* are bean-shaped masses of spongy tissue that are distributed throughout the body. Large clusters of them are found in the neck, armpits, abdomen, and groin. What do they do? Each lymph node contains filters that capture antigens and compartments that provide a home base for lymphocytes and other white blood cells. A network of *lymph vessels* that contains a clear fluid called *lymph* connects the lymph nodes. These vessels ultimately empty into the bloodstream. Although the lymph nodes and vessels play an important role in cleansing body cells of antigens, they can become a liability in some forms of cancer either by becoming infected with cancer or

HIGHLIGHT

When Immune Functions Are Absent

I can remember reading for the first time many years ago about a child who had to live in a large plastic "bubble" because he was born with virtually no major immune defenses. The condition he had is very rare and is called *severe combined immunodeficiency disease.* He lived in the bubble because it was germ free—exposure to microorganisms in the general environment would have been fatal. Transplants of healthy bone marrow tissue early in the child's life can cure this disorder (Coico, Sunshine, & Benjamini, 2003). More common inborn immune deficiencies involve the absence of only part of the system and can sometimes be treated with injections.

Having little or no immune defense was almost unheard of prior to the 1970s, and people were not very concerned about immune processes. All that changed in the 1980s as people became aware of the disorder called *acquired immune deficiency syndrome* (AIDS). This disorder is not inborn—it results from an infection when a virus (*human immunodeficiency virus,* or HIV) from an infected person's body fluid, such as blood or semen, contacts the body fluid of an uninfected person. This occurs in three major ways: through sexual activity if the body fluids become exposed to each other, in intravenous drug use if syringes are shared, and from an infected mother to her baby (UNAIDS, 2004). Receiving contaminated blood in a transfusion was once a major source of the virus, but in the United States and many other countries close monitoring of hospital blood supplies has sharply reduced this risk.

Although AIDS is a fatal disorder, it does not kill directly. It disables or destroys important components of the immune system—such as *helper T cells*—and leaves the victim defenseless against a variety of diseases, including pneumonia and a form of cancer called Kaposi's sarcoma (UNAIDS, 2004; Tortora & Grabowski, 2003). One of these diseases becomes the actual cause of death. Although researchers have made great progress in finding ways to prevent and treat AIDS, no fully successful methods exist yet.

AIDS is a worldwide epidemic: health agencies estimate that over 20 million people have died of AIDS since the epidemic began around 1980, about 38 million are currently infected with HIV, and 5 million are newly infected each year (UNAIDS, 2004). In the United States, nearly 890,000 people have been diagnosed with AIDS and over 500,000 have died from it; about 40,000 new infections occur each year (CDC, 2004). Developing countries have had the vast majority of HIV/AIDS cases, most of whom became infected through heterosexual contact. But in North America and Europe, infection has occurred mainly through sharing needles when injecting illicit drugs and practicing certain sexual acts, particularly anal intercourse. Prevention by changing high-risk behavior is essential, and studies of these changes have found encouraging results in developed countries, with gay males and intravenous drug users making substantial changes in their behavior to reduce their risk of infection. But more progress is needed in these groups and among people in the larger population, especially since most AIDS victims around the world have been neither gay nor drug users. We will discuss the topic of AIDS again in later chapters.

---

by distributing cancer cells to other parts of the body through the lymph and blood.

Lymphocytes and antigens that enter the blood are carried to the *spleen,* an organ in the upper left side of the person's abdomen. The spleen functions like an enormous lymph node except that blood, rather than lymph, travels through it. The spleen filters out antigens and serves as a home base for white blood cells. It also removes ineffective or worn-out red blood cells from the body. (Go to 💡.)

SOLDIERS OF THE IMMUNE SYSTEM

White blood cells play a key role in the immune system—they serve as soldiers in our counterattack against invading substances in the body. There are two types of white blood cells. Lymphocytes, as we have seen, are one type; phagocytes are the other.

Phagocytes are scavengers that patrol the body and engulf and ingest antigens. They are not choosy. They will eat anything suspicious that they find in the bloodstream, tissues, or lymphatic system. In the lungs, for instance, they consume particles of dust and other pollutants that enter with each breath. They can cleanse lungs that have been blackened with the contaminants of cigarette smoke, provided the smoking stops. Too much cigarette smoking, over too long a time, destroys phagocytes faster than they can be replenished. (Jaret, 1986, p. 715)

There are two types of phagocytes: *macrophages* become attached to tissues and remain there, and *monocytes* circulate in the blood (Coico, Sunshine, & Benjamini, 2003; Rhoades & Pflanzer, 1996). The fact that phagocytes "are not choosy" means that they are involved in *nonspecific immunity*—they respond to any kind of antigen.

Lymphocytes react in a more discriminating way, being tailored for attacks against specific antigens. The diagram in Figure 2–14 shows that, in addition to the process of nonspecific immunity, there are two types of *specific* immune processes: cell-mediated immunity and antibody-mediated "humoral" immunity. Let's examine these two specific immune processes and how they interrelate.

Cell-mediated immunity operates at the level of the cell. The soldiers in this process are lymphocytes called **T cells**—the name of these white blood cells reflects their having matured in the thymus. T cells are divided into several groups, each with its own important function:

- *Killer T cells* (also called CD8 cells) directly attack and destroy three main targets: transplanted tissue that is recognized as foreign, cancerous cells, and cells of the body that have already been invaded by antigens, such as viruses.

- *Memory T cells* "remember" previous invaders. At the time of an initial infection, such as with mumps, some T cells are imprinted with information for recognizing that specific kind of invader—the virus that causes mumps—in the future. Memory T cells and their offspring circulate in the blood or lymph for long periods of time—sometimes for decades— and enable the body to defend against subsequent invasions more quickly.

- *Delayed-hypersensitivity T cells* have two functions. They are involved in delayed immune reactions, particularly in allergies such as of poison ivy, in

which tissue becomes inflamed. They also produce protein substances called *lymphokines* that stimulate other T cells to grow, reproduce, and attack an invader.

- *Helper T cells* (also called CD4 cells) receive reports of invasions from other white blood cells that patrol the body, rush to the spleen and lymph nodes, and stimulate lymphocytes to reproduce and attack. The lymphocytes they stimulate are from both the cell-mediated and the antibody-mediated immunity (also called "humoral" immunity) processes.

- *Suppressor T cells* operate in slowing down or stopping cell-mediated and antibody-mediated immunity processes as an infection diminishes or is conquered. Suppressor and helper T cells serve to regulate cell-mediated and antibody-mediated immune processes.

What is antibody-mediated immunity, and how is it different from the cell-mediated process? **Antibody-mediated immunity** attacks bacteria, fungi, protozoa, and viruses while they are still in body fluids and before they have invaded body cells. Unlike the cell-mediated process of attacking infected cells of the body, the antibody-mediated approach focuses on the antigens directly. The soldiers in this approach are lymphocytes called **B cells.** Figure 2–14 shows that B cells give rise to *plasma cells* that produce antibodies. This process is often induced by helper T cells or inhibited by suppressor T cells.

How are antibodies involved? **Antibodies** are protein molecules called *immunoglobulins* (Ig) that attach to the surface of invaders and accomplish three results. First, they slow down the invader, making it an easier and more attractive target for phagocytes to destroy. Second, they recruit other protein substances that puncture the membrane of an invading microorganism, causing it to burst. Third, they find new invaders and form *memory B cells* that operate in the future like memory T cells. As you can see, antibodies are like sophisticated weapons in immune system wars. Researchers have identified five classes of antibodies—IgG, IgM, IgA, IgD, and IgE—each with its own special function and "territory" in the body. For example, IgA guards the entrances of the body in fluids, such as saliva, tears, and secretions of the respiratory tract.

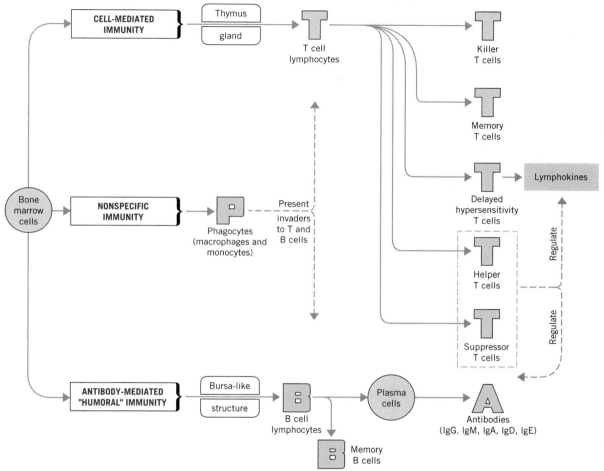

Figure 2–14 Components and interrelationships of the immune system. The bone marrow produces two types of white blood cells (leukocytes): *phagocytes* and *lymphocytes*. There are two kinds of lymphocytes: T *cells*, which are processed by the *thymus* gland; and B *cells*, which are processed by an as-yet-unknown *bursa*like structure. (B cells were first discovered in the "bursa of Fabricius" structure of birds.) See text for description. (*Sources*: Borysenko, 1984; Braveman, 1987; Coico, Sunshine, & Benjamini, 2003; Jaret, 1986; Rhoades & Pflanzer, 1996; Tortora & Grabowski, 2003.)

DEFENDING THE BODY WITH AN IMMUNE RESPONSE

Now that we have seen the soldiers and weaponry of the immune system, let's see how all of this is orchestrated in defending your body. Protection from disease actually involves a series of defenses (Coico, Sunshine, & Benjamini, 2003; Jaret, 1986; Rhoades & Pflanzer, 1996; Tortora & Grabowski, 2003). We will start at the beginning, as the invader tries to enter the body.

Your body's first line of defense is the skin and the mucous membranes that line the respiratory and digestive tracts. The skin serves as a barrier to entry, and mucous membranes are coated with fluids that contain antibodies and other antimicrobial substances. Even though these defenses are highly effective, large numbers of antigens get through, either by eluding the antibodies or by entering a wound in the skin or the mucous membrane. Once an antigen penetrates this barrier, it encounters the second line of defense, which includes nonspecific and specific immune processes. Phagocytes in your blood and tissues attack and consume invading substances of all types. They also have another important function, they present the antigen to B cells and helper T cells, as if to say, "Here's the enemy. Go get 'em!" The B cells respond to this message and to stimulation from helper T cells by giving rise to plasma cells that produce the needed antibodies. The role of the phagocytes is especially important if the antigen is new and the body has no memory B cells for this substance. Antibodies in body fluids attach to microorganisms, thereby aiding the phagocytes and other protein substances that can kill the invaders.

Antigens that manage to get through and invade body cells encounter the third line of defense in which killer T cells destroy the invaded cells. Phagocytes often initiate this process by presenting antigens to T cells, as we have seen. Once again, this is especially important if the antigen is new to the cell-mediated system and the body has no memory T cells for the substance. As the invasion subsides, suppressor T cells slow down the cell-mediated and antibody-mediated immune responses. Memory B and T cells are left in the blood and lymph, ready to initiate the immune response if the same antigen invades the body again.

You may be thinking, "This is a wonderful and complex system that responds when there are antigens in the body, but killer T cells also attack cancer cells. Why? Aren't cancer cells basically normal cells that multiply out of control?" Cancer cells have antigens on their surface to which T cells respond (Coico, Sunshine, & Benjamini, 2003). What scientists don't yet know is why some cancers escape destruction. One reason is that some cancer cells appear to release substances that suppress the immune response (Acevedo, Tong, & Hartsock, 1995; Mizoguchi et al., 1992). Another possibility is that the antigen is simply not easy for the immune system to recognize. As a result, the immune response may not be strong enough to stop the cells from multiplying wildly. Some researchers are studying approaches for treating cancer that are designed to strengthen the patient's own immune processes. In one of these approaches, for example, researchers manufacture antibodies that are sensitive to and seek out a specific type of cancer cell. These approaches are not yet perfected, but they are very promising.

LESS-THAN-OPTIMAL DEFENSES

If our immune systems always functioned optimally, we would become sick much less often. Why and in what ways do our defenses function less than optimally?

Developmental Changes

Immune system functioning changes over the life span, becoming increasingly effective throughout childhood and declining in old age (Coico, Sunshine, & Benjamini, 2003; Tortora & Grabowski, 2003). Newborns come into the world with relatively little immune defense. They have only one type of antibody (IgG), for example, which they receive prior to birth from their mothers through the placenta (the filterlike organ that permits the exchange of nutrients and certain other substances between the bloodstreams of the mother and baby). Infants who are nursed receive antibodies, particularly IgA, in their mother's milk (Ashburn, 1986).

In early infancy, children in technological societies generally begin a regular schedule of immunizations through the use of vaccines. Most vaccines contain dead or disabled disease microorganisms that get the body to initiate an immune response and produce memory lymphocytes, but do not produce the full-blown disease (AMA, 2003; Benjamini, Sunshine, & Leskowitz, 1996). The efficiency and complexity of the immune system develop very rapidly in childhood. As a result, the incidence of illness serious enough to keep children home from school declines with age (Ashburn, 1986).

Throughout adolescence and much of adulthood, the immune system generally functions at a high level. Then, as people approach old age, the effectiveness of the system tends to decline (Braveman, 1987; Tortora & Grabowski, 2003). Although the overall numbers of T cells, B cells, and antibodies circulating in the blood do not decrease, their potency diminishes in old age. Compared with the T cells and B cells of younger adults, those of elderly people respond weakly to antigens and are less likely to generate the needed supply of lymphocytes and antibodies to fight an invasion.

Lifestyles, Stress, and Immune Function

Unhealthful lifestyles, such as smoking cigarettes and being sedentary, have been associated with impaired immune function (Kusaka, Kondou, & Morimoto, 1992). Poor nutrition can also lead to less-than-optimal immune function (Coico, Sunshine, & Benjamini, 2003;

Braveman, 1987). Diets deficient in vitamins seem to diminish the production of lymphocytes and antibodies, for example.

Many people believe stress and illness often are related—and they are right. Research has confirmed this belief, showing, for instance, that people who experience high levels of stress contract more infectious diseases (Dougall & Baum, 2001). Is there a direct link between stress and immune function? Yes. Kiecolt-Glaser and her colleagues from a variety of disciplines have done research to examine this link. One study of first-year medical students who were scheduled to take a series of highly stressful final examinations assessed important variables in two sessions, 1 month before the finals and 1 month after their last major exam (Kiecolt-Glaser et al., 1984). In the first session, the researchers took a sample of blood from the students and had them fill out questionnaires that assessed their experience of loneliness and stress during the past year. In the second session, only a blood sample was taken. Analyses of the samples revealed that killer-T-cell activity was considerably lower in the second (high stress) blood sample than in the first and among students who scored high on the loneliness and stress questionnaires than for those who scored low. Another study analyzed blood samples of married and separated or divorced women (Kiecolt-Glaser et al, 1987). This study found weaker immune function among married women who reported less marital satisfaction than those who reported greater satisfaction

and among the separated or divorced women who refused to accept the fact of the separation or thought excessively about their ex-spouse than those who did not. Studies by other researchers support these results, finding, for example, that immune function is suppressed in individuals several weeks following the deaths of their spouses (Antoni, 1987).

Autoimmune Diseases

When your immune system functions optimally, it attacks foreign matter and protects the body. Sometimes this process goes awry, and the immune response is directed at parts of the body it should protect. Several disorders result from this condition—they are called *autoimmune diseases* (AMA, 2003; Coico, Sunshine, & Benjamini, 2003). One of these diseases is *rheumatoid arthritis*, in which the immune response is directed against tissues and bones at the joints. This causes swelling and pain and can leave the bones pitted. In *rheumatic fever*, the muscles of the heart are the target, often leaving the heart valves permanently damaged. *Multiple sclerosis* results when the immune system attacks the myelin sheath of neurons. Another autoimmune disease is *lupus erythematosus*, which affects various parts of the body, including the skin and kidneys. What causes autoimmune diseases? Although we are not certain of the causes, it is likely that heredity and immune responses to prior infections play important roles.

SUMMARY

The immune system responds to antigens by attacking and eliminating invading substances and microorganisms to protect us from infection and disease. It does this by using white blood cells, including phagocytes and two types of lymphocytes: B cells, which produce antibodies,

and T cells. These cells operate in different immune processes: antibody-mediated immunity uses B cells, cell-mediated immunity involves T cells, and nonspecific immunity uses phagocytes. Stress, poor nutrition, and HIV infection impair the effectiveness of the immune system.

KEY TERMS (SEPARATED BY MODULES)

MODULE 1
neurotransmitter
central nervous
  system

cerebrum
limbic system
thalamus
hypothalamus

cerebellum
brainstem
spinal cord

peripheral nervous
  system
somatic nervous
  system

autonomic nervous
  system
sympathetic
  nervous system
parasympathetic
  nervous system
MODULE 2
endocrine system
hormones
pituitary gland
adrenal glands

MODULE 3
digestive system
enzymes
metabolism
MODULE 4
respiratory system
MODULE 5
cardiovascular
  system
blood pressure

lipids
atherosclerosis
arteriosclerosis
MODULE 6
immune system
antigen
lymphocytes
phagocytes

cell-mediated
  immunity
T cells
antibody-mediated
  immunity
B cells
antibodies

3

STRESS—ITS MEANING, IMPACT, AND SOURCES

Experiencing Stress in Our Lives
What Is Stress?
Appraising Events as Stressful
Dimensions of Stress

Biopsychosocial Aspects of Stress
Biological Aspects of Stress
Psychosocial Aspects of Stress

Sources of Stress Throughout Life
Sources Within the Person
Sources in the Family
Sources in the Community and Society

Measuring Stress
Physiological Arousal
Life Events
Daily Hassles

Can Stress Be Good for You?

PROLOGUE

"Tell me what's been happening in your life in the past several months, Vicki," the college counselor probed in the student's first visit to his office. A nurse suggested that Vicki talk to a counselor because she has been physically run down for the past few months, has been sleeping poorly, and has had several viral infections. During this visit, she described many problems she has experienced. For one thing, this is her first year in college, and, although she goes home most weekends, she has never been away from her family, high school friends, and boyfriend Chris so long before—and she misses them.

Her relationship with Chris is a special problem. He decided to go to a college closer to home so that he could commute. They've been going together for 2 years, and he says he loves her, but Vicki isn't convinced. She feels a lot of jealousy, often imagining that he is seeing others on the side even though she has no evidence that he is. She calls him several times a week, saying she wants to hear his voice, but they both know deep down that she's calling to check up on him. They argue about her suspicions at least once a week. She says he's seeing others because "He's so good looking and I'm so fat." Keeping her weight down is a constant struggle that, in her view, she always loses. Actually, her weight is within the recommended healthful range for her height.

Vicki has also had other difficulties. She worries that she's preparing for the wrong career, argues often with other students about the noise on her dormitory floor, and is overcommitted with schoolwork, club activities on campus, and a part-time job. On top of all this, her car keeps breaking down, she's running out of money to fix it, and her illnesses are compounding her problems.

Vicki's situation is not uncommon. We all experience stress in our everyday lives, probably more than we would like. It occurs in a wide variety of situations and settings—in the family, in school, and on the job, for example. Sometimes the stress experience is brief, and sometimes it continues for a long time. Sometimes it is intense, and sometimes it is mild. It varies across time in a particular person, and it varies between individuals. An experience that is stressful for one person—such as taking a difficult examination—may not be stressful for another and may even be exciting or challenging for still another person.

In this chapter we discuss what stress is, where it comes from, and the impact it has. As we do so, you will find answers to questions you may have about stress. What makes an event stressful? Why does a particular event produce more stress in one person than in another? How does stress affect our bodies and our behavior? Does the experience of stress change across the life span?

EXPERIENCING STRESS IN OUR LIVES

When you hear people say they are "under a lot of stress," you have some idea of what they mean. Usually the statement means they feel unable to deal with the demands of their environment, and they feel tense and uncomfortable. You understand the meaning because you have had similar experiences, which you have labeled "stress." Because of the pervasiveness and commonality of these experiences in our lives, you might expect that defining the concept of stress would be simple. But it isn't. Let's see how psychologists have conceptualized stress and what the prevailing definition is today.

WHAT IS STRESS?

The condition of stress has two components: *physical*, involving direct material or bodily challenge, and *psychological*, involving how individuals perceive circumstances in their lives (Lovallo, 1997). These com-

ponents can be examined in three ways (Dougall & Baum, 2001; Hobfoll, 1989). One approach focuses on the environment: stress is seen as a *stimulus*, as when we have a demanding job or experience severe pain from arthritis or a death in the family. Physically or psychologically challenging events or circumstances are called **stressors.** The second approach treats stress as a *response*, focusing on people's reactions to stressors. We see an example of this approach when people use the word *stress* to refer to their state of tension, and when someone says, "I feel a lot of stress when I have to give a speech." Our responses can be psychological, such as your thought patterns and emotions when you "feel nervous," and physiological, as when your heart pounds, your mouth goes dry, and you perspire. The psychological and physiological response to a stressor is called **strain.**

The third approach describes stress as a *process* that includes stressors and strains, but adds an important dimension: the relationship between the person and environment (Lazarus, 1999; Lazarus & Folkman, 1984a, 1984b). This process involves continuous interactions and adjustments—called **transactions**—with the person and environment each affecting and being affected by the other. According to this view, stress is not just a stimulus or a response, but rather a process in which the person is an active agent who can influence the impact of a stressor through behavioral, cognitive, and emotional strategies. People differ in the amount of strain they experience from the same stressor, such as being stuck in traffic or losing a job. One person who is stuck in traffic and late for an important appointment keeps looking at his watch, honking his horn, and getting angrier by the minute; another person in the same circumstances stays calm, turns on the radio, and listens to music.

We will define **stress** as the circumstance in which *transactions* lead a person to *perceive a discrepancy* between the physical or psychological *demands* of a situation and the *resources* of his or her biological, psychological, or social systems (Lazarus & Folkman, 1984b; Lovallo, 1997; Trumbull & Appley, 1986). Let's look at the four components of this definition, starting at the end.

1. Stress taxes the person's biopsychosocial resources for coping with difficult events or circumstances. These resources are limited, as we saw when Vicki had depleted her ability to cope with her problems, became ill, and sought counseling. Sometimes the impact is focused mainly on our

biological system—for instance, when we tax our physical strength to lift something heavy. More typically, however, the strain has an impact on all three systems; in Vicki's stressful experience, her physical, psychological, and social resources were strained and became exhausted. Other stressful encounters that strain our biopsychosocial resources include participating in a competitive athletic event, being injured in an accident, or becoming nauseated before performing in a play.

2. The phrase *"demands of a situation"* refers to the amount of our resources the stressor appears to require. For instance, Vicki thought achieving the body weight she would need to keep Chris required tremendous willpower.

3. When there is a poor fit, or a mismatch, between the demands of the situation and the resources of the person, a *discrepancy* exists. This generally takes the form of the demands taxing or exceeding the resources, as in Vicki's belief that she did not have the willpower to keep her weight down. But the opposite discrepancy also occurs—that is, our resources may be underutilized—and this can be stressful, too. A worker who is bored by a lack of challenge in a job may find this situation stressful. An important point to keep in mind is that the discrepancy may be either *real* or just *believed* to exist. Suppose you had to take an exam and wanted to do well, but worried greatly that you would not. If you had procrastinated and did not prepare for the test, the discrepancy you see between the demands and your resources might be real. But if you had previously done well on similar exams, prepared thoroughly for this one, and scored well on a pretest in a study guide and yet still thought you would not do well, the discrepancy you see would not reflect the true state of affairs. Stress often results from inaccurate perceptions of discrepancies between environmental demands and the actual resources. Stress is in the eye of the beholder.

4. In our *transactions* with the environment, we assess demands, resources, and discrepancies between them—as Vicki might do if she notices Chris looking at an attractive woman. These transactions are affected by many factors, including our prior experiences and aspects of the current situation. Suppose you are on a track team and are running in a race. Relevant transactions for this race actually began long before the race started, such as during your previous wins and losses, your recent training and fitness, and your knowledge of and experience with your competitors. In the race, these prior transactions have an impact on the continuous transactions that occur: you assess your strength and energy reserves, the position you are in relative to the other runners, and the likelihood that another runner will show a surge of speed toward the end of the race.

APPRAISING EVENTS AS STRESSFUL

Transactions in stress generally involve an assessment process that Richard Lazarus and his coworkers call **cognitive appraisal** (Lazarus, 1999; Lazarus & Folkman, 1984b). Cognitive appraisal is a mental process by which people assess two factors: (1) whether a demand

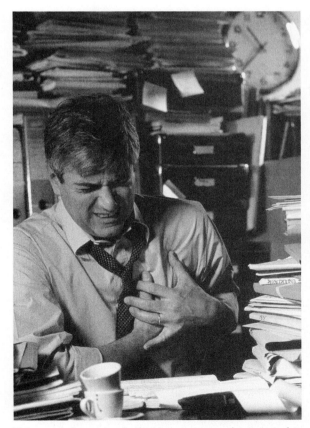

This man's face reveals that he appraises the pain in his chest as stressful.

threatens their physical or psychological well-being and (2) the resources available for meeting the demand. These two factors distinguish two types of appraisal—primary and secondary.

Primary and Secondary Appraisal

When we encounter a potentially stressful circumstance—for example, feeling symptoms of pain or nausea—we first try to assess the meaning of the situation for our well-being. This assessment process is called **primary appraisal.** In effect, this appraisal seeks answers to such questions as, "What does this mean to me?" and "Will I be okay or in trouble?" Your primary appraisal regarding the pain or nausea could yield one of three judgments:

- It *is irrelevant*—as you might decide if you had had similar symptoms before that lasted only a short while and were not followed by illness.
- It *is good* (called "benign-positive")—which might be your appraisal if you wanted very much to skip work or have a college exam postponed.
- It *is stressful*—as you might judge if you feared the symptoms were of a serious illness, such as botulism (a life-threatening type of food poisoning).

Circumstances we appraise as stressful receive further appraisal for three implications: harm-loss, threat, and challenge.

Harm-loss refers to the amount of damage that has already occurred, as when someone is incapacitated and in pain following a serious injury. Sometimes people who experience a relatively minor stressor think of it as a "disaster," thereby exaggerating its personal impact and increasing their feelings of stress (Ellis, 1987). *Threat* involves the expectation of future harm—for example, when hospitalized patients contemplate their medical bills, difficult rehabilitation, and loss of income. Stress appraisals seem to depend heavily on harm-loss and threat (Hobfoll, 1989). *Challenge* is the opportunity to achieve growth, mastery, or profit by using more than routine resources to meet a demand. For instance, a worker might view an offer of a higher-level job as demanding, but see it as an opportunity to expand her skills, demonstrate her ability, and make more money. Many people are happiest when they are engaged in complicated activities that bring them satisfaction.

Sometimes we experience stress even when the stressor does not relate to us directly—the transaction is *vicarious*. If we see other people in stressful circumstances, such as suffering from pain or a life-threatening illness, we may empathize with their feelings and feel vulnerable ourselves. A classic experiment demonstrated empathic appraisal by showing college students a film called *Subincision* (Speisman, Lazarus, Mordkoff, & Davison, 1964). The film showed a rite of passage for young adolescent boys in a primitive society in which the underside of the penis is cut deeply from the tip to the scrotum, using a sharp stone. Before seeing the film, the subjects were divided into four groups, so that each group would see the film a different way. Each group saw the film with either:

1. No sound track.
2. A sound track with a "trauma" narrative that emphasized the pain, danger, and primitiveness of the operation.
3. A narration that denied any pain and potential harm to the boys, describing them as willing participants in a joyful occasion who "look forward to the happy conclusion of the ceremony."
4. A "scientific" narration that encouraged the viewers to watch in a detached manner—for example, the narrator commented, "As you can see, the operation is formal and the surgical technique, while crude, is very carefully followed."

Did the different sound tracks affect the subjects' stress appraisals? Physiological (such as heart rate) and self-report measures of stress showed that, compared with the subjects who saw the film with no sound track, those who heard the trauma narration reacted with more stress, particularly during the film; those who heard the denial and scientific tracks displayed less stress. Thus, people can experience stress vicariously, and their reactions depend on the process of primary appraisal. As a dramatic real-life confirmation of this process, researchers found heightened stress reactions among people across the United States a few days after the September 11 terrorist attacks (Schuster et al., 2001).

Secondary appraisal refers to our assessment of the resources we have available for coping. Although these assessments occur continuously in our transactions, we are especially aware of our secondary appraisals when we judge a situation as potentially stressful and try to determine whether our resources are sufficient to meet the harm, threat, or challenge we face. Examples of secondary appraisal judgments include:

- I can't do it—I know I'll fail.
- I'll try, but my chances are slim.

- I can do it if Ginny will help.
- If this method fails, I can try a few others.
- I can do it if I work hard.
- No problem—I can do it.

The condition of stress that we experience often depends on the outcome of the appraisals we make. When we judge the fit between demands and resources to be close, we may experience little or no stress; but when our appraisals indicate a discrepancy, particularly if we appraise greater demands than resources, we may feel a great deal of stress.

Can stress occur without cognitive appraisals? According to some researchers, it can, particularly in emergency situations. Suppose you are in your car, stopped at a red light. In a split second you hear the squealing of brakes; your body tenses as you say, "Oh my God!"; and a car smashes yours in the rear. Your saying, "Oh my God!" is not really a cognitive appraisal—it's a reflexive response. But a stress reaction has already begun, as the tensing of your body indicates, and this is "*followed* by 'feelings' and appraisals" (Trumbull & Appley, 1986, p. 34). The stress reaction in serious emergencies often includes a state of shock in which the person is stunned, dazed, or disoriented for minutes or hours, or longer (Shontz, 1975). Because cognitive functioning is impaired, appraisal processes are probably limited during shock. When stress does not involve an emergency, cognitive appraisals appear to precede stress reactions (Tomaka et al., 1997).

What Factors Lead to Stressful Appraisals?

Appraising events as stressful depends on two types of factors—those that relate to the person and those that relate to the situation (Lazarus & Folkman, 1984b). Let's begin by looking at how personal factors can affect appraisals of stress.

Personal factors include intellectual, motivational, and personality characteristics. One example is self-esteem: people who have high self-esteem are likely to believe they have the resources to meet demands that require the strengths they possess. If they perceive an event as stressful, they may interpret it as a challenge rather than a threat. Another example relates to motivation: the more important a threatened goal, the more stress the person is likely to perceive (Paterson & Neufeld, 1987). One other example involves the person's belief system: as the psychologist Albert Ellis has noted, many people have irrational beliefs that increase their stress, for instance:

> Because I strongly desire to have a safe, comfortable, and satisfying life, the conditions under which I live *absolutely must* be easy, convenient and gratifying (and it is *awful* and I *can't bear it* and *can't be happy at all* when they are unsafe and frustrating)! (1987, p. 373)

A person who has such a belief is likely to appraise almost any sort of inconvenience as harmful or threatening.

What is it about situations that make them stressful? For instance, events that involve very *strong demands* and are *imminent* tend to be seen as stressful (Paterson & Neufeld, 1987). Thus, patients who expect to undergo a physically uncomfortable or painful medical procedure, such as surgery, tomorrow are likely to view their situation as being more stressful than, say, expecting to have a blood pressure test next week. Table 3.1 presents several other characteristics of events that make them stressful.

Table 3.1   *Characteristics of Stressful Situations*

Characteristic	Description/Example
Life transitions	Passing from one life condition or phase to another. Examples: starting day care or school, moving to a new community, becoming a parent, and retiring from a career.
Difficult timing	Events that happen earlier or later in life than usual or expected. Examples: having a child at 15 years of age and entering college at 40.
Ambiguity	A lack of clarity in a situation. Examples: unclear information for a worker about a function or task and for a patient about his or her health status, treatment options, or prognosis.
Low desirability	Some circumstances are undesirable to most people in virtually all respects. Examples: losing one's house in a fire and getting a traffic ticket.
Low controllability	Circumstances that seem to be outside the person's behavioral or cognitive influence. Examples: low *behavioral control*, such as not being able to do anything to prevent instances of back pain; low *cognitive control*, such as not being able to stop thinking about a traumatic experience.

Sources: Lazarus of Folkman, 1984a, 1984b; Moos & Schaefer, 1986; Paterson & Neufeld, 1987; Quick et al., 1997; Suls & Mullen, 1981; Thompson, 1981.

CLINICAL METHODS AND ISSUES

Posttraumatic Stress Disorder (PTSD)

Experiencing an extremely severe stressor that creates intense fear and horror can lead to a psychiatric condition called *posttraumatic stress disorder.* A person suffering from PTSD is highly aroused (with difficulty sleeping or concentrating), relives the event often, and is unresponsive to other people (Davison, Neale, & Kring, 2004). This disorder occurs frequently in people who have been injured in car accidents, exposed to war, forcibly raped, or subjected to intense, painful cancer treatment (Aaron, Zaglul, & Emery, 1999;

Boscarino, 1997; Foa, 1998; Jacobsen et al., 1998). Being a victim of PTSD may affect people's health: for instance, veterans with PTSD are more likely to develop various serious illnesses in the years after military discharge than veterans without the disorder (Boscarino, 1997; Deykin et al., 2001). Studies have shown that behavior modification therapy with behavioral and cognitive methods can prevent this disorder after a trauma and help people overcome it if it develops (Davison, Neale, & Kring, 2004; Foa, 1998).

DIMENSIONS OF STRESS

Psychologists who study stress or perform therapy to help people manage it assume that the amount of stress a person experiences increases with the frequency, intensity, and duration of the stressor (Cattanach & Rodin, 1988; Sarafino & Ewing, 1999). Evidence supports this assumption. Research has shown that stronger stressors produce greater physio-

logical strain (Steptoe, Cropley, & Joekes, 2000). Many people experience *chronic stress*—that is, it occurs extremely often or lasts a long time, such as when many stressors happen or thoughts about a trauma occur repeatedly over time (Dougall & Baum, 2001). Chronic stress makes people more susceptible to catching cold when exposed to infection than occasional stress (Cohen et al., 1998). (Go to 👤.)

If you have not read Chapter 2, The Body's Physical Systems, and your course has you read the modules from that chapter distributed to later chapters, read now **Modules 1** (The Nervous System) and **2** (The Endocrine System).

BIOPSYCHOSOCIAL ASPECTS OF STRESS

We've seen that stressors can produce strain in the person's biological, psychological, and social systems. Let's examine biopsychosocial reactions to stress more closely.

BIOLOGICAL ASPECTS OF STRESS

Anyone who has experienced a very frightening event, such as a near accident or other emergency, knows that there are physiological reactions to stress. For instance, our heartbeat and breathing rates increase immediately and, a little later, our skeletal muscles

may tremble, especially in the arms and legs. The body is aroused and motivated to defend itself, and the sympathetic nervous system and the endocrine system cause this arousal to happen. After the emergency passes, the arousal subsides. The physiological portion of the response to a stressor—or strain—is called **reactivity,** which researchers measure by comparison against a baseline, or "resting," level of arousal (Matthews, 1986). Genetic factors influence people's degree of reactivity to stressors (Williams et al., 2001). People who are under chronic stress show heightened reactivity when a stressor occurs, and their arousal takes more time to return to baseline levels (Gump & Matthews, 1999).

Many years ago the distinguished physiologist Walter Cannon (1929) provided a basic description of

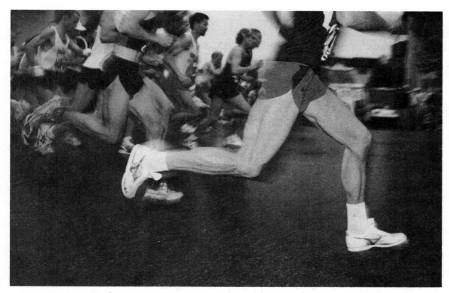

Physical exertion, such as in athletic competition, is a stressor that produces strain in the body.

how the body reacts to emergencies. He was interested in the physiological reaction people and animals make in response to a perceived danger. This reaction has been called the *fight-or-flight* response because it prepares the organism to attack the threat or to flee. In the fight-or-flight response, the perception of danger causes the sympathetic nervous system to stimulate the adrenal glands of the endocrine system to secrete epinephrine, which arouses the body. Cannon proposed that this arousal could have both positive and negative effects: the fight-or-flight response is adaptive because it mobilizes the organism to respond quickly to danger, but the state of high arousal can be harmful to health if it is prolonged.

General Adaptation Syndrome

What happens to the body when high stress levels are prolonged? Hans Selye studied this issue by sub-

jecting laboratory animals to a variety of stressors—such as very high or low environmental temperatures, X rays, insulin injections, and exercise—over a long period of time. He also observed people who experienced stress from being ill. Through this research, he discovered that the fight-or-flight response is only the first in a series of reactions the body makes when stress is long-lasting (Selye, 1956, 1976, 1985). Selye called this series of physiological reactions the **general adaptation syndrome** (GAS). As Figure 3–1 shows, the GAS consists of three stages:

1. **Alarm reaction.** The first stage of the GAS is like the fight-or-flight response to an emergency—its function is to mobilize the body's resources. At the very beginning of the alarm reaction, arousal—as measured by blood pressure, for example—and the disease resistance it produces

Figure 3–1 General adaptation syndrome with three stages. The superimposed graph illustrates changes in the body's degree of resistance against disease.

drop below normal for a moment but then rapidly rise to above normal. This fast-increasing arousal results from activation of the *hypothalamus–pituitary–adrenal axis*: the hypothalamus triggers the pituitary gland to secrete ACTH, which causes the adrenal glands to release epinephrine, norepinephrine, and cortisol into the bloodstream. By the end of this stage in the GAS, the body is fully mobilized. But the body cannot maintain this intense arousal for very long. Some organisms that have experienced a continuous and unrelieved alarm reaction to an extremely intense stressor have died within hours or days.

2. **Stage of resistance.** If a strong stressor continues but is not severe enough to cause death, the physiological reaction enters the stage of resistance. In this stage, the body tries to adapt to the stressor. Physiological arousal remains higher than normal, and the body replenishes the hormones released by the adrenal glands. Despite this continuous physiological arousal, the organism may show few outward signs of stress. But the ability to resist new stressors may become impaired. According to Selye, this impairment may eventually make the individual vulnerable to the health problems he called *diseases of adaptation*. These health problems include ulcers, high blood pressure, asthma, and illnesses that result from impaired immune function.

3. **Stage of exhaustion.** Prolonged physiological arousal produced by severe long-term or repeated stress is costly. It weakens the immune system and depletes the body's energy reserves until resistance is very limited. At this point, the stage of exhaustion begins. If the stress continues, disease and damage to internal organs are likely, and death may occur.

Two lines of evidence support the long-term effects the GAS describes. First, people who experience chronically high levels of stress show greater reactivity to stressors they encounter. Compared with other people, individuals under chronic stress respond to a stressor with greater increases in blood pressure and decrements in immune function (Lepore, Miles, & Levy, 1997; Pike et al., 1997). Second, having to adapt repeatedly to intense stressors may take a high physiologic toll that accumulates over time in a process called *allostatic load* (McEwen & Stellar, 1993). Studies of chronic stress have confirmed that high levels of allostatic load are related to poor health in children and the elderly (Johnston-Brooks et al., 1998; Seeman et al., 1997).

Do All Stressors Produce the Same Physical Reactions?

Many studies have demonstrated that stressors of various types increase the secretion of hormones by the adrenal glands (Baum, Grunberg, & Singer, 1982; Ciaranello, 1983). These stressors include cold temperatures, noise, pain, athletic competition, failure, taking examinations, flying in an airplane, and being in crowded situations.

Selye (1956) believed that the GAS is *nonspecific* with regard to the type of stressor. That is, the series of physiological reactions the GAS describes will occur regardless of whether the stress results from very cold temperature, physical exercise, illness, or the death of a loved one. However, although various stressors increase the secretion of adrenal hormones, the notion of nonspecificity does not take important psychosocial processes into account. Three lines of evidence suggest this is a problem.

First, some stressors appear to elicit a stronger *emotional* response than others do. This is important because the amount of hormone released in reaction to a stressor that involves a strong emotional response, as a *sudden* increase in environmental temperature might produce, appears to be different from the amount released with a less emotional stressor, such as a *gradual* increase in temperature. After conducting extensive studies of various stressors and hormones, John Mason concluded that he and his colleagues "have not found evidence that any single hormone responds to *all* stimuli in *absolutely* nonspecific fashion" (1975, p. 27). For instance, some stressors led to increases in epinephrine, norepinephrine, and cortisol, but other stressors increased only two of these hormones. He also pointed out that research conducted since Selye first described the GAS has shown that stressors are most likely to trigger the release of large amounts of all three of these hormones if the individual's response includes a strong element of emotion.

Second, findings of many studies conducted on stress led Marianne Frankenhaeuser to propose that the pattern of physiological arousal under stress depends on two factors: effort and distress. *Effort* involves the person's interest, striving, and determination, and *distress* involves anxiety, uncertainty, boredom, and dissatisfaction:

> *Effort with distress* tends to be accompanied by an increase of both catecholamine *and* cortisol excretion. This is the state typical of daily hassles. In working life, it commonly occurs among people engaged in repetitious, machine-paced jobs on the assembly line or in highly routinized work as, for example, at a computer terminal.
>
> *Effort without distress* is a joyous state, characterized by active and successful coping, high job involvement, and a high degree of personal control. It is accompanied by increased catecholamine secretion, whereas cortisol secretion may be suppressed.
>
> *Distress without effort* implies feeling helpless, losing control, giving up. It is generally accompanied by increased cortisol secretion, but catecholamines may be elevated, too. This is the endocrine profile typical of depressed patients. (1986, p. 107)

Because distress is an emotion, Frankenhaeuser's view ties in with and extends that of Mason.

Third, evidence indicates that cognitive appraisal processes appear to play a role in people's physiological reaction to stressors. This role is suggested by the results of a study by Katherine Tennes and Maria Kreye (1985). The researchers assessed elementary school children's cortisol levels in urine samples taken on regular school days and on days when achievement tests were given. The expected increase in cortisol on test days was found, but not for all children—their intelligence was an important factor. Intelligence test scores were obtained from school records. Cortisol levels increased on test days for children with above-average intelligence but not for children with low to average intelligence. The influence of intelligence suggests that the brighter children were more concerned about academic achievement and, as a result, appraised the tests as more threatening than did the other children.

To summarize, the basic structure of the GAS appears to be valid, but it incorrectly assumes that all stressors produce the same physiological reactions and fails to include the role of psychosocial factors in stress.

PSYCHOSOCIAL ASPECTS OF STRESS

At this juncture, we can begin to see how interwoven our biological, psychological, and social systems are in the experience of stress. Stressors produce physiological changes, but psychosocial factors also play a role. To give a more complete picture of the interplay among these systems, we will now examine the impact of stress on people's cognitive, emotional, and social systems.

Cognition and Stress

Many students have had this experience: While taking a particularly stressful exam in school, they may neglect or misinterpret important information in a question or have difficulty remembering an answer they had studied well the night before. It is infuriating to know that an answer is "on the tip of your tongue," especially since you will probably remember it after the test is over. High levels of stress affect people's memory and attention. Let's see how.

Stress can impair cognitive functioning, often by distracting our attention. Noise can be a stressor, which can be chronic for people who live in noisy environments, such as next to train tracks or highways (Lepore, 1997). How does chronic noise affect cognitive performance? Many people try to deal with this kind of stress by changing the focus of their attention from the noise to relevant aspects of a cognitive task—they "tune out" the noise. Evidence suggests that children who try to tune out chronic noise may develop generalized cognitive deficits because they have difficulty knowing which sounds to attend to and which to tune out (Cohen et al., 1986).

But stress can also enhance our attention, particularly toward the stressor. For instance, researchers had people watch a series of pictures while listening to a story about a boy and his mother who go to a hospital (Cahill et al., 1994). For some subjects, the story was emotional: the boy had a terrible accident, his feet were severed, and surgeons reattached the feet. For other subjects, the story was neutral: the boy went to the hospital to watch activities there. Before this experience, the subjects with each type of story received an injection of either a placebo or a drug that stops the action of epinephrine and norepinephrine. When tested a week later, the subjects who heard the emotional story remembered more details of it if they had gotten the placebo rather than the drug. But the drug had no effect on subjects' memory of the neutral story. These findings suggest that epinephrine and norepinephrine enhance the memory of stressors we experience.

Not only can stress affect cognition, but the reverse is true, too. In the opening story about Vicki, she kept imagining that her boyfriend was seeing other women, which was very distressing for her. Her thinking was making the stress chronic. Andrew Baum (1990) has studied this kind of thinking in individuals who were living near the Three Mile Island nuclear power plant in Pennsylvania when a major nuclear accident occurred. He found that some of these people still experienced stress from the incident years later, but others did not. One of the main factors differentiating these people was that those who continued to feel this stress had trouble keeping thoughts about the accident and their fears out of their minds. It seems likely that these thoughts perpetuated their stress and made it chronic.

Emotions and Stress

Long before infants can talk, they display what they feel by their motor, vocal, and facial expressions. You can test this with a little experiment: place a bit of a bitter food, such as unsweetened chocolate, in a newborn's mouth and watch the baby's face—the eyes squint, the brows drop and draw together, the mouth opens, and the tongue juts out. This is the facial expression for the emotion of disgust. Each emotion has a specific facial pattern. Using procedures like this one, researchers have shown that although newborn babies do not display all the emotional expressions they will develop, they do express several, such as disgust, distress, and interest (Izard, 1979).

Emotions tend to accompany stress, and people often use their emotional states to evaluate their stress. Cognitive appraisal processes can influence both the stress and the emotional experience (Lazarus, 1999; Scherer, 1986). For example, you might experience stress and fear if you came across a snake while walking in the woods, particularly if you recognized it as poisonous. Your emotion would not be joy or excitement, unless you were studying snakes and were looking for this particular type. Both situations would involve stress, but you might experience fear if your appraisal was one of threat, and excitement if your appraisal was one of challenge.

Fear is a common emotional reaction that includes psychological discomfort and physical arousal when we feel threatened. Of the various types and intensities of fears people experience in everyday life, psychologists classify many into two categories: phobias and anxiety. *Phobias* are intense and irrational fears that are directly associated with specific events and situations. Some people are afraid of being enclosed in small rooms, for instance, and are described as claustrophobic. *Anxiety* is a vague feeling of uneasiness or apprehension—a gloomy anticipation of impending doom—that often involves a relatively uncertain or unspecific threat. That is, the person may not be aware either of the situations that seem to arouse anxiety or of exactly what the "doom" entails. Patients awaiting surgery or the outcome of diagnostic tests generally experience high levels of anxiety. In other situations, anxiety may result from appraisals of low self-worth and the anticipation of a loss of either self-esteem or the esteem of others.

Stress can also lead to feelings of sadness or *depression*. We all feel depressed at times, although we may call the feeling "sad," "blue," or "unhappy." These feelings are a normal part of life for children and adults. The difference between normal depression and depression as a serious *disorder* is a matter of degree. Depression meets the criteria for a psychological disorder when it is severe, frequent, and long-lasting. People with this disorder tend to:

- Have a mostly sad mood nearly every day
- Appear listless, with loss of energy, pleasure, concentration, and interest
- Show poor sleeping habits and either poor appetite or markedly increased appetite
- Have thoughts of suicide, feeling hopeless about the future
- Have low self-esteem, often blaming themselves for their troubles (Davison, Neale, & Kring, 2004)

Having long-term disabling health problems, such as being paralyzed by a stroke, often leads to depressive disorders.

Another common emotional reaction to stress is *anger*, particularly when the person perceives the situation as harmful or frustrating. You can see this in the angry responses of a child whose favorite toy is taken away or an adult who is stuck in a traffic jam. Anger has important social ramifications—it can produce aggressive behavior, for instance.

Social Behavior and Stress

Stress changes people's behavior toward one another. In some stressful situations, such as train crashes, earthquakes, and other disasters, many people may work together to help each other survive. In other stressful situations, people may become less sociable or caring and more hostile and insensitive toward other individuals.

When stress and anger join, negative social behaviors often increase. Research has shown that stress-produced anger increases aggressive behavior, and these negative effects continue after the stressful event is over (Donnerstein & Wilson, 1976). This increased aggressive behavior has important implications in real life, outside the laboratory. Child abuse is a major social problem that poses a serious threat to children's health, physical development, and psychological adjustment. Studies have found a connection between parental stress and child abuse (Kempe, 1976; Kolbe et al., 1986). Prior to an act of battering, frequently the parent has experienced a stressful crisis, such as the loss of a job. A parent under high levels of stress is at risk of losing control. If, for example, the child runs around the house making a racket, a stressed parent may become very angry, lose control, and start beating the child.

Stress also affects helping behavior. This was shown in an experiment conducted in a shopping center (Cohen & Spacapan, 1978). After each subject completed either a difficult shopping task or an easy one in either a crowded or uncrowded shopping center, he or she walked through a deserted hallway to meet with the researcher. In the hallway, the subject encountered a woman who feigned dropping a contact lens—a situation in which the subject could provide help. Those subjects who had just experienced the most stress, having completed the difficult shopping task in crowded conditions, helped less often and for less time than those with the easy task in uncrowded conditions.

Gender and Sociocultural Differences in Stress

Does the experience of stress depend on a person's gender and sociocultural group membership? Apparently it does. Women generally report having experienced a greater number of major and minor stressors than men do (Davis, Matthews, & Twamley, 1999). Although this difference may result partly from women's greater willingness to say they experienced stress, it probably also reflects real variations in experiences. Because in today's two-income households, mothers still do most of the chores at home, they often have heavier daily workloads than men and greater physiological strain than women without children (Luecken et al., 1997; Lundberg & Frankenhaeuser, 1999).

Being a member of a minority group or being poor appears to increase the stressors people experience (Clark et al., 1999; Johnson et al., 1995). Research in the United States has shown that minority and poor individuals report having experienced a disproportionately large number of major stressors (Gottlieb & Green, 1987). For example, Black Americans report far more stressors than Hispanics, who in turn report more stress than do nonminority people.

There appear to be gender and sociocultural differences in physiological strain from stressors, too. Many studies have found that men show more reactivity than females when psychologically stressed (Collins & Frankenhaeuser, 1978; Kudielka et al., 1998; Ratliff-Crain & Baum, 1990). Men also seem to take longer for their physiological arousal to return to baseline levels after the stressor has ended (Earle, Linden, & Weinberg, 1999). But some evidence suggests that men and women differ in the events they find stressful, and the strength of reactivity compared with that of the opposite sex may be greater when the stressor is relevant to the person's gender (Weidner & Messina, 1998). For instance, men show greater reactivity than women do when their competence is challenged, and women show greater reactivity than men when their friendship or love is challenged (Smith et al., 1998).

Regarding sociocultural differences, some studies in the United States have found that Blacks show greater reactivity than Whites when under stress (McAdoo et al., 1990; Miller et al., 1995). And a study found that Black siblings were more similar to each other in their degree of reactivity than White siblings were, which suggests that heredity may play a role (Wilson et al., 1995). But the outcomes of other studies suggest that differences between Blacks and Whites vary depending on the stressor and the subjects' gender (Saab et al., 1997; Sherwood et al., 1995).

We've seen that the effects of stress are wide ranging and involve an interplay among our biological, psychological, and social systems. Even when the stressor is no longer present, the impact of the stress experience can continue. Some people experience more stress than others do, but we all find stress somewhere in our lives. Stress arises from many sources.

SOURCES OF STRESS THROUGHOUT LIFE

Babies, children, and adults all experience stress. The sources of stress may change as people develop, but the condition of stress can occur at any time throughout life. Where does stress come from, and what are its sources? To answer this question, we will examine sources that arise within the *person*, in the *family*, and in the *community* and *society*.

SOURCES WITHIN THE PERSON

Sometimes the source of stress is within the person. *Illness* is one way stress arises from within the individual. Being ill creates physical and psychological demands on the person, and the degree of stress these demands produce depends on the seriousness of the illness and the age of the individual, among other things. Why is the person's age important? For one thing, the ability of the body to fight disease normally improves in childhood and declines in old age (Coico, Sunshine, & Benjamini, 2003). Another reason is that the meaning of a serious illness for the individual changes with age. For example, young children have a limited understanding of disease and death. For this reason, their appraisal of stress that arises from their illness is likely to focus on current, rather than future, concerns—such as how well they feel at the moment and whether their activities are impaired (La Greca & Stone, 1985). Stress appraisals by ill adults typically include both current difficulties and concerns for the future, such as whether they may be disabled or may die.

Another way stress arises within the person is through the appraisal of opposing motivational forces, when a state of *conflict* exists. Suppose you are registering for next semester and find that two courses that you need meet at the same time. You can take only one. Which will you choose? You have a conflict—you are being pushed and pulled in two directions. Many conflicts are more momentous than this one. We may need to choose between two or more job offers, or different medical treatments, or houses we are thinking of buying, for instance. Conflict is a major source of stress.

The pushes and pulls of conflict produce two opposing tendencies: *approach* and *avoidance*. These two tendencies characterize three basic types of conflict (Miller, 1959):

1. *Approach/approach conflict* arises when we are attracted toward two appealing goals that are incompatible. For example, individuals who are trying to lose weight to improve either their health or appearance experience frequent conflicts when delicious, fattening foods are available. Although people generally resolve an approach/approach conflict fairly easily, the more important they perceive the decision to be, the greater the stress it is likely to produce.

2. *Avoidance/avoidance conflict* occurs when we are faced with a choice between two undesirable situations. For example, patients with serious illnesses may be faced with a choice between two treatments that will control or cure the disease, but have very undesirable side effects. People in avoidance/avoidance conflicts usually try to postpone or escape from the decision. When delaying or escaping is not possible, people often vacillate between the two alternatives, changing their minds repeatedly. Sometimes they get someone else to make the decision for them. People generally find avoidance/avoidance conflicts difficult to resolve and very stressful.

3. *Approach/avoidance conflict* arises when we see attractive and unattractive features in a single goal or situation. This type of conflict can be stressful and difficult to resolve. Consider, for instance, individuals who smoke cigarettes and want to quit. They may be torn between wanting to improve their health and wanting to avoid the weight gain and cravings they believe will occur if they quit.

As you may realize, conflicts can be more complicated than the examples we have considered. People often have to choose between two or more alternatives, recognizing that each has multiple attractive and unattractive features, as in buying a new house or car. In general, people are likely to find conflict stressful when the choices involve many features, when opposing motivational forces have fairly equal strength, and when the "wrong" choice can lead to very negative and permanent consequences. These conditions often apply when people face major decisions about their health.

SOURCES IN THE FAMILY

The behavior, needs, and personality of each member of a family have an impact on and interact with those of the other members of the family system, sometimes producing stress. Interpersonal discord can arise from financial problems, from inconsiderate behavior, or from opposing goals, such as which television program to watch. Living in an overcrowded household increases discord over privacy and the use of family resources, such as the bathroom. Of the many sources of stress in the family, we will focus on three: adding a new family member, divorce, and illness and death in the family.

An Addition to the Family

A new child in the family is a joyful event, but it also brings stress—particularly to the mother, of course, during pregnancy and after the birth. But an addition to the family is stressful to other family members, too. For instance, the father may worry about the health of his wife and baby or fear that his relationship with his wife may deteriorate, and both parents may feel the need to earn more money. The arrival of a new baby can also be stressful to other children in the family.

An important factor in parental stress relates to the child's personality. Each baby comes into the world with personality dispositions, which are called **temperaments** (Buss & Plomin, 1975; Thomas, Chess, & Birch, 1970). Pediatric nurses and physicians, well aware of the unique combinations of temperaments that babies show right from birth, describe infants broadly as "easy" babies and "difficult" ones. These terms do, in fact, capture the general dispositions of most infants fairly accurately on the basis of differences in the way babies react to feeding, cuddling, bathing, dressing, and so on.

Temperamentally difficult babies tend to cry a great deal—often very loudly—and efforts to soothe them do not work very well. They resist being introduced to new foods, routines, and people, and their patterns of sleep, hunger, and bowel movements are hard to predict from day to day. These behaviors are stressful for parents. Although only about 10% of babies are classified as "difficult," displaying most or all of these traits fairly consistently, many others show some of these traits at least occasionally. Although temperaments are fairly stable across time, with aspects of these traits continuing for many years, many difficult children show changes toward the development of easy traits (Carey & McDevitt, 1978; Thomas, Chess, & Birch, 1970).

Divorce

A divorce produces many stressful transitions for all members of the family as they deal with changes in their social, residential, and financial circumstances. In the case of the children, they may move to a new neighborhood, be left with new sitters, or have to take on new chores at home. The custodial parent may not be very available to the children because of work or other preoccupations. Adapting to divorce usually takes several years, and some family members may never adjust fully (Wallerstein, 1983). Parents can help their children adjust to a divorce by maintaining a loving, secure home life and (Sarafino & Armstrong, 1986):

- Telling the children in advance of the impending separation.
- Encouraging open communication and answering the children's questions truthfully but sensitively.
- Giving information, such as what changes will happen, at the children's levels of understanding.
- Recruiting help and advice from others, such as relatives, parent organizations, counselors, and the children's school personnel.
- Encouraging the children to have contact with both parents.

Family Illness, Disability, and Death

The following is a familiar story to many parents: In the middle of a frantic day at work, the parent receives a call from the school nurse, who says, "Your child is sick. You'll have to come and pick him up." Having a sick child adds to the stress in an already stressful day.

When children have a serious chronic illness, their families must adapt to unique and long-term stress (Johnson, 1985; Leventhal, Leventhal, & Van Nguyen, 1985; Quittner et al., 1998). Part of the stress stems from the amount of time needed to care for the child and from the reduced freedom family members have in their schedules. For example, a child with the respiratory disease called cystic fibrosis may need to have an adult thump his or her back two or three times a day to reduce the mucus that collects in the lungs (AMA, 2003). The family also faces many difficult decisions and must learn about the illness and how to care for the child. The medical needs of chronically ill children are expensive, and this burden adds to the family's stress. Relationships between family

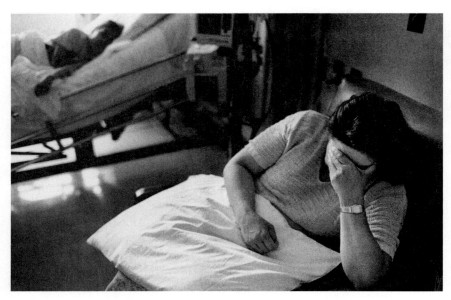

A mother overcome by the stress of dealing with her daughter's recurrent leukemia episodes and hospital treatments. Family stressors increase when children require special attention.

members may also suffer. The parents are likely to feel that having a chronically ill child reduces the time they have to devote to each other. In addition, other children in the family may feel isolated and deprived of parental attention.

Adult illness or disability is another source of family stress. The strain on their financial resources is especially severe if the sick adult is a principal breadwinner. Having a physically ill or disabled adult in the family restricts the family's time and personal freedom and produces very important changes in interpersonal relationships (Leventhal, Leventhal, & Van Nguyen, 1985; Michela, 1987). For example, suppose a man has a heart attack. His spouse may experience stress from fears that he may have another attack and from changes in his behavior, such as being more irritable and dependent. Although the couple may show increased affection for one another during convalescence, their sexual relations are generally curtailed—often because of fears that sex could induce another attack. And the roles of family members change: the healthy spouse and the children who are old enough take on many of the responsibilities and tasks of the recovering spouse. As the convalescing adult begins to show good physical recovery, the stress generally diminishes in the family.

Often the stress a family experiences when an adult is seriously ill depends on the sick person's age. For instance, advanced cancer in an elderly person has a very different meaning than the same illness in someone at 30 years of age, especially if the young adult has one or more children. In the latter case, the disease is inconsistent with the person's roles and threatens the family unit. Chronic illness is likely to produce intense frustration, distress, and anger if it is out of step with expectations and needs for the future (Leventhal, Leventhal, & Van Nguyen, 1985). But if an elderly person who is ill or disabled must live with and be cared for by relatives, the stress for all those in the household can be severe, especially if the person requires constant care and shows mental deterioration (Martire & Schulz, 2001). Elderly spouses who provide care for such individuals are often emotionally distressed and show heightened physiological strain, making them more susceptible to infectious disease (Vedhara et al., 1999).

Age is also an important factor in the experience of stress when a family member dies. Some children suffer the loss of a parent during the childhood years—one of the most traumatic events a child can face. Children under about 5 years of age seem to grieve for the lost parent less strongly and for a shorter time than older children and adolescents do (Garmezy, 1983). This age difference probably results from their different levels of understanding about the nature of death. Children's concept of death changes between 4 and 8 years of age (Lonetto, 1980; Speece & Brent, 1984). Young children often think death is reversible: the

HIGHLIGHT

Gender Differences in Caregiving?

If I mentioned to you that an elderly friend was receiving care at home from family members, would you picture most of those caregivers as women? Probably most people would, and studies have typically found more women than men are caregivers (Vitaliano, Zhang, & Scanlan, 2003). But some researchers have questioned the societal image of women being the main caregivers among family members.

To examine this issue, Baila Miller and Lynda Cafasso (1992) did a **meta-analysis**—a statistical research method that pools the results of prior studies to create an integrated overview of their findings. No new data are collected. The prefix *meta* means "after" or "among"—thus, researchers apply this method *after* a series of studies has been done and assess the overall relationships these studies found *among* relevant variables. Meta-analysis is a useful technique for revealing patterns in relationships and clarifying what has been found, *especially* when some studies found different results than others. This meta-analysis was based on 14 published studies that had investigated gender differences in caregiving for elderly individuals.

Miller and Cafasso decided to examine the data from these studies for gender differences in several aspects of the caregiving experience. These analyses revealed that female caregivers were somewhat more likely than males to:

- Carry out personal care activities, such as dressing, bathing, and grooming the elderly person.

- Do the household chores in the elderly person's dwelling.
- Report experiencing greater degrees of stress from the caregiving.

But these differences were not very great, and no gender differences were found for any of the other aspects of caregiving, including:

- The degree of caregiving involvement, which was based on the number of tasks the caregiver had to do, the extent of assistance the elderly person needed to perform tasks, and the number of hours spent in caregiving.
- The extent to which the elderly person was functionally impaired, or unable to carry out activities of daily living.
- The caregiver's involvement in managing the elderly person's finances.

The researchers concluded that their results contradict gender-role stereotypes of Western societies and indicate that females and males are fairly similar in the degree to which they provide care for elderly relatives, the types of caregiving tasks they do, and the stress they experience from caregiving.

---

person is simply living somewhere else—such as underground—and can come back. By about 8 years of age, most children understand that death is final and involves an absence of bodily functions.

An adult whose child or spouse dies suffers a tremendous loss (Kastenbaum & Costa, 1977; Kosten, Jacobs, & Kasl, 1985). Losing a child creates other losses—for example, bereaved mothers reported that they had lost important hopes and expectations for the future (Edelstein, 1984). Parents who lose their only child lose their identity and role as mothers and fathers, too. When a spouse dies, the surviving spouse also loses important hopes, expectations, and roles—as well as the one companion who made him

or her feel loved, wanted, special, and safe. Although the loss of a spouse is difficult at any age, it appears to be especially stressful in early adulthood (Ball, 1976–1977). (Go to 💡.)

SOURCES IN THE COMMUNITY AND SOCIETY

Interpersonal contacts people make outside the family provide many sources of stress. For instance, children experience stress at school and in competitive events, such as in sports and talent performances. Much of the stress adults experience is associated with their occupations, and a variety of environmental situations can be stressful. We will focus on how people's jobs and environments can be sources of stress.

Jobs and Stress

Almost all people at some time in their lives experience stress that relates to their occupations. Often these stressful situations are minor and brief and have little impact on the person. But for many people, the stress is intense and continues for long periods of time. What factors make jobs stressful?

The *demands of the task* can produce stress in two ways. First, the workload may be too high. Some people work very hard for long hours over long periods of time because they feel required to do so—for example, if they need the money or think their bosses would be unhappy if they did not. Studies have found

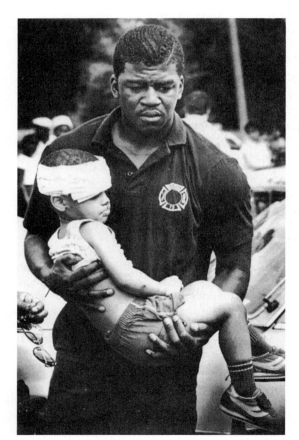

Firefighters have stressful jobs, partly because of their responsibility for people's lives. *Reprinted courtesy of Bunny Hoest.*

that excessive workloads are associated with increased rates of accidents and health problems (Mackay & Cox, 1978; Quick et al., 1997). Second, some kinds of job activities are more stressful than others. For example, repetitive manual action, as in cashier work, can be stressful and is linked to physical symptoms such as neck and shoulder pain (Lundberg et al., 1999). Also, jobs that underutilize workers' abilities can produce stress. As one worker put it:

> I sit by these machines and wait for one to go wrong, then I turn it off, and go and get the supervisor. They don't go wrong very much. Sometimes I think I'd like them to keep going wrong, just to have something to do. . . . It's bloody monotonous. (Mackay & Cox, 1978, p. 159)

Another kind of activity that can produce stress is the evaluation of an employee's job performance—a process that can be difficult for both the supervisor and the employee.

Jobs that involve a *responsibility for people's lives* can be very stressful. Medical personnel have heavy workloads and must deal with life or death situations frequently. Making a mistake can have dire consequences. In an intensive care unit of a hospital, emergency situations are common; decisions must be made instantly and carried out immediately and accurately. As part of the job,

> the nurse must reassure and comfort the man who is dying of cancer; she must change the dressings of a decomposing, gangrenous limb; she must calm the awakening disturbed "overdose" patient. . . . It is hard to imagine any other situation that involves such intimacy with the frightening, repulsive, and forbidden. . . . To all this is added the repetitive contact with death. (Hay & Oken, 1985, p. 108)

These and other conditions of jobs in the health professions take their toll, often leading to emotional exhaustion (Maslach, Schaufeli, & Leiter, 2001). Police and fire personnel face similar stressors in their jobs.

Several other aspects of jobs can increase workers' stress (Cottington & House, 1987; Hepburn, Loughlin, & Barling, 1997; Mackay & Cox, 1978; Quick et al., 1997). For example, stress can result from:

- *The physical environment* of the job. Stress increases when the job involves extreme levels of noise, temperature, humidity, or illumination.

- *Perceived insufficient control* over aspects of the job. People experience stress when they have little opportunity to learn new skills and to make decisions on their own (Fitzgerald et al., 2003).

- *Poor interpersonal relationships.* People's job stress increases when a coworker or customer is socially abrasive or treats them unfairly (Fitzgerald et al., 2003).

- *Perceived inadequate recognition or advancement.* Workers feel stress when they do not get the recognition or promotions they believe they deserve.

- *Job loss.* People experience stress when they lose their jobs or think they are likely to be fired or laid off. Research has found that job loss is associated with subsequent depression and health problems, particularly if the person encounters major financial difficulties (Price, Choi, & Vinokur, 2002).

Research has linked these aspects of jobs to physiological strain—particularly for high blood pressure and heart rate (Melin et al., 1999; Schnall et al., 1998; Steptoe, Cropley, & Joekes, 2000)—and eventual development of heart disease (Bosma et al., 1998).

Many elderly people approach *retirement* with expectations of blissful freedom and leisure. But it does not always turn out that way. Retirees often find that they have lost opportunities for social interaction and an important part of their identity. They may miss the power and influence they once had, the structure and routines of a job, and the feeling of being useful and competent (Bohm & Rodin, 1985; Bradford, 1986). The stress from these circumstances can affect not only the retirees, but their spouses too. What's more, many retirees have the added problem that their income is not sufficient for their needs.

Environmental Stress

Have you ever been at a big noisy event with thousands of people jammed into an arena and felt physiologically aroused, tense, and uncomfortable? Events like these can be stressful because of the noise and the crowded conditions (Evans, 2001). Crowded conditions reduce your control over interpersonal interaction and restrict your ability to move about freely or obtain resources, such as seats.

Some environmental conditions are intensely stressful—imagine how you would react to learning that a hazardous substance has seeped into the water supply where you live. How much of it have you and your family already drunk? Will you develop serious illnesses because of it in the future? Can the substance be removed? And after it is, will you believe there is no more danger? Can you sell your house now without suffering a great financial loss? Many people who are exposed to hazardous substances or other continuous threats in their environment worry for years about what will happen to them (Baum, 1988; Bland et al., 1996; Specter, 1996). Natural disasters, such as earthquakes, have the added difficulty of long-term disruptions in social relationships, which worsen the stress (Bland et al., 1997).

In the late 1970s, attention was focused on this type of situation at Love Canal in New York State, where a chemical dump site had contaminated a residential community. In many ways this situation is more stressful than a natural disaster—at least a tornado ends quickly, its damage can be assessed, and much of the damage can be repaired in time. At Love Canal, however, "the nightmare goes on and on" (Holden, 1980). Another example of the psychological effects of living in a hazardous environment comes from the nuclear accident at the Three Mile Island power plant in Pennsylvania. More than a year after the accident, researchers compared the stress of nearby residents to that of people who lived near a different nuclear facility that had not had an accident. This comparison revealed greater psychological and physiological evidence of stress among the residents around Three Mile Island than among those near the other facility (Fleming et al., 1982).

So far in this chapter we have seen that stress involves biopsychosocial reactions and that all sorts of circumstances can be stressors, including extreme temperatures, noise, taking an exam, being stuck in a traffic jam, having a painful medical test, getting married, and losing a job. The possible stimuli and reactions, and the appraisal processes that link them, make for an interesting question: If you were doing research and needed to know whether different people had experienced different amounts of stress, how could you assess this variable?

MEASURING STRESS

Researchers have used several different approaches for measuring stress. The three most commonly used approaches involve assessing people's physiological arousal, life events, and daily hassles.

(a)

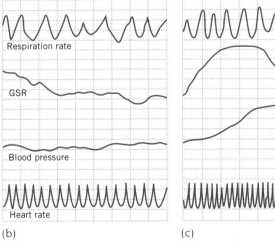

(b)   (c)

Figure 3–2 A typical polygraph (*a*) makes a graphical record of several indexes of arousal, including blood pressure, heart rate, respiration rate, and the galvanic skin response (the GSR measures skin conductance, which is affected by sweating). A comparison of the two graphs depicts the difference in arousal between someone who is calm (*b*) and someone who is under stress (*c*).

PHYSIOLOGICAL AROUSAL

Stress produces physiological arousal, which is reflected in the functioning of many of our body systems. One way to assess arousal is to use electrical/mechanical equipment to take measurements of blood pressure, heart rate, respiration rate, or galvanic skin response (GSR). Each of these indexes of arousal can be measured separately, or they can all be measured and recorded simultaneously by one apparatus called the **polygraph** (Figure 3–2). Miniaturized versions of these devices are available with recording units that can fit in a pocket, thereby allowing assessments during the person's daily life at home, at work, or in a stressful situation, such as while flying in an airplane or receiving dental treatment. Using one of these devices, researchers have shown that paramedics' blood pressure is higher during ambulance runs and at the hospital than during other work situations or at home (Goldstein, Jamner, & Shapiro, 1992).

Another way to measure arousal is to do biochemical analyses of blood, urine, or saliva samples to assess the level of hormones that the adrenal glands secrete profusely during stress (Kirschbaum & Hellhammer, 1999; van Eck & Nicolson, 1994). Using this approach, researchers can test for two classes of hormones: **corticosteroids,** the most important of which is cortisol, and **catecholamines,** which include epinephrine and norepinephrine. A chemist does the analysis using special procedures and equipment.

Using measures of physiological arousal to assess stress has several advantages (Baum, Grunberg, & Singer, 1982; Cacioppo, Petty, & Marshall-Goodell, 1985). Physiological measures are reasonably direct and objective, quite reliable, and easily quantified. But there are disadvantages as well. Assessing physiological arousal can be expensive, and the measurement technique may itself be stressful for some people, as may occur when blood is drawn or when electrical devices are attached to the body. Lastly, measures of physiological arousal are affected by the person's gender, body weight, activity prior to or during measurement, and consumption of various substances, such as caffeine.

LIFE EVENTS

If you wanted to know whether people were feeling stress, you might simply ask them. Using a self-report method is easy to do. But in doing research, you would probably want to get a more precise answer than, "Yes, I am," or even, "Yes, I'm under a lot of stress." For this reason, a number of different scales have been developed to measure people's stress and assign it a numerical value. One approach many scales have used is to develop a list of **life events**—major happenings that can occur in a person's life that require some degree of psychological adjustment. The scale assigns each event a value that reflects its stressfulness.

The Social Readjustment Rating Scale

A widely-used scale of life events is the *Social Readjustment Rating Scale* (SRRS) developed by Thomas Holmes and Richard Rahe (1967). To develop this scale, these researchers constructed a list of events they derived from clinical experience. Then they had hundreds of men and women of various ages and backgrounds rate the amount of adjustment each event would require, using the following instructions:

> *Use all of your experience* in arriving at your answer. This means personal experience where it applies as well as what you have learned to be the case for others. Some persons accommodate to change more readily than others; some persons adjust with particular ease or difficulty to only certain

events. Therefore, strive to give your opinion of the average degree of readjustment necessary for each event rather than the extreme. (p. 213)

The researchers used these ratings to assign values to each event and construct the scale shown in Table 3.2.

Table 3.2.   *Social Readjustment Rating Scale*

Rank	Life Event	Mean Value
1	Death of spouse	100
2	Divorce	73
3	Marital separation	65
4	Jail term	63
5	Death of close family member	63
6	Personal injury or illness	53
7	Marriage	50
8	Fired at work	47
9	Marital reconciliation	45
10	Retirement	45
11	Change in health of family member	44
12	Pregnancy	40
13	Sex difficulties	39
14	Gain of new family member	39
15	Business readjustment	39
16	Change in financial state	38
17	Death of close friend	37
18	Change to different line of work	36
19	Change in number of arguments with spouse	35
20	Mortgage over $10,000	31
21	Foreclosure of mortgage or loan	30
22	Change in responsibilities at work	29
23	Son or daughter leaving home	29
24	Trouble with in-laws	29
25	Outstanding personal achievement	28
26	Wife begin or stop work	26
27	Begin or end school	26
28	Change in living conditions	25
29	Revision of personal habits	24
30	Trouble with boss	23
31	Change in work hours or conditions	20
32	Change in residence	20
33	Change in schools	20
34	Change in recreation	19
35	Change in church activities	19
36	Change in social activities	18
37	Mortgage or loan less than $10,000	17
38	Change in sleeping habits	16
39	Change in number of family get-togethers	15
40	Change in eating habits	15
41	Vacation	13
42	Christmas	12
43	Minor violations of the law	11

Source: From Holmes & Rahe (1967, Table 3).

As you can see, the values for the life events in the SRRS range from 100 points for death of a spouse to 11 points for minor violations of the law. To measure the amount of stress people have experienced, respondents are given a survey form listing these life events and asked to check off the ones that happened to them during a given period of time, usually not more than the past 24 months. The researcher sums the values of the checked items to get a total stress score.

How commonly do life events like those in the SRRS occur? A study of nearly 2,800 adults used a modified version of the SRRS and found that 15% of the subjects reported having experienced none of the events during the prior year, and 18% reported five or more (Goldberg & Comstock, 1980). The three most frequent events reported were "took a vacation" (43%), "death of a loved one or other important person" (22%), and "illness or injury" (21%). The number of life events the subjects reported *decreased* with age from early adulthood to old age and *increased* with the number of years of schooling. Single, separated, and divorced people reported larger numbers of events than did married and widowed individuals.

Strengths and Weaknesses of the SRRS

When you examined the list of life events included in the SRRS, you probably noticed that many of the events were ones we have already discussed as stressors, such as the death of a spouse, divorce, pregnancy, and occupational problems. One of the strengths of the SRRS is that the items it includes represent a fairly wide range of events that most people do, in fact, find stressful. Also, the values assigned to the events were carefully determined from the ratings of a broad sample of adults. These values provide an estimate of the relative impact of the events, distinguishing fairly well between such stressors as "death of a close family member" and "death of a close friend." Another strength of the SRRS is that the survey form can be filled out easily and quickly.

One of the main uses of the SRRS has been to relate stress and illness. Many studies have addressed this issue by using retrospective approaches—for example, by asking subjects to recall events and illnesses they experienced over the past year. Other studies have combined retrospective and prospective methods—for instance, by having subjects report recent life events and then checking their medical records over the next months. Studies using these

approaches have generally found that people's illness and accident rates tend to increase following increases in stress (Holmes & Masuda, 1974; Johnson, 1986; Rahe & Arthur, 1978). But the correlation between subjects' scores on the SRRS and illness is only about .30—which means that the relationship is not very strong (Dohrenwend & Dohrenwend, 1984). One reason that the relationship is not stronger is that people get sick and have accidents for many reasons other than stress. But another factor is that the SRRS has several weaknesses.

Some researchers have criticized items in the SRRS as being vague or ambiguous (Hough, Fairbank, & Garcia, 1976). For example, "change in responsibilities at work" fails to indicate how much change and whether it involves more or less responsibility. As a result, someone whose responsibility has decreased a little gets the same score as someone whose responsibility has increased sharply. Similarly, "personal injury or illness" does not indicate the seriousness of the illness—someone who had the flu gets the same score as someone who became paralyzed. Vague or ambiguous items reduce the precision of an instrument and the correlation it is likely to have with other variables (Anastasi, 1982).

Another criticism is that the scale does not consider the meaning or impact of an event for the individual (Cohen, Kamarck, & Mermelstein, 1983; Lazarus & Folkman, 1984b). For example, two people who each had a mortgage for $50,000 would get the same score for "mortgage over $10,000" even though one of them made ten times the income of the other. Similarly, the score people get for "death of spouse" is the same regardless of their age, dependence on the spouse, and the length and happiness of the marriage. These items do not take the person's subjective appraisal into account, and this may also reduce the precision of the instrument.

One other problem with the SRRS is that it does not distinguish between desirable and undesirable events. Most people view some events, such as "marriage" or "outstanding personal achievement," as desirable; but "sex difficulties" and "jail term" are undesirable. Other items could be either desirable or undesirable, for example, "change in financial state"; the score people get is the same regardless of whether their finances improved or worsened. This is important because studies have found that undesirable life events are correlated with illness, but desirable events are not (McFarlane et al., 1983; Sarason et al., 1985).

Given the weaknesses of the SRRS, the correlations between its scores and illness may be considered all the more impressive. Because the overall approach it uses to measure stress is useful, researchers have constructed other life event scales in an effort to develop more precise instruments.

Other Life Events Scales

Several other life events scales have attempted to improve on the method of the SRRS; the most widely used of these scales is the *Life Experiences Survey* (LES, Sarason, Johnson, & Siegel, 1978). The LES contains 57 items that are stated relatively precisely, for example, "major change in financial status (a lot better off or a lot worse off)." Subjects rate each event on a 7-point scale, ranging from extremely negative (−3) to extremely positive (+3). The items perceived as positive or as negative can be examined separately or combined for a total change score.

Two other life-events scales are used less often. One is the PERI *Life-Events Scale*, which contains 102 items that describe events involving either a gain, a loss, or an ambiguous outcome (Dohrenwend et al., 1978). The other is the *Unpleasant Events Schedule* (UES; Lewinsohn et al., 1985), which contains 320 items and takes an hour to complete (although a shorter, 53-item form is also available).

The instruments we have discussed so far have been designed to measure stress mainly in adults. Other scales have been developed to measure stress in children and adolescents. The most widely used scale for children is the *Life Events Record*, which is very similar to the SRRS in its format and scoring (Coddington, 1972a, 1972b). The items are relevant to children, such as "divorce of parents" and "change to a different school," and are assigned separate values for children of different age groups. When children are not old enough to respond to the items themselves, their parents complete the scale for them. Because the Life Events Record has many of the same problems as the SRRS, other instruments for children have been developed (Johnson, 1986).

DAILY HASSLES

Not all of the stress we experience comes from major life events. Lesser events can also be stressful, as when we give a speech, misplace our keys during a busy day, or have our quiet disrupted by a loud party next door. These are called **daily hassles.** Some people experience more daily hassles than others do.

Richard Lazarus and his associates developed a scale to measure people's experiences with day-today unpleasant or potentially harmful events (Kanner et al., 1981). This instrument—called the *Hassles Scale*—lists 117 of these events that range from minor annoyances, such as "silly practical mistakes," to major problems or difficulties, such as "not enough money for food." Respondents indicate which hassles occurred in the past month and rate each event as "somewhat," "moderately," or "extremely" severe. Because the researchers felt that having *desirable* experiences may make hassles more bearable and reduce their impact on health, they also developed the *Uplifts Scale*, which lists 135 events that bring peace, satisfaction, or joy. The researchers tested 100 middle-aged adults monthly over a 9-month period and identified the most frequently occurring items. For hassles, they included "concerns about weight," "health of a family member," "too many things to do," and "misplacing or losing things"; for uplifts, they included "relating well to your spouse or lover" and "completing a task."

Are hassles and uplifts related to health? Studies have examined this issue. One study tested middle-aged adults, using four instruments: (1) the Hassles Scale; (2) the Uplifts Scale; (3) a life events scale that includes no desirable items; and (4) the Health Status Questionnaire, which contains questions regarding a wide variety of bodily symptoms and overall health (DeLongis et al., 1982). Hassles scores and life-events scores were associated with health status—both correlations were weak, but hassles were more strongly associated with health than life events were. Uplifts scores had virtually no association with health status. Other studies generally support these findings regarding the relationship of hassles and uplifts to health (Gortmaker, Eckenrode, & Gore, 1982; Holahan, Holahan, & Belk, 1984; Zarski, 1984).

In general, all measures of stress have strengths and shortcomings. Some evidence suggests that self-report measures of life events may be unreliable: A study had subjects fill out a scale regarding life events they experienced during the prior year and then fill out the same scale each month during the next year. The extent to which later reports agreed with the first measurement declined sharply over time (Raphael, Cloitre, & Dohrenwend, 1991). Stress is a difficult concept to define, and it is even more difficult to measure. Still, judging from the evidence that exists, stress has a moderate relationship to health and is one of many factors that contribute to the development of illness. (Go to 🍎.)

Hassles in Your Life

Table 3A.1 gives a list of common events you may sometimes find unpleasant because they make you irritated, frustrated, or anxious. The list was taken from the Hassles Assessment Scale for Students in College, which has respondents rate the *frequency* and *unpleasantness* of and *dwelling* on each event.

For this exercise, rate only the *frequency* of each event. Beside each item estimate how often it occurred during the past month, using the scale:

0 = never, **1** = rarely, **2** = occasionally, **3** = often, **4** = very often, **5** = extremely often.

Then add all of the ratings for a total score. You can evaluate your relative hassles with the following schedule: compared to the stress other college students have from hassles, a total score of 105 is about average, above 135 indicates much more stress, and below 75 indicates much less stress.

Table 3A.1 *Hassles Assessment Scale for Students in College (HASS/Col)*

_____ Annoying behavior of self (e.g., habits, temper)
_____ Accidents/clumsiness/mistakes of self (e.g., spilling beverage, tripping)
_____ Annoying social behavior of others (e.g., rude, inconsiderate, sexist/racist)
_____ Appearance of self (e.g., noticing unattractive features, grooming)
_____ Athletic activities of self (e.g., aspects of own performance, time demands)
_____ Bills/overspending: seeing evidence of
_____ Boredom (e.g., nothing to do, current activity uninteresting)
_____ Car problems (e.g., breaking down, repairs)
_____ Crowds/large social groups (e.g., at parties, while shopping)
_____ Dating (e.g., noticing lack of, uninteresting partner)
_____ Environment (e.g., noticing physical living or working conditions)
_____ Exams (e.g., preparing for, taking)
_____ Exercising (e.g., unpleasant routines, time to do)
_____ Extracurricular groups (e.g., activities, responsibilities)
_____ Facilities/resources unavailable (e.g., library materials, computers)
_____ Family: obligations or activities
_____ Family: relationship issues, annoyances
_____ Fears of physical safety (e.g., while walking alone, being on a plane or in a car)
_____ Fitness: noticing inadequate physical condition
_____ Food (e.g., unappealing or unhealthful meals)
_____ Forgetting to do things (e.g., to tape TV show, send cards, do homework)
_____ Friends/peers: relationship issues, annoyances
_____ Future plans (e.g., career or marital decisions)
_____ Getting up early (e.g., for class or work)
_____ Girl/boy-friend: relationship issues, annoyances
_____ Goals/tasks: not completing enough
_____ Grades (e.g., getting a low grade)
_____ Health/physical symptoms of self (e.g., flu, PMS, allergies, headaches)

_____ Housing: finding/getting or moving
_____ Injustice: seeing examples or being a victim of
_____ Job: searching for or interviews
_____ Job/work issues (e.g., demands or annoying aspects of)
_____ Lateness of self (e.g., for appointment or class)
_____ Losing or misplacing things (e.g., keys, books)
_____ Medical/dental treatment (e.g., unpleasant, time demands)
_____ Money: noticing lack of
_____ New experiences or challenges: engaging in
_____ Noise of other people or animals
_____ Oral presentations/public speaking
_____ Parking problems (e.g., on campus, at work, at home)
_____ Privacy: noticing lack of
_____ Professors/coaches (e.g., unfairness, demands of, unavailability)
_____ Registering for or selecting classes to take
_____ Roommate(s)/housemate(s): relationship issues, annoyances
_____ Schoolwork (e.g., working on term papers, reading tedious/hard material, low motivation)
_____ Sexually transmitted diseases (e.g., concerns about, efforts to reduce risk of STDs/HIV)
_____ Sports team/celebrity performance (e.g., favorite athlete or team losing)
_____ Tedious everyday chores (e.g., shopping, cleaning apartment)
_____ Time demands/deadlines
_____ Traffic problems (e.g., inconsiderate or careless drivers, traffic jams)
_____ Traffic tickets: getting (e.g., for moving or parking violations)
_____ Waiting (e.g., for appointments, in lines)
_____ Weather problems (e.g., snow, heat/humidity, storms)
_____ Weight/dietary management (e.g., not sticking to plans)

Source: Sarafino & Ewing (1999).

CAN STRESS BE GOOD FOR YOU?

Another reason measures of stress do not correlate very highly with illness may be that not all stress is unhealthy. Is it possible that some types or amounts of stress are neutral or, perhaps, *good* for you? There is reason to believe this is the case (McGuigan, 1999).

How much stress may be good for people? Some theories of motivation and arousal propose that people function best, and feel best, at what is, *for them,* an optimal level of arousal (Fiske & Maddi, 1961; Hebb, 1955). People differ in the amount of arousal that is optimal, but too much or too little arousal impairs their functioning. Figure 3–3 illustrates how stress, as a form of arousal, relates to the quality of functioning. How might different levels of stress affect functioning? Imagine that you are in class one day and your instructor passes around a surprise test. If the test would not be collected or count toward your final grade, you might be underaroused and answer the questions carelessly or not at all. But if it were to count as 10% of your grade, you might be under enough stress to perform well. And if it counted a lot, you might be overwhelmed by the stress and do poorly.

Are some types of stress better than others for people? Three prominent researchers on stress have taken very similar positions on this question, claiming that there are at least two kinds of stress that differ in their impact. Selye (1974, 1985), for instance, claimed that one kind of stress is harmful and damaging, and is called *distress*; another kind is beneficial or constructive, and is called *eustress* (from the Greek *eu,* which means "good"). Similarly, as we saw earlier, Frankenhaeuser (1986) has described two components of stress: *distress* and *effort.* Distress with or without effort is probably more damaging than effort without distress. And Lazarus has described three types of stress appraisals—*harm-loss, threat,* and *challenge*—and noted:

> Challenged persons are more likely to have better morale, because to be challenged means feeling positive about demanding encounters, as reflected in the pleasurable emotions accompanying challenge. The quality of functioning is apt to be better in challenge because the person feels more confident, less emotionally overwhelmed, and more capable of drawing on available resources than the person who is inhibited or blocked.

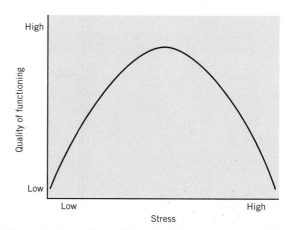

Figure 3–3 Quality of functioning at varying levels of stress. Functioning is poor at very low and very high levels of stress but is best at some moderate, "optimal" level. (Based on material in Hebb, 1955.)

> Finally, it is possible that the physiological stress response to challenge is different from that of threat, so that diseases of adaptation are less likely to occur. (Lazarus & Folkman, 1984b, p. 34)

There is a commonality to these three positions: to state it in its simplest form, there is good stress and

"I JUST READ THAT A CERTAIN AMOUNT OF STRESS IS GOOD FOR YOU."

bad stress—bad stress generally involves a strong negative emotional component. Cognitive appraisal processes play an important role in determining which kind of stress we experience.

Finally, in discussing whether stress is harmful, one other point should be made: individuals seem to differ in their susceptibility to the effects of stress. John Mason (1975) has proposed that these differences are like those that people show to the effects of viruses and bacteria. That is, not all people who are exposed to a disease-causing antigen, such as a flu virus, develop the illness—some individuals are more susceptible than others. Susceptibility to the effects of antigens and to stress varies from one person to the next and within the same individual across time. These differences result from biological variations within and between individuals, and from psychosocial variations, as we will see in the next chapter.

SUMMARY

Researchers have conceptualized stress in three ways. In one approach, stress is seen as a stimulus, and studies focus on the impact of stressors. Another approach treats stress as a response and examines the physical and psychological strains that stressors produce. The third approach proposes that stress is a process that involves continuous interactions and adjustments—or transactions—between the person and the environment. These three views lead to a definition of stress: the condition that results when person–environment transactions lead to a perceived discrepancy between the demands of a situation and the resources of the person's biological, psychological, and social systems.

Transactions that lead to the condition of stress generally involve a process of cognitive appraisal, which takes two forms: *primary appraisal* focuses on whether a demand threatens the person's well-being, and *secondary appraisal* assesses the resources available for meeting the demand. Primary appraisal produces one of three judgments: the demand is irrelevant, it is good, or it is stressful. A stressful appraisal receives further assessment for the amount of harm or loss, the threat of future harm, and the degree of challenge the demand presents. When primary and secondary appraisals indicate that the fit between demands and resources is close, we may experience little stress. But when we appraise a discrepancy—especially if the demands seem greater than our resources—we may feel a substantial amount of stress.

Whether people appraise events as stressful depends on factors that relate to the person and to the situation. Factors of the person include intellectual, motivational, and personality characteristics, such as the person's self-esteem and belief system. With regard to situational factors, events tend to be appraised as stressful if they involve strong demands, are imminent, are undesirable and uncontrollable, involve major life transitions, or occur at an unexpected time in the life span.

Stressors produce strain in the person's biological, psychological, and social systems. Emergency situations evoke a physiological fight-or-flight reaction, by which the organism prepares to attack the threat or flee. When stress is strong and prolonged, the physiological reaction goes through three stages: the alarm reaction, the stage of resistance, and the stage of exhaustion. This series of reactions is called the general adaptation syndrome. According to Selye, continuous high levels of stress can make the person vulnerable to diseases of adaptation, including ulcers and high blood pressure. Psychosocial factors influence reactivity, the physiological reaction to stressors.

Stress is linked to psychosocial processes. It can impair cognitive functioning and reduce people's helping behavior. Various emotions can accompany stress—these emotions include fear, anxiety, depression, and anger. Although the sources of stress may change as people develop, the condition of stress can occur at any time in the life span. Sometimes stress arises from within the person, such as when the person is ill or experiences conflict. Another source of stress is the family, such as if one of its members is seriously ill or dies; although women are more likely than men to be caretakers of elderly relatives, a meta-analysis found that the amount of care men and women give is similar. A new baby with a difficult temperament can be stressful for parents. Other sources of stress include the community and society—for example, from problems related to people's jobs or environmental hazards.

Researchers measure stress in three ways. One way assesses physiological arousal. Blood pressure, heart rate, respiration rate, and galvanic skin response can be measured with an apparatus called the polygraph. Biochemical analyses of blood or urine samples can test for corticosteroids (for example, cortisol) and catecholamines (for example, epinephrine and norepinephrine). Other methods to measure stress use surveys of people's experi-ence of life events and daily hassles. Although stress can contribute to the development of illness, many psycholo-gists believe that not all stress is harmful.

KEY TERMS

stressors	primary appraisal	alarm reaction	polygraph
strain	secondary appraisal	stage of resistance	corticosteroids
transactions	reactivity	stage of exhaustion	catecholamines
stress	general adaptation	temperaments	life events
cognitive appraisal	syndrome	meta-analysis	daily hassles

Note: If you read **Modules 1** and **2** (from Chap-ter 2) with the current chapter, you should include the key terms for those modules.

4

STRESS, BIOPSYCHOSOCIAL FACTORS, AND ILLNESS

Psychosocial Modifiers of Stress
Social Support
A Sense of Personal Control
A Hardy Personality
Type A and Type B Behavior Patterns

How Stress Affects Health
Stress, Behavior, and Illness
Stress, Physiology, and Illness
Psychoneuroimmunology

Psychophysiological Disorders
Digestive System Diseases
Asthma
Recurrent Headache
Other Disorders

Stress and Cardiovascular Disorders
Hypertension
Coronary Heart Disease
Stress and Cancer

PROLOGUE

They were best friends, Joan and Sally, on their way to an art museum a year ago when a car accident ended

their lives. Their husbands, Bob and Walt, were devastated, not only by their individual losses but also for each other's. These men were also friends—both worked as engineers for the same company and shared hobbies and other interests. The four of them used to double date often, leaving the kids with one babysitter. How did the terrible loss of their wives affect these men?

The initial impact of their loss was similar, but the amount of stress they experienced differed. Bob's stress was not as severe as Walt's. One thing that helped Bob was that he had an extended family that lived nearby. They provided consolation for his grief, a place to go to get out of the house and to socialize, and help in caring for his children. After school, the kids would go to either Bob's or Joan's parents' house, and Bob would pick them up on his way home from work. Sometimes he and the children would stay there for dinner. This helped save him time and money—both of which were in short supply. How was Bob doing a year later? He had made a good adjustment, had a good relationship with his children, was starting to date, and was in good health.

Walt was not as fortunate. For one thing, he had no nearby family to rely on. Unlike Bob, Walt had little emotional support in his grief, and being a single parent made his workload and financial situation very difficult. Walt had little time or money for socializing, and virtually all of his adult contacts were at work. Although he and Bob often had lunch together, their interests were drifting apart. Unlike Bob, Walt had never been very outgoing, and he felt awkward and insecure in meeting women. A year after Sally died, he was isolated and lonely. His relationship with his children was deteriorating, and so was his health. He had developed migraine headaches, neck problems, and high blood pressure. The stress in Walt's life was taking its toll.

This chapter examines the effects of stress on health. We begin by looking at psychosocial factors that can modify the stress people experience. Then we consider how stress affects health and the development of specific illnesses. And in this chapter we address many questions about stress and illness that are of great concern today. Why can some people experience one traumatic event after another without ill effects, but others cannot? Are hard-driving people more likely to have a heart attack than people who are easygoing? Can people actually "die of a broken heart"? Can stress retard people's recovery from illness?

PSYCHOSOCIAL MODIFIERS OF STRESS

People's reactions to stress vary from one person to the next and from time to time for the same person. These variations often result from psychological and social factors that seem to *modify* the impact of stressors on the individual. Let's look at some of these modifiers, beginning with the role of social support.

SOCIAL SUPPORT

We saw in the bereavement experiences of Bob and Walt how important social ties and relationships can be during troubled times. The social support Bob got from his family tempered the impact of his stressful loss and probably helped him adjust. **Social support** refers to the perceived comfort, caring, esteem, or help a person receives from other people or groups (Gentry & Kobasa, 1984; Wallston et al., 1983; Wills & Fegan, 2001). This support can come from many

different sources—the person's spouse or lover, family, friends, coworkers, physician, or community organizations. People with social support believe they are loved, valued, and part of a social network, such as a family or community organization that can help in times of need or danger.

Types of Social Support

What specifically does social support provide to the person? It appears to provide four basic functions (Cutrona & Russell, 1990; Schaefer, Coyne, & Lazarus, 1981; Wills & Fegan, 2001). *Emotional or esteem support* conveys empathy, caring, concern, positive regard, and encouragement toward the person. It provides comfort and reassurance with a sense of belongingness and of being loved in times of stress, as Bob

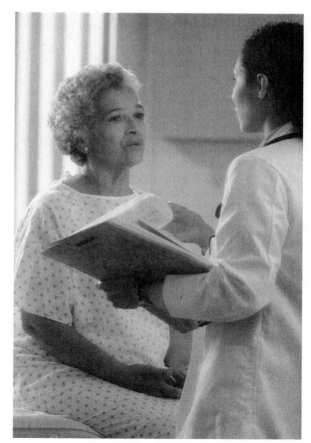

A patient receiving informational support from her physician.

received after the death of his wife. *Tangible or instrumental support* involves direct assistance, as when people give or lend the person money or help out with chores in times of stress. Bob's family helped with child care, for example, which reduced the demands on his time and finances. *Informational support* includes giving advice, directions, suggestions, or feedback about how the person is doing. For example, a person who is ill might get information from family or a physician on how to treat the illness. *Companionship support* refers to the availability of others to spend time with the person, thereby giving a feeling of membership in a group of people who share interests and social activities.

What type of support do people generally need and get? The answer depends on the stressful circumstances. For instance, Figure 4–1 shows that cancer patients find emotional and esteem support to be especially helpful, but patients with less serious chronic illnesses find the different types of support equally helpful (Martin et al., 1994). Another study had college students fill out a questionnaire, rating the degree to which their current relationships

provided them with different types of support, and then keep a daily record of their stress and social experiences for 2 weeks (Cutrona, 1986). The daily records revealed that most of the stressors were relatively minor, such as having car trouble or an argument with a roommate, but one-fifth of the students reported a severe event, such as a parent's diagnosis of cancer or the ending of a long-term romantic relationship. As you might expect, individuals received more social support following stressful events than at less stressful times. Tangible support occurred very infrequently, but informational and emotional/esteem support occurred often. Emotional/esteem support appeared to protect individuals from the negative emotional consequences of stress.

Who Gets Social Support?

Not everyone gets the social support they need. Many factors determine whether people receive support (Antonucci, 1985; Broadhead et al., 1983; Wortman & Dunkel-Schetter, 1987). Some factors relate to the potential *recipients* of support. People are unlikely to receive support if they are unsociable, don't help others, and don't let others know that they need help. Some people are not assertive enough to ask for help, or feel that they should be independent or not burden others, or feel uncomfortable confiding in others, or don't know whom to ask. Other factors relate to the potential *providers* of support. For instance, they may not have the resources needed, or may be under stress and in need of help themselves, or may simply be insensitive to the needs of others. Old age is a time when social support sometimes declines: the elderly may exchange less support because of the loss of a spouse or because they may feel reluctant to ask for help if they become unable to reciprocate. Whether people receive social support also depends on the size, composition, intimacy, and frequency of contact of individuals their *social network*—the linkages with people in their family and community (Schaefer, Coyne, & Lazarus, 1981; Wills & Fegan, 2001).

How can we assess people's social support, given the different types of support and the complex relationships that are involved? One highly regarded instrument is the *Social Support Questionnaire*, which consists of 27 items, such as, "Who helps you feel that you truly have something positive to contribute to others?" (Sarason et al., 1983). For each item, the respondents list the people they can rely on and then

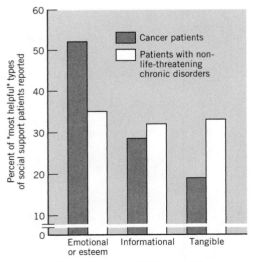

Figure 4–1 Percentage of patients with cancer and with non-life-threatening disorders (chronic headache or irritable bowel syndrome) whose reports of the "most helpful" social support they received described the emotional/esteem, instrumental, or tangible types of support. Notice that the cancer patients found emotional or esteem support especially helpful. (Data from Martin et al., 1994, Figure 1.)

ASSESS YOURSELF

How Much Emotional Support Do You Get?

Think of the ten people to whom you feel closest. For some of them, you may not feel a strong bond—but they are still among the closest ten people in your life. Write their initials in the following spaces:

_____ _____ _____ _____ _____

In the *corresponding* spaces below each of the following four questions, rate each person on a 5-point scale, where **1** = "not at all" and **5** = "extremely."

• How reliable is this person; is this person there when you need him or her?

_____ _____ _____ _____ _____

• How much does this person boost your spirits when you feel low?

_____ _____ _____ _____ _____

• How much does this person make you feel he or she cares about you?

_____ _____ _____ _____ _____

• How much do you feel you can confide in this person?

_____ _____ _____ _____ _____

Add together all of the ratings you gave across all of the people and questions. A total score between 12 and 15 is fairly typical and suggests that you can get a reasonably good level of emotional support when you need it. (*Source:* Based on material in Schaefer, Coyne, and Lazarus, 1981.)

indicate their overall degree of satisfaction with the support available. Using this instrument, these researchers have found that some people report high levels of satisfaction with support from a small number of close friends and relatives, but others seem to need a large social network. (Go to 🍎.)

Gender and Sociocultural Differences in Receiving Support

The amount of social support individuals receive appears to depend on their gender and sociocultural group membership. Some evidence suggests that women receive less support from their spouses than men do and seem to rely heavily on women friends for social support (Greenglass & Noguchi, 1996). These gender differences may result from the greater intimacy that seems to exist in the friendships of females than males and may reflect mainly differences in the emotional and esteem support males and females seek out and give (Heller, Price, & Hogg, 1990). Research on social networks in the United States has revealed interesting gender and sociocultural relationships (Gottlieb & Green, 1987): Black Americans have smaller social networks than Whites and Hispanics, and men's networks are larger than women's among Black and Hispanic groups but not among nonminority people. Hispanics tend to focus mainly on extended families as their networks, Whites have broader networks of friends and coworkers, and Blacks focus on family and church groups.

Social Support, Stress, and Health

A fortune cookie I received said, "Friendship is to people what sunshine is to flowers." Does the social support of friends, relatives, and other people affect our stress and health? Social support may reduce the stress people experience. For example, studies of job stress have shown that the greater the social support available to employees, the lower the psychological strain they report (Cottington & House, 1987; LaRocco, House, & French, 1980). Other research has found that blood pressure during work is lower for workers who have high social support than for those with less support (Karlin, Brondolo, & Schwartz, 2003). Social support has also been associated with reduced stress from a variety of other sources, such as living near the damaged nuclear power plant at Three Mile Island (Fleming et al., 1982).

Experiments have assessed people's physiological strain while they were engaged in a stressful activity (such as giving a speech or performing mental arithmetic) either alone or in the presence of one or more individuals. Strain was typically assessed as *cardiovascular reactivity*—that is, an increase in blood pressure and/or heart rate from a baseline level. Let's consider a few findings. First, while giving a speech, people show much less reactivity if a supportive person is present than if speaking alone (Lepore, Allen, & Evans, 1993; Uchino & Garvey, 1997). Second, reactivity is lower with a friend present than with a supportive stranger (Christenfeld et al., 1997). Third, reactivity is also lower in the presence of the person's pet than alone (Allen, Blascovich, & Mendes, 2002). Fourth, other findings suggest that the benefits of social support on reactivity depend on the person's gender and the type of support: when instrumental support is given, males show less reactivity than females; when emotional support is given, females show less reactivity than males (Wilson, Kliewer et al., 1999).

Having social support also seems to benefit people's health (Berkman, 1995). For instance, a prospective study had more than 4,700 men and women between 30 and 69 years of age report on four aspects of social support: marital status, contacts with family and friends, church membership, and formal and informal group associations (Berkman & Syme, 1979). Mortality data collected over the next 9 years revealed that the greater the degree of social support the subjects had, the lower the likelihood of their dying during the period of the study. Figure 4–2 shows an example of these findings. In each age category, individuals who had few contacts with friends and relatives had higher mortality rates than those with many contacts. This relationship applied to deaths from all causes and deaths from several specific diseases, including cancer and heart disease.

Because this research is quasi-experimental, the relationship found between social support and mortality is correlational. How do we know whether social support leads to better health and lower mortality, or whether the influence is the other way around? That is, could the people who had less social support be less active socially because they were already sick at the start of the study? Berkman and Syme provided some evidence that this was not the case. For instance, the subjects had been asked about past illnesses at the initial interview, and those with high levels of social support did not differ from those with low levels of support.

Figure 4–2   Percentage of adults who died within 9 years as a function of the number of contacts with friends and relatives and the subjects' ages at the start of the study, in 1965. (Data from Berkman & Syme, 1979, Table 2.)

But better evidence comes from a similar study of more than 2,700 adults who were medically examined at the start of the research (House, Robbins, & Metzner, 1982). This research found that people with less social support had higher mortality rates and that the initial health of those with low social support was the same as that of those with high support.

Researchers have also studied the association between social support and the likelihood that people will develop illnesses and recover quickly when they do. Early findings were inconsistent— probably because of variations in research methods, such as in the way support was defined and measured (Wallston et al., 1983; Wortman & Dunkel-Schetter, 1987). Newer research has found more consistently positive results, showing, for example, that heart disease and surgery patients with high levels of social support recover more quickly than comparable patients with less support (Berkman, 1995; Kulik & Mahler, 1989; Wills & Fegan, 2001). Although these findings suggest that social support reduces the likelihood of illness and speeds recovery, the connection between social support and health is not always very strong, probably because support is only one of many factors involved (Kobasa et al., 1985; Smith et al., 1994). Social support appears to have a strong impact on the health of some individuals and a weak influence on the health of others. For instance, some evidence indicates that the recovery of many patients who believe they can cope with the emotional demands of their illness does not benefit from social support (Wilcox, Kasl, & Berkman, 1994).

How May Social Support Affect Health?

We have seen that prolonged exposure to high levels of stress can lead to illness. To explain how social support may influence health, researchers have proposed two theories: the "buffering" and the "direct effects" (or "main effects") hypotheses (Wills & Fegan, 2001). According to the **buffering hypothesis,** social support affects health by *protecting* the person against the negative effects of high stress. A graphical illustration of the buffering hypothesis appears in Figure 4–3a. As the graph shows, this protective function is effective only or mainly when the person encounters a strong stressor. Under low-stress conditions, little or no buffering occurs. Research has shown that the buffering process does occur (Wills & Fegan, 2001). For example, a study of job stress found that social support had a much stronger association with lower blood pressure during stressful than nonstressful work times (Karlin, Brondolo, & Schwartz, 2003).

How may buffering work? Here are two ways. First, when people encounter a strong stressor, such as a major financial crisis, those who have high levels of social support may be less likely to appraise the situation as stressful than those with low levels of support. Individuals with high social support may expect that someone they know will help them, such as by lending money or giving advice on how to get it. Second, social support may modify people's response to a stressor after the initial appraisal. For instance, people with high social support might have someone provide a solution to the problem, convince them that the problem is not very important, or cheer them on to "look on the bright side." People with little social support are much less likely to have any of these advantages; the negative impact of the stress is therefore greater for them than for those with high levels of support.

The **direct effects hypothesis** maintains that social support benefits health and well-being regardless of the amount of stress people experience— the beneficial effects are similar under high- and low-stressor intensities, as depicted in Figure 4–3b. How do direct effects work? One way is that people with high levels of social support may have strong feelings of belongingness and self-esteem. The positive outlook this produces may be beneficial to health independently of stress: studies have found lower blood pressures in both daily life and laboratory tests among middle-aged and younger adults with higher

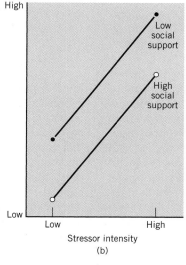

Figure 4–3 Illustration of two ways social support may benefit health and well-being. Graph (*a*) illustrates the buffering hypothesis, which proposes that social support modifies the negative health effects of high levels of stress. Graph (*b*) depicts the direct effects hypothesis, which proposes that the health benefits of social support occur regardless of stress.

levels of social support regardless of stress levels (Carels, Blumenthal, & Sherwood, 1998; Uchino et al., 1999). Other evidence suggests that high levels of support may encourage people to lead healthful lifestyles (Broman, 1993; Peirce et al., 2000). People with social support may feel, for example, that because others care about them and need them, they should exercise, eat well, and not smoke or drink heavily.

Does Social Support Always Help?

Social support does not always reduce stress and benefit health. Why? For one thing, although support may be offered or available to us, we may not *perceive* it as supportive (Dunkel-Schetter & Bennett, 1990; Wilcox, Kasl, & Berkman, 1994). This may happen because the help is insufficient, or we may not want help or are too emotionally distraught to notice it, for instance. When we do not perceive help as supportive, it is less likely to reduce our stress.

Another reason social support does not always help is that the type of support we receive may not *match* the needs that the stressor has produced. For example, if your car broke down, your passenger's emotional consolation probably would not reduce your stress very much. Carolyn Cutrona and Daniel Russell (1990) have outlined a pattern for matching support with need. Instrumental support is particularly valuable for stressful events that are *controllable*— that is, we can do something to achieve a goal or prevent the situation from becoming worse, such as when we feel ill. Emotional support is especially important for *uncontrollable* stressful events, such as when a loved one dies. But other types of support may also be needed—for instance, if the uncontrollable event involved losing your job, esteem and tangible support might help, too.

Marriage is often thought to convey protective health benefits by providing social support. Consistent with this idea, studies have found that married people live longer than divorced and never-married individuals (Berkman & Syme, 1979; House, Robbins, & Metzner, 1982). James Lynch (1990) has argued that being lonely or having a "broken heart" is a risk factor for heart disease because widowed, divorced, and never-married individuals have higher death rates from heart disease than married people do. But newer findings suggest that marriage by itself may not protect people's health. One study found that people who had not married by midlife were not at greater

risk of dying before 80 years of age and that differences in death rates for married and divorced people result in part from differences in their personality characteristics (Tucker et al., 1996). Another study found that marriage had a protective role in women's health only when their marital satisfaction was high (Gallo et al., 2003).

Lastly, in many circumstances social ties can harm a person's health. For one thing, individuals with frequent contacts with many people are more likely than others to develop infectious illnesses, such as colds, when they have high stress levels (Hamrick, Cohen, & Rodriguez, 2002). In other circumstances, social ties harm health when people encourage unhealthful behavior (Burg & Seeman, 1994; Kaplan & Toshima, 1990; Suls, 1982). We'll look at three examples. First, people may set a bad example. For instance, children are more likely to start smoking and drinking if their friends and family engage in these behaviors and less likely to use seat belts and eat a balanced diet if friends and family don't. Second, people may encourage individuals who are overweight or have high blood pressure to eat prohibited foods, saying, "A little more cheesecake can't hurt" or "You can make up for it by dieting next week." Third, families may be overprotective toward a person with a serious illness, such as heart disease, and discourage the patient's need to become more active or to go back to work. This can interfere with rehabilitation and make the patient increasingly dependent and disabled.

In summary, people receive various types of support from friends, family, and others in their lives. Social support usually tends to reduce people's stress and benefit their health. (Go to 🐦.)

A SENSE OF PERSONAL CONTROL

Another psychosocial factor that modifies the stress people experience is the degree of control people feel they have in their lives. People generally like the feeling of having some measure of control over the things that happen to them, and they take individual action when they want to influence events directly. In doing these things, people strive for a sense of **personal control**—the feeling that they can make decisions and take effective action to produce desirable outcomes and avoid undesirable ones (Wallston, 2001). Studies have found that people who have a strong sense of personal control report experiencing

CLINICAL METHODS AND ISSUES

Social Support, Therapy, and Cognitive Processes

Years ago, a reporter asked actress Melina Mercouri about psychotherapy in her native country; she replied that in Greece people don't need therapists, they have friends. Although her view oversimplifies the therapy process, therapy does include two features friends can provide: social support and the opportunity to *disclose* negative experiences and feelings. James Pennebaker and other researchers have found that people's talking or writing about traumatic or very emotional experiences for a few 15- to 30-minute sessions has beneficial effects that last for months. It reduces their stress and negative feelings, and it seems to improve their health, as reflected in the number of physician visits and episodes of chronic illness symptoms (Pennebaker, 1990; Smyth & Pennebaker, 2001). Other research has shown that less upsetting procedures, such as describing the benefits gained from traumatic events or the success in managing one's stress, can have similar effects (King & Miner, 2000; Leake, Friend, & Wadhwa, 1999). Why does disclosure help? An experiment tested this issue with college students who had identified a prior trauma from their lives that still bothered them and then kept journals for a month with different types of content (Ulrich & Lutgendorf, 2002). The results suggest that the benefits people experience after disclosure may arise from their finding meaning in and reconceptualizing distressing experiences.

less strain from stressors (McFarlane et al., 1983; Suls & Mullen, 1981).

Types of Control

How can feelings of personal control reduce the stress people experience? People can influence events in their lives and reduce their stress through four types of control (Cohen et al., 1986; Thompson, 1981). We'll focus on two of them. **Behavioral control** involves the ability to take concrete action to reduce the impact of a stressor. This action might reduce the intensity of the event or shorten its duration. For example, a pregnant woman who has taken natural childbirth classes can use special breathing techniques during delivery that reduce the pain of labor. **Cognitive control** is the ability to use thought processes or strategies to modify the impact of a stressor, such as by thinking about the event differently or focusing on a pleasant or neutral thought. While giving birth, for instance, the mother might think about the positive meanings the baby will give to her life, or she could focus her mind on an image, such as a pleasant day she had at the beach.

The two other types of control are *decisional control*, or being able to choose between alternative procedures or courses of action, and *informational control*, or the opportunity to get knowledge about a stressful

event—what will happen, why, and what the consequences are likely to be. Each of the four types of control can reduce stress, but one of them—cognitive control—seems to have the most consistently beneficial effect (Cohen et al., 1986; Thompson, 1981).

Beliefs about Oneself and Control

People differ in the degree to which they believe they have control over their lives. Some people believe they have a great deal of control, and others think they have almost none. The latter is shown in the case study of a chronically unemployed man named Karl, who was referred to therapy by the Veterans Administration and with some help

> applied for a job and got it. But this did not raise his expectancies of being able to get another job should he have to do so. Indeed, he attributed his success entirely to good fortune. He believed that the employer probably was partial to veterans or just happened to be in a good mood that day . . . [and] that the occurrence of reinforcement was outside his own personal control. (Phares, 1984, pp. 505–506)

People who believe they have control over their successes and failures are described as possessing an *internal* **locus of control.** That is, the control for these events lies within themselves—they are responsible. Other people, like Karl, who believe that their lives are controlled by forces outside themselves, for example, by luck, have an *external* locus of control (Rotter, 1966). A questionnaire called the I-E *Scale*, is used for measuring the degree of internality or externality of a person's beliefs about personal control.

Another important aspect of personal control is our sense of **self-efficacy**—the belief that we can succeed at a specific activity we want to do (Bandura, 1986, 2004). People estimate their chances of success in an activity, such as quitting smoking or running a mile, on the basis of their prior observations of themselves and others. They decide whether to attempt the activity according to their expectations that (1) the behavior, if properly carried out, would lead to a favorable outcome, and (2) they can perform the behavior properly. For example, you may know that by taking and doing well in a set of college honors courses you can graduate with that accomplishment recognized, such as with a special diploma or certificate. But if you think the likelihood of achieving that feat as "zilch," you are not likely to try. For people engaged in a stressful activity, those with strong self-efficacy for the activity show less psychological and physiological strain than do those with a weak sense of efficacy (Bandura, Reese, & Adams, 1982; Bandura et al., 1985; Holahan, Holahan, & Belk, 1984).

Determinants and Development of Personal Control

On what basis do people judge that they have control over things that happen in their lives? We make these assessments by using information we gain from our experiences throughout life (Bandura, 1986, 2004; DeVellis & DeVellis, 2001). An important information source is our own performance—the successes and failures we perceive in the activities we attempt. Infants begin to learn about personal control as they coordinate sensory experiences with their motor activity—for example, learning that they can make a noise with a rattle by shaking it.

Throughout the life span, we assess our personal control through the process of *social learning*, in which we learn by observing the behavior of others (Bandura, 1969, 1986). During childhood, people in the family and at school are particularly important in this process, with members serving as models of behavior, agents of reinforcement, and standards for comparison.

At the other end of the life span, people tend to be relatively external in locus of control—that is, beliefs that chance and powerful others affect their lives are greater in the elderly than in younger adults (Lachman, 1986). So, among adults who develop serious illnesses, those who are elderly are more inclined to prefer having professionals make health-related decisions for them (Woodward & Wallston, 1987).

You may have noticed that the information people use in determining their personal control is usually retrospective, can be very complex, and is not always clear-cut. As a result, the judgments we make about our control are not always very objective or based on fact. We sometimes develop what Ellen Langer (1975) calls an *illusion of control*—a belief in our control over an event that is really determined by chance, which has been confirmed in research (Wortman, 1975).

Gender and Sociocultural Differences in Personal Control

Gender and sociocultural differences in personal control often develop, depending on the social experiences individuals have. Sometimes parents and teachers inadvertently lead girls more than boys toward beliefs in external control and in low self-efficacy for certain activities (Dweck & Elliott, 1983). This socialization may carry over to old age: among elderly cardiac patients, men report greater self-efficacy than women for being able to walk various distances, a common rehabilitation behavior (Jenkins & Gortner, 1998). Because minority groups and poor people generally have limited access to power and economic advancement, they tend to have external locus of control beliefs (Lundin, 1987).

When People Lack Personal Control

What happens to people who experience high levels of stress over a long period of time and feel that nothing they do matters? They feel helpless—trapped and unable to avoid negative outcomes. A worker who cannot seem to please her boss no matter what she does, a student who cannot perform well on exams, or a patient who is unable to relieve his severe low back pain—each of these situations can produce apathy. As a result, these people may stop striving for these goals, come to believe they have no control over these and other events in their lives, and fail to exert control even when they could succeed. This is the condition Martin Seligman (1975) has called **learned helplessness**—which he describes as a principal characteristic of depression. Research has shown that people can learn to be helpless by being in uncontrollable situations that lead to repeated failure, such as in trying to stop an unpleasant noise (Hiroto & Seligman, 1975).

Seligman and his colleagues have extended the theory of learned helplessness to explain two important observations (Abramson, Seligman, & Teasdale, 1978). First, being exposed to uncontrollable negative events does not always lead to learned helplessness. Second, depressed people often report feeling a loss in self-esteem. The revised theory takes these issues into account by proposing that people who experience uncontrollable negative events apply a cognitive process called *attribution*, in which they make judgments regarding events, such as their own or others' actions, motives, feelings, or intentions. How does attribution work? When uncontrollable negative events happen, people consider possible judgments and causes by assessing three dimensions of the situation:

1. *Internal–external*. They consider whether this situation results from their own personal inability to control outcomes or from external causes that are beyond anyone's control. For example, suppose a boy receives physical therapy for a serious injury but cannot seem to meet the goals each week. He might attribute this failure either to his own lack of fortitude or to the rehabilitation program the physical therapist designed. Both judgments may make him stop trying. He is likely to suffer a loss of self-esteem if he attributes the difficulty to a lack of personal strength, but not if he attributes the difficulty to external causes.

2. *Stable–unstable*. They assess whether the situation results from a cause that is long-lasting (stable) or temporary (unstable). If they determine that it is long-lasting, as when people develop a chronic and disabling disease, they are more likely to feel helpless and depressed than if they think their condition is temporary.

3. *Global–specific*. They consider whether these events result from factors that have global and wide-ranging effects or specific and narrow effects. Someone who is unable to stop smoking cigarettes and arrives at a *global* judgment—for example, "I'm totally no good and weak-willed"—may feel helpless and depressed. But a similar person who makes a *specific* judgment, such as "I'm not good at controlling this part of my life," is less likely to feel helpless.

Thus, people who tend to attribute negative events in their lives to *stable* and *global* causes are at high risk for feeling helpless and depressed. If their judgments are also *internal*, their depressive thinking is likely to include a loss of self-esteem as well. People who believe bad events result from internal, stable, and global factors while good events result from external, unstable, and specific factors have a very *pessimistic* view of life (Kamen & Seligman, 1989).

How does lacking personal control affect people in real-life stressful conditions? Studies have examined this question with college students and children. For instance, of college students in dormitories, those who

This homeless woman probably sees little personal control in her life and feels very helpless.

lived on crowded floors reported more stress and less ability to control unwanted social interaction and showed more evidence of helplessness, such as giving up in competitive games, than those on uncrowded floors (Baum, Aiello, & Calesnick, 1978; Rodin & Baum, 1978). In a study of fifth-graders, students were given an impossible task to arrange blocks to match a pictured design (Dweck & Repucci, 1973). Children who attributed their failure to stable, uncontrollable factors, such as their own lack of ability, showed poorer performance on subsequent problems than those who attributed failure to unstable, modifiable factors, such as a lack of effort. Thus, the children's attributions were linked to their feelings of helplessness.

Personal Control and Health

Personal control and health may be related in two ways. First, people who have a strong sense of personal control may be more likely or able to maintain their health and prevent illness than those who have a weak sense of control. Second, once people become seriously ill, those who have a strong sense of control may adjust to the illness and promote their own rehabilitation better than those who have a weak sense of control. Both types of relationships have been examined.

To study these relationships, researchers have used several approaches to measure people's personal control. One of the best-developed health-related measures of personal control is the *Multidimensional Health Locus of Control Scales* (Wallston, Wallston, & DeVellis, 1978). This instrument contains 18 items divided into three scales that assess:

1. *Internal health locus of control*, or the belief that control for one's health lies within the person.

2. *Powerful-others' health locus of control*, the belief that one's health is controlled by other people, such as physicians.

3. *Chance locus of control*, or the belief that luck or fate controls health.

As you can see, the powerful-others and chance scales are directed toward assessing the degree to which people believe important external sources have control over their health.

Does a sense of personal control influence people's health? Studies have shown that pessimistic people—those who believe they have little control—

have poorer health habits, contract more illnesses, and are less likely to take active steps to treat their illness than people with a greater sense of control (Kamen & Seligman, 1989; Lin & Peterson, 1990). Personal control can also help people adjust to becoming seriously ill (Thompson & Kyle, in press). Patients with illnesses such as kidney failure or cancer who score high on internal or powerful-others' health locus of control suffer less depression than those with strong beliefs in the role of chance (Devins et al., 1981; Marks et al., 1986). The belief that either they or someone else can influence the course of their illness allows patients to be hopeful about their future. Moreover, patients with strong internal locus of control beliefs probably realize they have effective ways to control their stress.

Some types of control may be more effective than others in helping people adjust to serious illness. One study investigated the relationship between women's adjustment to breast cancer and their use of different types of control, three of which were cognitive, behavioral, and informational (Taylor, Lichtman, & Wood, 1984). Adjustment was most strongly associated with the women's use of cognitive control, such as by thinking about their lives differently and taking life more easily. Also, women who used behavioral control—for example, by exercising more than before—showed better adjustment than those who did not. But adjustment was not related to their use of informational control, such as by reading books on cancer. It may be that seeking information about the illness either leads the patients to materials that increase their fears or simply has little influence if the patients have no cognitive or behavioral possibilities for control.

Personal control also affects the patients' rehabilitation efforts; in particular, feelings of self-efficacy enhance their efforts. A study demonstrated this with older adult patients who had serious respiratory diseases, such as chronic bronchitis and emphysema (Kaplan, Atkins, & Reinsch, 1984). The patients were examined at a clinic and given individualized prescriptions for exercise. And they rated on a survey their self-efficacy—that is, their belief in their ability to perform specific physical activities, such as walking different distances, lifting objects of various weights, and climbing stairs. Correlational analyses revealed that the greater the patients' self-efficacy for doing physical activity, the more they adhered to the exercise prescription.

Health and Personal Control in Old Age

Here are two things we know about elderly people who live in nursing homes. First, they often show declines in their activity and health after they begin living in nursing homes. Second, residents of nursing homes frequently have few responsibilities or opportunities to influence their everyday lives. Could it be that the declines in activity and health among nursing-home residents result in part from their dependency and loss of personal control that the nursing home procedures seem to encourage?

Ellen Langer and Judith Rodin (1976) studied this issue by manipulating the amount of responsibility allowed residents of two floors of a modern, high-quality nursing home. The residents on the two floors were similar in physical and psychological health and prior socioeconomic status. On one floor, residents were given opportunities to have responsibilities—for example, they could select small plants to care for and were encouraged to make decisions about participating in activities and rearranging furniture. In comparison, residents of the other floor continued to have little personal control. For example, they were assigned to various activities without choice, and when they were given plants, they were told that the staff would take care of them. Assessments revealed that the residents who were given more responsibility became happier and more active and alert than the residents who had little control. A year and a half later the residents who were given responsibility were still happier and more active than those who had little control (Rodin & Langer, 1977). Moreover, comparisons of health data during these 18 months showed that the residents with responsibility were healthier and had half the rate of mortality than the residents with little control.

Other research with residents of a retirement home also demonstrated the importance of personal control for physical and psychological well-being and showed that withdrawing opportunities for personal control may impair people's health (Schulz, 1976; Schulz & Hanusa, 1978). The results of these studies suggest two important conclusions. First, personal control—even over relatively simple or minor events—can have a powerful effect on people's health and psychological condition. Second, health care workers and researchers need to consider the nature of the personal control they introduce and what the impact will be if it is removed.

To summarize the material on personal control, people differ in the degree to which they believe they have control over the things that happen in their lives. People who experience prolonged, high levels of stress and lack a sense of personal control tend to feel helpless. Having a strong sense of control seems to benefit people's health and help them adjust to becoming seriously ill. A sense of personal control contributes to people's hardiness, which is the next psychosocial modifier of stress we will examine.

A HARDY PERSONALITY

According to researchers Suzanne Kobasa and Salvatore Maddi, individual differences in personal control provide only part of the reason some people who are under stress get sick whereas others do not. They have proposed that a broader array of personality characteristics—called **hardiness**—differentiates people who do and do not get sick under stress (Kobasa & Maddi, 1977; Maddi, 1998; Ouellette & DiPlacido, 2001). Hardiness includes three characteristics: control, commitment, and challenge. (1) *Control* refers to people's belief that they can influence events in their lives—that is, a sense of personal control. (2) *Commitment* is people's sense of purpose or involvement in the events, activities, and people in their lives. For instance, people with a strong sense of commitment tend to look forward to starting each day's projects and enjoy getting close to people. (3) *Challenge* refers to the tendency to view changes as incentives or opportunities for growth rather than threats to security.

Hardiness, Coherence, and Resilience

Other researchers have described similar personality traits that, like hardiness, might protect people from the effects of stress. Aaron Antonovsky (1979, 1987) has described the *sense of coherence*, which involves the tendency of people to see their worlds as comprehensible, manageable, and meaningful. People's low sense of coherence has been linked to heightened stress and illness symptoms (Jorgensen, Frankowski, & Carey, 1999).

Another trait—*resilience*—seems to include high levels of three components: self-esteem, personal control, and optimism (Major et al., 1998). Resilient people appraise negative events as less stressful; they bounce back from life's adversities and recover their strength and spirit. For example, resilient children develop into competent, well-adjusted individuals even when they are growing up under extremely difficult conditions (Garmezy, 1983; Werner & Smith, 1982). The following case shows what this means:

> In the slums of Minneapolis . . . is a 10-year-old boy who lives in a dilapidated apartment with his father, an ex-convict now dying of cancer, his illiterate mother, and seven brothers and sisters, two of whom are mentally retarded. Yet his teachers describe him as an unusually competent child who does well in his studies and is loved by almost everyone in the school. (Pines, 1979, p. 53)

Resilient people seem to use positive emotions in the face of distress and find meaning in the experience (Tugade & Fredrickson, 2004). Although resilience was considered rare, it appears that probably most adults work through difficulties in their lives and do not suffer serious depression after a trauma, such as the loss of a close relative or friend (Bonanno, 2004).

Optimism—which may be part of resilience—is the point of view that good things are likely to happen. Optimists tend to experience life's difficulties with less distress than do pessimists (Scheier, Carver, & Bridges, 2001). They also tend to have better health habits, better mental and physical health, and faster recovery when they become ill than pessimists (Ouellette & DiPlacido, 2001).

Why are some individuals resilient and others not? Part of the answer may lie in their genetic endowments. Resilient people may have inherited traits, such as relatively easy temperaments, that enable them to cope better with stress and turmoil. Another part lies in their experiences. Resilient people who overcome a history of stressful events often have compensating experiences and circumstances in their lives, such as special talents or interests that absorb them and give them confidence and close relationships with friends or relatives. Hardiness, resilience, and coherence have a great deal in common and may be basically the same thing.

Hardiness and Health

Hardy people should remain healthier under stress than less hardy individuals because they are better able to deal with stressors and are less likely to become anxious and aroused by these events. As a result, the spiraling process that can lead from stress

to illness should not take hold. Studies have supported this prediction, finding that people who are high in hardiness tend to deal more effectively with stressful situations than low-hardiness people do—for example, by working through problems or transforming negative situations into positive ones (Ouellette & DiPlacido, 2001; Williams, Wiebe, & Smith, 1992). In addition, hardy people show less physiological strain when under stress than less hardy individuals (Contrada, 1989).

Does hardiness protect people's health? Research has found that individuals who are high in hardiness and sense of coherence report having developed fewer illnesses during extended stressful periods than people who are low on these traits (Kobasa et al., 1985; Ouellette & DiPlacido, 2001). And a prospective study found that people who have a strong sense of coherence had far lower mortality rates from cardiovascular disease and cancer over a 6-year period than people low on this trait (Surtees et al., 2003). But other studies have found conflicting results, and some evidence indicates that tests used in assessing hardiness may simply be measuring negative affect, such as the tendency to be anxious, depressed, or hostile (Funk, 1992). We saw in Chapter 1 that people with these personality characteristics are at risk for developing heart disease and other illnesses.

Although the status of the concept and measurement of hardiness is uncertain at this time, related aspects of personality are involved in maintaining health. Future research will need to clarify what these personality variables are and how they operate.

Hardiness in Old Age

Old age is a time when very difficult life events often occur, particularly reduced income, failing health and disability, and the loss of one's spouse and close friends. What are hardy people like in old age, and how did they get that way?

Elizabeth Colerick (1985) studied 70- to 80-year-old men and women for the quality she called *stamina*, which is similar to hardiness. This research was undertaken to determine how people who do and do not have stamina in later life deal with setbacks, such as the loss of a loved one. On the basis of questionnaires and interviews she identified two groups: one with high stamina and one with low stamina. She found that stamina in old age is characterized by "a triumphant, positive outlook during periods of adversity," as illustrated by the following interview excerpts from two different high-stamina people:

> The key to dealing with loss is not obvious. One must take the problem, the void, the loneliness, the sorrow and put it on the *back* of your neck and use it as a driving force. Don't let such problems sit out there in front of you, blocking your vision. . . . Use hardships in a positive way. (p. 999)
>
> I realize that setbacks are a part of the game. I've had 'em, I have them now, and I've got plenty more ahead of me. Seeing this—the big picture— puts it all into perspective, no matter how bad things get. (p. 999)

In contrast, low-stamina people described a negative outlook and feelings of helplessness and hopelessness in facing life events in old age. One woman who had undergone surgery for colon cancer said:

> I was certain that I would die on the table . . . never wake up. . . . I felt sure it was the end. Then I woke up with a colostomy and figured I have to stay inside the house the rest of my life. Now I'm afraid to go back to the doctor's and keep putting off my checkups. (p. 999)

Little research is available that bears directly on the question of how people become hardy. More research is needed on a variety of biopsychosocial factors that are likely to shape hardy personalities.

In summary, people with a high degree of hardiness, coherence, or resilience—or some related personality traits—may have some protection against the harmful effects of stress on health. The last psychosocial modifier of stress we will consider is people's tendency toward the Type A or B behavioral and emotional styles.

TYPE A AND TYPE B BEHAVIOR PATTERNS

The history of science has many stories about researchers accidently coming upon an idea that changed their focus and led to major discoveries. Such was the case for bacteriologist Alexander Fleming, for instance. When the bacteria cultures he was studying developed unwanted molds, he happened to notice some properties of the molds that led to the discovery of penicillin. Serendipity also led to the discovery of the "Type A" behavior pattern. Cardiologists Meyer Friedman and Ray Rosenman were studying the diets

of male heart disease victims and their wives when one of the wives exclaimed: "If you really want to know what is giving our husbands heart attacks, I'll tell you. It's stress, the stress they receive in their work, that's what's doing it" (Friedman & Rosenman, 1974, p. 56). These researchers began to study this possibility and noticed that heart patients were more likely than non-patients to display a pattern of behavior we now refer to as Type A.

Defining and Measuring Behavior Patterns

The **Type A behavior pattern** consists of three characteristics (Chesney, Frautschi, & Rosenman, 1985; Friedman & Rosenman, 1974):

1. *Competitive achievement orientation.* Type A individuals tend to be very self-critical and to strive toward goals without feeling a sense of joy in their efforts or accomplishments.

2. *Time urgency.* Type A people seem to be in a constant struggle against the clock. Often, they quickly become impatient with delays and unproductive time, schedule commitments too tightly, and try to do more than one thing at a time, such as reading while eating or watching TV.

3. *Anger/hostility.* Type A individuals tend to be easily aroused to anger or hostility, which they may or may not express overtly.

In contrast, the **Type B behavior pattern** consists of low levels of competitiveness, time urgency, and hostility. People with the Type B pattern tend to be more easygoing and "philosophical" about life—they are more likely to "stop and smell the roses."

Researchers measure people's Type A and Type B behavior either by using a standard interview procedure or by having people fill out surveys. The most widely-used interview procedure is the *Structured Interview*: a trained interviewer asks individuals a standard series of questions about their behavioral and emotional styles, particularly regarding their competitiveness, impatience, and hostility (Rosenman, Swan, & Carmelli, 1988; Tallmer et al., 1990). For instance, the interviewer asks, "When you play games with people your own age, do you play for the fun of it, or are you really in there to win?" Although the specific answers people give to these questions contribute to the assessment of their behavior pattern, their style of interaction with the interviewer also contributes. Some features of the interview are designed to encourage Type A behaviors, such as interrupting, annoying, or challenging the person. The most widely-used survey is the *Jenkins Activity Survey* (Jenkins, Zyzanski, & Rosenman, 1979). Some of its 52 items inquire about the person's usual way of responding to situations that can produce stress as a result of, for example, competition, time pressure, or frustration. This instrument is used for adults. A survey called the *Matthews Youth Test for Health* has been developed by which adults can rate Type A and B behavior in children (Matthews & Angulo, 1980).

Is one approach best for measuring Type A and B behaviors? Each approach has its own strengths and weaknesses (Carver, Diamond, & Humphries, 1985; O'Rourke et al., 1988; Powell, 1984). The Structured Interview has two strengths: it measures all three Type A characteristics (competitiveness, time urgency, and anger/hostility), and its scores have been associated fairly consistently with health outcomes, particularly heart disease. But the Structured Interview is time-consuming and expensive to use, and details of its procedure can affect the outcome (Tallmer et al., 1990). The strengths of self-report methods rest mainly in their time- and cost-efficiency; two weaknesses are that they do not measure anger/hostility well, and the relationship between health outcomes and Type A classification with existing self-report methods appears to be weak and inconsistent.

Behavior Patterns and Stress

Individuals who exhibit the Type A behavior pattern react differently to stressors than do those with the Type B pattern. Type A individuals respond more quickly and strongly to stressors, often interpreting them as threats to their personal control (Carver, Diamond, & Humphries, 1985; Glass, 1977).

We've seen that the response to a stressor—or strain—includes a physiological component called *reactivity*, such as increased blood pressure or cortisol levels compared against baseline levels. Do Type A individuals show greater reactivity to stressors than Type Bs? In general, yes. One study examined the reactivity of men each of whom competed in a video game against an individual who was a confederate of the researchers (Glass et al., 1980). Although the winner was supposed to receive a prize, the game was rigged so that a subject could never win. The men

were assigned to two groups, Type A or Type B, on the basis of a Structured Interview. Half of the men in each group played the game while being harassed and insulted by the confederate; for the remaining subjects, the confederate was silent. Several physiological measures were used, including blood pressure, heart rate, and plasma catecholamine levels. Although both Type A and Type B subjects showed substantial and equal increases in physiological arousal in the absence of harassment, the Type A subjects showed greater reactivity than the Type Bs in the harassment condition.

Gender, Sociocultural, and Age Differences in Type A Behavior

Is Type A behavior more common among males than females or among different ethnic groups? Because comparisons have produced inconsistent results, we don't really know (Thoresen & Pattillo, 1988). However, reactivity differences between Type A and Type B people are clear and show a role of gender: reactivity is greater for Type A individuals, especially males (Carver, Diamond, & Humphries, 1985; Contrada & Krantz, 1988). Other researchers have examined reactivity in Type A and Type B boys and girls and found results similar to those found with adults (Lawler et al., 1981; Lundberg, 1986; Thoresen & Pattillo, 1988). Thus, the tendency of Type A individuals to be highly reactive is greater in males than females and may begin in childhood.

Do Type A and B behaviors change over the life span? Longitudinal studies have found that although people's behavior patterns often change over time, many individuals exhibit the same pattern across many years. This has been shown for children and adults (Bergman & Magnusson, 1986; Carmelli et al., 1991; Carmelli, Rosenman, & Chesney, 1987). Also, cross-sectional studies have found that the Type A behavior pattern among Americans becomes more prevalent with age from childhood through middle age or so and then declines (Amos et al., 1987; Moss et al., 1986). But the decline in prevalence in old age could be the result of Type A individuals dying at earlier ages than Type Bs.

Other studies have been conducted to determine the origins of the Type A pattern and factors that influence its development. One approach for determining the origins of Type A behavior is to study how its development relates to the early *temperaments* of children. Behavior patterns and temperaments have similar characteristics, such as the impulsiveness and intensity with which the person reacts and his or her ease in adjusting to changes in the environment. One longitudinal study found that temperament ratings taken in early childhood were related to measures of Type A behavior taken 20 years later (Steinberg, 1985). Another longitudinal study examined this relationship in adults and found an association between measures of temperament and Type A behavior both at the beginning of the study and 10 years later (Carmelli, Rosenman, & Chesney, 1987). Thus, adult Type A behavior may have roots in the person's early temperament, which remains influential over time in at least some individuals.

Heredity also affects the development of Type A and B behavior. Research with identical (monozygotic) and fraternal (dizygotic) twins has found a genetic role in the development of both temperament (Buss & Plomin, 1975, 1986) and Type A behavior (Carmelli, Rosenman, & Chesney, 1987; Pedersen et al., 1989). That is, identical twins are more similar to each other in temperament and behavior patterns than are fraternal twins. And they are much more similar than fraternal twins in their reactivity to stressors, too (Ditto, 1993; Turner & Hewitt, 1992). Demographic and genetic variations in Type A behavior are important because of the relationships researchers have found between reactivity and health, such as in the development of heart disease.

If you have not read Chapter 2, The Body's Physical Systems, and your course has you read the modules from that chapter distributed to later chapters, read **Module 5** (The Cardiovascular System) now.

Type A Behavior and Health

How are people's health and behavior patterns related? Researchers have studied this issue in two ways. First, studies have examined whether Type A individuals are at greater risk than Type Bs for becoming sick with any of a variety of illnesses, such as asthma and indigestion, but the associations appear to be weak and inconsistent (Orfutt & Lacroix, 1988; Suls & Sanders, 1988).

Second, studies have focused on the Type A pattern as a risk factor for **coronary heart disease** (CHD)—illnesses involving the narrowing or blocking of the coronary arteries, which encircle the heart and supply blood to the heart muscle. These illnesses include *angina*, *arteriosclerosis*, and *myocardial infarction* (commonly called "heart attack"). Dozens of studies have been done to assess the link between Type A behavior and CHD. An example of research on this link comes from the Western Collaborative Group Study, a large-scale prospective study of 3,000 39- to 59-year-old initially healthy men who were tested for behavior patterns using the Structured Interview (Rosenman et al., 1976). A followup 8½ years later showed that the Type A individuals were twice as likely as Type Bs to have developed CHD and to have died of CHD.

Have other studies found similar results? An overall assessment shows mixed results because they depend on the way Type A behavior was measured: although the link is inconsistent when surveys are used to measure behavior patterns, the link is *clear in most studies using the Structured Interview* (Booth-Kewley & Friedman, 1987; Matthews, 1988; Smith & Gallo, 2001). Type A women and men, particularly white-collar workers, have a much greater chance of developing CHD than Type Bs do. Are survey measures of behavior patterns useful? They may have a different value: predicting the *timing* of a heart attack. Researchers followed for 9 years the health of men who had been tested with surveys of Type A behavior (Gallacher et al., 2003). They found that of the men who had heart attacks, those high in Type A were much more likely to have had the attack earlier in life than those low in Type A.

Type A's "Deadly Emotion"

Why is CHD associated with Type A when behavior patterns are measured with the Structured Interview but not with surveys? We saw earlier that the Structured Interview assesses all three components of Type A behavior well, but available surveys only assess competitive achievement and time urgency well—

they measure anger/hostility poorly. These discrepancies prompted researchers to examine the role of individual Type A components, which revealed that anger/hostility is the main aspect of Type A behavior in the link with CHD (Smith & Gallo, 2001; Williams & Barefoot, 1988). Anger/hostility is the Type A's deadly emotion: people who are chronically angry have an increased risk of developing CHD.

A study that supports this idea examined the records of 255 physicians who had taken a psychological test that included a scale for hostility while they were in medical school 25 years earlier (Barefoot, Dahlstrom, & Williams, 1983). For the physicians with high scores on the hostility scale, the rates of both CHD and overall mortality during the intervening years were several times higher than for those with low hostility scores. The researchers measured hostility with a widely-used test, the *Cook–Medley Hostility Scale*, which has 50 true/false items, such as "It is safer to trust nobody" and "Some of my family have habits that bother and annoy me very much" (Cook & Medley, 1954). This scale measures anger, as well as cynicism, suspiciousness, and other negative traits (Friedman, Tucker, & Reise, 1995). Other studies have clarified the hostility–CHD connection in two ways. First, chronically very high and very low anger expression may be damaging to cardiovascular health, but moderate anger expression may be protective (Eng et al., 2003; Linden et al., 2003). Second, hostility seems to be especially damaging when it is expressed outwardly and when it involves a cynical or suspicious mistrust of others (Everson et al., 1999; Knox et al., 1998; Siegman, 1993).

Why is hostility linked to CHD? Part of the answer seems to involve the stress-related hormone levels of chronically hostile people (Smith & Gallo, 2001). Frequent episodes of high arousal produce a lot of wear and tear on the cardiovascular system through the hormones released during arousal. Research has shown that chronically high levels of certain hormones, such as epinephrine and norepinephrine, can injure the heart and blood vessels. Another way wear and tear may lead to CHD in hostile people is through blood pressure (Smith & Gallo, 2001). For instance, hostile individuals have higher resting blood pressure; and when harassed or stressed, they show greater heart rate and blood pressure reactions (Everson, McKey, & Lovallo, 1995; Powch & Houston, 1996; Suls, Wan, & Costa, 1995). High blood pressure strains the heart and arteries. The role of hostility is particularly

important with social stressors: hostility seems to be more closely associated with reactivity to interpersonal stressors than to nonsocial stressors (Smith & Gallo, 2001).

These factors form only part of the process linking hostility to CHD. As psychologist Timothy Smith (1992) has pointed out, a person with cynical and suspicious beliefs about and behaviors toward other people is likely to provoke and worsen social conflicts and undermine his or her social support. A vicious circle emerges: as the social environment becomes less supportive and more stressful, the person's hostility and reactivity are maintained or increased. Research on college students confirmed this scenario, finding that hostile individuals tend to experience excessive anger in many situations and not to seek or accept social support (Houston & Vavak, 1991).

As a summary of the role of psychosocial modifiers of stress, we have seen that social support, personal control, hardiness, and the Type A and B behavior patterns are factors that can modify the impact of stress on health. High levels of social support, personal control, and hardiness are generally associated with reduced stress and resulting illnesses; Type A behavior, especially the anger/hostility component, is associated with increased stress and cardiovascular illness. The remainder of this chapter examines health problems that are affected by people's experience of stress. We begin by considering how stress leads to illness.

HOW STRESS AFFECTS HEALTH

Why does stress lead to illnesses in some individuals but not others? One answer: other factors influence the effects of stress. This idea forms the basis of the *diathesis–stress model*, the view that people's vulnerability to a physical or psychological disorder depends on the interplay of their predisposition to the disorder (the diathesis) and the amount of stress they experience (Davison, Neale, & Kring, 2003). The predisposition can result from organic structure and functioning, often genetically determined, or from prior environmental conditions, such as living in a community that promotes drug use. So, for example, chronically high levels of stress are especially likely to lead to CHD if the person's body produces high levels of cholesterol. Or adolescents are at high risk for abusing drugs if they are doing poorly in school and their friends use drugs. Or students are likely to catch cold around final exams week if their immune system functioning is impaired. This concept may explain why not all individuals in the following experiment caught cold.

Researchers conducted an interesting experiment: they gave people nasal drops that contained a "common cold" virus or a placebo solution and then quarantined them to check for infection and cold symptoms (Cohen, Tyrrell, & Smith, 1991). Before the nasal drops were administered, the subjects had filled out questionnaires to assess their stress. Of these people, 47% of those with high stress and 27% of those with low stress developed colds. Other studies have produced two related findings. First, people under chronic, severe stress are more vulnerable to catching cold when exposed to the virus than people under less stress (Cohen et al., 1998). Second, people who experience a lot of positive emotions, such as feeling energetic or happy, are less likely to catch cold when exposed to the virus than people with less of these emotions (Cohen et al., 2003).

What is it about stress that leads to illness? The causal sequence can involve two routes: (1) a direct route, resulting from the changes stress produces in the body's *physiology*, or (2) an indirect route, affecting health through the person's *behavior*. Let's look first at the behavioral route.

STRESS, BEHAVIOR, AND ILLNESS

Stress can affect behavior, which, in turn, can lead to illness or worsen an existing condition. We can see the behavioral links between stress and illness in many stressful situations, such as when a family undergoes a divorce. In many cases during the first year following the separation, the parent who has the children is less available and responsive to them than she or he was before, resulting in haphazard meals, less regular bedtimes, and delays in getting medical attention, for instance (Wallerstein, 1983).

People who experience high levels of stress tend to behave in ways that increase their chances of becoming ill or injured (Weidner et al., 1996; Wiebe & McCallum, 1986). For instance, compared with people with low stress, those with high stress are more likely to eat higher fat diets with less fruits and vegetables, engage in less exercise, smoke cigarettes, and consume more alcohol (Baer et al., 1987; Cartwright et al., 2003; Ng &

Jeffery, 2003). These behaviors are associated with the development of various illnesses. In addition, stress impairs sleep (Hall et al., 2004). The resulting inattention and carelessness probably play a role in the relatively high accident rates of people under stress. Studies have found that children and adults who experience high levels of stress are more likely to suffer accidental injuries at home, in sports activities, on the job, and while driving a car than individuals under less stress (Johnson, 1986; Quick et al., 1997).

STRESS, PHYSIOLOGY, AND ILLNESS

Stress produces many physiological changes in the body that can affect health, especially when stress is chronic and severe. In Chapter 3, we discussed the concept of *allostatic load* in which the strain involved in adapting repeatedly to intense stressors produces wear and tear on body systems that accumulate over time and lead to illness (McEwen & Stellar, 1993). Clear connections have been found between illness and the degree of reactivity people show in their cardiovascular, endocrine, and immune systems when stressed.

Cardiovascular System Reactivity and Illness

Cardiovascular reactivity includes any physiological change that occurs in the heart, blood vessels, and blood in response to stressors. People's degree of cardiovascular reactivity is very stable, showing little change when retested with the same stressors years later (Sherwood et al., 1997; Veit, Brody, & Rau, 1997).

Research has discovered links between chronically high cardiovascular reactivity and the development of CHD, hypertension, and stroke (Dougall & Baum, 2001; Everson et al., 2001; Manuck, 1994). For example, high levels of job stress are associated with high blood pressure and abnormally enlarged hearts (Schnall et al., 1990), and people's laboratory reactivity to stress in early adulthood is associated with their later development of high blood pressure (Menkes et al., 1989). The heightened blood pressure reactivity that people display in laboratory tests appears to reflect their reactivity in daily life (Turner et al., 1994).

Stress produces several cardiovascular changes that relate to the development of CHD. For instance, the blood of people who are under stress contains high concentrations of activated platelets (Malkoff et al., 1993; Patterson et al., 1994) and unfavorable levels of lipids, such as cholesterol (Patterson et al., 1995; Vitaliano, Russo, & Niaura, 1995). These changes in blood composition tend to promote atherosclerosis—the growth of plaques (fatty patches) on artery walls. As these plaques build up, they narrow and harden the arteries, thereby increasing blood pressure and the likelihood of a heart attack or stroke. Prospective studies have found that people who display high cardiovascular reactivity to stressors show faster progression of atherosclerosis than those with lower reactivity, especially if they experience chronic, severe stress in their lives (Everson et al., 1997; Lynch et al., 1998; Matthews et al., 1998). (Go to 💡.)

Endocrine System Reactivity and Illness

Part of reactivity involves activation of the *hypothalamus–pituitary–adrenal axis*, which releases endocrine hormones—particularly catecholamines and corticosteroids—during stress (Lundberg, 1999; Sternberg & Gold, 1997). The increased endocrine reactivity that people display in these tests appears to reflect their reactivity in daily life (Williams et al., 1991). One way in which high levels of these hormones can lead to illness involves their effects on the cardiovascular system. For example, an intense episode of stress with extremely high levels of these hormones can cause the heart to beat erratically and may lead to sudden cardiac death. In addition, chronically high levels of catecholamines and corticosteroids appear to increase atherosclerosis.

Stephen Manuck and his colleagues (1988, 1995) have demonstrated this link between stress and atherosclerosis in research with monkeys. In one study, some of the subjects were relocated periodically to different living groups, thereby requiring stressful social and psychological adjustments to retain their dominant social status; the remaining

---

HIGHLIGHT

Sudden "Voodoo" Death

Can a person die from extreme psychological distress? It seems so, at least on the basis of anecdotal evidence, as seen in the following case study:

> In 1967 a distraught woman, pleading for help, entered the Baltimore City Hospital a few days before her 23rd birthday. She and two other girls had been born of different mothers assisted by the same midwife in the Okefenokee Swamp on a Friday the 13th. The midwife cursed all three babies, saying one would die before her 16th birthday, another before her 21st birthday, and the third before her 23rd birthday. The first had died in a car crash during her 15th year; the second was accidentally shot to death in a nightclub fight on the evening of her 21st birthday. Now she, the third, waited in terror for her death. The hospital somewhat skeptically admitted her for observation. The next morning, two days before her 23rd birthday, she was found dead in her hospital bed—physical cause unknown. (Seligman, cited in Rosenhan & Seligman, 1984, p. 292.)

This woman died of **sudden cardiac death**—the abrupt death from cardiac dysfunction of a seemingly healthy person (AHA, 2004). Sudden death was originally called "voodoo death" (Cannon, 1942), perhaps because many of the cases described were from primitive cultures.

Sudden cardiac death usually results from heart failure of some sort and often involves two factors: a preexisting cardiovascular disorder and a severe physical or psychological stressor, such as extreme anger or fear (Allan & Scheidt, 1990; Kop, 1999; Möller et al., 1999). The underlying cardiovascular disorder may take two forms (AHA, 2004; Kop, 1999). First, the disorder may involve CHD or damage to the myocardium from a prior heart attack. Second, the disorder typically involves the occurrence of *cardiac arrhythmia*—an abnormal rhythm of the heart's functioning. Arrhythmias can take the form of an extremely high heart rate, called *tachycardia*, or of uncoordinated heartbeats, called *fibrillation*. Research has shown that emotional upset and arrhythmia are associated in daily life (Carels et al., 2003).

subjects stayed in stable groups. Regardless of whether the monkeys' diets had high or low levels of cholesterol, the stressed subjects who had to retain their dominant status developed greater atherosclerosis than the subjects in the low-stress condition. This effect of stress is probably very similar in humans. Disruptions of soldiers' social status in boot camp affect endocrine reactivity (Hellhammer et al., 1997). And as we saw earlier, people are more likely to develop atherosclerosis under chronically high stress than with less stress. But social support may help: people tend to exhibit lower endocrine reactivity with high levels of social support than with low levels (Seeman & McEwen, 1996).

If you have not read Chapter 2, The Body's Physical Systems, and your course has you read the modules from that chapter distributed to later chapters, read **Module 6** (The Immune System) now.

Immune System Reactivity and Illness

The release of catecholamines and corticosteroids during arousal affects health in another way: some of these hormones impair the functioning of the immune system (Dougall & Baum, 2001; Rozlog et al., 1999). For example, increases in cortisol and epinephrine are associated with decreased activity of T cells and B cells against antigens. This decrease in lymphocyte activity appears to be important in the development and progression of a variety of infectious diseases and cancer (Kiecolt-Glaser & Glaser, 1995; Vedhara et al., 1999). Among people with cancer, those with high levels of killer-T-cell activity have a better prognosis and disease course than those with low levels of activity (Dougall & Baum, 2001).

Immune processes also protect the body against cancers that result from excessive exposure to harmful chemical or physical agents called *carcinogens*, which include radiation (nuclear, X, and ultraviolet types), tobacco smoke, and asbestos (AMA, 2003). Carcinogens can damage the DNA in body cells, which may then develop into mutant cells and spread. Fortunately, people's exposure to carcinogens is generally at low levels and for short periods of time, and most DNA changes probably do not lead to cancer (Glaser et al., 1985). When mutant cells develop, the immune system attacks them with killer T cells. Actually, the body begins to defend itself against cancer even before a cell mutates by using enzymes to destroy chemical carcinogens or to repair damaged DNA. But research has shown that high levels of stress reduce the production of these enzymes and the repair of damaged DNA (Glaser et al., 1985; Kiecolt-Glaser & Glaser, 1986).

PSYCHONEUROIMMUNOLOGY

We have seen in this and earlier chapters that psychological and biological systems are interrelated—as one system changes, the others are often affected. The recognition of this interdependence and its connection to health and illness led researchers to form a new field of study called **psychoneuroimmunology.** This field focuses on the relationships between psychosocial processes and the activities of the nervous, endocrine, and immune systems (Ader & Cohen, 1985; Dunn, 1995; Marsland et al., 2001). These systems form a *feedback loop*: the nervous and endocrine systems send chemical messages in the form of neurotransmitters and hormones that increase or decrease immune function, and cells of the immune system produce chemicals, such as ACTH, that feed information back to the brain. The brain appears to serve as a control center to maintain a balance in immune function, since too little immune activity leaves the individual open to infection and too much activity may produce autoimmune diseases.

Emotions and Immune Function

People's emotions—both positive and negative—play a critical role in the balance of immune functions. Research has shown that pessimism, depression, and stress from major and minor events are related to impaired immune function (Dunn, 1995; Leonard, 1995; Marsland et al., 2001). For example, research compared immune variables of caregiver spouses of Alzheimer's disease patients with matched control subjects and found that the caregivers had lower immune function and reported more days of illness over the course of about a year (Kiecolt-Glaser et al., 1991). Another study compared individuals who received a flu vaccination and found that those who developed and maintained over 5 months a high level of flu antibodies had experienced less stress in the interim than those with fewer antibodies (Burns et al., 2003).

Positive emotions can also affect immune function, giving it a boost (Futterman et al., 1994; Stone et al., 1994). In the study by Arthur Stone and his coworkers, adult men kept daily logs of positive and negative events and gave saliva samples for analyses of antibody content. Negative events were associated with reduced antibodies only for the day the events occurred, but positive events enhanced antibody content for the day of occurrence and the next two.

Some stressful situations start with a crisis, and the ensuing emotional states tend to continue and suppress immune processes over an extended period of time. This was demonstrated with healthy elderly individuals who were taking part in a longitudinal study of the aging process (Willis et al., 1987). These people were asked to contact the researchers as soon as they were able if they experienced any major crisis, such as the diagnosis of a serious illness in or the death of a spouse or child; 15 of them did so. A month after the crisis, and again months later, the researchers assessed the people's cortisol and lymphocyte blood concentrations, recent diets, weights, and psychological distress. Because the subjects were already participating in the longitudinal study, comparable data were available from a time prior to the crisis. Analysis of these data revealed that lymphocyte concentrations, caloric intake, and body weight decreased, and cortisol concentrations and psychological distress increased, soon after the crisis. By the

time of the last assessment several months later, however, all of these measures had returned almost to the precrisis levels.

When people react to short-term, minor events, such as doing difficult math problems under time pressure, changes in the number and activity of immune cells occur for fairly short periods of time—minutes or hours (Delahanty et al., 1996). The degree of change depends on the event's characteristics—long-lasting and intense interpersonal events seem to produce especially large immune reductions (Herbert & Cohen, 1993). Of course, immune system reactivity varies from one person to the next, but a person's degree of response to a type of event seems to be much the same when tested weeks apart (Marsland et al., 1995). This suggests that an individual's reaction to specific stressors is fairly stable over time.

Psychosocial Modifiers of Immune System Reactivity

We saw earlier that psychosocial factors in people's lives may modify the stress they experience. Such factors seem to affect immune system responses, too. For instance, social support affects the immune function of people under long-term, intense stress. People who have strong social support have stronger immune systems and smaller immune impairments in response to stress than others with less support (Esterling, Kiecolt-Glaser, & Glaser, 1996; Kennedy, Kiecolt-Glaser, & Glaser, 1990; Levy et al., 1990). Similarly, people high in hardiness show stronger immune responses to antigens than low-hardiness people (Dolbier et al., 2001).

A related psychosocial modifier involves describing one's feelings about stressful events. An experiment

Reprinted with permission of United Features Syndicate, Inc.

with college students examined the effect of expressing such feelings on blood levels of antibodies against the Epstein-Barr virus, a widespread virus that causes mononucleosis in many of those who are infected (Esterling et al., 1994). The students were randomly assigned to three conditions that met in three weekly 20-minute sessions when they either described *verbally* or *in writing* a highly stressful event they had experienced or wrote about a trivial (nonstress-related) topic, such as the contents of their bedrooms. The students in each condition had the same level of immune control against the virus before the study. But blood samples taken a week after the last session revealed that immune control improved substantially in the verbal condition, moderately in the written condition, and declined slightly in the control (trivial topic) condition, as Figure 4–4 depicts. Other research has found that describing feelings about stressful events is more effective in enhancing immune function in cynically hostile than in nonhostile individuals (Christensen et al., 1996).

The influence of optimism on immune function appears to depend on whether the stress is short term or chronic. A study examined this issue with healthy women for 3 months (Cohen, Kearney et al., 1999). The impact of optimism varied with the intensity of short-term stressors: immune function declined among pessimistic women, but not optimistic women, as stressor intensity increased. Perhaps the optimists appraised their stress in a more positive way. During chronic stressors, optimists showed progressive declines in immune function over time, but pessimists did not. It may be that the persistence of stress disconfirms optimists' beliefs that they can control negative events, which then makes the stress less bearable.

Lifestyles and Immune Function

Do people's lifestyles affect the functioning of their immune systems? Some evidence suggests that they do. People with generally healthful lifestyles—including exercising, getting enough sleep, eating balanced meals, and not smoking—show stronger immune functioning than those with less healthful lifestyles (Kusaka, Kondou, & Morimoto, 1992). Other studies have found that sleeping poorly impairs immune function the next day (Irwin et al., 1994) and people who smoke are more susceptible than those who don't to catching colds (Cohen et al., 1993).

Conditioning Immune Function

Research on psychoneuroimmunology with animals has revealed that the influence of psychological processes on immune function is not limited to the effects of stress. The impact may be far more broad and pervasive. Robert Ader and Nicholas Cohen (1975, 1985) have shown that *immune suppression can be conditioned.* In their original research, they were actually studying how animals learn to dislike certain tastes. The procedure used a single conditioning trial: the subjects (rats) received saccharin-flavored water to drink (which they seemed to like) and then got an injection of a drug that induces nausea. To see if the rats' subsequent dislike of the taste depended on its strength, some subjects received more saccharin flavoring than others in this conditioning trial. Over the next several weeks, the drug was *not* used, but the animals continued to receive saccharin-flavored water. During this time, the researchers noticed a curious thing: a number of rats had fallen ill and died—and these animals tended to be the ones that had consumed the greatest amount of saccharin in the conditioning trial.

How did these deaths relate to immune suppression? Since the nausea-inducing drug used in the conditioning trial was also known to suppress immune function temporarily, Ader and Cohen hypothesized that the continued intake of saccharin water served as a conditioned stimulus, suppressing the ability of the

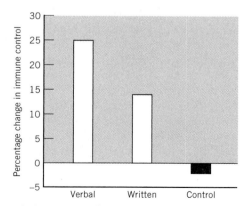

Figure 4–4   Percent change in immune control against the Epstein-Barr virus, as reflected in blood concentrations of specific antibodies, for subjects having sessions for verbal expression of stress feelings, written expression of stress feelings, or a control condition. (Based on data from Esterling et al., 1994, Figure 3.)

rats to fight infection. Subsequent experiments by these researchers and others confirmed this hypothesis and demonstrated that conditioning can raise or lower immune function and can influence both antibody-mediated and cell-mediated immune processes (Kusnecov, 2001). Similar conditioning effects have been demonstrated in humans, such as cancer patients who receive medications that impair immune function.

Psychoneuroimmunology is a very new and exciting field, and researchers are discovering fascinating connections between biological and psychosocial processes very quickly. They are also developing ways to apply this knowledge (Kusnecov, 2001). For instance, researchers have shown that conditioning can suppress immune function to help reduce allergies, such as hay fever, and organ transplant rejection, perhaps enabling patients to use less medication.

PSYCHOPHYSIOLOGICAL DISORDERS

The word *psychosomatic* has a long history and was coined to refer to symptoms or illnesses that are caused or aggravated by psychological factors, mainly emotional stress (Lipowski, 1986). Although many professionals and the general public still use this term, the concept has undergone some changes and now has a new name: **psychophysiological disorders,** which refers to physical symptoms or illnesses that result from the interplay of psychosocial and physiological processes. This definition clearly uses a biopsychosocial perspective. We will discuss several illnesses traditionally classified as psychosomatic. Some of these illnesses will be examined in greater detail in later chapters.

DIGESTIVE SYSTEM DISEASES

Ulcers and **inflammatory bowel disease** are two illnesses that involve wounds in the digestive tract that may cause pain and bleeding (AMA, 2003). Ulcers are found in the stomach and the duodenum, or upper section of the small intestine. Inflammatory bowel disease, which includes disorders such as *colitis*, can occur in the colon (large intestine) and the small intestine. Another digestive system illness, **irritable bowel syndrome,** produces abdominal pain, diarrhea, and constipation without organic evidence of disease (AMA, 2003). Although these diseases afflict mainly adults, similar symptoms occur in childhood (Blanchard, 2001).

Most ulcers are produced by a combination of gastric juices eroding the lining of the stomach and duodenum that has been weakened by bacterial infection (AMA, 2003). But stress plays a role, too (Levenstein, 2002). In a classic study, a patient (called Tom) agreed to cooperate in a lengthy and detailed examination of gastric function (Wolf & Wolff, 1947). Tom was unique in that many years earlier, at the age of 9, he had had a stomach operation that left an opening to the outside of the body. This opening, which provided the only way he could feed himself, was literally a window through which the inside of his stomach could be observed. When Tom was subjected to stressful situations, his stomach-acid production greatly increased. When he was under emotional tension for several weeks, there was a pronounced reddening of the stomach lining. Another study reported similar effects with a 15-month-old girl, Monica, who had a temporary opening to her stomach. Her highest levels of acid secretion occurred when she experienced rage (Engel, Reichsman, & Segal, 1956).

The physical causes of inflammatory bowel disease and irritable bowel syndrome are not yet known (AMA, 2003). Stress is related to flare-ups of these illnesses, but its specific role is currently unclear (Blanchard, 2001).

ASTHMA

Asthma is a respiratory disorder in which inflammation, spasms, and mucous obstruct the bronchial tubes and lead to difficulty breathing, with wheezing or coughing. This ailment is prevalent around the world—in the United States it afflicts about 6% of the population and is more common in children than in adults (AAFA, 2004; ALA, 2003). Asthma attacks appear to result from some combination of three factors: allergies, respiratory infections, and biopsychosocial arousal, such as from stress or exercise (ALA, 2003; Lehrer et al., 2002). In most cases, the cause of an attack is largely physical, but sometimes it may be largely psychosocial.

Professionals working with hospitalized children have noted an interesting phenomenon that suggests a role of psychosocial factors in asthma. About one-third of asthmatic children show reduced symptoms shortly after admission to the hospital even though their medication is not changed. When they return home, the symptoms reappear (Purcell, Weiss, & Hahn, 1972). Does this happen because the children are allergic to something in their own houses, such as dust, or because of other factors? This question was tested in an ingenious study with asthmatic children who were allergic to house dust (Long et al., 1958). Without the children knowing, the researchers vacuumed the children's homes and then sprayed the collected dust from each house into their individual hospital rooms. *None* of the children had respiratory difficulty when exposed to their home dust, which suggests that psychosocial factors may be involved. The results of other research indicate that stress can trigger asthma attacks (Lehrer et al., 2002; Miller & Wood, 1994; Sarafino, 1997).

RECURRENT HEADACHE

Many people suffer chronically from intense headaches. Although there are many types of recurrent headache, two of the most common are called tension-type and migraine headache. **Tension-type** (or *muscle contraction*) **headaches** seem to be caused by a combination of a central nervous system dysfunction and persistent contraction of the head and neck muscles (AMA, 2003; Holroyd, 2002). The pain it produces is a dull and steady ache that often feels like a tight band of pressure around the head. Recurrent tension-type headaches occur twice a week or more, and may last for hours, days, or weeks (Dalessio, 1994).

Migraine headaches seem to result from a dysfunction in the brainstem and the dilation of blood vessels surrounding the brain (AMA, 2003; Holroyd, 2002). The pain often begins on one side of the head near the temple, is sharp and throbbing, and lasts hours or, sometimes, days (Dalessio, 1994). Sometimes migraines begin with or follow an *aura*, a set of symptoms that signal an impending headache episode. These symptoms usually include sensory phenomena, such as seeing lines or shimmering in the visual field. This may be accompanied by dizziness, nausea, and vomiting. Recurrent migraine is marked by periodic debilitating symptoms, which occur about once a month, with headache-free periods in between (Dalessio, 1994).

Most adults and children have headaches at least occasionally, and tension-type headaches are common (AMA, 2003). The prevalence of migraine varies widely across cultures but is about 10% overall, is far greater in females than males, and increases with age from childhood to middle age and then declines (Stewart, Shechter, & Rasmussen, 1994). Many children experience their first headaches in the preschool years, and chronic headaches have been reported in boys and girls as young as 6 years of age (Andrasik, Blake, & McCarran, 1986). Figure 4–5 presents a drawing by an 11-year-old

Figure 4–5   Drawing by 11-year-old Meghan of her experience of migraine headache pain. The lower left-hand corner has a self-portrait with a dramatic facial expression. When a headache begins, Meghan typically retreats to her bedroom "to ride out the storm," lying down in a darkened room. (From Andrasik, Blake, & McCarran, 1986, Figure 18.1.)

girl named Meghan to describe her experience of migraine headache pain.

What triggers headaches? They often are brought on by hormonal changes, missing a meal, sunlight, sleeping poorly, and consuming certain substances, such as alcohol or chocolate. Research has also shown that stressors—particularly the hassles of everyday living—are common triggers of migraine and tension-type headaches (Köhler & Haimerl, 1990; Robbins, 1994). Yet some patients with chronic headache have attacks when they are not under great stress, and others fail to have headaches when they are under stress. Stress appears to be one of many factors that produce headaches, but the full nature of these causes is not yet known.

OTHER DISORDERS

There are several other psychophysiological disorders for which stress appears to be involved in triggering or aggravating episodes. One of these illnesses is *rheumatoid arthritis*—a chronic and very painful disease that produces inflammation and stiffness of the small joints, such as in the hands. It afflicts about 1% of the general population, and its victims are primarily women (AF, 2004). Another disorder, called *dysmenorrhea*, affects millions of women. It is characterized by painful menstruation, which may be accompanied by nausea, headache, and dizziness (AMA, 2003; Calhoun & Burnette, 1983). A third stress-related problem involves skin disorders, such as *hives, eczema,* and *psoriasis*, in which the skin develops rashes or becomes dry and flakes or cracks (AMA, 2003). In many cases, specific allergies are identified as contributing to episodes of these skin problems.

Although current evidence implicates both biological and psychosocial causes for each of the psychophysiological disorders we have considered, the evidence is sketchy and the nature of the interplay of these factors is unclear. The remainder of this chapter focuses on the role of stress in the development of cardiovascular disorders and cancer.

STRESS AND CARDIOVASCULAR DISORDERS

Earlier in this chapter, we saw that psychosocial modifiers of stress can affect health—for instance, the risk of developing CHD is greater for people with the Type A than the Type B behavior pattern. Such findings suggest that stress may be a factor in the development of cardiovascular disorders, the number-one cause of death in the United States and many other countries. We'll look at the role of stress in hypertension and CHD.

HYPERTENSION

Hypertension—the condition of having high blood pressure consistently over several weeks or more—is a major risk factor for CHD, stroke, and kidney disease (AHA, 2004; NKF, 2004). In the United States, more than one-fourth of adults are classified as hypertensive, having blood pressures at or above 140 (systolic) over 90 (diastolic). Because lesser elevations in blood pressure are now known to increase risk, current guidelines designate less than 120/80 as "normal," or conveying little risk, as shown in Table 4.1. Prevalence rates for hypertension increase in adulthood, particularly after about 40 years of age (NCHS, 2003). Some cases of hypertension are caused by, or are *secondary* to, disorders of other body systems or organs, such as the kidneys or endocrine system. Secondary hypertension can usually be cured by medical procedures. But the vast majority—over 90%—of hypertensive cases are classified as *primary* or *essential hypertension*, in which the mechanisms causing the high blood pressure are unknown.

Table 4.1   *Blood Pressure Categories* (values in mm Hg units)

Category	Systolic		Diastolic
Normal (recommended)	less than 120	*and*	less than 80
Prehypertension	120–139	*or*	80–89
Hypertension: Stage 1	140–159	*or*	90–99
Hypertension: Stage 2	160 or higher	*or*	100 or higher

Source: AHA, 2004.

To say that the causes for essential hypertension are unknown is somewhat misleading. In cases of essential hypertension, physicians are unable to identify any biomedical causes, such as infectious agents or organ damage. But many risk factors are associated with the development of hypertension—and there is evidence implicating the following as some of the risk factors for hypertension (AHA, 2004; Rutledge & Hogan, 2002):

- Obesity
- Dietary elements, such as high salt, fats, and cholesterol
- Excessive alcohol use
- Physical inactivity
- Family history of hypertension
- Psychosocial factors, such as chronic stress, anger, and anxiety

One interesting finding is that just the anxiety involved in having blood pressure tested can increase the reading in some individuals, leading to a false diagnosis of hypertension (McGrady & Higgins, 1990).

Stress, Emotions, and Hypertension

People's occupations provide sources of stress that can have an impact on their blood pressure. Traffic controllers at airports provide an example. Sidney Cobb and Robert Rose (1973) compared the medical records of thousands of men employed as air traffic controllers or as second-class airmen, separating the data for different age groups, since blood pressure increases with age. Comparisons for each age group revealed prevalence rates of hypertension among traffic controllers that were several times higher than those for airmen. The researchers also compared the records of traffic controllers who experienced high and low levels of stress, as measured by the traffic density at the air stations where they worked. Figure 4–6 depicts the results: for each age group, prevalence rates of hypertension were higher for traffic controllers working at high-stress locations than for those at low-stress sites.

Aspects of social environments, such as crowding and aggression, are also linked to stress and hypertension. Experiments with animals have shown that living in crowded, aggressive conditions induces chronic hypertension (Henry et al., 1993). Research with humans compared people living in crowded and

Figure 4–6 Prevalence of hypertension per 1,000 air traffic controllers as a function of stress and age. Hypertension rates increase with age and stress. (Data from Cobb & Rose, 1973, Table 3.)

uncrowded neighborhoods to see if these living conditions influence blood pressure (Fleming et al., 1987). The people from the two types of neighborhoods were similar in important characteristics, such as age, gender, and family income. While working on a stressful cognitive task, the subjects showed greater increases in heart rate and systolic and diastolic pressure if they lived in crowded neighborhoods. Other research has found that high cardiovascular reactivity may be a risk factor for, or even a cause of, hypertension (Fredrikson & Matthews, 1990; Manuck, 1994). Taken together, the evidence suggests that chronic stress plays a role in the development of hypertension.

But not all people with hypertension react to stressors of different types in the same way. Mats Fredrikson and Karen Matthews (1990) performed a *meta-analysis*, which as we saw in Chapter 3 is a statistical research method that pools the results of prior studies to clarify the findings. Some, but not all, studies had found greater cardiovascular reactivity—that is, blood pressure and heart rate responses—to stressors in people who are hypertensive than in people who are not. The meta-analysis focused on studies that tested hypertensive patients who were not currently taking antihypertensive drugs. Each study also had a control group with normal blood pressure and measured reactivity in a laboratory with a psychological stressor, such as performing mental arithmetic or watching a stressful film, rather than a physical one, such as exercising. Dozens of studies were found that met these criteria, and a computer analysis of the data revealed two previously unknown patterns. First, patients with relatively mild hypertension exhibit heart rate and blood pressure reactivity mainly to psychological stressors that require them to be *active*, such as doing arithmetic, rather than *passive*, as in watching a stressful film. Second, patients with more severe hypertension show reactivity to *all* types of psychological stressors. Many earlier studies had found no link between cardiovascular reactivity and hypertension because they tested mild hypertensives with passive stressors.

Studies on pessimism, anger, and hostility have revealed important links to the development of hypertension; we'll consider three of these links. First, blood pressure is higher in pessimistic than optimistic individuals (Räikkönen et al., 1999). Second, people who are hypertensive are more likely to be chronically hostile and resentful than are *normotensive* people, those with normal blood pressure (Diamond, 1982). Third, resting blood pressure is higher among individuals who ruminate or dwell on events that provoke anger than people who don't ruminate (Hogan & Linden, 2004). These findings indicate that chronically high levels of pessimism, anger, and hostility may contribute to the high blood pressure of many hypertensives.

Stress and Sociocultural Differences in Hypertension

The impact of stress on hypertension may be particularly relevant for Black people in the United States, who have a much higher prevalence rate of high blood pressure than Whites do (NCHS, 2003). In a study of Black and White people in Detroit, the highest blood pressure readings found were those of Blacks living in high-stress areas of the city—neighborhoods that were crowded and had high crime rates and low incomes (Harburg et al., 1973). But Blacks and Whites who lived in low-stress areas had similar blood pressures. Two other findings suggest that perceived racism is a stressor that plays a major role in the high rates of hypertension among African Americans. First,

Black women's blood pressure reactivity to stressors is higher among those who feel that racial discrimination underlies the mistreatment they've experienced than those who do not (Guyll, Matthews, & Bromberger, 2001). Second, blood pressure in waking daily life is higher among Black men and women who perceive frequent racism in their lives than those who do not (Steffen et al., 2003).

Few, if any, cases of essential hypertension are likely to be caused by emotional factors alone (Schneiderman & Hammer, 1985). Most cases of high blood pressure probably involve several of the determinants listed earlier in this section.

CORONARY HEART DISEASE

Epidemiologists have studied the distribution and frequency of CHD over many decades in many different cultures. The data they have collected suggest that CHD is, to some extent, a disease of modernized societies—that is, the incidence rate of heart disease is higher in technologically advanced countries than in other nations (Susser, Hopper, & Richman, 1983). In advanced societies, people live long enough to become victims of CHD, which afflicts mainly older individuals, and are more likely than those in less developed countries to have certain risk factors for CHD, such as obesity and low levels of physical activity. Last, the psychosocial stressors of advanced societies are different from those in other societies and may be more conducive to the development of heart disease. For instance, people in less advanced societies may have more social support to protect them from the effects of stress and perceive less reason for anger and hostility, which we've already seen can increase the risk of CHD.

The link between stress and CHD has considerable support, and we'll consider three examples. First, studies of occupational stress have shown that high workloads, job responsibility, and job dissatisfaction are associated with a high incidence of CHD (Cottington & House, 1987; Quick et al., 1997). Second, research has found higher levels of atherosclerosis in the arteries of African American women who perceived high levels of stress, unfair treatment, and racial discrimination in their lives than those who did not (Troxel et al. 2003). Third, studies have examined the relationship between heart disease and major life stressors, using prospective approaches. For instance, researchers carried out periodic followup assessments over an 8-year period of patients who had recovered from their first heart attacks (Theorell & Rahe, 1975). These patients were separated into two groups—those who did and those who did not have subsequent attacks. The group who suffered subsequent attacks—some of whom died—had experienced a substantial buildup in life events over the preceding year or so. But the group who had no recurrence of heart attack reported no increase in life events during the study.

What physical processes link stress and CHD? We've discussed three processes already. First, stress increases catecholamine and corticosteroid release by the endocrine glands; chronically high levels of these hormones can damage the arteries and heart, promote atherosclerosis, and lead to the development of hypertension and arteriosclerosis (hardening of the arteries). Second, stress can elicit cardiac arrhythmia, which can cause a cardiac episode and sudden death. Third, stress is associated with cigarette smoking and high levels of alcohol use, for example, which are behavioral risk factors for CHD. The stress–CHD connection often progresses from chronic stress to poor health habits to a condition called *metabolic syndrome*, which consists of being overweight and having hypertension, high cholesterol, and poor control of insulin levels; to CHD (Vitaliano et al., 2002). The stress-CHD link also involves immune reactions to stress, which seem to promote atherosclerosis (Kop, 2003). In later chapters we will examine in greater detail various risk factors and issues relating to CHD and the next stress-related illness, cancer.

STRESS AND CANCER

The idea that stress and other psychosocial factors contribute to the development of cancer has a long history. The physician Galen, who practiced in Rome during the second century A.D., believed that individuals who were sad and depressed, or "melancholy," were more likely to develop cancer than those who were happy, confident, and vigorous (Sklar & Anisman, 1981). Similar ideas have appeared in the writings of physicians in later eras.

Cancer is a term that refers to a broad class of disease in which cells multiply and grow in an unrestrained manner. As such, cancer does not refer to a single illness but to dozens of disease forms that share this characteristic (ACS, 2004; Williams, 1990).

It includes, for instance, *leukemias*, in which the bone marrow produces excessive numbers of white blood cells, and *carcinomas*, in which tumors form in the tissue of the skin and internal organ linings. Some cancers take longer to develop or follow more irregular courses in their development than others do. Although the causes of cancer are difficult to study because the disease has so many forms, some evidence suggests that stress may play a role in the beginnings and progression of cancer.

Early evidence linking stress and cancer came from research using retrospective methods (Sklar & Anisman, 1981). This research generally had cancer patients fill out life-events questionnaires to assess the stress they experienced during the year or so preceding the diagnosis. Although some studies found that the appearance of cancer was associated with self-reported high levels of prior stress, others did not (Delahanty & Baum, 2001). And problems with retrospective methods cloud the interpretation of the results of these studies. Because the cancer diagnoses were typically made years after the disease process started, the patients' cancers were probably present prior to and during the year for which they reported high levels of stress. Also, the patients' perceptions or recollections of prior stress may have been distorted by their knowledge that they have cancer. A better approach to study the role of stress in the development of cancer uses prospective methods: measure psychosocial factors and follow up on the subjects' health over time. Several prospective studies of women, for instance, found that those who developed breast cancer had reported more severe life events than those who did not develop cancer (Delahanty & Baum, 2001).

An overview of findings from research on cancer and stress published since the mid-1970s suggests four conclusions. First, the experience of moderate stress has little influence on later development of cancer (Delahanty & Baum, 2001). Second, cancer patients who have relapses within a given time period, such as a year, tend to have experienced more stressful life events or received less social support during that time than those who do not have relapses (Sabbioni, 1991; Watson & Ramirez, 1991). Third, cancer patients typically experience high levels of stress after diagnosis, and their immune functions are less able to fight the cancer if their stress remains high (Andersen, Golden-Kreutz, & DiLillo, 2001). Fourth, people who generally respond to stressors with appeasing, compliant, and unexpressive behaviors (sometimes called the Type C behavior pattern) seem more likely than others to develop cancer (Temoshok & Dreher, 1992).

The effects of stress on cancer seem to be influenced by many factors, such as the severity of the stress, whether it is chronic, the way the person reacts to it, and whether it is experienced before or after initiation of the disease. If stress plays a causal role in the development of cancer, it probably does so by impairing the immune system's ability to combat the disease and by increasing behavioral risk factors, such as smoking cigarettes.

SUMMARY

Researchers have identified several psychosocial factors that modify the impact of stress on the individual. One of these factors is social support—the perceived comfort, caring, esteem, or help a person receives from others. There are four basic types of support: emotional or esteem, tangible or instrumental, informational, and companionship. Whether people receive social support depends on characteristics of the recipients and providers of support and on the composition and structure of the social network.

Social support appears to reduce the stress people experience and enhance their health. The greater people's social support, the lower their mortality rates and likelihood of becoming ill. These benefits seem to accrue in accordance with the buffering and direct effects hypotheses. That is, social support may buffer a person against the negative effects of high levels of stress and may enhance health regardless of the level of stress by simply providing encouragement for leading healthful lifestyles, for instance.

Another psychosocial modifier of stress is people's sense of personal control over events in their lives, such as through behavioral and cognitive control. Personal control includes beliefs about one's locus of control—that is, whether control is internal or external to the person—and self-efficacy. People acquire a sense of personal control from their successes and failures and through the process of social learning. Individuals who experience prolonged, high levels of stress and have a weak sense of personal control tend to feel helpless. The cognitive process of attribution seems to be important in the development of learned helplessness. A strong sense of personal control tends to benefit people's health and help them adjust to a serious illness if it occurs. Hardiness is another psychosocial modifier of stress that may help people remain healthy when under stress.

One other psychosocial modifier of stress is people's tendency toward either the Type A or the Type B behavior pattern. The Type A behavior pattern consists of three characteristics: competitive achievement orientation, time urgency, and anger or hostility. Compared with Type Bs, Type A individuals respond more quickly and strongly to stressors both in their overt behaviors and in their physiological reactivity. The Type A pattern—particularly the anger/hostility component—is associated with the development of coronary heart disease (CHD) and hypertension. Both biological and psychosocial factors affect the development of the Type A and B behavior patterns.

Stress affects health in two ways. First, stress can affect health-related behaviors, such as alcohol and cigarette use. Second, it produces changes in the body's physical systems, as when the endocrine system releases catecholamines and corticosteroids, which can cause damage to the heart and blood vessels and impair immune system functioning. The physical effects of intense stress can even lead to sudden cardiac death. Psychoneuroimmunology is a new field of study that focuses on how psychosocial processes and the nervous, endocrine, and immune systems are interrelated. Stress also plays a role in many psychophysiological disorders, such as ulcers, inflammatory bowel disease, irritable bowel syndrome, asthma, and tension-type and migraine headache. In addition, stress is implicated in the development of hypertension, CHD, and cancer.

KEY TERMS

social support
buffering hypothesis
direct effects hypothesis
personal control
behavioral control
cognitive control
locus of control

self-efficacy
learned helplessness
hardiness
Type A behavior pattern
Type B behavior pattern
coronary heart disease
  (CHD)

sudden cardiac death
psychoneuroimmunology
psychophysiological
  disorders
ulcers
inflammatory bowel
  disease

irritable bowel syndrome
asthma
tension-type headaches
migraine headaches
hypertension

Note: If you read **Modules 5** and **6** (from Chapter 2) with the current chapter, you should include the key terms for those modules.

5

COPING WITH AND REDUCING STRESS

Coping with Stress
What Is Coping?
Functions and Methods of Coping

Reducing the Potential for Stress
Enhancing Social Support
Improving One's Personal Control
Organizing One's World Better
Exercising: Links to Stress and Health
Preparing for Stressful Events

Reducing Stress Reactions: Stress Management
Medication
Behavioral and Cognitive Methods
Massage, Meditation, and Hypnosis

Using Stress Management to Reduce Coronary Risk
Modifying Type A Behavior
Treating Hypertension

PROLOGUE

One morning while taking a shower, Cicely felt a small lump in her breast. She was sure it had not been there before. It didn't hurt, but she was momentarily alarmed—her mother had had breast cancer a few years before. "It could be a pimple or some other benign growth," she thought. Still, it was very worrisome. She decided not to tell her husband or her physician about it yet because as she thought, "it may not be anything." Over the next several days, she examined the lump daily. This was a very stressful time for her, and she slept poorly and seemed preoccupied. After a week without the lump changing, she decided to take action. She told her husband and made an appointment to see her physician.

Another woman, Beth, had a similar experience. Finding a lump on her breast alarmed her, but she didn't deal with the stress as rationally as Cicely did. Beth's initial fright led her to reexamine her breast just once, and in a cursory way. She told herself, "There isn't really a *lump* on my breast, it's just a rough spot." And she convinced herself that she should not touch it because, she thought, "That will only make it worse." During the next few months, Beth was quite worried about the "rough spot." She studiously avoided touching it, even while washing. She became increasingly moody, slept poorly, and developed many more headaches than usual. She also told her husband that she didn't like him to fondle her

116

breasts in lovemaking. When he asked why she was acting so differently in recent weeks, she denied anything was wrong. Beth finally mentioned the "rough spot" to a friend who convinced her to have her physician examine it.

People vary in the ways they deal with stress. Sometimes people confront a problem directly and rationally, as Cicely did, and sometimes they do not. For these two women, the way they dealt with their stress had the potential for affecting their health. Because Beth did not face up to the reality of the lump, she delayed seeking medical attention and experienced high levels of stress for a long time. If the lump were malignant, delaying treatment would allow the cancer to progress and spread. As we have seen, prolonged stress can have adverse health effects even in healthy people.

In this chapter we discuss the ways people can and do deal with stress. Through this discussion, you will find answers to questions you may have about the methods people use in handling stress. Are some methods for coping with stress more effective than others? How can people reduce the potential for stress in their lives? When people encounter a stressor, how can they reduce the strain it produces?

COPING WITH STRESS

Individuals of all ages experience stress and try to deal with it. During childhood years, people learn ways to manage feelings of stress that arise from the many fearful situations they experience (Sarafino, 1986). For instance, psychologist Lois Murphy (1974, p. 76) has described the progress and setbacks a 4-year-old named Molly had made in dealing with the terror she felt during thunderstorms. In her last steps at gaining control over her fear, she experienced two storms a few months apart. During the first storm, she awoke and didn't cry, "but I just snuggled in my bed," she said later. In the second storm, she showed no outward fear and comforted her frightened brother, saying, "I remember when I was a little baby and I was scared of thunder and I used to cry and cry every time it thundered." Like most children, Molly became better able to cope with the stress of storms as she grew older. What's more, in the last steps of her progress she showed pride in having mastered her fear.

WHAT IS COPING?

Because the emotional and physical strain that accompanies stress is uncomfortable, people are motivated to do things to reduce their stress. These "things" are what is involved in coping.

What is coping? Several definitions of coping exist (Lazarus & Folkman, 1984b). We'll use a definition based on how we defined stress in Chapter 3, when we saw that stress involves a *perceived discrepancy* between the demands of the situation and the resources of the person. **Coping** is the process by which people try to *manage the perceived discrepancy* between the demands and resources they appraise in a stressful situation. Notice the word *manage* in this definition. It indicates that coping efforts can be quite varied and do not necessarily lead to a solution of the problem. Although coping efforts can be aimed at correcting or mastering the problem, they may also simply help the person alter his or her perception of a discrepancy, tolerate or accept the harm or threat, or escape or avoid the situation (Lazarus & Folkman, 1984b; Moos & Schaefer, 1986). For example, a child who faces a stressful exam in school might cope by feeling nauseated and staying home.

We cope with stress through our cognitive and behavioral transactions with the environment. Suppose you are overweight and smoke cigarettes, and your physician has asked you to lose weight and stop smoking because several factors place you at very high risk for developing heart disease. You are faced with a threat: you may become disabled or die. This is stressful, but you don't think you can change your behavior. How might you cope with this problem? Some people would cope by seeking information about ways to improve their ability to change. Other people would simply find another doctor who is not so directive. Others would attribute their health to fate or "the will of God," and leave the problem "in His hands." Still others would try to deaden this and other worries with alcohol, which would add to the risk. People use many different methods to try to manage the appraised discrepancy between the demands of the situation and their resources.

The coping process is not a single event. Because coping involves ongoing transactions with the environment, the process is best viewed as a dynamic series

. . . of continuous appraisals and reappraisals of the shifting person–environment relationships. Shifts may be the result of coping efforts directed at changing the environment, or coping directed inward that changes the meaning of the event or increases understanding. They may also be the result of changes in the environment that are independent of the person and his or her coping activity. Regardless of its source, any shift in the person–environment relationship will lead to a reevaluation of what is happening, its significance, and what can be done. The reevaluation process, or reappraisal, in turn influences subsequent coping efforts. (Lazarus & Folkman, 1984b, pp. 142–143)

And so, in coping with the threat of serious illness, people who make efforts to change their lifestyles may receive encouragement and better relationships with their physician and family. But individuals who ignore the problem are likely to experience ever worsening health and relations with these people. Each shift in one direction or the other is affected by the transactions that preceded it and affects subsequent transactions.

FUNCTIONS AND METHODS OF COPING

You have probably realized by now that people have an enormous number of ways for coping with stress. As a result, researchers have attempted to organize coping approaches on the basis of their functions and the methods they employ. (Go to 🍎.)

Functions of Coping

According to Richard Lazarus and his colleagues, coping can serve two main functions (Lazarus, 1999; Lazarus & Folkman, 1984b). It can alter the *problem* causing the stress, or it can regulate the *emotional* response to the problem.

Emotion-focused coping is aimed at controlling the emotional response to the stressful situation. People can regulate their emotional responses through *behavioral* and *cognitive* approaches. Examples of *behavioral* approaches include using alcohol or drugs, seeking emotional social support from friends or relatives, and engaging in activities, such as sports or watching TV, which distract attention from the problem.

ASSESS YOURSELF

Your Focuses in Coping

Think about a very stressful personal crisis or life event you experienced in the last year—the more recent and stressful the event, the better for this exercise. How did you handle this situation and your stress? Some of the ways people handle stressful experiences are listed below. Mark an "X" in the space preceding each one you used.

_____ Tried to see a positive side to it

_____ Tried to step back from the situation and be more objective

_____ Prayed for guidance or strength

_____ Sometimes took it out on other people when I felt angry or depressed

_____ Got busy with other things to keep my mind off the problem

_____ Decided not to worry about it because I figured everything would work out fine

_____ Took things one step at a time

_____ Read relevant material for solutions and considered several alternatives

_____ Drew on my knowledge because I had a similar experience before

_____ Talked to a friend or relative to get advice on handling the problem

_____ Talked with a professional person (e.g., doctor, clergy, lawyer, teacher, counselor) about ways to improve the situation

_____ Took some action to improve the situation

Count how many of the first six ways you marked—these are examples of "emotion-focused" ways. How many of the second six—"problem-focused"—ways did you mark? When you read the upcoming text material entitled *Functions of Coping*, answer these questions: Did you use mostly emotion- or problem-focused methods? Why, and what functions did your methods serve? (*Source*: Based on material in Billings and Moos, 1981.)

Cognitive approaches involve how people think about the stressful situation. In one cognitive approach, people *redefine* the situation to put a good face on it, such as by noting that things could be worse, making comparisons with individuals who are less well off, or seeing something good growing out of the problem. We can see this approach in two statements of women with breast cancer (Taylor, 1983):

> What you do is put things into perspective. You find out that things like relationships are really the most important things you have—the people you know and your family—everything else is just way down the line. It's very strange that it takes something so serious to make you realize that. (p. 1163)
>
> The people I really feel sorry for are these young gals. To lose a breast when you're so young must be awful. I'm 73; what do I need a breast for? (p. 1166)

People who want to redefine a stressful situation can generally find a way to do it since there is almost always *some* aspect of one's life that can be viewed positively (Taylor, 1983).

Other emotion-focused cognitive processes include strategies Freud called "defense mechanisms," which involve distorting memory or reality in some way (Cramer, 2000). For instance, when something is too painful to face, the person may deny that it exists, as Beth did with the lump on her breast. This defense mechanism is called *denial*. In medical situations, individuals who are diagnosed with terminal diseases often use this strategy and refuse to believe they are really ill. This is one way by which people cope by using *avoidance* strategies. But strategies that promote avoidance of the problem are helpful mainly in the short run, such as during an early stage of a prolonged stress experience (Suls & Fletcher, 1985). This is so for individuals who are diagnosed with a serious illness, for instance. As a rule of thumb, the effectiveness of avoidance-promoting methods seems to be limited to the first couple of weeks of a prolonged stress experience. Thereafter, coping is better served by giving the situation attention.

People tend to use emotion-focused approaches when they believe they can do little to change the stressful conditions (Lazarus & Folkman, 1984b). An example is when a loved one dies—in this situation, people often seek emotional support and distract themselves with funeral arrangements and chores at home or at work. Other examples involve situations in which individuals believe their resources are not and cannot be adequate to meet the demands of the stressor. A child who tries very hard to be the "straight A" student his or her parents seem to want, but never succeeds, may reappraise the situation and decide, "I don't need their love." Coping methods that focus on emotions are important because they sometimes interfere with getting medical treatment or involve unhealthy behaviors, such as using cigarettes, alcohol, and drugs to reduce tension. People often use these substances in emotion-focused coping (Wills, 1986).

Problem-focused coping is aimed at reducing the demands of the stressful situation or expanding the resources to deal with it. Everyday life provides many examples of problem-focused coping, including quitting a stressful job, negotiating an extension for paying some bills, devising a new schedule for studying (and sticking to it), choosing a different career to pursue, seeking medical or psychological treatment, and learning new skills. People tend to use problem-focused approaches when they believe their resources or the demands of the situation are changeable

"I COULD HAVE OPENED THE JAR THAT WAY!"

Sometimes people don't cope effectively with stress. *Reprinted with special permission of King Features Syndicate, Inc.*

(Lazarus & Folkman, 1984b). For example, caregivers of terminally ill patients use problem-focused coping approaches more in the months prior to the death than during bereavement (Moskowitz et al., 1996).

To what extent do people use problem-focused and emotion-focused approaches in coping with stress in their lives? Andrew Billings and Rudolf Moos (1981) studied this issue by having nearly 200 married couples fill out a survey. The respondents described a recent personal crisis or negative life event that happened to them and then answered questions that were very similar to the ones you answered in the self-assessment exercise. The outcomes of this research revealed some interesting relationships. Both the husbands and the wives used more problem-focused than emotion-focused methods to cope with the stressful event. But the wives reported using more emotion-focused approaches than the husbands did. People with higher incomes and educational levels reported greater use of problem-focused coping than those with less income and education. Finally, individuals used much less problem-focused coping when the stress involved a death in the family than when it involved other kinds of problems, such as illness or economic difficulties.

Can problem-focused and emotion-focused coping be used together? Yes, and they often are. For instance, in one study patients with painful arthritis were asked to keep track of their daily use of problem- and emotion-focused coping (Tennen et al., 2000). Most often, they used the two types of coping together—and three quarters of the time that they used only one type, they used problem-focused coping. We can see an example of both types of coping in a man's experience when a coworker accused him of not sending out the appropriate letters for a job. In describing how he reacted to this stressful situation, he said he first confirmed that the coworker's accusation

> was not true, that everything [letters] had gone out. There's always a chance you might be wrong so I checked first. Then I told him. No, everything had gone out. My immediate reaction was to call him on the carpet first. He doesn't have any right to call me on something like this. Then I gave it a second thought and decided that that wouldn't help the situation. (Kahn et al., cited in Lazarus & Folkman, 1984b, p. 155)

This example illustrates problem-focused coping in confirming that the letters had gone out and emotion-focused coping in controlling his angry impulse "to call him on the carpet."

Coping Methods and Measurement

What specific methods—that is, skills and strategies—do people apply in stressful situations to alter the problem or regulate their emotional response? Researchers have described about 400 methods and incorporated sets of them into dozens of instruments to assess overall coping and categories of coping types (Skinner et al., 2003). Table 5.1 lists two dozen coping methods that are easy to conceptualize, without stating definitions, to give you a sense of the great variety of possible methods people can use.

Unfortunately, instruments to measure coping haven't been very useful so far. They were typically developed with the expectation that the scores would predict mental or physical health, but they don't (Coyne & Racioppo, 2000; Skinner et al., 2003). And they don't seem to be very accurate in measuring people's coping. Most measures of coping are retrospective, asking

Table 5.1   *Methods of Coping with Stressful Situations (listed alphabetically)*

Assistance seeking[p]	Hiding feelings[e]	Positive reappraisal[e]
Avoidance[e]	Humor[e]	Praying[e]
Confrontive assertion[p]	Increased activity[e]	Resigned acceptance[e]
Denial[e]	Information seeking[p]	Seeking meaning[e]
Direct action[p]	Intrusive thoughts[e]	Self-criticism[e]
Discharge (venting)[e]	Logical analysis[p]	Substance use[e]
Distraction (diverting attention)[e]	Physical exercise[e]	Wishful thinking[e]
Emotional approach[e]	Planful problem solving[p]	Worry[e]

Note: Superscripted letters refer to the method's most likely function, [p] = problem-focused and [e] = emotion-focused coping, but some methods may serve either function.
Source: Skinner et al., 2003, Table 3.

respondents about the methods used in the past week, month, or more. Do you remember exactly how you coped 2 weeks ago with a stressful event, such as a poor grade on a test or an argument with a close friend? A study tested this issue by having people report daily for a month on the coping strategies they used with the most negative event that occurred that day (Todd et al., 2004). They used a list and description of 16 strategies that comprise a widely used coping survey for the daily reports, and then at the end of the study they filled out the survey to report on the whole month. Comparisons of daily and full-month reports showed weak correspondence for about half of the coping methods, suggesting that assessments of coping pertaining to more than the past week or so are inaccurate for many methods.

Researchers are currently working to identify the coping methods that are most important—those that can be measured accurately and are related to psychological and health outcomes, such as people's development of and recovery from illnesses. Let's look at three of several directions that look promising (Folkman & Moskowitz, 2004).

1. *Role of positive emotions.* You may have noticed that the coping methods we've discussed so far are designed to deal directly with people's distress. But Susan Folkman (1997; Folkman & Moskowitz, 2004) has found that individuals who were caring for a dying spouse or partner and then lost that person report both positive and negative emotions occurring together during times of great stress. As an example, a gay man described the difficulty of tending for his partner during the extreme sweating episodes he, like many AIDS patients, had many times each day and noted that he feels "proud, pleased that I can comfort him. . . . We are still making our love for each other the focal point" (Folkman, 1997, p. 1213). According to Folkman, one way positive emotions help in dealing with stress is by sustaining the coping process.

2. *Positive reappraisal.* Researchers have noticed for many years that most people who are trying to cope with severe stress try to reappraise their life situation in a positive light, such as by finding meaning or benefits in the experience (Folkman, 1997; Sears, Stanton, & Danoff-Burg, 2003). They reappraise in many ways, such as

"when people whose loved ones have died from a disease become advocates for research on that

disease; finding that new or closer bonds with others have been formed because of having experienced or survived a natural disaster together; or finding that the event has clarified which goals or priorities are important and which are not." (Folkman, 1997, p. 1215)

According to Folkman, finding meaning and benefits provides an important avenue for experiencing positive emotions during stressful times.

3. *Engaging in emotional approach.* In emotional approach, people cope with stress by actively processing and expressing their feelings (Stanton et al., 2000). To assess emotional approach, people rate how often they engage emotional *processing* (in such activities as, "I take time to figure out what I'm really feeling" and "I delve into my feelings to get a thorough understanding of them") and emotional *expression* ("I take time to express my emotions"). The emotional approach probably includes the method of disclosure of negative experiences and feelings we discussed in Chapter 4 as a way of reducing stress and enhancing health.

There is growing evidence of the psychological and health benefits of coping that includes positive emotions, positive reappraisal, and emotional approach (Folkman & Moskowitz, 2004). For example, Stanton and her colleagues (2000) tested women with breast cancer for emotional approach soon after medical treatment and for psychological and health status 3 months later. They found that higher levels of emotional *expression* were associated with improved self-perceived health, increased vigor, fewer medical visits for cancer-related problems, and decreased distress. But high levels of emotional *processing* were associated with increased distress. It may be that emotional processing includes or leads to rumination, in which people have *intrusive thoughts* and images that perpetuate their stress (Baum, 1990). For example, people may think repeatedly about how they or others are to blame for their problems or have "flashbacks" of painful or traumatic events. People who often have intrusive thoughts report having poorer health habits and health than individuals who seldom have such thoughts (Nowack, 1989).

No single method of coping is uniformly applied or effective with all stressful situations (Ilfeld, 1980; Pearlin & Schooler, 1978). Research has revealed four findings about people's patterns in using different coping methods. First, people tend to be consistent in the way they cope with a particular type of stressor—that is, when faced with the same problem, they tend to use the same methods they used in the past (Stone & Neale, 1984). Second, people seldom use just one method to cope with a stressor. Their efforts typically involve a combination of problem- and emotion-focused strategies (Tennen et al., 2000). Third, the methods people use in coping with short-term stressors may be different from those they use under long-term stress, such as from a serious chronic illness (Aldwin & Brustrom, 1997). Fourth, although the methods people use to cope with stress develop from the transactions they have in their lives, a genetic influence is suggested by the finding that identical twins are more similar than fraternal twins in the coping styles they use (Busjahn et al., 1999).

Developing Methods of Coping

Psychologists assume that coping processes change across the life span. But the nature of these changes is unclear because there is little research, especially longitudinal studies, charting these changes (Aldwin & Brustrom, 1997; Lazarus & Folkman, 1984b).

Some aspects of the changes in coping that occur in the early years are known. Infants and toddlers being examined by their pediatricians are likely to cope by trying to stop the examination (Hyson, 1983). We saw earlier in the case of Molly that young children develop coping skills that enable them to overcome many of their fears, making use of their expanding cognitive abilities. Over the next several years, children come to rely increasingly on cognitive strategies for coping (Brown et al., 1986; Miller & Green, 1984). So, for example, they learn to think about something else as a way to distract themselves from stress. More and more, they regulate their feelings with emotion-focused methods, such as playing with toys or watching TV, especially when they can't do anything to solve the problem, such as a serious illness in their parents (Compas et al., 1996).

Few studies have examined changes in methods of coping from adolescence to old age. One study used interviews and questionnaires to compare the daily hassles and coping methods of middle-aged and elderly men and women (Folkman et al., 1987). The middle-aged individuals used more problem-focused coping, whereas the elderly people used more emotion-focused approaches. For example, the middle-aged people were more likely to report problem-focused actions ("Stood my ground and fought for what I wanted" and "I made a plan of action and followed it"). The elderly individuals were more likely to report emotion-focused methods ("Went on as if nothing happened" and "Wished that the situation would go away or somehow be over with").

Why do adults use less problem-focused and more emotion-focused coping as they get older? These changes probably result at least in part from differences in the kind of problems people must cope with as they age. The elderly individuals in this study were retired from full-time work and reported more stress relating to health and home maintenance than did the middle-aged people, who reported more stress relating to work, finances, and family and friends. The stressors encountered in middle age are more changeable than those in old age. But there was also a difference in the outlook of the two age groups: regardless of the source of stress, the elderly people appraised their problems as *less* changeable than the middle-aged individuals did. As we saw earlier, people tend to use problem-focused approaches when they believe the situation is changeable, and they rely on emotion-focused coping when they do not.

Gender and Sociocultural Differences in Coping

Studies of gender differences in coping have generally found that men are more likely to report using problem-focused strategies and women are more likely to report using emotion-focused strategies in dealing with stressful events. But when the men and women have similar occupations and education, no gender differences are found (Greenglass & Noguchi, 1996). These results suggest that societal sex roles play an important role in the coping patterns of men and women.

Billings and Moos (1981) found that people with higher incomes and educational levels report greater use of problem-focused coping than those with less income and education. This finding suggests that the social experiences of disadvantaged people lead many of them to believe they have little control over events in their lives. In general, disadvantaged individuals—a category that typically includes disproportionately more minority group members—are more likely to experience stressful events and are less likely to cope with them effectively than other people are (Gottlieb & Green, 1987).

We have examined many ways people cope with stress. Each method can be effective and adaptive for the individual if it neutralizes the current stressor and does not increase the likelihood of future stressful situations. In the next section, we consider how people can reduce the potential for stress for themselves and for others.

REDUCING THE POTENTIAL FOR STRESS

Can people become "immune" to the impact of stress to some extent? Some aspects of people's lives can reduce the potential for stressors to develop and help individuals cope with problems when they occur. Prevention is the first line of defense against the impact of stress. We will look at several ways people can help themselves and others prevent and cope with stress. The first approach makes use of the beneficial effects of social support.

ENHANCING SOCIAL SUPPORT

We have all turned to others for help and comfort when under stress at some time in our lives. If you have ever had to endure troubled times on your own, you know how important social support can be. But social support is not only helpful after stressors appear, it also can help avert problems in the first place. Consider, for example, the tangible support newlyweds receive, such as items they will need to set up a household. Without these items, the couple would be saddled either with the financial burden of buying the items or with the hassles of not having them.

Although people in all walks of life can lack the social support they need, some segments of the population have less than others (Antonucci, 1985; Broadhead et al., 1983; Ratliff-Crain & Baum, 1990). For instance:

- Although men tend to have larger social networks than women, women seem to use theirs more effectively for support.

- Many elderly individuals live in isolated conditions and have few people on whom to rely.

- Network size is related to social prestige, income, and education: the lower the prestige, income, and education level of individuals, the smaller their social networks tend to be.

Furthermore, the networks of people from lower socioeconomic classes are usually less diverse than those of people from higher classes; that is, lower-class networks contain fewer nonkin members. In contemporary American society, the traditional sources of support have shifted to include greater reliance on individuals in social and helping organizations. This is partly because extended family members today have different functions and live farther apart than they did many decades ago (Pilisuk, 1982).

Social support is a dynamic process. People's needs for, giving of, and receipt of support change over time. Whether an individual will receive or provide social support when it is needed depends on factors within that person, such as his or her temperament and interest in social affiliation (Broadhead et al., 1983; Wortman & Dunkel-Schetter, 1987). But research has found that people who experience high levels of chronic stress, such as when their health declines severely, often find that their social support resources deteriorate at the same time (Kaplan et al., 1997; Lepore, 1997; Wortman & Dunkel-Schetter, 1987). These results are disheartening because they suggest that people whose need for social support is greatest may be unlikely to receive it.

People can enhance their ability to give and receive social support by joining community organizations,

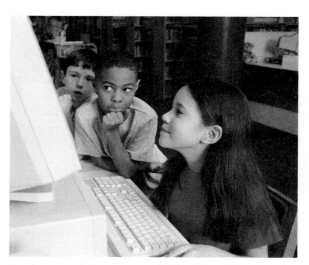

Teachers can help enhance children's social support by having them work together.

such as social, religious, special interest, and self-help groups. These organizations have the advantage of bringing together individuals with similar problems and interests, which can become the basis for sharing, helping, and friendship. In the United States, there are many widely known self-help groups, including Alcoholics Anonymous and Parents without Partners, and special-interest groups, including the American Association of Retired People and support groups for people with specific illnesses, such as arthritis or AIDS. Although groups like these are helpful, we don't yet know which ones work best for specific problems (Hogan, Linden, & Najarian, 2002). People are most likely to join a support group for a serious illness if it is embarrassing or stigmatizing, such as AIDS (Davison, Pennebaker, & Dickerson, 2000). Isolated people of all ages—especially the elderly—with all types of difficulties should be encouraged to join suitable organizations.

Communities can play a valuable role in enhancing people's resources for social support by creating programs to help individuals develop social networks, such as in occupational and religious settings, and by providing facilities for recreation and fitness, arranging social events, and providing counseling services. But social support may not be effective if the recipient interprets it as a sign of inadequacy or believes his or her personal control is limited by it. Providing effective social support requires sensitivity and good judgment. (Go to 💡.)

IMPROVING ONE'S PERSONAL CONTROL

When life becomes stressful, people who lack a strong sense of personal control may stop trying, thinking, "Oh, what's the use." Instead of feeling they have power and control, they feel helpless and afraid that their efforts will lead to failure and embarrassment. For instance, people with painful, disabling, or life-threatening chronic illnesses may stop trying to improve their conditions. When seriously-ill patients who feel little personal control face a new severe stressor, they show more emotional distress than others who feel more control (Benight et al., 1997). The main psychological help such people need is to bolster their self-efficacy and reduce their passiveness and helplessness (Smith & Wallston, 1992). A pessimistic outlook increases people's potential for stress and can have a negative effect on their health.

How can a person's sense of control be enhanced? The process can begin very early. Parents, teachers, and other caregivers can show a child their love and respect, provide a stimulating environment, encourage and praise the child's accomplishments, and set reasonable standards of conduct and performance that he or she can regard as challenges rather than threats. In adulthood, employers can help by giving workers some degree of control over aspects of their jobs, allowing them input in decisions about the hours they work, which tasks to work on, and ways to improve the quality of their work. In later life, nursing homes and families can allow elderly individuals to do things for themselves and have responsibilities, such as in cleaning, cooking, and arranging social activities. One woman described the prospect of living with her children in the following way: "I couldn't stand to live with my children, as much as I love them, because they always want to take over my life" (Shupe, 1985). For people with serious illnesses, health psychologists can help patients with little control by training them in effective ways to cope with stress (Thompson & Kyle, 2000).

ORGANIZING ONE'S WORLD BETTER

"Where did I put my keys?" you have surely heard someone ask frantically while running late to make an appointment. People often feel stress because they are running late or believe they don't have enough time to do the tasks of the day. They need to organize their worlds to make things happen efficiently. This can take the form of keeping an appointment calendar, designating certain places for certain items, or putting materials in alphabetized file folders, for instance. Organizing one's world reduces frustration, wasted time, and the potential for stress.

An important approach for organizing one's time is called **time management.** It consists of three elements (Lakein, 1973). The first element is to *set goals*. These goals should be reasonable or obtainable ones, and they should include long-term goals, such as graduating college next year, and short-term ones, such as getting good grades. The second element involves making daily *To Do* lists with priorities indicated, keeping the goals in mind. These lists should be composed each morning or late in the preceding day. Each list must be written—trying to keep the list in your head is unreliable and makes setting priorities difficult. The third element is to set up a *schedule* for

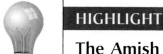

HIGHLIGHT

The Amish Way of Social Support in Bereavement

The Amish people in North America form a conservative religious sect that settled in Pennsylvania in the 18th century. Amish families generally live in colonies that now exist in many states and Canada. These families have a strongly religious orientation and a serious work ethic that revolves around farming. Their way of life is quite distinctive: they wear uniquely simple and uniform clothing; speak mainly a Pennsylvania-German dialect; and reject modern devices, using horse-driven buggies instead of automobiles, for example. Their social lives require their adherence to strict rules of conduct and obedience to patriarchal authority.

One feature of Amish life is that community members give assistance to one another in all times of need. Their way of dealing with death provides a good example, as Kathleen Bryer (1986) has studied and described. Before death, a person who is seriously ill receives care from his or her family. This care generally occurs at home rather than in a hospital. The Amish not only expect to give this care, but see it as a positive opportunity. A married woman who was asked about caring for a dying relative replied, "Oh yes, we had the chance to take care of all four of our old parents before they died. We are both so thankful for this" (p. 251). Death typically occurs in the presence of the family.

Upon someone's death, the Amish community swings into action. Close neighbors notify other members of the colony, and the community makes most of the funeral arrangements. The family receives visits of sympathy and support from other Amish families, some of whom come from other colonies far away and may not even know the bereaved family. In contrast to the social support most Americans receive in bereavement, Amish supportive efforts do not end shortly after the funeral—they continue at a high level for at least a year. Supportive activities include evening and Sunday visiting, making items and scrapbooks for the family, and organized quilting projects that create fellowship around a common task. Moreover, Amish individuals often give extraordinary help to bereaved family members. For instance, the sister of one widower came to live with him and care for his four children until he remarried. The community encourages widowed individuals to remarry in time, and they often do so.

An Amish funeral procession. The Amish provide social support to one another in many ways, particularly after a member dies.

the day, allocating estimated time periods to each item in the list. If an urgent new task arises during the day, the list should be adjusted to include it.

EXERCISING: LINKS TO STRESS AND HEALTH

You have probably heard from TV, radio, magazine, and newspaper reports that exercise and physical fitness can protect people from stress and its harmful effects on health. These reports cite a wide range of benefits of exercising ranging from increased intellectual functioning and personal control to decreased anxiety, depression, hostility, and tension. Do exercise and fitness reduce the potential for stress and its effects on health?

Correlational and retrospective studies of this question have found that people who exercise or are physically fit often report less anxiety, depression, and tension in their lives than do people who do not exercise or are less fit (Dishman, 1986; Holmes, 1993). Although these results are consistent with the view that exercise and fitness reduce stress, they present two problems of interpretation. First, the reduction in self-reported stress and emotion may have resulted partly from a placebo effect—that is, the subjects' expectations that psychological improvements would occur (Desharnais et al., 1993). Second, the results of correlational research do not tell us what causes what. Do exercise and fitness cause people to feel less stress? Or are people more likely to exercise and keep fit if they feel less stress and time pressures in their lives? Fortunately, there is stronger evidence for the beneficial effects of exercise and fitness on stress and health.

An experiment by Bram Goldwater and Martin Collis (1985) examined the effects of exercise on cardiovascular fitness and feelings of anxiety in healthy 19- to 30-year-old men who were randomly assigned to one of two groups. In one group, the men worked out 5 days a week in a vigorous fitness program, including swimming and active sports, such as soccer; the second group had a more moderate program with less demanding exercise activities. Both programs lasted for 6 weeks, and cardiovascular fitness and anxiety were tested before and after. Compared with the men in the moderate program, those in the vigorous program showed greater gains in fitness and reductions in anxiety. Other experiments have shown similar beneficial effects of exercise on depression and anxiety with men and women, but the program needs to last at least 2 or 3 months (Babyak et al., 2000; Phillips, Kiernan, & King, 2001).

Research has also assessed the role of exercise in cardiovascular function. Much of the evidence is correlational: people who exercise or are physically fit show less reactivity to stressors and are less likely to be hypertensive than individuals who do not exercise or are less fit (Blumenthal et al., 2002; Dimsdale, Alpert, & Schneiderman, 1986). But some studies have used experimental methods, which have found modest reductions in blood pressure (Blumenthal, Sherwood et al., 2002). One experiment recruited healthy 19- to 27-year-olds with sedentary occupations and had not regularly engaged in vigorous physical activity in the previous year (Jennings et al., 1986). During the next 4 months, these people spent 1 month at each of four levels of activity: normal (sedentary), below normal, above normal, and much above normal. Below-normal activity included 2 weeks of rest in a hospital setting; above-normal activity had three sessions of vigorous exercise weekly; and much above-normal activity included daily vigorous exercise. Each exercise period lasted 40 minutes. Measurements of heart rate and blood pressure were taken after each month. Compared with the normal sedentary activity level, the two above-normal activity conditions reduced heart rate by 12% and systolic and diastolic blood pressure by 8% and 10%. Below-normal activity levels did not alter heart rate or blood pressure.

Do exercise and fitness prevent people from developing stress-related illnesses? The results of several studies suggest they do (Phillips, Kiernan, & King, 2001). For example, one study used prospective methods by first assessing the subjects' recent life events and fitness, and then having them keep records concerning their health over the next 9 weeks (Roth & Holmes, 1985). The results revealed that individuals who reported high levels of stress had poorer subsequent health if they were not fit; stress had little impact on the health of fit subjects. Overall, the evidence is fairly strong that engaging in regular exercise can promote health by reducing stress.

PREPARING FOR STRESSFUL EVENTS

In this and previous chapters we have discussed many types of stressful events, ranging from being stuck in traffic to starting day care or school, being overloaded with work, going through a divorce, and experiencing a disaster. Preparing for these events often can reduce the potential for stress. For instance, parents can help prepare a child for starting day care by taking the child there in advance to see the place, meet the teacher, and play for a while (Sarafino, 1986).

Irving Janis (1958) pioneered the psychological study of the need to prepare people for stressful events, such as surgery. In general, research on preparing for surgery indicates that the higher the patients' *preoperative* fear, the worse their *postoperative* adjustment and recovery tend to be, as reflected in the following measures (Anderson & Masur, 1983; Johnson, 1983:

- The patient's self-reported pain
- The amount of medication taken to relieve pain
- Self-reported anxiety or depression
- The length of stay in the hospital after surgery
- Ratings by hospital staff of the patient's recovery or adjustment

These outcomes suggest that preparing patients to help them cope with their preoperative concerns should enhance later adjustment and recovery.

How can we prepare people psychologically for the stress of surgery? The most clearly effective methods are those designed to enhance the patients' feelings of *control* (Anderson & Masur, 1983; Mathews & Ridgeway, 1984). To promote *behavioral control*, for example, patients learn how to reduce discomfort or promote rehabilitation through specific actions they can take, such as by doing leg exercises to improve strength or deep breathing exercises to reduce pain. For *cognitive control*, patients learn ways to focus their thoughts on pleasant or beneficial aspects of the surgery rather than the unpleasant aspects. And for *informational control*, patients receive information about the procedures and/or sensations they will experience. Each of these methods can promote postoperative adjustment and recovery. (We will examine these methods in greater detail in Chapter 10, when we discuss hospital treatment.)

Although receiving preparatory information is usually helpful, sometimes it can have the opposite effect. As psychologist Suzanne Thompson has described:

> The Los Angeles City Council had placed cards in the city elevators assuring riders that they should stay calm, since "there is little danger of the car dropping uncontrollably or running out of air." . . . A year later the cards had to be removed because of complaints from elevator riders that the message made them anxious. Apparently most people had not worried about these dangers until they read the card meant to reassure them. (1981, p. 96)

Also, having too much information can be confusing and actually arouse fear. Young children often become more anxious when they receive a great deal of information about the medical procedures they will undergo (Miller & Green, 1984). With children in dental or medical settings, it is generally best not to give a lot of detail. Describing some sensory experiences to expect is especially helpful, such as the sounds of equipment of the tingly feeling from the dental anesthetic.

In summary, we have discussed several methods that are helpful in reducing the potential for stress and, thereby, benefiting health. These methods take advantage of the stress-moderating effects of social support, personal control, exercise, being well organized, and being prepared for an impending stressor. In the next section, we consider ways to reduce the reaction to stress once it has begun.

REDUCING STRESS REACTIONS: STRESS MANAGEMENT

People acquire coping skills through their experiences, which may involve strategies they have tried in the past or methods they have seen others use. But sometimes the skills they have learned are not adequate for a current stressor because it is so strong, novel, or unrelenting. In some cases, the approaches they have acquired reduce stress in the short run—as alcohol or drug use can do—but are not adaptive and increase stress in the long run. These problems in coping often arise in individuals whose potential for stress is high because of a lack of social support, personal control, and so on. But coping problems also happen among people whose potential for stress is relatively low. When people cannot cope effectively, they need help in learning new and adaptive ways of managing stress.

Many techniques are available to help individuals manage stress. These *stress management* techniques are mainly psychological, but *pharmacological* approaches are sometimes used under medical supervision.

MEDICATION

Of the many types of drugs physicians prescribe to help patients manage stress, we will consider two: benzodiazepines and beta-blockers, both of which reduce physiological arousal and feelings of anxiety (AMA, 2003; Shapiro, Krantz, & Grim, 1986). *Benzodiazepines*, which include drugs with the trade names Valium and Librium, activate a neurotransmitter that decreases neural transmission in the central nervous system. *Beta-blockers*, such as Inderal, are used to reduce anxiety and blood pressure. They block the activity stimulated by epinephrine and norepinephrine in the peripheral nervous system. Beta-blockers cause less drowsiness than benzodiazepines, probably because they act on the peripheral rather than central nervous system. Although many people use drugs for long-term control of stress and emotions, using drugs for stress should be a temporary measure. For instance, they might be used during an acute crisis, such as in the week or two following the death of a loved one, or while the patient learns new psychological methods for coping.

BEHAVIORAL AND COGNITIVE METHODS

Psychologists have developed methods they can train people to use in coping with stress. Some of these techniques focus mainly on the person's behavior, and some emphasize the person's thinking processes. People who use these methods usually find them helpful.

Relaxation

The opposite of arousal is relaxation—so relaxing should be a good way to reduce stress. "Perhaps so," you say, "but when stress occurs, relaxing is easier said than done." Actually, relaxing when under stress is not so hard to do when you know how. One way people can learn to control their feelings of tension is called **progressive muscle relaxation** (or just *progressive relaxation*), in which they focus their attention on specific muscle groups while alternately tightening and relaxing these muscles (Sarafino, 2001).

The idea of teaching people to relax their skeletal muscles to reduce psychological stress was introduced many years ago by Edmund Jacobson (1938). He found that muscle tension could be reduced much more if individuals were taught to pay attention to the sensations as they tense and relax individual groups of muscles. Although today there are various versions of the progressive muscle relaxation technique, they each outline a sequence of muscle groups for the person to follow. For example, the sequence might begin with the person relaxing the hands, then the forehead, followed by the lower face, the neck, the stomach, and, finally, the legs. For each muscle group, the person first tenses the muscles for 7 to 10 seconds, and then relaxes them for about 15 seconds, paying attention to how the muscles feel. This is usually repeated for the same muscle group two or three times in a relaxation session, which generally lasts 20 or 30 minutes. The tensing action is mainly important while the person is being trained and can be eliminated after he or she has mastered the technique (Sarafino, 2001). Relaxation works best in a quiet, nondistracting setting with the person lying down or sitting on comfortable furniture.

Stress management is applied mainly with adults, but children also experience stress without being able to cope effectively. Fortunately, many behavioral and cognitive methods are easy to learn and can be adapted so that an adult can teach a young child to use them (Siegel & Peterson, 1980). Relaxation exercises provide a good example. An adult could start by showing the child what relaxing is like by lifting and then releasing the arms and legs of a rag doll, allowing them to fall down. Then, the adult would follow a *protocol*, or script, giving instructions like those presented in Table 5.2. When children and

---

Table 5.2 *Progressive Muscle Relaxation Protocol for Children*

1. "OK. Let's raise our arms and put them out in front. Now make a fist with both your hands, really hard. Hold the fist tight and you will see how your muscles in your hands and arms feel when they are tight." (hold for 7–10 seconds)
   "That's very good. Now when I say relax, I want the muscles in your hands and arms to become floppy, like the rag doll, and your arms will drop to your sides. OK, relax." (about 15 seconds)
2. "Let's raise our legs out in front of us. Now tighten the muscles in your feet and legs, really hard. Make the muscles really tight, and hold it." (7–10 seconds)
   "Very good. Now relax the muscles in your feet and legs, and let them drop to the floor. They feel so good. So calm and relaxed." (15 seconds)
3. "Now let's do our tummy muscles. Tighten your tummy, really hard—and hold it." (7–10 seconds)
   "OK. Relax your tummy, and feel how good it feels. So comfortable." (15 seconds)
4. "Leave your arms at your side, but tighten the muscles in your shoulders and neck. You can do this by moving your shoulders up toward your head. Hold the muscles very tightly in your shoulders and neck." (7–10 seconds)
   "Now relax those muscles so they are floppy, and see how good that feels." (15 seconds)
5. "Let's tighten the muscles in our faces. Scrunch up your whole face so that all of the muscles are tight—the muscles in your cheeks, and your mouth, and your nose, and your forehead. Really scrunch up your face, and hold it." (7–10 seconds)
   "Now relax all the muscles in your face—your cheeks, mouth, nose, and forehead. Feel how nice that is." (15 seconds)
6. "Now I want us to take a very, very deep breath—so deep that there's no more room inside for more air. Hold the air in. (use a shorter time: 6–8 seconds)
   "That's good. Now slowly let the air out. Very slowly, until it's all out. . . . And now breathe as you usually do." (15 seconds)

Source: From Sarafino (1986, pp. 112–113).

adults first learn progressive muscle relaxation, they sometimes don't relax their muscles when told to do so. Instead of letting their arms and legs *fall* down, they *move* them down. They may also tense more muscles than required—for example, tightening facial muscles when they are asked to tense hand muscles. These errors should be pointed out and corrected.

Often, after individuals have thoroughly mastered the relaxation procedure, they can gradually shorten the procedure so they can apply a very quick version in times of stress, such as when they are about to give a speech (Sarafino, 2001). This quick version might have the following steps: (1) taking a deep breath, and letting it out; (2) saying to oneself, "Relax, feel nice and calm"; and (3) thinking about a pleasant thought for a few seconds. In this way, relaxation methods can be directly applied to help people cope with everyday stressful events.

Research has demonstrated that progressive muscle relaxation is highly effective in reducing stress (Carlson & Hoyle, 1993; Lichstein, 1988). What's more, people who receive training in relaxation show less cardiovascular reactivity to stressors and stronger immune function (Lucini et al., 1997; Sherman et al., 1997).

Systematic Desensitization

Although relaxation is often successful by itself in helping people cope, it is frequently used in conjunction with **systematic desensitization,** a useful method for reducing fear and anxiety (Sarafino, 2001). This method is based on the view that fears are learned by *classical conditioning*—that is, by associating a situation or object with an unpleasant event. This can happen, for example, if a person associates visits to the dentist with pain, thereby becoming "sensitized" to dentists. Desensitization is a classical conditioning procedure that *reverses* this learning by pairing the feared object or situation with either pleasant or neutral events, as Figure 5–1 outlines. According to Joseph Wolpe (1958, 1973), an originator of the desensitization method, the reversal comes about through the process of *counterconditioning*, whereby the *"calm"* response gradually replaces the *"fear"* response. Desensitization has been used successfully in reducing a variety of children's and adults' fears, such as fear of dentists, animals, high places, public speaking, and taking tests (Lichstein, 1988; Sarafino, 2001).

Figure 5–1 Classical conditioning in learning to fear dental visits and in reversing this learning. In conditioning the fear, the unconditioned stimulus (US) of pain elicits the unconditioned response (UR) of fear automatically. Learning occurs by pairing the dentist, the conditioned stimulus (CS), with the US so that the dentist begins to elicit fear. The reverse conditioning pairs the feared dentist with a US that elicits calm.

An important feature of the systematic desensitization method is that it uses a *stimulus hierarchy*—a graded sequence of approximations to the conditioned stimulus, the feared situation. The purpose of these approximations is to bring the person gradually in contact with the source of fear in about 10 or 15 steps. To see how a stimulus hierarchy might be constructed, we will look at the one in Table 5.3 that deals with the fear of dentists. The person would follow the instructions in each of the 14 steps. As you can see, some of the steps involve real-life, or *in vivo*, contacts with the feared situation, and some do not. Two types of non-real-life contacts, of varying degrees, can be included. One type uses *imaginal* situations, such as having the person think about calling the dentist. The other involves *symbolic* contacts, such as by showing pictures, films, or models of the feared situation.

Table 5.3   *Example of a Stimulus Hierarchy for a Fear of Dentists*

1. Think about being in the dentist's waiting room, simply accompanying someone else who is there for an examination.
2. Look at a photograph of a smiling person seated in a dental chair.
3. Imagine this person calmly having a dental examination.
4. Think about calling the dentist for an appointment.
5. Actually call for the appointment.
6. Sit in a car outside the dentist's office without having an appointment.
7. Sit in the dentist's waiting room and hear the nurse say, "The hygienist is ready for you."
8. Sit in the examination room and hear the hygienist say, "I see one tooth the dentist will need to look at."
9. Hear and watch the drill run, without its being brought near the face.
10. Have the dentist pick at the tooth with an instrument, saying, "That doesn't look good."
11. See the dentist lay out the instruments, including a syringe to administer an anesthetic.
12. Feel the needle touch the gums.
13. Imagine having the tooth drilled.
14. Imagine having the tooth pulled.

The systematic desensitization procedure starts by having the person do relaxation exercises. Then the steps in a hierarchy are presented individually, while the person is relaxed and comfortable (Sarafino, 2001). The steps follow a sequence from the least to the most fearful for the individual. Each step may elicit some wariness or fear behavior, but the person is encouraged to relax. Once the wariness at one step has passed and the person is calm, the next step in the hierarchy can be introduced. Completing an entire stimulus hierarchy and reducing a fairly strong fear can be achieved fairly quickly—it is likely to take several hours, divided into several separate sessions. In one study with dental-phobic adults who simply imagined each step in a hierarchy, the procedure successfully reduced their fear in six 1½-hour sessions (Gatchel, 1980). Individual sessions for reducing fears in children are usually much shorter than those used with adults, especially for a child who is very young and has a short attention span.

Biofeedback

Biofeedback is a technique in which an electromechanical device monitors the status of a person's physiological processes, such as heart rate or muscle

A biofeedback procedure for forehead muscle tension. One way to give feedback regarding the status of the muscles is with audio speakers, such as by sounding higher tones for higher levels of tension.

tension, and immediately reports that information back to the individual. This information enables the person to gain voluntary control over these processes through operant conditioning. If, for instance, the person is trying to reduce neck-muscle tension and the device reports that the tension has just decreased, this information reinforces whatever efforts the individual made to accomplish this decrease.

Biofeedback has been used successfully in treating stress-related health problems. For example, an experiment found that patients suffering from chronic headaches who were given biofeedback regarding muscle tension in their foreheads later showed less tension in those muscles and reported having fewer headaches than subjects in control groups (Budzynski et al., 1973). What's more, these benefits continued at a followup after 3 months. Biofeedback and progressive muscle relaxation are effective for treating headache and many other stress-related disorders (Gatchel, 2001; Holroyd & Penzien, 1986). Both biofeedback and progressive muscle relaxation techniques can help reduce stress, but some individuals may benefit more from one method than the other.

According to Virginia Attanasio, Frank Andrasik, and their colleagues (1985), children may be better candidates for biofeedback treatment than adults. In treating recurrent headache with biofeedback, these researchers noticed that children seem to acquire biofeedback control faster and show better overall improvement than adults. Part of this observation has been confirmed in research: the headaches of children and adults improve with biofeedback, but children's headaches improve more (Sarafino & Goehring, 2000). Why? Attanasio and her coworkers have offered some reasons. First, although a small proportion of children are frightened initially by the equipment and procedures, most are more enthusiastic than adults, often regarding biofeedback as a game. Some children become so interested and motivated in the game that their arousal interferes with relaxation if the therapist does not help them remain calm. Second, children are usually less skeptical about their ability to succeed in biofeedback training and to benefit from doing so. Adults often say, "Nothing else I've ever tried has worked, so why should biofeedback?" This difference in skepticism may reflect differences in experience: adults are likely to have had more failure experiences with other treatments than children. Third, children may be more likely than adults to practice their training at home, as they are instructed to do.

Although children have characteristics that make them well–suited to biofeedback methods, they also have some special difficulties (Attanasio et al., 1985). For one thing, children—particularly those below the age of 8—have shorter attention spans than adults. If biofeedback sessions last more than 20 minutes or so, it may be necessary to divide each session into smaller units with brief breaks in between. A related problem is that children sometimes perform disruptive behaviors during a session, disturbing the electrodes and wires or interrupting to talk about tangential topics, for instance. The therapist can reduce the likelihood of these unwanted behaviors, such as by providing rewards for being cooperative. The difficulties some children have in biofeedback training can usually be overcome.

Modeling

People learn not just by doing, but also by observing. They see what others do and the consequences of the behavior these models perform. As a result, this kind of learning is called **modeling,** and sometimes "observational" or "social" learning. People can learn fears and other stress-related behavior by observing fearful behavior in other individuals. In one study, children (with their parents' permission) learned to fear a Mickey Mouse figure by watching a short film showing a 5-year-old boy's fear reaction to plastic figures of Mickey Mouse and Donald Duck (Venn & Short, 1973). This learned fear reaction was pronounced initially—but declined a day or two later.

Since people can learn stressful reactions by observing these behaviors in others, modeling should be effective in reversing this learning and helping people cope with stressors too. A large body of research has confirmed that it is (Sarafino, 2001; Thelen et al., 1979). The therapeutic use of modeling is similar to the method of desensitization: the person relaxes while watching a model calmly perform a series of activities arranged as a stimulus hierarchy—that is, from least to most stressful. The modeling procedure can be presented *symbolically,* using films or videotapes, or *in vivo,* with real-life models and events. Using symbolic presentations, for example, Barbara Melamed and her coworkers have shown that modeling procedures can reduce the stress experienced by hospitalized 4- to 17-year-old children and improve their recovery from surgery (Melamed, Dearborn, & Hermecz, 1983; Melamed & Siegel, 1975). But the

CLINICAL METHODS AND ISSUES

The Case of "Bear"

We've seen that people's thought processes can affect their stress. Appraisals of stress are often based on thoughts that are not rational. To illustrate how irrational thoughts can increase stress and lead to psychological problems, consider the case of a college baseball player, nicknamed "Bear,"

who was not hitting up to expectations, and was very depressed about his poor performance. In talking with Bear, it quickly became apparent that his own expectations were unrealistic. For instance, Bear wanted to hit the ball so hard that it would literally be bent out of shape (if someone happened to find it in the next county!). After a particularly bad batting session, he would go home and continue to practice until he was immobilized with

exhaustion. Simply put, he believed that if an athlete was not performing well, this could only mean he was not trying hard enough. (Rimm & Masters, 1979, p. 40)

Bear's therapy involved progressive muscle relaxation and cognitive methods to help him realize two important things: First, although motivation and desire increase performance, they do so only up to a point, after which additional motivation impairs performance. Second, although hitting very well is "nice," hitting moderately well is not "terrible" or "intolerable." These realizations restructured Bear's thinking about his performance, and his batting average increased dramatically. Similar methods can help people reduce irrational thoughts that lead to their debilitating feelings of anxiety and depression (Sarafino, 2001).

child's age and prior experience with surgery were also important factors in the results. Children under the age of 8 who had had previous surgery experienced increased anxiety rather than less. These children may benefit from other methods to reduce stress, such as activities that simply distract their attention. (Go to 🌳).

Approaches Focusing on Cognitive Processes

Because stress results from cognitive appraisals that are frequently based on a lack of information, misperceptions, or irrational beliefs, some approaches to modify people's behavior and thought patterns have been developed to help them cope better with the stress they experience. To achieve this goal, these methods guide people toward what Arnold Lazarus (1971) has called a "restructuring" of their thought patterns. **Cognitive restructuring** is a process by which stress-provoking thoughts or beliefs are replaced with more constructive or realistic ones that reduce the person's appraisal of threat or harm.

What sorts of irrational beliefs do people have that increase stress? Two leading theorists have described a variety of erroneous thought patterns that

some people use habitually and frequently that lead to stress, and we'll consider two from each theorist. The beliefs described by Albert Ellis (1962, 1977, 1987) include:

- *Can't-stand-itis*—as in, "I *can't stand* not doing well on a test."

- *Musterbating*—for instance, "People *must* like me, or I'm worthless."

And the beliefs described by Aaron Beck (1976; Beck et al., 1990) include:

- *Arbitrary inference* (drawing a specific conclusion from insufficient, ambiguous, or contrary evidence). For example, a husband might interpret his wife's bad mood as meaning she is unhappy with something he did when she is actually just preoccupied with another matter.

- *Magnification* (greatly exaggerating the meaning or impact of an event). For instance, a recently retired person diagnosed with arthritis might describe it as a "catastrophe."

These ways of thinking affect stress appraisal processes, increasing the appraisal of threat or harm because the perspectives are so extreme. None of the circumstances that are the bases of these thoughts is "good," but they're probably not as bad as the thoughts imply.

A widely used cognitive restructuring approach to change maladaptive thought patterns is called **cognitive therapy** (Beck, 1976; Beck et al., 1990). Although it was developed originally to treat psychological depression, it is also being applied today for anxiety. Cognitive therapy attempts to help clients see that they are not responsible for all of the problems they encounter, the negative events they experience are usually not catastrophes, and their maladaptive beliefs are not logically valid. For instance, the following dialogue shows how a therapist tried to counter the negative beliefs of a woman named Sharon.

THERAPIST: . . . what evidence do you have that all this is true? That you are ugly, awkward? Or that it is not true? What data do you have?

SHARON: Comparing myself to people that I consider to be extremely attractive and finding myself lacking.

THERAPIST: So if you look at that beautiful person, you're less?

SHARON: Yeah.

THERAPIST: Or if I look at that perfect person, I'm less. Is that what you're saying? . . .

SHARON: Yeah. I always pick out, of course, the most attractive person and probably a person who spends 3 hours a day on grooming and appearance. . . . I don't compare myself to the run-of-the-mill. . . . (Freeman, 1990, p. 83)

One technique cognitive therapy uses, called *hypothesis testing*, has the person treat an erroneous belief as a hypothesis and test it by looking for evidence for and against it in his or her everyday life. Research has shown that cognitive therapy is clearly effective in treating depression (Hollon, Shelton, & Davis, 1993; Robins & Hayes, 1993) and appears to be a very promising approach for treating anxieties (Chambless & Gillis, 1993).

Another cognitive approach is designed to help clients solve problems in their lives. By a "problem" we mean a life circumstance, such as being stuck in traffic or feeling a worrisome chest pain, that requires a response based on thinking and planning. People experience stress when they face a problem and don't know what to do or how to do it. In **problem-solving training,** clients learn a strategy for identifying, discovering, or inventing effective or adaptive ways to address problems in everyday life (D'Zurilla, 1988; Nezu, Nezu, & Perri, 1989). They learn to watch for problems that can arise, define a problem clearly and concretely, generate a variety of possible solutions, and decide on the best course of action. Evidence indicates that problem-solving training reduces anxiety and other negative emotions (D'Zurilla, 1988).

Some cognitive-based approaches use a variety of methods to help people cope with stress. Donald Meichenbaum and his colleagues have developed a procedure called **stress-inoculation training** that is designed to teach people skills for alleviating stress and achieving personal goals (Meichenbaum & Cameron, 1983; Meichenbaum & Turk, 1982). The training program involves three phases. In the first phase, *conceptualization*, the person learns about the nature of stress and how people react to it. In the *skills acquisition and rehearsal* phase, the person learns behavioral and cognitive skills to use in emotion-focused and problem-focused coping. These skills can include relaxation, desensitization, seeking social support, and cognitive restructuring. In the last phase, *application and follow-through*, the person practices coping skills with actual or imagined stressors. The methods used in stress-inoculation training are well thought out and include a number of well-established techniques. Research has shown that stress-inoculation training can alleviate stress, but more evidence is needed to demonstrate its value relative to other approaches (Meichenbaum & Deffenbacher, 1988).

Multidimensional Approaches

The coping difficulties individuals have are often multidimensional and multifaceted. As a result, one particular technique may not be sufficient in helping that person, and the most effective approach usually draws upon many techniques. The method of stress inoculation training provides an example of an approach that teaches people to use a variety of techniques. When designing a multidimensional approach, the program for helping an individual cope better with stress would be tailored to the person's specific problems (Sarafino, 2001). The program may make use of any of the methods we have considered, many methods that would take this discussion too far afield, and the methods we are about to examine.

MASSAGE, MEDITATION, AND HYPNOSIS

Three additional techniques have been used in stress management. The first two we will consider—massage and meditation—are often classified as relaxation methods. The third technique, hypnosis, seems to produce an *altered state of consciousness* in which mental functioning differs from its usual pattern of wakefulness. Some people believe that meditation and massage are other ways by which we can alter consciousness.

Massage

Massage has several forms that vary in the degree of pressure applied. Some forms of massage use soothing strokes with light pressure, others involve a rubbing motion with moderate force, and still others use a kneading or pounding action. *Deep tissue massage* uses enough pressure to penetrate deeply into muscles and joints. Infants seem to prefer light strokes, but adults prefer more force (Field, 1996). When seeking a massage therapist, it is a good idea to ask about licensing and certification.

Massage therapy can reduce anxiety and depression (Moyer, Rounds, & Hannum, 2004). It also helps reduce hypertension, some types of pain, and asthma symptoms; some evidence indicates that it may bolster immune function (Field, 1996, 1998).

Meditation

Transcendental meditation is a method in the practice of yoga that was promoted by Maharishi Mahesh Yogi as a means of improving physical and mental health and reducing stress (Benson, 1984, 1991; Nystul, 1987). Individuals using this procedure are instructed to practice it twice a day, sitting upright but comfortably relaxed with eyes closed, and mentally repeating a word or sound (such as "om"), called a *mantra*, to prevent distracting thoughts from occurring.

Psychologists and psychiatrists have advocated similar meditation methods for reducing stress. For example, Herbert Benson has recommended that the person

> sit quietly in a comfortable position and close your eyes. . . . Deeply relax all your muscles. . . . Become aware of your breathing. As you breathe out, say the word *one* silently to yourself. . . . Maintain a

passive attitude and permit relaxation to occur at its own pace. Expect other thoughts. When these distracting thoughts occur, ignore them by thinking, "Oh well," and continue repeating, "One." (1984, p. 332)

The purpose of this procedure is to increase the person's ability in the face of a stressor to make a "relaxation response," which includes reduced physiological activity as an alternative to a stress response. According to Benson, the relaxation response enhances health, such as by reducing blood pressure, and may be achieved in many different ways. For example, a religious person might find that a meditative prayer is the most effective method for bringing forth the relaxation response.

Although meditation helps people relax, it has a broader purpose: to develop a clear and *mindful awareness*, or "insight" regarding the essence of one's experiences, unencumbered by cognitive or emotional distortions (Hart, 1987; Solé-Leris, 1986). Jon Kabat-Zinn (1982; Kabat-Zinn, Lipworth, & Burney, 1985) has emphasized the mindful awareness component of meditation to help individuals who suffer from chronic pain to detach themselves from the cognitive and emotional distortions they have with their pain. He trains patients to pay close attention to their pain and other sensations without reacting toward them in any way, thereby enabling the people to be aware of the pain itself with no thoughts or feelings about it. Using this technique leads to a reduction in the patients' reports of physical and psychological discomfort.

Many people believe that meditation enables people to reach a state of profound rest, as is claimed by popular self-help books (for example, Forem, 1974). Many quasi-experimental studies have examined this issue but found no consistent differences in blood pressure, heart rate, or respiration rate between experienced meditators while meditating and nonmeditators who were resting (Holmes, 1984; Lichstein, 1988). But two findings from other research are important here. First, Buddhist monks in Southeast Asia can dramatically alter their body metabolism and brain electrical activity through meditation (Benson et al., 1990). Second, people's blood pressure decreases while they meditate (Barnes et al., 1999).

Still, the main question of concern for stress management is whether meditation is a useful procedure for alleviating stress in daily life. Research has generally found that it is (Lichstein, 1988;

Shapiro, Schwartz, & Bonner, 1998; Williams et al., 2001). And practicing meditation on a regular basis appears to reduce blood pressure and enhance immune function (Barnes, Treiber, & Johnson, 2004; Davidson et al., 2003).

Hypnosis

The modern history of hypnosis began with its being called *animal magnetism* and *Mesmerism* in the 18th and 19th centuries. The Austrian physician Franz Anton Mesmer popularized its use in treating patients who had symptoms of physical illness, such as paralysis, without a detectable underlying organic disorder. Today, *hypnosis* is considered to be an altered state of consciousness that is induced by special techniques of suggestion and leads to varying degrees of responsiveness to directions for changes in perception, memory, and behavior (Orne, 1989).

People differ in *suggestibility*, or the degree to which they can be hypnotized. Perhaps 15 to 30% of the general population is easily and deeply hypnotizable (Evans, 1987; Hilgard, 1967). Suggestibility appears to change with age, being particularly strong among children between the ages of about 7 and 14, and then declining in adolescence to a level that remains stable throughout adulthood (Hilgard, 1967; Place, 1984). People who are reasonably suggestible can often learn to induce a hypnotic state in themselves—a process called *self-hypnosis*. Usually they learn to do this after they have experienced hypnosis under the supervision of a skilled hypnotist.

Because individuals who have been hypnotized usually claim that it is a relaxing experience, researchers have examined whether it can reduce stress. These studies have generally found that hypnosis is helpful in stress management, but not necessarily more effective than other relaxation techniques (Tapp, 1985; Wadden & Anderton, 1982). Other research has revealed that people who received training in and practiced regularly either hypnosis or relaxation showed enhanced immune function weeks later (Kiecolt-Glaser et al., 2001; McGrady et al., 1992).

In summary, we have seen that many different behavioral and cognitive methods, massage, meditation, and hypnosis offer useful therapeutic approaches for helping people cope with stress. Research is also revealing more and more clearly the important benefits of stress management in preventing illness.

USING STRESS MANAGEMENT TO REDUCE CORONARY RISK

Of the many risk factors that have been identified for CHD, a few of them—such as age and family history—are beyond the control of the individual. But many risk factors for CHD are directly linked to the person's experiences and behavior, which should be modifiable. One of these risk factors is stress. In the remainder of this chapter, we will consider how stress management techniques can be applied to reduce coronary risk.

MODIFYING TYPE A BEHAVIOR

When the Type A behavior pattern was established as a risk factor for CHD, researchers began to study ways to modify Type A behavior to reduce coronary risk. Ethel Roskies and her colleagues began a research and therapy program in the 1970s to modify Type A behavior. After some initial research, they designed and tested a multidimensional program that included progressive muscle relaxation, cognitive restructuring, and stress-inoculation training (Roskies, 1983; Roskies et al., 1986). The participants were Type A men who were randomly assigned to either the multidimensional program or to one of two physical exercise groups: an aerobic training (mostly jogging) and a weight-training program. After 10 weeks, the men were retested for Type A behavior and cardiovascular reactivity (blood pressure and heart rate) to stressors, such as doing mental arithmetic, to compare with measures taken earlier. One finding can be seen in Figure 5–2: the hostility component of Type A behavior decreased markedly in the multidimensional program but not in the exercise groups. These benefits can be quite durable: another study found that improvements in Type A behavior with a similar intervention were maintained at a 2-year followup (Karlberg, Krakau, & Undén, 1998).

Raymond Novaco (1975, 1978) has demonstrated the usefulness of stress-inoculation training with relaxation in helping people control their anger. He trained individuals who were both self-identified and clinically assessed as having serious problems controlling anger. In this treatment program, the subjects first learned about the role of arousal and cognitive processes in feelings of anger.

Figure 5–2 Hostility of Type A men measured by the Structured Interview method before and after a 10-week multidimensional, aerobic exercise, or weight-training treatment program. (Data from Roskies et al., 1986, Table 4.)

Then they learned muscle relaxation along with statements—like those in Table 5.4—they could say to themselves at different times in the course of angry episodes, such as at the point of "impact and confrontation." Finally, they practiced the techniques while imagining and role-playing realistic anger situations. The results showed that this treatment improved the subjects' ability to control anger, as measured by their self-reports and their blood pressure when provoked in the laboratory. Many studies have confirmed the success of interventions using cognitive and behavioral methods in decreasing anger (Beck & Fernandez, 1998), and research has shown that such interventions reduce both hostility and diastolic (resting) blood pressure in patients with CHD and mild hypertension (Gidron, Davidson, & Bata, 1999; Larkin & Zayfert, 1996).

Does decreasing Type A behavior with stress management techniques decrease the incidence of CHD? Researchers studied this issue with over 1,000 patients who had suffered a heart attack and who agreed to participate in the study for 5 years (Friedman et al., 1986; Powell & Friedman, 1986). They were *not* selected on the basis of their exhibiting

---

Table 5.4   *Examples of Anger Management Self-Statements Rehearsed in Stress-Inoculation Training*

Preparing for Provocation

"This could be a rough situation; but I know how to deal with it. I can work out a plan to handle this. Easy does it. Remember, stick to the issues and don't take it personally. There won't be any need for an argument. I know what to do."

Impact and Confrontation

"As long as I keep my cool, I'm in control of the situation. You don't need to prove yourself. Don't make more out of this than you have to. There is no point in getting mad. Think of what you have to do. Look for the positives and don't jump to conclusions."

Coping with Arousal

"Muscles are getting tight. Relax and slow things down. Time to take a deep breath. Let's take the issue point by point. My anger is a signal of what I need to do. Time for problem solving. He probably wants me to get angry, but I'm going to deal with it constructively."

Subsequent Reflection

a. *Conflict unresolved*: Forget about the aggravation. Thinking about it only makes you upset. Try to shake it off. Don't let it interfere with your job. Remember relaxation. It's a lot better than anger. Don't take it personally. It's probably not so serious.

b. *Conflict resolved*: I handled that one pretty well. That's doing a good job. I could have gotten more upset than it was worth. My pride can get me into trouble, but I'm doing better at this all the time. I actually got through that without getting angry.

Source: From Novaco (1978, p. 150).

Type A behavior, and they continued to be treated by their own physicians throughout the study. The subjects were randomly assigned to two intervention groups and a control group. One intervention, called *cardiac counseling*, presented information, such as about the causes of heart disease and the importance of altering standard coronary risk factors, such as cigarette smoking. (Type A behavior was not discussed.) The other intervention, called the *Type A/ cardiac group*, included the same cardiac counseling plus a multidimensional program, including progressive muscle relaxation and cognitive restructuring techniques, to modify Type A behavior. The results revealed that the Type A/cardiac group showed a much larger decrease in Type A behavior (measured with Structured Interview and questionnaire methods) than those in the other groups and had substantially lower rates of cardiac morbidity and mortality (Friedman et al., 1986). For example, subsequent heart attacks occurred in about 13% of the Type A/cardiac subjects, 21% of the cardiac counseling subjects, and 28% of the control subjects during the $4^1/_2$-year followup.

Research has investigated the possibility of using pharmacological approaches to modify Type A behavior. Beta-blockers appear to reduce Type A behavior (Schmieder et al., 1983). Although the use of beta-blockers may not be the treatment of choice for most Type A individuals, it may be an appropriate alternative for people who are at coronary risk who do not respond to behavioral and cognitive interventions (Chesney, Frautschi, & Rosenman, 1985).

TREATING HYPERTENSION

As we discussed in Chapter 4, essential hypertension is an important risk factor for CHD. Patients with diagnosed hypertension above the borderline level usually receive medical treatment that includes the use of prescription drugs, such as *diuretics*, which lower blood pressure by decreasing blood volume. In addition, physicians advise hypertensive patients to control their body weight, exercise regularly, and reduce their intake of cholesterol, sodium, caffeine, and alcohol (AHA, 2004). Sometimes physicians and others urge hypertensive patients "to try to relax" when hassles occur. But there is a danger in this advice: untrained people who make an effort to relax often end up increasing their blood pressure rather than decreasing it (Suls, Sanders, & Labrecque, 1986).

Because the development of essential hypertension has been linked to the amount of stress people experience, researchers have examined the utility of stress management techniques in treating high blood pressure. The findings suggest two conclusions. First, using a single technique, such as relaxation, to lower blood pressure often provides only limited success; stress management methods are more effective when combined in multidimensional programs (Larkin, Knowlton, & D'Alessandri, 1990; Spence et al., 1999). Second, a meta-analysis by Wolfgang Linden and Laura Chambers (1994) of dozens of studies found that multidimensional programs consisting of behavioral and cognitive methods for stress management are highly effective—as effective as diuretic drugs—in reducing blood pressure. It is now clear that psychological approaches have considerable value in treating hypertension, making effective treatment possible without drugs or with lower doses for most patients.

In an effort to improve the health of employees, many large companies have introduced voluntary stress management programs for their workers. Most studies of these programs have found that they produce improvements in measures of workers' psychological and physiological stress (Alderman, 1984; Sallis et al., 1987). Despite the success of stress management programs in reducing coronary risk by modifying Type A behavior and lowering blood pressure, they are not yet widely applied—partly because the evidence supporting the use of these programs is relatively new and partly because they cost money to run. Other reasons relate to the participants; although people typically recognize the seriousness of heart disease, Type A individuals probably don't see any connection between CHD and their hard-driving lifestyles (Roskies, 1983). Also, people with high blood pressure either don't know they have it or say they "feel good anyway." For these and similar reasons, many people who could benefit from stress management programs don't join one when it is available, drop out before completing the program, or don't adhere closely to its recommendations, such as to practice relaxation techniques at home (Alderman, 1984; Hoelscher, Lichstein, & Rosenthal, 1986).

SUMMARY

Coping is the process by which people try to manage the real or perceived discrepancy between the demands and resources they appraise in stressful situations. We cope with stress through transactions with the environment that do not necessarily lead to solutions to the problems causing the stress.

Coping serves two types of functions. The function of emotion-focused coping is to regulate the person's emotional response to stress. This regulation occurs through the person's behavior, such as using alcohol or seeking social support, and through cognitive strategies, such as denying unpleasant facts. People tend to rely on emotion-focused coping when they believe they cannot change the stressful conditions. The function of problem-focused coping is to reduce the demands of the stressor or expand the resources to deal with it, such as by learning new skills. People tend to use problem-focused coping when they believe they can change the situation. Adults report using more problem-focused than emotion-focused coping approaches when they experience stress. Some of these methods tend to increase the attention the person gives to the problem, and other methods promote avoidance of the problem. People tend to use a combination of methods in coping with a stressful situation.

Although coping changes across the life span, the exact nature of these changes is unclear. Young children's coping is limited by their cognitive abilities, which improve throughout childhood. During adulthood, a shift in coping function occurs as people approach old age—they rely less on problem-focused and more on emotion-focused coping. Elderly people seem to regard stressors as less changeable than middle-aged individuals do.

People can reduce the potential for stress in their lives and others' lives in several ways. First, they can increase the social support they give and receive by joining social, religious, and special-interest groups. Second, they can improve their own and others' sense of personal control and hardiness by giving and taking responsibility. Also, they can reduce frustration and waste less time by organizing their world better, such as through time management. And by exercising and keeping fit, they can reduce the experience of stress and the impact it has on their health. Finally, they can prepare for stressful events, such as a medical procedure, by improving their behavioral, cognitive, and informational control.

Sometimes the coping skills individuals have learned are not adequate for dealing with a stressor that is very strong, novel, or unrelenting. A variety of stress management techniques is available to help people who are having trouble coping effectively. One technique is pharmacological, that is, using prescribed drugs, such as beta-blockers. Stress management methods include progressive muscle relaxation, systematic desensitization, biofeedback, modeling, and several cognitive approaches. Cognitive therapy attempts to modify stress-producing, irrational thought patterns through the process of cognitive restructuring. Stress-inoculation training and problem-solving training are designed to teach people skills to alleviate stress and achieve personal goals. Stress-inoculation training is a multidimensional approach in that it uses a variety of techniques that are designed to reduce specific components of the person's problems. Beneficial effects on people's stress have been found for all of the behavioral and cognitive stress management methods, particularly relaxation. Massage, meditation, and hypnosis have shown promise for reducing stress, too. Stress management techniques can reduce coronary risk by modifying Type A behavior and by treating hypertension.

KEY TERMS

coping	time management	biofeedback	problem-solving
emotion-focused	progressive muscle	modeling	training
coping	relaxation	cognitive restruc-	stress-inoculation
problem-focused	systematic desensi-	turing	training
coping	tization	cognitive therapy	

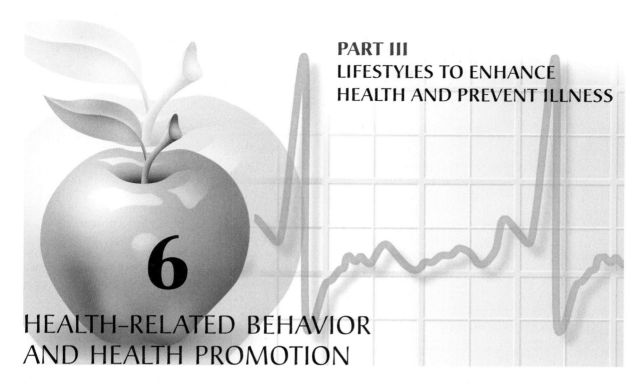

LIFESTYLES TO ENHANCE
HEALTH AND PREVENT ILLNESS

6

HEALTH-RELATED BEHAVIOR
AND HEALTH PROMOTION

Health and Behavior
Lifestyles, Risk Factors, and Health
Interdisciplinary Perspectives on Preventing
   Illness
Problems in Promoting Wellness

**What Determines People's Health-Related
Behavior?**
General Factors in Health-Related Behavior
The Role of Beliefs and Intentions
The Role of Less Rational Processes

**Developmental, Gender, and Sociocultural
Factors in Health**
Development and Health
Gender and Health
Sociocultural Factors and Health

Programs for Health Promotion
Methods for Promoting Health
Promoting Health in the Schools
Worksite Wellness Programs
Community-Based Wellness Programs
Prevention with Specific Targets: Focusing
   on AIDS

PROLOGUE

"It's getting worse—those health nuts are all over the place these days, telling me how to live my life," said Joshua between puffs on his cigarette. Things were not necessarily "worse," but they had changed. People were now much more health conscious. They were exercising more, eating more healthful diets, and using better hygiene. Does this story describe the contemporary scene in a technologically advanced country? It could, but it could also describe the mid-1800s in America. People of today are not the first to be interested in health and fitness.

In the 1800s, disease was widespread, epidemics were common, and physicians had few effective methods for preventing or treating illness. As a result, health reformers advocated that people change their lifestyles to protect their health (Collins, 1987; Leventhal, Prohaska, & Hirschman, 1985). These reformers were often imbued with patriotic or religious zeal. Some of them advocated vegetarian diets. Others proposed that people chew their food to a watery consistency, or stop smoking cigarettes and drinking, or get more exercise if they led sedentary lives. Often people who exercised wore loose-fitting gym suits and used a variety of apparatuses, such as rowing machines. It was a lot like today, wasn't it?

This part of the book contains three chapters concerned with behaviors that can enhance or compromise health. In the present chapter, we'll start with the health habits people practice and how their lifestyles affect their health. Then we turn to factors that influence the health-related behaviors individuals adopt and programs to help people lead more healthful lives. As we study these topics, you will find answers to questions you may have about health-related behavior and health promotion. Are people leading more healthful lives today than they did in the past? Why is it that some people take better care of themselves than others do? How effective are health-promotion programs that try to motivate healthful behavior through fear?

of developing fatal and chronic diseases, such as heart disease, cancer, and AIDS (WHO, 2004). Illness and early death could be substantially reduced if people would adopt lifestyles that promote wellness, such as eating healthful diets and not smoking.

The percentage of deaths resulting from any specific cause changes over time. Figure 6–1 depicts the pattern of changes in the United States that occurred after the late 1960s. These changes resulted partly from the modifications people made in behavioral risk factors for major chronic diseases. Of course, we can't live forever. If we made all of the recommended lifestyle changes and researchers found cures for most major diseases, people's average life expectancy in technologically advanced countries would rise several years to about 85 years, its likely upper limit (Olshansky, Carnes, & Cassel, 1990).

HEALTH AND BEHAVIOR

The role of behavior in health has been receiving increased attention in countries around the world because people's *health habits*—that is, their usual health-related behaviors—influence their likelihood

LIFESTYLES, RISK FACTORS, AND HEALTH

The typical person's lifestyle includes many behaviors that are risk factors for illness and injury. For instance, millions of Americans smoke cigarettes, drink excessively, use drugs, eat high-fat and high-cholesterol diets, eat too much and become overweight, have too

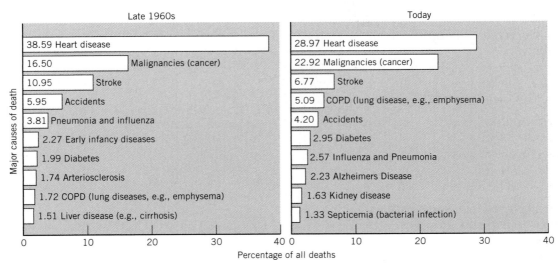

Figure 6–1 Percentage of all deaths caused by each of the 10 leading causes of death in the United States in the *late 1960s* (1968) and *today*. Notice that cancer and COPD deaths increased markedly after 1968 (partly due to cigarette smoking); heart disease and stroke deaths declined (partly due to recent lifestyle changes, such as in diet); deaths from diseases of early infancy declined markedly and are no longer in the top 10. (Data from USBC, 1971, Table 77; USBC, 2003, Table 116.)

little physical activity, and behave in unsafe ways, such as not using seat belts in automobiles. Many people realize these dangers and adjust their behavior to protect their health. Middle-aged adults who don't smoke and have favorable blood pressure and cholesterol levels can expect to live 6 years longer than they would otherwise (Stamler et al., 1999).

Health Behavior

Health behavior is any activity people perform to maintain or improve their health, regardless of their perceived health status or whether the behavior actually achieves that goal. Researchers have noted that people's health status influences the type of health behavior they perform and their motivation to do it (Kasl & Cobb, 1966a, b; Parsons 1951). To illustrate these differences, we will consider examples of behaviors people perform when they are well, experience symptoms, and are clearly sick.

Well behavior is any activity people undertake to maintain or improve current good health and avoid illness. These activities can include healthy people's exercising, eating healthful diets, having regular dental checkups, and getting vaccinations against diseases. But when people are well, they may not feel inclined to devote the effort and sacrifice that healthful behavior

entails. Thus, engaging in healthful behavior depends on motivational factors, particularly with regard to the individual's perception of a threat of disease, the value in the behavior in reducing this threat, and the attractiveness of the opposite behavior. Some unhealthful behaviors, such as drinking or smoking, are often seen as pleasurable or the "in" thing to do. As a result, many individuals do not resist beginning unhealthful behaviors and may reject efforts or advice to get them to quit.

Symptom-based behavior is any activity people who feel ill undertake to determine the problem and find a remedy. These activities usually include complaining about symptoms, such as stomach pains, and seeking help or advice from relatives, friends, and medical practitioners. Some people are more likely than others to engage in symptom-based behavior when symptoms appear, and there are many reasons for these differences. For instance, some individuals may be more afraid than others of physicians, hospitals, or the serious illness a diagnosis may reveal. Some people are stoic or unconcerned about the aches and pains they experience, and others do not seek medical care because they simply do not have the money to pay for it. Chapter 9 will examine these and other reasons why people do and do not use health care services.

Sick-role behavior refers to any activity people undertake to get well after deciding that they are ill and

People engage in health behaviors, such as using exercise bikes, to maintain or improve their fitness and avoid illness.

what the illness is. This behavior is based on the idea that sick people take on a special "role," making them exempt from their normal obligations and life tasks, such as going to work or school. You'd be showing sick-role behaviors if you got a prescription filled, used it as the physician directed, stayed home from work to recover, and had someone else do your household chores. Although this status ordinarily obligates patients to try to get well, many do not follow their recommended treatment, particularly if it is inconvenient or uncomfortable to do. Sometimes sick-role behaviors seem to serve emotional functions, as when patients moan or sigh and receive sympathy as a result.

How people behave when they are sick depends in large measure on what they have learned. As an example, a study of female college students assessed whether they had been encouraged during adolescence to adopt the sick role for menstruation or had observed their mothers exhibit menstrual distress. Compared with students who did not have these experiences, those who *did* reported more menstrual symptoms, disability, and clinic visits for these symptoms as adults (Whitehead et al., 1986). Other research has found cultural differences in the way people respond to their symptoms and go about trying to get well (Korol & Craig, 2001). For example, studies in the United States have found differences among groups of immigrants in their willingness to tolerate pain, but these differences diminish in succeeding generations (Chapman & Brena, 1985). (Go to 💡.)

HIGHLIGHT

Two Health Behaviors: Breast and Testicular Examinations

Breast cancer is a leading cause of women's deaths around the world. For women in the United States, one of every eight is likely to develop breast cancer at some time in her life, especially after the age of 50, and breast cancer is the second most frequent cause of cancer death (ACS, 2004). Compared with breast cancer, *testicular cancer* is much less prevalent, but several thousand cases are diagnosed each year in American men, mainly between the ages of 15 and 35 (ACS, 2004; Rosella, 1994). Breast and testicular cancers are treated with some combination of radiation therapy, chemotherapy, and surgery, and both cancers have very high cure rates if treated early.

Individuals can detect cancer of the breast or testicles in its early stages by self-examination. Breast and testicular self-examinations are done with the fingers, searching mainly for abnormal lumps. For breast self-examination (BSE), the woman lies on her back and, before examining a breast, places the arm of the same side of the body as that breast behind her head. With her other hand, she presses her middle three fingertips flatly against the breast tissue and moves them in small circles until she examines the entire breast. The method for testicular self-examination (TSE) is relatively simple. The man first locates the tubelike structures that extend behind the testicle. Then he rotates the entire surface of each testicle between the fingers and thumbs of both hands, looking for lumps. Unfortunately, people don't do BSEs and TSEs very often. The reasons they don't include not knowing how important early detection can be, being afraid they will find a malignant lump, or just forgetting and having no reminders (Aiken, Gerend, & Jackson, 2001; Craun & Deffenbacher, 1987; Moore, Barling, & Hood, 1998; Rosella, 1994).

How can we encourage the practice of BSE and TSE? One way is through the mass media, which can note the very high cure rates (over 90%) when detected in early stages and emphasize that treatment for cancer is often less extensive and disfiguring in earlier than later stages. For example, breast cancer in its early stages can often be treated without removing the entire breast. Two other ways of encouraging self-examinations involve health practitioners, such as nurses: they can provide information and training through individual and group contacts, such as at worksites and medical offices, and send reminders to do the examinations (Craun & Deffenbacher, 1987). It is especially important that men and women with family histories or other risk factors for cancer devise effective BSE or TSE reminders, such as by writing them in a calendar.

Practicing Health Behaviors

What health behaviors do people actually perform? Table 6.1 presents the results of a national survey of American men and women that focused on a limited set of clearly healthful behaviors. Although these data show important shortcomings in the health practices of people in the United States, data from other research reveal that most of these levels of health-related behavior represent clear improvements over the levels assessed about 10 years earlier (McGinnis & Lee, 1995).

Who practices healthful behavior and why? We are far from a complete answer to this question, but there are gender, sociocultural, and age differences in practicing health behaviors (Schoenborn, 1993; USBC, 1995). For instance, an international survey of adults in European countries found that women perform more healthful behaviors than men (Steptoe et al., 1994). One reason for such differences is that people seem to perform behaviors that are salient to them. For example, a study compared the health behaviors of medical and nonmedical students and found that the medical students exercised more and were much less likely to smoke cigarettes, drink alcohol excessively, and use drugs (Golding & Cornish, 1987).

You probably know some individuals who are highly health-conscious and others who display little concern about their health. To some extent individuals who practice certain behaviors that benefit their health also practice other healthful behaviors and continue to perform these behaviors over time (Schoenborn, 1993). Many people lead very healthful lifestyles, and the number of health behaviors individuals practice remains fairly constant over many years. But other people show little consistency in their health habits (Langlie, 1977; Mechanic, 1979). Research results suggest three conclusions. First, although people's health habits are fairly stable, they often change over time. Second, particular health behaviors are not strongly tied to each other. That is, if we know a person practices one specific health habit, such as using seat belts, we cannot accurately predict that he or she practices another specific habit, such as exercising. Third, health behaviors do not seem to be governed in each person by a single set of attitudes or response tendencies. Thus, a girl who uses seat belts to protect herself from injury may watch her weight in order to be attractive and may not smoke because she is allergic to it.

Why are health behaviors not more stable and strongly linked to each other? Here are a few reasons (Leventhal, Prohaska, & Hirschman, 1985). First, various factors at any given time in people's lives may differentially affect different behaviors. For instance, a person may have lots of social encouragement to eat too much ("You don't like my cooking?"), and, at the same time, to limit drinking and smoking. Second, people change as a result of experience. For example, many people did not avoid smoking until they learned that it is harmful. Third, people's life circumstances change. Thus, factors, such as peer pressure, that may have been important in initiating and maintaining exercising or smoking at one time may no longer be present, thereby increasing the likelihood that the habit will change.

INTERDISCIPLINARY PERSPECTIVES ON PREVENTING ILLNESS

The advances in health that have occurred over the years have come about through two avenues: efforts to prevent illness and improvements in medical diagnosis and treatment. We can illustrate three approaches in illness prevention, using tooth decay as an example. One approach involves *behavioral influence*, such as by

Table 6.1   *Percentages Reporting Selected Health-Related Behaviors or Characteristics*

Behavior/Characteristics	Men (%)	Women (%)
Eat breakfast almost every day	54.6	58.0
Rarely snack	25.6	25.4
Exercise or play sports regularly	44.0	37.3
Average two or more drinks per day	9.7	1.7
Smoke regularly	28.4	22.8
Overweight by at least 20%[a]	29.6	25.6

[a] Subjects reported height and weight data; researchers compared against standard recommendations for healthful weights.

Source: USBC (1995, Table 215).

encouraging and demonstrating good brushing and flossing techniques. Another applies *environmental measures*, which might involve fluoridating water supplies. The third approach uses *preventive medical efforts*, such as removing calculus from teeth and repairing cavities. In much of the world, the greatest impact on health promotion probably lies in influencing behavior, such as by reducing cigarette smoking, excessive alcohol use, and unhealthful dietary practices (Breslow, 1983).

We usually think of prevention as occurring before an illness takes hold. Actually, there are three levels of prevention, only one of which applies before a disease or injury occurs (Evans & Kazarian, 2001; Runyan, 1985; Sanson-Fisher, 1993). These levels are called *primary*, *secondary*, and *tertiary* prevention. Each level of prevention can include the efforts of oneself in our well, symptom-based, and sick-role behaviors; one's social network; and health professionals.

Primary Prevention

Primary prevention consists of actions taken to avoid disease or injury. In avoiding automobile injuries, for example, primary prevention activities might include our well behavior of using seat belts, a friend reminding us to use them, and public health reminders on TV to buckle up. Primary prevention can also be directed at improving people's diet, exercise, toothbrushing and flossing, and immunity against a contagious disease.

Primary prevention for an individual can begin before he or she is born, or even conceived. Today it is possible for *genetic counselors* to estimate the risk of a child's inheriting a genetic disorder and, in some cases, to diagnose genetic abnormalities in the unborn fetus (AMA, 2003). These estimates are based on the couple's family histories, biological tests for carriers of specific genes, and biological tests on the fetus. Prospective and expectant parents may use this information to help them make important family planning decisions. Genetic counseling and biological tests can be applied to determine the risk of many serious and potentially fatal problems, such as the metabolic disorder *Tay-Sachs disease*, the red blood cell disorder *sickle-cell anemia*, and *Duchenne muscular dystrophy*. Physicians can help in selecting genetic counselors. Another way parents can exercise primary prevention is to have their children immunized against several diseases, including diphtheria, tetanus, whooping cough, measles, rubella, mumps, and polio. Although world-

wide immunization rates increased greatly in the last decades of the 20th century, they remain lower in poorer than richer societies (WHO, 1999). In the United States, the percentage of preschool children with full immunization from controllable diseases has increased to over 75%, but Black children have lower immunization rates (USBC, 2003).

Three promising approaches to primary prevention exist. One involves having medical professionals give health-promotion advice to patients. Because physicians find it hard to incorporate this approach in their practices, nurses or other medical staff might be better able to do it (Glasgow et al., 2001; Radecki & Brunton, 1992). A system of reminders to provide such advice with individual patients can improve these activities (Anderson, Janes, & Jenkins, 1998). The second approach helps people recognize the need for improvements in their health behaviors by using questionnaires to assess their risk factors, such as their current health and lifestyle; family history of illness; and personal characteristics, such as age, weight, and sex (Weiss, 1984). Third, Websites are available that give health promotion information (for example, http://www.hc-sc.gc.ca).

Secondary Prevention

In **secondary prevention,** actions are taken to identify and treat an illness or injury early with the aim of stopping or reversing the problem. In the case of someone who has developed an ulcer, for example, secondary prevention activities include the person's symptom-based behavior of seeking medical care for abdominal pain, the physician's prescribing medication and dietary changes, and the patient's sick-role behavior of following the doctor's prescriptions. For other health problems, instances of secondary prevention might include examination of the mouth and jaw regions for early cancer detection during dental visits, free blood pressure measurements at shopping malls, and assessments of children's vision and hearing at school.

A common secondary prevention practice is the complete physical examination, often done each year. These checkups are costly in time and money because they include several imaging (such as X ray) and laboratory tests. Not all of these tests have proven useful, therefore, medical experts now recommend getting specific tests, each with recommended schedules ranging from 1 to 5 years, depending on the person's age (CU, 1998). For instance, the American

Cancer Society recommends that women should have *mammograms* (breast X ray) annually after the age of 40, but less frequently at younger ages (ACS, 2004). All adults over the age of 50 should have regularly scheduled colon inspections, such as a *sigmoidoscopy* every 5 years or so. Individuals who are not healthy or are considered to be at high risk—for example, because of past illnesses, family history, or hazardous work conditions—should be examined more often.

These medical examinations are recommended because they detect the disease earlier and save lives. In the case of mammograms, women who follow the recommended schedules after age 50 reduce their mortality rates by 26% in followups of 10 years or so after diagnosis (Kerlikowske et al., 1995). A national survey found that about 70% of American women over 40 years of age had had a mammogram in the prior 2 years, but the rate was much lower for poor and less educated women (USBC, 2003). Explicitly describing to a woman her relatively high risk of breast cancer due to her family history increases the likelihood that she will increase her frequency of mammograms (Curry et al., 1993). Among elderly middle- and upper-middle-class women, the main reasons for not having mammograms are the fear of pain and radiation (Fullerton et al., 1996).

Tertiary Prevention

When a serious injury occurs or a disease progresses beyond the early stages, the condition often leads to lasting or irreversible damage. **Tertiary prevention** involves actions to contain or retard this damage, prevent disability or recurrence, and rehabilitate the patient. For people with severe arthritis, for instance, tertiary prevention includes doing exercises for physical therapy and taking medication to control inflammation and pain. In the treatment of incurable forms of cancer, the goal may be simply to keep the patient reasonably comfortable and the disease in remission as long as possible. People who suffer disabling injuries may undergo intensive long-term physical therapy to regain the use of their limbs or develop other means for independent functioning.

PROBLEMS IN PROMOTING WELLNESS

The process of preventing illness and injury can be thought of as operating as a *system*, in which the individual, his or her family, health professionals, and the community each play a role. According to health psychologist Craig Ewart (1991b), many interrelated factors and problems can impair the effectiveness of each component in the system, and each component affects each other. Let's look at some of these factors, beginning with those within the individual.

Factors Within the Individual

People who consider ways to promote their own health often face an uphill battle with themselves. One problem is that many people perceive some healthful behaviors as less appealing or convenient than their unhealthful alternatives. Some people deal with this situation by maintaining a balance in their lives, setting reasonable limits on the unhealthful behaviors they perform. But other people do not, opting too frequently in favor of pleasure, sometimes vowing to change in the future: "I'll go on a diet next week," for example. They see little incentive to change immediately, especially if they think they are healthy. Even when individuals know they have health problems, many drop out of treatment or fail to follow some of the recommendations of their physician.

Four other factors within the individual are also important. First, adopting wellness lifestyles may require individuals to change longstanding behaviors that have become habitual and may involve addictions, as in cigarette smoking. Habitual and addictive behaviors are very difficult to modify. Second, people need to have certain cognitive resources, such as the knowledge and skills, to know what health behaviors to adopt, to make

"ENOUGH, LORETTA! YOU MUST BE HALFWAY TO ENGLAND BY NOW!"

Reprinted courtesy of Bunny Hoest.

plans for changing existing behavior and to overcome obstacles to change, such as having little time or no place to exercise. Third, individuals need sufficient self-efficacy regarding their ability to carry out the change. Without self-efficacy, their motivation to change will be impaired. Last, being sick or taking certain drugs can affect people's moods and energy levels, which may affect their cognitive resources and motivation.

Interpersonal Factors

Many social factors influence people's likelihood to adopt health behaviors. These factors include whether they have friends or family who model the behaviors and receive social support and encouragement for trying to change their lifestyles.

People living in a family system may encounter problems in their efforts to promote wellness. Some problems come about because the family is composed of individuals, each with his or her own motivations and habits. Suppose, for instance, that a member of a family wants to consume less cholesterol, but no one else is willing to stop eating high-cholesterol foods, such as butter, eggs, and red meats. Or suppose the person has begun exercising three times a week, but this regimen disrupts the daily routine of another family member. The interpersonal conflicts that circumstances like these can create in the family may undermine preventive efforts that the majority of family members support. Similar interpersonal conflicts can undermine prevention efforts among friends, classmates at school or college, and fellow employees at work.

Factors in the Community

People are more likely to adopt healthful behaviors if these behaviors are promoted or encouraged by community organizations, such as governmental agencies and the health care system. Health professionals face unique problems in trying to promote wellness. For instance, they need more accurate information regarding their patients' health-related behaviors and how to intervene to change unhealthful behaviors effectively. Also, medical practitioners have traditionally focused their attention on treating, rather than preventing, illness and injury. But this focus has begun to change, and physicians are becoming increasingly interested in prevention (Radecki & Brunton, 1992).

The larger community faces an enormous array of problems in trying to prevent illness and injury. These problems include having insufficient funds for public health projects and research, needing to adjust to and communicate with individuals of very different ages and sociocultural backgrounds, and providing health care for those who need it most. Also, people's health insurance may not cover preventive medical services. Among the most difficult problems communities face is trying to balance public health and economic priorities. For example, suppose the surrounding community of an industry is subjected to potentially unhealthful conditions, such as toxic substances. But the community depends heavily on that industry for jobs and tax revenue, and the cost of reducing the potential for harm would force the company out of business. What should the community do? Many such dilemmas exist in most societies throughout the world.

WHAT DETERMINES PEOPLE'S HEALTH-RELATED BEHAVIOR?

If people were all like Mr. Spock of the TV show *Star Trek*, the answer to the question of what determines people's health-related behavior would be simple: facts and logic, for the most part. These people would have no conflicting motivations in adopting wellness lifestyles to become as healthy as they can be. In this section we examine the complex factors that affect health-related behavior.

GENERAL FACTORS IN HEALTH-RELATED BEHAVIOR

The "average" person can describe healthful behaviors and generate a fairly complete list: "Don't smoke," "Don't drink too much, and don't drive if you do," "Eat balanced meals, and don't overeat," "Get regular exercise," and so on. But practicing these acts is another matter. Several processes affect people's health habits, and one factor is *heredity*. Genetic factors influence some health-related behaviors—excessive alcohol use provides a good example. Twin studies and adoption studies have confirmed that heredity plays a role in the development of alcoholism (Ciraulo & Renner, 1991; Schuckit, 1985). As we will see in Chapter 7, the exact nature of this role and the relative degree to which genetic and psychosocial factors are involved are unknown.

Learning

People also learn health-related behavior, particularly by way of *operant conditioning*, whereby behavior changes because of its consequences (Sarafino, 2001). Three types of consequences are important:

1. **Reinforcement.** When we do something that brings a pleasant, wanted, or satisfying consequence, the tendency to repeat that behavior is increased or *reinforced*. A child who receives something she wants, such as a nickel, for brushing her teeth at bedtime is more likely to brush again the following night. The nickel in this example is a positive reinforcer partly because it was wanted and partly because it was *added* to the situation. But reinforcement can also occur in a different way. Suppose you have a headache, you take aspirin, and the headache goes away. In this case, your headache was unpleasant and your behavior of taking aspirin *removed* it from the situation. The headache is called a "negative" reinforcer because it was *unwanted* or *unpleasant* and it was *taken away* from the situation. In both cases of reinforcement, the end result is a desirable state of affairs from the person's point of view.

2. **Extinction.** If the consequences that maintain a behavior are eliminated, the response tendency gradually weakens. The process or procedure of extinction exists only if no alternative maintaining stimuli (reinforcers) for the behavior have supplemented or taken the place of the original consequences. In the above example of tooth-brushing behavior, if the money is no longer given, the child may continue brushing if another reinforcer exists, such as praise from her parents or her own satisfaction with the appearance of her teeth.

3. **Punishment.** When we do something that brings an unpleasant consequence, the behavior tends to be suppressed. A child who gets a scolding from his parents for playing with matches is less likely to repeat that behavior, especially if his parents might see him. The influence of punishment on future behavior depends on whether the person expects the behavior will lead to punishment again. Take, for example, people who injure themselves (punishment) jogging—those who think they could be injured again are less likely to resume jogging than those who do not.

We've seen that people can learn by observing the behavior of others—a process called *modeling* (Bandura, 1969, 1986). In this kind of learning, the consequences the model receives affect the behavior of the observer. If a teenager sees people enjoying and receiving social attention for smoking cigarettes, these people serve as powerful models and increase the likelihood that the teenager will begin smoking too. But if models receive punishment for smoking, such as being avoided by classmates at school, the teenager may be less likely to smoke. In general, people are more likely to perform the behavior they observe if the model is *similar to themselves*—that is, of the same sex, age, or race—and is a *high-status person*, such as a physically attractive individual, movie star, or well-known athlete. Advertisers of products such as alcoholic beverages know these facts and use them in their commercials.

If a behavior becomes firmly established, it tends to be *habitual*; that is, the person often performs it automatically and without awareness. For example, a man who smokes and has a head cold might be engaged in an activity, catch a glimpse of a pack of cigarettes, and respond "by automatically reaching out, taking one, and starting to smoke without at all being aware of what he has done. Only when the irritation produced in his nose and throat . . . by the smoke 'captures his attention' is he likely to disengage in smoking behavior" (Hunt et al., 1979, p. 115). Even though the behavior may have been learned because it was reinforced by positive consequences, it is now less dependent on consequences and more dependent on antecedent cues (seeing a pack of cigarettes) with which it has been linked in the past (Sarafino, 2001). *Antecedents* are internal or external stimuli that precede and set the occasion for a behavior. A smoker who says, "I have to have a cigarette with my coffee after breakfast," is pointing out an antecedent. Behaviors that become habitual can be very difficult to change.

Habitual behaviors are hard to change, people need to develop well behaviors as early as possible and eliminate unhealthful activities as soon as they appear. Families play a major role in children's learning of health-related behaviors (Baranowski & Nader, 1985). Children observe, for example, the dietary, exercise, and smoking habits of other family members and may be encouraged to behave in similar ways. Children who observe and receive encouragement for healthful behaviors at home are more likely than others to develop good health habits.

Social, Personality, and Emotional Factors

Many health-related behaviors are affected by *social* factors (Baranowski & Nader, 1985; Burg & Seeman, 1994; Kirscht, 1983). We just saw that friends and family can encourage or discourage children's practice of health-related behaviors, such as smoking and exercising, by providing consequences, such as praise or complaints, for a behavior, modeling it, and conveying a value for good health. These social processes may also lead to gender differences in health behavior, such as the greater physical activity of American boys than girls. Very different patterns of encouragement may lead boys more than girls toward healthful physical activity.

Two other factors that are linked to health-related behavior are the person's *personality* and *emotional state*, particularly stress. One personality characteristic that is associated with practicing health behavior is conscientiousness. People who score high on a test of conscientiousness are more likely to take prescribed medications and follow the recommended schedule for getting mammograms than those who score low on this trait (Christensen & Smith, 1995; Siegler, Feaganes, & Rimer, 1995). The role of emotions can be seen in two ways. First, among women who have a close relative with breast cancer and are low in conscientiousness, those who are very distressed about cancer are especially unlikely to have a mammogram (Schwartz et al., 1999). A brief cognitive intervention to enhance coping skills can reduce cancer distress among women who have a close relative with cancer and substantially improve their preventive behavior (Audrain et al., 1999). Second, people who experience high levels of stress engage in less exercise and consume poorer diets and more alcohol and cigarettes than those who experience less stress (Baer et al., 1987; Cartwright et al., 2003; Ng & Jeffery, 2003). If you ask people why they smoke, for example, they often will say, "To relieve tension." Many people cite coping with stress as an important reason for continuing to smoke (Gottlieb, 1983).

Perception and Cognition

The *symptoms* people experience can influence their health-related behaviors. The way they react varies from ignoring the problem to seeking immediate professional care. Certainly when the perceived symptoms are severe—as with excruciating pain, obvious bone fractures, profuse bleeding, or very high fever—almost everyone who has access to a health care system will try to use it (Rosenstock & Kirscht, 1979). When symptoms are not so severe, people often adjust their health habits, such as by limiting certain foods and drink, to meet the needs of the health problem as they see it (Harris & Guten, 1979).

Cognitive factors play an important role in the health behaviors people perform. As we saw earlier, people must have correct knowledge about the health issue and the ability to solve problems that arise when trying to implement healthful behavior, such as how to fit an exercise routine into their schedules. People also make many judgments that have an impact on their health. They assess the general condition of their health: Is it good or bad? They also make decisions about other questions, such as: Should I cut back on the salt in my diet? If I begin an exercise program, will I stick to it? But the answers they produce can be based on misconceptions, as when hypertensive patients overestimate their ability to sense when their blood pressure is high (Baumann & Leventhal, 1985; Brondolo et al., 1999; Pennebaker & Watson, 1988). Hypertensive patients generally report that they can tell when their blood pressure is up, citing symptoms—headache, warmth or flushing face, dizziness, and nervousness—that are actually poor estimators of blood pressure. People's assessments of their blood pressure often correlate with their symptoms and moods, but not with their actual blood pressure. The potential harm in their erroneous beliefs is that patients often alter their medication-taking behavior, and sometimes drop out of treatment, on the basis of their subjective assessments of their blood pressure. Clearly, beliefs are important determinants of health behavior.

Another important belief that can impair health behavior is called *unrealistic optimism*. Neil Weinstein (1982) studied how optimistically people view their future health by asking them, "Compared to other people your age and sex, are your chances of getting lung cancer greater than, less than, or about the same as theirs?" He then had students fill out a questionnaire with a long list of health problems, rating each problem for their own likelihood of developing it, relative to other students of the same sex at the university. The results revealed that the students believed they were less likely than others to develop three-quarters of the health problems listed, including alcoholism, diabetes, heart attack, lung cancer, and venereal disease. They believed they were more susceptible than other students to only one of the health problems, that of ulcers. In a later study, Weinstein (1987) used similar questions in a mailed survey with 18- to 65-year-old adults in the general population. He found that these people were just as unrealistically optimistic as the students and that this optimism is based on illogical ideas—for instance, that they are at lower risk than other people if the health problem occurs rarely and has not happened to them yet. These factors do not affect one's risk relative to that of others.

Do people remain optimistic about their health when they are sick or when a threat of illness is clear? Evidently not. Using a procedure similar to Weinstein's, a study found that university students who were waiting for treatment at the student health center were less optimistic about their future health than were healthy students in a psychology course (Kulik & Mahler, 1987b). Another study was conducted with students in Poland, just after the radioactive cloud reached their community from the explosion of the atomic power plant at Chernobyl in the former Soviet Union (Dolinski, Gromski, & Zawisza, 1987). Although these people believed they were less likely than others to have a heart attack or be injured in an accident, they believed they were equally likely to develop cancer and *more* likely than others to suffer illness effects of the radiation over the next several years. Thus, in the face of a real threat, they showed "unrealistic pessimism" regarding their health.

Studies of optimistic and pessimistic beliefs are important for three reasons. First, they reveal that feelings of *invulnerability* are not a unique feature of adolescence (Cohn et al., 1995). Second, people who practice health behaviors tend to feel they would otherwise be at risk for associated health problems (Becker & Rosenstock, 1984). This means that people with unrealistically optimistic beliefs about their health are unlikely to take preventive action. Third, health professionals may be able to implement programs to address these beliefs in helping people see their risks more realistically. The next section examines the role of people's health beliefs in more detail.

THE ROLE OF BELIEFS AND INTENTIONS

Suppose your friend believed in *reflexology*, a "healing" method that involves massaging specific areas of the feet to treat illnesses. The belief that underlies this method is that each area of the foot connects to a specific area of the body—the toes connect to the head, for instance, and the middle of the arch links to certain endocrine glands (Livermore, 1991). For a patient with recurrent headaches, a reflexologist's treatment might include massaging the toes. Your friend would probably try ways to prevent and treat illness that are different from those most other people would try. Psychologists are interested in the role of health beliefs in people's practice of health behaviors. A widely–researched and accepted theory of why people do and do not practice these behaviors is called the health belief model (Becker, 1979; Becker & Rosenstock, 1984; Rosenstock, 1966). Let's see what this theory proposes.

The Health Belief Model

According to the **health belief model,** the likelihood that a person will take *preventive action*—that is, perform some health behavior—depends directly on the outcome of two assessments he or she makes. Figure 6–2 shows that one assessment pertains to the *threat* the person feels regarding a health problem, and the other weighs the *pros and cons* of taking the action.

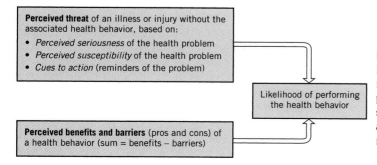

Perceived threat of an illness or injury without the associated health behavior, based on:
- *Perceived seriousness* of the health problem
- *Perceived susceptibility* of the health problem
- *Cues to action* (reminders of the problem)

Likelihood of performing the health behavior

Perceived benefits and barriers (pros and cons) of a health behavior (sum = benefits – barriers)

Figure 6–2 The health belief model. People's likelihood of taking preventive action is determined by two assessments they make: their perceived threat of the health problem and the sum of pros and cons they perceive in taking action. Many factors contribute to these assessments. (Adapted from Becker & Rosenstock, 1984, Figure 2.)

Three factors influence people's *perceived threat*—that is, the degree to which they feel threatened or worried by the prospect of a particular health problem:

- *Perceived seriousness* of the health problem. People consider how severe the organic and social consequences are likely to be if they develop the problem or leave it untreated. The more serious they believe its effects will be, the more likely they are to perceive it as a threat and take preventive action.

- *Perceived susceptibility* to the health problem. People evaluate the likelihood of their developing the problem. The more risk they perceive for themselves, the more likely they are to perceive it as a threat and take action.

- *Cues to action.* Being reminded or alerted about a potential health problem increases the likelihood of perceiving a threat and taking action. Cues to action can take many forms, such as a public service announcement of a dangerous storm approaching, a friend or relative developing an illness, a newspaper article about the illness, or a reminder phone call for an upcoming medical appointment.

Figure 6–2 shows that in weighing the pros and cons of performing a health behavior, people assess the *benefits*—such as being healthier or reducing health risks—and the *barriers* or costs they *perceive* in taking action. What barriers might people see in preventive action? For the health behavior of getting a physical checkup, the barriers might include financial considerations ("Can I afford the bills?"), psychosocial consequences ("People will think I'm getting old if I start having checkups"), and physical considerations ("My doctor's office is across town, and I don't have a car"). The outcome of weighing the benefits against the barriers is an assessed *sum*: the extent to which taking the action is more beneficial for them than not taking the action. This assessed sum combines with the perceived threat of illness or injury to determine the likelihood of preventive action. Thus, for the health behavior of having a medical checkup, people who feel threatened by an illness and believe the benefits of having a checkup outweigh the barriers are likely to go ahead with it. But people who do not feel threatened or assess that the barriers are too strong are unlikely to have the checkup. According to the

health belief model, these processes apply to primary, secondary, and tertiary prevention activities.

The theory also proposes that characteristics of individuals can influence their perceptions of benefits, barriers, and threat. These factors include the person's age, sex, race, ethnic background, social class, personality traits, and knowledge about or prior contact with the health problem. Thus, for example, people who are poor are likely to see strong barriers to getting medical treatment. Women, but not men, over 50 are likely to perceive a substantial risk of breast cancer. And elderly individuals whose close friends have developed severe cases of cancer or heart disease are more likely to perceive a personal threat of these illnesses than young adults whose friends are in good health.

Has research generally supported the health belief model's explanation of health-related behavior? The model has generated a great deal of research, much of which has upheld its predictions for a variety of health behaviors, including getting vaccinations, having regular dental visits, and taking part in exercise programs (Becker, 1979; Becker & Rosenstock, 1984; Curry & Emmons, 1994; Kirscht, 1983; Rosenstock & Kirscht, 1979). For instance, compared to people who do not take prescribed medication as directed or do not stick with dietary programs, those who *do* are more likely to believe they would be susceptible to the associated illness without the behavior and that the benefits of protective action exceed the barriers. Perceived barriers and perceived susceptibility (risk, which leads to perceived threat) appear to be the main elements in the theory for predicting health behavior, such as performing breast self-examinations (BSEs), and strong barriers may have more influence than susceptibility (Aiken, Gerend, & Jackson, 2001). Research has also supported the role of cues to action: women are more likely to perform BSEs if they receive reminders (Craun & Deffenbacher, 1987).

Despite the health belief model's success, it has some shortcomings. One shortcoming is that it does not account for health-related behaviors people perform habitually, such as tooth brushing—behaviors that probably originated and have continued without the person's considering health threats, benefits, and costs. Another problem is that there is no standard way of measuring its components, such as perceived susceptibility and seriousness. Different studies have used different questionnaires to measure the same factors, thereby making it difficult to compare the results across studies. These problems do not mean that the theory is wrong, but that it is incomplete. We now turn to another theory that focuses on the effect of people's beliefs on their practice of health-related behavior.

The Theory of Planned Behavior

Suppose you are having dinner at a restaurant with Dan, a friend who is overweight, and you wonder whether he will order dessert. How could you predict his behavior? That's simple—you could ask what he *intends* to do. According to the **theory of planned behavior** (Ajzen, 1985), an expanded version of the *theory of reasoned action* (Ajzen & Fishbein, 1980), people decide their intention in advance of most voluntary behaviors, and intentions are the best predictors of what people will do.

What determines people's intentions? The theory indicates that three judgments determine a person's intention to perform a behavior, which we'll illustrate with a girl named Ellie who has decided to start exercising:

- *Attitude regarding the behavior*, which is basically a judgment of whether or not the behavior is a good thing to do. Ellie has decided that exercising "would be a good thing for me to do." This judgment is based on two expectations: the likely *outcome* of the behavior (such as, "If I exercise, I will be healthier and more attractive") and whether the outcome would be *rewarding* (for example, "Being healthy and good looking will be satisfying and pleasant").

- *Subjective norm*. This judgment reflects the impact of social pressure or influence on the behavior's acceptability or appropriateness. Ellie has decided that exercising "is a socially appropriate thing for me to do." This decision is based on her beliefs regarding *others' opinions* about the behavior (such as, "My family and friends think I should exercise") and her *motivation to comply* with those opinions (as in, "I want to do what they want").

- *Perceived behavioral control*, or the person's expectation of success in performing the contemplated behavior (which is very similar to the concept of *self-efficacy*). Ellie thinks she can do the exercises and stick to the program.

The theory of planned behavior proposes that these judgments combine to produce an intention that

leads to performance of the behavior. If Ellie had the opposite beliefs, such as exercising is uncomfortable and she won't find time to exercise, she probably wouldn't generate an intention to exercise and thus would not do so.

Self-efficacy is an important component. When deciding to practice a health behavior, people appraise their efficacy on the basis of the effort required, complexity of the task, and other aspects of the situation, such as whether they are likely to receive help from other people (Schunk & Carbonari, 1984). Research has found that self-efficacy does influence people's health behavior. Cigarette smokers who believe they can't kick the habit typically don't try, but smokers who believe they can succeed in quitting often do (DiClemente, Prochaska, & Gilbertini, 1985). Similarly, individuals who believe they can succeed in losing weight are more likely to try and to succeed than those with less self-efficacy (Schifter & Ajzen, 1985). And patients recovering from serious illnesses, such as heart or respiratory disease, who believe they can perform a progressive program of recovery behaviors, such as walking various distances, are more likely to adhere to the program than those who have less self-efficacy (Jenkins & Gortner, 1998; Kaplan, Atkins, & Reinsch, 1984).

Studies have found support for the theory in explaining several health-related behaviors. A study by Richard Bagozzi (1981), for example, had possible donors for a Red Cross blood drive fill out a survey in the week prior to the drive to assess their intentions and attitudes, such as the degree of pleasantness or unpleasantness, toward giving blood. The Red Cross provided information on whether the people actually gave blood. As the theory predicts, attitudes about giving blood were related to the actual behavior through their impact on the people's intentions. Other studies have found that attitudes and intentions influence people's quitting smoking cigarettes (Norman, Conner, & Bell, 1999), exercising (Wurtele & Maddux, 1987), eating healthful diets (Conner, Norman, & Bell, 2002), and practicing testicular self-examination (TSEs) (Moore, Barling, & Hood, 1998). In addition, a study on using condoms for safer sex found that if preparatory behaviors, such as buying and carrying condoms, occur after the intention is made, the likelihood of actually using condoms in sex increases greatly (Bryan, Fisher, & Fisher, 2002).

What shortcomings does the theory of planned behavior have? One problem is that intentions and behavior are only moderately related—people do not always do what they plan (or *claim* they plan) to do. People's attitudes seem to predict some health-related behaviors, such as alcohol use, but not others, such as smoking and drunk driving (Stacy, Bentler, & Flay, 1994). Another problem is that the theory is incomplete; it does not include, for example, the important role of people's prior experience with the behavior. In the blood donation study we just described, the subjects were also asked about their past behavior in donating or not donating blood (Bagozzi, 1981). Of those subjects who said they intended to give blood, those who had given before were more likely to give than those who had not donated in the past. Similarly, other studies have found that people's history of performing a health-related behavior, such as exercising or using alcohol or drugs, is a strong predictor of their future practice of that behavior (Bentler & Speckart, 1979; Godin et al., 1987). Thus, for example, compared to adults who have engaged in little exercise in the past, those who have exercised are much more likely to carry out their promises to exercise in the future.

The health belief model and the theory of planned behavior provide valid explanations for parts of the process that determines people's practice of health-related behavior. At their core, both theories assume that people weigh perceived benefits and costs and behave according to the outcome of their analysis. But neither approach is sufficient, and both have limitations (Janis, 1984; Kirscht, 1983; Weinstein, 1988). One weakness in these theories is that they assume people think about risks in a detailed fashion, knowing what diseases are associated with different behaviors and estimating the likelihood of becoming seriously ill. In reality, people may modify their lifestyles, such as reducing coffee consumption, for very vague reasons, such as, "My doctor says coffee is bad for you." People appear to be especially inaccurate in estimating the degree of increased risk when the risks of illness, such as cancer, increase beyond moderate levels—for example, for individuals who smoke more than 15 cigarettes a day (Sastre, Mullet, & Sorum, 1999; Weinstein, 2000).

The Stages of Change Model

A wife's letter in an Ann Landers newspaper column once described her worry about her husband, who had suffered a heart attack but hadn't tried to lose

weight or exercise as his doctor recommended. This situation is not uncommon. Although there are probably many reasons why this man hadn't changed his behavior, one may be that he wasn't "ready." Readiness to change is the main focus of a theory called the **stages of change model** (also called the *transtheoretical model* because it includes factors described in other theories) (DiClemente et al., 1991; Prochaska & DiClemente, 1984; Prochaska, DiClemente, & Norcross, 1992). The model outlines five *stages* of intentional behavior change:

1. *Precontemplation.* People in this stage are not considering changing, at least during the next several months or so. These people may have decided against changing or just never thought about it.

2. *Contemplation.* During this stage, people are aware a problem exists and are seriously considering changing to a healthier behavior within the next several months. But they are not yet ready to make a commitment to take action.

3. *Preparation.* At this stage, individuals are ready to try to change and plan to pursue a behavioral goal, such as stopping smoking, in the next month. They may have tried to reach that goal in the past year without being fully successful. For instance, these people might have reduced their smoking by half but did not yet quit completely.

4. *Action.* This stage spans a period of time, usually 6 months, from the start of people's successful and active efforts to change a behavior.

5. *Maintenance.* People in this stage work to maintain the successful behavioral changes they achieved. Although this stage can last indefinitely, researchers often define its length as, say, 6 months, for followup assessment.

According to the stages of change model, people who are currently in one stage show different psychosocial characteristics from people in other stages. For instance, people in the precontemplation stage regarding an unhealthy behavior, such as eating a high-cholesterol diet, are likely to have less self-efficacy and see more barriers than benefits for changing that behavior than people in the more advanced stages. Efforts to change the behavior are not likely to succeed until these individuals advance through the stages. Is it possible to help them advance? One of the values of the stages of change model is that it describes important characteristics of people at each stage, enabling an intervention to *match* useful strategies to help individuals advance to the next stage (Perz, DiClemente, & Carbonari, 1996; Prochaska, DiClemente, & Norcross, 1992).

Let's consider an example of matching. Suppose you are a nurse providing care to an elderly woman with heart disease who doesn't exercise, even though her physician advised her to do so. If she is at the pre-contemplation stage, you might talk with her about why exercise would help her and why not exercising would harm her physically, for instance, and have her generate ways this activity would improve her general functioning. The goal at this point is just to get the person to consider changing the behavior. If she is at the contemplation stage, the goal might be to help her decide to change soon. Discussing the benefits and barriers she perceives in exercising, finding ways to overcome barriers, and showing her that she can do the physical activities would help.

The stages of change model is a very useful theory. Studies have confirmed that people at higher stages are more likely than others to succeed at adopting healthful behaviors, such as quitting cigarette smoking (Spencer et al., 2002), getting breast cancer testing (Rakowski et al., 1992), exercising (Marshall & Biddle, 2001), and using safer sex practices (Bowen & Trotter, 1995). Research has generally confirmed that matching an intervention to people's stage of readiness improves its success in helping to change unhealthful behaviors, such as smoking (Spencer et al., 2002).

In the preceding sections, we have examined many aspects of people's beliefs and intentions that appear to influence their health-related behavior. These aspects include people's perceived susceptibility to illness, perceived barriers and benefits to changing unhealthy behavior, ideas about what behaviors are socially acceptable and encouraged by family and friends, self-efficacy beliefs, and readiness to change. These factors seem sensible for individuals to consider, but the decisions they make are often *irrational* or *unwise*. The flawed decisions that people make about their health often result from motivational and emotional processes that are not addressed in the theories. For instance, these theories do

> not provide an adequate explanation for the widespread tendency of patients who have painful heart attacks to delay obtaining medical aid. . . . Typically, when the afflicted person thinks of the

> possibility that it might be a heart attack, he or she assumes that "it couldn't be happening to me." The patients' delay of treatment is not attributable to unavailability of medical aid or transportation delays; approximately 75% of the delay time elapses before a patient decides to contact a physician. (Janis, 1984, pp. 331–332)

Thus, theories that focus on rational thinking do not adequately consider the processes we're about to see that can override logical decision-making.

THE ROLE OF LESS RATIONAL PROCESSES

Although body builders generally know that using anabolic steroids can harm their health, some may try to justify using these substances to build muscles with statements like, "Experts have told us almost everything is bad for us and later found out lots of things aren't." Why are the decisions people make regarding health-related behavior not more rational? We'll look first at motivational factors that influence people's decisions.

Motivational Factors

Research findings indicate that people's desires and preferences influence the judgments they make of the validity and utility of new information, through a process called **motivated reasoning** (Kunda, 1990). In one form of motivated reasoning, individuals who prefer to reach a particular conclusion, such as to continue to eat fatty foods or smoke cigarettes, tend to use biased cognitive processes: they search for reasons to accept supportive information and discount disconfirming information. The reasons they choose seem "reasonable" to them, even if the logic is actually faulty. People's tendency to use biased reasoning processes appears to be fairly stable and consistent across a variety of situations (Sarafino, Groff, & DePaulo, 2000).

Studies have demonstrated nonrational thought processes in several types of health-related decisions. First, people with a chronic illness, such as diabetes, who tend to use illogical thought patterns in health-related situations tend not to follow medical advice for managing their illness (Christensen, Moran, & Weibe, 1999). Second, people who use defense mechanisms a lot to cope with stressful information are more likely than other individuals to deny that they are at risk for AIDS, especially if their risk of infection is high (Gladis et al., 1992). Perhaps their high feeling of threat motivates their use of denial. Similarly, individuals seem to use irrelevant information, such as a sexual partner's attractiveness, to judge the risks in having sex with that person (Blanton & Gerrard, 1997; Gold & Skinner, 1996). Third, people who smoke cigarettes give lower ratings of risk than nonsmokers do when asked to rate their own risk of developing smoking-related diseases, such as lung cancer (Lee, 1989; McCoy et al., 1992). Beliefs like these appear very resistant to change (Kreuter & Strecher, 1995; Weinstein & Klein, 1995).

False Hope and Willingness

Here are two features of health-related behaviors which the theories we've considered don't account for well. First, you've probably heard that most people who lose weight gain it back within a year or so, yet they try again at a later time. Similar patterns occur for other behavior changes, such as quitting smoking or starting to exercise. Second, many risky behaviors occur spontaneously, without the individuals having thought it through.

It's encouraging to know that people who don't maintain a healthier behavior try again, but why do they decide to retry if they've failed previously and are likely to fail again? The reason may be that they develop **false hopes,** believing without rational basis that they will succeed. They form false hopes for at least two reasons (Polivy & Herman, 2002). First, because they did succeed for a while, that success provides reinforcement for the efforts they made to that point. Second, they misinterpret their failures. The real reason most people fail to maintain a changed behavior is that they expected too large a change in their behavior, too great an effect it would have for them, and too quick and easy a process of change. But people who don't maintain a health behavior decide instead that they just didn't try hard enough for enough time—after all, they succeeded initially.

What risky behaviors occur without careful thought? Lots, maybe most. People often find themselves in unexpected situations that give them the opportunity to perform an attractive behavior, such as drinking a bit too much or having sex, but there's some risk. In this type of situation, the critical issue may not be whether they "intend" to engage in a risky behavior but whether they are *willing* to do it. In this context, **willingness** to engage in a risky behavior

depends on four factors (Gibbons et al., 1998). Two of the factors that increase willingness are positive subjective norms and attitudes toward the behavior, which we considered as elements of the theory of planned behavior. The other factors that increase willingness are having engaged in the behavior previously and having a positive *prototype* for the behavior—a favorable social image of the type of person who would perform the behavior.

Emotional Factors

Stress also affects the cognitive processes people use in making decisions. **Conflict theory** presents a model that accounts for both rational and irrational decision making, and stress is an important factor in this model (Janis, 1984; Janis & Mann, 1977). The model describes the cognitive sequence by which people make important decisions, including health-related decisions. According to conflict theory, the cognitive sequence people use in making a stable decision starts when an event challenges their current course of action or lifestyle. The challenge can be either a *threat*, such as a symptom of illness or a news story about the dangers of smoking, or an *opportunity*, such as the chance to join a free program at work to quit smoking. This produces an appraisal of the risk: if no risk is seen, the behavior stays the same and the decision-making process ends; but if the answer is "yes," the process continues—for instance, with a survey of alternatives for dealing with the challenge.

Conflict theory proposes that people experience stress with all major decisions, particularly those relating to health, because of the importance of and conflicts about what to do. People's coping with decisional conflict depends on their perceptions of the presence or absence of three factors: *risks, hope,* and *adequate time.* These three factors produce different coping patterns, two of which are:

- *Hypervigilance.* People sometimes see serious risks in their current behavior *and* those alternatives they have considered. If they believe they may still find a better solution *but* think they are rapidly running out of time, they experience high stress. These people tend to search frantically for a solution—and may choose an alternative hastily, especially if it promises immediate relief.

- *Vigilance.* People who perceive serious risks in all possibilities they have considered *but* believe they may find a better alternative and have the time to search experience only moderate levels of stress. Under these conditions, people tend to search thoroughly and make rational choices.

When the challenge is very serious, such as a physician's warning or obvious symptoms of illness, vigilance is the most adaptive coping pattern. Although the conflict theory has not been tested sufficiently to know its strengths and weaknesses, there is little question that the impact of stress is an important determinant of preventive action, particularly in people's symptom-based and sick-role behaviors.

We have examined how many different psychological and social factors can affect people's health behavior. We have not, however, considered the influence of age, sex, and sociocultural background, which we examine next.

DEVELOPMENTAL, GENDER, AND SOCIOCULTURAL FACTORS IN HEALTH

It comes as no surprise that people's health changes across the life span, that women and men possess some differences in health risks and needs, and that variations in preventive behavior occur between individuals of different social classes and ethnic backgrounds. What are some of these changes and - differences, and why do they exist? Let's examine these health issues, starting with the role of development.

DEVELOPMENT AND HEALTH

The biological, psychological, and social factors that affect people's health change throughout the life span, causing individuals to face different health risks and problems as they develop. For instance, adolescents and young adults are at relatively high risk for injury from automobile accidents, but older adults are at relatively high risk for hypertension and heart disease. As a result, people's preventive needs and goals change with age. Table 6.2 presents main preventive goals for each period in the life span. During the beginning of the life span, and sometimes toward the end, the individual may lack the ability to take preventive action, and other people assume that responsibility.

Table 6.2   *Prevention Goals over the Life Span*

Health Goals of Gestation and Infancy

- To allow the mother to have a healthy, full-term pregnancy and rapid recovery after a normal delivery.
- To facilitate the live birth of a normal baby, free of congenital or developmental damage.
- To help both mother and father achieve the knowledge and capacity to provide for the physical, emotional, and social needs of the baby.
- To establish immunity against specified infectious diseases.
- To detect and prevent certain other diseases and problems before irreparable damage occurs.

Health Goals of Childhood and Adolescence

- To facilitate the child's optimal physical, emotional, and social growth and development.
- To establish healthy behavioral patterns (in children) for nutrition, exercise, study, recreation, and family life, as a foundation for a healthy lifetime lifestyle.
- To reinforce healthy behavior patterns (in adolescents), and discourage negative ones, in physical fitness, nutrition, exercise, study, work, recreation, sex, individual relations, driving, smoking, alcohol, and drugs.

Health Goals of Adulthood

- To prolong the period of maximum physical energy and to develop full mental, emotional, and social potential.
- To anticipate and guard against the onset of chronic disease through good health habits and early detection and treatment where effective.
- To detect as early as possible any of the major chronic diseases, including hypertension, heart disease, diabetes, and cancer, as well as vision, hearing, and dental impairments.

Health Goals in Old Age

- To minimize handicapping and discomfort from the onset of chronic conditions.
- To prepare in advance for retirement.
- To prolong the period of effective activity and ability to live independently, and avoid institutionalization so far as possible.
- When illness is terminal, to assure as little physical and mental stress as possible and to provide emotional support to patient and family.

Source: Based on Breslow & Somers (1977).

During Gestation and Infancy

Each year millions of babies around the world are born with birth defects; in the United States alone, there are 150,000 cases, or 3.6 out of every 100 births annually (MDBDF, 2004). These defects range from

A pregnant woman receives an ultrasound procedure in prenatal care to check the development of her baby. Following medical advice during pregnancy can enhance the healthfulness of her baby's prenatal environment.

relatively minor physical or mental abnormalities to gross deformities; some are not apparent until months or years later, and some are fatal. Birth defects result from genetic abnormalities and harmful factors in the fetal environment.

A mother can control much of the fetal environment through her behavior. Early in gestation, a *placenta* and *umbilical cord* develop and begin to transmit substances to the fetus from the mother's bloodstream. These substances typically consist mostly of nourishment, but they can also include hazardous microorganisms and chemicals that happen to be in her blood. We will consider three main hazards. First, the mother may be malnourished because of inadequate food supplies or knowledge of nutritional needs. Babies born to malnourished mothers tend to have low birth weights, poorly developed immune and central nervous systems, and a high risk of mortality in the first weeks after birth (Chandra, 1991; Huffman & del Carmen, 1990; Smart, 1991). Second, certain infections the mother may contract during pregnancy can also attack her gestating baby, sometimes causing permanent injury or death (LaBarba, 1984; Moore, 1983). For example, *rubella* (German measles) in the first several weeks of pregnancy may cause the baby to die or be severely deformed; the mother can protect the fetus by being vaccinated.

Third, various substances the mother uses may enter her bloodstream and harm the baby (Cook,

Petersen, & Moore, 1990; LaBarba, 1984). Babies exposed prenatally to addictive drugs, such as cocaine and heroin, are far more likely than others to die in infancy or be born with very low weights or malformations, such as of the heart (Lindenberg et al., 1991; MDBDF, 2004). Also, cigarette smoke exposure from the mother's smoking or from her environment—for instance, if the father smokes—is associated with low birth weight and other health problems in babies (DiFranza & Lew, 1995; Eliopoulos et al., 1994; Martinez et al., 1994). And the mother's drinking alcohol, especially heavy drinking, can cause *fetal alcohol syndrome*, which has several symptoms: (1) low birth weight and retarded subsequent growth, (2) subnormal intelligence, and (3) certain facial characteristics, such as small eye openings (Burns & Arnold, 1990; NIAAA, 1993). Ideally, expectant mothers should use *none* of these substances. Health education for pregnant women can help, such as by getting those who smoke to quit (Windsor et al., 1993).

Birth catapults the newborn into a new world, where risks continue. The rate of infant mortality in some developing countries is extremely high, greater than 100 per 1,000 live births for the first year of life (WHO, 2004). Although infant mortality is greater in the United States than in many other industrialized countries, its rate has declined since 1980 from 12.6 to 6.8 per 1,000 live births (USBC, 2003). Out of these, approximately half die within the first week. In early infancy, the baby's immunity to disease depends largely on the white blood cells and antibodies passed on by the mother prenatally and in her milk if she breastfeeds (Moore, 1983). Due to the immunity it gives to the baby, breast milk is sometimes called "nature's vaccine." Parents should arrange for the baby to begin a vaccination program early in infancy for such diseases as diphtheria, whooping cough, and polio.

Childhood and Adolescence

In the second year of life, toddlers are walking and beginning to "get into everything," exposing them to risk of injury, such as contact with sharp objects and chemicals around the house. In the United States, accidental injury is the leading cause of death during childhood and adolescence (Cataldo et al., 1986; USBC, 2003). Parents, teachers, and other caregivers can reduce the likelihood of injury by teaching children safety behaviors, supervising them when possible, and decreasing their access to dangerous situations, such as keeping chemicals out of reach. The role of cognitive processes in the practice of health-related behavior has important implications here, since cognitive abilities are immature in early childhood and become more sophisticated as children get older. With these advances, children are more able to make decisions and assume responsibility for promoting their own health and safety (Burbach & Peterson, 1986; Maddux et al., 1986).

Adolescence is a critical time in the development of preventive behavior. Although teenagers have the cognitive ability to make the logical decisions leading to healthful behavior, they face many temptations and forces—especially peer pressure—that lead them in other directions (Jessor, 1984; La Greca & Stone, 1985; Leffert & Petersen, 1998). This is the time when they stand the greatest chance of starting to smoke, drink, use drugs, and have sexual relations. These risky behaviors are interrelated: teens who smoke and drink are more likely to use marijuana and have unsafe sex (Duncan, Strycker, & Duncan, 1999). Teens also learn to drive, and too often combine this new skill with drinking and using drugs. Most teenage deaths in developed countries result from accidents. In the United States, death rates for accidents rise sharply during the teenage years and are several times as high for 15- to 24-year-olds as for younger age groups (USBC, 2003). All these newly acquired behaviors involve substantial health risks, which teenagers are highly susceptible to taking.

Adulthood and Aging

When people reach adulthood, they become less likely than they were in adolescence to take new behavioral risks that may impair their health. In general, older adults are more likely than younger ones to practice various health behaviors, such as eating healthful diets and getting medical checkups, even though both age groups believe in the value of these behaviors in preventing serious illnesses, such as heart attack and cancer (Belloc & Breslow, 1972; Leventhal, Prohaska, & Hirschman, 1985). This age difference may exist because older adults perceive themselves as more vulnerable to these illnesses than younger adults and engage in preventive acts for that reason. Then again, it may be that these age-related increases in practicing healthful behaviors simply reflect an increased rate of survival of people who engage in these habits.

Old age is not what it used to be. Older people in industrialized countries live longer and are in better financial and physical condition than in the past (Horn & Meer, 1987). One health behavior that generally declines as adults get older is regular vigorous exercise (Leventhal, Prohaska, & Hirschman, 1985). Many elderly people avoid physical exercise because they tend to exaggerate the danger that exertion poses to their health, underestimate their physical capabilities, and feel embarrassed by their performance of these activities (Woods & Birren, 1984).

GENDER AND HEALTH

In most countries of the world, an average female's expected life span at birth is at least a few years longer than a male's (WHO, 2004). The gap in life expectancy is especially wide in developed countries: newborn females can expect to outlive males by about 8 years in France and Poland, 7 years in Finland and Spain, and 6 years in Austria and the United States (NCHS, 2003). For people in the United States who survive to 65 years of age, women's remaining life expectancy is 3.2 years longer than men's (NCHS, 2003). The reason why females live longer involves both biological and behavioral factors (Cataldo et al., 1986; Greenglass & Noguchi, 1996; Reddy, Fleming, & Adesso, 1992; Williams, 2003). Some of these factors are:

- Physiological reactivity, such as blood pressure and catecholamine release, when under stress is greater in men than in women, which may make men more likely to develop cardiovascular disease.

- Males have shorter life expectancies in almost all countries of the world, and boys have higher death rates than girls even in infancy. Biological factors may underlie part of these gender differences in mortality.

- Behavioral factors are implicated in the fact that boys have far higher rates of injury than girls—such as from drowning, bicycling, and pedestrian traffic accidents.

- In adolescence and adulthood, males have far higher rates of injury and death from automobile accidents than females do.

- Men smoke more and drink more than women do, thereby making men more susceptible to cardiovascular and respiratory diseases, some forms of cancer, and cirrhosis of the liver.

- It may be that men's jobs, household work, and leisure activities pose greater health hazards than women's, but little or no research has been done on these issues.

One of the few behavioral advantages men have is that they get more strenuous exercise than women do. The practice of many other health-related behaviors is similar for men and women.

Does the longer life span of women mean that they have fewer health problems than men? Actually, the opposite is true (NCHS, 2003; Reddy, Fleming, & Adesso, 1992; Williams, 2003). For example, American women have much higher rates than men of acute illnesses, such as respiratory and digestive ailments, and nonfatal chronic diseases, such as varicose veins, arthritis, anemia, and headache. They also use medical drugs and services much more than men, even when pregnancy and other reproductive conditions are not counted.

SOCIOCULTURAL FACTORS AND HEALTH

Have people's health behaviors been improving in different cultures? An international survey on improvements in health behaviors across 2 years found that the percentage of people who reported increased exercise and decreased alcohol and red meat intake was much greater among Americans than Britons, whose percentage was greater than that of the French (Retchin et al., 1992). People's health behaviors are improving in industrialized nations, but the rates vary across cultures.

Cultural differences also exist within nations. In America, most people feel they are in pretty good health: a national survey of males and females of all ages and backgrounds found that fewer than 10% claimed to be in only "fair" to "poor" health (NCHS, 2000). But this was not true for all segments of the population. Compared with the population as a whole, people were much more likely to rate their health as "fair" or "poor" if they were over 45 years of age, or from the lower social classes, or of African American or American Indian background. As it turns out, these lower assessments reflect real health problems of the individuals these groups comprise.

Social Class and Minority Group Background

The concept of *social class*, or *socioeconomic status*, describes differences in people's resources, prestige, and power within a society (Filsinger, 1987; Williams & Rucker, 1996). These differences are reflected in three main characteristics: income, occupational prestige, and education. The lowest social classes in industrialized societies contain people who live in poverty or are homeless. By almost any gauge of wellness, health correlates with social class (Adler et al., 1994; Anderson & Armstead, 1995; Marmot, Kogevinas, & Elston, 1987; Ostrove, Feldman, & Adler, 1999). For example, individuals from lower classes are more likely than those from higher classes to:

- Be born with very low birth weight
- Die in infancy or in childhood
- Die in adulthood before age 65
- Have poorer overall health and develop a long-standing illness in adulthood
- Experience days of restricted activity because of illness

Not coincidentally, individuals from the lower classes have poorer health habits and attitudes than those from higher classes. For instance, they smoke more, participate less in vigorous exercise, and are less likely to feel that people can actively promote their own health (Adler et al., 1994; Marmot, Kogevinas, & Elston, 1987; Williams & Rucker, 1996). Research has also shown that people from the lower classes have less knowledge about risk factors for disease. They are also less likely than individuals from upper classes to receive health information from the mass media (Ribisl et al., 1998). Members of minority groups usually are disproportionately represented in the lower social classes.

Minority group background is an important risk factor for poor health. Today a baby born in Cuba stands a better chance of reaching the age of one than the average African American newborn in the United States (USBC, 2003; WHO, 2004). The rate of infant mortality in America is twice as high for Blacks as it is for Whites. Among babies who survive the first year, the life expectancy for an African American baby is about 6 years shorter than that for a White baby in America (USBC, 2003). Moreover, regardless of that African American baby's gender, he or she is far more likely than a same-sex White baby to develop a major chronic disease in its lifetime and to die of that disease. Figure 6–3 compares racial mortality data for four major causes of death and shows that the death rates for the three most deadly diseases are far higher for Blacks than for Whites. Although American racial

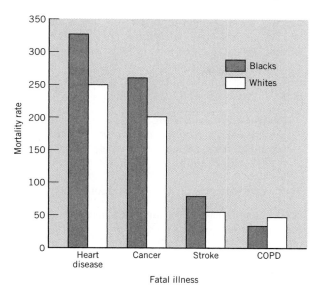

Figure 6–3 Death rates (per 100,000 individuals in the population) for Whites and Blacks in the United States, resulting from four leading chronic diseases (COPD is chronic obstructive lung disease). The rates are averaged for males and females and age-adjusted to take into account that mortality rates increase with age and that the average age of Blacks is less than that of Whites. (Data from NCHS, 2003, Tables 36, 37, 38, and 41.)

differences in health were much larger decades ago, they are still substantial and remain a dilemma and a national disgrace.

Three minority groups that have high levels of health problems and risks in the United States are Blacks, American Indians, and Hispanics. In general, the health problems and risk factors of Hispanics are intermediate, being neither as negative as those of Blacks and American Indians nor as positive as those of Whites (NCHS, 2003). Many individuals in these minority groups live in environments that do not encourage the practice of health behavior (Johnson et al., 1995; Whitefield et al., 2002). African Americans and Hispanics also share a vulnerability to three health problems: substance abuse, AIDS, and injury or death from violence (Whitefield et al., 2002; Yee et al., 1995). These individuals are more likely than whites to smoke, use drugs, and practice unsafe sex. Moreover, African Americans and Hispanics— especially young males—are several times more likely than their White counterparts to become victims of homicide. These problems are disturbing, and

correcting them will take a great deal of time, effort, and social change.

Promoting Health with Diverse Populations

How can societies help their diverse populations live healthful lives? Part of the solution would involve broad programs to reduce poverty. Communities contain people of different ages, genders, and sociocultural backgrounds, therefore, professionals who are trying to prevent and treat illness need to take a biopsychosocial perspective (Flack et al., 1995; Johnson et al., 1995; Landrine & Klonoff, 2001). You can see what this means in Table 6.3, which presents three types of issues that professionals can address to make their health-promotion services culturally sensitive. Ideally, programs to promote minority health would use a grassroots, culturally–relevant approach with trained health leaders from the community (Castro, Cota, & Vega, 1999). An example program, called *Por La Vita*, increased breast and cervical cancer testing in Hispanic women by identifying and training respected women of their community to provide weekly educational sessions on cancer prevention (Navarro et al., 1998). The remainder of this chapter focuses on techniques and program designs for enhancing health and preventing illness.

Table 6.3 *Cultural Diversity Issues for Professionals in Promoting Health*

- *Biological factors.* Sociocultural groups can differ in their physiological processes, as reflected in African Americans' high risk of developing the genetic blood disease of sickle-cell anemia. For instance, we saw in Chapter 4 that Black people show higher reactivity to stress, which may result from heredity or environmental factors, such as living under relatively high stress.
- *Cognitive and linguistic factors.* People of different sociocultural groups seem to have different ideas about the causes of illness, give different degrees of attention to their body sensations, such as pain, and interpret symptoms differently. For example, Hispanic Americans often believe in using "folk healing" practices, such as actions to drive away evil spirits. Professionals who try to refute these beliefs may drive their patients away. Language differences between professionals and the people they serve impair their ability to communicate with each other.
- *Social and emotional factors.* Sociocultural groups differ in the amount of stress they experience, their physiological reactivity to it, and the ways they cope with it. They also differ in their amount and use of social support.

PROGRAMS FOR HEALTH PROMOTION

In 1982, fast-food chains in New Orleans began using a gimmick to reverse a dangerous trend: more and more parents were not having their children vaccinated. The gimmick involved offering discount coupons for meals to parents whose children got immunized before the end of the summer. Other creative approaches to promote health have been used elsewhere with other goals. Let's look at some of these approaches.

METHODS FOR PROMOTING HEALTH

Interventions to promote health seek to encourage the practice of healthful behavior by teaching individuals what these behaviors are and how to perform them, and by persuading people to change their current unhealthful habits. An important step in this effort is motivating individuals to *want* to change, and this often requires modifying their health beliefs and attitudes. What methods do these programs use to encourage health behavior?

Providing Information

People who want to lead healthful lives need information—they need to know what to do and when, where, and how to do it. In reducing dietary cholesterol, people need to know what cholesterol is and that it can clog blood vessels, which can produce heart disease. They also need to know where they can have their blood tested for cholesterol level, what levels are high, how much cholesterol is in the foods they currently eat, which foods might be good substitutes for those they should eliminate from their diets, and how to prepare these foods. There are several sources of health information.

One source is the *mass media*. Television, radio, newspapers, and magazines can play a useful role in promoting health by presenting warnings and providing information, such as to help people avoid or stop smoking. One such approach simply provides information to the general population about the *negative consequences* of an activity—smoking, for instance—as public service advertisements often do. This approach has had limited success in changing behavior (Flay, 1987; Lau et al., 1980). One reason for the limited

success is that people often misunderstand the health reports they encounter (Yeaton, Smith, & Rogers, 1990). Another reason may be that they just don't want to change the behavior at issue: a noted newspaper columnist who did not want to change his diet railed against warnings, writing,

> Cholesterol, shmolesterol!... Almost everything [experts] say is good for you will turn out bad for you if you hang around long enough, and almost everything they say is bad for you will turn out not to matter. (Baker, 1989, p. A31; note that this quote is a good example of motivated reasoning!)

But when people already want to change an unhealthful habit, programs conducted on TV can be more effective (Freels et al., 1999). For example, a comprehensive program on TV, called Cable Quit, was successful in helping people stop smoking by showing them how to prepare to quit, helping them through the day they quit, describing ways to maintain their success, and giving them opportunities to call for advice (Valois, Adams, & Kammermann, 1996). Of those who started the program, 17% continued to abstain from smoking a year later.

Another source of health-promotion information is the *computer*, particularly via the Internet. People anywhere in the world who are already interested in promoting their health and have access to the Internet can contact a wide variety of Websites. Some are huge databases with information on all aspects of health promotion, and others provide detailed information on specific illnesses, such as cancer and arthritis, or support groups for health problems. People can learn how to avoid health problems and, if they become ill, what the illness is and how it can be treated.

A third source of health-promotion information is the *medical setting*, particularly the physician's office, which offers some advantages and disadvantages. Two advantages are that many individuals visit a physician at least once a year, and they respect health care workers as experts. Two disadvantages are that these efforts take up time in already busy practices and medical personnel may not know how to help people overcome problems they have in following prevention advice (Radecki & Brunton, 1992). Unfortunately, medical staff don't provide enough health-promotion advice. For example, less than half of patients who smoke report in surveys that their physician ever advised them to quit (Frank et al., 1991;

Thorndike et al., 1998). Due to the problem of time in busy practices, researchers have developed 5- to 10-minute counseling programs that medical staff can be trained to give in person or by telephone; having a system that cues the staff to give the program increases its delivery (Adams et al., 1998). These programs enhance many types of health behaviors, such as stopping smoking, reducing fat intake and weight, and getting cancer screening (Lichtenstein et al., 1996; Ockene et al., 1999; Rimer, 1998).

Medical professionals now have another avenue for providing health-promotion information. They can offer individuals who are at risk for inherited illnesses, such as some forms of cancer, estimates of their chances of getting the disease and opportunities to undergo tests, such as periodic examinations and genetic testing. But even when genetic testing is offered at no cost, less than half of individuals request the testing and results (Lerman et al., 1996, Lerman, Hughes et al., 1999). Are there psychological risks for people who receive this advice and undergo the tests? Making the decision to have genetic testing can be very agonizing because of the possibility that it will reveal a genetic risk and because it creates conflicts among family members who may not want the information. In breast cancer testing, for example, although most women who receive the test do not show adverse psychological effects, women who were already very anxious about health threats before receiving the opportunity for the test often become more distressed (Lerman, Audrain, & Croyle, 1994). More research is needed on ways to prevent these adverse effects and how best to provide all types of information for health promotion. (Go to 🌳.)

CLINICAL METHODS AND ISSUES
Dialogues to Help People Stop Smoking

Patients who smoke tend to express many common rationalizations for not quitting that their medical or psychological practitioner can discuss with them. Each of the following rationalizations has a reply the practitioner can give (Adapted from USDHHS, 1986a).

PATIENT: *I am under a lot of stress, and smoking relaxes me.*

STAFF (practitioner): Your body has become accustomed to nicotine, so you naturally feel more relaxed when you get the nicotine you have come to depend on. But nicotine is actually a stimulant that temporarily raises heart rate, blood pressure, and adrenaline level. After a few weeks of not smoking, most ex-smokers feel less nervous.

PATIENT: *Smoking stimulates me and helps me to be more effective in my work.*

STAFF: Difficulty in concentrating can be a symptom of nicotine withdrawal, but it is a short-term effect. Over time, the body and brain function more efficiently when you don't smoke, because carbon monoxide from cigarettes is displaced by oxygen in the bloodstream.

PATIENT: *I have already cut down to a safe level.*

STAFF: Cutting down is a good step toward quitting. But smoking at any level increases the risk of illness. And some smokers who cut back inhale more often and more deeply, thus maintaining nicotine dependence. It is best to quit smoking completely.

PATIENT: *I only smoke safe, low-tar/low-nicotine cigarettes.*

STAFF: Low-tar cigarettes still contain harmful substances. Many smokers inhale more often or more deeply and thus maintain their nicotine levels. Carbon monoxide intake often increases with a switch to low-tar cigarettes.

PATIENT: *I don't have the willpower to give up smoking.*

STAFF: It can be hard for some people to give up smoking, but for others it is much easier than they expect. Millions of people quit every year. It may take more than one attempt for you to succeed, and you may need to try different methods of quitting. I will give you all the support I can.

Similar dialogues can help people change other health-related behaviors too.

Features of Information to Enhance Motivation

Individuals do not necessarily follow advice and warnings on ways to promote their health. How can the information they receive enhance their motivation to adopt health behaviors?

One approach to enhance people's motivation to follow health promotion advice is to use *tailored content*—that is, the advice delivered in person, in print, or on the telephone is designed for a specific individual, based on characteristics of that person. For example, the message would refer to the person by name and might include personal or behavioral details, such as the person's age or smoking history, and a message geared to the person's readiness to adopt the proposed health behavior, such as stopping smoking, scheduling a mammogram, or losing weight. Tailoring the content appears to enhance the success of health-promotion information (Rimer et al., 1999; Skinner et al., 1999).

Another approach to enhance motivation is based on a concept called *message framing*, which refers to whether the information emphasizes the benefits (gains) or costs (losses) associated with a behavior or decision. For a health behavior, a gain-framed message would focus on attaining desirable consequences or avoiding negative ones. It might state, for example, "If you exercise, you will become more fit and less likely to develop heart disease." A loss-framed message would focus on getting undesirable consequences and avoiding positive ones; for instance, "If you do not get your blood pressure checked, you could increase your chances of having a heart attack or stroke, and you will not know that your blood pressure is good." A large body of evidence indicates that the best type of framing to use depends on the type of health behavior (Rothman & Salovey, 1997; Schneider et al., 2001). Gain-framed messages seem to work best for motivating behaviors that serve to prevent or recover from illness or injury; two such behaviors are using condoms and performing physical therapy. Loss-framed messages work best for behaviors that serve to detect a health problem early, as getting a mammogram can do.

A special case of loss-framed messages is when information arouses fear. According to the health belief model, people are likely to practice healthful behavior if they believe that by not doing so they are susceptible to serious health problems. In other words, fear motivates them to protect their health.

Studies have found that fear-arousing warnings can motivate people to adopt a variety of more healthful attitudes and behavior (Sutton & Hallett, 1988). But two issues about warnings are unclear. First, given the role of message framing, it may be that warnings, as loss-framed messages, may work better for early detection behaviors than for illness prevention behaviors. Second, how much fear should the message generate to be most successful? Some evidence suggests that too much fear may lead the person to use avoidance coping strategies—ignoring, minimizing, or denying the threat, especially when warnings are personally and directly threatening (Janis, 1984; Lee, 1989). More research is needed to identify conditions under which fear appeals work best.

What can be done to make fear messages more effective? Fear messages for changing unhealthful behavior are most persuasive if they:

- Emphasize the organic and social consequences— that is, the perceived seriousness—of developing the health problem (Banks et al., 1995; Kalichman & Coley, 1995).

- Provide specific instructions or training for performing the behavior (Albarracín et al., 2003; Sutton & Hallett, 1988).

- Help bolster people's self-confidence, or self-efficacy, for performing the behavior before urging them to begin the plan (Self & Rogers, 1990; Sutton & Hallett, 1988).

Motivational Interviewing

A one-on-one technique called **motivational interviewing,** a counseling style designed to help individuals explore and resolve their ambivalence in changing a behavior, was originally developed to help people overcome addictions, such as to alcohol and drugs (Miller & Rollnick, 1991). The counselor in the interview uses a "client-centered" style in which the client has control over the conversation, reflective listening and directive questioning to evoke the client's internal motivation for behavior change, and strategies to minimize client resistance to the process.

Motivational interviewing has been extended for use in health care settings to promote healthful behavior, such as to help a girl named Latisha to get her boyfriend to use condoms when they had sex. The following exchange ensued after she pointed out that he had used condoms in the past "when he got 'em."

INTERVIEWER: So if you had them around, would you be able to use them with him?

LATISHA: If I really wanted him to. He'd probably use it.

INTERVIEWER: All you'd have to do is ask him to use a condom, and he'd do it?

LATISHA: Well, I'd have to be nice about it, so he don't think I'm sayin' he's dirty or go around anymore. I'd have to be nice.

INTERVIEWER: It sounds like you know what he would be sensitive about. What could you say to make it sound nice? (Brown & Lourie, 2001, p. 262)

An interview like this one would then discuss the things she could say, the problems that could arise, and how she would deal with them.

The course of motivational interviewing can take one session or several and would typically lead the client to identify many of the elements of theories we've previously discussed, such as the benefits and barriers to the behavior change. They then work through identified problems that have made it harder to adopt the behavior in the past. Research has revealed promising outcomes of motivational interviewing, such as in helping patients follow the medication directions their physician prescribed and getting sexually active people to use condoms (Resnicow et al., 2002).

Behavioral Methods

Behavioral methods focus directly on enhancing people's performance of the preventive act itself by altering its antecedents and consequences. We can alter antecedents to promote healthful behavior in many ways, such as by providing specific instructions or training for performing the behavior, calendars to indicate when to perform infrequent preventive actions, and reminders of appointments. Research has shown that these techniques enhance the effectiveness of programs for health promotion (Sarafino, 2001).

To encourage healthful behavior by manipulating its consequences, we can provide reinforcers when the behavior occurs. Reinforcers can be useful for increasing health behavior, such as practicing good dental hygiene, but their effectiveness depends on the types of reward used, the age and sociocultural background of the individual, and the person's interest in performing the activity (Lund & Kegeles, 1984; Sarafino, 2001, 2004; Suls, 1984). For instance, people differ in their reward preferences—tickets for a Sting concert might be very enjoyable for you, but your friend might prefer hearing a symphony performed by the Philadelphia Orchestra; and attending either of these events might be very unpleasant for someone else. The consequences need to be matched to the person. There is also evidence that reward preferences change with age: kindergarten children tend to prefer material rewards (a charm, money, candy) over social rewards such as praise, but this preference seems to reverse by third grade (Witryol, 1971). For adults, monetary rewards seem to be particularly effective in encouraging health behaviors, such as breast self-examination (Solomon et al., 1998). Programs for health promotion need to consider the individual's point of view with regard to the preventive action and any consequences that the program introduces to enhance performance of that behavior.

Maintaining Healthy Behaviors

When people adopt a new behavior in place of one they performed for a long time, their success usually has some setbacks, or lapses (Sarafino, 2001). A *lapse* is an instance of backsliding; for instance, a person who quits smoking might have a cigarette one day. Lapses should be expected; they do not indicate failure. A more serious setback is a **relapse,** or falling back to one's original pattern of the undesirable behavior. Relapses are very common when people try to change longstanding habits, such as their eating and smoking behaviors.

Psychologists G. Alan Marlatt and Judith Gordon (1980) have proposed that for many individuals who quit a behavior, such as smoking, experiencing a lapse can destroy their confidence in remaining abstinent and precipitate a full relapse. This is called the **abstinence-violation effect.** Because these people are committed to total abstinence, they tend to feel guilty about any lapses, even with just one cigarette, and they see their violation as a sign of a personal failure. They might think, for instance, "I don't have any willpower at all and I cannot change." In programs to change behavior, relapses can be reduced by training individuals to cope with lapses and to maintain self-efficacy about the behavior and by providing "booster" sessions or contacts (Curry & McBride,

1994; Irvin et al., 1999). Contacts, even by phone, can reduce relapses substantially by providing counseling on dealing with difficult situations that could lead to lapses (Zhu et al., 1996).

Many types of programs have been carried out to promote health in different settings and with a variety of goals, methods, and populations. We will examine different types of interventions, beginning with health education efforts that are designed to reach children and adolescents in schools and establish healthful habits at early ages.

PROMOTING HEALTH IN THE SCHOOLS

Public and private schools have a unique opportunity to promote health. In developed nations, they have access to virtually all individuals during the years that are probably most critical in the development of health-related behavior. Teaching children about healthful and unhealthful behaviors can produce two benefits: they may avoid developing unhealthful

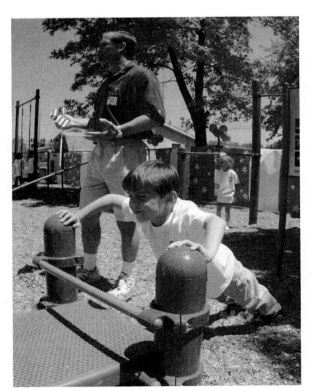

Schools can encourage fitness by providing exercise equipment and showing children how to use it, as in this Project Fit America program.

habits at a vulnerable time in the life span and acquire health behaviors that become habitual aspects of their lifestyles that may stay with them throughout their lives.

Are school programs effective? Some have been. An experiment in 22 American elementary schools introduced a curriculum with emphasis on nutrition and physical fitness (Walter et al., 1985). The schools were randomly assigned so that their students either participated in the program or served as a control group for that year. Relative to the control subjects, the children who participated in the program showed improvements in their blood pressure and cholesterol levels. Another study found that more children practiced safety behavior if they were taught about health and safety in a 4-year program than if they were not (Parcel, Bruhn, & Cerreto, 1986). But many schools do not provide health education at all, or their programs are poorly designed and funded and taught by teachers whose interests and training are in other areas (Kolbe & Iverson, 1984).

WORKSITE WELLNESS PROGRAMS

Wellness programs have spread rapidly in workplaces in industrialized countries. A national survey of American worksites with 50 or more employees found that over 90% offered some form of health-promotion activity, such as for fitness or diet (USDHHS, 2004). One-third of small worksites and 50% of large worksites offered comprehensive programs, which focus on lifestyle change and screen employees for health-promotion needs. Workers with poor health habits in the United States cost employers substantially more in health benefits and other costs of absenteeism than those with good habits. These savings offset and often exceed the expense of running a wellness program (Aldana, 2001). Psychologists who study or administer such programs are called *occupational health psychologists* (Quick, 1999).

Worksite wellness programs vary in their aims, but usually address some or all of several risk factors: hypertension, cigarette smoking, unhealthful diets obesity, poor physical fitness, alcohol abuse, and high levels of stress. These risk factors do not seem to be equally changeable. For example, worksite programs seem to achieve more healthful changes in dietary and exercise behaviors than in smoking (Biener et al., 1999; Emmons et al., 1999). Housing these interventions in workplaces has several advantages.

Worksite programs are convenient to attend, are fairly inexpensive for employees, can provide participants with reinforcement from the employer and coworkers, and can structure the environment to encourage healthful behavior, such as by making healthy food available in the cafeteria (Cohen, 1985). Although the number of employees who participate in worksite programs is not as high as one would hope, over 60% of American workers do (USDHHS, 2004). The number of workers who participate and stick with the programs increases markedly if the employer actively recruits them (Linnan et al., 2002).

Let's look at a model intervention and how effective it is. Johnson & Johnson, America's largest producer of health care products, began the *Live for Life* program in 1978. The program covers thousands of employees and is one of the most effective worksite programs yet developed (Fielding, 1990; Nathan, 1984). The program is designed to improve employees' health knowledge, stress management, and efforts to exercise, stop smoking, and control their weight. For each participating employee, Live for Life begins with a *health screen*—a detailed assessment of the person's current health and health-related behavior, which is shared with the individual later. After taking part in a lifestyle seminar, the employee joins professionally led *action groups* for specific areas of improvement, such as quitting smoking or controlling weight, focusing on how people can alter their lifestyle and maintain these improvements permanently. Followup contacts are made with each participant during the subsequent year. The company also provides a work environment that supports and encourages healthful behavior: it has designated no-smoking areas, established exercise facilities, and made nutritious foods available in the cafeteria, for example.

Evaluation of Live for Life involves ongoing studies, using quasi-experimental research methods. These studies generally compare the health and behavior of employees from different Johnson & Johnson companies that either did or did not offer the Live for Life program (Golaszewski, 2001; Fielding, 1990; Nathan, 1984). All the employees studied completed a health screen in the initial year and then again in later years. Compared with the employees at the companies where Live for Life was not offered, those where it *was* have shown greater improvements in their physical activity, weight, smoking behavior, ability to handle job stress, absenteeism, and health care costs.

COMMUNITY-BASED WELLNESS PROGRAMS

Community-based programs for health promotion are designed to reach large numbers of people and improve their knowledge and performance of preventive behavior (Thompson et al., 2003). These interventions may address an array of behaviors or just one and use any or all of the methods we have considered. They may, for instance, use the media and social organizations to provide information and advice regarding the risks factors for heart disease (smoking and poor diet and exercise), the dangers of drinking and driving, or the availability of free blood–pressure testing or vaccinations. Community-based programs may also provide incentives for performing the health behavior or reaching a goal, such as losing a certain amount of weight.

We'll look at an early example: an ambitious community-based program called the *Three Community Study* to get people to change their behavior and reduce their risk of cardiovascular disease (Farquhar et al., 1977; Meyer et al., 1980). For this study, the investigators selected three very similar towns in northern California. Two of these towns, which shared the same TV and radio stations, were chosen to receive an extensive 2-year mass-media campaign, consisting of warnings and information concerning diet, exercise, and smoking. The third town received no campaign and served as a control community because it was relatively distant and isolated from media in the other towns. To evaluate the success of the campaign, the researchers randomly selected several hundred men and women from each community, interviewed them annually, and took measurements, such as blood pressure, cholesterol, and weight, and combined these data to calculate each person's *overall risk* of cardiovascular disease. Analyses found that people's overall risk increased somewhat in the control community and decreased moderately in the two campaign towns. Subsequent followup research revealed that the program's long-term success was greatest with older people and lowest with individuals who were much younger, had little education, and were from the lower socioeconomic classes (Winkleby, Flora, & Kraemer, 1994).

At about the time that the Three Community Study occurred, other researchers conducted a similar study in Finland and found similar results (Salonen et al, 1981). Although the magnitudes of risk factor

ASSESS YOURSELF

Your Knowledge about AIDS

Answer the following true-false items by circling the T or F for each one.

T F 1. People who develop AIDS usually die within a couple of years.

T F 2. Blood tests can usually tell within a week after infection whether someone has received the AIDS virus.

T F 3. People do not get AIDS from using swimming pools or rest rooms after someone with AIDS does.

T F 4. Some people have contracted AIDS from insects, such as mosquitoes, that have previously bitten someone with AIDS.

T F 5. AIDS can now be prevented with a vaccine and cured if treated early.

T F 6. People who have the AIDS virus can look and feel well.

T F 7. Gay women (lesbians) get AIDS much more often than heterosexual women, but not as often as gay men.

T F 8. Health workers have a high risk of getting AIDS from or spreading the virus to their patients.

T F 9. Kissing or touching someone who has AIDS can give you the disease.

T F 10. AIDS is less contagious than measles.

Check your answers against the key below that is printed upside down—a score of **8** items correct is good, **9** is very good, and **10** is excellent. (*Sources:* Carey, Morrison-Beedy, & Johnson, 1998; DiClemente, Zorn, & Temoshok, 1987; Vener & Krupka, 1990).

Answers:

1. T, 2. F, 3. T, 4. F, 5. F, 6. T, 7. F, 8. F, 9. F, 10. T

---

improvement were not dramatic in either study, they showed that community-based programs offer promising approaches for health promotion and led to larger-scale, longer-term projects with more advanced methods (Farquhar, Maccoby, & Solomon, 1984). The effects have continued to be modest, such as reducing blood pressure by only a few points; but "small effects at the population level can have a large effect on disease" (Thompson et al., 2003, pp. 330–331). (Go to 🍎).

PREVENTION WITH SPECIFIC TARGETS: FOCUSING ON AIDS

Sometimes prevention programs focus on reducing people's risk of developing a specific health problem and center these efforts on specific segments of the population. One example of this approach is the Multiple Risk Factor Intervention Trial (MRFIT), a project that recruited and provided health-promotion programs for thousands of men across the United States who were at substantial risk for heart disease (Caggiula et al., 1981). Another example involves efforts to reduce the spread of infection with the *human immunodeficiency virus* (HIV), which causes *acquired immune*

deficiency syndrome (AIDS), an incurable and usually fatal disease. We'll focus on efforts to reduce HIV infection.

HIV Infection

The magnitude of the AIDS threat is astounding (UNAIDS, 2004): worldwide, over 20 million people have died of AIDS since 1980, 3 million died in 2003 alone; 38 million people are currently infected with HIV, and 5 million were newly infected in 2003. Over 160 countries have reported cases of AIDS, but the infection is unevenly distributed worldwide. The largest concentration of infections continues to be in sub-Saharan Africa, which has 70% of all individuals currently living with HIV/AIDS. The incidence is also high in many Asian countries, and the epidemic is increasing fastest in Eastern Europe. But the rate of infection in industrialized countries has declined since the mid-1990s. In the United States, over 500,000 people have died of AIDS, 900,000 have been diagnosed with the disease, and 40,000 new HIV infections occur each year (CDC, 2004a). Although new medical treatments can extend the lives of victims, AIDS is still a fatal disease that kills the large majority of those who develop it (UNAIDS, 2004).

There is no vaccine against the HIV virus, and there is not likely to be one in the near future. The virus spreads to an uninfected person only through contact of his or her body fluids with those of an infected person, generally either through sexual practices or when intravenous drug users share needles. The likelihood of infection increases if the person has wounds or inflammation from other sexually transmitted diseases, such as syphilis, herpes, or chlamydia (Peterman, 1990). Infected mothers sometimes transmit the virus to their babies during gestation, delivery, and later during breast-feeding (European Collaborative Study, 1991; Fathalla, 1990). Changing people's behavior is virtually the only means of reducing the risk of infection, and worldwide public health efforts for prevention have concentrated on using fear-arousing warnings and providing information.

These efforts also try to correct misconceptions about HIV transmission—for instance, that AIDS can only happen to homosexuals and drug users, that all gay men are infected, that mosquitoes can spread the virus, or that the virus can be transmitted through casual contact, such as by touching or hugging infected individuals or by sharing office equipment they have used (DiClemente, Zorn, & Temoshok, 1987). Many people also believe that health care personnel are usually at high risk of becoming infected when working with AIDS patients, but research has disconfirmed this. It is rare for health care workers to become infected, even when they are accidently stuck with a needle that had been used on an AIDS patient (Clever & LeGuyader, 1995; Henderson et al., 1990).

A large proportion of AIDS victims in the United States and other industrialized countries have been gay men. This is probably because many gay men have tended to be very promiscuous and have engaged regularly in certain sexual practices, especially anal intercourse, that involve a high risk of transmission (Kalichman, 1998). But many other gay men do not lead high-risk lifestyles, lesbians have a very low prevalence of AIDS, and the vast majority of victims in Africa are heterosexuals. A person's sexual orientation is not a guarantee of high or low risk—as many people came to realize in 1991 when basketball star Magic Johnson announced that he had the virus. Of new HIV infections in the United States today, 42% develop from sexual contact between men, 33% are from heterosexual sex, and 25% are from injection drug use (CDC, 2004a).

Why do people continue to engage in unsafe sex? Although ignorance and a lack of availability of protection are the main reasons in many developing countries, other factors are more influential in other cultures. Let's look at some of these factors:

- People are much more likely to have very unsafe sex if they are promiscuous or have sex while under the influence of alcohol or drugs (Kalichman et al., 2002; Leigh, 1990; Lowry et al., 1994). In men, intoxication seems to increase negative attitudes and decrease self-efficacy about using condoms and to increase the willingness to have unsafe sex when they are sexually aroused (Gordon & Carey, 1996; MacDonald et al., 2000).

- Unmarried partners are less likely to use condoms if they perceive their relationship to be close or serious (Cooper & Orcutt, 2000; Misovich, Fisher, & Fisher, 1997).

- Decision making in sexual situations is often subject to nonrational processes, such as denial or wishful thinking (Blanton & Gerrard, 1997; Gold, Skinner, & Hinchy, 1999; Thompson et al., 1999).

- Many individuals have maladaptive beliefs about their own low self-efficacy to use condoms and about the effect that doing so would have on sexual pleasure and spontaneity (Kelly et al., 1991, 1995; Wulfert, Wan, & Backus, 1996).

- Some people appear to gain greater reinforcement from sex when it involves risky behavior (Kelly & Kalichman, 1998).

- The advent of medical treatments that lower viral load and prolong life has led to overoptimism in many individuals, leading them to think that protection is not so necessary anymore (Halkitis & Wilton, 1999).

People's maladaptive beliefs are often clear when they recognize that their behavior contradicts what experts say, so they add qualifiers, such as, "I know that's what they say but . . ." or, "but in my case . . ." (Maticka-Tyndale, 1991).

Basic Messages to Prevent HIV Infection

Major efforts have been introduced in most countries around the world to prevent HIV infection by having the mass media and health organizations provide information about several basic behaviors (Carey, 1999; Kalichman, 1998). First, people should avoid or reduce having sex outside of long-term monogamous relationships or, otherwise, use "safer sex" practices with new partners. Safer sex involves selecting sexual partners carefully, avoiding practices that may injure body tissues, and using condoms in all forms of sexual intercourse. Second, not all people who have the virus know they do, and not all of those who know they do tell their sexual partners (Ciccarone et al., 2003; Simoni et al., 1995). Third, drug users should not share a needle or syringe; if they do, they should be sure it is sterile. Fourth, women who could have been exposed to the virus should have their blood tested for the HIV antibody before becoming pregnant and, if the test is positive, avoid pregnancy. Much of this information has been designed to arouse fear, and it has in many people.

Do informational efforts change people's HIV knowledge and behavior? In the United States, public health programs have been directed toward youth in the general population, intravenous drug users and their sexual partners, and gays and bisexuals. Adolescents and young adults of the general population are vulnerable to infection because of their relatively high levels of sexual promiscuity and drug use. Although providing information to teens increases their knowledge about AIDS (Holtzman et al., 1994), most sexually–experienced teenagers and young adults do not seem to take the precautions they should (Ku, Sonenstein, & Pleck, 1993; Leigh et al., 1994). Although informational programs that focus on getting adolescents to abstain from or reduce the frequency of sexual activity can help, efforts to promote condom use are more effective for teens who are sexually experienced (Jemmott, Jemmott, & Fong, 1999).

Providing information about AIDS has also reduced the risk behaviors of intravenous drug users, who learned that sharing needles can transmit HIV and that there are ways to protect themselves. In the United States, most of these people then began to use sterile needles, reduce their drug use, or use drugs in other ways, such as by inhaling. The risk of HIV infection among drug users decreases if they can buy needles legally or exchange used needles for new ones (Des Jarlais & Friedman, 2002; Ksobiech, 2003). But drug users' caution may not extend as readily into their sexual behavior: few drug users and their sexual partners use condoms (Krajick, 1988). Most drug users are heterosexual men, and their sexual partners often are women who know about the risks but feel powerless and are willing to go along with having unprotected sex (Logan, Cole, & Leukefeld, 2002).

Perhaps the best-organized efforts to change sexual practices have been directed at gay men, particularly in gay communities in large cities. This is partly because many gay social, political, and religious organizations existed before the AIDS epidemic began, and these groups became actively involved in public health campaigns to prevent the spread of the disease. These efforts have had a substantial impact on gay men's sexual behavior across the United States and in other parts of the world, such as Amsterdam, Holland (Kelly & Kalichman, 2002; Van Griensven et al., 1989). In San Francisco, for instance, gay and bisexual men significantly reduced several high-risk patterns of sexual behavior between 1982 and 1986 (Catania et al., 1991; Coates, 1990). These changes greatly decreased the spread of the virus: incidence rates of infection declined during that period from over 13% to about 1% per year. Today, much less than half of new infections in the United States are in gay men (CDC, 2004a). AIDS education and prevention campaigns with gay and bisexual men have produced "the most profound modifications of personal health-related behaviors ever recorded" (Stall, Coates, & Hoff, 1988, p. 878).

Focusing on Sociocultural Groups and Women

Although more needs to be done to reduce HIV risk in urban gay men and intravenous drug users around the world, efforts must be intensified among heterosexual women and disadvantaged sociocultural groups (Coates, 1990; Raj, Amaro, & Reed, 2001; Logan, Cole, & Leukefeld, 2002). For minority groups in the United States, particularly African Americans and Hispanics, there can be added problems of lesser knowledge about risky behavior and suspicions concerning information from health care systems they believe have treated them badly (Boulware et al., 2003; Raj, Amaro, & Reed, 2001). Women are often vulnerable to HIV infection when they are with a male partner who resists using condoms, are socially or economically dependent on the man, and have less power in their relationships (Sikkema, 1998). A woman's ability to protect herself from infection by asking for condom use under these circumstances is especially problematical if the man has violent tendencies and interprets such requests negatively—for example, that she doesn't care about him or thinks he has been unfaithful (Neighbors, O'Leary, & Labouvie, 1999).

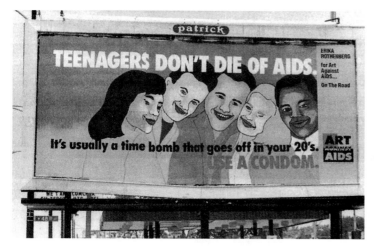

Efforts to prevent the spread of AIDS include using billboards to reach teenagers.

Interventions have been tested with large numbers of Hispanic and African American women who met in small-group sessions to enhance their motivation and interpersonal skills for adopting safer sex practices. Comparisons with women in control groups were made during subsequent months. Women who received the interventions were more likely to report using safer sex practices and to use coupons to redeem free condoms (Carey et al., 2000; Sikkema, Kelly et al., 2000); they were also less likely to develop STDs (chlamydia or gonorrhea) over the next year (Shain et al., 1999).

Making HIV Prevention More Effective

Many interventions provide individual counseling, such as motivational interviewing, to prevent HIV infection (Carey, 1999; Kelly & Kalichman, 2002). Although these methods are moderately effective in decreasing risky behavior, their success is mainly with men and women who are already infected (Weinhardt et al., 1999). Uninfected people who should reduce their risky sexual behavior often do not, and the reasons they don't seem to be similar for homosexual and heterosexual individuals. We need to keep in mind that the vast majority of today's new infections worldwide occur in individuals who are neither gay nor intravenous drug users (UNAIDS, 2004).

How can programs to reduce the spread of HIV infection be made more effective? Prevention programs must provide information about HIV transmission and prevention, use techniques to enhance people's motivation to avoid unsafe sex, and teach the skills needed to perform preventive acts (Fisher et al., 1996; Kalichman, 1998). Some ways to incorporate these features include:

- Tailoring the program to meet the needs of the sociocultural group being addressed (Raj, Amaro, & Reed, 2001).
- Giving strong emphasis to training in the actual skills individuals will need to resist having unsafe sex (Kalichman, Rompa, & Coley, 1996; St. Lawrence et al., 1995; St. Lawrence et al., 2002).
- Making sure the training is geared toward bolstering self-efficacy and advancing the individuals through the stages of change (Galavotti et al., 1995).
- Making use of respected or popular individuals as leaders to endorse the program and promote its acceptance by the group being addressed (Kelly et al., 1997).
- Encouraging infected individuals to disclose their HIV status to prospective sexual partners (Kalichman & Nachimson, 1999).
- Using techniques to reduce nonrational influences in sexual decisions. For example, having people give advice publicly that contradicts their own behavior can reduce their future use of denial (Eitel & Friend, 1999).

SUMMARY

People's behavior has an important impact on their health. Mortality from today's leading causes of death could be markedly reduced if people would adopt a few health behaviors, such as not smoking, not drinking excessively, eating healthful diets, and exercising regularly. Although some individuals are fairly consistent in their practice of health-related behaviors, these behaviors can be quite changeable over time. A person's practice of health behaviors does not seem to be governed by a single set of attitudes or response tendencies. Health-related behaviors that become well established often become habitual.

Health problems can be averted through three levels of prevention and can involve efforts by the individual and by his or her social network, physician, and other health professionals. Primary prevention consists of actions taken to avoid illness or injury. It can include public service announcements, genetic counseling, and a wide variety of health behaviors, such as using seat belts and performing breast or testicular self-examinations. Secondary prevention involves actions taken to identify and stop or reverse a health problem. It includes tests and treatments health professionals may conduct, as well as people's visiting a physician when ill and taking medication as prescribed. Tertiary prevention consists of actions taken to contain or retard damage from a serious injury or advanced disease, prevent disability, and rehabilitate the patient.

People acquire health-related behaviors through modeling and through operant conditioning, whereby behavior changes because of its consequences: reinforcement, extinction, and punishment. Other determinants of these behaviors include genetic, social, emotional, and cognitive factors. Errors in symptom perception and ideas people have about illnesses can lead to health problems. People's thinking about health and illness is not always logical—it often includes motivated reasoning, unrealistic optimism, and false hopes about their health. Unhealthful behaviors are not always planned and often depend on the person's willingness to be drawn into an attractive situation.

Some theories focus on the role of health beliefs to account for people's health-related behavior. The health belief model proposes that people take preventive action on the basis of their assessments of the threat of a health problem and the pros and cons of taking the action. Threat perceptions are based mainly on the person's perceived seriousness of and susceptibility to the health problem. Assessing the pros and cons of the action involves weighing its perceived benefits and barriers. These assessments combine to determine the likelihood of preventive action. The theory of planned behavior proposes that health-related behaviors are determined by people's intentions, which are a function of their attitudes regarding the behaviors, subjective norms, and self-efficacy. The stages of change model focuses on people's readiness to modify their behavior; conflict theory focuses on the role of stress in decisions.

People's age, sex, and sociocultural background also affect health-related behavior and need to be considered in programs for health promotion. Efforts to promote healthful behavior use information, fear-arousing warnings, motivational interviewing, and behavioral methods. But changes in behavior can be temporary; relapses can occur, partly via the abstinence-violation effect. Programs for health promotion can be effective in the schools and in worksites. Community-based wellness programs are designed to reach large numbers of people and improve their knowledge and practice of preventive behavior. The Three Community Study demonstrated that media campaigns can promote health, and subsequent research has also integrated extensive efforts by community organizations toward improving people's preventive actions, such as in stemming the spread of AIDS.

KEY TERMS

health behavior	extinction	stages of change	conflict theory
primary prevention	punishment	model	motivational interviewing
secondary prevention	health belief model	motivated reasoning	relapse
tertiary prevention	theory of planned	false hopes	abstinence-violation
reinforcement	behavior	willingness	effect

7
SUBSTANCE USE AND ABUSE

Substance Abuse
Addiction and Dependence
Processes Leading to Dependence

Smoking Tobacco
Who Smokes, and How Much?
Why People Smoke
Smoking and Health

Alcohol Use and Abuse
Who Drinks, and How Much?
Why People Use and Abuse Alcohol
Drinking and Health

Drug Use and Abuse
Who Uses Drugs, and Why?
Drug Use and Health

Reducing Substance Use and Abuse
Preventing Substance Use
Quitting a Substance without Therapy
Treatment Methods to Stop Substance Use and Abuse
Dealing with the Relapse Problem

PROLOGUE

The stakes were high when Jim signed an agreement to quit smoking for a year, beginning January 2nd. The contract was with a worksite wellness program at the large company where he was employed as a vice president. It called for money to be given to charity by either Jim or the company, depending on how well he abstained from smoking. For every day he did not smoke, the company would give $10 to the charity; and for each cigarette Jim smoked, he would give $25, with a maximum of $100 for any day.

Jim knew stopping smoking would not be easy for him—he had smoked more than a pack a day for the last 20 years, and he had tried to quit a couple of times before. In the contract, the company could have required that he submit to medical tests to verify that he did in fact abstain but were willing to trust his word and that of his family, friends, and coworkers. These people were committed to helping him quit, and they agreed to be contacted by someone from the program weekly and give honest reports. Did he succeed? Yes, but he had a few "lapses" that cost him $325. By the end of the year, Jim had not smoked for 8 months continuously.

People voluntarily use substances that can harm their health. This chapter focuses on people's use of three substances: tobacco, alcohol, and drugs. We'll examine who uses substances and why, how these substances can affect health, and what can be done to help prevent people from using and abusing them. We'll also address questions about substances and health. Do people smoke tobacco, drink alcohol, and use drugs more than in the past? Why do people start to smoke, or drink excessively, or use drugs? Why is it so difficult to quit these behaviors? If individuals succeed in stopping smoking, will they gain weight?

SUBSTANCE ABUSE

"I just can't get started in the morning without a cup of coffee and a cigarette—I must be addicted," you may have heard someone say. The term *addicted* used to have a very limited meaning, referring mainly to the excessive use of alcohol and drugs. It was common knowledge that these chemical substances have *psychoactive effects*: they alter the person's mood, cognition, or behavior. We now know that other substances, such as nicotine and caffeine, have psychoactive effects, too—but people are commonly said to be "addicted" also to eating, gambling, buying, and many other things. How shall we define addiction?

ADDICTION AND DEPENDENCE

Addiction is a condition, produced by repeated consumption of a natural or synthetic substance, in which the person has become physically and psychologically dependent on the substance (Baker et al., 2004). **Physical dependence** exists when the body has adjusted to a substance and incorporated it into the "normal" functioning of the body's tissues. For instance, the structure and function of brain cells and chemistry change (Torres & Horowitz, 1999). This state has two characteristics:

- **Tolerance** is the process by which the body increasingly adapts to a substance and requires larger and larger doses of it to achieve the same effect. At some point, these increases reach a plateau.

- **Withdrawal** refers to unpleasant physical and psychological symptoms people experience when they discontinue or markedly reduce using a substance on which the body has become physically dependent. The symptoms experienced depend on the particular substance used, and can include anxiety, irritability, intense cravings for the substance, hallucinations, nausea, headache, and tremors.

Substances differ in their *potential* for producing physical dependence: the potential is very high for heroin but appears to be lower for other substances, such as LSD (Baker et al., 2004; NCADI, 2000; Schuster & Kilbey, 1992).

Psychological dependence is a state in which individuals feel compelled to use a substance for the effect it produces, without necessarily being physically dependent on it. Despite knowing that the substance can impair psychological and physical health, they rely heavily on it—often to help them adjust to life and feel good—and spend much time obtaining and using it.

Dependence develops through repeated use (Cunningham, 1998). Users who are not physically dependent on a substance experience less tolerance and withdrawal (Schuckit et al., 1999). Being without the substance can elicit *craving*, a motivational state that involves a strong desire for it. Users who become addicted usually become psychologically dependent on the substance first; later they become physically dependent as their bodies develop a tolerance for it. Substances differ in the potential for producing psychological dependence: the potential is high for heroin and cocaine, moderate for marijuana, and lower for LSD (NCADI, 2000; Schuster & Kilbey, 1992).

The terms used in describing addiction and dependence vary somewhat (Baker et al., 2004), but diagnosing substance dependence and abuse depends on the extent and impact of clear and ongoing use (Davidson, Neale, & Kring, 2004). Psychiatrists and clinical psychologists diagnose **substance abuse** on the basis of three criteria:

- Failing to fulfill important obligations, such as in repeatedly neglecting a child or being absent from work.

- Putting oneself or others at repeated risk for physical injury, for instance, by driving while intoxicated.

- Having substance-related legal difficulties, such as being arrested for disorderly conduct.

Psychiatric classifications of disorders now include the pathological use of tobacco, alcohol, and drugs—the substances we'll focus on in this chapter.

PROCESSES LEADING TO DEPENDENCE

Researchers have identified many factors associated with substance use and abuse. In this section, we'll discuss factors that apply to all addictive substances, are described in the main theories of substance dependence, and for which there is clear evidence of a role in developing and maintaining dependence.

Reinforcement

We saw in Chapter 6 that reinforcement is a process whereby a consequence strengthens the behavior on which it is contingent. There are two types of reinforcement: positive and negative (Sarafino, 2001). In **positive reinforcement,** the consequence is an event or item the individual finds pleasant or wants that is introduced or *added* after the behavior occurs. For example, many cigarette smokers report that smoking produces a "buzz" or "rush" and feelings of elation (Baker, Brandon, & Chassin, 2004). Alcohol and drugs often have similar and other effects. In **negative reinforcement,** the consequence involves *reducing* or *removing* an aversive circumstance, such as pain or unpleasant feelings. For instance, tobacco, alcohol, and drugs relieve stress and other negative emotions at least temporarily (Baker et al., 2004). Positive and negative reinforcement both produce a wanted state of affairs, which occurs very soon after the behavior in substance use. Thus, one reason people abuse substances is that they come to rely on them increasingly to regulate their cognitive and emotional states (Holahan et al., 2001; Pomerleau & Pomerleau, 1989).

Avoiding Withdrawal

Because withdrawal symptoms are very unpleasant, people want to avoid them (Baker, Brandon, & Chassin, 2004). People who have used a substance long enough to develop a dependence on it are likely to keep on using it to prevent withdrawal, especially if they have experienced the symptoms. As an example of the symptoms, for people addicted to alcohol, the withdrawal syndrome (called *delirium*

tremens, "the DTs") often includes intense anxiety, tremors, and frightening hallucinations when their blood alcohol levels drop (Davidson, Neale, & Kring, 2004). Each substance has its own set of withdrawal symptoms.

Substance-Related Cues

When people use substances, they associate with their activity the specific internal and environmental stimuli that are regularly present. These stimuli are called *cues,* and they can include the sight and smell of cigarette smoke, the bottle and taste of beer, and the mental images of and equipment involved in taking cocaine. These associations occur by way of **classical conditioning:** a conditioned stimulus—say, the smell of cigarette smoke—comes to elicit a response through association with an unconditioned stimulus, the substance's effect, such as the "buzz" feeling. There may be more than one response, but an important one is craving: for people who are alcohol dependent, the odor of and words related to alcohol can elicit cravings for a drink (Schneider et al., 2001; Tapert et al., 2004).

Evidence now indicates that the role of cues in substance dependence involves physiological mechanisms. Let's look at two lines of evidence. First, learning the cues enables the body to anticipate and compensate for a substance's effects (McDonald & Siegel, 2004). For instance, for a frequent user of alcohol, an initial drink gets the body to prepare for more, which may lead to tolerance; and if an expected amount does not come for someone who is addicted, withdrawal symptoms occur. Second, studies have supported the *incentive-sensitization theory* of addiction, which proposes that a neurotransmitter called *dopamine* enhances the salience of stimuli associated with substance use so that they become increasingly powerful in directing behavior (Robinson & Berridge, 2001, 2003). These powerful cues grab the substance user's attention, arouse the anticipation of the reward gained from using the substance, and compel the person to get and use more of it.

Expectancies

People develop *expectancies,* or ideas about the outcomes of behavior, from their own experiences and from watching other people. Some expectancies are positive; that is, the expected outcome is desirable. For example, we may decide by watching others that drinking alcohol is "fun"—people who are drinking are often boisterous, laughing, and, perhaps, celebrating. These people may be family members, friends, and celebrities in movies—all of whom are powerful models. Even before tasting alcohol, children acquire expectancies about the positive effects of alcohol through social learning processes, such as by watching TV shows and advertisements (Dunn & Goldman, 1998; Grube & Wallack, 1994; Scheier & Botvin, 1997). Teenagers also perceive that drinking is "sociable" and "grown up," two things they generally want very much to be. As a result, when teens are offered a drink by their parents or friends, they are likely to see this as a very positive opportunity. Other expectancies are negative, such as that drinking can lead to a hangover. Similar processes operate for other substances, such as tobacco (Cohen et al., 2002).

Genetics

Heredity influences addiction. For example, twin studies have shown that identical twins are more similar in cigarette smoking behavior and in becoming dependent on tobacco than fraternal twins, and researchers have identified specific genes that are involved in this addictive process (Lerman & Berrettini, 2003). Dozens of twin and adoption studies, as well as research with animals, have clearly demonstrated a genetic influence in the development of alcohol problems (Ciraulo & Renner, 1991; NIAAA, 1993; Prescott & Kendler, 1999; Schuckit, 1985). For instance, twin studies in general have found that if one member of a same-sex twin pair is alcoholic, the risk of the other member being alcoholic is twice as great if the twins are identical rather than fraternal. And specific genes have been identified for this substance, too. What's more, the genes that affect smoking are not the same ones that affect drinking (Bierut et al., 2004).

If you have not read Chapter 2, The Body's Physical Systems, and your course has you read the modules from that chapter distributed to later chapters, read **Module 4** (The Respiratory System) now.

SMOKING TOBACCO

When Columbus explored the Western Hemisphere, he recorded in his journal that the inhabitants would set fire to leaves—rolled up or in pipes—and draw in the smoke through their mouths (Ashton & Stepney, 1982). The leaves these people used were tobacco, of course. Other early explorers tried smoking and, probably because they liked it, took tobacco leaves back to Europe in the early 1500s, where tobacco was used mainly for "medicinal purposes." Smoking for pleasure spread among American colonists and in Europe later in that century. In the 1600s, pipe smoking became popular, and the French introduced *snuff*, powdered tobacco that people consumed chiefly by inserting it in the nose and sniffing strongly. After inventors made a machine for mass-producing cigarettes and growers developed mellower tobacco in the early 1900s for easier inhaling, the popularity of smoking grew rapidly over the next 50 years.

Today there are about 1.3 billion smokers in the world (WHO, 2003). In the United States, cigarette smoking reached its greatest popularity in the mid-1960s, when about 53% of adult males and 34% of adult females smoked regularly (Shopland & Brown, 1985). Among adults between 20 and 45 years of age, smoking was even more prevalent: about 60% of the men and 40% of the women smoked regularly. Before that time, people generally didn't know about the serious health effects of smoking. But in 1964 the Surgeon General issued a report describing these health effects, and warnings against smoking began to appear in the American media and on cigarette packages. Since that time, the prevalence of adult smokers has dropped steadily, and today about 25% of the men and 21% of the women in the United States smoke (NCHS, 2003). Teen smoking has also declined: today 17% of high school seniors smoke daily (Johnston, O'Malley, & Bachman, 2003).

Do these trends mean cigarette manufacturers are on the verge of bankruptcy? Not at all—their profits are still quite high! In the United States, there are still about 48 million smokers, the retail price of cigarettes has increased, and manufacturers have sharply increased sales to foreign countries. At the same time that smoking has declined in many industrialized countries, it has been increasing in developing nations, such as in Asia and Africa (Fiore, Newcomb, & McBride, 1993; WHO, 2003).

WHO SMOKES, AND HOW MUCH?

Although huge numbers of people in the world smoke, most do not. In the United States, the adolescent and adult populations have about four times as many nonsmokers as smokers. Are some people more likely to smoke than others?

Age and Gender Differences in Smoking

Smoking varies with age. For example, few Americans begin to smoke regularly before 12 years of age (NCHS, 2000). But the great majority of people who will ever become regular smokers begin the habit before the age of 20 or so (Matarazzo, 1982; McGinnis, Shopland, & Brown, 1987). The habit generally develops gradually, and several years may pass before an individual's smoking rate reaches its eventual adult level (Pechacek et al., 1984). The percentage of Americans who smoke declines after about 40 years of age (NCHS, 2003), and many adults are *former* smokers.

Gender differences in smoking are quite large in some parts of the world: about 1 billion men and 250 million women smoke worldwide (WHO, 2003). Among Americans, the prevalence of smoking had always been far greater among males than females before the 1970s, but this gender gap has narrowed considerably for two reasons (McGinnis, Shopland, & Brown, 1987). First, much larger numbers of men than women stopped smoking after starting. Second, although the percentage of individuals who started smoking declined until 1990, it decreased more sharply for males than for females. Today, the percentage of high-school seniors who smoke is similar for girls and boys (Johnston, O'Malley, & Bachman, 2003). Cigarette advertising targeted at one gender or the other, such as by creating clever brand names and slogans, played a major part in these gender-related shifts in smoking (Pierce & Gilpin, 1995). A slogan designed to induce young females to smoke is:

"You've come a long way, baby," with its strong but still subtle appeal to the women's liberation movement. The "Virginia Slims" brand name artfully takes advantage of the increasingly well-documented research finding that, for many female

(and male) smokers, quitting the habit is associated with gaining weight. (Matarazzo, 1982, p. 6)

There is an important and hopeful point to keep in mind about the changes we have described in smoking behavior: they demonstrate that people can be persuaded to avoid or quit smoking.

Sociocultural Differences in Smoking

Large variations in smoking occur across cultures, with far higher rates in developing than in industrialized countries (WHO, 2003). Over 80% of the world's smokers live in developing countries, where, for example, 50% of the men smoke; nearly two-thirds of Chinese men smoke.

In the United States, ethnic groups differ in smoking rates (NCHS, 2003). The percentages of Blacks and Whites who smoke regularly have declined substantially since the 1960s, but these percentages depend on the people's ages and gender. Among men, far more Whites than Blacks smoke in early adulthood, but far more Blacks than Whites smoke after 45 years of age. Among women, far more Whites than Blacks smoke in early adulthood, but the percentages are similar after 45 years of age. Differences in smoking rates are also related to social class: the percentage of people who smoke tends to decline with increases in education, income, and job prestige class (McGinnis, Shopland, & Brown, 1987). Thus, the highest rates of smoking are likely to be found among adults who did not graduate from high school, have low incomes, and have blue-collar occupations, such as carpentry, maintenance work, and truck driving.

An examination of cigarette sales figures in the United States in the two decades after the mid-1960s reveals two curiously contrasting trends (Shopland & Brown, 1985). First, the number of cigarettes sold per adult person decreased sharply, corresponding to the decline in the percentage of smokers. Second, the total cigarette consumption in America *increased* markedly during most of that period. These trends seem inconsistent, but they are not: there were increases in the number of adults in the population, offsetting the effect of the decline in the percentage of adults who smoke, and in the proportion of smokers who smoke *heavily*, more than a pack a day (McGinnis, Shopland, & Brown, 1987). This means, of course, that the people who continued to smoke after the 1960s are the ones who needed to quit the most.

WHY PEOPLE SMOKE

Cigarette smoking is a strange phenomenon in some respects. If you ever tried to smoke, chances are you coughed the first time or two, found the taste unpleasant, and, perhaps, even experienced nausea. This is not the kind of outcome that usually makes people want to try something again. But many teenagers do, even though most teens say that smoking is unhealthy (Johnston, O'Malley, & Bachman, 2003). Given these circumstances, we might wonder why people start to smoke and why they continue.

Starting to Smoke

Smoking usually starts during the teenage years, and psychosocial factors provide the primary forces that lead adolescents to begin. Several aspects of the social environment are influential in shaping teenagers' attitudes, beliefs, and intentions about smoking. For instance, studies have found that adolescents are more likely to begin smoking if their parents and friends smoke (Conrad, Flay, & Hill, 1992; Hansen et al., 1987; Killen et al., 1997; Robinson & Klesges, 1997). Teens who try their first cigarette typically smoke it in the company of peers and with their encouragement (Leventhal, Prohaska, & Hirschman, 1985). And adolescents are more likely to start smoking if their favorite movie stars smoke on or off screen (Distefan et al., 1999). Thus, modeling and peer pressure are important determinants of smoking.

Personal characteristics, such as being rebellious and a risk-taker, seem to influence whether adolescents begin to smoke (Conrad, Flay, & Hill, 1992; Griffin et al., 1999; Robinson & Klesges, 1997). As psychologists Howard Leventhal and Paul Cleary have suggested, teenagers

who are less successful in school . . . , more rebellious, and doing less well in meeting expectations of parents and traditional authorities . . . are more likely to be attracted to smoking at an early age and begin using cigarettes as a means of defining themselves as tough, cool, and independent of authority. (1980, p. 384)

Expectancies are also important. Many teens believe that smoking can enhance their image (Robinson & Klesges, 1997). Studies have found that boys and girls between the ages of 11 and 15 often associate smoking with being attractive to and interested in the opposite sex, looking mature, and being "glamorous"

and "exciting" (Barton et al., 1982; Dinh et al., 1995). Teens who are very concerned with how others view them do not easily overlook social images, models, and peer pressure. The impact of the psychosocial factors we've considered on smoking seems to depend on the person's gender and sociocultural background. In the United States, for example, smoking by peers and family members is more closely linked to smoking in girls than boys and in White than Black teens (Flay, Hu, & Richardson, 1998; Robinson & Klesges, 1997).

Becoming a Regular Smoker

There is a rule of thumb about beginning to smoke that seems to have some validity: individuals who smoke their *fourth* cigarette are very likely to become regular smokers (Leventhal & Cleary, 1980). Although the vast majority of youngsters try at least one cigarette, most of them never get to the fourth one and don't go on to smoke regularly. Becoming a habitual smoker generally develops slowly, often taking a few years (Ary & Biglan, 1988; Chassin et al., 2000).

Why is it that some people continue smoking after the first tries and others don't? Part of the answer lies in the types of psychosocial influences that got them to start in the first place. Studies that tested thousands of adolescents in at least two different years have examined whether the teens' social environments and beliefs about smoking were related to changes in their smoking behavior (Chassin et al., 1991; Choi et al., 2002; Murray et al., 1983). Smoking tended to continue or increase if the teens:

- Had at least one parent who smoked.
- Perceived their parents as unconcerned or even encouraging about their smoking.
- Had siblings or friends who smoked and socialized with friends very often.
- Were receptive to tobacco advertisements, such as by naming a favorite one.
- Felt peer pressure to smoke, for example, reporting, "Others make fun of you if you don't smoke," and "You have to smoke when you're with friends who smoke."
- Held positive attitudes about smoking, such as, "Smoking is very enjoyable," and, "Smoking can help people when they feel nervous or embarrassed."

- Did not believe smoking would harm their health, for instance, feeling, "Smoking is dangerous only to older people," and, "Smoking is only bad for you if you have been smoking for many years."
- Believed they'd be able to quit smoking if they wanted to do so.

Other research has shown that teenagers usually smoke in the presence of other people, especially peers, and that smokers consume more cigarettes when in the company of someone who smokes at a high rate rather than a low rate (Antonuccio & Lichtenstein, 1980; Biglan et al., 1984). Adolescents who smoke also receive many more offers of cigarettes from friends than nonsmokers do (Ary & Biglan, 1988).

Reinforcement is another important factor in continuing to smoke. For many smokers, the taste of a cigarette provides positive reinforcement for smoking. Research has found that people who feel that the taste of a cigarette is the main reason for smoking smoke less than other smokers when their cigarettes are altered to taste less pleasant (Leventhal & Cleary, 1980). Negative reinforcement maintains smoking when people use the behavior as a means of coping with stress or other unpleasant emotional states (Baker et al., 2004). Smoking among adolescents is related to the amount of stress in their lives—the greater the stress, the more likely they are to smoke (Wills, 1986). In addition, adult smokers report less anxiety and greater ability to express their opinions if they smoke during stressful social interactions than if they do not smoke (Gilbert & Spielberger, 1987). But even if smokers perform better and feel more relaxed in stressful situations when they are allowed to smoke than when they are not, they do not necessarily perform better or feel more relaxed than nonsmokers do (Schachter, 1980). Some findings suggest that smoking may reduce stress temporarily but may increase it in the long run (Parrott, 1999). A study that tested this idea found support for it, but another did not (Orlando, Ellickson, & Jinnett, 2001; Wills, Sandy, & Yeager, 2002).

Biological factors are also involved in sustaining smoking behavior. The fact that adolescent smoking is strongly associated with parental and sibling smoking shows that smoking runs in families. Certainly part of this relationship results from social learning processes. But there are at least two biological routes. First, some evidence suggests that nicotine passed on by a smoking mother to her baby in pregnancy may make the child more susceptible to the addictive effects of nicotine (Kandel, Wu, & Davies, 1994). Second, we saw earlier that heredity plays a role and that specific genes are involved in tobacco dependence. What role do these processes play? As an example, heredity affects how easily and strongly a person becomes physically dependent on tobacco (Pomerleau et al., 1993). Also, people with a specific gene pattern are less likely to become smokers and be more able to quit if they start (Lerman, Caporaso et al., 1999).

The Role of Nicotine

People become physically dependent on tobacco because of the chemical substances their bodies take in when they use it. A person who smokes a pack a day takes more than 50,000 puffs a year, with each puff delivering chemicals into the lungs and bloodstream (Pechacek et al., 1984; USDHHS, 1986b). These chemicals include carbon monoxide, tars, and nicotine. Cigarette smoke has high concentrations of **carbon monoxide,** a gas that is readily absorbed by the bloodstream and rapidly affects the person's physiological functioning, such as by reducing the oxygen-carrying capacity of the blood. It is possible that these physiological changes influence whether people like or dislike smoking. **Tars** exist as minute particles of residue, suspended in smoke. Although tars have important health effects, there is no evidence that they affect people's desire to smoke. **Nicotine** is the addictive chemical in cigarette smoke and produces rapid and powerful physiological effects. Nicotine dependence does not necessarily take months or years to develop: a study found that some beginning smokers who had smoked infrequently experienced symptoms of dependence, such as craving (O'Loughlin et al., 2003).

Nicotine is a substance that occurs only in tobacco. When a person smokes, nicotine penetrates cell membranes of the mouth and nose on the way to the lungs, where alveoli quickly absorb it and transmit it to the blood (Pechacek et al., 1984; Baker, Brandon, & Chassin, 2004). In a matter of seconds the blood carries the nicotine to the brain, where it leads to the release of various chemicals that activate both the central and sympathetic nervous systems, which arouse the body, increasing the person's alertness, heart rate, and blood pressure. These and other consequences of nicotine form the basis for the positive and negative reinforcement effects of smoking. Then, while the person is smoking a cigarette, nicotine accumulates very rapidly in the blood. But it soon decreases through metabolism—in about 2 hours, half of the nicotine inhaled from a cigarette has dissipated.

Biological explanations of people's continued cigarette smoking have focused chiefly on the role of nicotine. One prominent explanation, called the **nicotine regulation model,** is based on the addictive quality of nicotine. According to this model, established smokers continue to smoke to maintain a certain level of nicotine in their bodies and to avoid withdrawal symptoms. Stanley Schachter and his associates (1977) provided evidence for this model in an ingenious series of studies with adult smokers. In one study, the researchers had subjects smoke low-nicotine cigarettes during one week and high-nicotine cigarettes during another week. As the model predicts, the subjects smoked more low- than high-nicotine cigarettes. This effect was especially strong for heavy smokers, who smoked 25% more of the low- than high-nicotine cigarettes. Consistent with these results, other researchers have found that people who regularly smoke ultralow-nicotine cigarettes do not consume less nicotine than those who smoke other cigarettes; ultralow smokers simply smoke more cigarettes (Maron & Fortmann, 1987).

Although the nicotine regulation model has received research support, it provides only part of the explanation for people's smoking behavior (Leventhal & Cleary, 1980). One reason is that people who quit smoking typically continue to crave it, and often return to smoking long after all the nicotine is gone from their bodies. Another reason is that some people, called "chippers," who smoke a few cigarettes a day regularly for years don't increase their use; that is, they don't show tolerance. These people usually don't experience withdrawal symptoms but absorb as much nicotine from a cigarette as heavier smokers do (Shiffman et al., 1990; Shiffman et al., 1995). Why do chippers continue to smoke? Each of the theories of addiction we considered earlier provides a cogent explanation. For instance, nicotine provides very powerful reinforcement of smoking behavior soon after the first puff of a cigarette (Baker, Brandon, & Chassin, 2004; Donny et al., 1998; McGehee et al., 1995).

Researchers today generally recognize that a complete explanation of the development and maintenance of smoking behavior involves the interplay of biological, psychological, and social factors (Fisher, Lichtenstein, & Haire-Joshu, 1993; Shadel et al., 2000).

An example of this interplay is seen in the finding that among depressed smokers, those with a specific gene rely more on smoking to cope than those without that gene (Lerman et al., 1998).

SMOKING AND HEALTH

"Warning: The Surgeon General has determined that cigarette smoking is dangerous to your health," states a cigarette pack sold in the United States. In the year 2000, annual deaths from smoking-related illnesses had risen to 4.9 million worldwide, and projections indicated that this rate would rise to 9 million a year by 2020 (WHO, 2003). Smoking reduces people's life expectancy by several years and increases their risk of many illnesses, particularly cancer and cardiovascular diseases (Thun et al., 1995). No other single behavior takes such a toll. To what extent do your odds of dying of lung cancer or heart disease increase if you smoke? Figure 7–1 shows that the odds increase greatly,

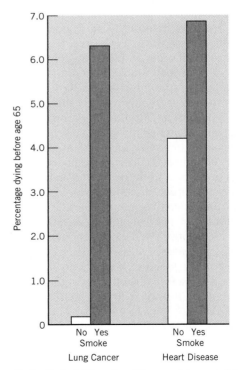

Figure 7–1 Probability of a 35-year-old man dying of lung cancer or heart disease before age 65 as a function of smoking heavily or not smoking. Data for women were less complete, but probably would reveal similar risk increases. (Data from Mattson, Pollack, & Cullen, 1987, p. 427.)

especially for lung cancer (Mattson, Pollack, & Cullen, 1987). The more you smoke, the worse your odds become—and if you quit, your odds improve steadily, in about 15 years becoming similar to those of people who never smoked (Godtfredsen et al., 2002; LaCroix et al., 1991). Smoking and, specifically, nicotine also impair immune function (McAllister-Sistilli et al., 1998).

Cancer

In the late 1930s, two important studies were done that clearly linked smoking and cancer for the first time (Ashton & Stepney, 1982). One study presented statistics showing that nonsmokers live longer than smokers. In the other study, researchers produced cancer in laboratory animals by administering cigarette tar. By producing cancer with experimental methods, these researchers demonstrated a causal link between cancer and a chemical in tobacco smoke and identified tar as a likely *carcinogen*, a substance that causes cancer. The evidence now is overwhelming that tobacco tars and probably other byproducts of tobacco smoke cause cancer (Denissenko et al., 1996; USDHHS, 1986b, 1989).

Hundreds of retrospective and prospective studies have consistently demonstrated the link between tobacco use and cancer in humans. Prospective research provides fairly strong evidence for a causal relationship because smokers and nonsmokers are identified and then followed over a long period of time to see if they develop cancer. Many large-scale prospective studies have linked smoking with cancers of various body sites, including the lung, mouth, esophagus, bladder, and kidney (Levy, 1985; Shopland & Burns, 1993). The last two may result because carcinogenic chemicals in tobacco smoke are absorbed into the blood and conveyed to the urine. Cancers of the mouth and esophagus can also result from using smokeless tobacco—chewing tobacco or snuff (Severson, 1993; USDHHS, 1989). Thus, carcinogenic substances exist not only in smoke but in tobacco itself.

As recently as the 1930s, lung cancer in America was quite uncommon and much less prevalent than many other forms of cancer, such as cancer of the breast, stomach, and prostate (ACS, 2004). Deaths from lung cancer at that time occurred at an annual rate of about 5 per 100,000 people in the population, whereas mortality rates for breast and stomach cancer were more than five times that high. Over the years, the mortality rates for most forms of cancer have

either declined or remained fairly constant, but not for lung cancer. The annual death rate per 100,000 population for lung cancer rose sharply in the second half of the 20th century; it is now over 78 for men and 41 for women. It is the deadliest form of cancer, being responsible for nearly three times more deaths yearly than cancer of the colon or rectum, the second most deadly form. Lung cancer claims about 156,000 lives in the United States each year (USBC, 2003).

The correspondence between the rises in lung cancer deaths and in smoking prevalence since the 1930s is quite striking (McGinnis, Shopland, & Brown, 1987; Shopland & Burns, 1993). The rate of mortality from lung cancer began to rise about 15 or 20 years after the rate of smoking started to rise, and these rates have paralleled each other ever since. During this time, the rates of smoking and of lung cancer were higher for males than for females, but since the mid-1960s, important gender-related changes have occurred. Smoking has decreased among men and increased among women, thus narrowing the gender gap—and corresponding changes in incidence rates of lung cancer are now evident: from 1980 to 2000 the rates declined steadily for men but increased for women (ACS, 2004).

How does smoking harm the lungs? When smoke recurrently passes through the bronchial tubes, the lining of the tubes begins to react to the irritation by increasing the number of cells just below the surface. Then,

> the fine, hairlike growths, or cilia, along the surface of the lining, whose function is to clear the lungs of foreign particles, begin to slow or stop their movement. In time, the cilia may disappear altogether, and as a consequence carcinogenic substances remain in contact with sensitive cells in the lining of the bronchi instead of being removed in the mucus. . . . At this stage, a *smoker's cough* may develop. It is a feeble attempt by the body to clear the lungs of foreign particles in the absence of functioning cilia. (La Place, 1984, p. 326)

Lung cancer usually originates in the bronchial tubes. In most cases, it probably develops because of the continual contact of carcinogens with the bronchial lining.

Smoking is a major risk factor for all forms of cancer, but its role is more direct and powerful in lung cancer than in other cancers. People's environments contain many other carcinogens, and smoking is not the only cause of these diseases. (Go to 💡.)

HIGHLIGHT

Does Someone Else's Smoking Affect Your Health?

"What do you mean I can't smoke in this bar! I'm a customer, and it isn't anybody else's business what I do to my body," a patron said indignantly to a bartender. Some customers of businesses have reacted strongly to smoking bans in a variety of public places. Why were these regulations introduced?

Not all tobacco smoke goes into the smoker's body, and much of that which does comes back out. All this excess smoke gets into the environment as *secondhand smoke* for others to consume. Breathing secondhand smoke is called **passive smoking.** In the mid-1980s, the United States Surgeon General issued a report on the effects of passive smoking that included three conclusions:

1. Involuntary smoking is a cause of disease, including lung cancer, in healthy nonsmokers.
2. Compared with the children of nonsmoking parents, children of parents who smoke have a higher frequency of respiratory infections, increased respiratory symptoms, and slightly smaller rates of increase in lung function as the lungs mature.
3. The simple separation of smokers and nonsmokers within the same air space may reduce, but does not eliminate, the exposure of nonsmokers to environmental tobacco smoke. (USDHHS, 1986b, p. 7)

The smoke that comes from the burning tip of a cigarette—or *sidestream smoke*—makes up most of environmental tobacco smoke and contains high concentrations of known carcinogens (Eriksen, LeMaistre, & Newell, 1988). Public places, such as worksites, have high levels of sidestream smoke when smoking is permitted (Hammond et al., 1995).

Evidence of the harmful effects of secondhand smoke is quite substantial. Some of the strongest evidence has linked passive smoking to lung cancer (Erikson, LeMaistre, & Newell, 1988; USDHHS, 1986b). Many studies of this relationship in various countries around the world have examined the development of cancer in nonsmokers who had spouses who smoked and generally found that passive smokers' risk of lung cancer increases, and sometimes doubles or triples. Studies have also found a higher risk of cardiovascular disease in nonsmoking spouses of smokers than nonsmokers (Humble et al., 1990).

Passive smoking also has other health effects. For instance, exposure to secondhand smoke also increases atherosclerosis (Howard et al., 1998; Penn & Snyder, 1993). What's more, for people with existing cardiovascular conditions, such as angina, and respiratory problems, such as asthma and hay fever, environmental tobacco smoke can bring on attacks or aggravate acute symptoms (Eriksen, LeMaistre, & Newell, 1988). Increasingly, people are becoming aware of the health effects of secondhand smoke and are making efforts to have smoke-free environments.

Cardiovascular Disease

Cardiovascular disease—including coronary heart disease (CHD) and stroke—is the leading cause of death by far in adults over age 60 worldwide (WHO, 2004). In the United States, it is responsible for over 35% of all deaths each year and claims more lives than cancer, accidents, and several other causes combined (USBC, 2003). When you point out these facts to some smokers, they say, "Well, you have to die of *something.*" Of course, that's true—but *when* you will die is the real issue. Cardiovascular disease takes many lives early: one in seven Americans it kills are under 65 years of age.

Many millions of Americans suffer from CHD and stroke. The risk of having a heart attack is twice as high for smokers as for nonsmokers (AHA, 2004; USDHHS, 1989). A prospective study examined the impact of smoking on the incidence of CHD across 8½ years in over 3,000 men who participated in the research, beginning when they were 39 to 59 years of age (Rosenman et al., 1976). Compared to nonsmokers, the incidence of CHD was more than 50% higher for men who smoked about a pack a day and over twice as high for those who smoked more than a pack a day. Two other points are important in the link between smoking and CHD. First, the greater risks for CHD

The pictures say it all.

Healthy lung   Smoker's lung (cancerous tumor)   Smoker's lung (emphysema)

An advertisement by the American Cancer Society that may motivate people to avoid starting or to quit smoking.

among smokers than among nonsmokers may be aggravated by stress, since smoking increases when people are under stress. Second, smokers tend to have lifestyles that include other risk factors for CHD, such as being physically inactive (Castro et al., 1989).

How does smoking cause cardiovascular disease? Researchers generally believe that the disease process involves several effects that the nicotine and carbon monoxide in cigarette smoke have on cardiovascular functioning (USDHHS, 1986a). Nicotine constricts blood vessels and increases heart rate, cardiac output, and both systolic and diastolic blood pressure. Carbon monoxide reduces the availability of oxygen to the heart, which may cause damage and lead to atherosclerosis. Studies have found that the more cigarettes people smoke per day the greater their level of serum cholesterol and size of plaques on artery walls (Muscat et al., 1991; Tell et al., 1994). After stopping smoking, cardiovascular risk factors, such as cholesterol levels, improve markedly within 2 months (Eliasson et al., 2001), and the risk of heart attack or stroke declines greatly in the next few years (Kawachi et al., 1993; Negri et al., 1994).

Other Illnesses

Smoking can lead to a variety of other illnesses—particularly emphysema and chronic bronchitis—which are classified together as *chronic obstructive pulmonary disease* (COPD) (ALA, 2003; Haas & Haas, 1990). People

with COPD experience permanently reduced airflow, which is especially evident when they try to exhale with force. Over 80% of cases of COPD in the United States are related to smoking (ALA, 2003; USDHHS, 1986a). As we saw earlier, recurrent smoking irritates and damages respiratory organs. Research has shown that more damage occurs from smoking high-tar than low-tar cigarettes and that regularly smoking nontobacco (marijuana) cigarettes also damages the respiratory system (Bloom et al., 1987; Paoletti et al., 1985). COPD can incapacitate its victims, often forcing relatively young individuals to retire from work. It causes over 2.7 million deaths each year worldwide, particularly among its victims who smoke (WHO, 2003).

Smoking may also increase acute respiratory infections. This has been shown in two ways. First, studies have found that children of smokers are more likely to develop pneumonia than are children of nonsmokers (USDHHS, 1986b). Second, when exposed to common cold viruses, smokers are much more likely to catch cold than nonsmokers, probably because their immune functions are impaired (Cohen et al., 1993).

ALCOHOL USE AND ABUSE

People's use of alcoholic beverages has a very long history, beginning before the eras of ancient Egypt, Greece, and Rome, when using wine and beer was very common. Its popularity continued through the centuries and around the world—except in cultures that strongly prohibited its use, as in Islamic nations—and eventually reached America in the colonial period. Colonial Americans arrived with

> the drinking habits and attitudes of the places they left behind. Liquor was viewed as a panacea; even the Puritan minister Cotton Mather called it "the good creature of God." By all accounts, these people drank, and drank hard. (Critchlow, 1986, p. 752)

But the Puritans also realized that excessive drinking led to problems for society, so they condemned drunkenness as sinful and enforced laws against it.

Over the next two centuries, attitudes about alcohol changed in many cultures. In the United States, the *temperance* movement began in the 18th century and pressed for total abstinence from alcohol. By the mid-1800s, the use of alcohol had diminished sharply and so had its reputation: many Americans at that time believed alcohol destroyed morals and created crime and degenerate behavior (Critchlow, 1986). These attitudes persisted and helped bring about Prohibition, beginning in 1920, when the production, transport, and sale of alcohol became unlawful. After the repeal of Prohibition, the use of alcohol increased, of course, and attitudes about alcohol softened. Americans today believe alcohol has both good and bad effects. (Go to 🍎.)

WHO DRINKS, AND HOW MUCH?

People's attitudes about and use of alcohol are tied to their own characteristics and backgrounds, such as their age, gender, and sociocultural experiences.

Age, Gender, and Alcohol Use

Age and gender affect people's experience with drinking alcoholic beverages in most societies. One reason for gender differences in drinking is that females experience more intoxication than males from the same amount of alcohol. This is because, even when body size is the same, females have smaller blood volume and metabolize alcohol less quickly than males (Tortora & Grabowski, 2003).

Drinking typically begins in adolescence and sometimes in childhood. In a survey of thousands of students across the United States, high school seniors' answers indicated that 78% had consumed an alcoholic drink at some time in their lives, 49% had had a drink in the last month, 50% had been drunk in the past year, and 29% had drunk five or more drinks in a row in the preceding 2 weeks (Johnston, O'Malley, & Bachman, 2003). Males reported more drinking than females. Nearly 39% of eighth-graders reported having had a drink in the past year. Although young people sometimes have alcohol at home with the parents present, such as at special occasions, most teenage drinking occurs in different circumstances. Even when it is illegal for high school and college students

Women in the temperance movement were very assertive, and some went to saloons to keep records of who bought drinks.

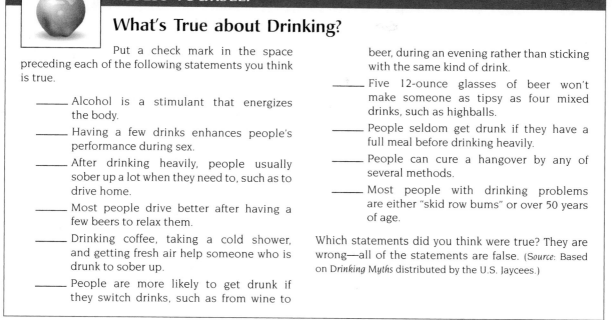

ASSESS YOURSELF

What's True about Drinking?

Put a check mark in the space preceding each of the following statements you think is true.

_____ Alcohol is a stimulant that energizes the body.

_____ Having a few drinks enhances people's performance during sex.

_____ After drinking heavily, people usually sober up a lot when they need to, such as to drive home.

_____ Most people drive better after having a few beers to relax them.

_____ Drinking coffee, taking a cold shower, and getting fresh air help someone who is drunk to sober up.

_____ People are more likely to get drunk if they switch drinks, such as from wine to

beer, during an evening rather than sticking with the same kind of drink.

_____ Five 12-ounce glasses of beer won't make someone as tipsy as four mixed drinks, such as highballs.

_____ People seldom get drunk if they have a full meal before drinking heavily.

_____ People can cure a hangover by any of several methods.

_____ Most people with drinking problems are either "skid row bums" or over 50 years of age.

Which statements did you think were true? They are wrong—all of the statements are false. (*Source*: Based on *Drinking Myths* distributed by the U.S. Jaycees.)

to purchase alcohol and to drink without parental supervision, many do so anyway. In adulthood, males continue to drink more than females (SAMHSA, 2003). Over 60% of young adult and middle-aged Americans drink, but the prevalence is lower in older groups.

Sociocultural Differences in Using Alcohol

Alcohol use varies widely across cultures around the world: people in Norway drink very little, and the French and Italians consume more, mainly wine, which they commonly have with meals (Criqui & Ringel, 1994). Table 7.1 gives comparison data for

four European countries on the amount of alcohol consumed per person and alcohol-related traffic accidents.

In the United States, sharp contrasts in drinking patterns can be made among its many different ethnic groups. The percentage of adults who drink is higher for White Americans than Hispanics, and higher for Hispanics than Blacks—the respective percentages are about 55%, 45%, and 40% (SAMHSA, 1999). Drinking prevalence is very high for Native Americans overall and very low for Asian Americans, especially those of Chinese origin (NIAAA, 1993). Of course, all ethnic groups consist of subgroups, and this is especially

Table 7.1   *Per Capita Alcohol Consumption and Rate of Alcohol-Related Accidents in Four European Countries*

Consumption and Accidents	United Kingdom	Russia	Germany	Italy
Pure alcohol consumed in liters per capita for people aged 15 and over in one year	10.39	10.58	12.89	9.14
Traffic accidents involving alcohol per 100,000 accidents	18.45	22.15	31.20	5.73

Source: WHO/Europe (2004).

important to point out for Native Americans, whose tribes number over 300. Different tribes hold different views toward drinking and show different patterns of alcohol use, with some having very high rates of heavy drinking.

Problem Drinking

In the United States, 120 million individuals age 12 and over drink alcohol at least occasionally (SAMHSA, 2003). Most of these people are light-to-moderate drinkers, consuming fewer than, say, 60 drinks a month. Many people drink much more heavily, but not all of these drinkers meet the criteria for substance abuse we described earlier. One definition of *heavy drinking* is engaging in **binge drinking**—that is, consuming five or more drinks on a single occasion—on five or more days in a month. By this definition, nearly 16 million Americans are heavy drinkers (SAMHSA, 2003). About 50% of 21-year-olds engage in binge drinking in a given month. Binge drinking occurs at very high levels on college campuses, especially among fraternity and sorority members (Goldberg, 1998). Of those individuals who develop problems associated with drinking, most—but not

all—do so within about 5 years of starting to drink regularly (Sarason & Sarason, 1984).

How many drinkers meet the criteria for substance abuse? Estimates have been made on the basis of the proportion of individuals at a given time who had ever displayed the problem. This statistic, called the *lifetime prevalence rate*, indicates that about 20% of men and 8% of women in the United States become alcohol abusers (Davison, Neale, & Kring, 2004). People who abuse alcohol—often called **problem drinkers**—drink heavily on a regular basis and suffer social and occupational impairments from it. Many of them frequently get drunk, drink alone or during the day, and drive under the influence. Although alcohol abuse is far more common in males than females, it is most likely to develop between the ages of 18 and 29 for both sexes (McCrady, 1988; NIAAA, 1993). More than half of those who abuse alcohol are physically dependent on it, or addicted to it, and are classified as **alcoholics.** These people have developed a very high tolerance for alcohol and often have blackout periods or substantial memory losses; many experience delirium tremens when they stop drinking. Although alcoholics often drink the equivalent of a fifth of whiskey (about 25 ounces) a day,

Drinking and celebrating often occur together, and this association conveys the message that drinking is fun.

8 ounces can sometimes be sufficient to produce addiction in humans (Davidson, 1985).

Who abuses alcohol? Many people have an image of the "typical" alcoholic as a scruffy looking, unemployed derelict with no family or friends. But this image is valid for only a small minority of people who abuse alcohol (Mayer, 1983; McCrady, 1988; USDHHS, 1990). Most problem drinkers are married, living with their families, and employed. Many women who are problem drinkers are homemakers and are married to men who drink heavily. Although individuals from the lower social classes—especially homeless people—are at greater risk than those from higher classes for abusing alcohol, large numbers of problem drinkers come from the higher classes and hold high-status jobs. Problem drinking is very rare in childhood; its prevalence increases in adolescence, rises sharply in early adulthood, and gradually declines across ages thereafter (NIAAA, 1993). Alcohol abuse is a major social problem that affects substantial numbers of people from almost all segments of many societies around the world. (Go to 🍎.)

WHY PEOPLE USE AND ABUSE ALCOHOL

In examining why people use and abuse alcohol, we need to consider why individuals start to drink in the first place. The chief reasons for starting to drink involve social and cultural factors, particularly the expectancies that form from watching other individuals enjoying themselves while drinking (Bandura, 1986; NIAAA, 1993; Wood, Vinson, & Sher, 2001).

Adolescents continue drinking partly for the same reasons they started, but these factors intensify and new ones come into play. For one thing, the role of peers increases. Although teenagers often begin occasional drinking under their parents' supervision, such as at celebrations, drinking increases with peers at parties or in cars. The percentage of American adolescents who drink is about 2% at the age of 12 years, 13% at age 14, and 36% at 17—and 26% of 17-year-olds engage in binge drinking (SAMHSA, 2003). In late adolescence and early adulthood, drinkers drink frequently and almost always socially, with friends at parties or in bars. The social aspect is important in two ways (McCarty, 1985; NIAAA, 1993). First, in social drinking, modeling processes affect behavior—for example, people tend to adjust their drinking rates to match those of their companions. Second, drinking socially creates a subjective norm in individuals that the behavior is appropriate and desirable.

With continued drinking, the strength of the behavior increases through positive and negative reinforcement, and substance-related cues develop (Baker, Brandon, & Chassin, 2004; Cunningham, 1998; NIAAA, 1993). Individuals may receive *positive* reinforcement for drinking if they like the taste of a drink or the feeling they get from it, or if they think they succeeded in

---

ASSESS YOURSELF

Do You Abuse Alcohol?

Ask yourself the following questions about your drinking:

- Do you usually have more than 14 drinks a week (assume a drink is one mixed drink with 1¼ ounces of alcohol, 12 ounces of beer, or the equivalent)?
- Do you often think about how or when you are going to drink again?
- Is your job or academic performance suffering by your drinking?
- Has your health declined since you started drinking a lot?

- Do family or friends mention your drinking to you?
- Do you sometimes stop and start drinking to "test" yourself?
- Have you been stopped for drunk driving in the past year?

If you answered "yes" to the first question, consider changing your drinking pattern. If you answered "yes" to any additional questions, consult your college's counseling office for their advice or help. (*Sources:* Based on TSC, 1992; and USDHHS, 1995) business deals or social relationships as a consequence of drinking. Having reinforcing experiences with drinking increases their expectancies for desirable consequences when deciding to drink in the future (Adesso, 1985; Stacy, 1997). In the case of *negative* reinforcement—that is, the reduction of an unpleasant situation—we've seen that people often use alcohol to reduce stress and unpleasant emotions. They may, for instance, drink to suppress their negative thoughts about themselves (Hull, Young, & Jouriles, 1986). But the effects of alcohol on people's anxiety and tension are not so simple. Although drinkers report that alcohol reduces tension and improves their mood, it seems to do so only with the first few drinks they consume in a series. After people consume many drinks, their anxiety and depression levels usually increase (Adesso, 1985; Davidson, 1985; Hull & Bond, 1986).

Why can most people drink in moderation, but others become problem drinkers? Part of the answer lies in psychosocial differences between these people. Compared to individuals who do not abuse alcohol, those who do are more likely to perceive fewer negative consequences for drinking (Hansen, Raynor, & Wolkenstein, 1991). They also tend to experience high levels of stress and live in environments that encourage drinking. For instance, adolescents who abuse alcohol are more likely to have experienced a major trauma, such as physical assault, and have family members who drink heavily (Kilpatrick et al., 2000). And heavy drinkers may form particularly strong substance-related cues: they develop heightened physiological reactions and positive feelings to alcohol-related stimuli, such as seeing or smelling liquor, especially when alcohol is available (Turkkan, McCaul, & Stitzer, 1989)

But a complete answer to why people become problem drinkers also includes developmental and biological factors. For instance,

- Heredity plays a much stronger role when the abuse begins before age 25 than after (Kranzler & Anton, 1994).

- People with a family history of alcoholism appear to develop a tolerance to alcohol, drinking increasing amounts to feel the same effects, more readily than other people (Morzorati et al., 2002).

- People with a specific gene pattern experience stronger cravings for alcohol after having a drink than other individuals do (Hutchinson et al., 2002).

- Some evidence suggests that people at high genetic risk for alcohol dependence find alcohol more rewarding each time they drink, but low-risk people do not (Newlin & Thompson, 1991).

Genetic factors seem to combine with psychosocial processes, especially conditioning, in the development of drinking problems.

DRINKING AND HEALTH

Drinking too much is associated with a wide range of health hazards both for the drinker and for the people the drinker may harm. Drinkers can harm others in several ways. Pregnant women who drink more than two drinks a day place their babies at substantial risk for health problems, such as being born with low birth weight or *fetal alcohol syndrome*, which can involve serious cognitive and physical defects (NIAAA, 1993; Wood, Vinson, & Sher, 2001). And drinking lesser amounts during pregnancy has been associated with impaired learning ability in the child. The safest advice to pregnant women is *not to drink at all*.

Drinking also increases the chance that individuals will harm themselves and others through accidents of various types, such as from unintentionally firing a gun to having a mishap while boating or skiing (Wood, Vinson, & Sher, 2001). Drunk driving is a major cause of death in the United States: about 28% of the nearly 44,000 traffic deaths each year are associated with alcohol use (DeJong & Hingson, 1998; USBC, 2003). Fortunately, the number of motor vehicle deaths and those related to alcohol use have declined greatly since the early 1980s. Consuming alcohol impairs cognitive, perceptual, and motor performance for several hours, particularly the first 2 or 3 hours after drinks are consumed. The degree of impairment people experience can vary widely from one person to the next and depends on the rate of drinking and the person's weight. Figure 7–2 gives the *average* impairment for driving—but for some individuals, one or two drinks may be too many to drive safely.

People's judging how many drinks they can have before engaging in a dangerous activity can be difficult for a couple of reasons. First, many people have misconceptions about the effects of alcohol, such as believing that drinking on a full stomach prevents drunkenness, or thinking, "I'll be OK as soon as I get behind the wheel." For instance, a study found that

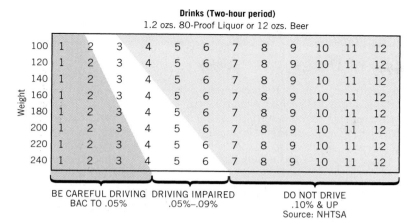

Drinks (Two-hour period)
1.2 ozs. 80-Proof Liquor or 12 ozs. Beer

Weight												
100	1	2	3	4	5	6	7	8	9	10	11	12
120	1	2	3	4	5	6	7	8	9	10	11	12
140	1	2	3	4	5	6	7	8	9	10	11	12
160	1	2	3	4	5	6	7	8	9	10	11	12
180	1	2	3	4	5	6	7	8	9	10	11	12
200	1	2	3	4	5	6	7	8	9	10	11	12
220	1	2	3	4	5	6	7	8	9	10	11	12
240	1	2	3	4	5	6	7	8	9	10	11	12

BE CAREFUL DRIVING   DRIVING IMPAIRED   DO NOT DRIVE
BAC TO .05%   .05%–.09%   .10% & UP
                                             Source: NHTSA

Figure 7–2 Chart developed by the National Highway Traffic Safety Administration (NHTSA) showing the *average* effects of blood alcohol concentration (BAC) on driving. Although alcohol impairment varies from one person to the next, three drinks (the equivalent of three 12-ounce bottles of beer) in a 2-hour period will make most adults' driving unsafe.

students underestimated the impact that alcohol has 2 or 3 hours after drinking, thought that later drinks in a series have less impact than the first couple, and downplayed the effects of beer and wine relative to mixed drinks (Jaccard & Turrisi, 1987). Second, people tend to "super-size" a drink they make for themselves, and still count it as "a single drink," especially if the glass is large (White et al., 2003). So if we try to gauge how intoxicated we're becoming by counting drinks, we may underestimate the effect.

Long-term, heavy drinkers place themselves at risk for developing several health problems (NIAAA, 1993; Wood, Vinson, & Sher, 2001). One of the main risks is for a disease of the liver called *cirrhosis*. Heavy drinking over a long period can cause liver cells to die off and be replaced by permanent, nonfunctional scar tissue. When this scar tissue becomes extensive, the liver is less able to cleanse the blood and regulate its composition. Cirrhosis causes thousands of deaths each year. Heavy drinking also presents other health risks: it has been linked to the development of some forms of *cancer, high blood pressure,* and *heart* and *brain damage.* The brain damage many alcoholics develop can impair their perceptual and memory functions (Parsons, 1986). The person who stops drinking may recover these functions gradually, but some impairments may persist for years or never fully disappear. As you might expect, long-term heavy drinkers have higher death rates than do other people (Schutte et al., 2003; Thun et al., 1997). But if they quit, their mortality risk declines greatly in several years.

Some people believe that drinking in moderation—having, say, a drink or two each day—is *good* for their health, and they may be right. Long-term prospective studies of many thousands of people have found that individuals who drink light or moderate amounts of alcohol, especially wine, each month have lower morbidity and mortality rates than those who drink heavily or who do not drink at all (Gronbæk et al., 2000; Sacco et al., 1999; Thun et al., 1997). Does moderate drinking *cause* better health? It appears that it does, largely by yielding substantial improvements in cardiovascular risk factors, such as blood cholesterol levels (Mukamal & Rimm, 2001). Although all types of alcohol, consumed as one or two drinks a day, can improve health, wine appears to have the strongest effects because of substances it contains (Corder et al., 2001; Klatsky et al., 2003; Stein et al., 1999). Another reason for the health benefits of moderate drinking is that alcohol affects the body's response to stress, reducing cardiovascular and endocrine (for example, catecholamine production) reactions (Levenson, 1986). But as we've seen, larger amounts of alcohol can impair health.

DRUG USE AND ABUSE

The word "drug" can refer to many substances, including prescription and nonprescription medicine, that people may take into their bodies. We will limit the

HIGHLIGHT

Types and Effects of Drugs

"Oh, I feel so light, like a feather," said Dolores, after taking several hits from a "joint." That lightness of feeling is a common effect people get from smoking a marijuana cigarette. Each drug has its own set of general psychological and physiological effects (Ciraulo & Shader, 1991; NCADI, 2000; Schuster & Kilbey, 1992). Some drugs are highly addictive, and others have little potential for producing physical dependence. Drugs are usually classified into four categories: stimulants, depressants, hallucinogens, and narcotics.

Stimulants are chemicals that produce physiological and psychological arousal, keeping the user awake and making the world seem to race by. This category of drugs includes *amphetamines, caffeine,* and *cocaine,* which can be inhaled, injected, or smoked ("crack"). Chronic use of stimulants can produce mental confusion, exhaustion, and weight loss—and can lead to psychological dependence. Physical dependence on amphetamines, cocaine, or caffeine can develop; the withdrawal symptoms often are subtle, but are still very influential on behavior.

Depressants decrease arousal and increase relaxation. People use these drugs to reduce anxiety and induce sleep. Depressants include various *tranquilizers* (such as Valium) and *barbiturates,* which are commonly called "downers." Excessive and chronic use of depressants interferes with motor and emotional stability and produces psychological dependence. Addiction can develop with long-term use of depressants and can occur rapidly for barbiturates.

Hallucinogens produce perceptual distortions, such as when the body or mind feels light. The most commonly used drug of this type is *marijuana,* which people use for the relaxation and intoxication it causes. Other hallucinogens, such as *mescaline,* LSD (*lysergic acid diethylamide*), and PCP (phencyclidine), often produce a feeling of exhilaration. Hallucinogens have a relatively low potential for causing physical dependence, but chronic use of these drugs can lead to psychological dependence.

Narcotics or *opiates* are sedatives that relieve pain. In many people, but not all, they produce a euphoric and relaxed feeling. The narcotics include *morphine, codeine,* and *heroin.* These drugs, especially heroin, generally cause intense physical *and* psychological dependence when used continually in large doses.

The effects of drugs can vary. The same dose of a drug may produce quite different reactions in different people and in the same person on different occasions (Bardo & Risner, 1985). Why? Physiological processes, such as metabolism and absorption by tissues, vary from one person to the next and within each individual over time. Partly because very young people and the elderly have lower rates of metabolism than others do, they tend to experience relatively strong reactions to drugs. Stress can also influence the effects of a drug, causing physiological changes that may increase a drug's impact.

---

term *drug* to mean psychoactive substances other than nicotine and alcohol that can cause physical or psychological dependence. Like smoking and drinking, the use of drugs has a long history—for example, the Chinese evidently used marijuana 27 centuries B.C. In the United States, addiction to narcotics was widespread among people of all ages in the 19th century. Many "patent medicines" in those days contained opium and were sold without government regulation. As a result, large numbers of people became addicted at early ages (Kett, 1977). Laws were enacted in the early 1900s against the use of narcotics in America. (Go to 💡.)

WHO USES DRUGS, AND WHY?

Drug use has become a serious problem in many countries of the world, especially in North America and Europe. Some individuals and segments of society are more likely than others to use drugs.

Age, Gender, and Sociocultural Differences in Drug Use

We have seen that smoking and drinking are more likely to begin in adolescence than at any other time in the life span. This developmental pattern is true for using most drugs, too. Three types of drugs that are exceptions to this pattern are tranquilizers, barbiturates, and painkillers (such as OxyContin): use commonly begins in adulthood, often with prescriptions from physicians (AMA, 2003; Ciraulo & Shader, 1991; Davison, Neale, & Kring, 2004).

One of the most popular drugs in the United States is marijuana. Its use often begins by the eighth grade, and individuals who eventually try it are likely to do so before they reach the eleventh grade (Johnston, O'Malley, & Bachman, 2003). Nearly half of American teenagers try it before they graduate high school. Teenagers' use of most other drugs tends to begin somewhat later and is much less prevalent—for instance, about 9% try cocaine before graduation. Drug use in the United States has fluctuated over time and has been decreasing in recent years. These changes have coincided with adolescents' beliefs about whether drugs are harmful, rather than changes in drug availability (Johnston, O'Malley, & Bachman, 2003). Drug use is far more prevalent in males than females at virtually all adolescent and adult ages and for almost all drug types, but the prevalence of drug use by different American ethnic groups varies with age and drug type (NCHS, 2000). For example, the prevalence of marijuana use by Whites, Blacks, and Hispanics is similar in the teenage years, but is higher among Whites and Blacks than Hispanics in early adulthood. The prevalence of cocaine use is higher among Whites and Hispanics than Blacks for teenagers, but the gap narrows sharply in early adulthood.

Many individuals engage in *polysubstance abuse*, that is, using more than one substance. Does using one substance lead to using another? The likelihood that individuals will progress from a less serious drug, such as marijuana, to a more serious drug, such as cocaine, is related to how heavily the earlier drug was used (Kandel & Faust, 1975; Newcomb & Bentler, 1986). Heavy users of a less serious drug are more likely to begin using more serious drugs than light users are. Similarly, smoking cigarettes and using alcohol have been linked to subsequent drug use (Petraitis et al., 1998).

Why Adolescents Use Drugs

Why do teens try marijuana and other drugs? They do so for many of the same reasons they start to drink or smoke cigarettes (Hansen et al., 1987; Stein, Newcomb, & Bentler, 1987). Two of the strongest factors in determining initial and early stages of drug use are availability and social learning. Teenagers see peers and important adults, such as parents and celebrities, model behaviors and attitudes that promote drug use. Studies have shown that adolescents are more likely to use marijuana and other drugs if their parents and friends use mood-altering substances, such as alcohol and marijuana (Petraitis et al., 1998; Stein, Newcomb, & Bentler, 1987). Teenagers' marijuana use seems to be affected more by their friends' than their parents' substance use, and the first introduction of most youths to marijuana is through a friend (Kandel, 1974).

After people start using drugs, they tend to continue if they like the experience—that is, if the drug makes them "feel good" or helps them feel *better* than they felt before taking it (Barrett, 1985). Many people claim that taking drugs reduces their anxiety and tension. In other words, drugs have reinforcing effects. Then, with continued use, drug-related cues become conditioned to the drug, can elicit effects like those the drug itself produces, and compel the user to use it again (Childress, 1996; Robinson & Berridge, 2003). People often use drugs in the presence of friends and other peers, therefore, social pressure and encouragement also tend to maintain and increase drug use.

Why do some individuals progress from drug use to *drug abuse*? Personality traits seem to be involved (Brook et al., 1986; Cox, 1985; Newcomb, Maddahian, & Bentler, 1986; Stein, Newcomb, & Bentler, 1987). Compared to individuals who use drugs occasionally, those who go on to abuse drugs tend to be *more* rebellious, impulsive, accepting of illegal behavior, and oriented toward sensation seeking; and they tend to be *less* socially conforming and less committed to a religion.

DRUG USE AND HEALTH

The effects of drug use and abuse on people's health are not as well documented as those of drinking and cigarette smoking. This is because drug use did not become widespread until the 1960s, it is still much less prevalent than drinking and smoking, and many drug users are unwilling to admit to researchers that they use drugs—a criminal offense—for fear of being prosecuted. Nevertheless, some health effects are known. For example, drugs taken by women during pregnancy cross the placenta and may harm the fetus; and babies born to addicted mothers are likely to be addicted, too (Cook, Petersen, & Moore, 1990). Also, each year millions of American teens drive under the influence of drugs (SAMHSA, 2003). And long-term marijuana smoking damages the user's lungs (Bloom et al., 1987).

The health effects of cocaine are becoming increasingly clear, particularly with regard to the cardiovascular system (AMA, 2003; Mittleman et al., 1999). Taking crack cocaine causes the person's blood vessels to constrict, heart rate to speed up, and blood pressure to increase suddenly. It can also trigger cardiac arrhythmia. These events can cause a stroke or myocardial infarction and can lead to death. Cocaine also produces many other health problems. For example, the more people use it in their mid-20s, the more likely they will have neurological symptoms and poor general health 10 years later (Chen, Scheier, & Kandel, 1996). What's more, poor health leads to continued cocaine use.

REDUCING SUBSTANCE USE AND ABUSE

How can we help prevent people from using or abusing substances and help them stop using tobacco, alcohol, and drugs if they start?

PREVENTING SUBSTANCE USE

The focus for prevention is on helping people avoid beginning to use specific substances in the first place. To be effective, prevention programs must consider two factors: *when* and *why* individuals start to use the substances. The first factor is straightforward and easily addressed. The likelihood of starting to use tobacco, alcohol, and drugs rises during the junior high school years, increases sharply in the high school years, and is very low in adulthood, therefore, prevention programs should begin early (Evans, 1984). Programs to prevent substance use are often conducted in schools and are introduced before children reach the age of 12 or so. To address why people start using substances, programs usually include features to combat the psychosocial factors we've already discussed that encourage use.

Early programs to prevent substance use usually focused on only one substance, but programs today recognize that use of tobacco, alcohol, and drugs be-

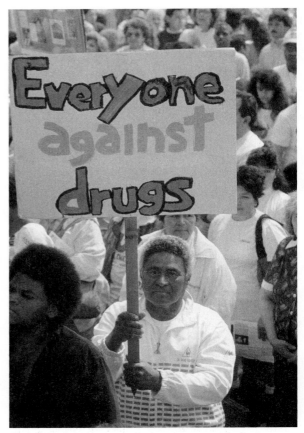

A demonstration against the use of drugs.

gins mainly during adolescence and for similar reasons. As a result, many programs now try to address all three substances, which seems to be an efficient strategy. A program of this type that does *not* seem to work is the widely–publicized Project DARE, in which police officers lead sessions in school to prevent substance use. Children who do and do not receive the program do not differ in their use of or attitudes about cigarettes, alcohol, marijuana, and other illicit drugs when assessed in late adolescence. (Lynam et al., 1999). The most common and effective prevention approaches have had three focuses: public policy and legal issues, health promotion and education, and family involvement; the last two are implemented by professionals trained in preventing substance use.

Public Policy and Legal Approaches

Governments apply public policy and legal approaches to reduce per capita consumption of tobacco, alcohol, and drugs by creating barriers to buying and using them. For tobacco, effective approaches include increasing the price of cigarettes through taxation and restricting the advertisement and purchase of cigarettes, such as by underage adolescents (Altman et al., 1999; Kaplan et al., 1995). For alcohol, two methods have been effective: increasing the price of alcoholic beverages through taxation and prohibiting underage individuals from buying or consuming alcohol (Ashley & Rankin, 1988; NIAAA, 1993). These methods reduce alcohol consumption and related automobile accidents among individuals in the late adolescent and early adulthood years. Another approach has not been very effective in reducing drinking: limiting the number of outlets where alcoholic beverages can be bought and restricting the times when they are on sale. For preventing drug use, the main approaches have been to outlaw possessing, selling, and consuming drugs.

Health Promotion and Education

Programs to prevent substance use originally focused on giving fear-arousing warnings of the health consequences of smoking, drinking, and using drugs (Des Jarlais et al., 1987; Evans, 1984). These programs did not take into account the past social experiences and current psychosocial forces that exert very strong influences on teenage behavior. Although knowing the health consequences can change children's beliefs and attitudes about using a substance, such as tobacco, it is usually not sufficient to stop them from starting (Bruvold, 1993; Flay, 1985). This failure points out the need for prevention programs to consider more fully *why* youth begin to use substances.

As we saw earlier, researchers have identified several psychosocial reasons as to why young people start using tobacco, alcohol, and drugs. Social influences and associated social skills appear to have stronger effects on teenage substance use than long-range health consequences that seem remote, both in time and in likelihood. Recognizing this, researchers have designed and tested school-based programs to deter teenage substance use by addressing psychosocial factors. For now, we'll consider programs to prevent smoking for examples of useful methods. One early program focused on the immediate consequences of smoking, such as how much it costs and its physiological effects (Evans, 1976; Evans et al., 1978). Films with same-age peers as narrators gave information to help students understand how modeling, peer pressure, and cigarette advertising influence their willingness to smoke and to teach them how to resist these forces. The purpose of the program was to provide the knowledge and skills to "immunize" teenagers against forces that lead to smoking. This psychosocial approach produced encouraging results and has served as the basis for developing increasingly effective methods for deterring smoking (Botvin & Epstein, 1999; Flay, 1985).

The psychosocial perspective became the foundation for two types of smoking prevention efforts:

- *Social influence approaches* focus on training skills to help individuals resist social pressures to smoke. They include (1) discussions and films regarding how peers, family members, and the media influence smoking by teenagers, (2) modeling and role-playing of specific refusal skills, such as saying, "No thank you, I don't smoke," and (3) requiring that each student decide his or her intention regarding whether or not to smoke and announce that decision publicly to classmates (Flay et al., 1985).

- *Life skills training approaches* address general social, cognitive, and coping skills. Because many individuals who begin smoking seem to lack these general skills, this approach focuses on improving (1) personal skills, including critical thinking for making decisions, techniques for coping with anxiety, and basic principles for changing their own behavior and (2) general social skills, including methods for being assertive and making conversation (Botvin, Renick, & Baker, 1983; Botvin & Wills, 1985).

Longitudinal studies have tested these approaches for smoking prevention for 1 to 6 years. Although the exact procedures varied somewhat from one study to the next, they were fairly similar. Most of the programs began when the children were in sixth or seventh grade (about age 12). They used a large number of schools, which were assigned to *program* or *control* groups in ways to assure comparability of the schools' size and social class across conditions. The programs gave information about the short- and long-term health and social consequences of smoking. And the subjects' self-reports of their smoking were verified, using biochemical analyses of saliva or breath samples.

Were these approaches successful? Compared with the control subjects, children who received each type of program were less likely to begin to smoke during the next couple of years or so (Botvin & Wills, 1985; Bruvold, 1993; Flay et al., 1985; Murray et al., 1987; Murray et al., 1988). But some long-term followup studies of teens in social influence programs found that the programs' beneficial effects don't last beyond 4 years or so: smoking surged in the juniors and seniors (Flay et al., 1989; Murray et al., 1989). And some psychosocial programs have had high attrition rates, particularly among smokers and those at high risk of becoming smokers (Biglan et al., 1987). Researchers have described ways to improve future programs:

- They should be long enough (at least five sessions) to have an impact, be administered correctly and fully, and have "booster" sessions every year or two (Botvin & Epstein, 1999).

- They may need to start before the fifth grade and focus on attitudes about smokers. A study found that by the time children enter fifth grade many already have positive attitudes about smokers; having these attitudes at that time was associated with beginning to smoke by the ninth grade (Dinh et al., 1995).

- Getting parents involved may also be useful. For example, if parents who smoke quit, their children will be much less likely to smoke, especially if quitting occurs before the child is 9 years old (Farkas et al., 1999).

Because of the successes psychosocial programs have had with smoking, they have been extended for preventing alcohol and drug use. These programs effectively reduce teenage drinking (Kivlahan et al., 1990; NIAAA, 1993) and marijuana use (Chou et al., 1998). A psychosocial program that addressed and followed tobacco, alcohol, and marijuana use over 18 months prevented seventh- and eighth-graders from starting to use substances they hadn't begun using and reduced the amount of substances the students were already using (Ellickson et al., 2003).

Family Involvement Approaches

In family involvement approaches, efforts are made to get parents more actively involved in supervising their children. Family involvement makes intuitive

sense, and the need for it is supported by three research findings. First, children of parents who provide little monitoring, rules, and supervision are four times more likely to try drugs in the future than children with actively involved parents (Chilcoat, Dishion, & Anthony, 1995). Second, children are far less likely to use a substance if they know their parents would disapprove of it and would punish that behavior (Komro et al., 2003; SAMHSA, 2003). Third, most parents of teenagers who use a substance are not aware of it: the percentages of parental awareness for each substance are 39% for tobacco use, 34% for alcohol use, and 11% for drugs (Williams et al., 2003).

Family involvement programs for preventing tobacco, alcohol, and marijuana use were introduced with the families of sixth–grade students, whose substance use was followed for 4 years (Spoth, Redmond, & Shin, 2001). The families were recruited from the general population; that is, they were not selected on the basis of the children's using or not using a substance. The programs were presented in several weekly sessions and were designed to teach parenting skills that should help the children delay starting to use the substances or reduce their current use of them. For example, the parents learned how to monitor the child's behavior and use appropriate discipline, teach the child ways to resist peer pressure to use substances, and reduce family conflict. Comparisons in tenth grade with a control group revealed that the children in the families with a prevention program were far less likely to have begun smoking, drinking, or using marijuana; and those who did use substances, used much less.

QUITTING A SUBSTANCE WITHOUT THERAPY

Alcohol and drug abuse have been viewed in most societies as deviant behaviors for centuries. And today, people in many societies are finding that cigarette smoking is not only harmful to their health, but it is like a deviant behavior. Many nonsmokers resent people smoking in their presence, and many smokers feel guilty when smoking because they know it offends others and believe it is unhealthy, irrational behavior. Still, most teenage and young adult smokers think they're at least as healthy as nonsmokers their age, and many are not concerned about potential health problems, even if they've already developed a smoker's cough (Prokhorov, 2003). Few substance abusers seek therapy to stop. For example, only about one third of alcoholics ever seek treatment (Cunningham & Breslin, 2004). Let's look at the process of quitting substances without therapy.

Stopping Smoking on One's Own

You probably know people who were smokers—perhaps heavy smokers—who have quit. Chances are they quit without any sort of professional help. Millions of people around the world stop smoking each year, and the vast majority do it on their own. But only a small percentage of individuals who begin smoking in adolescence quit in the next 20 years (Chassin et al., 2000). Are people effective at stopping on their own, and does it take enormous effort?

Stanley Schachter (1982) interviewed 16- to 79-year-old men and women about their experience in stopping smoking if they had ever smoked cigarettes regularly. These interviews revealed that over 60% of smokers who tried to quit eventually succeeded—virtually all had not smoked in the last 3 months, and the average length of abstinence was more than 7 years. Was it harder for the heavy smokers (smoking at least three-quarters of a pack a day) to quit than the light smokers? Yes, much harder. Nearly half of the heavy smokers who quit reported severe withdrawal symptoms, such as intense cravings, irritability, sleeplessness, and cold sweats; less than 30% reported having no difficulties. In contrast, almost all of the light smokers said quitting had been easy, even if they had failed! A similar study found very similar results (Rzewnicki & Forgays, 1987).

The results of these studies suggest that most people can stop smoking on their own, even if they smoke heavily. Other studies have clarified the process of quitting on one's own (Carey et al., 1993; Cohen et al., 1989; Curry, Wagner, & Grothaus, 1990; DiClemente et al., 1991; Gritz, Carr, & Marcus, 1991; Pallonen et al., 1990; Rose et al., 1996). Most people do not succeed in one attempt, but eventually succeed after several tries, and certain factors differentiate those people who do and don't succeed. Compared to smokers who do not succeed in quitting, those who do are likely to:

- Have decided that they want and are ready to quit.
- Feel confident that they can succeed.
- Have smoked less than a pack a day.

- Experience less stress.
- Feel less nicotine dependence and experience less craving for tobacco and fewer and less severe withdrawal symptoms, such as restlessness and tension.
- Be highly motivated, especially by *intrinsic* factors, such as a feeling of self-control or a concern about their health.
- Be willing to try again if they don't succeed. Many people fail the first few times they try, but learn from their mistakes.

People often decide to quit smoking when rules restricting smoking are introduced at work, especially if the worksite offers a program to help them stop. The above factors seem to affect their success, too (Fielding, 1991; Grunberg, 1991; Klesges et al., 1999).

What methods do smokers use when trying to quit? To answer this question, researchers interviewed participants in a month-long communitywide stop-smoking contest that had a grand prize of a trip to Disney World (Glasgow et al., 1985). These interviews revealed that:

- The vast majority of the men and women attempted to quit cold turkey rather than trying to reduce their smoking gradually before the contest began.
- Most participants used oral substitutes, such as candy or mints, in place of cigarettes.
- Most tried to go it alone, without involving other people, but many others used a buddy system or made bets with others.
- Most used cognitive strategies, such as telling themselves, "I don't need a cigarette," or reminding themselves of the health risks in smoking, the commitment they made to quit, or the possibility of winning a prize.
- A minority of individuals provided themselves with material rewards for sticking with quitting or punishment for backsliding.

Fifty-five participants—about 40%—remained abstinent throughout the month (which was verified through biochemical saliva or breath analyses). Quitting cold turkey rather than gradually and providing rewards for abstaining were more strongly related to successful quitting than some other methods the smokers used.

Stopping Alcohol and Drug Use on One's Own

Because little is known about quitting alcohol and drug use on one's own, we'll focus on problem drinkers' reducing their alcohol intake without treatment. What proportion of people who abuse alcohol recover without professional help? Researchers have estimated that about 20% markedly reduce or stop drinking on their own (Miller & Hester, 1980; Moyer & Finney, 2002). This estimate is based on data from studies of treatment effectiveness in which some problem drinkers were randomly assigned to control groups and stopped drinking with no treatment. How do drinkers who quit on their own differ from those who do not? Those who quit have higher self-esteem, fewer past experiences of intoxication, and social networks with members who drink less (Russell et al., 2001). And they have social support from a spouse and changed the way they weighed the pros and cons of drinking—for example, realizing "I was sick and tired of it, really weary of it" (Sobell et al., 1993).

Early Intervention

Early intervention efforts center on identifying people at high risk for substance abuse and then providing information to reduce that risk (Ashley & Rankin, 1988). Although early intervention can be used for smoking and drug use, we'll focus on alcohol use here. Most high-risk drinkers are identified on the basis of current drinking patterns or problems, such as being charged with drunk driving. Interventions have been far more successful for relatively *light* drinkers than heavy drinkers, who often get *worse* after an intervention (McGuire, 1982). If drinking problems are detected early, successful interventions can simply involve giving information and advice, and the individuals may be able to reduce their drinking to a moderate level (Ashley & Rankin, 1988; NIAAA, 1993; Sobell et al., 2002).

Early interventions have been successful with high-risk drinkers identified at colleges, in medical settings, and at worksites. In medical settings, for example, physicians identified high-risk drinkers by having patients fill out a health survey that included questions on drinking; some of these patients received information and advice on reducing their drinking (Fleming et al., 2000). Compared with high-risk drinkers who did not get the intervention, those

who got the intervention incurred lower expenses for health care and for legal and motor vehicle events over the next year. In worksites, many employers and unions provide *employee assistance programs* (EAPs) to help individuals who have personal problems, such as with drinking or stress (USDHHS, 1990). EAPs can be helpful, but they usually don't identify high-risk drinkers until the problem is severe, and workers are not likely to use them at all if they worry that counselors will leak information back to their bosses. The worksite should be a good place for preventing alcohol abuse because most individuals who abuse alcohol have jobs, and drinking is often related to stresses on the job (Mayer, 1983).

TREATMENT METHODS TO STOP SUBSTANCE USE AND ABUSE

Of the substance users who are willing to try to quit or reduce their use, the ones who seek help are likely to be psychologically and physically dependent on the substance, decreasing the chances that they will succeed. Therapists can design programs that use a variety of methods to help. (Go to 💡.)

Psychosocial Methods for Stopping Substance Abuse

Substance abuse involves entrenched behaviors that are difficult to stop, particularly if physical dependence has developed. In many cases, chemical approaches are useful to decrease craving and other withdrawal symptoms, as we'll see later. For now, we'll focus on psychosocial methods. Because the psychosocial processes leading to and maintaining substance abuse are similar for using tobacco, alcohol, and drugs, the approaches health psychologists apply to help people stop or reduce using them are basically the same for all three substances. We'll concentrate on methods for which there is good evidence for their success. Other methods have received much media attention but lack clear evidence of success: contrary to media hype, for example, *hypnosis* is not useful in treating alcohol and drug abuse, and the evidence for its utility in quitting smoking is mixed (Nash, 2001).

An initial issue in treating substance abuse is the person's desire and readiness to change. Although most people who seek treatment to stop or reduce their substance use want to change, not all do. Some

HIGHLIGHT ON ISSUES

Where Should Alcohol and Drug Abuse Treatment Occur, and What Should Be the Goals and Criteria for Success?

Because of their physical dependence when alcohol and drug abusers enter treatment, the first step in their recovery is **detoxification**—the drying out process to get an addicted person safely through the period of withdrawal from a substance. This is an essential step before treatment can proceed. Withdrawal symptoms can be severe, sometimes even causing death, therefore, detoxification often occurs in hospitals under medical supervision, using medication to control the symptoms (Ciraulo & Renner, 1991; Miller & Hester, 1985). Improved assessment procedures and detoxification methods today enable many addicted people to undergo detoxification at home if they receive careful assistance and support from trained individuals. After that, the question becomes: should treatment be carried out in a residential setting or on an outpatient basis? Most problem drinkers and drug users can be treated as outpatients. But with alcoholics, for example, those who are strongly addicted appear to benefit more from inpatient than outpatient care (Finney & Moos, 1997; NIAAA, 1993; Rychtarik et al., 2000). In the United States, most problem drinkers who receive treatment do so as outpatients (USBC, 2003).

Ideally, treatment should "cure" the person's substance problem forever, but at what point can therapists expect that their assessments of the success of treatment are likely to reflect durable effects? On this issue, there is considerable agreement among researchers: They generally recommend and use a minimum followup interval of 12 to 18 months to determine the success of treatment (Emrick & Hansen, 1983; Nathan, 1986). Many programs today also attempt to verify self-reports of substance use through other sources—reports by the ex-abuser's spouse or through blood or breath tests, for instance—and measure other outcomes of treatment, such as physical health, employment status, and legal problems encountered.

Due to legal and medical considerations, the treatment goal for tobacco and drug users is to quit completely. But what about alcohol use—should treatment aim to have drinkers become *permanently abstinent*, or can some return gradually to *controlled drinking*? This distinction generated a bitter controversy in the 1980s (Marlatt, 1983; Peele, 1984). According to some professionals, the research findings indicated that some problem drinkers—including alcoholics—could learn to drink in moderation after first becoming abstinent, but other professionals strongly challenged this view. Although the controversy is not completely resolved, it does appear that *some* problem drinkers can learn through treatment to drink in moderation (Miller & Hester, 1980; Peele, 1984). Problem drinkers who have the best prospects for controlled drinking:

- Are relatively young.
- Are socially stable, that is, married or employed.
- Have had a relatively brief history of alcohol abuse.
- Have *not* suffered severe withdrawal symptoms while becoming abstinent.
- Prefer trying to drink in moderation and have *not* made a personal commitment to abstinence as a goal.

In other words, the less severe the drinking problem, the better the chances of succeeding in controlled drinking. What's more, long-term alcoholics who choose abstinence as their goal have fewer drinking problems at 1-year followup than those who choose controlled drinking (Hodgins et al., 1997). For long-term alcoholics to pursue a goal of controlled drinking is unrealistic and probably not in their best interests (Nathan, 1986; Sandberg & Marlatt, 1991).

were coerced or required to enter therapy by their family, employer, or the justice system. And clients who do want to change vary in their degree of commitment. We saw in Chapter 6 that professionals can use the *stages of change model* to describe people's readiness to modify health-related behaviors. A critical transition occurs when the person's stage of readiness moves from *contemplation*, or thinking about changing, to *preparation* and *action*. According to psychologist William Miller (1989), this transition is like a door that opens for a period of time and closes if the substance abuser doesn't use it in that time. Using this approach can be encouraged in several ways, such as:

- Giving the person clear advice about why and how to change.
- Removing important barriers for change.
- Introducing external consequences, such as rewards for changing or real threats (for example, of being fired) if no change occurs.
- Offering help and showing a helping attitude.

Family members, friends, coworkers, physicians, or therapists can use these and other approaches to increase the person's motivation to change. Family members who receive training in motivational methods can be very successful in helping problem drinkers and drug users to decide to start therapy (Meyers et al., 2002; Miller, Meyers, & Tonigan, 1999). These methods are based on the technique of *motivational interviewing* we discussed in Chapter 6. Therapists also use motivational interviewing methods during treatment to enhance its success; these methods appear to be more effective with drinking and drug use than with smoking (Burke, Arkowitz, & Menchola, 2003).

Another effective psychosocial method for treating substance use is to provide the user with *positive reinforcement* for stopping or reducing use. Compared to treatments that don't include reinforcement, treatments that do use it are more successful in reducing the use of tobacco, alcohol, and a variety of drugs, including marijuana, cocaine, and opiates (Higgins, Heil, & Lussier, 2004). The reinforcers are mainly monetary based—for instance, vouchers that can be exchanged for desirable items—and programs usually spend several times more per client to treat opiate abuse than to treat smoking (about $150). Some researchers have designed and tested programs with reinforcers that cost less, as one study did with cocaine abusers who were randomly assigned to either a standard treatment or the same treatment with reinforcement (Petry & Martin, 2002). The clients in both conditions submitted urine samples two or three times a week, which was analyzed for opioids and cocaine. If they were abstinent—the sample was negative—they could participate in a lottery that determined whether they would win a prize and what it would be. Most prizes were small, such as a choice of a $1 coupon for fast food or some toiletries, and some were larger

(worth $20). Each drawing also offered a slim chance of winning a much larger prize, such as a small TV or a boombox. Compared to the clients with the standard treatment, those in the reinforcement condition were far more abstinent during the 12-week program and for the following 3 months. The reinforcement program cost $137 per client.

Therapists sometimes use **aversion strategies,** which use procedures to link unpleasant stimuli to substance use to discourage the behavior. For smoking, therapists have tried several types of unpleasant stimuli, but one type that seems to work well is making cigarette smoke itself unpleasant (Lichtenstein & Mermelstein, 1984). One way to make smoke unpleasant is called *satiation:* the person doubles or triples his or her usual smoking rate at home for some period of time. For some smokers, aversion strategies may be useful as a first step in a program for quitting. Aversion strategies have also been applied to treat alcohol abuse. An effective aversion strategy is to have the person take an **emetic drug,** such as *emetine*, that induces nausea when alcohol is consumed. In a typical half-hour session, the person first receives an injection of emetine and then repeatedly drinks an alcoholic beverage, each time quickly becoming nauseated and vomiting (Miller & Hester, 1980). The person undergoes several of these sessions, typically as an inpatient in a hospital, and then receives booster sessions periodically after discharge. A study of hundreds of problem drinkers who received emetine therapy revealed that 63% of the men and women remained abstinent during the 12 months after treatment, and half of these individuals remained abstinent for the next 2 years (Wiens & Menustik, 1983).

Because of the role of substance-related cues in maintaining smoking, drinking, and drug use, therapists use a method called **cue exposure** to counteract the classical conditioning that occurs with long-term substance use. Let's use drinking as an example. The cues, such as seeing a liquor bottle, are paired with substance use, drinking, and gain the ability to produce internal responses like those that happen when the person actually uses the substance. In using cue exposure to reduce these internal reactions to conditioned stimuli, therapists expose problem drinkers repeatedly to substance-related cues, such as holding a beer can, while not allowing them to drink. Cue exposure has had some success in treating substance abuse, particularly drinking (Blakey & Baker, 1980; Drummond & Glautier, 1994; Rohsenow et al., 2001).

Earlier we saw that one reason people use a substance is that they gain negative reinforcement from it: they use it to regulate emotional states—that is, to cope—and need to learn ways to deal with stress that are more adaptive. As a result, therapists often help substance abusers learn to manage their stress with behavioral and cognitive methods for *stress management* that we described in Chapter 5. These methods include:

- Progressive muscle relaxation, in which people alternately tighten and relax individual muscle groups.
- Meditation, an alternative relaxation method.
- Cognitive restructuring, in which people learn to replace stress-provoking thoughts with more constructive and realistic ones.

Cognitive–behavioral methods are among the most effective approaches in treating problem drinking (Finney & Moos, 1997; Stockwell & Town, 1989) and drug use (Maude-Griffin et al., 1998; Tims, Fletcher, & Hubbard, 1991). They are also useful in helping people stop smoking. (Go to ●.)

Self-Help Groups

Alcoholics Anonymous (AA) is a widely known self-help program that was founded in the 1930s by people with drinking problems (Bean-Bayog, 1991; McCrady & Irvine, 1989). The program now has thousands of chapters throughout the United States and around the world and has set up organizations to help alcoholics' families, such as *Alateen* for their adolescent children and *Al-Anon* for adults in the family. The AA philosophy includes two basic views. First, people who abuse alcohol are alcoholics and remain alcoholics for life, even if they never take another drink. Second, taking one drink after becoming abstinent can be enough to set off an alcoholic binge and, therefore, must be avoided. As a result, AA is committed to the goal of permanent and total abstinence, and their approach is aimed at helping their members resist even one drink. A similar organization for drug users is called Narcotics Anonymous.

Because the AA philosophy has its roots in evangelical Protestantism, the program emphasizes the individual's needs for spiritual awakening, public confession, and contrition (McCrady & Irvine, 1989; Peele, 1984). This philosophy can be seen in the Twelve Steps AA uses to help drinkers quit—for example, one step is, "Admitted to God, to ourselves, and to another human being the exact nature of our wrongs." Members attend frequent AA meetings, which use the Twelve Steps to promote frank discussions about the members' experiences with alcohol and difficulties resisting drinking. An important feature of the AA approach is that its members develop friendships with other ex-drinkers and get encouragement from each other and from knowing individuals who have succeeded.

Does AA work, and is it more effective than other approaches for helping drinkers quit? Until the late 1990s, AA's effectiveness was unknown because its membership is anonymous and the organization does not keep systematic information about people who attend. Today, there are two lines of evidence for its success. First, studies compared different methods conducted by professional therapists and found that treatments using the AA approach produced as much improvement as other treatments (Ouimette, Finney, & Moos, 1997; PMRG, 1998). Second, research has shown that the greater the duration and frequency of alcoholics' involvement in AA, the less their binge drinking and the better their social functioning in the following years (McKellar, Stewart, & Humphreys, 2003; Moos & Moos, 2004). But AA may not be the best approach for problem drinkers who do not believe in God: a study found that atheists and agnostics are less likely than believers to initiate and sustain AA participation (Tonigan, Miller, & Schermer, 2002). AA is being used more and more as an approach to prevent relapse after other forms of treatment (NIAAA, 1993).

Chemical Methods for Treating Substance Abuse

Treatments for substance abuse often use prescribed drugs that the person is required to take regularly to combat the conditions that maintain the behavior. Some of these drugs interact with the abused substance, such as alcohol, producing unpleasant reactions, such as nausea and vomiting. The chemical methods we are discussing here are different from the use of emetine that we described earlier, which is not taken on a regular basis but is instead used in conditioning sessions as an aversion strategy.

Different chemicals are used in treatments for different substances. In stopping tobacco use, the main chemical used is *nicotine*, which the person can administer as a gum, a patch placed on the skin, an inhaler, or

CLINICAL METHODS AND ISSUES

Behavioral Methods for Treating Substance Abuse

Psychologists apply behavioral methods to gain control over environmental conditions that sustain an undesirable behavior, such as smoking or drinking (Sarafino, 2001). These methods are based on the recognition that modifying behavior requires changing the *behavior itself* and its *antecedents* and *consequences*. For example, the consequences can be changed by introducing rewards for not using a substance and penalties for using it, as occurred for Jim at the start of this chapter. In designing a program to help clients stop or reduce substance use, four behavioral methods are often used.

* *Self-monitoring* is a procedure in which people record information pertaining to their problem behavior, such as how often they smoked or drank and the circumstances, place, and time of each instance. To encourage self-monitoring, a pencil and paper can be kept with the smokers' cigarettes. Although this technique by itself can produce a temporary decrease in the behavior, its utility is mainly in gathering information to be used in other techniques.

* *Stimulus control* procedures address the antecedents by altering elements of the environment that serve as *cues* and lead a person to perform the problem behavior. For example, many smokers report that they regularly have (and "*need* to have") a cigarette in certain situations, such as after meals, or with coffee or alcohol, or when talking on the phone, or while sitting in a favorite chair watching TV. And many problem drinkers are unable to resist having a drink when friends are drinking. Elements of these environments can be altered in many ways—for example, by making the substance less available, removing cues such as ashtrays,

or restricting the time spent in situations where the behavior occurs, such as watching TV or sitting at the table after meals. Stimulus control procedures can help a great deal: a study on quitting smoking found that getting rid of cigarettes is a critical factor in remaining abstinent on the first day (O'Connell et al., 2002).

* *Response substitution* involves replacing a problem behavior with an alternative response, particularly one that is incompatible with or not likely to be performed at the same time as the problem behavior. For instance, a smoker who "has to have a cigarette with coffee after breakfast" could skip coffee and take a shower right after breakfast. People are not likely to smoke in the shower (though some smokers do!).

* *Behavioral contracting* is a technique whereby certain conditions and consequences regarding the problem behavior are spelled out in a contract. Behavioral contracts usually indicate the conditions under which the behavior may or may not occur and specify what reinforcing and punishing consequences will be applied, and when. Contracts for quitting substance use often have the person deposit a substantial sum of money, which is then meted out if he or she meets certain goals.

Therapists often teach these and other techniques to clients so they can apply them themselves—an approach called **self-management** (Sarafino, 2001). Although each of the methods is useful in changing behavior, such as smoking or drinking, they are most effective when combined and used together.

a nasal spray. Using nicotine decreases withdrawal symptoms, such as sleeplessness, helps men and women achieve short-term and long-term quitting success, and is particularly effective for men (Cepeda-Benito, Reynoso, & Erath, 2004; Wetter et al., 1995).

And if an abstinent smoker chews nicotine gum when exposed to smoking cues, it reduces the resulting craving (Shiffman et al., 2003). Another useful chemical treatment for reducing smoking is *bupropion hydrochloride*, an antidepressant drug (Niaura & Abrams, 2002).

Two types of chemicals are used in treating alcohol abuse. One is an emetic drug called *disulfiram* (brand name Antabuse) that the person needs to take each day orally (Ciraulo & Renner, 1991; Schuckit 1996). In addition to producing nausea if the person drinks, it has some important side effects that can preclude its use—it causes drowsiness, raises blood pressure, and has physiological effects that make it inappropriate for people with heart and liver diseases. For those who can use it, disulfiram can be an effective therapy, but getting people to take the drug consistently is often a problem. The second chemical is *naltrexone*, a drug that blocks the "high" feeling that alcohol and narcotics produce (AMA, 2003). A study found that alcoholics treated with naltrexone experienced fewer days of heavy drinking and fewer drinks on days when they drank than a control group that received a placebo (Monti et al., 2001).

Several chemical agents can be used for treating narcotic addiction. The most widely used of these agents is *methadone*, a chemical that has physiological effects that are similar to those of opiates. However, methadone does not produce euphoria, and, when taken regularly, it prevents euphoria from occurring if the person then takes an opiate (O'Brien, 1996; Sindelar & Fiellin, 2001). Methadone is usually taken orally. Having a narcotics addict take methadone—or a similar agent, *levoalpha acetylmethadyl* (LAAM)—regularly as a substitute for the opiate is called *methadone maintenance*. Another chemical agent that blocks the euphoria from opiates taken after it is *buprenorphine*, which has advantages over methadone, such as its staying active longer (Sindelar & Fiellin, 2001). Naltrexone, which we just discussed for treating alcohol abuse, blocks opiate euphoria but isn't used often for narcotic abuse.

Multidimensional Programs

You may know someone who tried to quit smoking just by using a nicotine patch and failed. Research has shown that the psychosocial and chemical methods we've discussed are useful in stopping or reducing substance use, but none is highly effective *alone*. As a result, the methods are usually combined in a *multidimensional program* to improve their success. For instance, studies of treatments to stop smoking have found that programs combining cognitive–behavioral methods with the nicotine patch are far more effective than using either approach alone (Alterman, Gariti, & Mulvaney, 2001; Cinciripini et al., 1996). And research

on treatments for drug abuse has shown that combining methadone and psychological treatment is far more effective than methadone alone (McClellan et al., 1993).

Four other features should be considered in designing multidimensional programs to curb substance use. First, using biochemical analyses to verify self-reports of use and demonstrating these verification procedures at the *beginning* of treatment enhances the success of a program (Glynn, Gruder, & Jegerski, 1986). Second, a brief daily phone call to the clients improves their performance of certain procedures, such as keeping records of smoking (McConnell, Biglan, & Severson, 1984). Third, involving the client's family or significant person in the program improves the outcome (Carlson et al., 2002; Fals-Stewart & O'Farrell, 2003). Fourth, physician involvement helps. For example, people are more likely to try to quit smoking and stick with it if they are advised to stop by their physician, receive a prescription for nicotine, are shown on an apparatus how impaired their respiratory system is, or have been diagnosed with a serious smoking-related disease (Fiore, Jorenby, & Baker, 1997; Ockene et al., 1991, 1994; Risser & Belcher, 1990; USDHHS, 1986a).

DEALING WITH THE RELAPSE PROBLEM

Quitting substance use is one thing; staying quit is another. As Mark Twain noted, "To cease smoking is the easiest thing I ever did; I ought to know because I've done it a thousand times" (Grunberg & Bowen, 1985). The methods we have considered work well in helping people stop or reduce substance use, but preventing backsliding is a major problem.

The Relapse Problem

Regardless of how smokers quit, their likelihood of *relapse*—that is, returning to the full-blown pattern of behavior—is very high in the first weeks and months after stopping. Most people who quit smoking start again within a year, and most relapses occur in the first 3 months (Ockene et al., 2000). Estimates of relapse rates vary from 50 to 80%, depending on many factors, including the methods used in quitting, how heavily the person smoked, and characteristics of the individual and his or her environment (Curry & McBride, 1994; Ossip-Klein et al., 1986).

The problem of relapse is at least as severe in efforts to stop drinking and using drugs as it is in quitting smoking. Many of the more successful treatment approaches for alcohol abuse produce very high rates of success initially, but these rates decline sharply by the end of the first year and again during the next 2 years (Nathan, 1986). For drug use relapse, researchers have estimated that 60% or more individuals return to drug use after having quit (Donovan, 2003).

Why People Relapse

Withdrawal symptoms probably contribute strongly to immediate relapses. But these symptoms decline over time. For instance, nicotine withdrawal declines sharply in the first week or so after stopping (Gritz, Carr, & Marcus, 1991; Killen & Fortmann, 1994; Piasecki et al., 1997). Smokers who are trying to quit need reassurance that their cravings and negative feelings will diminish greatly in less than a month. What other factors lead people to return to using a substance they quit? We'll cite several (Witkiewitz & Marlatt, 2004):

* *Low self-efficacy.* Maintaining a sense of self-efficacy for staying abstinent is not always easy. As we saw in Chapter 6, people who quit a behavior and experience a lapse may lose their confidence in remaining abstinent and see their violation as a sign of a personal failure. These events can lead to a full relapse through the process called the *abstinence violation effect* (Marlatt & Gordon, 1980). Research has shown that self-efficacy during quitting is dynamic. When quitting smoking, for instance, it remains fairly high before a lapse and drops after the lapse; the sharper the drop, the more likely a relapse will occur (Shiffman et al., 2000).

* *Outcome expectancies for reinforcement.* People tend to relapse if they think that using the substance again would be rewarding, such as "Having a drink would taste great and make me feel so relaxed."

* *High craving.* The greater the craving, the more likely a relapse.

* *Low motivation.* People at lower levels of readiness to change when they try to quit are more likely to relapse than people at higher readiness levels.

* *Interpersonal issues.* Substance users who quit, but lack constructive social support, are more likely to relapse than others who have strong support.

* *Negative emotional states and poor coping.* Because people often use substances to regulate their emotional states, they tend to lack good coping skills to take the place of the substance when difficulties arise.

The role of emotion is particularly important: for example, people who experience high levels of stress are more likely to start smoking again than those who experience less stress (Lichtenstein et al., 1986; Shiffman et al., 1996). Ex-smokers who go back to smoking often report that acute episodes of anxiety or frustration at work or at home led to their relapse (Shiffman, 1986). Sheldon Cohen and Edward Lichtenstein (1990) examined the role of stress in relapse longitudinally among smokers who had decided to quit. The subjects were interviewed before quitting and at 1, 3, and 6 months after their quit date regarding their recent stress levels and smoking status, with biochemical verification. Those individuals who remained continuously abstinent over the full 6 months reported less and less stress at each interview, but those who relapsed early reported high levels of stress throughout. Some evidence also suggested that the abstinent subjects' reduced stress not only helped them succeed but may have resulted partly from succeeding, such as by increasing their feelings of self-efficacy and self-esteem.

Two other factors in relapse relate mainly to smoking. First, an interesting thing happens to smokers' beliefs when they relapse: they tend to lower their perceptions of the health risks of smoking. A study of people who relapsed after completing a treatment program to stop smoking found that they reported strong beliefs that smoking could harm their health when they entered the program, but after the relapse these beliefs decreased (Gibbons, McGovern, & Lando, 1991). Why? They probably used cognitive processes, such as motivated reasoning or denial, to cope with the fact that their attempt to quit smoking failed. This finding is important because it means people who relapse may not be ready to quit again until their beliefs change back again. Many smokers deny or minimize the health risks of smoking, thereby decreasing the likelihood that they will try to quit (Lee, 1989; Strecher, Kreuter, & Kobrin, 1995).

Second, some people who go back to smoking claim they did so because they were *gaining weight* (Jeffrey et al., 2000; Perkins, 1994). Smokers tend to weigh less than nonsmokers, and this difference is greater among middle-aged than younger individuals (Klesges, Zbikowski et al., 1998). When people stop smoking, most—but not all—do, in fact, tend to gain several pounds over the next few years (Klesges et al., 1997; Klesges, Ward et al., 1998; Williamson et al., 1991). They do so for two reasons (Klesges, Benowitz, & Meyers, 1991). First, ex-smokers often increase their caloric intake, sometimes by eating more fats and sweet-tasting carbohydrates. Second, the amount of energy they expend in metabolism declines, for at least a short time, after quitting. To prevent weight gain, many ex-smokers may need to control their diets, get more exercise, and perhaps use a nicotine supplement. Ex-smokers who use nicotine gum during the weeks after quitting gain much less weight than controls with a placebo gum (Doherty et al., 1996; Perkins, 1994).

Can Relapses Be Prevented?

Three approaches can reduce the occurrence of relapse in substance use treatment, and each continues after the formal treatment program ends. One approach uses a process called the **relapse prevention method,** which is based on G. Alan Marlatt's view that relapses develop through the cognitive events of the abstinence violation effect that follow a lapse (Marlatt & Gordon, 1980; Witkiewitz & Marlatt, 2004). The cognitive events involve mainly guilt and reduced self-efficacy. The relapse prevention method is basically a therapist-supervised self-management program in which the client takes the following steps:

1. *Learn to identify high-risk situations* by generating a list and descriptions of antecedent conditions in which lapses are most likely to occur.

2. *Acquire competent and specific coping skills* through training in specific behaviors and thought patterns that

will enable the person to deal with high-risk situations and avoid lapses. For example, people who get treatment for stopping smoking need to receive training in ways to cope with stress without relying on smoking as a coping strategy (Shadel & Mermelstein, 1993).

3. *Practice effective coping skills in high-risk situations* under a therapist's supervision. For example, a problem drinker might go with the therapist to a bar and practice ways to avoid drinking.

The second approach involves *booster sessions*—additional phases or sessions to shore up or refresh the treatment's effects. Evidence has shown that providing booster sessions or contacts and training on ways to cope with lapses and maintain self-efficacy reduces relapses (Brandon et al., 2000; Curry & McBride, 1994; Irvin et al., 1999). The relapse prevention method can also help individuals stay abstinent for a substance after quitting on their own (Brandon, Herzog, & Webb, 2003). The third approach that reduces relapse has clients continue using a chemical method after formal treatment ends; they'd continue to use nicotine if they quit smoking or methadone if they quit using a narcotic (Klesges, Benowitz, & Meyers, 1991; Stephens, Roffman, & Simpson, 1994).

SUMMARY

People's use of tobacco, alcohol, or drugs can affect their health, particularly if the substance is abused. Addiction is a condition through which the person has developed a physical and psychological dependence on the substance. People who are physically dependent on a substance have developed a tolerance for it and suffer withdrawal symptoms when they abruptly stop using it. Substance abuse exists when a person has shown a clear pattern of pathological use for at least a month, with resulting problems in social and occupational functioning. Processes in developing dependence include positive and negative reinforcement, classical conditioning of substance-related cues, and heredity.

Smoking tobacco is a worldwide problem. In the United States it became popular after the early 1900s, reached its greatest popularity in the mid-1960s, and then declined after its harmful health effects were publicized. Most people who become cigarette smokers begin

the habit in adolescence. Although a larger percentage of men than women smoke, this gap has decreased in recent years. Americans are more likely to smoke if they are from the lower rather than the higher social classes. Psychosocial factors influence whether individuals will start to smoke. Whether people go on to smoke on a regular basis is determined by biopsychosocial factors. The likelihood of individuals becoming regular smokers increases if they have peer and adult models of smoking, experience peer pressure to smoke, and find that smoking helps them relax and have less tension.

Cigarette smoke contains tars, carbon monoxide, and nicotine, a chemical that appears to produce physical dependence. One theory that describes why established smokers continue to smoke is the nicotine regulation model, which proposes that they smoke to maintain a certain level of nicotine in their bodies and to avoid withdrawal. Smoking reduces the person's life expectancy and increases the risk of lung cancer, other cancers, cardiovascular disease, and chronic obstructive pulmonary disease. Breathing secondhand smoke is called passive smoking and is also harmful to one's health.

Alcohol use varies widely across cultures and time periods. Americans drank alcohol at extremely high rates prior to the mid-1800s, when the temperance movement changed people's views. After the repeal of Prohibition, alcohol use began to increase gradually. Most American adults drink at least occasionally, and many adolescents and adults engage in binge drinking. Many individuals who drink abuse alcohol and are classified as problem drinkers, and those who are physically dependent on alcohol are classified as alcoholics. People who are addicted to alcohol suffer withdrawal symptoms when they quit drinking. Psychosocial factors—such as modeling, social pressure, and reinforcement—have a very powerful influence on drinking. Heredity plays an important role in the development of alcohol abuse. Heavy drinking is related to a variety of health problems, including fetal alcohol syndrome in babies of drinking mothers, automobile accidents, and such diseases as cirrhosis of the liver, cancer, high blood pressure, and brain damage.

Many people use and abuse drugs that can be classified as stimulants, depressants, hallucinogens, and narcotics. Drugs differ in their potential for producing physical and psychological dependence. Drug abuse is related to a number of psychosocial factors, such as modeling, social pressure, reinforcement, and personality traits. The health effects of drug use and abuse are becoming increasingly clear. For example, using cocaine produces cardiovascular reactions that can cause a potentially fatal myocardial infarction.

Programs to prevent smoking and alcohol and drug abuse attempt to address relevant psychosocial factors by providing information and teaching important social skills. These programs teach children and adolescents about the immediate and long-term consequences of the substances, the ways modeling and peer pressure influence their tendency to use substances, and the ways they can resist these forces. Some programs also teach general social, cognitive, and coping skills. Once people become regular users of tobacco, alcohol, or drugs, many are able to quit on their own, but many others are not, especially if they use the substances heavily. Alcoholics Anonymous and Narcotics Anonymous are self-help groups that enable many substance users to quit.

People who can't stop or reduce their substance use on their own or through a self-help group can receive professional treatment. Alcohol or drug abusers typically undergo detoxification. Effective psychosocial treatment approaches for substance use include reinforcing abstinence, aversion strategies (which can involve using an emetic drug for alcoholics), substance-related cue exposure, and self-management with behavioral and cognitive methods. Chemical treatments are also effective and include administering nicotine for smokers and methadone for narcotics users. Combining effective methods in a multidimensional approach improves treatment success. Many people who quit eventually resume using the substance. Relapse is common and can result if the person experiences high levels of stress, little helpful social support, and feelings of low self-efficacy. The relapse prevention method can reduce relapse rates, as can booster sessions and continuing chemical methods after formal treatment ends.

KEY TERMS

addiction	negative reinforcement	binge drinking	aversion strategies
physical dependence	classical conditioning	problem drinkers	emetic drug
tolerance	carbon monoxide	alcoholics	cue exposure
withdrawal	tars	stimulants	self-management
psychological	nicotine	depressants	relapse prevention
dependence	nicotine regulation	hallucinogens	method
substance abuse	model	narcotics	
positive reinforcement	passive smoking	detoxification	

Note: If you read **Module 4** (from Chapter 2) with the current chapter, you should include the key terms for that module.

8

NUTRITION, WEIGHT CONTROL AND DIET, EXERCISE, AND SAFETY

Nutrition
Components of Food
What People Eat
Nutrition and Health

Weight Control and Diet
Desirable and Undesirable Weights
Becoming Overly Fat
Dieting and Treatments to Lose Weight
Anorexia and Bulimia

Exercise
The Health Effects of Exercise
Who Gets Enough Exercise, Who Does Not—and Why?
Promoting Exercise Behavior

Safety
Accidents
Environmental Hazards

PROLOGUE

"Let's share something with each other," said the health expert to the members of a community workshop. "What excuses do we find ourselves using for not eating more healthfully, not exercising regularly, and not behaving in other ways that promote health, such as using seat belts? I'll start it off," she continued, "by confessing that I sometimes skip exercising because I run out of time. What excuses do you use?" The answers came quickly:

> "I never seem to have the energy to exercise."
>
> "My wife sprained her ankle jogging, and I know lots of other people who injured themselves exercising."
>
> "I don't have the time to prepare healthful meals."
>
> "My grandparents ate high-fat diets and lived past 85."
>
> "My kids hate vegetables and my husband insists on having meat for dinner."
>
> "Seat belts are uncomfortable to use and wrinkle my clothes."
>
> "I've had my habits for so long—it's hard to change."

People cite many reasons for not leading more healthful lifestyles. Some of the obstacles they describe can be overcome fairly easily, but others are more difficult. In most cases, people could find ways to overcome obstacles to healthful behavior if they believed it was important and were motivated to do so.

In this chapter, we discuss how nutrition, weight control, exercise, and safety habits are important to people's health. We also examine what people do and do not do in these areas of their lifestyles, as well as why they behave as they do and how they can change unhealthful behaviors. As we study these topics, we will consider important questions and problems people have in leading healthy lives. Which foods are healthful, and which are not? What determines people's preferences for different foods, such as sweets? Why do overweight individuals have such a hard time losing weight and keeping it off? What kinds of exercise benefit health? What hazards exist in our environments, and how can we protect ourselves from them?

NUTRITION

"You are what you eat," as the saying goes. This saying has at least two meanings. Most commonly, it means that the quality of your diet can determine how you look, act, and feel. Another meaning is that the same five types of chemicals—water, carbohydrates, fats, proteins, vitamins, and minerals—that

make up food also make up the human body and contribute to the cells' metabolic processes (Holum, 1994; Peckenpaugh, 2003). In this section, we will examine both meanings, beginning with the components of food and their importance in metabolic processes.

COMPONENTS OF FOOD

Healthful diets provide optimal amounts of all essential nutrients for the body's metabolic needs. Let's consider the five types of chemical components of food, besides water, that provide specific nutrients for body functioning.

1. *Carbohydrates* include simple and complex sugars that are major sources of energy for the body. Simple sugars include *glucose*, which is found in foods made of animal products, and *fructose*, which is found in fruits and honey. Diets may also provide more complex sugars, such as *sucrose* (table sugar), *lactose* in milk products, and *starch* in many plants.

2. *Lipids* or "fats" also provide energy for the body. Lipids include saturated and polyunsaturated fats, as well as cholesterol. Nutritionists recommend that diets contain not more than 30% of calories (nor less than 10%) from fat. To calculate a food's

Reading labels informs this mother and daughter of the food's content. Guidelines adopted in the 1990s for labeling packaged foods in the United States make nutritious choices easier for consumers.

percentage of calories from fat, you need to know its number of calories and grams of fat. Multiply the grams of fat by 9 (because a gram of fat has 9 calories), and divide that value by the number of calories.

3. *Proteins* are important mainly in the body's synthesis of new cell material. They are composed of organic molecules called *amino acids*; about half of the 20 or so known amino acids are essential for body development and functioning and must be provided by our diet.

4. *Vitamins* are organic chemicals that regulate metabolism and functions of the body. They are used in converting nutrients to energy, producing hormones, and breaking down waste products and toxins. Some vitamins (A, D, E, and K) are *fat-soluble*—they dissolve in fats and are stored in the body's fatty tissue. The remaining vitamins (B and C) are *water-soluble*—the body stores very little of these vitamins and excretes excess quantities as waste.

5. *Minerals* are inorganic substances, such as calcium, phosphorus, potassium, sodium, iron, iodine, and zinc, each of which is important in body development and functioning. For example, calcium and phosphorus are components of bones and teeth, potassium and sodium are involved in nerve transmission, and iron helps transport oxygen in the blood.

Food also contains *fiber*, which is not considered a nutrient because it is not used in metabolism but is still needed in the process of digestion. People can get all the nutrients and fiber they need by eating diets that consist of a variety of foods from five basic groups: grains, fruits, vegetables, milk products, and meats and fish. Breads and cereals made of whole grains have more fiber than those made of grains that are "enriched" or "fortified" with nutrients. You can see the relative amounts of foods from different categories to make a healthful diet by accessing the United States Department of Agriculture Website: http://www.cnpp.usda.gov.

Most people who eat healthfully do not need to supplement their diets with vitamins and other nutrients; one carrot, for instance, provides enough vitamin A to last 4 days. A class of vitamins called *antioxidants*—including vitamins A (carotene), C, and E that reduce the damage to cells from a process in metabolism called oxidation—are thought to reduce

the risk of several diseases, such as cancers and cardiovascular and eye diseases. Although some evidence exists for these benefits from vitamins A and C consumption, it is not yet definitive (Johnson, Meacham, & Kruskall, 2003), but a meta-analysis revealed no support for taking vitamin E in preventing cardiovascular disease (Vivekananthan et al., 2003). Some people who take supplements have an attitude of "the more the better." However, one can overdo taking some nutrients, leading to a "poisoning" if they accumulate in the body. For example, too much of vitamins A and D can pose serious health hazards to the liver and kidneys, respectively. Women who are pregnant have greater needs of all nutrients. Although most of their extra nutrients can come from dietary adjustments, they should also take recommended supplements, such as iron (Insel & Roth, 1998; Peckenpaugh, 2003). Pregnant women with a specific, detectable gene may need to take folic acid, a B vitamin, to prevent a severe birth defect called *spina bifida*, in which the spinal column doesn't close and often protrudes through the back (AMA, 2003).

Unprocessed foods are generally more healthful than processed foods, which often contain additives that benefit the food industry more than the consumer. Some additives lengthen the shelf life of the food, improve or maintain the texture of foods, or enhance the taste of foods, for example (Insel & Roth, 1998). Although most additives are not hazardous, some cause allergic reactions or may be carcinogenic. For instance, some people are sensitive to monosodium glutamate (MSG, a flavor enhancer), experiencing heightened blood pressure and sweating when they consume it. Children may be especially vulnerable to the effects of additives because their body systems are still forming and maturing rapidly and, pound-for-pound, they eat more than adults.

WHAT PEOPLE EAT

Diets vary by gender and culture. A survey of nearly 20,000 university students in 23 countries showed that women report eating healthier diets—less fat and more fruit and fiber—than men in almost all countries, but there are marked national differences in dietary practices (Wardle et al., 2004). Table 8.1 lists countries with the most and least healthful practices. For most of the 20th century, American diets had a fairly consistent trend: people consumed more and more sugar, animal fats, and animal proteins, while consuming less and

Table 8.1   *Two Countries among the Highest and the Lowest in Percentage of Individuals with Healthful Practices for Each of Three Dietary Components (Fat, Fruit, and Fiber)*[a]

Healthful Practices	Countries with High Practice (% of males, females)	Countries with Low Practice (% of males, females)
Dietary fat, avoid eating	Columbia (36.3, 55.7)	France (16.6, 38.2)
	Thailand (34.5, 59.2)	Korea (11.3, 13.2)
Dietary fruit, eat daily	Italy (57.9, 63.8)	Japan (11.9, 12.1)
	Spain (57.1, 64.0)	Korea (16.0, 33.3)
Dietary fiber, eat daily	Korea (38.7, 58.8)	Bulgaria (12.5, 25.4)
	Thailand (64.6, 78.6)	France (10.9, 28.7)

[a]The percentages were intermediate for the United States (33.1, 50.4 for fat; 31.7, 35.5 for fruit; 21.2, 20.4 for fiber) and England (29.8, 49.5 for fat; 35.8, 44.1 for fruit; 26.0, 38.7 for fiber).

Source: Wardle et al., 2004, abstracted from Table 2.

less fiber (Winikoff, 1983). Their consumption of vegetables, fruits, and cereals declined, while that of meats and sugary foods, such as soft drinks and processed goods, increased. The way food is prepared also changed and affected people's diets. Consider the potato: A baked or boiled potato by itself has few calories and almost no fat, but when french-fried or made into potato chips, its calorie and fat content skyrockets. Americans' increased use of processed and fast foods has contributed to the changes in their diets.

How healthful are people's diets in the United States today? One dimension of this question involves their consumption of sugars and animal fats, which is too high (USDA, 1999). Nutritionists and others concerned with people's health have been recommending that Americans reduce these components in their diets. Are Americans beginning to follow these recommendations? Yes, in some ways (USBC, 2003; USDA, 1999). Since 1980, people's consumption of red meats has declined, and they're eating more fish and poultry, cereals and grains, and fruits and vegetables. However, they've also increased their intake of sugars, soft drinks, and fats and oils. Although most Americans at all ages consume sufficient amounts of the essential nutrients, many adults consume too little calcium, magnesium, vitamin B6, vitamin E, and zinc (USDA, 1999). Some of these deficiencies are especially large among women and the elderly, and supplements of these nutrients may be warranted.

Why do people eat what they eat? Biopsychosocial factors determine diets (Drewnowski, 2002; Peckenpaugh, 2003). Newborn babies like sweet tastes and avoid bitter tastes; these preferences are inborn. Preschoolers use mainly two criteria, sweetness and familiarity, when choosing foods. Brain chemicals can

bias people to eat fatty foods and activate their brain pleasure centers when they do (Azar, 1994). But people's diets also depend on their individual and social experiences (French, Story, & Jeffery, 2001; Hearn et al., 1998). Some foods are more available than others at home, work, or school. Children receive certain foods, but not others, depending on cultural and economic conditions—and simply being exposed to a food may increase their liking of it. They also observe, in person and through TV commercials, how other people respond to a food and tend to become more attracted to it if they see others eat it and like it. Two other factors in people's diets are portion sizes and freedom to choose foods. The larger the portions, the more people eat (Rolls, Morris, & Roe, 2002). Food vending machines and à la carte cafeteria menus in schools lead to consuming more fat and less fruits and vegetables (Kubik et al., 2003).

Enormous numbers of children around the world simply do not have nutritious diets available to them for proper growth and development. Half or more children are stunted in growth from malnutrition in several countries, such as Ethiopia, Guatemala, and India (WHO, 1999). Children are much shorter if they live in very impoverished areas than in wealthier regions, even in the same countries (Meredith, 1978). Regional and social class differences in bodily growth result from many factors, including genetics, nutrition, and disease.

NUTRITION AND HEALTH

The mass media announces almost daily that many individuals eat diets that are not as healthful as they should be. Some people react by using foods and

Reprinted by permission: Tribune Media Services.

"...MAN, THE FDA IS REALLY CRACKING DOWN ON FOOD LABELING!....."

substances sold at health food stores. Although some of these products—such as whole grains—are beneficial, many supplements and other products are of dubious worth (Peckenpaugh, 2003). Some people attempt to improve their diets by becoming *vegetarians*. There are degrees of vegetarianism, ranging from simply avoiding red meats to strictly using only plant foods and no animal products whatsoever. When people avoid all animal products, they must plan very carefully to assure that their diets, and especially their children's, contain a balance of proteins and sufficient amount of essential vitamins and minerals (Peckenpaugh, 2003). In many nations of the world, dietary excesses are the main nutritional problem, especially in developing atherosclerosis, hypertension, and cancer.

Diet and Atherosclerosis

Cholesterol is the main dietary culprit in atherosclerosis, the deposit of fatty plaques in our blood vessels. As we saw in Chapter 2, cholesterol is a fatty substance. Our bodies produce most of the cholesterol in blood, and our diets provide the remainder. Whether cholesterol forms plaques in our blood vessels depends on the presence of different types of **lipoproteins,** which consist of fat and proteins. There are several types of lipoproteins, but two are most important: **low-density lipoprotein** (LDL) is related to *increased* plaque deposits; **high-density lipoprotein**

(HDL) is linked to *decreased* likelihood of plaque buildup (AMA, 2003; AHA, 2004). Cholesterol carried by LDL is called "bad cholesterol" because it mixes with other substances to form plaques, whereas cholesterol carried by HDL is called "good cholesterol" because it seems to carry LDL away to be processed or removed by the liver. There are many other types of dietary fat, three of which are clearly linked to health. *Triglycerides* are in most fats people consume and increase the risk of heart disease; *omega-3 fatty acids*, which occur at high levels in fish, reduce serum triglycerides and raise HDL; and *trans-fatty acids* are in processed oils, such as margarine, and increase LDL (Peckenpaugh, 2003).

How much cholesterol in the blood is too much? Normal levels of cholesterol increase with age in adulthood; they are measured in milligrams of cholesterol per 100 milliliters of blood serum. Experts once thought that long-term *total* serum cholesterol levels above 240 mg put people at high risk for heart disease or stroke, but they have refined this view (EPDET, 2001). *"Bad" cholesterol (LDL) is the real culprit,* and its risk depends on five other risk factors:

- *Age* (over 45 years for men, 55 for women)
- *Cigarette smoking*
- *High blood pressure*
- *Low "good" cholesterol* (HDL less than 40 mg)
- *Family history* of early cardiovascular disease

To determine one's heart attack or stroke risk, count up the person's risk factors and subtract 1 if his or her HDL is high (60 mg or higher). People with scores of 0 or 1 are at *low risk* and should keep LDL levels below 160 mg. People with higher scores should maintain much lower LDL levels, and those who already have heart disease should strive to keep LDL levels below 70 mg (AHA, 2004).

People's cholesterol levels are determined partly by heredity and partly by their lifestyles (Hopkins, 1992; McCaffery et al., 2001). Some evidence suggests that smoking cigarettes may increase LDL and decrease HDL levels (Muscat et al., 1991). Diet is an important factor; some foods, such as eggs, many milk products, and fatty meats, contain very high concentrations of cholesterol. The average daily consumption of cholesterol for Americans is 331 mg for men and 213 mg for women (USDA, 1999), but daily intake should not exceed 300 mg and should be much lower than that for those at moderate or high risk for cardiovascular disease. Children older than 5 years should follow diets like those recommended for adults; those whose parents or grandparents had heart disease at early ages should have their cholesterol levels and diets assessed. Atherosclerosis can begin in childhood, and children need to develop good eating habits early so that they don't have entrenched habits to overcome later (DISC, 1995). If dietary changes do not sufficiently lower patients' cholesterol levels, physicians may prescribe medication. *Statin* drugs (some brand names: Lipitor, Zocor) greatly reduce LDL but not HDL levels (AMA, 2003; Maron, Fazio, & Linton, 2000).

Does lowering serum cholesterol reduce cardiovascular illness? Yes. Studies have demonstrated that large reductions in serum cholesterol, produced with combined dietary and drug treatment, retard and slowly *reverse* atherosclerosis and reduce the risk of heart attacks (Karnik, 2001). Most people can lower their cholesterol intake markedly if they will modify their eating habits, sometimes by making very simple changes, such as by substituting low-cholesterol foods, such as cereals, for just four eggs per week—an egg contains over 200 mg of cholesterol. Most cereals, breads, fruits, nuts, and vegetables contain little or no cholesterol. Other ways include switching to fish or poultry in place of red meats, broiling or baking foods instead of frying, using low-fat dairy products, and using low-cholesterol vegetable fats for cooking. But people should be wary of processed foods that

don't specify the type of vegetable oil they use—these products often contain *saturated* fats (coconut or palm oils) instead of the more expensive polyunsaturated fats, such as corn or soybean oils. Oils that derive from certain plants, such as olives, consist of *monounsaturated* fats that contain no cholesterol and appear to *lower* serum LDL, but not HDL, cholesterol (Insel & Roth, 1998; Peckenpaugh, 2003).

There is a curious caution on the health effects of lowering people's cholesterol: although the evidence is inconsistent and inconclusive, some studies have found that markedly reduced serum cholesterol is associated with nonillness deaths, such as from accidents, suicide, and violence (Muldoon & Manuck, 1992; Muldoon, Manuck, & Matthews, 1990). However, we don't know why. Prospective studies have tested whether lowering cholesterol might, perhaps, increase people's negative moods in the following months or years and found that it does not (Bovbjerg et al., 1999; Coutu, Dupuis, & D'Antono, 2001).

Diet and Hypertension

People with blood pressures exceeding 140 systolic/ 90 diastolic are classified as hypertensive. Nearly 700 million people around the world and one-fourth of American adults are hypertensive (NCHS, 2003; WHO, 1999). Although medication can lower blood pressure, the first methods doctors advise usually involve lifestyle changes, especially losing weight and restricting certain foods in the diet. People who are at risk for developing hypertension can effectively reduce their risk by making such changes (Blumenthal et al., 2002).

Of all the substances in people's diets that could affect blood pressure, *sodium*—such as in salt (sodium chloride)—may play the strongest role. Consuming high levels of sodium can increase people's blood pressure and reactivity when stressed (Blumenthal et al., 2002; Falkner & Light, 1986). The body needs about 500 mg of sodium a day, and health experts recommend consuming less than 2,300 mg, the amount in 1 teaspoon of salt (Insel & Roth, 1998; USDA, 1999). American adults consume an average of 3,270 mg of sodium daily in foods that contain sodium before eating or cooking, as many processed meats, potato chips, and cereals do, for example. And many people add salt to foods. Because sodium can elevate blood pressure, physicians often place hypertensive patients on low-sodium diets. Although some people are more sensitive to the effects of sodium than others, the evidence is now clear that reducing dietary sodium lowers blood pressure in hypertensive people. Salt-sensitive individuals can lower their blood pressure by reducing sodium intake and by increasing potassium intake, which counteracts sodium effects (Blumenthal, Sherwood et al., 2002; West et al., 1999).

Caffeine is another dietary substance that can affect blood pressure. Most of the caffeine people consume generally comes from drinking caffeinated coffee, strong tea, and cola beverages. Caffeine increases people's reactivity to stress and raises their blood pressure during the days that it is consumed (James, 2004; Lane et al., 2002). Does caffeine consumption lead to hypertension and coronary heart disease? Although not all studies have found that it does, meta-analyses now indicate that the more caffeine people consume, the greater their risk of cardiovascular disease (James, 2004).

Diet and Cancer

Although some studies have found that diets high in saturated fat and low in fiber are associated with the development of cancer, particularly of the colon and prostate gland, the evidence across studies is inconsistent (Kolonel, 2001; Slattery & Caan, 2001). However, it remains advisable for people to consume little of fatty meats and much of vegetables, fruits, and high-fiber breads and cereals to reduce their risk of cancer.

Do vitamins protect people from cancer? Many fruits and vegetables are rich in *beta-carotene*, which the body converts to vitamin A; these foods are also good sources of vitamin C. Early studies yielded results suggesting that these vitamins may protect people from cancers, but the current evidence is not definitive (Johnson, Meacham, & Kruskall, 2003). On the basis of the early findings, some people began to take high doses of vitamin A and C supplements. Nutritionists recommend against this regimen, especially with vitamin A because it builds up in the body, and it is easy to overdose.

Interventions to Improve Dietary Components

Dietary interventions take many forms. They can focus on a single nutritional component, such as cholesterol, or promote a healthy overall diet of low fat and high vegetable and fruit content. And they can be provided as counseling sessions with individuals who have a known dietary or health problem and as large-scale programs for members of a group or community, such as employees or school students, using written or computer materials and group meetings. The most effective dietary interventions today incorporate or address elements of the theories of health-related behavior we considered in Chapter 6—for example, the person's perceived barriers and benefits of change (health belief model), self-efficacy (social-cognitive theory), and readiness to change (stages of change model) (Glanz, 2001). To maximize success, interventions can use behavioral and educational methods for the person, training and cooperation by members of the person's household, support groups, and a long-term followup program (Carmody et al., 1982). They should also address the person's strong preferences for high-fat, low-fiber foods and difficulties having healthful foods when not eating at home (Terry, Oakland, & Ankeny, 1991).

Let's look at a couple of examples of dietary interventions, one that focused on reducing cholesterol and a more recent one that addressed the overall diet. The program to reduce cholesterol was part of the Multiple Risk Factor Intervention Trial (MRFIT) and was designed to modify the diets of thousands of men over a period of 6 years (Caggiula et al., 1981; Dolecek et al., 1986). The men were between 35 and 57 years of age at the start of the study and were at risk of coronary heart disease because of high serum cholesterol levels, high blood pressure, and cigarette smoking. Half of them got the intervention and half were in a control group with "usual care" from their physicians. The intervention provided counseling and information each year about the benefits of and methods for modifying diets when the men and "their homemakers" attended group meetings. The MRFIT program was successful in modifying the men's diets substantially and lowering their serum cholesterol levels. The men who most needed to modify their diets tended to do so and achieved the greatest gains. Subsequent interventions applied more techniques, such as behavioral methods. A meta-analysis of many studies found that programs to reduce high serum cholesterol help people improve their diets and reduce cardiovascular risk (Brunner et al., 1997).

The intervention to modify overall diets recruited over 600 adult females from a large medical practice (an HMO) who were not already eating a low-fat diet and assigned them randomly to an intervention or control condition (Stevens et al., 2002). The intervention applied elements of the stages of change model, motivational interviewing, and social-cognitive theory to decrease fat and increase vegetable and fruit consumption. The women in the intervention received two individual counseling sessions that included a 20-minute computer program to assess and give feedback on their dietary habits and a discussion of their dietary goals and plans. They also received two counseling phone calls and healthful recipes and hints on shopping, snacking, and eating in restaurants. All the women's diets were assessed after a few months and revealed that they had improved—that is, contained much less fat and more vegetables and fruit—for women in the intervention but had gotten a little worse for those in the control condition.

What people include in their diets is clearly related to their risk of developing several major chronic diseases. Do people who receive an intervention and improve their intake of fat, vegetables, and fruit because they were at risk for illness dislike their new diets? No, and across years they report greater life satisfaction and confidence that they can promote their health than similar people without the intervention (Corle et al., 2001). Other dietary problems that affect health arise from consuming too many calories. Research with animals has shown that reducing calorie intake by 30% from standard nutritious diets decreases metabolism, slows the aging process, and increases longevity (Lane et al., 1996). Eating too much food can be unhealthful, as we are about to see.

If you have not read Chapter 2, The Body's Physical Systems, and your course has you read the modules from that chapter distributed to later chapters, read **Module 3** (The Digestive System) now.

WEIGHT CONTROL AND DIET

People in many cultures around the world are "weight conscious." In the United States, individuals often start being concerned about their weight in childhood, particularly if they are overweight and are teased and excluded from social groups (Brownell, 1986; Rozen, 2002). When children reach the teenage years, many become greatly preoccupied with their physical appearance and want to change how they look. They frequently express concerns about skin problems and about having a better figure or more athletic body, being taller or shorter, and being the "right" weight. People with less-than-ideal bodies are often thought of as lazy and self-indulgent, and many of them wish or strive for bodies they are biologically unable to achieve (Brownell, 1991).

DESIRABLE AND UNDESIRABLE WEIGHTS

We judge the desirability of our weight with two criteria. One is attractiveness. Being the "wrong" weight often affects people's self-esteem, and American females provide a clear example. A study of overweight 10- to 16-year-old Caucasians found that girls' self-esteem declined sharply and consistently

through those years, but boys' self-esteem declined only during the early years (Mendelson & White, 1985). Perhaps as overweight boys get older, some degree of bulk is considered "manly." And a survey of teenagers found that most of the girls and few boys were trying to *lose* weight, and many boys were trying to *gain* weight (Rosen & Gross, 1987). The greater concern among females than males about their weight—especially about being overweight—continues in adulthood (Forman et al., 1986). But cultural differences exist. Among overweight women, African-Americans are more satisfied with their bodies than Whites are (Flynn & Fitzgibbon, 1998).

The other criterion for judging weight is healthfulness, based on data from studies of morbidity and mortality rates of men and women. Individuals who stay within certain weight ranges for their height have far lower rates of chronic illness and longer life spans than others do. *Whether* individuals do anything about their weight and *what* they do can have important implications for their health.

Overweight and Obesity

No matter how fit we are, our bodies have some fat— and they should. Having fat is a problem only when we have too much. The question is, how much is too much? Determining how much fat a person's body has is not as easy as it may seem. Bulk or stockiness alone can be misleading since some stocky people simply have larger skeletal frames than others, or their bodies are more muscular. Until the mid-1990s, overweight was evaluated by the degree of excess over ideal weights, given in tables. Today, these judgments are based on the **body mass index** (BMI): people are classified as **overweight** if their BMI is 25 or higher, and **obese** if their BMI is greater than 30 (NCHS, 2003). You can find your approximate BMI in Table 8.2 or calculate it exactly: for American measurements, multiply your weight in pounds by 704.5 and divide *twice* by your height in inches (for metric measurements, simply divide your weight in kilograms twice by your height in meters). Although the BMI doesn't measure the amount of body fat an individual has, professionals can use complex methods that do (Perri, Nezu, & Viegener, 1992).

Sociocultural, Gender, and Age Differences in Weight Control

The prevalence of overly fat people varies with nationality, sociocultural factors, gender, and age. For example, the prevalence of obesity in adults is higher in the United States than in Britain and Canada, and is very low in China and Japan (Valdez & Williamson, 2002). Among Americans, nearly two-thirds of adults are overweight and almost half of these are obese; nearly one in six children and adolescents is overweight or obese (NCHS, 2003). More men than women are overweight, but more women are obese. The percentage of women who are overweight or obese is higher for African Americans and Hispanics than for Whites, and the percentage of overweight men is higher for Hispanics than for African Americans and Whites. Americans get heavier throughout the early- and middle-adulthood years, with the percentage of overweight people peaking between 55 and 64 years of age (NCHS, 2003). Research has revealed a disturbing trend: among children and the population as a whole in the United States and other developed nations, the percentage who are overly fat has increased substantially during the last few decades (NCHS, 2003; Wadden, Brownell, & Foster, 2002). The reason is simple. People are consuming more calories and engaging in less physical activity than in the past. For instance, in the three decades preceding 2000, Americans' daily consumption increased by 168 calories (7%) for men and 335 (22%) for women (CDC, 2004b).

Table 8.2   *Values of the Body Mass Index Calculated from Height and Weight, with Shading for Health-Related Categories: Underweight, Healthy Weight, Overweight, and Obese*

Height in ft. & in.	Weight in Pounds											
	130	140	150	160	170	180	190	200	210	220	230	240
4'6"	31	34	36	39	41	43	46	48	51	53	56	58
4'8"	29	31	34	36	38	40	43	45	47	49	52	54
4'10"	27	29	31	34	36	38	40	42	44	46	48	50
5'0"	25	27	29	31	33	35	37	39	41	43	45	47
5'2"	24	26	27	29	31	33	35	37	38	40	42	44
5'4"	22	24	26	28	29	31	33	34	36	38	40	41
5'6"	21	23	24	26	27	29	31	32	34	36	37	39
5'8"	20	21	23	24	26	27	29	30	32	34	35	37
5'10"	19	20	22	23	24	26	27	29	30	32	33	35
6'0"	18	19	20	22	23	24	26	27	28	30	31	33
6'2"	17	18	19	21	22	23	24	26	27	28	30	31
6'4"	16	17	18	20	21	22	23	24	26	27	28	29
6'6"	15	16	17	19	20	21	22	23	24	25	27	28

Underweight	Healthy weight	Overweight	Obese[a]
BMI = below 18.5	BMI = 18.5–24.9	BMI = 25.0–29.9	BMI = 30 or more

[a]People with BMIs of 40 or more are described as extremely or morbidly obese.

BECOMING OVERLY FAT

People add fat to their bodies by consuming more calories than they burn up through metabolism. Children who put on a lot of weight also eat much more fatty foods than others do (Robertson et al., 1999). The body stores excess calories as fat in *adipose tissue*, which consists of cells that vary in number and size (Logue, 1991). According to researcher Margaret Straw, the

> growth of adipose tissue throughout childhood and adolescence involves both an increase in cell size and in cell number. Thereafter, it appears that growth in adipose tissue is initially associated with an increase in cell size; if cell size becomes excessive, new adipose tissue is generated through an increase in the number of cells. (1983, p. 223)

There are two main reasons adults tend to gain weight as they get older. First, people often gain weight periodically, such as around holidays, without taking it all off; the balance accumulates across years (Yanovski et al., 2000). Second, physical activity and metabolism decline with age (Smith, 1984). To maintain earlier weight levels, people need to take in fewer calories

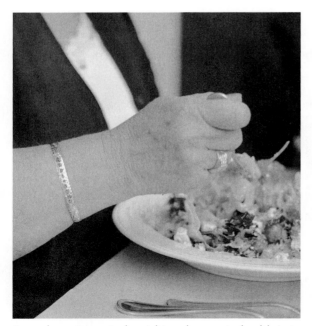

A good way to control weight and promote health is to eat foods that are low in calories and fat, such as salads with low fat dressings.

and exercise more as they get older. Both biological and psychosocial factors affect weight control.

Biological Factors in Weight Control

The metabolic rates of individuals can differ greatly, therefore, some thin people consume many more calories than some heavy people do and still stay slim. Fat tissue is less metabolically active than lean tissue, "so fatness itself can directly lower metabolic rate if fat tissue begins to replace lean tissue" (Rodin, 1981, p. 362). This means that people who are obese may continue to gain weight even if they don't increase caloric intake. Do heavy people eat more than normal-weight people? Yes, on average they do, and their diets contain more fats (Wing & Polley, 2001). Although some studies found that obese and normal-weight individuals do not differ in the amount or type of food they report having consumed (Braitman, Adlin, & Stanton, 1985; Shah & Jeffery, 1991), it is now clear that these groups of people differ in the accuracy of their reports. Underreporting dietary intake is very common and occurs more among heavy rather than normal-weight individuals, females than males, and people with little education (Klesges, Eck, & Ray, 1995; Lichtman et al., 1992).

Many people believe individuals become obese because of glandular problems. Although malfunctioning endocrine glands can cause extreme weight gains, this occurs in only a small percentage of obese people (Robinson & Lawler, 1977). Are other biological processes important in the development of obesity? Yes—two lines of evidence indicate that heredity plays a role: Researchers have identified defective genes in animals that disrupt the balance between metabolism and energy intake, and twin and adoption studies have consistently found a genetic link in obesity (Wing & Polley, 2001). In addition, relationships have been noted between the fatness of parents and that of their offspring (Whitaker et al., 1997). Only about 7% of normal-weight children with normal-weight parents become obese by 30 years of age, but obesity in the child or parents increases this risk. For offspring of normal weight in childhood, having an obese parent doubles the risk of becoming obese. For offspring who are obese in childhood, about 38% of those with normal-weight parents and 73% of those with an obese parent are obese in adulthood. However, keep in mind two points about genetics and obesity. First, these parent–child similarities may not be the result only of genetic factors—for instance, children learn many of their eating habits and physical activity patterns from their parents. Second, the recent surge in obesity around the world could not have resulted from changes in genes; they're due to environmental factors.

How does heredity affect our weight? Part of the answer seems to be described in **set-point theory,** which proposes that each person's body has a certain or "set" weight that it strives to maintain (Keesey, 1986; Keesey & Powley, 1975). The body tries to maintain its weight near the set-point by means of a thermostat-like physiological mechanism that seems to involve the hypothalamus. When a person's weight departs from the set-point, the body takes corrective measures, such as by increasing or decreasing metabolism. According to the theory, people whose caloric intake is either drastically reduced or increased for a few months should show rapid corresponding weight changes initially, but the weight should then show slower changes and reach a limit. Studies have found that these predictions are correct and that people quickly return to their original weight when they can eat what they want again (Leibel, Rosenbaum, & Hirsch, 1995; Sims, 1974, 1976). But set-point theory is incomplete: it doesn't explain, for instance, why some people who lose a lot of weight manage to keep it off.

How is the hypothalamus involved in regulating body weight? One way is by monitoring some aspect of fat cells; after obese people lose weight, they produce large amounts of an enzyme that makes it easier to store fat in cells and gain weight (Kern et al., 1990). It may be that the loss of fat in cells triggers the hypothalamus to initiate enzyme production to maintain the set-point. Another way the hypothalamus may affect weight control is by altering the level of insulin in the person's blood (Keesey & Powley, 1975). **Insulin** is a hormone produced by the pancreas that regulates the amount of sugar (glucose) in the blood and its conversion to fat, and promotes the storage of fat in adipose tissue (Rodin, 1981, 1985). Obese people tend to have high serum levels of insulin—a condition called *hyperinsulinemia.* High serum insulin levels increase one's sensations of hunger, perceived pleasantness of sweet tastes, and food consumption. Taken together, these findings indicate that weight gain results from a biopsychosocial process in which physiological factors interact with psychological and environmental factors (Rodin, 1985).

It seems likely that the setting and function of the set-point in regulating weight depend on the number and size of fat cells in the body. Because the number of fat cells increases mainly in childhood and adolescence, the diets of individuals during that time in the life span are likely to be very important. Obese children between 2 and 10 years of age have fat cells that are as large as those of adults (Knittle et al., 1981). As these children gain weight, they do so mainly by adding fat cells. Fat cell size for normal-weight children does not reach adult levels until age 12, and the number of their fat cells does not increase very much between 2 and 10 years of age. Also, it appears that the number of fat cells can increase, but *not* decrease (Brownell, 1982). Individuals who develop too many fat cells—a condition called *fat-cell hyperplasia*—may be doomed to a difficult struggle against a high set-point for the rest of their lives. When fat-cell-hyperplastic adults try to lose weight, their fat cells shrink and

> send out metabolic signals similar to those during food deprivation. As a result, bodily mechanisms respond as though the person were starving, resulting in, among other things, an increase in hunger and a decrease in basal metabolism so that energy stores (i.e., fat) are maintained more efficiently. (Buck, 1988, p. 467)

This suggests that children's dietary and exercise patterns may be critical in determining whether they become overly fat. Once a person's set-point becomes established, however, changing it appears to be difficult.

Psychosocial Factors in Weight Control

Psychosocial factors are also involved in weight control. For one thing, emotion affects eating and weight gain. Many people claim to eat more when they are anxious or upset, and evidence indicates that stress can induce eating (Logue, 1991). What's more, the foods people and animals eat when stressed tend to be sweet and high in fat—that is, "comfort foods" (Dallman et al., 2003; Oliver, Wardle, & Gibson, 2000). For individuals who are *restrained eaters*—that is, they watch their diets continuously and try to resist eating what they want—emotions can override or "disinhibit" these efforts temporarily, producing a bout of overeating (Herman & Polivy, 1980; Ruderman, 1986). Prospective research indicates that experiencing chronic negative emotion, such as depression, puts people at risk for binge eating and becoming obese

(Goodman & Whitaker, 2002; Stice, Presnell, & Spangler, 2002). **Binge eating** refers to episodes in which the person eats far more than most people would in a fairly short period, such as a couple of hours, and feels unable to control that behavior during that time (Garfinkel, 2002). Frequent binge eating is a common feature of individuals who seek treatment for obesity (Stice et al., 1999).

Lifestyle is an important factor, too. Regularly drinking a lot of alcohol adds calories to the diet and reduces the body's disposal of fat (Suter, Schutz, & Jequier, 1992; Tremblay et al., 1995). Watching television can affect weight control by decreasing people's physical activity and lowering the rate at which the body burns calories, and by presenting mainly low-nutrient, sweet foods in shows and commercials (Andersen, Crespo et al., 1998; Gortmaker, Dietz, & Cheung, 1990; Story & Faulkner, 1990). A study compared obese and normal-weight children's metabolic rates while they simply rested and while they watched the show "The Wonder Years" (Klesges et al., 1992). During the show, the children's metabolic rates dropped to *below* their resting rates—12% below for the normal-weight and 16% below for the obese individuals.

Another psychosocial factor in weight control is the person's sensitivity to food-related cues in the environment: obese people are more sensitive than nonobese people to certain cues (Schachter, 1971). For example, compared with the amount normal-weight people eat, obese individuals eat more when food tastes good, but eat less when it tastes bad. This stronger responsiveness to food cues appears to make obese individuals more susceptible to, say, the influence of a sales pitch when deciding whether to have a dessert. A study found that obese diners at a restaurant were more persuaded by a waitress's description or display of the dessert than nonobese diners (Herman, Olmstead, & Polivy, 1983). Because of this susceptibility to food-related cues, obese children may have difficulty controlling their eating at home. Studies examining family behaviors at mealtimes have shown that parents give more encouragement for eating and offer food more often to heavier children than to slimmer ones (Baranowski & Nader, 1985).

It is tempting to think that obese people are simply unrestrained eaters, but this doesn't seem to be so. For instance, a study found an important similarity between obese people and normal-weight, *restrained* eaters: they seem to share a low sensitivity to the fat content of food (Rolls, 1995). Yogurts were secretly spiked with different amounts of fat and given to subjects to eat before lunch. For both males and females, *unrestrained* eaters ate *less* at lunch if the yogurt contained a lot of fat, but *obese people* and *restrained* eaters did not adjust their intake at lunch to compensate for the fat in their yogurts. How these effects lead to the development of obesity is still unclear.

Overweight and Health

In a study of overweight–and normal-weight men and women, people were asked to rate their own health on a 10-point scale, where 1 equaled the "worst health" and 10 equaled the "best health" they could imagine (Laffrey, 1986). The ratings of the overweight and normal-weight individuals were about the same, averaging in the mid-7s. Are overweight and normal-weight people equally healthy?

Losing weight is an important goal in many people's lives that brings great joy when it is clear that the effort worked.

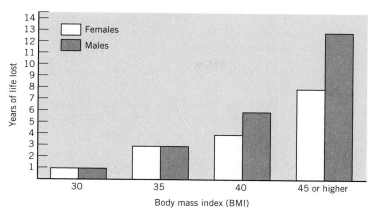

Figure 8–1 Years of life lost for obese Caucasian men and women in the United States as a function of their BMI in early adulthood. The number of years lost is the difference between the death ages for each BMI category and the life expectancies for same-age normal-weight people. Similar trends were found for African Americans, but the impact of BMI was less for the women and far greater for the men—for instance, among Blacks with BMIs at or above 45, the women lost about 5 years of life, and the men lost 20. (Abstracted from Fontaine et al., 2003, Figure 1.)

To answer this question, we need to consider three factors, one of which is the *degree of overweight*. Research has demonstrated that obesity is clearly associated with high cholesterol levels and developing hypertension, heart disease, stroke, diabetes, and cancer (AHA, 2004; Calle et al., 2003; Kurth et al., 2003; Wing & Polley, 2001). The greater the severity of obesity, the greater the person's risk of developing and dying from one of these diseases. Thus, a person whose BMI is over 32 has a much greater risk of morbidity and mortality from, say, heart disease than someone whose BMI is 26, whose risk may not be elevated very much. What's more, the greater the BMI of overweight people, the more years they lose from their life span, as shown in Figure 8–1 (Fontaine et al., 2003). Also, adults' medical costs are related to BMI: compared with costs for healthy-weight individuals, annual costs are 69% higher for severely obese and 43% higher for underweight people (Wang et al., 2003).

The two other factors in the health risks of being heavy are people's *fitness* and *distribution of fat* on the body. Among heavy people, those who are physically active and fit have much lower rates of death and of heart disease and diabetes than those who are sedentary (Blair & Brodney, 1999). Regarding body fat distribution, men's fat tends to collect in the abdominal region, but heavy women have more of their fat on the thighs, hips, and buttocks. Research has found higher rates of hypertension, diabetes, coronary heart disease, and mortality among people with higher, rather than lower, ratios of *waist to hip girth*—that is, their waist measurements compared to their hip measurements (Wing & Polley, 2001). The reason for height-

ened health risks when bodies are "rounded in the middle" is unclear, but it may be that abdominal fat breaks down and is released into the bloodstream more readily than other fat.

Preventing Overweight

Being obese presents disadvantages to the person's health and social relationships in childhood and adulthood (Wadden, Brownell, & Foster, 2002). Is it true, as many people believe, that children tend to outgrow weight problems, or that they will find it easy to lose weight when they are interested in dating? Probably neither belief is true for most children (Brownell, 1986; Jeffery, 1998). Losing weight after becoming obese is not easy at any age, and this is one reason it is important to try to prevent overweight.

Preventing overweight should begin in childhood. Beginning fairly early is important for two reasons. First, obesity in childhood is likely to continue into adult life (Serdula et al., 1993). As Figure 8–2 depicts, this likelihood depends on the age of the child—although only 14% of obese infants become obese adults, 70% of obese 10- to 13-year-olds do. Normal-weight children don't usually become obese adults. Another reason to begin early is to prevent the excess development of fat cells, which occurs in childhood and adolescence. Obese adults who were fat in childhood have the double burden of dealing with bigger fat cells and more of them. Still, there's a problem in preventing obesity in childhood: about one-third of mothers of overweight children claim their child is "at about the right weight" (Maynard et al., 2003).

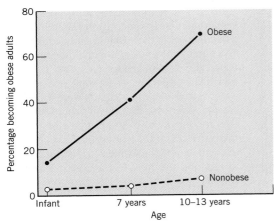

Figure 8–2   Percentage of obese and nonobese children who eventually become obese adults, as a function of age when weight status is assessed. (Data of Epstein, reported in Brownell, 1986, p. 313.)

Most children will not require special preventive efforts to control their weight. Those who will need these efforts are likely either to have a family history of obesity or to have become overweight already (Jeffery, 1998). Efforts to help control their weight need to focus on improving the diets and physical activity of the children, and should involve their families in the program (Baranowski & Hearn, 1997; Jeffery, 1998). Health and physical education programs in schools provide excellent opportunities to promote healthful eating and exercise habits. Studies have shown, for example, that children who receive instruction on healthful diets begin to bring more healthful lunches to school and throw fewer healthful foods away (Striegel-Moore & Rodin, 1985; Wadden & Brownell, 1984). Children who are at risk of becoming obese on the basis of family history or current overweight can be identified and given special attention and training in dietary and exercise behavior. School programs for preventing obesity are most effective when they include a variety of training methods, involve cafeteria and educational facilities and staff, and enlist the cooperation of the parents (Striegel-Moore & Rodin, 1985).

Parents provide almost all the food that comes into the house and most of the food their children eat. They also model and encourage eating and physical activity patterns. Nutritionists and other researchers have identified several ways parents can help their children avoid becoming overly fat (Peckenpaugh, 2003; Striegel-Moore & Rodin, 1985). These recommendations include:

- Encourage regular physical activity and restrict TV watching.
- Don't use unhealthful food rewards for eating a nonpreferred food (e.g., "You may have dessert if you eat your peas"); use praise as the reward instead.
- Decrease buying high-cholesterol and sugary foods of all kinds, including soft drinks, for use in the home or elsewhere; avoid fast-food restaurants.
- Use fruits, nuts, and other healthful foods as regular desserts, and reserve rich cakes and other less healthful desserts for special occasions or once-a-week treats.
- Make sure the child eats a healthful breakfast (with few eggs) each day and does not have high-calorie snacks at night. Calories consumed early in the day tend to be used as fuel; metabolism generally decreases later in the day, and calories consumed at night often become fat.
- Monitor the child's BMI on a regular basis.

Childhood is probably the ideal time to establish activity and dietary habits to prevent individuals from becoming overly fat. Parents, schools, and the mass media can play important roles in helping people control their weight. (Go to 💡.)

DIETING AND TREATMENTS TO LOSE WEIGHT

Many millions of people around the world are dieting on any given day of the year, especially in the spring when they are getting ready to bare their bodies in the summer. In the United States alone, nearly 44% of the women and 29% of the men are trying to lose weight (Serdula et al., 1999). Some individuals try to lose weight because they are concerned about the health risks of being overly fat: losing weight does in fact improve blood pressure and levels of lipids and lipoproteins (Datillo & Kris-Etherton, 1992; Linden & Chambers, 1994). But attractiveness motivates many people.

By American tastes, fatness is considered unattractive, particularly for females—and this confers important disadvantages for heavy people in social

HIGHLIGHT

Which "Carbs" to Avoid

The turn of the century brought a diet craze: avoid carbohydrates ("carbs"). In the process of digestion, carbs increase *glycemia*, or level of sugar in the blood. Avoiding carbs as a general diet strategy ignores the fact that carbohydrates differ in the speed and intensity of conversion to sugar. The physical effect on the body of an amount of carbs in a serving combined with the speed and intensity of conversion can be expressed with a measure called the **glycemic load** (Brand-Miller et al., 2003). Foods that contain a lot of carbs per serving and raise blood sugar quickly and markedly have high glycemic loads; these foods require strong insulin responses and are digested quickly. In contrast, foods with low glycemic loads make lower insulin demands and spread them out, are digested slowly, and delay feelings of hunger.

A study randomly assigned children to receive low or high glycemic-load breakfasts and found that those in the former condition ate less at lunch, where they could choose their diets freely (Warren, Henry, & Simonite, 2003).

Thus, not all carbs are equal in their effects, and we should try to avoid foods with high glycemic loads. Foods with low glycemic loads include most fruits, vegetables, nuts, and whole grains; foods with high glycemic loads include candies, russet potatoes (not new potatoes), and items containing refined grains, such as instant rice, corn flakes, and most cakes and pasta. Meats and most dairy products have low glycemic loads, but often contain high levels of cholesterol and saturated fats.

---

situations, such as dating. There is also a social stigma to being fat because many people *blame* heavy individuals for their condition, believing they simply lack willpower. Experiments have had high school and college girls rate the likeability and characteristics of girls they did not know (DeJong, 1980; Teachman et al., 2003). The ratings were less favorable for obese girls than for normal-weight girls and were especially low if the subjects thought the obese girl was to blame for her weight and was not trying to change it. The social aspects of overweight can be distressing to those who see themselves as being too heavy, and this often motivates them to try to lose weight.

Most people try to reduce their weight on their own by "going on a diet." In the United States, only about 20% of people who are trying to lose weight follow official guidelines to reduce calories and get 2½ hours of exercise a week; 35 to 40% use a poor dieting strategy of consuming less fat rather than fewer calories (Serdula et al., 1999). Using ineffective methods may account for a paradoxical finding: the more that teenage girls and boys try to control their weight, the greater their increases in weight in the long run (Field et al., 2003; Stice et al., 1999). Losing weight and keeping it off is difficult. The best approach for losing weight is to do it gradually and make lifestyle changes that the dieter and his or her

family can accept and maintain permanently. People are more likely to succeed at losing weight if they have constructive social support from their families and others in their social network and if they have a high degree of self-efficacy or confidence that they can do it (Edell et al., 1987; Wing & Polley, 2001).

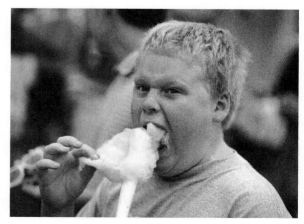

Given what we know about the development of obesity, this boy is likely to be an overweight adult and at heightened risk of developing heart disease and diabetes. And the treat he's eating won't help matters.

Although many overweight people succeed in making and sticking with the lifestyle changes needed to lose weight on their own, most do not (Rzewnicki & Forgays, 1987; Schachter, 1982). Many who do not succeed on their own feel they need help, and probably all people who seek help to lose weight have failed numerous times either to reduce or to maintain the new weight. What kinds of help do people seek, and what works?

Commercial and "Fad Diet" Plans

One kind of help millions of people try is the latest "miracle diet," which is often "guaranteed" to work in a short time. There never seems to be a shortage of these "crash" *fad diets*—many of which are not only ineffective, but are nutritionally unsound and often produce unpleasant and unhealthful side effects (Warshaw, 1992). Some fad diets prescribe a strict dietary regimen with virtually no deviations permitted—the "Scarsdale Diet" outlines specific meals to eat each day. Other fad diets have people eat certain types of food, such as only fruit, as in the "Beverly Hills diet," or foods that are high in protein and fat and low in carbohydrates and sugar, as in the "Atkins Diet." Several commercial plans sell low-calorie liquid or solid replacements for part or all of the person's diet, but provide little or no help in maintaining weight loss later. To the extent that people stick to these diets, they lose weight because they consume fewer calories (Seagle, Wyatt, & Hill, 2001). No crash diet is a substitute for adopting a healthful lifestyle of exercise and moderately sized, balanced meals.

Exercise

Physical activity is an important component in controlling weight. One of its benefits is that it increases metabolism, thereby helping the body to burn off an increased number of calories. Unfortunately, dieters often fail to exercise as part of losing weight because they notice that it takes a lot of exercise to use up a few hundred calories—for instance, they would have to jog about half an hour to burn off the 400 or so calories in a milkshake. But studies of dieting obese individuals have revealed a variety of benefits of exercise in weight control, and they seem to accumulate over time. One benefit of exercise occurs in the first few months: it focuses weight reduction mostly on body fat, while preserving lean tissue (Andersen et al., 1999). Over the next several months, combining exercise with

reduced caloric intake leads to greater weight losses than dieting alone (Epstein, Wing et al., 1985). After losing weight, continued physical activity—even frequent short bouts of walking instead of driving or climbing stairs instead of taking an elevator—helps in maintaining the reduced weight, and more vigorous exercise helps people lose even more (Andersen et al., 1999; Epstein et al., 1988).

Behavioral and Cognitive Methods

People who try to lose weight usually find that changing their eating patterns is very hard to do. Why? A major reason is that they don't know how to control antecedents and consequences in their environments that maintain their eating patterns. Behavioral methods have been developed to help dieters gain the control they need. Richard Stuart (1967) conducted a pioneering study of the utility of behavioral techniques, such as self-monitoring and stimulus control, in helping several obese women lose weight over a 12-month period. The results were impressive: each of the eight women who stayed with the program lost weight fairly consistently throughout the year, losing from 26 to 47 pounds.

The dramatic success of Stuart's program prompted dozens of other researchers to study the usefulness of behavioral methods in weight control. The outcome of these studies suggests the following conclusions (Perri, Nezu, & Viegener, 1992; Wing & Polley, 2001). First, behavioral techniques are generally helpful in losing weight, but they do not work with all people. Second, behavioral programs have very low dropout rates, and people who complete a program lose an average of about 10% of their original weight in the first 4 months. Third, although on average obese people who complete a behavioral program for weight control gain 40% of it back in the first year, many maintain their lower weight.

What techniques do behavioral programs for weight loss use? They are typically given in a group format with weekly meetings when participants submit records of their eating, are weighed, and receive information and feedback (Perri, Nezu, & Viegener, 1992; Wing & Polley, 2001). And they usually include the following components:

- *Nutrition* and *exercise counseling*.
- *Self-monitoring* by keeping careful records of the foods eaten, when, where, with whom, and under what circumstances.

- *Stimulus control* techniques, such as shopping for food with a list, storing food out of sight, and eating at home in only one room.

- *Altering the act of eating*, for example, by chewing the food very thoroughly before swallowing and putting utensils down on the table between mouthfuls.

- *Behavioral contracting*, or setting up a system of rewards for sticking to the diet.

In addition, rewarding overweight individuals for *not engaging in sedentary activities*, such as watching TV or playing computer games, and unplugging the TV and computer are very helpful in promoting weight loss (Epstein et al., 2004).

An important way to enhance the effectiveness of behavioral programs is to involve family and friends in the weight-reduction process, working as a team (Wing & Jeffery, 1999). Family-based behavioral programs were found highly effective in helping obese children and their parents lose weight together over a 10-year period (Epstein et al., 1994). The interventions were most successful when they focused on weight loss in both the parents and children, included exercise in the program, and had the children and parents reward each other for diet and exercise behavior.

Cognitive methods have also been used in weight loss programs. *Motivational interviewing*, which we've discussed in earlier chapters, is applied to increase the person's commitment to and self-efficacy for change; it is helpful in promoting weight loss (Burke, Arkowitz, & Menchola, 2003). Another method, called *problem-solving training*, is designed to teach people strategies to help them deal with everyday difficulties they encounter in sticking to their diets (Perri, Nezu, & Viegener, 1992). Individuals often have difficulty sticking to a diet at family celebrations, when eating at restaurants, and when under stress, for instance. The skills learned in problem-solving training enable people to find solutions to these difficulties. Overweight people who can generate these kinds of solutions tend to lose more weight and have fewer lapses than do others (Drapkin, Wing, & Shiffman, 1995). (Go to 🦶.)

CLINICAL METHODS AND ISSUES

Problem-Solving Training to Control Weight

The cognitive method called problem-solving training can help people deal with a variety of behavioral and emotional difficulties by teaching them how to generate solutions to specific problems in their lives (Sarafino, 2001). For example, when people try to follow a low-calorie diet, they often have trouble eating healthfully when they eat outside their own households, such as at restaurants, work, or sporting events. Here are some common problems these dieters face and examples of solutions they might produce.

PROBLEM: *I eat vending machine and restaurant food too much. How can I curb this?*

SOLUTIONS: Prepare lunch and take it to work; eat with others who do the same. Take low-calorie snacks with you to work, movies, sporting events, shopping malls, etc.

PROBLEM: *When I know I will be eating out, how can I choose a restaurant that will make it easier to stick to my diet?*

SOLUTIONS: Identify restaurants in advance that have healthy selections. Avoid going to all-you-can-eat buffet restaurants that have tempting high-calorie selections.

PROBLEM: *When faced with a restaurant menu that includes high-calorie foods, how can I restrict the calories I eat?*

SOLUTIONS: Learn about high- and low-calorie ingredients and preparation methods, such as frying versus grilling, and ask the waiter questions. Skim the menu to reject high-calorie selections; read only low-calorie options. If ordering a salad, ask for the dressing on the side; use only a little. If others are having dessert, either share one with another person or order fruit or sherbet. Ask about portion size; if too large, ask for smaller.

Self-Help Groups and Worksite Weight-Loss Programs

Although there are dozens of self-help organizations for weight control, *Weight Watchers* is among the most widely known of these groups. The Weight Watchers approach uses several behavioral techniques, such as self-monitoring, along with nutritional information and group meetings for social support. Different self-help organizations have their own mix of methods to help people lose weight (Chesney, 1984; Perri, Nezu, & Viegener, 1992). Little research has been done on the success of self-help groups; one study found that they produce moderate weight losses for those who complete them (Heshka et al., 2003). But dropout rates for self-help groups may be high, sometimes over 50% in the first 6 weeks alone (Stunkard, 1987).

Worksite weight-loss programs have been introduced and evaluated in a variety of businesses and industries. These programs generally used behavioral techniques but were not very successful (Foreyt & Leavesley, 1991). High dropout rates and small weight losses have been common, suggesting that inadequate motivation is a major problem. Evidence indicates that these problems can be reduced with two approaches: gearing the program to the workers' stages of readiness to change and providing incentives for participation (Gomel et al., 1993). Using teams in *weight-loss competitions* at worksites increases the amount of weight lost (Brownell et al., 1984; Wing & Polley, 2001). As an example, a company might offer a prize for the team achieving the greatest percentage of a previously set weight-loss goal. To help the teams do well, the company could provide information about nutrition, exercise, and behavioral methods, such as self-monitoring, stimulus control, and rewards.

Medically Supervised Approaches

Some approaches for losing weight involve medical procedures or require supervision by a physician. One such approach uses prescribed drugs, and two are currently available: *sibutramine* suppresses appetite, and *orlistat* decreases intestinal absorption of ingested fat. Each of these drugs produces moderate weight loss, and combining pharmacological and behavioral treatments is more effective than either alone (Phelan & Wadden, 2002; Wadden, Brownell, & Foster, 2002). Because of the side effects all such drugs seem to have, they are recommended only for people who are *obese*, some of whom may need to take them indefinitely (Stallone & Stunkard, 1991).

Another medical approach for losing weight involves placing the patient on a *very-low-calorie diet* (VLCD) regimen that contains fewer than 800 calories per day, usually as a liquid formula for 12 to 16 weeks (Seagle, Wyatt, & Hill, 2001; Wing & Polley, 2001). VLCDs are safe under careful medical supervision if the patients do not have certain medical conditions, such as heart disease. Although VLCDs produce rapid and substantial weight losses, much of it is regained when the patients return to regular foods, and the diet can have serious side effects, such as cardiac problems. VLCDs may be appropriate mainly for obese patients who have failed to control their weight with other methods and whose obesity poses an unusually high health risk, such as from diabetes (Seagle, Wyatt, & Hill, 2001).

The most drastic medical approaches for losing weight involve *bariatric surgery*, procedures that change the structure of the stomach or intestines (AMA, 2003). The two most common forms of bariatric surgery alter the stomach. One form simply installs a band around the upper part of the stomach to create a little chamber with a small opening to the rest of the stomach. Because the chamber holds only an ounce or so, the person feels full after ingesting a small amount. The second form reduces the size of the stomach by literally stapling part of it up and then attaching that section to the intestine, bypassing most of the original stomach. Although these approaches markedly reduce weight, they entail some surgical risk and may produce unpleasant side effects—for example, nausea, vomiting, and abdominal pain after eating. As a result, these methods are recommended only for patients who meet one of two criteria: BMI of 40 or more but otherwise healthy or BMI of 35 with another serious illness, such as diabetes (Brolin, 2002). Another surgical procedure called *liposuction* sucks adipose tissue from the body with a tube but is not a weight reduction method—its function is strictly cosmetic, "body sculpting." It is used for removing fat from specific regions of the body, such as the thighs or abdomen. Although the procedure is usually safe, complications can include blood clots or even death (AMA, 2003).

We have considered methods for losing weight that range from adjusting one's diet and exercising to using surgical procedures. Choosing the most appropriate approaches to use requires *matching* the methods to people's weight problems and characteristics, such as their metabolic function, dieting history, and financial resources (Brownell & Wadden, 1991). Someone who is overweight, say BMI = 27, might use a structured self-dieting approach or a worksite program, but someone with a BMI greater than 35 would probably need to use medically supervised approaches.

Relapse after Weight Loss

The problem of relapse after completing treatment to lose weight is similar to that which many people experience after quitting smoking, drinking, or using drugs. The situations in which people who have lost weight overeat usually involve *food cues*, such as being at a restaurant or having a special meal, *negative emotions*, such as stress or depression, and *boredom* (Wing & Polley, 2001). Individuals who maintain their reduced weight for a few years stand a very good chance of maintaining that weight in subsequent years (McGuire et al., 1999). When considering weight gain in the years after losing weight, keep in mind that people generally gain weight as they get older—1 or 2 pounds a year in middle-aged Americans, on average. A fair assessment of weight-loss success should also take into account *the weight dieters didn't gain* that other people do (Perri, Nezu, & Viegener, 1992).

Michael Perri and his colleagues (1988) demonstrated that followup treatment programs can be effective in reducing the relapse problem in weight control. In this study, obese men and women lost an average of 12.5 pounds in a behavioral program for dietary and exercise behaviors, and some received followup treatment. Assessments 18 months later revealed that the average weight loss the subjects maintained was 10.6 pounds for those who received followup treatment and only 3.6 pounds for those who did not. Data analysis revealed two critical components in the success of the followup treatments: (1) frequent therapist meetings to deal with specific problems individuals were having in maintaining their weight and (2) social influences of other members of a treatment group. These findings suggest that obese individuals who have lost weight may benefit from having continued meetings with therapists, relapse "hot lines" to call, and support groups. Perri and colleagues (2001) later demonstrated that problem-solving training after weight loss with behavioral methods was also effective in helping clients maintain the loss.

Most people who lose weight do not use effective ways to maintain the loss. If you wanted to lose weight and keep it off, what methods could you use? Here are some:

- When losing the weight, use behavioral techniques— such as self-monitoring and stimulus control—to diet and increase exercise. Choose a reasonable final weight goal, and plan to lose weight *gradually*, such as a pound a week or less.

- After reaching your weight goal, permanently eat a lower-calorie-and-fat diet than in the past. For carbohydrates, choose ones that have low glycemic loads. Stick to this diet fairly consistently throughout the week, including weekends (Gorin et al., 2004).

- Continue to exercise—it's the best predictor of long-term weight maintenance (Wing & Polley, 2001). Weigh yourself each time you exercise.

- Avoid situations that prompt lapses and reward good behavior. Occasional lapses are not a problem as long as you get back on track as soon as possible.

- Get social support from family and friends for maintaining your weight loss. Join a self-help or support group if you find that you have too many lapses.

(Go to 🍎.)

ANOREXIA AND BULIMIA

Although gaining weight by overeating is a very common problem with psychosocial relationships, it is not a psychiatric disorder. In contrast, two relatively unusual eating problems—*anorexia nervosa* and *bulimia nervosa*—are included as psychiatric disorders in the *Diagnostic and Statistical Manual of Mental Disorders* (DSM-IV) of the American Psychiatric Association (1994). People with these two disorders use extreme ways to keep their weight down. Anorexia is illustrated in the following case study of a 19-year-old, 5'3" tall coed named Frances who had been 20 pounds overweight 6 years earlier. She

> weighed 83 lbs upon admission [to therapy]. She reported eating very little food each day (estimated to be less than 500 kcal). She exercised for at least 3 hours each day by attending aerobics classes and running. When she did consume a normal meal, she purged it via self-induced vomiting. . . . She never binged (i.e., ate large quantities of food). She was obsessed with fears of weight gain. (Williamson, Cubic, & Fuller, 1992, p. 367)

ASSESS YOURSELF

Your Weight Control Patterns

For each of the following questions, put a check mark in the preceding space if your answer is "yes."

_____ Do you watch your calorie intake more carefully than anyone else you know?

_____ Is your BMI less than 19?

_____ Do you think gaining a few pounds during a holiday season would be a terrible thing?

_____ Have you ever eaten so much so quickly that you felt like you had lost control of your eating?

_____ If yes, has this happened more than about 10 times in the past year?

_____ Have you ever eaten a lot and then tried to "purge" the food by using laxatives, diuretics, or self-induced vomiting?

_____ If yes, has this happened more than about 10 times in the past year?

_____ Have you felt a lot of emotional distress in recent months?

_____ Do you often eat fewer than two meals a day?

_____ Do you regularly exercise more than 10 hours a week to lose weight?

How many "yes" answers did you give? A high number suggests that you may have an eating disorder. If your number is: from 3 to 5, you may want to consider getting professional help, especially if your situation seems to be getting worse; 6 or more, you should seek help right away. You can find help through your college's counseling office or by contacting professional organizations, such as the American Psychological Association and the American Psychiatric Association, which are in Washington, DC. (*Sources*: Based on material in Brownell, 1989; Davison, Neale, & Kring, 2004; Logue, 1991.)

When she was younger, she had been teased by peers and repeatedly criticized by her mother for being overweight. As Frances's case shows, **anorexia nervosa** is an eating disorder that involves a drastic reduction in food intake and an unhealthy loss of weight. People with this disorder are characterized by a weight at least 15% below normal (BMI at or less than 17.5), an intense fear of gaining weight, a distorted idea of their body shape, and, for females who have begun to menstruate, absence of a period (Rock & Kaye, 2001). The starvation in anorexia may be so extreme as to cause or contribute to the person's death—for instance, by causing extremely low blood pressure, heart damage, or cardiac arrhythmias (due to low levels of electrolytes, such as potassium) (Pomeroy & Mitchell, 2002).

Bulimia nervosa is characterized by recurrent episodes of *binge eating*, generally followed by *purging* by self-induced vomiting, laxative use, or other means to prevent gaining weight (Garfinkel, 2002; Pomeroy & Mitchell, 2002; Rock & Kaye, 2001). It was not recognized as a distinct syndrome until the late 1970s. This disorder can cause a wide range of medical problems, including inflammation of the digestive tract and cardiac problems, such as arrhythmias. Bulimic individuals are aware that their eating pattern is abnormal, are fearful of having lost control of their eating, and tend to be depressed and self-critical after a bulimic episode. Many individuals exhibit some bulimic behaviors, such as purging, but are not classified as bulimics because they engage in these behaviors infrequently.

It is difficult to know how prevalent eating disorders are. A study that compared women's medical records with returned surveys on eating disorders to the researchers found that many of those who did not return the survey did in fact have eating disorders (Beglin & Fairburn, 1992). Thus, existing data are likely to be underestimates. Estimates of prevalence for the general population are 0.5–1.0% for anorexia and 2% for bulimia, with more than 95% of diagnosed cases being females (Rock & Kaye, 2001). Anorexia is especially common among dance students, models, and athletes who feel pressured to control their weight (French & Jeffery, 1994).

Why People Become Anorexics and Bulimics

What causes the eccentric eating habits of anorexia and bulimia? The answer is still unclear, and researchers have suggested biological, psychological, and cultural factors that may be involved. There is evidence for genetic and physiological links to these disorders (Rock & Kaye, 2001). For example, studies have examined the occurrence of anorexia and bulimia in twins and found that these disorders are far more likely to appear in *both* twin members if they are identical twins rather than fraternal twins. Other research findings indicate that the functioning of neuroendocrine and neurotransmitter processes may be abnormal in eating-disordered individuals.

Cultural factors may provide the answer to two obvious questions about these eating disorders: Why is the prevalence of anorexia and bulimia particularly high among White females, and why has it increased in recent years? African American girls have lower prevalence rates of eating disorders than White girls, partly because they tend to be less concerned about their weight even when they are heavy (Abrams, Allen, & Gray, 1993). Beauty plays a central role in the sex-role stereotype of women in many cultures, and Western

cultures have witnessed recent changes in their ideals about female beauty (Striegel-Moore, 1997). These changes are evident in the body proportions of models and beauty pageant contestants. Years ago, the "ideally beautiful woman" had a figure that was more rounded, with larger bust and hip measurements. After 1960 or so, the ideal figure of a woman became much thinner, and the social pressures on women to be slender increased. Caucasian females are more likely than males to wish they were thinner and to diet, and these gender differences begin to show up by age 11 or so (Cohen, Brownell, & Felix, 1990). In social interactions with other children, parents, and teachers, girls more than boys are given the message: thin is better (Attie & Brooks-Gunn, 1987). And once the message is clear, they reach puberty, when girls add an average of over 20 pounds of fat to their bodies while boys add muscle. This is a no-win situation for adolescent girls. How do they deal with it?

When adolescents—especially females—start trying to control their weight, they typically adjust their diets in a normal manner, but for many teens the methods they use become more extreme, involving occasional fasting or purging. A study found that about 13% of 15-year-olds engaged in some form of purging behavior, mainly on a monthly basis or less, with the rate for females being twice as high as that for males (Killen et al., 1986). Prospective evidence indicates that individuals who become anorexic and bulimic typically start out dieting normally but have relatively strong concerns about their weight, and then begin using more extreme methods (French & Jeffery, 1994; Killen et al., 1994). Dieters with strong weight concerns may come to rely more and more on fasting and purging because these methods keep weight off. This pattern becomes entrenched in those who become bulimic, especially if they were overweight in childhood (Fairburn et al., 2003). Bulimics tend to binge after unpleasant experiences, particularly negative social interactions, which function as disinhibiting events (Steiger et al., 1999).

Why do these eating patterns become so compulsive? People who are extremely concerned about their weight tend to see themselves as round-faced and pudgy, even when others do not. Studies using ingenious apparatuses, such as special projectors, have shown that the great majority of women overestimate their size and generally perceive themselves to be one-fourth larger than they really are (Thompson, 1986). Although men make similar errors, they do so

"Beep-beep-beep...The number you are trying to reach, 173, has been changed. The new number is..."

Reprinted courtesy of Bunny Hoest.

to a much lesser degree—and, unlike women, many of these men may *want* to be larger. Overestimation of body size is particularly pronounced among anorexics and bulimics. Among anorexics, for example, the idea that they are overweight persists long after they have become slim. When they are reduced to skin and bones, anorexics still claim to be "too fat" and greatly overestimate their size (Askevold, 1975; Crisp & Kalucy, 1974). Interventions delivered on the Internet or in person can reduce the risk of developing eating disorders in people who are very dissatisfied with their body shapes (Celio et al., 2000; Stice & Shaw, 2004).

Treatments for Anorexia and Bulimia

Because anorexia nervosa involves a severe and health-threatening underweight condition, the first priority in treating this disorder is to restore the person's body weight and nutrition to as near normal as possible. This is often done in a hospital setting. Several approaches that include behavioral techniques and drug therapy are effective for putting weight on (Logue, 1991; Rock & Kaye, 2001; Williamson, Cubic, & Fuller, 1992). However, keeping the weight on is difficult; about half of previously treated anorexics continue to have eating problems and often show other social and emotional difficulties, such as depression. Treatments that include cognitive methods to alter irrational thinking, such as the person's distorted body image, may be more effective than other approaches, but little evidence exists on this issue (Vitousek, 2002).

Psychotherapy is more effective for bulimia than anorexia, particularly when it includes behavioral and cognitive methods (Compas et al., 1998; Fairburn, 2002; Rock & Kaye, 2001). These methods—such as self-monitoring, reinforcement, and cognitive restructuring—focus on reducing bingeing and purging behaviors. If a patient does not respond to these methods, *antidepressant drugs* may be added to elevate the person's mood (Compas et al., 1998). Treatment is less effective for bulimics who have very high initial rates of bingeing and purging and a history of substance abuse (Wilson, Loeb et al., 1999).

We have discussed the problems people have in controlling their weight through adjustments in their diets. We have also seen that exercise can play an important role in reducing body fat and, thereby, can enhance people's health. The next section examines exercise as a means of becoming fit and keeping well.

EXERCISE

Sometimes it seems that a fitness boom has occurred in many nations. For instance, the proportion of Americans who exercise doubled in the 20 years after the early 1960s (Serfass & Gerberich, 1984). Joggers and bicyclists today can be seen on roads and paths in cities and out in the country, and fitness clubs have sprung up everywhere. But in the United States and most other industrialized countries, adults' lifestyles still include very little or irregular physical activity (Dubbert 2002; Sallis & Owen, 1999). We've all heard that exercise is healthy. We'll see why in this section. (Go to 💡.)

This anorexic girl probably sees herself as 'too fat' despite her thinness.

HIGHLIGHT

Types and Amounts of Healthful Exercise

All physical activities—even just fidgeting—use energy and burn calories. *Exercise* is a special class of physical activity in which people exert their bodies in a structured and repetitive way for the sake of health or body development. There are several types of exercise, each with its own form of activity physical goals, and effects.

Isotonics, Isometrics, and Isokinetics

Isotonic exercise refers to a type of activity that builds strength *and* endurance by the person's moving a heavy object, exerting most of the muscle force in one direction. This type of exercise includes weight lifting and many calisthenics. In doing push-ups, for example, most of the exertion occurs in raising the body.

Isometric exercise builds mainly strength rather than endurance, and the person exerts muscle force against an *immovable* object. An example of an isometric exercise is the "chair lift": the person sits in a standard unupholstered chair, grasps the sides of the seat with both hands, and pulls upward, straining the arm muscles. The pulling doesn't move the seat. **Isokinetic exercise** builds strength *and* endurance by the person's exerting muscle force in more than one direction in the course of moving an object. An example would be in exerting substantial force to push forward and to pull it back. Isokinetic exercise typically requires special equipment, such as Nautilus machines.

Aerobics

The word *aerobic* literally means "with oxygen." What does oxygen have to do with exercise? When we exert ourselves physically, the energy for it comes from the metabolic process of burning fatty acids and glucose in the presence of oxygen. Continuous exertion at high intensity over many minutes requires a great deal of oxygen. Being "in shape" means the person consumes a high *volume of oxygen* (VO2) per heartbeat during physical exertion.

The term **aerobic exercise** refers to energetic physical activity that requires high levels of oxygen over an extended time, say, 20 minutes. Aerobic activities generally involve rhythmical actions that move the body over a distance or against gravity—as occurs in fast dancing, jogging, bicycling, swimming, or certain calisthenics. Performing aerobic activity with sufficient intensity and duration on a regular basis increases the body's ability to extract oxygen from the blood and burn fatty acids and glucose.

An Ideal Exercise Program for Health

How much and what kinds of exercise are best for fitness? The answer depends on the individual's age, current health and physical capacity, goals, interests, and opportunities, such as whether facilities or partners are available (Insel & Roth, 1998). Almost all individuals need to begin with a moderate *starter program* and progress in a gradual manner toward fitness, and people who are elderly or less fit should progress more slowly than others. Starting gradually avoids muscle soreness and injury and allows the body to adapt to increasing demands, such as in the use of oxygen.

An ideal exercise program would involve about three hours of exercise a week divided into three to five sessions, each having three phases (Blair et al., 1992; Insel & Roth, 1998):

1. *Warmup.* Each session should include two types of warmup activities: (1) stretching and flexibility exercises, for various major muscle groups, such as of the neck, back, shoulders, abdomen, and legs and (2) strength and endurance exercises, such as push-ups, pull-ups, and lifting.
2. *Aerobics.* The next 20 minutes or more involves rhythmical exercise of large muscle groups, performed vigorously enough to raise the heart (pulse) rate to a moderately high target range. The easiest way to estimate the target range for an adult is to use a formula based on the person's age: the *minimum* heart rate is 160 pulse beats per minute minus the person's age; the *maximum* is 200 minus age (La Place, 1984). Thus, 30-year-olds would maintain their heart rate between 130 and 170 beats per minute during aerobics.
3   *Cool-down.* The last few minutes of exercise should taper off in intensity to return the body to its

HIGHLIGHT

normal state. These exercises can include calisthenics or walking.

Although this ideal seems fairly rigid, there is room for variation. For instance, individuals who exercise at the upper end of their target range can use fewer or shorter exercise periods each week. People can also tailor the program to their goals and interests by varying the exercises they perform during each phase and across sessions. For instance, they can vary the aerobics they do, jogging on one day, skipping rope on another, swimming on another, and so on. If they want to firm their abdomens, they can focus on appropriate activities during the warmup and cool-down phases.

Is the Ideal Necessary to Benefit Health?

Not all people can or will get the ideal amount and type of physical activity. Can they benefit from less? Absolutely, and the activity needn't be "exercise." Individuals can get substantial health and fitness benefits from just 30 minutes of daily moderate activity—such as walking briskly, taking a leisurely bicycle ride, or gardening—and this activity can occur in, say, 10-minute periods rather than all at once (Phillips, Kiernan, & King, 2001). The closer to the ideal one gets, the greater the benefits. However, the most important strategy to maintain health is to *avoid* having an almost completely sedentary lifestyle.

THE HEALTH EFFECTS OF EXERCISE

If you asked fitness-conscious people why they exercise, they would probably give a variety of reasons: "Exercising helps me keep my weight down," "I like it when I'm in shape—and so does my boyfriend," "It helps me unwind and relieves my tension," "Being in shape keeps me sharp on my job," "I don't get sick as often when I'm fit," and "It makes people's hearts stronger, so they live longer." These answers describe several psychosocial and physical health benefits of exercising and are, for the most part, correct.

Three psychosocial benefits of exercise have been shown in many studies. First, engaging in regular vigorous exercise is associated with lower feelings of *stress* and anxiety, as we discussed in Chapter 5. Second, people who get involved in fitness programs report that their *work performance* and attitudes improve—they make fewer errors, for instance (Quick et al., 1997). Third, participating in regular exercise is linked to enhanced *self-concepts* of individuals, especially children (Dishman, 1986; Sallis & Owen, 1999). Self-concept enhancements may occur because individuals who exercise are better able to control their weight, maintain an attractive appearance, and engage successfully in physical activities and sports. These outcomes help people to feel a greater sense of esteem and to receive the many social advantages that accrue with being fit. But keep in mind that most studies of psychosocial benefits from exercise have used correlational or retrospective methods, making

it difficult to determine cause-effect relationships. Some evidence suggests that part of the self-reported benefits may have resulted from a placebo effect of the subjects' expecting that psychosocial benefits would occur (Desharnais et al., 1993).

Of the many physiological effects that physical activity produces, one effect is especially intriguing: vigorous exercise seems to increase the body's production of *endorphins*, which are morphinelike chemical substances. Studies have shown that endorphin levels in the blood are higher after exercise than before (Carr et al., 1981). Some researchers claim that the euphoric "runner's high" that many individuals feel after a very vigorous aerobic workout results from high levels of endorphins reaching the brain. These researchers have also proposed that these higher endorphin levels may be responsible for decreases in both the stress and sensations of pain many people feel during or after vigorous exercise. But evidence for these possibilities is unclear (Phillips, Kiernan, & King, 2001).

Exercise can enhance many aspects of people's physical fitness throughout the life span. In early childhood, aerobic exercise improves agility and cardiovascular function (Alpert et al., 1990). What about the other end of the life span, when people generally show a gradual decline in their physical work capacity—as reflected in their muscle flexibility, strength, and endurance? This decline occurs partly because many individuals get less exercise as they get older. An 18-year longitudinal study examined the physical work capacity of men who were over 50 years of age at the start of the study and who engaged in aerobic exercise regularly (Kasch, Wallace, & Van Camp, 1985). The work capacity of these men decreased only slightly across the 18 years, whereas individuals in the general population tend to show a 1 to 2% decrease per year. Also, the percentage of body fat and resting blood pressure of these men did not show the increases that usually occur during these years. This and other evidence indicates that engaging in aerobic exercise curbs the usual decline in fitness that people experience as they get older (Buchner et al., 1992).

The physical benefits from regular exercise are reflected also in people's health and longevity (Sallis & Owen, 1999). Vigorous exercise produces the greatest gains, but even several brisk walks a month can benefit longevity (Kujala et al., 1998). The main health benefits of exercise relate to preventing cardiovascular problems and some forms of cancer (Phillips, Kiernan, & King, 2001; Sallis & Owen, 1999). Many studies have demonstrated that individuals who regularly engage in vigorous physical activity are less likely to develop and die from coronary heart disease (CHD) than those who lead relatively sedentary lives (Powell et al., 1987). Although no experimental research has been done in which humans were randomly assigned to exercise and nonexercise conditions, research with animals and prospective studies with humans indicate that the link between physical activity and reduced risk of CHD is probably causal.

How does engaging in regular vigorous activity protect individuals against CHD? The benefits of exercise on blood pressure are clear from three findings. First, children and adults who are physically active have lower systolic and diastolic blood pressure than those who are not (Haskell, 1984; Panico et al., 1987). Second, prospective data indicate that people who are physically fit and active are less likely to develop hypertension than less-fit and inactive people (Blair et al., 1992). Third, experimental research has shown that exercise lowers blood pressure in both hypertensive and normotensive people (Arroll & Beaglehole, 1992; Braith et al., 1994; Kokkinos et al., 1995). Exercise may also prevent CHD in two other ways: by reducing the occurrence of arrhythmic heartbeats and by decreasing LDL while increasing HDL serum cholesterol. Some evidence supports each of these possibilities (Blair et al., 1992).

The risk of developing cancer has been linked to low physical activity; the evidence is fairly strong for colon cancer and more modest for other cancers, such as of the breast and prostate (Sallis & Owen, 1999). Although the reason for this link is unclear, part of it may involve the beneficial effect of both immediate and long-term exercise on the immune system. One study tested healthy, physically active 24- to 35-year-olds and 65- to 79-year-olds for the effects of a vigorous exercise session on immune function (Fiatarone et al., 1989). Natural killer cell number and function were similar in both age groups before the session and increased substantially in both groups in response to the exercise.

Not all effects of exercise are beneficial—there can be hazards as well. One hazard occurs when people jog or bicycle in traffic, of course, risking a collision. But the most common problems that arise involve injury to bones or muscles from other kinds of accidents and from overstraining the body (Sallis & Owen, 1999). For instance, high-impact exercises, such as jogging and tennis, can injure joints and lead to arthritis. Many injuries happen to people who do not exercise regularly or are beginners, mainly from overtaxing their bodies and from unsafe exercise conditions, such as having improper shoes. Exercising too long in very hot weather can lead to heat exhaustion—with symptoms of dizziness, rapid and weak pulse, and headache—or a more severe condition called heat stroke, which can be fatal.

Sudden cardiac death can occur when exercising. Autopsy reports for individuals who had died in association with exercising typically reveal that the cause was cardiac arrest, and most of them had cardiovascular problems that existed prior to the attack (Northcote, Flannigan, & Ballantyne, 1986). Most of these problems could have been detected by medical screening, and the deaths of these people might have been avoided through medical counseling. Cardiac arrest from exercising is unlikely—one case per 1.5 million sessions of physical exertion—and occurs much less frequently in people who exercise five times rather than once a week (Albert et al., 2004). Physicians and physical therapists can prescribe exercise programs for people with specific health problems, such as diabetes and CHD.

Another health hazard that relates to exercise is people's use of *anabolic steroids*—male hormones that build tissue—to increase muscle size and strength. Many more males than females use steroids, and most users are athletes (AMA, 2003; Strauss & Yesalis, 1991). Using steroids for an extended period has several negative health effects. It raises LDL and lowers HDL serum cholesterol and is related to liver and kidney tumors and to heart attacks and strokes. It also has a permanent masculinizing effect in women, increasing facial hair and lowering the voice, for instance. In males, it increases acne and balding and decreases the size and firmness of testes, at least temporarily. Some who use steroids share needles with others, putting each other at risk for HIV infection (DuRant et al., 1993).

Conclusions regarding the health effects of exercise are fairly clear. Frequent physical activity, especially vigorous exercise, is psychologically and physically healthful, particularly for preventing heart disease. People who begin exercise programs should guard against overtaxing their bodies, exercise under safe conditions with proper skills, and have periodic medical examinations to determine whether any underlying risks exist. Although more people exercise today than was the case decades ago, most adults in industrialized countries do not get enough regular and energetic physical activity to gain substantial health benefits.

WHO GETS ENOUGH EXERCISE, WHO DOES NOT—AND WHY?

Physical activity varies across cultures. Probably most people around the world have lifestyles that provide regular, vigorous, and sustained activity naturally, without actually doing exercises. They commute to work by bicycle, for instance, or have jobs that involve energetic work, as farmers, laborers, and homemakers often do. These people can get healthful amounts of physical activity if it occurs in at least three episodes a week, totaling about 3 hours (Blair et al., 1992). But most people in the United States and other industrialized nations have relatively sedentary life circumstances. Many individuals who could be physically active in their normal lifestyles choose not to be—they may take rest breaks rather than sustaining an activity or opt to use a machine instead of doing a task manually. The high levels of physical activity of early childhood decline sharply; only half of American adolescents are vigorously active on a regular basis (Marcus et al., 2000). Because little is known about people's everyday physical activities, we will focus our discussion on factors associated with doing and not doing exercises.

Gender, Age, and Sociocultural Differences in Exercise

Overall demographic patterns give a portrait of who exercises in the United States. Adults who exercise tend to have more income and education than those who don't exercise and are more likely to be men than women and White than Black or Hispanic (USBC, 2003). They also tend to have participated in exercise in the past (Dishman, 1991). Similar patterns exist in other industrialized countries, such as Australia (Sallis & Owen, 1999). Another factor is age—as adults get older, most tend to

> disengage from participating in physical activities due less, it appears, to decrements in physiological functioning ability than to cultural and psychosocial factors which persuade them that vigorous exercise is not appropriate for the elderly. Sedentary social role models, distorted body image, exaggerated notions of risk, expectations of disapproval, fear of failure, misinformation, and limited previous involvement in physical activities all conspire to limit the elderly's desire to be active. (Vertinsky & Auman, 1988, p. 16)

These forces against exercise are particularly strong among many of today's elderly women. Women seem to learn from past sex-role experiences that men are more socially and physically suited to vigorous activity than females. Although both male and female older people tend to underrate their physical capabilities and exaggerate their health risks in performing energetic exercise after middle age, women are especially prone to these beliefs (Vertinsky & Auman, 1988; Woods & Birren, 1984). Health care workers and organizations for the elderly have many opportunities to dispel incorrect beliefs about health risks, change sex-role stereotypes regarding exercise, and encourage active lifestyles.

Reasons for Not Exercising

When individuals are asked why they don't exercise, the most common reason they give is that they cannot find the time (Dishman, 1991; Godin et al., 1992). Actually, of course, most people could have the time but choose to use it in other ways. People also report not exercising because they have no convenient place to do it or because the weather or other environmental conditions make it unpleasant or impossible.

Whether people exercise is also related to the amount of stress in their lives, social influences, and their beliefs. People who exercise regularly tend to skip sessions when they experience high levels of stress (Stetson et al., 1997). Social influences on exercise involve modeling, encouragement, and reinforcement by peers and family. Adults who exercise tend to have spouses who encourage them to do so, and children and adolescents who exercise or engage in sports tend to have friends or family who also do so (Dishman, Sallis, & Orenstein, 1985; Gottlieb & Baker, 1986; Sallis et al., 1988). People's beliefs can influence exercising in at least three ways:

- Individuals with high self-efficacy about their ability to exercise are more likely to do so than those with low self-efficacy (Clark et al., 1995; Wilcox & Storandt, 1996).

- Perceived susceptibility to illness can spur people to exercise. People who received information describing their level of fitness or indicating they might be susceptible to health problems that could be prevented through exercise were more likely to start exercising than others who did not get such information (Godin et al., 1987; Wurtele & Maddux, 1987).

- Perceived barriers reduce exercise; enjoying exercise increases it (Brennan et al., 2003; Salmon et al., 2003). The barriers can be *personal*, such as feeling tired or having work commitments, or *environmental*, such as cost, weather, or safety.

People who do *not* exercise tend to have other risk factors for developing serious illnesses, such as by being overweight or smoking cigarettes. From the standpoint of performing health-protective behavior, people whose health would benefit most from physical activity seem to be the most resistant to starting or maintaining an exercise program. Quitting smoking may help: a study of smokers found that those who quit were more likely to start exercising than those who didn't (Perkins et al., 1993).

PROMOTING EXERCISE BEHAVIOR

A person who spends time watching youngsters play is likely to have the impression that children are innately very active—running, jumping, and climbing—and that they do not need to be encouraged to exercise, as older individuals do. Some children seem to find physical activity naturally reinforcing (Epstein et al., 1999). Although most children and adolescents are more active than adults, many children are not active enough (Marcus et al., 2000). People of all ages could benefit from school, park, and worksite recreation programs and facilities to promote exercise.

To obtain the full health benefits of physical activity, people need to exercise or be very active as a

People of all ages can benefit from exercise programs. These children are in an aerobics class.

permanent part of their normal lifestyles. Few people in industrialized societies achieve this ideal. Of individuals who are already exercising regularly at any given time, about half will quit in the coming year (Dishman, Sallis, & Orenstein, 1985). Table 8.3 presents several strategies that help people start and continue exercising. These strategies can be applied by individuals who decide on their own to start or by organized interventions to promote exercise in target populations, such as schoolchildren, workers, or the elderly. Note three additional points. First, we can promote physical activity by giving rewards for increased exercising *and* for decreased sedentary behavior (Epstein, Saelens, & O'Brien, 1995). Second, physicians can increase physical activity markedly in sedentary patients by giving verbal and written advice on specific behaviors and goals (Swinburn et al., 1998). Third, sedentary people who are willing to increase their activity are more likely to stick with an exercise routine that requires a high frequency (5 or more days per week) than a high intensity (Perri et al., 2002).

Interventions with various populations have been successful in promoting exercise, particularly if they included behavioral methods to modify the antecedents and consequences of physical activity (Sallis & Owen, 1999). Interventions since the late 1980s that have included strategies like those in Table 8.3 have reported higher rates of exercise adherence and fewer dropouts

"SURE, JOGGING TAKES THE YEARS OFF · · · ·
I HAVEN'T FELT THIS RIDICULOUS
SINCE I WAS 13."

Reprinted courtesy of Bunny Hoest.

Table 8.3   *Strategies to Promote Exercising*

- *Preassessment.* Before people begin an exercise program, they need to determine their purposes for exercising and the benefits they can expect. They should also assess their health status, preferably through a medical checkup.
- *Exercise selection.* The exercises included in the program should be tailored to meet the health needs of the individual and his or her interests and purposes, such as firming up certain parts of the body. People are more likely to stick with the program if it includes exercises that they enjoy doing.
- *Exercise conditions.* Before people start an exercise program, they should determine when and where they will exercise and arrange to get any equipment they will need. Some people seem to adhere to a program if they pick a fixed time for exercising and refuse to schedule anything else at that time; others can be more flexible and still make sure to exercise about every other day. The exercise conditions should be safe and convenient.
- *Goals.* Most people adhere to a program more closely if they write out a specific sequence of goals and consequences for exercise behavior in a behavioral contract. The goals should be graduated, beginning at a modest level. They should also be measurable—as body weight or number of push-ups would be—rather than vague, such as "to feel good."
- *Consequences.* Exercise should lead to reinforcement. Some individuals may need tangible reinforcers to maintain their exercise behavior in the early stages of the program. After these people get in shape, many will find that the enjoyment of exercise and the physical benefits are sufficient rewards.
- *Social influence.* People are more likely to start and stick with an exercise program if these efforts have the support and encouragement of family and friends. Exercising with a partner or in groups sometimes enhances people's motivation to continue in a program.
- *Record keeping.* People can enhance their motivation to exercise by keeping records of their weight and performance. Seeing on paper how far they have progressed can be very reinforcing.

Sources: Dishman, Sallis, & Orenstein, 1985; Oldridge, 1984; Sallis & Owen, 1999; Serfass & Gerberich, 1984.

than earlier programs (Marcus et al., 2000). Two other strategies appear to increase success. First, interventions that provide contact by telephone to assess progress and provide advice when there are problems are more successful than those that do not (Marcus et al., 2000). Second, an important factor in people's starting and sticking with an exercise routine is their *readiness* to do so, in terms of the stages of change model (see Chapter 6). People who are at the contemplation stage—that is, they're already considering the change—are more likely to start exercising and to exercise vigorously once they do than are people at the precontemplation stage (Armstrong et al., 1992). Interventions that are tailored to the motivational readiness of individuals to exercise are more effective than standard, nontailored programs (Marcus et al., 1998).

SAFETY

Unsafe conditions threaten people's health in virtually all environments, such as in traffic, at home, on the job, and at the beach. These conditions produce huge numbers of illnesses, injuries, and deaths each year. In most cases, these health problems could have been avoided if the victim or other people had used reasonable safety precautions. Sometimes people don't know how to prevent injury—as is often the case for elderly individuals who become injured when they fall—but safety training can reduce these injuries (Tinetti et al., 1994). Let's see what is known about the hazards people face and how to help people live safer lives.

ACCIDENTS

Each year in the United States, over 24 million injuries or poisonings occur that require medical attention (USBC, 2003). Some of these events are serious enough to cause long-term disability or death. More than 100,000 Americans die each year from unintentional injuries in accidents (USBC, 2003). By far the most frequent of these accidental fatalities involve traffic mishaps. More than 5,000 people die in accidents at their jobs each year, and thousands of other workers are seriously injured (NCHS, 2000). The industries with the highest mortality rates include construction and transportation, and the industries with the highest injury rates are transportation, construction, manufacturing, agriculture and

fishing, and mining. Government data reveal that accidental injury is:

- The fifth most frequent cause of death in the American population as a whole.
- The leading cause of death of individuals under age 45.
- Responsible for over 37% of all deaths of children 1 to 14 years of age (USBC, 2003).

Another way to see the relative impact of injury versus disease is to estimate the years of life lost by the victims of these causes of death. Using age 65 as a standard, we would subtract the age of death of each person who dies earlier and then sum the years lost for injuries and disease separately. Calculations like these reveal that the total number of years lost from unintentional and intentional (that is, homicide or suicide) injuries in the United States is about the same as from the total of the three most frequent causes of death in America: heart disease, cancer, and stroke (USDHHS, 1995). Over 60% of all injury deaths are unintentional.

How can accidental injuries be prevented? In discussing this question, we will focus on injuries in traffic mishaps because they account for about half of all accidental deaths and researchers have done many studies on methods to prevent traffic injuries. The death rates for motor vehicle accidents in the United States increase dramatically during adolescence, as depicted in Figure 8–3, and the rate of deaths from traffic mishaps among 15- to 24-year-olds is over twice as high for males as for females (NCHS, 2003). Safe-driving programs have been applied for two groups—teens learning to drive and adults with poor traffic records—to reduce traffic fatalities, but these interventions seem to have little effect on accidents (Robertson, 1986). Two other ways to reduce traffic accidents have been more effective. One approach capitalizes on research findings regarding drivers' perceptual and reaction abilities, with the goal of reducing their errors and enhancing their reaction time. For example, a study found that mounting an extra brake light above the trunk of vehicles reduced rear-end collisions by 50%. Another approach that is quite effective in reducing traffic deaths is not very popular with teenagers; it involves raising the legal driving age (Robertson, 1986).

Injuries and deaths can also be prevented if drivers and passengers will use protective equipment, such as seat belts in cars and helmets when riding motorcycles

Figure 8–3 The relationship between age and motor-vehicle-injury death rates in the United States. (Data from NCHS, 2003, Table 44.) Note, however, that the dramatic increase during adolescence primarily reflects the deaths of individuals who are *occupants* of motor vehicles; much of the upswing in old age reflects deaths of individuals who are *pedestrians* (Cataldo et al., 1986).

or bicycles (Latimer & Lave, 1987; Robertson, 1986; Waller, 1987). After seat belts were installed as standard equipment in cars, few people opted to use them. Safety programs have targeted parents and children. Educational programs for parents, offered through hospitals and pediatricians, have had mixed success (Cataldo et al., 1986; Christophersen, 1984). One successful program provided computer-assisted video instruction on using an infant safety seat to mothers before leaving the hospital after giving birth (Hletko et al., 1987). Observation by a parking lot attendant at the hospital 4 months later when mothers brought their babies for a checkup revealed that many more trained than untrained mothers had their infants correctly restrained. Safety training programs for parents are more successful when there are strong consequences for their behavior—reinforcement for safety action or punishment for inaction (Tremblay & Peterson, 1999).

A program to increase seat belt use was presented to children in preschools, using a theme character called "Bucklebear" (Chang et al., 1985). The children in several other preschools served as a control group who were matched to the experimental subjects for their prior seat belt use. Observations in the preschool parking lots 3 weeks after the program ended found that over 44% of the "Bucklebear" children and only about 22% of the control children were using seat belts. Other programs have addressed the use of bicycle helmets or car safety restraints; some included incentives for the parents, such as discounts to buy helmets (Tremblay & Peterson, 1999). After one of these programs, children in the community increased helmet use markedly and had fewer head injuries over the next several years.

Fewer than 15% of Americans were using seat belts by the early 1980s, despite public health announcements and other programs to promote this behavior (Latimer & Lave, 1987). As a result, many states began to pass laws requiring adults and children to use protective equipment in cars. Seat belt and safety seat use generally increased sharply, and traffic fatalities decreased after these laws went into effect (Latimer & Lave, 1987; Robertson, 1986; Waller, 1987). But the behaviors regressed after a while, and probably less than half of the people were complying with the laws by the time a year had passed. Although such laws are helpful, they may not be sufficient.

ENVIRONMENTAL HAZARDS

A 1987 newspaper poll in New Jersey asked people, "Do you use sunscreen in the summer?" One young man answered, "No. I don't use anything—never have, never will," and a young woman said, "Never, because the sun's not too hot in New Jersey." Another young woman said she uses only the weakest sunscreen because, "I want to have a gorgeous tan." Ever since the French fashion designer Coco Chanel made tanning fashionable, people in many parts of the world have come to believe tans are attractive and healthful. This belief develops by early adolescence (Broadstock, Borland, & Gason, 1992).

Today we know that excessive exposure to the sun's ultraviolet rays makes the skin age and can cause skin cancers, particularly in people who are fair skinned and burn easily (AMA, 2003; Harrison et al., 1994). Keep in mind that sunlamps and sunbeds have the same effect, and the more exposure to them the greater the chance of getting cancer (Westerdahl et al., 1994). Although most cases of skin cancer can be easily treated and cured, others cannot, especially if they are discovered late (ACS, 2004). Dermatologists and other health care practitioners recognize that

Parents can teach their children to use sunscreen, and make it fun!

most people will not stay out of the sun and that many strive for a "healthy" and attractive tan. As a result, these practitioners recommend that most people use sunscreens (SPF of 15 or more) when exposed to the sun for more than, say, an hour or so. But only about a third of American children and adolescents use sunscreen, and over 80% report having had a sunburn in the past year (Geller et al., 2002). Girls use sunscreen more than boys do, but they also use tanning beds more. Because skin appearance is a main motivator for tanning, researchers have tested interventions with appearance information to promote sunscreen use. Information has a greater influence on the likelihood of sunscreen use if it has gain-framed messages ("Using sunscreen increases your chances of maintaining healthy, young–looking skin") than loss-framed messages, which might state that not using sunscreen can cause cancer and prematurely aged skin (Detweiler et al., 1999).

Ultraviolet radiation is only one of many environmental hazards people need to guard against. Many harmful chemicals and gases exist in households,

worksites, and general communities. Some of these hazards and their effects are (AMA, 2003):

- *Lead* poisoning, which can damage children's nervous systems and impair intelligence if they ingest it, such as by mouthing objects painted with lead-based paints, drinking water from a plumbing system with poorly soldered lead joints, or drinking acidic beverages from lead-glazed ceramics.
- *Radon*, a radioactive odorless gas that can cause lung cancer with long-term exposure and enters dwellings from the ground. Ventilating a basement can reduce radon pollution.
- *Asbestos*, a substance that was used in buildings and equipment as a fire retardant. People who have regular contact with it risk developing lung cancer.
- *Radiation* poisoning, which can occur with one very high-level exposure or long-term lower exposure and causes cancer. It can be released into the environment from many sources, such as nuclear power plants, hospitals, and military facilities. A massive radiation release occurred in 1986 at the Soviet nuclear power plant in Chernobyl.

People who work with hazardous materials need to know what the substances are, what dangers they pose, and how to use them safely. Some states in America have enacted "Right to Know" laws that require (1) employers to notify and train employees regarding the safe use of hazardous materials and (2) community agencies to provide information about the exposure of residents to hazardous materials. If people know that a danger exists, they can try to take protective action (for example, by drinking bottled water), become involved in community change, and notify their physician so that appropriate tests can be done (Winett, King, & Altman, 1989).

People are becoming increasingly concerned about the chemicals and gases that pervade our lives. They should be vigilant—but they should also be aware of three things. First, not every chemical or gas is harmful. Second, exposure to toxic or carcinogenic substances poses little risk when the contact is infrequent and the dosage is small (Ames & Gold, 1990; Cohen & Ellwein, 1990). Third, some harmful substances may have benefits that outweigh their dangers. For example, chlorinating water has all but erased many of the waterborne infections that once threatened enormous numbers of lives. But chlorinated water often has very small amounts of the carcinogen *chloroform* in it. Given these circumstances, the benefits of chlorinating appear to outweigh the risks.

SUMMARY

In addition to water, food contains five types of chemical components: carbohydrates, lipids or "fats," proteins, vitamins, and minerals. People can get all the nutrients and fiber they need by eating diets that include grains, fruits, vegetables, milk products, and meats and fish. People's food preferences are determined by biological and psychosocial factors.

Diet is associated with the development of atherosclerosis, hypertension, and cancer. Cholesterol leads to atherosclerosis. Whether plaques form in our blood vessels depends on the presence of two types of cholesterol-carrying proteins: low-density lipoprotein and high-density lipoprotein. Low-density lipoprotein is often called "bad cholesterol" because it is the main culprit in plaque buildup. Genetic factors and the foods people eat determine serum cholesterol levels. Intervention programs can be effective in helping people reduce dietary cholesterol substantially. High blood pressure can result from consuming too much sodium.

Many people are very conscious of and concerned about their weight. Most concerns among Americans are with being too fat rather than too thin, particularly among females. We can determine whether individuals are at a healthy weight by calculating their body mass index (BMI): if their BMI exceeds 25, they are overweight; they are considered obese if their BMI is 30 or more. People become fat because they consume more calories than they burn up through metabolism. Heredity plays a role in weight control, probably by affecting the set-point for body weight. The nature of the set-point mechanism is not clear, but it may involve the hypothalamus and serum insulin levels. Psychosocial factors also affect weight control, especially in the role of emotions in binge eating.

Obesity is associated with the development of many illnesses, such as hypertension, coronary heart disease, and diabetes. These health risks depend on the person's fitness and amount and location of fat tissue. Risks decrease with fitness and increase as the degree of obesity increases and when fat is concentrated in the abdominal region, rather than mostly in the thighs, hips, and buttocks. Prevention of overweight should begin in childhood to avoid fat-cell hyperplasia. Eating low-calorie,

low-fat diets and avoiding carbohydrate foods with high glycemic loads can help people control their weight and protect their health.

Most heavy people try to reduce their weight on their own by going on a diet. Those who are not able to lose weight on their own often seek help, such as through self-help groups and weight-loss programs. Behavioral and cognitive methods are more effective than other approaches. In relatively extreme cases, drastic procedures with medical supervision may be warranted; these procedures include placing the patient on a very-low-calorie diet, using appetite-suppressing drugs, or performing surgery. Although many people who lose weight in cognitive-behavioral programs keep most of that weight off, others do not; relapse can be reduced if the programs make use of frequent followup meetings with weight-control therapists and social influences of other members in a treatment group.

Anorexia nervosa is an eating disorder that results in an unhealthy and extreme loss of weight. Bulimia nervosa is an eating disorder that involves recurrent episodes of binge eating and purging. Both of these disorders occur mainly in adolescence and early adulthood and are much more prevalent in females than in males. Treatment is more difficult and less successful for anorexia than for bulimia.

Three types of exercise are isotonic, isometric, and isokinetic. Aerobic exercise refers to energetic physical activity that involves rhythmical movement of large muscle groups and requires high levels of oxygen over a period of half an hour or so. Engaging regularly in vigorous exercise increases people's life spans and protects them against coronary heart disease, partly because it reduces blood pressure. People who exercise tend to be young and well-educated adults from the upper social classes.

Tens of thousands of Americans die each year in accidents, especially traffic mishaps. Death rates for motor vehicle accidents increase dramatically during adolescence. People also need to guard against many environmental hazards, including excessive exposure to sunlight and harmful chemicals and gases.

KEY TERMS

lipoproteins	overweight	binge eating	isotonic exercise
low-density lipoprotein	obese	glycemic load	isometric exercise
high-density lipoprotein	set-point theory	anorexia nervosa	isokinetic exercise
body mass index	insulin	bulimia nervosa	aerobic exercise

Note: If you read **Module 3** (from Chapter 2) with the current chapter, you should include the key terms for those modules.

9

USING HEALTH SERVICES

Types of Health Services
Specialized Functions of Practitioners
Office-Based and Inpatient Treatment
The American Health Care System
Health Care Systems in Other Countries

Perceiving and Interpreting Symptoms
Perceiving Symptoms
Interpreting and Responding to Symptoms

Using and Misusing Health Services
Who Uses Health Services?
Why People Use, Don't Use, and Delay Using
   Health Services
Using Complementary and Alternative Medicine
Misusing Health Services

The Patient–Practitioner Relationship
Patient Preferences for Participation in Medical
   Care
The Practitioner's Behavior and Style
The Patient's Behavior and Style

Compliance: Adhering to Medical Advice
Extent of the Nonadherence Problem
Why Patients Do and Do Not Adhere to Medical
   Advice

Patient–Practitioner Interactions
Increasing Patient Adherence

Focusing on Prevention

PROLOGUE

Jo's life had just undergone major changes—she had been promoted by her employer, and she had relocated to a new town with her two children. A year ago, she was diagnosed with high blood pressure and began taking a prescribed medication, which she supplements with sassafras and herbal tea that a clerk at a natural food store recommended. Having noticed that her supply of medication would run out in about a month, she decided to find a new physician soon. A coworker suggested she try Dr. Armstrong and, when asked, said that he was not like Jo's last physician, who would sweep into the examining room, hurriedly ask very specific short-answer questions, dominate the conversation, and rush on to the next patient.

The coworker was right: Dr. Armstrong was competent and caring. He started the visit by chatting a little with Jo to learn more about her and to establish a friendly relationship. Then he asked her about her health problem, did some physical tests, and discussed with her a few alternatives for treating her hypertension. She felt comfortable enough with him to tell him about the supplements she was using, and he responded that she could continue taking them if she'd like, but the evidence for their benefit was not yet very solid. He gave her a pamphlet about hypertension and the URL for the American Heart Association Web site so she could get more information if she wanted it. Jo left the office very much relieved and feeling secure in having found a good physician whom she and her children could talk to easily and trust.

With this chapter, our main focus in this book begins to *shift from primary to secondary prevention* efforts. Most health care systems engage chiefly in secondary and tertiary care, providing treatment to stop or reverse a problem or to retard damage it might cause and rehabilitate the person. In this chapter, we will see that the relationship formed between the patient and the health care *practitioner*, or health professional, can influence the actions they take in preventing and managing illness. The importance of this relationship will become clear as we discuss the kinds of health services available and the factors that affect when and how effectively people use these services. As we examine these topics, you'll find answers to questions you may have about people's use of health services. How do people decide they are sick and may need medical attention? How can patients influence their health care? Do people follow medical advice—and if not, why don't they comply?

TYPES OF HEALTH SERVICES

Systems of medical care delivery and management are complex in most societies, particularly in industrialized nations like the United States, where the medical system consists of an enormous variety of health services. To see the complex nature of health care systems, we will consider the specialized functions of health care workers, compare office-based and inpatient treatment, and contrast the American medical system with systems in other countries.

SPECIALIZED FUNCTIONS OF PRACTITIONERS

Medical care systems have staffs of health care workers who differ greatly in their roles and specialties. The American system, for instance, employs millions of professionals, including physicians of many types—general practitioners, pediatricians, cardiologists, neurosurgeons, dermatologists, gynecologists, psychiatrists, and so on—as well as nurses, dentists, optometrists, respiratory therapists, physical therapists, medical social workers, and dietitians, to name only a small number. Each type of practitioner provides a different type of health service, using specialized knowledge and skills.

Because each of these services involves an enormous amount of knowledge and skill that grows and changes very rapidly, individual practitioners cannot perform the services of several specialties simultaneously with a high degree of skill. The advantage in organizing the health care system into specialties is that patients can receive the greatest expertise available for each aspect of the treatment of each health problem. However, this great advantage has drawbacks. For instance, the many professionals who provide care for a particular individual do not always communicate with each other effectively, so that the physician in charge of the treatment may not have a full picture of the person's condition or progress. Also, because many practitioners work with a patient very briefly—performing just a few medical tests, for example—the contact these practitioners have with patients is often impersonal.

OFFICE-BASED AND INPATIENT TREATMENT

When we get sick and seek professional treatment, the first place we usually go is to our family physician at his or her office. This practitioner can treat the illness, refer us to a specialist for treatment, or arrange for hospitalization.

People with serious illnesses who require medical attention either on a continuous basis or with complex equipment or procedures generally receive treatment as inpatients in hospitals and nursing homes. *Hospitals* are the most complex medical facilities in medical care systems, employing highly sophisticated equipment and skilled practitioners from almost all specialty areas (AMA, 2003). As a result, they can provide a wide variety of services, ranging from emergency care to diagnostic testing, to curative treatment, to rehabilitation and social services. Many hospitals also offer health promotion facilities, such as wellness centers and weight-loss programs. Some hospitals have specialized missions, such as in providing care for children or for certain health problems—cancer, eye diseases, or orthopedic problems, for instance.

Nursing homes provide care for individuals who need relatively long-term medical and personal care, particularly if the patients or their families cannot provide this care (AMA, 2003; USBC, 2003). The large majority of patients in nursing homes are handicapped or frail, elderly individuals who often need help in day-to-day activities such as dressing and bathing themselves. The average nursing home in the United States is a moderate-sized facility, with about 100 beds. Nursing homes vary in the degree of skilled nursing and rehabilitative services they are prepared to provide. Although most American nursing homes provide high-quality care, many others do not. Quality ratings can be obtained through Medicare.

People with serious health problems in many nations have been relying less and less on inpatient services in recent years, using *outpatient* or *home health care* instead (AMA, 2003; USBC, 2003). The shift away from inpatient care has occurred because of the fast-rising costs of hospital and nursing home services and because technological advances have made it possible to maintain medical treatment with outpatients. Two examples of technological devices that provide outpatient treatment are *pacemakers*, which are installed in the body to send electrical pulses to regulate heartbeat, and *insulin pumps*, which inject insulin into the body on a specific schedule. Clients who use home care usually begin their treatment on an inpatient basis but are then discharged in the care of a home health care service.

Outpatient care offers some advantages over inpatient care. For one thing, home care is likely to be less expensive. Also, people usually prefer being at home, and can often return to work or school while receiving outpatient treatment. But for some patients—particularly the elderly—home health care can present problems if they lack needed help from family or friends and do not have the means of transportation to make periodic visits to their physicians.

THE AMERICAN HEALTH CARE SYSTEM

When most Americans get sick and need treatment, their health insurance pays for most of the costs. Employers provide insurance for most working people. Many other people are covered under governmental insurance programs: *Medicare* for the elderly and *Medicaid* for low-income people. But 15% of Americans are not insured, and the percent uninsured is much higher for Hispanics and Blacks than Whites (USBC, 2003). These people can't afford to get sick.

Most patients in nursing homes are elderly individuals who need long-term medical and personal care.

Several decades ago, private-practice physicians gave all office-based medical treatment in the United States, and each charged a fee for each service. American health insurance now structures medical care within two broad options: fee-for-service and managed-care programs. People who opt for *fee-for-service* programs can choose their physicians, and the insurance pays most (often 80%) of incurred charges. Practitioners who treat fee-for-service patients generally must accept the amount of payment insurance plans specify. The amount is often lower than the practitioner requests; because Medicaid plans usually pay very low amounts, many members have difficulty finding a practitioner who will provide treatment. *Managed-care* programs place important restrictions on their members' choices and services. Most managed-care and fee-for-service programs charge annual fees paid by members or their employers; fees are lower in managed-care plans. Over 70% of employed Americans opt for managed-care programs. Medicare began offering managed-care programs in the late 1990s (Luft, 1998; CU, 2001). Some managed-care programs provide financial incentives to their physicians for cost-saving behaviors, such as sending only a small number of patients to hospitals, which may foster suboptimal care.

One type of managed-care plan is the *health-maintenance organization* (HMO), in which members are entitled to use the services of any affiliated physician or hospital with little or no additional charges (CU, 2001; Miller & Luft, 1994). Some affiliated physicians practice in HMO clinics, but others have their own offices; others are salaried employees of the HMO, and still others receive payment based on the number of clients they see or the specific procedures they perform. If necessary, the primary care physician can arrange for the patient to be referred to a specialist or admitted to a hospital. The HMO pays for all treatments it arranges or recommends and negotiates with specific hospitals and physicians for discounted fee-for-service rates. Another type of managed-care plan—called the *preferred provider organization* (PPO)—is very similar to some HMOs. Each PPO consists of a network of affiliated physicians and hospitals that have agreed to discount their usual charges; members may go to any affiliated physician or hospital.

Do HMOs, PPOs, and fee-for-service plans provide the same quality of medical care? Arriving at a clear answer to this question presents some important problems. For one thing, plans vary greatly in their policies and structures, which change frequently. Also, the research comparing managed care and private-physician care has used quasi-experimental methods, and most of the HMOs studied have been large, well-established plans rather than newer, developing ones. Findings from research comparing fee-for-service and PPO plans against HMOs indicate that patients in HMOs (CU, 1999b, 2001; Miller & Luft, 1994):

- Have more trouble getting to see a physician when seriously ill.
- Are less likely to be admitted to a hospital, and when admitted, they are likely to leave sooner.
- Use more preventive examinations and procedures.
- Often face major obstacles getting treatment they need (HMOs vary in willingness to approve procedures), but medical care is comparable for most patients otherwise.
- Report being somewhat less satisfied with the care they received but much more satisfied with the costs to them.

But consumer organizations have found substantial variations in the quality of managed-care plans and recommend that people choose plans carefully (CU, 1999b). Although people can seek ratings of managed-care plans and answers to critical questions, such as whether the plan pays for emergency care received in other countries and allows doctors to refer members to specialists freely, there is reason to question the value of the ratings (Schauffler & Mordavsky, 2001).

Americans receive medical care that is among the very finest in the world, but the health care system has important flaws. Its costs are skyrocketing, it is not accessible to the many people who have inadequate or no insurance, and it is so complex and offers so many managed-care options that deciding to use these services can be intimidating to some people. Do other countries have health care systems that have solved these problems?

HEALTH CARE SYSTEMS IN OTHER COUNTRIES

Many countries, such as Canada and most of the European Union, have adopted health care systems that incorporate national health insurance programs for all of their citizens (Erdmann & Wilson, 2001;

Kazarian & Evans, 2001). The health care they provide is excellent and usually less complicated to use than America's. People in poorer countries generally have little or no coverage, and the ability to pay for service or private insurance is increasingly becoming a device to ration medical care, even in richer nations (WHO, 1999c).

How are the health care systems with national health insurance programs structured and financed? Each one is different—for instance, some systems provide insurance through the government, but others require employers to provide it. In some systems most physicians are employed by the government, but in others most doctors are privately employed. Let's look at the Canadian system as an example. It has the following features (CU, 1992):

- The Canadian system provides coverage for everyone in the nation, financed through payroll taxes. Each province pays its citizens' medical bills and determines its own policies, such as what types of care will be covered. In addition to office-based and hospital care, most provinces cover prescription drugs for people over age 65, long-term care, and mental health services. Private insurance is available for services not covered.
- Canadian physicians are typically employed privately and practice in their own offices. Patients may choose any doctor they wish.
- The fees physicians charge are determined by the province in negotiation with the medical association.

Compared with the American health care system, other systems are far less expensive in terms of costs per citizen and the percentage of each country's gross domestic product spent on health care (NCHS, 2000). Because of steadily increasing costs in most nations, efforts are being made around the world to slow these increases (WHO, 1999c). Funding problems in some countries, such as Britain, have sometimes led to long waits for care and the inability to get needed treatment (Lyall, 2000).

In any health care system, a critical step in seeking medical attention is finding a regular physician to contact when we are sick. He or she can either cure our illness or help us find other help within the system. Now, suppose someone who has a regular physician develops some symptoms—say, nausea and a moderately high fever. Will the person go to the doctor? An impor-

tant step in using health services involves deciding when we are sick enough to require medical attention in the first place. This is the topic of the next section.

PERCEIVING AND INTERPRETING SYMPTOMS

If you came down with a case of strep throat as a child, chances are the symptoms you experienced were obvious to you and your parents. You had a very sore throat, fever, and headache, for instance, and your physician prescribed a curative course of action. From experiences of this type, you learned that symptoms accompany illness, certain symptoms reliably signal certain illnesses, some symptoms are more serious than others, and when they go away, you're well again. As an adult, you decide whether to visit your physician on the basis of the symptoms you perceive and what they mean to you.

PERCEIVING SYMPTOMS

Perceiving symptoms of illness is more complicated than it may seem. It is true that we perceive internal states on the basis of physical sensations, and we are more likely to notice strong sensations than weak ones. But we do not assess our internal states very accurately. For example, people's estimates of their own heart rate, breathing function, and degree of nasal congestion correlate poorly with physiological measures of these states (Pennebaker, 1983; Rietveld & Brosschot, 1999). Individuals also have trouble perceiving external symptoms, such as whether a mole-like skin lesion is melanoma (Miles & Meehan, 1995). Partly because of people's low degree of accuracy in assessing signs of illness, the point at which people recognize a symptom can differ from one individual to the next and within the same person from one time to the next. Furthermore, people do not always notice a symptom—even a strong one—when it is there, and sometimes they may perceive a symptom that has no actual physical basis. Let's see what factors affect our perception of symptoms.

Individual Differences

"He's such a big baby; he notices every little ache and pain," you may have heard someone say. Why do some individuals report more symptoms than others do? One reason is that some people simply *have* more symptoms than others, of course. Another possibility is that people could differ in the sensations they experience from the same symptom, such as a specific intensity of a painful stimulus. But studies testing large numbers of normal individuals with stimuli of different temperatures have cast doubt on this possibility. They found that people seem to have a uniform threshold at which heat becomes painful—"almost all persons begin to feel pain when the tissue temperature rises to a level between 44°C and 46°C" (Guyton, 1985, p. 302). But individuals differ in the degree of pain they will tolerate before doing something about it, such as taking medication (Karoly, 1985; Melzack & Wall, 1982).

Some individuals seem to pay more attention to their internal states than others do (Pennebaker, 1983). They show a heightened awareness of or sensitivity to their body sensations. As a result, these people notice changes more quickly than individuals who tend to focus their attention on external happenings. But this does not mean internally focused individuals' perceptions of internal changes are more *accurate*. Indeed, research has found that they are more likely than externally focused people to overestimate their bodily changes, such as in heart rate (Pennebaker, 1983). And among patients who seek medical treatment, those who are internally focused tend to have less severe illness and perceive their recovery as slower than those who pay less attention to their internal states (Miller, Brody, & Summerton, 1987). Many internally focused individuals may pay *too much* attention to their internal states and, in so doing, magnify departures from normal bodily sensations.

Competing Environmental Stimuli

You may have heard anecdotes about athletes who were unaware of a major injury they had suffered during a competition until after the sporting event was over—*then* it hurt! The extent to which people pay attention to internal stimuli at any given time depends partly on the nature or degree of environmental stimuli present at that time.

When the environment contains a great deal of sensory information or is exciting, people become less likely to notice internal sensations. People are far more likely to report sensations or physical symp-toms when the external environment is boring or lacks information than when the environment captures their attention (Pennebaker, 1983). For instance, when watching a movie, they are more likely to notice an itch or a tickle in their throats during boring parts. Also, people who hold boring jobs or live alone tend to report more physical symptoms and use more aspirin and sleeping pills than those who hold interesting jobs or live with other people.

Psychosocial Influences

Because people are not very accurate in assessing their actual internal physical states, their perception of body sensations can be heavily influenced by cognitive, social, and emotional factors (Rietveld & Brosschot, 1999; Suls, Martin, & Leventhal, 1997). One way researchers have demonstrated the role of cognitive factors in symptom perception is in the effects of *placebos*, which are inert substances or sham treatments (Melzack & Wall, 1982; Roberts, 1995). For example, people who receive a placebo "drug" to reduce their pain, not knowing the drug is inert, often report that it relieves their symptoms or sensations.

Expectations can also increase the symptoms people perceive. For instance, patients who are taking an active medication sometimes show a *nocebo* phenomenon: they perceive side effects, such as dizziness or fatigue, that could not be the direct result of the drug (Barsky et al., 2002). In another example, Diane Ruble (1977) gave women a physiological "test" that she falsely described as accurately pinpointing the timing of their next menstruation (which was actually an average of a week away). Using the false test results, she told randomly selected women either that they were within a couple of days of beginning menstruation or that their menstruation was a week or more away. The women then filled out a questionnaire that asked about current premenstrual symptoms. The women who were told they were near menstruation reported more premenstrual symptoms—such as water retention and pain—than the other women. These findings indicate that the symptoms people perceive can result not only from actual physiological changes that occur in their bodies but from their beliefs, too.

The combined roles of cognitive, social, and emotional factors in symptom perception can be seen in two interesting phenomena. The first is called *medical student's disease*. As medical students learn about the symptoms of various diseases, more than two-thirds of them come to believe incorrectly that they have contracted one of these illnesses at one time or another (Mechanic, 1972). The second phenomenon, called *mass psychogenic illness*, involves widespread symptom perception across individuals, even though tests indicate that their symptoms have no medical basis in their bodies or in the environment, such as from toxic substances. An example of mass psychogenic illness began one morning at an electronics plant when a female production worker became faint, and another female worker who came to her aid also fainted (Colligan, 1979). Soon, other workers began reporting dizziness, headache, nausea, and difficulty breathing; 20 workers were taken to the hospital, and the building was evacuated. Two similar episodes occurred days later after the plant reopened. Medical and environmental tests after each episode revealed no abnormalities that could account for the symptoms experienced.

Why do such phenomena occur? Researchers have described several reasons (Colligan et al., 1979; Mechanic, 1972; Suls, Martin, & Leventhal, 1997). The perception of symptoms is heightened if:

- They involve common physical sensations, such as headache or dizziness, that are vague and very subjective in nature.
- Cognitive factors exaggerate these sensations, attaching to them more importance than they warrant.
- Modeling of the symptoms occurs.
- The people are feeling negative emotions, such as high stress. That is, medical student's disease and mass psychogenic illness tend to occur when people have been experiencing high levels of anxiety, heavy workloads, or disturbing interpersonal conflicts.

Gender and Sociocultural Differences

Women in pain research report feeling discomfort at lower stimulus intensities than men and request sooner that a painful stimulus be terminated (Fillingim, 2000). Why? There is evidence for several factors, such as differences in sex hormones and sex-role beliefs.

People of different cultural backgrounds seem to differ in their perceptions of and reactions to illness symptoms—for instance, displaying much more distress and disability to pain in some cultures than in others (Young & Zane, 1995). These differences may result from cultural norms for reinforcing stoical versus distressed and disabled behaviors when in pain. Let's consider three related findings. First, people of Asian cultures report more physical symptoms with psychological bases than people of other cultures (Chun, Enomoto, & Sue, 1996). Second, a study compared disability in individuals with long-term lower back pain conditions in six different countries (Sanders et al., 1992). American pain patients reported the greatest overall impairment, such as of their work and social activities. Italians and New Zealanders reported the second-largest impairments, followed by Japanese, Colombian, and Mexican pain patients. These differences did not result from differences in the severity or duration of the subjects' pain conditions. Third, among heart attack patients in the United States, Black individuals experience symptoms that are less typical than those of Whites and delay getting treatment longer (Lee et al., 1999).

In summary, people's perception of a symptom depends on the strength of the underlying physical sensation, their tendency to pay attention to their internal states, the degree to which external stimuli compete for their attention, and a variety of cognitive, social, and emotional processes. What individuals *do* when they perceive symptoms is the topic of the next section.

INTERPRETING AND RESPONDING TO SYMPTOMS

Psychiatrist George Engel (1980) described the case of a 55-year-old man whom he called Mr. Glover, who suffered his second heart attack 6 months after his first. He was at work, alone at his desk, when he experienced general discomfort, pressure over his chest, and pain down his left arm.

> The similarity of those symptoms to those of his heart attack six months earlier immediately came to mind . . . but he dismissed this in favor of "fatigue," "gas," "muscle strain," and, finally, "emotional tension." But the negation itself, "*not another heart attack,*" leaves no doubt that the idea "heart attack" was very much in his mind despite his apparent denial. Behaviorally, he alternated between sitting quietly to "let it pass," pacing about the office "to work it off," and taking Alka-Seltzer. (p. 539)

When Mr. Glover's boss noticed his strange behavior and sick appearance, she convinced him to let her take him to the hospital.

The role of people's prior experiences in their decision of what the symptoms they feel reflect and whether they warrant attention can be complex. Most often, past experience probably helps people make correct judgments. A study found, for instance, that one of the strongest factors in mothers' correct decisions to seek medical care for their children is prior experience—that is, whether the child or a relative had a similar problem in the past (Turk et al., 1985). But sometimes people's prior experiences and expectations can lead them to incorrect interpretations of their symptoms. Let's consider a few examples. For instance, if Mr. Glover had always led a healthy lifestyle and never been seriously ill, he might have thought, "It's so unlikely that I'm having a heart attack," and not sought treatment. Also, many elderly individuals assume that feeling weak is a symptom of old age rather than a sign of illness (Leventhal & Prohaska, 1986). And people who notice symptoms while under long-term, intense stress may attribute the symptoms to their stress reaction (Cameron, Leventhal, & Leventhal, 1995). Although these interpretations may sometimes be correct, they may also lead people to ignore symptoms that do, in fact, need treatment.

From direct experience and the things we read and hear, we develop ideas and expectations about illnesses—some are correct, some are not—and use this information to construct *cognitive representations* or **commonsense models** of those illnesses (Croyle & Barger, 1993; Lau & Hartman, 1983; Leventhal, Leventhal, & Contrada, 1998). These models can affect our health-related behavior and seem to involve four basic components of how people think about disease:

- *Illness identity*, which consists of the name and symptoms of the disease.

- *Causes and underlying pathology*, which are ideas concerning how one gets the disease ("I got a cold because a girl sneezed her germs in my face.") and what physiological events occur with it.

- *Time line*, which involves prognosis ideas, such as how long the disease takes to appear and lasts. For instance, symptoms of salmonella take many hours to appear after eating tainted food; some people know this, and others think the symptoms occur immediately.

- *Consequence*, which involves ideas about the seriousness, effects, and outcomes of an illness.

People use many types of information in constructing ideas about illnesses; for example, they seem to use illness *prevalence* in judging its seriousness (Jemmott, Croyle, & Ditto, 1988). Rare illnesses are seen as more serious. Commonsense models of illness are important because people with incorrect ideas may fail to adopt preventive behaviors, and if they develop a serious illness, they may not seek treatment, follow medical advice, or adapt well psychologically (Schiaffino, Shawaryn, & Blum, 1998).

Mr. Glover's reaction to the classic heart attack symptoms he was having was probably governed by emotion elicited by the memory of his earlier attack. Although fear can motivate a person toward health behavior, it can also motivate maladaptive avoidance behavior. As we saw in Chapter 6, *conflict theory* proposes that stress can interfere with rational decision making (Janis, 1984; Janis & Mann, 1977). Mr. Glover perceived severe risks in both seeking and not seeking medical care. He tried to deny the meaning of the symptoms, but that didn't seem to work, and the real meaning was still on his mind. As conflict theory predicts in these circumstances, he used a *hypervigilant* coping pattern: he believed he was fast running out of time and began to search frantically for a solution, as when he tried sitting quietly, pacing, and taking Alka-Seltzer.

Mr. Glover finally decided to go to the hospital after his boss persuaded him that his symptoms needed treatment. Before people decide to seek medical attention for their symptoms, they typically get advice from friends, relatives, or coworkers (Croyle & Barger, 1993; Suls, Martin, & Leventhal, 1997). These advisers form a **lay referral system,** an informal network of nonpractitioners who provide their own information and interpretations regarding the person's symptoms (Freidson, 1961). These people may respond to a request for help or just the ill person's appearance and might:

- Help interpret a symptom—such as, "Jim and his sister Lynn both had rashes like that. They were just allergic to a new soap their mother had bought."

- Give advice about seeking medical attention—as in, "MaryLou had a dizzy spell like the one you just had, and it was a mild stroke. You'd better call your doctor."

- Recommend a remedy—such as, "A little chicken soup, some aspirin, and bed rest, and you'll be fine in no time."
- Recommend consulting another lay referral person—as in, "Pat had the same problem. You should give him a call."

Although the lay referral system often provides good advice, laypersons are, of course, far more likely than practitioners to recommend actions that worsen the condition or delay the person's use of appropriate and needed treatment.

USING AND MISUSING HEALTH SERVICES

The pharmacist is often the first health professional that people consult when they have a health problem. A customer might ask, "My hands get these red patches that peel, and hand creams don't do any good. Do you have anything that'll help?" When pharmacists suggest an over-the-counter remedy, they usually recommend that the person see a physician if it doesn't work.

Most prospective patients try hard to avoid contacting their physicians. Despite these avoidance efforts, Americans consult their doctors' offices either

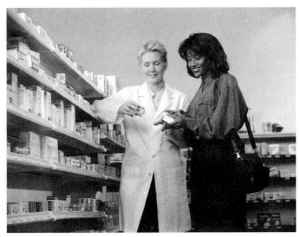

People with health problems often consult pharmacists for over-the-counter remedies before seeing their physician.

in person or by telephone 1½ billion times a year—about six contacts per person—for medical advice or treatment (NCHS, 2000). What are the most frequent *acute* and *chronic* conditions discussed in these contacts? The acute conditions are flu, common cold, fractures or dislocations, sprains or strains, wounds, and ear infections; the chronic conditions are hypertension, orthopedic problems, arthritis, diabetes, asthma, and heart disease. Of course, these illnesses are not evenly distributed over the population—and as you might expect, some segments of the population who become ill are more likely to use health services than others are.

WHO USES HEALTH SERVICES?

People with health risks, such as obesity and high stress, use health care substantially more than others do (Tucker & Clegg, 2002). Demographic and sociocultural factors are also related to health services use in the United States and probably most industrialized countries.

Age and Gender

One factor in using health services is *age*. In general, young children and the elderly have contact with physicians more often each year than adolescents and young adults do (NCHS, 2000). Young children visit physicians for general checkups and vaccinations, and they develop a variety of infectious childhood diseases. Physician contacts are less frequent from late childhood through early adulthood, but increase in the middle-age and elderly years as the incidence of chronic diseases rises.

Figure 9–1 depicts how physician contacts vary with age and with another important factor, the patient's *gender*. Women have a higher rate of physician contacts than men (NCHS, 2000). This gender difference begins to appear during adolescence. Although much of women's higher rates of physician contacts in early adulthood results from the medical care they require in pregnancy, the difference remains even when physician visits for pregnancy and childbirth are not counted (Reddy, Fleming, & Adesso, 1992; Verbrugge, 1985). The reasons for gender differences in using medical care are unclear, but there are several possible explanations. One obvious explanation is that women may simply develop more illnesses that require medical attention: they show

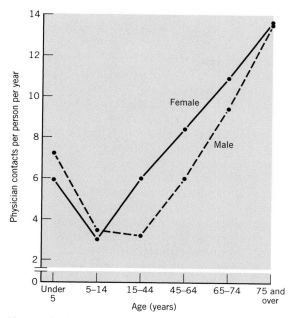

Figure 9–1 Average number of physician contacts (in person and by telephone) per person per year as a function of age and gender. (Data from NCHS, 2000, Table 75.)

higher rates of medical drug use and illness from acute conditions, such as respiratory infections, and from nonfatal chronic diseases, such as arthritis and migraine headache. Another reason is that men are more hesitant to admit having symptoms and to seek medical care for the symptoms they experience. In a study that asked men and women about recent experiences of various symptoms, women reported more of almost all symptoms, including ones that had no medical confirmation (Kroenke & Spitzer, 1998). Gender differences in reporting and, perhaps, perceiving symptoms probably reflects sex-role stereotypes; that is, American society encourages men more than women to ignore pain and to be tough and independent.

Sociocultural Factors in Using Health Services

The United States Department of Health and Human Services conducts periodic large-scale surveys to determine usage rates of health services by different segments of the American population. The results of

recent surveys lead to two important conclusions about sociocultural differences in usage (NCHS, 2000). First, the percentage of people who seek medical care at a physician's office or by telephone increases with family income. Second, African Americans and other individuals with low family incomes are far more likely than Whites and others with higher incomes to use outpatient clinics and hospital emergency rooms for medical care. This is probably because disadvantaged people are less likely to have regular physicians (Flack et al., 1995). Although there is clearly a gap between social classes in utilization of health services in America, it has narrowed since the mid-1960s, when the government introduced Medicare and Medicaid insurance programs for the elderly and poor, respectively. These programs account for much of the 25% increase in physician visits that occurred between 1968 and 1972 (USDHHS, 1985).

Despite the help these programs provide, the costs American patients must bear for medical treatment can still be substantial because public and private insurance programs generally do not cover all the expenses. Some kinds of treatment are excluded, and patients typically must pay part of the costs for those treatments that are covered. These circumstances are especially difficult for the poor because they tend to become sick more often and require longer hospital stays (NCHS, 2003). Worldwide, a lack of knowledge about prevention and poor access to health counseling and preventive services contributes to the high illness rates of low-income people (WHO, 1999).

Although medical insurance can help many low-income people get the treatment they need, there are reasons besides the expense of medical care for the gap between social classes and cultural groups in using health services (Flack et al., 1995; Penn et al., 1995; Rundall & Wheeler, 1979; Young & Zane, 1995). For one thing, individuals from the lower classes tend to perceive themselves as being less susceptible to illness than those from the higher classes do. As a result, low-income people are less likely to seek out preventive care. Second, people with low incomes and from minority groups are less likely to have regular sources of health care than others are. Often this situation develops because low-income regions are less able to attract physicians to provide health services there. In addition, people in the lower classes and from minority groups may feel less welcomed by and trustful of the health care system than other individuals. Third, in many countries language can be a barrier to health care for immigrants if they do not speak the dominant language and no translators are available. These and many other factors tend to reduce the likelihood that low-income individuals will use health services for preventive care and when they are ill. Public health informational programs need to combat cultural barriers that impede the use of health care and prevention services.

The title of this section is Who Uses Health Services? To answer this question, we can construct two portraits—one of the users and one of the nonusers of these services. The users of health services tend to be young children, women, and elderly individuals from the higher social classes. The nonusers are likely to be members of the lower classes and minority groups, particularly males in adolescence and early adulthood. But almost all people use health services at some time, and many upper-class individuals fail to get medical treatment when they should. Thus, although these portraits give us an image of *who* uses health services, they do not provide a good explanation of *why*.

WHY PEOPLE USE, DON'T USE, AND DELAY USING HEALTH SERVICES

Health psychologists and others who study health care have discovered many factors that influence whether and when individuals are likely to seek medical care. Some of these factors involve people's ideas and beliefs about treating illness.

Ideas, Beliefs, and Using Health Services

An ailing man who was considering whether or not to seek treatment thought, "Remember how the medicine Buddy's doctor gave him made him sicker? I don't trust doctors." Patients sometimes develop health problems as a *result* of medical treatment, and these problems are called **iatrogenic conditions.** The condition can result either from a practitioner's error or as a normal side effect or risk of the treatment, as may occur when people undergo surgery or begin to take a new medication. In Buddy's case, the medication he received caused an allergic reaction. Tens of thousands of people are killed each year in the United States alone as a result of medical errors in the hospital and adverse effects of drugs, either from prescription or filling errors

(Gerlin, 1999; Phillips & Bredder, 2002). Positive and negative stories we hear about the treatment patients received may influence our decisions to use medical services.

Not trusting practitioners can stop people from seeking the care they need. We will consider two issues of trust. First, individuals may avoid getting care because they worry about the confidentiality of information they disclose to or is found by their practitioners. For instance, a study found that most American adolescents have health concerns they want to keep private from their parents, and one-fourth said they would forgo treatment if their parents could find out about it (Cheng, 1993). Many gay men and women avoid medical care because of concerns about confidentiality or physician reaction to their sexual orientation (Mann, 1996). Second, minority group members have heard stories, some of which are true, of discriminatory practices and atrocities carried out by medical personnel against them (Landrine & Klonoff, 2001). One true story is that physicians in the United States falsely told Black men with syphilis that they were being treated and that the disease was "bad blood." This was done so that a research project, called the Tuskegee Syphilis Study, could chart the effects of untreated syphilis, which include blindness, brain damage, and death.

The Health Belief Model and Seeking Medical Care

In Chapter 6, we examined the role of health beliefs in taking preventive action, and we saw that the *health belief model* provides a useful framework for explaining why people do and do not practice healthful behaviors. How does the health belief model apply to people's seeking medical care when they notice symptoms?

According to the health belief model (refer back to Figure 6–2), symptoms initiate a decision-making process about seeking medical care. Part of this process involves assessing the *perceived threat* suggested by the symptoms (Becker & Rosenstock, 1984; Rosenstock & Kirscht, 1979). How much threat individuals perceive depends mainly on three factors. One factor is *cues to action*, which can include the symptoms themselves, advice sick people receive in lay referral, and information from the mass media, such as descriptions of cancer symptoms. Two other factors, *perceived susceptibility* and *perceived seriousness*, modify the concern the cues arouse: the threat individuals feel intensifies with increases in the perceived susceptibility to the particular illness and the perceived seriousness of the physical and social consequences of contracting the disease.

The health belief model also proposes that people assess whether the *perceived benefits* of getting treatment outweigh the *perceived barriers* to doing so. People who believe treatment can cure the symptoms or arrest the progression of the illness are more likely to seek medical care than those who believe otherwise. In assessing the barriers to medical care, people consider whether the treatment will have unpleasant side effects and will be costly, painful, and difficult to obtain. The assessed sum of benefits and barriers combines with the perceived threat to determine the likelihood of seeking care. People who feel threatened by their symptoms and believe the benefits of receiving treatment outweigh the barriers are likely to visit a practitioner. But individuals who do not feel threatened or assess that the barriers are too strong are likely to decide to delay treatment or avoid it altogether.

The results of research suggest that the factors described by the health belief model do influence people's decisions of whether and how soon to use health services (Becker & Rosenstock, 1984; Rosenstock & Kirscht, 1979). For example, among people who know about and have cancer symptoms, those who believe cancer cannot be treated effectively or cured tend to delay seeking medical care much longer than individuals who believe treatment can be successful (Antonovsky & Hartman, 1974). However, some studies have found only a weak relationship between factors in the health belief model and people's likelihood of using health services, which suggests that other variables are also important in decisions to seek treatment (Harris & Guten, 1979; Langlie, 1977).

Social and Emotional Factors and Seeking Medical Care

Earlier, we considered the case of Mr. Glover, who delayed medical treatment for clear symptoms of a heart attack, and we saw that social and emotional factors can play important roles in people's decisions about seeking treatment for their symptoms.

Strong emotional reactions to symptoms sometimes impede people's use of health services. Individuals may perceive a disease, such as cancer, to be so serious that they avoid medical attention for their symptoms because of the extreme anxiety and fear their perceptions generate. As a result, the threat these individuals perceive does not increase their likelihood of using health services but instead may decrease it: many people claim they would be reluctant to seek medical care for cancer symptoms because of their fear of pain from the disease or its treatment (Levin, Cleeland, & Dar, 1985). Expectations of pain play a role in people's fear of dental care, too—about 5% of Americans are so fearful that they avoid all kinds of dental treatment (Gatchel, 1980). People may also avoid medical care if they fear embarrassment, such as when adults have problems of bladder control.

Social factors influence people's tendencies to seek medical care for their symptoms. For example, many men believe getting medical care is a sign of weakness, violating their social role of being strong. But social factors can also encourage people to seek care, such as through the process of lay referral, which can serve as "social trigger" to seek treatment (Zola, 1973). One example is called *sanctioning*, in which someone asks or insists that an ill person have his or her symptoms treated. For instance, a man who had been having problems with his vision for a while finally went to a doctor after his wife prodded him to do so. Sometimes overt prodding isn't even necessary—sick individuals who simply believe significant others want them to seek treatment are more likely to do so than those who believe others think they should wait (Timko, 1987).

Stages in Delaying Medical Care

When symptoms of a potentially serious illness develop, seeking treatment promptly is imperative. **Treatment delay** refers to the time that elapses between when a person first notices a symptom and when he or she enters medical care. In medical emergencies, such as severe injury or a heart attack, people often seek help in a matter of minutes or hours, as Mr. Glover did. What determines how long people wait?

On the basis of interviews with patients at a clinic, researchers discovered that treatment delay occurs as a sequence of three stages (Safer et al., 1979). As the diagram in Figure 9–2 illustrates, the three stages are:

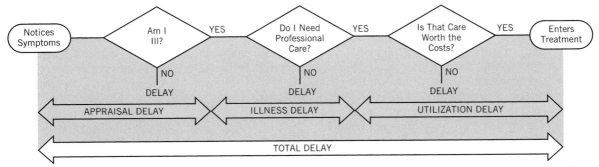

Figure 9–2   Treatment delay is conceptualized as having three stages: appraisal delay, illness delay, and utilization delay. (From Safer et al., 1979, Figure 1.)

1. *Appraisal delay*—the time a person takes to interpret a symptom as an indication of illness.

2. *Illness delay*—the time taken between recognizing one is ill and deciding to seek medical attention.

3. *Utilization delay*—the time after deciding to seek medical care until actually going in to use that health service.

The people's reasons for delaying treatment revealed that different factors were important in different stages of delay. During *appraisal delay*, the sensory experience of a symptom had the greatest impact on delay—for instance, patients recognized a symptom as an indication of illness more quickly if they experienced severe pain or bleeding than if they did not.

In the *illness delay* stage, thoughts about the symptom had the greatest impact. Thus, individuals decided to seek medical attention more quickly if the symptom was new rather than very familiar and if they didn't think much about the symptom and its implications. During *utilization delay*, perceptions of benefits and barriers were important—delay was shortest for those people who were less concerned about the cost of treatment, had severe pain, and felt that their symptoms could be cured. In addition, the researchers found that having a major nonillness problem or life event, such as a marriage or divorce, was an important factor that increased the *total* treatment delay.

Some people delay getting care for a long time, sometimes weeks or months, because they are not experiencing pain. This factor is potentially very important because pain is *not* a major symptom of many very serious diseases, such as hypertension. Pain is also not one of the main warning signs of cancer. Most people who notice a warning sign of cancer wait at least a month before visiting a physician, and between 35 and 50% delay for more than 3 months (Antonovsky & Hartman, 1974). A heart attack usually involves pain and requires treatment quickly: drugs can prevent myocardial damage if administered within, say, an hour or so after the attack begins. Do heart attack victims seek treatment quickly? Of heart attack victims, more than a third delay the decision for more than 3 hours, and those who seek treatment early are more likely to be men than women and have relatively high levels of problem-focused coping (Martin et al., 2004; O'Carroll et al., 2001; Walsh et al., 2004). People need to know what the symptoms of serious diseases are and realize that some illnesses do not have the signs

"You called me just in time. Another day or two, and you would have been up and around."

© 1991; Reprinted courtesy of Bunny Hoest and *Parade* Magazine.

people often rely on in deciding whether to seek medical care.

USING COMPLEMENTARY AND ALTERNATIVE MEDICINE

When Elena feels a cold coming on, she takes echinacea, an herb that is extracted from a plant. Many people in various parts of the world, including industrialized nations, try to prevent or treat illnesses with practices or products, such as massage or herbal methods, not currently considered part of conventional medicine. As a group, these methods are called **complementary and alternative medicine** (CAM); a method is *complementary* if used along with conventional treatments, and *alternative* if used in place of them. Although CAM methods are quite diverse, they can be classified into five types (NCCAM, 2004):

- *Manipulative and body-based methods* maneuver or move parts of the body, as occurs in chiropractic and massage procedures.

- *Biologically based methods* apply materials found in nature, such as herbal products and dietary supplements.

- *Mind–body interventions* use techniques for enhancing the mind's ability to manage body function and symptoms, as in progressive muscle relaxation and meditation.

- *Energy therapies* employ hypothesized or known physical energy fields, such as "biofields" believed to exist and surround the body and electric or magnetic fields.

- *Alternative medical systems*, such as traditional Chinese medicine and homeopathy, are complex theoretical approaches for treating illness that differ from and often preceded the development of the system of medicine practiced by professionals with MD degrees. These alternative systems often use one or more of the preceding four methods.

Although these methods are viewed as unconventional by medical societies in developed nations, they are often widely used, traditional treatments in other countries, such as China, Puerto Rico, and Haiti (Belluck, 1996; Bezkor & Lee, 1999). Some CAM procedures require the services of a practitioner, and others do not. Patients often fail to tell their physicians that they use CAM treatments.

Who uses CAM? Probably most people around the world who use them learned to do so through their religious or cultural backgrounds. Individuals in the United States who use CAM tend to be well educated, have beliefs and values that are consistent with the method's rationale, and have troublesome symptoms, such as pain or stress, that have not improved with standard medical care (Astin, 1998; CU, 2000; NCCAM, 2004). Over one-third of American adults use CAM, and the most frequently used methods are mind–body and biologically based methods interventions. A large-scale survey of thousands of North Americans regarding illness treatments in the prior 2 years found that most were satisfied with the medical care they received and, if they had tried CAM methods, had gotten better results from medical treatment for almost all illnesses (CU, 2000). Most CAM methods were not very successful, having helped the people "feel much better" in only 10 to 30% of cases, depending on the illness and method used. (Although there was no control group, a placebo would probably have gotten similar ratings.) Two alternative treatments, chiropractic and deep-tissue massage, were particularly successful for back pain.

A main feature of CAM methods is that they have little or no scientific evidence of their safety and effectiveness for treating specific disorders. Once sufficient evidence is found, they are adopted into conventional health care, as has occurred for the dietary supplements glucosamine sulfate to prevent and treat arthritis and folic acid to prevent birth defects (AMA, 2003; NCCAM, 2004). Some CAM treatments have been tested in careful experiments. At various points in this book, you will find evidence for the utility of relaxation techniques, deep-tissue massage, and biofeedback in treating pain and other chronic conditions, such as asthma and diabetes. Although spinal manipulation appears useful for treating back pain, it is not effective with tension headache (Bove & Nilsson, 1998). Many dietary supplements and herbal remedies are not very effective and some have serious side effects (CU, 1999a; CU, 2004), but a few have good evidence of success, such as in treating irritable bowel syndrome (Bensoussan et al, 1998). Some CAM methods have value, but others clearly do not. People who want to use a CAM

HIGHLIGHT

Fighting for Your Life

Not all victims of serious diseases who are getting medical care receive the most effective treatments available (Kolata, 1992). Although this situation sometimes occurs because a doctor is overworked or not competent, it's more likely to result from physicians' difficulty in keeping up with rapid advances in medical knowledge and from their reluctance to switch from a procedure that works reasonably well to one that may work better. What can people do to get the best possible treatment?

Patients and people close to them can join the fight for their lives by taking an active interest in their illnesses and health care (CU, 1995; Gipson, Liskevych, & Swillinger, 1996). Let's consider a hypothetical case of a man named Morry who has a serious illness, such as heart disease or cancer. Once he receives the diagnosis, he and his family can swing into action. They can:

- Get information about the disease and the usual courses of treatment. Information is readily available on the Internet and in books they can purchase in bookstores or use through public, college, and medical school libraries.

- Make a list of questions to ask for each meeting with physicians working on his case. If possible, Morry should have a relative or friend accompany him and take notes in physician visits. They should ask to know all possible treatment options, what each involves, what the risks are, and the likelihood of success. Be sure all uncertainties are cleared up before leaving each meeting.

- Broaden the sources of information. All major organizations—such as the American Heart Association and the American Cancer Society—have Internet sites with information about support groups, treatment methods, and physicians who specialize in treating the illness (most of these Websites are included in the reference list for this book). At least one of the physicians Morry consults for treatment options should be certified in the specialty and, preferably, on staff at a major university or teaching hospital. Many people consult only the original physician on their case, and this is a mistake.

- Use reputable information sources to find out about very new medical procedures (and even some risky experimental ones). Even though many newer approaches may provide the most effective treatment, not all physicians know about them or feel comfortable about recommending them.

Individuals with any serious illness can join the fight for their lives in these ways. When patients and people close to them take an active interest in their health care, they can play an informed role in discussions and negotiations with their physicians toward making decisions. Patients who do this can be satisfied that they are getting the best treatment available and feel a sense of efficacy in themselves and in their physicians.

each client, practitioners clearly need to assess and consider how much the person wants. (Go to 💡.)

THE PRACTITIONER'S BEHAVIOR AND STYLE

Imagine this test: you recently completed medical training and have just started a position in a clinic as a general practitioner. Your next patient this morning is waiting in an examination room, which you are preparing to enter. Your task will be to decide which one of the more than 1,300 disease entities known to medicine this person has (Mentzer & Snyder, 1982). Or maybe the person has no physical problem at all. You have 20 minutes.

Diagnosing and treating health problems are difficult tasks, which different physicians undertake with their own behaviors and styles of interacting with patients. Patrick Byrne and Barrie Long (1976) identified different styles of interacting by analyzing about 2,500 tape-recorded medical consultations with physicians in several countries, including England, Ireland, Australia, and Holland. Each physician tended to use a consistent style for all clients treated.

Most of the styles were classified as **doctor-centered,** in which the physician asked questions that required only brief answers—generally "yes" or "no"—and focused mainly on the first problem the person mentioned. These physicians tended to ignore attempts by patients to discuss other problems. Doctor-centered physicians seemed to be intent on establishing a link between the initial problem and some organic disorder, without being sidetracked. In contrast, physicians who used a **patient-centered** style took less controlling roles. They tended to ask open-ended questions, such as, "Can you describe the situations when the pain occurs?" that allow a patient to relate more information and introduce new facts that may be pertinent. They also tended to avoid using medical jargon and to allow clients to participate in some of the decision making.

The patient–practitioner relationship depends on the ability of the two participants to communicate with each other. But physicians sometimes impede communication by using *medical jargon* or technical terms. For example, telling hypertensive patients to "reduce sodium intake" is an accurate recommendation, but will they know what it means? Some people will know exactly what sodium is, others won't have any idea, and still others will think it only means table salt, not realizing that there are other sources of dietary sodium. Studies have found that most patients, particularly those from lower-class backgrounds, fail to understand many of the terms their physicians use—such terms as "mucus," "sutures," and "glucose," for instance (DiMatteo & DiNicola, 1982; IOM, 2004; McKinlay, 1975). Although jargon is useful for accuracy and for communicating among medical professionals, practitioners who use medical and technical terms in talking with clients without explaining the terms or checking comprehension can create confusion, incorrect ideas, and dissatisfaction in them.

John McKinlay (1975) assessed lower-class women's understanding of 13 terms their physicians used with them in a maternity ward. Although over two-thirds of the women understood the terms "breech" and "navel," almost none understood "protein" and "umbilicus"—and on the average, each of the 13 words was understood by only about 39% of the patients. McKinlay also had the physicians indicate for each word whether they thought "average lower-working-class women" would understand the term. The physicians expected even *less* comprehension than the clients showed, yet they used these terms often with these women.

Why would physicians use technical terms with a patient when they do not expect the person to understand? Sometimes they may do this "out of habit;" that is, the terms are so familiar to them that they forget the client is less medically sophisticated. Or they may feel—perhaps in a patronizing way—that the person "doesn't need to know." Other reasons for

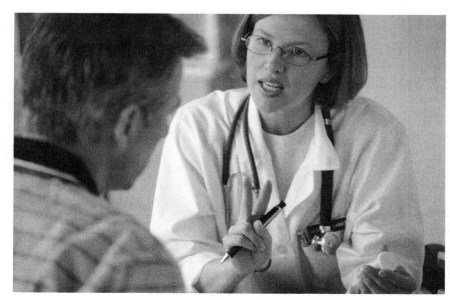

Patients tend to prefer a physician who gives clear explanations about illnesses and treatments, encourages them to ask questions, and conveys a feeling of concern for them.

using jargon may involve their perceptions of what would benefit the patient or the medical staff (DiMatteo & DiNicola, 1982; McKinlay, 1975). How might using jargon benefit the client? Sometimes physicians may feel that the person is better off not knowing exactly what the disease or its treatment may entail; knowing may produce too much stress or interfere with treatment, they may think. And how may using jargon with a patient benefit the medical staff? For one thing, using medical terms without explanations keeps interactions between the client and practitioners short. It may also reduce the chances that the client will react emotionally to the information, or ask questions about the treatment, or discover if errors have been made. Finally, using "big words" the client does not understand elevates the status of practitioners.

First and foremost, people prefer to have a practitioner whom they think is competent. But there are other factors that are important in the patient–practitioner relationship, too—especially the *sensitivity*, *warmth*, and *concern* the person perceives in the practitioner's behavior. People prefer and evaluate highly dentists and physicians who seem friendly and interested in them as persons, show empathy for their feelings, project a feeling of reassurance, and present a calm and competent image (DiMatteo et al., 1985; Hall et al., 1998; van Dulmen & Bensing, 2002). In contrast, practitioners who seem emotionally neutral are often evaluated less positively, perhaps because they appear detached and unconcerned. People assess these characteristics not just by the words the practitioner says, but by his or her body language—facial expressions, eye contact, and body positions (DiMatteo, 1985; Thompson, 1984).

The behavior and style of practitioners can have important implications for them and their patients. People tend to express greater satisfaction for physicians who give them a chance to talk, take the time to listen, give clear explanations about illnesses and treatments, and project a feeling of concern and reassurance than for doctors who do not (Feletti, Firman, & Sanson-Fisher, 1986; van Dulmen & Bensing, 2002). The greater satisfaction these patients feel appears to translate into a higher likelihood that they will keep appointments with their doctors (DiMatteo, Hays, & Prince, 1986).

Perhaps the most important implication of physicians' styles relates to the diagnostic information they receive from their patients. Physicians vary

greatly in their ability to elicit significant diagnostic information from their clients (Marvel et al., 1999; Roter & Hall, 1987). Physicians who ask more open-ended questions, allow clients to give a full answer, give more information about the cause and prognosis of the illness, and discuss more details about prevention and treatment receive more diagnostic facts from their clients than doctors who do less of these things. The additional facts doctors receive are not trivial ones, but ones other physicians judge to be important in diagnosing the person's illness. The first complaint or detail the client gives is often not the most significant one, and getting a full statement of the client's concerns takes only several additional seconds. Findings like these have led medical schools to introduce programs to educate future physicians regarding interviewing skills and psychosocial factors in treating patients (Carpenter, 2001; CU, 1995). (Go to 🍎.)

THE PATIENT'S BEHAVIOR AND STYLE

It takes two to tango, as the saying goes. Although the practitioner's behavior plays an important role in the relationship he or she forms with a patient, the client's behavior and style are important, too. Physicians reported in a survey, for instance, that patients sometimes do things that can be very troubling or unsettling for a doctor (Smith & Zimny, 1988). Some of these behaviors include:

- Expressing criticism or anger toward the physician.
- Ignoring or not listening to what the doctor is trying to say.
- Insisting on laboratory tests, medications, or procedures the physician thinks are unnecessary.
- Requesting that the doctor certify something, such as a disability, the physician thinks is untrue.
- Making sexually suggestive remarks or behaviors toward the physician.

If behaviors such as these lead to a breakdown in the relationship between the patient and practitioner, the quality of the medical care may suffer. Also, the potential for people to bring malpractice suits claiming incompetence or negligence in the physician's treatment can also affect the relationship, making physicians wary of patients and less satisfied with their careers (Kolata, 1990).

ASSESS YOURSELF

Do You Know Medical Terms' Meanings?

The following 10 medical terms were used in McKinlay's (1975) study of patients' understanding of medical jargon, which is described in the text. Match the terms with the definitions given below: in the space preceding each term, place the number for the corresponding definition.

———— antibiotic   ———— mucus

———— breech   ———— protein

———— enamel   ———— purgative

———— glucose   ———— suture

———— membrane   ———— umbilicus

1. The rump or back part.

2. A small scar on the abdomen; the navel.

3. A substance that makes up plant and animal tissue.

4. A simple sugar that the body manufactures from ingested food.

5. A joining together of separated tissue or bone, or a device to achieve this joining.

6. A sheet of tissue that covers or lines a body organ.

7. An agent that works against bacterial infections.

8. A hard, glossy coating or surface.

9. A substance or procedure that causes a cleansing of a body organ, as occurs in a bowel movement.

10. A secretion of body tissues.

Check your answers against the key below. Did you get them all correct? Would you have known as many of the definitions if they weren't given? Would your friends—especially ones who have not gone to college—know the terms?

Answers:

7, 1, 8, 4, 6, 10, 3, 9, 5, 2

Do patients do things that impair patient–practitioner communication? Yes. For one thing, people who are high in neuroticism may convey too much concern about their conditions and seem less credible and less in need of medical care (Ellington & Wiebe, 1999). But others may give no signs of concern when they are feeling a great deal of distress (Roter & Ewart, 1992). Also, sometimes clients describe their symptoms in unclear or misleading ways. As an example, two women who had developed the same condition, *hyperopia* (farsightedness), went to their physicians for medical care (Zola, 1973). In response to the practitioner's question, "What seems to be the trouble?" one client simply said, "I can't see to thread a needle or read the paper." The other patient answered, "I have a constant headache and my eyes seem to get all red and burny." Each patient's manner or focus in describing her problem was different, and neither expanded the description with significant facts when asked if she had anything to add.

Why do patients give unclear descriptions of their symptoms? Let's look at a few reasons. One reason

may lie in the way they perceive or interpret different symptoms. As we saw earlier, people differ in the attention they pay to internal states and the degree to which they associate different sensations with health problems. Second, individuals form different commonsense models of illness. When reporting symptoms to a doctor, people may describe only or mainly those problems they think are important, based on their own notions (Bishop & Converse, 1986). Third, clients may try either to emphasize or to downplay a symptom they believe may reflect a serious illness. For example, people high in hypochondriasis may try to maximize the physician's attention to a sensation they are worried about, whereas other patients may describe a worrisome symptom very casually or offhandedly in the hope that the doctor will agree that "it's nothing." Last, the person may be very young or lack a good command of the practitioner's primary language. The United States, for example, has always had large numbers of immigrants from many parts of the world who do not speak English well. Their English descriptions of their problems are likely to be inaccurate and incomplete (Giachello & Arrom, 1997). They are also unlikely to understand fully what their illnesses are or what they need to do to treat them.

What can be done to improve communication between patients and practitioners? Physicians' interviewing skills can be enhanced with training programs that teach how and when to summarize information, ask questions, and check for comprehension (Roter & Hall, 1989). Researchers have also found that a simple approach can improve clients' communication: while patients wait for their visits, they can fill out a form that has them list any symptoms and questions they have and encourages them to ask questions when they see the doctor (Thompson, Nanni, & Schwankovsky, 1990).

One thing to keep in mind about patient–practitioner communication is that often practitioners lack feedback for their work. For example, although a patient may visit the doctor again if symptoms persist or if the illness is serious or long term, physicians cannot be certain that *not* hearing from a person means a diagnosis was correct or the treatment was effective. And as we are about to see, practitioners usually cannot be sure to what extent a client is following the medical *regimen*—the treatment program or lifestyle change—they recommended.

COMPLIANCE: ADHERING TO MEDICAL ADVICE

"Now don't tell the doctor, but I don't always take my medicine when I'm supposed to," Amy whispered to a friend in her physician's waiting room. People don't always *adhere to*, or *comply with*, their practitioner's advice. **Adherence** and **compliance** are terms that refer to the degree to which patients carry out the behaviors and treatments their practitioners recommend. Most researchers have used these terms interchangeably, and we will, too. But *adherence* is a better term because the dictionary definition of the word *compliance*—"giving in to a request or demand" or "acquiescence"—suggests that the practitioner uses an authoritarian style and the person obeys reluctantly (DiMatteo & DiNicola, 1982; Shearer & Evans, 2001). The remainder of this chapter examines the extent to which clients fail to follow medical advice, why they do and do not comply, and what can be done to increase their adherence.

EXTENT OF THE NONADHERENCE PROBLEM

How widespread is the problem of noncompliance? Answering this question is actually more difficult than it may seem (Dunbar-Jacob & Schlenk, 2001; Shearer & Evans, 2001). First of all, failures to adhere may occur for many different types of medical advice. For instance, patients may fail to take medication as directed, not show up for appointments, skip or stop doing rehabilitation exercises, or "cheat a little" in following specific diet or other lifestyle changes advised by practitioners. Second, people can violate each of these types of advice in many different ways. In failing to take their medication as directed, for example, they might omit some doses, use a drug for the wrong reasons, take medication in the wrong amount or at the wrong time, or discontinue the drug before the prescribed course of therapy ends. Finally, there is the problem of determining whether a person has or has not complied. What is the most accurate and practical way to assess compliance?

Researchers assess patient adherence to medical recommendations in several ways, and each has advantages and disadvantages (Dunbar-Jacob & Schlenk, 2001; Rand & Weeks, 1998; Shearer & Evans, 2001). One of the easiest approaches for measuring compliance is to *ask a practitioner* who works with the client to estimate it. As it turns out, however, practitioners do not really know; they generally overestimate their patients' compliance and are poor at estimating which clients adhere better than others. Another simple approach is to *ask the patient*. But people tend to overreport their adherence, perhaps because they know they should "follow the doctor's orders." These two methods are very subjective and open to various forms of bias, including lying and wishful thinking. As a result, researchers who use these approaches today usually supplement them with reports of family members or medical personnel and with other methods that are more objective. Table 9.1 describes three relatively objective approaches for assessing adherence to using medication.

Despite the complexities in assessing adherence, we can provide some general answers to the question we started with: How widespread is noncompliance? Speaking in very broad terms, the average rate of nonadherence to medical advice is about 40%—that is, *two of every five patients fail to adhere* fairly closely to their

Table 9.1   *Objective Methods for Assessing Adherence to Using Medication*

- *Pill or quantity accounting,* in which the remaining medication is measured, such as by counting the number of pills left. This is compared against the quantity that should be left at that point in treatment if the patient has been following the directions correctly. Of course, this method does not reveal whether the person used the medication at the right times, and patients who expect an accounting and want to conceal their noncompliance can discard some of the contents.
- *Medication-recording dispensers* contain mechanical or electromechanical recording devices that can count and record the time when the dispenser is used. Although this approach is expensive to implement, it assesses compliance accurately as long as the patient does not deliberately create a ruse. If patients know about the device and want to avoid taking the medicine, they can operate the dispenser at the right time and discard the drug.
- *Biochemical tests,* such as of the patient's blood or urine. This approach can assess whether medication was used recently, but usually it cannot determine how much or when, and it can be very time-consuming and expensive to implement.

regimens (DiMatteo, 1985; Rand & Weeks, 1998). Conversely, the overall rate of *adherence* is about 60%. Adherence varies considerably, depending on the type of medical advice, the duration of the recommended regimen, and whether its purpose is to prevent an illness from occurring or to treat or cure an illness that has developed. An overview of the findings of research on compliance indicates the following conclusions (Dunbar-Jacob & Schlenk, 2001; Shearer & Evans, 2001):

- The average adherence rate for taking medicine to treat acute illnesses with short-term treatment regimens is about 67%; for chronic illnesses with long-term regimens, the rate drops to 50–55%.
- Adherence to taking medicine is higher in the days before and after visiting a doctor than at other times.
- Adherence to recommended changes in lifestyle, such as stopping smoking or altering one's diet, is generally quite variable and often very low.

But keep in mind two things about these conclusions. First, the percentages given may *overestimate* adherence because most studies have included in their samples only people who agreed to participate (Cluss & Epstein, 1985). It's likely that people who do not participate differ from those who do, such as by having lower health motivation. Second, the adherence rates cited do not reflect the *range* of noncompliance; some patients adhere exactly to a medical regimen, others do not comply at all, and probably most adhere to some degree.

WHY PATIENTS DO AND DO NOT ADHERE TO MEDICAL ADVICE

We have seen that practitioners do not generally know how well their clients adhere to medical advice. What do physicians think when they learn their patients have not followed their advice? They are concerned about the effects of noncompliance on the person's health, of course, and they tend to place most of the "blame" on the patients—their "uncooperative"

FRANK & ERNEST® by Bob Thaves

Reprinted by permission of United Features Syndicate, Inc.

personalities, inability to understand the advice, or difficult life situations (Davis, 1966). But as we will see, both the practitioners and patients influence adherence, and an individual's adherence depends on characteristics of (1) the *illness or regimen*, (2) the *person*, and (3) the *interactions* between the practitioner and patient.

Medical Regimens and Illness Characteristics

The medical regimens practitioners advise can differ in many ways, such as in their complexity, duration, cost, side effects, and the degree to which they require changes in the patient's habits. Let's see how each of these factors relates to compliance.

Some regimens require clients to *change longstanding habits*—for example, to begin and maintain exercising regularly, reduce the calories or certain components in their diets, stop smoking cigarettes, or cut down on drinking alcoholic beverages. We have seen in previous chapters that these changes can be very difficult for people to make. Recommendations by physicians can induce many patients to make changes in such habits, particularly if the individuals are at high risk for serious illness (Dolecek et al., 1986; Pederson, 1982). But studies have consistently found that people are much less likely to adhere to medical advice for changes in personal habits than to advice for taking medication (Haynes, 1976; Dunbar-Jacobs & Schlenk, 2001).

Some treatment regimens are more *complex* than others—such as by requiring the person to take two or more drugs, each with its own special instructions: "Take one of these pills after meals, and two of these other pills at bedtime, and one of these other pills every 8 hours." As you might expect, the greater the number of drugs and the more complex the medication schedule and dosage, the greater the likelihood the person will make an error, thereby failing to adhere to the regimen (Haynes, 1976; Shearer & Evans, 2001). Regimens also become difficult if they require a variety of complicated tasks, as, for example, individuals suffering from chronic *kidney disease* must do (Finn & Alcorn, 1986; NKF, 2000; Swigonski, 1987). Many of these patients must:

- Undergo *hemodialysis*, in which the blood is shunted from an artery to a filtering apparatus and returned to a vein. This procedure generally takes

4 to 6 hours three times a week, during which time the person may either sleep or engage in a sedentary activity, such as reading.

- Take large quantities of medication and vitamins—sometimes involving dozens of pills a day—while also strictly limiting fluid intake.

- Severely restrict their dietary intake of *sodium*, mainly salt; *potassium* and *phosphorus*, which are found in many fruits and vegetables; and *protein*, especially meats and dairy products.

In general, the more a client is required to do, the more likely compliance will suffer.

The duration, expense, and side effects of a medical regimen are also factors in people's adherence to their practitioner's advice. Studies have confirmed the role of *duration*—compliance tends to decline over time (Parrish, 1986; Varni & Babani, 1986). Short-term regimens are usually prescribed for acute illnesses and show beneficial effects fairly quickly and dramatically, but long-term regimens usually apply to chronic health problems and have slower and less obvious beneficial effects. The *expense* and *side effects* of treatment play a role, too. It may be that treatment expense may not prevent most people from adhering because they have sufficient incomes or insurance to pay for it or feel the benefits of the treatment are essential despite the cost. Similarly, most drugs do not have noticeable or worrisome side effects. But what happens, for instance, when individuals cannot afford their medicine or its side effects do become a problem? Some patients may reduce the dosage of the drug or discontinue using it entirely. The expense and side effects of treatment can impair adherence for many people (Murdaugh, 1998; Steinman, Sands, & Covinsky, 2001).

We might expect that individuals who have health problems that could disable them or threaten their lives would be more likely to adhere to their treatment regimens than people with less serious illnesses. Whether this idea is correct seems to depend on whose perspective of the severity of the health problem we consider—the practitioner's or the patient's. When comparisons are based on illness severity judged by *physicians*, clients with serious illnesses are no more likely to adhere than those with milder health problems (Becker & Rosenstock, 1984; Haynes, 1976). Perhaps this is because many very serious health problems, such as hypertension and atherosclerosis, have no symptoms that worry people greatly or interfere with their functioning; on the other hand, many less serious illnesses do have such symptoms. In contrast, when comparisons are based on illness severity judged by *patients* who have the health problem, clients who rate their illness as relatively serious generally show better adherence to their treatment regimens than those who perceive their illness to be less severe (Becker & Rosenstock, 1984).

Age, Gender, and Sociocultural Factors

Research has found little or no association between compliance in general and clients' specific personal and demographic characteristics, such as their age, gender, social class, race, and religion (Cluss & Epstein, 1985; Haynes, 1976). Does this mean these factors never affect compliance? Probably not. For one thing, although each of these factors is not *by itself* strongly related to adherence, when they are *joined*—for example, gender plus age plus social class—their combination shows a stronger association to compliance (Korsch, Fine, & Negrete, 1978). What's more, some of these factors may be related to adherence in some circumstances but not in others.

Consider the factor of *age*, which seems to affect adherence in different ways, depending on the illness. For example, research found that:

- For childhood cancer patients, problems in adherence to specific care procedures, such as using antibiotics correctly, were greater for younger than for older children (Manne et al., 1993). Although the parents mainly controlled these procedures, the child's age made a difference.

- Among child and adolescent diabetics, adolescents were less adherent to their special diets than children (Johnson et al., 1992).

- For adult arthritis patients, 47% of 55- to 84-year-olds and only 28% of 34- to 54-year-olds made no medication errors in several weeks of monitoring; middle-aged people with very busy lives made the most errors (Park et al., 1999).

Children become increasingly responsible for their own medical treatment as they get older (La Greca & Stone, 1985). Adolescents may be less likely than individuals from other age groups to comply with long-term treatments that single them out or make

them different from peers. And the elderly are more likely than other age groups to suffer from visual, hearing, and cognitive impairments that may lead to noncompliance (Murdaugh, 1998).

Gender and *sociocultural* influences on adherence may also depend on specific circumstances. For instance, women's concern about controlling their weight appears to interfere with using medication to control their blood sugar (Polonsky et al., 1994). And some cultural groups may have beliefs or customs that undermine adherence. As an example, among American Indians, the idea "of taking something all the time, like an antihypertensive drug, is foreign to some cultures where 'cure' is inherent to the healing process, thus making medications that must be taken continuously appear ineffective" (Baines, 1992).

Psychosocial Aspects of the Patient

We saw earlier that the seriousness of an illness and the costs of its treatment can affect compliance, depending on the patient's point of view. Perceived seriousness and perceived costs and benefits are two psychosocial factors that should have a familiar ring by now—we have examined them more than once before as components in the *health belief model*. The health belief model components are as important in explaining why people do and do not adhere to medical advice as they are in explaining other health-related behaviors, such as whether people are likely to adopt health behaviors or use health services (Becker, 1979; Becker & Rosenstock, 1984). Thus, a patient who feels threatened by an illness and believes the benefits of the recommended regimen outweigh the barriers is likely to adhere to his or her practitioner's advice. But individuals who do not feel threatened by the health problem or assess that the barriers of the regimen outweigh the benefits are unlikely to comply.

Sometimes not adhering to a treatment regimen may be *deliberate* and based on *valid reasons*, regardless of whether they are medically sound (Kaplan & Simon, 1990; Turk & Meichenbaum, 1991). This is called **rational nonadherence.** How can not adhering to medical advice be rational? Patients may be acting rationally when they fail to take medication as directed because they:

- Have reason to believe the medication isn't helping.

- Feel that its side effects are very unpleasant, worrisome, or seriously reducing the quality of their lives.
- Are confused about when to take it, or how much.
- Don't have the money to buy the next refill.
- Want to "see if the illness is still there" when they withdraw the medication.

These are not unreasonable motives—and sometimes the clients may be medically correct in not adhering, such as when they experience serious or unexpected side effects. A study of arthritis patients found the most common *intentional* reasons for not taking medication were the side effects and the cost (Lorish, Richards, & Brown, 1989). But most instances of nonadherence occur unintentionally: by forgetting (Dunbar-Jacob & Schlenk, 2001).

Patients' adherence to medical advice is often affected by *cognitive and emotional* factors operating at the time they receive the recommendations. Table 9.2 summarizes the findings of research on these factors. For people to comply with a treatment regimen, they must be cognitively and emotionally able to understand and remember what they are to do. The directions they receive are often complex and given at a time when they may not be listening as carefully as they should. Even when health information is given in writing, most adult patients may not understand it if it is written much above the fifth-grade reading level (Estey, Musseau, & Keehn, 1994).

Two other psychosocial factors that are associated with adherence are *self-efficacy* and *social support*. Generally speaking, people who feel they can carry out the regimen and receive the comfort, caring, and help they need from other individuals or groups are more likely to follow medical advice than clients who have less social support (Dunbar-Jacob &

Schlenk, 2001; DiMatteo, 2004). This support is most effective when the person has a cohesive family that gives tangible or instrumental support in caring for the health problem regimen. It comes from the patient's family, friends, or support groups, such as the many organizations founded to help people deal with specific illnesses. But for some people, such as kidney disease patients who must restrict fluid intake, social relationships can sometimes lead to nonadherence (Swigonski, 1987). This may happen because social gatherings often involve food and beverages—in meetings for lunch, dinner, drinks, or just a cup of coffee, for instance. Some evidence indicates that individuals who are low in conscientiousness are more likely to be led astray by social support than people who are high in conscientiousness (Moran, Christensen, & Lawton, 1997).

PATIENT–PRACTITIONER INTERACTIONS

The word "doctor" comes from the Latin *docere*, which means "to teach." Two features of good teaching involve explaining information in a clear and organized fashion and assessing whether the learner has learned or understands. Some medical practitioners are good teachers, and others are not:

> for example, there are documented cases of men consuming contraceptive drugs intended for their wives. The idea may be amusing, but the fact of an unwanted child was not. (Hunt & MacLeod, 1979, p. 315)

This example illustrates that physicians do not always make sure the patient understands what they have said. Successful communication in patient–practitioner interactions is essential if the client is to adhere to the advice.

Table 9.2   *Cognitive and Emotional Factors in Patients' Recall of Information from Physicians*

1. Patients forget much of what the doctor tells them.
2. Instructions and advice are more likely to be forgotten than other information.
3. The more a patient is told, the greater the proportion he or she will forget.
4. Patients will remember: (a) what they are told first and (b) what they consider most important.
5. More intelligent patients do not remember more than less intelligent patients.
6. Older patients remember just as much as younger ones.
7. Moderately anxious patients recall more of what they are told than highly anxious patients or patients who are not anxious.
8. The more medical knowledge a patient has, the more he or she will recall.

Source: Cassata, cited in DiMatteo & DiNicola (1982, p. 45).

Communicating with Patients

If your physician told you to "take one pill every 6 hours," does that mean you should wake up in the middle of each night to take one? Or would it be OK simply to take four pills a day, equally spaced during your waking hours? Would you ask? Sometimes the information people get from practitioners is not very clear. You might argue that the advice *was* clear: every 6 hours, on the dot. But practitioners need to anticipate unspoken questions—saying, for instance, "You'll need to wake up to take one because the infection may recur if the medicine wears off." If practitioners don't do this, patients usually answer these questions themselves, often incorrectly.

Many people leave their doctors' offices not knowing how to follow their treatment regimens. Bonnie Svarstad (1976) conducted a study in which she interviewed patients at a community health center, recorded their actual verbal interactions with their physicians, and checked their medication containers a week later. This study revealed four findings. First, the patients' knowledge about their treatment was deficient—for example, half did not know how long to continue the medication, and about one-fifth did not know the purpose of or how often to take the prescribed drugs. Second, the patients' poor knowledge often resulted from the physicians not providing the needed information. Third, the clients asked very few questions during the visits. Fourth, the more explicit the doctors' directions, the more the people complied, which was measured by pill counts at the patients' homes about a week later. Today, many pharmacies provide instructions.

Physicians spend very little time giving information to patients during a visit. One study that assessed hundreds of visits found that they lasted about 20 minutes on average, and the physicians spent only about 1 minute, or 5% of the time, giving information to the individuals about their illnesses or treatment (Waitzkin & Stoeckle, 1976). But the physicians themselves reported a very different picture of their interactions: when asked how much time they spent giving information, the doctors gave estimates that were several times higher than the records showed. Other researchers have conducted similar studies; averaging across these studies, it appears that doctors spend perhaps 10% of the time in consultations giving patients information (DiMatteo, 1985). A person's adherence to medical advice depends on the practitioner's communicating information. Good communication takes time and is much more likely to occur when the practitioner's style is more patient-centered than doctor-centered.

Adherence and the Patient–Practitioner Relationship

As we have seen, people generally prefer medical care that involves a patient-centered style. Research has shown that individuals who have good relationships with their physicians are more likely to adhere to the medical advice they give (DiMatteo, 1985; Garrity, 1981; Shearer & Evans, 2001). For example, researchers found that mothers who were very satisfied with the warmth, concern, and communication of information of their child's physician were three times more likely to adhere closely to the regimens than mothers who were dissatisfied (Francis, Korsch, & Morris, 1969). It may be that doctors who succeed in fostering compliance are those who use patient-centered styles.

To summarize, the reasons patients do and do not adhere to medical advice include characteristics of the illness and regimen, the clients and practitioners, and the way these people interrelate or communicate. While reading this material, you may have thought, "Couldn't many of the circumstances that lead to nonadherence be changed to enhance compliance?" The next section examines this question.

INCREASING PATIENT ADHERENCE

Implicit in our interest in enhancing adherence is the assumption that doing so is important—that it would benefit the person's health. How important is adherence to the patient's health? If it is very important, should health care workers aim for each client to comply perfectly to his or her regimen, or would a lesser degree of adherence be acceptable? We will address these questions briefly before considering ways to increase compliance.

Noncompliance and Health Outcomes

By not adhering to regimens recommended by their physicians, people increase their risk of developing health problems they don't already have or of prolonging or worsening their current illnesses. Hospital admissions are substantially higher for people who fail to follow medication regimens for serious conditions, such as hypertension (Dunbar-Jacobs & Schlenk, 2000). And prospective studies of people with serious illnesses have shown that individuals who adhered poorly to their medical regimens were much more likely to die during a 2-year followup period than people who adhered well. For example, one study found higher mortality rates in heart disease patients who adhered poorly to taking a drug to prevent arrhythmia (Irvine et al., 1999); another study found higher death rates among kidney disease patients who adhered poorly to dialysis treatments (Kimmel et al., 1998). Research with HIV patients has shown that even occasional deviations from the regimen allows the virus to rebound, giving it a chance to develop drug resistance (Catz et al., 2000).

But failing to follow a practitioner's orders exactly is not always detrimental to the client's health. One reason is that the effect of nonadherence is greater for serious and chronic illnesses than for less serious conditions (DiMatteo et al., 2002). Other reasons may be that some treatments are harmful and have side effects that produce iatrogenic conditions and that doctors sometimes prescribe unnecessary drugs or other procedures with nonmedical goals in mind, such as to avoid risking malpractice suits. But even when medically sound regimens are given—as in the great majority of cases—some people who follow their doctors' orders closely show little benefit from the treatment, whereas others who are much less compliant show substantial improvements in their health (Cluss & Epstein, 1985; Hayes et al., 1994).

The importance of following medical advice closely seems to depend on the particular health problem and the treatment prescribed. For hypertensive patients, for instance, consuming 80% of the medication prescribed to reduce their blood pressure is probably the minimum level of compliance needed to treat hypertension effectively. For other health problems, however, "an 80% rate of compliance may be unnecessary" (Epstein & Cluss, 1982, p. 952). And so, following the usual regimen of penicillin for treating rheumatic fever at only a 50% rate may be sufficiently effective. Unhealthful noncompliance might therefore be defined as "the point below which the desired preventive or therapeutic result is unlikely to be achieved with the medication prescribed" (Parrish, 1986, p. 456). Unfortunately, however, compliance cutoff points still need to be established for individual illnesses and treatments.

Although more research is needed to determine compliance cutoff points, two things should be clear. First, *perfect* adherence may not be necessary in many cases. Second, the current adherence levels of clients are very far from perfect.

Improving Physicians' Communication Skills

Probably most physicians in the past who have dealt with the compliance problem at all did so after the fact. Rather than trying to prevent noncompliance, they tried to correct it if and when they learned about it. How did they try to correct it? A study examined this question and found that the first step physicians used when a client failed to adhere was to give a "thorough explanation of the regimen and repeat it so that the patient understands" (Davis, 1966). As we have seen, explaining the regimen and making sure the person understands can prevent noncompliance in the first place.

Getting practitioners to improve their style of communicating with patients is not necessarily difficult to accomplish. One study presented a brief program to instruct physicians at a hospital clinic about the kinds of reasons hypertensive people have for not adhering to their regimens and about ways to detect and improve low compliance (Inui, Yourtee, & Williamson, 1976). Compared to doctors in a control group, the physicians who received the program subsequently spent more time giving information during patient visits—and, more importantly, their clients showed more knowledge about their regimens and illnesses, greater adherence in taking medications, and better blood pressure control. Often such changes in physician behavior last indefinitely (Roter & Hall, 1989). (Go to 👤.)

Improving Psychosocial Factors in Patients

Other approaches to promote adherence focus on modifying psychosocial factors in the patient. One method that seems to be effective at least for short-term regimens is to have the person state explicitly that he or she will comply. In an experiment with parents of children suffering from acute infections, parents who were asked to promise (all agreed) to give all of the medication doses had higher compliance rates than those who were not asked to promise to comply (Kulik & Carlino, 1987). And the children of the parents who promised showed greater recovery later from their illnesses.

CLINICAL METHODS AND ISSUES
How to Present Medical Information

Because patients often misunderstand or forget medical recommendations, practitioners are also learning specific techniques for presenting medical information. Several methods are particularly effective (Parrish, 1986; Schraa & Dirks, 1982; Shearer & Evans, 2001). These methods include:

- Orienting patients to the disease process and reason for the treatment in terms they can understand.
- Simplifying verbal instructions by using clear and straightforward language and sentences, without condescending.
- Using specific and concrete statements—such as, "You should walk a mile a day for the first week, and

2 miles after that," instead of, "You should get daily exercise."
- Breaking down a complicated or long-term regimen into smaller segments. The patient might begin the regimen by doing only part of it and then adding to it later. Or the regimen might involve a series of smaller goals that the client believes he or she can achieve.
- Emphasizing key information by stating why it is important and offering it early in the presentation.
- Using simple, written instructions.
- Having the patient repeat instructions or state them in his or her own words.
- Assessing the person's self-efficacy, motivation, and opportunities for social support in the regimen.

Social and motivational forces in a patient's life can have important effects on adherence, particularly when the regimen is long term or requires lifestyle changes. One helpful approach that we discussed in Chapter 6 is for practitioners to use *motivational interviewing* methods to identify the benefits and problems of adherence and to reduce resistance to implement the regimen (Resnicow et al., 2002; Shearer & Evans, 2001). Another approach is for the practitioner or client to recruit constructive sources of *social support* (Jenkins, 1979; Shearer & Evans, 2001). Family and friends who are committed to the regimen can promote compliance by having positive attitudes about the treatment activities and making sure they occur. Effective social support can also come from self-help and patient groups established to give information and assistance with specific health problems. Practitioners can help clients make contact with appropriate groups.

Several *behavioral methods* are also effective in enhancing patients' motivation to adhere to their treatment regimens (Burke, Dunbar-Jacob, & Hill, 1997; Epstein & Cluss, 1982; Jenkins, 1979; Roter et al., 1998). These methods include:

- *Tailoring the regimen*, in which activities in the treatment are designed to be compatible with

the patient's habits and rituals. For example, taking a pill at home at breakfast or while preparing for bed is easier to do and remember for most people than taking it in the middle of the day.
- *Providing prompts and reminders*, which serve as cues to perform recommended activities. These cues can include reminder phone calls for appointments or notes posted at home that remind the client to exercise. Innovative drug packaging can also help—for instance, some drugs today come in dispensers with dated compartments or built-in reminder alarms.
- *Self-monitoring*, in which the patient keeps a written record of regimen activities, such as the foods eaten each day.
- *Behavioral contracting*, whereby the practitioner and client negotiate a series of treatment activities and goals in writing and specify rewards the patient will receive for succeeding.

A major advantage of these methods is that the client can become actively involved in their design and execution (Turk & Meichenbaum, 1991). Furthermore, the patient can carry them out alone or with the aid of the practitioner, family, or friends.

The procedures we have examined for increasing patient compliance are often combined into a complex program, particularly to enhance medication adherence for people with chronic illnesses, such as hypertension or heart disease. But these programs have been only moderately effective so far, and new methods are needed (McDonald, Garg, & Haynes, 2002). Some current methods are easy for practitioners to incorporate into existing ways of working with clients, but others are time-consuming to apply and involve skills that are outside the expertise of most medical workers.

FOCUSING ON PREVENTION

Health care systems have focused mainly on secondary and tertiary prevention—that is, treating an illness to reverse the condition or to contain or slow its progress—and have developed processes for managing chronic diseases. This approach is called the *chronic care model*. Can the chronic care model be applied to promote primary prevention and help people avoid health problems? Researchers have proposed that it can if efforts for primary prevention in a health care organization incorporate six features of the chronic care model (Glasgow et al., 2001):

1. *Organization of care.* The administrators of the health care system give explicit and obvious priority to primary prevention, such as identifying smokers and helping them quit, and provide incentives for staff to engage in these efforts.

2. *Clinical information systems.* The organization requires regularly updated, easily accessed data in clients' files regarding the need for and status of preventive services so that clients and staff can receive performance feedback and reminders.

3. *Delivery-system design.* Physicians initiate preventive interventions, such as mailings and counseling for stopping smoking, which nonphysicians carry out.

4. *Decision support.* The organization provides its staff with guidelines, training, and reminders to identify clients who need intervention and to carry it out.

5. *Self-management support.* The health care system provides information and referrals to clients, and their families help them recognize the need for preventive services and for change in unhealthful behaviors.

6. *Community resources.* The health care system extends its prevention efforts into the community by making use of self-help organizations, such as for quitting smoking and losing weight, and supporting public health programs and laws.

The chronic care model provides a blueprint for designing prevention programs in health care organizations, some of which have already begun to use it and improve prevention.

SUMMARY

Health care systems for the delivery and management of medical care are complex, involving professionals with a variety of specialized functions. Inpatient treatment for people with serious illnesses occurs in hospitals; nursing homes provide care mainly for elderly individuals who need long-term medical and personal care. Practitioners give office-based treatment in private practice and in prepaid group plans, such as health-maintenance organizations. Although the health care systems in many countries provide insurance for all citizens, the American system does not.

People decide they are sick and in need of medical attention chiefly on the basis of the symptoms they perceive. They often consult a lay referral system before going to a physician. Some people seem to pay closer attention to their internal states than other individuals do and are, therefore, more likely to notice changes in physical sensations and to perceive these sensations as symptoms. Stimuli in the environment can interfere with or mask people's attention to internal sensations. Because people generally do not assess their internal states very accurately, psychosocial factors can have a strong influence on the perception of symptoms, which may account for the phenomena of medical student's disease and mass psychogenic illness. The common-sense models and other knowledge people extract from their experience generally help them to make appropriate decisions about seeking medical attention. But sometimes people's knowledge, such as with iatrogenic conditions, and their emotions, such as intense fear or anxiety, can lead them to interpret their symptoms incorrectly and lead to treatment delay.

Young children and the elderly use health services more than adolescents and young adults do, and women use more medical services and drugs than men do. Many people use complementary and alternative medicine methods to supplement or take the place of medical care. The health belief model has been useful in helping to explain why people use, don't use, and delay using health services. Many individuals wait months before seeking attention for symptoms of serious illnesses, such as cancer. In contrast, some people overuse health services. Hypochondriasis involves the tendency for a person to interpret real but benign bodily sensations as symptoms of illness despite reassurances by a doctor that they are harmless. This tendency is linked to emotional maladjustment, but it is not more common in old age than at other ages.

People generally express high levels of satisfaction with the care they receive from physicians who communicate with a patient-centered rather than a doctor-centered style. Patient-centered physicians tend to ask open-ended questions, avoid using medical jargon or technical terms, and allow clients to participate in some of the decision making regarding the treatment of their illness. These doctors are also likely to project feelings of concern and reassurance and to give clear explanations about illnesses and treatments. Of course, patients vary in their behaviors and styles, too, and may impair communication with their doctors because of the way they describe their symptoms.

Patient compliance with or adherence to medical advice varies greatly and noncompliance is very common. Individuals tend to be less compliant for long-term regimens to treat chronic diseases than for short-term regimens to treat acute illnesses, and they are particularly unlikely to adhere to recommendations to change longstanding habits. Also, the more complicated the regimen, the more likely adherence will suffer. Adherence is affected by various psychosocial factors, including rational nonadherence decisions and the patient's health beliefs, social support, and cognitive and emotional conditions when receiving medical advice. Patients are more likely to adhere closely to their regimens when their practitioners are patient-centered and explain their illnesses and treatments clearly. Behavioral methods and communication enhancement can improve people's adherence to medical advice.

KEY TERMS

commonsense models	treatment delay	hypochondriasis	adherence
lay referral system	complementary and	doctor-centered	compliance
iatrogenic conditions	alternative medicine	patient-centered	rational nonadherence

10

IN THE HOSPITAL: THE SETTING, PROCEDURES, AND EFFECTS ON PATIENTS

The Hospital—Its History, Setting, and Procedures
How the Hospital Evolved
The Organization and Functioning of Hospitals
Roles, Goals, and Communication
The Impact of the "Bottom Line"

Being Hospitalized
Relations with the Hospital Staff
Sick-Role Behavior in the Hospital

Emotional Adjustment in the Hospital
Coping Processes in Hospital Patients
Preparing Patients for Stressful Medical Procedures
When the Hospitalized Patient Is a Child

How Health Psychologists Assist Hospitalized Patients
Initial Steps in Helping
Tests for Psychological Assessment of Medical Patients
Promoting Patients' Health and Adjustment

PROLOGUE

"I had a fast-growing conviction that a hospital was no place for a person who was seriously ill," a patient once wrote. This patient was Norman Cousins, former editor of *Saturday Review*, whom we described in Chapter 1 as having developed and recovered from a typically incurable and painful crippling disease. His symptoms began with a fever and general achiness—the kinds of sensations we usually associate with minor illnesses. Within a week, however, his condition worsened, and he began to have difficulty moving his neck, legs, arms, and hands. He was soon hospitalized for the diagnostic tests that pinpointed his disease: ankylosis spondylitis.

What experiences did Cousins have that led to his negative view of hospitals? Here is one example he described (1985, pp. 55–56):

> I was astounded when four technicians from four different departments took four separate and substantial blood samples on the same day. That the hospital didn't take the trouble to coordinate the tests, using one blood specimen, seemed to me inexplicable and irresponsible.

He reacted by stating he would not give more than one sample every 3 days and that he expected different departments to draw from it. He also criticized other hospital practices, such as awakening patients from sleep to carry out regular routines. In his view, sleep in the hospital is an "uncommon blessing" that should not be interrupted casually.

Few people enjoy being hospitalized, even under the best of circumstances. Although many people probably have more positive feelings about their hospital experiences than those Cousins had, some have even worse impressions. We have all heard stories of mistakes being made or other situations that produced more serious health problems than those with which the patient was admitted to the hospital. This chapter focuses on the experience of being hospitalized. First we examine the hospital—its history, setting, and procedures—as well as the roles and points of view of the hospital staff. Then we consider what being hospitalized is like from the perspective of patients, and what can be done to assess and provide help for their psychological needs. As we study these topics, we will consider important questions that are of great concern to patients, their families, and practitioners. For instance, hospital personnel have difficult jobs—what impact does this have on them? How do people adjust to being hospitalized? What special needs do children have as patients, and how can

hospitals and parents help? How can practitioners reduce the stress individuals experience with unpleasant, painful, and surgical procedures?

THE HOSPITAL—ITS HISTORY, SETTING, AND PROCEDURES

Hospitals in industrialized countries around the world are typically large institutions with separate wards or buildings for different kinds of health problems and treatment procedures. These institutions have changed in their long history, and so have people's attitudes about them. People in the United States today are more likely than people years ago to view hospitals as places to go to get well rather than to die, even though most Americans are in hospitals when they die (Easterbrook, 1987). Let's see how hospitals began and evolved.

HOW THE HOSPITAL EVOLVED

Special places to care for the ill did not always exist. One of the earliest roots of this approach can be seen in the ancient Greeks' establishment of temples

Typical of hospitals prior to the 20th century, this women's ward had many beds close together in a huge room.

where sick people would pray and receive cures or advice from the god Aesculapius (Anderson & Gevitz, 1983). But the idea of having special facilities to house and treat the sick probably began with the Roman military, who established separate barracks for their ill and disabled soldiers.

The first institutions established to care for the sick were associated with Christian monasteries and had a broad charitable purpose—that of helping the less fortunate members of society. As a result, these facilities housed not only sick people, but also orphans, the poor, and even travelers who needed lodging. One of the earliest of these hospitals, the Hôtel-Dieu of Lyons in present-day France, was established in A.D. 542 (Anderson & Gevitz, 1983). The charitable purposes of hospitals in Western Europe continued with little change until the 18th and 19th centuries, when these institutions became more specialized in two ways. First, they began to restrict admissions to people who were both sick and judged to be members of the "worthy poor"—that is, individuals who could make contributions to society.

> Others, namely the aged, the very young, the physically handicapped, and the mentally deficient . . . were confined to abysmally kept poorhouses, irrespective of whether they were in need of medical attention. The second change was that hospitals became more medically specialized. Wards were established for different illness categories. . . . By keeping patients with the same or seemingly related ailments together, one could readily make far more detailed comparisons and thus advance learning. (Anderson & Gevitz, 1983, p. 307)

The American colonies used similar approaches to those used in Europe for the care of the sick. In 1751, Pennsylvania Hospital opened in Philadelphia as the first institution in the colonies devoted exclusively to treating disease. It was built as a result of a citizens' campaign led by Benjamin Franklin.

Until the 20th century, hospitals had always had a well-deserved bad reputation as places that gave miserable care and ministered exclusively to poor people, who often died from infections they did not have when they entered. Sick people from the upper and middle classes were treated at home. Therefore, this situation quickly changed with advances in medical knowledge and technology in the late 1800s. In 1873, there were only 178 hospitals in the United States; in 1909, there were over 4,300, and the increase in the number of hospital beds was seven times that which would be expected on the basis of population growth alone (Anderson & Gevitz, 1983). American hospitals in the early 20th century gained a much more positive reputation and were attracting patients from all social classes. Nowadays, the nation's hospitals admit over 32 million people as inpatients each year (USBC, 2003).

Hospitals today involve a wider variety of functions than ever before. They provide services to inpatients and outpatients to cure disease and repair injury, prevent illness, conduct diagnostic tests, and aid people's rehabilitation and life situations after being discharged. They are also involved in conducting research and teaching current and future medical personnel. To carry out these complex and varied functions, hospitals require organized hierarchies of personnel with specific roles and lines of authority.

THE ORGANIZATION AND FUNCTIONING OF HOSPITALS

Although the organizational structures of hospitals vary across nations, most share many aspects of the organization used in the United States. At the top of the structure is a board of trustees, whose members are generally upper-level business and professional people from the community (Anderson & Gevitz, 1983; APA, 1998). Most boards limit their role mainly to long-range planning and fund-raising. At the next level of authority, the chain of command splits into two parallel lines of responsibility. The hospital *administrators* are mainly in charge of the day-to-day business of the institution, such as in purchasing equipment and supplies, keeping records, and providing food and maintenance services. These functions often affect the medical care patients receive. The *medical staff* are responsible for patient care. Each of these two lines has its own hierarchy of authority. We will focus on the medical staff.

The head of the medical staff is a physician who usually has the title "Medical Director" or "Chief of Staff." The next level of authority consists of the staff (or "attending") physicians. In the majority of American hospitals, most staff physicians are not actually employed or paid by the institution. They are employed in private practice or affiliated with a private clinic or group health plan, and they provide services at the hospital for their clients from these sources

(Anderson & Gevitz, 1983; APA, 1998). Doctors not employed by the hospital get paid for their hospital services by billing each of their patients or by their clinics or health plan. To become a staff physician, a doctor must receive *admission privileges*, generally by applying to a committee of physicians at the hospital. As a condition for granting privileges, most hospitals require staff physicians to do certain tasks, such as teaching or providing emergency or clinic service. The main exception to this system of staff physicians occurs at "teaching hospitals," which are affiliated with medical schools. Although teaching hospitals grant admission privileges, they also have large staffs of doctors whom they employ; these doctors include (1) *residents*, who are recent medical school graduates, and (2) full-fledged physicians, whose duties include supervising the residents.

Nurses form the next rung in the hierarchy of medical staff in hospitals. They are salaried hospital employees who have two functions: caring for patients and managing the wards. Nurses are as important as doctors to a patient's recovery. They spend more time with the person, often explaining medical regimens and procedures when physicians do not. The medical staff also includes a great variety of allied health workers, such as physical therapists, respiratory therapists, laboratory technicians, pharmacists' assistants, and dietitians (Ginzberg, 1983). These workers often have less authority than nurses. At the bottom of the medical staff hierarchy are or-derlies and other workers whose roles require less advanced skills than those of the allied health workers. (Go to 🍎.)

ROLES, GOALS, AND COMMUNICATION

Picture this scene: as the ambulance crew wheels the victim of an automobile accident into the emergency room, the medical staff swings into action. Their specific actions and roles are dictated by the presenting health problems of the patient and would be different if the person had suffered serious burns in a fire or experienced symptoms of a heart attack, for instance. Nurses and orderlies know the usual procedures for patients with the presenting problems and begin to perform their roles without specific instruction—for example, a nurse may prepare to take a blood sample, and an orderly may wheel a piece of equipment into place. The physician is, of course, in charge and either conducts needed actions directly or orders others to do them.

Coordinating Patient Care

Years ago, the typical hospital patient received services from a small team of physicians and nurses who worked side by side in close communication throughout the person's stay (Benoliel, 1977). This situation rarely exists today. Instead, assessment and treatment procedures for a hospitalized person involve a

---

ASSESS YOURSELF

Who's Who in Physician Care

The medical staffs in hospitals contain a great variety of specialized personnel. If you were hospitalized, chances are you would receive care from at least two of the ten types of medical specialists listed below. Do you know what their specialty areas of illness or treatment are? For this matching task, write the number for each specialty area in the space preceding the corresponding type of specialist. Then use the answer key to find out how many you matched correctly.

_____ Anesthesiologist   _____ Gastroenterologist
_____ Cardiologist   _____ Hematologist
_____ Neurologist   _____ Otolaryngologist
_____ Orthopedist   _____ Proctologist
_____ Oncologist   _____ Radiologist

Specialty areas: **1.** Cancer; **2.** Blood; **3.** Nervous system; **4.** Colon and rectum; **5.** Painkilling drugs; **6.** Ear, nose, and throat; **7.** Bones and joints; **8.** X rays; **9.** Heart; **10.** Digestive system.

Answers, in order:

5, 9, 10, 2, 3, 7, 1, 6, 4, 8

wide array of personnel who have different specialties and carry out their roles separately, often with little contact with each other and with the patient. The danger in the current approach is that the patient's care can become *fragmented*, or uncoordinated, with seemingly no one in charge. Hospitals attempt to minimize this danger by giving a particular staff position, usually a nurse, responsibility for coordinating the care of each patient in a ward (Aiken, 1983; Benoliel, 1977). But *direct* communication is best and leaves less opportunity for errors.

Health Hazards in Hospitals

Communication among medical personnel is also important because hospitals contain many health hazards for personnel and patients. These hazards include chemicals that are used in treatment and other hospital procedures (Clever & Omenn, 1988). Hospitals need to maintain good channels of com-

munication to protect their workers and patients from excessive exposure to harmful chemicals and substances.

Another hazard in hospitals is the potential exposure of personnel and patients to disease-causing microorganisms (AMA, 2003). As we saw earlier, hospitals prior to the 20th century were places where infection spread quickly and widely, and patients often died of diseases they did not have when they entered. Although the spreading of infection in hospitals has been reduced, it hasn't been eliminated. Each year, 5 to 10% of American hospital patients—1½ to 3 million people—acquire a **nosocomial infection,** an infection that a patient contracts while in the hospital setting, and tens of thousands of them die from these infections (CU, 2004b). The rate of nosocomial infection is especially high in intensive care units and varies across nations: in Europe, it is much higher in Greece and Portugal than in Switzerland and Ireland (Vincent, 2003). To combat hospital infections,

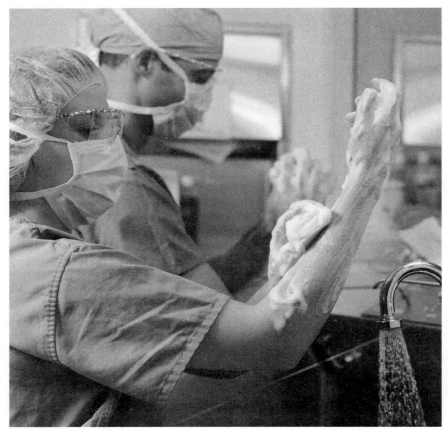

Hospitals try to reduce the spread of infection by establishing rules about medical staff wearing clean masks, clothing, and gloves.

guidelines for infection control have been developed and widely adopted. Guidelines in the United States, for instance, state that each hospital should have an Infection Control Committee headed by an epidemiologist to establish policies to control the spread of disease, and the medical staff should include an Infection Control Nurse (ICN). The ICN has the most direct role in curbing the spread of disease, being responsible for detecting and recording instances of nosocomial infections and taking measures to prevent them.

To reduce nosocomial infections, hospitals have established regulations regarding such issues as when medical workers must wash their hands or wear masks. But hospital personnel often fail to follow these rules (Vincent, 2003). A survey of about 8,000 nurses, ICNs, and epidemiologists at hospitals across the United States assessed whether medical workers adhere to infection control regulations and what is done when they do not (Raven & Haley, 1982). Physicians were considerably less likely to comply than were nurses and laboratory technicians. The ICNs were also asked how often they would "say something to a staff member" who violated infection control rules, such as by entering a strict isolation area without putting on a mask or by discarding an unprotected syringe in a waste basket. The ICNs were much more likely to correct nurses and technicians than to correct physicians.

Interventions with behavioral methods can increase markedly the infection control actions of nurses (DeVries, Burnette, & Redmon, 1991), but programs to improve such behaviors must be repeated periodically because their effects fade over time (Vincent, 2003). Hospitals also need to find constructive ways to enable a staff member at a lower level of the medical staff hierarchy to give feedback to individuals at higher levels regarding their nonadherence to infection control regulations.

THE IMPACT OF THE "BOTTOM LINE"

The costs of hospital services are very high, but health care systems around the world are trying to contain them. The Medicare system in the United States today helps contain medical costs, but it made the situation worse when it was first introduced because its procedures encouraged overcharging, keeping patients in the hospital, and performing many tests and procedures. In those days, maintaining a hospi-

tal's financial solvency was a relatively easy job for administrators.

This situation in America soon changed when Medicare adopted a payment method called the *prospective-payment system* (PPS) (APA, 1998; Lave, 1989). With the PPS approach, health problems are classified into "diagnostic-related groups," and the fee a hospital receives for treating a person with a particular health problem is predetermined. This fee reflects the average cost of treating individuals in the corresponding diagnostic-related group, based on past recovery rates for similar people. If the patient's condition does not respond to the treatment as readily as expected and requires extra care, the hospital usually bears the cost beyond the PPS allowance. But if the patient's condition responds better than expected, the hospital keeps the excess payment. The continually increasing costs of medical care and hospital administrators' concern for the "bottom line" have led to changes in hospital procedures.

How have hospital procedures changed? Although some American hospitals focus on treating patients who require long-term care, the great majority were established to treat people quickly and discharge them in good health (Lawrence & Gaus, 1983; USDHHS, 1985). Most hospitals keep patients for an average of less than 30 days and are classified as *short-stay hospitals*. As Figure 10–1 depicts, the rate at which short-stay hospitals admit and discharge patients increased from 1970 to 1980, when the average length of stay was about a week. Since 1980, both admissions and lengths of stay have declined sharply. These decreases reflect three important changes. First, people are having more procedures done on an outpatient basis. Second, medical procedures are becoming increasingly efficient. For example, new surgical methods for correcting orthopedic injuries entail little or no cutting of healthy tissue, so that recovery time and pain are greatly diminished. And emergency room diagnoses are being made more quickly with the aid of new, accurate tests, such as for heart attacks (Puleo et al., 1994). Third, patients are being released at earlier stages of recovery, so that a larger part of their recovery time is spent at home while receiving care as outpatients. Although there is some concern that people are being released too quickly from hospitals, for the most part patients have not been harmed by the PPS procedures (Ashton et al., 2003; Kahn et al., 1990; Lave, 1989).

Figure 10–1 United States hospital utilization from 1970 to 2001, as indicated by patient discharge rate and average length of stay at nonfederal "short-stay" hospitals. (Pre-1980 data from USDHHS, 1985, Figure 30; later data from USBC, 2003, Table 174. Note that a change in research methodology beginning in 1988 may be responsible for part of any differences seen between earlier and later data.)

People typically prefer being released from the hospital as early as possible. Being hospitalized is a negative experience in many ways—financially, physically, socially, and emotionally. Some hospitals in the United States and other countries are changing the look and feel of their wards, using the

recommendations of an organization called Program Planetree (CU, 1995). Wards have rooms with homelike furnishings and libraries with medical and health information, and the staff work as a team with a nurse-coordinator for each patient. The next section considers the impact on the patient of being hospitalized.

BEING HOSPITALIZED

Although being sick is unpleasant and being seriously ill is worse, being hospitalized adds many other negative aspects to a person's sick-role experience: it disrupts the individual's lifestyle, involves a high degree of dependency on others, and presents many events that can be extremely distressing. The unpleasantness may begin at admission, such as when a clerk in an American hospital asks questions about the patient's ability to pay for the medical services. As this example suggests, part of the unpleasantness of being hospitalized relates to the interactions between the patient and the hospital staff.

RELATIONS WITH THE HOSPITAL STAFF

Imagine that you have just been admitted to a hospital. How should you behave toward the staff if you don't get the care or information you want? Patients typically enter the hospital with a clear social role—that of being dependent for their very lives on the medical staff, who have most of the knowledge, authority, and power in their relationship (CU, 1995; Rodin & Janis, 1979; Taylor, 1979). The patient is a stranger in the hospital community and is likely to be unfamiliar with its structure, procedures, and terminology. These conditions often make the person feel uneasy in an already worrisome situation.

Psychosocial Issues of Patients

Anxiety is probably the most common and pervasive emotion of hospitalized people (Newman, 1984a). If their health problems have not yet been identified, they worry about what the problems are, what the outcomes will be, and how the illnesses will influence their lives. If the diagnoses have been made, they worry about many other matters, such as what the treatment will be like and the degree to which it will be successful. Many of the worries patients have stem from uncertainties that result from a lack of information. Although the lack of information may occur because tests have not yet been completed, sometimes it occurs because no one has taken the time to inform the person (CU, 1995). One hospital patient, for example, gave the following description of experiences with a physician who would:

> talk fast, he out-talks you—and rushes out of the room and then when he's out of the room you think, well, I was supposed to ask him what he's going to do about my medicine . . . you run in the hall and he has disappeared that fast. (Tagliacozzo & Mauksch, 1972, p. 177)

Hospitals are busy places, and the limited time of medical personnel accounts in part for their failure to provide the information patients may need. But not providing information may lead to misunderstandings that may impair the person's compliance with the advice of the medical staff or cause unnecessary emotional suffering.

Another common characteristic of the way practitioners interact with patients is called **depersonalization,** or treating the person as if he or she were either not present or not a person. Sociologist Erving Goffman referred to this characteristic as "nonperson treatment"—the patient is treated like "a possession someone has left behind" (1961, pp. 341–342). A psychologist has described a personal example of depersonalization as a patient for an eye injury. The physician

> abruptly terminated his conversation with me as soon as I lay down on the operating table. Although I had no sedative, or anesthesia, he acted as if I were no longer conscious, directing all his questions to a friend of mine—questions such as, What's his name?, What occupation is he in? . . . As I lay there, these two men were speaking about me as if I were not there at all. The moment I got off the table and was no longer a cut to be stitched, the surgeon resumed his conversation with me, and existence was conferred upon me again. (Zimbardo, 1970, p. 298)

Practitioners may treat patients as nonpersons to distance themselves from the fact that the body they are treating belongs to a thinking and worried person who can observe what is going on, ask questions, and behave in ways that can interfere with their work (Goffman, 1961). Medical workers may try to save themselves and the patient trouble, awkwardness, and anxiety by acting as if the person had dropped off the defective body at the hospital for repair and would pick it up when it was ready.

There are also many emotional factors that lead hospital workers to treat patients in a depersonalized manner. Hospital jobs entail heavy responsibilities and can be very hectic, particularly when many emergencies punctuate the day. These features can create high levels of stress, which may lead workers to give less personalized care. Practitioners need ways to protect themselves emotionally when a patient takes a turn for the worse or dies, which can be a crushing experience (Benoliel, 1977). Depersonalization probably helps practitioners feel less attached and emotionally affected when these events occur.

Burnout Among Health Care Professionals

Hour after hour, day after day, people who work with people who are suffering and distressed must cope with the stress these encounters produce. All jobs have stressful conditions of some kind, such as heavy workloads, deadlines, and interpersonal conflicts. But workers in certain professions—for example, police work, social work, and health care—have the added emotional burden of working continuously in emotionally charged situations that involve feelings of anxiety, fear, embarrassment, and hostility. This burden makes the risk of "burnout" greater in these professions than in most others. **Burnout** is a state of psychosocial and physical exhaustion that results from chronic exposure to high levels of stress and little personal control (Maslach & Jackson, 1982; Maslach, Schaufeli, & Leiter, 2001). Workers who experience burnout tend to show low levels of job satisfaction and high levels of absenteeism, job turnover, and alcohol and drug abuse.

What psychological characteristics contribute to burnout in workers? There are three psychosocial components of burnout:

- *Emotional exhaustion*—feeling drained of emotional resources and unable to help others on a psychological level.

- *Depersonalization*—a lack of personal regard for others, as shown by treating people as objects, having little concern for and sensitivity to their needs, and developing callous attitudes toward them.

- *Perceived inadequacy of professional accomplishment*—feeling low in self-efficacy and falling short of personal expectations for work performance.

Maslach and Jackson (1982) studied burnout in a large sample of workers in a variety of helping professions and in separate samples of nurses and physicians. Let's consider three findings from this research. First, the nurses, physicians, and workers in various helping professions reported fairly similar, high levels of emotional exhaustion. Second, differences were found among occupations for the two other components of burnout: the nurses showed the lowest degree of depersonalization, and the physicians reported the least dissatisfaction with their sense of accomplishment in their work. The low degree of depersonalization among nurses may reflect a sex difference in empathy toward people: almost all the nurses but few of the physicians were females. The relatively high sense of accomplishment among doctors may be the result of such factors as their high pay and status in the medical staff hierarchy. Third, the more time health care workers spent in direct care of patients, the greater was their risk of emotional exhaustion. For instance, physicians who spent almost all their time in direct care reported greater emotional exhaustion than those who spent some of their time in teaching or administrative duties.

What can hospitals do to help health care workers avoid or cope with burnout? We can describe two things. First, hospitals can provide opportunities for workers to mix direct care for patients and other tasks in their daily activities whenever possible. Second, hospitals can help establish support groups for their health care workers. Meetings of these groups can provide training in stress management and coping methods, like those we discussed in Chapter 5. Health care workers who receive such training and periodic booster sessions experience much less burnout than individuals without such training (Rowe, 1999).

SICK-ROLE BEHAVIOR IN THE HOSPITAL

Relations between patients and practitioners in the hospital are affected not only by the behavior of the medical staff, but by the patient's behavior, too. A hospital presents an unfamiliar and strange environment that requires psychological and social adjustments that most patients have difficulty making. They must get used to a lack of privacy, strict rules and time schedules, having their activities restricted, having little control over events around them, and being dependent on others. These things complicate their psychosocial transition to the sick role (Kasl & Cobb, 1966b). How are patients supposed to behave in the hospital?

When patients enter the hospital, they have ideas about how they should behave. Judith Lorber (1975) studied these ideas and the sick-role behavior of over 100 patients, mostly over 40 years of age, who entered a hospital for elective surgeries ranging from routine to very serious. Interviews at the start and end of their hospital stays assessed whether they thought patients should be *active* or *passive*, or "conforming." One finding of this study was that people with passive beliefs when they entered were less likely than those with active beliefs to argue with the staff and complain about minor discomforts.

Another purpose of this study was to examine the reactions of the medical staff to the patients' sick-role behaviors. At the end of each patient's stay, the medical staff rated the individual as a "good patient," "average patient," or "problem patient." They were also asked to provide verbal descriptions of the person's behavior and their reactions when the behavior occurred. In general, individuals rated as *good patients* were those who behaved passively, being cooperative, uncomplaining, and stoical; those rated as *problem patients* were seen as uncooperative, constantly complaining, overemotional, and dependent. Let's describe two patients. One was an overly passive "good" patient who "didn't want to bother" the nurses, even when she should have. As a result, the nurses' routines were disrupted by having to check on her status frequently to make sure she was all right. The other one was a "problem" patient, a man who had psychological and medical complications after his gallbladder was removed. Medical staff said he lied, called people names, and became so uncooperative that it was difficult for staff to carry out routine procedures.

Severe medical conditions can make patients' difficult behavior understandable, and so the staff in Lorber's study distinguished between two types of problem patients. One type consists of individuals who are very seriously ill, having severe complications or poor prognoses. Although these patients show problem behaviors and require a lot of attention, the staff often forgives their behavior because of their medical conditions. The second type consists of people who are not seriously ill but take up more staff time than is warranted by their conditions, and they complain or fail to cooperate a lot. It may be that patients who are not seriously ill behave disruptively as a reaction to their loss of freedoms and control (Taylor, 1979). For instance, a patient may not be allowed to walk for a while because of a leg injury, or watch television late because it would disturb other patients, or have visitors at certain times because their presence might make the work of the medical staff more difficult. People's angry responses to being controlled or believing their freedom is threatened are called **reactance** (Brehm, 1966). Although hospital staff usually try to deal with problem patients in a pleasant manner, they sometimes respond by administering sedatives and, for highly problematic cases, even arranging a premature discharge (Lorber, 1975).

Fortunately, the large majority of patients are not problem patients (Lorber, 1975). Most hospitalized people try to be considerate, recognizing that medical workers have difficult jobs. Other individuals behave as "good patients" because they are wary of the consequences of being disliked by the staff. These people do not want to appear to be "troublemakers," by being too demanding or too dependent. They may think an angered staff may "refuse to answer your bell" or "refuse to make your bed," for

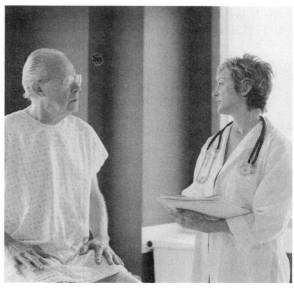

"Good patients" are cooperative, calm, and attentive in discussions with the medical staff.

instance. As a result, these patients may anxiously watch the clock when their medication does not arrive on time, rather than reminding the nurse (Tagliacozzo & Mauksch, 1972). We have discussed several factors that determine how people react to being hospitalized, and we turn now to the role of their emotional adjustment with their medical conditions and the medical treatment procedures they experience in the hospital.

"WE'LL HAVE YOU OUT OF HERE IN NO TIME, MR. LOCKHORN···THE NURSES HAVE HAD IT WITH YOU."   Reprinted courtesy of Bunny Hoest.

EMOTIONAL ADJUSTMENT IN THE HOSPITAL

Imagine you are in your 30s, waiting in your hospital room for surgery to remove the large tumor you have seen in X rays that is growing in your lung. Then imagine that the operation goes badly, not all of the tumor could be removed, and the radiation and chemotherapy treatments over the next several weeks leave you weak and nauseated for days at a time. This was the real experience of Fitzhugh Mullan, which he described in his 1983 book called *Vital Signs*. Being hospitalized with a serious illness or injury produces enormous stress and anxiety.

Hospitalized people must cope with their emotions, and they tend to adjust gradually. For example, most surgical patients experience anxiety levels that are especially high when they are admitted, remain quite high prior to the operation, and then decline steadily during the week or two after surgery (Newman, 1984a). But sometimes the anxiety levels of patients increase with time, as happened with a 25-year-old man who had suffered serious burns over 30% of his body. After 3 weeks of hospitalization, he became increasingly difficult and demanding. Interviews revealed the reason: he had

> a very exaggerated view of the nature of his injury, expecting it would render him a cripple for life and unable to support himself or his family. He feared discharge and the subsequent demands of his family. (Steiner & Clark, 1977, p. 138)

How a patient adjusts to his or her health problem and treatment in the hospital depends on many factors, such as the person's age, gender, and perceived characteristics of the illness or injury (Moos, 1982). For instance, young adults often have more difficulty coping with serious illnesses than older individuals do. Also, men tend to be more distressed than women by illnesses that reduce their vigor and physical abilities, but women often have an especially difficult time adjusting to disfigurement, such as facial injuries or losing one of their breasts.

COPING PROCESSES IN HOSPITAL PATIENTS

How would you try to cope with the stress and anxiety of being hospitalized? Two broad ways were discussed in Chapter 5: altering the cause of the stress and regulating the emotional response to the situation. Some situations that produce stress in the hospital can be altered by the patient's taking action, such as by asking for medication to reduce pain or by reading information about his or her health problem. Because these actions can reduce the demands of the stressor or expand the person's resources for dealing with it, they are examples of *problem-focused coping*.

Patients in the hospital experience many stressors they believe they cannot change. In some cases these beliefs are correct, as when a person whose spinal cord was severed in an accident must cope with not being able to walk. But in other cases they are incorrect, as when a patient does not realize that it may be possible to use another medication if the current one produces discomfort or other side effects. People who believe they can do nothing to change a stressor usually try to cope with their emotions and the situation by using methods classified as *emotion-focused coping*. Patients may try to regulate their emotions by denying unpleasant facts, performing distracting activities, or seeking social support, for example. Research has consistently shown that social support aids people's recovery from and adjustment to illness (Kulik & Mahler, 1989; Wallston et al., 1983; Wills & Fegan, 2001).

Cognitive Processes in Coping

One cognitive process many patients engage in after becoming ill or injured is attributing *blame*—trying to answer the question, "Who's at fault for my condition?" They often grapple with this issue while in the hospital. Some people blame mainly themselves, others blame someone else, and others attribute their conditions to luck or God's will. Does the way people attribute blame affect their success in coping with their conditions? We might expect, for instance, that people who blame themselves would have intense feelings of guilt and self-recrimination and, therefore, have more difficulty adjusting to their conditions than those who blame someone else. On the other hand, blaming someone else may induce intense feelings of anger and bitterness, which would impair adjustment.

Research has found that both types of blame are related to poor adjustment. The more blame for a traumatic event that individuals attribute to themselves or other people, the poorer their adjustment tends to be (Downey, Silver, & Wortman, 1990). But poor adjustment seems to be more strongly related to blaming others than to self-blame (Bulman & Wortman, 1977; Kiecolt-Glaser & Williams, 1987; Taylor, Lichtman, & Wood, 1984). Although it is unclear why adjustment is so difficult when patients blame someone else, the reason may be that these people feel an added sense of injustice if the person they blame did not suffer severe consequences too. These feelings are reflected in such statements as, "I'm paralyzed, but the driver only broke his leg," or, "I can't walk now, but the guy who shot me is now walking free" (Bulman & Wortman, 1977, p. 360). One thing to keep in mind about the cognitive processes used in ascribing blame is that they can be quite convoluted or disturbed; a young man set himself on fire and blamed his act on his father-in-law's saying bad things about him (Kiecolt-Glaser & Williams, 1987). But keep in mind that because this research has been correlational, variations in both blame and adjustment may be caused by some other factor.

Another cognitive process that patients engage in involves the assessment of their personal control. Patients enter the hospital with the expectation of losing some degree of personal control, either from the effects of the illness itself or from being dependent on the actions of the medical staff. Hospital environments encourage patients to believe their involvement in the treatment process is irrelevant— that they are *helpless*. People who feel helpless are likely to behave like "good patients" (Taylor, 1979). Some patients enter the hospital feeling quite helpless right from the start, but others try to exert control and fail. Through repeated failures in exerting control, many people learn to be helpless in the hospital, eventually making no effort to initiate changes when control is actually possible. One study of patients found, for instance, that feelings of helplessness and depression increased with time in the hospital, even as their health improved (Raps et al., 1982).

The connections among "good patient" behavior, helplessness, and depression can be seen in the case of a 50-year-old divorced man who had suffered burns over 40% of his body. When he returned to the hospital 6 months later for a followup visit, his hands were still stiff, and he was having many psychological problems. He had moved in with his very supportive daughter and son-in-law

in hopes that he would be able to take care of repair work that needed doing around the house.

When it became clear that he was not able to do any of these things to his satisfaction, he became increasingly depressed. . . . On reviewing his case it turned out that he had indeed been a very "good" patient, quiet and cooperative. He never asked any questions about the details or the implications of his illness. (Steiner & Clark, 1977, p. 139)

This case is consistent with the view of some researchers that a "so-called 'good patient' is often actually in a state of helplessness" (Taylor, 1979, p. 171), which may eventually lead to feelings of depression. Patients' emotional adjustment has serious links to health: regardless of the severity of people's illness, they are more likely to die in the hospital if they are depressed than if they are not (Cavanaugh et al., 2001).

Helping Patients Cope

Suppose you were having surgery with *full anesthesia*. Would it make any difference to your recovery if *during surgery* someone said to you, "How quickly you recover from your operation depends on you," and gave suggestions of things you should do to speed recovery? Perhaps. An experiment found that anesthetized patients who received this kind of information recovered more quickly and had fewer complications than control patients who got no suggestions during their operations (Evans & Richardson, 1988). These results and those of other studies indicate that people hear and understand at least broad meanings while anesthetized, especially emotionally negative information, even though they cannot say what they heard (Bennett, 1989; Gidron et al., 2002). This is important for two reasons: (1) medical staff often make negative remarks during surgery, and (2) it may be possible to help surgical patients cope by giving them constructive suggestions while they are anesthetized.

An effective way to help hospitalized people cope is to provide psychological counseling during their stays. Walter Gruen (1975) gave brief counseling sessions to heart attack patients almost every day during the 3 weeks or so that they were in the hospital. Compared with a control group, the subjects who received the counseling spent fewer days in intensive care and in the hospital, had fewer heart complications and less psychological depression during their stays, and showed fewer signs of anxiety problems when contacted about 4 months after discharge.

A circumstance in the hospital that may help a patient adjust to his or her illness and impending treatment is sharing a room with a person who is recovering after having a similar medical procedure. James Kulik and Heike Mahler (1987a) conducted an experiment with male patients who were scheduled for coronary bypass surgery. Upon admission, each man was assigned a roommate, based on room availability, for the 2 days prior to surgery. About half of them shared rooms with men who were also awaiting operations, and the remaining patients shared rooms with men who had already had operations and were recovering. Assessments showed that compared to the men who had preoperative roommates, those with roommates who had already undergone surgery were far less anxious before their operation, engaged in much more physical activity after surgery, and were able to leave the hospital an average of 1.4 days sooner.

Why did the type of roommate affect patients' adjustment? The findings of two studies may provide an answer. First, when patients have multiple roommates, they spend more time talking to roommates with a similar surgery status and health problem than to other roommates (Moore, Kulik, & Mahler, 1998). Second, having presurgery patients share a room may increase the anxiety of both individuals by some form of "emotional contagion" (Kulik, Moore, & Mahler, 1993). Perhaps presurgery patients try to alleviate their anxiety by talking to a similar roommate, but the information they share makes things worse for both.

PREPARING PATIENTS FOR STRESSFUL MEDICAL PROCEDURES

Preparing people psychologically for surgery has important implications for their recovery: among patients with similar medical conditions, the more anxiety they feel before surgery, the more difficult their adjustment and recovery are likely to be after surgery. People with high preoperative anxiety tend to report more pain, use more medication for pain, stay in the hospital longer, and report more anxiety and depression during their recovery than patients with less preoperative fear (Anderson & Masur, 1983; Johnson, 1983). What can psychologists do to reduce the

stress people experience in conjunction with medical procedures?

Psychological Preparation for Surgery

Although several methods seem to be useful in helping people cope with impending surgery, the most effective of these approaches are those that enhance patients' sense of *control* over the situation or the recovery process (Anderson & Masur, 1983; Mathews & Ridgeway, 1984; Thompson, 1981). These approaches are generally designed to give the person one or more of the following types of control:

- *Behavioral control*—being able to reduce discomfort or promote recovery during or after the medical procedure by performing certain actions, such as special breathing or coughing exercises.
- *Cognitive control*—knowing how to focus on the benefits of the medical procedure and not its unpleasant aspects.
- *Informational control*—gaining knowledge about the events and/or sensations to expect during or after the medical procedure.

Patients can acquire the knowledge for these types of control in many ways, such as through discussion with practitioners, reading, listening to tape recordings, or watching film or video recordings.

An experiment demonstrated the utility of *cognitive control* with individuals who were in the hospital to undergo major *elective* surgeries and were assigned to groups on a random basis (Langer, Janis, & Wolfer, 1975). One of the groups received training in cognitive control that pointed out how paying attention to negative aspects of an experience increases stress and taught them to focus on the positive aspects of their impending surgery when feeling distressed by the surgical experience. A comparison group spent an equal amount of time with a psychologist, but they only engaged in general conversation about the hospital experience. The records and nurses' ratings on the surgical ward revealed important benefits of training in cognitive control: the patients who received this training showed greater reductions in preoperative stress behavior, less postoperative stress, and fewer requests for medication after surgery than the comparison subjects.

Several other studies have demonstrated beneficial effects of enhancing surgical patients' *informational* and *behavioral control* (Anderson, 1987; Andrew, 1970; Johnson et al., 1978; Johnston & Vögele, 1993). In one of these experiments, Erling Anderson randomly assigned to three groups 60 adult male cardiac patients who were scheduled for coronary bypass surgery. One group had a general conversation with the researcher and received the *standard preparation* of the hospital, in which the patient and a nurse discussed two pamphlets that outlined the procedures related to the upcoming surgery. A second group received the standard preparation plus training in *informational control* that gave procedural and sensory information in two ways. These men (1) watched a videotape of former bypass patients in interviews going through preoperative tests and exercises, preparation for surgery, recovery, and discharge; and (2) were given an audiotape, describing sensations they might experience, that they could play in their rooms. The third group received training in both *informational and behavioral control*. They had the same preoperative training as the informational control group but were also taught how to perform various behaviors, such as coughing exercises and ways to turn in bed, that they would need to do after the operation.

Anderson had the patients fill out a questionnaire to measure their distress at three times: when they were admitted, the evening before surgery, and 1 week later. As Figure 10–2 shows, the anxiety levels in the three groups were almost identical on admission but then diverged after the different preparation methods were conducted. Both types of psychological preparation reduced the patients' anxiety substantially before and after the operation. Assessments were also made of the subjects' use of pain medication and length of stay in the hospital, but the three groups did not differ on these measures. Finally, the patients' blood pressures were monitored closely because dangerous levels of acute hypertension occur very commonly during the first 12 hours following bypass surgery. For this critical measure, psychological preparation had a very beneficial effect. Of the patients who received the standard preparation, 75% developed acute hypertension and required medication to dilate their blood vessels. In contrast, only 45% of subjects in the informational control group and 40% of those in the informational and behavioral control group had episodes of acute hypertension.

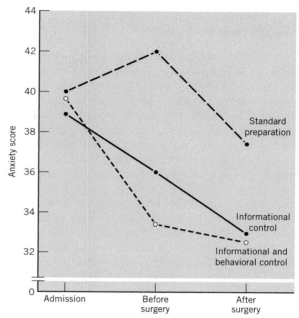

Figure 10–2 Anxiety levels of cardiac surgery patients as a function of the psychological preparation they received. Anxiety was measured by the State-Trait Anxiety Inventory at three times: on admission, the evening before surgery, and 1 week after the operation. (Adapted from Anderson, 1987, Figure 1.)

Similar benefits accrue with videotapes showing the hospital experiences of patients with comparable surgeries. For instance, men and women awaiting hip replacement who saw a videotape of a prior hip surgery patient subsequently showed less anxiety, lower serum cortisol levels, fewer instances of acute hypertension during the surgery, and less pain medication use than comparable patients without the videotape (Doering et al., 2000). Although psychological preparations that increase patients' sense of control when awaiting operations have obvious value, the materials and instructions must be clear and straightforward. Unclear information can lead to misconceptions and anxiety, producing more harm than good (Wallace, 1986). Patients may need to discuss the information with medical and psychological staff. Of course, surgery is only one of many types of stressful medical procedures that may occur in the hospital, and patients often dread experiencing each of them.

Psychological Preparations for Nonsurgical Procedures

How would you like to be awake while a physician inserts a thin, hollow tube called a *catheter* into one of your blood vessels, gently threads it toward your heart, and then injects dye through the catheter? This is a procedure called *cardiac catheterization*, which is used with people who show signs of cardiovascular disorders, such as damage to a major blood vessel or heart valve. The dye enables practitioners to see the damage with the aid of X-ray or other radiological devices. By using this procedure, physicians can determine whether to recommend other medical procedures, such as bypass or open-heart surgery. A patient undergoing cardiac catheterization receives tranquilizing medication and a local anesthetic for the area where the tube enters the body. This procedure is not painful, but can be unpleasant and produce strange and frightening sensations, such as "hot flashes" when dye is injected into the heart.

Preparing patients for unpleasant medical procedures helps reduce their anxiety and disruptive behavior during the procedures. Philip Kendall and his associates (1979) examined the effects of psychological preparation for cardiac catheterization on the anxiety experienced by male patients, about two-thirds of whom had undergone the procedure at least a year earlier. The men were randomly assigned to four groups. One group received training in *cognitive control* methods from a therapist, learning how to recognize signs of their own anxiety and ways to cope when these signs occur. Another group received preparation to enhance their *informational control*, learning about the procedures and sensations to expect through printed materials and discussions with therapists. Two other groups served as comparison (control) conditions. Analyses of the patients' self-reports and of hospital staff ratings showed that individuals who received the cognitive and the informational control preparations experienced less anxiety than those in the two comparison groups before and during catheterization.

As you may have surmised, the catheterization procedure requires that the patient be inactive. There are no actions the person can take to make the process occur more smoothly or pleasantly—that is, the patient has little or no behavioral control. This is true of many but not all aversive medical procedures.

One medical procedure in which patients can perform useful actions is called an *endoscopy*, which is used in diagnosing ulcers and other disorders of the digestive tract. The procedure's most aversive aspect is that a long, flexible, fiberoptic tube, almost half an inch in diameter, must be passed through the patient's mouth and down to the stomach and intestine. This tube remains in the digestive tract, transmitting images of the lining, for about 15 to 30 minutes. During this procedure, the person is awake but has received tranquilizing medication, and the throat has been swabbed with a local anesthetic. Preparing patients with informational control (describing endoscopy and sensations to expect) and behavioral control (teaching how to breathe and swallow during the procedure) methods reduces their emotional behavior and gagging during an endoscopy (Johnson & Leventhal, 1974).

In summary, psychological preparation benefits patients in surgical and nonsurgical medical procedures. Generally speaking, when these procedures offer little opportunity for the person to take helpful action, psychological preparation to promote informational and cognitive control may be especially effective. But when patients will undergo procedures in which they can take direct action to facilitate the process and reduce their own discomfort, preparation should usually include approaches to enhance behavioral control. (Go to 💡.)

Coping Styles and Psychological Preparation

People use many different styles in coping with stress, as we discussed in Chapter 5. When faced with stressful medical procedures, for instance, some individuals tend to cope by using *avoidance* strategies to minimize the impact of the situation. They may deny that a threat exists; refuse to seek or attend to threatening information, perhaps saying, "I don't want to know," or suppress unpleasant thoughts. In contrast, other individuals tend to use *attention* or "vigilant" strategies, seeking detailed information about the situation (Newman, 1984a). Studies have found that some patients who use avoidance strategies show better emotional adjustment to medical procedures, such as blood donation or dental surgery, than those who use attention strategies (Kaloupek, White, & Wong, 1984; Kiyak, Vitaliano, & Crinean, 1988). If this is so, how do people who use avoidance strategies

HIGHLIGHT

Lamaze Training as a Method of Psychological Preparation for a Medical Procedure

Some people believe that during childbirth the mother will experience intense and prolonged pain unless she is given tranquilizing and pain-reducing drugs and so the use of drugs is best for the mother and her baby. But these beliefs are questioned for two reasons. First, drugs given to the mother during childbirth pass through the placenta and can have unwanted effects, such as reducing oxygen flow to the fetus and impairing motor control in the newborn's first days (Feldman, 2000). Second, anthropologists have reported that women in cultures where childbirth is regarded as an easy and open process have shorter and less complicated labors than women in cultures where birth is regarded as fearful and private (Mead & Newton, 1967). Could it be that part of the difficulty many mothers have in childbirth is the result of the inadequate psychological preparation they receive?

Because of these considerations, many prospective parents opt for preparation involving "natural childbirth" methods, such as **Lamaze training.** Natural childbirth methods generally involve three components: preparation, participation, and minimal medication (Parfitt, 1977). Birth is essentially a process in which the muscles of the uterus contract in a rhythmical pattern to push the baby out. A fearful woman is likely to tighten her muscles, which then act against the natural muscular contractions and make labor more painful. A main purpose of natural childbirth methods is to prepare the woman to be more relaxed and better able to control her breathing and muscular activity to help in the process at each stage. In addition to the social support women in

Lamaze training get from the baby's father and the people in the training meetings, the method appears to enhance the mother's sense of control (Wideman & Singer, 1984). Lamaze training includes features that promote

- *Informational control*, such as by providing descriptions of the physiological processes in birth and the procedures and sensations to expect during labor and delivery.
- *Behavioral control*, for example, through instruction and practice in muscle relaxation and special breathing techniques.
- *Cognitive control*, such as by teaching the woman to stare at an object in the room or to concentrate on images or phrases during the childbirth process.

American hospitals generally cooperate with the procedures the method describes, such as having the father present.

Is Lamaze preparation beneficial? Although the results of studies suggest that it is, the evidence is not yet very clear (Feldman, 2000; Wideman & Singer, 1984). Women who receive Lamaze training use less painkilling medication during delivery and are less anxious about the birth procedure than those who do not; but these studies have used quasi-experimental designs and self-report methods. Part of the difficulty in interpreting these findings is that women who choose natural childbirth are different from those who do not—for example, they tend to be from higher social classes and report lower anxiety levels even before receiving the training.

react to psychological preparations to enhance their control?

Researchers have examined this question by using approaches to enhance informational control with patients who were classified as using avoidance or attention styles. Suzanne Miller and Charles Mangan (1983) conducted one of these studies with women who were scheduled to undergo an unpleasant but painless diagnostic test for gynecological

cancer. By random assignment, half of the avoidance subjects (called "blunters") and the attention subjects ("monitors") received extensive information regarding the procedures and sensations they would experience during the examination; the remaining women got very little information about the examination. Measures of the patients' distress were taken at three times: before receiving the information, after getting the information but before the examination, and after

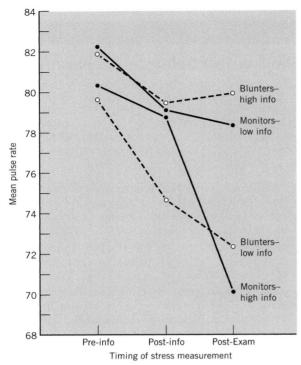

Figure 10–3 Effects of extensive information versus little information regarding an impending medical examination on the stress experienced by patients who use avoidance coping strategies (the "blunters") or attention strategies (the "monitors"). Pulse rate, the measure of stress, was taken for each subject at three times: before receiving the information, after the information, and after the examination. High pulse rate indicates more distress. (From Miller & Mangan, 1983, Figure 7.)

the examination. Figure 10–3 presents the results of this research, using the women's pulse rates as the measure of distress. These findings indicate that monitors who receive very little information and blunters who receive extensive information react negatively to the amount of information they receive, as shown by their continued high pulse rates after the examination.

Other research has confirmed these findings and shown that psychological preparation for medical procedures is most effective when its content is matched to the needs of the person (Carpenter, Gatchel, & Hasegawa, 1994; Litt, Nye, & Shafer, 1995; Ludwick-Rosenthal & Neufeld, 1993). In addition, the number of times people see the information seems to affect the amount of stress they experience. In one

study, patients awaiting endoscopic examinations filled out a questionnaire that assessed their coping styles and then watched a videotape that showed the procedures and sensations they could expect during their own endoscopies (Shipley et al., 1978). Some subjects watched the informational tape only once, and others viewed it three times. A comparison group watched an irrelevant tape. Measures of the patients' anxiety during their endoscopies included heart rate and questionnaire assessments by the patients and practitioners after the examinations. The study found that *avoidance copers* who saw the informational tape only once experienced more anxiety than those who saw it three times and those who watched the irrelevant tape. Of the *attention copers*, those who watched the irrelevant tape experienced the most anxiety, and those who viewed the informational tape three times had the least anxiety.

The benefits of psychological preparations for medical procedures seem to depend on the patients' coping styles, and it may be that different preparations are more helpful for people using avoidance strategies than for those using attention strategies. Although being exposed to information about impending medical procedures more than once appears to help all patients, it may be particularly beneficial to those who tend to cope by using avoidance strategies.

WHEN THE HOSPITALIZED PATIENT IS A CHILD

Over 2½ million individuals who are admitted to short-stay hospitals in the United States each year are under 15 years of age, and most of these children are under 5 (USBC, 2003). We have seen that adults become distressed by pain and illness, think hospitals are big and frightening places, and become anxious when undergoing unpleasant or painful medical procedures. So do children, but their level of psychosocial development may make some aspects of the hospital experience particularly difficult for them. For one thing, children are less able than adults to influence and understand what is happening to them. Children at young ages may also feel abandoned or unloved by being without their families, and some may believe that they were put in the hospital as punishment for misbehavior. What special adjustments do hospitalized children need to make, and how well do they cope? Answers to these questions depend partly on the child's age.

Hospitalization in the Early Years of Childhood

The experience of being hospitalized is distressing for children of all ages, but the reasons for their distress tend to change as they get older (La Greca & Stone, 1985; Sarafino, 1986). For children in toddlerhood and the preschool years—who are rarely inactive when healthy—a hospital stay that involves being immobilized can be very stressful. These children may protest loudly and struggle against medically necessary devices that restrain their movement (Smith & Autman, 1985). But the most salient source of stress of young children in the hospital is being separated from their parents.

Separation distress is the normal reaction of being upset and crying that young children exhibit when they are separated from their parents, particularly in unfamiliar surroundings (Ainsworth, 1973, 1979). Late in the first year of life, most infants begin showing this reaction, even in everyday short separations of a few minutes or hours. As Figure 10–4 illustrates, the tendency of children to show distress in situations of short-term separation peaks at

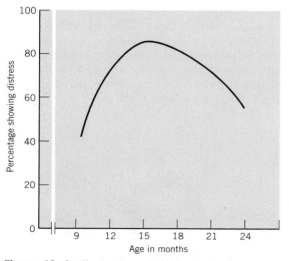

Figure 10–4 Illustration of children's tendency to exhibit separation distress when tested with short-term separations at different ages. (From Sarafino & Armstrong, 1986, Figure 5.3.) The graph represents approximate percentages at each age, averaged across cultures—for example, the reaction occurs in about 90% of American working-class infants and 70 to 80% of Guatemalan babies at 15 months (Super, 1981).

roughly 15 months of age. This is true of children from a wide variety of cultures around the world. After that age, the percentage of children showing distress with short-term separations declines universally (Super, 1981). Being hospitalized can involve prolonged periods of separation, with little parent–child contact for days, weeks, or longer. How well do toddlers and preschool-age children cope with long-term separation? Prolonged separation produces dramatic and, perhaps, long-lasting reactions in young children: it may begin with intense crying, calling, and searching for his or her parents, typically the mother, followed by behaviors suggesting *despair*—reduced activity, withdrawal, and apparent hopelessness (Bowlby, 1969, 1973).

After a prolonged or difficult stay in the hospital, young children often display anxious behavior at home. They may begin having nightmares or become very clinging and unwilling to let their mothers out of their sight. One child named Sara, for instance, had attended nursery school and was becoming quite independent for her age before having a difficult hospital experience that included receiving 22 injections in just 2 days. After she returned home, she was highly anxious. Her mother reported:

> She follows me everywhere! I can't even go to the bathroom alone. She wakes up screaming five or six times at night, shaking and crying, "The nurses are giving me shots! I can't run away! They're tying me down". . . and when I approach her, she backs away and shakes like a hurt puppy! (Ramsey, 1982, p. 332)

Sara's hospital experience was very traumatic. Subsequently, she seemed to be afraid that if she were separated from her mother, she would again be left alone and unprotected.

Preschoolers do not yet think very logically and, as a result, may have many misconceptions about their health problems and why things happen in the hospital (Eiser, 1985; Ramsey, 1982; Smith & Autman, 1985). They may, for example, believe their illnesses or the treatments they receive are punishments for having been bad. Perhaps these ideas come from adults saying, for instance, "You'll catch cold if you don't wear your coat" or "You'll get an upset stomach if you eat too much candy." Some adults even threaten children with going to the doctor or having an operation if they continue to disobey (Eiser, 1985).

In the hospital, young children may become worried when they see other patients with disfigurements, such as an amputation or extensive scars, and think one of these conditions may happen to themselves in the hospital.

Hospitalized School-Age Children

Advances in school-age children's psychosocial development enable them to cope with some aspects of hospitalization better than younger patients can. For instance, although prolonged separation from their parents can be difficult for older children, they usually tolerate it more easily than preschoolers can. The cognitive ability of school-age children progresses rapidly, but they sometimes retain earlier misconceptions about their illnesses or develop new ones. An older child's incorrect ideas can be seen in a nursing student's report about a 10-year-old hemophiliac patient:

> When I asked him what happened when he bled, he said, "Oh . . . there's a hemophiliac bug eating his way in and out of my blood vessels, and that's what makes me bleed." And when asked what caused his disease, he answered, "Well, it's 'cause I ate too much candy after my mom told me not to." (Ramsey, 1982, pp. 335–336).

Clearly, the idea that illness is a punishment can continue long after early childhood.

Four aspects of hospitalization seem to become increasingly difficult for children as they get older (Ramsey, 1982; Smith & Autman, 1985). One aspect involves feelings of personal control. As children get older and their greater cognitive and social abilities strengthen their sense of control, the limited independence and influence they experience in the hospital may become very irritating and distressing. Second, school-age children's increased cognitive abilities allow them to think about and worry about the outcomes of their illness or treatment, such as whether they will be physically harmed or even die. Third, being away from friends and schoolmates can lead to feelings of loneliness, boredom, and concern about losing friends or status in their social groups. Fourth, as children get older—particularly when they are entering puberty—they tend to become more embarrassed by exposing their bodies to strangers or needing help with "private" activities, such as toileting.

Studies conducted in industrialized nations in the 1950s revealed that most children who were hospitalized were very poorly prepared for the experience (Eiser, 1985). Most children were either told nothing about why they were there, or received only vague reasons, or learned why by overhearing others' conversations. This situation has changed since then, and children today are much better prepared for stays in the hospital. A survey in the United States, for example, found that the large majority of hospitals in the late 1990s provided the kinds of preparation we have described for children who will undergo surgery or other major procedures (O'Byrne, Peterson, & Saldana, 1997). (Go to 🧠.)

Helping Children Cope with Being Hospitalized

Many children suffer long-term fears from being hospitalized, particularly if they are relatively young, had more severe illnesses, and underwent more invasive procedures (Rennick et al., 2002). How can hospitals help? When a child is admitted to the hospital, one or both parents (or another very familiar adult) should accompany and remain with the child at least until he or she is settled into the room. Many parents stay much longer, taking advantage of opportunities hospitals provide today for a parent to "room-in" with the child, especially when the patient is very young or very seriously ill (Olivet, 1982). American pediatric hospitals typically have rooming-in options (Melamed & Bush, 1985).

Medical procedures and equipment are often very frightening to young children.

CLINICAL METHODS AND ISSUES

Preparing Children for Impending Hospitalization

Ideally, psychological preparation should begin before the child enters the hospital, if at all possible. Research has shown that children cope better with medical procedures if their parents give them information about their illnesses and treatment and try to allay their fears than if the parents do not (Melamed & Bush, 1985). Hospitals can initiate this process by discussing it with the parents and providing materials and services. Medical and psychological staff can inform parents about several ways to help their child cope with an impending hospital stay (Sarafino, 1986). Parents can:

• Explain the reason for the stay and what it will be like.

• Give the child opportunities to ask questions, answering them carefully and in a way he or she can understand.

• Read with the child a children's book that describes a child's hospital experience.

• Take the child to the hospital and explain some of the hospital routines, such as what to do about going to the bathroom and how he or she will be awakened in the morning and have breakfast in bed.

• Describe when the parents will be with the child.

• Maintain a calm and confident manner, thereby conveying the message that there is no need to be very frightened.

Parents should try not to appear agitated and anxious about the child's medical treatment because they can transmit their fear. Children of outwardly anxious parents do not cope as well with medical procedures as those with parents who are relatively calm (Bush et al., 1986; Melamed & Bush, 1985).

What kinds of psychological preparation can hospitals provide for children? American hospitals use several approaches (O'Byrne, Peterson, & Saldana, 1997). Printed leaflets, narrative presentations, and tours describing hospital routines and medical procedures are among the most commonly used methods. Another method involves using puppets in a play activity to demonstrate medical procedures, such as inducing anesthesia or taking an X ray. This approach may be especially appropriate for preschoolers and younger school age children. Two other commonly used approaches involve training in coping skills and relaxation, using methods like those we examined in Chapter 5.

One last approach hospitals often use with children involves a video or film presentation. This method was evaluated in an experiment by Barbara Melamed and Lawrence Siegel (1975) with 4- to 12-year-old children who were in the hospital for elective surgery, such as for hernias or tonsillectomies. The children were assigned to two groups, matching for age, sex, race, and type of operation. One group saw a film that was relevant to having surgery, and the other group saw a film about a boy who goes on a nature trip in the country. The relevant film, entitled *Ethan Has an Operation*, portrays the hospital experience of a 7-year-old boy,

> showing various events that most children encounter when hospitalized for elective surgery from the time of admission to time of discharge including the child's orientation to the hospital ward and medical personnel such as the surgeon and anesthesiologist; having a blood test and exposure to standard hospital equipment; separation from the mother, and scenes in the operating and recovery rooms. In addition to explanations of the hospital procedures provided by the medical staff, various scenes are narrated by the child, who describes his feelings and concerns. (Melamed & Siegel, 1975, p. 514)

Although Ethan exhibits visible apprehension initially, he overcomes his fear and has the operation without serious distress.

The researchers assessed the emotional adjustment of the children in the two groups the evening before surgery and at a followup visit about 3 weeks after the operation with three types of measures: the children's hand sweating, questionnaire self-reports of fear, and ratings of their emotional behavior by trained observers. The results with all three measures revealed that the children who saw the film about Ethan's operation experienced less anxiety before and after surgery than those who saw the irrelevant film. Several studies have found similar benefits in reducing children's medical fears with video presentations (Eiser, 1985; Miller & Green, 1984). What's more, video preparations for surgery are cost-effective: a study of children in the hospital for elective surgery found that those who received video preparation recovered more quickly than those who did not. The savings from being released from the hospital sooner amounted to several times the cost of providing the preparation (Pinto & Hollandsworth, 1989).

Although most children benefit from information about impending medical procedures presented by any of the methods we have considered, not all children do—and some are actually made *more* anxious by the preparation. Studies have shown that the effects of the preparation depend on its timing and on the child's age, coping style, and previous medical experience (Dahlquist et al., 1986; Melamed & Bush, 1985; Melamed, Dearborn, & Hermecz, 1983; Miller & Green, 1984). More specifically, children younger than age 7 or so seem to profit from information presented shortly before the medical procedure, whereas older children are more likely to benefit from information presented several days before. In addition, young children more so than older ones may be made more anxious by information if they have had prior difficult experiences with medical procedures. Also, some evidence indicates that children who tend to use avoidance strategies to cope with stressful events probably derive less benefit from information about medical procedures than those who use attention strategies.

Hospitals and medical workers usually try to make a child's stay as pleasant as they can. Pediatric nurses, for instance, receive training in the special needs of children and ways to introduce tests and equipment in a nonthreatening manner (Ramsey, 1982). When preparing to take the child's blood pressure with a sphygmomanometer, for example, the nurse might demonstrate its use on someone else and say, "When I squeeze this ball, the thing on the arm just becomes tight, like a belt. It doesn't hurt—it

just gets tight. . . . Now when I'm done, I make it get loose and take it off." Often when a young child undergoes stressful procedures, such as drawing blood, a parent is present. Although most techniques parents use to help reduce the child's distress don't work very well, one that does involves distracting attention from the procedure—for instance, by saying, "Look at this nice picture" (Manne et al., 1992, 1994). Hospital pediatric wards also arrange for children to play together when possible and try to have entertainment, such as a clown show, for their patients. For most hospitalized children who have positive health outcomes today, the stress of their hospital experience tends to be temporary and does not seem to produce serious long-term emotional problems (La Greca & Stone, 1985).

People of all ages can have difficulty coping with hospitalization and medical procedures. Psychological interventions can help promote positive emotional adjustment among patients and reduce the psychological problems that may be associated with their medical conditions.

HOW HEALTH PSYCHOLOGISTS ASSIST HOSPITALIZED PATIENTS

Some patients in hospitals have illnesses that result partly from psychosocial factors, such as Type A behavior or alcohol abuse, and some individuals develop psychosocial problems because of their illnesses, hospitalizations, or treatment regimens. In the former case, health psychologists are interested in correcting the factors that produced the disease to help these patients recover and prevent recurrences of their illnesses. In the latter case, health psychologists try to help clients cope with their illnesses, treatment regimens, possible disabilities or deformities, and, for terminal conditions, with impending death.

The potential importance of the help psychologists provide can be seen in research findings on psychological characteristics among people with cardiovascular disease. Depression is an important characteristic: compared with people who are not depressed, those who are very depressed show slower recovery and are much more likely to develop subsequent cardiac problems (Carney et al., 1988; Tennen, Eberhardt, & Affleck, 1999). Pessimism is also important: compared with optimistic people, coronary bypass patients who have a very pessimistic outlook are more likely to be hospitalized again for coronary problems in subsequent months (Scheier et al., 1999).

The number of psychologists working in hospitals in the United States and their role in treatment programs for patients have expanded greatly since the 1970s (APA, 1998; Enright et al., 1990; Sweet, 1991). Psychologists

- Consult with patients' specialists, such as cardiologists, neurologists, and pediatricians, to provide diagnostic and counseling services.

- Assess clients' needs for and provide psychological preparation to cope with surgery and other stressful procedures.

- Help patients adhere to medication and treatment regimens in the hospital.

- Provide behavioral programs for improving clients' self-care skills and compliance with medical and lifestyle regimens after discharge.

- Assist in rehabilitation processes, such as by promoting adherence to physical therapy, helping family members adjust to a patient's condition, and helping clients decide on new careers, if needed.

Let's look at how health psychologists assist patients, beginning with determining who needs and wants help.

INITIAL STEPS IN HELPING

Patients who need psychological help generally don't request it themselves—the request usually comes from a physician or nurse who has noticed signs of a psychological, social, or intellectual problem (Huszti & Walker, 1991). This is not an ideal situation, for most medical staff are not trained to identify signs of distress or behavioral problems. A study found that physicians are not very good at recognizing emotional problems in their clients—they tend to judge that such problems exist if they think the patient has a severe medical illness and is dissatisfied with the present treatment (Jones, Mabe, & Riley, 1989). A brief training seminar does not improve their judgments (Deshields et al., 1995).

After the psychologist receives the request to see a patient, he or she then consults the person who made the request and reviews the client's medical record. The next step is to interview the patient and/or relevant family members to arrive at an impression of what the problem is and its history and status (Sweet, 1991). Sometimes the resulting impression is sufficient for the psychologist to decide how to help, but frequently more information is needed and can be obtained by administering psychological tests.

TESTS FOR PSYCHOLOGICAL ASSESSMENT OF MEDICAL PATIENTS

Psychologists have developed hundreds of instruments to assess a wide variety of psychological characteristics of people. The tests the psychologist administers depend on the type of illness or problem the client seems to have (Derogatis et al., 1995; Sweet, 1991). For example, patients with serious head injuries and behavioral signs of neurological problems are especially likely to be assessed with tests of intelligence, academic skills, and specific perceptual and motor functions. Clients who will need to change existing or planned careers may be tested for vocational interests and abilities. Some of the most widely used instruments with hospital patients assess their psychosocial needs and problems (Piotrowski & Lubin, 1990). We will describe a few of these instruments.

The Minnesota Multiphasic Personality Inventory

One approach psychological tests use for assessing the needs and problems of individuals is to ask them questions about themselves to reveal aspects of their personalities. The most widely used personality test is the **Minnesota Multiphasic Personality Inventory** (MMPI), which was developed in the 1930s and updated in the 1980s as the MMPI-2 (Butcher et al., 1989; Davison, Neale, & Kring, 2004). This test has the person respond in a true–false format to about 500 statements, such as, "I would rather win than lose a game" and "I am worried about sex matters." The items in the test cover a great variety of topics.

Although the MMPI was developed to characterize the personalities that underlie or correspond with specific psychiatric disorders, portions of the test can supply important information about the emotional adjustment of medical patients. The instrument contains ten scales, each of which assesses features of psychiatric conditions and personality traits. Three of these scales are especially relevant toward providing psychological help for medical patients. These scales are:

- *Hypochondriasis*, which assesses people's preoccupation with and complaints about their physical health.
- *Depression*, which measures people's feelings of unhappiness, pessimism, and hopelessness.
- *Hysteria*, which assesses people's tendency to cope with problems by using avoidance strategies and developing physical symptoms.

The scores individuals obtain on these scales can suggest significant issues for the therapist to explore further. For one thing, individuals who score high on these three scales are prone to developing psychophysiological disorders, such as ulcers and chronic headaches (Gilberstadt & Duker, 1965). Also, patients with serious illnesses, such as cancer or heart disease, may fail to comply with their treatment regimens because of intense feelings of depression, which might be revealed by their scores on the depression scale of the MMPI (Green, 1985).

The MMPI can be usefully applied in psychological treatment in medical settings, but it has two important drawbacks: it takes about $1\frac{1}{2}$ hours to complete, and it measures many traits that are not pertinent to the treatment of most medical patients.

Specialized Tests for Medical Patients

In recent years, psychologists have developed new tests that are specifically designed to assess psychological characteristics associated with physical illness. These tests include measures of people's stress and Type A and Type B behavior patterns—two characteristics that are associated with heart disease, for instance. As we saw in Chapter 5, psychological methods can be applied effectively to reduce people's stress and modify their Type A behavior, thereby lowering their risk of heart attack. We turn now to a discussion of other psychological tests that were designed specifically for medical populations.

The **Millon Behavioral Medicine Diagnostic** (MBMD) is a self-report test that was developed to assess specific psychosocial factors and decision-making issues that are known to be relevant for medical patients (Pearson Assessments, 2004). It consists of 165 items that provide information regarding several factors, such as the client's coping style, negative health habits, and stress moderators. The MBMD also attempts to assess the client's reaction to his or her illness and predict difficulties with the treatment regimen. Although the MBMD is being used in medical settings, such as in pain treatment centers and cancer units, and it should prove to be a valuable tool, more research is needed to establish its utility.

The **Psychosocial Adjustment to Illness Scale** (PAIS) is another psychological test designed specifically for use with medical patients (Derogatis, 1977, 1986). The PAIS consists of just 46 items, and the person responds to each item on a 4-point scale, such as "not at all," "mildly," "moderately," or "markedly." This test is available in two forms—one that patients can fill out on their own and one that is administered by an interviewer. It was designed to assess seven psychosocial characteristics of the client's life, each of which has been associated with adjustment to medical illness. Table 10.1 outlines these characteristics. The results of several studies appear to confirm the ability of the PAIS to measure adjustment problems accurately in patients with a variety of serious illnesses, such as kidney disease, hypertension, and cancer (Derogatis, 1986).

Table 10.1   *Patients' Psychosocial Characteristics Assessed by the Psychosocial Adjustment to Illness Scale* (PAIS)

- *Health care orientation*—the nature of the patient's attitudes about health care in general, views regarding health care professionals, and expectancies about his or her health problem and its treatment.
- *Vocational environment*—the impact of the health problem on such issues as the person's vocational performance and satisfaction.
- *Domestic environment*—difficulties the health problem will present for the client and his or her family in the home environment.
- *Sexual relationships*—modifications in sexual activity as a result of the health problem.
- *Extended family relationships*—disruptions in relationships between the patient and family members outside of his or her immediate family.
- *Social environment*—the impact of the health problem on the client's socializing and leisure-time activities.
- *Psychological distress*—the effect of the health problem on such factors as the patient's self-esteem and feelings of depression, anxiety, and hostility.

In summary, psychologists have developed instruments specifically for the purpose of assessing the psychological needs and problems of medical patients. These tests offer considerable promise for aiding health psychologists and other health care workers in promoting the health and adjustment of their patients.

PROMOTING PATIENTS' HEALTH AND ADJUSTMENT

Once health psychologists determine the nature and extent of the client's difficulty, they decide which specific therapeutic techniques should be applied to address it. As we have seen in previous chapters and will see ahead, behavioral and cognitive methods have been applied with some success—sometimes with great success—in many primary, secondary, and tertiary prevention efforts. These techniques are useful in helping people improve their eating and exercise habits, stop smoking and curb their drinking, and reduce the stress and other negative emotional states they experience (Parker, 1995; Sarafino, 2001; Turk & Salovey, 1995).

Many hospitalized people develop severe psychosocial problems, particularly if their illnesses or injuries continue to be life threatening or leave them disfigured or handicapped. These individuals and their families often need help to overcome feelings of depression and counseling to anticipate and plan for the difficulties they are likely to experience. Several psychological approaches are helpful in dealing with patients' psychosocial problems. These approaches often involve group-discussion and cognitive-behavioral therapy to identify, examine, and replace negative thought patterns with more constructive ones (Davison, Neale, & Kring, 2004; Turk & Salovey, 1995).

The approaches health psychologists currently use in promoting patients' health and adjustment sometimes have important limitations, particularly in their continued effectiveness over long periods of time and in preventing relapse, such as in health-related lifestyle changes. Health psychologists are working to enhance their effectiveness in helping clients by improving the techniques they use, but they must also continue to develop stronger relationships with medical professionals, such as by expanding their knowledge of the language and rules of hospital settings (Huszti & Walker, 1991). More and more, medical and psychological staff are working together to improve these relationships for the benefit of their patients.

SUMMARY

The huge hospitals of today evolved from institutions in Europe that were established to give help to people with various needs—the sick, the poor, orphans, and even travelers who needed lodging. Well-to-do individuals received better care at home. In the early 20th century, hospitals gained a much better reputation and began to attract patients from all social classes.

The hospital medical staff has a typical hierarchy of authority with physicians at the top, followed by nurses and various allied health workers. The specialization and variety of hospital personnel can lead to fragmented health care. Good communication among hospital personnel not only improves the treatment patients receive but can help protect patients from potential hazards in the hospital, such as from nosocomial infection. The system of payment for medical care in the United States led to decreases in hospital admissions and the length of time patients stay there.

Being hospitalized is unpleasant to patients because of the disruptions it produces in their lifestyles, the high degree of dependency they have on others, the experience of aversive medical procedures, and the many worries they have about their conditions, treatment, and futures. Sometimes the treatment people receive is characterized by depersonalization. Working in emotionally charged situations with heavy workloads can lead to burnout among health care professionals, especially those who spend almost all of their time providing direct care to clients.

Some patients enter the hospital with the idea that the sick role involves being passive. These people are generally described by hospital staff as "good patients," being relatively cooperative, uncomplaining, and stoical. Other clients believe they should be more active in their sick-role behavior. Some of these people are described as "problem patients," showing little cooperation, voicing many complaints, and being very dependent and emotional. When problem patients are very seriously ill, their difficult behavior is usually understandable to the medical staff. But other problem patients take up more time and attention than their conditions seem to warrant, and may display angry reactance behavior in response to having their freedoms or control curtailed.

Patients engage in problem-focused and emotion-focused coping techniques to adjust to the stress and anxiety that they experience in the hospital. Some of their anxiety stems from their impending surgery and other medical procedures, such as cardiac catheterization and endoscopy. High levels of anxiety before surgery impair people's physical recovery after the operation. Reducing the anxiety connected with medical procedures can be accomplished through methods of psychological preparation that provide clients with behavioral, cognitive, and informational control. Lamaze training for childbirth seems to provide these kinds of preparation.

Although most patients benefit from methods of psychological preparation that enhance control, some benefit more than others. One factor that seems to affect the success of these methods is whether the patient's coping style tends toward avoidance rather than attention strategies. Children's separation distress in the hospital can be reduced if parents visit often or room in. Children can also benefit from psychological preparation for medical procedures, but the success of providing children with information depends on its timing and on their ages, coping styles, and previous medical experience.

The role of psychologists in the overall treatment effort for hospitalized people has increased in recent years, particularly in preparing clients for surgery and other medical procedures, helping them adjust to their medical conditions, and enhancing their adherence to treatment regimens after discharge. To identify the needs and problems of patients, psychologists administer tests, such as the Minnesota Multiphasic Personality Inventory, and instruments developed specifically for use with medical clients, such as the Millon Behavioral Medicine Diagnostic and the Psychosocial Adjustment to Illness Scale.

KEY TERMS

nosocomial infection	Lamaze training	Millon Behavioral Medi-	Psychosocial Adjustment
depersonalization	separation distress	cine Diagnostic	to Illness Scale
burnout	Minnesota Multiphasic		
reactance	Personality Inventory		

11

THE NATURE AND SYMPTOMS OF PAIN

What Is Pain?
The Qualities and Dimensions of Pain
Perceiving Pain

Theories of Pain
Early Theories of Pain
The Gate-Control Theory of Pain

Biopsychosocial Aspects of Pain
Neurochemical Transmission and Inhibition of Pain
Personal and Social Experiences and Pain
Emotions, Coping Processes, and Pain

Assessing People's Pain
Self-Report Methods
Behavioral Assessment Approaches
Psychophysiological Measures

Pain in Children
Pain and Children's Sensory and Cognitive
    Development
Assessing Pain in Children

PROLOGUE

"Wouldn't it be wonderful never to experience pain," many people have thought when they or others they have known were suffering. Pain hurts, and people typically dislike it and try to avoid it. But being able to sense pain is critical to our survival—without it, how would we know when we are injured? We could have a sprained ankle or an ulcer, for instance, without realizing it, and not seek treatment. And how would we know we are about to be injured, such as when we approach a hot flame without seeing it? Pain serves as a signal to take protective action.

Are there people who do not feel pain? Yes—several disorders can reduce or eliminate the ability to sense pain. People with a condition called *congenital insensitivity to pain*, which is present from birth, may report only a "tingling" or "itching" sensation when seriously injured. A young woman with this disorder seemed normal in every way, except that she had never felt pain. As a child she had bitten off the tip of her tongue while chewing food, and had suffered third-degree burns after kneeling on a hot radiator to look out of a window. When examined by a psychologist . . . in the laboratory, she reported . . . no pain when parts of her body were subjected to strong electric shock, to hot water at temperatures that usually produce reports of burning pain, or to a prolonged ice-bath. Equally astonishing was the fact that she showed no changes in blood pressure, heart rate, or respiration when these stimuli were presented. Furthermore, she could not remember ever sneezing or coughing, the gag reflex could be elicited only with great difficulty, and the cornea reflexes (to protect the eyes) were absent. (Melzack, quoted in Bakal, 1979, p. 141)

This disorder contributed to her death at the age of 29. People with congenital insensitivity to pain often die young because injuries or illnesses, such as acute appendicitis, go unnoticed (Chapman, 1984; Manfredi et al., 1981).

Health psychologists study pain because it influences whether individuals seek and comply with medical treatment and because being in pain can be very distressing, particularly when it is intense or enduring. In this chapter, we examine the nature and symptoms of pain, and the effects it has on its victims when it is severe. As we consider these topics, you will find answers to questions you may have about pain. What is pain, and what is the physical basis for it? Can people feel pain when there is no underlying physical disorder? Do psychosocial factors affect our experience of pain? Since pain is a subjective experience, how do psychologists assess how much pain a person feels?

WHAT IS PAIN?

Pain is the sensory and emotional experience of discomfort, which is usually associated with actual or threatened tissue damage or irritation (AMA, 2003). Virtually all people experience pain, and at all ages—from the pains of birth for mother and baby, to those of colic and teething in infancy, to those of injury and illness in childhood and adulthood. Some pain becomes chronic, as with arthritis, problems of the lower back, migraine headache, or cancer.

People's experience with pain is important for several reasons. For one thing, no medical complaint is more common than pain. According to researcher Paul Karoly, pain is the "most pervasive symptom in medical practice, the most frequently stated 'cause' of disability, and the single most compelling force underlying an individual's choice to seek or avoid medical care" (1985, p. 461). As we saw in Chapter 9, people are more likely to seek medical treatment without delay if they feel pain. Also, severe and prolonged

pain can come to dominate the lives of its victims, impairing their general functioning, ability to work, social relationships, and emotional adjustment. Finally, pain has enormous social and economic effects on all societies of the world. In the United States in any given year, a third or more people suffer from one or more continuous or recurrent painful conditions that require medical care, and tens of millions of these people are partially or completely disabled by their conditions (Turk, 2001; Von Korff, Dworkin, & Le Resche, 1990). Americans spend tens of billions of dollars each year on pain-related expenses, such as for treatment, loss of income, disability payments, and litigation.

THE QUALITIES AND DIMENSIONS OF PAIN

Our sensations of pain can be quite varied and have many different qualities. We might describe some pains as "sharp" and others as "dull," for example—and sharp pains can have either a stabbing or pricking feel. Some pains involve a burning sensation, and others have a cramping, itching, or aching feel. And some pains are throbbing, or constant, or shooting, or pervasive, or localized. Often the feelings we experience depend on the kinds of irritation or damage that has occurred and the location. For instance, when damage occurs deep within the body, individuals usually report feeling a "dull" or "aching" pain; but damage produced by a brief noxious event to the skin is often described as "sharp" (McClintic, 1985; Schiffman, 1996).

The painful conditions people experience also differ in how the pain originates and how long it lasts. We will consider two dimensions that describe these differences, beginning with the degree to which the origin of the pain can be traced to tissue damage.

Organic Versus Psychogenic Pain

People who suffer physical injuries, such as a serious burn, experience pain that is clearly linked to tissue damage. When discomfort is mainly from tissue damage, it is described as *organic pain*. For other pains, no tissue damage appears to exist—at least, medical examinations fail to find an organic basis. The discomfort involved in these pains seems to result primarily from psychological processes. For this reason, this type of discomfort is described as *psychogenic pain.* I once witnessed an extreme example of psychogenic pain in a schizophrenic man; he claimed—and *really* looked like—he was "feeling" stings from being "shot by enemy agents with ray guns."

Not long ago, researchers considered organic and psychogenic pain to be separate entities, with psychogenic pain not involving "real" sensations. As pain researcher Donald Bakal has noted, a practitioner's reference to pain as "psychogenic"

> was taken to mean "due to psychological causes," which implied that the patient was "imagining" his pain or that it was not really pain simply because an organic basis could not be found. Psychogenic pain is not experienced differently, however, from that arising from physical disease or injury. Psychogenic and organic pain both hurt. (1979, p. 167)

Researchers now recognize that virtually all pain experiences involve an interplay of both physiological and psychological factors. As a result, the dimension of pain involving organic and psychogenic causes is viewed as a continuum rather than a dichotomy. Different pain experiences simply involve different mixtures of organic and psychogenic factors. A mixture of these factors seems clear in the findings that many people with tissue damage experience little or no pain, others without damage report severe pain, and the role of psychological factors in people's pain increases when the condition is long lasting (Turk, 2001). When

people experience chronic pain with no detectable physical basis, psychiatrists diagnose the condition as a *pain disorder* (classified within *somatoform disorders*) and often assume the origin is mainly psychogenic (Davison, Neale, & Kring, 2004). Keep in mind, however, that failing to find a physical basis for someone's pain does not necessarily mean there is none. Unfortunately, many health care workers still think pain that has no demonstrated physical basis is purely psychogenic, and their patients struggle to prove that "the pain isn't just in my head, Doc" (Karoly, 1985).

Acute Versus Chronic Pain

Experiencing pain either continuously or frequently over a period of many months or years is different from having occasional and isolated short-term bouts with pain. The length of experience an individual has had with a painful condition is an important dimension in describing his or her pain.

Most of the painful conditions people experience are temporary—the pain arrives and then subsides in a matter of minutes, days, or even weeks, often with the aid of painkillers or other treatments prescribed by a physician. If a similar painful condition occurs in the future, it is not connected in a direct way to the earlier experience. This is the case for most everyday headaches, for instance, and for the pain typically produced by such conditions as toothaches, muscle strains, accidental wounds, and surgeries.

By permission of Johnny Hart and Creators Syndicate, Inc.

Acute pain refers to the discomfort people experience with temporary painful conditions that last less than 6 months or so (Chapman, 1991; Turk, Meichenbaum, & Genest, 1983). Patients with acute pain often have higher than normal levels of anxiety while the pain exists, but their distress subsides as their conditions improve and their pain decreases (Fordyce & Steger, 1979).

When a painful condition lasts for more than a few months, it is called *chronic*. People with chronic pain continue to have high levels of anxiety and tend to develop feelings of hopelessness and helplessness because various medical treatments have not helped. Pain interferes with their daily activities, goals, and sleep (Affleck et al., 1998), and it can come to dominate their lives. These effects can be seen in the following passage:

> Pain patients frequently say that could stand their pain much better if they could only get a good night's sleep. . . . They feel worn down, worn out, exhausted. They find themselves getting more and more irritable with their families, they have fewer and fewer friends, and fewer and fewer interests. Gradually, as time goes by, the boundaries of their world seem to shrink. They become more and more preoccupied with their pain, less and less interested in the world around them. Their world begins to center around home, doctor's office, and pharmacy. (Sternbach, quoted in Bakal, 1979, p. 165)

Although pain itself can interfere with sleep, intrusive thoughts and worry before getting to sleep may be a more important factor (Smith et al., 2000). Another problem of people with chronic pain is that many leave their jobs for emotional and physical reasons and must live on reduced incomes at the same time that their medical bills are piling up. The experience of pain is very different when the condition is chronic than when it is acute.

The effects of chronic pain also depend on whether the underlying condition is *benign* (harmless) or is *malignant* (injurious) and worsening and whether the discomfort exists *continuously* or occurs in frequent and intense *episodes*. Using these factors, Dennis Turk, Donald Meichenbaum, and Myles Genest (1983) have described three types of chronic pain:

1. **Chronic-recurrent pain** stems from benign causes and is characterized by repeated and intense episodes of pain separated by periods without pain. Two examples of chronic-recurrent pain are migraine headaches and tension-type (muscle-contraction) headaches; another example is *myofascial pain*, a syndrome that typically involves shooting or radiating, but dull, pain in the jaw and muscles of the head and neck, and sometimes the back (AMA, 2003; Hare & Milano, 1985).

2. **Chronic-intractable-benign pain** refers to discomfort that is typically present all of the time, with varying levels of intensity, and is not related to an underlying malignant condition. Chronic low back pain often has this pattern.

3. **Chronic-progressive pain** is characterized by continuous discomfort, is associated with a malignant condition, and becomes increasingly intense as the underlying condition worsens. Two of the most prominent malignant conditions that frequently produce chronic-progressive pain are rheumatoid arthritis and cancer.

As we shall see later in this chapter and in the next one, the type of pain people experience influences their psychosocial adjustment and the treatment they receive to control their discomfort. (Go to 💡.)

PERCEIVING PAIN

Of the several perceptual senses the human body uses, the sense of pain has three unique properties (Chapman, 1984; Melzack & Wall, 1982). First, although nerve fibers in the body sense and send signals of tissue damage, the receptor cells for pain are different from those of other perceptual systems, such as vision, which contain specific receptor cells that transmit only messages about a particular type of stimulation—light, for the visual system. The body has no *specific* receptor cells that transmit *only* information about pain. Second, the body senses pain in response to many types of noxious stimuli, such as physical pressure, lacerations, and intense heat or cold. Third, the perception of pain almost always includes a strong emotional component. As we are about to see, perceiving pain involves a complex interplay of physiological and psychological processes.

The Physiology of Pain Perception

To describe the physiology of perceiving pain, we will trace the bodily reaction to tissue damage, as when the body receives a cut or burn. The noxious stimulation

HIGHLIGHT

Acute Pain in Burn Patients

Almost every day we hear or read about people being seriously burned, such as in a fire or through scalding. Each year in the United States, over 2 million individuals receive burn injuries, and 300,000 of these injuries are serious (AMA, 2003). People with serious burns suffer acute pain both from their injuries and from the treatment procedures that must be performed.

Medical workers describe the severity of a burn on the basis of its location and with two measures of its damage (AMA, 2003). One measure estimates the amount of skin *area* affected in terms of the percentage of the body surface burned; the other assesses the *depth* of the burn, expressed in three "degrees":

1. *First-degree burns* involve damage restricted to the epidermis, or outermost layer of skin. The skin turns red but does not blister—as, for example, in most cases of sunburn.

2. *Second-degree burns* are those that include damage to the dermis, the layer below the epidermis. These burns are quite painful, often form blisters, and can result from scalding and fire.

3. *Third-degree burns* destroy the epidermis and dermis down to the underlying layer of fat, and may extend to the muscle and bone. These burns usually result from fire. Because the nerve endings are generally damaged in third-degree burns, there is generally no pain sensation in these regions initially.

Practitioners assess the depth of a burn by its appearance and the sensitivity of the region to pain.

Hospital treatment for patients with severe burns progresses through three phases (AMA, 2003; Wernick, 1983). The first few days after the burn is called the *emergency phase*, during which medical staff assess the severity of the burn and work to maintain the patient's body functions and defenses, such as in preventing infection and keeping a balance of fluids and electrolytes. The *acute phase* extends from the end of the emergency phase until the burned area is covered with new skin. This process can take from several days to several months, depending on the severity of the burn. The pain is constant during most or all of this phase, particularly when nerve endings begin to regenerate in third-degree burns. Suffering is generally

> greatest during "tankings," in which the patient is lowered on a stretcher into a large tub. The old dressings are removed and the patient is gently scrubbed to remove encrusted medication. Debridement, which is usually necessary during the early weeks of hospitalization, involves the vigorous cutting away of dead tissue in burned areas. The process, which may last for more than an hour and involve several people working on different parts of the body simultaneously, ends when fresh medication and new dressings are applied. (Wernick, 1983, p. 196)

These and many other painful medical procedures occur very frequently, and burn patients must also do exercises for physical or occupational therapy. Last, the *rehabilitation phase* begins at about the time of discharge from the hospital and continues until the scar tissue has matured. Although the pain has now subsided, itching in the healed area (which should not be scratched) can be a source of discomfort, as can using devices and doing exercises to prevent scarring and contractures (skin shrinkage that can restrict the person's range of motion).

Analgesic medication is the main approach for controlling acute pain in the hospital (AMA, 2003). However, psychological approaches can also help burn patients cope with their pain so that they need less medication. Robert Wernick (1983) used a program of psychological preparation with adult severe-burn patients to enhance the patients' sense of informational, behavioral, and cognitive control over their discomfort, especially with regard to the tanking and debridement procedures. Although these patients were not specifically asked to reduce their use of drugs, they subsequently requested much less medication than patients in a comparison (control) group who received the standard hospital preparation. Similar preparation methods have also been successful with children (Tarnowski, Rasnake, & Drabman, 1987).

instantly triggers chemical activity at the site of injury, releasing chemicals—which include *serotonin*, *histamine*, and *bradykinin*—that promote immune system activity, cause inflammation at the injured site, and activate endings of nerve fibers in the damaged region, signaling injury. Afferent neurons of the peripheral nervous system carry the signal of injury to the spinal cord, which carries the signal to the brain. The afferent nerve endings that respond to pain stimuli and signal injury are called **nociceptors** (Chapman, 1984; Tortora & Grabowski, 2003). These fibers "have no special structure for detecting injury; they are simply free nerve endings" (Chapman, 1984, p. 1261). They exist in skin, blood vessels, muscles, joints, and other body structures.

Pain signals are carried by afferent peripheral fibers of two types: A-delta and C fibers. A-*delta fibers* are coated with myelin, a fatty substance that enables neurons to transmit impulses very quickly. These fibers are associated with sharp, well-localized, and distinct pain experiences. C *fibers* transmit impulses more slowly—because they are not coated with myelin—and seem to be involved in experiences of diffuse dull, burning, or aching pain sensations (Chapman, 1984; Tortora & Grabowski, 2003). Signals from A-delta and C fibers follow different paths when they reach the brain (Bloom, Lazerson, & Hofstadter, 1985; Guyton, 1985). The brain regions we'll mention are shown in Figures 2–3 and 2–4 in Chapter 2. A-delta signals, which reflect sharp pain, go all the way to motor and sensory areas. This suggests that these signals receive special attention in our sensory awareness, probably so that we can respond to them quickly. C fiber signals, which reflect burning or aching pain, terminate mainly in the brainstem and forebrain, with their remaining impulses connecting with a diffuse network of neurons. Signals of dull pain are less likely to command our immediate attention than those of sharp pain, but are more likely to affect our mood, general emotional state, and motivation.

So far, the description we have given of physiological reactions to tissue damage makes it seem as though the process of perceiving pain is rather straightforward. But it actually is not. One phenomenon that complicates the picture is that pains originating from internal organs are often perceived as coming from other parts of the body, usually near the surface of the skin. This is called **referred pain** (AMA, 2003; Tortora & Grabowski, 2003). The pain people often feel in a heart attack provides one of the most

widely known examples of this phenomenon; the pain is referred to the shoulders, pectoral area of the chest, and arms. Other examples of referred pain include:

- Pain perceived in the right shoulder resulting from a problem in the liver or gallbladder.
- Pain in the upper back originating in the stomach.
- Pain in the neck and left shoulder that results from a problem in the diaphragm.

Referred pain results when sensory impulses from an internal organ and the skin use the same pathway in the spinal cord (AMA, 2003; Tortora & Grabowski, 2003). Because people are more familiar with sensations from the skin than from internal organs, they tend to perceive the spinal cord impulses as coming from the skin. Another issue that complicates our understanding of pain perception is that people feel pains that have no detectable physical basis, as the next section discusses.

Pain Without Detectable Body Damage

Some pains people experience are quite mysterious, since they occur with no detectable "reason"—for instance, no noxious stimulus is present. Most of these pain experiences belong to one of three syndromes: neuralgia, causalgia, and phantom limb pain. These syndromes often begin with tissue damage, such as from an injury, but the pain persists long after healing is complete, may spread and increase in intensity, and may become stronger than the pain experienced with the initial damage (AMA, 2003; Melzack & Wall, 1982).

Neuralgia is an extremely painful syndrome in which the patient experiences recurrent episodes of intense shooting or stabbing pain along the course of a nerve (AMA, 2003; Chapman, 1984; Melzack & Wall, 1982). Sometimes neuralgia begins after an infection, such as of shingles (herpes zoster). In one form of this syndrome, called *trigeminal neuralgia*, excruciating spasms of pain occur along the trigeminal nerve that projects throughout the face. Episodes of neuralgia occur very suddenly and without any apparent cause. Curiously, attacks of neuralgia can be provoked more readily by innocuous stimuli than by noxious ones. For instance, drawing a cotton ball across the skin can trigger an attack, but a pin prick does not.

Another mysterious pain syndrome is *causalgia*, which is characterized by recurrent episodes of severe burning pain (AMA, 2003; Melzack & Wall, 1982;

Weisenberg, 1977). A patient with causalgia might report, for instance, that the pain feels "like my arm is pressed against a hot stove." In this syndrome, the pain feels as though it originates in a region of the body where the patient had at some earlier time been seriously wounded, such as by a gunshot or stabbing. Curiously, only a small minority of severely wounded patients develop causalgia—but for those who do, the pain persists long after the wound has healed and damaged nerves have regenerated. Episodes of causalgia can be unpredictable and often occur spontaneously. Like neuralgia, attacks of causalgia can be triggered by minor stimuli, such as a gentle touch or a puff of air.

Phantom limb pain is an especially puzzling phenomenon because the patient—an amputee or someone whose peripheral nervous system is irreparably damaged—feels pain in a limb that either is no longer there or has no functioning nerves (AMA, 2003; Chapman, 1984; Melzack, 1997). After an amputation, for instance, most patients claim to have sensations of their limb still being there—such as by feeling it "move"—and most of these individuals report feeling pain, too. Phantom limb pain generally persists for months or years, can be quite severe, and

sometimes resembles the pain produced by the injury that required the amputation. Individuals with phantom limb pain may experience either recurrent or continuous pain and may describe it as shooting, burning, or cramping. For example, many patients who feel pain in a phantom hand report sensing that the hand is tightly clenched and its fingernails are digging into the palm.

Why do people feel pain when no noxious stimulation is present? Perhaps the answer relates to the neural damage that precedes the condition (Hare & Milano, 1985). But then why is it that the large majority of patients who suffer obvious neural damage do not develop these curious pain syndromes? Although the puzzle is far from being solved, the explanation will almost surely involve both physiological and psychological factors.

The Role of the "Meaning" of Pain

Some people evidently like pain—at least under some, usually sexual, circumstances—and are described as *masochists*. For them, pain seems to have a different meaning than it does for most people. Some psychologists believe individuals may come to like

For many wounded soldiers, their pain seemed to be reduced by the knowledge that they were going home.

pain through classical conditioning, that is, by participating in or viewing activities that associate pain with pleasure in a sexual context (Wincze, 1977). Most of the evidence for the view that the meaning of pain can change by its association with pleasure comes from research with animals. For example, Ivan Pavlov (1927) demonstrated that the dogs' negative reactions to aversive stimuli, such as electric shocks or skin pricks, changed if the stimuli repeatedly preceded presentation of food. Eventually, the dogs would try to approach the aversive stimuli, which now signaled that food, not danger, was coming.

Physician Henry Beecher (1956) described a dramatic example of how the meaning of pain affects people's experience of it. During World War II, he had examined soldiers who had recently been very seriously wounded and were in a field hospital for treatment. Of these men, only 49% claimed to be in "moderate" or "severe" pain, and only 32% requested medication when asked if they "wanted something to relieve it." Some years later, Beecher conducted a similar examination—this time with civilian men who had just undergone surgery. Although the surgical wounds were in the same body regions as those of the soldiers, the soldiers' wounds had been more extensive. Nevertheless, 75% of the civilians claimed to be in "moderate" or "severe" pain and 83% requested medication. (The painkillers used for the soldiers and civilians were narcotics.)

Why did the soldiers—who had more extensive wounds—perceive less pain than the civilians? Beecher described the meaning the injuries had for the soldiers, who

> had been subjected to almost uninterrupted fire for weeks. Notable in this group of soldiers was their optimistic, even cheerful, state of mind. . . . They thought the war was over for them and that they would soon be well enough to be sent home. It is not difficult to understand their relief on being delivered from this area of danger. The battlefield wound marked the end of disaster for them. (1956, p. 1069)

For the civilian surgical patients, however, the wound marked the *start* of a personal problem, and their condition represented a major disruption in their lives.

We discussed in Chapter 9 how people's perceptions of body sensations are influenced by cognitive, social, and emotional factors—for instance, that they

are less likely to notice pain when they are distracted by competing environmental stimuli, such as while participating in competitive sports. Psychological factors play an important role in perceiving pain, and theories of pain need to take these factors into account.

THEORIES OF PAIN

You have probably seen demonstrations in which hypnotized people were instructed that they would not feel pain—they were then stuck by a pin and did not react. When people under hypnosis do not react to noxious stimulation, do they still perceive the pain—only "it doesn't matter" to them? Similarly, do patients who seem relaxed while under the influence of painkillers actually perceive their pain? Some theories of pain would answer "yes" to these questions (Karoly, 1985). Let's look at two of these theories as we begin to examine how to explain pain perception.

EARLY THEORIES OF PAIN

In the early 1900s, the dominant theories of pain took a very mechanistic view of pain perception. They proposed that if an appropriate stimulus activates a receptor, the signal travels to the spinal cord and then the brain, and sensation results (Korol & Craig, 2001; Melzack & Wall, 1982; Weisenberg, 1977). *Specificity theory* argued, for example, that the body has a separate sensory system for perceiving pain—just as it does for hearing and vision. This system was thought to contain its own special receptors for detecting pain stimuli, its own peripheral nerves and pathway to the brain, and its own area of the brain for processing pain signals. However, this structure is not correct.

Another view of pain, called *pattern theory*, proposed that there is no separate system for perceiving pain and that the receptors for pain are shared with other senses, such as of touch. According to this view, people feel pain when certain patterns of neural activity occur, such as when appropriate types of activity reach excessively high levels in the brain. These patterns occur only with intense stimulation. Because strong and mild stimuli of the same sense modality produce different patterns of neural activity, being hit hard feels painful, but being caressed does not.

None of the early theories adequately explained pain perception (Korol & Craig, 2001; Melzack & Wall, 1982). Pattern theory has been criticized because it requires that the stimuli triggering pain must be intense. Thus, it cannot account for the fact that innocuous stimuli can trigger episodes of causalgia and neuralgia. Perhaps the most serious problem with the early theories is that they do not attempt to explain why the experience of pain is affected by psychological factors, such as the person's ideas about the meaning of pain, beliefs about the likelihood of pain, and attention to (or distraction from) noxious events. Partly because these theories overlook the role of psychological factors, they incorrectly predict that a person must feel just as much pain when hypnotized as when not hypnotized, even though he or she does not show it. Research findings indicate that people who are instructed not to feel pain actually do feel less pain when deeply hypnotized than when in the normal waking state (Hilgard & Hilgard, 1983). (Go to 💡.)

HIGHLIGHT

Inducing Pain in Laboratory Research

To conduct an experiment dealing with pain, researchers sometimes need to create a physically painful situation for human participants. How can they accomplish this in a standard way without harming the people? Several approaches have been used safely; two common methods are the *cold-pressor* and *muscle-ischemia* procedures (Turk, Meichenbaum, & Genest, 1983).

The Cold-Pressor Procedure

The cold-pressor procedure basically involves immersing the person's hand and forearm in ice water for a few minutes. A special apparatus is used, like the one illustrated in Figure 11H–1, so that the researcher can maintain a standard procedure across all people they test. The apparatus consists of an armrest mounted on an ice chest filled with water, which is maintained at a temperature of 2°C (35.6°F). Water at this temperature produces a continuous pain that subjects describe as "aching" or "crushing." A pump circulates the water to prevent it from warming in local areas around the arm.

Before using the apparatus, the person's arm is immersed in a bucket of room-temperature water for 1 minute. The researcher also explains the cold-pressor

Microswitch starts photo timer in monitoring room

Hinge

Webbing

Plastic cord

Insulated ice chest

Water immersion line

Counterweight

Figure 11H–1 Apparatus for the cold-person procedure.

HIGHLIGHT

procedure, solicits questions, and indicates that some temporary discoloration of the arm is common. When the procedure is over and the person's arm is removed from the apparatus, the researcher notes that the discomfort will decrease rapidly but that it sometimes increases first for a short while (Turk, Meichenbaum, & Genest, 1983). When using this procedure, the person's pain may be assessed in several ways, such as by self-ratings or by the length of time he or she is willing to endure the discomfort.

An experiment had people experience the cold-pressor procedure twice to test the role of coping methods in pain perception (Girodo & Wood, 1979). Before the second procedure, subjects in different groups received different types of training for coping with pain. We will focus on two groups. One group was trained to cope by making positive *self-statements*; they were taught a list of 20 statements, such as, "No matter how cold it gets, I can handle it," and "It's not the worst thing that can happen." For the other group, training involved the same self-statements, but they also received an *explanation* of how using these statements can enhance their personal control and help them cope with the pain. Immediately after each cold-pressor procedure, the people rated their experience of pain on a scale. Pain ratings *decreased* from the first to the second test for subjects who received the explanation for making the statements and *increased* for those who did not receive the explanation. These results suggest that people's beliefs about the purpose of using self-statements may affect their experience of pain.

The Muscle-Ischemia Procedure

The condition of *ischemia*—or insufficient blood flow—is an important stimulus for the experience of pain when circulation is blocked in internal organs (AMA, 2003). The pain people experience in a heart attack, for instance, results from poor blood flow in the blood vessels to the heart muscle.

The muscle-ischemia procedure typically involves reducing blood flow to the muscles of the arm. This is accomplished by wrapping the cuff of a sphygmomanometer (blood pressure testing device) around the arm, inflating it, and maintaining the pressure at a high level—240 mm Hg (Turk, Meichenbaum, & Genest, 1983). This pressure produces pain without causing damage and can be applied safely for 50 minutes or so. Before the procedure begins, the arm is raised over the

subject's head for 1 minute to drain excess venous blood. The researcher also informs the person that the procedure is safe and harmless, but that it is uncomfortable and may produce temporary numbness, throbbing, changes in arm temperature, and discoloration of the arm and hand. When the cuff is removed, the person raises the arm over his or her head for a few minutes to allow blood flow to return gradually and comfortably. As with the cold-pressor procedure, measures of muscle-ischemia pain can include self-ratings and endurance.

Another way to measure muscle-ischemia pain uses a variation of the procedure we described; that is, the cuff is inflated only to the point when the subject first reports discomfort. This approach assesses the individual's pain *threshold*. Using this method, researchers found that people's pain thresholds, or cuff pressures at which they reported discomfort, were much (50%) higher for individuals who were listening to a comedy recording (by Lily Tomlin) or practicing relaxation than for people in control groups (Cogan et al., 1987). Thus, listening to comedy and practicing relaxation reduces the experience of pain. Other researchers have assessed pain thresholds and found almost no correlation for different types of pain *within* individuals (Janal et al., 1994). This suggests that most people cannot be characterized as "stoical" or "sensitive" to pain in general.

Pain Research and Ethical Standards

When conducting any kind of research with human participants, psychologists are obliged to follow the ethical standards set forth by the American Psychological Association (separate guidelines apply for animal studies). Some of the standards are especially pertinent for research with aversive stimuli. First of all, researchers should make certain that any aversive stimulus they use is not actually harmful. In addition, all participants should:

- Be informed of any features of the study that might affect their willingness to participate.
- Receive clear answers to their questions.
- Be allowed to choose freely, and without undue influence, whether to participate and whether to quit at any point.

If a participant is a child, researchers should also obtain consent from an appropriate guardian, usually a parent.

THE GATE-CONTROL THEORY OF PAIN

In the 1960s, Ronald Melzack and Patrick Wall (1965, 1982) introduced the **gate-control theory** of pain perception. This theory integrated useful ideas from earlier theories and improved on them in several ways, particularly by describing a physiological mechanism by which psychological factors can affect people's experience of pain. As a result, the gate-control theory can account for many phenomena in pain perception that have vexed earlier theories. For instance, it does not have to predict that hypnotized people must feel noxious stimulation (Karoly, 1985).

The Gating Mechanism

At the heart of the gate-control theory is a neural "gate" that can be opened or closed in varying degrees, thereby modulating incoming pain signals before they reach the brain. The theory proposes that the *gating mechanism* is located in the spinal cord—

more specifically, in the *substantia gelatinosa* of the *dorsal horns*, which are part of the *gray matter* that runs the length of the core of the spinal cord. Figure 11–1 depicts how the gate-control process works. You can see in both diagrams of the figure that signals of noxious stimulation enter the gating mechanism (substantia gelatinosa) of the spinal cord from *pain fibers* (A-delta and C fibers). After these signals pass through the gating mechanism, they activate *transmission cells*, which send impulses to the brain. When the output of signals from the transmission cells reaches a critical level, the person perceives pain; the greater the output beyond this level, the greater the pain intensity.

The two diagrams in the figure outline how the gating mechanism controls the output of impulses by the transmission cells. When pain signals enter the spinal cord and the gate is open, the transmission cells send impulses freely; but to the extent that the gate is closed, the output of the transmission cells is inhibited. What controls the opening and closing of

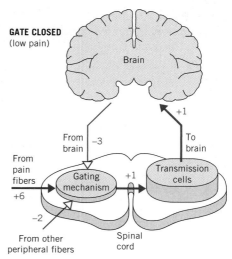

Figure 11–1 Two diagrams to illustrate gate-control theory predictions when strong pain signals arrive from *pain fibers* (A-delta and C) at the spinal cord, along with signals from other *peripheral fibers* (A-beta) and the *brain*. The diagram on the left depicts what conditions might exist when the gate is *open*, and the person feels strong pain; the one on the right shows a scenario when the gate is *closed*, and the person feels little pain. The thick arrows indicate "stimulation" conditions that tend to open the gate and send pain signals through, and the thin ones indicate the opposite, "inhibition," effect. The numbers that accompany each arrow represent hypothetical values for the degrees of pain *stimulation* (positive numbers) or *inhibition* (negative numbers). Pain signals enter the spinal cord and pass through a gating mechanism before activating transmission cells, which send impulses to the brain. (From information in Melzack & Wall, 1965, 1982.)

the gate? The gate-control theory proposes that three factors are involved:

1. *The amount of activity in the pain fibers.* Activity in these fibers tends to open the gate. The stronger the noxious stimulation, the more active the pain fibers.

2. *The amount of activity in other peripheral fibers.* Some peripheral fibers, called A-*beta fibers*, carry information about harmless stimuli or mild irritation, such as touching, rubbing, or lightly scratching the skin. Activity in A-beta fibers tends to close the gate, inhibiting the perception of pain when noxious stimulation exists. This would explain why gently massaging or applying heat to sore muscles decreases the pain.

3. *Messages that descend from the brain.* Neurons in the brainstem and cortex have efferent pathways to the spinal cord, and the impulses they send can open or close the gate. The effects of some brain processes, such as those in anxiety or excitement, probably have a general impact, opening or closing the gate for *all* inputs from *any* areas of the body. But the impact of other brain processes may be very specific, applying to only some inputs from certain parts of the body. The idea that brain impulses influence the gating mechanism helps to explain why people who are hypnotized or distracted by competing environmental stimuli may not notice the pain of an injury.

The theory proposes that the gating mechanism responds to the combined effects of these three factors. Table 11.1 presents a variety of conditions in people's lives that seem to open or close the gate. For instance, anxiety and boredom are conditions that tend to open the gate, and positive emotions and distraction tend to close it.

Evidence on the Gate-Control Theory

The gate-control theory has stimulated a great deal of research and has received strong support from the findings of many, but not all, of these studies (Melzack, 2004; Winters, 1985). One study, for instance, confirmed the theory's prediction that impulses from the brain can inhibit the perception of pain. David Reynolds (1969) conducted this study with rats as subjects. He first implanted an electrode in the midbrain portion of each rat's brainstem, varying the exact location from one rat to the next. Then he made sure they could feel pain by

Table 11.1 *Conditions That Can Open or Close the Pain Gate*

Conditions That Open the Gate
- Physical conditions
  - Extent of the injury
  - Inappropriate activity level
- Emotional conditions
  - Anxiety or worry
  - Tension
  - Depression
- Mental conditions
  - Focusing on the pain
  - Boredom; little involvement in life activities

Conditions That Close the Gate
- Physical conditions
  - Medication
  - Counterstimulation (e.g., heat or massage)
- Emotional conditions
  - Positive emotions (e.g., happiness or optimism)
  - Relaxation
  - Rest
- Mental conditions
  - Intense concentration or distraction
  - Involvement and interest in life activities

Source: Based on material by Karol et al., cited in Turk, Meichenbaum, & Genest (1983).

applying a clamp to their tails—and all reacted. Several days later, he tested whether stimulation through the electrode would block pain. While providing continuous, mild electrical stimulation, he again applied the clamp. Although most of the subjects did show a pain reaction, those with electrodes in a particular region of the midbrain—the **periaqueductal gray** area—did not. The electrical stimulation had produced a state of not being able to feel pain, or *analgesia*, in these rats. Then Reynolds used these few rats for a dramatic demonstration: he performed abdominal surgery on them while they were awake and with only the analgesia produced through electrode stimulation. Subsequent studies by other researchers have confirmed that stimulation to the periaqueductal gray area can induce analgesia in animals and in humans. Moreover, they have determined that morphine works as a painkiller by activating the brainstem to send impulses down the spinal cord (Chapman, 1984; Melzack & Wall, 1982; Winters, 1985).

The gate-control theory clearly takes a biopsychosocial perspective in explaining how people perceive pain. You'll see many features of this theory as you read the material in the next section.

BIOPSYCHOSOCIAL ASPECTS OF PAIN

Why does electrical stimulation to the periaqueductal gray area of the brainstem produce analgesia? The search for an answer to this question played an important part in major discoveries about the neurochemical bases of pain. We will begin this section by examining some of these discoveries and seeing that the neurochemical substances that underlie acute pain are linked to psychosocial processes. Then we will consider how psychosocial factors are related to the experience of chronic pain.

NEUROCHEMICAL TRANSMISSION AND INHIBITION OF PAIN

The phenomenon whereby stimulation to the brainstem produces insensitivity to pain has been given the name **stimulation-produced analgesia** (SPA). To understand how SPA occurs, we need to see how transmission cells are activated to send pain signals to the brain. This activation is triggered by a neurotransmitter called *substance* P that is secreted by pain fibers and crosses the synapse to the transmission cells (Chapman, 1984; Tortora & Grabowski, 2003). SPA occurs when another chemical blocks the pain fibers' release of substance P. Let's see how this happens and what this other chemical is.

What Stimulating the Periaqueductal Gray Area Does

Stimulation to the periaqueductal gray area starts a neurochemical chain reaction that seems to take the course shown in Figure 11–2. The impulse travels down the brainstem to the spinal cord, where the neurotransmitter *serotonin* activates nerve cells called "inhibitory interneurons." Impulses in these interneurons then cause the release of the neurotransmitter *endorphin* at the pain fibers; endorphin inhibits these fibers from releasing substance P (Tortora & Grabowski, 2003; Winters, 1985). Endorphin is a chemical belonging to a class of opiatelike substances called **endogenous opioids** that the body produces naturally; *enkephalin* is another of these chemicals. (*Endogenous* means "developing from within," and *oid* is a suffix meaning "resembling.") Endogenous opioids and opiates (morphine and heroin) appear to function in much the same way in reducing pain (Snyder, 1977; Winters,

Figure 11–2 Illustration of the chain of activity involved in SPA. Stimulation to the periaqueductal gray area of the brain starts a sequence of electrochemical reactions, eventually leading to inhibition (shown by shaded arrows) of the pain fibers' release of substance P, thereby reducing pain messages from the transmission cells to the brain.

1985). Many neurons in the central nervous system have receptors that are sensitive to both opiates and opioids and allow these chemicals to bind to them. Evidence now indicates that people with chronic pain have diminished levels of endogenous opioids in their blood, which may partly explain why their pain gets worse and why they are highly sensitive to acute pain (Bruehl, McCubbin, & Harden, 1999).

How Opiates and Opioids Work

Researchers have studied the action of opiates and endogenous opioids by using the drug *naloxone*, which acts in opposition to opiates and opioids, and prevents them from working as painkillers (Schiffman, 1996; Winters, 1985). In fact, physicians administer naloxone to counteract the effects of heroin in addicts who have taken an overdose of the narcotic. In studying the action of opioids, researchers have examined whether these chemicals are involved in the phenomenon of SPA and found that naloxone blocks the analgesic effects of electrical stimulation to the periaqueductal gray area: animals with naloxone react strongly to the pain, but those without naloxone do not (Akil, Mayer, & Liebeskind, 1976). Furthermore, research with humans found that injecting naloxone in patients who have undergone tooth extractions increases their pain (Levine, Gordon, & Fields, 1978).

These findings indicate that endogenous opioids are involved in producing SPA.

The body clearly contains its own natural painkilling substances, but the ways by which they reduce pain are more complicated than they once appeared (Cannon et al., 1982; Melzack & Wall, 1982). Three issues are relevant. First, studies have found that naloxone does not always block SPA. Second, some research findings suggest that neurotransmitters may have different effects for momentary pain than for pain lasting for an hour or more; most research has been with pain that lasts only seconds or minutes. Third, when morphine is given to control pain, tolerance to the drug occurs quickly for momentary pain but does *not* seem to occur for longer-lasting acute pain and for chronic severe pain, such as that experienced by some cancer patients. These patients generally don't increase their doses, even across months or years of use (Melzack & Wall, 1982). Just why these differences in tolerance occur is unclear.

Having internal pain-relieving chemicals in the body serves an adaptive function. It enables people to regulate the pain they experience to some extent so that they can attend to other matters, such as taking immediate action to survive serious injuries. Pain activates this analgesic system (Winters, 1985). However, most of the time, high levels of endogenous opioid activity are not needed and would be maladaptive since chronic analgesia would undermine the value of pain as a warning signal. Perhaps because pain and emotions are closely linked, studies have found that psychological stress can trigger endogenous opioid activity (Bloom, Lazerson, & Hofstadter, 1985; Winters, 1985). The release of endogenous opioids in times of stress may help to explain how injured athletes in competition and soldiers on the battlefield continue to function with little or no perception of pain. The connection between stress, coping, and opioid activity points to the interplay between biological and psychosocial factors in people's experience of pain. (Go to 💡.)

PERSONAL AND SOCIAL EXPERIENCES AND PAIN

Imagine this scene: little Stevie is a year old and is in the pediatrician's office to receive a standard immunization shot, as he has done before. As the physician approaches with the needle, Stevie starts to cry and tries to kick the doctor. He is reacting in anticipation of pain—something he learned through *classical conditioning* when he had received vaccinations before.

Learning and Pain

We learn to associate pain with antecedent cues and its consequences, especially if the pain is severe and repeated, as it usually is with chronic pain (Martin, Milech, & Nathan, 1993). Many individuals who suffer from migraine headaches, for example, often can tell when headaches are on the way because they experience symptoms, such as dizziness, that precede the pain. These symptoms become conditioned stimuli that tend to produce distress, a conditioned response, and may heighten the perception of pain when it arrives. Also, words or concepts that describe the pain people have experienced can become conditioned stimuli and produce conditioned responses. A study of people who do and do not have migraine headaches measured their physiological arousal in response to pain-related words, such as "throbbing," "sickening," "stabbing," "scalding," and "itching" (Jamner & Tursky, 1987). Migraine sufferers displayed much stronger physiological reactions to these words—especially the words that described their own experience with pain—than those without migraines did. Other findings indicate that people who suffer from chronic pain, such as headaches, show lower discomfort thresholds for pain and nonpain stimuli than others do (Ukestad & Wittrock, 1996). Perhaps they learn to notice and react more strongly to low levels of discomfort.

Learning also influences the way people behave when they are in pain. People in pain behave in characteristic ways—they may moan, grimace, or limp, for instance. These actions are called **pain behaviors,** and they can be classified into four types (Turk, Wack, & Kerns, 1985):

- *Facial or audible expression of distress*, as when people clench their teeth, moan, or grimace.
- *Distorted ambulation or posture*, such as moving in a guarded or protective fashion, stooping while walking, or rubbing or holding the painful area.
- *Negative affect*, such as being irritable.
- *Avoidance of activity*, as when people lie down frequently during the day, stay home from work, or refrain from motor or strenuous behavior.

HIGHLIGHT

Placebos and Pain

You have probably heard of physicians prescribing a medicine that actually consisted of "sugar pills" when they could not find a physical cause for a patient's complaints or did not know of any medication that would help. You may also have heard that this treatment sometimes works—the patient claims the symptoms are reduced. An inert substance or procedure that produces an effect is called a *placebo*. Studies have shown that placebos can often be effective in treating a wide variety of ailments, including coughs, nausea, and hypertension, at least on a temporary basis (Agras, 1984; Roberts, 1995). And an effective placebo need not be a substance: an experiment found that of patients who got sham surgery for arthritis of the knee or real surgery, nearly 40% of each group claimed to have less pain and better movement (Moseley et al., 2002).

Placebos can also be effective in treating pain (Melzack & Wall, 1982). They do not always work, but they seem to produce substantial relief in about half as many patients as do real drugs, such as aspirin or morphine. The effect of placebos depends on the patient's belief that they will work—for instance, they are more effective:

* With large doses—such as more capsules or larger ones—than with smaller doses.
* When injected than when taken orally.
* When the practitioner indicates explicitly and strongly that they will work.

Unfortunately, however, the effectiveness of placebos in treating pain tends to decline with repeated use.

Why do placebos reduce pain? A widely accepted theory is that psychological processes in the patient trigger the release of endogenous opioids in the body, thereby inhibiting the transmission of pain signals. Two of these triggering processes are *expectancies* and *classical conditioning* (Stewart-Williams, 2004). These are the same processes we discussed in Chapter 7 that lead to dependence on substances, such as drugs and alcohol. In both processes, people acquire from past experience a connection between active treatments and their effects, such as reduced pain, so that something resembling an active treatment—the placebo—can lead to the effect. Earlier in the current chapter, we saw the role of endogenous opioids in stimulation-produced analgesia (SPA); this role is important in placebos, too. Research with double-blind procedures has shown that placebos do, in fact, elicit the body's production of endogenous opioids and that people who receive naloxone to block the transmission of pain signals report more discomfort than those who do not get naloxone with pain from muscle-ischemia and actual tooth extractions (Benedetti et al., 2003; Fields & Levine, 1984; Johansen, Brox, & Flaten, 2003).

The effects of placebos are fascinating and important, but they also present major ethical dilemmas for practitioners. Is it appropriate to use placebo drugs or procedures to treat symptoms and illnesses—and if so, when and under what circumstances?

Pain behaviors are a part of the sick role, and people in pain may begin to exaggerate these behaviors because, they think, "No one believes me" (Hendler, 1984). Regardless of why the behaviors start, they are often strengthened or maintained by reinforcement in *operant conditioning* (Fordyce, 1976; Turk, 2001). When pain persists and becomes chronic, these behaviors often become part of the person's habits and lifestyle. People with entrenched patterns of pain behavior usually feel powerless to change.

How are pain behaviors reinforced? Although being sick or in pain is unpleasant, it sometimes has benefits, or "secondary gains." Someone who is in pain may be relieved of certain chores around the

house or of going to work, for instance. Also, when a person has a painful condition that flares up in certain circumstances, such as when lifting heavy objects, he or she may begin to avoid these activities. In both of these situations, pain behavior is reinforced if the person does not like doing these activities in the first place: getting out of doing them is rewarding. Another way pain behavior and other sick-role behaviors may be reinforced is if the person receives disability payments. Studies of injured or ill patients who differ in the financial compensation they receive have found that those with greater compensation tend to remain hospitalized and miss work longer, report more chronic pain, and show less success from pain treatments (Chapman, 1991; Ciccone, Just, & Bandilla, 1999; Rohling, Binder, & Langhinrichsen-Rohling, 1995). Part of these differences probably reflects a willingness of those receiving compensation to take more time to recover and try to prevent a relapse. Many pain patients who receive disability compensation show substantial emotional and behavioral improvements from pain rehabilitation programs (Trabin, Rader, & Cummings, 1987).

Social Processes and Pain

People who suffer with pain also receive attention, care, and affection from family and friends, which can provide social reinforcement for pain behavior. Researchers have demonstrated this relationship with both child and adult patients. Karen Gil and her colleagues (1988) videotaped parents' reactions to the pain behavior of their children who had a chronic skin disorder with severe itching that should not be scratched since it can cause peeling and infection. An analysis revealed that the children's scratching *increased*, rather than decreased, when parents paid attention to scratching, and paying attention to the children when they were *not* scratching seemed to reduce their scratching behavior.

Studies have assessed how patients' pain behaviors relate to their receiving social rewards, such as being able to avoid disliked social activities or getting solicitous care from a spouse, that is, high levels of help and attention (Ciccone, Just, & Bandilla, 1999; Newton-John, 2002). Receiving higher levels of social reward is associated with patients reporting more pain and showing more disability and less activity, such as in visiting friends or going shopping. In one study, patients with chronic pain were interviewed about their spouses' solicitousness regarding their pain behavior (Block, Kremer, & Gaylor, 1980). The interviews occurred in meetings in which the patients were aware of being observed through a one-way mirror and of who was observing: their spouse or a hospital employee. The degree of pain the patients described depended on whether the spouse or the employee was observing and whether the patient thought the spouse was solicitous. Patients who felt their spouses were solicitous reported *more* pain when their spouses watched than when the employee did. In contrast, patients who felt their spouses were not solicitous reported

less pain when their spouses watched than when the employee did.

Findings on parents' and spouses' reactions to chronic pain behavior and the social climate within the family system illustrate how each family member's behavior impacts on the behavior of the others (Kerns & Weiss, 1994; Romano, Turner, & Jensen, 1997; Turk, 2001). When families lack cohesion or the members are highly solicitous to pain behavior without encouraging the patient to become active, they tend to promote sick-role behavior. These conditions can develop into a vicious circle—for example, solicitousness may lead to more pain behavior, which elicits more solicitousness, and so on. Showing care and concern when people are in pain is, of course, important and constructive. But the patient's diminished activity may lead to physical deterioration, such as through muscle atrophy, and to progressively more pain and less activity. These social processes in the family system of pain patients are gradual and insidious—they tend to increase the patients' dependency and decrease their self-efficacy and self-esteem. Self-efficacy is important because people who believe they cannot control their pain very well experience more pain and use more medication than those who believe they can control it (Turk, 1996).

Gender, Sociocultural Factors, and Pain

Studies have found gender and sociocultural differences in the experience of pain. Men and women differ in the types of pain they experience and reactions to pain. In cold-pressor tests, women have lower thresholds and give higher ratings for pain, and some evidence suggests this may result in part from different effects of endogenous opioids (al'Absi et al., 2004; Myers et al., 2001). Women also have higher incidence rates of pain from arthritis, migraine headache, myofacial neuralgia, and causalgia, but men have a greater incidence of back pain and cardiac pain (Bodnar, 1998). Women report more than men that pain interfered with their daily activities (Lester, Lefebvre, & Keefe, 1994).

Surveys of adults in different countries who suffer from chronic low back pain revealed greater work and social impairments among Americans, followed by Italians and New Zealanders, and then by Japanese, Colombian, and Mexican individuals (Sanders et al., 1992). Pain research has also compared people from different ethnic groups in the United States. African Americans showed less tolerance for muscle-ischemia pain and reported higher levels of chronic pain than Whites (Edwards et al., 2001). And Blacks reported more pain after dental surgery than people of European, Asian, or Hispanic backgrounds, and women in each group reported more pain than men (Faucett, Gordon, & Levine, 1994). But other studies have found no ethnic pain differences, and knowing of actual differences is of little value for a practitioner treating individual people (Korol & Craig, 2001).

EMOTIONS, COPING PROCESSES, AND PAIN

People in chronic pain experience high levels of anger, fear, and sadness (Fernandez, Clark, & Rudick-Davis, 1998). Pain and emotion are intimately linked, and cognitive processes mediate this link. In a study of these relationships, Gerry Kent (1985) had dental patients fill out a brief dental anxiety scale while waiting for their appointments. Then they rated the pain they expected in their visits. After the appointment, the patients rated the pain they actually experienced and rated it again by mail 3 months later. The results revealed that anxiety played a role in their expectations of pain and in their memories of it 3 months later. The patients with high dental anxiety expected *and* later remembered four times as much pain as they experienced. In contrast, the low-anxiety patients expected and remembered less than twice as much pain as they experienced. These findings suggest that high-anxiety patients' memories of pain are determined more by what they expect than by what they feel.

Does Emotion Affect Pain?

Investigations using self-report methods have found that migraine and muscle-contraction headaches tend to occur after periods of heightened stress and that Type A individuals have more frequent chronic headaches than others do (Köhler & Haimerl, 1990; Wittrock & Myers, 1998; Woods et al., 1984). These studies indicate that stress and headache are related. Has any research shown that stress causes headaches?

Convincing evidence that stress can cause headaches comes from a study with adults who suffered from either chronic headache or only occasional headaches (Gannon et al., 1987). Before testing a

Pain is an important factor in dentistry: it motivates patients to seek treatment, but the discomfort during visits makes them feel uneasy about going in the future.

subject, a researcher attached sensors to the person's body to take physiological measurements, such as of heart rate. Soon, the subjects were given a stressful task—calculating arithmetic problems, such as 349 + 229, for an hour—and told that a buzzer would sound if their performance fell below a norm. Actually, the buzzer sounded periodically regardless of their performance. What effect did these conditions have? More than two-thirds of the chronic headache sufferers and only one-fourth of the occasional sufferers reported developing headaches during the stress task. Ratings of headache pain increased throughout the stress condition and decreased later while they sat quietly. The headaches tended to resemble tension-type headaches and be preceded by sustained physiological arousal. These are important findings that indicate that stress can cause headaches.

Emotions are also related to other kinds of pain, but the degree to which emotions cause the pain is still in question. For example, the feelings of stress people with sickle-cell disease experience appear to result from the discomfort they experience on previous days, and lead to pain on subsequent days, but feeling positive moods seems to offset the effects of negative moods (Gil et al., 2004; Zautra et al., 2001). On the other hand, people with recurrent low back pain report higher levels of anxiety and tension than pain-free control subjects do, but these mood states do not worsen in the day or so preceding pain attacks (Feuerstein, Carter, & Papciak, 1987). Pain is itself very stressful, and many people with chronic pain consider their discomfort—the actual pain and the physical limitations it produces—to be the most prominent stressor in their lives (Turner, Clancy, & Vitaliano, 1987). Health psychologists who work with pain patients often try to assess how well they cope with their pain. (Go to 🌳.)

Coping with Pain

Part of the stress that chronic pain patients experience stems from their common belief that they have little personal control over their pain, aside from avoiding activities they believe can trigger an attack or make it worse. As a result, they tend to deal with their stress by using emotion-focused coping strategies. That is, rather than trying to alter the problem itself, they try to regulate their emotional responses to it. Some of the more common coping methods adults and children with chronic pain use include hoping or praying the pain will get better someday and diverting their attention, such as by counting numbers or running a song through their heads (Gil, Wilson, & Edens, 1997; Keefe & Dolan, 1986). These approaches are not very effective in reducing chronic pain.

How effectively do people cope with pain? Studies that tested pain patients with the MMPI have found some fairly consistent outcomes (Cox, Chapman, & Black, 1978; Rappaport et al., 1987; Rosen et al., 1987). These outcomes lead to three conclusions. First, individuals who suffer from various types of chronic pain, such as severe headache and low back pain, often show a characteristic MMPI profile with extremely high scores on hypochondriasis, depression, and hysteria—the neurotic triad scales, as Figure 11–3 illustrates. But their scores on the seven other MMPI scales tend to be well within the normal range. Second, this pattern appears to hold regardless of whether their pain has a known organic source. In other words, people whose pain might be classified as psychogenic by a physician tend to show similar problems of adjustment on the MMPI as those whose

CLINICAL METHODS AND ISSUES
Assessing Difficulty Coping with Pain

One way a psychologist can evaluate the coping difficulties of pain patients is to assess their emotional adjustment with psychological tests, particularly the Minnesota Multiphasic Personality Inventory (MMPI). As we saw in Chapter 10, this test contains several scales, three of which are especially relevant for medical patients. These three scales assess: *hypochondriasis*, the tendency toward being preoccupied with physical symptoms and health; *depression*, feelings of unhappiness, pessimism, and hopelessness; and *hysteria*, the tendency to cope with problems by developing physical symptoms and using avoidance methods, such as denial. Because the MMPI is given and scored in a standardized manner and has been administered to large samples of people, norms exist that allow psychologists to compare an individual's scores on the different scales with those of the general population. For instance, a score of 70 or above on any scale occurs in less than 5% of the population and is considered extreme and clinically significant (Anastasi, 1982). Psychologists generally refer to hypochondriasis, depression, and hysteria as the *neurotic triad* because clients with neurotic disorders often have high scores on these three scales. By combining information from psychological tests and other sources, such as interviews, psychologists can identify and help patients who are having difficulty coping with the stress of pain conditions.

Figure 11–3 Illustration of MMPI profiles comparing chronic pain and acute pain patients. Chronic pain patients typically show abnormally high scores (70 or above) on the "neurotic triad" scales (Hs = hypochondriasis, D = depression, Hy = hysteria), but not on the seven other MMPI scales. These data were averaged across mean scores presented in two studies (Cox, Chapman & Black, 1978; Rosen et al., 1987).

pain has a clear organic basis. Third, individuals with acute pain, such as patients recovering from injuries, sometimes have moderately elevated scores on the neurotic triad scales, but these scores and those for the remaining MMPI scales are generally well within the normal range. These findings make sense and reflect the differential psychological impact of pain that patients expect will end soon versus pain they fear will never end. Keep in mind also that people with chronic-recurrent pain conditions show worse psychological symptoms during pain episodes than during pain-free periods (Holroyd et al., 1993).

It is clear that being in frequent, severe discomfort is related to having high scores on the MMPI neurotic triad scales, but does chronic pain cause maladjustment? Yes, it can: people whose pain has ended show substantial reductions in various measures of psychological disturbance (Melzack & Wall, 1982). Depression is very common in chronic pain patients, and two factors are involved. One factor is the stress these people experience without being able to change their situations (Anderson et al., 1985; Turk & Holzman, 1986). They develop a sense of helplessness, which leads to depression. The other factor is that they may begin to *catastrophize*, or have

frequent negative thoughts about their plight (Lackner, Quigley, & Blanchard, 2004; Turk, 2001). But maladjustment can also lead to pain: people who are depressed are somewhat more likely than others to develop a chronic pain condition in the future, and people with chronic pain are much more likely than others to become depressed (Magni et al., 1994). Pain and maladjustment involve interactive processes, with each feeding on the other over time, but chronic pain is more likely to lead to maladjustment than the other way around. Also keep in mind that not all patients with severe chronic pain become maladjusted; many adapt to their conditions much better than others do (Klapow et al., 1993; Linton et al., 1994). Coping well with chronic pain is a struggle that unfolds over time, as this arthritis patient noted:

> Over time I've figured out that I can do things to bring on the pain and things that could limit it. I also figured out that my flares won't last forever, although while they're happening it seems like forever. It took quite a while to figure that out. (Tennen & Affleck, 1997, p. 274)

To summarize, the process by which people perceive pain involves a complex chain of physiological and neurochemical events. These events can be affected by psychosocial processes, such as people's beliefs about whether a drug will reduce their discomfort. Pain also affects and can be influenced by people's learning, cognition, social experiences, and emotion. Although people can indicate through their behavior that they are feeling pain, the pain they perceive is actually a private and subjective experience. How can researchers and clinicians who work with patients who have painful symptoms assess the level and type of pain these individuals perceive? We turn now to answering this question.

ASSESSING PEOPLE'S PAIN

Researchers and clinicians have developed a variety of techniques for assessing people's pain. Although virtually all these methods can be applied both in research and in treating pain patients, some techniques are used more often in research, whereas others are used mostly to supplement a detailed medical history in clinical practice. In either setting, it is a good idea to use two or more different measurement techniques to enhance the accuracy of the assessment (Bradley, 1994). We'll organize our discussion by classifying ways to measure pain into three groups: self-report methods, behavioral assessment approaches, and psychophysiological measures.

SELF-REPORT METHODS

An obvious approach to measure people's pain is to ask them to describe the discomfort, either in their own words or by filling out a rating scale or questionnaire. In treating a patient's pain, health care workers ask where the pain is, what it feels like, how strong it is, and when it tends to occur. With chronic pain patients, medical and psychological professionals often incorporate this kind of questioning within the structure of a clinical interview.

Interview Methods in Assessing Pain

To treat chronic pain effectively, professionals need more information than just a description of the pain. Interviews with the patient and key others, such as family members and coworkers, provide a rich source of background information in the early phases of treatment (Bradley & McKendree-Smith, 2001; Chapman, 1991; Karoly, 1985). These discussions ordinarily focus on such issues as:

- The history of the pain problem, including when it started, how it progressed, and what approaches have been used for controlling it.
- The patient's emotional adjustment, currently and before the pain syndrome began.
- The patient's lifestyle before the pain condition began: recreational interests, exercise patterns, diet, and so on.
- The pain syndrome's impact on the patient's current lifestyle, interpersonal relations, and work.
- The social context of pain episodes, such as happenings in the family before an attack and how family members respond when the pain occurs.
- Factors that seem to trigger attacks or make them worse.
- How the patient typically tries to cope with the pain.

The information obtained in these interviews can also be supplemented by having the patient and key others fill out questionnaires.

Pain Rating Scales and Diaries

A direct, simple, and commonly used way to assess pain is to have individuals rate some aspect of their discomfort on a scale (Chapman et al., 1985; Jensen & Karoly, 2001). This approach is used very often to measure how strong the pain is; three different types of scales for rating pain intensity are illustrated in Figure 11–4. One type is the *visual analog scale*, which has people rate their pain by marking a point on a line of a standard length (usually 100 mm) that has labels only at each end. This type of scale is very easy for people to use and can be used with children as young as 5 years of age (Karoly, 1985). The *box scale* has individuals choose one number from a series of numbers that represent levels of pain within a specified range. The *verbal rating scale* has people describe their pain by choosing a word or phrase from several that are given.

Because rating scales are so easy and quick to use, people can rate their pain frequently. Averaging these ratings across time gives a more accurate picture of the pain the person generally experiences than individual ratings do (Jensen & McFarland, 1993). Repeated ratings can also reveal changes in pain over time, such as during everyday activities or during the course of an experiment. Patients could rate their pain each waking hour of each day for, say,

VISUAL ANALOG SCALE

BOX SCALE

VERBAL RATING SCALE

| No pain | Some pain | Considerable pain | Worst pain possible |

Figure 11–4 Illustrations of the visual analog, box, and verbal rating scales. Example instructions are as follows: *visual analog scale*—"Mark a point on the line to show how strong your pain is"; *box scale*—"Rate the level of your pain by circling one number on the scale, where 0 means 'no pain' and 10 means 'worst pain possible'"; *verbal rating scale*—"Circle the one phrase that best describes your pain." The labels and number of choices on a scale can be different from those shown here.

2 weeks, also indicating whenever they take pain medication. Before starting this procedure, they would learn what to say if someone saw them doing the rating, ways to remind themselves to do each hourly rating, and what to do if they forgot (Turk, Meichenbaum, & Genest, 1983). One use of repeated ratings is in showing the ebbs and flows of pain intensity that patients often experience. For instance, one patient's wife

> believed that her husband was experiencing incapacitating and severe pain every waking hour of his life. This belief contributed to her preventing him from participating in any but the simplest chores around the house. Their social life had deteriorated, and the couple had grown increasingly depressed over the course of 4 years. Upon hearing that her husband experienced only moderate pain most of the time, that he indeed felt capable of various tasks, and that he actually resented his wife's efforts at pampering him, she was helped to alter her behavior. (Turk, Meichenbaum, & Genest, 1983, pp. 218–219)

Repeated ratings during each day may also reveal patterns in the timing of severe pain. Is the pain most severe in the evening, or on certain days? If so, are there aspects of the environment that may be responsible and, perhaps, changeable?

Pain ratings can also be used in a *pain diary*, which is a detailed record of a person's pain experiences. As Figure 11–5 illustrates, the pain diary a patient keeps would include pain ratings and information about the time and circumstances of pain episodes, any medications taken, and comments about each episode. (Go to 🍎.)

PAIN QUESTIONNAIRES

Pain is only partly described by the intensity of the discomfort people feel—the experience of pain has many qualities and dimensions. Ronald Melzack began to recognize the multidimensional nature of pain through his interactions with pain patients. He described in an interview how this realization emerged from talks he had with a woman who suffered from phantom limb pain. She

> would describe burning pains that were like a red-hot poker being shoved through her toes and her ankle. She would cry out from the pain in her legs. Of course, there were no legs. Well, that made me realize the utter subjectivity of pain— no objective physical measure is very likely to capture that. . . . I began to write down the words she used to describe her pain. I realized that the words describing the *emotional-motivational*

PAIN DIARY for	*Ed*				

Date: **3-5-97**   Did you change your medication today? If yes, describe _____ *No*

Pain Rating Scale: No pain | 0 | 1 | 2 | 3 | 4 | 5 | Unbearable pain

Time	Pain rating and body location.	Activity at start of pain.	What medicine did you take, and how much?	Pain rating after 1 or 2 hours.	Comments and other problems.
8:30 pm	4/lower back	Leaned over to turn on bath water	Asprin (2)	3–helped a little	Could stand up and walk better
11:00pm	2/lower back, dull ache	Lying flat on back in bed	Ibuprofen (Motrin)(2)	1–helped	Couldn't sleep at first; got to sleep by 1:00

Figure 11–5 A pain diary. The chronic pain patient keeps a daily record of important information about pain episodes.

Describing Your Pain

Use the questionnaire in Figure 11A–1 to assess an acute or a chronic pain you have experienced. Try to choose a painful condition that you either currently have, had recently, or remember vividly from the past. If the pain you assess is not current, answer the questions as if it is. Do this now.

Ronald Melzack (1975) developed this questionnaire and described its scoring system, which is too complex to do here. You can get a sense of the pain you assessed in two ways: (1) Review the answers you chose—for instance, questions 2 and 3 of Part 4 tell you its range of intensity. (2) Refer back to your answers as you read the description of the McGill Pain Questionnaire in the text.

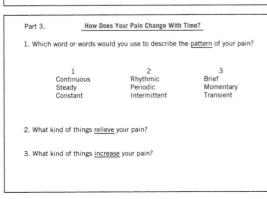

Part 1.   **Where Is Your Pain?**

Please mark on the drawing below, the areas where you feel pain. Put E if external, or I if internal, near the areas which you mark. Put EI if both external and internal.

Part 2.   **What Does Your Pain Feel Like?**

Some of the words below describe your <u>present</u> pain. Circle <u>ONLY</u> those words that best describe it. Leave out any category that is not suitable. Use only a single word in each appropriate category–the one that applies best.

1	2	3	4
Flickering	Jumping	Pricking	Sharp
Quivering	Flashing	Boring	Cutting
Pulsing	Shooting	Drilling	Lacerating
Throbbing		Stabbing	
Beating		Lancinating	
Pounding			

5	6	7	8
Pinching	Tugging	Hot	Tingling
Pressing	Pulling	Burning	Itchy
Gnawing	Wrenching	Scalding	Smarting
Cramping		Searing	Stinging
Crushing			

9	10	11	12
Dull	Tender	Tiring	Sickening
Sore	Taut	Exhausting	Suffocating
Hurting	Rasping		
Aching	Splitting		
Heavy			

13	14	15	16
Fearful	Punishing	Wretched	Annoying
Frightful	Grueling	Blinding	Troublesome
Terrifying	Cruel		Miserable
	Vicious		Intense
	Killing		Unbearable

17	18	19	20
Spreading	Tight	Cool	Nagging
Radiating	Numb	Cold	Nauseating
Penetrating	Drawing	Freezing	Agonizing
Piercing	Squeezing		Dreadful
	Tearing		Torturing

Part 3.   **How Does Your Pain Change With Time?**

1. Which word or words would you use to describe the <u>pattern</u> of your pain?

1	2	3
Continuous	Rhythmic	Brief
Steady	Periodic	Momentary
Constant	Intermittent	Transient

2. What kind of things <u>relieve</u> your pain?

3. What kind of things <u>increase</u> your pain?

Part 4.   **How Strong Is Your Pain?**

People agree that the following 5 words represent pain of increasing intensity. They are:

1	2	3	4	5
Mild	Discomforting	Distressing	Horrible	Excruciating

To answer each question below, write the number of the most appropriate word in the space beside the question.

1. Which word describes your pain right now?   _____
2. Which word describes it at its worst?   _____
3. Which word describes it when it is least?   _____
4. Which word describes the worst toothache you ever had?   _____
5. Which word describes the worst headache you ever had?   _____
6. Which word describes the worst stomach-ache you ever had?   _____

Figure 11A–1   The McGill Pain Questionnaire. (*Source*: Melzack, 1975.)

component of her pain—"exhausting, sickening, terrifying, punishing"—were very different from those for the *sensory* component—"shooting, scalding, splitting, cramping." Later I came to see there was also an *evaluative* component, such as "it's unbearable" or "it's annoying." I wrote down the words other patients used, too, but I didn't know what to do with them. (Warga, 1987, p. 53, italics added)

Melzack determined that pain involves three broad dimensions—*affective* (emotional-motivational), *sensory*, and *evaluative*—by conducting a study in which subjects sorted over 100 pain-related words into separate groups of their own making (Melzack & Torgerson, 1971).

Melzack's research also indicated that each of the three dimensions consisted of subclasses. For instance, the sensory dimension included a subclass with the words "hot," "burning," "scalding," and "searing"—words relating to temperature. Notice that these four words connote increasingly hot temperatures, with searing being the hottest. Similarly, the affective dimension included a subclass of three words relating to fear: "fearful," "frightful," "terrifying." Then, by determining the degree of pain reflected by each word, Melzack (1975)—a professor at McGill University—was able to construct an instrument to measure pain. This test is called the **McGill Pain Questionnaire** (MPQ), which you filled out in the Assess Yourself exercise.

Part 2 of the MPQ presents a list of descriptive words, separated into a total of 20 subclasses. The test instructs the person to select from each subclass the best word to describe his or her pain. Each word in each class has an assigned value based on the degree of pain it reflects. Let's look, for instance, at subclass 7, which ranges from "hot" to "searing." Selecting "searing" would contribute the highest number of points from this subclass to the person's pain score ("hot" would contribute the lowest number). The sum of these points across the 20 subclasses is called the *pain rating index.* Part 4 of the MPQ contains a series of verbal rating scales; the one that rates "your pain right now" yields a separate score called the *present pain intensity.*

The MPQ appears to have many strengths as an instrument for assessing chronic pain, both for research and for clinical purposes (Melzack & Katz, 2001). For one thing, research has confirmed that the experience of pain is multidimensional. Also, individuals with similar pain syndromes tend to choose the same patterns of words to describe their pain. But people suffering from very different types of pain—for example, toothache, arthritis, cancer, and phantom limb pain—choose different patterns of words in the MPQ to describe their different pain experiences. The main limitation of the MPQ is that it requires a fairly strong English vocabulary (Chapman et al., 1985; Karoly, 1985). For instance, it includes a few words, such as "taut" and "lancinating," that many people may not know. Moreover, sometimes respondents must make very fine distinctions between words, as with "throbbing," "beating," and "pounding." Even if an interviewer is present to define the words, the MPQ may be of limited use with people who have poor English skills and children under about 12 years of age.

The MPQ is the best-known and most widely used pain questionnaire, but others are available. One of these, the *Multidimensional Pain Inventory*, accurately assesses people's pain and its psychosocial effects (Kerns, Turk, & Rudy, 1985; Jacob & Kerns, 2001).

BEHAVIORAL ASSESSMENT APPROACHES

Because people tend to exhibit pain behaviors when they are in discomfort, it should be possible to assess their pain by observing their behavior. A person is likely to show different types and patterns of behavior if the pain is intense as compared to moderate, if it involves a headache as opposed to low back pain, and if chronic pain is recurrent than if it is intractable. Psychologists have developed procedures for assessing pain behavior in two types of situations: in *everyday activities* and in *structured clinical sessions*.

Assessing Pain Behavior in Structured Clinical Sessions

Procedures are available whereby health care workers can assess the pain behavior of patients in structured sessions that are usually conducted in hospital settings. They are structured by the specific pain behaviors to be assessed and the tasks the patient is asked to perform. One approach of this kind has been developed into a pain assessment instrument—the UAB *Pain Behavior Scale*—for use by nurses during their standard routines, such as in early morning rounds (Richards et al., 1982). The nurse has the patient perform several activities and rates each of 10 behaviors, such as the patient's mobility and use of medication, on a 3-point scale: "none," "occasional," and "frequent." These ratings are converted into numerical values and summed for a total score.

Structured clinical sessions have been used in assessing discomfort in individuals with a variety of pain conditions, including arthritis and low back pain (Keefe, Williams, & Smith, 2001; Öhlund et al., 1994). Each session has patients perform a standard set of activities. In one study, patients with low back pain were asked to walk, pick up an object on the floor, remove their shoes while sitting, and perform several exercises, such as trunk rotations, toe touching, and sit-ups (Kleinke & Spangler, 1988). The patients were videotaped, and trained assessors rated their performance for several pain behaviors, such as guarded movement, rubbing the pain area, grimacing, and sighing. Pain behaviors can be assessed in this manner easily and reliably, and these assessments correlate well with patients' self-ratings of pain.

Assessing Pain Behavior in Everyday Activities

How does the pain patient behave in everyday activities, especially at home? Does the person spend much time in bed, complain of discomfort a lot, seek help frequently in moving, or walk with a limp most of the time? How much of these behaviors does the person exhibit? Behavioral assessments of everyday activities like these can be made.

Family members or key others in the patient's life are usually the best people to make these everyday assessments of pain behavior. These people must, of course, be willing to help and be trained to make careful observations and keep accurate records. Researcher Wilbert Fordyce (1976) designed a procedure whereby the assessor—say, the client's spouse—compiles a list of five to ten behaviors that generally signal when the patient is in pain. Then the spouse is trained to watch for these behaviors, to keep track of the amount of time the patient exhibits them, and to monitor how people, including the assessor, react to the client's pain behavior. This procedure is useful not only in assessing the patient's pain experiences but in determining their impact on his or her life and the social context that may maintain pain behaviors. As a

This woman's pain behavior can be used in assessing her discomfort.

supplement to this procedure, the assessor can keep a pain diary about the patient's severe pain episodes, recording the date and time, as well as where the episode occurred, such as in the car or at home in bed (Turk, Meichenbaum, & Genest, 1983). The assessor can also describe what he or she:

- Noticed as behaviors that suggested the patient was in pain.
- Thought and felt during the episode.
- Did in order to help, along with a rating of the action's effectiveness, ranging on a scale from "did not help at all" to "seemed to stop the pain completely."

These supplemental procedures provide additional data that can be of value in dealing with interpersonal issues that influence the pain experience.

PSYCHOPHYSIOLOGICAL MEASURES

Another approach for assessing pain involves taking measurements of physiological activity, since pain has both sensory and emotional components that can produce changes in bodily functions. *Psychophysiology* is the study of mental or emotional processes as reflected by changes they produce in physiological activity (Lykken, 2004).

One psychophysiological measure researchers have used for assessing pain uses an apparatus called an *electromyograph* (EMG) to measure the electrical activity in muscles, which reflects their tension. Because *muscle tension* is associated with various pain states, such as headaches and low back pain, we might expect EMG recordings of the affected muscles when physically or psychologically stressed to be greater for pain patients than pain-free controls, and they are (Flor, 2001). But when the muscles are inactive, no consistent difference is found. Does EMG level reflect pain level? Yes, but only when assessments are taken over an extended period of time (Flor, 2001). When EMG and pain levels are measured for a brief period, the correlation between the two is not reliable.

Researchers have also attempted to assess people's pain with measures of *autonomic activity*, such as of heart rate and skin conductance, but these measures do not seem to be very useful (Chapman et al., 1985; Flor, 2001). This is because changes in autonomic activity are more strongly related to people's ratings of pain than to the strength of the pain stimulus, are inconsistently associated with chronic pain, and readily occur in the absence of the sensation of pain, such as when people feel stressed. As a result, interpreting variations in autonomic activity as reflecting pain is often difficult.

The last psychophysiological measure of pain we will consider involves the electrical activity of the brain, as measured by an *electroencephalograph* (EEG). When a person's sensory system detects a stimulus, such as a clicking sound from earphones, the signal to the brain produces a change in EEG voltage. Electrical changes produced by stimuli are called *evoked potentials* and show up in EEG recordings as sharp surges or peaks in the graph. Pain stimuli produce evoked potentials that vary in magnitude—the amplitudes of the surges increase with the intensity of the stimuli, decrease when subjects take analgesics, and correlate with people's subjective reports of pain (Chapman et al., 1985; Flor, 2001).

Even though psychophysiological measures provide objective assessments of bodily changes that occur in response to pain, these changes may also be affected by other factors, such as attention, diet, and stress. In clinical situations, measures of muscle tension, autonomic activity, and evoked potential are probably best used as supplements to self-report and behavioral assessment approaches (Chapman et al., 1985).

PAIN IN CHILDREN

We have focused in this chapter mainly on the experience of pain by adults, but children experience almost all of the types of discomfort and pain syndromes that adults have (Lavigne, Schulein, & Hahn, 1986b; McGrath & Hillier, 1996). And some children suffer from an arthritislike condition in their arms and legs that is unique to their age group. The condition usually occurs among 6- to 10-year-olds and is often called "growing pains," which may be a misnomer because the disease is not related to growth (AMA, 2003).

Although less is known about the pain people experience in childhood than at other times in their lives, much research since the early 1980s has focused on children's pain (Jeans, 1983; McGrath & Hillier, 1996). Before then, some practitioners believed that babies feel relatively little pain because their nervous systems are immaturely developed and their reactions to pain often differ from those of older individuals. As a result, minor surgery, such as circumcision, was commonly done on infants with little or no anesthesia. But this situation changed rapidly as a result of new research. Let's see what is known today about pain in children.

PAIN AND CHILDREN'S SENSORY AND COGNITIVE DEVELOPMENT

Although the issue of whether babies are as sensitive as adults to pain is not yet resolved, one thing is clear: newborn babies feel pain. The fact that they typically cry when slapped on the rump if they do not start to breathe after birth certainly suggests that they feel pain. Is clearer evidence available?

Better evidence that babies perceive pain comes from studies with newborns as they undergo noxious medical procedures, such as when the foot is pierced to draw a blood sample. One of these studies found

Very young children in acute pain do not have sufficient language to express what they are feeling and need special efforts to reduce their distress.

that babies' reactions to the noxious stimulus included a "pain" facial expression: they had their eyes squeezed, brows contracted, tongue taut, and mouth open (Grunau & Craig, 1987). This pattern is comparable to the expression adults display when in pain. Another study found that newborns' crying varied with the intensity of the noxious procedure (Porter, Miller, & Marshall, 1986). Highly noxious procedures elicited cries with certain characteristics, such as relatively high-pitched peak tones, that adults judged as indicating "urgency."

One difficulty young children have in expressing their experience of pain is that their language abilities are very limited. Toddlers may know the word "hurt," but they do not usually have many other words to describe their pain (McGrath & Hillier, 1996; Mills, 1989). Instead of telling adults of their pain, they may display other pain behaviors, such as crying, rubbing the affected area, or clenching their jaws. Mary Ellen Jeans (1983) interviewed 5- to 13-year-old children to determine their knowledge about pain. When asked to describe pain, the 5-year-olds used only 5 different adjectives, on average, but older children used more: the 13-year-olds used an average of 26.

ASSESSING PAIN IN CHILDREN

When a patient has symptoms that include pain, the physician usually needs to know its location, intensity, quality, duration, and temporal patterning. This information helps in making an accurate diagnosis. Although children's ability to provide this information is limited, especially if they are young, researchers have developed measures that use self-report, behavioral, and physiological methods (Bush & DeLuca, 2001; McGrath & Gillespie, 2001). Interviewing children requires considerable skill in developing rapport with them, asking the right questions in ways they can understand, and knowing what their answers mean.

What kinds of self-report methods are available to assess children's pain? One approach uses rating scales to describe the intensity of their pain (McGrath & Gillespie, 2001). With children under about 5 years of age, pain assessments are usually made on the basis of pain behavior, such as vocalizations and facial expressions. Older children can understand and use visual analog scales and verbal rating scales if the choices are labeled in ways they can understand, such as with faces indicating graded degrees of distress. Other approaches are designed to measure multiple dimensions of child and adolescent pain experiences, two of which are the Pediatric Pain Questionnaire (Varni & Thompson, 1986) and the Children's Comprehensive Pain Questionnaire (McGrath & Hillier, 1996). These instruments assess the pain itself and its psychosocial effects, such as how the child and family reacted to the pain. Adults may help the children fill out portions of the questionnaires when they lack needed language skills.

Behavioral and physiological assessment approaches also provide valuable ways to measure children's pain, especially in early childhood (Bush & DeLuca, 2001; McGrath & Gillespie, 2001). The most obvious behavioral approach simply involves having the child or parents report the child's pain behaviors in pain diaries. Other behavioral assessments can use structured clinical sessions in which health care workers rate or record the occurrence of pain behavior. Methods for physiological assessment are like those we considered earlier.

Children's pain experiences are affected by a variety of psychosocial factors, particularly the social environment in which pain occurs (Bush & DeLuca, 2001). Parents serve as models and agents of reinforcement for the pain behavior of their children. But little is known about the personality and family characteristics of children that may contribute to the intensity and frequency of their pain (Jeans, 1983; Lavigne, Schulein, & Hahn, 1986). Now that researchers have methods to assess children's pain, they can do the research that is needed.

SUMMARY

Although pain is typically unpleasant, it is a critical sense for survival because it warns us of actual or threatened tissue damage. It is the most frequent medical complaint of patients and the most commonly stated reason for disability. Pain includes both sensory and emotional components, and it has many different qualities. Sometimes it feels sharp and localized, other times it's dull and pervasive, sometimes it has a burning sensation, and other times it has a cramping or aching feeling.

Pain experiences also vary along a continuum, ranging from those that are mostly organic in origin to those that are mostly psychogenic. Virtually all pain experiences involve an interplay of both physiological and psychological processes, but the mixture of organic and psychogenic factors varies. Most pain conditions involve acute pain, which may last just a moment or as long as a few months and eventually disappears. Other pain conditions last longer and are described as chronic. Long-lasting pain can be classified as chronic-recurrent, chronic-intractable-benign, and chronic-progressive pain.

The body's tissues contain chemical substances that are released at the site where an injury occurs, thereby activating afferent nociceptors, which are free nerve endings. Pain signals are carried toward the central nervous system by A-delta fibers, which carry signals of sharp and well-localized pain rapidly to motor and sensory areas of the cortex, and C fibers, which carry information about dull and diffuse pain slowly to the forebrain.

The process of pain perception involves three curious and fascinating phenomena. The first is called referred pain, whereby pain originating from internal organs is perceived as coming from other parts of the body.

The second involves pain with no detectable physical basis. Neuralgia, causalgia, and phantom limb pain are syndromes that involve intense pain even though no noxious stimulus is present. Third, the meaning of pain affects people's experience of it. Individuals for whom pain means a personal disaster is almost over and better things are coming seem to perceive less pain than do people with similar wounds who believe the personal disaster is just beginning.

The gate-control theory of pain proposes that neural signals of pain pass through a gate that can modulate the signals before they reach the brain. The degree to which the gate is open or closed depends on three factors: the amount of activity in the pain fibers, the amount of activity in other peripheral fibers, and messages that descend from the brain. This theory allows for the influence of psychological factors in pain perception. The phenomenon of stimulation-produced analgesia supports this theory, demonstrating that stimulation to the periaqueductal gray area of the brainstem can block the sensation of noxious stimulation elsewhere in the body. The findings of research with a drug called naloxone indicate that this phenomenon depends on the action of endogenous opioids—a class of neurochemicals that includes endorphin and enkephalin. The effect of placebos in reducing pain also depends on opioids.

Psychological processes play an important role in the experience of pain. People in pain generally display pain behaviors, such as moaning, guarded movement, or avoidance of activity. These behaviors are often reinforced—for instance, when they result in the person being relieved of doing disliked activities or receiving special attention, care, and affection. Pain and stress are intimately linked: pain is stressful, and stress can produce pain—at least headache pain. People often have difficult times coping with chronic pain, which can lead to psychological maladjustment.

A person's pain can be assessed in several ways. Self-report methods include interviews, rating scales, and pain questionnaires. The McGill Pain Questionnaire assesses three dimensions of pain: affective, sensory, and evaluative. Behavioral assessment approaches can measure pain in the person's everyday activities and in structured clinical sessions. Psychophysiological measures of pain assess muscle tension, autonomic activity, and evoked potentials of the brain. Children can perceive pain when they are born. Methods to assess pain and its psychosocial effects in children have been developed.

KEY TERMS

pain
acute pain
chronic-recurrent pain
chronic-intractable-
  benign pain

chronic-progressive pain
nociceptors
referred pain
gate-control theory

periaqueductal gray
stimulation-produced
  analgesia

endogenous opioids
pain behaviors
McGill Pain Questionnaire

12

MANAGING AND CONTROLLING CLINICAL PAIN

Clinical Pain
Acute Clinical Pain
Chronic Clinical Pain

Medical Treatments for Pain
Surgical Methods for Treating Pain
Chemical Methods for Treating Pain

Behavioral and Cognitive Methods for Treating Pain
The Operant Approach
Relaxation and Biofeedback
Cognitive Methods

Hypnosis and Interpersonal Therapy
Hypnosis as a Treatment for Pain
Interpersonal Therapy for Pain

Physical and Stimulation Therapies for Pain
Stimulation Therapies
Physical Therapy

Pain Clinics
Multidisciplinary Programs
Evaluating the Success of Pain Clinics

PROLOGUE

"Ouch! My foot hurts," the little girl cried as she tried to walk. The nurse responded quickly, saying, "I'm sorry it hurts. Show me where it hurts. . . . Let's get some exercise some other time." This 3-year-old girl was a patient who had had a difficult life. She was in her tenth month of hospitalization after receiving second- and third-degree burns to her legs and buttocks from having been immersed in scaldingly hot water. Some evidence indicated that the burn had been deliberately inflicted and that she was a victim of child abuse.

After all these months this little girl's discomfort was not over. She still needed physical therapy and plastic surgery and still had to wear uncomfortable knee-extension splints to prevent contractures. But her therapy was not going well. What had become clear was that the hospital staff was inadvertently reinforcing her pain behavior by comforting her and allowing her to avoid disliked activities. James Varni and Karen Thompson have described how this situation was not in the child's long-term best interests, having disrupted her physical, social, and emotional rehabilitation:

> Physical therapy was essentially terminated because of the patient's interfering pain behaviors.

319

Two patterns emerged when the patient was placed in her bedroom in the crib with knee extension splints on. First, the child would struggle until she had removed the splints, resulting in further contractures and the need for additional plastic surgery. Second, if she failed to remove the splints, her crying would intensify to the point of screaming. At times she would fall asleep, exhausted, and continue sobbing well into the naptime hour. Other times, she would continue screaming until, in consideration of the other children, the nursing staff would remove her to a separate room for the reminder of the hour. (1986, p. 382)

Her rehabilitation and interactions with adults and other children were being limited because of her behavior, and she was clearly not coping well with her situation.

What can be done to help patients who, like this girl, have developed chronic pain behaviors that interfere with their rehabilitation? In this chapter, we will examine how she was helped and what methods are effective in reversing chronic pain behaviors. We will also discuss a variety of techniques and programs for treating and helping patients control the pain experience. As we study these issues, we will try to answer other questions you may have about dealing with pain. Do effective treatments for acute pain also work with chronic pain? What role do drugs have in treating pain, and how can patients decrease drug use? Do such methods as hypnosis and acupuncture really work in reducing pain? What are pain clinics, and are they effective in treating pain?

CLINICAL PAIN

Not all of our pain experiences receive professional treatment, and not all of them require it. The term **clinical pain** refers to any pain that receives or requires professional treatment. The pain may be either acute or chronic and may result from known or unknown causes (Sanders, 1985). Clinical pain calls for treatment in and of itself, and not only because it may be a symptom of a progressive disease, such as arthritis or cancer. Relieving pain is important for humanitarian reasons, of course—and doing so also produces medical and psychosocial benefits for the patient.

Let's look at medical and psychosocial issues that are associated with controlling clinical pain, beginning with acute pain.

ACUTE CLINICAL PAIN

By preventing or relieving acute pain, practitioners make medical procedures go more smoothly, reduce patients' stress and anxiety, and help them recover more quickly. Much of the acute pain people experience in today's world has little survival value (Chapman, 1984). What survival value would there be in feeling the pain as a dentist drills a tooth or a surgeon removes an appendix? How would people's survival be enhanced by feeling the intense pain that accompanies normal healing while resting in a hospital during the days after surgery?

When competent medical care is available, these pains are not useful. Yet during recovery after surgery in the United States, many patients experience higher-than-necessary pain (Chapman, 1984; Williams, 1996). As a result, the American Pain Society recommends that practitioners assess patients' pain intensity and satisfaction with pain relief after surgery (Haythornthwaite & Fauerbach, 2001). On a visual analog scale (see Figure 11–4) with a 100 mm long line, ratings of 45 to 74 reflect moderate pain and 75 to 100 reflect severe pain; reducing pain ratings by one-third suggests a change that is meaningful for the patient (Jensen, Chen, & Brugger, 2003). Inadequately reduced pain after surgery can cause physiological reactions that can lead to medical complications and even death. For instance, high pain and muscle spasms that may arise from abdominal and chest surgery can prevent patients from breathing deeply and coughing, allowing bacterial infections to take hold in the lungs and cause pneumonia (Chapman, 1984).

CHRONIC CLINICAL PAIN

When pain persists and becomes chronic, patients begin to perceive its nature differently. Although in the acute phase the pain was very aversive, they expected it to end and did not see it as a permanent part of their lives. As the pain persists, they tend to become discouraged and angry and are likely to seek the opinions of other physicians. This can be constructive. However, when this is not successful, and as patients come to see less and less connection between their discomfort and any known or treatable disorder, increasing hopelessness and despair may lead them to resort to consulting quacks (Chapman, 1984).

The transition from acute to chronic pain is a critical time when many of these patients develop feelings of helplessness and psychological disorders, such as depression, especially if the pain is disabling (Epping-Jordan et al., 1998; Gatchel, 1996). The neurotic triad—hypochondriasis, depression, and hysteria—often becomes a dominant aspect of their personalities (Gatchel, 1996; Rosen et al., 1987). These changes typically parallel alterations in the patients' lifestyles, employment status, and family lives—as the following letter from a wife to her husband's therapist reflects:

> perhaps if I could explain my husband's attitudes it might help you understand his problems. . . . The questionnaire you gave him to complete and send back became a tremendous ordeal for him. Why, I'll never know, because the questions were simple, but in the state of mind he is in, everything gets to be a chore. . . . Since his back operation five years ago he has become increasingly impatient and progressively slower with no ambition at all to even try to help himself. He had made himself an invalid and it has become very difficult for me or my family to tolerate his constant complaining. He blames me, blames our two sons, who he says don't help him around the house when in fact he does little or nothing to help himself. He does exactly the same things day after day with projects he starts and never completes and always because of his health. . . . To dwell on his illness is what he wants and only that he will do, believe me. He needs psychiatry of some kind. (Flor & Turk, 1985, p. 268)

A study of people who had suffered for years with severe chronic-recurrent and chronic-intractable-benign pain found that about half had considered suicide because of their conditions (Hitchcock, Ferrell, & McCaffery, 1994). Chronic pain often creates a broad array of long-term psychosocial problems and impaired interrelationships, which distinguish its victims from those of acute pain (Weir et al. 1994).

Individuals who receive treatment for their pain after it has progressed and become chronic tend to exhibit certain physical and psychosocial symptoms that characterize a "chronic pain syndrome." According to psychologist Steven Sanders (1985), these symptoms include:

- Associated tissue damage or irritation, which may be minor or major.
- Persistent pain complaints and other pain behaviors, such as grimacing or guarded movement, when in discomfort.
- Disrupted daily activity patterns, characterized either by a general reduction or by recurrent large fluctuations.
- Disrupted social, marital, employment, and recreational activities.
- Excessive use of drugs or repeated use of surgical procedures to relieve pain.
- Disturbed sleep patterns.
- Increased anxiety and depression.

Chronic pain patients usually exhibit the first two symptoms and at least one of the remaining ones. Generally speaking, the more symptoms the patient presents, the greater the impact the pain has had and the greater the maladjustment it has produced.

Because of the differences between acute pain and chronic pain in their duration and the effects they have on their victims, these conditions usually require different treatment methods. Health care professionals need to distinguish between acute and chronic pain conditions and provide the most appropriate pain relief techniques for the patient's needs (Gatchel, 1996). Failing to do so can make the condition worse. Keeping this caution in mind, we'll turn our attention for the remainder of this chapter to the many medical, psychological, and physical techniques available to help control patients' pain.

MEDICAL TREATMENTS FOR PAIN

A few centuries ago, peasants in Western cultures commonly treated pain by piercing the affected area of the body with a "vigorous" twig of a tree, believing that the twig would absorb the pain from the body (Turk, Meichenbaum, & Genest, 1983). Then, to prevent anyone from getting the pain from that twig, they buried it deep in the ground. Other early practices for controlling pain were not so farfetched, but they were crudely applied, even by physicians. In 19th-century America, alcoholic beverages and "medicines" laced with opium were readily available (Critchlow, 1986; Kett, 1977). Many people used these substances to

Readily available elixirs in 19th-century America often contained such substances as opium and cocaine.

alleviate pain, and physicians commonly employed them as anesthetics for surgery before ether was introduced. Today when patients suffer from pain, physicians try to reduce the discomfort in two ways—chemically and surgically.

SURGICAL METHODS FOR TREATING PAIN

Treating chronic pain with surgical methods is a relatively radical approach, and some surgical procedures are more useful than others. In some procedures, the surgery removes or disconnects portions of the peripheral nervous system or the spinal cord, thereby preventing pain signals from reaching the brain. These are extreme procedures—and if they are successful, they produce numbness and, sometimes, paralysis in the region of the body served by the affected nerves. But these procedures seldom provide long-term relief from the pain, which is often replaced after some days or months by pain and other sensations that are worse than the original condition (Hare & Milano, 1985; Melzack & Wall, 1982). Because of the poor prospects of permanent relief and the risks involved in these surgical procedures, they are rarely used today.

Other surgical procedures for relieving pain do not remove or disconnect nerve fibers and are much more successful. One example is the *synovectomy*, a technique whereby a surgeon removes membranes that become inflamed in arthritic joints (AMA, 2003; Anderson et al., 1985). Another example is *spinal fusion*, a procedure that joins two or more adjacent vertebrae to treat severe back pain (AMA, 2003). Surgery is often used in the United States to treat back pain, but there is little evidence that it produces better long-term pain reduction than nonsurgical methods. They are used at a far lower rate in other developed countries, such as Denmark and England (Cherkin et al., 1994; Turk, 2002). Surgery for chronic skeletal pain conditions is most appropriate when the person is severely disabled and nonsurgical treatment methods have failed. Physicians and patients usually prefer other medical approaches, such as chemical methods.

CHEMICAL METHODS FOR TREATING PAIN

Although medical research has led to many advances in treating pain since the 1800s, this progress has been slow. The field of medicine has focused much more on developing methods for curing disease than on reducing pain (Melzack & Wall, 1982). Let's look at the use of chemical methods for treating acute and chronic pain. (Go to 💡.)

Using Chemicals for Acute Pain

Many pharmaceuticals are very effective for relieving acute pain, such as occurs after surgery. Physicians choose the specific drug and dosage by considering many factors, such as how intense the pain is and its location and cause. Their effective use of these chemicals, giving as much pain relief as they safely can, depends on characteristics of the drug, the patients, and sociocultural factors. In some countries, such as in Latin America, using narcotics for pain relief is extremely rare (DePalma, 1996). Other cultures have become much more accepting of narcotic pain control.

Many hospital patients in pain are *undermedicated*, and those who receive too little pain relief tend to be children and minority group members, even when compared against other patients with the same medical condition (Bush & DeLuca, 2001; Cleeland et al., 1994; Ng et al., 1996). For instance, when the patient is a child, practitioners tend to administer painkillers less frequently, give doses below the recommended level, and discontinue it earlier, especially if the drug is a narcotic. The reasons for these age and sociocultural differences are unclear. In the case of children, it

HIGHLIGHT

Types of Pain-Relieving Chemicals

The most common medical approaches for treating pain today involve the use of various chemicals, some of which are used mainly in hospitals. Four types of chemicals are commonly used in treating pain (Winters, 1985; Zeltzer et al., 1997).

1. *Peripherally active analgesics* make up one type of pain-relieving chemical. As the name implies, these drugs reduce pain by their action in the peripheral nervous system, such as by inhibiting the synthesis of neurochemicals that sensitize nociceptors to algogenic substances released at the site of tissue damage. These analgesics include *aspirin*, *acetaminophen* (brand names Tylenol and Datril), and *ibuprofen* (Advil and Motrin). Aspirin was first manufactured in the late 1800s and is by far the best-known and most widely used drug in this class; Americans take many billions each year. Aspirin is a remarkable drug, being a very effective analgesic for mild-to-moderate pain, while also reducing fever and inflammation. Using aspirin on an occasional basis has no adverse effects, but heavy use can irritate the stomach lining. Peripherally acting analgesics provide substantial pain relief for many pain conditions, especially arthritis and other conditions that involve inflammation.

2. *Centrally acting analgesics* are narcotics (opioids) that bind to opiate receptors in the central nervous system and inhibit nociceptor transmission or alter the perception of pain stimuli. These drugs are derived either directly from the opium poppy—as are codeine and morphine—or synthetically, such as heroin, methadone, and the brand-name drugs Percodan and Demerol. Narcotics are very effective in reducing severe acute pain, but patients who use them on a long-term basis report only about a one-third reduction in pain (Turk, 2002). Physicians and patients often worry about the potential these drugs have for producing tolerance, in which the individual requires increasingly large doses, and for causing addiction with long-term use. However, the risk of addiction to opioids used for pain relief is not as great as many people believe, and practitioners are obliged to monitor use carefully (DEA, 2004).

3. *Local anesthetics*, such as novocaine, lidocaine, and bupivacaine, make up the third category of chemicals for relieving pain. Although local anesthetics can be applied topically, they are much more potent when injected at the site where the pain originates, as a dentist does before drilling or pulling a tooth. These chemicals block nerve cells in the region from generating impulses—and they often continue to relieve pain for hours or days after the chemical action has worn off (AMA, 2003; Hare & Milano, 1985). Long-term use of currently available local anesthetics is not recommended because of their serious side effects (Melzack & Wall, 1982).

4. *Indirectly acting drugs* affect nonpain conditions, such as emotions, that produce or contribute to pain. These drugs include depressants (tranquilizers and sedatives) and antidepressants. Although depressants reduce anxiety and help patients sleep, they do not relieve pain and can produce psychological and physical dependence with long-term use. Drugs classed as *antidepressants* not only reduce psychological depression, but they also markedly relieve chronic pain in about one-third of individuals (Turk, 2002).

---

may be that practitioners believe children feel less pain than adults or are more likely to become addicted to a drug (Bush, Holmbeck, & Cockrell, 1989). Or children may simply request less medication, perhaps because they dislike injections or taking pills more than adults do. Similar reasons may explain the ethnic differences.

The conventional ways for administering painkilling chemicals involve giving injections or pills, and these are given under one of two arrangements: a prescribed schedule or "as needed" (called PRN for the Latin *pro re nata*) by the patient. But two other methods are available today (AMA, 2003; Zeltzer et al., 1997). In one of these methods—called an *epidural block*—practitioners inject narcotics or local anesthetics epidurally, that is, near the membrane that surrounds the spinal cord. These chemicals then prevent pain signals from being transmitted to the brain. The second technique is called *patient-controlled analgesia*. This procedure allows the patient to determine how much painkiller, such as morphine, he or she needs, and get it without delay. The patient simply pushes a button to activate a computerized pump that dispenses a preset dose of the chemical through a needle that remains inserted continuously. Practitioners monitor the patient's use of the drug and set limits on the rate and amount of its use.

Do patients abuse the opportunity to control their use of narcotics for pain control? Current evidence suggests that the risk of abuse is low for most patients, at least under certain circumstances. A study by Marc Citron and his colleagues (1986) examined this issue in hospitalized men with severe cancer pain who were placed on a patient-controlled analgesia procedure for about 2 days. A physician preset for each patient the dosage of morphine the pump would deliver and a lockout time, that is, the interval after a dose when no more morphine would be available (about 30 minutes). The patients' rate of morphine use actually *declined* over time rather than increased, being used far more heavily in the first few hours than it was later: after the first 4 hours, the rate dropped sharply to less than 40% of the earlier rate. These patients were free to take much more medication, but they did not. Similar results have been found with male and female adolescent patients following surgery (Tyler, 1990). But there is a caution in using patient-controlled analgesia with patients who are relatively young, have high levels of anxiety, or have low levels of social support. They tend to use more of the drug than other acute pain patients do (Gil et al., 1990).

Using Chemicals for Chronic Pain

Chronic pain occurs most commonly with disorders that are not life threatening, such as arthritis, but it can also occur with cancer, which practitioners generally view differently for pain relief. Using opioids for managing moderate to severe cancer pain is widely accepted today (DEA, 2004). But despite guidelines to treat pain more aggressively, many cancer patients receive inadequate analgesic drugs (Cleeland et al., 1994). Why? Part of the reason is that cancer patients—especially older, less educated ones—often fear they will become addicted if the drug is a narcotic and believe that "good" patients don't complain (Ward et al., 1993). Practitioners need to discuss these issues with their patients and correct misconceptions.

Should narcotics be used in treating chronic noncancer pain? Practitioners first consider other treatment methods—other chemicals or methods discussed later in this chapter—but if those don't provide enough relief, they can consider long-term opioid treatment with careful monitoring (DEA, 2004). Narcotics provide effective pain relief for many patients with a variety of chronic pain conditions (Jadad et al., 1992; Turk, 2002). For example, researchers tested drug therapy, combining methadone and an antidepressant, over a 2-year period for men and women patients with long-term, severe phantom limb pain (Urban et al., 1986). These people were in pain almost constantly and had tried a variety of treatments for pain relief in the past. They began the drug therapy as hospital inpatients, reported at discharge that their pain had been reduced by about two thirds, and maintained this level of pain reduction throughout the next 2 years with very low daily doses of each drug.

These findings are very important and indicate that narcotics in low doses can provide effective pain relief without requiring progressively larger doses or leading to addiction. Because of a growing body of similar findings, American practitioners are using narcotics more than in the past for patients who are severely disabled by their chronic pain conditions, such as rheumatoid arthritis and severe back injury (Turk, Brody, & Okifuji, 1994). But increases in using narcotics for chronic pain are occurring cautiously for at least three reasons. First, the findings we have described need to be confirmed with a greater variety of subjects and types of pain conditions. Despite the low risk that drug abuse appears to have for most pain patients, it probably poses a high risk for *some* patients. Second, studies need to determine specifically how taking daily doses of narcotics alters patients' lives and functioning. Third, researchers need to find out why tolerance and addiction to narcotics are less likely when they are taken for pain relief. Is it because the doses are so small, for instance, or that the practitioners monitor and set limits on the drug use? Or is it that the patients believe they may lose their painkillers if they use them too much?

Chemical methods alone are usually not sufficient for controlling pain. The need for other approaches in helping pain patients is suggested in the research findings on three psychosocial factors. First, chronic headache patients tend to use maladaptive ways of coping with everyday stressors more than people without chronic headaches (Mosley et al., 1990). Second, arthritis patients with high feelings of helplessness before drug treatment begins report poorer treatment success in reducing pain and disability than do comparable low-helplessness patients (Nicassio et al., 1993). Third, many patients in research who receive *placebo* drugs with double-blind procedures report substantial pain relief (Andrasik, Blake, & McCarran, 1986; Feuerstein & Gainer, 1982). Because placebo effects result from psychological processes, we might expect that psychological methods might also relieve pain. As we saw in the gate-control theory in Chapter 11, separating physiological and psychosocial aspects of a person's pain experience is artificial.

To summarize, medical treatments of pain focus mainly on using chemical approaches to reduce discomfort. For chronic pain patients, these approaches can be enhanced when combined with pain control methods that other health care professions provide.

Collaborating with Other Professionals

Because psychosocial factors are so important in people's experience of chronic pain, many medical practitioners treat pain patients by joining forces with psychologists and other health care professionals, such as social workers and physical and occupational therapists. When introducing a team approach to chronic pain patients, physicians need to describe the rationale for it and the functions each professional can provide. For instance,

> pain patients might balk at the suggestion that they see a psychologist. They typically believe, generally quite correctly, that their problems have a physical basis. Hence, the relevance of a psychological consultation may not be evident to the patient. The meaning of the referral also may be unclear. The patient may infer that the physician making the referral believes the problem to be somehow less than real, or believes the patient to be seriously maladjusted psychologically. Patients who interpret the referral this way are likely to be guarded with the psychologist. (Cameron & Shepel, 1986, p. 242)

The physician should state clearly that (1) he or she realizes the patient is "obviously living in a great deal of pain," (2) patients can help themselves control their pain by working with these other professionals, and (3) the physician will be an active part of the team.

Psychologists conduct therapy with patients individually and in groups. Table 12.1 describes some advantages of a group format in helping patients cope with their pain and disability. The pain group provides a forum for talking about their worst fears and conflicts to people who share these concerns and understand. Patients often say, "I'm afraid the pain will get worse," "I was beginning to believe I was imagining the pain," and "I can't do things because of the pain,

---

Table 12.1 *Advantages of Group Psychotherapy Over Individual Therapy in Treating Pain*

1. *Efficiency.* Although each patient has unique problems, chronic pain sufferers also face common difficulties, such as depression and addiction to medication. As a result, they often need similar types of advice and information. Group meetings use the therapist's time more efficiently.

2. *Reduced isolation.* Chronic pain sufferers are typically isolated from extended social contact. This situation can lead to a sense of alienation, which involves feelings of being different from others and of anger and suspicion toward them. Group meetings can help to overcome these feelings.

3. *Credible feedback for patients.* Pain patients often resist feedback or advice from therapists, saying such things as, "You don't know what it's like to live with pain 24 hours a day!" In their eyes, the type of feedback other patients can give may be more believable.

4. A *new reference group for patients.* Patients in a pain group develop new social networks of individuals who are comparable to themselves and who can provide social pressure to conform to the realities and constructive "rules" of living with pain and physical limitations.

5. A *different perspective for the therapist.* Watching the patient relate to other individuals in a group provides the therapist with certain kinds of information that may aid in identifying specific problems therapy should address, such as maladaptive coping styles.

Source: Based on Gentry & Owens (1986).

and I feel guilty, helpless, frustrated, and angry" (Hendler, 1984). Patients in the group may answer, for instance, "You hurt whether you go shopping or not; so the choice isn't between having pain or not, it's between whether you go shopping or stay home!" (Gentry & Owens, 1986). These people can say things to each other that others could not, without seeming cruel. Group members can also disconfirm each other's misconceptions, share their own ways for managing pain on a day-to-day basis, give each other hope and social support, and detect and confront each others' pain games, such as when patients engage in pain behaviors that bring them attention and sympathy.

The goals of psychological treatments for pain include helping clients' reduce their frequency and intensity of pain, improve their emotional adjustment to the pain they have, increase their social and physical activity, and reduce their use of analgesic drugs. Physicians usually want to minimize their patients' use of medication, especially when drugs are to be taken on a long-term basis.

BEHAVIORAL AND COGNITIVE METHODS FOR TREATING PAIN

Gate-control theory changed the way many health care workers conceptualize pain by proposing that pain can be controlled not only by biochemical methods that alter sensory input directly, but by modifying motivational and cognitive processes, too. This more complex view of pain provided the rationale for psychologists to develop techniques to help patients *cope more effectively* with the pain and other stressors they experience and *reduce their reliance on drugs* for pain control. Some of these techniques use behavioral and cognitive methods, such as by changing patients' pain behaviors through techniques of operant conditioning.

THE OPERANT APPROACH

At the start of this chapter, we considered the case of a 3-year-old girl whose pain behaviors hampered her rehabilitation after she suffered severe burns months earlier. The help therapists provided was successful. It used an *operant approach*, in which therapists apply operant conditioning techniques to modify patients' behaviors.

The approach the therapists used with this girl involved extinction procedures for her pain behavior and reinforcement for appropriate, or "well," behavior (Varni et al., 1986; Varni & Thompson, 1986). Observations of the child's social environment revealed that the hospital staff reinforced her pain behaviors—crying, complaining of pain, resisting the nurse's efforts to put her splints on, and so forth—by giving attention to those behaviors and allowing her to avoid uncomfortable or disliked activities, such as physical therapy. To change this situation, the therapists instructed the hospital staff to:

- Ignore the pain behaviors they paid attention to in the past; this method is extinction.
- Provide rewards for compliant behavior—telling her, for instance, "If you don't cry while I put your splints on, you can have some cookies when I'm finished," or, "If you do this exercise, we can play a game."
- Praise her if she helps in putting on the splints, sleeps through naptime, goes for a period of time without complaining, or does an exercise.

Changing the consequences of her behavior in these ways had a dramatic effect: her pain behaviors decreased sharply, and she began to comply with requests to do exercises, make positive comments about her accomplishments, and assist in putting on her splints.

The operant approach to treating pain can be adapted for use with individuals of all ages, in hospitals and at home—and elements of the operant approach can be introduced before pain behavior becomes chronic. But treatment programs using this approach are usually applied with patients whose chronic pain has already produced serious difficulties in their lives. These programs typically have two main goals: the first is to reduce the patient's reliance on medication. This can be achieved, with the patient's approval, by mixing the painkiller with a flavored syrup, called a "pain cocktail," and giving it on a fixed schedule, such as every 4 hours, rather than whenever the patient requests it (Fordyce, 1976). Because receiving the painkiller is not tied to requesting it, any reinforcing effect the drug may have on that pain behavior is eliminated. Then, over a period of several weeks, the dosage of medication in the cocktail is gradually reduced until the syrup contains little or no drugs.

The second goal of the operant approach is to reduce the disability that generally accompanies chronic pain conditions. This is accomplished by altering the consequences for behavior so that they promote "well" behavior and discourage pain behavior, as we just saw in the program with the young burn patient. The chief feature of this approach is that the therapist trains people in the patient's social environment to monitor and keep a record of pain behaviors, try not to reinforce them, and systematically reward physical activity. The reinforcers may be of any kind—attention, praise and smiles, candy, money, or the opportunity to watch TV, for example—and may be formalized within a behavioral contract (Fordyce, 1976). The therapist periodically reviews the record of pain behavior to determine whether changes in the program are needed.

Is the operant approach effective? Studies have shown that operant techniques can successfully decrease patients' pain reports and medication use and increase their activity levels (Morley, Eccleston, & Williams, 1999; Roelofs et al., 2002). Although these findings are promising, some limitations should be mentioned. First, after the operant intervention ends and rewards are discontinued, some patients revert to their old pattern of inactivity and pain behavior. Second, not all chronic pain patients are likely to benefit from operant methods. For one thing, the goals of this approach seem more appropriate for patients with chronic-recurrent or chronic-intractable-benign pain than for those with chronic-progressive pain, such as in cancer patients. Also, patients are less likely to show behavioral improvements if they or people in their social environment are unwilling to participate and if they receive disability compensation (Fordyce, 1976). Despite these limitations, it seems clear that the operant approach can be a very useful component in treatment programs for many acute and chronic pain patients.

RELAXATION AND BIOFEEDBACK

Many people experience chronic episodes of pain resulting from underlying physiological processes that can be triggered by stress. If these patients could control their stress or the physiological processes that cause pain, they should be able to decrease the frequency or intensity of discomfort they experience. We saw in Chapter 4 that stress is one of many factors that can produce episodes of migraine and tension-

type headache. Until recently, researchers thought that stress triggers migraine headache by dilating arteries surrounding the brain and triggers tension-type headache by persistently contracting muscles of the scalp, neck, and shoulders (Andrasik, 1986). However, it is now clear that nervous system dysfunction is involved, such as sensitization or inflammation of nerves in the face and arteries around the brain (AMA, 2003; Holroyd, 2002).

Although the exact role of stress in these processes is not yet known, researchers have applied progressive muscle relaxation and biofeedback to reduce stress and related physiological processes in an effort to decrease headaches. These treatments are usually conducted in weekly sessions that span about 2 or 3 months (see, for example, Blanchard et al., 1986). We saw in Chapter 5 that individuals using the technique of *progressive muscle relaxation* focus their attention on specific muscle groups while alternately tightening and relaxing these muscles. In *biofeedback* procedures, people learn to exert voluntary control over a bodily function, such as heart rate, by monitoring its status with information from electronic devices (Sarafino, 2001). Of the many physiological processes people can learn to control through biofeedback, we'll consider one: to treat tension-type headaches, patients learn to control the tension of specific muscle groups, such as those in the forehead or neck. They learn by receiving biofeedback from an electromyograph (EMG) device, which measures electrical activity in those muscles. Therapists urge patients to practice these skills at home and use them when they feel pain episodes beginning—doing so improves treatment success (Gauthier, Côté, & French, 1994).

Do Relaxation and Biofeedback Help Relieve Pain?

Relaxation and biofeedback methods relieve pain. This broad conclusion comes from reviews and meta-analyses of studies that examined the effectiveness of these procedures (Bogaards & ter Kuile, 1994; Holroyd & Penzien, 1986; Morley, Eccleston, & Williams, 1999; Penzien, Rains, & Andrasik, 2002; Roelofs et al., 2002). But several points need to be made about this conclusion. First, although studies have demonstrated that relaxation and biofeedback treatments can help alleviate many types of pain, such as arthritic, phantom limb, and low back pain, the large majority of studies testing these treatments have focused on headache pain. Treatment with relaxation or biofeedback reduces the frequency of migraine and tension-type headaches by about 40 to 50% (Holroyd, 2002).

Second, progressive muscle relaxation and biofeedback treatments are about equally effective in relieving headache pain, but EMG biofeedback is somewhat more effective than relaxation (Holroyd, 2002). Studies have examined the success of these procedures by assessing whether the patients' daily records at the end of treatment showed decreases in the headache pain (its frequency, intensity, and duration) and by comparing the headache pain of patients who received these treatments with those who were in control groups. In one type of control group, the subjects receive no training but monitor their headache pain with daily records. In another type of control condition, subjects keep records and receive a placebo treatment, such as by taking sham medication or by receiving biofeedback sessions that give false feedback about changes in their bodily functions. Generally speaking, treatment with relaxation or biofeedback is about twice as effective in relieving pain as placebo conditions, which are more effective than just monitoring headache pain (Holroyd & Penzien, 1986). Figure 12–1 depicts these effects for tension-type (muscle-contraction) headache sufferers, averaged across subjects in many studies.

Third, the graph in Figure 12–1 suggests that headache sufferers get more pain relief when biofeedback and progressive muscle relaxation are combined, but these differences are not reliable because patients vary greatly in the amount of benefit they get from these treatments. For instance, among individuals who received relaxation treatment only, the percentage by which their pain improved ranged from 17 to 94%; among those who had the combined treatment, improvements ranged from 29 to 88% (Holroyd & Penzien, 1986). This variability is important: it reflects that many patients—especially middle-aged and elderly ones—seem to gain relatively little relief with these treatments (Blanchard & Andrasik, 1985; Holroyd & Penzien, 1986). Since biofeedback treatment is relatively expensive to conduct, being able to predict who will benefit from it most would be useful. Some evidence suggests, for example, that most children and those individuals of all ages who show certain psychophysiological patterns, such as a high correlation between their pain and EMG levels, may be better candidates for biofeedback treatment than other people (Keefe & Gil, 1985; Sarafino & Goehring, 2000).

Fourth, although the pain relief patients experience with progressive muscle relaxation or biofeedback treatment may result from the specific skills they have learned for controlling physiological processes, other psychological factors also seem to play a role. Consider, for instance, two findings. One is that placebo conditions often produce more relief than simply monitoring headache pain (Andrasik, 1986). The other is that massage therapy over a period of time can reduce chronic pain (Moyer, Rounds, & Hannum, 2004). Why? Patients' thoughts, beliefs, and spontaneous cognitive strategies probably account for these findings and contribute to part of the success of relaxation and biofeedback treatments in controlling pain (Turk, Meichenbaum, & Genest, 1983).

Figure 12–1 Percentage of change in headache pain, pretreatment to posttreatment, across many studies with patients suffering from chronic *muscle-contraction* (tension-type) headaches. Treatments consisted of EMG biofeedback, or relaxation, or EMG biofeedback and relaxation combined. Control conditions consisted of placebo biofeedback or simply monitoring headache pain. (Data from Holroyd & Penzien, 1985, Table IV.)

Are the Improvements from Relaxation and Biofeedback Durable?

After a patient completes the treatment for chronic pain, how long do the effects of the treatment last? Do the effects wear off in a few weeks or months? This is an issue of great importance in health psychology. As we saw in earlier chapters, interventions do not always last, such as in cases of alcohol abuse, and relapse often occurs. Pain researchers have addressed this issue by conducting a 5-year followup investigation on chronic headache patients who completed training for either progressive muscle relaxation or for both relaxation and biofeedback (Blanchard et al., 1986; Blanchard, Andrasik, et al., 1987; Blanchard, Appelbaum, et al., 1987).

The subjects in this research were adult patients who had suffered many years either from muscle-contraction (tension-type) headache or from "vascular" headache, which includes both migraine and combined (migraine plus tension-type) headache. All patients received relaxation training in ten sessions, spanning 8 weeks. Those people whose headache pain had not improved by at least 60% were offered additional treatment with biofeedback. All subjects had an audiotape to guide their practice of relaxation, and the vascular patients who received training in temperature biofeedback were given a temperature-monitoring device to use at home. The patients kept daily "headache diaries" with four ratings each day of their headache pain. Psychological assessment before and after the treatment revealed that their feelings of depression and anxiety decreased substantially (Blanchard et al., 1986). For 6 months after completing the treatment, the patients received treatment booster sessions if they desired them.

A difficulty in doing longitudinal research is that the number of original subjects who are available and willing to participate declines over time. At the time of the last annual followup, a little more than half of the patients could be located and agreed to participate. Figure 12–2 presents the people's ratings of headache pain during each of seven 4-week periods: pretreatment, post-treatment, and years 1 through 5 in the followup. As you can see, the treatment effects were quite durable for these patients. What about the patients who did not continue through the 5-year followup? Although there is no way of knowing for sure, the researchers presented evidence to suggest that the treatments were durable for them, too (Blanchard, Andrasik, et al., 1987; Blanchard, Appelbaum, et al.,

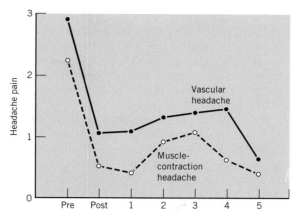

Figure 12–2 Averaged ratings of headache pain for muscle-contraction (tension-type) and vascular (migraine and combined) headache patients who successfully completed treatment and continued to participate in the followup. The graphs depict these ratings at pretreatment, post-treatment, and followup years 1 through 5. (Data from Blanchard, Appelbaum, et al., 1987, Table 1.)

1987). And findings of other followup studies confirm that completing relaxation training or both relaxation and biofeedback training provides durable headache relief for at least 2 years (Blanchard, 1987).

Progressive muscle relaxation and biofeedback techniques are very helpful in controlling the discomfort many chronic pain patients experience, but these treatments do not provide all the pain relief most patients need. Because chronic pain involves a complex interplay of sensory and psychosocial factors, therapists generally use these techniques along with several other approaches, especially cognitive therapies that address the thought patterns that occur when people experience pain.

COGNITIVE METHODS

What do people think about when they experience pain? In an acute pain situation, some people focus on the ordeal and how uncomfortable and miserable they are, but others do not (Turk & Rudy, 1986). For example, researchers asked children and adolescents what they think about when getting an injection at their dentist's office (Brown et al., 1986). Over 80% of the subjects reported thoughts that focused on negative emotions and pain, such as, "This hurts, I hate shots," "I'm scared," and "My heart is pounding and I feel shaky." One-fourth of the subjects had thoughts of escaping or avoiding the situation, as in, "I want to run away." Thoughts like these focus the person's attention on unpleasant aspects of the experience and make the pain worse (Keefe et al., 1994; Turk & Rudy, 1986).

Not all people who experience acute pain focus on the ordeal and discomfort; many use cognitive strategies to modify their experience. For instance, by 10 years of age, many children report that they try to cope with pain in a dental situation by thinking about something else or by saying to themselves such things as, "It's not so bad" or "Be brave" (Brown et al., 1986). But even when children know ways to cope with pain and recommend them for others to use, they don't necessarily use those skills themselves (Peterson et al., 1999). Although coping skills tend to improve as children get older, many patients in adulthood still exaggerate the fearful aspects of the painful medical procedures they experience (Chaves & Brown, 1987).

How do people cope with chronic pain? Some approaches they use involve *active coping*, in which they try to keep functioning by ignoring their pain or keeping busy with an interesting activity. Other approaches involve *passive coping*, such as taking to one's bed or curtailing social activities. For many chronic pain patients, a vicious circle develops in which passive coping leads to feelings of helplessness and depression, which leads to more passive coping, and so on (Smith & Wallston, 1992). Family and friends influence people's coping patterns by reinforcing some behaviors but not others (Menefee et al., 1996). The impact of chronic pain also depends on they way patients view their conditions (Jensen et al., 1999; Williams & Keefe, 1991). Those who believe their pain will last a very long time, is a sign of a disabling injury, and has unknown causes tend to show more pain behaviors and cope poorly, thinking the worst about their conditions and feeling that active coping strategies will not work. On the other hand, patients who believe that they understand the nature of their pain and that their conditions will improve tend to use active coping strategies. Those who cope well are more likely to return to work despite their pain (Linton & Buer, 1995).

To help people cope effectively with pain, medical and psychological practitioners need to assess and address their patients' beliefs. Cognitive techniques for treating pain involve active coping strategies, and many of these methods are, in fact, quite effective in helping people cope with pain. These techniques can be classified into three basic types: *distraction*, *imagery*, and *redefinition* (Fernandez, 1986; McCaul & Malott, 1984). We will examine these methods and consider their usefulness for people with acute and chronic pain.

Distraction

At your dentist's office, do the examination rooms have colorful pictures or large windows with nice views on all the walls that a patient can see while in the dental chair? My dentist's rooms do, and I use the pictures and windows to distract my attention when I feel the need. **Distraction** is the technique of focusing on a nonpainful stimulus in the immediate environment to divert one's attention from discomfort (Fernandez, 1986). We can be distracted from pain in many ways, such as by looking at a picture, listening to someone's voice, singing a song, counting ceiling tiles, playing a video game, or doing mathematics problems.

Not all distraction attempts are likely to work in relieving pain. Research on acute pain has shown that these strategies are more effective if the pain is mild or moderate than if it is strong (McCaul & Malott, 1984). Three aspects of the distraction task seem to affect how well it works. One aspect is the amount of attention the task receives; the greater the attention the task requires, the lower the pain ratings. Experiments with college students with the cold-pressor procedure found this effect, particularly when the ratings of pain were taken several minutes after the arm was removed from the cold water rather than while it was in the water (Christenfeld, 1997; McCaul, Monson, & Maki, 1992). The distraction tasks involved watching and reacting to numbers or colored lights on a panel or screen. High-distraction tasks required frequent or complex reactions to the stimuli.

The second factor that seems to affect whether distraction relieves pain is the extent to which the task is interesting or engrossing. Researchers compared the pain and coping behavior of 10-year-old children when receiving immunization injections under three conditions: standard care, application of a local anesthetic, or distraction (Cohen, Blount et al., 1999). The distraction task was engrossing: it involved watching a movie of the child's choice and answering a nurse's questions, such as "Which one is the good guy?" The children showed less distress and better coping under the distraction condition than under the standard care or anesthetic conditions. Similar distracting tasks have been applied successfully with infants and with preschoolers undergoing repeated injections (Cohen, 2002; Dahlquist et al., 2002).

The third factor in whether distraction relieves pain is its credibility to the person. A study demonstrated this by having college students undergo the cold-pressor procedure while listening to distracting stimuli through earphones (Melzack, Weisz, & Sprague, 1963). During the cold-pressor test, the students in one condition listened to a clearly noticeable sound, such as music, after having been told that they could control its volume and that dentists had found that loud sound helps reduce pain. Students in another condition got similar instructions, but they tried to listen for a low-intensity "hum" that really didn't exist. The subjects who heard the noticeable sound kept their hands in the cold water longer than those who listened for the hum. Since there was no sound, the students probably didn't believe the technique would work.

Because of the role of credibility in using distraction methods, therapists may need to help patients understand how these techniques can work. One therapist described the following approach for doing this:

> First, I ask the patient to be aware of the sensations in his thighs as he sits in his chair. I note that those sensations are real, and they have a physical basis, but they are not normally experienced because other things occupy his attention. Then I suggest that he think of a TV set: he could block out the channel 9 signal by tuning in channel 11; the channel 9 signal is still there, but not being tuned in. I suggest that while his pain signals are real, he can learn to "tune them out." . . . A number of pain patients have reported that they frequently think of the TV metaphor when experiencing pain and take appropriate action to "tune out." (Cameron, quoted in Turk, Meichenbaum, & Genest, 1983, p. 284)

By providing plausible explanations for a recommended technique, therapists can increase its effectiveness and the likelihood that the patient will use it.

Distraction strategies are useful for reducing acute pain, such as that experienced in some medical or dental procedures, and they can also provide relief for chronic pain patients in some circumstances (McCaul & Malott, 1984). Singing a song or staring intently at a stimulus can divert the person's attention for a short while—and this may be a great help, such as for an arthritis sufferer who experiences heightened pain when climbing stairs. People who want to use distraction for moderate levels of continuous pain may get longer-lasting relief by engaging in an extended engrossing activity, such as watching a movie or reading a book.

Imagery

Sometimes when children are about to receive injections, their parents will say something like, "It'll be easier if you think about something nice, like the fun things we did at the park." **Nonpain imagery**—sometimes called *guided imagery*—is a strategy whereby the person tries to alleviate discomfort by conjuring up a mental scene that is unrelated to or incompatible with the pain (Fernandez, 1986). The most common type of imagery people use involves scenes that are pleasant to them—they think of "something nice." This scene might involve being at the beach or in the country, for instance. Therapists usually encourage, or "guide," the person to include aspects of different senses: vision, hearing, taste, smell, and touch. As an example, the scene at the beach could include the sight and smell of the ocean water, the sound of the waves, and the warm, grainy feel of the sand. The person generally tries to keep the imagined event in mind as long as possible.

The imagery technique is in many ways like distraction. The main difference is that imagery is based on the person's imagination rather than on real objects or events in the environment. As a result, individuals who use imagery do not have to depend on the environment to provide a suitably distracting stimulus. They can develop one or more scenes that work reliably, which they "carry" around in their heads. They can then call one of these scenes up for pain relief whenever they need it. Imagery seems to work best when it attracts high levels of the person's attention or involvement, and it is likely to work better with mild or moderate pain than with strong pain (McCaul & Malott, 1984; Turk, Meichenbaum, & Genest, 1983). Although imagery clearly helps in reducing acute pain, the extent of this technique's usefulness with longer-lasting pain episodes is unclear. One limitation with using imagery in pain control is that some individuals are less adept in imagining scenes than others (Melzack & Wall, 1982).

Redefinition

The third type of cognitive strategy for reducing discomfort is **pain redefinition,** in which the person substitutes constructive or realistic thoughts about the pain experience for thoughts that arouse feelings of threat or harm (Fernandez, 1986; McCaul & Malott, 1984). Therapists can help people redefine their pain experiences in several ways. One approach involves teaching clients to engage in an internal dialogue, using positive self-statements that take basically two forms (Fernandez, 1986):

- *Coping statements* emphasize the person's ability to tolerate the discomfort, as when people say to themselves, "It hurts, but you're in control," or, "Be brave—you can take it."
- *Reinterpretative statements* are designed to negate the unpleasant aspects of the discomfort, as when people think, "It's not so bad," "It's not the worst thing that could happen," or, "It hurts, but think of the benefits of this experience."

This last statement can be particularly appropriate for persons undergoing painful medical procedures.

Two other methods can help people redefine their pain experiences. First, therapists can provide information about the sensations to expect in medical procedures, thereby reducing the pain that patients experience when undergoing these procedures (Anderson & Masur, 1983). The information therapists provide can also help clients remember more accurately the amount of pain they experienced in these procedures in the past and how well they coped (Chen et al., 1999). Since many patients exaggerate the discomfort they will feel and misremember past pain experiences, providing realistic information helps them redefine the experiences before they occur. Second, therapists can help individuals see that some of their beliefs are illogical and are making the discomfort worse. (Go to 🔍.)

The Value of Cognitive Strategies in Controlling Pain

Studies have found that cognitive strategies effectively reduce *acute* pain (Fernandez & Turk, 1989;

Manne et al., 1994). Distraction and imagery seem to be particularly useful with mild or moderate pain, and redefinition appears to be more effective with strong pain (McCaul & Malott, 1984). How helpful are cognitive methods for treating *chronic* pain? The answer is likely to depend on many factors, such as the severity of the pain, the type of illness, and the methods used. Redefinition may be more effective in relieving chronic pain than distraction is. A study compared these two techniques in reducing the chronic pain of patients who were receiving physical rehabilitation for a variety of medical problems, including arthritis, amputation, and spinal cord injury (Rybstein-Blinchik, 1979). Although both techniques were effective, patients who received redefinition training reported less pain and exhibited less pain behavior than those who were trained in distraction.

Because each behavioral and cognitive strategy we've considered can be helpful in treating clinical pain, programs for chronic pain sufferers generally combine different types of methods. One study, for instance, used a program that combined imagery, redefinition, and progressive muscle relaxation training to treat chronic low back pain patients (Turner, 1982). Some people received this program, others received a program of only relaxation training, and a third group served as controls. Compared with the control subjects, the patients in both programs reported much less pain, depression, and disability by the end of treatment, and these improvements were similar for the people in both programs. A followup on the patients in the two programs more than 1½ years later revealed that the benefits of the treatments were maintained, as measured by the people's ratings of pain and reports of health care use. However, the patients who received the program combining cognitive strategies and relaxation also showed a marked improvement in their employment, working 60% more hours per week than those who had the program of relaxation only.

Programs combining behavioral and cognitive methods are at least as effective as chemical methods in reducing chronic tension-type headaches (Holroyd, 2002). What's more, a review of research and a meta-analysis have shown that cognitive-behavioral programs are effective in treating chronic pain conditions, such as headache, arthritis, and

CLINICAL METHODS AND ISSUES

Guiding a Client to Pain Redefinition

The following dialogue illustrates how a clinical health psychologist can guide a client with illogical beliefs toward pain redefinition. "Mrs. D," a 56-year-old patient, worried that her chronic-recurrent head pain was actually caused by a tumor, which repeated neurological tests had failed to reveal. The therapist suggested that they examine those thoughts, and she replied:

MRS. D: Yes, I know they're not true but I cannot help it.

THERAPIST: You don't think you have control over your thoughts?

MRS. D: Yes, they just come to me.

T: Well, let's come back to the idea that your thoughts are automatic. First, let's break down your flood of negative thoughts and look at each part separately. Do you really think that you have a tumor?

MRS. D: I don't know. I guess not (pause) but it's hard not to worry about it. My head hurts so bad.

T: Yes, I know. So how do you convince yourself that you don't have a tumor or something else seriously wrong?

MRS. D: Well, as you know I've been examined many times by the best neurologists around. They say I'm OK. Also, my pain always goes away and I've never had any other neurological problems. My only problem is the pain. But, it's

hard to remember these facts when my pain is so awful.

T: It's much easier to be positive about your condition when you're not suffering. Nevertheless, rationally, you really are convinced that there's nothing seriously wrong.

MRS. D: I guess so. If only I could remember that when my pain starts coming on.

T: So the goal of our work today could be to figure out a strategy to increase the likelihood that you'll remember the positive thoughts during a pain episode.

MRS. D: Yes, that sounds good.

T: Let's start by generating a list of accurate statements about your pain. Then we can talk about ways you can cue yourself to remember the list when you begin to feel pain. You already mentioned a couple of beliefs about your pain; that is, that there's nothing seriously wrong, that the pain always goes away, and that, other than the pain, you feel pretty healthy. Can you think of other accurate and positive thoughts? (Holzman, Turk, & Kerns, 1986, pp. 45–46)

In this example, the therapist helped the client examine the logic of her thought patterns and generate a list of ideas she believed that were incompatible with her irrational fears. They later rehearsed these beliefs so that she could use them as self-statements when pain episodes occurred.

---

low back pain, but programs with only behavioral methods may sometimes be sufficient (Compas et al., 1998; Morley, Eccleston, & Williams, 1999). To summarize, several behavioral and cognitive methods can help people control acute and chronic pain. These methods include operant techniques, progressive muscle relaxation and biofeedback, and the cognitive strategies of distraction, imagery, and redefinition. Behavioral and cognitive methods are often most helpful when used in combination. (Go to 🍎.)

HYPNOSIS AND INTERPERSONAL THERAPY

You may have noticed that the behavioral and cognitive methods we just described for relieving pain sound familiar—and they should. For the most part, they involve psychological procedures derived from the stress reduction techniques we considered in Chapter 5. Because people's experiences of pain include an emotional component and are stressful,

ASSESS YOURSELF

Would Behavioral or Cognitive Methods Help *Your* Pain?

For each of the following questions about your recent experiences relating to pain, put a check mark in the preceding space if your answer is "yes."

_____ Have you been experiencing strong pain three or more days a week for more than a month?

_____ Do you take painkillers four or more days a week?

_____ Do you often take painkillers to prevent pain before it begins?

_____ Has your pain been getting worse?

_____ Have you canceled or avoided making social plans in the past month because you thought your pain would interfere with them?

_____ Do you ever drink alcohol to relieve your pain or the stress it produces?

_____ Have you seen more than three physicians about your pain?

_____ Are you afraid of performing physical activities, feeling they could elicit or aggravate your pain condition?

_____ Has your pain caused you to feel depressed and helpless for more than a couple of weeks or so?

_____ Do family or friends either seem annoyed by your pain or often ask how your pain is doing?

If you have been suffering from pain but have not yet seen a physician about it, see one soon. If you have seen your physician about the pain repeatedly but the treatments have not worked, consider supplementing your medical therapy with behavioral and cognitive approaches, especially if you answered "yes" to three or more of the above questions. If you answered "yes" to five or more questions, consider contacting a *multidisciplinary pain clinic*, as described toward the end of this chapter. (*Source*: Based on material in Tunks and Bellissimo, 1991.)

and because behavioral and cognitive methods are effective in reducing stress, psychologists have adapted these techniques to help people control their pain. Other psychological approaches have also been applied to relieve pain. These approaches include hypnosis and interpersonal therapy.

HYPNOSIS AS A TREATMENT FOR PAIN

In the mid-1800s, before ether was discovered, dramatic reports began to appear of physicians performing major surgery on individuals, using hypnosis as the sole method of analgesia (Bakal, 1979; Barber, 1986). In one such case of a woman with breast cancer, a surgeon made an incision halfway across her chest and removed the tumor as well as several enlarged glands in her armpit. During the procedure, the woman conversed with the surgeon and showed no signs of feeling pain. Another physician reported having done hundreds of surgeries with hypnosis as the only analgesic and argued that the patients experienced no pain.

Can Hypnosis Eliminate Acute Pain?

Were all of these operations painless? Probably not—although many patients *claimed* to feel no pain, some showed other pain behaviors, such as facial expressions, suggesting they were suppressing their agony (Bakal, 1979). Nevertheless, hypnosis can reduce the intensity of acute pain, but it is not highly effective for all individuals (Hilgard & Hilgard, 1983; Patterson & Jensen, 2003; Zeltzer et al., 1997). People vary in their ability to be hypnotized, and those who can be hypnotized very easily and deeply seem to gain more pain relief from hypnosis than those who are less hypnotically susceptible (Freeman et al., 2000; Milling, Levine, & Meunier, 2003).

How does hypnosis reduce pain? Although the mechanisms underlying pain relief from hypnosis are not clear, part of the answer seems to involve physiological changes that occur in the brain and spinal cord of people who are highly suggestible when they are hypnotized (Patterson & Jensen, 2003). Other factors may involve the deep relaxation people experience when hypnotized—as we saw earlier, relaxation can relieve pain—and cognitive factors, such as by producing states of heightened attention to internal images (Barber, 1986; Turk, Meichenbaum, & Genest, 1983). Studies have shown that hypnosis and cognitive-behavioral methods produce similar pain relief and that combining these methods does not enhance their effects (Liossi & Hatira, 1999; Milling, Levine, & Meunier, 2003).

Hypnosis is a dramatic and unusual phenomenon. Laboratory research on acute pain, induced by cold-pressor or muscle-ischemia procedures, has found that (Barber, 1982):

- When hypnotized, the people who gain the most pain relief from suggestions of analgesia tend to be those who are highly responsive to other suggestions, such as that their arm is becoming light.

- Whether under hypnosis or not, individuals who are told to try not to feel pain tend to use distraction and redefinition techniques.

- Contrary to the common myths about hypnosis, people usually show as much pain reduction using cognitive strategies, such as imagery and redefinition, as they do under hypnosis.

It may be that some patients who were supposedly hypnotized actually were not, and they may have applied cognitive strategies to reduce the pain.

Can Hypnosis Relieve Chronic Pain?

Hypnosis can reduce chronic pain. Although most relevant studies have tested patients with recurrent headache, some have shown that hypnosis also helps with other pain conditions, such as low back pain and cancer pain (Patterson & Jensen, 2003). In general, hypnosis is about as effective as relaxation therapy, and, interestingly, regardless of which of these therapies people receive, their pain relief is greatest if they are high in hypnotic suggestibility. These findings lead to an important question: What is it about being highly suggestible that helps people apply psychological methods to control their pain?

INTERPERSONAL THERAPY FOR PAIN

Interpersonal therapy uses psychoanalytic and cognitive-behavioral perspectives to help people deal with emotional difficulties, such as adjusting to chronic pain, by changing the way they interact with and perceive their social environments (Davison, Neale, & Kring, 2004). The underlying theory is that people's emotional difficulties arise from the way they relate to others, particularly family members. Therapy sessions involve discussions to help clients gain insights into their own motivations and how their behavior toward other people affects their own emotional adjustment. In the case of chronic pain patients, the insights often relate to feelings they and their families have about the pain condition, how they deal with pain behavior, and changes that have developed in the interpersonal relationships of these people.

An example of this approach involves showing patients how their pain behavior is part of "pain games" they play with other people (Szasz, cited in Bakal, 1979). In these games, individuals with chronic pain seem to take on roles in which they continually seek to confirm their identities as suffering persons, maintain their dependent lifestyles, and receive various secondary gains, such as attention and sympathy. These patients are probably not aware of what is actually happening in these games, and the purpose of this psychotherapeutic approach is to make them aware. The assumption is that once patients gain an insight into how their behavior patterns are affecting their lives, they can give up the games if they want to and are shown how.

Therapies leading to insight can also help chronic pain patients and their families understand the problems they experience in their relationships within the family system (Flor & Turk, 1985; Kerns & Payne, 1996). For instance, when a spouse suffers from chronic pain, both spouses experience feelings of frustration, anger, helplessness, and guilt that they often do not communicate openly to each other. These feelings can result from changes in their roles, general style of communication, and sexual relationship. The following excerpt shows how a therapist was able to help a pain patient, John Cox, and his wife gain insights about their feelings and behavior. The three of them were discussing a pain episode John had had while he watched TV with his wife, and the therapist (T) asked the wife how she reacted when she realized he was in pain:

Mrs. Cox: I really felt sorry for John, but I didn't know what to do. I just tried to watch the show and not say anything to him. At those times I feel . . . so helpless.

T: Mr. Cox, it sounds as if your wife tried to avoid talking about your pain. She sounds sort of helpless and frustrated. . . . How did you feel about her response?

MR. COX: I think I got kind of mad at her because she seemed to be ignoring me, not really caring how I was feeling.

T: Mr. Cox, what do you think she should have done at that time?

MR. COX: I don't really know.

T: Mr. Cox, do you think there was anything she could have done to make you feel better?

MR. COX: Not really.

T: . . . Perhaps at such times ignoring your pain may be the most she can do. . . .

MR. COX: Perhaps.

T: Perhaps?

MR. COX: Well maybe she did know how I was feeling, but I felt upset that she didn't tell me. (Turk, Meichenbaum, & Genest, 1983, pp. 244–245)

Insights such as these help family members understand each others' feelings and points of view, and this understanding can help to break down the long-standing confusion and conflicts that have developed over time. Improvements in family relationships can enable the therapist to enhance the cooperation of each member in the treatment process (Kerns & Payne, 1996). Also, interpersonal therapy appears to be useful in treating depression, a common problem among pain patients (Davison, Neale, & Kring, 2004).

In summary, hypnosis and interpersonal therapy offer promising techniques in the treatment of chronic pain. Thus far in our discussion of methods for reducing pain we have considered a variety of medical and psychological techniques. In the next section, we will see how physical therapy and certain skin stimulation methods can also play important roles in controlling pain.

PHYSICAL AND STIMULATION THERAPIES FOR PAIN

Anthropologists and medical historians have noted that most, if not all, cultures in recorded history have learned that people can "fight pain with pain" (Melzack

& Wall, 1982). One pain can cancel another—a brief or moderate pain can cancel a longer-lasting or stronger one. For example, you might reduce the pain of an injection by pressing your thumbnail into your forefinger as the shot is given. Reducing one pain by creating another is called **counter-irritation.** People in ancient cultures developed a counter-irritation procedure called *cupping* to relieve headaches, backaches, and arthritic pain. In this procedure, one or more heated glass cups are inverted and pressed on the skin. As the air in the cup cools, it creates a vacuum, causing the skin to be bruised as it is drawn up into the cup. This method is still used in some parts of the world today (Melzack & Wall, 1982).

The principle of counter-irritation is the basis for present-day stimulation therapies for reducing pain. After examining these pain control methods, we will discuss the important role other physical approaches can play in reducing pain.

STIMULATION THERAPIES

Why does counter-irritation relieve pain? One reason is that people actively distract their attention from the stronger pain to the milder one. Another explanation comes from gate-control theory. Recall that activity in the peripheral fibers that carry signals about mildly irritating stimuli tends to close the gate, thereby inhibiting the transmission cells from sending pain signals to the brain. Counter-irritation, such as massaging a sore muscle, activates these peripheral fibers, and this may close the gate and soothe the pain.

This gate-control view of how counter-irritation works led to the development of a pain control technique called **transcutaneous electrical nerve stimulation** (TENS). This technique involves placing electrodes on the skin near where the patient feels pain and stimulating that area with mild electric current, which is supplied by a small portable device. Anecdotal evidence suggests that TENS can reduce acute muscular and postoperative pain (Chapman, 1984; Hare & Milano, 1985). For example, a 9-year-old boy began receiving TENS while still unconscious after kidney surgery and then awoke, not feeling any pain. He thought the surgery had not occurred and that the hospital staff was not telling the truth when they said it did. When

asked why it couldn't be true, he asserted confidently, "Because I haven't got any bandages." We asked him to feel his belly, since his hands were outside of the bedclothes. When he did, an expression of astonishment came over his face. (Chapman, 1984, p. 1265)

Then, he claimed to feel pain and began to cry. Despite this dramatic anecdote, evidence today indicates that TENS is not effective in reducing acute pain (Johnson, 2001). And its success in treating chronic pain is unclear. When TENS does relieve discomfort for some chronic conditions, such as phantom limb pain, its effects are often short-lived (Hare & Milano, 1985; Zeltzer et al., 1997).

Another stimulation therapy that is used today for reducing pain is **acupuncture,** a technique in which fine metal needles are inserted under the skin at special locations and then twirled or electrically charged to create stimulation. Acupuncture has been used in China for at least the past 2,000 years and was originally based on the idea that pain occurs when the life forces of yin and yang are out of balance (AMA, 2003; Bakal, 1979; CU, 1994). Although acupuncturists do not necessarily believe this rationale any longer, many, but not all, still determine the placement of the needles on the basis of charts that show hundreds of insertion points on the body. These acupuncturists believe that stimulation at several specific points relieves pain in associated parts of the body. On the nose and ear, for example, certain points are associated with the small intestine, whereas other points are associated with the kidney, or heart, or abdomen.

Does acupuncture work? Its ability to produce high levels of analgesia for acute pain in some individuals has been clearly and dramatically demonstrated; for instance, surgeons have performed major surgery on patients with only acupuncture anesthesia. But research findings point to several conclusions about its effects and its limitations (Bakal, 1979; Chapman, 1984; Melzack & Wall, 1982):

- Even in China, physicians perform only a small percentage (less than 10%) of surgeries with acupuncture analgesia, and these operations are straightforward ones with little likelihood of complications.
- Patients must volunteer for the procedure, and then their physicians select appropriate candidates very carefully and make sure these patients are well indoctrinated.
- Acupuncture is rarely effective for surgical patients in Western cultures.

- Laboratory studies have shown that acupuncture produces only mild analgesia in most people.
- The degree of analgesia acupuncture produces depends on the intensity of the stimulation, and not on its being applied at the exact points described on acupuncture charts.
- Pain patients who benefit most from acupuncture tend to be those who are also easily and deeply hypnotizable.

Acupuncture does *not* provide long-term relief for most chronic pain patients, but some evidence indicates that it is useful in treating headache and low back pain (Mayer, 2000; Zeltzer et al., 1997).

It is tempting to conclude from these findings that acupuncture works simply through suggestion or distraction effects, but this seems unlikely because the technique also produces analgesia in animals,

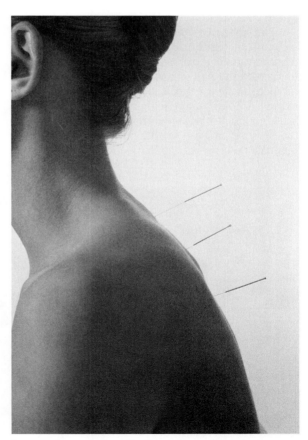

Acupuncture can be effective in reducing pain in some individuals.

such as monkeys and mice (Melzack & Wall, 1982). Psychological factors cannot provide a full explanation. Gate-control theory provides two plausible reasons for the effects of acupuncture: stimulation from the needles may close the gate by activating peripheral fibers or the release of opioids, such as endorphins (Bakal, 1979; Zeltzer et al., 1997).

PHYSICAL THERAPY

Physical therapy is an important rehabilitation component for many medical conditions—for instance, after injury or surgery, patients perform exercises to enhance muscular strength and tissue flexibility to restore their range of motion. Physical therapists have a variety of techniques they can incorporate into individualized treatment programs to help patients who suffer from acute and chronic pain conditions. Exercise is a common feature in these programs (AMA, 2003; Zeltzer et al., 1997).

The therapist and patient generally plan the program together, setting daily or weekly goals that promote very gradual but steady progress. The progress is tailored to the patient's needs, being fast enough to promote a feeling of accomplishment but slow enough to prevent overexertion, reinjury, or failure. In cases of acute injury, such as serious damage to the knee joint, the exercise program might span a year or two. The rationale for using exercise to control pain depends on the type of health problem the patient has. With arthritis, for instance, exercise helps by maintaining the flexibility of the joints and preventing them from becoming deformed (Minor & Sanford, 1993). Other approaches in physical therapy, such as massage, traction, and applying heat or cold to the painful area of the body, seem to provide temporary pain relief (Tunks & Bellissimo, 1991). The spinal manipulation treatment people get from *chiroproactic* and *osteopathic* specialists, especially for neck and lower back pain, is not generally considered to be physical therapy, but it appears to relieve back pain (Andersson et al., 1999; Bove & Nilsson, 1998).

Physical therapy programs are widely used in treating two highly prevalent chronic pain conditions, arthritis and low back pain (Minor & Sanford, 1993; Moffet et al., 1999). For both of these conditions, exercise is probably the most important physical therapy approach for achieving long-term pain relief. For instance, programs for low back pain that gradually increase exercise produce substantial improvements in self-reports of pain and ability to perform physical activities, such as standing and lifting weights (Alaranta et al., 1994; Moffet et al., 1999). Sometimes physical therapy is combined with behavioral methods in treating chronic pain to gain the benefits of each approach, and treatments for low back pain provide a good example again. A study compared the benefits of two 10-week programs—one with physical therapy, the other with behavioral and cognitive

Physical therapy not only promotes rehabilitation for this patient suffering from a leg injury but may also help in reducing his pain.

methods—for adults with chronic low back pain (Heinrich et al., 1985). Both groups experienced similar reductions in pain across many months, and each group showed improvements that were specific to the programs they received. At the end of the programs and at followup, subjects in the physical therapy group showed better physical functioning, and those in the behavioral-cognitive group showed better psychosocial adjustment. Other research has combined these methods and found that low back pain patients show less pain behavior, disability, and self-reported pain with both physical and behavioral-

cognitive therapy than with either approach alone (Turner et al., 1990).

In this chapter we have described many different types of treatment, including medical, psychological, and physical therapies, and we have seen that each method can help to alleviate clinical pain. Some methods seem to be more effective than others, especially for particular pain conditions. Typically, no single approach is sufficient by itself. Therefore, specialists who provide treatment in pain clinics often apply several methods in combination. (Go to 🍎.)

HIGHLIGHT

Physical Activity and Back Pain

The spine has an intricate structure, with each of its many sections of bone, called *vertebrae*, being cushioned from adjacent sections by rubbery *disks* of connective tissue. Each vertebra is connected to adjacent ones by antler-shaped *facet joints* that enable the vertebrae to pivot against one another (Tortora & Grabowski, 2003). But the spine depends on the muscles of the back and abdomen for support, without which it would just topple over. When all these muscles are strong and in good working order, they balance each other's action and keep the body's weight centered on the spine. However, when these muscles are weak or the back muscles are under

excessive or prolonged tension—sometimes due to emotional stress—back problems tend to occur.

A 10-year longitudinal study of men and women found evidence suggesting that low back pain progresses over time through a vicious circle: poor muscle function may lead to low back disorders, which lead to poorer muscle function, and so on (Leino, Aro, & Hasan, 1987). Although back pain can arise from such conditions as arthritis and ruptured disks, this is not typical—medical examinations fail to find underlying physical causes in the large majority of back cases (Chapman, 1984; Deyo et al., 1991). Most backaches seem to arise from

Figure 12H–1   Six stretching and strengthening exercises to protect from low back pain.

---

muscle or ligament strains, lack of proper exercise, and normal wear and tear on facet joints. These problems tend to increase with age for many reasons—for instance, people's muscular conditioning usually declines as they get older, the effects of wear and tear accumulate, and the disks gradually dry out and provide less cushioning for the vertebrae. People whose jobs require frequent heavy lifting are more likely than other workers to develop low back pain (Kelsey & Hochberg, 1988). Exercise can help protect people from back problems, but it needs to consist of *proper* activities. People who do the wrong kinds of exercises do not get this protection, and those who overexert themselves can precipitate back pain.

What kinds of physical activity can help protect against back problems? Proper exercise involves a program of back-strengthening and stretching activities, along with abdominal exercises. Many different exercises are available for these purposes, and Figure 12H–1 presents a few easy ones. What

should people do when they develop backaches? Medical advice in the past called for getting lots of bed rest and taking aspirin. But this advice has changed as a result of new research (Deyo et al., 1991; USDHHS, 1994). Most backaches resolve themselves in a few days or weeks with or without medical attention. Physicians today recommend that the person *become active as soon as possible*—walking and exercising cautiously—even if it hurts a little. People with back pain should consult their doctor when the pain is:

- Linked to a known injury, such as from a fall.
- Severe enough to disable the sufferer and awaken him or her at night.
- Not relieved by changing position or lying down.
- Accompanied by nausea, fever, difficulty or pain in urinating, loss of bladder or bowel control, numbness or weakness in a leg or foot, or pain that shoots down the leg.

PAIN CLINICS

Before the 1970s, if a person's pain lingered, and physicians could not determine its cause or find a remedy for the discomfort, that patient was left with virtually no reasonable treatment alternatives. In desperation, such people often tried extreme medical approaches that could lead to drug addiction or irreversible nerve damage, or they may have turned to charlatans. Although many people with chronic pain still use ill-conceived, desperate measures to gain relief from their discomfort, effective alternatives are available today, as we have seen. Effective pain control treatments can now be obtained through **pain clinics** (or *pain centers*), which are institutions or organizations that have been developed specifically for the treatment of chronic pain conditions.

The concept of having special institutions for treating pain originated with John Bonica, an anesthesiologist who founded the first pain clinic at the University of Washington Medical School (Fordyce, 1976; Melzack & Wall, 1982). Soon other professionals followed suit, and by the late 1990s there were per-

haps a thousand pain clinics in the United States alone (Turk & Stacey, 2000). The structure, methods, and quality of pain clinics vary widely. Many pain clinics are private organizations, whereas others are affiliated with medical schools, university departments of behavioral medicine, and hospitals. Many provide inpatient treatment, and others focus on outpatient care; and many incorporate a variety of treatment methods, whereas others provide basically one approach, such as acupuncture, hypnosis, biofeedback, or TENS (Follick et al., 1985; Kanner, 1986; Turk & Stacey, 2000). Pain centers accredited by the Commission on Accreditation of Rehabilitation Facilities in Tucson, Arizona, typically offer high-quality treatment (Chapman, 1991).

MULTIDISCIPLINARY PROGRAMS

A theme that has appeared more than once in this chapter is that no single method for treating chronic pain is likely to succeed. In fact, one physician has advised avoiding clinics that focus on applying a single approach, such as biofeedback or nerve block methods (Kanner, 1986). *Multidisciplinary pain clinics* (or *centers*)—those that combine and integrate several effective approaches—are likely to succeed for the largest percentage of patients and provide the greatest pain relief for each individual. Clinics that use multidisciplinary programs generally use assessment and treatment procedures for each patient that involve medical, psychosocial, physical therapy, occupational therapy, and vocational factors and approaches (Follick et al., 1985; Turk & Stacey, 2000).

Assessment procedures are used in determining the factors that are contributing to the patient's condition, identifying the specific problems to address in the program, and customizing the program to match the needs of the patient (Chapman, 1991; Turk & Stacey, 2000). Although the goals and objectives of different multidisciplinary programs vary, they typically include:

* Reducing the patient's experience of pain.
* Improving physical and lifestyle functioning.
* Decreasing or eliminating drug intake.
* Enhancing social support and family life.
* Reducing the patient's use of medical services.

Multidisciplinary programs generally integrate specific treatment components to achieve each goal (Follick et al., 1985). These programs include, for example, procedures to decrease the patient's reliance on medication and physical exercises to increase the person's strength, endurance, flexibility, and range of motion. They provide counseling to improve family relationships and to enable the patient to find full-time employment when possible. And they offer a range of psychological services to reduce the experience of pain, decrease pain behavior, and improve the patient's psychological adjustment to the pain condition.

EVALUATING THE SUCCESS OF PAIN CLINICS

How effective are multidisciplinary pain clinics? To answer this question, we'll start by examining the procedures and results of two pain programs. Each program (1) was conducted by a hospital-affiliated pain clinic, (2) provided treatment on an inpatient basis for 4 weeks with weekends off, (3) treated several patients at a time with a variety of treatment techniques, and (4) had staff to provide medical, psychological, physical, and occupational therapy. Each program also used a medication reduction procedure, physical therapy, relaxation and biofeedback training, cognitive-behavioral group therapy, family involvement and training, and other methods.

In the first of these programs, the patients were men and women who had suffered intractable pain from known injuries or diseases, such as arthritis, for at least a year and were unemployed because of their pain conditions (Cinciripini & Floreen, 1982). All subjects received the full program. The researchers assessed the patients' behavior and functioning at the start and at the end of the program, and in followups 6 and 12 months after. By the end of this program, the patients' activity levels had increased and their pain experiences, pain behaviors, and drug use had decreased sharply. Indeed, 90% of the patients were now free of analgesic medication. The subjects who participated in the followup assessments reported that they continued to be active, and about half were employed. Moreover, their pain continued to diminish: before treatment their average pain rating was 4.6 on a 10-point scale; by the end of the program it was 2.2, and after a year it was 1.2.

The second program compared a *treatment group* that completed the program with a *control group* that met all the criteria for acceptance into the program but declined to participate solely because they lacked insurance coverage (Guck et al., 1985). Followup assessments comparing the treatment and control subjects 1 to 5 years later revealed impressive outcomes: the treatment group reported experiencing far less pain, less evidence of depression, and less interference from pain in various activities, such as household chores, socializing, sexual relations, exercise, and sleep. Almost two-thirds of the treatment group and only one-fifth of the controls were employed, and far fewer treatment subjects used painkilling drugs.

Meta-analyses of dozens of studies have shown that people suffering with chronic pain who receive treatment at multidisciplinary pain centers report much less subsequent pain and are far more likely to return to work than individuals who have standard pain treatment (Cutler et al., 1994; Flor, Fydrich, & Turk, 1992). What's more, the cost of the treatment is only a small fraction of the medical and disability payments patients would receive for a year (Stieg & Turk, 1988). Other research has found evidence indicating that reductions in pain helplessness and catastrophizing during multidisciplinary treatment lead to later decreases in pain severity and anxiety (Burns et al., 2003). Of course, not all pain patients benefit from this treatment, but most do.

SUMMARY

Pain that receives or requires professional attention is called clinical pain. Practitioners try to reduce acute clinical pain for humanitarian reasons and for practical reasons, such as to enable medical procedures to be carried out smoothly, reduce patients' stress, and help patients recover quickly and without complications. Although the medical treatment for pain may involve surgery if all other methods have failed, it usually involves pharmaceuticals selected from four types: peripherally acting analgesics; centrally acting analgesics; local anesthetics; and indirectly acting drugs, such as sedatives, tranquilizers, and antidepressants. These chemical methods are used extensively for relieving acute pain; they can be administered in several ways, such as by epidural block or patient-controlled analgesia.

One of the main goals of behavioral and cognitive methods for treating chronic pain is to reduce the patient's drug consumption. The operant approach focuses on reducing pain behaviors through extinction procedures and increasing other behavior through reinforcement. Therapists apply progressive muscle relaxation and biofeedback to reduce the stress and muscle tension that can cause or aggravate patients' pain experiences. Research has shown that relaxation and biofeedback training produce effective and long-lasting relief for many chronic pain patients. Cognitive techniques focus on changing thought patterns that increase the intensity or frequency of pain experiences. Distraction and nonpain imagery methods appear to be effective chiefly for mild or moderate acute pain or for brief episodes of heightened chronic pain. Pain redefinition can involve clarifying what a pain experience will be like, using positive self-statements, and correcting faulty beliefs and logic. Redefinition can help reduce strong pain and chronic pain.

Hypnosis seems to relieve pain, particularly for individuals who can be deeply hypnotized. In general, people can reduce their pain as effectively with cognitive strategies in the waking state as with hypnosis. Interpersonal therapy strives to help people achieve insight into the social and motivational factors underlying their emotional difficulties. For pain patients, this may involve making them aware of what is happening in the pain games they play or of how others feel about their pain conditions.

Counter-irritation is a procedure whereby a brief or moderate pain cancels a longer-lasting or stronger one. A pain control technique based on this procedure, called transcutaneous electrical nerve stimulation, is not as effective as researchers had thought. Acupuncture is an ancient Asian procedure for reducing pain; it produces high levels of analgesia for acute pain in some patients but not in most. Although it does not provide long-term relief for most chronic pain patients, it appears useful in treating headache and low back pain. Physical therapy includes such approaches as exercise, massage, traction, and the application of heat and cold to painful regions. Spinal manipulation techniques appear to reduce headache and low back pain. Proper exercise can protect individuals from low back pain.

Pain clinics are institutions developed specifically for treating chronic pain. Multidisciplinary pain clinics use a variety of methods to provide highly effective and long-lasting pain relief, while also rehabilitating patients physically, psychologically, socially, and vocationally.

KEY TERMS

clinical pain	pain redefinition	transcutaneous electrical	acupuncture
distraction	counter-irritation	nerve stimulation	pain clinics
nonpain imagery			

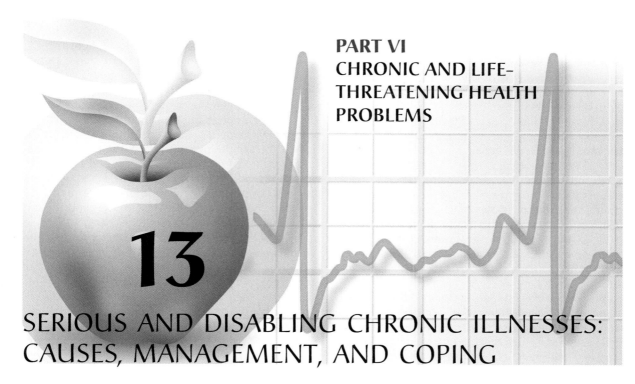

13

SERIOUS AND DISABLING CHRONIC ILLNESSES: CAUSES, MANAGEMENT, AND COPING

Adjusting to a Chronic Illness
Initial Reactions to Having a Chronic Condition
Influences on Coping with a Health Crisis
The Coping Process

Impacts of Different Chronic Conditions
Asthma
Epilepsy
Nervous System Injuries
Diabetes
Arthritis
Alzheimer's Disease

Psychosocial Interventions for People with Chronic Conditions
Educational, Social Support,
    and Behavioral Methods
Relaxation and Biofeedback
Cognitive Methods
Interpersonal and Family Therapy

PROLOGUE

"It's not fair," 12-year-old Joe complained. "Why can't I eat the stuff I like? Other kids can. Why do I have to check my blood every day and take shots? Nobody else has to do that." He voiced these complaints as he left the emergency room after suffering severe stomach cramps because he was not adhering to his medical regimen. Hospital tests recently determined that Joe has diabetes, and he was not adjusting well to the regimen his physician instructed him to follow. His parents tried to explain that not following the regimen could have serious health consequences, but Joe didn't believe those problems would happen. When his noncompliance led to his being rushed to the hospital with severe abdominal pain and difficulty breathing, he finally believed the warnings and began to adhere to his regimen.

Different individuals react differently to developing a chronic illness. Their reactions depend on many factors, such as their coping skills and personalities, the social support they have, the nature and consequences of their illnesses, and the impact of the illnesses on their daily functioning. At the very least, having a chronic condition entails frequent impositions on the patients and their families. Chronically ill people may suffer periodic episodes of feeling poorly and need to have regular medical checkups, restrict their diets or other aspects of their lifestyles, or administer daily treatment, for instance. Many chronic conditions entail more than just impositions—they produce frequent pain or lead to disability or even death. Most of us will develop at least one of these illnesses in our lifetimes, and one of them, such as cancer or cardiovascular disease, will probably take our lives.

This chapter and the next focus mainly on *tertiary prevention* for chronic illness—to retard its progression, prevent disability, and rehabilitate the person, physically and psychologically. We examine how people react to and cope with chronic health problems and what can be done to help these people cope effectively. In contrast to the next chapter, which deals with illnesses that have high rates of mortality and on processes relating to dying and death, the present chapter concentrates on health problems that are less likely to result in death but often lead to disability. This chapter begins by discussing people's reactions to having a chronic condition and then examines the experiences of and psychosocial interventions for individuals living with various health problems. These discussions address many questions that are of great concern to patients, to their families and friends, and probably to you. How do individuals react after their initial shock of learning that they have a chronic illness? What kinds of health problems usually involve the most difficult adjustments for people? How do patients' chronic conditions impact on their families? What can families, friends, and therapists do to help chronically ill people adapt effectively to their conditions?

ADJUSTING TO A CHRONIC ILLNESS

"I felt like I'd been hit in the stomach by a sledge-hammer"—this is how many patients describe their first reaction upon learning that they have a disabling or life-threatening illness. Questions without immediate answers flash through their minds: Is the diagnosis right, and, if so, what can we do about it? Will I be disabled, disfigured, or in pain? Will I die? How soon will these consequences happen? What will happen to my family? Do I have adequate medical and life insurance?

INITIAL REACTIONS TO HAVING A CHRONIC CONDITION

The first reaction most individuals experience when a physician diagnoses a chronic health problem is *shock*—they are stunned or bewildered and behave in

an automatic and detached fashion (Shontz, 1975). The shock may last only a short while or may continue for weeks, shock occurs to some degree in any crisis situation people experience, and it is likely to be most pronounced when the crisis comes without warning. Then, after a period of using emotion-focused strategies, such as denial and grief, reality begins to intrude: the symptoms remain or get worse, additional diagnoses confirm the original one, and it becomes clear that adjustments need to be made. Patients tend to contact reality a little at a time until they reach some form of adjustment to the problem and its implications. Not all people react this way; some may be "cool and collected," whereas others may be "paralyzed" with anxiety or may become "hysterical" (Silver & Wortman, 1980).

People who use denial and other avoidance strategies do so to control their emotional responses to a stressor, especially when they believe they can do nothing to change the situation (Croyle & Ditto, 1990; Lazarus & Folkman, 1984b). But the usefulness of this approach has limits, and excessive avoidance can soon become maladaptive to patients' physical and psychological well-being (Roesch & Weiner, 2001; Suls & Fletcher, 1985). For example, when hospitalized people receive information about their conditions and future risk factors, those individuals who use avoidance strategies heavily gain less information about their conditions than those who use these strategies to a lesser degree (Shaw et al., 1985). How can they make decisions about their treatment rationally if they fail to take in the information practitioners present? What factors influence how people cope with their health problems? The next section provides some answers to this question.

INFLUENCES ON COPING WITH A HEALTH CRISIS

Healthy people tend to take their health for granted. When a serious illness or injury occurs, their daily activities and social roles are disrupted. Regardless of whether the condition is temporary or chronic, the first phases in coping with it are similar. But there is an important difference: chronic health problems usually require that patients and their families make permanent behavioral, social, and emotional adjustments. Learning of a serious chronic illness quickly changes the way they view themselves and their lives.

The plans they had for tomorrow and for the next days, weeks, and years may be affected. Did they plan to go on a trip this weekend? They may change their minds now. Did they plan to complete a college education, or enter a specific career field, or get married and have children, or move to a new community when they retire? Some of these ideas for the future may evaporate after the diagnosis. Adjustment to life-threatening or potentially disabling illness or injury may require major coping efforts (Cohen & Lazarus, 1979). And often no one can tell for certain exactly what the course of the illness will be.

Why do some individuals cope differently from others after learning they have a chronic health problem? **Crisis theory** describes factors that influence how people adjust during a crisis, such as having an illness (Moos, 1982; Moos & Schaefer, 1986). Figure 13–1 presents a diagram of the theory, showing that the outcome of the crisis—or the adjustment the person makes—depends on the coping process, which in turn depends on three contributing influences: *illness-related* factors, *background and personal* factors, and *physical and social environmental* factors. We will look at these contributing influences, and then see how they affect the coping process the patient uses.

Illness-Related Factors

Some health problems present a greater threat to the person than others do—for example, they may be more disabling, disfiguring, painful, or life-threatening. The greater the threat patients perceive for any of these circumstances, the more difficulty they're likely to have coping with their conditions (Cohen & Lazarus, 1979; Moos, 1982). Adjusting to being disfigured can be extremely difficult, particularly when it involves the person's face. Many individuals whose faces are badly scarred withdraw from social encounters, sometimes completely. Often people who see the disfigurement react awkwardly, and some show feelings of revulsion. Even children react more negatively to people's facial disfigurements than to injuries to other parts of the body, such as when people are crippled or missing a limb (Richardson et al., 1961).

Patients also have difficulty coping with illness-related factors that involve annoying or embarrassing changes in bodily functioning or that draw attention to their conditions (Bekkers et al., 1995). People with some illnesses, for instance, may need artificial devices for excreting fecal or urinary wastes that are noticeable either visibly or by their odors. Other chronically ill people must treat their conditions with ointments that may have odors or equipment that is visible or makes noise. Still others may experience periodic seizures or muscle spasms that can be embarrassing. Many people with chronic illnesses feel self-conscious about their health problems—or even stigmatized by them—and want to hide them from others (Scambler, 1984).

Various other aspects of treatment regimens can make adjustment very difficult, too. For instance, some treatments are painful or involve medications that produce serious side effects—either by leading to additional health problems or by interfering with the patient's daily functioning, such as by making the person immobile or drowsy. Other regimens may have treatment schedules and time commitments

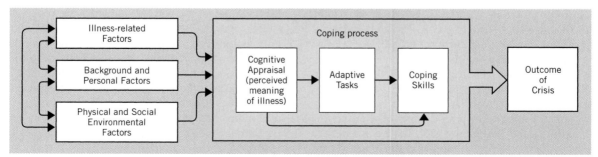

Figure 13–1 A diagram of the crisis theory's description of factors and the coping process patients use in the first phases of adjusting psychologically to a serious illness. Arrows denote the flow of effects. (Adapted from Moos, 1982, Figure 1.)

that require patients and their families to make substantial changes in their lifestyles and make it difficult for the person to find or hold a job. Each of these factors can impair people's adjustment to chronic health problems.

Background and Personal Factors

People who cope well with chronic health problems tend to have hardy or resilient personalities that allow them to see a good side in difficult situations (Pollock, Christian, & Sands, 1991). As an example, a 16-year-old boy named Ralfie, whose body had wasted away to 50 pounds from a rare spinal-muscular disease, stated:

> When I take a bath and look at myself naked, I think, "God Jesus." I'm disappointed when it comes to my body, but when it comes to my inside, my personality, my sense of humor, I'm proud of the way I am. I think I'm a nicer person. The girls always tell me, "You're very special. You're different than the other guys." (Hurley, 1987, p. 34)

People with chronic diseases who are like Ralfie can often find purpose and quality in their lives, maintain their self-esteem, and resist feeling helpless and hopeless.

The ways individuals cope with chronic health problems also depend on many other background and personal factors, such as their age, gender, social class, philosophical or religious commitments, emotional maturity, and self-esteem (Moos & Schaefer, 1986). With respect to gender differences, for instance, men are more likely than women to have difficulty with health problems that restrict their vigor or physical abilities (Moos, 1982). Having a chronic illness often means that the individual must take on a dependent and passive role for a long period of time. For men, this can be especially difficult since it is inconsistent with the assertive and independent roles they generally occupy in most societies of the world.

The timing of a health problem in the person's life span also affects the impact on him or her. Young children are not likely to understand the nature of their illnesses, the treatment regimens they must follow, and the long-term implications of their conditions (Burbach & Peterson, 1986). Their concerns are likely to focus on restrictions that are imposed on their lifestyles and activities, the frightening medical procedures they experience, and possible separations from their parents. Adolescents can understand

information about their illnesses and treatment, but their needing to be like and feel accepted by their peers can lead to difficulties in coping with their health problems (La Greca & Stone, 1985). Because of these motivations, adolescents may deny important aspects of their conditions and neglect their medical care to avoid appearing different from their friends.

In adulthood, too, the difficulties individuals have in coping with chronic health problems change with age (Mages & Mendelsohn, 1979; Moos, 1982). When people develop disabling or life-threatening illnesses or injuries in early adulthood, they tend to resent not having had the chance to develop their lives in the direction they planned—to get married, to have children, or to enter a particular career. In contrast, middle-aged patients may have problems adjusting to the disruption of established roles and lifestyles and to being unable to finish tasks they have started, such as building up a business. In old age, people who develop chronic illnesses may resent not being able to enjoy the leisure they feel they earned in their lifetimes of work and self-sacrifice.

Another personal factor that affects how people cope with health problems is their self-blame for their condition. People who believe they are personally responsible for developing a chronic illness and its symptoms tend to cope poorly with their condition, showing higher levels of depression in subsequent months than patients with less self-blame (Schiaffino, Shawaryn, & Blum, 1998). People's beliefs about the causes, effects, and treatments of their illnesses are often wrong and can affect their adjustment to a health problem.

Physical and Social Environmental Factors

Many physical and social features of our environments can affect the way we adjust to chronic health problems (Moos, 1982). The physical aspects of a hospital environment, for instance, are usually very dull and confining for patients, thereby depressing their general morale and mood. For some individuals, the home environment may not be much better. Many patients have difficulty getting around their houses or performing self-help tasks, such as buttoning clothes or opening food containers, and lack special equipment or tools that can help them do these tasks and be more self-sufficient. These people's adjustment to their health problems can be impaired as long as these situations persist.

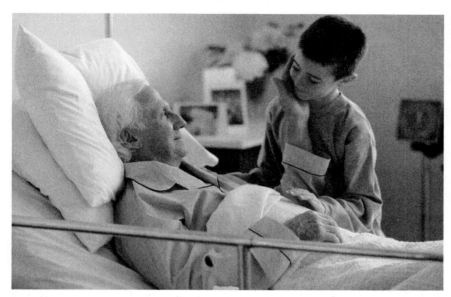

Sources of social support for patients usually involve their families, but also include friends and people from support groups and religious organizations.

The patient's social environment functions as a system, with the behavior of each person affecting the others (Kerns & Weiss, 1994; Revenson, 1994). The presence of social support, for example, generally helps patients and their families and friends cope with their illnesses. Individuals who live alone and have few friends, or who have poor relationships with the people they live with, tend to adjust poorly to chronic ill health (Gentry & Kobasa, 1984; Wallston et al., 1983). But it is also true that sometimes people in a patient's social network may undermine effective coping by providing bad examples or poor advice (Suls, 1982). The degree to which each member of the social system adjusts in constructive ways to the illness affects the adjustment of the others. The primary source of social support for most people who are ill typically comes from their immediate families (Miller & Cafasso, 1992). But friends and neighbors also help, and patients may join *support groups* for people with specific medical problems. These groups can provide informational and emotional support.

Figure 13–1 shows that the three contributing influences in crisis theory are interrelated. The patient's social class or cultural background, for instance, may affect his or her self-consciousness about or access to special devices and equipment to promote self-sufficiency. These contributing factors combine to influence the coping process the person uses to deal with the crisis.

THE COPING PROCESS

Crisis theory proposes that coping begins with the patient's *cognitive appraisal* of the meaning or significance of the health problem to his or her life. The outcome of this appraisal leads the individual to formulate an array of *adaptive tasks* and to apply various *coping skills* to deal with these tasks. Let's see what these tasks and skills are.

The Tasks and Skills of Coping

According to Moos (1982), people who are ill need to address two types of adaptive tasks in the coping process:

- *Tasks related to the illness or treatment*, which involve learning to (1) cope with the symptoms or disability the health problem causes, (2) adjust to the hospital environment and medical procedures needed to treat the problem, and (3) develop and maintain good relationships with their practitioners.

- *Tasks related to general psychosocial functioning*, which involve striving to (1) control negative feelings and retain a positive outlook for the future, (2) maintain a satisfactory self-image and sense of competence, (3) preserve good relationships with family and friends, and (4) prepare for an uncertain future.

These tasks can be very difficult for patients, particularly when their health problems may lead to disability, disfigurement, or death. Still, many people with poor prognoses for their health manage to adapt successfully and make the most of their new circumstances. Patients are likely to adapt well to a chronic condition if their family members participate actively in their treatment regimens, encourage them to be self sufficient, and respond to their needs in a caring and sensitive manner.

What coping skills do patients and their families employ to deal with these adaptive tasks? Table 13.1 describes several useful strategies that they commonly use. Each of these skills can help in achieving the goals of adaptive tasks and in leading to a positive outcome of the crisis. Is one approach best? Some coping skills may be more appropriate for dealing with some tasks than with others (Moos, 1982). As a result, people generally use these skills selectively, often in combination. For instance, seeking information may help patients deal with the symptoms, and setting reasonable goals may help them do exercises and reduce their incapacitation. Individuals who have adjusted successfully to each phase of the crises are ready to deal effectively with subsequent phases in their adjustment to their health problems.

Long-Term Adaptation to Chronic Health Problems

Chronic disorders last for a very long time—patients and their families need to adapt to the illnesses and to whether they worsen, stay the same, or improve over time. The term **adaptation** refers to the process of making changes in order to adjust constructively to life's circumstances. For example, almost all chronically ill individuals will limit certain activities, substitute one activity for another, or take action to assure that an activity can occur in some form, such as more slowly or for less time (Gignac, Cott, & Badley, 2002). These adaptive changes can enhance the quality of life for themselves and their families by promoting their effective physical, psychological, and social functioning. What does "quality of life" mean? **Quality of life** refers to the degree of excellence people appraise their lives to contain. People around the world appraise excellence with similar criteria, such as performing daily activities, energy or discomfort, positive and negative feelings, personal control, interpersonal relations, pleasant activities, personal and intellectual growth, and material possessions (Gill & Feinstein, 1994; Power et al., 1999).

Individuals who show effective long-term adaptation to chronic illness often have psychological resources that enable them to apply appropriate coping strategies to deal with the problems they face. When chronically ill people can expect to live for many years, they need to make many decisions, such as career selections, by examining their options based on realistic assessments of their conditions. People who continue to rely heavily on avoidance coping strategies, such as denial, are less likely to adapt effectively than those who use strategies that

Table 13.1 *Coping Strategies for Chronic Health Problems*

- *Denying or minimizing* the seriousness of the situation. As we have seen, this approach can be beneficial in the early phases of adjusting to a health problem. Patients may benefit from this approach by using it selectively to put aside their emotions temporarily, thereby saving them from feeling overwhelmed and giving them time to organize other personal coping resources.
- *Seeking information* about the health problem and treatment procedures.
- *Learning to provide one's own medical care* such as self-administering insulin shots. With this approach, patients gain a sense of control and personal effectiveness with respect to their conditions.
- *Setting concrete, limited goals* such as in exercising or in going to shows or social gatherings, and maintaining regular routines as well as possible. By doing this, patients and their families have things to look forward to and opportunities to achieve goals they consider meaningful.
- *Recruiting instrumental and emotional support* from family, friends, and practitioners by expressing needs and feelings.
- *Considering possible future events* and stressful circumstances in order to know what lies ahead and to be prepared for unexpected difficulties.
- *Gaining a manageable perspective* on the health problem and its treatment by finding a long-term "purpose" or "meaning" for the experience. Patients often do this by applying religious beliefs or by recognizing how the experience has changed them in positive ways.

Source: Based on Moos (1982).

allow them to consider their situations more carefully and objectively (Roesch & Weiner, 2001; Suls & Fletcher, 1985).

To summarize, most people tend to react to becoming seriously ill with shock, but they eventually deal with critical adaptive tasks they identify through the process of cognitive appraisal. The importance of each adaptive task depends on the person's personality, the physical and social environment, and the specific chronic health problem to which he or she must adjust.

IMPACTS OF DIFFERENT CHRONIC CONDITIONS

What is it like to live with a chronic health problem? To some extent, the answer depends on the illness. Beginning with this section, we will consider the impact of specific chronic medical conditions and treatments on patients and their families. The particular health problems we will examine were selected to illustrate disorders of different body systems and widely different adjustment difficulties. Some of the health problems tend to develop at much earlier ages than others; some require much more complex treatment regimens than others; and some produce more pain and disability than others. People who are disabled by illness are more likely than others to adjust poorly to their condition and become clinically depressed (Williamson, 2000). At the end of the chapter, we will consider psychosocial approaches to help chronically ill people adapt to their condition.

Although the medical problems we will discuss here include some that can be life-threatening, none of these chronic conditions is among the most deadly illnesses people around the world develop—particularly heart disease, cancer, stroke, and AIDS, which we will examine in the next chapter. We will use a *life-span perspective* to order the health problems in this chapter: illnesses that generally begin in childhood will be presented first, and illnesses that usually begin in old age will be considered last. As we have seen, the impact of a health problem and the way people cope with it depend partly on the patient's age. We will start by considering the impact of asthma, a chronic respiratory disorder that generally begins in the early childhood years.

ASTHMA

We all experience respiratory disorders at one time or another. If we are fortunate, these disorders are limited to occasional bouts with winter colds and the flu. But millions of people are not so fortunate—they suffer from chronic respiratory problems. In some cases, these problems involve constant breathing impairments that vary in intensity from one day to the next. In other cases, the victims breathe normally most of the time but suffer recurrent episodes of impaired breathing. Some chronic respiratory illnesses, such as *emphysema*, result largely from environmental causes, such as cigarette smoking. Others do not. Some chronic respiratory disorders become severe enough to disable their victims and may even claim their lives. This can happen with *asthma*.

What Is Asthma?

Imagine being at home reading one evening and noticing that a slight whistling, wheezing sound starts to accompany each breath you take. Soon the sound becomes louder and your breathing becomes labored. You try opening your mouth to breathe, but very little air goes in or out. When your chest begins to contract from the effort and your heart pounds rapidly, you are quite frightened and worry, "Will my next gasp for air be my last?" This is what a major asthma attack is like. Victims of extreme attacks may begin to turn blue and look as if they are about to die, and some do die.

Asthma is a respiratory disorder involving episodes of impaired breathing when the airways become inflamed and obstructed. This disease is very prevalent around the world; in the United States alone, about 17 million people—6% of the population—suffer from asthma (AAFA, 2004; ALA, 2003). The disorder may emerge at any age, but prevalence rates are much higher for children than adults. Fortunately, most childhood cases of asthma become less severe over time (Burg & Ingall, 1985), and one-fourth of children who develop asthma no longer have symptoms by the time they reach adulthood (ALA, 2003). Each year, over 4,000 asthmatics in the United States die from asthma attacks (USBC, 2003). The death rates for children are several times higher for African Americans than Whites (Akinbami & Schoendorf, 2002). Because Blacks have lower incomes than Whites and are less likely to have regular physicians, they tend to use hospital emergency rooms as their main source of treatment for asthma and seek help mainly when attacks are severe.

Asthma is a leading cause of short-term disability in the United States, resulting in millions of restricted-activity days in which patients either remain in bed or are unable to carry out their usual major activities, such as going to work or school. Each year, asthma results in:

- 14.5 million lost work days and 14 million lost school days.
- 2 million emergency room visits.
- 465,000 hospitalizations (ALA, 2003).

Asthma is clearly a major health problem. Let's see what causes asthma attacks.

The Physiology, Causes, and Effects of Asthma

Asthma episodes typically begin when the immune system is activated to react in an allergic manner, producing antibodies that cause the bronchial tubes and other affected body tissues to release a chemical called *histamine*. This chemical causes irritation to those tissues. In an asthma attack, these events cause the bronchial tubes to become obstructed as their smooth muscles become inflamed, develop spasms, and produce mucus (AAFA, 2000; Evans, 1990). These events last, perhaps, an hour or two and can lead to tissue damage, thereby increasing the likelihood of more frequent and severe future attacks. For some asthmatics, airway inflammation becomes constant.

What causes asthma attacks to happen? We do not have a full answer to this question, but we do know that attacks usually occur in the presence of certain conditions, called *triggers* (Evans, 1990). Asthma triggers can include *personal factors*, such as having a respiratory infection or feelings of anger or anxiety; *environmental conditions*, such as air pollution, pollen, or cold temperature; and *physical activities*, such as strenuous exercise (ALA, 2003; Sarafino & Goldfedder, 1995). The triggers that lead to attacks are different for different asthmatics, and some individuals have attacks only when two or more triggers occur at the same time (Evans, 1990). The main triggers for many asthmatics are allergens—substances, such as pollens or molds, that are known to cause allergic reactions. However, other asthmatics do not have any known allergies, and other factors, such as physical exercise

or cold air, are the main triggers for them. Tests for allergic reactions usually involve injecting a small amount of the allergen under the skin and checking to see if the skin in that area becomes inflamed.

Researchers demonstrated the important role of immune processes in the development of allergic reactions with a study involving transplanted bone marrow, the tissue that produces white blood cells (Agosti et al., 1988). The subjects were cancer patients who needed the transplants as part of their treatment. Each subject and donor was given skin tests with 17 allergen extracts—including house dust, cat hair, mites, and ragweed—before the transplant and one year after. In some of the pretransplant tests, the donor showed a positive allergic reaction but the subject did not. When tested again a year later, the subjects now showed reactions in 44.5% of the tests. In other pretransplant tests, neither the donor nor the patient showed an allergic reaction. This situation served as a control condition—and a year later the subjects showed reactions in only 3% of these tests. These findings indicate that bone marrow contains allergen-specific antibodies and that the donors' allergies were passed on to the patients. This research also found cases of asthma being transmitted from donors to people with no history of the disease.

What causes the condition of asthma to develop? Twin studies and other genetic research have shown that heredity clearly plays a role in determining whether individuals develop asthma (Sarafino, 2000). Research has also found evidence linking genetic factors to the severity of the condition and some of the specific triggers that are involved (Sarafino & Goldfedder, 1995). Other important factors include the person's history of respiratory infection and exposure to cigarette smoke. Individuals who contract serious viral infections in infancy or early childhood are more likely to develop asthma than individuals who do not (Li & O'Connell, 1987; Sarafino & Dillon, 1998). Children are more likely to develop asthma if their parents smoke (Hu et al., 1997). It may be that infections and smoke damage the respiratory system, making it highly sensitive to certain triggering conditions.

Medical Regimens for Asthma

Medical approaches provide the cornerstone of treatment for asthma (ALA, 2003; Evans, 1990). Asthma regimens consist of three components, the first being to *avoid known triggers* of attacks. The second component involves medication. To treat an acute attack, patients mainly use *bronchodilators*, which open constricted airways. To prevent attacks, patients can use *anti-inflammatories*, such as inhaled corticosteroids, which, when used regularly, reduce the sensitivity and inflammation of the airways when a trigger occurs. Steroids that are inhaled in low doses have little risk of undesirable side effects; they are usually applied three or four times a day.

The third component of asthma regimens is *exercise*. In the past, physicians advised many asthmatics to avoid exercise because it could induce an attack (Stockton, 1988). But it now appears that the less these people exercise, the worse their conditions get. Many physicians today recommend treatment regimens that carefully combine fitness training and the use of medication. Asthma's potential for producing disability and, sometimes, death, makes it important that patients adhere to their regimens. Although adhering to asthma regimens reduces attacks and incidents of wheezing, many asthmatics fail to take medication to prevent attacks and use medication during an attack incorrectly (Cluss & Fireman, 1985).

Psychosocial Factors in Asthma

We saw in Chapter 4 that psychosocial factors, including stress, can produce or aggravate an asthmatic episode, and we have just seen that emotional states, such as being angry or excited, can trigger attacks. Experimental research has shown that watching an exciting movie can trigger attacks in some children (Miller & Wood, 1994).

Studies have also found that *suggestion* can induce asthma symptoms. In one study, researchers had asthmatics inhale several doses of a placebo solution, with each succeeding dose labeled as containing an increasingly strong level of an allergen (Luparello et al., 1968). Nearly half of the subjects developed symptoms, either as full asthma attacks or as spasms of the bronchial muscles. Another study confirmed the effect of suggestion, but also showed that the asthmatic reaction could be negated if the people were first given another placebo that was described as a new asthma drug (Butler & Steptoe, 1986). In other words, the first suggestion blocked the second one. And another study found that false feedback indicating that the airways are becoming obstructed increases breathlessness in people with asthma (Rietveld & Brosschot, 1999). Although there is little question that psychosocial factors can influence asthma attacks, we do not know how these factors work and which asthmatics are more affected by them. It is possible that psychosocial factors make asthmatics more sensitive to allergens or other conditions that trigger their attacks.

Frequent asthma episodes are costly to the family and disrupt these people's lives and functioning. Living with this disorder adds to the stress asthmatics and their families experience, and studies have found that the rate of maladjustment, especially anxiety disorders, is higher among people with than without asthma (Lehrer et al., 2002). This relationship probably involves two causal directions: living with asthma may lead to emotional problems and maladjustment increases asthmatic episodes. Some asthmatics are chronically short of breath and have frequent attacks, and others have long attack-free periods. The psychosocial impact of asthma depends on many factors, such as how severe and disabling the condition is, and these factors probably play a role in asthmatics' low levels of adherence to taking medication and avoiding triggers, such as cigarette smoke (Cabana et al., 2004; Lehrer et al., 2002).

EPILEPSY

Epilepsy is a condition marked by recurrent, sudden seizures that result from electrical disturbances of the cerebral cortex (AMA, 2003; EFA, 2004; Fraser, 1999). Although the form of seizures can vary greatly, a common and very severe form is the *tonic-clonic*, or *grand mal*, which has two phases. It begins with a very brief "tonic" phase, in which the person loses consciousness and the body is rigid. It then progresses to a longer "clonic" phase that lasts 2 or 3 minutes and includes muscle spasms and twitching. The body may then relax until the person awakens. Sometimes before tonic-clonic seizures epileptics experience an *aura*, which consists of unexplained sounds, smells, or other sensations. In mild forms of seizures, the person may just stare blankly for a few seconds and show slight facial twitching.

Estimates of the prevalence of epilepsy vary somewhat, but it afflicts about 1% of people worldwide (Tortora & Grabowski, 2003). In the United States, more than 2½ million people have epilepsy, over 180,000 new cases are diagnosed each year, and one-third of cases are diagnosed by 20 years of age

(EFA, 2004). But many people with epilepsy are undiagnosed and untreated. What causes epilepsy? Sometimes physicians find a specific neurological defect that is the cause of an epileptic's disorder, but usually they do not (Hauser & Hesdorffer, 1990). Risk factors for developing epilepsy include a strong family history of the condition, severe head injury, infections of the central nervous system, and stroke. Most people with epilepsy eventually become seizure-free for at least 5 years. (Go to 💡.)

Medical Regimens for Epilepsy

Anticonvulsant drugs provide the main medical treatment for epilepsy (AMA, 2003; EFA, 2004; Fraser, 1999). These medications must be taken regularly to maintain the most effective serum concentrations throughout the day. In cases when medication does not control the seizures, physicians consider other methods, such as implanting a device that stimulates the vagal nerve or surgery if the seizures result from clear neurological defects. Neuropsychologists conduct tests to pinpoint the affected area of the brain and minimize cognitive and motor impairments the surgery might produce (DeAngelis, 1990). After surgery, as many as 80% of patients become

seizure-free in the next few years (Fraser, 1999). But undergoing surgery without becoming seizure-free may lead to subsequent psychosocial difficulties, such as heightened anxiety and depression (Rose, Derry, & McLachlan, 1995).

Psychosocial Factors in Epilepsy

Because individuals who are having epileptic episodes lose control of their behavior and "act strange," their condition stigmatizes them among people who do not understand it (Scambler, 1984). This stigma is clear in the experience of a college freshman named Kurt when he witnessed a severe epileptic attack for the first time. He described that a kitchen worker in the college dining hall

had collapsed in a convulsion. Four students quickly piled on top of him. His arms and legs jerked violently and, in the process of trying to hold him down, the students seemed to be smothering him. The young man's face, twisted and red, made him appear to be in great pain and, somehow, inhuman. Yet I could see myself in his place—I had just found out that I had epilepsy.

I did not want to say anything, but I thought the four students, in their panic, might kill the

---

HIGHLIGHT

What to Do for a Seizure

People react negatively to seeing a grand mal attack for many reasons, one of which may be that they don't know what to do to help. Actually, there is little one *can* do other than to remain calm and try to protect the epileptic from injury as he or she falls or flails about during the tonic or clonic phases. If you witness a seizure, the following five actions are recommended (Eichenwald, 1987; EFA, 2004):

1. Prevent injury from falls or flailing. Break the fall if possible and provide a cushion, such as a coat, between the person's head and the ground.

2. Do *not* put anything in the person's mouth. Many people believe they must put a spoon or other object in the mouth to prevent the epileptic from

swallowing his or her tongue, which actually cannot happen. Loosen tight clothing around the neck. Turn the person on his or her side so that saliva does not obstruct breathing.

3. Do *not* restrain the person. If you believe the epileptic could be injured while flailing near a hard object, try to move the object.

4. If the person does not come out of the attack in about 5 minutes, call an ambulance.

5. After the person wakes up, describe what happened and see if he or she needs help when ready to leave. Epileptics are often disoriented after an attack. For the most part, the role of the bystander requires calm and composed caring and common sense.

young man. So I told the largest of them, who by then had a headlock on the kitchen worker, to let go. The student brushed off my concern and seemed irritated that I should bother him at such a time. I paused, then repeated my statement in louder tones. The student was angry. "Look, kid, I'm a pre-med. I know what I'm doing. What makes you think you know so much?" I opened my mouth, but no words came out. Instead, I walked to a corner and leaned against a wall. As the young man's convulsions grew more violent, I whispered an apology to him and began to cry. (Eichenwald, 1987, p. 30)

Kurt had been advised to keep his epilepsy a secret, or people would fear and discriminate against him. Long ago, many people believed individuals with the condition were possessed by the devil. Although few people in advanced societies today shun victims of epilepsy, witnessing an attack may still arouse feelings of fear and aversion.

Aside from the reactions their attacks produce in people, what other problems do epileptics face as a result of their illness? Having strong seizures, especially with a loss of consciousness, is sometimes associated with important cognitive and motor impairments that can limit eligibility for certain activities and jobs, such as those that involve high memory loads or danger from heights or machinery (Fraser, 1999). An example of the discrimination epileptics have experienced comes from the case of Kurt, the freshman we just discussed. Because of his condition, he was expelled from the prestigious college he attended. As it turned out, however, he was reinstated after the United States Department of Health and Human Services ruled that dismissal was discriminatory. He graduated in 1983.

Epilepsy seems to be related to psychosocial processes in two ways. First, some evidence suggests that emotional arousal, such as of anxiety, may increase the likelihood or severity of epileptic episodes (Goldstein, 1990). Second, epileptics and their families sometimes adjust poorly to the disorder, especially if episodes are frequent and severe (Fraser, 1999; Hauser & Hesdorffer, 1990). Emotional difficulties, such as with anxiety or depression, often lead clients to drop out of rehabilitation programs. Many of the adjustment problems that epileptics face can be reduced through counseling when the diagnosis is made and through the work of support groups.

NERVOUS SYSTEM INJURIES

A woman named Leslie who suffered a *brain injury* in a car accident awoke after 17 days in a coma very disoriented; in her words,

> I didn't know who I was, what happened to me. All of a sudden you wake up in this bed one day and these people are hurting you, bending your leg and such. And you think it's a dream or a nightmare of some kind. (Leonard, 1990, p. 49)

This was the start of her long recovery. Many thousands of people suffer injuries to the brain or spinal cord each year, leaving them debilitated for life. Neuropsychologists and health psychologists play important roles in assessing these patients' impairments and helping them adapt to their conditions (Bleiberg, Ciulla, & Katz, 1991). In this section, we will focus on the impact of having a spinal cord injury.

Prior to the 1940s, medical practitioners knew almost nothing about treating people who suffered a severe injury to the spinal cord (Hendrick, 1985). In World War I, 80% of the soldiers who received such injuries died within 2 weeks, and little attempt was made to rehabilitate those who survived. But in World War II, England established special medical units to develop and provide comprehensive care and rehabilitation for people with spinal cord injuries. These medical units served as a model for others to be developed in countries around the world.

The Prevalence, Causes, and Physical Effects of Spinal Cord Injuries

The term **spinal cord injury** refers to neurological damage in the spine that results in the loss of motor control, sensation, and reflexes in associated body areas. The damage may be caused by disease or by an injury that compresses, tears, or severs the cord (AMA, 2003; NSCIA, 2004). When the cord is badly torn or severed, the damage is permanent because little or no nerve tissue will regenerate; but if the cord is compressed or has an abrasion, some function may be recovered when the pressure is removed or healing occurs. As we saw in Chapter 2, the degree to which the person's function is impaired depends on the amount of damage and its location. If the cord is completely severed in the neck region, *quadriplegia* results. If a lower portion is severed, *paraplegia* results. If the cord is not completely severed, partial function remains.

Millions of people around the world are living with spinal cord injuries; in the United States, there are about 250,000 people with this affliction, and about 11,000 new cases occur each year (NSCIA, 2004). About half of these people are quadriplegics. The great majority of Americans who receive spinal cord injuries are males, and most of them are under 30 years of age at the time. The most common cause is motor vehicle accidents, and the remainder result mainly from falls, sporting activities, and wounds, such as from a gunshot or stabbing.

The physical effects patients experience after spinal cord injuries change over time, and the full extent of spinal cord damage may not be clear for some time. Long-term prognoses are difficult to make during the first 6 months or so (Hendrick, 1985). If the cord is not severed, considerable functional recovery may occur over a long period of time. If the cord is severed, some autonomic functions will recover, but other functions will not. People who survive severe damage to the higher regions of the cord are typically fully paralyzed and unable to breathe without a respirator. Once the condition of spinal cord injury patients has stabilized, the process of rehabilitation begins. Most of these patients enter rehabilitation expecting to regain total function and are not prepared to cope with the reality of permanent functional losses. A major goal for psychologists at this time is to help these people adjust to the demands and limitations of the rehabilitation process (Bleiberg, Ciulla, & Katz, 1991).

Physical Rehabilitation

The process of physical rehabilitation for people with spinal cord injuries is geared toward helping them regain as much physical function as the neurological damage will allow and become as independent in their functioning as possible. This process focuses initially on training the patients to develop bladder and bowel control and on assisting them in moving paralyzed limbs to maintain their range of motion (Hendrick, 1985). Although many of these people will eventually be able to control their bladder functions, others will not and will need to use catheters or other devices. Hygienic bladder care is extremely important because a common cause of death in these patients is kidney failure from repeated infections (Frank, 2001; NSCIA, 2004).

The next phase of rehabilitation extends the focus of physical therapy toward maintaining and improving

"Actor Christopher Reeve resumed an active life for several years after a horse-riding accident rendered him quadriplegic, but he died in 2004 of complications from his condition."

the function of muscles over which the person has some control (Hendrick, 1985). For example, quadriplegics receive special attention toward improving respiration; paraplegics do exercises to strengthen the upper body. When some neural connection to affected parts of the body remains, therapy with biofeedback to "reeducate" the muscles in those areas appears to help some, but not all, patients (Klose et al., 1993). The last phase of physical rehabilitation extends the therapy as much as possible to include activities of daily living: performing self-care activities independently and using devices to compensate for permanent physical losses. Some devices today are highly sophisticated and use computers, allowing paralyzed individuals to turn on lights, answer the telephone, and operate computer keyboards with voice commands.

Psychosocial Aspects of Spinal Cord Injury

Most people with spinal cord injuries have a long life ahead—for example, the average years of life ahead for those injured at age 20 is about 38 years for quadriplegics and 45 years for paraplegics (NSCIA, 2004). Most victims who were employed prior to the injury are working again within a year or so (Heinemann, 1999).

The victims' main challenges after spinal cord injury are to make the most of their remaining abilities and lead as full a life as possible. This can be very difficult for many with spinal cord injuries because they often suffer from chronic pain conditions as a complication of the injury and lack the resources to help them live and function independently (Mariano, 1992; Tate, Maynard, & Forchheimer, 1993).

What can health care workers, family, and friends do to help? A lot depends on the way they respond to the person's condition. John Adams and Erich Lindemann (1974) described and contrasted the case studies of two young men, 17 and 18 years of age, who had suffered spinal cord injuries that rendered them quadriplegic. One adapted well: he was able to accept the injury and cope with no longer being a fine athlete. He turned his energies toward academic pursuits and eventually became a history teacher and coached a local basketball team from his wheelchair. The other patient provides a striking contrast. He was never able to accept the injury or the permanence of his condition. He became extremely withdrawn and depressed. At one point he was spending "much time in bed with the curtains drawn and frequently with the sheet over his head." Years later, he was readmitted to the hospital after taking an overdose of medication and was still clinging to the hope that he would walk again. Why did these young men adapt so differently to their similar physical conditions? Part of the answer may be in their strikingly different social environments. The patient who adapted well had family and friends who could accept his paralysis and help him redefine his self-concept. For instance, his parents installed ramps in their home and widened doorways to accommodate a wheelchair. The other patient's family and friends were not able to accept his condition or provide the support he needed to help him adapt.

Family and friends can also help by providing social support without being overprotective and "taking over" when the patient has difficulty performing self-help tasks. Having a disabled individual in the household increases the stress of all family members. They need to make many adjustments in daily living and, while doing so, try not to make the person feel like a burden. If the patient is a husband or wife, his or her spouse faces difficult adjustments (Hendrick, 1985). Role changes occur immediately—at least for a while, and perhaps permanently. The healthy spouse, with or without the help of other family members, must suddenly take on full responsibility for providing the family's income, maintaining the household, caring for the children, and caring for the disabled person. Sexual problems brought on by the patient's injury may become a major source of stress in the marital relationship.

Many people believe that all individuals who become paralyzed below the waist lose all sexual function and interest. This belief is not correct (Frank, 2001; NSCIA, 2004). Males usually lose their fertility. But although they initially lose the ability to have an erection, they often regain it to some degree. Females generally retain their fertility after paralysis, and about half become able to achieve orgasm. The most serious barriers to sexual function in people with spinal cord injuries appear to be psychosocial rather than physical. These patients and their sexual partners can overcome many of these barriers through counseling and education, such as in ways to position themselves during sex acts and to heighten the degree of stimulation they achieve.

Disabled people also experience many unpleasant thoughts about themselves, their future, their relations with other people in general, and physical barriers in society (Eisenberg, 1984). They find that many places they once liked to go to are inaccessible by wheelchair, for example. Furthermore, people in general act strangely toward them—staring, or quickly averting their eyes, or behaving awkwardly or uncomfortably in their presence. These experiences tend to reduce the self-esteem of disabled people, many of whom have heightened levels of depression and drug and alcohol use (Heinemann, 1999). Adapting to becoming disabled takes time, and a couple of years may pass before many individuals with spinal cord injuries report improvements in their adjustment and quality of life (Krause & Crewe, 1991).

DIABETES

"Too much of a good thing is wonderful," the late actress Mae West once said. Although her rule might possibly apply for some good things, glucose in the blood is not one of them. The body needs glucose to fuel metabolic processes, but too much of it in the blood over a long period of time—a condition called *hyperglycemia*—is the mark of *diabetes mellitus*. The body normally controls blood sugar levels with the hormone *insulin*, which the pancreas produces. In the disorder of diabetes, however, abnormal levels of glucose accumulate in the blood because the pancreas does not produce sufficient insulin (ADA, 2004; AMA, 2003; Kilo & Williamson, 1987).

Diabetes is a prevalent illness around the world; it is among the most common chronic conditions in the United States, with 13 million currently diagnosed cases and over 5 million people who are not aware that they have the disorder (ADA, 2004). Prevalence rates for diagnosed diabetes increase with age throughout the life span, being many times higher among middle-aged and elderly adults than among children and adolescents. The rates for American adults are:

- 1.9% between 18 and 44 years of age.
- 9.5% between 45 and 64.
- 17.3% between 65 and 74.

Women from Hispanic, African, and Native American groups are at especially high risk of dying from diabetes (USDHHS, 1995).

The Types and Causes of Diabetes

Diabetes is not a single disease—it occurs in two major patterns that require different kinds of treatment and may have somewhat different causes. The two forms of diabetes are:

- **Type 1 diabetes** (formerly called *insulin-dependent diabetes mellitus*) typically develops in childhood or adolescence and accounts for only 5 to 10% of diabetes cases. In this form of diabetes, autoimmune processes have destroyed cells of the pancreas that normally produce insulin, and people afflicted with it require insulin injections to prevent acute and very serious complications (AMA, 2003; Kilo & Williamson, 1987). An acute complication that occurs without insulin in type 1 diabetes is called *ketoacidosis*, in which high levels of fatty acids in the blood lead to kidney malfunctions, thereby causing wastes to accumulate and poison the body. The symptoms of ketoacidosis are subtle at first but advance to an episode of nausea, vomiting, abdominal pain, and labored breathing. If left untreated, ketoacidosis can lead to coma and death in a matter of days or weeks.
- **Type 2 diabetes** is very prevalent, accounting for the vast majority of diabetes cases. In this form of diabetes, the pancreas produces at least some insulin, and treatment may not require insulin injections. Most, but not all, people with type 2

diabetes can manage their glucose levels with diet and medication (AMA, 2003). Although type 2 diabetes can develop at any age, it usually appears after age 40. Most type 2 patients are very overweight, and many produce substantial amounts of insulin—sometimes more than normal—but their bodies seem to "resist" the glucose-controlling action of insulin (Kohrt et al., 1993). Normal-weight type 2 patients seem to produce reduced levels of insulin. In either case, hyperglycemia results.

What causes the pancreas to reduce its production of insulin? Although the causes are not well understood, most diabetics probably inherit some form of susceptibility to the effects of environmental conditions that could affect insulin production (ADA, 2004; Kilo & Williamson, 1987). In type 1, one environmental condition seems to involve a viral infection that stimulates the immune system to attack pancreas cells (Conrad et al., 1994). For type 2, evidence exists for three possible conditions: diets high in fat and sugar, stress, and an overproduction of a protein that impairs the metabolism of sugars and carbohydrates (Maddux et al., 1995; Surwit, 1993). A 3-year intervention in which people at high risk for diabetes ate less fat, exercised moderately, and took a drug for treating diabetes reduced their development of type 2 diabetes by nearly 60% (Knowler et al., 2002). (Go to 🍎.)

Health Implications of Diabetes

Diabetes can be a direct cause of death; in the United States it claims over 70,000 lives each year (USBC, 2003). Many of these deaths result from acute complications that can be prevented by appropriate medical care. Few diabetics die of acute complications if they follow the recommended medical regimens for controlling glucose levels (Santiago, 1984).

But the deaths that are caused directly by diabetes constitute only part of the serious health effects of this disease (ADA, 2004; AMA, 2003; Kilo & Williamson, 1987). One health problem diabetes can lead to is *neuropathy*, or nerve disease. High blood glucose levels appear to cause chemical reactions that can destroy the myelin sheath that insulates nerve fibers. When this occurs in peripheral fibers, such as in the feet, the person may lose sensation in the affected area or have abnormal sensations, such as chronic pain. The risk of other health problems also increases markedly among people who have di-

ASSESS YOURSELF

Do You Have Diabetes?

About half of the people who have diabetes don't know it. To tell if you might have this disorder, put a check mark in the space preceding each of the following warning signs that are true for you.

_____ Very frequent urination.

_____ Frequent excessive thirst.

_____ Often hungry, even after eating.

_____ Unexplained large weight loss.

_____ Chronically tired.

_____ Occasional blurry vision.

_____ Wounds heal very slowly.

_____ Tingling or numbness in your feet.

_____ Waist measurement greater than half your height.

If you check three or more of these signs, see your doctor—one or two signs alone may not mean anything is wrong. But the more signs you checked, the greater the chance that you have diabetes. (*Source*: Based on *Signs and Symptoms of Diabetes* distributed by the American Diabetes Association.)

abetes. These problems include blindness, kidney disease, gangrene (and as a result, amputation), heart disease, and stroke. The way diabetes contributes to these health problems is through its effects on the vascular system (AMA, 2003; Kilo & Williamson, 1987). High levels of glucose in the blood lead to a thickening of arterial walls as a result of atherosclerosis: in large blood vessels, it can cause gangrene in a limb or heart disease; in small blood vessels and capillaries, it can cause blindness and stroke. The long-term health risks of diabetes are quite serious, and patients and their families worry about them greatly (Wilkinson, 1987).

Medical Regimens for Diabetes

Ideally, the treatment for diabetes would enable the body to perform or simulate the normal biochemical activities for processing and maintaining normal levels of glucose. Normal and diabetic serum glucose levels in the hours after eating are shown in Figure 13–2. Medical regimens today compensate for these differences, but they do not enable the body to function exactly as it normally does, such as in continuously monitoring the need for insulin and secreting this hormone in precisely needed bursts.

The main approach for treating diabetes entails a balancing act with medication, diet, and regular exercise. Can diabetics reduce their long-term health risks by keeping their blood glucose levels within the normal range? Yes, these risks can be markedly reduced—with complications occurring much later

and far less often—if diabetics control their blood glucose levels by carefully following prescribed treatment regimens (ADA, 2004; Santiago, 1984; Wang, Lau, & Chalmers, 1993). But the *full extent* of the reduced risk is unclear because long-term complications of diabetes take many years or decades to develop, and many diabetics with good blood glucose control are not always able to keep their glucose levels consistently in the normal range. Today's treatments for diabetes allow patients to have better control over their blood sugar than in the past, but

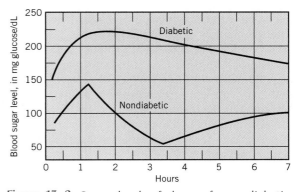

Figure 13–2 Serum levels of glucose for nondiabetics and unmedicated diabetics in the hours after consuming glucose. The data come from a standardized procedure in which subjects consume a specified amount of glucose per kilogram of body weight. (From Holum, 1994, Figure 26.4.)

these new methods are still not perfect. And many diabetics who have regimens that could provide good control over their blood glucose do not adhere to them closely.

Do Diabetics Adhere to their Regimens?

Noncompliance with the treatment regimen is a major problem in managing diabetes. Years ago, reviews of studies on this issue found most people with diabetes tested their glucose levels incorrectly, administered wrong doses of insulin, and failed to follow the recommended diets carefully (Wing et al., 1986). And the situation appears to be worse today: researchers found that blood sugar control among type 2 diabetics decreased from 1988 to 2000 (Koro et al., 2004). People with diabetes generally do *try* to adhere to their regimens, but they do not always succeed. One reason some fail may be that they rely on symptoms they perceive, such as dizziness or emotional states, to assess their glucose levels (Cox et al., 1993; Meltzer et al., 2003). Although many diabetics can make crude estimates of their actual glucose levels on the basis of perceived symptoms, these judgments are usually not very accurate.

Some research has found that people with diabetes have more difficulty following dietary and exercise advice than the more "medical" aspects of their regimens—testing their glucose levels and taking their insulin on time (Glasgow, McCaul, & Schafer, 1987). The patients' self-reports indicated they had complied fairly closely with their insulin and testing regimens. However, self-report data can be misleading. In two studies, for instance, researchers secretly inserted memory chips in blood glucose testing devices of adult and adolescent diabetics but also had the subjects keep records of their testing (Mazze et al., 1984; Wilson & Endres, 1986). The results showed that many subjects' records were inaccurate—at least according to the memory chips' records. The records did *not* contain data for some tests the subjects had done and *did* contain data for tests that they did not actually perform. (Go to 💡.)

Psychosocial Factors in Diabetes Care

A 60-year-old diabetic named Beth had not been able to get her glucose levels under control (Holt, 1995). Part of the problem was that she was mentally retarded and didn't understand how to plan her diet at home. A home-care nurse discovered an approach to help: they made up recipe cards for each meal, with pictures of its foods and a shopping list—and it worked! Not understanding how to interpret glucose test results and adjust the regimen accordingly is a common problem even among people with normal cognitive abilities (Patrick et al., 1994).

We saw in Chapter 9 that compliance with medical recommendations tends to be low when the regimen is complex, must be followed for a long time, requires changes in the person's lifestyle, and is designed to prevent rather than cure illness. Treatment regimens for diabetes have all of these characteristics. In addition, psychosocial factors in patients' lives are related to compliance. Two of these factors are social support and self-efficacy. A study found that diabetics' self-reports of adherence to dietary, exercise, and glucose testing aspects of their regimens increased with their perceived social support (Wilson et al., 1986). But the role of social support is unclear because it was not related to actual glucose control measured by analysis of blood samples. Research on diabetics' self-efficacy has shown that the greater their self-efficacy for following the diabetes regimen, the higher their subsequent self-reports of adherence and the better their actual glucose control (Johnston-Brooks, Lewis, & Garg, 2002; Skelly et al., 1995).

Coping processes are also important in diabetes care. Stress impairs blood sugar control in many diabetics (Kramer et al., 2000), especially in those who have sedentary lifestyles (Aikens et al., 1997). The effects of stress may occur in two ways. First, when people are under stress, the adrenal glands release epinephrine and cortisol into the bloodstream (Surwit, Feinglos, & Scovern, 1983). *Epinephrine* causes the pancreas to decrease insulin production; *cortisol* causes the liver to increase glucose production and body tissues to decrease their use of glucose. These biochemical reactions to stress clearly worsen the glucose regulation problems of diabetics. Second, stress can affect blood glucose levels indirectly by reducing adherence to diabetes regimens (Goldston et al., 1995). Many diabetics do not cope well with their condition and suffer from severe depression (Kovacs, 1997). The more that diabetes interferes with their daily activities and reduces their feelings of personal control, the more depressed they feel (Talbot et al., 1999). And the more depressed they feel, the worse their glucose control and the greater their risk of resulting health problems, such as blindness (de Groot et al., 2001; Van Tilburg et al., 2001).

HIGHLIGHT

Self-Managing Diabetes

Managing diabetes requires self-care activities that focus mainly on four components: self-monitoring of blood glucose, taking insulin or other medication, diet, and exercise.

Monitoring Blood Glucose and Taking Insulin or Medication

Patients typically estimate the sugar content of their blood by pricking their finger to get a drop of blood that a blood-glucose meter analyzes (AMA, 2003). Depending on the treatment regimen, these tests may be done just once a day or several times, often before each meal and at bedtime.

Many diabetics can use medication to help control their blood glucose levels. Different types of chemicals work in different ways; for instance, some drugs increase insulin production in the pancreas, whereas others reduce the liver's production of glucose (AMA, 2003; Kilo & Williamson, 1987). Other patients must use *insulin*, usually by injection. In the early 1920s, a physician named Frederick Banting devised a method that made it possible to extract insulin from the pancreas glands of slaughtered pigs and cattle. The insulin used today can be from these sources, or it can be synthetic. The physician's decision on the frequency and dosage of insulin depends on many factors, such as the person's size, age, food intake, and activity level (AMA, 2003). Some diabetics are able to use a device called an insulin pump that can be implanted in the body and delivers small amounts of insulin continuously, with extra doses at mealtimes.

One of the difficulties in using insulin is knowing how much to inject—taking too much may be as dangerous as taking too little. Using too much insulin can produce *hypoglycemia*, the condition of having too little sugar in blood. Severe hypoglycemia can cause insulin shock, in which the person lapses into a coma (Kilo & Williamson, 1987). When hypoglycemia is less severe, it can impair cognitive and emotional functioning, making the person excited, irritable, and confused (AMA, 2003). Diabetics dread these episodes, and so do their families (Wilkinson, 1987). With careful training, people with diabetes can reduce these episodes by adjusting their insulin doses accurately to keep glucose levels within the normal range.

Diet and Exercise

The diets recommended for diabetics are designed to help them maintain normal blood glucose levels, achieve or maintain a healthful weight, and limit foods that may raise their already high risk of developing heart disease (AMA, 2003). To maintain normal glucose levels, patients usually need to reduce their intake of foods that contain sugar and some other carbohydrates. People who take insulin must also maintain consistency in timing their meals and, usually, in their calorie intake each day. Once they take their insulin, they generally need to eat within a range of time thereafter to prevent an episode of hypoglycemia.

Because physical activity burns up glucose as fuel, exercise is another important part of the treatment of diabetes. Engaging in physical activity after meals inhibits glucose production by the liver and increases glucose use by the muscles (Zinman, 1984). Regular exercise also complements dietary efforts to reduce body weight and maintain overall fitness. But unplanned vigorous activity can cause an episode of hypoglycemia. People with diabetes who engage in vigorous activity should eat a sufficient number of calories to last through the event or carry packets of medication to adjust their blood sugar quickly (Kilo & Williamson, 1987).

Following a regimen to treat diabetes is difficult, but the risks of not doing so are very serious. It takes a good deal of planning, strong efforts to maintain the routine with only occasional departures, and the confidence of patients and their families that they can do it.

People's everyday lives present many circumstances that make it difficult to adhere to diabetes regimens (Glasgow, McCaul, & Schafer, 1986). Diabetics may feel that testing their glucose levels at work or school is embarrassing, or forget to take their testing materials with them, or have difficulty getting up on weekend mornings to take their injections on time, or make mistakes in judgments about what they can eat, for example. Four other issues can be important. First, because some temporary weight gain tends to occur when diabetics get their glucose under control, many female patients, in an effort to control their weight, fail to take their insulin (Polonsky et al., 1994). Second, a regimen's dietary recommendations may be incompatible with the food habits of patients in certain ethnic groups (Raymond & D'Eramo-Melkus, 1993). Third, diabetics often feel frustrated when they "didn't cheat," but their glucose control is off target for some other reason, such as being under stress. Fourth, because diabetes is not a painful condition, patients may not feel that following the regimen closely is critical (Kilo & Williamson, 1987).

One other psychosocial situation that can lead to noncompliance arises when the patient and the physician have different goals of treatment. A study demonstrated this by having doctors and the parents of diabetic children serve as subjects and asking them to assess hypothetical glucose test profiles (Marteau et al., 1987). The doctors were asked to pick the one profile they would be "happiest to see" for a child at their clinic; the parents were asked to pick the one they would be "happiest to see" for *their* own child. The results showed that the vast majority of physicians, but only about half of the parents, chose a profile reflecting a normal glucose level. More than a third of the parents chose either a mild or a moderate *hyperglycemic* profile. This suggests that doctors focus on preventing long-term complications, and parents may be more interested in preventing *hypoglycemic* episodes and promoting the day-to-day well-being and activity of their children. Not surprisingly, the children's actual glucose levels more closely matched the goals of their parents than those of physicians. Because much smaller deviations from normal blood sugar levels result in symptoms of hypoglycemia than in those of hyperglycemia, parents and diabetics may choose to err on the side of higher glucose levels (Varni & Babani, 1986).

When the Diabetic Is a Child or Adolescent

Most parents of diabetic children cope well with the disease (Eiser, 1985). Many family stressors remain, however, and stem from having to deal with occasional diabetic crises, take the child in for medical examinations, give glucose tests and injections, and make and monitor dietary adjustments. Parents also worry more than their diabetic children about future health complications.

Diabetic children younger than, say, 8 or 10 years of age have little understanding about their conditions

and tend to dislike most the aspects of their regimen that set them apart from other children—for example, the glucose monitoring and rigid eating patterns and restrictions (Eiser, 1985). Most of these activities can be done at home or privately. Maintaining the diabetes treatment regimen during childhood is essentially the parents' responsibility, but children can learn to select appropriate foods by 8 years of age, give themselves injections by 9 or 10, and perform glucose testing by 12 (Eiser, 1985). As adolescence approaches, parents allow their children more and more responsibility for managing the diabetes regimen. But children who are given too much responsibility are less adherent and have poorer glucose control than those whose parents stay involved (Gonder-Frederick, Cox, & Ritterband, 2002). And the quality of diabetes care is often lower in adolescence than in the preadolescent years (Anderson et al., 1990; Johnson et al., 1990). Adherence to glucose monitoring and diet declines with age in adolescence; blood sugar control also decreases. Although adolescent diabetics can generate solutions that would enable them to adhere, they often succumb to peer pressure, such as to drink (Thomas, Peterson, & Goldstein, 1997). Noncompliance is probably not the only reason for decreased glucose control in adolescence: hormonal changes may make controlling blood glucose more difficult (Eiser, 1985).

Teenagers' adherence to their diabetes regimens is relatively high among those who have high levels of self-esteem and social competence and have good relations with their parents (Hanson, Henggeler, & Burghen, 1987; Jacobson et al., 1994; Miller-Johnson et al., 1994). Teens who feel less sure of themselves may neglect their self-care activities partly because they may feel a greater need to avoid appearing different from their peers.

ARTHRITIS

Before developing a severe case of arthritis, Ron had been active in athletics for most of his 50 years of life, having played and coached college football and become an avid golfer and tennis player (McIlwain et al., 1991). Playing sports became increasingly difficult over a period of 5 years because of pain in his knee and hip, and he eventually stopped playing completely. After 2 months of treatment with medication and exercise, he was able to resume these activities without severe pain.

Musculoskeletal disorders affecting the body's muscles, joints, and connective tissues near the joints are classified as *rheumatic diseases*, which include over 100 conditions that cause pain, stiffness, or inflammation (AF, 2004). Rheumatic diseases that affect mainly the joints are called **arthritis.** Disorders of the bones and joints have probably always plagued humans and almost all other animals—archaeologists have found evidence of arthritis in the fossil bones of dinosaurs and prehistoric bears, for instance (Achterberg-Lawlis, 1988).

The Types and Causes of Rheumatic Diseases

Osteoarthritis is a disease in which the joints degenerate, mainly as a result of wear and tear (AF, 2004; AMA, 2003). It afflicts over 20 million Americans and is by far the most common rheumatic condition. People's risk of developing this condition increases with age and body weight and is associated with certain occupations in which particular joints are subjected to repeated heavy use (Kelsey & Hochberg, 1988). For instance, weavers and cotton pickers often develop osteoarthritis of the hands, whereas ballet dancers tend to have the condition in their feet.

Fibromyalgia produces pain and stiffness mainly in the muscles and other soft tissue (AF, 2004; Lee & Abramson, 1999). *Gout* can affect any of the body's joints but is most common in the big toe. In this disease, the body produces more uric acid than the kidneys can process, and the excess acid circulates in the blood and leaves crystalline deposits at the joints (AF, 2004; AMA, 2003). *Rheumatoid arthritis* is a disease that involves extreme inflammation of joint tissues and also affects the heart, blood vessels, and lungs when it reaches advanced stages (AF, 2004; AMA, 2003). It is potentially the most serious arthritic condition, being the most crippling and painful type. It often spreads to all of the body's joints. Although the mechanisms that lead to rheumatoid arthritis are unclear, they seem to involve an autoimmune response that attacks the tissues and bones of the joints (Lee & Abramson, 1999; Coico, Sunshine & Benjamini, 2003).

An estimated 70 million Americans suffer from a rheumatic disease (AF, 2004). Each rheumatic disease appears to have its own pattern of causes, including genetic factors and viral infections (McIlwain et al., 1991). Although arthritis can appear at any age, it becomes far more prevalent as people get older. As Figure 13–3 shows, arthritis afflicts nearly half of

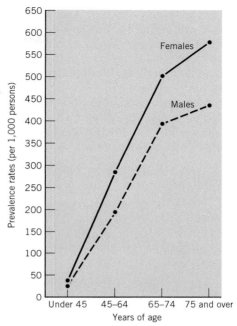

Figure 13–3 Prevalence rates of arthritis per 1,000 males and females in the United States at each age range. (Data from USBC, 1999, Table 232.)

Americans over 65 years of age and occurs more often among females than males. But three points should be made about the data in the figure. First, these data probably underestimate the actual number of people who have the disorder because mild cases often are not reported to health agencies (Kelsey & Hochberg, 1988). Second, the figure does not show that, whereas females are much more likely than males to develop most rheumatic diseases, males are more likely to develop gout (AF, 2004). Third, nearly 300,000 American children have arthritis; many have *juvenile rheumatoid arthritis*. An encouraging point about juvenile rheumatoid arthritis is that most patients do *not* suffer serious disability in their adult lives; for many, the disorder disappears in several years (AMA, 2003; Burg & Ingall, 1985).

The Effects and Treatment of Arthritis

Arthritis is a leading cause of disability around the world. Any type of arthritis can disable its victims on a short-term or long-term basis. Of the major chronic diseases that afflict people in the United States, arthritis is the leading cause of disability in people over age 15 and is second, behind heart disease, in causing work disability (AF, 2004). Elderly people have more functional limitations from osteoarthritis of the knee than from most other chronic illnesses (Guccione et al., 1994).

In the case of rheumatoid arthritis, some patients experience only mild episodes of inflammation and pain in a few joints, but others suffer intense pain in many joints, often showing the following progression:

- The lubricating fluid leaks out of the joints, usually in the knees, ankles, shoulders, elbows, and wrists.
- Cartilage is destroyed, and joint function is reduced.
- The conversion of organic matter into minerals for bones decreases near the joints.
- Bone erosions take place near the joints.
- Joints become dislocated and sometimes fused, producing deformities. (Anderson et al., 1985)

Some of the people whose rheumatoid arthritis progresses to the later stages show associated damage to other organ systems, developing vascular or heart valve diseases, for example.

What treatments can be used in managing the pain and functional impairment of arthritis? People with arthritis typically take some form of pain-relieving medication, especially aspirin and other drugs, such as ibuprofen, that reduce inflammation (AMA, 2003; Lee & Abramson, 1999; McIlwain et al., 1991). Other drugs may be used for more severe cases, and when these do not reduce the pain, surgeons may replace affected joints with artificial ones. People can also reduce arthritic pain and impairment by maintaining proper body weight and, especially for people with gout, limiting certain foods and alcohol (McIlwain et al., 1991). Physical therapy is very important in treating arthritis and can include exercise, applying heat or cold, and using devices to prevent joint damage and assist patients in performing daily activities (Lee & Abramson, 1999; Minor & Sanford, 1993). For example, a 58-year-old woman with rheumatoid arthritis whose hand pain and weakness made doing household tasks difficult received physical therapy with three components (Philips, 1989). First, she did *exercises* to increase hand strength and range of motion. Second, she wore *splints* at night to reduce pain and swelling. Third, she received *advice on devices* that make

daily activities easier, such as a cart to transport things, purses that hang from the shoulder instead of the hand, and handles with large diameters. Many arthritis sufferers use complementary and alternative medicine methods, such as acupuncture and herbal therapy, especially if they are dissatisfied with medical procedures (Vecchio, 1994).

Studies of compliance for medical treatment regimens have shown that people with arthritis adhere closely to recommendations for the more powerful drugs but not for milder ones, such as aspirin, and they adhere less closely to physical therapy than to taking medication (Anderson et al., 1985). Many patients dislike physical therapy, seeing its negative aspects, rather than its positive ones (Jensen & Lorish, 1994). They feel, for instance, that exercising is boring and its value is not obvious.

Psychosocial Factors in Arthritis

Any chronic pain condition is distressing for the patients and their families, and the distress is worse if the pain is severe and frequent. If the pain is disabling, the condition produces a great deal of stress for patients and their families. Evidence indicates that a vicious circle occurs for many patients: arthritis symptoms increase the person's stress which, in turn, increases symptoms (Dougall & Baum, 2001).

People with severe rheumatoid arthritis experience at least some pain virtually every day, and on many days it is intense (Affleck et al., 1991). This pain can interfere in many everyday activities: as one patient stated,

> There are times when I'm downright miserable, like when I can't even pick up a pot off the stove. Every once in a while, I have to miss work for a week or two because I simply can't keep my knee in a position to drive a car. (Tennen & Affleck, 1997, p. 264)

People with severe arthritis are more likely to feel helpless and depressed than those with milder conditions. One study, for instance, examined over 200 patients' disabilities and feelings of helplessness about their conditions over a 1-year period (Nicassio et al., 1985). Their self-reports showed that their feelings of helplessness correlated with changes in their ability to perform daily activities, such as dressing, turning faucets on and off, and getting in and out of a car. Other studies have confirmed the link between arthritis severity and feelings of helplessness and

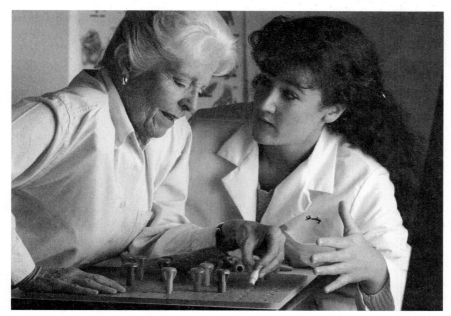

Physical therapy for a patient with arthritic hands can involve enjoyable activities that exercise the affected joints.

found that these feelings lead to maladjustment and depression (Nicassio et al., 1993; Parker et al., 1991; Smith & Wallston, 1992; Smith, Peck, & Ward, 1990; Zautra et al., 1995).

Of course, not all individuals with severe arthritis experience serious emotional difficulties. Some arthritic people with severe pain feel a greater sense of personal control over their conditions than others do, and this may benefit their emotional adjustment. Researchers examined this relationship by interviewing adults with rheumatoid arthritis regarding their mood states and their perceptions of personal control over their illness (Affleck et al., 1987). These interviews revealed three main findings. First, the subjects generally thought their practitioners had greater control over the *course* of the disease than they did themselves. Second, of the patients who had relatively active symptoms, those who believed they could control their *daily symptoms* reported less mood disturbance than those who did not. Third, the people who saw themselves as *active partners* in decisions about their medical care and treatment showed better adjustment to their illness. These findings are also important because people with arthritis who understand their treatment and believe it can help are more likely to adhere closely to their medical regimens than those individuals who do not (Jette, 1984).

What impact does the arthritis condition have on the psychological status of the patient's family? The severity of the disease by itself seems to have little impact. Spouses of arthritis patients seem to adapt similarly to different levels of disease severity—the feelings of distress or depression they report relate mainly to their perceptions of the quality of the marriage and of social support (Manne & Zautra, 1990). Social processes affect the spouse and patient in two ways. First, as arthritis severity increases, spouses who perceive little social support in their lives report *more* depression, while spouses with high levels of social support report *less* depression (Revenson & Majerovitz, 1991). Second, arthritis patients who cope by expressing negative emotions a lot and perceive their spouses as reacting negatively to their pain show poorer adjustment and disease status over time than others (Griffin et al., 2001).

ALZHEIMER'S DISEASE

For a long time, Martha, the wife of 75-year-old Alfred, denied her husband was sick, making excuses for his forgetful and odd behavior. Then

one evening, they were out dining with friends. During the meal, Alfred refused to remove his overcoat and wouldn't talk to anyone. Instead, he clanged his fork on his plate, put his napkin in his soup, and tried to eat his salad with his knife. When Martha whispered to him to put down his silverware, he yelled at her. She burst into tears. Finally, one of the male dinner guests led Alfred from the table, leaving a humiliated, mortified wife to confront a reality that could no longer be ignored: Alfred had Alzheimer's disease. (McCahon, 1991, p. 44)

Dementia is a term that refers to a progressive loss of cognitive functions that often occurs in old age. By far, the most common form of dementia is **Alzheimer's disease,** a brain disorder characterized by a deterioration of attention, memory, and personality. Figure 13–4 illustrates the cognitive deficits of an Alzheimer victim. An estimated 4 million Americans have Alzheimer's disease, and the prevalence rate increases sharply with each 10-year increase in age after 65: whereas probably 3% of individuals ages 65 to 74 have the disease, nearly half of those 85 and older have it (ADEAR, 2004; AMA, 2003). Some individuals show symptoms of the disease in their 40s (Gruetzner, 1992).

The cognitive functions of people with Alzheimer's disease do not disappear all at once. Perhaps the most critical functions to go at first are *attention* and *memory*. Peter Vitaliano and his colleagues (1986) conducted a 2-year followup study of Alzheimer vic-tims with mild impairment and found that their main deficits initially were in their attentive and memory abilities. The extent of these deficits was strongly associated with the degree of their impairment 2 years later. As the disease progresses over several years, the effects of the disorder become more pronounced (Haley, 1998). Personality changes often emerge, with the victims becoming less spontaneous and more apathetic and withdrawn. Self-care deteriorates, and behavior problems appear, as when these individuals wander and become lost. At some point, they may become frequently disoriented with regard to time, their location, and their identity. These declines develop faster if the patients suffer a severe loss of language or have a history of alcohol abuse or of neurological disorders, such as from a stroke or Parkinson's disease (Bracco et al., 1994; Teri, Hughes, & Larson, 1990).

The Causes and Treatment of Alzheimer's Disease

What causes Alzheimer's disease? A promising answer seems to involve a characteristic that differentiates the brains of Alzheimer victims from those of other elderly individuals: Alzheimer brains contain extensive *lesions*, consisting of gnarled and tangled nerve and protein fibers (AMA, 2003). Evidence now

Figure 13–4 Illustration of cognitive deficits in Alzheimer's disease. A graphic artist with this disorder was asked to copy the drawing of a hand shown on the left. The hand he drew was much smaller and had distortions in spatial relationships, misplaced fingernails, and an incorrect number of fingers.

indicates that genetic defects may cause these large deposits to occur. For instance, one study examined stored tissue samples from many members of a family across three generations (Murrell et al., 1991). All members with the genetic defect also had Alzheimer's disease, and no member who did not have the defect had the disease. And a likely gene involved in early onset of the disease has been identified (Levy-Lahad et al., 1995). Two other findings are also important. First, one study found that people with the brain lesions that characterize the disease are far more likely to develop Alzheimer symptoms if they have had strokes, even fairly mild ones, than if they have not (Snowdon et al., 1997). Second, factors associated with lower heart disease risk, such as regular physical activity and moderate drinking, are also linked to lower risk of Alzheimer's disease (Lindsay et al., 2002; Ruitenberg et al., 2003). It seems likely that this disease can result from genetic defects and several environmental factors.

Diagnosis of Alzheimer's disease should be made at specialized centers, is based mainly on tests of mental ability and physiological signs, and is nearly 90% accurate, as compared with autopsy findings of brain structure (ADEAR, 2004; Haley, 1998). No treatment exists yet to prevent Alzheimer's disease, but some medications can slow its progression and improve symptoms.

Psychosocial Effects of Alzheimer's Disease

Most victims of Alzheimer's disease live at home and receive care from their spouses or adult children (Gruetzner, 1992; Haley, 1998). In the early stages of the disease, family members and others may be able to help maximize the person's functioning, such as by marking objects clearly and giving social support. But many families either don't know or deny that the person has Alzheimer's disease. As patients lose more and more of their cognitive function, their inability to do simple tasks and remember everyday things becomes very frustrating and often leads to feelings of helplessness, which may account for their high rates of depression (Migliorelli et al., 1995).

Alzheimer patients' behavior becomes increasingly problematic as the disease progresses, producing great stress in their families. People with this disease may, for instance, accuse a family member of hiding things they cannot find, develop sleep disturbances and stay awake most of the night, get lost after wandering out of the house, lose control of their bowels and bladder, or become bedridden (Gruetzner, 1992; Haley, 1998). The demands in caring for Alzheimer patients can become physically and emotionally overwhelming, particularly when the caregivers are elderly spouses in failing health or grown children who have many career and family pressures of their own. The stress these caregivers experience is likely to affect their own health. Studies comparing caregivers with control subjects have found that caregivers have lower immune function, poorer overall health, higher stress hormones, and higher mortality rates (Kiecolt-Glaser et al., 1991; Schulz & Beach, 1999; Vedhara et al., 1999; Vitaliano, Zhang, & Scanlan, 2003). Some evidence suggests that the health effects are worse in caregivers with low levels of social support and high distress from dementia-related behaviors. The emotional and physical effects on Alzheimer caregivers appear similar in different cultures, such as in the United States and China (Patterson et al., 1998).

In the Alzheimer's case we saw earlier, Martha provided care for Alfred at home for a few years until his condition got too difficult for her to handle (McCahon, 1991). When she placed Alfred in a nursing home, she felt "defeated, inadequate, and guilty" for doing so. She visited him almost daily and eventually developed psychological problems because watching him deteriorate and realizing that he had, in effect, died years ago was so stressful. Alzheimer's patients usually need care for 5 to 10 years of decline (Haley, 1998). The slow decline, severe dementia-related behavior problems, and knowledge that it will only end when the patient dies generally makes Alzheimer's disease more difficult for families to adapt to than the other chronic illnesses we considered. The families often feel that watching the process is like watching an endless funeral.

We have examined in this chapter what it is like to live with each of a wide variety of chronic health problems. Some of these disorders begin earlier in the life span than others, some are more visible to people than are others, some involve more difficult treatment regimens than others, and some are more painful, disabling, or life-threatening than others. Each of these differences is important in determining patients' and their families' adaptation to the health problems and the psychosocial help they may need from professionals.

PSYCHOSOCIAL INTERVENTIONS FOR PEOPLE WITH CHRONIC CONDITIONS

Before people actually experience specific chronic illnesses in their families, they usually have some ideas about how serious the health problems are. How do they feel about an illness after someone in the family develops it? Is it worse than they expected, or not as bad, or about the same? The answers to these questions should have a bearing on how well the family adjusts to health problems. One study had parents whose children had either diabetes, asthma, epilepsy, or no chronic illness rate how serious each of the three health problems would be if their children were to develop it or had it now (Marteau & Johnston, 1986). The ratings revealed two interesting findings: (1) the lowest ratings of seriousness the parents gave were for the health problems their own children had and (2) parents whose children did not have chronic illnesses rated each of the health problems as being very serious. These findings indicate that parents who live with chronic illnesses in their children tend to have less negative views of the health problems than parents whose children do not have those illnesses. The prospect of a health problem is frightening, but most families adjust fairly well if a child develops a chronic illness (Cadman et al., 1991).

As we have seen, not all people adjust well to chronic health conditions. The types of adjustment problems that commonly develop with chronic conditions are outlined in Table 13.2. The problems patients and their families experience depend on many factors, such as how visible, painful, disabling, or life-threatening the illness is. Another factor is the patient's age (O'Dougherty & Brown, 1990). In the early childhood years, victims of chronic illness may become excessively dependent if the parents are overprotective, such as by not allowing an epileptic child to play in a wading pool with careful supervision. In later childhood and adolescence, chronically ill indi-

viduals may experience academic and social difficulties that impair their friendships, self-confidence, and self-esteem. Adults who develop a chronic condition may have difficulties if their illness leads them to stop working or change jobs, alter their parenting role, or change or stop their sexual relations.

Ideally, intervention programs to help individuals with chronic health problems involve interdisciplinary teams of professionals—physicians, nurses, psychologists, physical and occupational therapists, vocational counselors, social workers, and recreational therapists—working in an integrated manner toward the overall goals of rehabilitation (Bleiberg, Ciulla, & Katz, 1991). Psychologists contribute to this process by helping each client cope with the psychosocial implications of his or her medical condition and by using behavioral and cognitive principles to enhance the person's participation in and adherence to the therapeutic regimen. We will consider many useful psychosocial approaches, most of which can be used either with individuals or in groups and for a variety of illnesses.

EDUCATIONAL, SOCIAL SUPPORT, AND BEHAVIORAL METHODS

The first thing chronically ill people and their families need to help them adapt to a health problem is correct *information* about the disease and its prognosis and treatment. Part of the problem Martha had dealing with Alfred's Alzheimer's disease is that she was led to believe initially that he would "be a vegetable" in a matter of months. But Alfred's deterioration went on for years, as it does for most Alzheimer victims. She needed better information and might also have benefited from community services for Alzheimer families. For instance, many American communities have *respite centers* where Alzheimer patients can get occasional day care and temporary overnight care, giving the family a break from the caregiving burden (Gruetzner, 1992).

Table 13.2   *Types of Adjustment Problems in Chronic Illness*

- *Physical*—being unable to cope with disability or pain.
- *Vocational*—having difficulty revising educational and career plans or finding a new job.
- *Self-concept*—being unable to accept one's changed body image, self-esteem, and level of achievement or competence.
- *Social*—having difficulty with losing enjoyable activities or finding new ones and coping with changed relationships with family, friends, and sexual partners.
- *Emotional*—experiencing high levels of denial, anxiety, or depression.
- *Compliance*—failing to adhere to the rehabilitation regimen.

Effective systems of social support are also important for patients' and their families' adaptation to chronic health problems. People with chronic medical conditions usually receive this support from family or friends, but it can also come from *support groups* that offer patients and family information and opportunities to meet with people who are in the same boat. These groups give sensitive emotional support and share their own experiences and ways of dealing with everyday problems and difficult decisions, such as whether to place the patient in a nursing home (Gruetzner, 1992; Kapust & Weintraub, 1984). Contact information for support groups in specific geographical areas can be obtained through physicians, local community service agencies, or organizations for any particular illness. All major illness-related organizations now have Websites that provide information about support groups and about the disease and its treatment. (The Website for this book gives links to many of these Websites.)

In Chapter 9, we discussed how adherence to medical regimens is often a problem for people with chronic conditions. One way to enhance adherence involves improving practitioners' communication of information about the procedures and the importance of following the treatment. Other approaches use *behavioral methods*, such as tailoring the regimen to make it as compatible as possible with the person's habits, using prompts and reminders, having patients keep records of their self-care activities, and providing a system of rewards through the method of behavioral contracting. These methods can help improve compliance, such as with different aspects of diabetes regimens (Goodall & Halford, 1991; Wing et al., 1986). As an example, a program used self-monitoring and behavioral contracting methods for 8 weeks to improve regimen adherence in three noncompliant 16- to 18-year-old type 1 diabetes patients: Kathy, Tom, and Kim (Schafer, Glasgow, & McCaul, 1982). Adherence and glucose control improved greatly in both Kathy and Tom. Kim's self-care did not improve, probably because she came from a family with severe marital and family problems, and therapy had failed to resolve their conflicts. Family problems can have an overriding influence and undermine efforts to improve compliance with medical recommendations.

Another example of using behavioral methods to enhance compliance with medical regimens involves the physical rehabilitation process for individuals with spinal cord injuries. Reinforcement techniques are very effective in improving these patients' performance of therapeutically beneficial behaviors (Brucker, 1983). These behaviors include:

- Increasing daily fluid intake to prevent urinary tract infections.
- Changing one's sitting or lying position frequently to reduce the occurrence of bedsores.
- Using orthopedic devices to improve limb functioning.
- Performing exercises to increase strength and endurance.

Reinforcement can be given, for instance, by praising the client for each measurable improvement, such as in arm strength, and periodically updating the person's graph that charts these improvements.

The goal of most training and education programs is to enable patients and their families to self-manage the condition effectively, and this is best achieved by combining information with behavioral and cognitive methods. **Self-management** programs provide information and train patients in behavioral and cognitive skills to enhance their ability to carry out their regimens, create and adapt to the new behaviors or life roles the health condition requires, and cope with their emotions (Lorig & Holman, 2003). An important feature of self-management approaches is that they teach problem-solving skills so that the individuals can deal effectively with day-to-day circumstances and decisions, such as what to do when their ride to a doctor's office is canceled. Self-management programs can be provided by professionals in medical settings or by trained laypersons, such as in support groups. For example, the Arthritis Self-Management Program (Lorig et al., 1998) was designed to help arthritis sufferers cope with their illness and comply with their treatment. It is now offered in several countries by the Arthritis Foundation. The program involves six weekly group meetings in which individuals with arthritis receive training in:

- Exercising, including which exercises to do and exactly how to do them.
- Protecting their joints, such as through changing the way they lift heavy objects.
- Relaxation techniques to control stress.
- Appropriate diets for their illness.
- Self-monitoring and behavioral contracting to promote their complying with regimen activities.

The program is often conducted by a layperson who has arthritis. Programs like this one help arthritis patients to reduce pain and enhance their health status (Lorig & Holman, 2003; Lorig et al., 1998). What's more, in the first year alone, the savings in health care costs is more than seven times the cost of providing such programs for arthritis patients (Cronan, Groessl, & Kaplan, 1997). Similar programs have been developed for other illnesses, such as asthma and heart disease (Lorig & Holman, 2003).

RELAXATION AND BIOFEEDBACK

We have seen that stress and anxiety can aggravate some chronic conditions, such as by decreasing diabetics' ability to metabolize glucose and by triggering or worsening asthma attacks. Psychologists use stress management techniques—especially *progressive muscle relaxation* and *biofeedback*—to help patients control these psychosocial factors and the underlying body processes (Parker, 1995).

These approaches are useful for several chronic conditions—for instance, they help diabetic patients manage their stress and blood glucose levels (Surwit, Feinglos, & Scovern, 1983; Wing et al., 1986). People with epilepsy can also benefit from relaxation and biofeedback training. In using relaxation, they are taught to recognize sensations and events that are associated with attacks and to apply relaxation techniques when those situations occur. In using biofeed-back, epileptics receive training with feedback from an electroencephalograph (EEG) device, which measures electrical brain activity (Goldstein, 1990). Although not all patients benefit from this approach, many do, but there is no good way yet to determine in advance who will benefit from using biofeedback to reduce seizures and who will not. Epileptics who receive biofeedback therapy usually require many hours of costly training with a psychologist or other highly trained individual, using expensive equipment and computer analyses. (Go to 🔳.)

COGNITIVE METHODS

Cognitive processes affect a person's management of chronic health problems in at least two ways: they guide the individual's medical decisions and behaviors, and they affect the emotional adjustment to the condition. Therapists use *cognitive methods* to help clients change their thought processes and feelings (Sarafino, 2001). We will discuss two cognitive methods, problem-solving training and cognitive restructuring, which can be used with individual clients or in groups.

In Chapter 5, we discussed *problem-solving training* as a method to help clients reduce the anxiety and other negative emotions they experience when they don't know how to solve many of their everyday difficulties. This approach also helps them manage their medical condition by teaching them new

---

CLINICAL METHODS AND ISSUES

Treating Asthma with Biofeedback and Relaxation

Asthma provides a good example of how biofeedback and relaxation can help manage a chronic condition. In using *biofeedback* with asthmatics, an apparatus gives feedback regarding airflow in breathing so that the asthma patient can learn to control the diameter of the bronchial airways (Sarafino, 1997). One way to measure airflow has the person breathe through a device that varies the air pressure and assesses airway resistance to these variations: the greater the resistance, the poorer the airflow. The feedback tells the person when changes occur; it can be presented as corresponding numbers on a gauge or as different levels of (1) brightness of a light or (2) pitch or loudness of tones. Although airflow improvements are slight initially, feedback over several training sessions helps the person make them stronger, eventually enabling the person to increase airflow when an attack begins. Training in *progressive muscle relaxation* is used to help the person reduce the role of tension in either initiating an asthma attack or making it worse if one occurs. Studies have generally found that these methods provide useful supplements to medical treatments for asthma (Sarafino, 1997).

strategies for thinking through medical problem situations that arise and making good decisions, such as in managing diabetes (Hill-Briggs, 2003). As an example, diabetes patients often need to deal with situations in which appropriate foods may not be available. In problem-solving training, they would learn how to watch for or predict these situations, identify what form the problem is likely to take (for instance, most foods may be sweet), generate a variety of possible solutions, and decide on the best course of action. The solutions may involve actions to take before the situation, such as packing their own food, or while there, such as asking which foods have sugar in them and choosing from the others.

In *cognitive restructuring*, clients discuss incorrect thoughts and beliefs and learn ways to cope better by thinking more constructively or realistically. We have seen that many chronically ill people and their families experience strong feelings of helplessness, hopelessness, and depression. In the case of caregivers, such as for Alzheimer's disease or cancer patients, they are far more likely to suffer severe levels of depression than are similar individuals who are not caregivers, particularly if they are women and elderly (Pinquart & Sörensen, 2003). Their depression is related to the degree of stress or burden they perceive in their caregiving role, such as from the patient's memory and behavioral problems. Many people who are disabled or have chronic pain also become severely depressed, often because of their restricted daily activities (Talbot et al., 1999). Cognitive approaches can help people identify distorted thoughts ("I never get to do anything I like anymore"), replace those thoughts with more accurate ones, and learn how to increase their ability to perform activities, such as by scheduling them in reasonable amounts. Cognitive methods are very effective in treating depression (Sarafino, 2001).

As with all aspects of illness management, the success of the approach depends on how carefully and conscientiously the patient carries out the methods. For example, researchers studied the effects of cognitive and behavioral techniques in helping arthritis patients manage their pain (Parker et al., 1988). An *intervention* group received training in relaxation, pain redefinition, and distraction techniques; they also met periodically in groups to discuss their pain behavior and family dynamics. This group was compared with two others: a *placebo* group

received an educational program of films and written materials on arthritis and met in support groups without discussing cognitive or behavioral methods; and a *control* group received only standard care for people with arthritis. All subjects completed psychosocial measures and had their disease status evaluated by medical personnel at the start of the study and again after 6 and 12 months. At the last assessment, the intervention subjects rated the extent to which they continued to practice the techniques they were taught. Although no difference was found between the groups in their reports of pain and helplessness at 6 and 12 months, the intervention subjects who reported a high degree of adherence to the cognitive-behavioral methods reported much less pain and helplessness than the placebo and control subjects. These results suggest that long-term *adherence* may be critical for chronically ill people to benefit from cognitive–behavioral interventions.

INTERPERSONAL AND FAMILY THERAPY

We saw in Chapter 12 that *interpersonal therapy* is designed to help people change the way they interact with and perceive their social environments by gaining insights about their feelings and behavior toward other people. This approach is especially useful in helping patients deal with their anxieties and changed self-concepts or relationships with family and friends (Bleiberg, Ciulla, & Katz, 1991). As an example, one hospitalized quadriplegic man who became difficult to deal with each night revealed in group therapy that he felt very vulnerable and helpless at nighttime, which frightened him. By learning that other patients had similar feelings, he began to cope better with his disability and the day-to-day social problems it created (Eisenberg, 1984). Interpersonal therapy has also been used in helping chronically ill people deal with sexual difficulties and understand the thoughts, needs, and problems their friends and family members face.

Family therapy typically has the family meet as a group and draws on cognitive, behavioral, and interpersonal methods to examine and change interaction patterns among family members (Davison, Neale, & Kring, 2004; Kerns, 1995; Patterson & Garwick, 1994). A family with a chronically ill member might meet to review household and medical-regimen responsibilities, discuss grievances, and plan ways to alter daily routines. If the patient is a child, they may discuss, for instance:

- Jealousies siblings may feel if the patient seems to be getting more or special attention.
- Activities the chronically ill person can engage in successfully to build his or her feelings of competence and self-esteem.
- How to tell friends and relatives about the illness so they will understand what it is, the limitations it imposes on the patient, and what to do if an episode occurs.
- How and when the ill person could take responsibility for or improve self-care.

Parents and their ill children often do not communicate about sharing responsibilities for the patients'

care (Anderson et al., 1990). As a result, each person incorrectly assumes someone else is taking care of a task.

Sometimes a patient's *recovery* can present family problems. For example, a husband whose wife's epilepsy was greatly improved with surgery "felt secure when his wife with epilepsy was dependent on him" but became uncomfortable when she could function on her own and take advantage of new opportunities (DeAngelis, 1990). Family therapy can help to uncover and resolve anxieties that develop when the family dynamics and modes of interaction change in either a positive or negative direction.

In summary, psychosocial intervention can apply many approaches to address many different adjustment problems that chronically ill people and their families face. In most cases, using more than one approach provides the optimal help these people need.

SUMMARY

The initial reaction of individuals when diagnosed with chronic illnesses is usually shock, in which they are bewildered and behave in an automatic fashion. Avoidance coping is likely if people believe they can do nothing to change the situation.

Crisis theory provides a model that describes how patients adjust to learning they have chronic health problems. According to this model, their adjustment depends on the coping processes they use, which, in turn, depend on illness-related, background and personal, and physical and social environmental factors. Patients begin the coping process with a cognitive appraisal of the meaning or significance of the health problem to their lives. This appraisal leads to their formulating adaptive tasks, such as adjusting to their symptoms or maintaining positive relations with family or friends, and applying various coping skills to deal with these tasks. These coping skills include denying or minimizing the implications of their conditions, learning how to provide their own treatment, maintaining regular routines as well as possible, and discussing the future. Long-term adaptation to chronic health problems occurs when the patient and his or her family make adjustments that enhance the patient's quality of life by promoting effective physical, psychological, and social functioning.

Some chronic conditions usually begin early in the life span, and asthma is one of them. Asthma is a respiratory disorder that produces periodic attacks of extremely labored breathing. Episodes are generally

triggered by certain circumstances. For many asthmatics, the triggers are allergens, such as pollen. Other asthma triggers include respiratory infections, weather conditions, air pollution, and emotions, such as stress and anger. Although asthma is treated mainly with medication to prevent and combat attacks, exercise can be useful. Psychosocial factors are also important.

Epilepsy is a disorder in which electrical disturbances in the brain produce seizures that vary in intensity. In tonic-clonic attacks, the epileptic loses consciousness and exhibits muscle spasms. Sometimes specific neurological defects are identified as causing the disorder. Drugs provide the main form of treatment, but sometimes surgery is useful. Psychosocial processes are important because emotions may trigger episodes and lead to clients dropping out of rehabilitation. Spinal cord injuries occur most often in adolescence or early adulthood, are generally caused by accidents, and render the person paraplegic or quadriplegic. Rehabilitation programs are geared toward helping these individuals regain as much physical function and independence as possible.

Other chronic health problems are more likely to begin in middle adulthood and old age than at other times in the life span. One of those chronic diseases is diabetes, in which the blood contains high levels of glucose. Some people with this disorder have type 1 diabetes and must inject insulin daily to prevent very serious acute and long-term health complications; this type usually begins in childhood or adolescence. But the vast majority of diabetics have type 2 diabetes, and most of them can use medication and diet to control their blood sugar.

Disorders that affect the joints and connective tissues are called rheumatic diseases. Some rheumatic diseases produce painful inflammation and stiffness of the joints; they are called arthritis. Four common rheumatic diseases are osteoarthritis, fibromyalgia, rheumatoid arthritis, and gout. Although each of these diseases can lead to disability, rheumatoid arthritis is usually the most crippling and painful of the four. Treatment is mainly through drugs, but also includes physical therapy and maintaining proper body weight.

Alzheimer's disease involves a progressive deterioration of the person's cognitive functions, beginning with attention and memory. Since there is no effective treatment for this disorder, therapy focuses on maximizing the patient's functioning and helping the family cope.

Many chronically ill people and their families have difficulty adjusting to the health problem and its medical regimen. They can be helped with psychosocial interventions that involve education, support services, behavioral methods, relaxation and biofeedback, cognitive methods, and interpersonal and family therapy. Self-management programs combine these techniques to help patients adhere to their regimens, adapt to their new roles, and cope with their emotions.

KEY TERMS

crisis theory	asthma	type 1 diabetes	Alzheimer's disease
adaptation	epilepsy	type 2 diabetes	self-management
quality of life	spinal cord injury	arthritis	

14

HEART DISEASE, STROKE, CANCER, AND AIDS: CAUSES, MANAGEMENT, AND COPING

Coping with and Adapting to High-Mortality Illness
Adapting While the Prospects
   Seem Good
Adapting in a Recurrence or Relapse

Heart Disease
Who Is at Risk of Heart Disease,
   and Why?
Medical Treatment and Rehabilitation
   of Cardiac Patients
The Psychosocial Impact of Heart Disease
Psychosocial Interventions for Heart
   Disease

Stroke
Causes, Effects, and Rehabilitation
   of Stroke
Psychosocial Aspects of Stroke

Cancer
The Prevalence and Types of Cancer
The Sites, Effects, and Causes of Cancer
Diagnosing and Treating Cancer
The Psychosocial Impact of Cancer
Psychosocial Interventions for Cancer
Childhood Cancer

AIDS
Risk Factors, Effects, and Treatment of AIDS
The Psychosocial Impact of AIDS
Psychosocial Interventions for AIDS

Adapting to a Terminal Illness
The Patient's Age
Psychosocial Adjustments to Terminal Illness

The Quality of Life in Death
Medical and Psychological Care
   of Dying Patients
A Place to Die—Hospital, Home, or Hospice?

The Survivors: And Life Goes On

PROLOGUE

Deep down, in the "wishing" part of his mind, Jack thought he was immortal. Oh, he acknowledged that he'd die someday, but that day would *forever* be a long way off, he believed. He lived his life accordingly, even though he had almost every known major risk factor for heart disease. He was 30 pounds over-weight, ate high-cholesterol food with abandon, smoked two packs of cigarettes a day, got little exercise, experienced a lot of anger that he had trouble expressing, and had a father who had died of a heart attack at the age of 48. Jack had felt especially invulnerable 2 years ago on his 49th birthday, almost believing that, because he had lived past his father's age of death, the Grim Reaper might somehow never find him.

Jack's beliefs were jolted a couple of months ago—he had a heart attack that put him in the hospital. He was stunned at first. "This can't be happening to *me*," he thought. Soon it sank in that it *was* happening to him, and he felt anger and a sense of grief and helplessness. Although this realization was depressing to him for a while, he had always taken pride in his "fighting spirit." A month later Jack announced, "I'm gonna change my life," and he did! He gave up smoking, changed his diet, and started an exercise program. Just as important, he gradually changed his outlook on life. He now realizes how much the people in his life mean to him and how important he is to them, and he is working to get closer to them.

The majority of deaths in developed countries result from three chronic diseases: heart disease, cancer, and stroke (WHO, 1999). In the United States, the death *rate* for heart disease has declined by half since 1970, but it is still the number-one killer by far; cancer is second, and stroke is third (NCHS, 2003; USBC, 2003). People know these are the leading causes of death—and for many patients and their families, being diagnosed with one of these diseases *means* death. AIDS emerged in the 1980s as a major killer, and public attention has focused on how it is spread and the huge numbers of people who are infected with the virus and die each year around the world. These four very different, high-mortality illnesses are the focus of this chapter.

Although many people deal with having high-mortality chronic illnesses in positive and constructive ways, not all do. In this chapter we will examine how patients and their families react to and cope with health problems that have a high likelihood of taking their lives, especially when the illnesses are terminal. As we study these difficult circumstances, we will provide answers to questions you may have. What's it like to live with heart disease, stroke, cancer, or AIDS? How do these illnesses affect the patient's functioning, and what treatment regimens do they entail? What special problems exist when the victim is a child? What can be done to help terminally ill people and their loved ones cope?

COPING WITH AND ADAPTING TO HIGH-MORTALITY ILLNESS

Many healthy individuals who wonder how much longer they are likely to live look up the statistical life expectancy for people their age and gender and probably adjust that figure on the basis of the longevity of other people in their families. But estimates of a person's life expectancy are very imprecise, and this is true even for people with health conditions that threaten their lives. Public opinion aside, having a high-mortality disease does not usually mean a person will die in a matter of a few weeks or months. Many cancer patients, for instance, survive for 10 or 20 years before the disease takes their lives, and some are totally cured. Still, no one can tell for sure what the course of the disease will be, and these individuals and their families must adapt to this uncertainty.

ADAPTING WHILE THE PROSPECTS SEEM GOOD

Since none of us knows for sure what lies ahead for us, we all live with some degree of uncertainty. But for patients with high-mortality illnesses, the uncertainty for them and their families is more real and urgent. Even though they may have good prospects for the future, either in the short run or more permanently, the diagnosis changes them.

Mortality is the main issue of concern to patients in the first few months of convalescence with a seriously life-threatening illness. During this time, patients often show optimistic attitudes, hope they will be cured, but begin to view their plans for the future more tentatively (Moos, 1982). They also tend to switch from using avoidance coping to active problem-focused approaches. Jack, the man we described who had had a heart attack, showed these adjustments when he changed his lifestyle and his outlook regarding the people in his life. Lifestyle changes are typically part of the rehabilitation programs people with heart disease, stroke, cancer, and AIDS are asked to follow. Self-help and support groups that interact either in group meetings or online are available for patients with these illnesses to discuss and get advice about problems and stressors in their daily lives (Davison, Pennebaker, & Dickerson, 2000). As a patient's recovery progresses, he or she is able to return more and more to a regular routine, often gaining great satisfaction by once again being able to do simple household or self-help activities.

Having activities to occupy the day is important to convalescing people with high-mortality health problems. These activities give them some respite from thinking about their conditions. Patients often try to isolate the diseases from the rest of their lives by focusing on other things, such as preparing to do projects around the house or to return to work, but they sometimes overestimate what they can do. For example, a man named Clay who had suffered a serious stroke described making plans the "glorious day" he left the hospital—projects to do,

> museums and galleries to visit, friends I had wanted to meet for lunch. It was not until several days later that I realized I simply couldn't do them. I didn't have the mental or physical strength, and I sank into depression. (Dahlberg, 1977, p. 124)

Patients need to be encouraged to develop reasonable plans and to carry them out, especially with regard to going back to work or getting training to enter a new job, if necessary.

Sometimes the helplessness that chronically ill people feel and the nurturance their families give lead to a cycle of continued dependence that persists when the patients are able to begin doing things for themselves. This was starting to happen with Clay after his stroke, and his wife realized it. So she gradually began to leave things undone that he had previously taken care of, ask him to do things she thought he could do, and act in indecisive ways so he would take over. Gentle nudges by family members, like those from Clay's wife, can help patients become more self-sufficient, thereby making them feel useful and bolstering their self-esteem.

In the process of adapting to high-mortality illnesses over a long period of time, some individuals make helpful cognitive adjustments, such as positive reappraisals of their life situations. For instance, the champion cyclist Lance Armstrong said of his cancer experience the day he went for the diagnosis, he left home

> as one person and came home another. . . . The truth is that cancer was the best thing that ever happened to me. I don't know why I got the illness, but it did wonders for me, and I wouldn't want to walk away from it. (Sears, Stanton, & Danoff-Burg, 2003, p. 487)

Women with breast cancer have described similar reappraisals, often centering on three themes (Taylor, 1983; Taylor, Lichtman, & Wood, 1984). First, many find *meaning* in their illness experiences, either by determining why the illnesses happened or by rethinking their attitudes and priorities. One woman said, for instance,

> I have much more enjoyment each day, each moment. I am not so worried about what is or isn't or what I wish I had. All those things you get entangled with don't seem to be part of my life right now. (Taylor, 1983, p. 1163)

Second, some individuals gain a *sense of control* over their illnesses, such as by engaging in activities that reduce their risk of their conditions getting worse or increase their knowledge about their care. A spouse said of his wife:

> She got books, she got pamphlets, she studied, she talked to cancer patients, she found out everything that was happening to her, and she fought it. She went to war with it. She calls it taking in her covered wagons and surrounding it. (1983, p. 1164)

Third, some patients *restore their self-esteem*, often by comparing themselves with less fortunate people. For example, a married woman compared herself with others who may be dating and having to tell the man about the cancer.

These cognitive adjustments seem to promote adaptation: the greater the degree of patients' positive reappraisals after cancer diagnosis, the better their perceived health and psychosocial functioning months later (Sears, Stanton, & Danoff-Burg, 2003). But many individuals do not achieve high adjustment levels, particularly if they perceive low levels of social support in the months after diagnosis (Helgeson, Snyder, & Seltman, 2004).

ADAPTING IN A RECURRENCE OR RELAPSE

One thing that makes high-mortality diseases so dangerous is that the deadly medical conditions they produce have high rates of recurrence or relapse. Patients correctly recognize their heightened vulnerability and worry about it, and so do their families. Convalescing individuals tend to be very watchful for symptoms and changes in their conditions even if they are optimistic about their health. When a recurrence or relapse occurs, patients and their families rightly perceive this event as a bad sign—it typically indicates that the prognosis is now worse than before, since additional damage has occurred. Patients focus again on the illness, trying to forestall deterioration in their general functioning and quality of life. They undergo a new round of hospitalization, medical procedures, and, perhaps, surgery. Patients and their families go through the kinds of coping processes they experienced in the original bout, but they are likely to be less hopeful than they were before (Moos, 1982).

Living with any high-mortality disease can be quite stressful, but each disease creates a pattern of stress that is unique. We turn now to consider how people adapt to living with specific high-mortality health problems, starting with heart disease.

HEART DISEASE

Coronary heart disease refers to illnesses that result from the narrowing and blocking of the coronary arteries, which enmesh the heart and supply it with oxygen-rich blood. As we've seen in earlier chapters, blood vessels become narrowed as plaque builds up in the condition called *atherosclerosis*. Blockage can occur if a clot of plaque or blood platelets develops and gets lodged in an artery, preventing blood flow.

Brief reductions of oxygenated blood to the heart can produce painful cramps, called **angina pectoris,** in the chest and arm, back, or neck (AMA, 2003). This is most likely during exercise or stress, and little or no permanent damage occurs if the blockage ends quickly. But if reduced blood supply is severe or prolonged, part of the muscle tissue of the heart (myocardium) may be destroyed—a condition called **myocardial infarction,** or "heart attack." Table 14.1 describes common symptoms of a heart attack. Many people with heart disease develop *congestive heart failure*, which has three permanent features: the heart is enlarged, the pumping capacity is reduced, and the person becomes short of breath with little exertion. Heart disease is prevalent in developed countries. In the United States, each year about 1.2 million people suffer a heart attack; more than 40% of the victims die (AHA, 2004). Many of these people die before they reach a hospital because they delay getting help and the heart damage increases with each hour up to

Table 14.1   *Symptoms of a Heart Attack*

Many victims delay going to the hospital for hours because they don't know the symptoms of a heart attack, which are:

- Uncomfortable pressure, fullness, squeezing, or pain in the center of the chest that lasts for more than a few minutes.
- Pain or discomfort spreading to the shoulders, neck, or arms.
- Shortness of breath.
- Lightheadedness, fainting, sweating, or nausea.

Not all of these symptoms always happen in a heart attack; if some start to occur, the person should get medical care immediately. Prompt treatment can often prevent serious myocardial damage.

Source: AHA (2004).

about 6 (AMA, 2003). More than a third of heart attack victims delay deciding to get help for more than 3 hours (Martin et al., 2004; Walsh et al., 2004). The greater the damage, the worse the person's condition and prognosis.

WHO IS AT RISK OF HEART DISEASE, AND WHY?

Several demographic, lifestyle, and physiological characteristics are associated with developing heart disease.

Age, Gender, and Sociocultural Risk Factors

The prevalence rates for heart disease increase as people get older, particularly after about 45 years of age, and American men have far higher death rates than women from heart disease at all ages (NCHS, 2003). The link between heart disease and sociocultural factors can be seen in the death rate data for different ethnic groups in the United States. Among both men and women, heart disease death rates are two to three times higher for Blacks than for Asian Americans, with the rates for Whites, Native Americans, and Hispanics being intermediate (NCHS, 2003). Interestingly, a study of death rates around 1990 in New York City revealed that Blacks who were born in the Southern United States had far higher mortality rates from cardiovascular disease than those born in the North, whose death rates were similar to those of Whites (Fang, Madhavan, & Alderman, 1996). And cross-cultural research has found that men and women in Russia have extremely high death rates from cardiovascular disease, while the French and Japanese have very low rates (AHA, 1995). These findings suggest an important role of lifestyle in heart disease.

Lifestyle and Biological Risk Factors

Part of the reason for age, sex, and sociocultural differences in risk of heart disease lies in biological and lifestyle variations. For example, *hypertension*—the condition of having high blood pressure consistently over an extended period of time—is a major risk factor for heart disease (AHA, 2004). Nearly 30% of adult Americans are hypertensive (NCHS, 2003). High blood pressure has no overt symptoms, but its presence indicates that the heart is working harder than normal. When this continues over a long period of time, the heart becomes enlarged and has more and more difficulty meeting the demands of the body. High blood pressure also increases the development of atherosclerosis, causing blood vessels to become narrowed and less elastic. This increases the risk of a blood clot or piece of plaque becoming lodged in an artery and causing a myocardial infarction. Prevalence rates for hypertension increase with age and are higher in Black than White Americans (NCHS, 2003).

Several other lifestyle and biological risk factors are important in heart disease (AHA, 2004). They include:

- Family history of heart disease
- Diabetes
- High blood pressure
- Cigarette smoking
- High LDL and low HDL cholesterol levels
- Physical inactivity
- Obesity
- Stress

The great majority of people who have heart attacks have at least one of the listed risk factors (Greenland et al., 2003). Which factors are most important? A study examined all of the listed factors except the first across 52 countries and about 30,000 people, half of whom had had a heart attack, and found that high LDL with low HDL was the strongest risk factor, and smoking was second (Yusuf et al., 2004). The next most important factors were stress, obesity, diabetes,

and hypertension. These risks are modifiable: people who stop smoking and reduce their cholesterol intake and blood pressure halve their risk of dying of heart disease (Jousilahti et al., 1995).

Negative Emotions and Heart Disease

Prospective studies have shown that men and women who experience chronic high levels of hostility, depression, or anxiety are more likely than others to develop heart disease and hypertension (Weidner & Mueller, 1999). The link between negative emotions and heart disease involves two avenues. First, people tend to have less healthful lifestyles when they experience negative emotions. Second, negative emotions have physiological effects that promote heart disease. Some of the clearest physiological links have been shown among people with the Type A behavior pattern. When in stressful situations, Type A individuals—particularly those who experience frequent high levels of anger and hostility—often show high physiological *reactivity*, which includes increased blood pressure, catecholamine, and corticosteroid levels (Smith, 1992).

Type A people chronically produce high levels of catecholamines and corticosteroids, especially when under stress (Pope & Smith, 1991; Suarez et al., 1991). Chronic high levels of these hormones in the blood can damage the heart and blood vessels. Evidence now suggests that epinephrine (a catecholamine) increases the formation of platelet clots in the blood, which can block arteries and cause a heart attack (Markovitz & Matthews, 1991). Although heart attacks can happen at any time in any 24-hour day, they are most likely to occur on Mondays, at least for working people, and in the morning hours from 6 to 11 A.M. (Muller et al., 1987; Somers et al., 1993; Willich et al., 1994). They are least likely to occur during sleep at night. The increased risk in the morning probably occurs because dreaming shortly before awakening and becoming active after awakening increase blood pressure and catecholamines, which increase platelet clotting.

MEDICAL TREATMENT AND REHABILITATION OF CARDIAC PATIENTS

Many cardiac patients have not had a heart attack, but tests and symptoms indicate that they have heart disease, such as significant blockage in one or more coronary artery. These individuals usually receive long-term pharmacological therapy to protect against a heart attack and stop or reverse atherosclerosis; they may also receive one of two invasive procedures (AMA, 2003). One procedure is called *balloon angioplasty*, in which a tiny balloon is inserted in the blocked artery and inflated to open the blood vessel. A metal mesh *stent* is then placed permanently at the site to keep the vessel open. The other procedure—called *bypass surgery*—shunts around the diseased section of artery with a healthy vessel taken from another part of the person's body.

People who suffer a heart attack are likely to get similar treatments, but their condition is an emergency: because little heart damage typically occurs in the first hour or so after an attack starts, immediate treatment is critical (AMA, 2003). Their treatment starts with emergency care and continues with a program of rehabilitation.

Initial Treatment for Heart Attack

When heart attack victims enter the hospital, medical treatment focuses on preventing or limiting damage to the myocardium. Part of this treatment generally involves using *clot-dissolving medication* to free blocked arteries. Most patients are then placed in *coronary care units*, where medical staff can monitor their physiological functioning closely. The risk of another attack is high during the first few days. These people usually require other procedures, such as angioplasty or bypass surgery, too.

As you might expect, most heart attack patients experience extremely high levels of anxiety in the first day or two of coronary care. Many of these people cope with this crisis through *denial*, and those who use denial tend to be less anxious in the first few days than those who do not (Froese et al., 1974). Regardless of whether the patients use denial, their anxiety levels soon start to decline. After a few days, the anxiety levels of those who do and do not use denial are similar, but still higher than normal. These fairly high anxiety levels tend to persist for the remainder of their hospital stays (Cay, Philip, & Dugard, 1972; Froese et al., 1974). The heart attack patients with the greatest difficulty coping are not necessarily the ones who are the most seriously ill—instead, they tend to be those who were experiencing distress and social problems before the heart attack.

Excessive anxiety, depression, or denial can impair recovery, and psychological intervention may be needed (Erdman, 1990). For example, some patients may deny they had a heart attack and insist on leaving the hospital too early. Many patients anticipate psychosocial problems ahead, particularly in relation to their work. A program for rehabilitation generally begins after the first week, when cardiac patients are transferred to a general ward.

Rehabilitation of Cardiac Patients

Rehabilitation programs for heart attack patients are designed to promote recovery and reduce risk factors for having another attack (Erdman, 1990). These programs provide patients with information on such topics as lifestyle changes and restrictions they should follow, medications to take, and symptoms to expect. Many patients will experience recurrent angina pectoris pain for many months or even years after discharge (AMA, 2003; Rey, 1999). These episodes can be very frightening. Sometimes the pain requires medical attention, but the patients do not seem to suffer tissue damage, and they often can simply take medication to control it. For some patients, the pain can be quite severe and even disabling (Rey, 1999; Wielgosz et al., 1984). Tests often reveal no substantial artery blockage or ventricle impairment, but the pain persists (Ketterer et al., 1996).

To reduce the likelihood of another infarction, most cardiac patients receive advice on lifestyle changes, such as to:

• Quit smoking.

• Lose weight.

• Exercise.

• Reduce dietary fat and cholesterol.

• Reduce high alcohol consumption.

Because stress and hostility are linked to heart disease, training in stress management may be of value for many cardiac patients (Williams, 2001). Many heart attack victims who make healthful changes in their lifestyles and attitudes live longer than comparable people who have not had infarctions. Some cardiac patients find it easy to adhere to their rehabilitation programs; others do not and may resent the restrictions their conditions impose. In addition, coronary patients who perceive little social support in their lives and have low self-efficacy for carrying out their medical regimens show less adherence to the regimens and slower recovery than others do (Bastone & Kerns, 1995; Wills & Fegan, 2001).

Exercise is a very important aspect of rehabilitation programs for cardiac patients. A program of physical activity needs to be introduced gradually and tailored to each person's physical condition. It often begins in the hospital with supervised short-distance walking. In the following weeks, the physical activities become more and more vigorous and long-lasting, and are likely to include long-distance walking, calisthenics, and often jogging, bicycling, or swimming. Cardiac patients who adhere to their exercise programs gain substantial relevant benefits (Miller, Balady, & Fletcher, 1997). They reduce their risk of dying in the next few years by 20 to 25% and their symptoms, such as of angina pectoris and congestive heart failure. And they lower their risk for a subsequent heart attack—for instance, by reducing their blood pressure and levels of cholesterol, negative emotions, and cardiovascular reactivity to stress.

Unfortunately, many cardiac patients never begin an exercise program and about 50% of those who do discontinue it within the first 6 months (Dishman, 1982; Dishman, Sallis, & Orenstein, 1985). Compliance is likely to be higher if the rehabilitation program provides a special place, like a wellness center, for people to exercise, instead of having them exercise on their own. Cardiac patients may also have a difficult time making other lifestyle changes, particularly in their diets and in stopping smoking. Dietary changes to reduce fat and cholesterol are often hard

to make because they have an impact on family life (Croog, 1983). With respect to stopping smoking, studies have found that only perhaps 30 to 40% of individuals who suffer myocardial infarctions quit or substantially reduce their smoking (Ockene et al., 1985; Rigotti et al., 1991). An important influence in whether patients follow a cardiac regimen is self-efficacy: the higher their self-efficacy early in rehabilitation for making each change, the greater their improvements in physical and psychosocial functioning at the end of the program (Evon & Burns, 2004).

THE PSYCHOSOCIAL IMPACT OF HEART DISEASE

"Is it OK for me to drive a car, do chores around the house, or lift heavy things?" heart attack patients often ask their doctors, fearing that overexertion could bring on another attack (Erdman, 1990). The extent of patients' disability is likely to affect how well they and their families adjust to their conditions.

Being able to work has a special meaning to individuals who suffer from chronic health problems, and heart attack victims often view going back to work as an important sign that they are recovering (Croog, 1983). Advice about returning to work depends on how severe the heart condition is and the physical requirements of the job (Rey, 1999). In the past, individuals were advised to wait at least 60 days before

The treadmill stress test is used in examining heart function during strenuous exercise and to assess the ability of heart patients to engage in physical activity.

going back to work, but jobs in industrialized countries are less physically demanding now. Most heart attack patients can resume working in a few weeks without risking another cardiac episode (Dennis et al., 1988). Physicians often advise people with heart disease to cut back on the amount of physical effort and stress they experience on the job. Following this advice may mean finding a new job, which may be difficult to do, particularly for people over age 50 or so. If their cardiac condition requires restrictions on the activities they do on the job, they may experience interpersonal problems with coworkers. Patients who are near retirement age may simply leave the workforce if they can. Nevertheless, most cardiac patients—roughly 80%—do go back to work within the year following the heart attack, often with jobs requiring less productivity or shorter hours than previously (Doehrman, 1977; Shanfield, 1990). Compared to individuals who do not return to work, those who do return tend to be younger, in better physical condition, better educated, and employed in white-collar jobs. Delaying or failing to go back to work is often associated with long-lasting emotional difficulty.

Cardiac illness and family relationships are closely interrelated: cardiac patients with strong social support recover faster and survive longer than those with less support (Berkman, 1995; Wills & Fegan, 2001). For many heart patients, family difficulties—such as quarreling over financial or sexual problems—existed prior to the infarction, and these difficulties often become worse (Croog & Fitzgerald, 1978; Swan, Carmelli, & Rosenman, 1986). The illness may make these problems worse. Also, a "cycle of guilt and blame" may develop (Croog, 1983). For example, a husband who has a myocardial infarction may blame his wife or children for his condition, and they may agree and feel guilty. But even when harmonious relations exist before the attack, the illness adds to the stress of all members of the family. One marital difficulty that may arise after a heart attack relates to sexual activity, which often never returns to the level that existed prior to the attack (Krantz & Deckel, 1983; Michela, 1987). Either or both spouses may fear that having sex could precipitate another attack, even though this risk is very low, especially if the patient exercises regularly (Muller et al., 1996). The marital satisfaction of both partners generally benefits by having little or no sex initially and then increasing its frequency gradually, with the advice of the patient's doctor (Michela, 1987).

Families have an enormous impact on the process of cardiac rehabilitation: patients adjust better, adhere more closely to their regimens, and recover sooner if their efforts receive family encouragement (Kaplan & Toshima, 1990; Krantz & Deckel, 1983). But the danger exists that families will promote *cardiac invalidism*, in which people with heart disease become increasingly dependent and helpless. The beliefs a spouse has about the patient's physical capabilities can aid or retard rehabilitation. Two research findings about their beliefs are important. First, family members increase their estimates of the physical ability of cardiac patients by seeing and personally experiencing the physical feats the patients can actually perform, such as on a treadmill (Taylor et al., cited in Bandura, 1986). These family members are likely to provide more effective encouragement for the person to become increasingly active. Family members who do not have this experience continue to have low estimates of the patient's ability, even after receiving medical counseling to the contrary. Second, the more similar the patient's and spouse's positive beliefs about heart disease, such as of its timeline and consequences, the better the patient's physical and psychosocial functioning months later (Figueiras & Weinman, 2003).

What are the long-term emotional consequences of heart disease? During the first weeks or months after having a heart attack, most patients have higher-than-normal levels of anxiety and depression, but their distress tends to decline during the next year or two (Carney et al., 1995; Doehrman, 1977). Most eventually adjust fairly well, especially if they have high levels of social support (Holahan et al., 1997). But if very high levels of anxiety and depression continue beyond a few months, these emotions become signs of poor adaptation and tend to be linked to decreased compliance with the cardiac regimen and deterioration in the person's physical condition. Patients with severe depression or anxiety in the weeks after a heart attack are much more likely to suffer subsequent cardiac problems, such as arrhythmias, or to die in the next year than those who are less distressed (Carney et al., 1988; Frasure-Smith et al., 1999; Moser & Dracup, 1996). Similarly, patients who, after undergoing a successful angioplasty, feel optimistic about the future and have a strong sense of personal control and self-esteem are less likely than others to suffer a heart attack or require bypass surgery or another angioplasty in the next several months (Helgeson & Fritz, 1999).

PSYCHOSOCIAL INTERVENTIONS FOR HEART DISEASE

Interventions to enhance people's recovery from and long-term adaptation to having heart disease have used health and regimen education, psychosocial counseling, or both to improve their compliance with the cardiac regimen, enhance their adjustment to the illness, and reduce their risk of future cardiac problems. Two meta-analyses have been conducted with data from many interventions using these approaches (Dusseldorp et al., 1999; Linden, Stossel, & Maurice, 1996). In most interventions, nurses or physicians provided the education and counseling. Analyses comparing patients who received usual medical care with those who had the interventions revealed two important findings. First, the programs reduced several risk factors, improving blood pressure, cholesterol levels, body weight, eating habits, exercise, and smoking. Second, the interventions produced substantial reductions in mortality and recurrence of heart problems in the subsequent year or two. The programs that were more successful in reducing risk factors were also more effective in reducing mortality and heart problems.

Because of the role of negative emotions, especially depression, in the subsequent cardiac problems and mortality of heart disease patients, research has assessed the impact of treating their emotional difficulties. For example, an intervention provided patients with information about their conditions and treatment, training in relaxation to reduce stress, and counseling for their fears and anxieties while they were still in the hospital (Oldenburg, Perkins, & Andrews, 1985). Individuals who received this program showed far better psychosocial adjustment during the next year than those who received standard care. Other studies have shown that stress management training can reduce the number of angina pectoris attacks by nearly 40% compared against attacks of clients who received standard medical care (Bundy et al., 1994). And as we saw in Chapter 5, training in stress management can reduce Type A behavior, lower blood pressure, and reduce coronary risk (Friedman et al., 1986; Powell & Friedman, 1986). These benefits suggest that training to help patients anticipate and manage stressful situations can be a useful component in cardiac rehabilitation programs. Does psychotherapy improve depressed cardiac patients'

health and survival? The answer is not clear: research has produced conflicting results so far (Cossette, Frasure-Smith, & Lespérance, 2001; Lett et al., 2003).

In a now-famous intervention, Dean Ornish and his colleagues (1990) tested a multicomponent program of dietary, exercise, and stress management approaches for cardiac rehabilitation. The patients volunteered and were randomly assigned to receive either the program or standard medical care. The program had the people eat a mainly vegetarian diet, eliminate caffeine and restrict alcohol intake, stop smoking, get moderate exercise regularly, meet regularly as support groups, and use stress management methods, including relaxation and meditation. Medical assessments were made at the start of the study and at the end of a year. Comparisons of the groups showed that atherosclerosis and reports of chest pain worsened for the people who received standard medical care but improved for those in the intervention program. Although the results don't indicate which features of the program worked, they show that changes in lifestyle can unclog arteries. Other studies have not only confirmed these findings but found that intensive diminution of lifestyle risk factors reduces subsequent cardiac problems and hospitalizations (Haskell et al., 1994; Ornish et al., 1998; Superko & Krauss, 1994).

To summarize, recovery after a heart attack presents difficult physical and psychosocial challenges for patients and their families. Effective cardiac rehabilitation programs have individuals adhere to regimens of exercise, diet, medication, and stress management. These programs can reverse the disease process. The long-term impact of heart disease often involves emotional, vocational, and marital problems that may require therapeutic interventions to enhance adaptation.

STROKE

Sitting at the breakfast table, Neil began to feel faint and weak, his vision dimmed, and the right side of his body became numb and tingly. As he realized he was having a stroke, he tried to say so, but the words would not come out. Soon he lost consciousness. As Table 14.2 shows, these are common symptoms of a **stroke**—a condition in which damage occurs in some area of the brain when the blood supply to that area is disrupted, depriving it of oxygen. Stroke is a leading cause of death worldwide (WHO, 1999); in the United

Table 14.2 *Symptoms of Stroke*

Individuals who experience any of the following warning signs of a stroke should see a physician immediately.

- Sudden numbness or weakness of the face, arm, or leg, especially on one side of the body.
- Sudden confusion, trouble speaking or understanding.
- Sudden trouble seeing in one or both eyes.
- Sudden trouble walking, dizziness, loss of balance or coordination.
- Sudden, severe headache with no known cause.

Source: AHA (2004).

States each year, 700,000 new or recurrent strokes occur and claim over 160,000 lives (AHA, 2004; USBC, 2003).

CAUSES, EFFECTS, AND REHABILITATION OF STROKE

The disruption in blood supply that causes strokes occurs in two ways (AHA, 2004; AMA, 2003). In an *ischemic stroke*, damage results when the blood supply in a cerebral artery is sharply reduced or cut off, such as by a blood clot (a *thrombus*) or a piece of plaque (an *embolus*). In a *hemorrhagic stroke*, a blood vessel ruptures and bleeds into the brain. A stroke caused by a hemorrhage generally occurs rapidly and causes the person to lose consciousness; most of the damage it produces happens in a few minutes. In contrast, an ischemic stroke tends to occur more slowly, and the person is less likely to lose consciousness. Strokes from hemorrhages occur much less frequently but are much more likely to cause extensive damage and death than those from infarctions (AHA, 2004; AMA, 2003).

Age, Gender, and Sociocultural Risk Factors for Stroke

The incidence of stroke is very low prior to the middle-age years; from then on, its death rates in the United States triple in each successive decade (NCHS, 2003). Men are more likely than women to develop a stroke and die from it. We can see a role of sociocultural factors in death rate data for different ethnic groups in the United States: among both men and women, stroke death rates are far higher for Blacks than for Whites and Asian, Hispanic, and Native Americans (NCHS, 2003).

As in heart disease, part of the reason for age, sex, and sociocultural differences in the risk of stroke lies in biological and lifestyle variations. For example,

high blood pressure is a risk factor for stroke, and the prevalence rates for hypertension increase with age and are much higher in Black than White Americans (NCHS, 2003).

Lifestyle and Biological Risk Factors for Stroke

Several lifestyle and biological factors can increase the risk of a person having a stroke, and some of them can be changed or treated (AHA, 2004). In addition to age, gender, and race, these risk factors are:

- High blood pressure.
- Cigarette smoking.
- Heart disease, diabetes, and their risk factors, such as high cholesterol, obesity, and physical inactivity.
- Family history of stroke.
- High red blood cell count, which makes the blood thicker and more likely to form clots.
- Drinking more than a couple of alcoholic drinks per day.
- "Mini-strokes" called *transient ischemic attacks* that may occur one or more times before a full stroke.

Negative emotions also appear to be involved: prospective studies have found that people who are depressed are more likely than others to develop a stroke and die from one in the next two decades (Everson et al., 1998; Jonas & Mussolino, 2000). Many of the risk factors for a stroke are the same as those for heart disease. As a result, people who have had strokes are usually asked to make similar lifestyle changes to those of people who have had heart attacks: lose weight, stop smoking, exercise, and reduce dietary fat and cholesterol.

Stroke Effects and Rehabilitation

Strokes vary in severity. People who survive moderate or severe strokes generally suffer some degree of motor, sensory, cognitive, or speech impairment as a result of the brain damage. If enough cells are affected, the functions controlled by the damaged area of the brain can be severely disrupted. The extent and type of impairment stroke patients suffer and their medical treatment—drugs and surgery—can vary greatly, depending on the amount and location of damage (AHA, 2004; AMA, 2003). Getting immediate treatment is critical because clot-dissolving drugs can limit the damage from a stroke. The following discussion applies to strokes that produce at least moderately severe damage.

Although the initial deficits experienced by stroke victims can be permanent, these people often show considerable improvement over time. Medical treatment and physical, occupational, and speech therapy can help patients regain some of the functions they lost. Functional impairments are usually more easily overcome in hemorrhagic than ischemic strokes (AHA, 2004). Hemorrhages often impair functioning partly by creating pressure on neurons. If that pressure is relieved, such as if the body reabsorbs the pool of blood, the person may gradually recover some of the lost functioning.

Stroke is one of the most disabling chronic illnesses (AHA, 2004; Guccione et al., 1994). The most common deficits stroke patients experience involve motor action (Diller, 1999; Newman, 1984b). For these patients, some degree of paralysis occurs immediately, and the person usually cannot move the arm and leg on one side of the body. Which side is paralyzed depends on which side of the brain is damaged: the left hemisphere of the brain controls movement of the right side of the body; the right hemisphere controls the left side. As a result, paralysis occurs on the side of the body opposite to the hemisphere that sustained damage in the stroke. Because of the paralysis, these patients often cannot walk, dress themselves, or perform many usual self-help activities. Most of the gains these people show in the first month appear to happen spontaneously (AHA, 2004). Although most patients will be able to get around on their own and perform self-care, such as bathing and dressing, after 6 months without formal rehabilitation, engaging in rehabilitation activities reduces their disability (Diller, 1999). Biofeedback and intensive physical therapy can markedly improve motor function in stroke victims (Dobkin, 2004; Moreland & Thompson, 1994). For complex sequences of behavior, many patients benefit from constructing and practicing verbal instructions (O'Callaghan & Couvadelli, 1998). For instance, to transfer from a wheelchair to a bed, the person might say, "I position the wheelchair facing the bed; perpendicular to it," "Next, I put on the brakes," and so on.

Other common deficits many stroke patients face involve cognitive functions—language, learning, memory, and perception. The specific type of impairment they have depends on which side of the brain was damaged. In most people, the left hemisphere contains the areas that handle language processes, including speech and writing (Tortora & Grabowski,

2003). Thus, damage on the left side often causes language and learning deficits. A common language disorder in stroke patients is *aphasia*, which is marked by difficulty in understanding or using words. There are two kinds of aphasia: *receptive aphasia* refers to a difficulty in understanding verbal information; *expressive aphasia* involves a problem in producing language, even though the person can make the component sounds. For example, the individual may not be able to differentiate between two verbalized words, such as "coal" and "cold." Or the patient may have difficulty remembering a sequence of things he or she is told to do—such as, "Touch your right ear with your left hand, and touch your left eyebrow with your right hand."

What deficits are associated with damage on the right side of the brain? The right hemisphere usually processes visual imagery, emotions, and the perception of patterns, such as melodies (Tortora & Grabowski, 2003). As a result, visual disorders are common with right-brain damage (Diller, 1999). In the disorder called *visual neglect*, patients fail to process information on the left side of the normal visual field. For example, they may not notice food on the left side of a tray, items on the left side of a menu, or a minus sign in an arithmetic task (see Figure 14–1). This problem also impairs their ability to perceive distances correctly and causes them to bump into objects or doorframes on the left side of the visual field, making them accident-prone. Sometimes patients with this disorder feel they are "going crazy" when they hear someone speaking but cannot see the person because he or she is standing in the left side of the visual field. The discrepancy between what they hear and what they see makes them wonder if they are hallucinating.

The specific location of damage in the brain also can determine emotional disorders that stroke

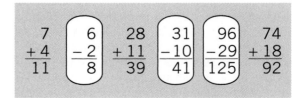

Figure 14–1 An illustration of arithmetic errors (circled items) a stroke patient with a visual disorder might make at the start of rehabilitation. In this case, the patient fails to scan to the left and assumes all of the problems involve addition. Rehabilitation can help patients overcome this deficit.

patients may show. Some studies have found associations between (1) specific left-hemisphere damage and patients' degree of depression and (2) specific right-hemisphere damage and patients' ability to interpret and express effect (Bleiberg, 1986; Newman, 1984b). An example of an emotional disorder some stroke patients have is called *emotional lability*, which can occur in varying degrees (AHA, 2004; Bleiberg, 1986). Some people with this disorder may laugh or cry with little or no provocation, realizing and being surprised by the discrepancy; others with milder disorders may display the appropriate emotion, but at excessive levels, such as sobbing when thinking mildly sad thoughts. In other emotional disorders, stroke patients may be unable to interpret other people's emotions correctly and may react oddly to them. (Go to ⬤.)

PSYCHOSOCIAL ASPECTS OF STROKE

Recovery from a severe stroke is a long and arduous process. The initial physical and cognitive deficits are extremely frightening, but many patients are heartened by early gains in their functioning. Although patients with all chronic illnesses often rely on avoidance strategies to cope during the early phases of convalescence, denial seems to be more common among patients who have had strokes than those with heart disease or cancer (Krantz & Deckel, 1983). Stroke patients who continue to deny their current or possible future limitations often retard their progress in rehabilitation.

Instead, they need a balance of reality and hope: stroke patients who feel a sense of control over their condition at the end of the first month show better recovery months later than others do (Johnston et al., 1999).

When a stroke produces physical or cognitive deficits, the emotional adjustments can be very difficult. Stroke patients are very prone to depression (Bleiberg, 1986; Krantz & Deckel, 1983; Newman, 1984b). Those who are depressed in the first weeks remain in the hospital much longer and show less improvement from the rehabilitation program before they leave (Tennen, Eberhardt, & Affleck, 1999). As patients see the gains in recovery slowing down and begin to realize the extent of their impairment, they may feel hopeless and helpless. At this point, the more severe their condition, the stronger the depression they develop (Diller, 1999). Intervention with cognitive-behavioral therapy is effective in treating depression (Sarafino, 2001).

Although stroke usually afflicts individuals who are beyond retirement age, many of its victims are employed when the illness occurs and suffer impairments that prevent them from returning to work. The results of followup studies suggest that less than half of patients who were working prior to the stroke return to work within 6 months, often at reduced hours (Diller, 1999). Some stroke victims who do not return to work are old enough to retire early with pensions, but others must leave the workforce under less favorable circumstances, which can be financially and emotionally trying.

The impairments produced by stroke have important social effects on patients and their families,

---

CLINICAL METHODS AND ISSUES

Stroke Rehabilitation for Visual Neglect

Like people in general, stroke patients with visual neglect initially take for granted that what they see reflects the full size of their normal visual field. Because they think they see the whole field, they first need to have their visual deficits clearly demonstrated. One way psychologists can do this involves placing paper money on a

  table in front of the patient. The large bills are purposely put on the impaired side. The patient is asked to pick up all of the money on the table. Naturally, a large sum of money remains on the table after the patient says that he or she has

completed the task. Having the patient turn his or her head to see all the money that was left on the table is one way to begin to teach the patient that . . . this difficulty can be overcome by turning the head. (Gordon & Diller, 1983, p. 119)

Rehabilitation then proceeds from very simple tasks, such as turning the head to track squares in a ceiling, to more difficult ones, such as tracking objects that move from the right to the left side of the visual field, so that the patient turns the head automatically (Diller, 1999). The therapist can provide cues before the response and reinforcement when it occurs.

particularly when the patients are severely paralyzed or have aphasia (Evans et al., 1992; Newman, 1984b). Some families adjust to the patient's condition reasonably well, as in the following case:

> Mrs. M. had always taken charge of bookkeeping and running the family. When her husband had a stroke, she adapted very well to his aphasia, inventing ways to communicate with him. When he developed cancer five years later, she helped him keep track of his medications by putting them in little cups at the beginning of the day, with coded instructions on how many to take and when to take them. In this way, Mr. M., who worried that he hadn't taken his medication, could keep track of it when she wasn't there. (Gervasio, 1986, p. 115)

But other families do not adjust well to the changing role relationships, and marital harmony often declines. In addition, social contacts and leisure activities with friends also drop off for both the stroke patient and his or her spouse (Newman, 1984b). Although the decrease in social and leisure activities worsens with the extent of the victim's disability, it is often substantial even when the person has made a good recovery. Family therapy and support groups can help stroke patients and their families adapt, but these approaches often need to address practical problems, such as not having transportation, before trying to resolve interpersonal problems (Evans et al., 1992; Krantz & Deckel, 1983).

In summary, stroke is a high-mortality illness that involves neurological damage as a result of disrupted blood flow to the brain. Survivors of stroke often suffer substantial physical and cognitive impairments, but medical treatment and physical, occupational, and speech therapy can help these people regain many of their lost abilities. The more severe the remaining deficits after rehabilitation, the more likely patients are to experience psychosocial problems.

CANCER

Cancer is probably the disease most people fear most—the word "cancer" itself scares many people, and they often overestimate the deaths that cancer causes (Burish et al., 1987). Receiving mammogram results indicating possible breast cancer can leave some women with high levels of anxiety months after further tests disconfirm the suspicion (Lerman et al.,

1991). But most women's distress from false-positive cancer tests is not very severe or long-lasting (Wardle et al., 1993). Although most practitioners recognize how people feel about cancer and are reluctant to discuss the disease and its effects with their patients, they are more likely today than in the past to share details about serious medical conditions with their patients (Andersen, Golden-Kreutz, & DiLillo, 2001; Laszlo, 1987).

THE PREVALENCE AND TYPES OF CANCER

A basic characteristic of life and growth is that body cells reproduce in an orderly and controlled fashion. Scientists know what the normal pattern of tissue growth looks like. Irregularities in this process can cause unrestricted cell growth, usually forming a tumor called a *neoplasm* (AMA, 2003; Tortora & Grabowski, 2003). *Oncogenes* regulate cell division, but genetic processes and carcinogens can damage them, causing unrestricted growth. Some neoplasms are harmless, or benign, but others are malignant.

Cancer is a disease of the cells characterized by uncontrolled cell proliferation that usually forms a malignant neoplasm. There are many forms of cancer, and the large majority can be classified into five types based on the kind of tissue in which it develops (Tortora & Grabowski, 2003; Williams, 1990):

- *Carcinomas*, which are malignant neoplasms in cells of the skin and the lining of body organs, such as the digestive, respiratory, and reproductive tracts. About 85% of human cancers are carcinomas.

- *Melanomas*, or neoplasms of a special type of skin cell that produces the skin pigment called melanin.

- *Lymphomas*, or cancers of the lymphatic system.

- *Sarcomas*, which are malignant neoplasms of the muscle, bone, or connective tissue.

- *Leukemias*, or cancers of the blood-forming organs, such as the bone marrow, that lead to an extreme proliferation of white blood cells.

An important characteristic of cancer cells is that they do not adhere to each other as strongly as normal cells do (AMA, 2003; Williams, 1990). As a result, they may separate and spread to other parts of the body through the blood or lymph systems. This migration is called *metastasis*, as is the new neoplasm (plural is *metastases*).

Cancer is a leading cause of death worldwide (WHO, 1999). In the United States, it is the second most frequent cause of death, and its death rates increased sharply in the second half of the 20th century (NCHS, 2003). The data on American cancer mortality and morbidity are sobering: each year cancer takes more than 550,000 lives, and nearly 1.4 million new cases are diagnosed (ACS, 2004). About 60% of these newly diagnosed people can expect to live at least 5 years—most of these people will be *cured* having virtually the same life expectancy as someone who never had the disease. Although cancer can strike any area of the body, as Figure 14–2 shows, almost all of the increase in cancer death rates since 1950 is from neoplasms in one body site: the lung.

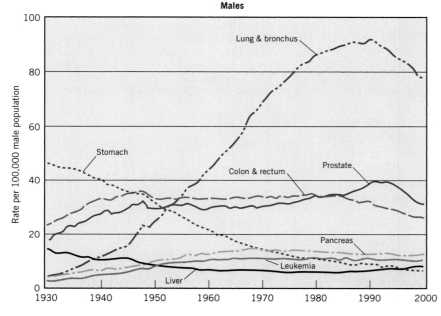

Figure 14–2 Age-adjusted death rates for selected cancer sites per 100,000 females and males in the United States between 1930 and 2000. (From ACS, 2004.) Notice three things: First, mortality rates for most forms of cancer have either declined or remained fairly constant; lung cancer is the dramatic exception. Second, the increases in lung cancer deaths for males and females correspond to gender differences in the prevalence of cigarette smoking. Third, corresponding to declines in smoking rates, the death rates for lung cancer are now declining for males and have leveled off for females.

THE SITES, EFFECTS, AND CAUSES OF CANCER

What are the physical effects of cancer, and how does it kill? Cancer progresses by enlarging and spreading to different sites; its growth at each site interferes with normal development and functioning. As the disease progresses, it can produce pain, often because the tumor creates pressure on normal tissue and nerves or blocks the flow of body fluids (Melzack & Wall, 1982). Substantial pain afflicts 40% of cancer victims in intermediate stages of the disease and 70 to 90% of those with advanced cancer (Greenwald, Bonica, & Bergner, 1987; Ward et al., 1993). The disease leads to death in direct and indirect ways. In the direct route, the cancer spreads over time to a vital organ, such as the brain, liver, or lungs; it then competes for and takes most of the nutrients the organ tissues need to survive, thereby causing the organ to fail. Cancer kills indirectly in two ways: the disease itself weakens the victims, and both the disease and the treatment can impair the patient's appetite and ability to fight infection (Laszlo, 1987).

Prognosis and Causes of Cancer

The prognosis for cancer depends on how early it is detected and its location (ACS, 2004; Williams, 1990). Table 14.3 describes cancers of common sites, listed in order of their yearly incidence in the United States.

We have seen in earlier chapters that cancer is caused by the interplay of genetic and environmental factors, and that high stress can promote progression of the disease. Environmental factors include smoking tobacco, diet, ultraviolet radiation, and household and worksite chemical hazards, among others. Some research has also found a link between certain viral infections and the development of some cancers, such as in the cervix and in the liver (Tortora & Grabowski, 2003; Williams, 1990). In cervical cancer, viral transmission probably occurs during intercourse. Because not all women who are exposed to the viruses develop cancer, it seems likely that the effects of the infections depend on or combine with genetic and environmental factors to produce the disease.

Age, Gender, and Sociocultural Factors in Cancer

The risk of developing cancer typically increases with age, especially from the middle-age years onward. For

Table 14.3 *Common Cancer Sites and Facts of the United States*

- *Skin cancer.* With over 1 million cases diagnosed in the skin each year, it is the organ with the highest cancer incidence by far in the United States. The vast majority of these cancers are *basal cell* and *squamous cell carcinomas*, and cure is almost assured with early detection. (For this reason, these cases are often not included in incidence data.) But about 5% of skin cancers are *melanomas*, which are more serious because they metastasize quickly. Still, 90% of melanoma patients survive at least 5 years.
- *Prostate cancer.* Today, 230,000 diagnoses are made of neoplasms of the prostate gland in male reproductive systems each year. The 5-year survival rate for prostate cancer is about 97% and increases to 100% if detected in its early stages. These rates are unclear because diagnosis usually occurs after the men are over 65 years of age.
- *Breast cancer.* The incidence of breast cancer is about 217,000 cases a year. Early detection permits over 97% of breast cancer patients to survive at least 5 years, but this rate drops to 79% if the cancer has begun to spread.
- *Lung cancer.* Nearly 174,000 new cases of lung cancer are diagnosed annually, and the incidence is far greater among males than among females, probably because of men's higher smoking rates in the past. The 5-year survival rate is only 15% overall and 49% if the disease is discovered while still localized. In lung cancer, neoplasms tend to metastasize while still small, and, for this reason, they generally have already spread by the time they are discovered.
- *Colorectal cancer.* Neoplasms of the colon or rectum account for over 147,000 cancer diagnoses each year. The 5-year survival rates are about 62% overall and 90% when detected early (less than 40% of cases) in recommended tests.
- *Uterine and cervical cancer.* Neoplasms of the uterus or cervix of the female reproductive system can be either *invasive*, which have an incidence of about 51,000 cases a year, or precancerous *carcinomas in situ*, which are discovered very early with Pap tests and are usually fully curable. For invasive cases detected early, the 5-year survival rate is 92%.

Source: ACS (2004).

all types of cancer combined, incidence rates for the disease quadruple from 40 to 80 years of age (Mor et al., 1985). Taking age into account, the incidence rates of cancer in the United States are much higher for males than females (ACS, 2004). Two of the most common newly diagnosed malignancies are prostate cancer for men and breast cancer for women.

The link between cancer and sociocultural factors can be seen in the death rate data for different ethnic groups in the United States. Cancer incidence and death rates are far higher for Blacks than for Asian, Hispanic, and Native Americans, with the rates for Whites being intermediate (ACS, 2004). Although the cancer incidence rates are not so discrepant for Blacks and Whites, survival rates are much lower in Blacks partly because their diagnoses occur later (Meyerowitz et al., 1998). Research has compared cancer rates for Japanese people who either stayed in Japan or moved to Hawaii and adopted Western habits but did not intermarry (Williams, 1990). For almost all cancer types, the incidence for those in Hawaii was more similar to that of local Caucasians than to people in Japan, which strongly supports a role of environmental factors in cancer development.

DIAGNOSING AND TREATING CANCER

People can increase the likelihood of early rather than late detection of certain cancers by knowing the warning signs of cancer and having or doing regular examinations, which are listed in Table 14.4.

Diagnosing cancer can involve three medical procedures (AMA, 2003; Laszlo, 1987; Nguyen et al.,

Table 14.4   *Early Cancer Detection: Examinations and Warning Signs*

Examinations

Physician- or self-administered examinations are available for early detection of the following cancer sites:

- Breast
- Skin
- Colon or rectum
- Testes
- Prostate
- Uterus or cervix

Warning Signs of Cancer: "CAUTION"

If you have any of the following signs, see your doctor soon. Notice that the first letters spell "caution."

- **C**hange in bowel or bladder habits.
- **A** sore that does not heal.
- **U**nusual bleeding or discharge.
- **T**hickening or lump in the breast or elsewhere.
- **I**ndigestion or difficulty swallowing.
- **O**bvious change in a wart or mole.
- **N**agging cough or hoarseness.

Sources: ACS (1989, 2004).

1994). First, *blood* or *urine tests* can suggest the presence of cancer by revealing telltale signs, such as unusual levels of certain hormones or enzymes. Second, *radiological imaging,* through X-ray and other techniques, allows physicians to see the structure of internal organs and whether a tumor exists. Third, in a *biopsy* a physician takes out a small piece of suspicious tissue and have it analyzed. Even when the tissue is deep within the abdomen, a sample can generally be removed with minor surgical procedures and a local anesthetic.

Types of Medical Treatment

The ideal goal of cancer treatment is to cure the disease—to free the person from it forever. This ideal is possible when all the neoplasms are found and eliminated (Laszlo, 1987). If not all of the cancer is eliminated, the patient's symptoms may disappear for a time—or "go into remission"—only to return at a later date. Sometimes physicians can be reasonably certain that all of the cancer was removed, but often they cannot be sure. This is why they use the individual's survival for at least 5 years as a gauge of a treatment's success. There are basically three types of treatment for cancer—surgery, radiation, and chemotherapy—that may be used singly or in combination. When choosing the treatment components, patients and practitioners consider many factors, such as the size and site of the neoplasm, whether it has metastasized, and how the treatment will affect the patient's quality of life. One factor that may affect treatment choices, perhaps inappropriately, is the patient's age: research some years ago found that victims under age 60 were more likely than older ones to receive radiation or chemotherapy in their treatment for cancers with similar stages and sites of neoplasms (Mor et al., 1985).

From a medical standpoint, *surgery* is frequently the preferred treatment for eliminating a neoplasm, such as in breast or colorectal cancer (AMA, 2003; Williams, 1990). If the cancer is localized, surgery often can be completely effective by itself; if the cancer has spread, surgery may be useful in removing large clusters of cancerous cells, leaving the remainder for radiation or chemotherapy treatment. Sometimes the surgeon removes large portions of tissue near the neoplasm because of the possibility that the cancer has spread to those areas, too. In patients with colorectal cancer, for example, the surgeon may remove

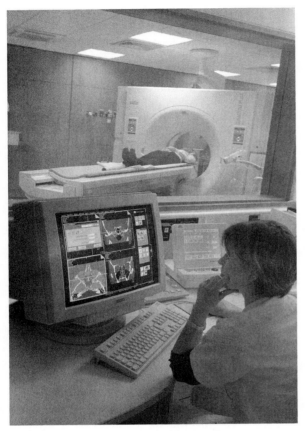

While the patient lies on a table in a large apparatus in the background, a radiological image of his brain appears on the monitor.

picture when the term *radiation therapy* is used. External beam therapy is usually given several times in a week and may be continued for up to several weeks. The second approach is called *internal radiation therapy* and involves placing a radioactive substance inside the body, near or into the tumor, by surgery or injection. Although radiation therapy is painless, it can have problematic side effects, depending on the area of the body radiated and the dose. Because radiation affects both healthy and malignant cells, the affected area may suffer irritation, burns, or hair loss, for example. The person may experience nausea, vomiting, loss of appetite, sterility, and reduced bone marrow function, particularly if the radiated area is large or is in the abdomen. In the days preceding radiation treatment, individuals often worry about these side effects and report heightened anxiety (Andersen, Golden-Kreutz, & DiLillo, 2001).

In *chemotherapy*, patients receive powerful drugs, usually orally or by injection, that circulate through the body to kill cells that divide very rapidly (AMA, 2003; Williams, 1990). The intended targets, of course, are cancerous cells, most of which reproduce rapidly. Different forms of cancer respond more readily to some types of drugs than to others. One problem with chemotherapy is that the drugs also kill many normal cells that divide rapidly, which can produce adverse side effects, including reduced immunity to infection, sores in the mouth, hair loss, nausea and vomiting, and damage to internal organs (ACS, 2004, AMA, 2003; Williams, 1990). Most of these effects are temporary—for instance, lost hair typically grows back.

Side Effects of Treatment

For many patients, two side effects of cancer treatment are especially difficult. First, most people who undergo repeated radiation or chemotherapy experience severe and long-lasting *fatigue* that often gets worse after the treatment ends (Cella et al., 1998; Jacobsen & Thors, 2003). Second, chemotherapy often produces periods of *nausea and vomiting* during and soon after each treatment; these periods can be so aversive and prolonged that patients have discontinued treatment, knowing that doing so could shorten their lives (Carey & Burish, 1988). The nausea and vomiting often have two effects: anticipatory nausea and learned food aversion.

In *anticipatory nausea*, patients who have received a few treatments and are about to receive the drug

a long section of the colon even though the neoplasm seems to be restricted to a small area. But the practice of removing large amounts of nearby tissue is changing, particularly in the treatment of breast cancer: a *mastectomy*—the removal of the entire breast—is not necessary in many, if not most, cases (ACS, 2004; Jacobson et al., 1995). Instead, a woman may choose to have a *lumpectomy*, in which just the tumor is removed, followed by radiation treatment.

Radiation in high doses damages the DNA of cells, and malignant cells are much less able than normal cells to repair the damage. In treating cancer, radiation is used in two ways (AMA, 2003; Laszlo, 1987). One approach, *external beam therapy*, involves directing a beam of intense radiation at the malignant tissue for a period of seconds or minutes. This is the most commonly used method and the one most people again begin vomiting before it is given. Some even become nauseated and throw up when they arrive at the hospital or while thinking about the upcoming treatment at home the night before. Anticipatory nausea appears to develop in about 25 to 50% of chemotherapy patients who have received repeated treatments (Andrykowski, 1990; Carey & Burish, 1988). These patients seem to learn this reaction through classical conditioning, whereby the drug itself is the unconditioned stimulus that reflexively produces the unconditioned response of nausea. By association, other related events, such as seeing the hospital or thinking about the procedure, become conditioned stimuli and can elicit nausea in the absence of the drug (Bovbjerg et al., 1992; Jacobsen et al., 1995). Anticipatory nausea is more likely to develop in people who, before treatments start, expect they will become nauseated than in those who do not expect nausea (Montgomery et al., 1998). Using behavioral methods, such as relaxation techniques, can help to reduce the nausea (Redd & Jacobsen, 2001).

Cancer patients who receive chemotherapy or radiation therapy often report that they develop a distaste for some foods they once liked, which is called a *learned food aversion*. The food becomes distasteful because the person associates it with symptoms of nausea and vomiting. Learned food aversion is a medical problem because cancer patients often experience a loss of appetite, which can lead to excessive weight loss. Research with chemotherapy patients has revealed several interesting findings (Mattes, Arnold, & Boraas, 1987a, 1987b). First, 55% of the patients developed aversions to foods consumed within the 24 hours preceding and following treatments. Second, many of these aversions formed after only one treatment, and subsequent treatments produced fewer and fewer new dislikes. Third, the amount of time (up to 24 hours) between eating the food and receiving the treatment did not affect whether an aversion would develop. Fourth, compared with individuals whose side effects did not include vomiting, subjects who vomited developed more learned food aversions, but receiving drugs to prevent vomiting did not help prevent aversions from forming. Fifth, the aversions generally lasted less than a month and included many of the foods the patients previously ate frequently and liked a great deal.

Can something be done to prevent cancer patients from learning to dislike foods they normally eat? One promising approach involves having a patient consume a strongly flavored, unfamiliar food between his or her last meal and the chemotherapy treatment. Why? The purpose is to create a scapegoat—that is, to direct the learning process to this new food and allow *it* to become disliked, instead of foods in the patient's normal diet. Research has shown that this approach works for many adult and child cancer patients (Broberg & Bernstein, 1987; Mattes, Arnold, & Boraas, 1987b). Individuals who form aversions to the scapegoat foods are much less likely to develop dislikes to foods in normal diets.

Cancer treatment not only can be unpleasant, it can be complex and demanding. Most cancer patients must also take medications at home, and many must return to their clinics frequently for laboratory tests, keep diaries of their food intake, or adhere to dietary and other changes in living habits. Do these conditions lead cancer patients to show poor compliance with their treatment regimens? Most adults seem to adhere well to cancer regimens, but adolescents and minority group individuals from the lower classes do not (Nehemkis & Gerber, 1986; Tebbi et al., 1986). Adherence to medical regimens depends on and affects psychosocial factors in patients' lives.

THE PSYCHOSOCIAL IMPACT OF CANCER

Like all chronic illnesses, cancer involves a series of threats and difficulties that change, often getting worse over time. Cancer creates unique stressors for patients and their families. These patients have a disease they recognize as a "real killer," and one that can lead to intense pain, disability, and disfigurement. The treatment decisions they make are complex—having to balance health benefits against distressing side effects, such as toxic reactions or disfigurement—and can lead to adjustment problems if the outcomes are not as expected (Stanton et al., 1998).

Even among patients who go into remission and adapt well in the first months or years, the threat of a recurrence looms—and if the disease flares up, the distress is worse than with the initial illness (Andersen, Golden-Kreutz, & DiLillo, 2001). What's more, some patients experience medical procedures that, for them, can be more aversive than the disease itself. How well patients adapt to having cancer can affect the progression of the disease. Those who have high levels of hopelessness and depression do not survive as long as others do (Brown et al., 2003; Watson et al., 1999). Cancer patients who feel high levels of stress

The social support of the cancer patient in the foreground is evident from his friends' having shaved their heads to help him feel more comfortable about losing his hair as a result of chemotherapy.

and do not cope well show poor immune system activity; some evidence suggests that cancers worsen more quickly if immune functions are impaired (Kiecolt-Glaser & Glaser, 1986; Redd et al., 1991).

Given all of the stress associated with having cancer, most patients show a remarkable amount of resilience and adapt fairly well (van't Spijker, Trijsburg, & Duivenvoorden, 1997). Even among hospitalized cancer patients, studies have generally found that less than half show significant emotional difficulties, and most of these involve relatively transient problems—chiefly anxiety and depressed mood—that are usually responsive to psychological therapy (Burish et al., 1987). This incidence of emotional problems may seem high, but keep in mind that hospitalization itself elevates emotional difficulties, and the patients may have been highly anxious or depressed before the illness. Psychologists often consider it "normal" for cancer patients to have some elevations in depression and anxiety. Given the life circumstances of these patients, deciding when these reactions are appropriate and when they are dysfunctional is likely to be difficult and based on arbitrary criteria.

Although adaptation to cancer can be very difficult for patients during the first several months and if their conditions worsen, their ability to adjust to their illnesses appears to improve with time during remission or after a cure (Burish et al., 1987; Glanz & Lerman, 1992). By 2 years or so, their psychosocial functioning stabilizes at levels similar to those they had prior to the diagnosis. Studies have compared the psychosocial adjustment of breast cancer patients who had been diagnosed and treated months earlier and women from the general population (Cordova et al., 2001; Craig, Comstock, & Geiser, 1974). The patients and the other women showed similar levels of depression, happiness, optimism for the future, and perceived health. As we saw earlier, people with cancer often cope by using positive reappraisal strategies.

The adaptation of people with cancer depends on many aspects of their illnesses and psychosocial situations. For example, the emotional adjustment cancer victims achieve depends on their ages and physical conditions—those who are middle-aged or physically impaired seem to fare worse than those who are older or less impaired (Vinokur et al., 1990). Patients who become most severely depressed tend to be those who are physically disabled by the disease or in pain (Burish et al., 1987; Spiegel, Sands, & Koopman, 1994). The site of the cancer is also important, and its impact often depends on the patient's age and gender. Cancer in some sites relates to sexual function, physically and psychologically, particularly for prostate and testicular cancer in men and for breast and gynecological cancer in women. Men with prostate cancer often become impotent and experience urinary incontinence; testicular cancer renders the man sterile.

The effect of age can be seen in the cases of two testicular cancer victims, a middle-aged married man with grown children and a younger man who had begun a career and developed a strong relationship with a woman 2 years before the diagnosis (Mages & Mendelsohn, 1979). The younger man was more distressed because his social network was less secure and his sterility meant that he would not have children of his own. A similar pattern of concerns affects women of different ages with cancer of the breast, cervix, and uterus (Andersen, Woods, & Copeland, 1997; Glanz & Lerman, 1992; Spencer et al., 1999). Their difficulties may be compounded if cancer or its treatment disfigures their bodies or alters their physical ability to function sexually, but breast-conserving surgery reduces disfigurement and adjustment problems (Moyer, 1997). Keep in mind, however, that sexual problems do not occur only among patients with cancers in sex-related organs. Many patients with cancers in other sites may also experience sexual problems as a result of their medical regimens, such as when chemotherapy causes fatigue (Burish et al., 1987; Redd et al., 1991).

Many cancer patients experience psychosocial problems that stem from changes in their relationships with family members and friends. Patients who perceive little social support and negative behaviors from significant people tend to have adjustment problems in part because they do not feel others want to talk about the cancer experience (Lepore & Helgeson, 1998; Manne, 1999). Although patients may withdraw from social contact because they feel socially awkward or embarrassed by their conditions, two other reasons are probably more common (Bloom, Kang, & Romano, 1991). First, patients' physical conditions and treatment may interfere with their seeing friends and family. Second, people may begin to avoid the patient—for instance, because they may feel personally vulnerable in his or her presence (Wortman & Dunkel-Schetter, 1979). They may also worry that they will "break down," or "betray their feelings," or "say the wrong thing" in front of the patient. When these people and the patient do get together, everyone may behave awkwardly.

PSYCHOSOCIAL INTERVENTIONS FOR CANCER

Psychosocial approaches for helping individuals cope with their cancers can begin in the diagnostic interview with the physician (Roberts et al., 1994). The physician can promote positive adaptation to the illness by discussing the diagnosis while the patient is alert with a spouse or other significant person present, expressing concern and giving the people some time to react emotionally and compose themselves, and then presenting information about the prognosis and treatment options. Medical personnel can also help by providing information on ways to manage the disease and difficult aspects of treatment and advice on improving the patient's diet and physical activity (Helgeson et al., 1999; Pinto, Eakin, & Maruyama, 2000).

Psychosocial interventions have been applied to deal with several difficulties of cancer patients, and we will focus on interventions to reduce patients' nausea from chemotherapy, lessen their physical pain, and improve their emotional adjustment and quality of life. Two successful approaches to reduce nausea are relaxation and systematic desensitization (Redd & Jacobsen, 2001). For example, one study found that training patients to use progressive muscle relaxation and imagery before and during chemotherapy sessions sharply reduced the development of nausea after the first session (Burish & Jenkins, 1992). Another study showed that systematic desensitization can help people who have already developed anticipatory nausea (Morrow et al., 1992). Patients used relaxation techniques while they imagined increasingly difficult scenes relating to chemotherapy, such as driving to the clinic or entering the waiting room. These individuals reported much less nausea and vomiting in subsequent chemotherapy sessions. Not all patients benefit from these techniques, partly because they don't believe psychosocial approaches will help (Carey & Burish, 1988).

Cancer pain is a serious problem when the illness is in advanced stages, especially in the last months before death (Butler et al., 2003). Although treatment with narcotic drugs is very useful, psychosocial interventions can also help. For example, researchers compared cancer pain patients who were randomly assigned to three groups (Dalton et al., 2003). A control group received usual medical care and two experimental groups received cognitive-behavioral treatment—one used a standard approach and the other was tailored to address specific difficulties assessed with psychological tests. The cognitive-behavioral treatments used a variety of methods, such as relaxation and problem-solving training. The patients in both of these groups, especially the tailored treatment group, reported having less pain and engaging in more daily activities than the usual care group.

Other interventions have been applied successfully to improve cancer patients' adjustment to their illnesses and quality of life (Meyer & Mark, 1995). For example, a cognitive-behavioral stress management program had breast cancer patients meet weekly for 2 hours in groups to discuss their difficulties and to learn methods, such as relaxation and coping strategies, that they could apply at home (Antoni et al., 2001; McGregor et al., 2004). The program improved their adjustment in two ways: it reduced the prevalence of depression, and it increased their use of positive reappraisal strategies, such as seeing benefits to their condition. These effects were strongest among women whose optimism was low at the start. The program also enhanced the women's immune functions. Because of the social problems cancer patients face, they and their families may benefit from family therapy and attending support groups that include education and group discussion (Helgeson & Cohen, 1996; Tovian, 1991). (Go to .)

CHILDHOOD CANCER

Cancer strikes tens of thousands of children around the world each year. In the United States, *leukemia* is the most common form of cancer in childhood, with 2,700 new cases annually (ACS, 2004). The 5-year survival rate for childhood leukemia is 78%; the main form of treatment is chemotherapy, which produces much the same side effects in children as in adults, including chronic nausea and vomiting. Losing their hair can be a very traumatic and embarrassing experience to most children and teenagers even though it does grow back (Spinetta, 1982). If a child receives treatment and a relapse does not occur in the first 5 years after diagnosis, the chances are very high that the leukemia will never recur (Laszlo, 1987).

The treatment program for leukemia is grueling. It begins on an inpatient basis with an "induction" phase, in which the patients receive combinations of drugs in high doses to produce a full remission, and radiation may be used to prevent the disease from developing in the brain (AMA, 2003; Williams, 1990). Chemotherapy then continues at regular intervals on an outpatient basis for the next 2 or 3 years in a "maintenance" phase. Many leukemia patients require a *bone marrow transplant*, an extremely painful process in which a large needle is inserted into the child's hip bone to remove the marrow and replace it with a donor's marrow. Although painkilling drugs help somewhat, the patients still feel intense pain. Children's pain and distress in this procedure can be

---

HIGHLIGHT

Can Psychosocial Interventions Improve Cancer Survival?

Around 1990, some very exciting research findings were published, indicating that psychosocial interventions can improve cancer survival. In one of the studies, patients attended weekly group meetings for a year where they could discuss their feelings and coping strategies and learn self-hypnosis to manage pain (Spiegel et al., 1989). A 10-year followup revealed that the patients who received the intervention lived nearly 18 months longer than others in a control group. Other similar interventions also produced positive results (Fawzy, Cousins et al., 1990; Fawzy, Kemeny et al., 1990). Assessments made 6 months after the intervention revealed that the subjects had better immune function and reported more vigor, better coping behavior, and less depression than control subjects. A followup 6 years later revealed that 29% of the controls and only 9% of the intervention subjects had died (Fawzy et al., 1993).

These outcomes were very encouraging, but several years later two similar efforts were not successful (Cunningham et al., 1998; Edelman et al., 1999). Although we don't yet know why the results conflict, a meta-analysis of eight studies, including the ones we discussed, found that psychosocial interventions did not prolong cancer patients' survival (Chow, Tsao, & Harth, 2004). If psychosocial methods are eventually developed that can enhance survival, they are likely to do so by improving immune function and reducing physiological stress reactions (Andersen, Farrar et al., 1998; Cruess et al., 2000).

reduced with psychological methods, such as showing them a film of a child coping realistically and teaching them to use techniques to distract their attention from the pain (Jay et al., 1987; Reeb & Bush, 1996).

What are the psychosocial effects of having cancer on children and their families? In an overall sense, the effects are like those with adult patients: the initial trauma is extremely difficult, but adjustment tends to improve over time (Eiser, 1985; Koocher et al., 1980). Two factors that are important in children's psychosocial adaptation to cancer are the age at the onset of the disease and the time since the diagnosis. The earlier the diagnoses and treatment occurred in the children's lives and the longer they survive in remission, the better their long-term adjustment tends to be. Another psychosocial issue in childhood cancer is that these patients often lag behind other children in academic skills, particularly during the first few years of school (Allen & Zigler, 1986; Eiser, 1985). These deficits probably result from their missing many school days and the psychosocial and physical effects of their medical treatment.

AIDS

Acquired immune deficiency syndrome—AIDS—is a very different high-mortality chronic illness from the others we have discussed in at least three ways. First, AIDS is a new disease and was virtually unknown before 1980. Second, it is an infectious disease that is caused by a virus (HIV) and is spread through the shared contact of blood or semen. Third, although the death rate from AIDS is fairly low in developed countries, it is a worldwide epidemic, its annual mortality statistics are very high, many millions of people are already infected with the virus, and the large majority of these people will probably die as a result of AIDS. Most of these people are heterosexuals with high rates of unsafe sex in developing countries (CDC, 2004a; UNAIDS, 2004).

RISK FACTORS, EFFECTS, AND TREATMENT OF AIDS

The risk factors for AIDS involve ways by which an infected person's blood or semen contacts the body

fluid of an uninfected person. This contact almost always occurs in one of three main ways:

- Sexual activity that exposes each person's body fluids to the other's. Exposure is more likely if the genital area has wounds or inflammation from a sexually transmitted disease (Peterman, 1990).
- Sharing contaminated syringes in drug use.
- Birth by an infected mother.

We saw in Chapter 6 that public health efforts have reduced these risks, especially among gay men and drug users in technologically advanced countries. But many people around the world still engage in risky behavior.

Age, Gender, and Sociocultural Factors in AIDS

The likelihood of becoming infected and developing AIDS depends on the person's age, gender, and sociocultural background. Worldwide, there are 38 million people living with HIV/AIDS; of the 5 million newly infected individuals per year, 800,000 are children (UNAIDS, 2004). In the United States, the rate of HIV infection is much higher among 20- to 45-year-old adults than other age groups and about three times higher in men than women; males have constituted over 80% of all AIDS cases since the epidemic began (CDC, 2004a). American death rate data reveal sociocultural differences: for males and females, AIDS death rates are many times higher for Blacks and Hispanics than for Whites and Native Americans, whose rates are higher than for Asian Americans (NCHS, 2003). Hispanic AIDS data reflect infections mainly among those of Puerto Rican descent (Flack et al., 1995). By far, the largest concentrations of HIV infection in the world today are in sub-Saharan Africa (UNAIDS, 2004).

FROM HIV INFECTION TO AIDS

When HIV infection occurs, several years may pass before the person's immune function is impaired—mainly from reduced numbers of helper T cells—and symptoms appear (Coico, Sunshine, & Benjamini, 2003). During the period before symptoms emerge, the virus appears to hide in the person's lymph tissue, multiplying there and battling the immune system (Cole & Kemeny, 1997; Pantaleo et al., 1993).

The diagnosis of AIDS is made only once the victim's condition has reached a certain criterion. Before 1993, the criterion required that the person have contracted one of several opportunistic diseases associated with the loss of immune function. These illnesses include *Pneumocystis carinii pneumonia* and *Kaposi's sarcoma*, a previously rare form of cancer. In 1993, the U.S. Centers for Disease Control changed the criterion to involve a low level of helper T cells (also called CD4 cells) in the person's blood. Years before reaching either of these criteria, however, the victim may have learned from a blood test that he or she was infected with HIV. There is now an accurate method to test a person's "viral load," an assessment of the number of viral particles in a blood sample, that reflects the amount of HIV in the body.

Between the time of infection and the AIDS diagnosis, the victim's immune system begins to falter, producing a variety of recurrent symptoms, such as spiking fever, night sweats, diarrhea, fatigue, and swollen lymph glands. Prior to this stage, called AIDS-*related complex* (ARC), the only way individuals with HIV can tell they are infected is by having a blood test. If the diagnosis comes after symptoms appear, the immune system is already severely weakened and struggles to fight repeated bouts of opportunistic diseases.

Medical Treatment for People with HIV/AIDS

Most, but not all, opportunistic diseases in AIDS can be medically treated effectively, such as with antibiotics, but sometimes victims become hypersensitive, or allergic, to the medications, and no therapy is available that their bodies will tolerate (AMA, 2003; Osborn, 1988). For patients whose immune systems continue to falter, the prognosis is poor. Their bodies become severely weakened, and they gradually waste away. Many AIDS patients develop a brain disorder when the HIV invades the central nervous system and causes it to deteriorate—a condition called *encephalopathy*. These patients gradually lose their cognitive functions, become disoriented and confused, and eventually lapse into comas.

The main treatment for AIDS uses drugs called *antiretroviral agents*. From the mid-1980s to the mid-1990s, the main drug was AZT (*azidothymidine*, or *zidovudine*), which slows HIV reproduction in the early stages and prolongs survival, but does not cure the disease (AMA, 2003; Osborn, 1988). By the mid-1990s, new antiretroviral drugs appeared; some, called *protease inhibitors*, suppress HIV reproduction and dramatically reduce the viral load in many, but not all, HIV-infected individuals (UNAIDS, 2004). Antiretroviral drug regimens may not work for all strains of HIV and usually involve a combination of drugs taken on a complex schedule that must be adhered to strictly. If a regimen fails, another set of similar drugs may work. Although these drugs have maintained low viral loads in many patients, it is too early to tell what the long-term effects will be. Even if the drugs are successful, the treatment is expensive ($15,000 a year) and can have serious side effects. Many people who use antiretroviral drugs do not adhere to the regimen well enough because of its complexity and side effects and because of patients' emotional difficulties, drug abuse, and poor social support (Catz et al., 2000; Gonzalez et al., 2004; Mellins et al., 2002). The cost makes these drugs unavailable for the large majority of AIDS patients around the world.

AIDS is fatal to the vast majority of its victims; most die within 3 years of the AIDS diagnosis (Cole & Kemeny, 1997). About 5 or 10% of HIV-infected people have survived for 15 years or more after the diagnosis without progressing to AIDS (UNAIDS, 2004). How do these people resist AIDS? The answer seems to involve biological and psychosocial differences between those who do and those who do not continue to survive. For one thing, researchers have discovered genetically driven processes that modulate the body's production of proteins and enzymes that slow down or speed up HIV progression (Hendel et al., 1999). Also, HIV victims who have high reactivity to stress and cope poorly show poorer immune function and faster progression of the disease than others do (Cole & Kemeny, 1997). Because AIDS is a new disease, most existing knowledge about patients' treatment and survival is tentative. A new and hopeful finding has emerged: a study found with several subjects that starting antiviral treatment very soon after infection and having brief interruptions once the virus was controlled enabled the body to develop immune defenses to fight the infection without further treatment (Rosenberg et al., 2000). If these effects are replicated with large numbers of subjects, the challenge will be in getting people to be tested early.

THE PSYCHOSOCIAL IMPACT OF AIDS

Every epidemic arouses fear—but when so little is known about the disease except that it is so deadly,

A caregiver hands medicine to his lover dying of AIDS.

people tend to react in extreme ways to protect themselves and the people they love. The American news media in the 1980s had frequent stories of AIDS patients being fired from their jobs, children with AIDS not being allowed to attend school, families with an AIDS patient being driven from their homes, and health care workers refusing to treat AIDS patients. Although stories like these are less common now, AIDS still arouses fear and discrimination in many people around the world (Herek, 1999; Herek & Capitanio, 1999). Many Americans still believe AIDS patients are being punished by God for their misbehavior, and in some developing nations, people with HIV are shunned by neighbors and medical workers. In one case, a woman was beaten to death for revealing her illness.

Because of the fears about AIDS, and because the disease is often associated with homosexuality and drug abuse in industrialized countries, AIDS patients and their families—which includes lovers—often feel stigmatized (Flaskerud, 1988; Herek, 1999). One of the first questions they consider is, "Should I tell anyone—and if so, who?" Some with HIV infections don't even tell their immediate family (Simoni et al., 1995). They worry that family, friends, neighbors, and coworkers will reject them. This may lead to their being secretive and withdrawn, thereby cutting off the social support they will need as the disease progresses.

For some families, learning of the AIDS diagnosis comes at the same time they first learn that the patient—their child or spouse—is gay, or bisexual, or a drug user. Moreover, spouses or lovers fear that the patient has already infected them, too. All these factors fuel the stigma associated with the disease, which has three health effects. First, some societies have resisted acknowledging the disease, thereby allowing it to spread. Second, the stigma leads some people to delay being tested for HIV and getting care and to avoid telling partners if they are infected (Chesney & Smith, 1999). Third, the progression of people's HIV disease appears to slow after they disclose their illness to others (Sherman et al., 2000).

Adapting to HIV and AIDS depends on access to effective treatment. Using effective antiretroviral agents after many months of less effective care reduces patients' distress, and these reductions seem to result mainly from decreases in physical symptoms and limitations (Rabkin et al., 2000). Many people without access to effective treatment still manage to adapt well to their conditions eventually, but others don't fare so well (Rotheram-Borus et al., 1996). Some fear they will be abandoned by those they love and suffer pain, debilitation, and disfigurement (Flaskerud, 1988). And cycles of AIDS-related diseases can arouse feelings of hopelessness and helplessness. Depression may become severe, especially among those patients who try to cope mainly with avoidance strategies, believe their illness is punishment for past wrongdoings, and have been rejected by people they care about (Ciesla & Roberts, 2001; Maj, 1990). Preventing and treating emotional distress is important because depressed HIV patients subsequently show faster disease progression and shorter survival than those who are not depressed (Ironson et al., 1994; Mayne et al., 1996; Patterson et al., 1996).

PSYCHOSOCIAL INTERVENTIONS FOR AIDS

Psychosocial efforts for AIDS need to begin when patients are tested for HIV (Sheridan, 1991). These individuals usually decide to get tested because they believe they could have the virus. They need carefully presented information to help reduce anxiety during the time before getting the results. Those who test HIV-positive will need counseling regarding the illness, treatment, and the many organizations and support groups available today to help AIDS patients and their families cope. Interventions for individuals with and without access to effective antiretroviral treatment need to focus on different issues. Because antiretroviral regimens are complex and must be strictly followed, interventions for people taking the drugs must monitor and promote adherence (Ekstrand & Chesney, 2002).

Many people with HIV and AIDS need psychosocial interventions for other problems, including emotional distress, pain management, and sleep disorders (Sikkema & Kelly, 1996). Interventions have focused on reducing anxiety and depression among patients who did *not* have effective antiretroviral drugs. For example, Michael Antoni and his colleagues (1990, 1991) recruited gay men who didn't know their HIV status and randomly assigned them to intervention and control groups. Intervention began weeks before HIV testing and consisted of aerobic exercise, relaxation training, and group meetings that included cognitive restructuring methods to modify maladaptive beliefs. For individuals who tested positive, those who received the intervention showed substantially less anxiety and depression and much stronger immune function, and these benefits increased with the amount of relaxation practice they did. Other studies have found that similar interventions also enhance immune function and reduce anxiety and depression for people with advanced HIV or AIDS (Antoni et al., 2000; Lutgendorf et al., 1997; Maj, 1990). Can psychosocial methods also help individuals with HIV who are using antiretroviral drugs? Recall from Chapter 4 that talking or writing about negative experiences appears to improve people's health: an experiment found that HIV patients who wrote about a very traumatic experience had markedly lower viral loads in the next months than those who wrote about a neutral topic (Petrie et al., 2004).

In this chapter, we have examined what it is like to live with and adapt to four very different high-mortality health problems. Each of these diseases can disable its victims and progress to the point that the patients and their loved ones are aware that the disease is terminal and death is imminent.

ADAPTING TO A TERMINAL ILLNESS

When people talk about the hypothetical prospects of dying, you will often hear them say, "I hope I go quickly and without pain." Some people might argue that there are no good ways to die, but almost everyone would agree that a slow and painful death is the worst way. By definition, a terminal illness entails a slow death. The patient typically suffers a progressive deterioration in the feeling of well-being and ability to function and may also experience chronic pain. Although dying from a terminal illness generally takes several weeks, it sometimes takes as little as a few days or as long as several months (Hinton, 1984). One factor that affects how people adapt to a terminal illness is the age of the victim.

THE PATIENT'S AGE

"Tragic" and "untimely" are words people often use to describe a young person's terminal illness or death. Death is more "appropriate" at 80 years of age than at 20. Let's consider how people adapt to terminal illness at different times in the life span.

A Terminally Ill Child

What does "dying" mean? Death is a very abstract concept and, as such, it is not well understood by young children (Lonetto, 1980; Speece & Brent, 1984). Prior to about 5 years of age, children think death is like living in another place and the person can come back.

They may also believe people can avoid death. For instance, a child might conceive of death as a monster and argue that "you won't die if you run faster than the monster or trick it." By about 8 years of age, most children understand that death happens to everyone, is final, and involves the absence of bodily functions.

Most children at early ages have some experience with dying—for instance, in the death of a close person, such as a grandparent or neighbor, or of a pet. Dying is not an easy topic for many adults to discuss, and they usually try to spare children the realities of death, saying that the dead person "has gone away," or "is in heaven, with Jesus," or "is only sleeping" (Koch, 1977; Sarafino, 1986). When a child has a terminal illness, parents sometimes decide not to tell him or her so that the child will have less emotional suffering. However, dying school-age children seem to realize that their illnesses are extremely serious even when they are not told, and they exhibit far greater anxiety than seriously ill children who are not dying (Spinetta, 1974). Child specialists today generally believe children should know as much about their illnesses as they can comprehend and should be told in an open, honest, and sensitive manner (La Greca & Stone, 1985).

A Terminally Ill Adolescent or Young Adult

Adolescents and young adults who develop terminal illnesses realize how unlikely dying at their ages is and feel angry about the "senselessness" and "injustice" of it and about not having a chance to develop their lives. As one dying college student put it, "Now a perfectly good person with an awful lot to give is going to die. A young person is going to die. His death is going to be senseless" (Shneidman, 1977, p. 77). He was having a very difficult time coping with his impending death, and a therapist was called in to help him because of his shouting and quarrelsome behavior in the hospital.

Having a terminal illness seems especially untimely when victims have young children. This condition is a threat to the family unit, and the patients feel guilty at not being able to care for their children and cheated out of the joys of seeing them develop. Because death at this point is so untimely, young adults seem to experience more anger and emotional distress when they have life-threatening illnesses than older individuals do (Leventhal, Leventhal, & Van Nguyen, 1985).

Terminal Illness in Middle-Aged and Older Adults

As people develop beyond the early adulthood years, the likelihood of contracting a high-mortality chronic illness—especially heart disease, cancer, or stroke—increases sharply. Although dying may not be easy at any point in the life span, it seems to become less difficult as people progress from middle age to old age. Studies have found, for instance, that adults become less and less afraid of death as they get older (Bengston, Cuellar, & Ragan, 1977; Kalish & Reynolds, 1976). Why is this?

Researcher Richard Kalish (1985) has outlined several reasons why the elderly have an easier time than younger individuals in facing impending death. As people get older, developing a terminal illness becomes less unexpected, less of a shock. The elderly know their remaining years are few, they realize that they will probably die of a chronic illness, and they think and talk more about poor health and death than most younger people do. Most of their peers and many relatives are suffering from declining health or have died. They often have made financial preparations, and some have even made plans or given instructions regarding the terminal care they would prefer and their funeral arrangements. In addition, older individuals have had longer pasts than younger people, which have allowed them the time to achieve more. People who review their pasts and believe they have accomplished important things and lived good lives tend to have less difficulty adapting to terminal illnesses than others do (Mages & Mendelsohn, 1979).

PSYCHOSOCIAL ADJUSTMENTS TO TERMINAL ILLNESS

As we have seen, most people with life-threatening chronic illnesses manage to adapt reasonably well to their conditions over time after the initial crises, and so do the closest people in their lives. But when their conditions worsen and progress to a terminal phase, new crises emerge that require intense coping efforts.

How People Cope with Terminal Illness

How do terminally ill people and their families cope, and what types of stress do they experience? The principal coping mechanism people use during the phase of terminal illness is denial (Hackett & Weisman,

1985; Hinton, 1984). As we saw in Chapter 5, emotion-focused coping is especially useful when the individuals cannot do anything to change their situations. Unfortunately, when people mutually avoid facing the imminent death, they may not discuss with each other how they feel or have any way to "say their good-byes."

Psychiatrist John Hinton (1984) has described three types of stress terminal patients experience. First, they must cope with the physical effects of their worsening conditions, such as pain, difficulty breathing, sleeplessness, or loss of bowel control. Second, their conditions severely alter their styles of living, restricting their activity and making them highly dependent on others. Perhaps two-thirds of terminally ill people are restricted in their activities during the last 3 months of their lives, and one-fifth of these patients are confined to bed. Third, they typically realize that the end of their lives is near, even when they are not told so. If they are in a hospital, they may think about never going home again or no longer being able to experience the intimacy they used to have with those they love.

Thinking about someone who is dying typically arouses feelings of sadness in people, but these people may not realize how well many terminally ill people come to face and accept dying. Hinton (1984) has noted similarities between people who are dying and those with diminished lives—such as the frail, disabled, or bereaved: they can still get pleasure from their lives despite earlier thoughts that such circumstances would be unbearable. The quality of life for such persons can be fairly good if they have a sense of fulfillment, such as from the family they'll leave behind or their career. Most people adapt to dying with little anger or depression if they are in little pain, receive sensitive and caring social support, feel satisfied with their lives, and have a history of coping well with life's problems and crises (Carey, 1975; Hinton, 1984; Kalish, 1985). Often, patients adapt better than their loved ones. For instance, spouses of dying people often experience increased health problems, depression, and memory difficulties (Howell, 1986). Support groups and family therapy can be of great help to dying individuals and their families.

Does Adapting to Dying Happen in "Stages"?

"Time changes things," people say. Since time passes in the process of dying from a terminal illness, we might expect that patients' reactions would change as they come to terms with their impending deaths. Do these changes occur in a predictable pattern, as a series of stages? On the basis of interviews with over 200 terminally ill people, Elisabeth Kübler-Ross (1969) proposed that people's adjustment to dying usually follows a pattern, passing through a sequence of *five* stages. Table 14.5 outlines these stages. Not all the patients she interviewed showed this pattern—a few, for example, continued to deny that they were dying to the very last. But the pattern of adjustments seemed sufficiently regular for Kübler-Ross to propose that coping in most dying people begins with denial and advances through the stages in order.

Do Kübler-Ross's stages correctly reflect the emotional reactions most dying patients experience as they cope with terminal illnesses? Available evidence does not support the idea that most individuals adjust to dying with a predictable and orderly

Table 14.5   *Kübler-Ross's Stages of Adjustment to Dying*

1. *Denial.* The first reaction to the prognosis of death involves refusing to believe it is true. Terminally ill patients say, "No, it can't be true," or "There must be some mistake," or "The lab reports must have gotten mixed up." Denial can be a valuable first reaction by giving patients time to mobilize other coping strategies and motivation to get second opinions. According to Kübler-Ross, denial soon fades in most patients and is replaced by anger.

2. *Anger.* The patients now realize, "Oh, yes, it is me, it was not a mistake," and are outraged and irate, asking, "Why me?" or, "Why couldn't it have been that miserable no-good guy down the street?" They resent others who are healthy and may show their anger in outbursts toward almost anyone—nurses, doctors, and family.

3. *Bargaining.* At this point, patients try to change their circumstances by offering to "make a deal." Most of the bargains they try to negotiate are with God, for example, thinking, "Oh, God, I promise to be a better person if you'll just make me well."

4. *Depression.* When bargaining no longer helps and patients feel their time is running out, hopelessness and depression set in. They grieve for things they had in the past and for things they will miss in the future. According to Kübler-Ross, even though depression is painful and may last for a prolonged period, it is helpful because part of the grieving process involves becoming detached from the things in the patient's world. Being detached enables the last stage—acceptance—to occur.

5. *Acceptance.* Patients who live long enough may reach the last stage in which they are no longer depressed, but feel a quiet calm and readiness for death.

Source: Kübler-Ross (1969).

sequence of coping reactions (Hinton, 1984; Kalish, 1985; Silver & Wortman, 1980; Zisook et al., 1995). An overview of this evidence indicates that some terminal patients do follow an orderly and predictable sequence of adjustment, but most people's emotions and coping patterns fluctuate. Some people may go through a specific stage, such as anger, more than once during their adjustment; others have more than one emotional reaction simultaneously; and some seem to skip stages. Some evidence indicates that people who achieve an "acceptance" of their impending death die much sooner than those who do not reach this stage (Reed et al., 1994).

Despite these shortcomings, Kübler-Ross's work has had many positive effects. For one thing, it has been influential in stimulating people's awareness and discussion of the dying process and the needs of terminal patients. It has also led to important and very beneficial changes in the care and treatment of dying people, thereby improving the quality of the last weeks and days of their lives.

THE QUALITY OF LIFE IN DEATH

The medical community and patients' families face one dilemma after another in trying to do what's best for a dying person. Medical technology has made it possible to keep some patients alive only in a legal sense, and societies have begun to question whether these people are alive in a humane sense. The news media describe patients lying in comas for years, dependent on life-support systems to stay alive, but with virtually no likelihood of recovery. An artificial respirator can make a person breathe, and other devices can keep the heart going. The vast majority of American physicians favor withdrawing life-support systems from hopelessly ill or irreversibly comatose individuals if the patients or their families request it (Shogren, 1988). In most of the United States, a person who anticipates these circumstances may issue a "living will" that instructs practitioners not to use extraordinary life-support measures.

A principal issue that enters into people's judgments about terminal care is the patient's quality of life. What kind of medical and psychological care do dying patients need? Who should be responsible for that care, and where should it be given? These are the main issues we consider in this section. (Go to 🍎.)

MEDICAL AND PSYCHOLOGICAL CARE OF DYING PATIENTS

The terminal phase of care begins when medical judgment indicates that the patient's condition is worsening and no treatment is available to reverse or arrest the progress toward death (AMA, 2003; Benoliel, 1977). At this point, medical treatment is mainly *palliative*; that is, it focuses on reducing pain and discomfort. This phase of treatment can be very distressing not only to the patients and their families, but to medical personnel, who entered the medical field to save lives. Terminally ill people in the United States can request that the specific instruction, "Do Not Resuscitate," be entered on their hospital charts. If they begin to die—for instance, if the person's heart stops beating—the medical staff is not to interfere. Should terminally ill adults be told they are dying? The great majority of dying patients want to know so that they can be prepared psychologically and legally (Abrahm, 2003). Because some patients would prefer not to know, physicians can probe sensitively to assess the person's wishes. Those who prefer not to know may be given the option of having their families handle all decisions (Blackhall et al., 1995).

Individuals who work with dying people on a daily basis must come to grips with the feelings of failure and loss they experience when patients die (Benoliel, 1977; Maguire, 1985). To protect themselves from this pain and to perform efficiently in their heavy workloads, medical staff may distance themselves psychologically from terminally ill people. By doing this, doctors and nurses avoid dealing with the psychological problems these patients are having. How do staff members distance themselves? They may simply not ask about the person's feelings or adjustment, or they may provide false reassurance, saying, "I'm sure you'll feel better soon," when they believe otherwise. The staff may also use selective attention, as illustrated in the following interaction:

SURGEON: Well, how are you today?

PATIENT: (dying of breast cancer): I'm very worried about what is happening to me. I'm beginning to think I'm not going to get better this time. The pain in my hip is getting worse.

SURGEON: Tell me more about this pain in your hip. (Maguire, 1985, p. 1711)

ASSESS YOURSELF

Your Living Will Choices

Fill out the *Health Care Living Will and Proxy* below, indicating what your wishes would be if you were unable to make decisions about your medical treatment, such as if you were in a coma. What specific treatments would you *want* or *not want* to receive? Whom would you choose as your agent or "proxy" in making decisions if you were unable to make them? This person should be an adult who is familiar with your personal and health care views—someone you would trust to make the decisions you would make.

If this were a legal document, you and two witnesses would need to sign it. Some living wills are much more complicated than this one, having the person make dozens of choices regarding many different medical procedures that might be considered in very different scenarios. One concern in being so specific is that knowledge about treatments can change: suppose evidence on a treatment's effectiveness changes between the time a patient rejects it in the will and the scenario actually occurs? What then?

HEALTH CARE LIVING WILL AND PROXY

TO MY FAMILY, PHYSICIANS, AND OTHER CONCERNED PARTIES:
I, _____
(the *principal*), being of sound mind, make the following advance directives to be carried out if I become unable to make or communicate decisions about my medical treatment.

LIVING WILL
I request the withdrawal or withholding of life-sustaining procedures, consistent with my desire that I be permitted to die naturally if the situation occurs that I am either (1) near death with no reasonable likelihood of recovery or (2) in a coma or vegetative state and my physicians believe that there is no significant possibility of my ever regaining consciousness or higher functions of my brain. Under these circumstances, I specifically:

1. DO NOT want the following treatments I have *initialed*.

  • Cardiac resuscitation _____
  • Artificial respiration _____
  • Artificial feeding or fluids _____
  • Other (specify) _____

2. DO want the following conditions I have *initialed*.

  • Medication to relieve pain _____
  • To die at home, if possible _____
  • Other (specify) _____

PROXY
I designate here (1) a *first proxy,* _____ (name), to make decisions in accordance with the wishes and conditions specified above, or as he or she otherwise knows, and (2) a *second proxy,* _____ (name), as a substitute if the first proxy is unable, unwilling, or unavailable to act as my health care proxy.

Although this patient mentioned both physical and psychological difficulties, the physician followed up only on the physical one. This may lead the patient to conclude that it is not appropriate to discuss psychological problems with medical staff.

Although many people are able to approach death with a feeling of acceptance and peacefulness, others become very troubled, often depressed. What can be done to help dying patients cope? Practitioners can try to assess depression in a preliminary way, such as by asking patients sensitively whether they have "felt depressed a lot recently" and what they "think is ahead with the illness." Answers that affirm emotional difficulty, can be confirmed in more extensive evaluations (Abrahm, 2003). Depressed patients can receive antidepressant drugs and psychotherapy to provide emotional support and help them to use positive reappraisal strategies. Health care workers may also be able to provide information about support groups that have developed specifically to improve the quality of life for people with terminal illnesses. And professionally led group therapy can help terminal patients face their impending deaths with less anxiety and depression and a greater sense of control over their remaining periods of life (Levy, 1983).

A PLACE TO DIE—HOSPITAL, HOME, OR HOSPICE?

Most people in developed nations die in hospitals or nursing homes (Hays et al., 1999). Although hospitals can provide a great deal of expertise, technical equipment, and efficient caregiving, they are usually not "psychologically comfortable" places for people. The environment there is unfamiliar, and patients have little control over their daily routine and activities, and they lack access to such things as photo albums or musical recordings, for example, that they have relied on in the past for enjoyment and to enrich their experiences. Moreover, most of the people there are strangers, not family or friends. As a result, many terminally ill people would rather die at home, and many do. Is this a reasonable alternative?

Home Care for the Dying Patient

Whether home care is a reasonable alternative for a dying person depends on his or her condition and the quality of care available at home. Can patients receive good terminal care at home? Yes, most can. Terminally ill people receive very good care if they have regular contact at home with a medical team and if family members are trained (Malkin, 1976; Zimmer, Juncker, & McCusker, 1985). Unfortunately, many dying patients may not have the option of home care because they lack family members who are able to provide the care they need or the financial resources that may be required.

Caring for a terminally ill person at home can be physically and emotionally exhausting (Hinton, 1984). There may be only one individual at home who can provide the care, and all of the burden falls on that person's shoulders. If the patient requires continuous attention, the life of that one caretaker may become limited to coping with the dying person's needs. This may go on for weeks or, sometimes, months. Even when there is more than one person available to help, their lives are to some extent restricted by the needs of the patient. Some terminally ill people are bedridden and need to be fed and bathed, for instance. Despite these hardships, many

people who have cared for dying persons at home claim it is extremely rewarding to know they have done everything they could to make the last days or weeks as pleasant as possible for someone they love.

Hospice Care for the Dying Patient

Is it possible to combine the strengths of a professional support system with the warm and loving care one can get at home, thereby helping terminal patients die comfortably and with dignity? This question led to the development of the concept of **hospice care,** which involves a medical and social support system to provide an enriched quality of life—through physical, psychosocial, and spiritual care—for terminally ill people and their families (Abrahm, 2003; Cioppa, 1984; HFA, 2004). In hospice care, the staff consists of a medically supervised team of professionals and volunteers. Much of the physical care the staff provides is designed to reduce discomfort and pain, often with the use of drugs.

The hospice care approach originated in Great Britain, largely through the efforts of physician Cicely Saunders, who was originally trained as a nurse and social worker (HFA, 2004; Torrens, 1985). Originally, hospices were designed as separate institutions for the purpose of caring for dying patients on an inpatient basis. But as the philosophy of hospice care spread to the United States and Canada, the organizational structure for delivering this care began to broaden. Hospice services in North America are available today both at *home* and at hundreds of *inpatient facilities*, many of which are housed in hospitals or nursing homes. When home hospice care is used, services are provided on a part-time, regularly scheduled basis and staff are available on-call 24 hours a day, 7 days a week (Cioppa, 1984).

Inpatient facilities generally try to make the environment as much like home as possible, often including a kitchen and family room area. If the facility is in a hospital, existing policies are adjusted to satisfy the goals of the program. These adjustments often provide for flexible visiting hours and regulations, freedom to wear one's own clothes, family members to prepare and share meals with alcoholic beverages, psychological and spiritual counseling, and assistance in completing unfinished business (Cioppa, 1984).

Cicely Saunders (1986) has outlined several "essential elements" in the hospice approach, some of which deal with psychosocial issues. First, people who are dying should be in a *place of choice* as they end their lives. They and their families should decide whether that place should be at home or in an inpatient setting. Most people prefer to be at home (Hays, Gold, Flint, & Winer, 1999). Second, the care given during the terminal phase should enable patients to *maximize their potential*, so that they perform to the limits of their physical, cognitive, and social potential, particularly as active members of their families. Third, the care should *address all family members' needs*, which may involve resolving interpersonal discord and feelings of anxiety, guilt, and depression. Fourth, *followup care* is available for family members to receive help through and after the period of bereavement.

Does hospice care help patients and their families cope better with the dying process than conventional care does? The testimonials from patients and family members are massive and glowing, describing the programs as enormously supportive and enriching. And a study found that the quality of life is better with inpatient hospice care than standard hospital care (Viney et al., 1994). Evidence from the small number of carefully controlled studies of inpatient hospice and conventional care suggests that both provide similar pain control and daily activities, but hospice patients show less anxiety and greater satisfaction with their care (Torrens, 1985).

THE SURVIVORS: AND LIFE GOES ON

Whether a person dies suddenly and unexpectedly or with warning over a long time, there are survivors who must then come to terms with the death and eventually pick up the pieces of their lives. Suffering a loss through death is called *bereavement*. Feelings of *grief* and the expression of these feelings in *mourning* characterize this state.

People adapt to their bereavement in their own individual ways. This process takes time, usually at least a year, but it does not seem to follow any particular pattern or stages, and there is no good rule of thumb to predict how long it will take (Joyce, 1984; Silver & Wortman, 1980; Zisook et al., 1995). Each grieving person needs to adjust at his or her own pace, and urgings to "start living again" may be insensitive and unproductive when they occur early in the adjustment process. A longitudinal study of individuals whose spouses succumbed to serious illnesses revealed that their psychological distress was similar before and soon after the death, remained high for about a year, and was greater for middle-aged than elderly individuals (Hays, Kasl, & Jacobs, 1994). Other findings indicate that adjustment is very difficult

A hospice staff member attends a terminally ill patient. Hospice care can be given at home or in inpatient facilities that look more like a home than a hospital.

when the death is sudden, such as from an accident or violence, and that for people with heavy caregiving strain experiences, the amount of stress after the death stays about the same as it was before (CFAH, 2003). Several types of psychosocial interventions, such as individual therapy and support groups, can help people who are having difficulty adjusting to their losses (CFAH, 2003; Zisook et al., 1995).

The AIDS epidemic has revealed two important issues about bereavement in gay individuals. First, many experienced a series of bereavements within a few years—often losing long-term partners and most of their friends—without completing their mourning between deaths. Coping with terminal illness repeatedly takes a severe emotional toll, and each death adds to the toll with increased demoralization, sleep problems, and stress reactions (Martin, 1988; Martin & Dean, 1993). Second, gay individuals who have lost their lovers receive less social support from others, such as bosses and coworkers, than heterosexuals do. For example, a man who was troubled by his partner's death and performing below par at work reported that his getting little understanding from his boss "makes me feel depressed, angry, and used. . . . I really loved him and I do miss him" (Moskowitz et al., 1996, p. 49). Most people in the larger society probably do not realize that gay couples' relationships can be so strong and loving.

Some people think that coming to terms with the loss of someone we love means we forget that person— he or she no longer means anything to us. This is not so. People who eventually adapt to the loss may feel recurrent moments or periods of sadness years later, especially on anniversaries or other significant dates (Joyce, 1984). A mother who lost her infant child years ago wrote:

My mind does not mourn yesterday
It mourns today
The images that pass before my eyes
Do not recall the infant son
But see you running through my house
A teenage child in search of food and gym shoes
and maybe me.
I do not mourn you for what you were,
But for what can't be . . .
(Anonymous, cited in Silver & Wortman, 1980, p. 337)

The death of a child is one of the most tragic events that can happen to a family, and parents often experience grief for many years after the loss (CFAH, 2003).

When a parent dies, the surviving children need special attention and understanding. Often the surviving parent is so caught up in his or her own shock and grief that the children's emotional needs are not adequately addressed. Many surviving parents say little about the death and exclude young children from the mourning process. It is not unusual for children to show little sense of loss or outward grief when a close family member dies (Koch, 1977; Sarafino, 1986). Young children do not understand fully what death is, and older children may be so confused and shocked by the tragedy that they are simply numbed emotionally. Their outward calmness should not be seen as a sign that they do not love the dead person. Sometimes their grief comes out later, and sometimes it happens privately.

Still, most people are resilient and adapt to their loss in time (Bonanno, 2004). During the first weeks after the death of a spouse, the surviving husband or wife usually receives a great deal of attention from friends and relatives. But soon this changes, and the bereaved person must gradually become involved again in work and leisure activities, in maintaining old friendships and developing new ones, and, perhaps, in finding a new mate. One man described his experience as a widower in the following way:

Having to "date" in the early 40s, or older, and after long years of marriage is, for many, an unnerving experience. I suggest there is something even worse—not getting out and having companionship.

How the widower chooses to begin his new social and sex life depends, of course, on his personality, his philosophy, and the sort of companionship he wants. . . . I had friends and relatives who put forward suggestions and invited me to dinner parties. I found most of these either tedious or painful. One night . . . however I did meet a beautiful woman. She was a widow, with one child. . . . We are a complete household again and throughout the home there once again is the sound of laughter, of music and, best of all, the rich sound of meaningful conversation between children and their parents. (Lindeman, 1976, pp. 285–286)

Of course, not all stories of people's coping with the loss of someone they love have happy endings. Some bereaved individuals never adjust to the loss. But with the help and support of others and a determined drive on their own part, most people can build a new and once-again enriching life. The social support bereaved people need can come from family and friends, but support groups may be especially helpful.

SUMMARY

People with a high-mortality illness realize their lives are threatened, and they and their families must adapt to living with uncertainty and watching for symptoms and changes in their conditions. Families can help patients adapt by encouraging them to be active, rather than encouraging helplessness and dependence. In adapting to illness over a long period of time, patients make cognitive adjustments by making positive reappraisals, such as finding meaning in their illness experiences, and gaining a sense of control over their illnesses. A recurrence or relapse of the condition creates a new and difficult crisis.

Most deaths in developed countries result from three chronic diseases: heart disease, cancer, and stroke. Coronary heart disease may show up in an episode of angina pectoris or of myocardial infarction. The prevalence of heart disease increases with age, and the death rate is greater in men than women. Cardiac rehabilitation involves the use of medication, a program of exercise, stress management, and changes in diet and other aspects of lifestyle, especially if the person smokes, drinks too much, or is overweight. Many heart patients fail to comply with the exercise programs and lifestyle changes. Most cardiac patients who were employed before the illness eventually return to work, often in less demanding jobs. Some people with heart disease need special interventions to enhance adaptation.

A stroke can cause damage to the brain and can occur by cutting off the blood supply or by a hemorrhage. Depending on the amount and location of neurological damage, patients may suffer motor and cognitive deficits, such as in language and perception, and emotional disorders. Some impairments recover with time and rehabilitation, but others are permanent. Stroke patients are very prone to depression.

Although there are many varieties of cancer, most can be classified into five types: carcinomas, melanomas, lymphomas, sarcomas, and leukemias. Untreated neoplasms eventually metastasize and spread to other parts of the body. Medical treatment consists of surgery, radiation, and chemotherapy, each of which has important drawbacks. Chemotherapy, in particular, causes nausea and vomiting that is associated with anticipatory nausea and learned food aversions. Despite the great stress cancer victims experience, most show a remarkable ability to adapt in remission or after a cure. Some, however, become very depressed and withdraw from social contact, but usually benefit from psychosocial interventions. Leukemia is the most common form of cancer in childhood.

Acquired immune deficiency syndrome is caused by HIV infection, which impairs the immune system, leaving the victims subject to opportunistic diseases. Most people with AIDS die within 3 years of that diagnosis if they do not receive effective antiretroviral treatment. Because AIDS is an infectious disease, many people have reacted to its outbreak with alarm and discrimination, making adaptation all the more difficult. Psychosocial intervention can reduce anxiety and depression and enhance immune function.

If and when a chronic condition deteriorates and no cure is likely, the illness is considered terminal. One factor that affects how people adapt to terminal illness is the age of the patient. Young children have little understanding of the meaning of death; by about 8 years of age, children's understanding is fairly complete. Adolescents and young adults react to their impending deaths with very strong feelings of anger and emotional distress. As adults get older, they become less fearful of death. Dying people may react to their conditions with denial, anger, bargaining, depression, and acceptance. The hospice care approach provides physical, psychosocial, and spiritual care for dying patients and their families during the terminal phase and in bereavement.

KEY TERMS

angina pectoris	stroke	acquired immune	hospice care
myocardial infarction	cancer	deficiency syndrome	

15

WHAT'S AHEAD FOR HEALTH PSYCHOLOGY?

Goals for Health Psychology
Enhancing Illness Prevention and Treatment
Improving Efforts for Helping Patients Cope
Documenting the Efficacy and Cost–Benefit Ratio of Care
Enhancing Psychologists' Acceptance in Medical Settings

Careers and Training in Health Psychology
Career Opportunities
Training Programs

Issues and Controversies for the Future
Environment, Health, and Psychology
Quality of Life
Ethical Decisions in Medical Care

Future Focuses in Health Psychology
Life-Span Health and Illness
Sociocultural Factors in Health
Gender Differences and Women's Health Issues

Factors Affecting Health Psychology's Future

PROLOGUE

"Oh, this looks very good," the palm reader said as she studied Marty's hand. She explained: "Your life line is very long, which usually means you will have a long and prosperous life. At first I thought this break here in the line meant you might have a serious health problem in your 50s, but these lines here at your wrist suggest otherwise. You'll have a long and healthy life!" Marty was relieved. He had come to have his fortune told rather than being tested for HIV. He knew that his past behavior put him at risk for HIV infection, but he couldn't bring himself to reveal this to the palm reader. Unreasoned behavior is not uncommon when people are very anxious.

Predicting the future is always a chancy enterprise. Still, because the field of health psychology is at an early stage in its development, many people wonder what the field and its goals will be like in the future. This chapter will try to predict what's ahead for health psychology, and our crystal ball will involve the views of noted researchers and trends that seem clear in recent research. As we consider what the crystal ball suggests, we will try to answer questions you may have about the field's prospects. What role will future health psychologists play in medical care? Will career opportunities and training programs for health psychologists flourish? How will the field's goals, issues, and perspectives change? What factors will affect the success and direction of health psychology in the coming years?

GOALS FOR HEALTH PSYCHOLOGY

Health and health care systems around the world have changed dramatically over the last several decades. People in most parts of the world today are living longer and are more likely to develop chronic illnesses than ever before. Many current health problems result from or are aggravated by people's long-standing habits, such as smoking cigarettes and coping poorly with stress, that medical professionals lack sufficient skills and time to change. The field of health psychology has made enormous advances, generating new knowledge and applying information gained from many disciplines to supplement medical efforts in promoting health. Let's look at some major goals that lie ahead for health psychology.

ENHANCING ILLNESS PREVENTION AND TREATMENT

We have seen that efforts to prevent health problems should try to reduce unhealthful behaviors. These efforts can be directed toward health-protective activity while the person is well, when symptoms appear, or once an illness is identified and treatment starts.

Health-related behaviors that become features of people's lifestyles have received a great deal of attention in health psychology. Because these behaviors affect whether people develop illnesses, efforts have been directed toward preventing unhealthful behaviors from developing and changing behaviors that already exist. Unhealthful lifestyles seem to be harder to change than to prevent (Wright & Friedman, 1991). We have seen that psychologists' efforts to change lifestyle behaviors, such as smoking, exercising, and eating habits, have focused mainly on cognitive and behavioral approaches. Although these approaches are often very effective in producing initial changes, the behaviors frequently revert to unhealthful patterns later. Relapse is a critical problem that researchers are working to reduce, and it will certainly be an important focus for health psychology in the future.

Once people notice symptoms or are diagnosed with serious health conditions, they often—but by no means always—engage in symptom-based and sick-role behaviors to protect their health. For instance, they may go to physicians, take medication, or even follow medical advice that involves changing their lifestyles. Researchers have identified many psychosocial factors that influence whether people will seek health care and adhere to medical regimens. We know, for example, that individuals often decide to reject or delay seeking medical attention because they don't know the symptoms of serious diseases, such as cancer or diabetes. And people are less likely to adhere to medical advice if the regimens involve complex or long-term behavioral changes and if their physicians do not seem caring or explain the illnesses and treatment clearly. Although we know some methods to reduce these problems, these methods often require extra time or effort that medical professionals are just beginning to incorporate into their practices.

Advances in Research and Theory

Health psychologists in the future will continue their search for ways to improve people's health behaviors before illness develops, use of health care services, and disease management after illness develops. New research methods and theories we have discussed in this book will promote these efforts. For example, the method called *ecological momentary assessment* has enabled researchers to examine people's behavior and feelings in daily life. And theories have appeared that attempt to explain why people do or do not change unhealthful behaviors, building on knowledge gained from earlier theories, especially the health belief model. The *stages of change model*, which outlines a series of stages in people's readiness to change health-related behaviors, is an example. This and other theories have generated important research that will contribute to our understanding of ways to promote healthier lifestyles. Research and theory of the future need to expand their focus in at least two ways (Smith, Orleans, & Jenkins, 2004). First, they need to incorporate more levels of factors to represent the biological, psychological, and social systems that work together in affecting health. Second, they need to give more attention to life-span changes in the nature of health threats.

Advances in Technology

Technological advances will play an increasing role in preventing and managing illness (Saab et al., 2004). For example, Internet sites have been developed to provide medical information and two-way video and audio communication to individuals in numerous countries and inaccessible areas. This process, called *telehealth* or *telemedicine*, provides diagnostic and treatment services and advice on lifestyle changes (Celler, Lovell, & Basilakis, 2003). For instance, a parent can use a device to scan a child's injured leg and send the image electronically to the hospital where the child had been treated so they can monitor recovery. Technological advances can also be used to implement interventions to change unhealthful behaviors. For instance, software has been developed and used to help problem drinkers stop or reduce their alcohol intake (Squires & Hester, 2004).

IMPROVING EFFORTS FOR HELPING PATIENTS COPE

Major advances have been made in using psychosocial methods to help people cope with various difficulties in their lives. Stress management programs are being applied widely with nonpatient populations, such as in worksite wellness programs, to help prevent illness.

People with serious medical conditions often must cope with pain, anxiety and fear, and depression. Psychosocial interventions are being applied more and more widely with patients in pain clinics, hospitals, and other medical settings. Years ago, the main function of psychologists in medical settings involved administering and interpreting tests of patients' emotional and cognitive functioning (Wright & Friedman, 1991). But this situation has changed, and psychologists are focusing much more on a broader array of activities, such as training medical students and interns and applying interventions to help patients cope with illnesses and medical treatment. The health psychologists' role is likely to continue to expand in hospitals and outpatient rehabilitation programs for people with chronic health problems, such as heart disease and arthritis (Nicassio, Myerowitz, & Kerns, 2004).

DOCUMENTING THE EFFICACY AND COST–BENEFIT RATIO OF CARE

Should health care organizations and employers provide psychosocial interventions to prevent illness and help patients cope? Perhaps most people would answer, "Yes, because it's the humane thing to do." But with today's spiraling medical costs, the answer is more commonly based on two factors: the intervention's *efficacy*, or degree to which it has the needed

effect, and *cost–benefit*, or the extent to which it saves more money in the long run than it costs (Graham et al., 1998; Kaplan & Groessl, 2002). Bottom-line issues are often weighed heavily in deciding whether to offer wellness or psychosocial programs at work and in medical settings.

Health psychologists recognize the importance of documenting the efficacy of approaches they use, and they do careful research to compare different approaches against each other and control groups. But psychologists seldom calculate the financial costs and benefits of interventions. Often the costs of providing an intervention are easily assessed, but the full benefits are not. At a worksite, for instance, what benefits of a wellness program could you assess in dollars to compare with the costs of running it? You might assess worker absenteeism or medical insurance claims, but these variables would reflect only part of the benefits. They wouldn't reflect other important financial gains, such as increases in workers' job satisfaction and resulting productivity. In medical settings, measuring the benefits of psychosocial interventions can be easier. For example, you could assign dollar values to the reduced time intervention patients spend recovering in the hospital and compare these data against the cost of the program.

Many psychosocial interventions for promoting health and helping patients cope have the potential for producing far more financial benefits than costs. More and more evidence is becoming available to document these effects (Aldana, 2001; Kaplan & Groessl, 2002). We considered research in Chapter 10 showing, for example, that hospital patients who receive help in coping with medical procedures recover more quickly and use less medication than those who don't receive such help. Table 15.1 lists some specific behavioral and health problems, with studies showing that psychosocial-educational interventions produced financial savings that were far greater than their costs. Other research has shown that the benefits of worksite wellness programs outweigh their costs (Golaszewski, 2001). Although most psychosocial methods with documented efficacy have not yet been subjected to cost–benefit analyses, health psychologists in the future will probably give much more attention to these analyses than they have in the past. They will also need to develop more effective methods to help people change unhealthful lifestyles—such as to eat healthful diets and exercising—and demonstrate

Table 15.1. *Studies of Psychosocial-Educational Interventions showing Very Favorable Cost-Benefit Ratios for Reducing Specific Behavioral and Health Problems*

Problem	Population	Studies
Behavior		
Drinking	Men and women, general	Fleming et al., 2000
Drug abuse	Clients in residential treatment	French, Salome, & Carney, 2002
Smoking	Men and women, general	Alterman, Gariti, & Mulvaney, 2001; Curry et al., 1998
Smoking	Pregnant women	Windsor et al., 1993
Health		
Arthritis	Elderly men and women patients	Cronan, Groessl, & Kaplan, 1997
Asthma	Children and adult patients	Liljas & Lahdensuo, 1997
Back pain	Employee patients	Turk, 2002
Heart disease	Men patients	Blumenthal, Babyak et al., 2002

that the benefits of these methods outweigh the costs.

ENHANCING PSYCHOLOGISTS' ACCEPTANCE IN MEDICAL SETTINGS

A woman wrote an article in the late 1980s and described her experience when she developed breast cancer. Her physicians advised her to get treatment from a variety of medical professionals but

> at no point did anyone in the medical fraternity recommend that I see a mental health professional to help me cope with the emotional impact of breast cancer. Perhaps they didn't realize that breast cancer had an emotional impact. But I did. So, I went to see a psychologist, ironically the one specialist not covered by my insurance. It was worth the cash out of pocket. (Kaufman, cited in Cummings, 1991, p. 119)

Although gaining acceptance by the medical profession has progressed steadily since the 1980s, it continues to be a challenge for health psychology (Suls & Rothman, 2004).

Part of the difficulty health psychologists have faced in gaining acceptance in medical settings stems from their past role and training. Before 1970, psychological services were usually seen as tangential to the medical needs of most patients, and psychologists had little or no training in physiological systems, medical illnesses and treatments, and the organization and protocols of hospitals. But these conditions have changed. Today, health psychologists are receiv-

ing the training they need to work effectively in medical settings. And more and more physicians are coming to recognize the importance of psychosocial factors in their patients' health, adherence to treatment regimens, and rehabilitation. Physicians also realize that they do not have the skills or time to address many of these factors.

Initial relations between medical staff and health psychologists still tend to be strained in some settings, particularly when one function of the psychologist may be to teach physicians and interns the "people skills" that are important for interviewing patients and communicating with them effectively. This kind of training may get a mixed reception, especially from some medical staff who feel these skills are not part of medicine (Christensen & Levinson, 1991). Even after medical and psychological staff have collaborated for a long time and seen that a biopsychosocial approach to health care can benefit patients, be intellectually stimulating, and lead to developing new techniques, their different styles and points of view can lead to conflicts (McDaniel & Campbell, 1986). For example, psychologists generally want to talk directly with the attending physician to describe subtle and complex issues relating to a patient's treatment plan, but medical specialists typically communicate with each other in writing, such as with notes in a hospital chart. Differences like these can be resolved. Beginning in 2001 guidelines from the Accreditation Council for Graduate Medical Education have required the training of future physicians to include skills in teamwork and partnering with professionals in nonmedical fields (Daw, 2001).

CLINICAL METHODS AND ISSUES

Psychologists in the Primary Care Team

In the late 1990s, some American managed-care programs, such as HMOs, began to include psychologists as members of the medical care team (D. Bruns, personal communication, September 1, 1998). Why? Program administrators came to realize that psychological factors, such as stress and emotional problems, play a pivotal role in the symptoms most patients present in their health care visits. The psychologists interview these patients and provide help, such as with brief counseling or training in stress and pain management.

What about patients—how do they feel about receiving psychological services? Their view is likely to depend on the way the physician and psychologist introduce these services. If a patient thinks the services are offered because his or her physician thinks he or she is "crazy" or that the problem "is all in your head," the patient is likely to have negative attitudes and will fail to cooperate. People are more likely to view psychosocial interventions positively if the services are introduced as part of a standard "team approach" with a biopsychosocial orientation. (Go to 🙍.)

CAREERS AND TRAINING IN HEALTH PSYCHOLOGY

Most health psychologists follow one of two career categories: working mainly in clinical capacities with patients or working mainly in academic or research capacities (Altman & Cahn, 1987; Sweet, Rozensky, & Tovian, 1991). Many health psychologists have careers that combine these areas, being involved in both clinical and academic or research activities, and some do administrative work, such as in governmental agencies or programs to promote health.

CAREER OPPORTUNITIES

The opportunities for careers in health psychology in the United States have been good, especially in health care settings—hospitals and clinics (DeAngelis, 1995). For example, the number of psychologists working in health care more than doubled from about 20,000 in 1974 to over 45,000 in 1985 (Enright et al., 1990). States have passed laws enabling psycholo-

gists to obtain full staff status in hospitals, giving them the same privileges as physicians. Psychologists have traditionally held lesser status levels, with little influence on hospital policy (Rozensky, 1991). What the job market will be in the future for health psychologists is hard to predict, but career opportunities in a variety of settings will probably continue to grow.

Besides hospitals, where else do health psychologists work? Some of the more prominent sites are:

- Colleges and universities
- Medical schools
- Health maintenance organizations
- Rehabilitation centers
- Pain centers
- Private practice and consultancy offices

Sometimes job descriptions for these settings are broad, making eligible even professionals from nonpsychology fields, such as nursing, public health, or social work. Although this can increase the competition for those jobs, broad job descriptions can increase the number of opportunities for psychologists, too.

TRAINING PROGRAMS

What kind of training is available and necessary in health psychology? Training is offered at three educational levels: *undergraduate* courses in health psychology or behavioral medicine, *graduate* programs, and *postdoctoral* programs. Because health psychologists typically hold doctoral degrees, dozens of graduate programs now exist in the United States and other countries specifically for that training. Postdoctoral programs are available in health psychology or behavioral medicine, particularly for people with doctoral degrees that did not focus on the relationship between health and psychology.

Graduate training programs in health psychology are quite diverse (Belar, 1988, 1991; HP, 2000). Some are highly interdisciplinary programs that are designed solely for this field. They often specialize in training students either for research careers or for direct clinical service to patients. Other programs provide graduate training in traditional psychology areas, such as clinical or social psychology, and contain special tracks or emphases relating to health. Common to all these programs is a solid grounding in psychology, along with training in research methods, biopsychosocial processes in health and disease, and health care terminology and organization. Programs that educate students for direct clinical service to patients generally include medical courses, such as in physiology and pharmacology. The future may see greater standardization of health psychology training programs in the United States and around the world, as some professionals have recommended (Methorst, Jansen, & Kerkhof, 1991).

Information about graduate and postdoctoral training programs in health psychology can be obtained by contacting the following professional organizations:

* American Psychological Association, Division of Health Psychology, 750 First Street N.E., Washington, DC 20002-4242.

  Web Page: http://www.health-psych.org
* Society of Behavioral Medicine, 7600 Terrace Avenue, Suite 203, Middleton, WI 53562.

  Web Page: http://www.sbm.org

The European Health Psychology Society (http://www.ehps.net) does not currently give information about education and training, but the delegates they list may be able to help for their specific countries.

ISSUES AND CONTROVERSIES FOR THE FUTURE

Findings from research and clinical experience will enable health psychologists to help societies resolve important issues and controversies in the future. We will look at several examples, beginning with the impact of environmental conditions on health and psychology.

ENVIRONMENT, HEALTH, AND PSYCHOLOGY

Each of the environments in which people live around the world contains conditions that have the potential to harm or benefit the health and psychological status of its inhabitants. For example, some communities contain barriers to physical activity; others encourage it (Salmon et al., 2003). We also read and hear in the news media that the environment is becoming increasingly polluted with toxic substances, which may be released accidently or deliberately into the air, ground, or bodies of water. The environments in which people live are also becoming more crowded and noisy. What effects do these conditions have? How can we reduce harmful environmental conditions? Some answers use a public health approach: because cigarette smoke pollutes the air and can lead to illnesses in those who breathe it, some psychologists have called for governmental control of tobacco products (Kaplan et al., 1995).

Many toxic environmental pollutants are produced as byproducts either of manufacturing or of generating energy. For instance, some manufacturing industries produce highly toxic cyanide or mercury as byproducts, which have made their ways into the environment. What direct effects on health does long-term exposure to low levels of pollutants have? How stressful is it to live or work in contaminated environments, and how much does this stress affect health? How much does the stress of crowding and noise affect health? Health psychologists can help in efforts to answer these questions and find ways to change behaviors that produce these problems (Weinman, 1990). Although we have some information on these questions, much more research will be needed in the future before we can provide accurate answers.

QUALITY OF LIFE

People's *quality of life* has become a significant issue in medical care because (1) it is reduced by becoming sick and by staying sick and (2) it is an important consideration in prevention efforts before and after an illness occurs. Efforts to maintain people's good health also maintain their quality of life, and efforts to help patients recover quickly and fully lessen the negative impact of the illness on their lives. For people who are ill, their quality of life enters into decisions about the medical and psychological treatment they will receive. Are they in pain? If so, what type of painkilling medication should they get, and how much? If they're distressed, what psychosocial methods are likely to improve their emotional status?

Life-or-death medical decisions are often heavily influenced by appraisals of patients' current and future quality of life. Current quality of life is especially important if there is virtually no hope of the patient's recovery. In such cases, the views of the patient, family, and medical staff are likely to come down to a judgment of whether living in the current state is better than not living at all. Future quality of life is important in medical decisions that can enable the patient to survive, but will leave him or her with seriously impaired physical, psychological, and social capacities. For example, the family of an elderly man with a disabling cardiovascular condition felt he would be better off not living

> if he was just going to be a vegetable. They said his whole life revolved around working in his yard and playing bridge; these were the things in life that gave him joy. Now the doctors were not giving any hope that he would ever get back to what he was before; the best that could be hoped for was that he would be able to sit in a wheelchair. They said they didn't want that for him, and . . . he wouldn't want that for himself either. (Degner & Beaton, 1987, p. 64)

Decisions to withhold heroic medical efforts clearly involve humane concerns, but financial considerations are important, too (Spurgeon et al., 1990). Heroic medical efforts and aftercare are extremely expensive. With the enormous pressures to contain the cost of health care, are these expenses always justified even when the resulting quality of life will be poor?

Making medical and psychological decisions based on a patient's current or future quality of life is difficult, partly because researchers need to determine the best ways to measure it. One approach that some people favor to help make these decisions uses a scale called *quality-adjusted life years* (QALYs, pronounced "KWAL-eez"). To calculate the QALYs for a medical treatment, we would assess how long a person is likely to live after receiving the treatment, multiply each year by its quality of life, and total these data (Bradley, 1993; Kaplan, 1994). Using QALYs, we could rank the value of different treatments for a particular person or in general, perhaps even taking the cost per QALY into

account, and decide whether to provide the treatment. At the heart of this approach is the measurement of quality of life. Although there are dozens of questionnaires to assess quality of life, the qualities they measure vary widely (Gill & Feinstein, 1995; Wilson & Cleary, 1995). Which should we use? Health psychologists will play an important role in resolving how best to use quality of life assessments in making treatment decisions.

ETHICAL DECISIONS IN MEDICAL CARE

Suppose you are an obstetrician delivering a baby when you realize that complications you see developing will surely kill the baby and, maybe, the mother, too. Suppose also that the mother flatly refuses a Caesarean delivery for religious reasons. What do you do? The typical medical response is to seek an immediate court order to override her decision. The decisions made in this case and the quality of life decisions we just considered all involve ethical issues. Many hospitals today have *bioethics committees* to discuss ethical issues in health care, make policy, and recommend action regarding specific cases. The ethical issues these committees consider often involve the patient's right to choose treatments, to withhold or withdraw treatment, or to die (Bouton, 1990). We will examine two other important issues: the role of technology in medical decisions and the role of physicians in helping patients die.

Technology and Medical Decisions

The technological advances we have seen in our lives over the past few decades have been quite remarkable. Many of these advances have been in medical technology, and they have sometimes raised important ethical questions.

One of these technological advances is a computer program that calculates the odds that individual patients will die in intensive care or after they leave it (Seligmann & Sulavik, 1992). Why might this be a problem? Decisions about whether intensive care treatment will help the patient survive are made every day, based on physicians' broad estimates, such as, "Her chances look bleak." With the computer program, physicians can get precise estimates of the person's odds of dying if he or she continues in intensive care, say 42%, versus if he or she is transferred, say 78%. In this example, transferring the patient would greatly increase the odds that he or she would die. The comparison helps in making the decision. The ethical problems relate to how these numbers will be used. Should physicians tell families these numbers? Will physicians and families weigh these data too heavily in their decisions? Will hospitals release these data to insurance companies, which could then decide to limit coverage when scores reach a certain level? Health psychologists can play a role in some of these decisions, especially those relating to families having and using these data (Weinman, 1990).

Other ethical dilemmas arise in deciding whether to provide an organ transplant for patients. Over 25,000 transplants are done each year in the United States (USBC, 2003). Health psychologists help medical practitioners to select candidates who are best able to benefit from the surgery and the scarce organs—people who are able to cope with the stress and behave appropriately to maintain their health with the new organ. To help make these decisions, psychologists screen potential candidates—some patients will be clearly up to the task, and some will not, such as candidates for liver transplant who have not been able to control their drinking. Others will be in between and may benefit from interventions of behavioral contracting and therapy to help them cope better (Olbrisch et al., 2002).

Advances in genetics technology may also present ethical problems. For instance, geneticists can identify individuals who are likely to develop serious diseases, such as cystic fibrosis and some forms of cancer, and may soon be able to identify individuals who are vulnerable to environmental causes of cancer and heart disease (Detjen, 1991; Lerman, Audrain, & Croyle, 1994). Who should be tested for these risks, and who should have access to the results? Insurance companies would like this information, and some are already turning down applicants for insurance on the basis of known family histories of certain diseases.

Assisted Dying: Suicide and Euthanasia

Some people with serious illnesses come to the decision that they want to end their lives. Should physicians help them in their wishes? This is a very controversial issue for society in general and in the medical community. Among physicians, some feel they should not help because of certain beliefs they hold, such as that life is sacred or that medical workers should only save lives and not take them. Other physicians feel they should participate in this act if the patient is actually beyond all help and the decision was not made because of psychological depression that could be reduced (Sears & Stanton, 2001). Depressed people who want to end their lives may change their minds if the depression is relieved (Zisook et al., 1995).

Some physicians have helped patients end their lives in two ways (Meier et al., 1998; Sears & Stanton, 2001). In *assisted suicide*, the patient takes the final act, but the physician knowingly prescribes the needed drugs or describes the methods and doses required. Because of the legal consequences for physicians who help people take their lives, a book called *Final Exit* was published in 1991 describing procedures physicians would recommend. In *euthanasia*, the physician (or someone else) takes the final act, usually by administering a drug that ends the life. Laws permit euthanasia in the Netherlands and physician-assisted suicide in Oregon under carefully specified and monitored circumstances. When societies decide that it is acceptable for physicians to help a patient end his or her life, laws can require psychological assessment of the person's emotional status, ability to make sound decisions, and likelihood of benefiting from psychosocial intervention (Sears & Stanton, 2001). (Go to 🍎.)

FUTURE FOCUSES IN HEALTH PSYCHOLOGY

The research that contributes to our knowledge in health psychology comes from many different fields. But early studies gave a relatively narrow view of the biopsychosocial processes involved in health and illness because of the people researchers tended to recruit as subjects: in studies of Type A behavior, for example, they often were 18- to 60-year-old White American males. Two reasons for this focus are that these people were readily available and some researchers incorrectly believed that the findings would easily generalize to other populations. In the 1980s, studies began to focus on including subjects representing a wider range of people. This trend will surely continue in the future.

ASSESS YOURSELF

Some Ethical Dilemmas: What Do You Think?

Each of the following cases describes a decision involving an ethical dilemma that is related to health. Circle the Y for "yes" or the N for "no" preceding each case to indicate whether you agree with the decision.

Y N A 47-year-old woman developed cirrhosis of the liver as a result of long-term alcoholism. She promised to stop drinking if she could receive a liver transplant. Her request was denied because of likely future drinking.

Y N An overweight, chain-smoking, sedentary 51-year-old man with high blood pressure had his first heart attack 7 years ago. His request for a heart transplant was denied because of continuing risk factors.

Y N A 28-year-old married woman with a hereditary crippling disease that is eventually fatal decided to become pregnant, knowing that there was a 50% chance that she would pass on the disease to her baby and she would not consider having an abortion.

Y N A 37-year-old executive was told by his boss that he would have to pay half of the costs of his employer-provided health insurance if he did not quit smoking and lower his cholesterol.

Y N An obese 20-year-old woman who refused to try to lose weight was expelled from nursing school, despite having good grades and clinical evaluations, because it was said she would "set a poor example for patients."

Y N A 24-year-old man was denied employment as a bank clerk because he was overweight and smoked cigarettes.

Y N A 30-year-old woman was denied a promotion to a job that involved working in an area with gases that could harm an embryo if she were to become pregnant.

Y N A year after a boy developed leukemia, the company that provided his family's health insurance quadrupled their premium.

These dilemmas are all based on real examples from the news media. Because they all involve controversies, there is no key to the "right" answers. But you might want to ask friends or classmates what they think.

LIFE-SPAN HEALTH AND ILLNESS

We have seen that the health problems people have and the extent to which they use health services change with age. Very young and elderly individuals use health services more than others do, and the elderly are much more likely to have chronic health problems than younger people are.

From Conception to Adolescence

Children's prenatal environments have a major effect on their health. Enormous numbers of babies are born each year with illnesses or defects that develop because of prenatal exposure to harmful conditions or chemicals, particularly when mothers use alcohol, drugs, or tobacco during pregnancy. The health problems these babies develop can last for years or for life. Health psychologists study ways to improve babies' prenatal environments, such as by educating and counseling prospective parents (Weinman, 1990). Although these approaches help, we need to find more effective ways to prevent these health problems from developing.

Childhood and adolescence are important periods in the life span because many health beliefs and habits form during these years (Smith, Orleans, & Jenkins, 2004). But very little research has examined how these beliefs and habits develop. We do know that efforts to promote health should be introduced early, before unhealthful beliefs and habits develop. Early childhood is clearly the time to intervene for some behaviors, such as for proper diets, exercise, dental care, and seat belt use. In later childhood, interventions should focus on preventing accidents, cigarette and drug use, and unsafe sex. We saw in Chapter 7, for example, that programs to prevent children from starting to smoke cigarettes have had some success. We have also seen that behaviors that put people at high risk for AIDS can be changed substantially, thereby reducing their risk. Efforts to prevent the spread of HIV need to be intensified and applied worldwide. To design more effective health promotion programs, we will need to focus more research—especially longitudinal studies—on how health behaviors form and change in childhood and adolescence.

Adulthood and Old Age

By the time people reach adulthood, most health-related values and behaviors are ingrained and difficult to change. People's lifestyles during the early adulthood and middle-age years tend to continue and affect whether or when they will develop major chronic illnesses, particularly heart disease and cancer. The earlier people change unhealthful behaviors, the lower their health risks are likely to be. In addition, prolonged emotional difficulties, particularly depression, are linked to future illness, such as heart disease. Among elderly people with similar physical health, those who are depressed show sharper physical declines, such as in walking speed, over the next few years than nondepressed elders do (Penninx et al., 1998).

People in most areas of the world are living longer, and the proportion of elderly individuals is increasing. As the world population ages, the proportion of individuals with disabling or life-threatening illnesses will surely grow, thereby requiring more health services and psychosocial interventions. In the United States, for example, an unusually high birth rate after World War II created a very large generation of people called "Baby Boomers," who are starting to swell the ranks of the elderly. How will health care systems around the world respond to the added loads? This potential makes it even more crucial that we find ways to prevent or change risky lifestyles, particularly with regard to diet, exercise, and substance use. We will also need to improve ways to help families cope with the difficulties of caring for elderly relatives. The number of studies dealing with health issues in old age published each year has increased since 1980 and will continue to be a major focus of health psychologists in the future.

SOCIOCULTURAL FACTORS IN HEALTH

Sociocultural differences in the United States and around the world are related to health and health behavior. For instance, Americans from the lower social classes and from Black and Hispanic minority groups tend to have poorer health and health habits than Whites and those from higher classes. These differences have been clear for a long time. Although researchers have begun to investigate why these differences exist and what can be done to reduce them, our knowledge on these issues is not very specific. For example, we don't know how cultural customs and socioeconomic factors shape the everyday lives of different ethnic groups (Anderson & Armstead, 1995; Yali & Revenson, 2004). And so we tend to make broad conclusions, as when we say people in a minority group "live in environments that do not encourage the practice of health-protective behavior." Health psychology must give greater emphasis to sociocultural issues so that we can provide specific and useful solutions in the future.

Cross-cultural research also needs more emphasis. We have spotty information about cultural differences in lifestyles, perceiving symptoms of illness, and using health services, but most research on these differences is old and very incomplete. Although some books and journal articles address ethnic differences within countries, especially the United States, few examine differences across countries (Kazarian & Evans, 2001). In the poorer nations of the world, where infectious diseases and malnutrition are often rampant, one in ten children under the age of 5 die each year (WHO, 1999). The number of people infected with HIV in Africa and other developing areas of the world is astounding and growing rapidly. The countries with the most urgent need to change behavioral risk factors have not yet recognized that principles of health psychology can help promote public health. In addition, health psychologists need to conduct research to determine how to adapt the principles that work in the United States and other industrialized countries to the needs of other cultures.

GENDER DIFFERENCES AND WOMEN'S HEALTH ISSUES

Health issues relating to women and gender differences were also neglected in health psychology research until the 1980s (Matthews et al., 1997). Since that time, studies have examined women's health behaviors, such as diet, smoking, and exercise, and issues that are specific to women, such as screening for cervical and breast cancer (Rimer, McBride, & Crump, 2001). Research has also studied differences between males and females in a wide variety of characteristics, such as reactions to stress, Type A and B behavior patterns, risk of AIDS and of heart disease, weight regulation, and tobacco and alcohol use. Gender-related research has become a main focus of health psychology today and for the future. This research is making clearer the uniqueness of women and men in their health and health-protective behaviors and the special interventions they are likely to need to promote their health.

FACTORS AFFECTING HEALTH PSYCHOLOGY'S FUTURE

The picture of health psychology's future that we have considered is based on trends and needs, which can change in the future. The prospects for our discipline will depend on forces and events in society, medical fields, and psychology. What factors are likely to affect the role and direction of health psychology in the future?

Some factors can have a broad impact on health psychology, affecting the amount and type of research, clinical intervention, and health promotion activities that we do. One of these factors is monetary (Tovian, 2004): How much financial support will there be for these activities? During hard economic times, cutbacks in governmental and private funding may reduce this support. But there is another side to this coin—health care costs around the world are increasing, and many health experts believe that two of the best ways to decrease these costs involve improving people's health behaviors and helping those individuals who become ill to recover quickly. Research findings have enabled health psychologists to help reduce costs in both of these ways. Funding will also depend on how health insurance and services are structured. Health care systems are changing rapidly in many countries. The changes that emerge will

probably continue or strengthen support for psychosocial interventions with favorable research evidence regarding their cost–benefit ratios.

Another factor that can have a broad impact on health psychology's future is education and training in this discipline (Weinman, 1990). Undergraduate courses in health psychology can reach students from various nonpsychology fields, such as nursing, premed, and sociology. Students who have a positive view of the role and success of health psychology are likely to promote its research, application, and interdisciplinary contacts in the future. If these students go into medical fields, they are likely to be receptive to learning about psychosocial methods by which they and health psychologists can promote the health of their patients. These circumstances can enhance acceptance of health psychologists in medical settings.

Developments in medicine will also influence the future of health psychology (Weinman, 1990). New and growing health problems generally require psychosocial interventions to reduce people's risk factors for these illnesses and help patients and their families cope. This can be seen clearly in the role of health psychology in addressing these kinds of issues in AIDS and Alzheimer's disease, for instance. Health psychologists often have an important role to play when new medical treatments are found, particularly if these treatments are unpleasant or if they may impair the patient's quality of life.

As you can see, many factors can affect the future of health psychology. The field has made dramatic and rapid advances in its short history, but we still have much to learn. Although we sometimes head in the wrong direction, we can take heart and humor from the following perspective:

> Life is a test,
> It is only a test.
> If this were your actual life,
> You would have been given better instructions!
> (Anonymous, cited in Pattishall, 1989, p. 47)

SUMMARY

Major changes have occurred in health and health care systems around the world in the past several decades. People are living longer today and are more likely to develop chronic illnesses that result from or are aggra-

vated by their long-standing health habits. Health psychology has made major advances in helping to prevent or change these behaviors. The field has also developed effective psychosocial methods to help patients and their families cope with chronic illnesses. For many of the interventions health psychologists use, research has demonstrated favorable cost–benefit ratios. These successes have helped to promote the acceptance of health psychologists in medical settings.

Career opportunities for health psychologists have expanded rapidly, and the employment outlook for the future continues to look good. The availability of training in health psychology has grown at the undergraduate, graduate, and postgraduate levels. This training is solidly based in psychology and includes a substantial amount of information on biopsychosocial processes in health and illness and on medical terminology and procedures.

Health psychology has begun to address important health issues and controversies that societies will need to resolve in the future. These issues and controversies include the impact of environmental factors on people's health and psychological status, patients' quality of life, and ethical decisions in medical care. Some ethical questions relate to the use of technological advances in health care and whether physicians should participate in helping hopelessly ill patients end their lives. Health psychology has also begun to focus its attention on life-span, sociocultural, and gender issues in health. Forces and events in society, medicine, and psychology will affect the future role and direction of health psychology.

GLOSSARY

abstinence-violation effect A cognitive process whereby a relapse occurs when people feel guilt and reduced self-efficacy if they experience a lapse in efforts to change their behavior.

acquired immune deficiency syndrome (AIDS) An infectious disease that disables the immune system. Individuals with AIDS are susceptible to a variety of life-threatening diseases.

acupuncture A pain-control technique in which fine metal needles are inserted under the skin at certain locations and then activated.

acute pain The discomfort patients experience with temporary medical conditions, lasting less than about 6 months.

adaptation The changes people undergo in making positive adjustments to circumstances in their lives.

addiction The condition of physical and psychological dependence on using a substance.

adherence The degree to which patients follow the medical recommendations of practitioners. Also called *compliance*.

adoption studies Research with subjects adopted at very early ages, comparing their characteristics with corresponding traits of their adoptive and natural parents to assess the influence of heredity.

adrenal glands Endocrine glands that secrete several hormones, such as cortisol, epinephrine, and norepinephrine, that are involved in stress reactions.

aerobic exercise (air-OH-bik) Sustained and energetic physical activity in which the body uses high volumes of oxygen over many minutes.

alarm reaction The first stage in the general adaptation syndrome when the body's resources are mobilized.

alcoholics People who drink alcohol heavily and are addicted to it.

Alzheimer's disease A chronic and progressive brain disorder marked by a loss of cognitive functions, such as memory.

angina pectoris (an-JEYE-nah, or AN-ji-nah, PEK-to-ris) A condition marked by chest pain that generally results from a brief or incomplete blockage of the blood supply to heart tissue.

anorexia nervosa (an-or-EX-ee-ah ner-VOE-sah) An eating disorder marked by self-starvation and an extreme and unhealthy loss of weight.

antibodies Protein molecules created to protect against specific antigens in body fluids.

antibody-mediated immunity The immune process that employs antibodies to attack antigens while they are still in body fluids and before they have invaded the cells.

antigen Any substance that can trigger the immune system to respond.

arteriosclerosis (ar-TEER-ee-o-skleh-ROE-sis) A condition in which fatty patches have accumulated to and hardened on artery walls, thereby reducing the elasticity of these walls.

arthritis A category of painful and potentially disabling chronic conditions that involve inflammation of the joints.

asthma A psychophysiological disorder of the respiratory system in which bronchial inflammation and spasms lead to episodes of difficult breathing.

atherosclerosis (ATH-eh-roe-skleh-ROE-sis) The condition in which fatty patches (plaques) form on artery walls.

autonomic nervous system A division of the peripheral nervous system that carries messages between the central nervous system and the internal organs. It has two parts: the sympathetic and parasympathetic nervous systems.

aversion strategies Methods that use unpleasant stimuli to discourage undesirable behaviors.

B cells Lymphocytes that lead to the formation of antibodies.

behavioral control A form of personal control involving the ability to reduce the impact of a stressor by taking concrete action.

behavioral medicine An interdisciplinary field introduced in the early 1970s to study the relationships between behavior and health.

behavioral methods Psychological techniques that use mainly operant and classical conditioning principles to change behavior.

binge drinking Consuming five or more alcoholic drinks in a single drinking session, such as during a party.

binge eating An episode of consuming much more food than most people would in a short period of time.

biofeedback A process by which individuals can acquire voluntary control over a physiological function by monitoring its status.

biomedical model The view that illness results from physical causes, such as infection or injury; psychosocial processes are not viewed as causal factors.

biopsychosocial model The view that health and illness involve the interplay of biological, psychological, and social factors in people's lives.

blood pressure The force of the blood against the inner walls of the arteries.

body mass index (BMI) A calculated measure of the ratio of weight to height; people with a BMI of 30 or more are considered obese.

brainstem The lowest portion of the brain, located at the top of the spinal cord, consisting of the midbrain, reticular system, pons, and medulla.

buffering hypothesis The view that the health benefits of social support come from its reducing the negative health effects of high stress levels.

bulimia nervosa (buh-LIM-ee-ah ner-VOE-sah) An eating disorder marked by repeated binge eating, usually followed by purging.

burnout An emotional and behavioral impairment resulting from exposure to high levels of occupational stress.

cancer A class of malignant diseases in which cells proliferate in an unrestricted manner, usually forming a tumor.

carbon monoxide A gas that is a constituent of cigarette smoke.

cardiovascular system A network of organs that circulates blood to supply oxygen and nutrients to the body's cells and removes wastes and other substances.

catecholamines (kat-eh-KOL-a-meenz) A class of hormones, including epinephrine and norepinephrine, secreted by the adrenal glands.

cell-mediated immunity The immune process that operates at the cellular level, using T cells to attack infected cells.

central nervous system That part of the nervous system consisting of the brain and spinal cord.

cerebellum (ser-uh-BEL-um) A large portion of the brain that coordinates motor activities and maintains body balance.

cerebrum (ser-EE-brum) The upper and largest portion of the human brain. It has primary control over motor and mental activity.

chronic diseases Illnesses that persist and generally get worse over a long period of time.

chronic-intractable-benign pain Long-term continuous, but variable, discomfort stemming from benign causes.

chronic-progressive pain Long-term continuous discomfort that worsens as the underlying malignant condition progresses.

chronic-recurrent pain Long-term repeated and intense episodes of discomfort stemming from benign causes.

classical conditioning A learning process in which a stimulus gains the ability to elicit a particular response by its repeated pairing with an unconditioned stimulus that already elicits that response.

clinical pain Any pain symptoms that receive or require professional treatment.

cognitive appraisal The mental process people use in assessing whether a demand is threatening and what resources are available to meet the demand.

cognitive control A form of personal control involving the ability to reduce the impact of a stressor by using thought processes.

cognitive methods Psychological techniques that focus on changing people's feelings and thought processes.

cognitive restructuring A therapeutic process for replacing thoughts that provoke stress with ones that do not.

cognitive therapy A cognitive restructuring approach that has clients test hypotheses about maladaptive beliefs they hold about events in their lives.

cohort effect The influence of different subjects having been born and raised in different eras.

commonsense models Cognitive representations people develop regarding specific illnesses.

complementary and alternative medicine Methods not included in conventional medicine to prevent or treat illnesses: they are complementary if used along with conventional methods and alternative if used instead of them.

compliance See *adherence*.

conflict theory An explanation of health-related behavior that includes both rational and emotional factors.

coping The process by which people try to manage the stress they experience.

coronary heart disease (CHD) A class of illnesses that result when a narrowing or blockage of the coronary arteries restricts the blood supply to the heart muscle (myocardium).

correlation coefficient A statistic that reflects the degree and direction of relationship between two variables; it can range from $+1.00$ through $.00$ to -1.00.

correlational studies Nonexperimental research conducted to determine the degree and direction of relationship between variables.

corticosteroids (cor-ti-koe-STEH-royds) A class of hormones, including cortisol, secreted by the adrenal glands.

counter-irritation A technique whereby one pain is reduced by creating another one.

crisis theory A model describing the factors that affect people's adjustment to having serious illnesses. The theory proposes that coping processes are influenced by three types of factors: illness-related, background and personal, and physical and social environmental.

cross-sectional approach   Method of studying developmental trends by observing different groups of subjects of different ages within a relatively short period of time.

cue exposure   A method to counteract the ability of stimuli linked to substance use to elicit use.

daily hassles   Everyday annoyances or unpleasant events.

depersonalization   A behavioral style of some practitioners that involves treating a patient as if he or she were not there or not a person.

depressants   Drugs that induce relaxation and sleep.

detoxification   The process of getting an addicted individual safely through withdrawal after discontinuing the use of a substance.

digestive system   The network of organs that processes ingested food by breaking it down for the body's use and excreting the remains.

direct effects hypothesis   The view that the health benefits of social support accrue regardless of whether people experience high or low levels of stress.

distraction   A pain management technique in which people divert their focus to nonpain stimuli in the environment.

doctor-centered   The behavioral style of some physicians in which interactions with patients are highly controlled by the practitioner and focus on the symptoms or treatment rather than the person.

double-blind   An experimental procedure whereby neither the subject nor the researcher knows which research treatment the subject is receiving.

emetic drug   (eh-MEH-tik) A chemical that induces nausea when a person drinks alcohol.

emotion-focused coping   Approaches people use for managing stress that are aimed at regulating their emotional responses.

endocrine system   An array of glands that secrete hormones into the bloodstream.

endogenous opioids   (en-DAH-je-nus OH-pee-oydz) Opiatelike substances the body produces naturally that reduce the sensation of pain.

enzymes   (EN-zymz) Substances that increase the speed of chemical reactions in cells.

epidemic   The situation in which the occurrence of a health problem has increased rapidly.

epilepsy   A chronic condition of the nervous system that produces recurrent seizures.

experiment   A controlled study in which variables are manipulated and observed to assess cause-effect relationships.

extinction   In operant conditioning, a process by which a previously reinforced behavior no longer receives reinforcement, making it less likely to occur in the future.

false hopes   Nonrational beliefs that positive outcomes of a behavior change are likely.

gate-control theory   An explanation of pain perception that proposes that a neural gate in the spinal cord can modulate incoming pain signals. The opening and closing of the gate is influenced by messages that descend from the brain and by the amount of activity in pain fibers and in other peripheral fibers.

general adaptation syndrome (GAS)   The sequence of physiological reactions to prolonged and intense stress. The sequence consists of the alarm reaction, the stage of resistance, and the stage of exhaustion.

glycemic load   (gleye-SEE-mik) A measure of the speed and intensity of carbohydrate conversion to sugar in the blood.

hallucinogens   (ha-LOO-sin-a-jins) Drugs that can produce perceptual and cognitive distortions.

hardiness   An array of personality characteristics that enables individuals to withstand stress and not succumb to its negative health effects.

health   A positive state of physical, mental, and social well-being that changes in degree over time.

health behavior   Any behavior people perform with the intention of promoting or maintaining well-being regardless of the state of their health.

health belief model   An explanation of people's health-related behavior based on their perception of the threat of illness or injury and the pros and cons of taking action.

health psychology   A field of psychology introduced in the late 1970s to examine the causes of illnesses and to study ways to promote and maintain health, prevent and treat illness, and improve the health care system.

high-density lipoprotein (HDL)   A cholesterol-carrying protein that is associated with decreased cholesterol deposits in blood vessels.

hormones   Chemical substances secreted by endocrine glands that affect body functions and behavior.

hospice care   A philosophy and procedure for enriching the quality of life of terminally ill patients and their families.

hypertension   The condition of persistent high blood pressure.

hypochondriasis   (hy-poe-kon-DRY-uhsis) The tendency of some individuals to be excessively concerned and vigilant regarding their health and body sensations.

hypothalamus A part of the forebrain that contains control centers for many body functions, such as eating, drinking, and sexual activity.

iatrogenic conditions (eye-a-tro-JEN-ik) Health problems that develop as a result of medical treatment.

illness/wellness continuum A model that describes health and sickness as overlapping concepts that vary in degree rather than being separate categories.

immune system The organs and structures that protect the body against harmful substances or agents, such as bacteria and viruses.

incidence The number of *new* cases reported during a given period of time, such as the previous year.

infectious diseases Illnesses caused by the body being invaded by microorganisms, such as bacteria or viruses.

inflammatory bowel disease A psychophysiological disorder involving wounds in the large or small intestine.

insulin A hormone secreted by the pancreas that speeds the conversion of blood sugar to fat.

irritable bowel syndrome A digestive system disease with symptoms of pain, diarrhea, and constipation but no evidence of organic disorder.

isokinetic exercise (eye-so-kin-EH-tic) A type of activity that involves exerting muscle force in more than one direction while moving an object.

isometric exercise (eye-so-MET-rik) A type of activity that involves exerting muscle force against an object that does not move.

isotonic exercise (eye-so-TAH-nik) A type of activity that involves exerting most of the muscle force in one direction.

Lamaze training An educational and procedural program for natural childbirth that involves preparation, participation, and minimal medication.

lay referral system An informal network of individuals who provide advice or information regarding a person's symptoms and health.

learned helplessness A condition of apathy or inactivity that results from repeated experiences with unavoidable stress.

life events Major occurrences in people's lives that require some degree of psychological adjustment.

limbic system A set of structures in the forebrain that seems to play a role in emotional expression.

lipids (LIH-pidz) Fatty materials, such as the cholesterol found in blood.

lipoproteins (LIP-oh-pro-teenz or LY-po-pro-teenz) Proteins that transport cholesterol in the blood.

locus of control A generalized belief people have about the causes of events in their lives—whether the causes are within or outside their control.

longitudinal approach Method of studying developmental changes in the same subjects by making repeated observations over a long period of time.

low-density lipoprotein (LDL) A cholesterol-carrying protein that is associated with increased cholesterol deposits in blood vessels.

lymphocytes (LIM-foe-sites) Various types of white blood cells that have several important functions in the body's immune response.

McGill Pain Questionnaire (MPQ) A self-report instrument for assessing people's pain.

meta-analysis A statistical technique that combines the results from earlier studies to generate an overview of those findings.

metabolism The chemical reactions of the body's cells that synthesize new cell material, regulate body processes, and create energy.

migraine headache Recurrent head pain that results from the constriction and dilation of blood vessels in the head.

Millon Behavioral Medicine Diagnostic (MBMD) A test that assesses several relevant characteristics of medical patients, such as their basic coping styles and hypochondriacal tendencies.

mind/body problem The issue in psychology and philosophy regarding the relationship between processes and functions of the mind and those of the body.

Minnesota Multiphasic Personality Inventory (MMPI) A lengthy test that assesses a variety of psychological problems, such as hypochondriasis, depression, and hysteria.

modeling Learning by watching the behavior of other people.

morbidity The condition of illness, injury, or disability.

mortality Death, usually with reference to large populations.

motivated reasoning Cognitive process whereby people's desires or preferences influence their decisions about the validity and utility of new information.

motivational interviewing A client-centered counseling style of leading a person to recognizing the need to change a behavior and to become committed to the change.

myocardial infarction (my-oh-KAR-dee-al in-FARK-shun) Damage to the heart muscle (myocardium) that results from severe or prolonged blockage of blood supply to the tissue. Commonly called a *heart attack*.

narcotics Drugs that relieve pain, act as sedatives, and may produce euphoria. These substances are also called *opiates* and usually lead to addiction with continued use.

negative reinforcement A process in which reducing or stopping an undesired stimulus as a consequence of making a behavior strengthens that behavior.

neurotransmitter A chemical involved in the transmission of impulses across the synapse from one neuron to another.

nicotine A chemical in cigarette smoke that appears to produce physical dependence.

nicotine regulation model An explanation of continued cigarette smoking based on the body's dependence on nicotine.

nociceptors (noe-see-SEP-torz) Afferent nerve endings that respond to pain stimuli in the damaged region of the body.

nonpain imagery A pain management method that involves picturing a mental scene that is unrelated to or incompatible with feeling discomfort.

nosocomial infection (noe-soe-KOE-mee-al) An infection a patient acquires while in the hospital.

obese The weight classification of individuals whose *body mass index* exceeds a value of 30 as a result of excess fat (formerly based on weight more than 20% over the desirable range).

overweight The weight classification of individuals whose *body mass index* exceeds a value of 25 as a result of excess fat (formerly based on weight 10–20% over the desirable range).

pain Sensory and emotional discomfort, usually related to actual or threatened tissue damage.

pain behaviors Characteristic ways people behave when they are in pain.

pain clinics Centers specializing in the treatment of chronic pain.

pain redefinition A pain management technique in which thoughts about pain that arouse a sense of threat are replaced with other thoughts that are more constructive or realistic.

parasympathetic nervous system A division of the autonomic nervous system that helps the body conserve energy and restore the normal body state after arousal.

passive smoking Breathing the smoke in the environment from someone else's cigarette or other smoking product.

patient-centered The behavioral style of some physicians in which their interactions encourage patients to share information and participate in medical decisions.

periaqueductal gray (per-ee-ak-weh-DUK-tal) A region of the midbrain that plays a major role in the perception of and reaction to pain stimuli.

peripheral nervous system The network of nerve fibers that carry messages between the central nervous system and the skin, skeletal muscles, and internal organs. This network has two parts: the somatic and autonomic nervous systems.

personal control The feeling people have that they can make decisions and take action to produce favorable events and avoid unfavorable ones.

personality Cognitive, affective, or behavioral predispositions of people in different situations and over time.

phagocytes (FAG-oh-sites) Certain types of white blood cells that engulf and ingest any kind of invading particles.

physical dependence A state in which the body has become accustomed to the presence of a substance in its physiological functioning.

pituitary gland An endocrine gland that has connections to the brain and secretes hormones that stimulate other endocrine glands to secrete.

placebo An inactive substance or procedure that may cause a change in an individual's behavior or health.

polygraph An electromechanical device that assesses the body's arousal by measuring and recording several physiological indexes, such as blood pressure and respiration rate, simultaneously.

positive reinforcement A process in which adding or introducing a consequence for a behavior strengthens that behavior.

prevalence The total number of cases existing at a given moment in time.

primary appraisal The cognitive process people use in assessing the meaning of an event or situation for their well-being.

primary prevention Actions undertaken to avoid health problems before they occur.

problem drinkers People who are psychologically dependent on alcohol and drink heavily.

problem-focused coping Approaches people use for managing stress aimed at reducing the discrepancy between their resources and the demands of the situation.

progressive muscle relaxation A stress reduction technique in which people are trained to alternate between tightening and relaxing specific muscle groups.

prospective approach A research strategy whereby characteristics of subjects are measured and later examined for their relationships to future conditions, such as health problems.

psychological dependence A state in which a person feels compelled to use a substance for the pleasant effect it produces.

psychoneuroimmunology (psy-ko-noo-roe-ih-myu-NOL-oh-jee) A field of study focusing on relationships between psychosocial processes and nervous, endocrine, and immune system functioning.

psychophysiological disorders Physical symptoms or illnesses resulting from some combination of psychosocial and physiological processes.

Psychosocial Adjustment to Illness Scale (PAIS) A test of several psychosocial aspects of a patient's life that are related to adjustment to medical illness.

psychosomatic medicine A field introduced in the 1930s to study the relationships between people's symptoms of illness and their emotions.

punishment A process by which a consequence of an operant behavior suppresses that response.

quality of life Individuals' appraisals of the degree to which their lives contain features that they find satisfying or meaningful.

quasi-experimental studies Nonexperimental research in which subjects are categorized or separated into two or more groups on the basis of existing characteristics and then compared regarding other variables.

rational nonadherence Noncompliance with medical regimens for valid, but not necessarily medically beneficial, reasons.

reactance People's angry responses to restrictions on their freedom of action or choice.

reactivity The physiological component of the response to stress.

referred pain The experience of discomfort as coming from an area of the body other than where the injury exists.

reinforcement A process whereby a consequence of an operant response strengthens or maintains that behavior.

relapse Regressing to the full-blown pattern of an unwanted behavior after beginning to change it.

relapse prevention method A self-management program to help maintain improved behavior by teaching the person how to identify and deal effectively with situations that tend to lead to relapses.

respiratory system A network of organs that supply oxygen for metabolism and expel carbon dioxide.

retrospective approach A research strategy whereby the histories of subjects are examined for their relationships to recent conditions, such as health problems.

risk factors Characteristics or conditions that occur more often among individuals who develop particular diseases or injuries than among those who do not.

secondary appraisal The cognitive process people use in assessing the resources they have to meet demands.

secondary prevention Actions undertaken to identify or treat a health problem early with the aim of arresting or reversing the condition.

self-efficacy People's belief that they can succeed at something they want to do.

self-management Methods used in helping people gain control over the conditions in their environment that encourage undesirable behaviors.

separation distress Emotional upset often shown by infants and young children when separated from their primary caretakers, typically their parents.

set-point theory An explanation of weight regulation that proposes that each person has a "set" physiologically based weight level that the body strives to maintain.

social support The perceived comfort, caring, esteem, or help an individual receives from other people or groups.

sociocultural Relating to or involving social and cultural features or processes.

somatic nervous system A division of the peripheral nervous system that transmits sensory and motor impulses.

spinal cord The major neural pathway that carries impulses between the brain and the peripheral nervous system.

spinal cord injury Neurological damage in the spine that impairs motor and sensory function.

stage of exhaustion The third stage in the general adaptation syndrome, when the body's energy reserves are severely depleted.

stage of resistance The second stage in the general adaptation syndrome, when the body tries to adapt to the stressor.

stages of change model A theory of intentional behavior that describes people's readiness to change with five potential stages: precontemplation, contemplation, preparation, action, and maintenance.

stimulants Drugs that activate the nervous system, producing physiological and psychological arousal.

stimulation-produced analgesia (SPA) A phenomenon whereby stimulation to the brainstem causes insensitivity to pain.

strain The psychological and physiological response to a stressor.

stress The condition that results when person–environment transactions lead the individual to perceive a discrepancy between the demands of a situation and his or her resources.

stress-inoculation training A cognitive–behavioral approach for stress management that teaches people a variety of skills for alleviating stress and achieving personal goals.

stressors Events or circumstances a person perceives as threatening or harmful.

stroke A condition involving brain damage that results from a disruption in the blood supply to that area of the brain.

substance abuse The prolonged overuse of a substance, involving a clear pattern of pathological use and heightened social and occupational problems.

sudden cardiac death The abrupt death from cardiac dysfunction of a person who seemed healthy.

sympathetic nervous system A division of the autonomic nervous system that enables the body to mobilize and expend energy during physical and emotional arousal.

system A continuously changing entity that consists of constantly interrelated components.

systematic desensitization A classical conditioning technique for reducing fear or anxiety by replacing it with a calm response.

tars Tiny particles in cigarette smoke.

T cells A class of lymphocytes; some attack antigens directly, and some work to regulate other immune functions.

temperaments Basic personality characteristics or dispositions that individuals show right from birth, allowing many of them to be classified broadly as "easy" or "difficult."

tension-type headache Recurrent head pain that results from persistent muscle tension in the head and neck. Also called *muscle-contraction* headache.

tertiary prevention Actions undertaken to contain or slow the progress of damage from a serious or established health problem.

thalamus A structure in the forebrain that serves as a relay station for sensory impulses to and commands from the cerebrum.

theory A tentative explanation of phenomena.

theory of planned behavior An explanation of people's health-related behavior. Their behavior depends on their intention, which is based on their attitudes regarding the behavior and beliefs about the subjective norm and behavioral control.

time management Methods for managing stress that involve organizing one's time.

tolerance A gradual decrease in the body's response to a drug, thereby requiring larger and larger doses to achieve the same effect.

transactions The continuous interplay and adjustments of the person and environment.

transcutaneous electrical nerve stimulation (TENS) (tranz-kyu-TAIN-ee-us) A counter-irritation pain control technique that involves electrically stimulating an area near where the patient feels pain.

treatment delay The elapsed time between noticing a symptom and getting medical care.

twin studies Research to assess the influence of heredity in determining a characteristic by focusing on differences between identical and fraternal twins.

type 1 diabetes The health problem of having chronically elevated blood sugar levels because the pancreas produces little or no insulin. People with type 1 diabetes typically require daily insulin supplements. Formerly called *insulin-dependent diabetes mellitus* (IDDM).

type 2 diabetes The health problem of having chronically elevated blood sugar levels even though the pancreas does produce at least some insulin. Most people with type 2 diabetes can manage their conditions without insulin supplements. Formerly called *non-insulin-dependent diabetes mellitus* (NIDDM).

Type A behavior pattern A behavioral or emotional style characterized by high levels of competitiveness, time urgency, and anger or hostility.

Type B behavior pattern A behavioral or emotional style characterized by low levels of competitiveness, time urgency, and anger or hostility.

ulcers A psychophysiological disorder involving wounds to the stomach or upper section of the small intestine.

variable A measurable characteristic of people, objects, or events that may change in quantity or quality.

willingness A factor that affects health-related behavior: the more disposed or open people are toward engaging in a specific unplanned risky behavior, the more likely they are to do so when the opportunity arises.

withdrawal Physical and psychological symptoms that occur when people stop taking a substance on which the body has become physically dependent.

REFERENCES*

AAFA (Asthma and Allergy Foundation of America) (2004). *Asthma.* Retrieved (5–12–2004) from http://www.aafa.org.

AARON, J., ZAGLUL, H., & EMERY, R. E. (1999). Posttraumatic stress disorder in children following acute physical injury. *Journal of Pediatric Psychology, 24,* 335–343.

ABRAHM, J. L. (2003). Update in palliative medicine and end-of-life care. *Annual Review of Medicine, 54,* 53–72.

ABRAMS, K. K., ALLEN, L., GRAY, J. J. (1993). Disordered eating attitudes and behaviors, psychological adjustment, and ethnic identity: A comparison of black and white female college students. *International Journal of Eating Disorders, 14,* 49–57.

ABRAMSON, L. Y., SELIGMAN, M. E. P., & TEASDALE, J. D. (1978). Learned helplessness in humans: Critique and reformulation. *Journal of Abnormal Psychology, 87,* 49–74.

ACEVEDO, H. F., TONG, J. Y., & HARTSOCK, R. J. (1995). Human chorionic gonadotropin-beta subunit gene expression in cultured human fetal cells of different types and origins. *Cancer, 76,* 1467–1475.

ACHTERBERG-LAWLIS, J. (1988). Musculoskeletal disorders. In E. A. Blechman & K. D. Brownell (Eds.), *Handbook of behavioral medicine for women* (pp. 222–235). New York: Pergamon.

ACS (American Cancer Society) (1989). *Cancer facts and figures—1989.* Atlanta: Author.

ACS (American Cancer Society) (2004). *Cancer facts and figures—2004.* Retrieved (5–11–2004) from http://www.cancer.org.

ADA (American Diabetes Association) (2000). *Diabetes Info* (Type 1 diabetes; Type 2 diabetes; Diabetes facts and figures). Retrieved (3–24–2000) from http://www.diabetes.org.

ADA (American Diabetes Association) (2004). *All about diabetes* (Type 1 diabetes; Type 2 diabetes; National diabetes fact sheet). Retrieved (5–18–2004) from http://www.diabetes.org.

ADAMS, A., OCKENE, J. K., WHEELER, E. V., & HURLEY, T. G. (1998). Alcohol counseling: Physicians will do it. *Journal of General Internal Medicine, 13,* 692–698.

ADAMS, J. E., & LINDEMANN, E. (1974). Coping with long-term disability. In G. V. Coelho, D. A. Hamburg, & J. E. Adams (Eds.), *Coping and adaptation* (pp. 127–138). New York: Basic Books.

ADEAR (Alzheimer's Disease Education and Referral Center) (2004). *About AD.* Retrieved (5–25–2004) from http://www.alzheimers.org.

ADER, R. (1997). The role of conditioning in pharmacotherapy. In A. Harrington (Ed.), *The placebo effect* (pp. 138–165). Cambridge, MA: Harvard University Press.

ADER, R., & COHEN, N. (1975). Behaviorally conditioned immunosuppression. *Psychosomatic Medicine, 37,* 333–340.

ADER, R., & COHEN, N. (1985). CNS-immune system interactions: Conditioning phenomena. *Behavioral and Brain Sciences, 8,* 379–395.

ADESSO, V. J. (1985). Cognitive factors in alcohol and drug use. In M. Galizio & S. A. Maisto (Eds.), *Determinants of substance abuse: Biological, psychological, and environmental factors* (pp. 179–208). New York: Plenum.

ADLER, N. E., BOYCE, T., CHESNEY, M. A., COHEN, S., FOLKMAN, S., KAHN, R. L., et al. (1994). Socioeconomic status and health: The challenge of the gradient. *American Psychologist, 49,* 15–24.

ADLER, N. E., & STONE, G. C. (1979). Social science perspectives on the health system. In G. C. Stone, F. Cohen, & N. E. Adler (Eds.), *Health psychology—A handbook* (pp. 19–46). San Francisco: Jossey-Bass.

AF (Arthritis Foundation) (2004). *Disease center: Facts about arthritis, rheumatoid arthritis, osteoarthritis, fibromyalgia, and gout.* Retrieved (5–25–2004) from http://www.arthritis.org.

AFFLECK, G., TENNEN, H., PFEIFFER, C., & FIFIELD, J. (1987). Appraisals of control and predictability in adapting to a chronic disease. *Journal of Personality and Social Psychology, 53,* 273–279.

AFFLECK, G., TENNEN, H., URROWS, S., & HIGGINS, P. (1991). Individual differences in the day-to-day experience of chronic pain: A prospective daily study of rheumatoid arthritis patients. *Health Psychology, 10,* 419–426.

AFFLECK, G., TENNEN, H., URROWS, S., HIGGINS, P., ABELES, M., HALL, C., et al. (1998). Fibromyalgia and women's pursuit of personal goals: A daily process analysis. *Health Psychology, 17,* 40–47.

AGOSTI, J. M., SPRENGER, J. D., LUM, L. G., WITHERSPOON, R. P., FISHER, L. D., STORB, R., et al. (1988). Transfer of allergen-specific IgE-mediated hypersensitivity with allogenic bone marrow transplantation. *New England Journal of Medicine, 319,* 1623–1628.

---

*Authorship for references with more than six authors is cited with the format: first six authors et al.

AGRAS, W. S. (1984). The behavioral treatment of somatic disorders. In W. D. Gentry (Ed.), *Handbook of behavioral medicine* (pp. 479–530). New York: Guilford.

AHA (American Heart Association) (1995). *Heart and stroke facts: 1996 statistical supplement.* Dallas, TX: Author.

AHA (American Heart Association) (2004). *Heart and stroke encyclopedia.* Retrieved (8–12–2004) from http://www.americanheart.org.

AIKEN, L. H. (1983). Nurses. In D. Mechanic (Ed.), *Handbook of health, health care, and the health professions* (pp. 407–431). New York: Free Press.

AIKEN, L. S., GEREND, M. A., & JACKSON, K. M. (2001). Subjective risk and health protective behavior: Cancer screening and cancer prevention. In A. Baum, T. A. Revenson, & J. E. Singer (Eds.), *Handbook of health psychology* (pp. 727–746). Mahwah, NJ: Erlbaum.

AIKENS, K. S., AIKENS, J. E., WALLANDER, J. L., & HUNT, S. (1997). Daily activity level buffers stress-glycemia associations in older sedentary NIDDM patients. *Journal of Behavioral Medicine, 20,* 379–390.

AINSWORTH, M. D. S. (1973). The development of infant-mother attachment. In B. M. Caldwell & H. N. Ricciutl (Eds.), *Review of child development research* (Vol. 3, pp. 1–94). Chicago: University of Chicago Press.

AINSWORTH, M. D. S. (1979). Infant-mother attachment. *American Psychologist, 34,* 932–937.

AJZEN, I. (1985). From intentions to actions: A theory of planned behavior. In J. Kuhl & J. Beckman (Eds.), *Action control: From cognition to behavior* (pp. 11–39). New York: Springer Verlag.

AJZEN, I., & FISHBEIN, M. (1980). *Understanding attitudes and predicting social behavior.* Englewood Cliffs, NJ: Prentice-Hall.

AKIL, H., MAYER, D. J., & LIEBESKIND, J. C. (1976). Antagonism of stimulation-produced analgesia by naloxone, a narcotic antagonist. *Science, 191,* 961–962.

AKINBAMI, L. J., & SCHOENDORF, K. C. (2002). Trends in childhood asthma: Prevalence, health care utilization, and mortality. *Pediatrics, 110,* 315–322.

ALA (American Lung Association) (2003). *Fact sheets: Asthma in adults, asthma & children, and chronic obstructive pulmonary disease* (COPD). Retrieved (5–11–2004) from http://www.lungusa.org.

AL'ABSI, M., WITTMERS, L. E., ELLESTAD, D., NORDEHN, G., KIM, S. W., KIRSCHBAUM, C., et al. (2004). Sex differences in pain and hypothalamic-pituitary-adrenocortical responses to opioid blockade. *Psychosomatic Medicine, 66,* 198–206.

ALARANTA, H., RYTÖKOSKI, U., RISSANEN, A., TALO, S., RÖNNEMAA, T., PUUKKA, P., et al. (1994). Intensive physical and psychosocial training program for patients with chronic low back pain: A controlled clinical trial. *Spine, 19,* 1339–1349.

ALBARRACÍN, D., MCNATT, P. S., KLEIN, C. T. F., HO, R. M., MITCHELL, A. L., & KUMKALE, G. T. (2003). Persuasive communications to change actions: An analysis of behavioral and cognitive impact in HIV prevention. *Health Psychology, 22,* 166–177.

ALBERT, C. M., MITTLEMAN, M. A., CHAE, C. U., LEE, I.-M., HENNEKENS, C. H., & MANSON, J. E. (2004). Triggering of sudden death from cardiac causes by vigorous exertion. *New England Journal of Medicine, 343,* 1355–1361.

ALDANA, S. G. (2001). Financial impact of health promotion programs: A comprehensive review of the literature. *American Journal of Health Promotion, 15,* 296–320.

ALDERMAN, M. H. (1984). Worksite treatment of hypertension. In J. D. Matarazzo, S. M. Weiss, J. A. Herd, N. E. Miller, & S. M. Weiss (Eds.), *Behavioral health: A handbook of health enhancement and disease prevention* (pp. 862–869). New York: Wiley.

ALDWIN, C. M., & BRUSTROM, J. (1997). Theories of coping with chronic stress: Illustrations from the health psychology and aging literatures. In B. H. Gottlieb (Ed.), *Coping with chronic stress* (pp. 75–103). New York: Plenum.

ALEXANDER, F. (1950). *Psychosomatic medicine: Its principles and applications.* New York: Norton.

ALLAN, R., & SCHEIDT, S. (1990). Life style: Its effect and modification for the prevention of sudden cardiac death. In J. B. Kostis & M. Sanders (Eds.), *The prevention of sudden cardiac death* (pp. 261–294). New York: Wiley.

ALLEN, K., BLASCOVICH, J., MENDES, W. B. (2002). Cardiovascular reactivity and the presence of pets, friends, and spouses: The truth about cats and dogs. *Psychosomatic Medicine, 64,* 727–739.

ALLEN, L., & ZIGLER, E. (1986). Psychosocial adjustment of seriously ill children. *Journal of the American Academy of Child Psychiatry, 25,* 708–712.

ALPERT, B., FIELD, T., GOLDSTEIN, S., & PERRY, S. (1990). Aerobics enhances cardiovascular fitness and agility in preschoolers. *Health Psychology, 9,* 48–56.

ALTERMAN, A. I., GARITI, P., & MULVANEY, F. (2001). Short- and long-term smoking cessation for three levels of intensity of behavioral treatment. *Psychology of Addictive Behaviors, 15,* 261–264.

ALTMAN, D. G., & CAHN, J. (1987). Employment options for health psychologists. In G. C. Stone, S. M. Weiss, J. D. Matarazzo, N. E. Miller, J. Rodin, C. D. Belar, M. J. Follick, & J. E. Singer (Eds.), *Health psychology: A discipline and a profession* (pp. 231–244). Chicago: University of Chicago Press.

ALTMAN, D. G., WHEELIS, A. Y., McFARLANE, M., LEE, H., & FORTMANN, S. P. (1999). The relationship between tobacco access and use among adolescents: A four community study. *Social Science & Medicine*, 48, 759–775.

AMA (American Medical Association) (2003). *American Medical Association complete medical encyclopedia*. New York: Random House.

AMERICAN PSYCHIATRIC ASSOCIATION (1994). *Diagnostic and statistical manual of mental disorders* (4th ed.). Washington, DC: Author.

AMES, B. N., & GOLD, L. S. (1990). Too many rodent carcinogens: Mitogenesis increases mutogenesis. *Science*, 249, 970–971.

AMOS, C. I., HUNTER, S. M., ZINKGRAF, S. A., MINER, M. H., & BERENSON, G. S. (1987). Characterization of a comprehensive Type A measure for children in a biracial community: The Bogalusa Heart Study. *Journal of Behavioral Medicine*, 10, 425–439.

ANASTASI, A. (1982). *Psychological testing* (5th ed.). New York: Macmillan.

ANDERSEN, B. L., FARRAR, W. B., GOLDEN-KREUTZ, D., KUTZ, L. A., MACCALLUM, R., COURTNEY, M. E., et al. (1998). Stress and immune responses after surgical treatment for regional breast cancer. *Journal of the American Cancer Institute*, 90, 30–36.

ANDERSEN, B. L., GOLDEN-KREUTZ, D. M., & DILILLO, V. (2001). Cancer. In A. Baum, T. A. Revenson, & J. E. Singer (Eds.), *Handbook of health psychology* (pp. 709–725). Mahwah, NJ: Erlbaum.

ANDERSEN, B. L., WOODS, X. A., & COPELAND, L. J. (1997). Sexual self-schema and sexual morbidity among gynecological cancer survivors. *Journal of Consulting and Clinical Psychology*, 65, 221–229.

ANDERSEN, R. E., CRESPO, C. J., BARTLETT, S. J., CHESKIN, L. J., & PRATT, M. (1998). Relationship of physical activity and television watching with body weight and level of fatness among children: Results from the Third National Health and Nutrition Survey. *Journal of the American Medical Association*, 279, 938–942.

ANDERSEN, R. E., WADDEN, T. A., BARTLETT, S. J., ZEMEL, B., VERDE, T. J., & FRANCKOWIAK, S. C. (1999). Effects of lifestyle activity vs structured aerobic exercise in obese women: A randomized trial. *Journal of the American Medical Association*, 281, 335–340.

ANDERSON, B. J., AUSLANDER, W. F., JUNG, K. C., MILLER, J. P., & SANTIAGO, J. V. (1990). Assessing family sharing of diabetes responsibilities. *Journal of Pediatric Psychology*, 15, 477–492.

ANDERSON, E. A. (1987). Preoperative preparation for cardiac surgery facilitates recovery, reduces psychological distress, and reduces the incidence of acute postoperative hypertension. *Journal of Consulting and Clinical Psychology*, 55, 513–520.

ANDERSON, K. O., BRADLEY, L. A., YOUNG, L. D., McDANIEL, L. K., & WISE, C. M. (1985). Rheumatoid arthritis: Review of psychological factors related to etiology, effects, and treatment. *Psychological Bulletin*, 98, 358–387.

ANDERSON, K. O., & MASUR, F. T. (1983). Psychological preparation for invasive medical and dental procedures. *Journal of Behavioral Medicine*, 6, 1–40.

ANDERSON, L. A., JANES, G. R., & JENKINS, C. (1998). Implementing preventive services: To what extent can we change provider performance in ambulatory care? A review of the screening, immunization, and counseling literature. *Annals of Behavioral Medicine*, 20, 161–167.

ANDERSON, N. B., & ARMSTEAD, C. A. (1995). Toward understanding the association of socioeconomic status and health: A new challenge for the biopsychosocial approach. *Psychosomatic Medicine*, 57, 213–225.

ANDERSON, O. W., & GEVITZ, N. (1983). The general hospital: A social and historical perspective. In D. Mechanic (Ed.), *Handbook of health, health care, and the health professions* (pp. 305–317). New York: Free Press.

ANDERSSON, G. B. J., LUCENTE, T., DAVIS, A. M., KAPPLER, R. E., LIPTON, J. A., & LEURGANS, S. (1999). A comparison of osteopathic spinal manipulation with standard care for patients with low back pain. *New England Journal of Medicine*, 341, 1426–1431.

ANDRASIK, F. (1986). Relaxation and biofeedback for chronic headaches. In A. D. Holzman & D. C. Turk (Eds.), *Pain management: A handbook of psychological treatment approaches* (pp. 213–239). New York: Pergamon.

ANDRASIK, F., BLAKE, D. D., & McCARRAN, M. S. (1986). A biobehavioral analysis of pediatric headache. In N. A. Krasnegor, J. D. Arasteh, & M. F. Cataldo (Eds.), *Child health behavior: A behavioral pediatrics perspective* (pp. 394–434). New York: Wiley.

ANDREW, J. M. (1970). Recovery from surgery with and without preparatory instruction for three coping styles. *Journal of Personality and Social Psychology*, 15, 223–226.

ANDRYKOWSKI, M. A. (1990). The role of anxiety in the development of anticipatory nausea in cancer chemotherapy: A review and synthesis. *Psychosomatic Medicine*, 52, 458–475.

ANTONI, M. H. (1987). Neuroendocrine influences in psychoimmunology and neoplasia: A review. *Psychology and Health*, 1, 3–24.

ANTONI, M. H., BAGGETT, L., IRONSON, G., LaPERRIERE, A., AUGUST, S., KLIMAS, N., et al. (1991). Cognitive-behavioral stress management intervention buffers distress responses and immunologic changes following notification of HIV-1 seropositivity. *Journal of Consulting and Clinical Psychology, 59,* 906–915.

ANTONI, M. H., CRUESS, D. G., CRUESS, S., LUTGENDORF, S., KUMAR, M., IRONSON, G., et al. (2000). Cognitive-behavioral stress management intervention effects on anxiety, 24-hr urinary norepinephrine output, and T-cytotoxic/suppressor cells over time among symptomatic HIV-infected gay men. *Journal of Consulting and Clinical Psychology, 68,* 31–45.

ANTONI, M. H., LEHMAN, J. M., KILBOURN, K. M., BOYERS, A. E., CULVER, J. L., ALFERI, S. M. et al. (2001). Cognitive–behavioral stress management intervention decreases the prevalence of depression and enhances benefit finding among women under treatment for early-stage breast cancer. *Health Psychology, 20,* 20–32.

ANTONI, M. H., SCHNEIDERMAN, N., FLETCHER, M. A., GOLDSTEIN, D. A., IRONSON, G., & LAPERRIERE, A. (1990). Psychoneuroimmunology and HIV-1. *Journal of Consulting and Clinical Psychology, 58,* 38–49.

ANTONOVSKY, A. (1979). *Health, stress, and coping.* San Francisco: Jossey-Bass.

ANTONOVSKY, A. (1987). *Unraveling the mystery of health: How people manage stress and stay well.* San Francisco: Jossey-Bass.

ANTONOVSKY, A., & HARTMAN, H. (1974). Delay in the detection of cancer: A review of the literature. *Health Education Monographs, 2,* 98–128.

ANTONUCCI, T. C. (1985). Personal characteristics, social support, and social behavior. In R. H. Binstock & E. Shanas (Eds.), *Handbook of aging and the social sciences* (2nd ed., pp. 94–128). New York: Van Nostrand-Reinhold.

ANTONUCCIO, D. O., & LICHTENSTEIN, E. (1980). Peer modeling influences on smoking behavior of heavy and light smokers. *Addictive Behaviors, 5,* 299–306.

APA (American Psychological Association: Practice Directorate) (1998). *Practicing psychology in hospitals and other health care facilities.* Washington, DC: Author.

ARMSTRONG, C. A., SALLIS, J. F., HOVELL, M. F., & HOFSTETTER, C. R. (1992, March). *Predicting exercise adoption: A stages of change analysis.* Paper presented at the meeting of the Society of Behavioral Medicine, New York.

ARROLL, B., & BEAGLEHOLE, R. (1992). Does physical activity lower blood pressure: A critical review of the clinical trials. *Journal of Clinical Epidemiology, 45,* 439–447.

ARY, D. V., & BIGLAN, A. (1988). Longitudinal changes in adolescent cigarette smoking behavior: Onset and cessation. *Journal of Behavioral Medicine, 11,* 361–382.

ASHBURN, S. S. (1986). Biophysical development of the toddler and the preschooler. In C. S. Schuster & S. S. Ashburn (Eds.), *The process of human development: A holistic life-span approach* (2nd ed., pp. 195–214). Boston: Little, Brown.

ASHLEY, M. J., & RANKIN, J. G. (1988). A public health approach to the prevention of alcohol-related health problems. *Annual Review of Public Health, 9,* 233–271.

ASHTON, C. M., SOUCHEK, J., PETERSON, N. J., MENKE, T. J., COLLINS, T. C., KIZER, K. W. et al. (2003). Hospital use and survival among Veterans Affairs beneficiaries. *New England Journal of Medicine, 349,* 1637–1646.

ASHTON, H., & STEPNEY, R. (1982). *Smoking: Psychology and pharmacology.* London: Tavistock.

ASKEVOLD, F. (1975). Measuring body image. *Psychotherapy and Psychosomatics, 26,* 71–77.

ASTIN, J. A. (1998). Why patients use alternative medicine: Results of a national study. *Journal of the American Medical Association, 279,* 1548–1553.

ATTANASIO, V., ANDRASIK, F., BURKE, E. J., BLAKE, D. D., KABELA, E., & MCCARRAN, M. S. (1985). Clinical issues in utilizing biofeedback with children. *Clinical Biofeedback and Health, 8,* 134–141.

ATTIE, I., & BROOKS-GUNN, J. (1987). Weight concerns as chronic stressors in women. In R. C. Barnett, L. Biener, & G. K. Baruch (Eds.), *Gender and stress* (pp. 218–254). New York: Free Press.

AUDRAIN, J., RIMER, B., CELLA, D., STEFANEK, M., GARBER, J., PENNANEN, M., et al. (1999). The impact of a brief coping skills intervention on adherence to breast self-examination among first-degree relatives of newly diagnosed breast cancer patients. *Psycho-Oncology, 8,* 220–229.

AUERBACH, S. M. (2000). Should patients have control over their own health care?: Empirical evidence and research issues. *Annals of Behavioral Medicine, 22,* 246–259.

AUERBACH, S. M., MARTELLI, M. F., & MERCURI, L. G. (1983). Anxiety, information, interpersonal impacts, and adjustment to a stressful health care situation. *Journal of Personality and Social Psychology, 44,* 1284–1296.

AZAR, B. (1994, November). Eating fat: Why does the brain say, "Ahhh"? *American Psychological Association Monitor,* p. 20.

BABYAK, M., BLUMENTHAL, J. A., HERMAN, S., KHATRI, P., DORAISWAMY, M., MOORE, et al. (2000). Exercise treatment for major depression: Maintenance of therapeutic benefit at 10 months. *Psychosomatic Medicine, 62,* 633–638.

BAER, P. E., GARMEZY, L. B., MCLAUGHLIN, R. J., POKORNY, A. D., & WERNICK, M. J. (1987). Stress, coping, family conflict, and adolescent alcohol use. *Journal of Behavioral Medicine, 10,* 449–466.

BAGOZZI, R. P. (1981). Attitudes, intentions, and behavior: A test of some key hypotheses. *Journal of Personality and Social Psychology, 41,* 606–627.

BAINES, D. R. (1992). Issues in cultural sensitivity: Examples from the Indian peoples. In D. M. Becker, D. R. Hill, J. S. Jackson, D. M. Levine, F. A. Stillman, & S. M. Weiss (Eds.), *Health behavior research in minority populations: Access, design, and implementation* (pp. 230–232). Bethesda, MD: National Heart, Lung, and Blood Institute.

BAKAL, D. A. (1979). *Psychology and medicine: Psychological dimensions of health and illness.* New York: Springer.

BAKER, R. (1989, January 29). The cholesterol thing. *New York Times,* p. A31.

BAKER, T. B., BRANDON, T. H., & CHASSIN, L. (2004). Motivational influences on cigarette smoking. *Annual Review of Psychology, 55,* 463–491.

BAKER, T. B., PIPER, M. E., McCARTHY, D. E., MAJESKIE, M. R., & FIORE, M. C. (2004). Addiction motivation reformulated: An affective processing model of negative reinforcement. *Psychological Review, 111,* 33–51.

BALL, J. F. (1976–1977). Widow's grief: The impact of age and mode of health. *Omega, 7,* 307–333.

BANDURA, A. (1969). *Principles of behavior modification.* New York: Holt, Rinehart & Winston.

BANDURA, A. (1986). *Social foundations of thought and action: A social cognitive theory.* Englewood Cliffs, NJ: Prentice-Hall.

BANDURA, A. (2004). Self-efficacy. In W. E. Craighead & C. B. Nemeroff (Eds.), *The concise Corsini encyclopedia of psychology and behavioral science* (3rd ed., pp. 860–862). Hoboken, NJ: Wiley.

BANDURA, A., REESE, L., & ADAMS, N. E. (1982). Microanalysis of action and fear arousal as a function of differential levels of perceived self-efficacy. *Journal of Personality and Social Psychology, 43,* 5–21.

BANDURA, A., TAYLOR, C. B., WILLIAMS, S. L., MEFFORD, I. N., & BARCHAS, J. D. (1985). Catecholamine secretion as a function of perceived coping self-efficacy. *Journal of Consulting and Clinical Psychology, 53,* 406–414.

BANKS, S. M., SALOVEY, P., GREENER, S., ROTHMAN, A. J., MOYER, A., BEAUVAIS, J. et al. (1995). The effects of message framing on mammography utilization. *Health Psychology, 14,* 178–184.

BARANOWSKI, T., & HEARN, M. D. (1997). Health behavior interventions with families. In D. S. Gochman (Ed.), *Handbook of health behavior research IV: Relevance for professionals and issues for the future* (pp. 303–323). New York: Plenum.

BARANOWSKI, T., & NADER, P. R. (1985). Family health behavior. In D. C. Turk & R. D. Kerns (Eds.), *Health, illness, and families: A life-span perspective* (pp. 51–80). New York: Wiley.

BARBER, J. (1986). Hypnotic analgesia. In A. D. Holzman & D. C. Turk (Eds.), *Pain management: A handbook of psychological treatment approaches* (pp. 151–167). New York: Pergamon.

BARBER, T. X. (1982). Hypnosuggestive procedures in the treatment of clinical pain: Implications for theories of hypnosis and suggestive therapy. In T. Millon, C. J. Green, & R. B. Meagher (Eds.), *Handbook of clinical health psychology* (pp. 521–560). New York: Plenum.

BARDO, M. T., & RISNER, M. E. (1985). Biochemical substrates of drug abuse. In M. Galizio & S. A. Maisto (Eds.), *Determinants of substance abuse: Biological, psychological, and environmental factors* (pp. 65–99). New York: Plenum.

BAREFOOT, J. C., DAHLSTROM, W. G., & WILLIAMS, R. B. (1983). Hostility, CHD incidence and total mortality: A 25-year follow-up study of 255 physicians. *Psychosomatic Medicine, 45,* 559–563.

BARNES, V. A., TREIBER, F. A., & JOHNSON, M. H. (2004). Impact of transcendental meditation on ambulatory blood pressure in African-American adolescents. *American Journal of Hypertension, 17,* 366–369.

BARNES, V. A., TREIBER, F. A., TURNER, R., DAVIS, H., & STRONG, W. B. (1999). Acute effects of transcendental meditation[1] on hemodynamic functioning in middle-aged adults. *Psychosomatic Medicine, 61,* 525–531.

BARRETT, R. J. (1985). Behavioral approaches to individual differences in substance abuse. In M. Galizio & S. A. Maisto (Eds.), *Determinants of substance abuse: Biological, psychological, and environmental factors* (pp. 125–175). New York: Plenum.

BARSKY, A. J., & AHERN, D. K. (2004). Cognitive behavior therapy for hypochondriasis: A randomized controlled trial. *Journal of the American Medical Association, 291,* 1464–1470.

BARSKY, A. J., & KLERMAN, G. L. (1983). Overview: Hypochondriasis, bodily complaints, and somatic styles. *American Journal of Psychiatry, 140,* 273–283.

BARSKY, A. J., SAINTFORT, R., ROGERS, M. P., & BORUS, J. F. (2002). Nonspecific medication side effects and the nocebo phenomenon. *Journal of the American Medical Association, 287,* 622–627.

BARTON, J., CHASSIN, L., PRESSON, C. C., & SHERMAN, S. J. (1982). Social image factors as motivators of smoking initiation in early and middle adolescence. *Child Development, 53,* 1499–1511.

BASTONE, E. C., & KERNS, R. D. (1995). Effects of self-efficacy and perceived social support on recovery-related behaviors after coronary artery bypass graft surgery. *Annals of Behavioral Medicine, 17,* 324–330.

BAUM, A. (1988, April). Disasters, natural & otherwise. *Psychology Today,* pp. 56–60.

BAUM, A. (1990). Stress, intrusive imagery, and chronic distress. *Health Psychology, 9,* 653–675.

BAUM, A., AIELLO, J. R., & CALESNICK, L. E. (1978). Crowding and personal control: Social density and the development of learned helplessness. *Journal of Personality and Social Psychology, 36,* 1000–1011.

BAUM, A., GRUNBERG, N. E., & SINGER, J. E. (1982). The use of physiological and neuroendocrinological measurements in the study of stress. *Health Psychology, 1,* 217–236.

BAUMANN, L. J., & LEVENTHAL, H. (1985). "I can tell when my blood pressure is up, can't I?" *Health Psychology, 4,* 203–218.

BEAN-BAYOG, M. (1991). Alcoholics anonymous. In D. A. Ciraulo & R. I. Shader (Eds.), *Clinical manual of chemical dependence* (pp. 359–375). Washington, DC: American Psychiatric Press.

BECK, A. T. (1976). *Cognitive therapy and the emotional disorders.* New York: International Universities Press.

BECK, A. T., FREEMAN, A., & ASSOCIATES. (1990). *Cognitive therapy of personality disorders.* New York: Guilford.

BECK, R., & FERNANDEZ, E. (1998). Cognitive-behavioral therapy in the treatment of anger: A meta-analysis. *Cognitive Therapy and Research, 22,* 63–74.

BECKER, M. H. (1979). Understanding patient compliance: The contributions of attitudes and other psychosocial factors. In S. J. Cohen (Ed.), *New directions in patient compliance* (pp. 1–31). Lexington, MA: Heath.

BECKER, M. H., & ROSENSTOCK, I. M. (1984). Compliance with medical advice. In A. Steptoe & A. Mathews (Eds.), *Health care and human behaviour* (pp. 175–208). London: Academic Press.

BEECHER, H. K. (1956). Relationship of significance of wound to pain experienced. *Journal of the American Medical Association, 161,* 1609–1613.

BEGLIN, S. J., & FAIRBURN, C. G. (1992). Women who choose not to participate in surveys on eating disorders. *International Journal of Eating Disorders, 12,* 113–116.

BEKKERS, M. J. T. M., van KNIPPENBERG, F. C. E., van den BORNE, H. W., POEN, H., BERGSMA, J., & vanBERGE-HENEGOUWEN, G. P. (1995). Psychosocial adaptation to stoma surgery: A review. *Journal of Behavioral Medicine, 18,* 1–31.

BELAR, C. D. (1988). Education in behavioral medicine: Perspectives from psychology. *Annals of Behavioral Medicine, 10,* 11–14.

BELAR, C. D. (1991). Issues in training clinical health psychologists. In M. A. Jansen & J. Weinman (Eds.), *The international development of health psychology* (pp. 91–97). Chur, Switzerland: Harwood.

BELAR, C. D. (1997). Clinical health psychology: A specialty for the 21st century. *Health Psychology, 16,* 411–416.

BELLOC, N. B., & BRESLOW, L. (1972). Relationship of physical health status and health practices. *Preventive Medicine, 1,* 409–421.

BELLUCK, P. (1996, May 9). Mingling two worlds of medicine. *New York Times,* pp. B1, 4.

BENEDETTI, F., POLLO, A., LOPIANO, L., LANOTTE, M., VIGHETTI, S., & RAINERO, I. (2003). Conscious expectation and unconscious conditioning in analgesic, motor, and hormonal placebo/nocebo responses. *Journal of Neuroscience, 23,* 4315–4323.

BENGSTON, V. L., CUELLAR, J. B., & RAGAN, P. K. (1977). Stratum contrasts and similarities in attitudes toward death. *Journal of Gerontology, 32,* 76–88.

BENIGHT, C. C., ANTONI, M. H., KILBOURN, K., IRONSON, G., KUMAR, M. A., FLETCHER, M. A., et al. (1997). Coping self-efficacy buffers psychological and physiological disturbances in HIV-infected men following a natural disaster. *Health Psychology, 16,* 248–255.

BENNETT, H. L. (1989, Fall/Winter). Report of the First International Symposium on Memory and Awareness in Anaesthesia. *Health Psychologist,* pp. 3–4.

BENNETT, W. I. (1987, December 13). Monitoring drugs for the aged. *New York Times Magazine,* pp. 73–74.

BENOLIEL, J. Q. (1977). Nurses and the human experience of dying. In H. Feifel (Ed.), *New meanings of death* (pp. 123–142). New York: McGraw-Hill.

BENSON, H. (1984). The relaxation response and stress. In J. D. Matarazzo, S. M. Weiss, J. A. Herd, N. E. Miller, & S. M. Weiss (Eds.), *Behavioral health: A handbook of health enhancement and disease prevention* (pp. 326–337). New York: Wiley.

BENSON, H. (1991). Mind/body interactions including Tibetan studies. In The *Dalai Lama,* H. Benson, R. A. F. Thurman, H. E. Gardner, & D. Goleman (Eds.), *Mindscience: An East-West dialogue* (pp. 37–48). Boston: Wisdom.

BENSON, H., MALHOTRA, M. S., GOLDMAN, R. F., JACOBS, G. D., & HOPKINS, P. J. (1990). Three case reports of the metabolic and electroencephalographic changes during advanced Buddhist meditation techniques. *Behavioral Medicine, 16,* 90–94.

BENSOUSSAN, A., TALLEY, N. J., HING, M., MENZIES, R., GUO, A., & NGU, M. (1998). Treatment of irritable bowel syndrome with Chinese herbal medicine: A randomized controlled trial. *Journal of the American Medical Association, 280,* 1585–1589.

BENTLER, P. M., & SPECKART, G. (1979). Models of attitude-behavior relations. *Psychological Review, 86,* 452–464.

BERGMAN, L. R., & MAGNUSSON, D. (1986). Type A behavior: A longitudinal study from childhood to adulthood. *Psychosomatic Medicine, 48,* 134–142.

BERKMAN, L. F. (1995). The role of social relations in health promotion. *Psychosomatic Medicine, 57,* 245–254.

BERKMAN, L. F., & SYME, S. L. (1979). Social networks, host resistance, and mortality: A nine-year follow-up study of Alameda County residents. *American Journal of Epidemiology, 109,* 186–204.

BEZKOR, M. F., & LEE, M. H. M. (1999). Alternative medicine and its relationship to rehabilitation. In M. G. Eisenberg, R. L. Glueckauf, & H. H. Zaretsky (Eds.), *Medical aspects of disability: A handbook for the rehabilitation professional* (2nd ed., pp. 587–597). New York: Springer.

BIENER, L., GLANZ, K., MCLERRAN, D., SORENSEN, G., THOMPSON, B., BASEN-EENGQUIST, K., et al. (1999). Impact of the Working Well Trial on the worksite smoking and nutrition environment. *Health Education and Behavior, 26,* 478–494.

BIERUT, L. J., RICE, J. P., GOATE, A., HINRICHS, A. L., SACCONE, N. L., FOROUD, T., et al. (2004). A genomic scan for habitual smoking in families of alcoholics: Common and specific genetic factors in substance dependence. *American Journal of Medical Genetics, 124A,* 19–27.

BIGLAN, A., MCCONNELL, S., SEVERSON, H. H., BAVRY, J., & ARY, D. (1984). A situational analysis of adolescent smoking. *Journal of Behavioral Medicine, 7,* 109–114.

BIGLAN, A., SEVERSON, H., ARY, D., FALLER, C., GALLISON, C., THOMPSON, R., et al. (1987). Do smoking prevention programs really work? Attrition and the internal and external validity of an evaluation of a refusal skills training program. *Journal of Behavioral Medicine, 10,* 159–171.

BILLINGS, A. G., & MOOS, R. H. (1981). The role of coping responses and social resources in attenuating the stress of life events. *Journal of Behavioral Medicine, 4,* 139–157.

BISHOP, G. D., & CONVERSE, S. A. (1986). Illness representations: A prototype approach. *Health Psychology, 5,* 95–114.

BLACK, F. L. (1992). Why did they die? *Science, 258,* 1739–1740.

BLACKHALL, L. J., MURPHY, S. T., FRANK, G., MICHEL, V., & AZEN, S. (1995). Ethnicity and attitudes toward patient autonomy. *Journal of the American Medical Association, 274,* 820–825.

BLAIR, S. N., & BRODNEY, S. (1999). Effects of physical inactivity and obesity on morbidity and mortality: Current evidence and research issues. *Medicine and Science in Sports and Exercise, 31*(Suppl.), S646–S662.

BLAIR, S. N., KOHL, H. W., GORDON, N. F., & PAFFEN-BARGER, R. S. (1992). How much physical activity is good for health? *Annual review of public health, 13,* 99–126.

BLAKEY, R., & BAKER, R. (1980). An exposure approach to alcohol abuse. *Behaviour Research and Therapy, 18,* 319–325.

BLANCHARD, E. B. (1987). Long-term effects of behavioral treatment of chronic headache. *Behavior Therapy, 18,* 375–385.

BLANCHARD, E. B. (2001). *Irritable bowel syndrome: Psychosocial assessment and treatment.* Washington, DC: American Psychological Association.

BLANCHARD, E. B., & ANDRASIK, F. (1985). *Management of chronic headaches: A psychological approach.* New York: Pergamon.

BLANCHARD, E. B., ANDRASIK, F., APPELBAUM, K. A., EVANS, D. D., MYERS, P., & BARRON, K. D. (1986). Three studies of the psychologic changes in chronic headache patients associated with biofeedback and relaxation therapies. *Psychosomatic Medicine, 48,* 73–83.

BLANCHARD, E. B., ANDRASIK, F., GUARNIERI, P., NEFF, D. F., & RODICHOK, L. D. (1987). Two-, three-, and four-year follow-up on the self-regulatory treatment of chronic headache. *Journal of Consulting and Clinical Psychology, 55,* 257–259.

BLANCHARD, E. B., APPELBAUM, K. A., GUARNIERI, P., MORRILL, B., & DENTINGER, M. P. (1987). Five year prospective follow-up on the treatment of chronic headache with biofeedback and/or relaxation. *Headache, 27,* 580–583.

BLAND, S. H., O'LEARY, E. S., FARINARO, E., JOSSA, F., KROGH, V., VIOLANTI, J. M., et al. (1997). Social network disturbances and psychological distress following earthquake evacuations. *Journal of Nervous and Mental Disease, 185,* 188–194.

BLAND, S. H., O'LEARY, E. S., FARINARO, E., JOSSA, F., & TREVISAN, M. (1996). Long-term psychological effects of natural disasters. *Psychosomatic Medicine, 58,* 18–24.

BLANTON, H., & GERRARD, M. (1997). Effect of sexual motivation on men's risk perception for sexually transmitted disease: There must be 50 ways to justify a lover. *Health Psychology, 16,* 374–379.

BLEIBERG, J. (1986). Psychological and neuropsychological factors in stroke management. In P. E. Kaplan & L. J. Cerullo (Eds.), *Stroke rehabilitation* (pp. 197–232). Boston: Butterworth.

BLEIBERG, J., CIULLA, R., & KATZ, B. I. (1991). Psychological components of rehabilitation programs for brain-injured and spinal-cord-injured patients. In J. J. Sweet, R. H. Rozensky, & S. M. Tovian (Eds.), *Handbook of clinical psychology in medical settings.* New York: Plenum.

BLOCK, A. R., KREMER, E., & GAYLOR, M. (1980). Behavioral treatment of chronic pain: The spouse as a discriminative cue for pain behavior. *Pain, 9,* 243–252.

BLOOM, F. E., LAZERSON, A., & HOFSTADTER, L. (1985). *Brain, mind, and behavior.* New York: Freeman.

BLOOM, J. R., KANG, S. H., & ROMANO, P. (1991). Cancer and stress: The effect of social support as a resource. In C. L. Cooper & M. Watson (Eds.), *Cancer and stress: Psychological, biological and coping studies* (pp. 95–124). Chichester: Wiley.

BLOOM, J. W., KALTENBORN, W. T., PAOLETTI, P., CAMILLI, A., & LEBOWITZ, M. D. (1987). Respiratory effects of non-tobacco cigarettes. *British Medical Journal,* 295, 1516–1518.

BLUMENTHAL, J. A., BABYAK, M., WEI, J., O'CONNOR, C., WAUGH, R., EISENSTEIN, E. et al. (2002). Usefulness of psychosocial treatment of mental stress-induced myocardial ischemia in men. *American Journal of Cardiology,* 89, 164–168.

BLUMENTHAL, J. A., SHERWOOD, A., GULLETTE, E. C. D., GEORGIADES, A., & TWEEDY, D. (2002). Biobehavioral approaches to the treatment of essential hypertension. *Journal of Consulting and Clinical Psychology,* 70, 569–589.

BODMER, W. F., BAILEY, C. J., BODMER, J., BUSSEY, H. J. R., ELLIS, A., GORMAN, P., et al. (1987). Localization of the gene for familial adenomatous polyposis on chromosome 5. *Nature,* 328, 614–616.

BODNAR, R. J. (1998). Pain. In E. A. Blechman & K. D. Brownell (Eds.), *Behavioral medicine and women: A comprehensive handbook* (pp. 695–699). New York: Guilford.

BOFFEY, P. M. (1987, April 16). Gains against cancer since 1950 are overstated, Congress is told. *New York Times,* pp. A1, B10.

BOGAARDS, M. C., & TER KUILE, M. M. (1994). Treatment of recurrent tension headache: A meta-analytic review. *Clinical Journal of Pain,* 10, 174–190.

BOHM, L. C., & RODIN, J. (1985). Aging and the family. In D. C. Turk & R. D. Kerns (Eds.), *Health, illness, and families: A life-span perspective* (pp. 279–310). New York: Wiley.

BONANNO, G. A. (2004). Loss, trauma, and human resilience: Have we underestimated the human capacity to thrive after extremely aversive events? *American Psychologist,* 59, 20–28.

BOOTH-KEWLEY, S., & FRIEDMAN, H. S. (1987). Psychological predictors of heart disease: A quantitative review. *Psychological Bulletin,* 101, 343–362.

BORYSENKO, J. (1984). Stress, coping, and the immune system. In J. D. Matarazzo, S. M. Weiss, J. A. Herd, N. E. Miller, & S. M. Weiss (Eds.), *Behavioral health: A handbook of health enhancement and disease prevention* (pp. 248–260). New York: Wiley.

BOSCARINO, J. A. (1997). Diseases among men 20 years after exposure to severe stress: Implications for clinical research and medical care. *Psychosomatic Medicine,* 59, 605–614.

BOSMA, H., PETER, R., SIEGRIST, J., & MARMOT, M. (1998). Two alternative job stress models and the risk of coronary heart disease. *American Journal of Public Health,* 88, 68–74.

BOTVIN, G. J., & EPSTEIN, J. A. (1999). Preventing cigarette smoking among children and adolescents. In D. F. Seidman & L. S. Covey (Eds.), *Helping the hard-core smoker: A clinician's guide* (pp. 51–71). Mahwah, NJ: Erlbaum.

BOTVIN, G. J., RENICK, N. L., & BAKER, E. (1983). The effects of scheduling format and booster sessions on a broad-spectrum psychosocial approach to smoking prevention. *Journal of Behavioral Medicine,* 6, 359–379.

BOTVIN, G. J., & WILLS, T. A. (1985). Personal and social skills training: Cognitive-behavioral approaches to substance abuse prevention. In C. S. Bell & R. Battjes (Eds.), *Prevention research: Deterring drug abuse among children and adolescents* (NIDA Research Monograph 63). Washington, DC: U.S. Government Printing Office.

BOULWARE, L. E., COOPER, L. A., RATNER, L. E., LaVEIST, T. A., & POWE, N. R. (2003). Race and trust in the health care system. *Public Health Reports,* 118, 358–365.

BOUTON, K. (1990, August 5). Painful decisions: The role of the medical ethicist. *New York Times Magazine,* pp. 22–25, 53, 65.

BOVBJERG, D. H., REDD, W. H., JACOBSEN, P. B., MANNE, S. L., TAYLOR, K. L., SURBONE, A., et al. (1992). An experimental analysis of classically conditioned nausea during cancer chemotherapy. *Psychosomatic Medicine,* 54, 623–637.

BOVBJERG, V. E., MCCANN, B. S., RETZLAFF, B. M., WALDEN, C. E., & KNOPP, R. H. (1999). Effect of cholesterol-lowering diets on indices of depression and hostility. *Annals of Behavioral Medicine,* 21, 98–101.

BOVE, G. & NILSSON, N. (1998). Spinal manipulation in the treatment of episodic tension-type headache. *Journal of the American Medical Association,* 280, 1576–1579.

BOWEN, A. M., & TROTTER, R. (1995). HIV risk in intravenous drug users and crack cocaine smokers: Predicting stage of change for condom use. *Journal of Consulting and Clinical Psychology,* 63, 238–248.

BOWLBY, J. (1969). *Attachment and loss. Vol. 1: Attachment.* New York: Basic Books.

BOWLBY, J. (1973). *Attachment and loss. Vol. 2: Separation.* New York: Basic Books.

BRACCO, L., GALLATO, R., GRIGOLETTO, F., LIPPI, A., LEPORE, V., BINO, G., et al. (1994). Factors affecting the course and survival in Alzheimer's disease. *Archives of Neurology,* 51, 1213–1219.

BRADFORD, L. P. (1986). Can you survive retirement? In R. H. Moos (Ed.), *Coping with life crises: An integrated approach* (pp. 211–219). New York: Plenum.

BRADLEY, G. W. (1993). *Disease, diagnosis, & decisions.* New York: Wiley.

BRADLEY, L. A. (1994). Pain measurement in arthritis. *Arthritis Care and Research, 6,* 178–186.

BRADLEY, L. A., & McKENDREE-SMITH, N. L. (2001). Assessment of psychological status using interviews and self-report instruments. In D. C. Turk & R. Melzack (Eds.), *Handbook of pain assessment* (2nd ed., pp. 292–319). New York: Guilford.

BRAITH, R. W., POLLOCK, M. L., LOWENTHAL, D. T., GRAVES, J. E., & LIMACHER, M. C. (1994). Moderate- and high-intensity exercise lowers blood pressure in normotensive subjects 60 to 79 years of age. *American Journal of Cardiology, 73,* 1124–1128.

BRAITMAN, L. E., ADLIN, E. V., & STANTON, J. L. (1985). Obesity and caloric intake: The National Health and Nutrition Examination Survey of 1971–1975 (HANES I). *Journal of Chronic Diseases, 9,* 727–732.

BRAND-MILLER, J., WOLEVER, T. M. S., FOSTER-POWELL, K., & COLAGIURI, S. (2003). *The new glucose revolution.* New York: Marlow.

BRANDON, T. H., COLLINS, B. N., JULIANO, L. M., & LAZEV, A. B. (2000). Preventing relapse among former smokers: A comparison of minimal interventions through telephone and mail. *Journal of Consulting and Clinical Psychology, 68,* 103–113.

BRANDON, T. H., HERZOG, T. A., & WEBB, M. S. (2003). It ain't over till it's over: The case for offering relapse-prevention interventions to former smokers. *American Journal of the Medical Sciences, 326,* 197–200.

BRAVEMAN, N. S. (1987). Immunity and aging: Immunologic and behavioral perspectives. In M. W. Riley, J. D. Matarazzo, & A. Baum (Eds.), *Perspectives in behavioral medicine: The aging dimension* (pp. 93–124). Hillsdale, NJ: Erlbaum.

BREHM, J. W. (1966). *A theory of psychological reactance.* New York: Academic Press.

BRENNAN, L. K., BAKER, E. A., HAIRE-JOSHU, D., & BROWNSON, R. C. (2003). Linking perceptions of the community to behavior: Are protective social factors associated with physical activity? *Health Education and Behavior, 30,* 740–755.

BRESLOW, L. (1983). The potential of health promotion. In D. Mechanic (Ed.), *Handbook of health, health care, and the health professions* (pp. 50–66). New York: Free Press.

BRESLOW, L., & SOMERS, A. R. (1977). The lifetime health-monitoring program. *New England Journal of Medicine, 296,* 601–608.

BROADHEAD, W. E., KAPLAN, B. H., JAMES, S. A., WAGNER, E. H., SCHOENBACH, V. J., GRIMSON, R. et al. (1983). The epidemiologic evidence for a relationship between social support and health. *American Journal of Epidemiology, 117,* 521–537.

BROADSTOCK, M., BORLAND, R., & GASON, R. (1992). Effects of suntan on judgements of healthiness and attractiveness by adolescents. *Journal of Applied Social Psychology, 22,* 157–172.

BROBERG, D. J., & BERNSTEIN, I. L. (1987). Candy as a scapegoat in the prevention of food aversions in children receiving chemotherapy. *Cancer, 60,* 2344–2347.

BROLIN, R. E. (2002). Bariatric surgery and long-term control of morbid obesity. *Journal of the American Medical Association, 288,* 2793–2796.

BROMAN, C. L. (1993). Social relationships and health-related behavior. *Journal of Behavioral Medicine, 16,* 335–350.

BRONDOLO, E., ROSEN, R. C., KOSTIS, J. B., & SCHWARTZ, J. E. (1999). Relationship of physical symptoms and mood to perceived and actual blood pressure in hypertensive men: A repeated-measures design. *Psychosomatic Medicine, 61,* 311–318.

BROOK, J. S., WHITEMAN, M., GORDON, A. S., & COHEN, P. (1986). Dynamics of childhood and adolescent personality traits and adolescent drug use. *Developmental Psychology, 22,* 403–414.

BROWN, J. M., O'KEEFFE, J., SANDERS, S. H., & BAKER, B. (1986). Developmental changes in children's cognition to stressful and painful situations. *Journal of Pediatric Psychology, 11,* 343–357.

BROWN, K. W., LEVY, A. R., ROSBERGER, Z., & EDGAR, L. (2003). Psychological distress and cancer survival: A follow-up 10 years after diagnosis. *Psychosomatic Medicine, 65,* 636–643.

BROWN, L. K., & LOURIE, K. J. (2001). Motivational interviewing and the prevention of HIV among adolescents. In P. M. Monti, S. M. Colby, & T. A. O'Leary (Eds.), *Adolescents, alcohol, and substance abuse: Reaching teens through brief interventions* (pp. 244–274). New York: Guilford.

BROWNELL, K. D. (1982). Obesity: Understanding and treating a serious, prevalent, and refractory disorder. *Journal of Consulting and Clinical Psychology, 50,* 820–840.

BROWNELL, K. D. (1986). Social and behavioral aspects of obesity in children. In N. A. Krasnegor, J. D. Arasteh, & M. F. Cataldo (Eds.), *Child health behavior: A behavioral pediatrics perspective* (pp. 310–324). New York: Wiley.

BROWNELL, K. D. (1989, June). When and how to diet. *Psychology Today,* pp. 40–46.

BROWNELL, K. D. (1991). Personal responsibility and control over our bodies: When expectation exceeds reality. *Health Psychology, 10,* 303–310.

BROWNELL, K. D., COHEN, R. Y., STUNKARD, A. J., FELIX, M. R. J., & COOLEY, N. B. (1984). Weight loss competitions at the work site: Impact on weight, morale and cost-effectiveness. *American Journal of Public Health, 74,* 1283–1285.

BROWNELL, K. D., & WADDEN, T. A. (1991). The heterogeneity of obesity: Fitting treatments to individuals. *Behavior Therapy, 22,* 153–177.

BRUCKER, B. S. (1983). Spinal cord injuries. In T. G. Burish & L. A. Bradley (Eds.), *Coping with chronic disease: Research and applications* (pp. 285–311). New York: Academic Press.

BRUEHL, S., MCCUBBIN, J. A., & HARDEN, R. N. (1999). Theoretical review: Altered pain regulatory systems in chronic pain. *Neuroscience and Biobehavioral Reviews, 23,* 877–890.

BRUNNER, E., WHITE, I., THOROGOOD, M., BRISTOW, A., CURLE, D., & MARMOT, M. (1997). Can dietary interventions change diet and cardiovascular risk factors? A meta-analysis of randomized controlled trials. *American Journal of Public Health, 87,* 1415–1422.

BRUVOLD, W. H. (1993). A meta-analysis of adolescent smoking prevention programs. *American Journal of Public Health, 83,* 872–880.

BRYAN, A., FISHER, J. D., & FISHER, W. A. (2002). Tests of the mediational role of preparatory safer sex behavior in the context of the theory of planned behavior. *Health Psychology, 21,* 71–80.

BRYER, K. B. (1986). The Amish way of death: A study of family support systems. In R. H. Moos (Ed.), *Coping with life crises: An integrated approach* (pp. 245–256). New York: Plenum.

BUCHNER, D. M., BERESFORD, S. A. A., LARSON, E. B., LACROIX, A. Z., & WAGNER, E. H. (1992). Effects of physical activity on health status in older adults II: Intervention studies. *Annual Review of Public Health, 13,* 469–488.

BUCK, R. (1988). *Human motivation and emotion* (2nd ed.). New York: Wiley.

BUDZYNSKI, T. H., STOYVA, J. M., ADLER, C. S., & MULLANEY, D. J. (1973). EMG biofeedback and tension headache: A controlled outcome study. *Psychosomatic Medicine, 35,* 484–496.

BULMAN, R. J., & WORTMAN, C. B. (1977). Attributions of blame and coping in the "real world": Severe accident victims react to their lot. *Journal of Personality and Social Psychology, 35,* 351–363.

BUNDY, C., CARROLL, D., WALLACE, L., & NAGLE, R. (1994). Psychological treatment of chronic stable angina pectoris. *Psychology and Health, 10,* 69–77.

BURBACH, D. J., & PETERSON, L. (1986). Children's concepts of physical illness: A review and critique of the cognitive-developmental literature. *Health Psychology, 5,* 307–325.

BURG, I. N., & INGALL, C. G. (1985). The immune system. In L. L. Hayman & E. M. Sporing (Eds.), *Handbook of pediatric nursing* (pp. 424–477). New York: Wiley.

BURG, M. M., & SEEMAN, T. E. (1994). Families and health: The negative side of social ties. *Annals of Behavioral Medicine, 16,* 109–115.

BURISH, T. G., & JENKINS, R. A. (1992). Effectiveness of biofeedback and relaxation training in reducing the side effects of cancer chemotherapy. *Health Psychology, 11,* 17–23.

BURISH, T. G., MEYEROWITZ, B. E., CAREY, M. P., & MORROW, G. R. (1987). The stressful effects of cancer in adults. In A. Baum & J. E. Singer (Eds.), *Handbook of psychology and health* (Vol. 5, pp. 137–173). New York: Erlbaum.

BURKE, B. L., ARKOWITZ, H., & MENCHOLA, M. (2003). The efficacy of motivational interviewing: A meta-analysis of controlled clinical trials. *Journal of Consulting and Clinical Psychology, 71,* 843–861.

BURKE, L. E., DUNBAR-JACOB, J. M., & HILL, M. N. (1997). Compliance with cardiovascular disease prevention strategies: A review of the research. *Annals of Behavioral Medicine, 19,* 239–263.

BURNS, E. M., & ARNOLD, L. E. (1990). Biological aspects of stress: Effects on the developing brain. In L. E. Arnold (Ed.), *Childhood stress* (pp. 73–108). New York: Wiley.

BURNS, J. W., GLENN, B., BRUEHL, S., HARDEN, R. N., & LOFLAND, K. (2003). Cognitive factors influence outcome following multidisciplinary chronic pain treatment: A replication and extension of a cross-lagged panel analysis. *Behaviour Research and Therapy, 41,* 1163–1182.

BURNS, V. E., CARROLL, D., DRAYSON, M., WHITHAM, M., & RING, C. (2003). Life events, perceived stress and antibody responses to influenza vaccination in young, healthy adults. *Journal of Psychosomatic Research, 55,* 569–572.

BURNSIDE, I. G., TOBIAS, H. S., & BURSILL, D. (1982). Electromyographic feedback in the remobilization of stroke patients: A controlled trial. *Archives of Physical Medicine and Rehabilitation, 63,* 217–222.

BUSH, J. P., & DELUCA, C. J. (2001). The biopsychosocial construct of pain: Developmental considerations and implications for clinical practice. *Journal of Psychological Practice, 7,* 57–76.

BUSH, J. P., HOLMBECK, G. N., & COCKRELL, J. L. (1989). Patterns of PRN analgesic drug administration in children following elective surgery. *Journal of Pediatric Psychology, 14,* 433–448.

BUSH, J. P., MELAMED, B. G., SHERAS, P. L., & GREENBAUM, P. E. (1986). Mother-child patterns of coping with anticipatory medical stress. *Health Psychology, 5,* 137–157.

BUSJAHN, A., FAULHABER, H.-D., FREIER, K., & LUFT, F. C. (1999). Genetic and environmental influences on coping styles: A twin study. *Psychosomatic Medicine, 61,* 469–475.

BUSS, A. H., & PLOMIN, R. (1975). *A temperamental theory of personality development.* New York: Wiley.

BUSS, A. H., & PLOMIN, R. (1986). The EAS approach to temperament. In R. Plomin & J. Dunn (Eds.), *The study of temperament: Changes, continuities and challenges* (pp. 67–79). Hillsdale, NJ: Erlbaum.

BUTCHER, J. N., DAHLSTROM, W. G., GRAHAM, J. R., TELLEGEN, A., & KRAEMER, B. (1989). *Minnesota Multiphasic Personality Inventory-2: Manual for administration and scoring.* Minneapolis: University Minnesota Press.

BUTLER, C., & STEPTOE, A. (1986). Placebo responses: An experimental study of psychophysiological processes in asthmatic volunteers. *British Journal of Clinical Psychology, 25,* 173–183.

BUTLER, L. D., KOOPMAN, C., CORDOVA, M. J., GARLAN, R. W., DiMICELI, S., & SPIEGEL, D. (2003). Psychosocial distress and pain significantly increase before death in metastatic breast cancer patients. *Psychosomatic Medicine, 65,* 416–426.

BYRNE, P. S., & LONG, B. E. L. (1976). *Doctors talking to patients.* London: Her Majesty's Stationery Office.

CABANA, M. D., SLISH, K. K., LEWIS, T. C., BROWN, R. W., NAN, B., LIN, X. et al. (2004). Parental management of asthma triggers within a child's environment. *Journal of Allergy and Clinical Immunology, 114,* 352–357.

CACIOPPO, J. T., PETTY, R. E., & MARSHALL-GOODELL, B. (1985). Physical, social, and inferential elements of psychophysiological measurement. In P. Karoly (Ed.), *Measurement strategies in health psychology* (pp. 263–300). New York: Wiley.

CADMAN, D., ROSENBAUM, P., BOYLE, M., & OFFORD, D. R. (1991). Children with chronic illness: Family and parent demographic characteristics and psychosocial adjustment. *Pediatrics, 87,* 884–889.

CAGGIULA, A. W., CHRISTAKIS, G., FARRAND, M., HULLEY, S. B., JOHNSON, R., LASSER, N. L., et al. (1981). The Multiple Risk Intervention Trial (MRFIT): IV. Intervention on blood lipids. *Preventive Medicine, 10,* 443–475.

CAHILL, L., PRINS, B., WEBER, M., & McGAUGH, J. L. (1994). β-adrenergic activation and memory for emotional events. *Nature, 371,* 702–704.

CALHOUN, K. S., & BURNETTE, M. M. (1983). Etiology and treatment of menstrual disorders. *Behavioral Medicine Update, 5*(4), 21–26.

CALLE, E. E., RODRIGUEZ, C., WALKER-THURMOND, K., & THUN, M. J. (2003). Overweight, obesity, and mortality from cancer in a prospectively studied cohort of U.S. adults. *New England Journal of Medicine, 348,* 1625–1638.

CAMERON, L., LEVENTHAL, E. A., & LEVENTHAL, H. (1995). Seeking medical care in response to symptoms and life stress. *Psychosomatic Medicine, 57,* 1–11.

CAMERON, R., & SHEPEL, L. F. (1986). The process of psychological consultation in pain management. In A. D. Holzman & D. C. Turk (Eds.), *Pain management: A handbook of psychological treatment approaches* (pp. 240–256). New York: Pergamon.

CAMPBELL, T., & CHANG, B. (1981). Health care of the Chinese in America. In G. Henderson & M. Primeaux (Eds.), *Transcultural health care* (pp. 163–172). Menlo Park, CA: Addison-Wesley.

CANNON, J. T., PRIETO, G. J., LEE, A., & LIEBESKIND, J. C. (1982). Evidence for opioid and non-opioid forms of stimulation-produced analgesia in the rat. *Brain Research, 243,* 315–321.

CANNON, W. B. (1929). *Bodily changes in pain, hunger, fear and rage* (2nd ed.). New York: Appleton.

CANNON, W. B. (1942). Voodoo death. *American Anthropologist, 44,* 169–181.

CARELS, R. A., BLUMENTHAL, J. A., & SHERWOOD, A. (1998). Effect of satisfaction with social support on blood pressure in normotensive and borderline hypertensive men and women. *International Journal of Behavioral Medicine, 5,* 76–85.

CARELS, R. A., CACCIAPAGLIA, H., PÉREZ-BENÍTEZ, C. I., DOUGLASS, O., CHRISTIE, S., & O'BRIEN, W. H. (2003). The association between emotional upset and cardiac arrhythmia during daily life. *Journal of Consulting and Clinical Psychology, 71,* 613–618.

CAREY, M. P. (1999). Prevention of HIV infection through sexual behavior change: Progress report focusing on downstream, midstream, and upstream strategies. *American Journal of Health Promotion, 14,* 104–111.

CAREY, M. P., BRAATEN, L. S., MAISTO, S. A., GLEASON, J. R., FORSYTH, A. D., DURANT, L. E., et al. (2000). Using information, motivational enhancement, and skills training to reduce risk of HIV infection for low-income urban women: A second randomized clinical trial. *Health Psychology, 19,* 3–11.

CAREY, M. P., & BURISH, T. G. (1988). Etiology and treatment of the psychological side effects associated with cancer chemotherapy: A critical review and discussion. *Psychological Bulletin, 104,* 307–325.

CAREY, M. P., KALRA, D. L., CAREY, K. B., HALPERIN, S., & RICHARDS, C. S. (1993). Stress and unaided smoking cessation: A prospective investigation. *Journal of Consulting and Clinical Psychology, 61,* 831–838.

CAREY, M. P., MORRISON-BEEDY, D., & JOHNSON, B. T. (1998). The HIV-Knowledge Questionnaire. In C. M. Davis, W. L. Yarber, R. Bauserman, G. Schreer, & S. L. Davis (Eds.), *Handbook of sexually related measures* (pp. 313–315). Thousand Oaks, CA: Sage.

CAREY, R. G. (1975). Living until death: A program of service and research for the terminally ill. In E. Kübler-Ross (Ed.), *Death: The final stage of growth* (pp. 75–86). Englewood Cliffs, NJ: Prentice-Hall.

CAREY, W. B., & McDEVITT, S. C. (1978). Stability and change in individual temperament diagnoses from infancy to early childhood. *Journal of the American Academy of Child Psychiatry*, 17, 331–337.

CARLSON, C. R., & HOYLE, R. H. (1993). Efficacy of abbreviated muscle relaxation training: A quantitative review of behavioral medicine research. *Journal of Consulting and Clinical Psychology*, 61, 1059–1067.

CARLSON, L. E., GOODEY, E., BENNETT, M. H., TAENZER, P., & KOOPMANS, J. (2002). The addition of social support to a community-based large-group behavioral smoking cessation intervention: Improved cessation rates and gender differences. *Addictive Behaviors*, 27, 547–559.

CARMELLI, D., DAME, A., SWAN, G., & ROSENMAN, R. (1991). Long-term changes in Type A behavior: A 27-year follow-up of the Western Collaborative Group Study. *Journal of Behavioral Medicine*, 14, 593–606.

CARMELLI, D., ROSENMAN, R. H., & CHESNEY, M. A. (1987). Stability of the Type A Structured Interview and related questionnaires in a 10-year follow-up of an adult cohort of twins. *Journal of Behavioral Medicine*, 10, 513–525.

CARMODY, T. P., FEY, S. G., PIERCE, D. K., CONNOR, W. E., & MATARAZZO, J. D. (1982). Behavioral treatment of hyperlipidemia: Techniques, results, and future directions. *Journal of Behavioral Medicine*, 5, 91–116.

CARNEY, R. M., FREEDLAND, K. E., RICH, M. W., & JAFFE, A. S. (1995). Depression as a risk factor for cardiac events in established coronary heart disease: A review of possible mechanisms. *Annals of Behavioral Medicine*, 17, 142–149.

CARNEY, R. M., RICH, M. W., FREEDLAND, K. E., SAINI, J., TeVELDE, A., SIMEONE, C., et al. (1988). Major depressive disorder predicts cardiac events in patients with coronary artery disease. *Psychosomatic Medicine*, 50, 627–633.

CARPENTER, D. J., GATCHEL, R. J., & HASEGAWA, T. (1994). Effectiveness of a videotaped behavioral intervention for dental anxiety: The role of gender and need for information. *Behavioral Medicine*, 20, 123–132.

CARPENTER, S. (2001, November). Curriculum overhaul gives behavioral medicine a higher profile. *Monitor on Psychology*, pp. 78–79.

CARR, D. B., BULLEN, B. A., SKRINAR, G. S., ARNOLD, M. A., ROSENBLATT, M., BEITINS, I. Z., et al. (1981). Physical conditioning facilitates the exercise-induced secretion of beta-endorphin and beta-lipotropin in women. *New England Journal of Medicine*, 305, 560–563.

CARTWRIGHT, M., WARDLE, J., STEGGLES, N., SIMON, A. E., CROKER, H., & JARVIS, M. J. (2003). Stress and dietary practices in adolescents. *Health Psychology*, 22, 362–369.

CARVER, C. S., DIAMOND, E. L., & HUMPHRIES, C. (1985). Coronary prone behavior. In N. Schneiderman & J. T. Tapp (Eds.), *Behavioral medicine: The biopsychosocial approach* (pp. 437–465). Hillsdale, NJ: Erlbaum.

CASTRO, F. G., COTA, M. K., & VEGA, S. C. (1999). Health promotion in Latino populations: A sociocultural model for program planning, development, and evaluation. In R. M. Huff & M. V. Kline (Eds.), *Promoting health in multicultural populations: A handbook for practitioners* (pp. 137–168). Thousand Oaks, CA: Sage.

CASTRO, F. G., NEWCOMB, M. D., McCREARY, C., & BAEZCONDE-GARBANATI, L. (1989). Cigarette smokers do more than just smoke cigarettes. *Health Psychology*, 8, 107–129.

CATALDO, M. F., DERSHEWITZ, R. A., WILSON, M., CHRISTOPHERSEN, E. R., FINNEY, J. W., FAWCETT, S. B., et al. (1986). Childhood injury control. In N. A. Krasnegor, J. D. Arasteh, & M. F. Cataldo (Eds.), *Child health behavior: A behavioral pediatrics perspective* (pp. 217–253). New York: Wiley.

CATANIA, J. A., COATES, T. J., STALL, R., BYE, L., KEGELES, S. M., CAPELL, F. et al. (1991). Changes in condom use among homosexual men in San Francisco. *Health Psychology*, 10, 190–199.

CATTANACH, L., & RODIN, J. (1988). Psychological components of the stress process in bulimia. *International Journal of Eating Disorders*, 7, 75–88.

CATZ, S. L., KELLY, J. A., BOGART, L. M., BENOTSCH, E. G., & McAULIFFE, T. L. (2000). Patterns, correlates, and barriers to medication adherence among persons prescribed new treatments for HIV disease. *Health Psychology*, 19, 124–133.

CAVANAUGH, S. V. A., FURLANETTO, L. M., CREECH, S. D., & POWELL, L. H. (2001). Medical illness, past depression, and present depression: A predictive triad for in-hospital mortality. *American Journal of Psychiatry*, 158, 43–48.

CAY, E. L., VETTER, N., PHILIP, A. E., & DUGARD, P. (1972). Psychosocial status during recovery from an acute heart attack. *Journal of Psychosomatic Research*, 16, 425–435.

CDC (Centers for Disease Control and Prevention, U.S. Public Health Service) (2004a). HIV/AIDS *prevention—*

Basic statistics. Retrieved (5–11–2004) from http://www.cdc.gov.

CDC (Centers for Disease Control and Prevention, U.S. Public Health Service) (2004b). *Trends in intake of energy and micronutrients—United States, 1971–2000*. Retrieved (8–18–2004) from http://www.cdc.gov.

CELIO, A. A., WINZELBERG, A. J., WILFLEY, D. E., EPPSTEIN-HERALD, D., SPRINGER, E. A., DEV, P., et al. (2000). Reducing risk factors for eating disorders: Comparison of an Internet- and classroom-delivered psychoeducational program. *Health Psychology*, 68, 650–657.

CELLA, D., PETERMAN, A., PASSIK, S., JACOBSEN, P., & BREITBART, W. (1998). Progress toward guidelines for the management of fatigue. *Oncology*, 12, 369–377.

CELLER, B. G., LOVELL, N. H., & BASILAKIS, J. (2003). Using information technology to improve the management of chronic disease. *Medical Journal of Australia*, 179, 242–246.

CEPEDA, BENITO, A., REYNOSO, J. T., & ERATH, S. (2004). Meta-analysis of the efficacy of nicotine replacement therapy for smoking cessation: Differences between men and women. *Journal of Consulting and Clinical Psychology*, 72, 712–722.

CFAH (Center for the Advancement of Health) (2003). *Report on bereavement and grief research*. Retrieved (5–18–2004) from http://www.cfah.org.

CHAMBLESS, D. L., & GILLIS, M. M. (1993). Cognitive therapy of anxiety disorders. *Journal of Consulting and Clinical Psychology*, 61, 248–260.

CHANDRA, R. K. (1991). Interactions between early nutrition and the immune system. In D. J. P. Barker (Chair, Ciba Foundation Symposium, No. 156), *The childhood environment and adult disease*. New York: Wiley.

CHANG, A., DILLMAN, A. S., LEONARD, E., & ENGLISH, P. (1985). Teaching car passenger safety to preschool children. *Pediatrics*, 76, 425–428.

CHAPMAN, C. R. (1984). New directions in the understanding and management of pain. *Social Science and Medicine*, 19, 1261–1277.

CHAPMAN, C. R., CASEY, K. L., DUBNER, R., FOLEY, K. M., GRACELY, R. H., & READING, A. E. (1985). Pain measurement: An overview. *Pain*, 22, 1–31.

CHAPMAN, S. L. (1991). Chronic pain: Psychological assessment and treatment. In J. J. Sweet, R. H. Rozensky, & S. M. Tovian (Eds.), *Handbook of clinical psychology in medical settings*. New York: Plenum.

CHAPMAN, S. L., & BRENA, S. F. (1985). Pain and society. *Annals of Behavioral Medicine*, 7(3), 21–24.

CHASSIN, L., PRESSON, C. C., PITTS, S. C., & SHERMAN, S. J. (2000). The natural history of cigarette smoking from adolescence to adulthood in a Midwestern

community sample: Multiple trajectories and their psychosocial correlates. *Health Psychology*, 19, 223–231.

CHASSIN, L., PRESSON, C. C., SHERMAN, S. J., & EDWARDS, D. A. (1991). Four pathways to young-adult smoking status: Adolescent social-psychological antecedents in a Midwestern community sample. *Health Psychology*, 10, 409–418.

CHAVES, J. F., & BROWN, J. M. (1987). Spontaneous cognitive strategies for the control of clinical pain and stress. *Journal of Behavioral Medicine*, 10, 263–276.

CHEN, E., ZELTZER, L. K., CRASKE, M. G., & KATZ, E. R. (1999). Alteration of memory in the reduction of children's distress during repeated aversive medical procedures. *Journal of Consulting and Clinical Psychology*, 67, 481–490.

CHEN, K., SCHEIER, L. M., & KANDEL, D. B. (1996). Effects of chronic cocaine use on physical health: A prospective study in a general population sample. *Drug and Alcohol Dependence*, 43, 23–37.

CHEN, Y., CHEN, C-F., RILEY, D. J., ALLRED, D. C., CHEN, P-H., VON HOFF, D., et al. (1995). Aberrant subcellular localization of BRCA1 in breast cancer. *Science*, 270, 789–791.

CHENG, T. L., SAVAGEAU, J. A., SATTLER, A. L., & DEWITT, T. G. (1993). Confidentiality in health care: A survey of knowledge, perceptions, and attitudes among high school students. *Journal of the American Medical Association*, 269, 1404–1407.

CHERKIN, D. C., DEYO, R. A., LOESER, J. D., BUSH, T., & WADDELL, G. (1994). An international comparison of back surgery rates. *Spine*, 19, 1201–1206.

CHESNEY, M. A. (1984). Behavior modification and health enhancement. In J. D. Matarazzo, S. M. Weiss, J. A. Herd, N. E. Miller, & S. M. Weiss (Eds.), *Behavioral health: A handbook of health enhancement and disease prevention* (pp. 338–350). New York: Wiley.

CHESNEY, M. A., FRAUTSCHI, N. M., & ROSENMAN, R. H. (1985). Modifying Type A behavior. In J. C. Rosen & L. J. Solomon (Eds.), *Prevention in health psychology* (pp. 130–142). Hanover, NH: University Press of New England.

CHESNEY, M. A., & SMITH, A. W. (1999). Critical delays in HIV testing and care. *American Behavioral Scientist*, 42, 1162–1174.

CHILCOAT, H. D., DISHION, T. J., & ANTHONY, J. C. (1995). Parent monitoring and the incidence of drug sampling in urban elementary school children. *American Journal of Epidemiology*, 141, 25–31.

CHILDRESS, A. R. (1996, March). *Cue reactivity and drug craving*. Paper presented at the meeting of the Society of Behavioral Medicine, Washington, DC.

CHOI, W. S., AHLUWALIA, J. S., HARRIS, K. J., & OKUYEMI, K. (2002). Progression to established smoking: The influence of tobacco marketing. *American Journal of Preventive Medicine, 22,* 228–233.

CHOU, C.-P., MONTGOMERY, S., PENTZ, M. A., ROHRBACH, L. A., JOHNSON, C. A., FLAY, B. R., et al. (1998). Effects of a community-based prevention program on decreasing drug use in high-risk adolescents. *American Journal of Public Health, 88,* 944–948.

CHOW, E., TSAO, M. N., & HARTH, T. (2004). Does psychosocial intervention improve survival in cancer? A meta-analysis. *Palliative Medicine, 18,* 25–31.

CHRISTENFELD, N. (1997). Memory for pain and the delayed effects of distraction. *Health Psychology, 16,* 327–330.

CHRISTENFELD, N., GERIN, W., LINDEN, W., SANDERS, M., MATHUR, J., DEICH, J. D., et al. (1997). Social support effects on cardiovascular reactivity: Is a stranger as effective as a friend? *Psychosomatic Medicine, 59,* 388–398.

CHRISTENSEN, A. J., EDWARDS, D. L., WIEBE, J. S., BENOTSCH, E. G., McKELVEY, L., ANDREWS, M., et al. (1996). Effect of verbal self-disclosure on natural killer cell activity: Moderating influence of cynical hostility. *Psychosomatic Medicine, 58,* 150–155.

CHRISTENSEN, A. J., MORAN, P. J., & WEIBE, J. S. (1999). Assessment of irrational health beliefs: Relation to health practices and medical regimen adherence. *Health Psychology, 18,* 169–176.

CHRISTENSEN, A. J., & SMITH, T. W. (1995). Personality and patient adherence: Correlates of the five-factor model in renal dialysis. *Journal of Behavioral Medicine, 18,* 305–313.

CHRISTENSEN, J., & LEVINSON, W. (1991). Implementing a behavioral medicine program in an internal medicine residency: A description of curriculum content, resources and barriers encountered. In M. A. Jansen & J. Weinman (Eds.), *The international development of health psychology* (pp. 145–155). Chur, Switzerland: Harwood.

CHRISTOPHERSEN, E. R. (1984). Preventing injuries to children: A behavioral approach to child passenger safety. In J. D. Matarazzo, S. M. Weiss, J. A. Herd, N. E. Miller, & S. M. Weiss (Eds.), *Behavioral health: A handbook of health enhancement and disease prevention* (pp. 990–1002). New York: Wiley.

CHUN, C.-A., ENOMOTO, K., & SUE, S. (1996). Health care issues among Asian Americans: Implications of somatization. In P. M. Kato & T. Mann (Eds.), *Handbook of diversity issues in health psychology* (pp. 347–365). New York: Plenum.

CIARANELLO, R. D. (1983). Neurochemical aspects of stress. In N. Garmezy & M. Rutter (Eds.), *Stress, coping,*

and development in children (pp. 85–105). New York: McGraw-Hill.

CICCARONE, D. H., KANOUSE, D. E., COLLINS, R. L., MIE, A., CHEN, J. L., MORTON, S. C. et al. (2003). Sex without disclosure of positive HIV serostatus in a US probability sample of persons receiving medical care for HIV infection. *American Journal of Public Health, 93,* 949–954.

CICCONE, D., JUST, N., & BANDILLA, E. B. (1999). A comparison of economic and social reward in patients with chronic nonmalignant back pain. *Psychosomatic Medicine, 61,* 552–563.

CIESLA, J. A., & ROBERTS, J. E. (2001). Meta-analysis of the relationship between HIV infection and risk for depressive disorders. *American Journal of Psychiatry, 158,* 725–730.

CINCIRIPINI, P. M., CINCIRIPINI, L. G., WALLFISCH, A., HAQUE, W., & VAN VUNAKIS, H. (1996). Behavior therapy and the transdermal nicotine patch: Effects on cessation outcome, affect, and coping. *Journal of Consulting and Clinical Psychology, 64,* 314–323.

CINCIRIPINI, P. M., & FLOREEN, A. (1982). An evaluation of a behavioral program for chronic pain. *Journal of Behavioral Medicine, 5,* 375–389.

CIOPPA, A. L. (1984). Hospice care. In S. N. McIntire & A. L. Cioppa (Eds.), *Cancer nursing: A developmental approach* (pp. 595–601). New York: Wiley.

CIRAULO, D. A., & RENNER, J. A. (1991). Alcoholism. In D. A. CIRAULO & R. I. SHADER (Eds.), *Clinical manual of chemical dependence* (pp. 1–93). Washington, DC: American Psychiatric Press.

CIRAULO, D. A., & SHADER, R. I. (Eds.) (1991). *Clinical manual of chemical dependence.* Washington, DC: American Psychiatric Press.

CITRON, M. L., JOHNSTON-EARLY, A., BOYER, M., KRASNOW, S. H., HOOD, M., & COHEN, M. H. (1986). Patient-controlled analgesia for severe cancer pain. *Archives of Internal Medicine, 146,* 734–736.

CLARK, D. O., PATRICK, D. L., GREMBOWSKI, D., & DURHAM, M. L. (1995). Socioeconomic status and exercise self-efficacy in late life. *Journal of Behavioral Medicine, 18,* 355–376.

CLARK, R., ANDERSON, N. B., CLARK, V. R., & WILLIAMS, D. R. (1999). Racism as a stressor for African Americans. *American Psychologist, 54,* 805–816.

CLEELAND, C. S., GONIN, R., HATFIELD, A. K., EDMONSON, J. H., BLUM, R. H., STEWART, J. A., et al. (1994). Pain and its treatment in outpatients with metastatic cancer. *New England Journal of Medicine, 330,* 592–596.

CLEVER, L. H., & LeGUYADER, Y. (1995). Infectious health risks for health care workers. *Annual Review of Public Health, 16,* 141–164.

CLEVER, L. H., & OMENN, G. S. (1988). Hazards for health care workers. *Annual Review of Public Health, 9*, 273–303.

CLUSS, P. A., & EPSTEIN, L. H. (1985). The measurement of medical compliance in the treatment of disease. In P. Karoly (Ed.), *Measurement strategies in health psychology* (pp. 403–432). New York: Wiley.

CLUSS, P. A., & FIREMAN, P. (1985). Recent trends in asthma research. *Annals of Behavioral Medicine, 7*(4), 11–16.

COATES, T. J. (1990). Strategies for modifying sexual behavior for primary and secondary prevention of HIV disease. *Journal of Consulting and Clinical Psychology, 58*, 57–69.

COBB, S., & ROSE, R. M. (1973). Hypertension, peptic ulcer, and diabetes in air traffic controllers. *Journal of the American Medical Association, 224*, 489–492.

CODDINGTON, R. D. (1972a). The significance of life events as etiological factors in the diseases of children—I: A survey of professional workers. *Journal of Psychosomatic Research, 16*, 7–18.

CODDINGTON, R. D. (1972b). The significance of life events as etiological factors in the diseases of children—II: A study of a normal population. *Journal of Psychosomatic Research, 16*, 205–213.

COGAN, R., COGAN, D., WALTZ, W., & McCUE, M. (1987). Effects of laughter and relaxation on discomfort thresholds. *Journal of Behavioral Medicine, 10*, 139–144.

COHEN, F., KEARNEY, K. A., ZEGANS, L. S., KEMENY, M. E., NEUHAUS, J. M., & STITES, D. P. (1999). Different immune system changes with acute and persistent stress for optimists vs pessimists. *Brain, Behavior, and Immunity, 13*, 155–174.

COHEN, F., & LAZARUS, R. S. (1979). Coping with the stresses of illness. In G. C. Stone, F. Cohen, & N. E. Adler (Eds.), *Health psychology—A handbook* (pp. 217–254). San Francisco: Jossey-Bass.

COHEN, L. L. (2002). Reducing infant immunization distress through distraction. *Health Psychology, 21*, 207–211.

COHEN, L. L., BLOUNT, R. L., COHEN, R. J., SCHAEN, E. R., & ZAFF, J. F. (1999). Comparative study of distraction versus topical anesthesia for pediatric pain management during immunizations. *Health Psychology, 18*, 591–598.

COHEN, L. M., McCARTHY, D. M., BROWN, S. A., & MYERS, M. G. (2002). Negative affect combines with smoking outcome expectancies to predict smoking behavior over time. *Psychology of Addictive Behaviors, 16*, 91–97.

COHEN, R. Y., BROWNELL, K. D., & FELIX, M. R. J. (1990). Age and sex differences in health habits and beliefs of schoolchildren. *Health Psychology, 9*, 208–224.

COHEN, S., DOYLE, W. J., TURNER, R. B., ALPER, C. M., & SKONER, D. P. (2003). Emotional style and susceptibility to the common cold. *Psychosomatic Medicine, 65*, 652–657.

COHEN, S., EVANS, G. W., STOKOLS, D., & KRANTZ, D. S. (1986). *Behavior, health, and environmental stress.* New York: Plenum.

COHEN, S., FRANK, E., DOYLE, W. J., SKONER, D. P., RABIN, B. S., & GWALTNEY, J. M. (1998). Types of stressors that increase susceptibility to the common cold in healthy adults. *Health Psychology, 17*, 214–223.

COHEN, S., KAMARCK, T., & MERMELSTEIN, R. (1983). A global measure of perceived stress. *Journal of Health and Social Behavior, 24*, 385–396.

COHEN, S., & LICHTENSTEIN, E. (1990). Perceived stress, quitting smoking, and smoking relapse. *Health Psychology, 9*, 466–478.

COHEN, S., LICHTENSTEIN, E., PROCHASKA, J. O., ROSSI, J. S., GRITZ, E. R., CARR, C. R. et al. (1989). Debunking myths about self-quitting: Evidence from 10 prospective studies of persons who attempt to quit smoking by themselves. *American Psychologist, 44*, 1355–1365.

COHEN, S., & RODRIGUEZ, M. S. (1995). Pathways linking affective disturbances and physical disorders. *Health Psychology, 14*, 374–380.

COHEN, S., & SPACAPAN, S. (1978). The aftereffects of stress: An attentional interpretation. *Environmental Psychology and Nonverbal Behavior, 3*, 43–57.

COHEN, S., TYRELL, D. A. J., RUSSELL, M. A. H., JARVIS, M. J., & SMITH, A. P. (1993). Smoking, alcohol consumption, and susceptibility to the common cold. *American Journal of Public Health, 83*, 1277–1283.

COHEN, S., TYRRELL, D. A. J., & SMITH, A. P. (1991). Psychological stress and susceptibility to the common cold. *New England Journal of Medicine, 325*, 606–612.

COHEN, S. M., & ELLWEIN, L. B. (1990). Cell proliferation in carcinogenesis. *Science, 249*, 1007–1011.

COHEN, W. S. (1985). Health promotion in the workplace: A prescription for good health. *American Psychologist, 40*, 213–216.

COHN, L. D., MACFARLANE, S., YANEZ, C., & IMAI, W. K. (1995). Risk-perception: Differences between adolescents and adults. *Health Psychology, 14*, 217–222.

COICO, R., SUNSHINE, G., & BENJAMINI, E. (2003). *Immunology: A short course* (5th ed.). Hoboken, NJ: Wiley.

COLE, S. W., & KEMENY, M. E. (1997). Psychobiology of HIV infection. *Critical Reviews in Neurobiology, 11*, 289–321.

COLERICK, E. J. (1985). Stamina in later life. *Social Science and Medicine, 21*, 997–1006.

COLLIGAN, M. J., URTES, M., WISSEMAN, C., ROSENSTEEL, R. E., ANANIA, T. L., & HORNUNG, R. W. (1979). An investigation of apparent mass psychogenic illness in an electronics plant. *Journal of Behavioral Medicine*, 2, 297–309.

COLLINS, A., & FRANKENHAEUSER, M. (1978). Stress responses in male and female engineering students. *Journal of Human Stress*, 4, 43–48.

COLLINS, G. (1987, April 29). Keeping fit wasn't easy in 1837, either. *New York Times*, pp. C1, 12.

COMPAS, B. E., HAAGA, D. A. F., KEEFE, F. J., LEITENBERG, H., & WILLIAMS, D. A. (1998). Sampling of empirically supported psychological treatments from health psychology: Smoking, chronic pain, cancer, and bulimia nervosa. *Journal of Consulting and Clinical Psychology*, 66, 89–112.

COMPAS, B. E., WORSHAM, N. L., EY, S., & HOWELL, D. C. (1996). When mom or dad has cancer: II. Coping, cognitive appraisals, and psychological distress in children of cancer patients. *Health Psychology*, 15, 167–175.

CONEL, J. L. (1939–1963). *The postnatal development of the human cerebral cortex* (Vols. 1–7). Cambridge, MA: Harvard University Press.

CONNER, M., NORMAN, P., & BELL, R. (2002). The theory of planned behavior and healthy eating. *Health Psychology*, 21, 194–201.

CONRAD, B., WEIDMANN, E., TRUCCO, G., RUDERT, W. A., BEHBOO, R., RICORDI, C., et al. (1994). Evidence for superantigen involvement in insulin-dependent diabetes mellitus aetiology. *Nature*, 371, 351–355.

CONRAD, K. M., FLAY, B. R., & HILL, D. (1992). Why children start smoking cigarettes: Predictors of onset. *British Journal of Addiction*, 87, 1711–1724.

CONTRADA, R. J. (1989). Type A behavior, personality hardiness, and cardiovascular responses to stress. *Journal of Personality and Social Psychology*, 57, 895–903.

CONTRADA, R. J., & GUYLL, M. (2001). On who gets sick and why: The role of personality and stress. In A. Baum, T. A. Revenson, & J. E. Singer (Eds.), *Handbook of health psychology* (pp. 59–84). Mahwah, NJ: Erlbaum.

CONTRADA, R. J., & KRANTZ, D. S. (1988). Stress, reactivity, and Type A behavior: Current status and future directions. *Annals of Behavioral Medicine*, 10, 64–70.

COOK, P. S., PETERSEN, R. C., & MOORE, D. T. (1990). *Alcohol, tobacco, and other drugs may harm the unborn*. Rockville, MD: U.S. Department of Health and Human Services.

COOK, W. W., & MEDLEY, D. M. (1954). Proposed hostility and pharisaic-virtue scores for the MMPI. *Journal of Applied Psychology*, 38, 414–418.

COOPER, M. L., & ORCUTT, H. K. (2000). Alcohol use, condom use, and partner type among heterosexual adolescents and young adults. *Journal of Studies on Alcohol*, 61, 413–419.

CORDER, R., DOUTHWAITE, J. A., LEES, D. M., KHAN, N. Q., VISEU DOS SANTOS, A. C., WOOD, E. G. et al. (2001). Endothelin-1 synthesis reduced by red wine. *Nature*, 414, 863–864.

CORDOVA, M. J., CUNNINGHAM, L. L. C., CARLSON, C. R., & ANDRYKOWSKI, M. A. (2001). Posttraumatic growth following breast cancer: A controlled comparison study. *Health Psychology*, 20, 176–185.

CORLE, D. K., SHARBAUGH, C., MATESKI, D. J., COYNE, T., PASKETT, E. D., CAHILL, J. et al. (2001). Self-rated quality of life measures: Effects of change to a low-fat, high-fiber, fruit and vegetable enriched diet. *Annals of Behavioral Medicine*, 23, 198–207.

COSSETTE, S., FRASURE-SMITH, N., & LESPÉRANCE, F. (2001). Clinical implications of a reduction in psychological distress on cardiac prognosis in patients participating in a psychosocial intervention program. *Psychosomatic Medicine*, 63, 257–266.

COSTA, P. T., & MCCRAE, R. R. (1980). Somatic complaints in males as a function of age and neuroticism: A longitudinal analysis. *Journal of Behavioral Medicine*, 3, 245–257.

COSTA, P. T., & MCCRAE, R. R. (1985). Hypochondriasis, neuroticism, and aging. *American Psychologist*, 40, 19–28.

COTTINGTON, E. M., & HOUSE, J. S. (1987). Occupational stress and health: A multivariate relationship. In A. Baum & J. E. Singer (Eds.), *Handbook of psychology and health* (Vol. 5, pp. 41–62). Hillsdale, NJ: Erlbaum.

COUSINS, N. (1985). Anatomy of an illness (as perceived by the patient). In A. Monat & R. S. Lazarus (Eds.), *Stress and coping: An anthology* (2nd ed, pp. 55–66). New York: Columbia University Press.

COUTU, M.-F., DUPUIS, G., & D'ANTONO, B. (2001). The impact of cholesterol lowering on patients' moods. *Journal of Behavioral Medicine*, 24, 517–536.

COX, D. J., GONDER-FREDERICK, L., ANTOUN, B., CRYER, P. E., & CLARKE, W. L. (1993). Perceived symptoms in the recognition of hypoglycemia. *Diabetes Care*, 16, 519–527.

COX, G. B., CHAPMAN, C. R., & BLACK, R. G. (1978). The MMPI and chronic pain: The diagnosis of psychogenic pain. *Journal of Behavioral Medicine*, 1, 437–443.

COX, W. M. (1985). Personality correlates of substance abuse. In M. Galizio & S. A. Maisto (Eds.), *Determinants of substance abuse: Biological, psychological, and environmental factors* (pp. 209–246). New York: Plenum.

COYNE, J. C., & RACIOPPO, M. W. (2000). Never the twain shall meet?: Closing the gap between coping research and clinical intervention research. *American Psychologist*, 55, 655–664.

CRAIG, T. G., COMSTOCK, G. W., & GEISER, P. B. (1974). The quality of survival in breast cancer: A case-control comparison. *Cancer, 33,* 1451–1457.

CRAMER, P. (2000). Defense mechanisms in psychology today: Further processes for adaptation. *American Psychologist, 55,* 637–646.

CRAUN, A. M., & DEFFENBACHER, J. L. (1987). The effects of information, behavioral rehearsal, and prompting on breast self-exams. *Journal of Behavioral Medicine, 10,* 351–365.

CRIQUI, M. H., & RINGEL, B. L. (1994). Does diet or alcohol explain the French paradox? *Lancet, 344,* 1719–1723.

CRISP, A. H., & KALUCY, R. S. (1974). Aspects of the perceptual disorder in anorexia nervosa. *British Journal of Medical Psychology, 47,* 349–361.

CRITCHLOW, B. (1986). The powers of John Barleycorn: Beliefs about the effects of alcohol on social behavior. *American Psychologist, 41,* 751–764.

CRONAN, T. A., GROESSL, E., & KAPLAN, R. M. (1997). The effects of social support and education interventions on health care costs. *Arthritis Care and Research, 10,* 99–110.

CROOG, S. H. (1983). Recovery and rehabilitation of heart patients: Psychosocial aspects. In D. S. Krantz, A. Baum, & J. E. Singer (Eds.), *Handbook of psychology and health* (Vol. 3, pp. 295–334). Hillsdale, NJ: Erlbaum.

CROOG, S. H., & FITZGERALD, E. F. (1978). Subjective stress and serious illness of a spouse: Wives of heart patients. *Journal of Health and Social Behavior, 19,* 166–178.

CROYLE, R. T., & BARGER, S. D. (1993). Illness cognition. In S. Maes, H. Leventhal, & M. Johnston (Eds.), *International review of health psychology* (Vol. 2, pp. 29–52). New York: Wiley.

CROYLE, R. T., & DITTO, P. H. (1990). Illness cognition and behavior: An experimental approach. *Journal of Behavioral Medicine, 13,* 31–52.

CRUESS, D. G., ANTONI, M. H., MCGREGOR, B. A., KILBOURN, K. M., BOYERS, A. E., ALFIERI, S. M., et al. (2000). Cognitive-behavioral stress management reduces serum cortisol by enhancing benefit finding among women being treated for early stage breast cancer. *Psychosomatic Medicine, 62,* 304–308.

CU (Consumers Union) (1992, September). Health care in crisis: The search for solutions. *Consumer Reports,* pp. 579–592.

CU (Consumers Union) (1994, January). Acupuncture. *Consumer Reports,* pp. 54–59.

CU (Consumers Union) (1995, February). How is your doctor treating you? *Consumer Reports,* pp. 81–88.

CU (Consumers Union). (1998, August). Checkups: Are you getting what you need? *Consumer Reports,* pp. 17–19.

CU (Consumers Union). (1999a, March). Herbal Rx: The promise and pitfalls. *Consumer Reports,* pp. 44–48.

CU (Consumers Union). (1999b, August). How does your HMO stack up? *Consumer Reports,* pp. 23–29.

CU (Consumers Union). (2000, May). The mainstreaming of alternative medicine. *Consumer Reports,* pp. 17–25.

CU (Consumers Union) (2001, October). Are you in the right plan? *Consumer Reports,* pp. 27–31.

CU (Consumers Union) (2004a, May). Dangerous supplements still at large. *Consumer Reports,* pp. 12–17.

CU (Consumers Union) (2004b, October). Hospital infections: Consumers drive a movement. *Consumer Reports,* p. 61.

CUMMINGS, N. A. (1991). Arguments for the financial efficacy of psychological services in health care settings. In J. J. Sweet, R. H. Rozensky, & S. M. Tovian (Eds.), *Handbook of clinical psychology in medical settings* (pp. 113–126). New York: Plenum.

CUNNINGHAM, A. J., EDMONDS, C. V. I., JENKINS, G. P., POLLACK, H., LOCKWOOD, G. A., & WARR, D. (1998). A randomized controlled trial of the effects of group psychological therapy on survival in women with metastatic breast cancer. *Psycho-Oncology, 7,* 508–517.

CUNNINGHAM, C. L. (1998). Drug conditioning and drug-seeking behavior. In W. O'Donahue (Ed.), *Learning and behavior therapy* (pp. 518–544). Boston: Allyn & Bacon.

CUNNINGHAM, J. A., & BRESLIN, F. C. (2004). Only one in three people with alcohol abuse or dependence ever seek treatment. *Addictive Behaviors, 29,* 221–223.

CURRY, S. J., & EMMONS, K. M. (1994). Theoretical models for predicting and improving compliance with breast cancer screening. *Annals of Behavioral Medicine, 16,* 302–316.

CURRY, S. J., GROTHAUS, L. C., MCAFEE, T., & PABINIAK, C. (1998). Use and cost effectiveness of smoking-cessation services under four insutance plans in a health maintenance organization. *New England Journal of Medicine, 339,* 673–679.

CURRY, S. J., & MCBRIDE, C. M. (1994). Relapse prevention for smoking cessation: Review and evaluation of concepts and interventions. *Annual Review of Public Health, 15,* 345–366.

CURRY, S. J., TAPLIN, S. H., ANDERMAN, C., BARLOW, W. E., & MCBRIDE, C. (1993). A randomized trial of the impact of risk assessment and feedback on participation in mammography screening. *Preventive Medicine, 22,* 350–360.

CURRY, S., WAGNER, E. H., & GROTHAUS, L. C. (1990). Intrinsic and extrinsic motivation for smoking cessation. *Journal of Consulting and Clinical Psychology, 58,* 310–316.

CUTLER, R. B., FISHBAIN, D. A., ROSOMOFF, H. L., ABDEL-MOTY, E., KHALIL, T. M., & ROSOMOFF, R. S. (1994). Does nonsurgical pain center treatment of chronic pain return patients to work?: A review and meta-analysis of the literature. *Spine*, 19, 643–652.

CUTRONA, C. E. (1986). Behavioral manifestations of social support: A microanalytic investigation. *Journal of Personality and Social Psychology*, 51, 201–208.

CUTRONA, C. E., & RUSSELL, D. W. (1990). Type of social support and specific stress: Toward a theory of optimal matching. In B. A Sarason, I. G. Sarason, & G. R. Pierce (Eds.), *Social support: An interactional view* (pp. 319–366). New York: Wiley.

CVENGROS, J. A., CHRISTENSEN, A. J., & LAWTON, W. J. (2004). The role of control and preference for control in adherence to a chronic medical regimen. *Annals of Behavioral Medicine*, 27, 155–161.

DAHLBERG, C. C. (1977, June). Stroke. *Psychology Today*, pp. 121–128.

DAHLQUIST, L. M., GIL, K. M., ARMSTRONG, F. D., DELAWYER, D. D., GREENE, P., & WUORI, D. (1986). Preparing children for medical examinations: The importance of previous medical experience. *Health Psychology*, 5, 249–259.

DAHLQUIST, L. M., PENDLEY, J. S., LANDTHRIP, D. S., JONES, C. L., & STEUBER, C. P. (2002). Distraction intervention for preschoolers undergoing intramuscular injections and subcutaneous port access. *Health Psychology*, 21, 94–99.

DALESSIO, D. J. (1994). Diagnosing the severe headache. *Neurology*, 44(Suppl. 3), S6–12.

DALLMAN, M. F., PECORARO, N., AKANA, S. F., LA FLEUR, S. E., GOMEZ, F., HOUSHYAR, H. et al. (2003). Chronic stress and obesity: a new view of "comfort food." *Proceedings of the National Academy of Sciences*, 100, 11696–11701.

DALTON, J. A., KEEFE, F. J., CARLSON, J., & YOUNGBLOOD, R. (2003). Tailoring cognitive-behavioral treatment for cancer pain. *Pain Management Nursing*, 5, 3–18.

DATILLO, A. M., & KRIS-ETHERTON, P. M. (1992). Effects of weight reduction on blood lipids and lipoproteins: A meta-analysis. *American Journal of Clinical Nutrition*, 56, 320–328.

DAVIDSON, R. J., KABAT-ZINN, J., SCHUMACHER, J., ROSENKRANZ, M., MULLER, D., SANTORELLI, S. F., et al. (2003). Alterations in brain and immune function produced by mindfulness meditation. *Psychosomatic Medicine*, 65, 564–570.

DAVIDSON, R. S. (1985). Behavioral medicine and alcoholism. In N. Schneiderman & J. T. Tapp (Eds.), *Behavioral medicine: The biopsychosocial approach* (pp. 379–404). Hillsdale, NJ: Erlbaum.

DAVIS, M. C., MATTHEWS, K. A., & TWAMLEY, E. W. (1999). Is life more difficult on Mars or Venus? A meta-analytic review of sex differences in major and minor life events. *Annals of Behavioral Medicine*, 21, 83–97.

DAVIS, M. S. (1966). Variations in patients' compliance with doctors' orders: Analysis of congruence between survey responses and results of empirical investigations. *Journal of Medical Education*, 41, 1037–1048.

DAVISON, G. C., NEALE, J. M. & KRING, A. M. (2004). *Abnormal psychology, with cases* (9th ed.). Hoboken, NJ: Wiley.

DAVISON, K. P., PENNEBAKER, J. W., & DICKERSON, S. S. (2000). Who talks? The social psychology of illness suport groups. *American Psychologist*, 55, 205–217.

DAW, J. (2001). New rule will change the psychologist–physician relationship. *Monitor on Psychology*, 32, pp. 66–69.

DEA (Drug Enforcement Administration of United States Department of Justice) (2004). *Frequently asked questions and answers for health care professionals and law enforcement personnel*. Retrieved (9–16–2004) from http://www.dea.gov.

DEANGELIS, T. (1990, October). Psychologists involved with epilepsy treatment. *American Psychological Association Monitor*, p. 24.

DEANGELIS, T. (1995, October). Primary-care collaborations growing. *American Psychological Association Monitor*, p. 22.

DEARDORFF, W. W. (1996). Board certification: What do you mean you're not board certified? *Health Psychologist*, 18(3), 10–11.

DEGNER, L. F., & BEATON, J. I. (1987). *Life-death decisions in health care*. New York: Hemisphere.

DE GROOT, M., ANDERSON, R., FREEDLAND, K. E., CLOUSE, R. E., & LUSTMAN, P. J. (2001). Association of depression and diabetes complications: A meta-analysis. *Psychosomatic Medicine*, 63, 619–630.

DEJONG, W. (1980). The stigma of obesity: The consequences of naive assumptions concerning the causes of physical deviance. *Journal of Health and Social Behavior*, 21, 75–87.

DEJONG, W., & HINGSON, R. (1998). Strategies to reduce driving under the influence of alcohol. *Annual Reviews*, 19, 359–378.

DELAHANTY, D. L., DOUGALL, A. L., HAWKEN, L., TRAKOWSKI, J. H., SCHMITZ, J. B., JENKINS, F. J., et al. (1996). Time course of natural killer cell activity and lymphocyte proliferation in response to two acute stressors in healthy men. *Health Psychology*, 15, 48–55.

DELONGIS, A., COYNE, J. C., DAKOF, G., FOLKMAN, S., & LAZARUS, R. S. (1982). Relationship of daily hassles, uplifts, and major life events to health status. *Health Psychology*, 1, 119–136.

DENISSENKO, M. F., PAO, A., TANG, M.-S., & PFEIFER, G. P. (1996). Preferential formation of benzo[a]pyrene adducts at lung cancer mutational hotspots in P53. *Science*, 274, 430–432.

DENNIS, C., HOUSTON-MILLER, N., SCHWARTZ, R. G., AHN, D. K., KRAEMER, H. C., GOSSARD, D., et al. (1988). Early return to work after uncomplicated myocardial infarction: Results of a randomized trial. *Journal of the American Medical Association*, 260, 214–220.

DEPALMA, A. (1996, June 19). In Mexico, pain relief is a medical and political issue. *New York Times*, p. A6.

DEROGATIS, L. R. (1977). *Psychological Adjustment to Illness Scale*. Baltimore, MD Clinical Psychometric Research.

DEROGATIS, L. R. (1986). The Psychological Adjustment to Illness Scale (PAIS). *Journal of Psychosomatic Research*, 30, 77–91.

DEROGATIS, L. R., FLEMING, M. P., SUDLER, N. C., & DELLAPIETRA, L. (1995). Psychological assessment. In P. M. Nicassio & T. W. Smith (Eds.), *Managing chronic illness: A biopsychosocial perspective* (pp. 59–116). Washington, DC: American Psychological Association.

DESCARTES, R. (1664). *Traite de l'Homme*. Paris: Angot.

DESHARNAIS, R., JOBIN, J., CÔTÉ, C., LÉVESQUE, L., & GODIN, G. (1993). Aerobic exercise and the placebo effect: A controlled study. *Psychosomatic Medicine*, 55, 149–154.

DESHIELDS, T., CARMIN, C., ROSS, L., & MANNEN, K. (1995, March). *Diagnosis of psychological disorders in primary care patients by medicine residents*. Paper presented at the meeting of the Society of Behavioral Medicine, San Diego.

DES JARLAIS, D. C., & FRIEDMAN, S. R. (2002). Strategies for working with injecting drug users: The role of health psychologists in harm reduction. In M. A. Chesney & M. H. Antoni (Eds.), *Innovative approaches to health psychology: Prevention and treatment lessons from AIDS* (pp. 97–114). Washington, DC: American Psychological Association.

DES JARLAIS, D. C., FRIEDMAN, S. R., CASRIEL, C., & KOTT, A. (1987). AIDS and preventing initiation into intravenous (IV) drug use. *Psychology and Health*, 1, 179–194.

DETJEN, J. (1991, November 10). Will genetics revolution mark some as victims? *Philadelphia Inquirer*, pp. A1, 18.

DETWEILER, J. B., BEDEL, B. T., SALOVEY, P., PRONIN, E., & ROTHMAN, A. J. (1999). Message framing and sunscreen use: Gain-framed messages motivate beach goers. *Health Psychology*, 18, 189–196.

DEVELLIS, B. M., & DEVELLIS, R. F. (2001). Self-efficacy and health. In A. Baum, T. A. Revenson, & J. E. Singer (Eds.), *Handbook of health psychology* (pp. 235–247). Mahwah, NJ: Erlbaum.

DEVINS, G. M., BINIK, Y. M., HOLLOMBY, D. J., BARRÉ, P. E., & GUTTMANN, R. D. (1981). Helplessness and depression in end-stage renal disease. *Journal of Abnormal Psychology*, 90, 531–545.

DEVRIES, J. E., BURNETTE, M. M., & REDMON, W. K. (1991). AIDS prevention: Improving nurses' compliance with glove wearing through performance feedback. *Journal of Applied Behavior Analysis*, 24, 705–711.

DEYKIN, E. Y., KEANE, T. M., KALOUPEK, D., FINDKE, G., ROTHENDLER, J., SIEGFRIED, M., et al. (2001). Posttraumatic stress disorder and the use of health services. *Psychosomatic Medicine*, 63, 835–841.

DEYO, R. A., CHERKIN, D., CONRAD, D., & VOLINN, E. (1991). Cost, controversy, crisis: Low back pain and the health of the public. *Annual Review of Public Health*, 12, 141–156.

DIAMOND, E. L. (1982). The role of anger and hostility in essential hypertension and coronary heart disease. *Psychological Bulletin*, 92, 410–433.

DICLEMENTE, C. C., PROCHASKA, J. O., FAIRHURST, S. K., VELICER, W. F., VELASQUEZ, M. M., & ROSSI, J. S. (1991). The process of smoking cessation: An analysis of precontemplation, contemplation, and preparation stages of change. *Journal of Consulting and Clinical Psychology*, 59, 295–304.

DICLEMENTE, C. C., PROCHASKA, J. O., & GILBERTINI, M. (1985). Self-efficacy and the stages of self-change of smoking. *Cognitive Therapy and Research*, 9, 181–200.

DICLEMENTE, R. J., ZORN, J., & TEMOSHOK, L. (1987). The association of gender, ethnicity, and length of residence in the Bay Area to adolescents' knowledge and attitudes about acquired immune deficiency syndrome. *Journal of Applied Social Psychology*, 17, 216–230.

DIEHR, P., KOEPSELL, T., CHEADLE, A., PSATY, B. M., WAGNER, E., & CURRY, S. (1993). Do communities differ in health behaviors? *Journal of Clinical Epidemiology*, 46, 1141–1149.

DIFRANZA, J. R., & LEW, R. A. (1995). Effect of maternal cigarette smoking on pregnancy complications and sudden infant death syndrome. *Journal of Family Practice*, 40, 385–394.

DILLER, L. (1999). Hemiplegia. In M. G. Eisenberg, R. L. Glueckauf, & H. H. Zaretsky (Eds.), *Medical aspects of disability: A handbook for the rehabilitation professional* (2nd ed., pp. 528–547). New York: Springer.

DIMATTEO, M. R. (1985). Physician-patient communication: Promoting a positive health care setting. In J. C. Rosen & L. J. Solomon (Eds.), *Prevention in health psychology* (pp. 328–365). Hanover, NH: University Press of New England.

DIMATTEO, M. R. (2002). Patient adherence and medical treatment outcomes: A meta-analysis. *Medical Care*, 40, 791–811.

DIMATTEO, M. R. (2004). Social support and patient adherence to medical treatment: A meta-analysis. *Health Psychology*, 23, 207–218.

DiMatteo, M. R., & DiNicola, D. D. (1982). *Achieving patient compliance: The psychology of the medical practitioner's role.* New York: Pergamon.

DiMatteo, M. R., Hays, R. D., & Prince, L. M. (1986). Relationship of physicians' nonverbal communication skill to patient satisfaction, appointment noncompliance, and physician workload. *Health Psychology,* 5, 581–594.

DiMatteo, M. R., Linn, L. S., Chang, B. L., & Cope, D. W. (1985). Affect and neutrality in physician behavior: A study of patients' values and satisfaction. *Journal of Behavioral Medicine,* 8, 397–409.

Dimsdale, J. E., Alpert, B. S., & Schneiderman, N. (1986). Exercise as a modulator of cardiovascular reactivity. In K. A. Matthews, S. M. Weiss, T. Detre, T. M. Dembroski, B. Falkner, S. B. Manuck, & R. B. Williams (Eds.), *Handbook of stress, reactivity, and cardiovascular disease* (pp. 365–384). New York: Wiley.

Dinh, K. T., Sarason, I. G., Peterson, A. V., & Onstad, L. E. (1995). Children's perception of smokers and nonsmokers: A longitudinal study. *Health Psychology,* 14, 32–40.

DISC (Writing group for the DISC Collaborative Research Group) (1995). Efficacy and safety of lowering dietary intake of fat and cholesterol in children with elevated low-density lipoprotein cholesterol: The Dietary Intervention Study in Children (DISC). *Journal of the American Medical Association,* 273, 1429–1435.

Dishman, R. K. (1982). Compliance/adherence in health-related exercise. *Health Psychology,* 1, 237–267.

Dishman, R. K. (1986). Mental health. In V. Seefeldt (Ed.), *Physical activity and well-being* (pp. 304–341). Reston, VA: American Alliance for Health, Physical Education, Recreation, and Dance.

Dishman, R. K. (1991). Increasing and maintaining exercise and physical activity. *Behavior Therapy,* 22, 345–378.

Dishman, R. K., Sallis, J. F., & Orenstein, D. R. (1985). The determinants of physical activity and exercise. *Public Health Reports,* 100, 158–171.

Distefan, J. M., Gilpin, E. A., Sargent, J. D., & Pierce, J. P. (1999). Do movie stars encourage adolescents to start smoking? Evidence from California. *Preventive Medicine,* 28, 1–11.

Ditto, B. (1993). Familial influences on heart rate, blood pressure, and self-report anxiety responses to stress: Results from 100 twin pairs. *Psychophysiology,* 30, 635–645.

Dobkin, B. H. (2004). Strategies for stroke rehabilitation. *Lancet Neurology,* 3, 528–536.

Doehrman, S. R. (1977). Psycho-social aspects of recovery from coronary heart disease: A review. *Social Science and Medicine,* 11, 199–218.

Doering, S., Katzlberger, F., Rumpold, G., Roessler, S. Hofstoetter, M. S., Schatz, D. S., et al. (2000). Videotape preparation of patients before hip replacement surgery reduces stress. *Psychosomatic Medicine,* 62, 365–373.

Doherty, K., Militello, F. S., Kinnunen, T., & Garvey, A. J. (1996). Nicotine gum dose and weight gain after smoking cessation. *Journal of Consulting and Clinical Psychology,* 64, 799–807.

Dohrenwend, B. S., & Dohrenwend, B. P. (1984). Life stress and illness: Formulation of the issues. In B. S. Dohrenwend & B. P. Dohrenwend (Eds.), *Stressful life events and their contexts* (pp. 1–27). New Brunswick, NJ: Rutgers University Press.

Dohrenwend, B. S., Krasnoff, L., Askenasy, A. R., & Dohrenwend, B. P. (1978). Exemplification of a method for scaling life events: The PERI Life Events Scale. *Journal of Health and Social Behavior,* 19, 205–229.

Dolbier, C. L., Cocke, R. R., Leiferman, J. A., Steinhardt, M. A., Schapiro, S. J., Nehete, P. N., et al. (2001). Differences in functional immune responses of high vs. low hardy healthy individuals. *Journal of Behavioral Medicine,* 24, 219–229.

Dolecek, T. A., Milas, N. C., Van Horn, L. V., Farrand, M. E., Gorder, D. D., Duchene, A. G., et al. (1986). A long-term nutrition experience: Lipid responses and dietary adherence patterns in the Multiple Risk Factor Intervention Trial. *Journal of the American Dietetic Association,* 86, 752–758.

Dolinski, D., Gromski, W., & Zawisza, E. (1987). Unrealistic pessimism. *Journal of Social Psychology,* 127, 511–516.

Donnerstein, E., & Wilson, D. W. (1976). Effects of noise and perceived control on ongoing and subsequent aggressive behavior. *Journal of Personality and Social Psychology,* 34, 774–781.

Donny, E. C., Caggiula, A. R., Mielke, M. M., Jacobs, K. S., Rose, C., & Sved, A. F. (1998). Acquisition of nicotine self-administration in rats: The effects of dose, feeding schedule, and drug contingency. *Psychopharmacology,* 136, 83–90.

Donovan, D. M. (2003). Relapse prevention in substance abuse treatment. In J. L. Sorensen, R. A. Rawson, J. Guydish, & J. E. Zweben (Eds.), *Drug abuse treatment through collaboration: Practice and research partnerships that work* (pp. 121–137). Washington, DC: American Psychological Association.

Dougall, A. L., & Baum, A. (2001). Stress, health, and illness. In A. Baum, T. A. Revenson, & J. E. Singer (Eds.), *Handbook of health psychology* (pp. 321–337). Mahwah, NJ: Erlbaum.

DOWNEY, G., SILVER, R. C., & WORTMAN, C. B. (1990). Reconsidering the attribution-adjustment relation following a major negative event: Coping with the loss of a child. *Journal of Personality and Social Psychology, 59*, 925–940.

DRAPKIN, R. G., WING, R. R., & SHIFFMAN, S. (1995). Responses to hypothetical high risk situations: Do they predict weight loss in a behavioral treatment program or the context of dietary lapses? *Health Psychology, 14*, 427–434.

DREWNOWSKI, A. (2002). Taste, taste preferences, and body weight. In C. G. Fairburn & K. D. Brownell (Eds.), *Eating disorders and obesity: A comprehensive handbook* (pp. 50–54). New York: Guilford.

DRUMMOND, D. C., & GLAUTIER, S. (1994). A controlled trial of cue exposure treatment in alcohol dependence. *Journal of Consulting and Clinical Psychology, 62*, 809–817.

DUBBERT, P. M. (2002). Physical activity and exercise: Recent advances and current challenges. *Journal of Consulting and Clinical Psychology, 70*, 526–536.

DUNBAR-JACOB, J., & SCHLENK, E. (2001). Patient adherence to treatment regimen. In A. Baum, T. A. Revenson, & J. E. Singer (Eds.), *Handbook of health psychology* (pp. 571–580). Mahwah, NJ: Erlbaum.

DUNCAN, S. C., STRYCKER, L. A., & DUNCAN, T. E. (1999). Exploring associations in developmental trends of adolescent substance use and risky sexual behavior in a high-risk population. *Journal of Behavioral Medicine, 22*, 21–34.

DUNKEL-SCHETTER, C., & BENNETT, T. L. (1990). Differentiating the cognitive and behavioral aspects of social support. In B. R. Sarason, I. G. Sarason, & G. R. Pierce (Eds.), *Social support: An interactional view* (pp. 267–296). New York: Wiley.

DUNN, A. J. (1995). Psychoneuroimmunology: Introduction and general perspectives. In B. Leonard & K. Miller (Eds.), *Stress, the immune system and psychiatry* (pp. 1–16). New York: Wiley.

DUNN, M. E., & GOLDMAN, M. S. (1998). Age and drinking-related differences in the memory organization of alcohol expectancies in 3rd-, 6th-, 9th-, and 12th-grade children. *Journal of Consulting and Clinical Psychology, 66*, 579–585.

DUSSELDORP, E., VAN ELDEREN, T., MAES, S., MEULMAN, J., & KRAAIJ, V. (1999). A meta-analysis of psychoeducational programs for coronary heart disease patients. *Health Psychology, 18*, 506–519.

DWECK, C. S., & ELLIOTT, E. S. (1983). Achievement motivation. In P. H. Mussen (Ed.), *Handbook of child psychology* (4th ed., Vol. 4, pp. 643–692). New York: Wiley.

DWECK, C. S., & REPUCCI, N. D. (1973). Learned helplessness and reinforcement responsibility in children. *Journal of Personality and Social Psychology, 25*, 109–116.

D'ZURILLA, T. J. (1988). Problem-solving therapies. In K. S. Dobson (Ed.), *Handbook of cognitive-behavioral therapies* (pp. 85–135). New York: Guilford.

EARLE, T. L., LINDEN, W., & WEINBERG, J. (1999). Differential effects of harassment on cardiovascular and salivary cortisol stress reactivity and recovery in women and men. *Journal of Psychosomatic Research, 46*, 124–141.

EASTERBROOK, G. (1987, January 26). The revolution. *Newsweek*, pp. 40–74.

EDELL, B. H., EDINGTON, S., HERD, B., O'BRIEN, R. M., & WITKIN, G. (1987). Self-efficacy and self-motivation as predictors of weight loss. *Addictive Behaviors, 12*, 63–66.

EDELMAN, S., LEMON, J., BELL, D. R., & KIDMAN, A. D. (1999). Effects of group CBT on the survival time of patients with metastatic breast cancer. *Psycho-Oncology, 8*, 474–481.

EDELSTEIN, L. (1984). *Maternal bereavement: Coping with the unexpected death of a child*. New York: Praeger.

EDWARDS, R. R., DOLEYS, D. M., FILLINGIM, R. B., & LOWREY, D. (2001). Ethnic differences in pain tolerance: Clinical implications in a chronic pain population. *Psychosomatic Medicine, 63*, 316–323.

EFA (Epilepsy Foundation of America) (2004). *Answer place: Epilepsy and seizure statistics; First aid for generalized tonic clonic (grand mal) seizures*. Retrieved (5–18–2004) from http://www.efa.org.

EICHENWALD, K. (1987, January 11). Braving epilepsy's storm. *The New York Times Magazine*, pp. 30–36.

EISENBERG, M. G. (1984). Spinal cord injuries. In H. B. Roback (Ed.), *Helping patients and their families cope with medical problems* (pp. 107–129). San Francisco: Jossey-Bass.

EISER, C. (1985). *The psychology of childhood illness*. New York: Springer-Verlag.

EITEL, P., K, & FRIEND, R. (1999). Reducing denial and sexual risk behaviors in college students: A comparison of a cognitive and a motivational approach. *Annals of Behavioral Medicine, 21*, 12–19.

EKSTRAND, M. L., & CHESNEY, M. A. (2002). Adhering to complex medication regimens. In M. A. Chesney & M. H. Antoni (Eds.), *Innovative approaches to health psychology: Prevention and treatment lessons from AIDS* (pp. 283–306) Washington, DC: American Psychological Association.

ELIASSON, B., HJALMARSON, A., KRUSE, E., LANDFELDT, B., & WESTIN, Å. (2001). Effect of smoking reduction and cessation on cardiovascular risk factors. *Nicotine and Tobacco Research, 3*, 249–255.

ELIOPOULOS, C., KLEIN, J., PHAN, M. K., KNIE, B., GREENWALD, M., CHITAYAT, D., et al. (1994). Hair concentrations of nicotine and cotinine in women and their newborn infants. *Journal of the American Medical Association*, 271, 621–623.

ELLICKSON, P. L., McCAFFREY, D. F., GHOSH-DASTIDAR, B., & LONGSHORE, D. L. (2003). New inroads in preventing adolescent drug use: Results from a large-scale trial of Project ALERT in middle schools. *American Journal of Public Health*, 93, 1830–1836.

ELLINGTON, L., & WIEBE, D. J. (1999). Neuroticism, symptom presentation, and medical decision making. *Health Psychology*, 18, 634–643.

ELLIS, A. (1962). *Reason and emotion in psychotherapy*. New York: Lyle Stuart.

ELLIS, A. (1977). The basic clinical theory of rational-emotive therapy. In A. Ellis & R. Grieger (Eds.), *Handbook of rational-emotive therapy* (pp. 3–34). New York: Springer.

ELLIS, A. (1987). The impossibility of achieving consistently good mental health. *American Psychologist*, 42, 364–375.

EMMONS, K., LINNAN, L. A., SHADEL, W. G., MARCUS, B., & ABRAMS, D. B. (1999). The Working Healthy Project: A worksite health-promotion trial targeting physical activity, diet, and smoking. *Journal of Occupational and Environmental Medicine*, 41, 545–555.

EMRICK, C. D., & HANSEN, J. (1983). Assertions regarding effectiveness of treatment for alcoholism. *American Psychologist*, 38, 1078–1088.

ENG, P. M., FITZMAURICE, G., KUBZANSKY, L. D., RIMM, E. B., & KAWACHI, I. (2003). Anger expression and risk of stroke and coronary heart disease among male health professionals. *Psychosomatic Medicine*, 65, 100–110.

ENGEL, G. L. (1977). The need for a new medical model: A challenge for biomedicine. *Science*, 196, 129–136.

ENGEL, G. L. (1980). The clinical application of the biopsychosocial model. *American Journal of Psychiatry*, 137, 535–544.

ENGEL, G. L., REICHSMAN, R., & SEGAL, H. L. (1956). A study of an infant with a gastric fistula: I. Behavior and the rate of total hydrochloric acid secretion. *Psychosomatic Medicine*, 18, 374–398.

ENRIGHT, M. F., RESNICK, R., DeLEON, P. H., SCIARA, A. D., & TANNEY, F. (1990). The practice of psychology in hospital settings. *American Psychologist*, 45, 1059–1065.

EPDET (Expert Panel on Detection, Evaluation, and Treatment of High Blood Cholesterol in Adults) (2001). Executive summary of the Third Report of the National Cholesterol Education Program (NCEP) Expert Panel on Detection, Evaluation, and Treatment of High Blood Cholesterol in Adults (Adult Treatment Panel III). *Journal of the American Medical Association*, 285, 2486–2497.

EPPING-JORDAN, J. E., WAHLGREN, D. R., WILLIAMS, R. A., PRUITT, S. D., SLATER, M. A., PATTERSON, T. L., et al. (1998). Transition to chronic pain in men with low back pain: Predictive relationships among pain intensity, disability, and depressive symptoms. *Health Psychology*, 17, 421–427.

EPSTEIN, L. H., & CLUSS, P. A. (1982). A behavioral medicine perspective on adherence to long-term medical regimens. *Journal of Consulting and Clinical Psychology*, 50, 950–971.

EPSTEIN, L. H., KILANOWSKI, C. K., CONSALVI, A. R., & PALUCH, R. A. (1999). Reinforcing value of physical activity as a determinant of child activity level. *Health Psychology*, 18, 599–603.

EPSTEIN, L. H., PALUCH, R. A., KILANOWSKI, C. K., & RAYNOR, H. A. (2004). The effect of reinforcement or stimulus control to reduce sedentary behavior in the treatment of pediatric obesity. *Health Psychology*, 23, 371–380.

EPSTEIN, L. H., SAELENS, B. E., & O'BRIEN, J. G. (1995). Effects of reinforcing increases in active behavior versus decreases in sedentary behavior for obese children. *International Journal of Behavioral Medicine*, 2, 41–50.

EPSTEIN, L. H., VALOSKI, A., WING, R. R., & McCURLEY, J. (1994). Ten-year outcomes of behavioral family-based treatment for childhood obesity. *Health Psychology*, 13, 373–383.

EPSTEIN, L. H., WING, R. R., PENNER, B. C., & KRESS, M. J. (1985). Effect of diet and controlled exercise on weight loss in obese children. *Journal of Pediatrics*, 107, 358–361.

EPSTEIN, L. H., WING, R. R., VALOSKI, A., & DEVOS, D. (1988). Long-term relationship between weight and aerobic-fitness change in children. *Health Psychology*, 7, 47–53.

ERDMAN, R. A. M. (1990). Myocardial infarction and cardiac rehabilitation. In A. A. Kaptein, H. M. van der Ploeg, B. Garssen, P. J. G. Schreurs, & R. Beunderman (Eds.), *Behavioural medicine: Psychological treatment of somatic disorders* (pp. 127–146). Chichester: Wiley.

ERDMANN, Y., & WILSON, R. (2001). Managed care: A view from Europe. *Annual Review of Public Health*, 22, 273–292.

ERIKSEN, M. P., LeMAISTRE, C. A., & NEWELL, G. R. (1988). Health hazards of passive smoking. *Annual Review of Public Health*, 9, 47–70.

ESTERLING, B. A., ANTONI, M. H., FLETCHER, M. A., MARGULIES, S., & SCHNEIDERMAN, N. (1994). Emotional disclosure through writing or speaking modulates latent Epstein-Barr virus antibody titers. *Journal of Consulting and Clinical Psychology*, 62, 130–140.

ESTERLING, B. A., KIECOLT-GLASER, J. K., & GLASER, R. (1996). Psychosocial modulation of cytokine-induced natural killer cell activity in older adults. *Psychosomatic Medicine, 58,* 264–272.

ESTEY, A., MUSSEAU, A., & KEEHN, L. (1994). Patient's understanding of health information: A multihospital comparison. *Patient Education and Counseling, 24,* 73–78.

EUROPEAN COLLABORATIVE STUDY (1991). Children born to women with HIV-1 infection: Natural history and risk of transmission. *Lancet, 337,* 253–260.

EVANS, C., & RICHARDSON, P. H. (1988). Improved recovery and reduced postoperative stay after therapeutic suggestions during general anaesthesia. *Lancet, 332,* 491–493.

EVANS, D. R., & KAZARIAN, S. S. (2001). Health promotion, disease prevention, and quality of life. In S. S. Kazarian & E. R. Evans (Eds.), *Handbook of cultural health psychology* (pp. 85–112). San Diego: Academic Press.

EVANS, F. J. (1987). Hypnosis. In R. J. Corsini (Ed.), *Concise encyclopedia of psychology* (pp. 554–555). New York: Wiley.

EVANS, G. W. (2001). Evironmental stress and health. In A. Baum, T. A. Revenson, & J. E. Singer (Eds.), *Handbook of health psychology* (pp. 365–385). Mahwah, NJ: Erlbaum.

EVANS, R. (1990, August/September). What you should know about childhood asthma. *Asthma and Allergy Advance* (reprint), pp. 1–4.

EVANS, R. I. (1976). Smoking in children: Developing a social psychological strategy of deterrence. *Preventive Medicine, 5,* 122–127.

EVANS, R. I. (1984). A social inoculation strategy to deter smoking in adolescents. In J. D. Matarazzo, S. M. Weiss, J. A. Herd, N. E. Miller, & S. M. Weiss (Eds.), *Behavioral health: A handbook of health enhancement and disease prevention* (pp. 765–774). New York: Wiley.

EVANS, R. I., ROZELLE, R. M., MITTELMARK, M. B., HANSEN, W. B., BANE, A. L., & HAVIS, J. (1978). Deterring the onset of smoking in children: Knowledge of immediate physiological effects and coping with peer pressure, media pressure, and parent modeling. *Journal of Applied Social Psychology, 8,* 126–135.

EVANS, R. L., HENDRICKS, R. D., HASELKORN, J. K., BISHOP, D. S., & BALDWIN, D. (1992). The family's role in stroke rehabilitation: A review of the literature. *American Journal of Physical Medicine & Rehabilitation, 71,* 135–139.

EVERSON, S. A., KAPLAN, G. A., GOLDBERG, D. E., LAKKA, T. A., SIVENIUS, J., & SALONEN, J. T. (1999). Anger expression and incident stroke: Prospective evidence from the Kuopio Ischemic Heart Disease Study. *Stroke, 30,* 523–528.

EVERSON, S. A., LYNCH, J. W., CHESNEY, M. A., KAPLAN, G. A., GOLDBERG, D. E., SHADE, S. B., et al. (1997). Interaction of workplace demands and cardiovascular reactivity in progression of carotid atherosclerosis: Population based study. *British Medical Journal, 314,* 553–558.

EVERSON, S. A., LYNCH, J. W., KAPLAN, G. A., LAKKA, T. A., SIVENIUS, J., & SALONEN, J. T. (2001). Stress-induced blood pressure reactivity and incident stroke in middle-aged men. *Stroke, 32,* 1263–1270.

EVERSON, S. A., MCKEY, B. S., & LOVALLO, W. R. (1995). Effect of trait hostility on cardiovascular responses to harassment in young men. *International Journal of Behavioral Medicine, 2,* 172–191.

EVERSON, S. A., ROBERTS, R. E., GOLDBERG, D. E., & KAPLAN, G. A. (1998). Depressive symptoms and increased risk of stroke mortality over a 29-year period. *Archives of Internal Medicine, 158,* 1133–1138.

EVON, D. M., & BURNS, J. W. (2004). Process and outcome in cardiac rehabilitation: An examination of cross-lagged effects. *Journal of Consulting and Clinical Psychology, 72,* 605–616.

EWART, C. K. (1991b). Social action theory for a public health psychology. *American Psychologist, 46,* 931–946.

FAIRBURN, C. G. (2002). Cognitive-behavioral therapy for bulimia nervosa. In C. G. Fairburn & K. D. Brownell (Eds.), *Eating disorders and obesity: A comprehensive handbook* (pp. 302–307). New York: Guilford.

FAIRBURN, C. G., STICE, E., COOPER, Z., DOLL, H. A., NORMAN, P. A., & O'CONNOR, M. E. (2003). Understanding persistence in bulimia nervosa: A 5-year naturalistic study. *Journal of Consulting and Clinical Psychology, 71,* 103–109.

FALKNER, B., & LIGHT, K. C. (1986). The interactive effects of stress and dietary sodium on cardiovascular reactivity. In K. A. Matthews, S. M. Weiss, T. Detre, T. M. Dembroski, B. Falkner, S. B. Manuck, & R. B. Williams (Eds.), *Handbook of stress, reactivity, and cardiovascular disease* (pp. 329–341). New York: Wiley.

FALS-STEWART, W., & O'FARRELL, T. J. (2003). Behavioral family counseling and naltrexone for male opioid-dependent patients. *Journal of Consulting and Clinical Psychology, 71,* 432–442.

FANG, J., MADHAVAN, S., & ALDERMAN, M. H. (1996). The association between birthplace and mortality from cardiovascular causes among black and white residents of New York City. *New England Journal of Medicine, 335,* 1545–1551.

FARKAS, A. J., DISTEFAN, J. M., CHOI, W. S., GILPIN, E. A., & PIERCE, J. P. (1999). Does parental smoking cessation discourage adolescent smoking? *Preventive Medicine, 28,* 213–218.

FARQUHAR, J. W., MACCOBY, N., & SOLOMON, D. S. (1984). Community applications of behavioral medicine. In W. D. Gentry (Ed.), *Handbook of behavioral medicine* (pp. 437–478). New York: Guilford.

FARQUHAR, J. W., MACCOBY, N., WOOD, P. D. ALEXANDER, J. K., BREITROSE, H., BROWN, B. W., et al. (1977). Community education for cardiovascular health. *Lancet*, 1192–1195.

FATHALLA, M. F. (1990). Relationship between contraceptive technology and HIV transmission: An overview. In N. J. Alexander, H. L. Gabelnick, & J. M. Spieler (Eds.), *Heterosexual transmission of AIDS*. New York: Wiley-Liss.

FAUCETT, J., GORDON, N., & LEVINE, J. (1994). Differences in postoperative pain severity among four ethnic groups. *Journal of Pain and Symptom Management, 9,* 383–389.

FAWZY, F. I., COUSINS, N. FAWZY, N. W., KEMENY, M. E., ELASHOFF, R., & MORTON, D. (1990). A structured psychiatric intervention for cancer patients: I. Changes over time in methods of coping and affective disturbance. *Archives of General Psychiatry, 47,* 720–725.

FAWZY, F. I., FAWZY, N. W., HYUN, C. S., ELASHOFF, R., GUTHRIE, D., FAHEY, J. L., et al. (1993). Malignant melanoma: Effects of an early structured psychiatric intervention, coping, and affective state on recurrence and survival 6 years later. *Archives of General Psychiatry, 50,* 681–689.

FAWZY, F. I., KEMENY, M. E., FAWZY, N. W., ELASHOFF, R., MORTON, D., COUSINS, N., et al. (1990). A structured psychiatric intervention for cancer patients: II. Changes over time in immunological measures. *Archives of General Psychiatry, 47,* 729–735.

FELDMAN, M., & RICHARDSON, C. T. (1986). Role of thought, sight, smell, and taste of food in the cephalic phase of gastric acid secretion in humans. *Gastroenterology, 90,* 428–433.

FELDMAN, P. J., COHEN, S., DOYLE, E. J., SKONER, D. P., & GWALTNEY, J. M. (1999). The impact of personality on the reporting of unfounded symptoms and illness. *Journal of Personality and Social Psychology, 77,* 370–378.

FELDMAN, R. S. (2000). *Development across the life span* (2nd ed.). Upper Saddle River, NJ: Prentice Hall.

FELETTI, G., FIRMAN, D., & SANSON-FISHER, R. (1986). Patient satisfaction with primary-care consultations. *Journal of Behavioral Medicine, 9,* 389–399.

FERNANDEZ, E. (1986). A classification system of cognitive coping strategies for pain. *Pain, 26,* 141–151.

FERNANDEZ, E., CLARK, T. S., & RUDICK-DAVIS, D. (1998). A framework for conceptualizing and assessment of affective disturbance in pain. In A. R. Block, E. F. Kremer, & E. Fernandez (Eds.), *Handbook of pain syndromes: Biopsychosocial perspectives* (pp. 123–147). Mahwah, NJ: Erlbaum.

FERNANDEZ, E., & TURK, D. C. (1989). The utility of cognitive coping strategies for altering pain perception: A meta-analysis. *Pain, 38,* 123–135.

FEUERSTEIN, M., CARTER, R. L., & PAPCIAK, A. S. (1987). A prospective analysis of stress and fatigue in recurrent low back pain. *Pain, 31,* 333–344.

FEUERSTEIN, M., & GAINER, J. (1982). Chronic headache: Etiology and management. In D. M. Doleys, R. L. Meredith, & A. R. Ciminero (Eds.), *Behavioral medicine: Assessment and treatment strategies* (pp. 199–249). New York: Plenum.

FIATARONE, M. A., MORLEY, J. E., BLOOM, E. T., BENTON, D., SOLOMON, G. F., & MAKINODAN, T. (1989). The effect of exercise on natural killer cell activity in young and old subjects. *Journal of Gerontology: Medical Sciences, 44,* M37–45.

FIELD, A. E., AUSTIN, S. B., TAYLOR, C. B., MALSPEIS, S., ROSNER, B., ROCKETT, H. R. et al. (2003). Relation between dieting and weight change among preadolescents and adolescents. *Pediatrics, 112,* 900–906.

FIELD, T. M. (1996). Touch therapies across the life span. In P. M. Kato & T. Mann (Ed.), *Handbook of diversity issues in health psychology* (pp. 49–67). New York: Plenum.

FIELD, T. M. (1998). Massage therapy effects. *American Psychologist, 53,* 1270–1281.

FIELDING, J. E. (1990). The challenges of work-place health promotion. In S. M. Weiss, J. E. Fielding, & A. Baum (Eds.), *Perspectives in behavioral medicine: Health at work* (pp. 13–28). Hillsdale, NJ: Erlbaum.

FIELDING, J. E. (1991). Smoking control at the workplace. *Annual Review of Public Health, 12,* 209–234.

FIELDS, H. L., & LEVINE, J. D. (1984). Placebo analgesia—A role for endorphins? *Trends in Neurosciences, 7,* 271–273.

FIGUEIRAS, M. J., & WEINMAN, J. (2003). Do similar patient and spouse perceptions of myocardial infarction predict recovery? *Psychology and Health, 18,* 201–216.

FILLINGIM, R. B. (2000). Sex, gender, and pain: Women and men really are different. *Current Review of Pain, 4,* 24–30.

FILSINGER, E. E. (1987). Social class. In R. J. Corsini (Ed.), *Concise encyclopedia of psychology* (pp. 1053–1054). New York: Wiley.

FINN, P. E., & ALCORN, J. D. (1986). Noncompliance to hemodialysis dietary regimens: Literature review and treatment recommendations. *Rehabilitation Psychology, 31,* 67–78.

FINNEY, J. W., & MOOS, R. H. (1997). Psychosocial treatments for alcohol use disorders. In P. E. Nathan & J. M. Gorman (Eds.), *A guide to treatments that work* (pp. 156–166). New York: Oxford University Press.

FIORE, M. C., JORENBY, D. E., & BAKER, T. B. (1997). Smoking cessation: Principles and practice based upon the AHCPR Guideline, 1996. *Annals of Behavioral Medicine*, 19, 213–219.

FIORE, M. C., NEWCOMB, P., & McBRIDE, P. (1993). Natural history and epidemiology of tobacco use and addiction. In C. T. Orleans & J. Slade (Eds.), *Nicotine addiction: Principles and management*. New York: Oxford University Press.

FISHER, E. B., LICHTENSTEIN, E., & HAIRE-JOSHU, D. (1993). Multiple determinants of tobacco use and cessation. In C. T. Orleans & J. Slade (Eds.), *Nicotine addiction: Principles and management*. New York: Oxford University Press.

FISHER, J. D., FISHER, W. A., MISOVICH, S. H., KIMBLE, D. L., & MALLOY, T. E. (1996). Changing AIDS risk behavior: Effects of an intervention emphasizing AIDS risk reduction information, motivation, and behavioral skills in a college student population. *Health Psychology*, 15, 114–123.

FISKE, D. W., & MADDI, S. R. (1961). A conceptual framework. In D. W. Fiske & S. R. Maddi (Eds.), *Functions of varied experience*. Homewood, IL: Dorsey.

FITZGERALD, S. T., HAYTHORNTHWAITE, J. A., SUCHDAY, S., & EWART, C. K. (2001). Anger in young Black and White workers: Effects of job control, dissatisfaction, and support. *Journal of Behavioral Medicine*, 26, 283–296.

FLACK, J. M., AMARO, H., JENKINS, W., KUNITZ, S., LEVY, J., MIXON, M., et al. (1995). Panel I: Epidemiology of minority health. *Health Psychology*, 14, 592–600.

FLASKERUD, J. H. (1988). AIDS: Psychosocial aspects. *Health Values*, 12(4), 44–52.

FLAY, B. R. (1985). Psychosocial approaches to smoking prevention: A review of findings. *Health Psychology*, 4, 449–488.

FLAY, B. R. (1987). Mass media and smoking cessation: A critical review. *American Journal of Public Health*, 77, 153–160.

FLAY, B. R., HU, F. B., & RICHARDSON, J. (1998). Psychosocial predictors of different stages of cigarette smoking among high school students. *Preventive Medicine*, 27, A9–A18.

FLAY, B. R., KOEPKE, D., THOMSON, S. J., SANTI, S., BEST, A., & BROWN, K. S. (1989). Six-year follow-up of the first Waterloo school smoking prevention trial. *American Journal of Public Health*, 79, 1371–1376.

FLAY, B. R., RYAN, K. B., BEST, J. A., BROWN, K. S., KERSELL, M. W., D'AVERNAS, J. R., et al. (1985). Are social-psychological smoking prevention programs effective? The Waterloo Study. *Journal of Behavioral Medicine*, 8, 37–59.

FLEMING, I., BAUM, A., DAVIDSON, L. M., RECTANUS, E., & McARDLE, S. (1987). Chronic stress as a factor in physiologic reactivity to challenge. *Health Psychology*, 6, 221–237.

FLEMING, M. F., MUNDT, M. P., FRENCH, M. T., MANWELL, L. B., STAUFFACHER, E. A., & BARRY, K. L. (2000). Benefit-cost analysis of brief physician advice with problem drinkers in primary care settings. *Medical Care*, 38, 7–18.

FLEMING, R., BAUM, A., GISRIEL, M. M., & GATCHEL, R. J. (1982). Mediating influences of social support on stress at Three Mile Island. *Journal of Human Stress*, 8, 14–22.

FLOR, H. (2001). Psychophysiological assessment of the patient with chronic pain. In D. C. Turk & R. Melzack (Eds.), *Handbook of pain assessment* (2nd ed., pp. 76–96). New York: Guilford.

FLOR, H., FYDRICH, T., & TURK, D. C. (1992). Efficacy of multidisciplinary pain treatment centers: A meta-analytic review. *Pain*, 49, 221–230.

FLOR, H., & TURK, D. C. (1985). Chronic illness in an adult family member: Pain as a prototype. In D. C. Turk & R. D. Kerns (Eds.), *Health, illness, and families: A life-span perspective* (pp. 255–278). New York: Wiley.

FLYNN, K. J., & FITZGIBBON, M. (1998). Body images and obesity risk among black females: A review of the literature. *Annals of Behavioral Medicine*, 20, 13–24.

FOA, E. B. (1998). Rape and posttraumatic stress disorder. In E. A. Blechman & K. D. Brownell (Eds.), *Behavioral medicine and women: A comprehensive handbook* (pp. 742–745). New York: Guilford.

FOGEL, E. R. (1987). Biofeedback-assisted musculoskeletal therapy and neuromuscular re-education. In M. S. Schwartz (Ed.), *Biofeedback: A practitioner's guide* (pp. 560–593). New York: Guilford.

FOLKMAN, S. (1997). Positive psychological states and coping with severe stress. *Social Science and Medicine*, 45, 1207–1221.

FOLKMAN, S., LAZARUS, R. S., PIMLEY, S., & NOVACEK, J. (1987). Age differences in stress and coping processes. *Psychology and Aging*, 2, 171–184.

FOLKMAN, S., & MOSKOWITZ, J. T. (2004). Coping: Pitfalls and promise. *Annual Review of Psychology*, 55, 745–774.

FOLLICK, M. J., AHERN, D. K., ATTANASIO, V., & RILEY, J. F. (1985). Chronic pain programs: Current aims, strategies, and needs. *Annals of Behavioral Medicine*, 7(3), 17–20.

FONTAINE, K. R., REDDEN, D. T., WANG, C., WESTFALL, A. O., & ALLISON, D. B. (2003). Years of life lost due to obesity. *Journal of the American Medical Association*, 289, 187–193.

FORDYCE, W. E. (1976). *Behavioral methods for chronic pain and illness*. St. Louis: Mosby.

FORDYCE, W. E., & STEGER, J. C. (1979). Behavioral management of chronic pain. In O. F. Pomerleau & J. P. Brady (Eds.), *Behavioral medicine: Theory and practice.* Baltimore, MD: Williams & Wilkins.

FOREM, J. (1974). *Transcendental meditation.* New York: Dutton.

FOREYT, J. P., & LEAVESLEY, G. (1991). Behavioral treatment of obesity at the work site. In S. M. Weiss, J. E. Fielding, & A. Baum (Eds.), *Perspectives in behavioral medicine: Health at work* (pp. 99–115). Hillsdale, NJ: Earlbaum.

FORMAN, M. R., TROWBRIDGE, F. L., GENTRY, E. M., MARKS, J. S., & HOGELIN, G. C. (1986). Overweight adults in the United States: The behavioral risk factor surveys. *American Journal of Clinical Nutrition, 44,* 410–416.

FOX, D. K., HOPKINS, B. L., & ANGER, W. K. (1987). The long-term effects of a token economy on safety performance in open-pit mining. *Journal of Applied Behavior Analysis, 20,* 215–224.

FRANCIS, V., KORSCH, B. M., & MORRIS, M. J. (1969). Gaps in doctor-patient communication. *New England Journal of Medicine, 280,* 535–540.

FRANK, E., WINKLEBY, M. A., ALTMAN, D. G., ROCKHILL, B., & FORTMANN, S. P. (1991). Predictors of physicians' smoking cessation advice. *Journal of the American Medical Association, 266,* 3139–3144.

FRANK, R. G. (2001). Rehabilitation. In A. Baum, T. A. Revenson, & J. E. Singer (Eds.), *Handbook of health psychology* (pp. 581–590). Mahwah, NJ: Erlbaum.

FRANKENHAEUSER, M. (1986). A psychobiological framework for research on human stress and coping. In M. H. Appley & R. Trumbull (Eds.), *Dynamics of stress: Physiological, psychological, and social perspectives* (pp. 101–116). New York: Plenum.

FRASER, R. T. R. M 1999). Epilepsy. In M. G., Eisenberg, R. L. Glueckauf, & H. H. Zaretsky (Eds.), *Medical aspects of disability: A handbook for the rehabilitation professional* (2nd ed., pp. 225–244). New York: Springer.

FRASURE-SMITH, N., LESPÉRANCE, F., JUNEAU, M., TALAJIC, M., & BOURASSA, M. G. (1999). Gender, depression, and one-year prognosis after myocardial infarction. *Psychosomatic Medicine, 61,* 26–37.

FREDRIKSON, M., & MATTHEWS, K. A. (1990). Cardiovascular responses to behavioral stress and hypertension: A meta-analytic review. *Annals of Behavioral Medicine, 12,* 30–39.

FREELS, S. A., WARNECKE, R. B., PARSONS, J. A., JOHNSON, T. P., FLAY, B. R., & MORENA, O. F. (1999). Characteristics associated with exposure to and participation in a televised smoking cessation intervention program for women with high school or less education. *Preventive Medicine, 28,* 579–588.

FREEMAN, A. (1990). Cognitive therapy. In A. S. Bellack & M, Hersen (Eds.), *Handbook of comparative treatments for adult disorders* (pp. 64–87). New York: Wiley.

FREEMAN, R., BARABASZ, A., BARABASZ, M., & WARNER, D. (2000). Hypnosis and distraction differ in their effects on cold pressor pain. *American Journal of Clinical Hypnosis, 43,* 137–148.

FREIDSON, E. (1961). *Patients' views of medical practice.* New York: Russell Sage Foundation.

FRENCH, M. T., SALOME, H. J., & CARNEY, M. (2002). Using the DATCAP and ASI to estimate the costs and benefits of residential addiction treatment in the State of Washington. *Social Science & Medicine, 55,* 2267–2282.

FRENCH, S. A., & JEFFERY, R. W. (1994). Consequences of dieting to lose weight: Effects on physical and mental health. *Health Psychology, 13,* 195–212.

FRENCH, S. A., STORY, M., & JEFFERY, R. W. (2001). Environmental influences on eathing and physical activity. *Annual Review of Public Health, 22,* 309–335.

FRIEDMAN, H. S., TUCKER, J. S., & REISE, S. P. (1995). Personality dimensions and measures potentially relevant to health: A focus on hostility. *Annals of Behavioral Medicine, 17,* 245–253.

FRIEDMAN, H. S., TUCKER, J. S., SCHWARTZ, J. E., TOMLINSON-KEASEY, C., WINGARD, D. L., & CRIQUI, M. H. (1995). Psychosocial and behavioral predictors of longevity. The aging and death of the "Termites." *American Psychologist, 50,* 69–78.

FRIEDMAN, M., & ROSENMAN, R. H. (1974). *Type A behavior and your heart.* New York: Knopf.

FRIEDMAN, M., THORESEN, C. E., GILL, J. J., ULMER, D., POWELL, L. H., PRICE, V. A., et al. (1986). Alteration of Type A behavior and its effect on cardiac recurrences in post myocardial infarction patients: Summary results of the Recurrent Coronary Prevention Project. *American Heart Journal, 112,* 653–665.

FROESE, A., HACKETT, T. P., CASSEM, N. H., & SILVERBERG, E. L. (1974). Trajectories of anxiety and depression in denying and nondenying acute myocardial infarction patients during hospitalization. *Journal of Psychosomatic Research, 18,* 413–420.

FULLERTON, J. T., KRITZ-SILVERSTEIN, D., SADLER, G. R., & BARRETT-CONNOR, E. (1996). Mammography usage in a community-based sample of older women. *Annals of Behavioral Medicine, 18,* 67–72.

FUNK, S. C. (1992). Hardiness: A review of theory and research. *Health Psychology, 11,* 335–345.

FUTTERMAN, A. D., KEMENY, M. E., SHAPIRO, D., & FAHEY, J. L. (1994). Immunological and physiological changes associated with induced positive and negative mood. *Psychosomatic Medicine, 56,* 499–511.

GALAVOTTI, C., CABRAL, R. J., LANSKY, A., GRIMLEY, D. M., RILEY, G. E., & PROCHASKA, J. O. (1995). Validation of measures of condom and other contraceptive use among women at high risk for HIV infection and unintended pregnancy. *Health Psychology*, 14, 570–578.

GALLACHER, J. E. J., SWEETNAM, P. M., YARNELL, J. W. G., ELWOOD, P. C., & STANSFELD, S. A. (2003). Is Type A behavior really a trigger for coronary heart disease events? *Psychosomatic Medicine*, 65, 339–346.

GALLO, L. C., TROXEL, W. M., MATTHEWS, K. A., & KULLER, L. H. (2003). Marital status and quality in middle-aged women: Associations with levels and trajectories of cardiovascular risk factors. *Health Psychology*, 22, 453–463.

GANNON, L. R., HAYNES, S. N., CUEVAS, J., & CHAVEZ, R. (1987). Psychophysiological correlates of induced headaches. *Journal of Behavioral Medicine*, 10, 411–423.

GARFINKEL, P. E. (2002). Classification and diagnosis of eating disorders. In C. G. Fairburn & K. D. Brownell (Eds.), *Eating disorders and obesity: A comprehensive handbook* (pp. 155–161). New York: Guilford Press.

GARMEZY, N. (1983). Stressors of childhood. In N. Garmezy & M. Rutter (Eds.), *Stress, coping, and development in children* (pp. 43–84). New York: McGraw-Hill.

GARRITY, T. F. (1981). Medical compliance and the clinician-patient relationship: A review. *Social Science and Medicine*, 15, 215–222.

GATCHEL, R. J. (1980). Effectiveness of two procedures for reducing dental fear: Group-administered desensitization and group education and discussion. *Journal of the American Dental Association*, 101, 634–638.

GATCHEL, R. J. (1996). Psychological disorders and chronic pain: Cause-and-effect relationships. In R. J. Gatchel & D. C. Turk (Eds.), *Psychological approaches to pain management: A practitioner's handbook* (pp. 33–52). New York: Guilford.

GATCHEL, R. J. (2001). Biofeedback and self-regulation of physiological activity: A major adjunctive treatment modality in health psychology. In A. Baum, T. A. Revenson, & J. E. Singer (Eds.), *Handbook of health psychology* (pp. 95–103). Mahwah, NJ: Erlbaum.

GAUTHIER, J., CÔTÉ, G., & FRENCH, D. (1994). The role of home practice in the thermal biofeedback treatment of migraine headache. *Journal of Consulting and Clinical Psychology*, 62, 180–184.

GELLER, A. C., COLDITZ, G., OLIVERIA, S., EMMONS, K., JORGENSEN, C., AWEH, G. N. et al. (2002). Use of sunscreen, sunburning rates, and tanning bed use among more than 10,000 US children and adolescents. *Pediatrics*, 109, 1009–1014.

GENTRY, W. D. (1984). Behavioral medicine: A new research paradigm. In W. D. Gentry (Ed.), *Handbook of behavioral medicine* (pp. 1–12). New York: Guilford.

GENTRY, W. D., & KOBASA, S. C. O. (1984). Social and psychological resources mediating stress-illness relationships in humans. In W. D. Gentry (Ed.), *Handbook of behavioral medicine* (pp. 87–116). New York: Guilford.

GENTRY, W. D., & OWENS, D. (1986). Pain groups. In A. D. Holzman & D. C. Turk (Eds.), *Pain management: A handbook of psychological treatment approaches* (pp. 100–112). New York: Pergamon.

GERACE, R. A., & VORP, R. (1985). Epidemiology and behavior. In N. Schneiderman & J. T. Tapp (Eds.), *Behavioral medicine: The biopsychosocial approach* (pp. 25–44). Hillsdale, NJ: Erlbaum.

GERLIN, A. (1999, September 12). Health care's deadly secret: Accidents routinely happen. *Philadelphia Inquirer*, pp. A1, A20.

GERVASIO, A. H. (1986). Family relationships and compliance. In K. E. Gerber & A. M. Nehemkis (Eds.), *Compliance: The dilemma of the chronically ill* (pp. 98–127). New York: Springer.

GIACHELLO, A. L., & ARROM, J. O. (1997). Health service access and utilization among adolecsent minorities. In D. K. Wilson, J. R. Rodrigue, & W. C. Taylor (Eds.), *Health-promoting and health-compromising behaviors among minority adolescents* (pp. 303–320). Washington, DC: American Psychological Association.

GIBBONS, F. X., GERRARD, M., BLANTON, H., & RUSSELL, D. W. (1998). Reasoned action and social reaction: Willingness and intention as independent predictors of health risk. *Journal of Personality and Social Psychology*, 74, 1164–1180.

GIBBONS, F. X., MCGOVERN, P. G., & LANDO, H. A. (1991). Relapse and risk perception among members of a smoking cessation clinic. *Health Psychology*, 10, 42–45.

GIDRON, Y., BARAK, T., HENIK, A., GURMAN, G., & STEINER, O. (2002). Implicit learning of emotional information under anesthesia. *Cognitive Neuroscience and Neuropsychology*, 13, 139–142.

GIDRON, Y., DAVIDSON, K., & BATA, I. (1999). The short-term effects of a hostility-reduction intervention on male coronary heart disease patients. *Health Psychology*, 18, 416–420.

GIGNAC, M. A. M., COTT, C., & BADLEY, E. M. (2002). Adaptation to disability: Applying selective optimization with compensation to the behaviors of older adults with osteoarthritis. *Psychology and Aging*, 17, 520–524.

GIL, K. M., CARSON, J. W., PORTER, L. S., SCIPIO, C., BEDIAKO, S. M., & ORRINGER, E. (2004). Daily mood and stress predict pain, health care use, and work activity in African American adults with sickle-cell disease. *Health Psychology, 23,* 267–274.

GIL, K. M., GINSBERG, B., MUIR, M., SYKES, D., & WILLIAMS, D. A. (1990). Patient-controlled analgesia in postoperative pain: The relation of psychological factors to pain and analgesic use. *Clinical Journal of Pain, 6,* 137–142.

GIL, K. M., KEEFE, F. J., SAMPSON, H. A., McCASKILL, C. C., RODIN, J., & CRISSON, J. E. (1988). Direct observation of scratching behavior in children with atopic dermatitis. *Behavior Therapy, 19,* 213–227.

GIL. K. M., WILSON, J. J., & EDENS, J. L. (1997). The stability of pain coping strategies in young children, adolescents, and adults with sickle cell disease over an 18-month period. *Clinical Journal of Pain, 13,* 110–115.

GILBERSTADT, H., & DUKER, J. (1965). *A handbook for clinical and actuarial MMPI interpretation.* Philadelphia: Saunders.

GILBERT, D. G., & SPIELBERGER, C. D. (1987). Effects of smoking on heart rate, anxiety, and feelings of success during social interaction. *Journal of Behavioral Medicine, 10,* 629–638.

GILL, T. M., & FEINSTEIN, A. R. (1994). A critical appraisal of the quality of quality-of-life measurements. *Journal of the American Medical Association, 272,* 619–626.

GINZBERG, E. (1983). Allied health resources. In D. Mechanic (Ed.), *Handbook of health, health care, and the health professions* (pp. 479–494). New York: Free Press.

GIPSON, M., LISKEVYCH, T., & SWILLINGER, E. (1996). *Managing your health care: Making the most of your medical resources.* Ventura, CA: Pathfinder.

GIRODO, M., & WOOD, D. (1979). Talking yourself out of pain: The importance of believing that you can. *Cognitive Therapy and Research, 3,* 23–33.

GLADIS, M. M., MICHELA, J. L., WALTER, H. J., & VAUGHAN, R. D. (1992). High school students' perceptions of AIDS risk: Realistic appraisal or motivated denial? *Health Psychology, 11,* 307–316.

GLANZ, K. (2001). Current theoretical bases for nutrition intervention and their uses. In A. M. Coulston, C. L. Rock, & E. R. Monsen (Eds.), *Nutrition in the prevention and treatment of disease* (pp. 83–93). San Diego: Academic Press.

GLANZ, K., & LERMAN, C. (1992). Psychosocial impact of breast cancer: A critical review. *Annals of Behavioral Medicine, 14,* 204–212.

GLASER, R., THORN, B. E., TARR, K. L., KIECOLT-GLASER, J. K., & D'AMBROSIO, S. M. (1985). Effects of stress on methyltransferase synthesis: An important DNA repair enzyme. *Health Psychology, 4,* 403–412.

GLASGOW, R. E., KLESGES, R. C., MIZES, J. S., & PECHACEK, T. F. (1985). Quitting smoking: Strategies used and variables associated with success in a stop-smoking contest. *Journal of Consulting and Clinical Psychology, 53,* 905–912.

GLASGOW, R. E., McCAUL, K. D., & SCHAFER, L. C. (1986). Barriers to regimen adherence among persons with insulin-dependent diabetes. *Journal of Behavioral Medicine, 9,* 65–77.

GLASGOW, R. E., McCAUL, K. D., & SCHAFER, L. C. (1987). Self-care behaviors and glycemic control in Type I diabetes. *Journal of Chronic Diseases, 40,* 399–412.

GLASGOW, R. E., ORLEANS, C. T., WAGNER, E. H., CURRY, S. J., & SOLBERG, L. I. (2001). Does the chronic care model serve also as a template for improving prevention? *Milbank Quarterly, 79,* 579–612.

GLASS, D. C. (1977). *Behavior patterns, stress, and coronary heart disease.* Hillsdale, NJ: Erlbaum.

GLASS, D. C., KRAKOFF, L. R., CONTRADA, R., HILTON, W. F., KEHOE, K., MANNUCCI, E. G., et al. (1980). Effect of harassment and competition upon cardiovascular and plasma catecholamine responses in Type A and Type B individuals. *Psychophysiology, 17,* 453–463.

GLYNN, S. M., GRUDER, C. L., & JEGERSKI, J. A. (1986). Effects of biochemical validation of self-reported cigarette smoking on treatment success and on misreporting abstinence. *Health Psychology, 5,* 125–136.

GODIN, G., DESHARNAIS, R., JOBIN, J., & COOK, J. (1987). The impact of physical fitness and health-age appraisal upon exercise intentions and behavior. *Journal of Behavioral Medicine, 10,* 241–250.

GODIN, G., DESHARNAIS, R., VALOIS, P., LEPAGE, L., JOBIN, J., & BRADET, R. (1992, March). *Perceived barriers to exercise among different populations.* Paper presented at the meeting of the Society of Behavioral Medicine, New York.

GODIN, G., VALOIS, P., SHEPHARD, R. J., & DESHARNAIS, R. (1987). Prediction of leisure-time exercise behavior: A path analysis (LISREL V) model. *Journal of Behavioral Medicine, 10,* 145–158.

GODTFREDSEN, N. S., HOLST, C., PRESCOTT, E., VESTBO, J., & OSLER, M. (2002). Smoking reduction, smoking cessation, and mortality: A 16-year follow-up of 19,732 men and women from the Copenhagen Center for Prospective Population Studies. *American Journal of Epidemiology, 156,* 994–1001.

GOFFMAN, E. (1961). *Asylums.* Garden City, NY: Doubleday.

GOLASZEWSKI, T. (2001). Shining lights: Studies that have most influenced the understanding of health promotion's financial impact. *American Journal of Health Promotion, 15,* 332–340.

GOLD, R. S., & SKINNER, M. J. (1996). Judging a book by its cover: Gay men's use of perceptible characteristics to infer antibody status. *International Journal of STD & AIDS, 7,* 39–43.

GOLD, R. S., SKINNER, M. J., & HINCHY, J. (1999). Gay men's stereotypes about who is HIV-infected: A further study. *International Journal of STD & AIDS, 10,* 1–6.

GOLDBERG, C. (1998, September 11). Little drop in college binge drinking. *New York Times,* p. A14.

GOLDBERG, E. L., & COMSTOCK, G. W. (1980). Epidemiology of life events: Frequency in general populations. *American Journal of Epidemiology, 111,* 736–752.

GOLDING, J. F., & CORNISH, A. M. (1987). Personality and life-style in medical students: Psychopharmacological aspects. *Psychology and Health, 1,* 287–301.

GOLDSTEIN, I. B., JAMNER, L. D., & SHAPIRO, D. (1992). Ambulatory blood pressure and heart rate in healthy male paramedics during a workday and a nonworkday. *Health Psychology, 11,* 48–54.

GOLDSTEIN, L. H. (1990). Behavioural and cognitive-behavioural treatments for epilepsy: A progress review. *British Journal of Clinical Psychology, 29,* 257–269.

GOLDSTON, D. B., KOVACS, M., OBROSKY, D. S., & IYENGAR, S. (1995). A longitudinal study of life events and metabolic control among youths with insulin-dependent diabetes mellitus. *Health Psychology, 14,* 409–414.

GOLDWATER, B. C., & COLLIS, M. L. (1985). Psychologic effects of cardiovascular conditioning: A controlled experiment. *Psychosomatic Medicine, 47,* 174–181.

GOMEL, M., OLDENBURG, B., SIMPSON, J. M., & OWEN, N. (1993). Work-site cardiovascular risk reduction: A randomized trial of health risk assessment, education, counseling, and incentives. *American Journal of Public Health, 83,* 1231–1238.

GONDER-FREDERICK, L. A., COX, D. J., & RITTERBAND, L. M. (2002). Diabetes and behavioral medicine: The second decade. *Journal of Consulting and Clinical Psychology, 70,* 611–625.

GONZALEZ, J. S., PENEDO, F. J., ANTONI, M. H., DURAN, R. E., FERNANDEZ, M. I., McPHERSON-BAKER, S. et al. (2004). Social support, positive states of mind, and HIV treatment adherence in men and women living with HIV/AIDS. *Health Psychology, 23,* 413–418.

GOODALL, T. A., & HALFORD, W. K. (1991). Self-management of diabetes mellitus: A critical review. *Health Psychology, 10,* 1–8.

GOODMAN, E., & WHITAKER, R. C. (2002). A prospective study of the role of depression in the development and persistence of adolescent obesity. *Pediatrics, 109,* 497–504.

GORDON, C. M., & CAREY, M. P. (1996). Alcohol's effects on requisites for sexual risk reduction in men: An initial experimental investigation. *Health Psychology, 15,* 56–60.

GORDON, W. A., & DILLER, L. (1983). Stroke: Coping with a cognitive deficit. In T. G. Burish & L. A. Bradley (Eds.), *Coping with chronic disease: Research and applications* (pp. 113–135). New York: Academic Press.

GORIN, A. A., PHELAN, S., WING, R. R., & HILL, J. O. (2004). Promoting long-term weight control: Does dieting consistency matter? *Journal of Obesity Related Metabolic Disorders, 28,* 278–281.

GORTMAKER, S. L., DIETZ, W. H., & CHEUNG, L. W. Y. (1990). Inactivity, diet, and the fattening of America. *Journal of the American Dietetic Association, 90,* 1247–1252, 1255.

GORTMAKER, S. L., ECKENRODE, J., & GORE, S. (1982). Stress and the utilization of health services: A time series and cross-sectional analysis. *Journal of Health and Social Behavior, 23,* 25–38.

GOTTLIEB, N. H. (1983). The effect of health beliefs on the smoking behavior of college women. *Journal of American College Health, 31,* 214–221.

GOTTLIEB, N. H., & BAKER, J. A. (1986). The relative influence of health beliefs, parental and peer behaviors and exercise program participation on smoking, alcohol use and physical activity. *Social Science and Medicine, 22,* 915–927.

GOTTLIEB, N. H., & GREEN, L. W. (1987). Ethnicity and lifestyle health risk: Some possible mechanisms. *American Journal of Health Promotion, 2,* 37–45, 51.

GRAHAM, J. D., CORSO, P. S., MORRIS, J. M., SEGUI-GOMEZ, M., & WEINSTEIN, M. C. (1998). Evaluating the cost-effectiveness of clinical and public health measures. *Annual Review of Public Health, 19,* 125–152.

GRANT, J. C. B. (1972). *An atlas of anatomy.* Baltimore, MD: Williams & Wilkins.

GREEN, C. J. (1985). The use of psychodiagnostic questionnaires in predicting risk factors and health outcomes. In P. Karoly (Ed.), *Measurement strategies in health psychology* (pp. 301–334). New York: Wiley.

GREENGLASS, E. R., & NOGUCHI, K. (1996, August). *Longevity, gender and health: A psychocultural perspective.* Paper presented at the meeting of the International Society of Health Psychology in Montreal.

GREENLAND, P., KNOLL, M. D., STAMLER, J., NEATON, J. D., DYER, A. R., GARSIDE, D. B., et al. (2003). Major risk factors as antecedents of fatal and nonfatal coronary heart disease events. *Journal of the American Medical Association, 290,* 891–897.

GREENWALD, H. P., BONICA, J. J., & BERGNER, M. (1987). The prevalence of pain in four cancers. *Cancer, 60,* 2563–2569.

GRIFFIN, K. W., BOTVIN, G. J., DOYLE, M. M., DIAZ, T., & EPSTEIN, J. A. (1999). A six-year follow-up study of determinants of heavy cigarette smoking among high-school seniors. *Journal of Behavioral Medicine*, 22, 271–284.

GRIFFIN, K. W., FRIEND, R., KAELL, A. T., & BENNETT, R. S. (2001). Distress and disease status among patients with rheumatoid arthritis: Roles of coping styles and perceived responses from support providers. *Annals of Behavioral Medicine*, 23, 133–138.

GRITZ, E. R., CARR, C. R., & MARCUS, A. C. (1991). The tobacco withdrawal syndrome in unaided quitters. *British Journal of Addiction*, 86, 57–69.

GROB, G. N. (1983). Disease and environment in American history. In D. Mechanic (Ed.), *Handbook of health, health care, and the health professions* (pp. 3–22). New York: Free Press.

GRØNBÆK, M., BECKER, U., JOHANSEN, D., GOTTSCHAU, A., SCHNOHR, P., HEIN, H. O., et al. (2000). Type of alcohol consumed and mortality from all causes, coronary heart disease, and cancer. *Annals of Internal Medicine*, 133, 411–419.

GRUBE, J. W., & WALLACK, L. (1994). Television beer advertising and drinking knowledge, beliefs, and intentions among schoolchildren. *American Journal of Public Health*, 84, 254–259.

GRUEN, W. (1975). Effects of brief psychotherapy during the hospitalization period on the recovery process in heart attacks. *Journal of Consulting and Clinical Psychology*, 43, 223–232.

GRUETZNER, H. (1992). *Alzheimer's: A caregiver's guide and sourcebook*. New York: Wiley.

GRUNAU, R. V. E., & CRAIG, K. D. (1987). Pain expression in neonates: Facial action and cry. *Pain*, 28, 395–410.

GRUNBERG, N. E. (1991). Cigarette smoking at work: Data, issues, and models. In S. M. Weiss, J. E. Fielding, & A. Baum (Eds.), *Perspectives in behavioral medicine: Health at work* (pp. 75–98). Hillsdale, NJ: Erlbaum.

GRUNBERG, N. E., & BOWEN, D. J. (1985). Coping with the sequelae of smoking cessation. *Journal of Cardiopulmonary Rehabilitation*, 5, 285–289.

GUCCIONE, A. A., FELSON, D. T., ANDERSON, J. J., ANTHONY, J. M., ZHANG, Y., WILSON, P. W. F., et al. (1994). The effects of specific medical conditions on the functional limitations of elders in the Framingham Study. *American Journal of Public Health*, 84, 351–358.

GUCK, T. P., SKULTETY, F. M., MEILMAN, P. W., & DOWD, E. T. (1985). Multidisciplinary pain center follow-up study: Evaluation with a no-treatment control group. *Pain*, 21, 295–306.

GUMP, B. B., & MATTHEWS, K. A. (1999). Do background stressors influence reactivity to and recovery from acute stressors? *Journal of Applied Social Psychology*, 29, 469–494.

GUYLL, M., MATTHEWS, K. A., & BROMBERGER, J. T. (2001). Discrimination and unfair treatment: Relationship to cardiovascular reactivity among African American and European American women. *Health Psychology*, 20, 315–325.

GUYTON, A. C. (1985). *Anatomy and physiology*. Philadelphia: Saunders.

HAAS, F., & HAAS, S. S. (1990). *The chronic bronchitis and emphysema handbook*. New York: Wiley.

HACKETT, T. P., & WEISMAN, A. D. (1985). Reactions to the imminence of death. In A. Monat & R. S. Lazarus (Eds.), *Stress and coping: An anthology* (2nd ed., pp. 248–255). New York: Columbia University Press.

HAFEN, B. Q. (1981). *Nutrition, food, and weight control*. Boston: Allyn & Bacon.

HALEY, W. E. (1998). Alzheimer's disease: A general review. In E. A. Blechman & K. D. Brownell (Eds.), *Behavioral medicine and women: A comprehensive handbook* (pp. 546–550). New York: Guilford.

HALKITIS, P. N., & WILTON, L. (1999, Fall). Optimism and HIV treatment advances: The impact on sexual risk-taking among gay men. *The Health Psychologist*, 21, 10–12.

HALL, J. A., MILBURN, M. A., ROTER, D. L., & DALTROY, L. H. (1998). Why are sicker patients less satisfied with their medical care? Tests of two explanatory models. *Health Psychology*, 17, 70–75.

HALL, M., VASKO, R., BUYSSE, D., OMBAO, H., CHEN, Q., CASHMERE, J. D., et al. (2004). Acute stress affects heart rate variability during sleep. *Psychosomatic Medicine*, 66, 56–62.

HAMMOND, S. K., SORENSON, G., YOUNGSTROM, R., & OCKENE, J. K. (1995). Occupational exposure to environmental tobacco smoke. *Journal of the American Medical Association*, 274, 956–960.

HAMRICK, N., COHEN, S., & RODRIGUEZ, M. S. (2002). Being popular can be healthy or unhealthy: Stress, social network diversity, and incidence of upper respiratory infection. *Health Psychology*, 21, 294–298.

HANSEN, W. B., GRAHAM, J. W., SOBEL, J. L., SHELTON, D. R., FLAY, B. R., & JOHNSON, C. A. (1987). The consistency of peer and parent influences on tobacco, alcohol, and marijuana use among young adolescents. *Journal of Behavioral Medicine*, 10, 559–579.

HANSEN, W. B., RAYNOR, A. E., & WOLKENSTEIN, B. H. (1991). Perceived personal immunity to the consequences of drinking alcohol: The relationship between behavior and perception. *Journal of Behavioral Medicine*, 14, 205–224.

HANSON, C. L., HENGGELER, S. W., & BURGHEN, G. A. (1987). Social competence and parental support as mediators of the link between stress and metabolic control in adolescents with insulin-dependent diabetes mellitus. *Journal of Consulting and Clinical Psychology*, 55, 529–533.

HARBURG, E., ERFURT, J. C., HAUENSTEIN, L. S., CHAPE, C., SCHULL, W. J., & SCHORK, M. A. (1973). Socio-ecological stress, suppressed hostility, skin color, and black-white male blood pressure: Detroit. *Psychosomatic Medicine*, 35, 276–296.

HARE, B. D., & MILANO, R. A. (1985). Chronic pain: Perspectives on physical assessment and treatment. *Annals of Behavioral Medicine*, 7(3), 6–10.

HARRIS, D. M., & GUTEN, S. (1979). Health-protective behavior: An exploratory study. *Journal of Health and Social Behavior*, 20, 17–29.

HARRIS, J. R., PEDERSON, N. L., McCLEARN, G. E., PLOMIN, R., & NESSELROADE, J. R. (1992). Age differences in genetic and environmental influences for health from the Swedish Adoption/Twin Study of Aging. *Journal of Gerontology*, 47, P213–220.

HARRISON, S. L., MacLENNAN, R., SPEARE, R., & WRONSKI, I. (1994). Sun exposure and melanocytic naevi in young Australian children. *Lancet*, 1994, 1529–1532.

HART, W. (1987). *The art of living: Vipassana meditation*. New York: HarperCollins.

HASKELL, W. L. (1984). Overview: Health benefits of exercise. In J. D. Matarazzo, S. M. Weiss, J. A. Herd, N. E. Miller, & S. M. Weiss (Eds.), *Behavioral health: A handbook of health enhancement and disease prevention* (pp. 409–423). New York: Wiley.

HASKELL, W. L., ALDERMAN, E. L., FAIR, J. M., MARON, D. J., MACKEY, S. F., SUPERKO, H. R., et al. (1994). Effects of intensive multiple risk factor reduction on coronary atherosclerosis and clinical cardiac events in men and women with coronary artery disease: The Stanford Coronary Risk Intervention Project (SCRIP). *Circulation*, 89, 975–990.

HAUG, M. R., & LAVIN, B. (1981). Practitioner or patient—Who's in charge? *Journal of Health and Social Behavior*, 22, 212–229.

HAUSER, W. A., & HESDORFFER, D. C. (1990). *Facts about epilepsy*. Landover, MD: Epilepsy Foundation of America.

HAY, D., & OKEN, D. (1985). The psychological stresses of intensive care unit nursing. In A. Monat & R. S. Lazarus (Eds.), *Stress and coping: An anthology* (2nd ed., pp. 107–117). New York: Columbia University Press.

HAYES, R. D., KRAVITZ, R. L., MAZEL, R. M., SHERBOURNE, C. D., DiMATTEO, M. R., ROGERS, W. H., et al. (1994). The impact of patient adherence on health outcomes for patients with chronic disease in the Medical Outcomes Study. *Journal of Behavioral Medicine*, 17, 347–360.

HAYNES, R. B. (1976). A critical review of the "determinants" of patient compliance with therapeutic regimens. In D. L. Sackett & R. B. Haynes (Eds.), *Compliance with therapeutic regimens* (pp. 26–40). Baltimore, MD: Johns Hopkins University Press.

HAYS, J. C., GOLD, D. T., FLINT, E. P., & WINER, E. P. (1999). Patient preference for place of death: A qualitative approach. In B. de Vries (Ed.), *End of life issues: Interdisciplinary and multidimensional perspectives* (pp. 3–21). New York: Springer.

HAYS, J. C., KASL, S. V., & JACOBS, J. C. (1994). The course of psychological distress following threatened and actual conjugal bereavement. *Psychological Medicine*, 24, 917–927.

HAYTHORTHWAITE, J. A., & FAUERBACH, J. A. (2001). Assessment of acute pain, pain relief, and patient satisfaction. In D. C. Turk & R. Melzack (Eds.), *Handbook of pain assessment* (2nd ed., pp. 417–430). New York: Guilford.

HEARN, M. D., BARANOWSKI, T., BARANOWSKI, J., DOYLE, C., SMITH, M., LIN, L. S., et al. (1998). Environmental influences on dietary behavior among children: Availability and accessibility of fruits and vegetables enable consumption. *Journal of Health Education*, 29, 26–32.

HEBB, D. O. (1955). Drives and the C.N.S. (conceptual nervous system). *Psychological Review*, 62, 243–254.

HEINEMANN, A. W. (1999). Spinal cord injury. In M. G. Eisenberg, R. L. Glueckauf, & H. H. Zaretsky (Eds.), *Medical aspects of disability: A handbook for the rehabilitation professional* (2nd ed., pp. 499–527). New York: Springer.

HEINRICH, R. L., COHEN, M. J., NALIBOFF, B. D., COLLINS, G. A., & BONNEBAKKER, A. D. (1985). Comparing physical and behavior therapy for chronic low back pain on physical abilities, psychological distress, and patients' perceptions. *Journal of Behavioral Medicine*, 8, 61–78.

HELGESON, V. S., & COHEN, S. (1996). Social support and adjustment to cancer: Reconciling descriptive, correlational, and intervention research. *Health Psychology*, 15, 135–148.

HELGESON, V. S., COHEN, S., SCHULZ, R., & YASKO, J. (1999). Education and peer discussion group interventions and adjustment to breast cancer. *Archives of General Psychiatry*, 56, 340–347.

HELGESON, V. S., & FRITZ, H. L. (1999). Cognitive adaptation as a predictor of new coronary events after percutaneous transluminal coronary angioplasty. *Psychosomatic Medicine*, 61, 488–495.

HELGESON, V. S., SNYDER, P., & SELTMAN, H. (2004). Psychological and physical adjustment to breast cancer over 4 years: Identifying distinct trajectories of change. *Health Psychology*, 23, 3–15.

HELLER, K., PRICE, R. H., & HOGG, J. R. (1990). The role of social support in community and clinical interventions. In B. R. Sarason, I. G. Sarason, & G. R. Pierce (Eds.), *Social support: An interactional view* (pp. 482–507). New York: Wiley.

HELLHAMMER, D. K., BUCHTAL, J., GUTBERLET, I., & KIRSCHBAUM, C. (1997). Social hierarchy and adrenocortical stress reactivity in men. *Psychoneuroendocrinology, 22,* 643–650.

HENDEL, H., CAILLAT-ZUCMAN, S., LEBUANEC, H., CARRINGTON, M., O'BRIEN, S., ANDRIEU, J. M., et al. (1999). New class I and II HLA alleles strongly associated with opposite patterns of progression to AIDS. *Journal of Immunology, 162,* 6942–6946.

HENDERSON, D. K., FAHEY, B. J., WILLY, M., SCHMITT, J. M., CAREY, K., KOZIOL, D. E., et al. (1990). Risk for occupational transmission of human immunodeficiency virus type I (HIV-1) associated with clinical exposures: A prospective evaluation. *Annals of Internal Medicine, 113,* 740–746.

HENDERSON, G., & PRIMEAUX, M. (1981). Religious beliefs and healing. In G. Henderson & M. Primeaux (Eds.), *Transcultural health care* (pp. 185–195). Menlo Park, CA: Addison-Wesley.

HENDLER, N. H. (1984). Chronic pain. In H. B. Roback (Eds.), *Helping patients and their families cope with medical problems* (pp. 79–106). San Francisco: Jossey-Bass.

HENDRICK, S. S. (1985). Spinal cord injury and neuromuscular reeducation. In N. Schneiderman & J. T. Tapp (Eds.), *Behavioral medicine: The biopsychosocial approach* (pp. 589–614). Hillsdale, NJ: Erlbaum.

HENRY, J. H., LIU, Y-Y., NADRA, W. E., QIAN, C-G., MORMEDE, P., LEMAIRE, V., et al. (1993). Psychosocial stress can induce chronic hypertension in normotensive strains of rats. *Hypertension, 21,* 714–723.

HEPBURN, C. G., LOUGHLIN, C. A., & BARLING, J. (1997). Coping with chronic work stress. In B. H. Gottlieb (Ed.), *Coping with chronic stress* (pp. 343–366). New York: Plenum.

HERBERT, T. B., & COHEN, S. (1993). Stress and immunity in humans: A meta-analytic review. *Psychosomatic Medicine, 55,* 364–379.

HERD, J. A., & WEISS, S. M. (1984). Overview of hypertension: Its treatment and prevention. In J. D. Matarazzo, S. M. Weiss, J. A. Herd, N. E. Miller, & S. M. Weiss (Eds.), *Behavioral health: A handbook of health enhancement and disease prevention* (pp. 789–805). New York: Wiley.

HEREK, G. M. (1999). AIDS and stigma. *American Behavioral Scientist, 42,* 1106–1116.

HEREK, G. M., & CAPITANIO, J. P. (1999). AIDS stigma and sexual prejudice. *American Behavioral Scientist, 42,* 1130–1147.

HEREK, G. M., & GLUNT, E. K. (1988). An epidemic of stigma: Public reactions to AIDS. *American Psychologist, 43,* 886–891.

HERMAN, C. P., OLMSTEAD, M. P., & POLIVY, J. (1983). Obesity, externality, and susceptibility to social influence: An integrated analysis. *Journal of Personality and Social Psychology, 45,* 926–934.

HERMAN, C. P., & POLIVY, J. (1980). Restrained eating. In A. J. Stunkard (Ed.), *Obesity.* Philadelphia: Saunders.

HERSHEY, G. K. K., FRIEDRICH, M. F., ESSWEIN, L. A., THOMAS, M. L., & CHATLIA, T. A. (1997). The association of atopy with a gain-of-function mutation in the (alpha) subunit of the interluken-4 receptor. *New England Journal of Medicine, 337,* 1720–1725.

HESHKA, S., ANDERSON, J. W., ATKINSON, R. L., GREENWAY, F. L., HILL, J. O., PHINNEY, S. D. et al. (2003). Weight loss with self-help compared with a structured commercial program: A randomized trial. *Journal of the American Medical Association, 289,* 1792–1798.

HFA (Hospice Foundation of America) (2004). *What is hospice?* Retrieved (5–18–2004) from http://www. hospicefoundation.org.

HIGGINS, S. T., HEIL, S. H., & LUSSIER, J. P. (2004). Clinical implications of reinforcement as a determinant of substance use disorders. *Annual Review of Psychology, 55,* 431–461.

HILGARD, E. R. (1967). Individual differences in hypnotizability. In J. E. Gordon (Ed.), *Handbook of clinical and experimental hypnosis.* New York: Macmillan.

HILGARD, E. R., & HILGARD, J. R. (1983). *Hypnosis in the relief of pain* (rev. ed.). Los Altos, CA: Kaufmann.

HILL-BRIGGS, F. (2003). Problem solving in diabetes self-management: A model of chronic illness self-management behavior. *Annals of Behavioral Medicine, 25,* 182–193.

HINTON, J. (1984). Coping with terminal illness. In R. Fitzpatrick, J. Hinton, S. Newman, G. Scambler, & J. Thompson (Eds.), *The experience of illness* (pp. 227–245). London: Tavistock.

HIROTO, D. S., & SELIGMAN, M. E. P. (1975). Generality of learned helplessness in man. *Journal of Personality and Social Psychology, 31,* 311–327.

HITCHCOCK, L. S., FERRELL, B. R., & MCCAFFERY, M. (1994). The experience of chronic nonmalignant pain. *Journal of Pain and Symptom Management, 9,* 312–318.

HLETKO, P. J., ROBIN, S. S., HLETKO, J. D., & STONE, M. (1987). Infant safety seat use: Reaching the hard to reach. *American Journal of Diseases in Children, 141,* 1301–1304.

HOBFOLL, S. E. (1989). Conservation of resources: A new attempt at conceptualizing stress. *American Psychologist, 44,* 513–524.

HODGINS, D. C., LEIGH, G., MILNE, R., & GERRISH, R. (1997). Drinking goal selection in behavioral self-management of chronic alcoholics. *Addictive Behaviors*, 22, 247–255.

HOELSCHER, T. J., LICHSTEIN, K. L., & ROSENTHAL, T. L. (1986). Home relaxation practice in hypertension treatment: Objective assessment and compliance induction. *Journal of Consulting and Clinical Psychology*, 54, 217–221.

HOGAN, B. E., & LINDEN, W. (2004). Anger response styles and blood pressure: At least don't ruminate about it! *Annals of Behavioral Medicine*, 27, 38–49.

HOGAN, B. E., LINDEN, W., & NAJARIAN, B. (2002). Social support interventions: Do they work? *Clinical Psychology Review*, 22, 381–440.

HOLAHAN, C. J., MOOS, R. H., HOLAHAN, C. K., & BRENNAN, P. L. (1997). Social context, coping strategies, and depressive symptoms: An expanded model with cardiac patients. *Journal of Personality and Social Psychology*, 72, 918–928.

HOLAHAN, C. J., MOOS, R. H., HOLAHAN, C. K., CRONKITE, R. C., & RANDALL, P. K. (2001). Drinking to cope, emotional distress and alcohol use and abuse: A ten-year model. *Journal of Studies on Alcohol*, 62, 190–198.

HOLAHAN, C. K., HOLAHAN, C. J., & BELK, S. S. (1984). Adjustment in aging: The roles of life stress, hassles, and self-efficacy. *Health Psychology*, 3, 315–328.

HOLDEN, C. (1980). Love Canal residents under stress. *Science*, 208, 1242–1244.

HOLLON, S. D., SHELTON, R. C., & DAVIS, D. D. (1993). Cognitive therapy for depression: Conceptual issues and clinical efficacy. *Journal of Consulting and Clinical Psychology*, 61, 270–275.

HOLMES, D. S. (1984). Meditation and somatic arousal reduction. *American Psychologist*, 39, 1–10.

HOLMES, D. S. (1993). Aerobic fitness and the response to psychological stress. In P. Seraganian (Ed.), *Exercise psychology: The influence of physical exercise on psychological processes* (pp. 39–63). New York: Wiley.

HOLMES, T. H., & MASUDA, M. (1974). Life change and illness susceptibility. In B. S. Dohrenwend & B. P. Dohrenwend (Eds.), *Stressful life events: Their nature and effects*. New York: Wiley.

HOLMES, T. H., & RAHE, R. H. (1967). The Social Readjustment Rating Scale. *Journal of Psychosomatic Research*, 11, 213–218.

HOLROYD, K. A. (2002). Assessment and psychological management of recurrent headache disorders. *Journal of Consulting and Clinical Psychology*, 70, 656–677.

HOLROYD, K. A., FRANCE, J. L., NASH, J. M., & HURSEY, K. G. (1993). Pain state as artifact in the psychological assessment of recurrent headache sufferers. *Pain*, 53, 229–235.

HOLROYD, K. A., & PENZIEN, D. B. (1986). Client variables and the behavioral treatment of recurrent tension headache: A meta-analytic review. *Journal of Behavioral Medicine*, 9, 515–536.

HOLT, J. (1995, December). Motivating Beth. *American Journal of Nursing*, 95, pp. 60, 62.

HOLTZMAN, D., LOWRY, R., KANN, L., COLLINS, J. L., & KOLBE, L. J. (1994). Changes in HIV-related information sources, instruction, knowledge, and behaviors among U.S. high school students, 1989 and 1990. *American Journal of Public Health*, 84, 388–393.

HOLUM, J. R. (1994). *Fundamentals of general, organic, and biological chemistry* (5th ed.). New York: Wiley.

HOLZMAN, A. D., TURK, D. C., & KERNS, R. D. (1986). The cognitive-behavioral approach to the management of chronic pain. In A. D. Holzman & D. C. Turk (Eds.), *Pain management: A handbook of psychological treatment approaches* (pp. 31–50). New York: Pergamon.

HOPKINS, P. N. (1992). Effects of dietary cholesterol on serum cholesterol: A meta-analysis and review. *American Journal of Clinical Nutrition*, 55, 1060–1070.

HORN, J. C., & MEER, J. (1987, May). The vintage years. *Psychology Today*, pp. 76–84, 89–90.

HOUGH, R. L., FAIRBANK, D. T., & GARCIA, A. M. (1976). Problems in the ratio measurement of life stress. *Journal of Health and Social Behavior*, 17, 70–82.

HOUSE, J. S., ROBBINS, C., & METZNER, H. L. (1982). The association of social relationships and activities with mortality: Prospective evidence from the Tecumseh Community Health Study. *American Journal of Epidemiology*, 116, 123–140.

HOUSTON, B. K., & VAVAK, C. R. (1991). Cynical hostility: Developmental factors, psychosocial correlates, and health behaviors. *Health Psychology*, 10, 9–17.

HOWARD, G., WAGENKNECHT, L. E., BURKE, G. L., DIEZ-ROUX, A., EVANS, G. W., MCGOVERN, P., et al. (1998). Cigarette smoking and progression of atherosclerosis: The Atherosclerosis Risk in Communities (ARIC) Study. *Journal of the American Medical Association*, 279, 119–224.

HOWELL, D. (1986). The impact of terminal illness on the spouse. *Journal of Palliative Care*, 2, 22–30.

HP (Health Psychology, Division 38 of the American Psychological Association) (2000). *Doctoral training programs in health psychology*. Retrieved (10–13–2004) from http://www.health-psych.org.

HU, F. B., PERSKY, V., FLAY, B. R., & RICHARDSON, J. (1997). An epidemiological study of asthma prevalence and related factors among young adults. *Journal of Asthma*, 34, 67–76.

HUFFMAN, L. C., & DEL CARMEN, R. (1990). Prenatal stress. In L. E. Arnold (Ed.), *Childhood stress* (pp. 141–172). New York: Wiley.

HULL, J. G., & BOND, C. F. (1986). Social and behavioral consequences of alcohol consumption and expectancy: A meta-analysis. *Psychological Bulletin, 99,* 347–360.

HULL, J. G., YOUNG, R. D., & JOURILES, E. (1986). Applications of the self-awareness model of alcohol consumption: Predicting patterns of use and abuse. *Journal of Personality and Social Psychology, 51,* 790–796.

HUMBLE, C., CROFT, J., GERBER, A., CASPER, M., HAMES, C. G., & TYROLER, H. A. (1990). Passive smoking and 20-year cardiovascular disease mortality among nonsmoking wives, Evans County, Georgia. *American Journal of Public Health, 80,* 599–601.

HUNT, E. B., & MACLEOD, C. M. (1979). Cognition and information processing in patient and physician. In G. C. Stone, F. Cohen, & N. E. Adler (Eds.), *Health psychology—A handbook* (pp. 303–332). San Francisco: Jossey-Bass.

HUNT, W. A., MATARAZZO, J. D., WEISS, S. M., & GENTRY, W. D. (1979). Associative learning, habit, and health behavior. *Journal of Behavioral Medicine, 2,* 111–124.

HURLEY, D. (1987, August). A sound mind in an unsound body. *Psychology Today,* pp. 34–43.

HUSSUSSIAN, C. J., STRUEWING, J. P., GOLDSTEIN, A. M., HIGGINS, P. A. T., ALLY, D. S., SHEAHAN, M. D., et al. (1994). Germline p16 mutations in familial melanoma. *Nature Genetics, 8,* 15–21.

HUSZTI, H. C., & WALKER, C. E. (1991). Critical issues on consultation and liaison. In J. J. Sweet, R. H. Rozensky, & S. M. Tovian (Eds.), *Handbook of clinical psychology in medical settings* (pp. 165–185). New York: Plenum.

HUTCHINSON, K. E., MCGEARY, J., SMOLEN, A., BRYAN, A., & SWIFT, R. M. (2002). The DRD4 VNTR polymorphism moderates craving after alcohol consumption. *Health Psychology, 21,* 139–146.

HYSON, M. C. (1983). Going to the doctor: A developmental study of stress and coping. *Journal of Child Psychology and Psychiatry, 24,* 247–259.

IHGSC (International Human Genome Sequencing Consortium) (2001). Initial sequencing and analysis of the human genome. *Nature, 409,* 860–921.

ILFELD, F. W. (1980). Coping styles of Chicago adults: Description. *Journal of Human Stress, 6,* 2–10.

INSEL, P. M., & ROTH, W. T. (1998). *Core concepts in health* (8th ed.). Mountain View, CA: Mayfield.

INUI, T. S., YOURTEE, E. L., & WILLIAMSON, J. W. (1976). Improved outcomes in hypertension after physician tutorials. *Annals of Internal Medicine, 84,* 646–651.

IOM (Institute of Medicine) (2004). *Health literacy: A prescription to end confusion.* Retrieved (6–18–2004) from http://www.iom.edu.

IRONSON, G., FRIEDMAN, A., KLIMAS, N., ANTONI, M., FLETCHER, M. A., LAPERRIERE, A., et al. (1994). Distress, denial, and low adherence to behavioral interventions predict faster disease progression in gay men infected with human immunodeficiency virus. *International Journal of Behavioral Medicine, 1,* 90–105.

IRVIN, J. E., BOWERS, C. A., DUNN, M. E., & WANG, M. C. (1999). Efficacy of relapse prevention: A meta-analytic review. *Journal of Consulting and Clinical Psychology, 67,* 563–570.

IRVINE, J., BAKER, B., SMITH, J., JANDCIU, S., PAQUETTE, M., CAIRNS, J. et al. (1999). Poor adherence to placebo or amiodarone therapy predicts mortality: Results from the CAMIAT study. *Psychosomatic Medicine, 61,* 566–575.

IRWIN, M., MASCOVICH, A., GILLIN, J. C., WILLOUGHBY, R., PIKE, J., & SMITH, T. L. (1994). Partial sleep deprivation reduces natural killer cell activity in humans. *Psychosomatic Medicine, 56,* 493–498.

IZARD, C. E. (1979). Emotions as motivations: An evolutionary developmental perspective. In H. E. Howe & R. A. Dienstbier (Eds.), *Nebraska Symposium on Motivation 1978* (Vol. 26, pp. 163–200). Lincoln, NE: University of Nebraska Press.

JACCARD, J., & TURRISI, R. (1987). Cognitive processes and individual differences in judgments relevant to drunk driving. *Journal of Personality and Social Psychology, 53,* 135–145.

JACOB, M. C., & KERNS, R. D. (2001). Assessment of the psychosocial context of the experience of chronic pain. In D. C. Turk & R. Melzack (Eds.), *Handbook of pain assessment* (2nd ed., pp. 362–385). New York: Guilford.

JACOBSEN, P. B., BOVBJERG, D. H., SCHWARTZ, M. D., HUDIS, C. A., GILEWSKI, T. A., & NORTON, L. (1995). Conditioned emotional distress in women receiving chemotherapy for breast cancer. *Journal of Consulting and Clinical Psychology, 63,* 108–114.

JACOBSEN, P. B., & THORS, C. L. (2003). Fatigue in the radiation therapy patient; Current management and investigations. *Seminars in Radiation Oncology, 13,* 372–380.

JACOBSEN, P. B., WIDOWS, M. R., HANN, D. M., ANDRYKOWSKI, M. A., KRONISH, L. E., & FILEDS, K. K. (1998). Posttraumatic stress disorder symptoms after bone marrow transplantation for breast cancer. *Psychosomatic Medicine, 60,* 366–371.

JACOBSON, A. M., HAUSER, S. T., LAVORI, P., WILLETT, J. B., COLE, C. F., WOLFSDORF, J. I., et al. (1994). Family environment and glycemic control: A four-year prospective study of children and adolescents with insulin-dependent diabetes mellitus. *Psychosomatic Medicine, 56,* 401–409.

JACOBSON, E. J. (1938). *Progressive relaxation.* Chicago: University of Chicago Press.

JACOBSON, J. A., DANFORTH, D. N., COWAN, K. H., D'ANGELO, T., STEINBERG, S. M., PIERCE, L., et al. (1995). Ten-year results of a comparison of conservation with mastectomy in the treatment of stage I and II breast cancer. *New England Journal of Medicine, 332,* 907–911.

JADAD, A. R., CARROLL, D., GLYNN, C. J., MOORE, R. A., & McQUAY, H. J. (1992). Morphine responsiveness of chronic pain: Double-blind randomised crossover study with patient-controlled anesthesia. *Lancet, 339,* 1367–1371.

JAMES, G. D., YEE, L. S., HARSHFIELD, G. A., BLANK, S. G., & PICKERING, T. G. (1986). The influence of happiness, anger, and anxiety on the blood pressure of borderline hypertensives. *Psychosomatic Medicine, 48,* 502–508.

JAMES, J. E. (2004). Critical review of dietary caffeine and blood pressure: A relationship that should be taken more seriously. *Psychosomatic Medicine, 66,* 63–71.

JAMNER, L. D., & TURSKY, B. (1987). Syndrome-specific descriptor profiling: A psychophysiological and psychophysical approach. *Health Psychology, 6,* 417–430.

JANAL, M. N., GLUSMAN, M., KUHL, J. P., & CLARK, W. C. (1994). On the absence of correlation between responses to noxious heat, cold, electrical, and ischemic stimulation. *Pain,* 403–411.

JANIS, I. L. (1958). *Psychological stress.* New York: Wiley.

JANIS, I. L. (1984). The patient as decision maker. In W. D. Gentry (Ed.), *Handbook of behavioral medicine* (pp. 326–368). New York: Guilford.

JANIS, I. L., & MANN, L. (1977). *Decision making: A psychological analysis of conflict, choice, and commitment.* New York: Free Press.

JANSON-BJERKLIE, S., CARRIERI, V. K., & HUDES, M. (1986). The sensations of pulmonary dyspnea. *Nursing Research, 35,* 154–159.

JARET, P. (1986, June). Our immune system: The wars within. *National Geographic, 169,* 702–735.

JAY, S. M., ELLIOTT, C. H., KATZ, E., & SIEGEL, S. E. (1987). Cognitive-behavioral and pharmacologic interventions for children's distress during painful medical procedures. *Journal of Consulting and Clinical Psychology, 55,* 860–865.

JEANS, M. E. (1983). Pain in children—A neglected area. In P. Firestone, P. J. McGrath, & W. Feldman (Eds.), *Advances in behavioral medicine for children and adolescents* (pp. 23–37). Hillsdale, NJ: Erlbaum.

JEFFERY, R. W. (1998). Prevention of obesity. In G. A. Bray, C. Bouchard, & W. P. T. James (Eds.), *Handbook of obesity* (pp. 819–829). New York: Marcel Dekker.

JEFFERY, R. W., HENNRIKUS, D. J., LANDO, H. A., MURRAY, D. M., & LIU, J. W. (2000). Reconciling conflicting findings regarding postcessation weight concerns and success in smoking cessation. *Health Psychology, 19,* 242–246.

JEMMOTT, J. B., CROYLE, R. T., & DITTO, P. H. (1988). Commonsense epidemiology: Self-based judgments from laypersons and physicians. *Health Psychology, 7,* 55–73.

JEMMOTT, J. B., JEMMOTT, L. S., & FONG, G. T. (1999). Abstinence and safer sex HIV risk-reduction interventions for African American adolescents: A randomized controlled trial. *Journal of the American Medical Association, 279,* 1529–1536.

JENKINS, C. D. (1979). An approach to the diagnosis and treatment of problems of health related behaviour. *International Journal of Health Education, 22*(Suppl. 2), 1–24.

JENKINS, C. D., ZYZANSKI, S. J., & ROSENMAN, R. H. (1979). *The Jenkins Activity Survey for Health Prediction.* New York: The Psychological Corporation.

JENKINS, L. S., & GORTNER, S. R. (1998). Correlates of self-efficacy expectations and prediction of walking behavior in cardiac surgery elders. *Annals of Behavioral Medicine, 20,* 99–103.

JENNINGS, G., NELSON, L., NESTEL, P., ESLER, M., KORNER, P., BURTON, D., et al. (1986). The effects of changes in physical activity on major cardiovascular risk factors, hemodynamics, sympathetic function, and glucose utilization in man: A controlled study of four levels of activity. *Circulation, 73,* 30–40.

JENSEN, G. M., & LORISH, C. D. (1994). Promoting patient cooperation with exercise programs. *Arthritis Care and Research, 7,* 181–189.

JENSEN, M. P., CHEN, C., & BRUGGER, A. M. (2003). Interpretation of visual analog scale ratings and change scores. *Journal of Pain, 4,* 407–414.

JENSEN, M. P., & KAROLY, P. (2001). Self-report scales and procedures for assessing pain in adults. In D. C. Turk & R. Melzack (Eds.), *Handbook of pain assessment* (2nd ed., pp. 15–34). New York: Guilford.

JENSEN, M. P., & McFARLAND, C. A. (1993). Increasing the reliability and validity of pain intensity measurement in chronic pain patients. *Pain, 55,* 195–203.

JENSEN, M. P., ROMANO, J. M., TURNER, J. A., GOOD, A. B., & WALD, L. H. (1999). Patient beliefs predict patient functioning: Further support for a cognitive-behavioral model of chronic pain. *Pain, 81,* 95–104.

JESSOR, R. (1984). Adolescent development and behavioral health. In J. D. Matarazzo, S. M. Weiss, J. A. Herd, N. E. Miller, & S. M. Weiss (Eds.), *Behavioral health: A handbook of health enhancement and disease prevention* (pp. 69–90). New York: Wiley.

JETTE, A. M. (1984). Understanding and enhancing patient cooperation with arthritis treatments. In G. K. Riggs & E. P. Gall (Eds.), *Rheumatic diseases: Rehabilitation and management* (pp. 299–307). Boston: Butterworth.

JOHANSEN, O., BROX, J., & FLATEN, M. A. (2003). Placebo and nocebo responses, cortisol, and circulating beta-endorphin. *Psychosomatic Medicine, 65,* 786–790.

JOHNSON, C. A., HANSEN, W. B., COLLINS, L. M., & GRAHAM, J. W. (1986). High-school smoking prevention: Results of a three-year longitudinal study. *Journal of Behavioral Medicine, 9,* 439–452.

JOHNSON, J. E. (1983). Psychological interventions and coping with surgery. In A. Baum, S. E. Taylor, & J. E. Singer (Eds.), *Handbook of psychology and health* (Vol. 4, pp. 167–187). Hillsdale, NJ: Erlbaum.

JOHNSON, J. E., & LEVENTHAL, H. (1974). Effects of accurate expectations and behavioral instructions on reactions during a noxious medical examination. *Journal of Personality and Social Psychology, 29,* 710–718.

JOHNSON, J. E., RICE, V. H., FULLER, S. S., & ENDRESS, M. P. (1978). Sensory information, instruction in a coping strategy, and recovery from surgery. *Research in Nursing and Health, 1,* 4–17.

JOHNSON, J. H. (1986). *Life events as stressors in childhood and adolescence.* Newbury Park, CA: Sage.

JOHNSON, K., ANDERSON, N. B., BASTIDA, E., KRAMER, B. J., WILLIAMS, D., & WONG, M. (1995). Panel II. Macrosocial and environmental influences on minority health. *Health Psychology, 14,* 601–612.

JOHNSON, L. J., MEACHAM, S. L., & KRUSKALL, L. J. (2003). The antioxidants—vitamin C, vitamin E, and carotenoids. *Journal of Agromedicine, 9,* 65–82.

JOHNSON, M. I. (2001). Transcutaneous electrical nerve stimulation (TENS) and TENS-like devices: Do they provide pain relief? *Pain Reviews, 8,* 121–158.

JOHNSON, S. B. (1985). The family and the child with chronic illness. In D. C. Turk & R. D. Kerns (Eds.), *Health, illness, and families: A life-span perspective* (pp. 220–254). New York: Wiley.

JOHNSON, S. B., FREUND, A., SILVERSTEIN, J., HANSEN, C. A., & MALONE, J. (1990). Adherence-health status relationships in childhood diabetes. *Health Psychology, 9,* 606–631.

JOHNSON, S. B., KELLY, M., HENRETTA, J. C., CUNNINGHAM, W. R., TOMER, A., & SILVERSTEIN, J. H. (1992). A longitudinal analysis of adherence and health status in childhood diabetes. *Journal of Pediatric Psychology, 17,* 537–553.

JOHNSON, S. K., DELUCA, J., & NATELSON, B. H. (1999). Chronic fatigue syndrome: Reviewing the research findings. *Annals of Behavioral Medicine, 21,* 258–271.

JOHNSTON, L. D., O'MALLEY, P. M., & BACHMAN, J. G. (2003). *Monitoring the Future: National survey results on drug use from the Monitoring the Future Study, 1975–2002. Volume I: Secondary school students.* (NIH Publication No. 03-5375). Bethesda, MD: National Institute on Drug Abuse.

JOHNSTON, M., MORRISON, V., MACWALTER, R., & PARTRIDGE, C. (1999). Perceived control, coping and recovery from disability following stroke. *Psychology and Health, 14,* 181–192.

JOHNSTON, M., & VÖGELE, C. (1993). Benefits of psychological preparation for surgery: A meta-analysis. *Annals of Behavioral Medicine, 15,* 245–256.

JOHNSTON-BROOKS, C. H., LEWIS, M. A., EVANS, G. W., & WHALEN, C. K. (1998). Chronic stress and illness in children. *Psychosomatic Medicine, 60,* 597–603.

JOHNSTON-BROOKS, C. H., LEWIS, M. A., & GARG, S. (2002). Self-efficacy impacts self-care and HbA1c in young adults with type 1 diabetes. *Psychosomatic Medicine, 64,* 43–51.

JONAS, B. S., & MUSSOLINO, M. E. (2000). Symptoms of depression as a prospective risk factor for stroke. *Psychosomatic Medicine, 62,* 463–471.

JONES, L. R., MABE, P. A., & RILEY, W. T. (1989). Physician interpretation of illness behavior. *International Journal of Psychiatry in Medicine, 19,* 237–248.

JORGENSEN, R. S., FRANKOWSKI, J. J., & CAREY, M. P. (1999). Sense of coherence, negative life events, and appraisal of physical health. *Personality and Individual Differences, 27,* 1079–1089.

JOUSILAHTI, P., VARTIAINEN, E., TUOMILEHTO, J., PEKKANEN, J., & PUSKA, P. (1995). Effect of risk factors and changes in risk factors on coronary mortality in three cohorts of middle-aged people in Eastern Finland. *American Journal of Epidemiology, 141,* 50–60.

JOYCE, C. (1984, November). A time for grieving. *Psychology Today,* pp. 42–46.

KABAT-ZINN, J. (1982). An outpatient program in behavioral medicine for chronic pain patients based on the practice of mindfulness meditation: Theoretical considerations and preliminary results. *General Hospital Psychiatry, 4,* 33–47.

KABAT-ZINN, J., LIPWORTH, L., & BURNEY, R. (1985). The clinical use of mindfulness meditation for the self-regulation of chronic pain. *Journal of Behavioral Medicine, 8,* 163–190.

KAHN, K. L., KEELER, E. B., SHERWOOD, M. J., ROGERS, W. H., DRAPER, D., BENTOW, S. S., et al. (1990). Comparing outcomes of care before and after implementation of the DRG-based prospective payment system. *Journal of the American Medical Association, 264,* 1984–1988.

KALICHMAN, S. C. (1998). *Preventing AIDS: A sourcebook for behavioral interventions.* Mahwah, NJ: Erlbaum.

KALICHMAN, S. C., & COLEY, B. (1995). Context framing to enhance HIV-antibody-testing messages targeted at African American women. *Health Psychology, 14,* 247–254.

KALICHMAN, S. C., & NACHIMSON, D. (1999). Self-efficacy and disclosure of HIV-positive serostatus to sex partners. *Health Psychology*, 18, 281–287.

KALICHMAN, S. C., ROMPA, D., & COLEY, B. (1996). Experimental component analysis of a behavioral HIV-AIDS prevention intervention for inner-city women. *Journal of Consulting and Clinical Psychology*, 64, 687–693.

KALICHMAN, S. C., WEINHARDT, L., DiFONZO, K., AUSTIN, J., & LUKE, W. (2002). Sensation seeking and alcohol use as markers of sexual transmission risk behavior in HIV-positive men. *Annals of Behavioral Medicine*, 24, 229–235.

KALISH, R. A. (1985). The social context of death and dying. In R. H. Binstock & E. Shanas (Eds.), *Handbook of aging and the social sciences* (pp. 149–170). New York: Van Nostrand-Reinhold.

KALISH, R. A., & REYNOLDS, D. K. (1976). *Death and ethnicity: A psychocultural study.* Los Angeles: University of Southern California Press.

KALOUPEK, D. G., WHITE, H., & WONG, M. (1984). Multiple assessment of coping strategies used by volunteer blood donors: Implications for preparatory training. *Journal of Behavioral Medicine*, 7, 35–60.

KAMEN, L. P., & SELIGMAN, M. E. P. (1989). Explanatory style and health. In M. Johnston & T. Marteau (Eds.), *Applications in health psychology* (pp. 73–84). New Brunswick, NJ: Transaction.

KANDEL, D. (1974). Inter- and intragenerational influences of adolescent marijuana use. *Journal of Social Issues*, 30, 107–135.

KANDEL, D., & FAUST, R. (1975). Sequence and stages in patterns of adolescent drug use. *Archives of General Psychiatry*, 32, 923–932.

KANDEL, D. B., WU, P., & DAVIES, M. (1994). Maternal smoking during pregnancy and smoking by adolescent daughters. *American Journal of Public Health*, 84, 1407–1413.

KANNER, A. D., COYNE, J. C., SCHAEFER, C., & LAZARUS, R. S. (1981). Comparison of two modes of stress measurement: Daily hassles and uplifts versus major life events. *Journal of Behavioral Medicine*, 4, 1–39.

KANNER, R. (1986). Pain management. *Journal of the American Medical Association*, 256, 2110–2114.

KAPLAN, R. M. (1994). The Ziggy theorem: Toward an outcomes-focused health psychology. *Health Psychology*, 13, 451–460.

KAPLAN, R. M., ATKINS, C. J., & REINSCH, S. (1984). Specific efficacy expectations mediate exercise compliance in patients with COPD. *Health Psychology*, 3, 223–242.

KAPLAN, R. M., & GROESSL, E. J. (2002). Applications of cost-effectiveness methodologies in behavioral medicine. *Journal of Consulting and Clinical Psychology*, 70, 482–493.

KAPLAN, R. M., ORLEANS, C. T., PERKINS, K. A., & PIERCE, J. P. (1995). Marshalling the evidence for greater regulation and control of tobacco products: A call for action. *Annals of Behavioral Medicine*, 17, 3–14.

KAPLAN, R. M., PATTERSON, T. L., KERNER, D., GRANT, I. et al. (1997). Social support: Cause or consequence of poor health outcomes in men with HIV infection? In G. R. Pierce, B. Lakey, I. G. Sarason, & B. R. Sarason (Eds.), *Sourcebook for social support and personality* (pp. 279–301). New York: Plenum.

KAPLAN, R. M., & SIMON, H. J. (1990). Compliance in medical care: Reconsideration of self-predictions. *Annals of Behavioral Medicine*, 12, 66–71.

KAPLAN, R. M., & TOSHIMA, M. T. (1990). The functional effects of social relationships on chronic illnesses and disability. In B. R. Sarason, I. G. Sarason, & G. R. Pierce (Eds.), *Social support: An interactional view* (pp. 427–453). New York: Wiley.

KAPUST, L. R., & WEINTRAUB, S. (1984). Living with a family member suffering from Alzheimer's disease. In H. B. Roback (Ed.), *Helping patients and their families cope with medical problems* (pp. 453–480). San Francisco: Jossey-Bass.

KARLBERG, L., KRAKAU, I., & UNDÉN, A.-L. (1998). Type A behavior intervention in primary health care reduces hostility and time pressure: A study in Sweden. *Social Science and Medicine*, 46, 397–402.

KARLIN, W. A., BRONDOLO, E., & SCHWARTZ, J. (2003). Workplace social support and ambulatory cardiovascular activity in New York City traffic agents. *Psychosomatic Medicine*, 65, 167–176.

KARNIK, R. (2001). The value of lipid lowering in patients with coronary heart disease. *Journal of Clinical and Basic Cardiology*, 4, 31–34.

KAROLY, P. (1985). The assessment of pain: Concepts and procedures. In P. Karoly (Ed.), *Measurement strategies in health psychology* (pp. 461–516). New York: Wiley.

KASCH, F. W., WALLACE, J. P., & VAN CAMP, S. P. (1985). Effects of 18 years of endurance exercise on the physical work capacity of older men. *Journal of Cardiopulmonary Rehabilitation*, 5, 308–312.

KASL, S. V., & COBB, S. (1966a). Health behavior, illness behavior, and sick role behavior: I. Health and illness behavior. *Archives of Environmental Health*, 12, 246–266.

KASL, S. V., & COBB, S. (1966b). Health behavior, illness behavior, and sick role behavior: II. Sick role behavior. *Archives of Environmental Health*, 12, 531–541.

KASTENBAUM, R., & COSTA, P. T. (1977). Psychological perspectives on death. *Annual Review of Psychology*, 28, 225–249.

KAWACHI, I., COLDITZ, G. A., STAMPFER, M. J., WILLETT, W. C., MANSON, J. E., ROSNER, B., et al. (1993). Smoking cessation and decreased risk of stroke in women. *Journal of the American Medical Association, 269,* 232–236.

KAZARIAN, S. S., & EVANS, D. R. (2001). Health psychology and culture: Embracing the 21st century. In S. S. Kazarian & E. R. Evans (Eds.), *Handbook of cultural health psychology* (pp. 3–43). San Diego: Academic Press.

KEATING, N. L., GREEN, D. C., KAO, A. C., GAZMARARIAN, J. A., WU, V. Y., & CLEARY, P. D. (2002). How are patients' specific ambulatory care experiences related to trust, satisfaction, and considering changing physicians? *Journal of General Internal Medicine, 17,* 29–39.

KEEFE, F. J., & DOLAN, E. (1986). Pain behavior and pain coping strategies in low back pain and myofascial pain dysfunction syndrome patients. *Pain, 24,* 49–56.

KEEFE, F. J., & GIL, K. M. (1985). Recent advances in the behavioral assessment and treatment of chronic pain. *Annals of Behavioral Medicine, 7*(3), 11–16.

KEEFE, F. J., HAUCK, E. R., EGERT, J., RIMER, B., & KORNGUTH, P. (1994). Mammography pain and discomfort: A cognitive-behavioral perspective. *Pain, 56,* 247–260.

KEEFE, F. J., WILLIAMS, D. A., & SMITH, S. J. (2001). Assessment of pain behaviors. In D. C. Turk & R. Melzack (Eds.), *Handbook of pain assessment* (2nd ed., pp. 170–187). New York: Guilford.

KEESEY, R. E. (1986). A set point theory of obesity. In K. D. Brownell & J. P. Foreyt (Eds.), *Handbook of eating disorders: The physiology, psychology, and treatment of the eating disorders* (pp. 63–87). New York: Basic Books.

KEESEY, R. E., & POWLEY, T. L. (1975). Hypothalamic regulation of body weight. *American Scientist, 63,* 558–565.

KELLNER, R. (1985). Functional somatic symptoms and hypochondriasis: A survey of empirical studies. *Archives of General Psychiatry, 42,* 821–833.

KELLY, J. A., KALICHMAN, S. C. (1998). Reinforcement value of unsafe sex as a predictor of condom use and continued HIV/AIDS risk behavior among gay and bisexual men. *Health Psychology, 17,* 328–335.

KELLY, J. A., & KALICHMAN, S. C. (2002). Behavioral research in HIV/AIDS primary and secondary prevention: Recent advances and future directions. *Journal of Consulting and Clinical Psychology, 70,* 626–639.

KELLY, J. A., KALICHMAN, S. C., KAUTH, M. R., KILGORE, H. G., HOOD, H. V., CAMPOS, P. E., et al. (1991). Situational factors associated with AIDS risk behavior lapses and coping strategies used by gay men who successfully avoid lapses. *American Journal of Public Health, 81,* 1335–1338.

KELLY, J. A., MURPHY, D. A., SIKKEMA, K. J., MCAULIFFE, T. L., ROFFMAN, R. A., SOLOMON, L. J., et al. (1997). Randomized, controlled, community-level HIV-prevention intervention for sexual-risk behaviour among homosexual men in U.S. cities. *Lancet, 350,* 1500–1505.

KELLY, J. A., SIKKEMA, K. J., WINETT, R. A., SOLOMON, L. J., ROFFMAN, R. A., HECKMAN, T. G., et al. (1995). Factors predicting continued high-risk behavior among gay men in small cities: Psychological, behavioral, and demographic characteristics related to unsafe sex. *Journal of Consulting and Clinical Psychology, 63,* 101–107.

KELSEY, J. L., & HOCHBERG, M. C. (1988). Epidemiology of chronic musculoskeletal disorders. *Annual Review of Public Health, 9,* 379–401.

KEMPE, C. H. (1976). Child abuse and neglect. In N. B. Talbot (Ed.), *Raising children in modern America: Problems and prospective solutions* (pp. 173–188). Boston: Little, Brown.

KENDALL, P. C., WILLIAMS, L., PECHACEK, T. F., GRAHAM, L. E., SHISSLAK, C., & HERZOFF, N. (1979). Cognitive-behavioral and patient education interventions in cardiac catheterization procedures: The Palo Alto Medical Psychology Project. *Journal of Consulting and Clinical Psychology, 47,* 49–58.

KENNEDY, S., KIECOLT-GLASER, J. K., & GLASER, R. (1990). Social support, stress, and the immune system. In B. R. Sarason, I. G. Sarason, & G. R. Pierce (Eds.), *Social support: An interactional view* (pp. 253–266). New York: Wiley.

KENT, G. (1985). Memory of dental pain. *Pain, 21,* 187–194.

KERLIKOWSKE, K., GRADY, D., RUBIN, S. M., SANDROCK, C., & ERNSTER, V. L. (1995). Efficacy of screening mammography: A meta-analysis. *Journal of the American Medical Association, 273,* 149–154.

KERN, P. A., ONG, J. M., SAFFARI, B., & CARTY, J. (1990). The effects of weight loss on the activity and expression on adipose-tissue lipoprotein lipase in very obese humans. *New England Journal of Medicine, 322,* 1053–1059.

KERNS, R. D. (1995). Family assessment and intervention. In P. M. Nicassio & T. W. Smith (Eds.), *Managing chronic illness: A biopsychosocial perspective* (pp. 207–244). Washington, DC: American Psychological Association.

KERNS, R. D., & PAYNE, A. (1996). Treating families of chronic pain patients. In R. J. Gatchel & D. C. Turk (Eds.), *Psychological approaches to pain management: A practitioner's handbook* (pp. 283–304). New York: Guilford.

KERNS, R. D., TURK, D. C., & RUDY, T. E. (1985). The West Haven–Yale Multidimensional Pain Inventory. *Pain, 23,* 345–356.

KERNS, R. D., & WEISS, L. H. (1994). Family influences on the course of chronic illness: A cognitive-behavioral transactional model. *Annals of Behavioral Medicine, 16,* 116–121.

KETT, J. F. (1977). *Rites of passage: Adolescence in America 1790 to present.* New York: Basic Books.

KETTERER, M. W., BRYMER, J., RHOADS, K., KRAFT, P., KENYON, L., FOLEY, B., et al. (1996). Emotional distress among males with "syndrome X." *Journal of Behavioral Medicine, 19,* 455–466.

KIECOLT-GLASER, J. K., DURA, J. R., SPEICHER, C. E., TRASK, O. J., & GLASER, R. (1991) Spousal caregivers of dementia victims: Longitudinal changes in immunity and health. *Psychosomatic Medicine, 53,* 345–362.

KIECOLT-GLASER, J. K., FISHER, L. D., OGROCKI, P., STOUT, J. C., SPEICHER, C. E., & GLASER, R. (1987). Marital quality, marital disruption, and immune function. *Psychosomatic Medicine, 49,* 13–34.

KIECOLT-GLASER, J. K., GARNER, W., SPEICHER, C., PENN, G. M., HOLLIDAY, J., & GLASER, R. (1984). Psychosocial modifiers of immunocompetence in medical students. *Psychosomatic Medicine, 46,* 7–14.

KIECOLT-GLASER, J. K., & GLASER, R. (1986). Psychological influences on immunity. *Psychosomatics, 27,* 621–624.

KIECOLT-GLASER, J. K., & GLASER, R. (1995). Psychoneuroimmunology and health consequences: Data and shared mechanisms. *Psychosomatic Medicine, 57,* 269–274.

KIECOLT-GLASER, J. K., MARUCHA, P. T., ATKINSON, C., & GLASER, R. (2001). Hypnosis as a modulator of cellular immune dysregulation during acute stress. *Journal of Consulting and Clinical Psychology, 69,* 674–682.

KIECOLT-GLASER, J. K., & WILLIAMS, D. A. (1987). Self-blame, compliance, and distress among burn patients. *Journal of Personality and Social Psychology, 53,* 187–193.

KILLEN, J. D., & FORTMANN, S. P. (1994). Craving is associated with smoking relapse: Findings from three prospective studies. *Experimental and Clinical Psychopharmacology, 5,* 137–142.

KILLEN, J. D., ROBINSON, T. N., HAYDEL, K. F., HAYWARD, C., WILSON, D. M., HAMMER, L. D., et al. (1997). Prospective study of risk factors for the initiation of cigarette smoking. *Journal of Consulting and Clinical Psychology, 65,* 1011–1016.

KILLEN, J. D., TAYLOR, C. B., HAYWARD, C., WILSON, D. M., HAYDEL, K. F., HAMMER, L. D., et al. (1994). Pursuit of thinness and onset of eating disorder symptoms in a community sample of adolescent girls: A three-year prospective analysis. *International Journal of Eating Disorders, 16,* 227–238.

KILLEN, J. D., TAYLOR, C. B., TELCH, M. J., SAYLOR, K. E., MARON, D. J., & ROBINSON, T. N. (1986). Self-induced vomiting and laxative and diuretic use among teenagers. *Journal of the American Medical Society, 255,* 1447–1449.

KILO, C., & WILLIAMSON, J. R. (1987). *Diabetes: The facts that let you regain control of your life.* New York: Wiley.

KILPATRICK, D. G., ACIERNO, R., SAUNDERS, B., RESNICK, H. S., BEST, C. L., & SCHNURR, P. P. (2000). Risk factors for adolescent substance abuse and dependence: Data from a national sample. *Journal of Consulting and Clinical Psychology, 68,* 19–30.

KIMMEL, P. L., PETERSON, R. A., WEIHS, K. L., SIMMENS, S. J., ALLEYNE, S., CRUZ, I., et al. (1998). Psychosocial factors, behavioral compliance and survival in urban hemodialysis patients. *Kidney International, 54,* 245–254.

KINDELAN, K., & KENT, G. (1987). Concordance between patients' information preferences and general practitioners' perceptions. *Psychology and Health, 1,* 399–409.

KING, L. A., & MINER, K. N. (2000). Writing about the perceived benefits of traumatic events: Implications for physical health. *Personality and Social Psychology Bulletin, 26,* 220–230.

KIRSCHBAUM, D., & HELLHAMMER, D. (1999). Noise and stress—Salivary cortisol as a non-invasive measure of allostatic load. *Noise and Health, 4,* 57–65.

KIRSCHT, J. P. (1983). Preventive health behavior: A review of research and issues. *Health Psychology, 2,* 277–301.

KIVLAHAN, D. R., MARLATT, G. A., FROMME, K., COPPEL, D. B., & WILLIAMS, E. (1990). Secondary prevention with college drinkers: Evaluation of an alcohol skills training program. *Journal of Consulting and Clinical Psychology, 58,* 805–810.

KIYAK, H. A., VITALIANO, P. P., & CRINEAN, J. (1988). Patients' expectations as predictors of orthognathic surgery outcomes. *Health Psychology, 7,* 251–268.

KLAPOW, J. C., SLATER, M. A., PATTERSON, T. L., DOCTOR, J. N., ATKINSON, J. H., & GARFIN, S. R. (1993). An empirical evaluation of multidimensional clinical outcome in chronic low back pain patients. *Pain, 55,* 107–118.

KLATSKY, A. L., FRIEDMAN, G. D., ARMSTRONG, M. A., & KIPP, H. (2003). Wine, liquor, beer, and mortality. *American Journal of Epidemiology, 158,* 585–595.

KLEINKE, C. L., & SPANGLER, A. S. (1988). Psychometric analysis of the audiovisual taxonomy for assessing pain behavior in chronic back-pain patients. *Journal of Behavioral Medicine, 11,* 83–94.

KLESGES, R. C., BENOWITZ, N. L., & MEYERS, A. W. (1991). Behavioral and biobehavioral aspects of smoking and smoking cessation: The problem of postcessation weight gain. *Behavior Therapy, 22,* 179–199.

KLESGES, R. C., ECK, L. H., & RAY, J. W. (1995). Who underreports dietary intake in a dietary recall? Evidence from the Second National Health and Nutrition Examination Survey. *Journal of Consulting and Clinical Psychology, 63,* 438–444.

KLESGES, R. C., HADDOCK, C. K., LANDO, H., & TALCOTT, G. W. (1999). Efficacy of forced smoking cessation and an adjunctive behavioral treatment on long-term smoking rates. *Journal of Consulting and Clinical Psychology, 67,* 952–958.

KLESGES, R. C., SHUSTER, M. L., KLESGES, L. M., & WERNER, K. (1992, March). *The effects of television viewing on metabolic rate in normal weight and obese children.* Paper presented at the meeting of the Society of Behavioral Medicine, New York.

KLESGES, R. C., WARD, K. D., RAY, J. W., CUTTER, G., JACOBS, D. R., & WAGENKNECHT, L. E. (1998). The prospective relationships between smoking and weight in a young, biracial cohort: The Coronary Artery Risk Development in Young Adults Study. *Journal of Consulting and Clinical Psychology, 66,* 987–993.

KLESGES, R. C., WINDERS, S. E., MEYERS, A. W., ECK, L. H., WARD, K. D., HULTQUIST, C. M., et al. (1997). How much weight gain occurs following smoking cessation? A comparison of weight gain using both continuous and point prevalence abstinence. *Journal of Consulting and Clinical Psychology, 65,* 286–291.

KLESGES, R. C., ZBIKOWSKI, S. M., LANDO, H. A., HADDOCK, C. K., TALCOTT, G. W., & ROBINSON, L. A. (1998). The relationship between smoking and body weight in a population of young military personnel. *Health Psychology, 17,* 454–458.

KLOSE, K. J., NEEDHAM, B. M., SCHMIDT, D., BROTON, J. G., & GREEN, B. A. (1993). An assessment of the contribution of electromyographic biofeedback as an adjunct therapy in the physical training of spinal cord injured persons. *Archives of Physical Medicine and Rehabilitation, 74,* 453–456.

KNITTLE, J., MERRITT, R. J., DIXON-SHANIES, D., GINSBERG-FELLNER, F., TIMMERS, K. I., & KATZ, D. P. (1981). Childhood obesity. In R. M. Suskind (Ed.), *Textbook of pediatric nutrition* (pp. 415–434). New York: Raven Press.

KNOWLER, W. C., BARRETT-CONNOR, E., FOWLER, S. E., HAMMAN, R. F., LACHIN, J. M., WALKER, E. A. et al. (2002). Reduction in the incidence of type 2 diabetes with lifestyle intervention or metformin. *New England Journal of Medicine, 346,* 393–403.

KNOX, S. S., SIEGMUND, K. D., WEIDNER, G., ELLISON, R. C., ADELMAN, A., & PATON, C. (1998). Hostility, social support, and coronary heart disease in the National Heart, Lung, and Blood Institute Family Heart Study. *American Journal of Cardiology, 82,* 1192–1196.

KOBASA, S. C., & MADDI, S. R. (1977). Existential personality theory. In R. Corsini (Ed.), *Current personality theories* (pp. 243–276). Itasca, IL: Peacock.

KOBASA, S. C. O., MADDI, S. R., PUCCETTI, M. C., & ZOLA, M. A. (1985). Effectiveness of hardiness, exercise and social support as resources against illness. *Journal of Psychosomatic Research, 29,* 525–533.

KOCH, J. (1977, August). When children meet death. *Psychology Today,* pp. 64–66, 79–80.

KÖHLER, T., & HAIMERL, C. (1990). Daily stress as a trigger of migraine attacks: Results of thirteen single-subject studies. *Journal of Consulting and Clinical Psychology, 58,* 870–872.

KOHRT, W. M., KIRWAN, J. P., STATEN, M. A., BOUREY, R. E., KING, D. S., & HOLLOSZY, J. O. (1993). Insulin resistance in aging is related to abdominal obesity. *Diabetes, 42,* 273–281.

KOKKINOS, P. F., NARAYAN, P., COLLERAN, J. A., PITTARAS, A., NOTARGIACOMO, A., REDA, D., et al. (1995). Effects of regular exercise on blood pressure and left ventricular hypertrophy in African-American men with severe hypertension. *New England Journal of Medicine, 333,* 1462–1467.

KOLATA, G. (1990, February 20). Wariness is replacing trust between health and patient. *New York Times,* pp. A1, D15.

KOLATA, G. (1992, May 10). Confronting new ideas, doctors often hold on to the old. *New York Times,* p. E6.

KOLBE, L. J., GREEN, L. FOREYT, J., DARNELL, L., GOODRICK, K., WILLIAMS, H., et al. (1986). Appropriate functions of health education in schools: Improving health and cognitive performance. In N. A. Krasnegor, J. D. Arasteh, & M. F. Cataldo (Eds.), *Child health behavior: A behavioral pediatrics perspective* (pp. 171–216). New York: Wiley.

KOLBE, L. J., & IVERSON, D. C. (1984). Comprehensive school health education programs. In J. D. Matarazzo, S. M. Weiss, J. A. Herd, N. E. Miller, & S. M. Weiss (Eds.), *Behavioral health: A handbook of health enhancement and disease prevention* (pp. 1094–1116). New York: Wiley.

KOLONEL, L. N. (2001). Nutrition and prostate cancer. In A. M. Coulston, C. L. Rock, & E. R. Monsen (Eds.), *Nutrition in the prevention and treatment of disease* (pp. 373–386). San Diego: Academic Press.

KOMRO, K. A., MCCARTY, M. C., FORSTER, J. L., BLAINE, T. M., & CHEN, V. (2003). Parental, family, and home characteristics associated with cigarette smoking among adolescents. *American Journal of Health Promotion, 17,* 291–299.

KOOCHER, G. P., O'MALLEY, J. E., GOGAN, J. L., & FOSTER, D. J. (1980). Psychological adjustment among pediatric cancer survivors. *Journal of Child Psychology and Psychiatry, 21,* 163–173.

KOP, W. J. (1999). Chronic and acute psychological risk factors for clinical manifestations of coronary artery disease. *Psychosomatic Medicine, 61,* 476–487.

KOP, W. J. (2003). The integration of cardiovascular behavioral medicine and psychoneuroimmunology:

New developments based on converging research fields. *Brain, Behavior, and Immunity, 17,* 233–237.

KORNACK, D. R., & RAKIC, P. (2001). Cell proliferation without neurogenesis in adult primate neocortex. *Science, 294,* 2127–2130.

KORO, C. E., BOURGEOIS, N., BOWLIN, S. J., & FEDDER, D. O. (2004). Glycemic control from 1988 to 2000 among U.S. adults diagnoses with type 2 diabetes. *Diabetes Care, 27,* 17–20.

KOROL, C. T., & CRAIG, K. D. (2001). Pain from the perspectives of health psychology and culture. In S. S. Kazarian & E. R. Evans (Eds.), *Handbook of cultural health psychology* (pp. 241–265). San Diego: Academic Press.

KORSCH, B. M., FINE, R. N., & NEGRETE, V. F. (1978). Noncompliance in children with renal transplants. *Pediatrics, 61,* 872–876.

KOSTEN, T. R., JACOBS, S. C., & KASL, S. V. (1985). Terminal illness, bereavement, and the family. In D. C. Turk & R. D. Kerns (Eds.), *Health, illness, and families: A lifespan perspective* (pp. 311–337). New York: Wiley.

KOVACS, M. (1997). Depression in patients with diabetes. *Contemporary Internal Medicine, 9,* 53–58.

KRAJICK, K. (1988, May). Private passions and public health. *Psychology Today,* pp. 50–58.

KRAMER, J. R., LEDOLTER, J., MANOS, G. N., & BAYLESS, M. L. (2000). Stress and metabolic control in diabetes mellitus: Methodological issues and an illustrative analysis. *Annals of Behavioral Medicine, 22,* 17–28.

KRANTZ, D. S., & DECKEL, A. W. (1983). Coping with coronary heart disease and stroke. In T. G. Burish & L. A. Bradley (Eds.), *Coping with chronic disease: Research and applications* (pp. 85–112). New York: Academic Press.

KRANTZ, D. S., LUNDBERG, U., & FRANKENHAEUSER, M. (1987). Stress and Type A behavior: Interactions between environmental and biological factors. In A. Baum & J. E. Singer (Eds.), *Handbook of psychology and health* (Vol. 5, pp. 203–228). Hillsdale, NJ: Erlbaum.

KRANZLER, H. R., & ANTON, R. F. (1994). Implications of recent neuropsychopharmacologic research for understanding the etiology and development of alcoholism. *Journal of Consulting and Clinical Psychology, 62,* 1116–1126.

KRAUSE, J. S., & CREWE, N. M. (1991). Chronologic age, time since injury, and time of measurement: Effect on adjustment after spinal cord injury. *Archives of Physical Medicine and Rehabilitation, 72,* 91–100.

KREUTER, M. W., & STRECHER, V. J. (1995). Changing inaccurate perceptions of health risk: Results from a randomized trial. *Health Psychology, 14,* 56–63.

KRIEG, A. M., YI, A.-K., MATSON, S., WALDSCHMIDT, T. J., BISHOP, G. A., TEASDALE, R., et al. (1995). CpG motifs in bacterial DNA trigger direct B-cell activation. *Nature, 374,* 546–549.

KROENKE, K., & SPITZER, R. L. (1998). Gender differences in the reporting of physical and somatoform symptoms. *Psychosomatic Medicine, 60,* 150–155.

KSOBIECH, K. (2003). A meta-analysis of needle sharing, lending, and borrowing behaviors of needle exchange program attenders. AIDS *Education and prevention, 15,* 257–268.

KU, L., SONENSTEIN, F. L., & PLECK, J. H. (1993). Young men's risk behaviors for HIV infection and sexually transmitted diseases, 1988 through 1991. *American Journal of Public Health, 83,* 1609–1615.

KUBIK, M. Y., LYTLE, L. A., HANNAN, P. J., PERRY, C. L., & STORY, M. (2003). The association of the school food environment with dietary behaviors of young adolescents. *American Journal of Public Health, 93,* 1168–1173.

KÜBLER-ROSS, E. (1969). *On death and dying.* New York: Macmillan.

KUDIELKA, B. M., HELLHAMMER, J., HELLHAMMER, D. H., WOLF, O. T., PIRKE, K.-M., VARADI, E., et al. (1998). Sex differences in endocrine and psychological responses to psychosocial stress in healthy elderly subjects and the impact of a 2-week dehydroepiandrosterone treatment. *Journal of Clinical Endocrinology and Metabolism, 83,* 1756–1761.

KUJALA, U. M., KAPRIO, J., SARNA, S., & KOSKENVUO, M. (1998). Relationship of leisure-time physical activity and mortality: The Finnish twin cohort. *Journal of the American Medical Association, 279,* 440–444.

KULIK, J. A., & CARLINO, P. (1987). The effect of verbal commitment and treatment choice on medication compliance in a pediatric setting. *Journal of Behavioral Medicine, 10,* 367–376.

KULIK, J. A., & MAHLER, H. I. M. (1987a). Effects of preoperative roommate assignment on preoperative anxiety and recovery from coronary-bypass surgery. *Health Psychology, 6,* 525–543.

KULIK, J. A., & MAHLER, H. I. M. (1987b). Health status, perceptions of risk, and prevention interest for health and nonhealth problems. *Health Psychology, 6,* 15–27.

KULIK, J. A., & MAHLER, H. I. M. (1989). Social support and recovery from surgery. *Health Psychology, 8,* 221–238.

KULIK, J. A., MOORE, P. J., & MAHLER, H. I. M. (1993). Stress and affiliation: Hospital roommate effects on preoperative anxiety and social interaction. *Health Psychology, 12,* 118–124.

KUNDA, Z. (1990). The case for motivated reasoning. *Psychological Bulletin, 108,* 480–498.

KURTH, T., GAZIANO, J. M., BERGER, K., KASE, C. S., REXRODE, K. M., COOK, N. R. et al. (2003). Body mass index and the risk of stroke in men. *Archives on Internal Medicine, 163,* 2557–2662.

KUSAKA, Y., KONDOU, H., & MORIMOTO, K. (1992). Healthy lifestyles are associated with higher natural killer cell activity. *Preventive Medicine, 21,* 602–615.

KUSNECOV, A. W. (2001). Behavioral conditioning of the immune system. In A. Baum, T. A. Revenson, & J. E. Singer (Eds.), *Handbook of health psychology* (pp. 105–115.). Mahwah, NJ: Erlbaum.

LABARBA, R. C. (1984). Prenatal and neonatal influences on behavioral health development. In J. D. Matarazzo, S. M. Weiss, J. A. Herd, N. E. Miller, & S. M. Weiss (Eds.), *Behavioral health: A handbook of health enhancement and disease prevention* (pp. 41–55). New York: Wiley.

LACHMAN, M. E. (1986). Personal control in later life: Stability, change, and cognitive correlates. In M. M. Baltes & P. B. Baltes (Ed.), *The psychology of control and aging* (pp. 207–236). Hillsdale, NJ: Erlbaum.

LACKNER, J. M., QUIGLEY, B. M., & BLANCHARD, E. B. (2004). Depression and abdominal pain in IBS patients: The mediating role of catastrophizing. *Psychosomatic Medicine, 66,* 435–441.

LACROIX, A. Z., LANG, J., SCHERR, P., WALLACE, R. B., CORNONI-HUNTLEY, J., BERKMAN, L., et al. (1991). Smoking and mortality among older men and women in three communities. *New England Journal of Medicine, 324,* 1619–1625.

LAFFREY, S. C. (1986). Normal and overweight adults: Perceived weight and health behavior characteristics. *Nursing Research, 35,* 173–177.

LA GRECA, A. M., & STONE, W. L. (1985). Behavioral pediatrics. In N. Schneiderman & J. T. Tapp (Eds.), *Behavioral medicine: The biopsychosocial approach* (pp. 255–291). Hillsdale, NJ: Erlbaum.

LAKEIN, A. (1973). *How to get control of your time and life.* New York: New American Library.

LANDRINE, H., & KLONOFF, E. A. (2001). Cultural diversity and health psychology. In A. Baum, T. A. Revenson, & J. E. Singer (Eds.), *Handbook of health psychology* (pp. 851–891). Mahwah, NJ: Erlbaum.

LANE, J. D., PIEPER, C. F., PHILLIPS-BUTE, B. G., BRYANT, J. E., & KUHN, C. M. (2002). Caffeine affects cardiovascular and neuroendocrine activation at work and home. *Psychosomatic Medicine, 64,* 595–603.

LANE, M. A., BAER, D. J., RUMPLER, W. V., WEINDRUCH, R., INGRAM, D. K., TILMONT, E. M., et al. (1996). Calorie restriction lowers body temperature in rhesus monkeys, consistent with a postulated anti-aging mechanism in rodents. *Proceedings of the National Academy of Sciences, 93,* 4159–4164.

LANGER, E. J. (1975). The illusion of control. *Journal of Personality and Social Psychology, 32,* 311–328.

LANGER, E. J., JANIS, I. L., & WOLFER, J. A. (1975). Reduction of psychological stress in surgical patients. *Journal of Experimental Social Psychology, 11,* 155–165.

LANGER, E. J., & RODIN, J. (1976). The effects of choice and enhanced personal responsibility for the aged: A field experiment in an institutional setting. *Journal of Personality and Social Psychology, 34,* 191–198.

LANGLIE, J. K. (1977). Social networks, health beliefs, and preventive health behavior. *Journal of Health and Social Behavior, 18,* 244–260.

LA PLACE, J. (1984). *Health* (4th ed.). Englewood Cliffs, NJ: Prentice-Hall.

LARKIN, K. T., KNOWLTON, G. E., & D'ALESSANDRI, R. (1990). Predicting treatment outcome to progressive relaxation training in essential hypertensive patients. *Journal of Behavioral Medicine, 13,* 605–618.

LARKIN, K. T., & ZAYFERT, C. (1996). Anger management training with mild essential hypertensive patients. *Journal of Behavioral Medicine, 19,* 415–433.

LAROCCO, J. M., HOUSE, J. S., & FRENCH, J. R. P. (1980). Social support, occupational stress, and health. *Journal of Health and Social Behavior, 21,* 202–218.

LASZLO, J. (1987). *Understanding cancer.* New York: Harper & Row.

LATIMER, E. A., & LAVE, L. B. (1987). Initial effects of the New York State auto safety belt law. *American Journal of Public Health, 77,* 183–186.

LAU, R. R., & HARTMAN, K. A. (1983). Common sense representations of common illnesses. *Health Psychology, 2,* 167–185.

LAU, R., KANE, R., BERRY, S., WARE, J., & ROY, D. (1980). Channeling health: A review of the evaluation of televised health campaigns. *Health Education Quarterly, 7,* 56–89.

LAVE, J. R. (1989). The effect of the Medicare prospective payment system. *Annual Review of Public Health, 10,* 141–161.

LAVIGNE, J. V., SCHULEIN, M. J., & HAHN, Y. S. (1986). Psychological aspects of painful medical conditions in children. II. Personality factors, family characteristics and treatment. *Pain, 27,* 147–169.

LAWLER, K. A., ALLEN, M. T., CRITCHER, E. C., & STANDARD, B. A. (1981). The relationship of physiological responses to the coronary-prone behavior pattern in children. *Journal of Behavioral Medicine, 4,* 203–216.

LAWRENCE, D. B., & GAUS, C. R. (1983). Long-term care: Financing and policy issues. In D. Mechanic (Ed.), *Handbook of health, health care, and the health professions* (pp. 365–378). New York: Free Press.

LAZARUS, A. A. (1971). *Behavior therapy and beyond.* New York: McGraw-Hill.

LAZARUS, R. S. (1999). *Stress and emotion: A new synthesis.* New York: Springer.

LAZARUS, R. S., & FOLKMAN, S. (1984a). Coping and adaptation. In W. D. Gentry (Ed.), *Handbook of behavioral medicine* (pp. 282–325). New York: Guilford.

LAZARUS, R. S., & FOLKMAN, S. (1984b). *Stress, appraisal, and coping.* New York: Springer.

LAZARUS, R. S., & LAUNIER, R. (1978). Stress-related transactions between person and environment. In L. A. Pervin & M. Lewis (Eds.), *Perspectives in interactional psychology.* (pp. 287–327) New York: Plenum.

LEAHEY, T. H. (1987). *A history of psychology: Main currents in psychological thought* (2nd ed.). Englewood Cliffs, NJ: Prentice-Hall.

LEAKE, R., FRIEND, R., & WADHWA, N. (1999). Improving adjustment to chronic illness through strategic self-presentation: An experimental study on a renal dialysis unit. *Health Psychology, 18,* 54–62.

LEE, C. (1989). Perceptions of immunity to disease in adult smokers. *Journal of Behavioral Medicine, 12,* 267–277.

LEE, H., BAHLER, R., TAYLOR, A., ALONZO, A., & ZELLER, R. A. (1999). Clinical symptoms of myocardial infarction and delayed treatment-seeking behavior in Blacks and Whites. *Journal of Applied Biobehavioral Research, 3,* 135–159.

LEE, S. H., & ABRAMSON, S. B. (1999). Rheumatic diseases. In M. G. Eisenberg, R. L. Glueckauf, & H. H. Zaretsky (Eds.), *Medical aspects of disability: A handbook for the rehabilitation professional* (2nd ed., pp. 472–498). New York: Springer.

LEE, W.-H., MORTON, R. A., EPSTEIN, J. I., BROOKS, J. D., CAMPBELL, P. A., BOVA, G. S., et al. (1994). Cytidine methylation of regulatory sequences near the π-class glutathione S-transferase gene accompanies human prostatic carcinogenesis. *Proceedings of the National Academy of Sciences USA, 91,* 11733–11737.

LEFFERT, N., & PETERSEN, A. C. (1998). Healthy adolescent development: Risks and opportunities. In P. M. Kato & T. Mann (Eds.), *Handbook of diversity issues in health psychology* (pp. 117–140). New York: Plenum.

LEHRER, P., FELDMAN, J., GIARDINO, N., SONG, H.-Y., & SCHMALING, K. (2002). Psychological aspects of asthma. *Journal of Consulting and Clinical Psychology, 70,* 691–711.

LEIBEL, R. L., ROSENBLUM, M., & HIRSCH, J. (1995). Changes in energy expenditure resulting from altered body weight. *New England Journal of Medicine, 332,* 621–628.

LEIGH, B. C. (1990). The relationship of substance use during sex to high-risk sexual behavior. *Journal of Sex Research, 27,* 199–213.

LEIGH, B. C., MORRISON, D. M., TROCKI, K., & TEMPLE, M. T. (1994). Sexual behavior of American adolescents: Results from a U.S. national survey. *Journal of Adolescent Health, 15,* 117–125.

LEINO, P., ARO, S., & HASAN, J. (1987). Trunk muscle function and low back disorders: A ten-year follow-up study. *Journal of Chronic Diseases, 40,* 289–296.

LENNEBERG, E. H. (1967). *Biological foundations of language.* New York: Wiley.

LEONARD, B. E. (1995). Stress and the immune system: Immunological aspects of depressive illness. In B. E. Leonard & K. Miller (Eds.), *Stress, the immune system and psychiatry* (pp. 113–136). New York: Wiley.

LEONARD, E. A. (1990, April 9). How the brain recovers. *Newsweek,* pp. 48–50.

LEPORE, S. J. (1997). Social-environmental influences on the chronic stress process. In B. H. Gottlieb (Ed.), *Coping with chronic stress* (pp. 133–160). New York: Plenum.

LEPORE, S. J., ALLEN, K. A. M., EVANS, G. W. (1993). Social support lowers cardiovascular reactivity to an acute stressor. *Psychosomatic Medicine, 55,* 518–524.

LEPORE, S. J., & HELGESON, V. S. (1998). Social constraints, intrusive thoughts, and mental health after prostate cancer. *Journal of Social and Clinical Psychology, 17,* 89–106.

LEPORE, S. J., MILES, H. J., & LEVY, J. S. (1997). Relation of chronic and episodic stressors to psychological distress, reactivity, and health problems. *International Journal of Behavioral Medicine, 4,* 39–59.

LERMAN, C., AUDRAIN, J., & CROYLE, R. T. (1994). DNA-testing for heritable breast cancer risks: Lessons from traditional genetic counseling. *Annals of Behavioral Medicine, 16,* 327–333.

LERMAN, C., & BERRETTINI, W. (2003). Elucidating the role of genetic factors in smoking behavior and nicotine dependence. *American Journal of Medical Genetics, 118B,* 48–54.

LERMAN, C., CAPORASO, N. E., AUDRAIN, J., MAIN, D., BOWMAN, E. D., LOCKSHIN, B., et al. (1999). Evidence suggesting the role of specific genetic factors in cigarette smoking. *Health Psychology, 18,* 14–20.

LERMAN, C., CAPORASO, N. E., MAIN, D., AUDRAIN, J., BOYD, N. R., BOWMAN, E. D., et al. (1998). Depression and self-medication with nicotine: The modifying influence of the dopamine D4 receptor gene. *Health Psychology, 17,* 56–62.

LERMAN, C., HUGHES, C., TROCK, B. J., MYERS, R. E., MAIN, D., BONNEY, A., et al. (1999). Genetic testing in families with heredity nonpolyposis colon cancer. *Journal of the American Medical Association, 17,* 1618–1622.

LERMAN, C., NAROD, S., SCHULMAN, K., HUGHES, C., GOMEZ-CAMINERO, A., BONNEY, G., et al. (1996). BRAC1 testing in families with hereditary breast-ovarian cancer: A prospective study of patient decision making and outcomes. *Journal of the American Medical Association, 275,* 1885–1892.

LERMAN, C., TROCK, B., RIMER, B. K., BOYCE, A., JEPSON, C., & ENGSTROM, P. F. (1991). Psychological and behavioral implications of abnormal mammograms. *Annals of Internal Medicine, 114,* 657–661.

LESTER, N., LEFEBVRE, J. C., & KEEFE, F. J. (1994). Pain in young adults: I. Relationship to gender and family history. *Clinical Journal of Pain, 10,* 282–289.

LETT, H. S., BLUMENTHAL, J. A., BABYAK, M. A., SHERWOOD, A., STRAUMAN, T., ROBINS, C., et al. (2003). Depression as a risk factor for coronary artery disease: Evidence, mechanisms, and treatment. *Psychosomatic Medicine, 66,* 305–315.

LEVENSON, R. W. (1986). Alcohol, reactivity, and the heart: Implications for coronary health and disease. In K. A. Matthews, S. M. Weiss, T. Detre, T. M. Dembroski, B. Falkner, S. B. Manuck, & R. B. Williams (Eds.), *Handbook of stress, reactivity, and cardiovascular disease* (pp. 345–364). New York: Wiley.

LEVENSTEIN, S. (2002). Psychosocial factors in peptic ulcer and inflammatory bowel disease. *Journal of Consulting and Clinical Psychology, 70,* 739–750.

LEVENTHAL, E. A., & PROHASKA, T. R. (1986). Age, symptom interpretation, and health behavior. *Journal of the American Geriatrics Society, 34,* 185–191.

LEVENTHAL, H., & CLEARY, P. D. (1980). The smoking problem: A review of research and theory in behavioral risk modification. *Psychological Bulletin, 88,* 370–405.

LEVENTHAL, H., LEVENTHAL, E. A., & CONTRADA, R. J. (1998). Self regulation, health, and behavior: A perceptual-cognitive approach. *Psychology & Health, 13,* 717–733.

LEVENTHAL, H., LEVENTHAL, E. A., & VAN NGUYEN, T. (1985). Reactions of families to illness: Theoretical models and perspectives. In D. C. Turk & R. D. Kerns (Eds.), *Health, illness, and families: A life-span perspective* (pp. 108–145). New York: Wiley.

LEVENTHAL, H., PROHASKA, T. R., & HIRSCHMAN, R. S. (1985). Preventive health behavior across the life span. In J. C. Rosen & L. J. Solomon (Eds.), *Prevention in health psychology* (pp. 191–235). Hanover, NH: University Press of New England.

LEVIN, D. N., CLEELAND, C. S., & DAR, R. (1985). Public attitudes toward cancer pain. *Cancer, 56,* 2337–2339.

LEVINE, J. D., GORDON, N. C., & FIELDS, H. L. (1978, September 23). The mechanism of placebo analgesia. *Lancet,* 654–657.

LEVY, S. M. (1983). The process of death and dying: Behavioral and social factors. In T. G. Burish & L. A. Bradley (Eds.), *Coping with chronic disease: Research and*

applications (pp. 425–446). New York: Academic Press.

LEVY, S. M. (1985). *Behavior and cancer.* San Francisco: Jossey-Bass.

LEVY, S. M., HERBERMAN, R. B., WHITESIDE, T., SANZO, K., LEE, J., & KIRKWOOD, J. (1990). Perceived social support and tumor estrogen/progesterone receptor status as predictors of natural killer cell activity in breast cancer patients. *Psychosomatic Medicine, 52,* 73–85.

LEVY-LAHAD, E., WASCO, W., POORKAJ, P., ROMANO, D. M., OSHIMA, J., PETTINGELL, W. H., et al. (1995). Candidate gene for the chromosome 1 familial Alzheimer's disease locus. *Science, 269,* 973–977.

LEWINSOHN, P. M., MERMELSTEIN, R. M., ALEXANDER, C., & MACPHILLAMY, D. J. (1985). The Unpleasant Events Schedule: A scale for the measurement of aversive events. *Journal of Clinical Psychology, 41,* 483–498.

LI, J. T. C., & O'CONNELL, E. J. (1987). Viral infections and asthma. *Annals of Allergy, 59,* 321–331.

LICHSTEIN, K. L. (1988). *Clinical relaxation strategies.* New York: Wiley.

LICHTENSTEIN, E., HOLLIS, J. F., SEVERSON, H. H., STEVENS, V. J., VOGT, T. M., GLASGOW, R. E., et al. (1996). Tobacco cessation interventions in health care settings: Rationale, model, outcomes. *Addictive Behaviors, 21,* 709–720.

LICHTENSTEIN, E., & MERMELSTEIN, R. J. (1984). Review of approaches to smoking treatment: Behavior modification strategies. In J. D. Matarazzo, S. M. Weiss, J. A. Herd, N. E. Miller, & S. M. Weiss (Eds.), *Behavioral health: A handbook of health enhancement and disease prevention* (pp. 695–712). New York: Wiley.

LICHTENSTEIN, E., WEISS, S. M., HITCHCOCK, J. L., LEVETON, L. B., O'CONNELL, K. A., & PROCHASKA, J. O. (1986). Task Force 3: Patterns of smoking relapse. *Health Psychology, 5*(Supplement), 29–40.

LICHTENSTEIN, P., HOLM, N. V., VERKASALO, P. K., ILIADOU, A., KAPRIO, J., KOSKENVUO, M., et al. (2000). Environmental and heritable factors in the causation of cancer—Analyses of cohorts of twins from Sweden, Denmark, and Finland. *New England Journal of Medicine, 343,* 78–85.

LICHTMAN, S. W., PISARSKA, K., BERMAN, E. R., PESTONE, M., DOWLING, H., OFFENBACHER, E., et al. (1992). Discrepancy between self-reported and actual caloric intake and exercise in obese subjects. *New England Journal of Medicine, 327,* 1893–1898.

LILIAS, B., & LAHDENSUO, A. (1997). Is asthma self-management cost-effective? *Patient Education and Counseling, 32,* S97–S104.

LIN, E. H., & PETERSON, C. (1990). Pessimistic explanatory style and response to illness. *Behavior Research and Therapy, 28,* 243–248.

LINDEMAN, B. (1976). Widower, heal thyself. In R. H. Moos (Ed.), *Human adaptation: Coping with life crises* (pp. 275–286). Lexington, MA: Heath.

LINDEN, W., & CHAMBERS, L. (1994). Clinical effectiveness of non-drug treatment for hypertension: A meta-analysis. *Annals of Behavioral Medicine, 16,* 35–45.

LINDEN, W., HOGAN, B. E., RUTLEDGE, T., CHAWLA, A., LENZ, J. W., & LEUNG, D. (2003). There is more to anger coping than "in" or "out." *Emotion, 3,* 12–29.

LINDEN, W., STOSSEL, C., & MAURICE, J. (1996). Psychosocial interventions for patients with coronary artery disease. *Archives of Internal Medicine, 156,* 745–752.

LINDENBERG, C. S., ALEXANDER, E. M., GENDROP, S. C., NENCIOLI, M., & WILLIAMS, D. G. (1991). A review of the literature on cocaine abuse in pregnancy. *Nursing Research, 40,* 69–75.

LINDSAY, J., LAURIN, D., VERREAULT, R., HÉBERT, R., HELLIWELL, B., HILL, G. B. et al. (2002). Risk factors for Alzheimer's disease: A prospective analysis from the Canadian Study on Health and Aging. *American Journal of Epidemiology, 156,* 445–453.

LINNAN, L. A., EMMONS, K. M., KLAR, N., FAVA, J. L., LaFORGE, R. G., & ABRAMS, D. B. (2002). Challenges to improving the impact of worksite cancer prevention programs: comparing reach, enrollment, and attrition using active versus passive recruitment strategies. *Annals of Behavioral Medicine, 24,* 157–166.

LINTON, S. J., ALTHOFF, B., MELIN, L., LUNDIN, A., BODIN, L., MÄGI, A., et al. (1994). Psychological factors related to health, back pain, and dysfunction. *Journal of Occupational Rehabilitation, 4,* 1–10.

LINTON, S. J., & BUER, N. (1995). Working despite pain: Factors associated with work attendance versus dysfunction. *International Journal of Behavioral Medicine, 2,* 252–262.

LIOSSI, C., & HATIRA, P. (1999). Clinical hypnosis versus cognitive behavioral training for pain management with pediatric cancer patients undergoing bone marrow aspirations. *International Journal of Clinical and Experimental Hypnosis, 47,* 104–116.

LIPOWSKI, Z. J. (1986). What does the word "psychosomatic" really mean? A historical and semantic inquiry. In M. J. Christie & P. G. Mellett (Eds.), *The psychosomatic approach: Contemporary practice and wholeperson care* (pp. 17–38). New York: Wiley.

LITT, M. D., NYE, C., & SHAFER, D. (1995). Preparation for oral surgery: Evaluating elements of coping. *Journal of Behavioral Medicine, 18,* 435–459.

LIVERMORE, B. (1991, December). What reflexology can do for you. *Self,* p. 50.

LOGAN, T. K., COLE, J., & LEUKEFELD, C. (2002). Women, sex, and HIV: Social and contextual factors, meta-analysis of published interventions, and implications for practice and research. *Psychological Bulletin, 128,* 851–885.

LOGUE, A. W. (1991). *The psychology of eating and drinking: An introduction* (2nd ed.). New York: Freeman.

LONETTO, R. (1980). *Children's conceptions of death.* New York: Springer.

LONG, R. T., LAMONT, J. H., WHIPPLE, B., BANDLER, L., BLOM, G. E., BURGIN, L., & JESSNER, L. (1958). A psychosomatic study of allergic and emotional factors in children with asthma. *American Journal of Psychiatry, 114,* 890–899.

LORBER, J. (1975). Good patients and problem patients: Conformity and deviance in a general hospital. *Journal of Health and Social Behavior, 16,* 213–225.

LORIG, K., GONZÁLEZ, V. M., LAURENT, D. D., MORGAN, L., & LARIS, B. A. (1998). Arthritis Self-Management Program variations: Three studies. *Arthritis Care and Research, 11,* 448–454.

LORIG, K. R., & HOLMAN, H. R. (2003). Self-management education: History, definition, outcomes, and mechanisms. *Annals of Behavioral Medicine, 26,* 1–7.

LORISH, C. D., RICHARDS, B., & BROWN, S. (1989). Missed medication doses in rheumatic arthritis patients: Intentional and unintentional reasons. *Arthritis Care and Research, 2,* 3–9.

LOVALLO, W. R. (1997). *Stress and health: Biological and psychological interactions.* Thousand Oaks, CA: Sage.

LOWRY, R., HOLTZMAN, D., TRUMAN, B. I., KANN, L., COLLINS, J. L., & KOLBE, L. J. (1994). Substance use and HIV-related sexual behaviors among U.S. high school students: Are they related? *American Journal of Public Health, 84,* 1116–1120.

LUCINI, D., COVACCI, G., MILANI, R., MELA, G. S., MALLIANI, A., & PAGANI, M. (1997). A controlled study of the effects of mental relaxation on autonomic excitatory responses in healthy subjects. *Psychosomatic Medicine, 59,* 541–552.

LUDWICK-ROSENTHAL, R., & NEUFELD, R. W. J. (1993). Preparation for undergoing an invasive medical procedure: Interacting effects of information and coping style. *Journal of Consulting and Clinical Psychology, 61,* 156–164.

LUECKEN, L. J., SUAREZ, E. C., KUHN, C. M., BAREFOOT, R. B., BLUMENTHAL, J. A., SIEGLER, I. C., & WILLIAMS, R. B. (1997). Stress in employed women: Impact of marital status and children at home on neurohormone output and home strain. *Psychosomatic Medicine, 59,* 352–359.

LUFT, H. S. (1998). Medicare and managed care. *Annual Review of Public Health, 19,* 459–475.

LUND, A. K., & KEGELES, S. S. (1984). Rewards and adolescent health behavior. *Health Psychology, 3,* 351–369.

LUNDBERG, U. (1986). Stress and Type A behavior in children. *Journal of the American Academy of Child Psychiatry*, 25, 771–778.

LUNDBERG, U. (1999). Coping with stress: Neuroendocrine reactions and implications for health. *Noise and Health*, 4, 67–74.

LUNDBERG, U., DOHNS, I. E., MELIN, B., SANDSJÖ, L., PALMERUD, G., EKSTRÖM, M., et al. (1999). Psychophysiological stress responses, muscle tension, and neck shoulder pain among supermarket cashiers. *Journal of Occupational Health Psychology*, 4, 245–255.

LUNDBERG, U., & FRANKENHAEUSER, M. (1999). Stress and workload in men and women in high-ranking positions. *Journal of Occupational Health Psychology*, 4, 142–151.

LUNDIN, R. W. (1987). Locus of control. In R. J. Corsini (Ed.), *Concise encyclopedia of psychology* (pp. 670–672). New York: Wiley.

LUPARELLO, T. J., LYONS, H. A., BLEECKER, E. R., & McFADDEN, E. R. (1968). Influences of suggestion on airway reactivity in asthmatic subjects. *Psychosomatic Medicine*, 30, 819–825.

LUTGENDORF, S. K., ANTONI, M. H., IRONSON, G., KLIMAS, N., KUMAR, M., STARR, K., et al. (1997). Cognitive-behavioral stress management decreases dysphoric mood and herpes simplex virus-type 2 antibody titers in symptomatic HIV-seropositive gay men. *Journal of Consulting and Clinical Psychology*, 65, 31–43.

LYALL, S. (2000, February 10). In Britain's health service, sick itself, cancer care is dismal. *New York Times*, pp. A1, A20.

LYKKEN, D. T. (2004). Psychophysiology. In W. E. Craighead & C. B. Nemeroff (Eds.), *The concise Corsini encyclopedia of psychology and behavioral science* (3rd ed., pp. 768–769). Hoboken, NJ: Wiley.

LYNAM, D. R., MILICH, R., ZIMMERMAN, R., NOVAK, S. P., LOGAN, T. K., MARTIN, C., et al. (1999). Project DARE: No effects at 10-year follow-up. *Journal of Consulting and Clinical Psychology*, 67, 590–593.

LYNCH, J. J. (1990). The broken heart: The psychobiology of human contact. In R. Ornstein & C. Swencionis (Eds.), *The healing brain: A scientific reader* (pp. 75–87). New York: Guilford.

LYNCH, J. W., EVERSON, S. A., KAPLAN, G. A., SALONEN, R., SALONEN, J. T. (1998). Does low socioeconomic status potentiate the effects of heightened cardiovascular responses to stress on the progression of carotid atherosclerosis? *American Journal of Public Health*, 88, 389–394.

MACDONALD, T. K., MACDONALD, G., ZANNA, M. P., & FONG, G. T. (2000). Alcohol, sexual arousal, and intentions to use condoms in young men: Applying alcohol myopia theory to risky sexual behavior. *Health Psychology*, 19, 290–298.

MACKAY, C., & COX, T. (1978). Stress at work. In T. Cox (Ed.), *Stress* (pp. 147–173). Baltimore: University Park Press.

MADDI, S. R. (1998). Hardiness. In E. A. Blechman & K. D. Brownell (Eds.), *Behavioral medicine and women: A comprehensive handbook* (pp. 152–155). New York: Guilford.

MADDUX, B. A., SBRACCIA, P., KUMAKURA, S., SASSON, S., YOUNGREN, J., FISHER, A., et al. (1995). Membrane glycoprotein PC-1 and insulin resistance in non-insulin-dependent diabetes mellitus. *Nature*, 373, 448–451.

MADDUX, J. E., ROBERTS, M. C., SLEDDEN, E. A., & WRIGHT, L. (1986). Developmental issues in child health psychology. *American Psychologist*, 41, 25–34.

MAGES, N. L., & MENDELSOHN, G. A. (1979). Effects of cancer on patients' lives: A personological approach. In G. C. Stone, F. Cohen, & N. E. Adler (Eds.), *Health psychology—A handbook* (pp. 255–284). San Francisco: Jossey-Bass.

MAGNI, G., MORESCHI, C., RIGATTI-LUCHINI, S., & MERSKEY, H. (1994). Prospective study on the relationship between depressive symptoms and chronic musculoskeletal pain. *Pain*, 56, 289–297.

MAGUIRE, P. (1985). Barriers to psychological care of the dying. *British Medical Journal*, 291, 1711–1713.

MAHLER, H. I. M., & KULIK, J. A. (1991). Health care involvement preferences and social-emotional recovery of male coronary-artery-bypass patients. *Health Psychology*, 10, 399–408.

MAJ, M. (1990). Psychiatric aspects of HIV-1 infection and AIDS. *Psychological Medicine*, 20, 547–563.

MAJOR, B., RICHARDS, C., COOPER, M. L., COZZARELLI, C., & ZUBEK, J. (1998). Personal resilience, cognitive appraisals, and coping: An integrative model of adjustment to abortion. *Journal of Personality and Social Psychology*, 74, 735–752.

MALKIN, S. (1976). Care of the terminally ill. *Canadian Medical Association Journal*, 115, 129–130.

MALKOFF, S. B., MULDOON, M. F., ZEIGLER, Z. R., & MANUCK, S. B. (1993). Blood platelet responsivity to acute mental stress. *Psychosomatic Medicine*, 55, 477–482.

MANFREDI, M., BINI, G., CRUCCU, G., ACCORNERO, N., BERADELLI, A., & MEDOLAGO, L. (1981). Congenital absence of pain. *Archives on Neurology*, 38, 507–511.

MANN, T. (1996). Why do we need a health psychology of gender or sexual orientation. In P. M. Kato & T. Mann (Eds.), *Handbook of diversity issues in health psychology* (pp. 187–198). New York: Plenum.

MANNE, S. L. (1999). Intrusive thoughts and psychological distress among cancer patients: The role of spouse avoidance and criticism. *Journal of Consulting and Clinical Psychology, 67,* 539–546.

MANNE, S. L., BAKEMAN, R., JACOBSEN, P. B., GORFINKLE, K., BERNSTEIN, D., & REDD, W. H. (1992). Adult-child interaction during invasive medical procedures. *Health Psychology, 11,* 241–249.

MANNE, S. L., BAKEMAN, R., JACOBSEN, P. B., GORFINKLE, K., & REDD, W. H. (1994). An analysis of a behavioral intervention for children undergoing venipuncture. *Health Psychology, 13,* 556–566.

MANNE, S. L., JACOBSEN, P. B., GORFINKLE, K., GERSTEIN, F., & REDD, W. H. (1993). Treatment adherence difficulties among children with cancer: The role of parenting style. *Journal of Pediatric Psychology, 18,* 47–62.

MANNE, S. L., & ZAUTRA, A. J. (1990). Couples coping with chronic illness: Women with rheumatoid arthritis and their healthy husbands. *Journal of Behavioral Medicine, 13,* 327–342.

MANUCK, S. B. (1994). Cardiovascular reactivity in cardiovascular disease: "Once more unto the breach." *International Journal of Behavioral Medicine, 1,* 4–31.

MANUCK, S. B., KAPLAN, J. R., ADAMS, M. R., & CLARKSON, T. B. (1988). Effects of stress and the sympathetic nervous system on coronary artery atherosclerosis in the cynomolgus macaque. *American Heart Journal, 116,* 328–333.

MANUCK, S. B., MARSLAND, A. L., KAPLAN, J. R., & WILLIAMS, J. K. (1995). The pathogenicity of behavior and its neuroendocrine mediation: An example from coronary artery disease. *Psychosomatic Medicine, 57,* 275–283.

MARCUS, B. H., BOCK, B. C., PINTO, B. M., FORSYTH, L. H., ROBERTS, M. B., & TRAFICANTE, R. M. (1998). Efficacy of an individualized, motivationally-tailored physical activity intervention. *Annals of Behavioral Medicine, 20,* 174–180.

MARCUS, B. H., DUBBERT, P. M., FORSYTH, L. H., MCKENZIE, T. L., STONE, E. J., DUNN, A. L., et al. (2000). Physical activity behavior change: Issues in adoption and maintenance. *Health Psychology, 19,* 32–41.

MARIANO, A. J. (1992). Chronic pain and spinal cord injury. *Journal of Clinical Pain, 8,* 87–92.

MARKOVITZ, J. H., & MATTHEWS, K. A. (1991). Platelets and coronary heart disease: Potential psychophysiologic mechanisms. *Psychosomatic Medicine, 53,* 643–668.

MARKS, G., RICHARDSON, J. L., GRAHAM, J. W., & LEVINE, A. (1986). Role of health locus of control beliefs and expectations of treatment efficacy in adjustment to cancer. *Journal of Personality and Social Psychology, 51,* 443–450.

MARLATT, G. A. (1983). The controlled-drinking controversy: A commentary. *American Psychologist, 38,* 1097–1110.

MARLATT, G. A., & GORDON, J. R. (1980). Determinants of relapse: Implications for the maintenance of behavior change. In P. O. Davidson & S. M. Davidson (Eds.), *Behavioral medicine: Changing health lifestyles* (pp. 410–452). New York: Brunner/Mazel.

MARMOT, M. G., KOGEVINAS, M., & ELSTON, M. A. (1987). Social/economic status and disease. *Annual Review of Public Health, 8,* 111–135.

MARON, D. J., FAZIO, S., & LINTON, M. F. (2000). Current perspectives on statins. *Circulation, 101,* 207.

MARON, D. J., & FORTMANN, S. P. (1987). Nicotine yield and measures of cigarette smoke exposure in a large population: Are lower-yield cigarettes safer? *American Journal of Public Health, 77,* 546–549.

MARSHALL, S. J., & BIDDLE, S. J. H. (2001). The transtheoretical model of behavior change: A meta-analysis of applications to physical activity and exercise. *Annals of Behavioral Medicine, 23,* 229–246.

MARSLAND, A. L., BACHEN, E. A., COHEN, S., & MANUCK, S. B. (2001). Stress, immunity, and susceptibility to infectious disease. In A. Baum, T. A. Revenson, & J. E. Singer (Eds.), *Handbook of health psychology* (pp. 683–695). Mahwah, NJ: Erlbaum.

MARSLAND, A. L., MANUCK, S. B., FAZZARI, T. V., STEWART, C. J., & RABIN, B. S. (1995). Stability of individual differences in cellular immune responses to acute psychological stress. *Psychosomatic Medicine, 57,* 295–298.

MARTEAU, T. M., & JOHNSTON, M. (1986). Determinants of beliefs about illness: A study of parents of children with diabetes, asthma, epilepsy, and no chronic illness. *Journal of Psychosomatic Research, 30,* 673–683.

MARTEAU, T. M., JOHNSTON, M., BAUM, J. D., & BLOCH, S. (1987). Goals of treatment in diabetes: A comparison of doctors and parents of children with diabetes. *Journal of Behavioral Medicine, 10,* 33–48.

MARTIN, J. L. (1988). Psychological consequences of AIDS-related bereavement among gay men. *Journal of Consulting and Clinical Psychology, 56,* 856–862.

MARTIN, J. L., & DEAN, L. (1993). Effects of AIDS-related bereavement and HIV-related illness on psychological distress among gay men: A 7-year longitudinal study, 1985–1991. *Journal of Consulting and Clinical Psychology, 61,* 94–103.

MARTIN, P. R., MILECH, D., & NATHAN, P. R. (1993). Towards a functional model of chronic headaches: Investigation of antecedents and consequences. *Headache, 33,* 461–470.

MARTIN, R., DAVIS, G. M., BARON, R. S., SULS, J., & BLANCHARD, E. B. (1994). Specificity in social support: Perceptions of helpful and unhelpful provider behaviors among irritable bowel, headache, and cancer patients. *Health Psychology, 13,* 432–439.

MARTIN, R., LEMOS, K., ROTHROCK, N., BELLMAN, S. B., RUSSELL, D., TRIPP-REIMER, T. et al. (2004). Gender disparities in common sense models of illness among myocardial infarction victims. *Health Psychology, 23,* 345–353.

MARTINEZ, F. D., WRIGHT, A. L., TAUSSIG, L. M., & THE GROUP HEALTH MEDICAL ASSOCIATES (1994). The effect of paternal smoking on the birthweight of newborns whose mothers did not smoke. *American Journal of Public Health, 84,* 1489–1491.

MARTIRE, L. M., & SCHULZ, R. (2001). Informal caregiving to older adults: Health effects of providing and receiving care. In A. Baum, T. A. Revenson, & J. E. Singer (Eds.), *Handbook of health psychology* (pp. 477–491). Mahwah, NJ: Erlbaum.

MARVEL, M. K., EPSTEIN, R. M., FLOWERS, K., & BECKMAN, H. B. (1999). Soliciting the patient's agenda: Have we improved? *Journal of the American Medical Association, 281,* 283–287.

MARX, M. H., & HILLIX, W. A. (1963). *Systems and theories in psychology.* New York: McGraw-Hill.

MASLACH, C., & JACKSON, S. E. (1982). Burnout in health professions: A social psychological analysis. In G. S. Sanders & J. Suls (Eds.), *Social psychology of health and illness* (pp. 227–251). Hillsdale, NJ: Erlbaum.

MASLACH, C., SCHAUFELI, W. B., & LEITER, M. P. (2001). Job burnout. *Annual Review of Psychology, 52,* 397–422.

MASON, J. W. (1975). A historical view of the stress field. *Journal of Human Stress, 1,* 22–36.

MATARAZZO, J. D. (1982). Behavioral health's challenge to academic, scientific, and professional psychology. *American Psychologist, 37,* 1–14.

MATHEWS, A., & RIDGEWAY, V. (1984). Psychological preparation for surgery. In A. Steptoe & A. Mathews (Eds.), *Health care and human behaviour* (pp. 231–259). London: Academic Press.

MATICKA-TYNDALE, E. (1991). Sexual scripts and AIDS prevention: Variations in adherence to safer-sex guidelines by heterosexual adolescents. *Journal of Sex Research, 28,* 45–66.

MATTES, R. D., ARNOLD, C., & BORAAS, M. (1987a). Learned food aversions among cancer chemotherapy patients. *Cancer, 60,* 2576–2580.

MATTES, R. D., ARNOLD, C., & BORAAS, M. (1987b). Management of learned food aversions in cancer patients receiving chemotherapy. *Cancer Treatment Reports, 71,* 1071–1078.

MATTHEWS, K. A. (1986). Summary, conclusions, and implications. In K. A. Matthews, S. M. Weiss, T. Detre, T. M. Dembroski, B. Falkner, S. B. Manuck, & R. B. Williams (Eds.), *Handbook of stress, reactivity, and cardiovascular disease* (pp. 461–473). New York: Wiley.

MATTHEWS, K. A. (1988). Coronary heart disease and Type A behaviors: Update on and alternative to the Booth-Kewley and Friedman (1987) quantitative review. *Psychological Bulletin, 104,* 373–380.

MATTHEWS, K. A., & ANGULO, J. (1980). Measurement of the Type A behavior pattern in children: Assessment of children's competitiveness, impatience-anger, and aggression. *Child Development, 51,* 466–475.

MATTHEWS, K. A., OWENS, J. F., KULLER, L. H., SUTTON-TYRRELL, K., LASSILA, H. C., & WOLFSON, S. K. (1998). Stress-induced pulse pressure change predicts women's carotid atherosclerosis. *Stroke, 29,* 1525–1530.

MATTHEWS, K. A., SHUMAKER, S. A., BOWEN, D. J., LANGER, R. D., HUNT, J. R., KAPLAN, R. M., et al. (1997). Women's Health Initiative: Why now? What is it? What's new? *American Psychologist, 52,* 101–116.

MATTSON, M. E., POLLACK, E. S., & CULLEN, J. W. (1987). What are the odds that smoking will kill you? *American Journal of Public Health, 77,* 425–431.

MAUDE-GRIFFIN, P. M., HOHENSTEIN, J. M., HUMFLEET, G. L., REILLY, P. M., TUSEL, D. J., & HALL, S. M. (1998). Superior efficacy of cognitive-behavioral therapy for urban crack cocaine abusers: Main and matching effects. *Journal of Consulting and Clinical Psychology, 66,* 832–836.

MAYER, D. J. (2000). Acupuncture: An evidence-based review of the clinical literature. *Annual Review of Medicine, 51,* 49–63.

MAYER, W. (1983). Alcohol abuse and alcoholism: The psychologist's role in prevention, research, and treatment. *American Psychologist, 38,* 1116–1121.

MAYNARD, L. M., GALUSKA, D. A., BLANCK, H. M., & SERDULA, M. K. (2003). Maternal perceptions of weight status of children. *Pediatrics, 111,* 1226–1231.

MAYNE, T. J., VITTINGHOFF, E., BARRETT, D. C., CHESNEY, M. A., & COATES, T. J. (1996, March). *Depressive affect and HIV survival.* Paper presented at the meeting of the Society of Behavioral Medicine in Washington, DC.

MAZZE, R. S., SHAMOON, H., PASMANTIER, R., LUCIDO, D., MURPHY, J., HARTMANN, K., et al. (1984). Reliability of blood glucose monitoring by patients with diabetes mellitus. *American Journal of Medicine, 77,* 211–217.

MCADOO, W. G., WEINBERGER, M. H., MILLER, J. Z., FEINBERG, N. S., & GRIM, C. E. (1990). Race and gender influence hemodynamic responses to psychological and physical stimuli. *Journal of Hypertension, 8,* 961–967.

MCALLISTER-SISTILLI, C. G., CAGGIULA, A. R., KNOPF, S., ROSE, C. A., MILLER, A. L., & DONNY, E. C. (1998). The effects of nicotine on the immune system. *Psychoneuroendocrinology, 23,* 175–187.

MCCAFFERY, J. M., POGUE-GEILE, M. F., MULDOON, M. F., DEBSKI, T. T., WING, R. R., & MANUCK, S. B. (2001). The nature of the association between diet and serum lipods in the community: A twin study. *Health Psychology*, 20, 341–350.

McCahon, C. P. (1991). Why did Martha want her husband to deteriorate? *Nursing*, 21(4), 44–46.

McCarty, D. (1985). Environmental factors in substance abuse: The microsetting. In M. Galizio & S. A. Maisto (Eds.), *Determinants of substance abuse: Biological, psychological, and environmental factors* (pp. 247–281). New York: Plenum.

McCaul, K. D., & Malott, J. M. (1984). Distraction and coping with pain. *Psychological Bulletin*, 95, 516–533.

McCaul, K. D., Monson, N., & Maki, R. H. (1992). Does distraction reduce pain-produced distress among college students? *Health Psychology*, 11, 210–217.

McClellan, A. T., Arndt, I. O., Metzger, D. S., Woody, G. E., & O'Brien, C. P. (1993). The effects of psychosocial services in substance abuse treatment. *Journal of the American Medical Association*, 269, 1953–1959.

McClintic, J. R. (1985). *Physiology of the human body* (3rd ed.). New York: Wiley.

McConnell, S., Biglan, A., & Severson, H. H. (1984). Adolescents' compliance with self-monitoring and physiological assessment of smoking in natural environments. *Journal of Behavioral Medicine*, 7, 115–122.

McCoy, S. B., Gibbons, F. X., Reis, T. J., Gerrard, M., Luus, C. A. E., & Von Wald Sufka, A. (1992). Perceptions of smoking risk as a function of smoking status. *Journal of Behavioral Medicine*, 15, 469–488.

McCrady, B. S. (1988). Alcoholism. In E. A. Blechman & K. D. Brownell (Eds.), *Handbook of behavioral medicine for women* (pp. 356–368). New York: Pergamon.

McCrady, B. S., & Irvine, S. (1989). Self-help groups. In R. K. Hester & W. R. Miller (Eds.), *Handbook of alcoholism treatment approaches: Effective alternatives* (pp. 153–169). New York: Pergamon.

McDaniel, S., & Campbell, T. L. (1986). Physicians and family therapists: The risk of collaboration. *Family Systems Medicine*, 4, 4–8.

McDonald, H. P., Garg, H. P., & Haynes, R. B. (2002). Interventions to enhance patient adherence to medication prescriptions. *Journal of the American Medical Association*, 288, 2868–2879.

McDonald, R. V., & Siegel, S. (2003). Intra-administration associations and withdrawal symptoms: Morphine-elicited morphine withdrawal. *Experimental and Clinical Psychopharmacology*, 12, 3–11.

McEwen, B. S., & Stellar, E. (1993). Stress and the individual: Mechanisms leading to disease. *Archives of Internal Medicine*, 153, 2093–2101.

McFarlane, A. H., Norman, G. R., Streiner, D. L., & Roy, R. G. (1983). The process of social stress: Stable, reciprocal, and mediating relationships. *Journal of Health and Social Behavior*, 24, 160–173.

McGehee, D. S., Heath, M. J. S., Gelber, S., Devay, P., & Role, L. W. (1995). Nicotine enhancement of fast excitatory transmission in CNS by presynaptic receptors. *Science*, 269, 1692–1696.

McGinnis, J. M. (1994). The role of behavioral research in national health policy. In J. A. Blumenthal, K. Matthews, & S. M. Weiss (Eds.), *New frontiers in behavioral medicine: Proceedings of the national conference* (pp. 217–222). Washington, DC: National Institutes of Health.

McGinnis, J. M., & Lee, P. R. (1995). Healthy People 2000 at mid decade. *Journal of the American Medical Association*, 273, 1123–1129.

McGinnis, J. M., Shopland, D., & Brown, C. (1987). Tobacco and health: Trends in smoking and smokeless tobacco consumption in the United States. *Annual Review of Public Health*, 8, 441–467.

McGrady, A., Conran, P., Dickey, D., Garman, D., Farris, E., & Schumann-Brzezinski, C. (1992). The effects of biofeedback-assisted relaxation on cell-mediated immunity, cortisol, and white blood cell count in healthy adult subjects. *Journal of Behavioral Medicine*, 15, 343–354.

McGrady, A., & Higgins, J. T. (1990). Effect of repeated measurements of blood pressure in essential hypertension: Role of anxiety. *Journal of Behavioral Medicine*, 13, 93–101.

McGrath, P. A., & Gillespie, J. (2001). Pain assessment in children and adolescents. In D. C. Turk & R. Melzack (Eds.), *Handbook of pain assessment* (2nd ed., pp. 97–118). New York: Guilford.

McGrath, P. A., & Hillier, L. M. (1996). Controlling children's pain. In R. J. Gatchel & D. C. Turk (Eds.), *Psychological approaches to pain management: A practitioner's handbook* (pp. 331–370). New York: Guilford.

McGregor, B. A., Antoni, M. H., Boyers, A., Alferi, S. M., Blomberg, B. B., & Carver, C. S. (2004). Cognitive–behavioral stress management increases benefit finding and immune function among women with early-stage breast cancer. *Journal of Psychosomatic Research*, 56, 1–8.

McGuigan, F. J. (1999). *Encyclopedia of stress*. Boston: Allyn & Bacon.

McGuire, F. L. (1982). Treatment of the drinking driver. *Health Psychology*, 1, 137–152.

McGuire, M. T., Wing, R. R., Klem, M. L., Lang, W., & Hill, J. O. (1999). What predicts weight regain in a group of successful weight losers? *Journal of Consulting and Clinical Psychology*, 67, 177–185.

McIlwain, H. H., Silverfield, J. C., Burnette, M. C., & Bruce, D. F. (1991). *Winning with arthritis*. New York: Wiley.

McKellar, J., Stewart, E., & Humphreys, K. (2003). Alcoholics Anonymous involvement and positive alcohol-related outcomes: Cause, consequence, or just a correlate? A prospective 2-year study of 2,319 alcohol-dependent men. *Journal of Consulting and Clinical Psychology, 71,* 302–308.

McKinlay, J. B. (1975). Who is really ignorant—Physician or patient? *Journal of Health and Social Behavior, 16,* 3–11.

MDBDF (March of Dimes Birth Defects Foundation) (2004). *National perinatal statistics.* Retrieved (5-18-2004) from http://www.modimes.org.

Mead, M., & Newton, N. (1967). Cultural patterning of perinatal behavior. In S. A. Richardson & A. F. Guttmacher (Eds.), *Childbearing: Its social and psychological aspects* (pp. 142–244). Baltimore: Williams & Wilkins.

Mechanic, D. (1972). Social psychologic factors affecting the presentation of bodily complaints. *New England Journal of Medicine, 286,* 1132–1139.

Mechanic, D. (1979). The stability of health and illness behavior: Results from a 16-year follow-up. *American Journal of Public Health, 69,* 1142–1145.

Meichenbaum, D., & Cameron, R. (1983). Stress inoculation training: Toward a general paradigm for training coping skills. In D. Meichenbaum & M. E. Jaremko (Eds.), *Stress reduction and prevention* (pp. 115–154). New York: Plenum.

Meichenbaum, D., & Deffenbacher, J. L. (1988). Stress inoculation training. *Counseling Psychologist, 16,* 69–90.

Meichenbaum, D., & Turk, D. (1982). Stress, coping, and disease: A cognitive-behavioral perspective. In R. W. J. Neufield (Ed.), *Psychological stress and psychopathology.* New York: McGraw-Hill.

Meier, D. E., Emmons, C.-A., Wallenstein, S., Quill, T., Morrison, R. S., & Cassel, C. K. (1998). A national survey of physician-assisted suicide and euthanasia in the United States. *New England Journal of Medicine, 338,* 1193–1201.

Melamed, B. G., & Bush, J. P. (1985). Family factors in children with acute illness. In D. C. Turk & R. D. Kerns (Eds.), *Health, illness, and families: A life-span approach* (pp. 183–219). New York: Wiley.

Melamed, B. G., Dearborn, M., & Hermecz, D. A. (1983). Necessary conditions for surgery preparation: Age and previous experience. *Psychosomatic Medicine, 45,* 517–525.

Melamed, B. G., & Siegel, L. J. (1975). Reduction of anxiety in children facing hospitalization and surgery by use of filmed modeling. *Journal of Consulting and Clinical Psychology, 43,* 511–521.

Melin, B., Lundberg, U., Söderlund, J., & Granqvist, M. (1999). Psychological and physiological stress reactions of male and female assembly workers: A comparison between two different forms of work organization. *Journal of Organizational Behavior, 20,* 47–61.

Mellins, C. A., Havens, J. F., McCaskill, E. O., Leu, C. S., Brudney, K., & Chesney, M. A. (2002). Mental health, substance use and disclosure are significantly associated with the medical treatment adherence of HIV-infected mothers. *Psychology, Health & Medicine, 7,* 451–460.

Meltzer, L. J., Johnson, S. B., Pappachan, S., & Silverstein, J. (2003). Blood glucose estimations in adolescents with type 1 diabetes: Predictors of accuracy and error. *Journal of Pediatric Psychology, 28,* 203–211.

Melzack, R (1975). The McGill Pain Questionnaire: Major properties and scoring methods. *Pain, 1,* 277–299.

Melzack, R. (1997). Phantom limbs. *Scientific American, 7*(1, Special issue), 84–91.

Melzack, R. (2004). Gate control theory of pain. In W. E. Craighead & C. B. Nemeroff (Eds.), *The concise Corsini encyclopedia of psychology and behavioral science* (3rd ed., pp. 389–390). Hoboken, NJ: Wiley.

Melzack, R., & Katz, J. (2001). The McGill pain Questionnaire: Appraisal and current status. In D. C. Turk & R. Melzack (Eds.), *Handbook of pain assessment* (2nd ed., pp. 35–52). New York: Guilford.

Melzack, R., & Torgerson, W. S. (1971). On the language of pain. *Anesthesiology, 34,* 50–59.

Melzack, R., & Wall, P. D. (1965). Pain mechanisms: A new theory. *Science, 150,* 971–979.

Melzack, R., & Wall, P. D. (1982). *The challenge of pain.* New York: Basic Books.

Melzack, R., Weisz, A. Z., & Sprague, L. T. (1963). Stratagems for controlling pain: Contributions of auditory stimulation and suggestion. *Experimental Neurology, 8,* 239–247.

Mendelson, B. K., & White, D. R. (1985). Development of self-body-esteem in overweight youngsters. *Developmental Psychology, 21,* 90–96.

Menefee, L. A., Haythornthwaite, J. A., Clark, M. R., & Koenig, T. (1996, March). *The effect of social responses on pain coping strategies.* Paper presented at the meeting of the Society of Behavioral Medicine, Washington, DC.

Menkes, M. S., Matthews, K. A., Krantz, D. S., Lundberg, U., Mead, L. A., Qaqish, B., et al. (1989). Cardiovascular reactivity to the cold pressor test as a predictor of hypertension. *Hypertension, 14,* 524–530.

Mentzer, S. J., & Snyder, M. L. (1982). The doctor and the patient: A psychological perspective. In G. S. Sanders & J. Suls (Eds.), *Social psychology of health and illness* (pp. 161–181). Hillsdale, NJ: Erlbaum.

Meredith, H. V. (1978). *Human body growth in the first ten years of life.* Columbia, SC: The State Printing Company.

METHORST, G. J., JANSEN, M. A., & KERKHOF, A. J. F. M. (1991). Training in health psychology: An international look. In M. A. Jansen & J. Weinman (Eds.), *The international development of health psychology* (pp. 111–122). Chur, Switzerland: Harwood.

MEYER, A. J., NASH, J. D., MCALISTER, A. L., MACCOBY, N., & FARQUHAR, J. W. (1980). Skills training in a cardiovascular health education campaign. *Journal of Consulting and Clinical Psychology, 48,* 129–142.

MEYER, T. J., & MARK, M. M. (1995). Effects of psychosocial interventions with adult cancer patients: A meta-analysis of randomized experiments. *Health Psychology, 14,* 101–108.

MEYEROWITZ, B. E., RICHARDSON, J., HUDSON, S., & LEEDHAM, B. (1998). Ethnicity and cancer outcomes: Behavioral and psychosocial considerations. *Psychological Bulletin, 123,* 47–70.

MEYERS, R. J., MILLER, W. R., SMITH, J. E., & TONIGAN, J. S. (2002). A randomized trial of two methods for engaging treatment-refusing drug users through concerned significant others. *Journal of Consulting and Clinical Psychology, 70,* 1182–1185.

MICHELA, J. L. (1987). Interpersonal and individual impacts of a husband's heart attack. In A. Baum & J. E. Singer (Eds.), *Handbook of psychology and health* (Vol. 5, pp. 225–301). Hillsdale, NJ: Erlbaum.

MIGLIORELLI, R., TESÓN, A., SABE, L., PETRACCHI, M., LEIGUARDA, R., & STARKSTEIN, S. E. (1995). Prevalence and correlates of dysthymia and major depression among patients with Alzheimer's disease. *American Journal of Psychiatry, 152,* 37–44.

MILES, F., & MEEHAN, J. W. (1995). Visual discrimination of pigmented skin lesions. *Health Psychology, 14,* 171–177.

MILLER, B., & CAFASSO, L. (1992). Gender differences in caregiving: Fact or artifact? *Gerontologist, 32,* 498–507.

MILLER, B. D., & WOOD, B. L. (1994). Psychophysiologic reactivity in asthmatic children: A cholinergically mediated confluence of pathways. *Journal of the American Academy of Child and Adolescent Psychiatry, 33,* 1236–1245.

MILLER, N. E. (1959). Liberalization of basic S-R concepts: Extensions to conflict behavior, motivation, and social learning. In S. Koch (Ed.), *Psychology: A study of a science* (Vol. 2, pp. 196–292). New York: McGraw-Hill.

MILLER, N. E. (1978). Biofeedback and visceral learning. *Annual Review of Psychology, 29,* 373–404.

MILLER, R. H., & LUFT, H. S. (1994). Managed care plans: Characteristics, growth, and premium performance. *Annual Review of Public Health, 15,* 437–459.

MILLER, S. B., TURNER, J. R., SHERWOOD, A., BROWNLEY, K. A., HINDERLITER, A. L., & LIGHT, K. C. (1995). Parental history of hypertension and cardiovascular response to stress in black and white men. *International Journal of Behavioral Medicine, 2,* 339–357.

MILLER, S. M., BRODY, D. S., & SUMMERTON, J. (1987). Styles of coping with threat: Implications for health. *Journal of Personality and Social Psychology, 54,* 142–148.

MILLER, S. M., & GREEN, M. L. (1984). Coping with stress and frustration: Origins, nature, and development. In M. Lewis & C. Saarni (Eds.), *The socialization of emotions* (Vol. 5, pp. 263–314). New York: Plenum.

MILLER, S. M., & MANGAN, C. E. (1983). Interacting effects of information and coping style in adapting to gynecologic stress: Should the doctor tell all? *Journal of Personality and Social Psychology, 45,* 223–236.

MILLER, T. D., BALADY, G. J., & FLETCHER, G. F. (1997). Exercise and its role in the prevention and rehabilitation of cardiovascular disease. *Annals of Behavioral Medicine, 19,* 220–229.

MILLER, W. R. (1989). Increasing motivation for change. In R. K. Hester & W. R. Miller (Eds.), *Handbook of alcoholism treatment approaches: Effective alternatives* (pp. 67–80). New York: Pergamon.

MILLER, W. R., & HESTER, R. K. (1980). Treating the problem drinker: Modern approaches. In W. R. Miller (Ed.), *The addictive behaviors: Treatment of alcoholism, drug abuse, smoking, and obesity.* New York: Pergamon.

MILLER, W. R., & HESTER, R. K. (1985). Inpatient alcoholism treatment: Who benefits? *American Psychologist, 41,* 794–805.

MILLER, W. R., MEYERS, R. J., & TONIGAN, J. S. (1999). Engaging the unmotivated in treatment for alcohol problems: A comparison of three strategies for intervention through family members. *Journal of Consulting and Clinical Psychology, 67,* 688–697.

MILLER, W. R., & ROLLNICK, S. (1991). *Motivational interviewing: Preparing people to change addictive behaviors.* New York: Guilford.

MILLER-JOHNSON, S., EMERY, R. E., MARVIN, R. S., CLARKE, W., LOVINGER, R., & MARTIN, M. (1994). Parent-child relationships and the management of insulin-dependent diabetes mellitus. *Journal of Consulting and Clinical Psychology, 62,* 603–610.

MILLING, L. S., LEVINE, M. R., & MEUNIER, S. A. (2003). Hypnotic enhancement of cognitive-behavioral interventions for pain: An analogue treatment study. *Health Psychology, 22,* 406–413.

MILLS, N. M. (1989). Pain behaviors in infants and toddlers. *Journal of Pain and Symptom Management, 4,* 184–190.

MINOR, M. A., & SANFORD, M. K. (1993). Physical interventions in the management of pain in arthritis. *Arthritis Care and Research, 6,* 197–206.

MISOVICH, S. J., FISHER, J. D., & FISHER, W. A. (1997). Close relationships and elevated HIV risk behavior: Evidence and possible underlying psychological processes. *Review of General Psychology, 1,* 72–107.

MITTLEMAN, M. A., MINTZER, D., MACLURE, M., TOFLER, G. H., SHERWOOD, J. B., & MULLER, J. E. (1999). Triggering of myocardial infarction by cocaine. *Circulation, 99,* 2737–2741.

MIZOGUCHI, H., O'SHEA, J. J., LONGO, D. L., LOEFFLER, C. M., MCVICAR, D. W., & OCHOA, A. C. (1992). Alterations in signal transduction molecules in T lymphocytes from tumor-bearing mice. *Science, 258,* 1795–1798.

MOFFET, J. K., TORGERSON, D., BELL-SYER, S., JACKSON, D., LLEWLYN-PHILLIPS, H., FARRIN, A., et al. (1999). Randomized controlled trial of exercise for low back pain: Clinical outcomes, costs, and preferences. *British Medical Journal, 319,* 279–283.

MÖLLER, J., HALLQVIST, J., DIDERICHSEN, F., THEORELL, T., REUTERWALL, C., & AHLBOM, A. (1999). Do episodes of anger trigger myocardial infarction? A case-crossover analysis in the Stockholm Heart Epidemiology Program (SHEEP). *Psychosomatic Medicine, 61,* 842–849.

MONTGOMERY, G. H., & BOVBJERG, D. H. (2003). Expectations of chemotherapy-related nausea: Emotional and experiential predictors. *Annals of Behavioral Medicine, 25,* 48–54.

MONTI, P. M., ROHSENOW, D. J., SWIFT, R. M., GULLIVER, S. B., COLBY, S. M., MUELLER, T. I. et al. (2001). Naltrexone and cue exposure with coping and communication skills training for alcoholics: Treatment process and 1-year outcomes. *Alcoholism: Clinical and Experimental Research, 25,* 1634–1647.

MOORE, M. L. (1983). *Realities of childbearing* (2nd ed.). Philadelphia: Saunders.

MOORE, P. J., KULIK, J. A., & MAHLER, H. I. M. (1998). Stress and multiple potential affiliates: Does misery choose miserable company? *Journal of Applied Biobehavioral Research, 3,* 81–95.

MOORE, S. M., BARLING, N. R., & HOOD, B. (1998). Predicting testicular and breast self-examination behaviour: A test of the theory of reasoned action. *Behaviour Change, 15,* 41–49.

MOOS, R. H. (1982). Coping with acute health crises. In T. Millon, C. Green, & R. Meagher (Eds.), *Handbook of clinical health psychology* (pp. 129–151). New York: Plenum.

MOOS, R. H., & MOOS, B. S. (2004). Long-term influence of duration and frequency of participation in Alcoholics Anonymous o individuals with alcohol use disorders. *Journal of Consulting and Clinical Psychology, 72,* 81–90.

MOOS, R. H., & SCHAEFER, J. A. (1986). Life transitions and crises: A conceptual overview. In R. H. Moos (Ed.), *Coping with life crises: An integrated approach* (pp. 3–33). New York: Plenum.

MOR, V., MASTERSON-ALLEN, S., GOLDBERG, R. J., CUMMINGS, F. J., GLICKSMAN, A. S., & FRETWELL, M. D. (1985). Relationships between age at diagnosis and treatments received by cancer patients. *Journal of the American Geriatrics Society, 33,* 585–589.

MORAN, P. M., CHRISTENSEN, A. J., & LAWTON, W. J. (1997). Social support and conscientiousness in hemodialysis adherence. *Annals of Behavioral Medicine, 19,* 333–338.

MORELAND, J., & THOMPSON, M. A. (1994). Efficacy of electromyographic biofeedback compared with conventional physical therapy for upper-extremity function in patients following stroke: A research overview and meta-analysis. *Physical Therapy, 74,* 534–547.

MORLEY, S., ECCLESTON, C., & WILLIAMS, A. (1999). Systematic review and meta-analysis of randomized controlled trials of cognitive behaviour therapy and behaviour therapy for chronic pain in adults, excluding headache. *Pain, 80,* 1–13.

MORROW, G. R., ASBURY, R., HAMMON, S., DOBKIN, P., CARUSO, L., PANDYA, K., & et al. (1992). Comparing the effectiveness of behavioral treatment for chemotherapy-induced nausea and vomiting when administered by oncologists, oncology nurses, and clinical psychologists. *Health Psychology, 11,* 250–256.

MORZORATI, S. L., RAMCHANDANI, V. A., FLURY, L., LI, T.-K., & O'CONNOR, S. (2002). Self-reported subjective perception of intoxication reflects family history of alcoholism when breath alcohol levels are constant. *Alcoholism: Clinical and Experimental Research, 26,* 1299–1306.

MOSELEY, J. B., O'MALLEY, K., PETERSEN, N. J., MENKE, T. J., BRODY, B. A., KUYKENDALL, D. H. et al. (2002). A controlled trial of arthroscopic surgery for osteoarthritis of the knee. *New England Journal of Medicine, 347,* 81–88.

MOSER, D. K., & DRACUP, K. (1996). Is anxiety early after myocardial infarction associated with subsequent ischemic and arrhythmic events? *Psychosomatic Medicine, 58,* 395–401.

MOSKOWITZ, J. T., FOLKMAN, S., COLLETTE, L., & VITTINGHOFF, E. (1996). Coping and mood during AIDS-related caregiving and bereavement. *Annals of Behavioral Medicine, 18,* 49–57.

MOSLEY, T. H., PENZIEN, D. B., JOHNSON, C. A., WITTROCK, D., RUBMAN, S., PAYNE, T. J., et al. (1990, April). *Coping with stress in headache sufferers and no-headache controls.* Paper presented at the meeting of the Society of Behavioral Medicine, Chicago.

MOSS, G. E., DIELMAN, T. E., CAMPANELLI, P. C., LEECH, S. L., HARLAN, W. R., VAN HARRISON, R., et al. (1986).

Demographic correlates of SI assessments of Type A behavior. *Psychosomatic Medicine*, 48, 564–574.

MOYER, A. (1997). Psychosocial outcomes of breast-conserving surgery versus mastectomy: A meta-analytic review. *Health Psychology*, 16, 284–298.

MOYER, A., & FINNEY, J. W. (2002). Outcomes for untreated individuals involved in randomized trials of alcohol treatment. *Journal of Substance Abuse Treatment*, 23, 247–252.

MOYER, C. A., ROUNDS, J., & HANNUM, J. W. (2004). A meta-analysis of massage therapy research. *Psychological Bulletin*, 130, 3–18.

MUKAMAL, K. J., & RIMM, E. B. (2001). Alcohol's effects on the risk for coronary heart disease. *Alcohol Research and Health*, 25, 255–261.

MULDOON, M. F., & MANUCK, S. B. (1992). Health through cholesterol reduction: Are there unforeseen risks? *Annals of Behavioral Medicine*, 14, 101–108.

MULDOON, M. F., MANUCK, S. B., & MATTHEWS, K. A. (1990). Lowering cholesterol concentrations and mortality: A quantitative review of primary prevention trials. *British Medical Journal*, 301, 309–314.

MULLAN, F. (1983). *Vital signs: A young doctor's struggle with cancer.* New York: Farrar, Straus, & Giroux.

MULLER, J. E., LUDMER, P. L., WILLICH, S. N., TOFLER, G. H., AYLMER, G., KLANGOS, I., et al. (1987). Circadian variation in the frequency of sudden cardiac death. *Circulation*, 75, 131–138.

MULLER, J. E., MITTLEMAN, M. A., MACLURE, M., SHERWOOD, J. B., TOFLER, G. H., et al. (1996). Triggering myocardial infarction by sexual activity: Low absolute risk and prevention by regular physical exertion. *Journal of the American Medical Association*, 275, 1405–1409.

MURDAUGH, C. L. (1998). Problems with adherence in the elderly. In S. A. Shumaker, E. B. Schron, J. K. Ockene, & W. L. McBee (Eds.), *The handbook of health behavior change* (2nd ed., pp. 357–376). New York: Springer.

MURPHY, L. B. (1974). Coping, vulnerability, and resilience in childhood. In G. V. Coelho, D. A. Hamburg, & J. E. Adams (Eds.), *Coping and adaptation* (pp. 69–100). New York: Basic Books.

MURRAY, D. M., DAVIS-HEARN, M., GOLDMAN, A. I., PIRIE, P., & LUEPKER, R. V. (1988). Four- and five-year follow-up results from four seventh-grade smoking prevention strategies. *Journal of Behavioral Medicine*, 11, 395–405.

MURRAY, D. M., PIRIE, P., LEUPKER, R. V., & PALLONEN, U. (1989). Five- and six-year follow-up results from four seventh-grade smoking prevention strategies. *Journal of Behavioral Medicine*, 12, 207–218.

MURRAY, D. M., RICHARDS, P. S., LUEPKER, R. V., & JOHNSON, C. A. (1987). The prevention of cigarette smoking in children: Two- and three-year follow-up comparisons of four prevention strategies. *Journal of Behavioral Medicine*, 10, 595–611.

MURRAY, M., SWAN, A. V., JOHNSON, M. R. D., & BEWLEY, B. R. (1983). Some factors associated with increased risk of smoking by children. *Journal of Child Psychology and Psychiatry*, 24, 223–232.

MURRELL, J., FARLOW, M., GHETTI, B., & BENSON, M. D. (1991). A mutation in the amyloid precursor protein associated with hereditary Alzheimer's disease. *Science*, 254, 97–99.

MUSCAT, J. E., HARRIS, R. E., HALEY, N. J., & WYNDER, E. L. (1991). Cigarette smoking and plasma cholesterol. *American Heart Journal*, 121, 121–141.

MYERS, C. D., ROBINSON, M. E., RILEY, J. L., & SHEFFIELD, D. (2001). Sex, gender, and blood pressure: Contributions to experimental pain report. *Psychosomatic Medicine*, 63, 545–550.

NASH, M. R. (2001). The truth and the hype of hypnosis. *Scientific American*, 285(1), 46–53.

NASH, S. S., & SMITH, M. J. (1982). Perception and coordination. In M. J. Smith, J. A. Goodman, N. L. Ramsey, & S. B. Pasternack (Eds.), *Child and family: Concepts in nursing practice* (pp. 1033–1088). New York: McGraw-Hill.

NATHAN, P. (1984). Johnson & Johnson's Live for Life: A comprehensive positive lifestyle change program. In J. D. Matarazzo, S. M. Weiss, J. A. Herd, N. E. Miller, & S. M. Weiss (Eds.), *Behavioral health: A handbook of health enhancement and disease prevention* (pp. 1064–1070). New York: Wiley.

NATHAN, P. E. (1986). Outcomes of treatment for alcoholism: Current data. *Annals of Behavioral Medicine*, 8(2–3), 40–46.

NAVARRO, A. M., SENN, K. L., McNICHOLAS, L. J., KAPLAN, R. M., ROPPÉ, B., & CAMPO, M. C. (1998). *Por La Vita* model intervention enhances use of cancer screening tests among Latinas. *American Journal of Preventive Medicine*, 15, 32–41.

NCADI (National Clearinghouse for Alcohol and Drug Information) (2000). *Drugs of abuse.* Retrieved (3–23–2000) from http://www.samhsa.gov.

NCCAM (National Center for Complementary and Alternative Medicine) (2004). *Health Information.* Retrieved (8–28–2004) from http://nccam.nih.gov.

NCHS (National Center for Health Statistics) (2000). *Health, United States, 1999.* Retrieved (3–21–2000) from http://www.cdc.gov/nchs.

NCHS (National Center for Health Statistics) (2003). *Health, United States, 2003.* Retrieved (4–6–2004) from http://www.cdc.gov/nchs.

NEGRI, E., LA VECCHIA, C., D'AVANZO, B., NOBILI, A., LA MALFA, R. G., et al. (1994). Acute myocardial infarction:

Association with time since stopping smoking in Italy. *Journal of Epidemiology and Community Health*, 48, 129–133.

NEHEMKIS, A. M., & GERBER, K. E. (1986). Compliance and the quality of survival. In K. E. Gerber & A. M. Nehemkis (Eds.), *Compliance: The dilemma of the chronically ill* (pp. 73–97). New York: Springer.

NEIGHBORS, C. J., O'LEARY, A., & LABOUVIE, E. (1999). Domestically violent and nonviolent male inmates' responses to their partners' requests for condom use: Testing a social-information processing model. *Health Psychology*, 18, 427–431.

NEWCOMB, M. D., & BENTLER, P. M. (1986). Cocaine use among adolescents: Longitudinal associations with social context, psychopathology, and use of other substances. *Addictive Behaviors*, 11, 263–273.

NEWCOMB, M. D., MADDAHIAN, E., & BENTLER, P. M. (1986). Risk factors for drug use among adolescents: Concurrent and longitudinal analyses. *American Journal of Public Health*, 76, 525–531.

NEWLIN, D. B., & THOMSON, J. B. (1991). Chronic tolerance and sensitization to alcohol in sons of alcoholics. *Alcoholism: Clinical and experimental research*, 15, 399–405.

NEWMAN, S. (1984a). Anxiety, hospitalization, and surgery. In R. Fitzpatrick, J. Hinton, S. Newman, G. Scambler, & J. Thompson (Eds.), *The experience of illness* (pp. 132–153). London: Tavistock.

NEWMAN, S. (1984b). The psychological consequences of cerebrovascular accident and head injury. In R. Fitzpatrick, J. Hinton, S. Newman, G. Scambler, & J. Thompson (Eds.), *The experience of illness* (pp. 179–202). London: Tavistock.

NEWTON-JOHN, T. R. O. (2002). Solicitousness and chronic pain: A critical review. *Pain Reviews*, 9, 7–27.

NEZU, A. M., NEZU, C. M., & PERRI, M. G. (1989). *Problem-solving therapy for depression: Theory, research, and clinical guidelines*. New York: Wiley.

NG, B., DIMSDALE, J. E., SHRAGG, P., & DEUTSCH, R. (1996). Ethnic differences in analgesic consumption for post-operative pain. *Psychosomatic Medicine*, 58, 125–129.

NG, D. M., & JEFFERY, R. W. (2003). Relationships between perceived stress and health behaviors in a sample of working adults. *Health Psychology*, 22, 638–642.

NGUYEN, M., WATANABE, H., BUDSON, A. E., RICHIE, J. P., HAYES, D. F., & FOLKMAN, J. (1994). Elevated levels of an angiogenic peptide, basic fibroblast factor, in the urine of patients with a wide spectrum of cancers. *Journal of the National Cancer Institute*, 86, 356–361.

NIAAA (National Institute on Alcohol Abuse and Alcoholism) (1993). *Alcohol and health* (8th Special Report to the U.S. Congress; Publication No. 94–3699). Washington, DC: U.S. Government Printing Office.

NIAURA, R., & ABRAMS, D. B. (2002). Smoking cessation: Progress, priorities, and prospectus. *Journal of Consulting and Clinical Psychology*, 70, 494–509.

NICASSIO, P. M., MEYEROWITZ, B. E., & KERNS, R. D. (2004). The future of health psychology interventions. *Health Psychology*, 23, 132–137.

NICASSIO, P. M., RADOJEVIC, V., WEISMAN, M. H., CULBERTSON, A. L., LEWIS, C., & CLEMMEY, P. (1993). The role of helplessness in the response to disease-modifying drugs in rheumatoid arthritis. *Journal of Rheumatology*, 20, 1114–1120.

NICASSIO, P. M., WALLSTON, K. A., CALLAHAN, L. F., HERBERT, M., & PINCUS, T. (1985). The measurement of helplessness in rheumatoid arthritis: The development of the Arthritis Helplessness Index. *Journal of Rheumatology*, 12, 462–467.

NKF (National Kidney Foundation) (2004). *A to Z guide*. Retrieved (6–1–2004) from http://www.kidney.org.

NORMAN, P., CONNER, M., & BELL, R. (1999). The theory of planned behavior and smoking cessation. *Health Psychology*, 18, 89–94.

NORTHCOTE, R. J., FLANNIGAN, C., & BALLANTYNE, D. (1986). Sudden death and vigorous exercise—A study of 60 deaths associated with squash. *British Heart Journal*, 55, 198–203.

NOVACO, R. W. (1975). *Anger control: The development and evaluation of an experimental treatment*. Lexington, MA: Heath.

NOVACO, R. W. (1978). Anger and coping with stress: Cognitive behavioral interventions. In J. P. Foreyt & D. P. Rathjen (Eds.), *Cognitive behavior therapy: Research and application* (pp. 135–161). New York: Plenum.

NOWACK, K. M. (1989). Coping style, cognitive hardiness, and health status. *Journal of Behavioral Medicine*, 12, 145–158.

NSCIA (National Spinal Cord Injury Association) (2004). *Fact Sheets (Facts and figures at a glance; SCI rehabilitation; Sexual function for men with SCI)*. Retrieved (5–18–2004) from http://www.spinalcord.org.

NYSTUL, M. S. (2004). Transcendental meditation. In W. E. Craighead & C. B. Nemeroff (Eds.), *Concise Corsini encyclopedia of psychology and behavioral science* (3rd ed., pp. 998–1000). New York: Wiley.

O'BRIEN, C. P. (1996). Recent developments in the pharmacotherapy of substance abuse. *Journal of Consulting and Clinical Psychology*, 64, 677–686.

O'BYRNE, K. K., PETERSON, L., & SALDANA, L. (1997). Survey of pediatric hospitals' preparation programs: Evidence for the impact of health psychology research. *Health Psychology*, 16, 147–154.

O'CALLAGHAN, M. E., & COUVADELLI, B. (1998). Use of self-instructional strategies with three neurologically impaired adults. *Cognitive Therapy and Research*, 22, 91–107.

O'CARROLL, R. E., SMITH, K. B., GRUBB, N. R., FOX, K. A. A., & MASTERSON, G. (2001). Psychological factors associated with delay in atending hospital following a myocardial infarction. *Journal of Psychosomatic Research*, 51, 611–614.

OCKENE, I. S., HEBERT, J. R., OCKENE, J. K., SAPERIA, G. M., STANEK, E., NICOLOSI, R., et al. (1999). Effect of physician-delivered nutrition counseling training and an office support program on saturated fat intake, weight, and serum lipid measurements in a hyperlipidemic population: Worcester Area Trial for Counseling in Hyperlipidemia (WATCH). *Archives of Internal Medicine*, 159, 725–731.

OCKENE, J. K., EMMONS, K. M., MERMELSTEIN, R. J., PERKINS, K. A., BONOLLO, D. S., VOORHEES, C. C., et al. (2000). Relapse and maintenance issues for smoking cessation. *Health Psychology*, 19, 17–31.

OCKENE, J. K., HOSMER, D., RIPPE, J., WILLIAMS, J., GOLDBERG, R. J., DECOSIMO, D., et al. (1985). Factors affecting cigarette smoking status in patients with ischemic heart disease. *Journal of Chronic Diseases*, 38, 985–994.

OCKENE, J. K., KRISTELLER, J., GOLDBERG, R., AMICK, T. L., PEKOW, P. S., HOSMER, D., et al. (1991). Increasing the efficacy of physician-delivered smoking interventions. *Journal of General Internal Medicine*, 6, 1–8.

OCKENE, J. K., KRISTELLER, J. L., PBERT, L., HEBERT, J. R., LUIPPOLD, R., GOLDBERG, R. J., et al. (1994). The Physician-Delivered Smoking Intervention Project: Can short-term interventions produce long-term effects for a general outpatient population? *Health Psychology*, 13, 278–281.

O'CONNELL, K. A., GERKOVICH, M. M., BOTT, M. J., COOK, M. R., & SHIFFMAN, S. (2002). The effect of anticipatory strategies on the first day of smoking cessation. *Psychology of Addictive Behaviors*, 16, 150–156.

O'DOUGHERTY, M., & BROWN, R. T. (1990). The stress of childhood illness. In L. E. Arnold (Ed.), *Childhood stress* (pp. 325–350). New York: Wiley.

ÖHLUND, C., LINDSTRÖM, I., ARESKOUG, B., EEK, C., PETERSON, L.-E., & NACHEMSON, A. (1994). Pain behavior in industrial subacute low back pain: Part I. Reliability: Concurrent and predictive validity of pain behavior assessments. *Pain*, 58, 201–209.

OLBRISCH, M. E., BENEDICT, S. M., ASHE, K., & LEVENSON, J. L. (2002). Psychological assessment and care of organ transplant patients. *Journal of Consulting and Clinical Psychology*, 70, 771–783.

OLDENBURG, B., PERKINS, R. J., & ANDREWS, G. (1985). Controlled trial of psychological intervention in myocardial infarction. *Journal of Consulting and Clinical Psychology*, 53, 852–859.

OLDRIDGE, N. B. (1984). Adherence to adult exercise fitness programs. In J. D. Matarazzo, S. M. Weiss, J. A. Herd, N. E. Miller, & S. M. Weiss (Eds.), *Behavioral health: A handbook of health enhancement and disease prevention* (pp. 467–487). New York: Wiley.

OLIVER, G., WARDLE, J., & GIBSON, E. L. (2000). Stress and food choice: A laboratory study. *Psychosomatic Medicine*, 62, 853–865.

OLIVET, L. W. (1982). Basic needs of the hospitalized child. In M. J. Smith, J. A. Goodman, N. L. Ramsey, & S. B. Pasternack (Eds.), *Child and family: Concepts of nursing practice* (pp. 342–408). New York: McGraw-Hill.

O'LOUGHLIN, J., DIFRANZA, J., TYNDALE, R. F., MESHEFEDJIAN, G., MCMILLAN-DAVEY, E., CLARKE, P. B. S. et al. (2003). Nicotine-dependence symptoms are associated with smoking frequency in adolescents. *American Journal of Preventive Medicine*, 25, 219–225.

OLSHANSKY, S. J., CARNES, B. A., & CASSEL, C. (1990). In search of Methuselah: Estimating the upper limits to human longevity. *Science*, 250, 634–640.

ORFUTT, C, & LACROIX, J. M. (1988). Type A behavior pattern and symptom reports: A prospective investigation. *Journal of Behavioral Medicine*, 11, 227–237.

ORLANDO, M., ELLICKSON, P. L., & JINNETT, K. (2001). The temporal relationship between emotional distress and cigarette smoking during adolescence and young adulthood. *Journal of Consulting and Clinical Psychology*, 69, 959–970.

ORNE, M. T. (1989). On the construct of hypnosis: How its definition affects research and its clinical application. In G. D. Burrows & L. Dennerstein (Eds.), *Handbook of hypnosis and psychosomatic medicine*. Amsterdam: Elsevier.

ORNISH, D., BROWN, S. E., SCHERWITZ, L. W., BILLINGS, J. H., ARMSTRONG, W. T., PORTS, T. A., et al. (1990). Can lifestyle changes reverse coronary heart disease: The Lifestyle Heart Trial. *Lancet*, 336, 129–133.

ORNISH, D., SCHERWITZ, L. W., BILLINGS, J. H., GOULD, K. L., MERRITT, T. A., SPARLER, S., et al. (1998). Intensive lifestyle changes for reversal of coronary heart disease. *Journal of the American Medical Association*, 280, 2001–2007.

O'ROURKE, D. F., HOUSTON, B. K., HARRIS, J. K., & SNYDER, C. R. (1988). The Type A behavior pattern: Summary, conclusions, and implications. In B. K. Houston & C. R. Snyder (Eds.), *Type A behavior pattern: Research, theory, and intervention* (pp. 312–334). New York: Wiley.

OSBORN, J. E. (1988). The AIDS epidemic: Six years. *Annual Review of Public Health*, 9, 551–583.

OSSIP-KLEIN, D. J., BIGELOW, G., PARKER, S. R., CURRY, S., HALL, S., & KIRKLAND, S. (1986). Task Force 1: Classification and assessment of smoking behavior. *Health Psychology*, 5(Supplement), 3–11.

OSTROVE, J. M., FELDMAN, P., & ADLER, N. E. (1999). Relations among socioeconomic status indicators and health for African-Americans and whites. *Journal of Health Psychology, 4,* 451–463.

OUELETTE, S. C., & DIPLACIDO, J. (2001). Personality's role in the protection and enhancement of health: Where the research has been, where it is stuck, how it might move. In A. Baum, T. A. Revenson, & J. E. Singer (Eds.), *Handbook of health psychology* (pp. 175–193). Mahwah, NJ: Erlbaum.

OUIMETTE, P. C., FINNEY, J. W., & MOOS, R. H. (1997). Twelve-step and cognitive-behavioral treatment for substance abuse: A comparison of treatment effectiveness. *Journal of Consulting and Clinical Psychology, 65,* 230–240.

PALLONEN, U. E., MURRAY, D. M., SCHMID, L., PIRIE, P., LUEPKER, R. V. (1990). Patterns of self-initiated smoking cessation among young adults. *Health Psychology, 9,* 418–426.

PANICO, S., CELENTANO, E., KROGH, V., JOSSA, F., FARINARO, E., TREVISAN, M. et al. (1987). Physical activity and its relationship to blood pressure in school children. *Journal of Chronic Diseases, 40,* 925–930.

PANTALEO, G., GRAZIOSI, C., DEMAREST, J. F., BUTINI, L., MONTRONI, M., FOX, C. H. et al. (1993). HIV infection is active and progressive in lymphoid tissue during the clinically latent stage of the disease. *Nature, 362,* 355–358.

PAOLETTI, P., CAMILLI, A. E., HOLBERG, C. J., & LEBOWITZ, M. D. (1985). Respiratory effects in relation to estimated tar exposure from current and cumulative cigarette consumption. *Chest, 88,* 849–855.

PARCEL, G. S., BRUHN, J. G., & CERRETO, M. C. (1986). Longitudinal analysis of health and safety behaviors among school children. *Psychological Reports, 59,* 265–266.

PARFITT, R. R. (1977). *The birth primer.* Philadelphia: Running Press.

PARK, D. C., HERTZOG, C., LEVENTHAL, H., MORRELL, R. W., LEVENTHAL, E., BIRCHMORE, D., et al. (1999). Medication adherence in rheumatoid arthritis patients: Older is wiser. *Journal of the American Geriatric Society, 47,* 172–183.

PARKER, J. C. (1995). Stress management. In P. M. Nicassio & T. W. Smith (Eds.), *Managing chronic illness: A biopsychosocial perspective* (pp. 285–312). Washington, DC: American Psychological Association.

PARKER, J. C., FRANK, R. G., BECK, N. C., SMARR, K. L., BUESCHER, K. L., PHILLIPS, L. R. et al. (1988). Pain management in rheumatoid arthritis patients: A cognitive-behavioral approach. *Arthritis and Rheumatism, 31,* 593–601.

PARRISH, J. M. (1986). Parent compliance with medical and behavioral recommendations. In N. A. Krasnegor,

J. D. Arasteh, & M. F. Cataldo (Eds.), *Child health behavior: A behavioral pediatrics perspective* (pp. 453–501). New York: Wiley.

PARROTT, A. C. (1999). Does cigarette smoking *cause* stress? *American Psychologist, 54,* 817–820.

PARSONS, O. A. (1986). Alcoholics' neuropsychological impairment: Current findings and conclusions. *Annals of Behavioral Medicine, 8*(2–3), 13–19.

PARSONS, T. (1951). *The social system.* New York: Free Press.

PATERSON, R. J., & NEUFELD, R. W. J. (1987). Clear danger: Situational determinants of the appraisal of threat. *Psychological Bulletin, 101,* 404–416.

PATRICK, A. W., GILL, G. V., MACFARLANE, I. A., CULLEN, A., POWER, E., & WALLYMAHMED, M. (1994). Home glucose monitoring in type 2 diabetes: Is it a waste of time? *Diabetic Medicine, 11,* 62–65.

PATTERSON, D. R., & JENSEN, M. P. (2003). Hypnosis and clinical pain. *Psychological Bulletin, 129,* 495–521.

PATTERSON, J. M., & GARWICK, A. W. (1994). The impact of chronic illness on families: A family systems perspective. *Annals of Behavioral Medicine, 16,* 131–142.

PATTERSON, S. M., MATTHEWS, K. A., ALLEN, M. T., & OWENS, J. F. (1995). Stress-induced hemoconcentration of blood cells and lipids in healthy women during acute psychological stress. *Health Psychology, 14,* 319–324.

PATTERSON, S. M., ZAKOWSKI, S. G., HALL, M. H., COHEN, L., WOLLMAN, K., & BAUM, A. (1994). Psychological stress and platelet activation: Differences in platelet reactivity in healthy men during active and passive stressors. *Health Psychology, 13,* 34–38.

PATTERSON, T. L., SEMPLE, S. J., SHAW, W. S., YU, E., HE, Y., ZHANG, M. Y., et al. (1998). The cultural context of caregiving: A comparison of Alzheimer's caregivers in Shanghai, China and San Diego, California. *Psychological Medicine, 28,* 1071–1084.

PATTERSON, T. L., SHAW, W. S., SEMPLE, S. J., CHERNER, M., MCCUTCHAN, J. A., ATKINSON, J. H., et al. (1996). Relationship of psychosocial factors to HIV disease progression. *Annals of Behavioral Medicine, 18,* 30–39.

PATTISHALL, E. G. (1989). The development of behavioral medicine: Historical models. *Annals of Behavioral Medicine, 11,* 43–48.

PAVLOV, I. P. (1927). *Conditioned reflexes.* New York: Oxford University Press.

PEARLIN, L. I., & SCHOOLER, C. (1978). The structure of coping. *Journal of Health and Social Behavior, 19,* 2–21.

PEARSON ASSESSMENTS (2004). Millon Behavioral Medicine Diagnostic. Retrieved (9–7–2004) from http://assessments.ncspearson.com.

PECHACEK, T. F., FOX, B. H., MURRAY, D. M., & LUEPKER, R. V. (1984). Review of techniques for measurement of smoking behavior. In J. D. Matarazzo, S. M. Weiss, J. A. Herd, N. E. Miller, & S. M. Weiss (Eds.), *Behavioral health: A handbook of health enhancement and disease prevention* (pp. 729–754). New York: Wiley.

PECHACEK, T. F., MURRAY, D. M., LUEPKER, R. V., MITTELMARK, M. B., JOHNSON, C. A., & SHUTZ, J. M. (1984). Measurement of adolescent smoking behavior: Rationale and methods. *Journal of Behavioral Medicine, 7,* 123–140.

PECKENPAUGH, N. J. (2003). *Nutrition essantials and diet therapy* (9th ed.). Philadelphia: Saunders.

PEDERSEN, N. L., LICHTENSTEIN, P., PLOMIN, R., DEFAIRE, U., MCCLEARN, G. E., & MATTHEWS, K. A. (1989). Genetic and environmental influences for Type A-like measures and related traits: A study of twins reared apart and twins reared together. *Psychosomatic Medicine, 51,* 428–440.

PEDERSON, L. L. (1982). Compliance with physician advice to quit smoking: A review of the literature. *Preventive Medicine, 11,* 71–84.

PEELE, S. (1984). The cultural context of psychological approaches to alcoholism: Can we control the effects of alcohol? *American Psychologist, 39,* 1337–1351.

PEIRCE, R. S., FRONE, M. R., RUSSELL, M., COOPER, M. L., & MUDAR, P. (2000). A longitudinal model of social contact, social support, depression, and alcohol use. *Health Psychology, 19,* 28–38.

PENN, A., & SNYDER, C. A. (1993). Inhalation of sidestream cigarette smoke accelerates development of arteriosclerotic placques. *Circulation, 88*(Part 1), 1820–1825.

PENN, N. E., KAR, S., KRAMER, J., SKINNER, J., & ZAMBRANA, R. E. (1995). Panel VI: Ethnic minorities, health care systems, and behavior. *Health Psychology, 14,* 641–646.

PENNEBAKER, J. W. (1983). Accuracy of symptom perception. In A. Baum, S. E. Taylor, & J. Singer (Eds.), *Handbook of psychology and health* (Vol. 4, pp. 189–217). Hillsdale, NJ: Erlbaum.

PENNEBAKER, J. W. (1990). *Opening up: The healing power of confiding in others.* New York: William Morrow.

PENNEBAKER, J. W., & WATSON, D. (1988). Blood pressure estimation and beliefs among normotensives and hypertensives. *Health Psychology, 7,* 309–328.

PENNINX, B. W. J. H., GURALNIK, J. M., FERRUCCI, L., SIMONSICK, E. M., DEEG, D. J. H., & WALLACE, R. B. (1998). Depressive symptoms and physical decline in community-dwelling older persons. *Journal of the American Medical Association, 279,* 1720–1726.

PENZIEN, D. B., RAINS, J. C., & ANDRASIK, F. (2002). Behavioral management of recurrent headache: Three decades of experience and empiricism. *Applied Psychophysiology and Biofeedback, 27,* 163–181.

PERKINS, K. A. (1994). Issues in the prevention of weight gain after smoking cessation. *Annals of Behavioral Medicine, 16,* 46–52.

PERKINS, K. A., ROHAY, J., MEILAHN, E. N., WING, R. R., MATTHEWS, K. A., & KULLER, L. H. (1993). Diet, alcohol, and physical activity as a function of smoking status in middle-aged women. *Health Psychology, 12,* 410–415.

PERRI, M. G., ANTON, S. D., DURNING, P. E., KETTERSON, T. U., SYDEMAN, S. J., BERLANT, N. E. et al. (2002). Adherence to exercise prescriptions: Effects of prescribing moderate versus higher levels of intensity and frequency. *Health Psychology, 21,* 452–458.

PERRI, M. G., MCALLISTER, D. A., GANGE, J. J., JORDAN, R. C., MCADOO, W. G., & NEZU, A. M. (1988). Effects of four maintenance programs on the long-term management of obesity. *Journal of Consulting and Clinical Psychology, 56,* 529–534.

PERRI, M. G., NEZU, A. M., MCKELVEY, S. F., SHERMER, R. L., RENJILIAN, D. A., & VIEGENER, B. J. (2001). Relapse prevention training and problem-solving training in the long-term management of obesity. *Journal of Consulting and Clinical Psychology, 69,* 722–726.

PERRI, M. G., NEZU, A. M., & VIEGENER, B. J. (1992). *Improving the long-term management of obesity.* New York: Wiley.

PERZ, C. A., DICLEMENTE, C. C., & CARBONARI, J. P. (1996). Doing the right thing at the right time? The interaction of stages and processes of change in successful smoking cessation. *Health Psychology, 15,* 462–468.

PETERMAN, T. A. (1990). Facilitators of HIV transmission during sexual contact. In N. J. Alexander, H. L. Gabelnick, & J. M. Spieler (Eds.), *Heterosexual transmission of AIDS.* New York: Wiley-Liss.

PETERSON, L., CROWSON, J., SALDANA, L., & HOLDRIDGE, S. (1999). Of needles and skinned knees: Children's coping with medical procedures and minor injuries for self and other. *Health Psychology, 18,* 197–200.

PETRAITIS, J., FLAY, B. R., MILLER, T. Q., TORPY, E. J., & GREINER, B. (1998). Illicit substance use among adolescents: A matrix of prospective predictors. *Substance Use and Misuse, 33,* 2561–2604.

PETRIE, K. J., FONTANILLA, I., THOMAS, M. G., BOOTH, R. J., & PENNEBAKER, J. W. (2004). Effect of written emotional expression on immune function in patients with human immunodeficiency virus infection: A randomized trial. *Psychosomatic Medicine, 66,* 272–275.

PETRY, N. M., & MARTIN, B. (2002). Low-cost contingency management for treating cocaine- and opioid-abusing methadone patients. *Journal of Consulting and Clinical Psychology, 70,* 398–405.

PHARES, E. J. (1984). *Introduction to personality.* Columbus, OH: Merrill.

PHELAN, S., & WADDEN, T. A. (2002). Combining behavioral and pharmacological treatments for obesity. *Obesity Research*, 10, 560–574.

PHILIPS, C. A. (1989). Rehabilitation of the patient with rheumatoid hand involvement. *Physical Therapy*, 69, 1091–1098.

PHILLIPS, D. P., & BREDDER, C. C. (2002). Morbicity and mortality from medical errors: An increasingly serious public health problem. *Annual Review of Public Health*, 23, 135–150.

PHILLIPS, W. T., KIERNAN, M., & KING, A. C. (2001). The effects of physical activity on physical and psychological health. In A. Baum, T. A. Revenson, & J. E. Singer (Eds.), *Handbook of health psychology* (pp. 627–657). Mahwah, NJ: Erlbaum.

PIASECKI, T. M., KENFORD, S. L., SMITH, S. S., FIORE, M. C., & BAKER, T. B. (1997). Listening to nicotine: Negative affect and the smoking withdrawal conundrum. *Psychological Science*, 8, 184–189.

PIERCE, J. P., & GILPIN, E. A. (1995). A historical analysis of tobacco marketing and the uptake of smoking by youth in the United States: 1890–1977. *Health Psychology*, 14, 500–508.

PIKE, J. L., SMITH, T. L., HAUGER, R. L., NICASSIO, P. M., PATTERSON, T. L., McCLINTIC, T. L., et al. (1997). Chronic life stress alters sympathetic, neuroendocrine, and immune responsivity to an acute psychological stressor in humans. *Psychosomatic Medicine*, 59, 447–457.

PILISUK, M. (1982). Delivery of social support: The social inoculation. *American Journal of Orthopsychiatry*, 52, 20–31.

PINES, M (1979, January). Superkids. *Psychology Today*, pp. 53–63.

PINQUART, M., & SÖRENSEN, S. (2003). Differences between caregivers and noncaregivers in psychological health and physical health: A meta-analysis. *Psychology and Aging*, 18, 250–267.

PINTO, B. M., EAKIN, E., & MARUYAMA, N. C. (2000). Health behavior changes after a cancer diagnosis: What do we know and where do we go from here? *Annals of Behavioral Medicine*, 22, 38–52.

PINTO, R. P., & HOLLANDSWORTH, J. G. (1989). Using videotape modeling to prepare children psychologically for surgery: Influence of parents and costs versus benefits of providing preparation services. *Health Psychology*, 8, 79–95.

PIOTROWSKI, C., & LUBIN, B. (1990). Assessment practices of health psychologists: Survey of APA Division 38 clinicians. *Professional Psychology: Research and Practice*, 21, 99–106.

PLACE, M. (1984). Hypnosis and the child. *Journal of Child Psychology and Psychiatry*, 25, 339–347.

PMRG (Project Match Research Group) (1998). Matching alcoholism treatments to client heterogeneity: Treatment main effects and matching effects on drinking during treatment. *Journal of Studies on Alcohol*, 59, 631–639.

POLIVY, J., & HERMAN, C. P. (2002). If at first you don't succeed: False hopes of self-change. *American Psychologist*, 57, 677–689.

POLLOCK, S. E., CHRISTIAN, B. J., & SANDS, D. (1991). Responses to chronic illness: Analysis of psychological and physiological adaptation. *Nursing Research*, 39, 300–304.

POLONSKY, W. H., ANDERSON, B. J., LOHRER, P. A., APONTE, J. E., JACOBSON, A. M., & COLE, C. F. (1994). Insulin omission in women with IDDM. *Diabetes Care*, 17, 1178–1185.

POMERLEAU, O. F., COLLINS, A. C., SHIFFMAN, S., & POMERLEAU, C. S. (1993). Why some people smoke and others do not: New perspectives. *Journal of Consulting and Clinical Psychology*, 61, 723–731.

POMERLEAU, O. F., & POMERLEAU, C. S. (1989). A biobehavioral perspective on smoking. In T. Ney & A. Gale (Eds.), *Smoking and human behavior* (pp. 69–90). New York: Wiley.

POMEROY, D., & MITCHELL, J. E. (2002). Medical complications of anorexia nervosa and bulimia nervosa. In C. G. Fairburn & K. D. Brownell (Eds.), *Eating disorders and obesity: A comprehensive handbook* (pp. 278–285). New York: Guilford.

POPE, M. K., & SMITH, T. W. (1991). Cortisol excretion in high and low cynically hostile men. *Psychosomatic Medicine*, 53, 386–392.

PORGES, S. W. (1995). Cardiac vagal tone: A physiological index of stress. *Neuroscience and Behavioral Reviews*, 19, 225–233.

PORTER, F. L., MILLER, R. H., & MARSHALL, R. E. (1986). Neonatal pain cries: Effects of circumcision on acoustic features and perceived urgency. *Child Development*, 57, 790–802.

POWCH, I. G., & HOUSTON, B. K. (1996). Hostility, anger-in, and cardiovascular reactivity in white women. *Health Psychology*, 15, 200–208.

POWELL, K. E., THOMPSON, P. D., CASPERSEN, C. J., & KENDRICK, J. S. (1987). Physical activity and the incidence of coronary heart disease. *Annual Review of Public Health*, 8, 253–287.

POWELL, L. H. (1984). The Type A behavior pattern: An update on conceptual, assessment, and intervention research. *Behavioral Medicine Update*, 6(4), 7–10.

POWELL, L. H., & FRIEDMAN, M. (1986). Alteration of Type A behaviour in coronary patients. In M. J. Christie & P. G. Mellett (Eds.), *The psychosomatic approach: Contemporary practice of whole-person care* (pp. 191–214). New York: Wiley.

POWER, M., BULLINGER, M., HARPER, A., and the World Health Organization Quality of Life Group (1999). The World Health Organization WHOQOL-100: Tests of the universality of quality of life in 15 different cultural groups worldwide. *Health Psychology, 18*, 495–505.

PRESCOTT, C. A., & KENDLER, K. S. (1999). Genetic and environmental contributions to alcohol abuse and dependence in a population-based sample of male twins. *American Journal of Psychiatry, 156*, 34–40.

PRICE, R. H., CHOI, J. N., & VINOKUR, A. D. (2002). Links in the chain of adversity following job loss: How financial strain and loss of personal control lead to depression, impaired functioning, and poor health. *Journal of Occupational Health Psychology, 7*, 302–312.

PROCHASKA, J. O., & DICLEMENTE, C. C. (1984). *The transtheoretical approach: Crossing traditional boundaries of therapy.* Homewood, IL: Dow Jones/Irwin.

PROCHASKA, J. O., DICLEMENTE, C. C., & NORCROSS, J. C. (1992). In search of how people change: Applications to addictive behaviors. *American Psychologist, 47,* 1102–1114.

PROKHOROV, A. V., WARNEKE, C., DE MOOR, C., EMMONS, K. M., MULLIN-JONES, M., ROSENBLUM, C. et al. (2003). Self-reported health status, health vulnerability, and smoking behavior in college students: Implications for intervention. *Nicotine and Tobacco Research, 5,* 545–552.

PULEO, P. R., MEYER, D., WATHEN, C., TAWA, C. B., WHEELER, S., HAMBURG, R. J., et al. (1994). Use of rapid assay of subforms of creatine kinase MB to diagnose or rule out acute myocardial infarction. *New England Journal of Medicine, 331*, 561–566.

PURCELL, K., WEISS, J., & HAHN, W. (1972). Certain psychosomatic disorders. In B. B. Wolman (Ed.), *Manual of child psychopathology* (pp. 706–740). New York: McGraw-Hill.

QUICK, J. C. (1999). Occupational health psychology: Historical roots and future directions. *Health Psychology, 18*, 82–88.

QUICK, J. C., QUICK, J. D., NELSON, D. L., & HURRELL, J. J. (1997). *Preventive stress management in organizations.* Washington, DC: American Psychological Association.

QUITTNER, A. L., ESPELAGE, D. L., OPIPARI, L. C., CARTER, B., EID, N., & EIGEN, H. (1998). Role strain in couples with and without a child with a chronic illness: Associations with marital satisfaction, intimacy, and daily mood. *Health Psychology, 17*, 112–124.

RABKIN, J. G., FERRANDO, S. J., SHU-HSING, L., SEWELL, M., & MCELHINEY, M. (2000). Psychological effects of HAART: A 2-year study. *Psychosomatic Medicine, 62*, 413–422.

RADECKI, S. E., & BRUNTON, S. A. (1992). Health promotion/disease prevention in family practice residency training: Results of a national survey. *Family Medicine, 24*, 534–537.

RAHE, R. H., & ARTHUR, R. J. (1978). Life change and illness studies: Past history and future directions. *Journal of Human Stress, 4*, 3–15.

RÄIKKÖNEN, K., MATTHEWS, K. A., FLORY, J. D., OWENS, J. F., & GUMP, B. B. (1999). Effects of optimism, pessimism, and trait anxiety on ambulatory blood pressure and mood during everyday life. *Journal of Personality and Social Psychology, 76*, 104–113.

RAJ, A., AMARO, H., & REED, E. (2001). Culturally tailoring HIV/AIDS prevention programs: Why, when, and how. In S. S. Kazarian & E. R. Evans (Eds.), *Handbook of cultural health psychology* (pp. 195–239). San Diego: Academic Press.

RAKOWSKI, W., DUBE, C. E., MARCUS, B. H., PROCHASKA, J. O., VELICER, W. F., & ABRAMS, D. B. (1992). Assessing elements of women's decisions about mammography. *Health Psychology, 11*, 111–118.

RAMSEY, N. L. (1982). Effects of hospitalization on the child and family. In M. J. Smith, J. A. Goodman, N. L. Ramsey, & S. B. Pasternack (Eds.), *Child and family: Concepts of nursing practice* (pp. 317–341). New York: McGraw-Hill.

RAND, C. S., & WEEKS, K. (1998). Measuring adherence with medication regimens in clinical care research. In S. A. Shumaker, E. B. Schron, J. L., Ockene, & W. L. McBee (Eds.), *The handbook of health behavior change* (2nd ed., pp. 114–132). New York: Springer.

RAPHAEL, B. G. (1999). Hematological disorders. In M. G. Eisenberg, R. L., Glueckauf, & H. H. Zaretsky (Eds.), *Medical aspects of disability: A handbook for the rehabilitation professional* (pp. 273–286). New York: Springer.

RAPHAEL, K. G., CLOITRE, M., & DOHRENWEND, B. P. (1991). Problems of recall and misclassification with checklist methods of measuring stressful life events. *Health Psychology, 10*, 62–74.

RAPPAPORT, N. B., MCANULTY, D. P., WAGGONER, C. D., & BRANTLEY, P. J. (1987). Cluster analysis of Minnesota Multiphasic Personality Inventory (MMPI) profiles in a chronic headache population. *Journal of Behavioral Medicine, 10*, 49–60.

RAPS, C. S., PETERSON, C., JONAS, M., & SELIGMAN, M. E. P. (1982). Patient behavior in hospitals: Helplessness, reactance, or both? *Journal of Personality and Social Psychology, 42*, 1036–1041.

RATLIFF-CRAIN, J., & BAUM, A. (1990). Individual differences and health: Gender, coping, and stress. In H. S. Friedman (Ed.), *Personality and disease* (pp. 226–253). New York: Wiley.

RAVEN, B. H., & HALEY, R. W. (1982). Social influence and compliance of hospital nurses with infection control policies. In J. R. Eiser (Ed.), *Social psychology and behavioral medicine* (pp. 413–438). New York: Wiley.

RAYMOND, N. R., D'ERAMO-MELKUS, G. (1993). Non-insulin-dependent diabetes and obesity in the black and Hispanic population: Culturally sensitive management. *Diabetes Educator, 19,* 313–317.

REDD, W. H., & JACOBSEN, P. (2001). Behavioral intervention in comprehensive cancer care. In A. Baum, T. A. Revenson, & J. E. Singer (Eds.), *Handbook of health psychology* (pp. 757–776). Mahwah, NJ: Erlbaum.

REDD, W. H., SILBERFARB, P. M., ANDERSEN, B. L., ANDRYKOWSKI, M. A., BOVBJERG, D. H., BURISH, T. G., et al. (1991). Physiologic and psychobehavioral research in oncology. *Cancer, 67,* 813–822.

REDDY, D, M., FLEMING, R., & ADESSO, V. J. (1992). Gender and health. In S. Maes, H. Leventhal, & M. Johnston (Eds.), *International review of health psychology* (Vol. 1, pp. 3–32). New York: Wiley.

REEB, R. N., & BUSH, J. P. (1996). Preprocedural psychological preparation in pediatric oncology: A process-oriented intervention study. *Children's Health Care, 25,* 265–279.

REED, G. M., KEMENY, M. E., TAYLOR, S. E., WANG, H-Y., & VISSCHER, B. R. (1994). Realistic acceptance as a predictor of decreased survival time in gay men with AIDS. *Health Psychology, 13,* 299–307.

REINIS, S., & GOLDMAN, J. M. (1980). *The development of the brain: Biological and functional perspectives.* Springfield, IL: Charles C. Thomas.

RENNICK, J. E., JOHNSTON, C. C., DOUGHERTY, G., PLATT, R., & RITCHIE, J. A. (2002). Children's psychosocial responses after critical illnesses and exposure to invasive technology. *Journal of Developmental and Behavioral Pediatrics, 23,* 133–144.

RESNICOW, K., DIIORIO, C., SOET, J. E., BORELLI, B., HECHT, J., & ERNST, D. (2002). Motivational interviewing in health promotion: It sounds like something is changing. *Health Psychology, 21,* 444–451.

RETCHIN, S. M., WELLS, J. A., VALLERON, A.-J., & ALBRECHT, G. L. (1992). Health behavior changes in the United States, the United Kingdom, and France. *Journal of General Internal Medicine, 7,* 615–622.

REVENSON, T. A. (1994). Social support and marital coping with chronic illness. *Annals of Behavioral Medicine, 16,* 122–130.

REVENSON, T. A., & MAJEROVITZ, S. D. (1991). The effects of chronic illness on the spouse: Social resources as stress buffers. *Arthritis Care and Research, 4,* 63–72.

REY, M. J. (1999). Cardiovascular disorders. In M. G. Eisenberg, R. L. Glueckauf, & H. H. Zaretsky (Eds.), *Medical aspects of disability: A handbook for the rehabilitation professional* (pp. 154–184). New York: Springer.

REYNOLDS, D. V. (1969). Surgery in the rat during electrical anesthesia induced by focal brain stimulation. *Science, 164,* 444–445.

RHOADES, R., & PFLANZER, R. (1996). *Human physiology* (3rd ed.). Fort Worth: Saunders.

RIBISL, K. M., WINKLEBY, M. A., FORTMANN, S. P., & FLORA, J. A. (1998). The interplay of socioeconomic status and ethnicity on Hispanic and White men's cardiovascular disease risk and health communication patterns. *Health Education Research, 13,* 407–417.

RICHARDS, J. S., NEPOMUCENO, C., RILES, M., & SUER, Z. (1982). Assessing pain behavior: The UAB Pain Behavior Scale. *Pain, 14,* 393–398.

RICHARDSON, S. A., GOODMAN, N., HASTORF, A. H., & DORNBUSCH, S. M. (1961). Cultural uniformity in reaction to physical disabilities. *American Sociological Review, 26,* 241–247.

RIETVELD, S., & BROSSCHOT, J. F. (1999). Current perspectives on symptom perception in asthma: A biomedical and psychological review. *International Journal of Behavioral Medicine, 6,* 120–134.

RIGOTTI, N. A., SINGER, D. E., MULLEY, A. G., & THIBAULT, G. E. (1991). Smoking cessation following admission to a coronary care unit. *Journal of General Internal Medicine, 6,* 305–311.

RIMER, B. K. (1998). Interventions to enhance cancer screening: A brief review of what works and what is on the horizon. *Cancer, 83,* 1770–1774.

RIMER, B. K., CONAWAY, M., LYNA, P., GLASSMAN, B., YARNALL, K. S. H., LIPKUS, I. et al. (1999). The impact of tailored interventions on a community health center population. *Patient Education and Counseling, 37,* 125–140.

RIMER, B. K., MCBRIDE, C. M., & CRUMP, C. (2001). Women's health promotion. In A. Baum, T. A. Revenson, & J. E. Singer (Eds.), *Handbook of health psychology* (pp. 519–539). Mahwah, NJ: Erlbaum.

RIMM, D. C., & MASTERS, J. C. (1979). *Behavior therapy: Techniques and empirical findings* (2nd ed.). New York: Academic Press.

RISSER, N. L., & BELCHER, D. W. (1990). Adding spirometry, carbon monoxide, and pulmonary symptom results to smoking cessation counseling: A randomized trial. *Journal of General Internal Medicine, 5,* 16–22.

ROBBINS, L. (1994). Precipitating factors in migraine: A retrospective review of 494 patients. *Headache, 34,* 214–216.

ROBERTS, A. H. (1995). The powerful placebo revisited: Magnitude of nonspecific effects. *Mind/Body Medicine, 1,* 35–43.

ROBERTS, C. S., COX, C. E., REINTGEN, D. S., BAILE, W. F., & GILBERTINI, M. (1994). Influence of physician communication on newly diagnosed breast patients' psychologic adjustment and decision-making. *Cancer, 74,* 336–341.

ROBERTSON, L. S. (1986). Behavioral and environmental interventions for reducing motor vehicle trauma. *Annual Review of Public Health, 7,* 13–34.

ROBERTSON, S. M., CULLEN, D. W., BARANOWSKI, J., BARANOWSKI, T., HU, S., & DE MOOR, C. (1999). Factors related to adiposity among children aged 3 to 7 years. *Journal of the American Dietetic Association, 99,* 938–943.

ROBINS, C. J., & HAYES, A. M. (1993). An appraisal of cognitive therapy. *Journal of Consulting and Clinical Psychology, 61,* 205–214.

ROBINSON, C. H., & LAWLER, M. R. (1977). *Normal and therapeutic nutrition* (15th ed.). New York: Macmillan.

ROBINSON, L. A., & KLESGES, R. C. (1997). Ethnic and gender differences in risk factors for smoking onset. *Health Psychology, 16,* 499–505.

ROBINSON, T. E., & BERRIDGE, K. C. (2001). Incentive-sensitization and addiction. *Addiction, 96,* 103–114.

ROBINSON, T. E., & BERRIDGE, K. C. (2003). Addiction. *Annual Review of Psychology, 54,* 25–53.

ROCK, C. L., & KAYE, W. H. (2001). Eating disorders: Anorexia nervosa, bulimia nervosa, and binge eating disorder. In A. M. Coulston, C. L. Rock, & E. R. Monsen (Eds.), *Nutrition in the prevention and treatment of disease* (pp. 685–700). San Diego: Academic Press.

RODENHUIS, S., VAN DE WETERING, M. L., MOOR, W. J., EVERS, S. G., VAN ZANDWIJK, N., & BOS, J. L. (1987). Mutational activation of the K-ras oncogene. *New England Journal of Medicine, 317,* 929–935.

RODIN, J. (1981). Current status of the internal-external hypothesis for obesity: What went wrong? *American Psychologist, 36,* 361–372.

RODIN, J. (1985). Insulin levels, hunger, and food intake: An example of feedback loops in body weight regulation. *Health Psychology, 4,* 1–24.

RODIN, J., & BAUM, A. (1978). Crowding and helplessness: Potential consequences of density and loss of control. In A. Baum & Y. M. Epstein (Eds.), *Human response to crowding* (pp. 390–401). Hillsdale, NJ: Erlbaum.

RODIN, J., & JANIS, I. L. (1979). The social power of health-care practitioners as agents of change. *Journal of Social Issues, 35,* 60–81.

RODIN, J., & LANGER, E. J. (1977). Long-term effects of a control-relevant intervention with the institutionalized aged. *Journal of Personality and Social Psychology, 35,* 897–902.

ROELOFS, J., BOISSEVAIN, M. D., PETERS, M. L., DE JONG, J. R., & VLAEYEN, J. W. S. (2002). Psychological treatments for chronic low back pain: Past, present, and beyond. *Pain Reviews, 9,* 29–40.

ROESCH, S. C., & WEINER, B. (2001). A meta-analytic review of coping with illness: Do causal attributions matter? *Journal of Psychosomatic Research, 50,* 205–219.

ROHLING, M. L., BINDER, L. M., & LANGHINRICHSEN-ROHLING, J. (1995). A meta-analytic review of the association between financial compensation and the experience and treatment of chronic pain. *Health Psychology, 14,* 537–547.

ROHSENOW, D. J., MONTI, P. M., RUBONIS, A. V., GULLIVER, S. B., COLBY, S. M., BINKOFF, J. A. et al. (2001). Cue exposure with coping skills training and communication skills training for alcohol dependence: 6- and 12-month outcomes. *Addiction, 96,* 1161–1174.

ROLLS, B. J. (1995). Carbohydrates, fats, and satiety. *American Journal of Clinical Nutrition, 61*(Suppl.), 960S–967S.

ROLLS, B. J., MORRIS, E. L., & ROE, L. S. (2002). Portion size of food affects energy intake in normal-weight and overweight men and women. *American Journal of Clinical Nutrition, 76,* 1207–1213.

ROMANO, J. M., TURNER, J. A., & JENSEN, M. P. (1997). The family environment in chronic pain patients: Comparison to controls and relationship to patient functioning. *Journal of Clinical Psychology in Medical Settings, 4,* 383–395.

ROSE, J. S., CHASSIN, L., PRESSON, C. C., & SHERMAN, S. J. (1996). Prospective predictors of quit attempts and smoking cessation in young adults. *Health Psychology, 15,* 261–268.

ROSE, K. J., DERRY, P. A., & MCLACHLAN, R. S. (1995). Patient expectations and postoperative depression, anxiety, and psychosocial adjustment after temporal lobectomy: A prospective study. *International Journal of Behavioral Medicine, 2,* 27–40.

ROSE, R. J. (1986). Familial influences on cardiovascular reactivity to stress. In K. A. Matthews, S. M. Weiss, T. Detre, T. M. Dembroski, B. Falkner, S. B. Manuck, & R. B. Williams (Eds.), *Handbook of stress, reactivity, and cardiovascular disease* (pp. 259–272). New York: Wiley.

ROSELLA, J. D. (1994). Testicular cancer health education: An integrative review. *Journal of Advanced Nursing, 20,* 666–671.

ROSEN, J. C. (2002). Obesity and body image. In C. G. Fairburn & K. D. Brownell (Eds.), *Eating disorders and obesity: A comprehensive handbook* (pp. 399–402). New York: Guilford.

ROSEN, J. C., & GROSS, J. (1987). Prevalence of weight reducing and weight gaining in adolescent boys and girls. *Health Psychology, 6,* 131–147.

ROSEN, J. C., GRUBMAN, J. A., BEVINS, T., & FRYMOYER, J. W. (1987). Musculoskeletal status and disability of

MMPI profile subgroups among patients with low back pain. *Health Psychology, 6,* 581–598.

ROSENBERG, E. S., ALTFELD, M., POON, S. H., PHILLIPS, M. N., WILKES, B. M., ELDRIDGE, R. L., et al. (2000). Immune control of HIV-1 after early treatment of acute infection. *Nature, 407,* 523–526.

ROSENHAN, D. L., & SELIGMAN, M. E. P. (1984). *Abnormal psychology.* New York: Norton.

ROSENMAN, R. H., BRAND, R. J., SHOLTZ, R. I., & FRIEDMAN, M. (1976). Multivariate prediction of coronary heart disease during 8.5 year follow-up in the Western Collaborative Group Study. *American Journal of Cardiology, 37,* 903–910.

ROSENMAN, R. H., SWAN, G. E., & CARMELLI, D. (1988). Definition, assessment, and evolution of the Type A behavior pattern. In B. K. Houston & C. R. Snyder (Eds.), *Type A behavior pattern: Research, theory, and intervention* (pp. 8–31). New York: Wiley.

ROSENSTOCK, I. M. (1966). Why people use health services. *Millbank Memorial Fund Quarterly, 44,* 94–127.

ROSENSTOCK, I. M., & KIRSCHT, J. P. (1979). Why people seek health care. In G. C. Stone, F. Cohen, & N. E. Adler (Eds.), *Health psychology—A handbook* (pp. 161–188). San Francisco: Jossey-Bass.

ROSKIES, E. (1983). Stress management for Type A individuals. In D. Meichenbaum & M. E. Jaremko (Eds.), *Stress reduction and prevention* (pp. 261–288). New York: Plenum.

ROSKIES, E., SERAGANIAN, P., OSEASOHN, R., HANLEY, J. A., COLLU, R., MARTIN, N., et al. (1986). The Montreal Type A Intervention Project: Major findings. *Health Psychology, 5,* 45–69.

ROTER, D. L., & EWART, C. K. (1992). Emotional inhibition in essential hypertension: Obstacle to communication during medical visits? *Health Psychology, 11,* 163–169.

ROTER, D. L., & HALL, J. A. (1987). Physicians' interviewing styles and medical information obtained from patients. *Journal of General Internal Medicine, 2,* 325–329.

ROTER, D. L., & HALL, J. A. (1989). Studies of doctor-patient interaction. *Annual Review of Public Health, 10,* 163–180.

ROTER, D. L., HALL, J. A., MERSICA, R., NORDSTROM, B., CRETIN, D., & SVARSTAD, B. (1998). Effectiveness of interventions to improve patient compliance: A meta-analysis. *Medical Care, 36,* 1138–1161.

ROTH, D. L., & HOLMES, D. S. (1985). Influence of physical fitness in determining the impact of stressful life events on physical and psychologic health. *Psychosomatic Medicine, 47,* 164–173.

ROTHERAM-BORUS, M. J., MURPHY, D. A., REID, H. M., & COLEMAN, C. L. (1996). Correlates of emotional distress among HIV+ youths: Health status, stress, and personal resources. *Annals of Behavioral Medicine, 18,* 16–23.

ROTHMAN, A. J., & SALOVEY, P. (1997). Shaping perceptions to motivate healthy behavior: The role of message framing. *Psychological Bulletin, 121,* 3–19.

ROTTER, J. B. (1966). Generalized expectancies for the internal versus external control of reinforcement. *Psychological Monographs, 90(1),* 1–28.

ROWE, M. M. (1999). Teaching health-care providers coping: Results of a two-year study. *Journal of Behavioral Medicine, 22,* 511–527.

ROZENSKY, R. H. (1991). Psychologists, politics, and hospitals. In J. J. Sweet, R. H. Rozensky, & S. M. Tovian (Eds.), *Handbook of clinical psychology in medical settings* (pp. 59–79). New York: Plenum.

ROZLOG, L. A., KIECOLT-GLASER, J. K., MARUCHA, P. T., SHERIDAN, J. F., & GLASER, R. (1999). Stress and immunity: Implications for viral disease and wound healing. *Journal of Periodontology, 70,* 786–792.

RUBLE, D. N. (1977). Premenstrual symptoms. A reinterpretation. *Science, 197,* 291–292.

RUDERMAN, A. J. (1986). Dietary restraint: A theoretical and empirical review. *Psychological Bulletin, 99,* 247–262.

RUITENBERG, A., VAN SWIETEN, J. C., WITTEMAN, J. C. M., MEHTA, K. M., VAN DUIJN, C. M., HOFMAN, A. et al. (2003). Alcohol consumption and risk of dementia: The Rotterdam Study. *Lancet, 359,* 281–286.

RUNDALL, T. G., & WHEELER, J. R. C. (1979). The effect of income on use of preventive care: An evaluation of alternative explanations. *Journal of Health and Social Behavior, 20,* 397–406.

RUNYAN, C. W. (1985). Health assessment and public policy within a public health framework. In P. Karoly (Ed.), *Measurement strategies in health psychology* (pp. 601–622). New York: Wiley.

RUSSELL, M., PEIRCE, R. S., CHAN, A. W. K., WIECZOREK, W. F., MOSCATO, B. S., & NOCHAJSKI, T. H. (2001). Natural recovery in a community-based sample of alcoholics: Study design and descriptive data. *Substance Use and Abuse, 36,* 1417–1441.

RUTLEDGE, T., & HOGAN, B. E. (2002). A quantitative review of prospective evidence linking psychological factors with hypertension development. *Psychosomatic Medicine, 64,* 758–766.

RYAN, R. S., & TRAVIS, J. W. (1981). *The wellness workbook.* Berkeley, CA: Ten Speed Press.

RYBSTEIN-BLINCHIK, E. (1979). Effects of different cognitive strategies on chronic pain experience. *Journal of Behavioral Medicine, 2,* 93–101.

RYCHTARIK, R. G., CONNORS, G. J., WHITNEY, R. B., MCGILLICUDDY, N. B., FITTERLING, J. M., & WIRTZ, P. W. (2000). Treatment settings for persons with alcoholism:

Evidence for matching clients to inpatient versus outpatient care. *Journal of Consulting and Clinical Psychology*, 68, 277–289.

RZEWNICKI, R., & FORGAYS, D. G. (1987). Recidivism and self-cure of smoking and obesity: An attempt to replicate. *American Psychologist*, 42, 97–100.

SAAB, P. G., LLABRE, M. M., SCHNEIDERMAN, N., HURWITZ, B. E., McDONALD, P. G., EVANS, J., et al. (1997). Influence of ethnicity and gender on cardiovascular responses to active coping and inhibitory-passive coping challenges. *Psychosomatic Medicine*, 59, 434–446.

SAAB, P. G., McCALLA, J. R., COONS, H. L., CHRISTENSEN, A. J., KAPLAN, R., JOHNSON, S. B. et al. (2004). Technological and medical advances: Implications for health psychology. *Health Psychology*, 23, 142–146.

SABBIONI, M. E. E. (1991). Cancer and stress: A possible role for psychoneuroimmunology in cancer research? In C. L. Watson & M. Watson (Eds.), *Cancer and stress: Psychological, biological, and coping studies* (pp. 3–26). New York: Wiley.

SACCO, R. L., ELKIND, M., BODEN-ALBALA, B., LIN, I.-F., KARGMAN, D. E., HAUSER, W. A., et al. (1999). The protective effect of moderate alcohol consumption on ischemic stroke. *Journal of the American Medical Association*, 281, 53–60.

SACKS, D. A., & KOPPES, R. H. (1986). Blood transfusion and Jehovah's Witnesses: Medical and legal issues in obstetrics and gynecology. *American Journal of Obstetrics and Gynecology*, 154, 483–486.

SAELENS, B. E., SALLIS, J. F., & FRANK, L. D. (2003). Environmental correlates of walking and cycling: Findings from the transportation, urban design, and planning literature. *Annals of Behavioral Medicine*, 25, 80–91.

SAFER, M. A., THARPS, Q. J., JACKSON, T. C., & LEVENTHAL, H. (1979). Determinants of three stages of delay in seeking care at a medical clinic. *Medical Care*, 17, 11–29.

SALLIS, J. F., & OWEN, N. (1999). *Physical activity and behavioral medicine*. Thousand Oaks, CA: Sage.

SALLIS, J. F., PATTERSON, T. L., BUONO, M. J., ATKINS, C. J., & NADER, P. R. (1988). Aggregation of physical activity habits in Mexican-American and Anglo families. *Journal of Behavioral Medicine*, 11, 31–41.

SALLIS, J. F., TREVORROW, T. R., JOHNSON, C. C., HOVELL, M. F., & KAPLAN, R. M. (1987). Worksite stress management: A comparison of programs. *Psychology and Health*, 1, 237–255.

SALMON, J., OWEN, N., CRAWFORD, D., BAUMAN, A., & SALLIS, J. F. (2003). Physical activity and sedentary behavior: A population-based study of barriers, enjoyment, and preference. *Health Psychology*, 22, 178–188.

SALONEN, J. T., HEINONEN, O. P., KOTTKE, T. E., & PUSKA, P. (1981). Change in health behaviour in relation to estimated coronary heart disease risk during a community-based cardiovascular disease prevention programme. *International Journal of Epidemiology*, 10, 343–354.

SAMHSA (Substance Abuse and Mental Health Services Administration) (2003). *Overview of findings from the 2002 National Survey of Drug Use and Health*. Retrieved (5–18–2004) from http://www.samhsa.gov.

SANDBERG, G. G., & MARLATT, G. A. (1991). Relapse prevention. In D. A. Ciraulo & R. I. Shader (Eds.), *Clinical manual of chemical dependence* (pp. 377–399). Washington, DC: American Psychiatric Press.

SANDERS, S. H. (1985). Chronic pain: Conceptualization and epidemiology. *Annals of Behavioral Medicine*, 7(3), 3–5.

SANDERS, S. H., BRENA, S. F., SPIER, C. J., BELTRUTTI, D., McCONNELL, H., & QUINTERO, O. (1992). Chronic low back pain patients around the world: Cross-cultural similarities and differences. *Journal of Clinical Pain*, 8, 317–323.

SANSON-FISHER, R. (1993). Primary and secondary prevention of cancer: Opportunities for behavioural scientists. In S. Maes, H. Leventhal, & M. Johnston (Eds.), *Interdisciplinary review of health psychology* (Vol. 2, pp. 117–146). New York: Wiley.

SANTIAGO, J. V. (1984). Effect of treatment on the long term complications of IDDM. *Behavioral Medicine Update*, 6(1), 26–31.

SARAFINO, E. P. (1986). *The fears of childhood: A guide to recognizing and reducing fearful states in children*. New York: Human Sciences Press.

SARAFINO, E. P. (1997). *Behavioral treatments for asthma: Biofeedback-, respondent-, and relaxation-based approaches*. Lewiston, NY: Edwin Mellon Press.

SARAFINO, E. P. (2000). Connections among parent and child atopic illnesses. *Pediatric Allergy and Immunology*, 11, 80–86.

SARAFINO, E. P. (2001). *Behavior modification: Principles of behavior change* (2nd ed.). Mountain View, CA: Mayfield.

SARAFINO, E. P. (2004). Rewards and intrinsic interest. In W. E. Craighead & C. B. Nemeroff (Eds.), *The concise Corsini encyclopedia of psychology and behavioral science* (3rd ed., pp. 818–820). Hoboken, NJ: Wiley.

SARAFINO, E. P. (2005). *Research methods: Using processes and procedures of science to understand behavior*. Upper Saddle River, NJ: Prentice Hall.

SARAFINO, E. P., & ARMSTRONG, J. W. (1986). *Child and adolescent development* (2nd ed.). St. Paul, MN: West.

SARAFINO, E. P., & DILLON, J. M. (1998). Relationships among respiratory infections, triggers of attacks, and asthma severity in children. *Journal of Asthma*, 35, 497–504.

SARAFINO, E. P., & EWING, M. (1999). The Hassles Assessment Scale for Students in College: Measuring the frequency and unpleasantness of and dwelling on stressful events. *Journal of American College Health, 48,* 75–83.

SARAFINO, E. P., & GOEHRING, P. (2000). Age comparisons in acquiring biofeedback control and success in reducing headache pain. *Annals of Behavioral Medicine, 22,* 10–16.

SARAFINO, E. P., & GOLDFEDDER, J. (1995). Genetic factors in the presence, severity, and triggers of asthma. *Archives of Disease in Childhood, 73,* 112–116.

SARAFINO, E. P., GROFF, A., & DEPAULO, D. J. (2000). *The Scale of Information Processing Diligence: Development and psychometric evaluation.* Unpublished manuscript.

SARASON, I. G., JOHNSON, J. H., & SIEGEL, J. M. (1978). Assessing the impact of life changes: Development of the Life Experiences Survey. *Journal of Consulting and Clinical Psychology, 46,* 932–946.

SARASON, I. G., LEVINE, H. M., BASHAM, R. B., & SARASON, B. R. (1983). Assessing social support: The Social Support Questionnaire. *Journal of Personality and Social Psychology, 44,* 127–139.

SARASON, I. G., & SARASON, B. R. (1984). *Abnormal psychology* (4th ed.). Englewood Cliffs, NJ: Prentice Hall.

SARASON, I. G., SARASON, B. R., POTTER, E. H., & ANTONI, M. H. (1985). Life events, social support, and illness. *Psychosomatic Medicine, 47,* 156–163.

SASTRE, M. T. M., MULLET, E., & SORUM, P. C. (1999). Relationship between cigarette dose and perceived risk of lung cancer. *Preventive Medicine, 28,* 566–571.

SAUNDERS, C. (1986). A philosophy of terminal care. In M. J. Christie & P. G. Mellett (Eds.), *The psychosomatic approach: Contemporary practice of whole-person care* (pp. 427–436). New York: Wiley.

SCAMBLER, G. (1984). Perceiving and coping with stigmatizing illness. In R. Fitzpatrick, J. Hinton, S. Newman, G. Scambler, & J. Thompson (Eds.), *The experience of illness* (pp. 203–226). London: Tavistock.

SCARR, S., & KIDD, K. K. (1983). Developmental behavior genetics. In P. H. Mussen (Ed.), *Handbook of child psychology* (4th ed., Vol. 2, pp. 345–434). New York: Wiley.

SCHACHTER, S. (1971). Some extraordinary facts about obese humans and rats. *American Psychologist, 26,* 129–144.

SCHACHTER, S. (1980). Urinary pH and the psychology of nicotine addiction. In P. O. Davidson & S. M. Davidson (Eds.), *Behavioral medicine: Changing health lifestyles* (pp. 70–93). New York: Brunner/Mazel.

SCHACHTER, S. (1982). Recidivism and self cure of smoking and obesity. *American Psychologist, 37,* 436–444.

SCHACHTER, S., SILVERSTEIN, B., KOZLOWSKI, L. T., PERLICK, D., HERMAN, C. P., & LIEBLING, B. (1977). Studies of the interaction of psychological and pharmacological determinants of smoking. *Journal of Experimental Psychology: General, 106,* 3–40.

SCHAEFER, C., COYNE, J. C., & LAZARUS, R. S. (1981). The health-related functions of social support. *Journal of Behavioral Medicine, 4,* 381–406.

SCHAFER, L. C., GLASGOW, R. E., & MCCAUL, K. D. (1982). Increasing the adherence of diabetic adolescents. *Journal of Behavioral Medicine, 5,* 353–362.

SCHAUFFLER, H. H., & MORDAVSKY, J. K. (2001). Consumer reports in health care: Do they make a difference? *Annual Review of Public Health, 22,* 69–89.

SCHEIER, L. M., & BOTVIN, G. J. (1997). Expectancies as mediators of the effects of social influences and alcohol knowledge on adolescent alcohol use: A prospective analysis. *Psychology of Addictive Behaviors, 11,* 48–64.

SCHEIER, M. F., & CARVER, C. S. (2001). Adapting to cancer: The importance of hope and purpose. In A. Baum & B. L. Anderson (Eds.), *Psychosocial interventions for cancer* (pp. 15–36). Washington, DC: American Psychological Association.

SCHEIER, M. F., CARVER, C. S., & BRIDGES, M. W. (2001). Optimism, pessimism, and psychological well-being. In E. C. Chang (Ed.), *Optimism and pessimism: Implications for theory, research and practice.* Washington, DC: American Psychological Association.

SCHEIER, M. F., MATTHEWS, K. A., OWENS, J. F., SCHULZ, R., BRIDGES, M. W., MAGOVERN, G. J., et al. (1999). Optimism and rehospitalization after coronary artery bypass graft surgery. *Archives of Internal Medicine, 159,* 829–835.

SCHERER, K. R. (1986). Voice, stress, and emotion. In M. H. Appley & R. Trumbull (Eds.), *Dynamics of stress: Physiological, psychological, and social perspectives* (pp. 157–179). New York: Plenum.

SCHIAFFINO, K. M., SHAWARYN, M. A., & BLUM, D. (1998). Examining the impact of illness representations on psychological adjustment to chronic illnesses. *Health Psychology, 17,* 262–268.

SCHIFFMAN, H. R. (1996). *Sensation and perception: An integrated approach* (4th ed.). New York: Wiley.

SCHIFTER, D. E., & AJZEN, I. (1985). Intention, perceived control, and weight loss: An application of the theory of planned behavior. *Journal of Personality and Social Psychology, 45,* 843–851.

SCHMIEDER, R., FRIEDRICH, G., NEUS, H., RÜDEL, H., & VON EIFF, A. W. (1983). The influence of beta-blockers on cardiovascular reactivity and Type A behavior pattern in hypertensives. *Psychosomatic Medicine, 45,* 417–423.

SCHNALL, P. L., PIEPER, C., SCHWARTZ, J. E., KARASEK, R. A., SCHLUSSEL, Y., DEVEREUX, R. B., et al. (1990). The relationship between "job strain," workplace diastolic blood pressure, and left ventricular mass index: Results of a case-control study. *Journal of the American Medical Association, 263,* 1929–1935.

SCHNALL, P. L., SCHWARTZ, J. E., LANDSBERGIS, P. A., WARREN, K., & PICKERING, T. G. (1998). A longitudinal study of job strain and ambulatory blood pressure: Results from a three-year follow-up. *Psychosomatic Medicine, 60,* 697–706.

SCHNEIDER, A. M., & TARSHIS, B. (1975). *An introduction to physiological psychology.* New York: Random House.

SCHNEIDER, F., HABEL, U., WAGNER, M., FRANKE, P., SALLOUM, J. M., SHAH, N. J. et al. (2001). Subcortical correlates of craving in recently abstinent alcoholic patients. *American Journal of Psychiatry, 158,* 1075–1083.

SCHNEIDER, T. R., SALOVEY, P., APANOVITCH, A. M., PIZARRO, J., MCCARTHY, D., ZULLO, J. et al. (2001). The effects of message framing and ethnic targeting on mammography use among low-income women. *Health Psychology, 20,* 256–266.

SCHNEIDERMAN, N., & HAMMER, D. (1985). Behavioral medicine approaches to cardiovascular disorders. In N. Schneiderman & J. T. Tapp (Eds.), *Behavioral medicine: The biopsychosocial approach* (pp. 467–507). Hillsdale, NJ: Erlbaum.

SCHOENBORN, C. A. (1993). The Alameda Study—25 years later. In S. Maes, H. Leventhal, & M. Johnston (Eds.), *International review of health psychology* (Vol. 2, pp. 81–116). New York: Wiley.

SCHRAA, J. C., & DIRKS, J. F. (1982). Improving patient recall and comprehension of the treatment regimen. *Journal of Asthma, 19,* 159–162.

SCHUCKIT, M. A. (1985). Genetics and the risk for alcoholism. *Journal of the American Medical Association, 254,* 2614–2617.

SCHUCKIT, M. A. (1996). Recent developments in the pharmacotherapy of alcohol dependence. *Journal of Consulting and Clinical Psychology, 64,* 669–676.

SCHUCKIT, M. A., DAEPPEN, J.-B., DANKO, G. P., TRIPP, M. L., SMITH, T. L., LI, T.-K. HESSELBROCK, V. M. et al. (1999). Clinical implications for four drugs of the DSM-IV distinction between substance dependence with and without a physiological component. *American Journal of Psychiatry, 156,* 41–49.

SCHULZ, R. (1976). Effects of control and predictability on the physical and psychological well-being of the institutionalized aged. *Journal of Personality and Social Psychology, 33,* 563–573.

SCHULZ, R., & BEACH, S. R. (1999). Caregiving as a risk factor for mortality: The Caregiver Effects Study. *Journal of the American Medical Association, 282,* 2215–2219.

SCHULZ, R., & HANUSA, B. H. (1978). Long-term effects of control and predictability-enhancing interventions: Findings and ethical issues. *Journal of Personality and Social Psychology, 36,* 1194–1201.

SCHUNK, D. H., & CARBONARI, J. P. (1984). Self-efficacy models. In J. D. Matarazzo, S. M. Weiss, J. A. Herd, N. E. Miller, & S. M. Weiss (Eds.), *Behavioral health: A handbook of health enhancement and disease prevention* (pp. 230–247). New York: Wiley.

SCHUSTER, C. R., & KILBEY, M. M. (1992). Prevention of drug abuse. In J. M. Last & R. B. Wallace (Eds.), *Maxcy-Rosenau-Last public health and preventive medicine* (13th ed., pp. 769–786). Norwalk, CT: Appleton & Lange.

SCHUSTER, M. A., STEIN, B. D., HAYCOX, L. H., COLLINS, R. L., MARSHALL, G. N., ELLIOTT, M. N. et al. (2001). A national survey of stress reactions after the September 11, 2001, terrorist attacks. *New England Journal of Medicine, 345,* 1507–1512.

SCHUTTE, K. K., NICHOLS, K. A., BRENNAN, P. L., & MOOS, R. H. (2003). A ten-year follow-up of older problem drinkers: Risk of relapse and implications of successfully maintained remission. *Journal of Studies on Alcohol, 64,* 367–374.

SCHWARTZ, M. D., TAYLOR, K. L., WILLARD, K. S., SIEGEL, J. E., LAMDAN, R. M., & MORAN, K. (1999). Distress, personality, and mammography utilization among women with a family history of breast cancer. *Health Psychology, 18,* 327–332.

SEAGLE, H. M., WYATT, H., & HILL, J. O. (2001). Obesity: Overview of treatments and interventions. In A. M. Coulston, C. L. Rock, & E. R. Monsen (Eds.), *Nutrition in the prevention and treatment of disease* (pp. 465–480). San Diego: Academic Press.

SEARS, S. R., & STANTON, A. L. (2001). Physician-assisted dying: Review of issues and roles for health psychologists.

SEARS, S. R., STANTON, A. L., & DANOFF-BURG, S. (2003). The yellow brick road and the Emerald City: Benefit finding, positive reappraisal coping, and posttraumatic growth in women with early-stage breast cancer. *Health Psychology, 22,* 487–497.

SEEMAN, T. E., & MCEWEN, B. S. (1996). Impact of social environment characteristics on neuroendocrine regulation. *Psychosomatic Medicine, 58,* 459–471.

SEEMAN, T. E., SINGER, B. H., ROWE, J. W., HORWITZ, R. I., & MCEWEN, B. S. (1997). Price of adaptation—allostatic load and its health consequences. *Archives of Internal Medicine, 157,* 2259–2268.

SELF, C. A., & ROGERS, R. W. (1990). Coping with threats to health: Effects of persuasive appeals on depressed, normal, and antisocial personalities. *Journal of Behavioral Medicine, 13,* 343–357.

SELIGMAN, M. E. P. (1975). *Helplessness: On depression, development, and death.* San Francisco: Freeman.

SELIGMANN, J., & SULAVIK, C. (1992, April 27). Software for hard issues. *Newsweek*, p. 55.

SELYE, H. (1956). *The stress of life.* New York: McGraw-Hill.

SELYE, H. (1974). *Stress without distress.* Philadelphia: Lippincott.

SELYE, H. (1976). *Stress in health and disease.* Reading, MA: Butterworth.

SELYE, H. (1985). History and present status of the stress concept. In A. Monat & R. S. Lazarus (Eds.), *Stress and coping: An anthology* (2nd ed., pp. 17–29). New York: Columbia University Press.

SERDULA, M. K., IVERY, D., COATES, R. J., FREEDMAN, D. S., WILLIAMSON, D. F., & BYERS, T. (1993). Do obese children become obese adults? A review of the literature. *Preventive Medicine, 22,* 167–177.

SERDULA, M. K., MOKDAD, A. H., WILLIAMSON, D. F., GALUSKA, D. A., MENDLEIN, J. M., & HEATH, G. W. (1999). Prevalence of attempting weight loss and strategies for controlling weight. *Journal of the American Medical Association, 282,* 1353–1358.

SERFASS, R. C., & GERBERICH, S. G. (1984). Exercise for optimal health: Strategies and motivational considerations. *Preventive Medicine, 13,* 79–99.

SEVERSON, H. H. (1993). Smokeless tobacco: Risks, epidemiology, and cessation. In C. T. Orleans & J. Slade (Eds.), *Nicotine addiction: Principles and management.* New York: Oxford University Press.

SHADEL, W. G., & MERMELSTEIN, R. (1993). Cigarette smoking under stress: The role of coping expectancies among smokers in a clinic-based smoking cessation program. *Health Psychology, 12,* 443–450.

SHADEL, W. G., SHIFFMAN, S., NIAURA, R., NICHTER, M., & ABRAMS, D. B. (2000). Current models of nicotine dependence: What is known and what is needed to advance understanding of tobacco etiology among youth. *Drug and Alcohol Dependence, 59*(Suppl.), S9–S22.

SHAH, M., & JEFFERY, R. W. (1991). Is obesity due to overeating and inactivity, or to a defective metabolic rate? A review. *Annals of Behavioral Medicine, 13,* 73–81.

SHAIN, R. N., PIPER, J. M., NEWTON, E. R., PERDUE, S. T., RAMOS, R., CHAMPION, J. D., et al. (1999). A randomized, controlled trial of a behavioral intervention to prevent sexually transmitted disease among minority women. *New England Journal of Medicine, 340,* 93–100.

SHANFIELD, S. B. (1990). Return to work after an acute myocardial infarction: A review. *Heart & Lung, 19,* 109–117.

SHAPIRO, A. P., KRANTZ, D. S., & GRIM, C. E. (1986). Pharmacologic agents as modulators of stress. In K. A. Matthews, S. M. Weiss, T. Detre, T. M. Dembroski, B. Falkner, S. B. Manuck, & R. B. Williams (Eds.), *Handbook of stress, reactivity, and cardiovascular disease* (pp. 401–416). New York: Wiley.

SHAPIRO, S. L., SCHWARTZ, G. E., & BONNER, G. (1998). Effects of mindfulness-based stress reduction on medical and premedical students. *Journal of Behavioral Medicine, 21,* 581–599.

SHAW, R. E., COHEN, F., DOYLE, B., & PALESKY, J. (1985). The impact of denial and repressive style on information gain and rehabilitation outcomes in myocardial infarction patients. *Psychosomatic Medicine, 47,* 262–273.

SHEARER, H. M., & EVANS, D. R. (2001). Adherence to health care. In S. S. Kazarian & E. R. Evans (Eds.), *Handbook of cultural health psychology* (pp. 113–138). San Diego: Academic Press.

SHERIDAN, K. (1991). Psychosocial services for persons with human immunodeficiency virus disease. In J. J. Sweet, R. H. Rozensky, & S. M. Tovian (Eds.), *Handbook of clinical psychology in medical settings* (pp. 587–600). New York: Plenum.

SHERMAN, B. F., BONANNO, G. A., WIENER, L. S., & BATTLES, H. B. (2000). When children tell their friends they have AIDS: Possible consequences for psychological well-being and disease progression. *Psychosomatic Medicine, 62,* 238–247.

SHERMAN, J. J., CARLSON, C. R., McCUBBIN, J. A., & WILSON, J. F. (1997). Effects of stretch-based progressive relaxation training on the secretion of salivary immunoglobulin A in orofacial pain patients. *Journal of Orofacial Pain, 11,* 115–124.

SHERWOOD, A., GIRDLER, S. S., BRAGDON, E. E., WEST, S. G., BROWNLEY, K. A., HINDERLITER, A. L., et al. (1997). Ten-year stability of cardiovascular responses to laboratory stressors. *Psychophysiology, 34,* 185–191.

SHERWOOD, A., MAY, C. W., SIEGEL, W. C., & BLUMENTHAL, J. A. (1995). Ethnic differences in hemodynamic responses to stress in hypertensive men and women. *American Journal of Hypertension, 8,* 552–557.

SHIFFMAN, S. (1986). A cluster-analytic classification of smoking relapse episodes. *Addictive Behaviors, 11,* 295–307.

SHIFFMAN, S., BALABANIS, M. H., PATY, J. A., ENGBERG, J., GWALTNEY, C. J., LIU, K. S., et al. (2000). Dynamic effects of self-efficacy on smoking lapse and relapse. *Health Psychology, 19,* 315–323.

SHIFFMAN. S., FISCHER, L. B., ZETTLER-SEGAL, M., & BENOWITZ, N. L. (1990). Nicotine exposure among nondependent smokers. *Archives of General Psychiatry, 47,* 333–336.

SHIFFMAN, S., HICKCOX, M., PATY, J. A., GNYS, M., KASSEL, J. D., & RICHARDS, T. J. (1996). Progression from a smoking lapse to relapse: Prediction from abstinence violation effects, nicotine dependence, and lapse characteristics. *Journal of Consulting and Clinical Psychology, 64,* 993–1002.

SHIFFMAN, S., PATY, J. A., GNYS, M., KASSEL, J. D., & ELASH, C. (1995). Nicotine withdrawal in chippers and regular smokers: Subjective and cognitive effects. *Health Psychology, 14,* 301–309.

SHIFFMAN, S., SHADEL, W. G., NIAURA, R., KHAYRALLAH, M. A., JORENBY, D. E., RYAN, C. F. et al. (2003). Efficacy of acute administration of nicotine gum in relief of cue-provoked cigarette craving. *Psychopharmacology, 166,* 343–350.

SHIFFMAN, S., & STONE, A. A. (1998). Introduction to the special section: Ecological momentary assessment in health psychology. *Health Psychology, 17,* 3–5.

SHIPLEY, R. H., BUTT, J. H., HORWITZ, B., & FARBRY, J. E. (1978). Preparation for a stressful medical procedure: Effect of amount of stimulus preexposure and coping style. *Journal of Consulting and Clinical Psychology, 46,* 499–507.

SHNEIDMAN, E. S. (1977). The college student and death. In H. Feifel (Ed.), *New meanings of death* (pp. 67–86). New York: McGraw-Hill.

SHOGREN, E. (1988, June 3). Physicians favor death with "dignity." *Philadelphia Inquirer,* p. D14.

SHONTZ, F. C. (1975). *The psychological aspects of physical illness and disability.* New York: Macmillan.

SHOPLAND, D. R., & BROWN, C. (1985). Changes in cigarette smoking prevalence in the U.S.: 1955 to 1983. *Annals of Behavioral Medicine, 7*(2), 5–8.

SHOPLAND, D. R., & BURNS, D. M. (1993). Medical and public health implications of tobacco addiction. In C. T. Orleans & J. Slade (Eds.), *Nicotine addiction: Principles and management.* New York: Oxford University Press.

SHUPE, D. R. (1985). Perceived control, helplessness, and choice: Their relationship to health and aging. In J. E. Birren & J. Livingston (Eds.), *Cognition, stress, and aging.* Englewood Cliffs, NJ: Prentice-Hall.

SIEGEL, L. J., & PETERSON, L. (1980). Stress reduction in young dental patients through coping skills and sensory information. *Journal of Consulting and Clinical Psychology, 48,* 785–787.

SIEGLER, I. C., FEAGANES, J. R., & RIMER, B. K. (1995). Predictors of adoption of mammography in women under age 50. *Annals of Behavioral Medicine, 14,* 274–278.

SIEGMAN, A. W. (1993). Cardiovascular consequences of expressing, experiencing, and repressing anger. *Journal of Behavioral Medicine, 16,* 539–569.

SIKKEMA, K. J. (1998). HIV prevention. In E. A. Blechman & K. D. Brownell (Eds.), *Behavioral medicine and women: A comprehensive handbook* (pp. 198–202). New York: Guilford.

SIKKEMA, K. J., & KELLY, J. A. (1996). Behavioral medicine interventions can improve the quality-of-life and health of persons with HIV disease. *Annals of Behavioral Medicine, 18,* 40–48.

SIKKEMA, K. J., KELLY, J. A., WINETT, R. A., SOLOMON, L. J., CARGILL, V. A., ROFFMAN, R. A., et al. (2000). Outcomes of a randomized community-level HIF prevention intervention for women living in 18 low-income housing developments. *American Journal of Public Health, 90,* 57–63.

SILVER, R. L., & WORTMAN, C. B. (1980). Coping with undesirable life events. In J. Garber & M. E. P. Seligman (Eds.), *Human helplessness: Theory and applications* (pp. 279–375). New York: Academic Press.

SIMONI, J. M., MASON, H. R. C., MARKS, G., RUIZ, M. S., REED, D., & RICHARDSON, J. L. (1995). Women's self-disclosure of HIV infection: Rates, reasons, and reactions. *Journal of Consulting and Clinical Psychology, 63,* 474–478.

SIMS, E. A. H. (1974). Studies in human hyperphagia. In G. A. Bray & J. E. Bethune (Eds.), *Treatment and management of obesity* (pp. 28–43). New York: Harper & Row.

SIMS, E. A. H. (1976). Experimental obesity, dietary-induced thermogenesis, and their clinical implications. *Clinics in Endocrinology and Metabolism, 5,* 377–395.

SINDELAR, J. L., & FIELLIN, D. A. (2001). Innovations in treatment for drug abuse: Solutions to a public health problem. *Annual Review of Public Health, 22,* 249–272.

SKELLY, A. H., MARSHALL, J. R., HAUGHEY, B. P., DAVIS, P. J., & DUNFORD, R. G. (1995). Self-efficacy and confidence in outcomes as determinants of self-care practices in inner-city, African-American women with non-insulin-dependent diabetes. *Diabetes Educator, 21,* 38–46.

SKINNER, C. S., CAMPBELL, M. K., RIMER, B. K., CURRY, S., & PROCHASKA, J. O. (1999). How effective is tailored print communication? *Annals of Behavioral Medicine, 21,* 290–298.

SKINNER, E. A., EDGE, K., ALTMAN, J., & SHERWOOD, H. (2003). Searching for the structure of coping: A review and critique of category systems for classifying ways of coping. *Psychological Bulletin, 129,* 216–269.

SKLAR, L. S., & ANISMAN, H. (1981). Stress and cancer. *Psychological Bulletin, 89,* 369–406.

SKOLNICK, A. S. (1986). *The psychology of human development.* San Diego: Harcourt Brace Jovanovich.

SLATTERY, M. L., & CAAN, B. J. (2001). Nutrition and colon cancer. In A. M. Coulston, C. L. Rock, & E. R. Monsen (Eds.), *Nutrition in the prevention and treatment of disease* (pp. 357–372). San Diego: Academic Press.

SMART, J. L. (1991). Critical periods in brain development. In D. J. P. Barker (Chair, Ciba Foundation Symposium,

No. 156), *The childhood environment and adult disease*. New York: Wiley.

SMITH, C. A., & WALLSTON, K. A. (1992). Adaptation in patients with chronic rheumatoid arthritis: Application of a general model. *Health Psychology*, 11, 151–162.

SMITH, C. E., FERNENGEL, K., HOLCORFT, C., GERALD, K., & MARIEN, L. (1994). Meta-analysis of the associations between social support and health outcomes. *Annals of Behavioral Medicine*, 16, 352–362.

SMITH, E. L. (1984). Special considerations in developing exercise programs for the older adult. In J. D. Matarazzo, S. M. Weiss, J. A. Herd, N. E. Miller, & S. M. Weiss (Eds.), *Behavioral health: A handbook of health enhancement and disease prevention* (pp. 525–546). New York: Wiley.

SMITH, J. B., & AUTMAN, S. H. (1985). The experience of hospitalization. In L. L. Hayman & E. M. Sporing (Eds.), *Handbook of pediatric nursing* (pp. 78–124). New York: Wiley.

SMITH, M. T., PERLIS, M. L., SMITH, M. S., GILES, D. E., & CARMODY, T. P. (2000). Sleep quality and presleep arousal in chronic pain. *Journal of Behavioral Medicine*, 23, 1–13.

SMITH, R. C., & ZIMNY, G. H. (1988). Physicians' emotional reactions to patients. *Psychosomatics*, 29, 392–397.

SMITH, T. W. (1992). Hostility and health: Current status of a psychosomatic hypothesis. *Health Psychology*, 11, 139–150.

SMITH, T. W., & GALLO, L. C. (2001). Personality traits as risk factors for physical illness. In A. Baum, T. A. Revenson, & J. E. Singer (Eds.), *Handbook of health psychology* (pp. 139–173). Mahwah, NJ: Erlbaum.

SMITH, T. W., GALLO, L. C., GOBLE, L., NGU, L. Q., & STARK, K. A. (1998). Agency, communion, and cardiovascular reactivity during marital interaction. *Health Psychology*, 17, 537–545.

SMITH, T. W., ORLEANS, C. T., & JENKINS, C. D. (2004). Prevention and health promotion: Decades of progress, new challenges, and an emerging agenda. *Health Psychology*, 23, 126–131.

SMITH, T. W., PECK, J. R., & WARD, J. R. (1990). Helplessness and depression in rheumatoid arthritis. *Health Psychology*, 9, 377–389.

SMITH, T. W., TURNER, C. W., FORD, M. H., HUNT, S. C., BARLOW, G. K., STULTS, B. M., et al. (1987). Blood pressure reactivity in adult male twins. *Health Psychology*, 6, 209–220.

SMYTH, J. M., & PENNEBAKER, J. W. (2001). What ar the health effects of disclosure? In A. Baum, T. A. Revenson, & J. E. Singer (Eds.), *Handbook of health psychology* (pp. 339–348). Mahwah, NJ: Erlbaum.

SNOW, L. F. (1981). Folk medical beliefs and their implications for care of patients: A review based on studies among black Americans. In G. Henderson & M. Primeaux (Eds.), *Transcultural health care* (pp. 78–101). Menlo Park, CA: Addison-Wesley.

SNOWDON, D. A., GREINER, L. H., MORTIMER, J. A., RILEY, K. P., GREINER, P. A., & MARKESBERY, W. R. (1997). Brain infarction and the clinical expression of Alzheimer disease. *Journal of the American Medical Association*, 277, 813–817.

SNYDER, S. H. (1977). Opiate receptors and internal opiates. *Scientific American*, 236, 44–56.

SOBEL, D. S. (1990). The placebo effect: Using the body's own healing mechanisms. In R. Ornstein & C. Swencionis (Eds.), *The healing brain: A scientific reader* (pp. 63–74). New York: Guilford.

SOBELL, L. C., SOBELL, M. B., LEO, G. I., AGRAWAL, S., JOHNSON-YOUNG, L., & CUNNINGHAM, J. A. (2002). Promoting self-change with alcohol abusers: A community-level mail intervention based on natural recovery studies. *Alcoholism: Clinical and Experimental Research*, 26, 936–948.

SOBELL, L. C., SOBELL, M. B., TONEATTO, T., & LEO, G. I. (1993). What triggers the resolution of alcohol problems without treatment? *Alcoholism: Clinical and Experimental Research*, 17, 217–224.

SOLÉ-LERIS, A. (1986). *Tranquility and insight*. Boston: Shambhala.

SOLOMON, L. J., FLYNN, B. S., WORDEN, J. K., MICKEY, R. M., SKELLY, J. M., GELLER, B. M., et al. (1998). Assessment of self-reward strategies for maintenance of breast self-examination. *Journal of Behavioral Medicine*, 21, 83–102.

SOMERS, V. K., DYKEN, M. E., MARK, A. L., & ABBOUD, F. M. (1993). Sympathetic-nerve activity during sleep in normal subjects. *New England Journal of Medicine*, 328, 303–307.

SPECTER, M. (1996, March 31). 10 years later, through fear, Chernobyl still kills in Belarus. *New York Times*, pp. 1, 6.

SPEECE, M. W., & BRENT, S. B. (1984). Children's understanding of death: A review of three components of a death concept. *Child Development*, 55, 1671–1686.

SPEISMAN, J. C., LAZARUS, R. S., MORDKOFF, A., & DAVISON, L. (1964). Experimental demonstration of stress based on ego-defense theory. *Journal of Abnormal and Social Psychology*, 68, 367–380.

SPENCE, J. D., BARNETT, P. A., LINDEN, W., RAMSDEN, V., & TAENZER, P. (1999). Recommendations on stress management. *Canadian Medical Association Journal*, 160(9 Suppl.), S46–S50.

SPENCER, L., PAGELL, F., HALLION, M. E., & ADAMS, T. B. (2002). Applying the transtheoretical model to tobacco cessation and prevention: A review of the literature. *American Journal of Health Promotion*, 17, 7–71.

SPENCER, S. M., LEHMAN, J. M., WYNINGS, C., ARENA, P., CARVER, C. S., ANTONI, M. H., et al. (1999). Concerns about breast cancer and relations to psychosocial well-being in a multiethnic sample of early-stage patients. *Health Psychology, 18*, 159–168.

SPIEGEL, D., BLOOM, J. R., KRAEMER, H. C., & GOTTHEIL, E. (1989). Effect of psychosocial treatment on survival of patients with metastatic breast cancer. *Lancet, 334*, 888–891.

SPIEGEL, D., SANDS, S., & KOOPMAN, C. (1994). Pain and depression in patients with cancer. *Cancer, 74*, 2570–2578.

SPINETTA, J. J. (1974). The dying child's awareness of death: A review. *Psychological Bulletin, 81*, 256–260.

SPINETTA, J. J. (1982). Behavioral and psychological research in childhood cancer. *Cancer, 50*, 1939–1943.

SPOTH, R. L., REDMOND, C., & SHIN, C. (2001). Randomized trial of brief family interventions for general populations: Adolescent substance use outcomes 4 years following baseline. *Journal of Consulting and Clinical Psychology, 69*, 627–642.

SPURGEON, P., BROOME, A., EARLL, L., & HARRIS, B. (1990). Health psychology in a broader context. In P. Bennett, J. Weinman, & P. Spurgeon (Eds.), *Current developments in health psychology* (pp. 331–345). Chur, Switzerland: Harwood.

SQUIRES, D. D., & HESTER, R. K. (2004). Using technical innovations in clinical practice: The Drinker's Check-Up program. *Journal of Clinical Psychology/In Session, 60*, 159–169.

STACY, A. W. (1997). Memory activation and expectancy as prospective mediators of alcohol and marijuana use. *Journal of Abnormal Psychology, 106*, 61–73.

STACY, A. W., BENTLER, P. M., & FLAY, B. R. (1994). Attitudes and health behavior in diverse populations: Drunk driving, alcohol use, binge eating, marihuana use, and cigarette use. *Health Psychology, 13*, 73–85.

STALL, R. D., COATES, T. J., & HOFF, C. (1988). Behavioral risk reduction for HIV infection among gay and bisexual men: A review of results from the United States. *American Psychologist, 43*, 878–885.

STALLONE, D. D., & STUNKARD, A. J. (1991). The regulation of body weight: Evidence and clinical implications. *Annals of Behavioral Medicine, 13*, 220–230.

STAMLER, J., STAMLER, R., NEATON, J. D., WENTWORTH, D., DAVIGLUS, M. L., GARSIDE, D., et al. (1999). Low risk-factor profile and long-term cardiovascular and noncardiovascular mortality and life expectancy. *Journal of the American Medical Association, 282*, 2012–2018.

STANTON, A. L., DANOFF-BURG, S., CAMERON, C. L., BISHOP, M., COLLINS, C. A., KIRK, S. B. et al. (2000). Emotionally expressive coping predicts psychological and physical adjustment to breast cancer. *Journal of Consulting and Clinical Psychology, 68*, 875–882.

STANTON, A. L., ESTES, M. A., ESTES, N. C., CAMERON, C. L., DANOFF-BURG, S., & IRVING, L. M. (1998). Treatment decision making and adjustment to breast cancer: A longitudinal study. *Journal of Consulting and Clinical Psychology, 66*, 313–322.

STEFFEN, P. R., MCNEILLY, M., ANDERSON, N., & SHERWOOD, A. (2003). Effects of perceived racism and anger inhibition on ambulatory blood pressure in African Americans. *Psychosomatic Medicine, 65*, 746–750.

STEIGER, H., GAUVIN, L., JABALPURWALA, S., SÉGUIN, J. R., & STOTLAND, S. (1999). Hypersensitivity to social interaction in bulimic syndromes: Relationship to binge eating. *Journal of Consulting and Clinical Psychology, 67*, 765–775.

STEIN, J. A., NEWCOMB, M. D., & BENTLER, P. M. (1987). An 8-year study of multiple influences on drug use and drug use consequences. *Journal of Personality and Social Psychology, 53*, 1094–1105.

STEIN, J. H., KEEVIL, J. G., WIEBE, D. A., AESCHLIMANN, S., & FOLTS, J. D. (1999). Purple grape juice improves endothelial function and reduces the susceptibility of LDL cholesterol to oxidation in patients with coronary artery disease. *Circulation, 100*, 1050–1055.

STEINBERG, L. (1985). Early temperamental antecedents of adult Type A behaviors. *Developmental Psychology, 21*, 1171–1180.

STEINER, H., & CLARK, W. R. (1977). Psychiatric complications of burned adults: A classification. *Journal of Trauma, 17*, 134–143.

STEINMAN, M. A., SANDS, L. P., & COVINSKY, K. E. (2001). Self-restriction of medications due to cost in seniors without prescription coverage. *Journal of General Internal Medicine, 16*, 793–799.

STEPHENS, R. S., ROFFMAN, R. A., & SIMPSON, E. E. (1994). Treating adult marijuana dependence: A test of the relapse prevention model. *Journal of Consulting and Clinical Psychology, 62*, 92–99.

STEPTOE, A., CROPLEY, M., & JOEKES, K. (2000). Task demands and the pressures of everyday life: Associations between cardiovascular reactivity and work blood pressure and heart rate. *Health Psychology, 19*, 46–54.

STEPTOE, A., WARDLE, J., VINCK, J., TUOMISTO, M., HOLTE, A., & WICHSTRØM, L. (1994). Personality and attitudinal correlated of healthy and unhealthy lifestyles in young adults. *Psychology and Health, 9*, 331–343.

STERNBERG, E. M., & GOLD, P. W. (1997). The mind–body interaction in disease. *Scientific American, 7*(Special Issue, No. 1), 8–15.

STETSON, B. A., RAHN, J. M., DUBBERT, P. M., WILNER, B. I., & MERCURY, M. G. (1997). Prospective evaluation of the effects of stress on exercise adherence in community-residing women. *Health Psychology, 16,* 515–520.

STEVENS, V. J., GLASGOW, R. E., TOOBERT, D. J., KARANJA, N., & SMITH, K. S. (2002). Randomized trial of a brief dietary intervention to decrease consumption of fat and increase consumption of fruits and vegetables. *American Journal of Health Promotion, 16,* 129–135.

STEWART, D. E., ABBEY, S. E., SHNEK, Z. M., IRVINE, J., & GRACE, S. L. (2004). Gender differences in health information needs and decisional preferences in patients recovering from an acute ischemic coronary event. *Psychosomatic Medicine, 66,* 42–48.

STEWART, W. F., SHECHTER, A., & RASMUSSEN, B. K. (1994). Migraine prevalence: A review of population-based studies. *Neurology, 44*(Suppl. 4), S17–23.

STEWART-WILLIAMS, S. (2004). The placebo puzzle: Putting together the pieces. *Health Psychology, 23,* 198–206.

STICE, E., CAMERON, R. P., KILLEN, J. D., HAYWARD, C., & TAYLOR, C. B. (1999). Naturalistic weight-reduction efforts prospectively predict growth in relative weight and onset of obesity among female adolescents. *Journal of Consulting and Clinical Psychology, 67,* 967–974.

STICE, E., PRESNELL, K., & SPANGLER, D. (2002). Risk factors for binge eating onset in adolescent girls: A 2-year prospective investigation. *Health Psychology, 21,* 131–138.

STICE, E., & SHAW, H. (2004). Eating disorder prevention programs: A meta-analytic review. *Psychological Bulletin, 130,* 206–227.

STIEG, R. L., & TURK, D. C. (1988). Chronic pain syndrome: Demonstrating the cost-benefit of treatment. *Clinical Journal of Pain, 4,* 58–63.

ST. LAWRENCE, J. S., CROSBY, R. A., BRASFIELD, T. L., & O'BANNON, R. E. (2002). Reducing STD and HIV risk behavior of substance-dependent adolescents. A randomized controlled trial. *Journal of Consulting and Clinical Psychology, 70,* 1010–1021.

ST. LAWRENCE, J. S., JEFFERSON, K. W., ALLEYNE, E., & BRASFIELD, T. L. (1995). Comparison of education versus behavioral skills training interventions in lowering sexual HIV-risk behavior of substance-dependent adolescents. *Journal of Consulting and Clinical Psychology, 63,* 154–157.

STOCKTON, W. (1988, March 7). Fresh research tells asthmatics to stay active. *New York Times,* p. C9.

STOCKWELL, T., & TOWN, C. (1989). Anxiety and stress management. In R. K. Hester & W. R. Miller (Eds.), *Handbook of alcoholism treatment approaches: Effective alternatives* (pp. 222–230). New York: Pergamon.

STOLBERG, S. G. (1998, August 2). Superbugs. *The New York Times Magazine,* pp. 42–47.

STONE, A. A., & NEALE, J. M. (1984). New measure of daily coping: Development and preliminary results. *Journal of Personality and Social Psychology, 46,* 892–906.

STONE, A. A., NEALE, J. M., COX, D. S., NAPOLI, A., VALDIMARSDOTTIR, H., & KENNEDY-MOORE, E. (1994). Daily events are associated with a secretory immune response to an oral antigen in men. *Health Psychology, 13,* 440–446.

STONE, G. C. (1979). Health and the health system: A historical overview and conceptual framework. In G. C. Stone, F. Cohen, & N. E. Adler (Eds.), *Health psychology—A handbook* (pp. 1–17). San Francisco: Jossey-Bass.

STORY, M., & FAULKNER, P. (1990). The prime time diet: A content analysis of eating behavior and food messages in television program content and commercials. *American Journal of Public Health, 80,* 738–740.

STRAUSS, R. H., & YESALIS, C. E. (1991). Anabolic steroids in the athlete. *Annual Review of Medicine, 42,* 449–457.

STRAW, M. K. (1983). Coping with obesity. In T. G. Burish & L. A. Bradley (Eds.), *Coping with chronic disease: Research and applications* (pp. 219–258). New York: Academic Press.

STRECHER, V. J., KREUTER, M. W., & KOBRIN, S. C. (1995). Do cigarette smokers have unrealistic perceptions of their heart attack, cancer, and stroke risks? *Journal of Behavioral Medicine, 18,* 45–54.

STRIEGEL-MOORE, R. H. (1997). Risk factors for eating disorders. *Annals of the New York Academy of Sciences, 817,* 98–109.

STRIEGEL-MOORE, R., & RODIN, J. (1985). Prevention of obesity. In J. C. Rosen & L. J. Solomon (Eds.), *Prevention in health psychology* (pp. 72–110). Hanover, NH: University Press of New England.

STRONG, J. P., MALCOM, G. T., McMAHAN, C. A., TRACY, R. E., NEWMAN, W. P., HERDERICK, E. E., et al. (1999). Prevalence and extent of atherosclerosis in adolescents and young adults: Implications for prevention from the Pathobiological Determinants of Atherosclerosis in Youth Study. *Journal of the American Medical Association, 281,* 727–735.

STUART, R. B. (1967). Behavioral control of overeating. *Behavior Research and Therapy, 5,* 357–365.

STUNKARD, A. J. (1987). Conservative treatments for obesity. *American Journal of Clinical Nutrition, 45,* 1142–1154.

SUAREZ, E. C., WILLIAMS, R. B., KUHN, C. M., ZIMMERMAN, E. H., & SCHANBERG, S. M. (1991). Biobehavioral basis of coronary-prone behavior in middle-aged men. Part II: Serum cholesterol, the Type A behavior pattern, and hostility as interactive modulators of physiological reactivity. *Psychosomatic Medicine, 53,* 528–537.

SULS, J. (1982). Social support, interpersonal relations, and health: Benefits and liabilities. In G. S. Sanders

& J. Suls (Eds.), *Social psychology of health and illness* (pp. 255–277). Hillsdale, NJ: Erlbaum.

SULS, J. (1984). Levels of analysis and efforts to modify adolescent health behavior: A commentary on Lund and Kegeles. *Health Psychology, 3,* 371–375.

SULS, J., & FLETCHER, B. (1985). The relative efficacy of avoidant and nonavoidant coping strategies: A meta-analysis. *Health Psychology, 4,* 249–288.

SULS, J., MARTIN, R., & LEVENTHAL, H. (1997). Social comparison, lay referral, and the decision to seek medical care. In B. P. Buunk & F. X. Gibbons (Eds.), *Health, coping, and well-being: Perspectives from social comparison theory* (pp. 195–226). Mahwah, NJ: Erlbaum.

SULS, J., & MULLEN, B. (1981). Life change and psychological distress: The role of perceived control and desirability. *Journal of Applied Social Psychology, 11,* 379–389.

SULS, J., & ROTHMAN, A. (2004). Evolution of the biopsychosocial model: Prospects and challenges for health psychology. *Health Psychology, 23,* 119–125.

SULS, J., & SANDERS, G. S. (1988). Type A behavior as a general risk factor for physical disorder. *Journal of Behavioral Medicine, 11,* 210–226.

SULS, J., SANDERS, G. S., & LABRECQUE, M. S. (1986). Attempting to control blood pressure without systematic instruction: When advice is counterproductive. *Journal of Behavioral Medicine, 9,* 567–576.

SULS, J., WAN, C. K., & COSTA, P. T. (1995). Relationship of trait anger to resting blood pressure: A meta-analysis. *Health Psychology, 14,* 444–456.

SUPER, C. N. (1981). Cross-cultural research on infancy. In H. C. Trandis & A. Heron (Eds.), *Handbook of cross-cultural psychology: Developmental psychology* (Vol. 4, pp. 17–53). Boston: Allyn & Bacon.

SUPERKO, H. R., & KRAUSS, R. M. (1994). Coronary artery disease regression: Convincing evidence for the benefit of aggressive lipoprotein management. *Circulation, 90,* 1056–1069.

SURTEES, P., WAINWRIGHT, N., LUBEN, R., KHAW, K.-T., & DAY, N. (2003). Sense of coherence and mortality in men and women in the EPIC-Norfolk United Kingdom Prospective Cohort Study. *American Journal of Epidemiology, 158,* 1202–1209.

SURWIT, R. S. (1993). Of mice and men: Behavioral medicine in the study of type II diabetes. *Annals of Behavioral Medicine, 15,* 227–235.

SURWIT, R. S., FEINGLOS, M. N., & SCOVERN, A. W. (1983). Diabetes and behavior: A paradigm for health psychology. *American Psychologist, 38,* 255–262.

SUSSER, M., HOPPER, K., & RICHMAN, R. (1983). Society, culture, and health. In D. Mechanic (Ed.), *Handbook of health, health care, and the health professions* (pp. 23–49). New York: Free Press.

SUTER, P. O., SCHUTZ, Y., & JEQUIER, E. (1992). The effect of ethanol on fat storage in healthy subjects. *New England Journal of Medicine, 326,* 983–987.

SUTTON, S., & HALLETT, R. (1988). Understanding the effects of fear-arousing communications: The role of cognitive factors and the amount of fear aroused. *Journal of Behavioral Medicine, 11,* 353–360.

SVARSTAD, B. (1976). Physician-patient communication and patient conformity with medical advice. In D. Mechanic (Ed.), *The growth of bureaucratic medicine.* New York: Wiley.

SWAN, G. E., CARMELLI, D., & ROSENMAN, R. H. (1986). Spouse-pair similarity on the California Psychological Inventory with reference to husband's coronary heart disease. *Psychosomatic Medicine, 48,* 172–186.

SWEET, J. J. (1991). Psychological evaluation and testing services in medical settings. In J. J. Sweet, R. H. Rozensky, & S. M. Tovian (Eds.), *Handbook of clinical psychology in medical settings* (pp. 291–313). New York: Plenum.

SWEET, J. J., ROZENSKY, R. H., & TOVIAN, S. M. (1991). Clinical psychology in medical settings: Past and present. In J. J. Sweet, R. H. Rozensky, & S. M. Tovian (Eds.), *Handbook of clinical psychology in medical settings* (pp. 3–9). New York: Plenum.

SWIGONSKI, M. E. (1987). *Bio-psycho-social factors affecting coping and compliance with the hemodialysis treatment regimen.* University Microfilms International. (Order No. 8803518).

SWINBURN, B. A., WALTER, L. G., ARROL, B., TILYARD, M. W., & RUSSELL, D. G. (1998). The Green Prescription Study: A randomized controlled trial of written exercise advice provided by general practitioners. *American Journal of Public Health, 88,* 288–291.

TAGLIACOZZO, D. L., & MAUKSCH, H. O. (1972). The patient's view of the patient's role. In E. G. Jaco (Ed.), *Patients, physicians, and illness* (2nd ed., pp. 172–185). New York: Free Press.

TALBOT, F., NOUWEN, A., GINGRAS, J., BÉLANGER, A., & AUDET, J. (1999). Relations of diabetes intrusiveness and personal control to symptoms of depression among adults with diabetes. *Health Psychology, 18,* 537–542.

TALLMER, J., SCHERWITZ, L., CHESNEY, M., HECKER, M., HUNKELER, E., SERWITZ, J., et al. (1990). Selection, training, and quality control of Type A interviewers in a prospective study of young adults. *Journal of Behavioral Medicine, 13,* 449–466.

TANNER, J. M. (1970). Physical growth. In P. H. Mussen (Ed.), *Carmichael's manual of child psychology* (3rd ed., Vol. 1, pp. 77–155). New York: Wiley.

TANNER, J. M. (1978). *Foetus into man.* Cambridge, MA: Harvard University Press.

TAPERT, S. F., BROWN, G. G., BARATTA, M. V., & BROWN, S. A. (2004). fMRI BOLD response to alcohol stimuli in alcohol dependent young women. *Addictive Behaviors*, 29, 33–50.

TAPP, J. T. (1985). Multisystems interventions in disease. In N. Schneiderman & J. T. Tapp (Eds.), *Behavioral medicine: The biopsychosocial approach* (pp. 219–254). Hillsdale, NJ: Erlbaum.

TARNOWSKI, K. J., RASNAKE, L. K., & DRABMAN, R. S. (1987). Behavioral assessment and treatment of pediatric burn injuries: A review. *Behavior Therapy*, 18, 417–441.

TATE, D. G., MAYNARD, F., & FORCHHEIMER, M. (1993). Predictors of psychologic distress one year after spinal cord injury. *American Journal of Physical Medicine and Rehabilitation*, 72, 272–275.

TAYLOR, S. E. (1979). Hospital patient behavior: Reactance, helplessness, or control? *Journal of Social Issues*, 35, 156–184.

TAYLOR, S. E. (1983). Adjustment to threatening events: A theory of cognitive adaptation. *American Psychologist*, 38, 1161–1173.

TAYLOR, S. E., LICHTMAN, R. R., & WOOD, J. V. (1984). Attributions, beliefs about control, and adjustment to breast cancer. *Journal of Personality and Social Psychology*, 46, 489–502.

TEACHMAN, B. A., GAPINSKI, K. D., BROWNELL, K. D., RAWLINS, M., & JEYARAM, S. (2003). Demonstrations of implicit anti-fat bias: The impact of providing causal information and evoking sympathy. *Health Psychology*, 22, 68–78.

TEBBI, C. K., CUMMINGS, K. M., ZEVON, M. A., SMITH, L., RICHARDS, M., & MALLON, J. (1986). Compliance of pediatric and adolescent cancer patients. *Cancer*, 58, 1179–1184.

TELL, G. S., POLAK, J. F., WARD, B. J., KITTNER, S. J., SAVAGE, P. J., ROBBINS, J., et al. (1994). Relation of smoking with carotid artery wall thickness and stenosis in older adults: The Cardiovascular Health Study. *Circulation*, 90, 2905–2908.

TEMOSHOK, L., & DREHER, H. (1992). *The Type C connection: The behavioral links to cancer and your health* (pp. 203–225). New York: Random House.

TENNEN, H., & AFFLECK, G. (1997). Social comparison as a coping process: A critical review and application to chronic pain disorders. In B. P. Buunk & F. X. Gibbons (Eds.), *Health, coping, and well-being: Perspectives from social comparison theory* (pp. 263–298). Mahwah, NJ: Erlbaum.

TENNEN, H., AFFLECK, G., ARMELI, S., & CARNEY, M. A. (2000). A daily process approach to coping: Linking theory, research, and practice. *American Psychologist*, 55, 626–636.

TENNEN, H., EBERHARDT, T. L., & AFFLECK, G. (1999). Depression research methodologies at the social-clinical interface: Still hazy after all these years. *Journal of Social and Clinical Psychology*, 18, 121–159.

TENNES, K., & KREYE, M. (1985). Children's adrenocortical responses to classroom activities and tests in elementary school. *Psychosomatic Medicine*, 47, 451–460.

TERI, L., HUGHES, J. P., & LARSON, E. B. (1990). Cognitive deterioration in Alzheimer's disease: Behavioral and health factors. *Journal of Gerontology: Psychological Sciences*, 45, P58–63.

TERRY, R. D., OAKLAND, M. J., & ANKENY, K. (1991). Factors associated with adoption of dietary behavior to reduce heart disease risk among males. *Journal of Nutrition Education*, 23, 154–160.

THELEN, M. H., FRY, R. A., FEHRENBACH, P. A., & FRAUTSCHI, N. M. (1979). Therapeutic videotape and film modeling: A review. *Psychological Bulletin*, 86, 701–720.

THEORELL, T., & RAHE, R. H. (1975). Life change events, ballistocardiography, and coronary death. *Journal of Human Stress*, 1, 18–24.

THOMAS, A., CHESS, S., & BIRCH, H. G. (1970, August). The origin of personality. *Scientific American*, pp. 102–109.

THOMAS, A. M., PETERSON, L., & GOLDSTEIN, D. (1997). Problem solving and diabetes regimen adherence by children and adolescents with IDDM in social pressure situations: A reflection of normal development. *Journal of Pediatric Psychology*, 22, 541–561.

THOMPSON, B., CORONADO, G., SNIPES, S. A., & PUSCHEL, K. (2003). Methodologic advances ans ongoing challenges in designing community-based health promotion programs. *Annual Review of Public Health*, 24, 315–340.

THOMPSON, J. (1984). Communicating with patients. In R. Fitzpatrick, J. Hinton, S. Newman, G. Scambler, & J. Thompson (Eds.), *The experience of illness* (pp. 87–108). London: Tavistock.

THOMPSON, J. K. (1986, April). Larger than life. *Psychology Today*, pp. 38–44.

THOMPSON, S. C. (1981). Will it hurt less if I can control it? A complex answer to a simple question. *Psychological Bulletin*, 90, 89–101.

THOMPSON, S. C., KENT, D. R., THOMAS, C., & VRUNGOS, S. (1999). Real and illusory control over exposure to HIV in college students and gay men. *Journal of Applied Social Psychology*, 29, 1128–1150.

THOMPSON, S. C., & KYLE, D. J. (2000). The role of perceived control in coping with the losses associated with chronic illness. In J. H. Harvey & E. D. Miller (Eds.), *Loss and trauma: General and close relationship perspectives*. Philadelphia: Bruner/Mazel.

THOMPSON, S. C., NANNI, C., & SCHWANKOVSKY, L. (1990). Patient-oriented interventions to improve communication in a medical office visit. *Health Psychology, 9,* 390–404.

THORESEN, C. E. (1984). Overview. In J. D. Matarazzo, S. M. Weiss, J. A. Herd, N. E. Miller, & S. M. Weiss (Eds.), *Behavioral health: A handbook of health enhancement and disease prevention* (pp. 297–307). New York: Wiley.

THORESEN, C. E., & PATTILLO, J. R. (1988). Exploring the Type A behavior pattern in children and adolescents. In B. K. Houston & C. R. Snyder (Eds.), *Type A behavior pattern: Research, theory, and intervention* (pp. 98–145). New York: Wiley.

THORNDIKE, A. N., RIGOTTI, N. A., STAFFORD, R. S., & SINGER, D. E. (1998). National patterns in the treatment of smokers by physicians. *Journal of the American Medical Association, 279,* 604–608.

THUN, M. J., DAY-LALLY, C. A., CALLE, E. E., FLANDERS, W. D., & HEATH, C. W. (1995). Excess mortality among cigarette smokers: Changes in a 20-year interval. *American Journal of Public Health, 85,* 1223–1230.

THUN, M. J., PETO, R., LOPEZ, A. D., MONACO, J. H., HENLEY, S. J., HEATH, C. W., et al. (1997). Alcohol consumption and mortality among middle-aged and elderly U.S. adults. *New England Journal of Medicine, 337,* 1705–1714.

TIMKO, C. (1987). Seeking medical care for a breast cancer symptom: Determinants of intentions to engage in prompt or delay behavior. *Health Psychology, 6,* 305–328.

TIMS, F. M., FLETCHER, B. W., & HUBBARD, R. L. (1991). Treatment outcomes for drug abuse clients. In R. W. Pickens, C. G. Leukefeld, & C. R. Schuster (Eds.), *Improving drug abuse treatment* (pp. 93–113). Rockville, MD: National Institute on Drug Abuse.

TINETTI, M. E., BAKER, D. I., MCAVAY, G., CLAUS, E. B., GARRETT, P., GOTTSCHALK, M., et al. (1994). A multifactorial intervention to reduce the risk of falling among elderly people living in the community. *New England Journal of Medicine, 331,* 821–827.

TODD, M., TENNEN, H., CARNEY, M. A., ARMELI, S., & AFFLECK, G. (2004). Do we know how we cope? Relating daily coping reports to global and time-limited retrospective assessments. *Journal of Personality and Social Psychology, 86,* 310–319.

TOMAKA, J. BLASCOVICH, J., KIBLER, J., & ERNST, J. M. (1997). Cognitive and physiological antecedents to threat and challenge appraisal. *Journal of Personality and Social Psychology, 73,* 63–72.

TONIGAN, J. S., MILLER, W. R., & SCHERMER, C. (2002). Atheists, agnostics and Alcoholics Anonymous. *Journal of Studies on Alcohol, 63,* 534–541.

TORRENS, P. R. (1985). Hospice care: What have we learned? *Annual Review of Public Health, 6,* 65–83.

TORRES, G., & HOROWITZ, J. M. (1999). Drugs of abuse and brain gene expression. *Psychosomatic Medicine, 61,* 630–650.

TORTORA, G. J., & GRABOWSKI, S. R. (2003). *Principles of anatomy and physiology* (10th ed.). New York: Wiley.

TOTMAN, R. (1982). Psychosomatic theories. In J. R. Eiser (Ed.), *Social psychology and behavioral medicine* (pp. 143–175). New York: Wiley.

TOVIAN, S. M. (1991). Integration of clinical psychology into adult and pediatric oncology programs. In J. J. Sweet, R. H. Rozensky, & S. M. Tovian (Eds.), *Handbook of clinical psychology in medical settings* (pp. 331–352). New York: Plenum.

TOVIAN, S. M. (2004). Health services and health care economics: The health psychology marketplace. *Health Psychology, 23,* 138–141.

TRABIN, T., RADER, C., & CUMMINGS, C. (1987). A comparison of pain management outcomes for disability compensation and non-compensation patients. *Psychology and Health, 1,* 341–351.

TRAPP, B. D., PETERSON, J., RANSOHOFF, R. M., RUDICK, R., MORK, S., & BO, L. (1998). Axonal transection in the lesions of multiple sclerosis. *New England Journal of Medicine, 338,* 278–285.

TREMBLAY, A., WOUTERS, E., WENKER, M., ST-PIERRE, S., BOUCHARD, C., & DESPRÉS, J.-P. (1995). Alcohol and a high-fat diet: A combination favoring overfeeding. *American Journal of Clinical Nutrition, 62,* 639–644.

TREMBLAY, G. C., & PETERSON, L. (1999). Prevention of childhood injury: Clinical and public health policy challenges. *Clinical Psychology Review, 19,* 415–434.

TROXEL, W. M., MATTHEWS, K. A., BROMBERGER, J. T., & SUTTON-TYRELL, K. (2003). Chronic stress burden, discrimination, and subclinical carotid artery disease in African American and Caucasian women. *Health Psychology, 22,* 300–309.

TRUMBULL, R., & APPLEY, M. H. (1986). A conceptual model for examination of stress dynamics. In M. H. Appley & R. Trumbull (Eds.), *Dynamics of stress: Physiological, psychological, and social perspectives* (pp. 21–45). New York: Plenum.

TSC (Trenton State College) (1992). *Alcohol & drug education program.* Trenton, NJ: Author.

TUCKER, J. S., FRIEDMAN, H. S., WINGARD, D. L., & SCHWARTZ, J. E. (1996). Marital history at midlife as a predictor of longevity: Alternative explanations to the protective effect of marriage. *Health Psychology, 15,* 94–101.

TUCKER, L. A., & CLEGG, A. G. (2002). Differences in health care costs and utilization among adults with selected lifestyle-related risk factors. *American Journal of Health Promotion, 16,* 225–233.

TUGADE, M. M., & FREDRICKSON, B. L. (2004). Resilient individuals use positive emotions to bounce back from negative emotional experiences. *Journal of Personality and Social Psychology, 86,* 320–333.

TUNKS, E., & BELLISSIMO, A. (1991). *Behavioral medicine: Concepts and procedures.* New York: Pergamon.

TURK, D. C. (1996). Biopsychosocial perspective on chronic pain. In R. J. Gatchel & D. C. Turk (Eds.), *Psychological approaches to pain management: A practitioner's handbook* (pp. 3–32). New York: Guilford.

TURK, D. C. (2001). Physiological and psychological bases of pain. In A. Baum, T. A. Revenson, & J. E. Singer (Eds.), *Handbook of health psychology* (pp. 117–137). Mahwah, NJ: Erlbaum.

TURK, D. C. (2002). Clinical effectiveness and cost-effectiveness of treatments for patients with chronic pain. *Clinical Journal of Pain, 18,* 355–365.

TURK, D. C., BRODY, M. C., & OKIFUJI, E. A. (1994). Physicians' attitudes and practices regarding the long-term prescribing of opioids for non-cancer pain. *Pain, 59,* 201–208.

TURK, D. C., & HOLZMAN, A. D. (1986). Commonalities among psychological approaches in the treatment of chronic pain: Specifying the meta-constructs. In A. D. Holzman & D. C. Turk (Eds.), *Pain management: A handbook of psychological treatment approaches* (pp. 257–267). New York: Pergamon.

TURK, D. C., LITT, M. D., SALOVEY, P., & WALKER J. (1985). Seeking urgent pediatric treatment: Factors contributing to frequency, delay, and appropriateness. *Health Psychology, 4,* 43–59.

TURK, D. C., & MEICHENBAUM, D. (1991). Adherence to self-care regimens: The patient's perspective. In J. J. Sweet, R. H. Rosensky, & S. M. Tovian (Eds.), *Handbook of clinical psychology in medical settings* (pp. 249–266). New York: Plenum.

TURK, D. C., MEICHENBAUM, D., & GENEST, M. (1983). *Pain and behavioral medicine: A cognitive-behavioral perspective.* New York: Guilford.

TURK, D. C., & RUDY, T. E. (1986). Assessment of cognitive factors in chronic pain: A worthwhile enterprise? *Journal of Consulting and Clinical Psychology, 54,* 760–768.

TURK, D. C., & SALOVEY, P. (1995). Cognitive-behavioral treatment of illness behavior. In P. M. Nicassio & T. W. Smith (Eds.), *Managing chronic illness: A biopsychosocial perspective* (pp. 245–284). Washington, DC: American Psychological Association.

TURK, D. C., & STACEY, B. R. (2000). Multidisciplinary pain centers in the treatment of chronic back pain. In J. W. Frymoyer, T. B. Ducker, N. M. Hadler, J. P. Kostuik, J. N. Weinstein, & T. S. Whitcloud (Eds.), *The adult spine: Principles and practice* (2nd ed.). Philadelphia: Lippincott Williams & Wilkins.

TURK, D. C., WACK, J. T., & KERNS, R. D. (1985). An empirical examination of the "pain-behavior" construct. *Journal of Behavioral Medicine, 8,* 119–130.

TURK-CHARLES, S., MEYEROWITZ, B. E., & GATZ, M. (1997). Age differences in information-seeking among cancer patients. *International Journal of Aging and Human Development, 45,* 85–98.

TURKKAN, J. S., McCAUL, M. E., & STITZER, M. L. (1989). Psychophysiological effects of alcohol-related stimuli: II. Enhancement with alcohol availability. *Alcoholism: Clinical and Experimental Research, 13,* 392–398.

TURNER, J. A. (1982). Comparison of group progressive-relaxation training and cognitive-behavioral group therapy for chronic low back pain. *Journal of Consulting and Clinical Psychology, 50,* 757–765.

TURNER, J. A., CLANCY, S., McQUADE, K. J., & CARDENAS, D. D. (1990). Effectiveness of behavioral therapy for chronic low back pain: A component analysis. *Journal of Consulting and Clinical Psychology, 58,* 573–579.

TURNER, J. A., CLANCY, S., & VITALIANO, P. P. (1987). Relationships of stress, appraisal and coping, to chronic low back pain. *Behavior Research and Therapy, 25,* 281–288.

TURNER, J. R., & HEWITT, J. K. (1992). Twin studies of cardiovascular response to psychological challenge: A review and suggested future directions. *Annals of Behavioral Medicine, 14,* 12–20.

TURNER, J. R., WARD, M. M., GELLMAN, M. D., JOHNSTON, D. W., LIGHT, K. C., & VAN DOORNEN, L. J. P. (1994). The relationship between laboratory and ambulatory cardiovascular activity: Current evidence and future directions. *Annals of Behavioral Medicine, 16,* 12–23.

TYLER, D. C. (1990). Patient-controlled analgesia in adolescents. *Journal of Adolescent Health Care, 11,* 154–158.

UCHINO, B. N., & GARVEY, T. S. (1997). The availability of social support reduces cardiovascular reactivity to acute psychological stress. *Journal of Behavioral Medicine, 20,* 15–27.

UCHINO, B. N., HOLT-LUNSTAD, J., UNO, D., BETANCOURT, R., & GARVEY, T. S.(1999). Social support and age-related differences in cardiovascular function: An examination of potential mediators. *Annals of Behavioral Medicine, 21,* 135–142.

UKESTAD, L. K., & WITTROCK, D. A. (1996). Pain perception and coping in female tension headache sufferers and headache-free controls. *Health Psychology, 15,* 65–68.

ULRICH, P. H., & LUTGENDORF, S. K. (2002). Journaling about stressful events: Effects of cognitive processing and emotional expression. *Annals of Behavioral Medicine, 24,* 244–250.

UNAIDS (Joint United Nations Programme on HIV/AIDS) (2004). *Questions & answers*. Retrieved (5–3–2004) from http://www.unaids.org.

URBAN, B. J., FRANCE, R. D., STEINBERGER, E. K., SCOTT, D. L., & MALTBIE, A. A. (1986). Long-term use of narcotic/antidepressant medication in the management of phantom limb pain. *Pain*, 24, 191–196.

USBC (United States Bureau of the Census) (1971). *Statistical Abstract of the United States: 1971.* (92nd ed.). Washington, DC: U.S. Government Printing Office.

USBC (United States Bureau of the Census) (1995). *Statistical Abstracts of the United States: 1994* (114th ed.). Washington, DC: U.S. Government Printing Office.

USBC (United States Bureau of the Census) (1999). *Statistical Abstracts of the United States: 1998* (118th ed.). Retrieved (2–28–2000) from http://www.census.gov.

USBC (United States Bureau of the Census) (2003). *Statistical Abstracts of the United States: 2003.* Retrieved (4–6–2004) from http://www.census.gov.

USDA (United States Department of Agriculture) (1999). *America's eating habits: Changes and consequences.* Retrieved (3–24–2000) from http://www.usda.gov.

USDHHS (United States Department of Health and Human Services) (1981). *Medicines and you* (Publication No. NIH 81-2140). Washington, DC: U.S. Government Printing Office.

USDHHS (United States Department of Health and Human Services) (1982). *Changes in mortality among the elderly: United States, 1940–78* (Publication No. PHS 82-1406). Washington, DC: U.S. Government Printing Office.

USDHHS (United States Department of Health and Human Services) (1985). *Charting the nation's health: Trends since 1960* (Publication No. PHS 85-1251). Washington, DC: U.S. Government Printing Office.

USDHHS (United States Department of Health and Human Services) (1986a). *Clinical opportunities for smoking intervention: A guide for the busy physician* (Publication No. NIH 86-2178). Washington, DC: U.S. Government Printing Office.

USDHHS (United States Department of Health and Human Services) (1986b). *The health consequences of involuntary smoking: A report of the Surgeon General* (Publication No. CDC 87-8398). Washington, DC: U.S. Government Printing Office.

USDHHS (United States Department of Health and Human Services) (1987). *Vital statistics of the United States, 1984: Life tables* (Publication No. PHS 87-1104). Washington, DC: U.S. Government Printing Office.

USDHHS (United States Department of Health and Human Services) (1989). *Reducing the health consequences of smoking: 25 years of progress. A report of the Surgeon General* (DHHS Publication No. CDC 89-8411). Rockville, MD: Office on Smoking and Health.

USDHHS (United States Department of Health and Human Services) (1990). *Alcohol and health* (Publication No. ADM 90-1656). Rockville, MD: National Institute on Alcohol Abuse and Alcoholism.

USDHHS (United States Department of Health and Human Services) (1994). *Acute low back pain problems in adults: Assessment and treatment.* (Quick reference guide for clinicians: Number 14). Washington, DC: U.S. Government Printing Office.

USDHHS (United States Department of Health and Human Services) (1995). *Health United States: 1994* (Publication No. PHS 95-1232). Washington, DC: U.S. Government Printing Office.

USDHHS (United States Department of Health and Human Services) (2004). *Healthy workforce: 2010.* Retrieved (7–16–2004) from http://www.prevent.org.

USDL (United States Department of Labor) (2004). *Occupational outlook handbook, 2004–05.* Retrieved (5–3–2004) from http://www.bls.gov.

VALDEZ, R., & WILLIAMSON, D. F. (2002). Prevalence and demographics of obesity. In C. G. Fairburn & K. D. Brownell (Eds.), *Eating disorders and obesity: A comprehensive handbook* (pp. 417–421). New York: Guilford.

VALOIS, R. F., ADAMS, K. G., & KAMMERMANN, S. K. (1996). One-year evaluation results from CableQuit: A community cable television smoking cessation pilot program. *Journal of Behavioral Medicine*, 19, 479–499.

VAN DULMEN, A. M., & BENSING, J. M. (2002). Health promoting effects of the physician–patient encounter. *Psychology, Health & Medicine*, 7, 289–300.

VAN ECK, M. M., & NICOLSON, N. A. (1994). Perceived stress and salivary cortisol in daily life. *Annals of Behavioral Medicine*, 16, 221–227.

VAN GRIENSVEN, G. J. P., DE VROOME, E. M. M., GOUDSMIT, J., & COUTINHO, R. E. (1989). Changes in sexual behaviour and the fall in incidence of HIV infection among homosexual men. *British Medical Journal*, 298, 218–221.

VAN TILBURG, M. A. L., MCCASKILL, C. C., LANE, J. D., EDWARDS, C. L., BETHEL, A., FEINGLOS, M. N. et al. (2001). Depressed mood is a factor in glycemic control in type 1 diabetes. *Psychosomatic Medicine*, 63, 551–555.

VAN'T SPIJKER, A., TRIJSBURG, R. W., & DUIVENVOORDEN, H. J. (1997). Psychological sequelae of cancer diagnosis: A meta-analytic review of 58 studies after 1980. *Psychosomatic Medicine*, 59, 280–293.

VARNI, J. W., & BABANI, L. (1986). Long-term adherence to health care regimens in pediatric chronic disorders. In N. A. Krasnegor, J. D. Arasteh, & M. F. Cataldo (Eds.), *Child health behavior: A behavioral pediatrics perspective* (pp. 502–520). New York: Wiley.

VARNI, J. W., JAY, S. M., MASEK, B. J., & THOMPSON, K. L. (1986). Cognitive-behavioral assessment and management of pediatric pain. In A. D. Holzman & D. C. Turk (Eds.), *Pain management: A handbook of psychological treatment approaches* (pp. 168–192). New York: Pergamon.

VARNI, J. W., & THOMPSON, K. L. (1986). Biobehavioral assessment and management of pediatric pain. In N. A. Krasnegor, J. D. Arasteh, & M. F. Cataldo (Eds.), *Child health behavior: A behavioral pediatrics perspective* (pp. 371–393). New York: Wiley.

VECCHIO, P. C. (1994). Attitudes to alternative medicine by rheumatology outpatient attenders. *Journal of Rheumatology, 21,* 147–147.

VEDHARA, K., COX, N. K. M., WILCOCK, G. K., PERKS, P., HUNT, M., ANDERSON, S., et al. (1999). Chronic stress in elderly carers of dementia patients and antibody response to influenza vaccination. *Lancet, 353,* 627–631.

VEIT, R., BRODY, S., & RAU, H. (1997). Four-year stability of cardiovascular reactivity to psychological stress. *Journal of Behavioral Medicine, 20,* 447–460.

VENER, A. M., & KRUPKA, L. R. (1990). AIDS knowledge and attitudes revisited (1987–1989). *American Biology Teacher, 52,* 461–466.

VENN, J. R., & SHORT, J. G. (1973). Vicarious classical conditioning of emotional responses in nursery school children. *Journal of Personality and Social Psychology, 28,* 249–255.

VERBRUGGE, L. M. (1985). Gender and health: An update on hypotheses and evidence. *Journal of Health and Social Behavior, 26,* 156–182.

VERTINSKY, P., & AUMAN, J. T. (1988). Elderly women's barriers to exercise, Part I: Perceived risks. *Health Values, 12*(4), 13–19.

VINCENT, J.-L. (2003). Nosocomial infections in adult intensive-care units. *Lancet, 361,* 2068–2077.

VINEY, L. L., WALKER, B. M., ROBERTSON, T., LILLEY, B., & EWAN, C. (1994). Dying in palliative care units and in hospital: A comparison of the quality of life of terminal cancer patients. *Journal of Consulting and Clinical Psychology, 62,* 157–164.

VINOKUR, A. D., THREATT, B. A., VINOKUR-KAPLAN, D., & SATARIANO, W. A. (1990). The process of recovery from breast cancer for younger and older patients: Changes during the first year. *Cancer, 65,* 1242–1254.

VITALIANO, P. P., RUSSO, J., BREEN, A. R., VITIELLO, M. V., & PRINZ, P. N. (1986). Functional decline in the early stages of Alzheimer's disease. *Journal of Psychology and Aging, 1,* 41–46.

VITALIANO, P. P., RUSSO, J., & NIAURA, R. (1995). Plasma lipids and their relationships with psychosocial factors in older adults. *Journal of Gerontology, 50B,* P18–24.

VITALIANO, P. P., SCANLAN, J. M., ZHANG, J., SAVAGE, M. V., HIRSCH, I. B., & SIEGLER, I. C. (2002). A path model of chronic stress, the metabolic syndrome, and coronary heart disease. *Psychosomatic Medicine, 64,* 418–435.

VITALIANO, P. P., ZHANG, J., & SCANLAN, J. M. (2003). Is caregiving hazardous to one's physical health? A meta-analysis. *Psychological Bulletin, 129,* 946–972.

VITOUSEK, K. B. (2002). Cognitive-behavioral therapy for anorexia nervosa. In C. G. Fairburn & K. D. Brownell (Eds.), *Eating disorders and obesity: A comprehensive handbook* (pp. 308–313). New York: Guilford.

VIVEKANANTHAN, D. P., PENN, M. S., SAPP, S. K., HSU, A., & TOPOL, E. J. (2003). Use of antioxidant vitamins for the prevention of cardiovascular disease: meta-analysis of randomized trials. *Lancet, 361,* 2017–2023.

VON KORFF, M., DWORKIN, S. F., & LE RESCHE, L. (1990). Graded chronic pain status: An epidemiologic evaluation. *Pain, 40,* 279–291.

WADDEN, T. A., & ANDERTON, C. H. (1982). The clinical use of hypnosis. *Psychological Bulletin, 91,* 215–243.

WADDEN, T. A., & BROWNELL, K. D. (1984). The development and modification of dietary practices in individuals, groups, and large populations. In J. D. Matarazzo, S. M. Weiss, J. A. Herd, N. E. Miller, & S. M. Weiss (Eds.), *Behavioral health: A handbook of health enhancement and disease prevention* (pp. 608–631). New York: Wiley.

WADDEN, T. A., BROWNELL, K. D., & FOSTER, G. D. (2002). Obesity: Responding to the global epidemic. *Journal of Consulting and Clinical Psychology, 70,* 510–525.

WAITZKIN, H., & STOECKLE, J. D. (1976). Information control and the micropolitics of health care: Summary of an ongoing research project. *Social Science and Medicine, 10,* 263–276.

WALLACE, L. M. (1986). Communication variables in the design of pre-surgical preparatory information. *British Journal of Clinical Psychology, 25,* 111–118.

WALLER, J. A. (1987). Injury: Conceptual shifts and preventive implications. *Annual Review of Public Health, 8,* 21–49.

WALLERSTEIN, J. S. (1983). Children of divorce: Stress and developmental tasks. In N. Garmezy & M. Rutter (Eds.), *Stress, coping, and development in children* (pp. 265–302). New York: McGraw-Hill.

WALLSTON, B. S., ALAGNA, S. W., DEVELLIS, B. M., & DEVELLIS, R. F. (1983). Social support and physical illness. *Health Psychology, 2,* 367–391.

WALLSTON, K. A. (1993). Health psychology in the USA. In S. Maes, H. Leventhal, & M. Johnston (Eds.), *International review of health psychology* (Vol. 2, pp. 215–228). Chichester, UK: Wiley.

WALLSTON, K. A. (2001). Conceptualization and operationalization of perceived control. In A. Baum, T. A.

Revenson, & J. E. Singer (Eds.), *Handbook of health psychology* (pp. 49–58). Mahwah, NJ: Erlbaum.

WALLSTON, K. A., WALLSTON, B. S., & DeVELLIS, R. (1978). Development of the Multidimensional Health Locus of Control (MHLC) Scales. *Health Education Monographs,* 6, 161–170.

WALSH, J. C., LYNCH, M., MURPHY, A. W., & DALY, K. (2004). Factors influencing the decision to seek treatment for symptoms of myocardial infarction: An evaluation of the self-regulatory model of illness behavior. *Journal of Psychosomatic Research,* 56, 67–73.

WALTER, H. J., HOFMAN, A., CONNELLY, P. A., BARRETT, L. T., & KOST, K. L. (1985). Primary prevention of chronic disease in children: Changes in risk factors after one year of intervention. *American Journal of Epidemiology,* 122, 772–781.

WANG, F., SCHULTZ, A. B., MUSICH, S., McDONALD, T., HIRSCHLAND, D., & EDINGTON, D. W. (2003). The relationship between National Heart, Lung, and Blood Institute wtight guidelines and concurrent medical costs in a manufacturing population. *American Journal of Health Promotion,* 17, 183–189.

WANG, P. H., LAU, J. & CHALMERS, T. C. (1993). Meta-analysis of effects of intensive blood-glucose control on late complications of type I diabetes. *Lancet,* 341, 1306–1309.

WARD, S. E., GOLDBERG, N., MILLER-MCCAULRY, V., MUELLER, C., NOLAN, A., PAWLIK-PLANK, D., et al. (1993). Patient-related barriers to management of cancer pain. *Pain,* 52, 319–324.

WARDLE, F. J., COLLINS, W., PERNET, A. L., WHITEHEAD, M. I., BOURNE, T. H., & CAMPBELL, S. (1993). Psychological impact of screening for familial ovarian cancer. *Journal of the National Cancer Institute,* 85, 653–657.

WARDLE, J., HAASE, A. M., STEPTOE, A., NILLAPUN, M., JONWUTIWES, K., & BELLISLE, F. (2004). Gender differences in food choice: The contribution of health beliefs and dieting. *Annals of Behavioral Medicine,* 27, 107–116.

WARGA, C. (1987, August). Pain's gatekeeper. *Psychology Today,* pp. 50–56.

WARREN, J. M., HENRY, C. J. K., & SIMONITE, V. (2003). Low glycemic index breakfasts and reduced food intake in preadolescent children. *Pediatrics,* 112, e414–e419.

WARSHAW, R. (1992, March 8). Fat chance. *Philadelphia Inquirer Magazine.* pp. 26–31.

WATSON, M., HAVILAND, J. S., GREER, S., DAVIDSON, J., & BLISS, J. M. (1999). Influence of psychological response on survival in breast cancer: A population-based cohort study. *Lancet,* 354, 1331–1336.

WATSON, M., & RAMIREZ, A. (1991). Psychological factors in cancer prognosis. In C. L. Cooper & M. Watson

(Eds.), *Cancer and stress: Psychological, biological, and coping studies* (pp. 47–72). New York: Wiley.

WEIDNER, G., KOHLMANN, C.-W., DOTZAUER, E., & BURNS, L. R. (1996). The effect of academic stress on health behaviors in young adults. *Anxiety, Stress, and Coping,* 9, 123–133.

WEIDNER, G., & MESSINA, C. R. (1998). Cardiovascular reactivity to mental stress. In K. Orth-Gomer, M. Chesney, & N. K. Wegner (Ed.), *Women, stress, and heart disease* (pp. 219–236). Mahwah, NJ: Erlbaum.

WEIDNER, G., & MUELLER, H. (1999). Emotions and heart disease. In M. B. Goldman & M. C. Hatch (Eds.), *Women and health* (pp. 789–797). San Diego: Academic Press.

WEINHARDT, L. S., CAREY, M. P., JOHNSON, B. T., & BICKHAM, N. L. (1999). Effects of HIV counseling and testing on sexual risk behavior: Meta-analytic review of published research, 1985–1997. *American Journal of Public Health,* 89, 1397–1405.

WEINMAN, J. (1990). Health psychology: Progress, perspectives and prospects. In P. Bennett, J. Weinman, & P. Spurgeon (Eds.), *Current developments in health psychology* (pp. 9–33). Chur, Switzerland: Harwood.

WEINSTEIN, N. D. (1982). Unrealistic optimism about susceptibility to health problems. *Journal of Behavioral Medicine,* 5, 441–460.

WEINSTEIN, N. D. (1987). Unrealistic optimism about susceptibility to health problems: Conclusions from a community-wide sample. *Journal of Behavioral Medicine,* 10, 481–500.

WEINSTEIN, N. D. (1988). The precaution adoption process. *Health Psychology,* 7, 355–386.

WEINSTEIN, N. D. (2000). Perceived probability, perceived severity, and health-protective behavior. *Health Psychology,* 19, 65–74.

WEINSTEIN, N. D., & KLEIN, W. M. (1995). Resistance of personal risk perceptions to debiasing interventions. *Health Psychology,* 14, 132–140.

WEIR, R., BROWNE, G., ROBERTS, J., TUNKS, E., & GAFNI, A. (1994). The Meaning of Illness Questionnaire: Further evidence for its reliability and validity. *Pain,* 58, 377–386.

WEISENBERG, M. (1977). Pain and pain control. *Psychological Bulletin,* 84, 1008–1044.

WEISS, S. M. (1984). Health hazard/health risk appraisals. In J. D. Matarazzo, S. M. Weiss, J. A. Herd, N. E. Miller, & S. M. Weiss (Eds.), *Behavioral health: A handbook of health enhancement and disease prevention* (pp. 275–294). New York: Wiley.

WERNER, E. E., & SMITH, R. S. (1982). *Vulnerable but invincible: A study of resilient children.* New York: McGraw-Hill.

WERNICK, R. I. (1983). Stress inoculation in the management of clinical pain: Applications to burn pain.

In D. Meichenbaum & M. E. Jaremko (Eds.), *Stress reduction and prevention* (pp. 191–217). New York: Plenum.

WEST, S. G., LIGHT, K. C., HINDERLITER, A. L., STANWYCK, C. L., BRAGDON, E. E., & BROWNLEY, K. A. (1999). Potassium supplementation induces beneficial cardiovascular changes during rest and stress in salt sensitive individuals. *Health Psychology, 18*, 229–240.

WESTERDAHL, J., OLSSON, H., MÅSBÄCK, A., INGVAR, C., JONSSON, N., BRANDT, L., et al. (1994). Use of sunbeds or sunlamps and malignant melanoma in Southern Sweden. *American Journal of Epidemiology, 140*, 691–699.

WETTER, D. W., FIORE, M. C., BAKER, T. B., & YOUNG, T. B. (1995). Tobacco withdrawal and nicotine replacement influence objective measures of sleep. *Journal of Consulting and Clinical Psychology, 63*, 658–667.

WHITAKER, R. C., WRIGHT, J. A., PEPE, M. S., SEIDEL, K. D., & DIETZ, W. H. (1997). Predicting obesity in young adulthood from childhood and parental obesity. *New England Journal of Medicine, 337*, 869–873.

WHITE, A. M., KRAUS, C. L., McCRACKEN, L. A., & SWARTZWELDER, H. S. (2003). Do college students drink more than they think? Use of a free-pour paradigm to determine how college students define standard drinks. *Alcoholism: Clinical and Experimental Research, 27*, 1750–1756.

WHITEHEAD, W. E., BUSCH, C. M., HELLER, B. R., & COSTA, P. T. (1986). Social learning influences on menstrual symptoms and illness behavior. *Health Psychology, 5*, 13–23.

WHITFIELD, K. E., WEIDNER, G., CLARK, F., & ANDERSON, N. B. (2002). Sociodemographic diversity and behavioral medicine. *Journal of Consulting and Clinical Psychology, 70*, 463–481.

WHO (World Health Organization) (1999). *World health report*. Retrieved (2–28–2000) from http://www.who.org.

WHO (World Health Organization) (2003). *Tobacco control country profiles* (2nd ed.). Retrieved (4–6–2004) from http://www.who.org.

WHO (World Health Organization) (2004). *World health report*. Retrieved (7–13–2004) from http://www.who.org.

WHO/Europe (World Health Organization Regional Office for Europe) (2004). *Health for All (HFA) database: Alcohol and drugs*. Retrieved (4–2–2004) from http://www.euro.who.int/alcoholdrugs.

WIDEMAN, M. V., & SINGER, J. E. (1984). The role of psychological mechanisms in preparation for childbirth. *American Psychologist, 39*, 1357–1371.

WIEBE, D. J., & McCALLUM, D. M. (1986). Health practices and hardiness as mediators in the stress-illness relationship. *Health Psychology, 5*, 425–438.

WIELGOSZ, A. T., FLETCHER, R. H., McCANTS, C. B., McKINNIS, R. A., HANEY, T. L., & WILLIAMS, R. B. (1984). Unimproved chest pain in patients with minimal or no coronary disease: A behavioral phenomenon. *American Heart Journal, 108*, 67–72.

WIENS, A. N., & MENUSTIK, C. E. (1983). Treatment outcome and patient characteristics in an aversion therapy program for alcoholism. *American Psychologist, 38*, 1089–1096.

WILCOX, S., & STORANDT, M. (1996). Relations among age, exercise, and psychological variables in a community sample of women. *Health Psychology, 15*, 110–113.

WILCOX, V. L., KASL, S. V., & BERKMAN, L. F. (1994). Social support and physical disability in older people after hospitalization: A prospective study. *Health Psychology, 13*, 170–179.

WILKINSON, G. (1987). The influence of psychiatric, psychological and social factors on the control of insulin-dependent diabetes mellitus. *Journal of Psychosomatic Research, 31*, 277–286.

WILLIAMS, C. J. (1990). *Cancer biology and management: An introduction*. New York: Wiley.

WILLIAMS, D. A. (1996). Acute pain management. In R. J. Gatchel & D. C. Turk (Eds.), *Psychological approaches to pain management: a practitioner's handbook* (pp. 55–77). New York: Guilford.

WILLIAMS, D. A., & KEEFE, F. J. (1991). Pain beliefs and the use of cognitive-behavioral coping strategies. *Pain, 46*, 185–190.

WILLIAMS, D. R. (2003). The health of men: Structured inequalities and opportunities. *American Journal of Public Health, 93*, 724–731.

WILLIAMS, D. R., & RUCKER, T. (1996). Socioeconomic status and the health of racial minority populations. In P. M. Kato & T. Mann (Eds.), *Handbook of diversity issues in health psychology* (pp. 407–423). New York: Plenum.

WILLIAMS, K. A., KOLAR, M. M., REGER, B. E., & PEARSON, J. C. (2001). Evaluation of a wellness-based mindfulness stress reduction intervention: A controlled trial. *American Journal of Health Promotion, 15*, 422–432.

WILLIAMS, P. G., WIEBE, D. J., & SMITH, T. W. (1992). Coping processes as mediators of the relationship between hardiness and health. *Journal of Behavioral Medicine, 15*, 237–255.

WILLIAMS, R. B. (2001). Hostility (and other psychosocial risk factors): Effects on health and the potential for successful behavioral approaches to prevention and treatment. In A. Baum, T. A. Revenson, & J. E. Singer (Eds.), *Handbook of health psychology* (pp. 661–668). Mahwah, NJ: Erlbaum.

WILLIAMS, R. B., & BAREFOOT, J. C. (1988). Coronary-prone behavior: The emerging role of the hostility complex. In B. K. Houston & C. R. Snyder (Eds.), *Type A behavior pattern: Research, theory, and intervention* (pp. 189–211). New York: Wiley.

WILLIAMS, R. B., MARCHUK, D. A., GADDE, K. M., BAREFOOT, J. C., GRINCHNIK, K. et al. (2001). Central nervous system serotonin function and cardiovascular resonses. *Psychosomatic Medicine, 63,* 300–305.

WILLIAMS, R. B., SUAREZ, E. C., KUHN, C. M., ZIMMERMAN, E. A., & SCHANBERG, S. M. (1991). Biobehavioral basis of coronary-prone behavior in middle-aged men. Part I: Evidence for chronic SNS activation in Type As. *Psychosomatic Medicine, 53,* 517–527.

WILLIAMS, R. J., MCDERMITT, D. R., BERTRAND, L. D., & DAVIS, R. M. (2003). Parental awareness of adolescent substance use. *Addictive Behaviors, 28,* 803–809.

WILLIAMSON, D. A., CUBIC, B. A., & FULLER, R. D. (1992). Eating disorders. In S. E. Turner, K. S., Calhoun, & H. E. Adams (Eds.), *Handbook of clinical behavior therapy* (2nd ed., pp. 355–372). New York: Wiley.

WILLIAMSON, D. F., MADANS, J., ANDA, R. F., KLEINMAN, J. C., GIOVINO, G. A., & BYERS, T. (1991). Smoking cessation and severity of weight gain in a national cohort. *New England Journal of Medicine, 324,* 739–745.

WILLIAMSON, G. M. (2000). Extending the activity restriction model of depressed affect: Evidence from a sample of breast cancer patients. *Health Psychology, 19,* 339–347.

WILLICH, S. N., LÖWEL, H., LEWIS, M., HÖRMANN, A., ARNTZ, H.-R., & KEIL, U. (1994). Weekly variation of acute myocardial infarction: Increased Monday risk in the working population. *Circulation, 90,* 87–93.

WILLIS, L., THOMAS, P., GARRY, P. J., & GOODWIN, J. S. (1987). A prospective study of response to stressful life events in initially healthy elders. *Journal of Gerontology, 42,* 627–630.

WILLS, T. A. (1986). Stress and coping in early adolescence: Relationships to substance use in urban school samples. *Health Psychology, 5,* 503–529.

WILLS, T. A., & FEGAN, M. F. (2001). Social networks and social support. In A. Baum, T. A. Revenson, & J. E. Singer (Eds.), *Handbook of health psychology* (pp. 209–234). Mahwah, NJ: Erlbaum.

WILLS, T. A., SANDY, J. M., & YEAGER, A. M. (2002). Stress and smoking in adolescence: A test of directional hypotheses. *Health Psychology, 21,* 122–130.

WILSON, D. K., HOLMES, S. D., ARHEART, K., & ALPERT, B. S. (1995). Cardiovascular reactivity in black and white siblings versus matched controls. *Annals of Behavioral Medicine, 17,* 207–212.

WILSON, D. K., KLIEWER, W., BAYER, L., JONES, D., WELLEFORD, A., HEINEY, M., et al. (1999). The influence of gender and emotional versus instrumental support on cardiovascular reactivity in African-American adolescents. *Annals of Behavioral Medicine, 21,* 235–243.

WILSON, D. P., & ENDRES, R. K. (1986). Compliance with blood glucose monitoring in children with type 1 diabetes mellitus. *Behavioral Pediatrics, 108,* 1022–1024.

WILSON, G. T., LOEB, K. L., WALSH, B. T., LABOUVIE, E., PETKOVA, E., LIU, X., et al. (1999). Psychological versus pharmacological treatments for bulimia nervosa: Predictors and processes of change. *Journal of Consulting and Clinical Psychology, 67,* 451–459.

WILSON, I. B., & CLEARY, P. D. (1995). Linking clinical variables with health-related quality of life. *Journal of the American Medical Association, 273,* 59–65.

WILSON, W., ARY, D. V., BIGLAN, A., GLASGOW, R. E., TOOBERT, D. J., & CAMPBELL, D. R. (1986). Psychosocial predictors of self-care behaviors (compliance) and glycemic control in non-insulin-dependent diabetes mellitus. *Diabetes Care, 9,* 614–622.

WINCZE, J. P. (1977). Sexual deviance and dysfunction. In D. C. Rimm & J. W. Somervill (Eds.), *Abnormal psychology.* New York: Academic Press.

WINDSOR, R. A., LOWE, J. B., PERKINS, L. L., SMITH-YODER, D., ARTZ, L., CRAWFORD, M. et al. (1993). Health education for pregnant smokers: Its behavioral impact and cost benefit. *American Journal of Public Health, 83,* 201–206.

WINETT, R. A., KING, A. C., & ALTMAN, D. G. (1989). *Health psychology and public health: An integrative approach.* New York: Pergamon.

WING, R. R., EPSTEIN, L. H., NOWALK, M. P., & LAMPARSKI, D. M. (1986). Behavioral self-regulation in the treatment of patients with diabetes mellitus. *Psychological Bulletin, 99,* 78–89.

WING, R. R., & JEFFERY, R. W. (1999). Benefits of recruiting participants with friends and increasing social support for weight loss and maintenance. *Journal of Consulting and Clinical Psychology, 67,* 132–138.

WING, R. R., & POLLEY, B. A. (2001). Obesity. In A. Baum, T. A. Revenson, & J. E. Singer (Eds.), *Handbook of health psychology* (pp. 263–279). Mahwah, NJ: Erlbaum.

WINIKOFF, B. (1983). Nutritional patterns, social choices, and health. In D. Mechanic (Ed.), *Handbook of health, health care, and the health professions* (pp. 81–98). New York: Free Press.

WINKLEBY, M. A., FLORA, J. A., & KRAEMER, H. C. (1994). A community-based heart disease intervention: Predictors of change. *American Journal of Public Health, 84,* 767–772.

WINTERS, R. (1985). Behavioral approaches to pain. In N. Schneiderman & J. T. Tapp (Eds.), *Behavioral medicine: The biopsychosocial approach* (pp. 565–587). Hillsdale, NJ: Erlbaum.

WITKIEWITZ, K., & MARLATT, G. A. (2004). Relapse prevention for alcohol and drug problems: That was Zen, this is Tao. *American Psychologist, 59,* 224–235.

WITRYOL, S. L. (1971). Incentives and learning in children. In H. W. Reese (Ed.), *Advances in child development and behavior* (Vol. 6, pp. 2–61). New York: Academic Press.

WITTROCK, D. A., & MYERS, T. C. (1998). The comparison of individuals with recurrent tension-type headache and headache-free controls in physiological response, appraisal, and coping with stressors: A review of the literature. *Annals of Behavioral Medicine*, 20, 118–134.

WOLF, S., & WOLFF, H. G. (1947). *Human gastric function* (2nd ed.). New York: Oxford University Press.

WOLPE, J. (1958). *Psychotherapy by reciprocal inhibition.* Stanford, CA: Stanford University Press.

WOLPE, J. (1973). *The practice of behavior therapy* (2nd ed.). New York: Pergamon.

WOOD, M. D., VINSON, D. C., & SHER, K. J. (2001). Alcohol use and misuse. In A. Baum, T. A. Revenson, & J. E. Singer (Eds.), *Handbook of health psychology* (pp. 281–318). Mahwah, NJ: Erlbaum.

WOODS, A. M., & BIRREN, J. E. (1984). Late adulthood and aging. In J. D. Matarazzo, S. M. Weiss, J. A. Herd, N. E. Miller, & S. M. Weiss (Eds.), *Behavioral health: A handbook of health enhancement and disease prevention* (pp. 91–100). New York: Wiley.

WOODS, P. J., MORGAN, B. T., DAY, B. W., JEFFERSON, T., & HARRIS, C. (1984). Findings on a relationship between Type A behavior and headaches. *Journal of Behavioral Medicine*, 7, 277–286.

WOODWARD, N. J., & WALLSTON, B. S. (1987). Age and health care beliefs: Self-efficacy as a mediator of low desire for control. *Psychology and Aging*, 2, 3–8.

WOOSTER, R., BIGNELL, G., LANCASTER, J., SWIFT, S., SEAL, S. MANGION, J., et al. (1995). Identification of the breast cancer susceptibility gene BRCA2. *Nature*, 378, 789–792.

WORTMAN, C. B. (1975). Some determinants of perceived control. *Journal of Personality and Social Psychology*, 31, 282–294.

WORTMAN, C. B., & DUNKEL-SCHETTER, C. (1979). Interpersonal relationships and cancer: A theoretical analysis. *Journal of Social Issues*, 35, 120–155.

WORTMAN, C. B., & DUNKEL-SCHETTER, C. (1987). Conceptual and methodological issues in the study of social support. In A. Baum & J. E. Singer (Eds.), *Handbook of psychology and health* (Vol. 5, pp. 63–108). Hillsdale, NJ: Erlbaum.

WRIGHT, L., & FRIEDMAN, A. G. (1991). Challenge of the future: Psychologists in medical settings. In J. J. Sweet, R. H. Rozensky, & S. M. Tovian (Eds.), *Handbook of clinical psychology in medical settings* (pp. 603–614). New York: Plenum.

WULFERT, E., WAN, C. K., & BACKUS, C. A. (1996). Gay men's safer sex behavior: An integration of three models. *Journal of Behavioral Medicine*, 19, 345–366.

WURTELE, S. K., & MADDUX, J. E. (1987). Relative contributions of protection motivation theory components in predicting exercise intentions and behavior. *Health Psychology*, 6, 453–466.

YALI, A. M., & REVENSON, T. A. (2004). How changes in population demographics will impact health psychology: Incorporating a broader notion of cultural competence into the field. *Health Psychology*, 23, 147–155.

YANOVSKI, J. A., YANOVSKI, S. Z., SOVIK, K. N., NGUYEN, T. T., O'NEIL, P. M., & SEBRING, N. G. (2000). A prospective study of holiday weight gain. *New England Journal of Medicine*, 342, 861–867.

YEATON, W. H., SMITH, D., & ROGERS, K. (1990). Evaluating understanding of popular press reports of health research. *Health Education Quarterly*, 72, 223–234.

YEE, B. W. K., CASTRO, F. G., HAMMOND, W. R., JOHN, R., WYATT, G. E., & YUNG, B. R. (1995). Panel IV: Risk-taking and abusive behaviors among ethnic minorities. *Health Psychology*, 14, 622–631.

YOUNG, K., & ZANE, N. (1995). Ethnocultural influences in evaluation and management. In P. M. Nicassio & T. W. Smith (Eds.), *Managing chronic illness: A biopsychosocial perspective* (pp. 163–206). Washington, DC: American Psychological Association.

YUSUF, S., HAWKEN, S., ÔUNPUU, S., DANS, R., AVEZUM, A., LANAS, F. et al. (2004). Effect of potentially modifiable risk factors associated with myocardial infarction in 52 countries (the INTERHEART Study): A case-control study. *Lancet*, 364, 937–952.

ZARSKI, J. J. (1984). Hassles and health: A replication. *Health Psychology*, 3, 243–251.

ZAUTRA, A. J., BURLESON, M. H., SMITH, C. A., BLALOCK, S. J., WALLSTON, K. A., DEVELLIS, R. F., et al. (1995). Arthritis and perceptions of quality of life: An examination of positive and negative affect in rheumatoid arthritis patients. *Health Psychology*, 14, 399–408.

ZAUTRA, A. J., SMITH, B., AFFLECK, G., & TENNEN, H. (2001). Examinations of chronic pain and affect relationships: Applications of a dynamic model of affect. *Journal of Consulting and Clinical Psychology*, 69, 786–795.

ZELTZER, L. K., BUSH, J. P., CHEN, E., & RIVERAL, A. (1997). A psychobiologic approach to pediatric pain: Part II: Prevention and treatment. *Current Problems in Pediatrics*, 27, 264–284.

ZHU, S.-H., STRECH, V., BALABANIS, M., ROSBROOK, B., SADLER, G., & PIERCE, J. P. (1996). Telephone counseling for smoking cessation: Effects of single-session and multiple-session interventions. *Journal of Consulting and Clinical Psychology*, 64, 202–211.

ZIMBARDO, P. G. (1970). The human choice: Individuation, reason, and order versus deindividuation, impulse, and chaos. In W. J. Arnold & D. Levine (Eds.), *Nebraska symposium on motivation*, 1969 (Vol. 17, pp. 237–307). Lincoln, NE: University of Nebraska Press.

ZIMMER, J. G., JUNCKER, A. G., & McCUSKER, J. (1985). A randomized controlled study of a home health care team. *American Journal of Public Health, 75,* 134–141.

ZINMAN, B. (1984). Diabetes mellitus and exercise. *Behavioral Medicine Update, 6*(1), 22–25.

ZISOOK, S., PETERKIN, J. J., SHUCHTER, S. R., & BARDONE, A. (1995). Death, dying, and bereavement. In P. M. Nicassio & T. M. Smith (Eds.), *Managing chronic illness: A biopsychosocial perspective* (pp. 351–390). Washington, DC: American Psychological Association.

ZOLA, I. K. (1973). Pathways to the doctor—From person to patient. *Social Science and Medicine, 7,* 677–689.

PHOTO CREDITS

CHAPTER 1

Page 3: Corbis-Bettmann. Page 5: John Verano, National Museum of Natural History. courtesy Smithsonian Institution. Page 7: From R. Melzack and P. Wall (1965). "Pain mechanisms: A new theory." *Science*, 150: 971–979. Page 14: Gilles Mingasson/Getty Images News and Sport Services. Page 15: Reprinted courtesy of Bunny Hoest.

CHAPTER 2

Page 45: Susumu Nishinaga/Photo Researchers.

CHAPTER 3

Page 62: Mauro Fermariello/Photo Researchers. Page 64: Anne W. Krause/Corbis Images. Page 74: David H. Wells/Corbis Images. Page 76: Jim Mahoney/The Image Works. Page 78: Richard T. Nowitz/Photo Researchers. Page 81: Reprinted courtesy of Bunny Hoest.

CHAPTER 4

Page 87: Jose Luis Pelaez/Corbis Stock Market. Page 95: Pat Benic/Corbis-Bettmann. Page 106: Reprinted by permission of United Feature Syndicate, Inc. Page 109: From F. Andrasik, D. D. Blake, & M. S. McCarran (1986).

CHAPTER 5

Page 119: Reprinted courtesy of Bunny Hoest. Page 123: Rob&Sas/Corbis Images. Page 125: © AP/Wide World Photos. Page 130: Bob Daemmrich/The Image Works.

CHAPTER 6

Page 141: The Image Bank/Getty Images. Page 145: Reprinted courtesy of Bunny Hoest. Page 156: Paul Campbell/Taxi/Getty Images. Page 164: ©AP/Wide World Photos.

CHAPTER 7

Page 181: Courtesy The American Cancer Society, Inc. All rights reserved. Page 182: Corbis-Bettmann Images. Page 184: Larry Gatz/The Image Bank/Getty Images. Page 190: Joseph Sohm; ChromoSohm Inc./Corbis Images.

CHAPTER 8

Page 204: Don Mason/Corbis Images. Page 207: Reprinted by permission of Tribune Media Services. Page 212: T. R. Tharp/Corbis Images. Page 214: PhotoDisc, Inc./Getty Images. Page 217: Stephen Wilkes/The Image Bank/Getty Images. Page 223: Reprinted courtesy of Bunny Hoest. Page 224: PhotoEdit. Page 229: Ariel Skelly/Corbis Images. Page 230: Reprinted courtesy of Bunny Hoest. Page 233: Kevin Mackintosh/Stone/Getty Images.

CHAPTER 9

Page 238: Bruce Ayres/Stone/Getty Images. Page 244: Corbis Images. Page 248: © 1991 Reprinted courtesy of Bunny Hoest. Page 251: Reprinted courtesy of Bunny Hoest. Page 253: LWA-Stephen Welstead/Corbis Images. Page 257: FRANK & ERNEST reprinted by permission of United Feature Syndicate, Inc.

CHAPTER 10

Page 267: Culver Pictures, Inc. Page 270: PhotoDisc, Inc./Getty Images. Page 275 (top): PhotoDisc, Inc./Getty Images. Page 275 (bottom): Reprinted courtesy of Bunny Hoest. Page 284: Corbis Images.

CHAPTER 11

Page 293: Reproduced by permission of Johnny Hart and Creators Syndicate, Inc. Page 297: Corbis-Bettmann. Page 307: Age Fotostock America, Inc. Page 314: Robert Brenner/ PhotoEdit. Page 316: Alan Delaney/Stone/Getty Images.

CHAPTER 12

Page 322: Courtesy The New York Historical Society. Page 337: Simon Bottomley/Taxi/Getty Images. Page 338: AJPhoto/Photo Researchers.

CHAPTER 13

Page 347: Rob Lewine/Corbis Images. Page 354: Richard Ellis/The Image Works. Page 363: Barros & Barros/The Image Bank/Getty Images.

CHAPTER 14

Page 378: AJ Photos/Hop American/Photo Researchers. Page 388: Edwige/Photo Researchers. Page 390: © Houston Chronicle. Page 395: Geoff Manasse/IPN/ Aurora & Quanta Productions. Page 402: Al Campanie/ The Image Works.

SUBJECT INDEX

A

A-delta fibers, 296, 301
AA, 197
Abdominal pain, 45
Absorption, 44
Abstinence violation effect, 163, 200
Accidental injuries, 231–232
Acetaminophen, 323
ACTH, 41
Active coping, 330
Acupuncture, 21, 337
Acute clinical pain, 320
Acute pain, 294
Adaptation, 348
A-delta fibers, 296, 301
Addiction, 172. See also Substance abuse
Adherence, 256–264, 367
Admission privileges, 269
Adolescence, 155, 157. See also Age
Adoption studies, 28
Adrenal glands, 41
Adrenalin, 41
Adulthood, 157
Advance directives, 400
Advil, 323
Aerobic exercise, 225
Afferent, 37
Afferent neurons, 38
African Americans. See Cultural differences
Age. See also Children
    adherence to medical advice, 259
    cancer, 386
    cholesterol, 207
    coping, 122
    drug use, 189
    exercise, 157, 208
    hardiness, 98–99
    health services, 244
    heart disease, 375
    HIV/AIDS, 393
    motor vehicle fatalities, 232
    personal control, 97
    reaction to death, 74
    smoking, 175
    stroke, 381

type A behavior, 100
    weight control, 211
AIDS, 55, 191–192, 393–396, 403
AIDS awareness, 166
AIDS-related complex (ARC), 394
Alarm reaction, 67
Alateen, 197
Alcohol use and abuse, 181–187. See also Substance abuse
    assess yourself, 183, 185
    binge drinking, 184, 185
    brain damage, 187
    drunk driving, 187
    Europe, 183
    health, 186–187
    historical overview, 182
    problem drinking, 184–185
    sociocultural differences, 183–184
    why such abuse?, 185–186
Alcoholics, 184–185
Alcoholics anonymous (AA), 197
All-Anon, 197
Allergens, 54
Allergies, 54
Allostatic load, 68, 103
Alternative medical systems, 249
Alveoli, 47
Alzheimer's disease, 363–365
American Psychosomatic Society, 10
Amino acids, 44, 205
Amish, 125
Amphetamines, 188
Anabolic steroids, 227–228
Analgesia, 302
Analgesics, 323
Anatomy. See Body systems
Anemia, 52
Aneurysm, 53
Anger, 70
Anger/hostility, 99, 102
Anger-management self-statements, 136
Angina pectoris, 53, 375
Animal magnetism, 135
Anorexia nervosa, 222–224
Antecedents, 147

Anthropology, 18
Anti-inflammatories, 351
Antibodies, 56
Antibody-mediated immunity, 56
Anticipatory nausea, 388–389
Anticonvulsant drugs, 352
Antidepressants, 224, 323
Antigens, 53–54
Antioxidants, 205
Antiretroviral agents, 394
Anxiety, 70
Aorta, 43, 49
Aphasia, 382
Application and follow-through, 133
Appraisal delay, 248
Approach/approach conflict, 72
Approach/avoidance conflict, 72
Arbitrary inference, 132
ARC, 394
Arousal, 78–79
Arrhythmia, 104
Arteries, 49
Arteriosclerosis, 52
Arthritis, 360–363
Arthritis Self-Management Program, 367
Asbestos, 233
Aspirin, 44, 323, 362
Assess yourself
    AIDS awareness, 166
    alcohol abuse, 185
    alcohol awareness, 166
    calories burnt while resting, 47
    coping, 118
    describing your pain, 312
    diabetes, 357
    emotional support, 89
    hassles, 82
    lifestyle, 8
    living will, 400, 413
    medical terminology, 255
    pain reduction, 334
    physician care, 269
    weight control problems, 222
Assisted suicide, 412
Asthma, 48–49, 108–109, 349–351, 368

Ataxia, 36
Atherosclerosis, 52, 207–208, 375
Atkins diet, 218
Atriums, 49, 50
Attention copers, 282
Attribution, 95
Aura, 109, 351
Autoimmune diseases, 59
Autonomic activity, 315
Autonomic nervous system, 37–39
Aversion strategies, 196
Avoidance, 119
Avoidance/avoidance conflict, 72
Avoidance copers, 282
Axon, 32
Azidothymidine, 394
AZT, 394

B

B cells, 56
Babies, 73
Back pain, 339–340
Bacteria, 53–54
Bad cholesterol, 207
Balloon angioplasty, 377
Barbiturates, 188
Bariatric surgery, 220
Basal cell carcinoma, 386
Basal metabolic rate (BMR), 47
Behavior modification, 12
Behavior patterns, 99–102
Behavioral contracting, 198, 219, 263
Behavioral control, 93
Behavioral influence, 143–144
Behavioral medicine, 11–12
Behavioral methods, 12
Behaviorism, 11
Beliefs, 149–153
Benign-positive, 64
Benzodiazepines, 127
Bereavement, 402
Beriberi, 2
Beta-blockers, 127
Beta-carotene, 209
Beverly Hills diet, 218
Binge drinking, 184, 185
Binge eating, 214
Biochemical tests, 257
Bioethics committees, 411

Biofeedback, 11
  chronic illness, 368
  clinical pain, 327–329
  forehead muscle tension, 130
  paralysis, 37
  stress, 130–131
Biological factors, 13
Biomedical model, 7
Biopsy, 387
Biopsychosocial perspective, 13–16
Birth defects, 155–156
Black lung disease, 48
Blinding, 22–23
Blood, 51–52
Blood pressure, 50–51. *See also*
      Hypertension
Blood vessels, 49, 50
Blood volume, 50
Blunters, 281
BMI, 211
BMR, 47
Body mass index (BMI), 211
Body sculpting, 220
Body surface area (BSA), 47
Body systems, 31–60
  cardiovascular system, 49–53
  digestive system, 42–46
  endocrine system, 40–42
  immune system, 53–59. *See also*
      Immune system
  nervous system, 32–40. *See also*
      Nervous system
  respiratory system, 47–49
Bone marrow, 54
Bone marrow transplant, 392
Booster sessions, 201
Bowel disease, 108
Box scale, 310
Brain, 34–36
Brain injury, 353
Brainstem, 36
Breast cancer, 142, 386
Breast self-examination (BSE), 142
Breastfeeding, 156
Bronchial tubes, 47, 48
Bronchitis, 49
Bronchodilators, 351
BSA, 47
BSE, 142
Bucklebear, 232
Buffering hypothesis, 91
Bulimia nervosa, 222–224

Buprenorphine, 199
Bupropion hydrochloride, 198
Burn patients, 295
Burnout, 273–274
Bypass surgery, 377

C

C fibers, 296, 301
Cable Quit, 160
Caffeine, 188, 209
CAM methods, 249–250
Cancer, 384–393
  age, 386
  breast, 386
  BSE, 142
  cervical, 386
  children, 392–393
  colorectal, 386
  death rates, 384–385
  defined, 384
  diagnosis, 387
  diet, 209
  digestive tract, 45
  exercise, 227
  forms of, 384
  gender, 386
  killer-T-cell activity, 105
  lung, 49, 179, 386
  medical treatment, 387–389
  prognosis, 386, 387
  prostate, 386
  psychosocial impact, 389–391
  psychosocial intervention, 391–392
  skin, 232–233, 386
  smoking, 179
  sociocultural differences, 386–387
  stress, 113–114
  TSE, 142
  uterine, 386
Can't-stand-itis, 132
Capillaries, 44
Carbohydrase, 42
Carbohydrates, 204, 217
Carbon monoxide, 177
Carcinogens, 105
Carcinoma, 113, 384
Carcinomas in situ, 386
Cardiac arrhythmia, 104
Cardiac catheterization, 280

Cardiac counseling, 137
Cardiac invalidism, 379
Cardiac output, 24, 50
Cardiovascular disorders, 52–53,
   375–380
  age, 375
  anatomy, 49–53
  biological risk factors, 376
  blood pressure, 50–51. *See also*
    Hypertension
  cardiac counseling, 137
  emotions, 376
  exercise, 227
  gender differences, 375
  life style of heart attack, 376
  medical treatment, 376–377
  psychosocial impact, 378–380
  psychosocial interventions, 380
  rehabilitation, 377–378
  smoking, 180–181
  sociocultural differences,
    375–376
  stress, 103–104, 112–113
  stress management, 135–137
  sudden cardiac death, 104
  symptoms of heart attack, 375
  type A personality, 101, 102
Cardiovascular reactivity, 103–104
Cardiovascular system, 49–53
Caregiving, 75
Case study, 27
Catalase, 42
Catecholamine, 79, 113
Catheter, 280
Causalgia, 296–297
Causes of death, 140
CD4 cells, 56
CD8 cells, 56
Cell-mediated immunity, 56
Centrally acting analgesics, 323
Cerebellum, 36
Cerebral cortex, 34, 35
Cerebrum, 34
Cervical cancer, 386
CFS, 250
Chair lift, 225
Challenge, 64, 83, 97
Chemotherapy, 388
Child abuse, 71
Children
  adolescence. *See* Adolescence.
  cancer, 392–393

chronic illness, 370
  diabetes, 360
  health, 155–156
  hospitalization, 282–286
  life events scales, 81
  muscle relaxation, 128
  pain, 315–317
  terminal illness, 396–397
Children's Comprehensive Pain
    Questionnaire, 316
Chippers, 178
Chlorinated water, 233–234
Chloroform, 234
Cholesterol, 21–22, 52, 207–208
Christian Scientists, 21
Chromosome, 27
Chronic bronchitis, 49
Chronic care model, 264
Chronic clinical pain, 320–321
Chronic diseases, 4
Chronic fatigue syndrome (CFS),
   250
Chronic illness, 74, 343–371
  adjusting to, 344–349, 366
  Alzheimer's disease, 363–365
  arthritis, 360–363
  asthma, 349–351, 368
  behavioral treatments, 367–368
  cognitive treatments, 368–369
  coping process, 347–349
  diabetes, 355–360
  education, 366
  epilepsy, 351–353
  family therapy, 369–370
  interpersonal therapy, 369
  long-term adaptation, 348–349
  nervous system injuries, 353–355
  relaxation/biofeedback, 368
  social support, 347, 367
  spinal cord injury, 353–355
Chronic-intractable-benign pain,
   294
Chronic obstructive pulmonary
   disease (COPD), 181
Chronic pain, 294
Chronic-progressive pain, 294
Chronic-recurrent pain, 294
Chronic stress, 66
Cigarette smoking, 174–181. *See also*
   Substance abuse
  age differences, 175
  cancer, 179

COPD, 181
  gender differences, 175
  health, 178–181
  heart disease, 180–181
  newborn's health, 156
  nicotine, 177–178
  passive smoking, 180
  prevention, 191
  rationalizations, 161
  sociocultural differences, 175
  starting to smoke, 176–177
  statistics/usage, 174
  weight gain, 200
Cirrhosis, 45, 187
Classical conditioning, 11, 129, 173,
   305
Clinical health psychology, 13
Clinical pain, 319–342. *See also* Pain
   and discomfort
  acupuncture, 337
  acute/chronic, 320–321
  back pain, 339–340
  chemical treatments, 322–325
  cognitive treatments, 329–333
  defined, 320
  distraction, 330–331
  group psychotherapy, 325
  hypnosis, 334–335
  imagery, 331–332
  interpersonal therapy, 335–336
  medical treatments, 321–326
  multidisciplinary programs,
    340–341
  pain clinics, 340–341
  physical therapy, 338–339
  redefinition, 332, 333
  relaxation/biofeedback, 327–329
  stimulation therapies, 336–338
  surgical treatment, 322
  team approach to treatment,
    325–326
Clot-dissolving medication, 377
Cocaine, 189, 190
Codeine, 188
Cognition, 13
Cognitive control, 93
Cognitive methods, 12
Cognitive restructuring, 132–133,
   369
Cognitive therapy, 133
Coherence, 97
Cohort effect, 26

Cold-pressor procedure, 299–300
Colorectal cancer, 386
Commitment, 97
Commonsense models, 243
Community, 14
Community-based wellness
    programs, 165–166
Community organizations, 123–124
Companionship support, 88
Comparison group, 22
Competitive achievement
    orientation, 99
Complementary and alternative
    medicine (CAM), 249
Compliance, 256–264, 367
Conceptualization, 133
Conditioned stimulus (CS), 129
Conditioning immune function,
    107–108
Conditioning methods, 11
Conditioning techniques, 129
Conflict, 72
Conflict theory, 154
Congenital insensitivity to pain, 291
Congestive heart failure, 53, 375
Conscientiousness, 147
Contemplation, 152
Control, 97. See also Personal control
Control group, 22, 341
Conversion hysteria, 10
Cook-Medley Hostility Scale, 102
COPD, 181
Coping
    active/passive, 330
    chronic illness, 347–349
    emotion-focused, 118–119
    functions of, 118–120
    gender differences, 122
    high-mortality illness, 373–375
    methods of, 120–122
    pain, 308–309
    patient in hospital, 276–278,
        280–282
    problem-focused, 119–120
    sociocultural differences, 122
    stress, 117–123. See also Stress
        management
Coping statements, 332
Coronary care units, 377
Coronary heart disease (CHD), 101.
    See also Cardiovascular
    disorders

Correlation coefficient, 24
Correlational studies, 24
Corticosteroid, 79, 113, 351
Corticotropin-releasing factor, 40
Cortisol, 41, 100, 105
Cost-benefit analysis, 407–408
Counter-irritation, 336
Counterconditioning, 129
Cranial nerves, 39
Craving, 172, 200
Crisis theory, 345
Cross-cultural differences. See
    Cultural differences
Cross-sectional approach, 26
CS, 129
Cue exposure, 196
Cues to action, 150
Cultural differences, 18–21, 159
    adherence to medical advice, 259
    alcohol abuse, 183–184
    atherosclerosis, 112
    cancer, 386–387
    drug use, 189
    eating disorders, 223
    exercise, 228
    health, 158–159
    health services, 245–246
    heart disease, 375–376
    HIV/AIDS, 168–169, 393
    hypertension, 112
    pain, 306–307
    perception of illness, 242
    personal control, 94
    religion, 21
    smoking, 175
    social class, 158
    social support, 89
    stress, 71
    stroke, 381
    weight control, 211
Cupping, 336
Cystic fibrosis, 73

D

Daily hassles, 81, 82
DARE, 190
Datril, 323
Death and dying, 74–75
    advance directives, 400
    bereavement, 402–404
    home care, 401

hospice care, 401–402
    medical/psychological care,
        399–401
    quality of life in death, 399–402
    stages of adjustment to dying, 398
    survivors, 402–404
    terminal illness, 396–399
Decisional control, 93
Deep tissue massage, 134
Defense mechanisms, 119
Delayed-hypersensitivity T cells, 56
Delirium tremens (DTs), 173
Dementia, 364
Dendrites, 32
Denial, 119
Dentists, fear of, 130
Dependence, 172–174
Dependent variable, 22
Depersonalization, 273
Depressants, 323
Depression, 70, 286, 309
Desensitization, 129–130
Determinants of health-related
        behavior
    beliefs/intentions, 149–153
    emotional factors, 148, 154–155
    false hope/willingness, 154
    general factors, 146–149
    learning, 147–148
    less rational processes, 153–155
    motivational factors, 153–154
    perception/cognition, 148–149
    personality, 148
    social factors, 148
Detoxification, 195
Development and health, 155–157
Diabetes, 42, 355–360
Diagnostic-related groups, 271
Diastolic pressure, 50
Diathesis-stress model, 102
Diencephalon, 34
Diet. See Nutrition; Weight control
Dietary diseases, 2
Dietary interventions, 209–210
Dietitian, 19
Digestive system, 42–46
Direct effects hypothesis, 91
Disease. See Illness
Diseases of adaptation, 68
Distraction, 330–331
Distress, 69, 83
Disulfiram, 199

Diuretics, 137
Divorce, 70
Dizygotic (DZ) twins, 27–28
DNA, 27
Doctor-centered, 253
Doctor-patient relationship. *See*
    Patient-practitioner
    relationship
Dopamine, 173
Double-blind, 23
Downers, 188
Drug use and abuse, 187–190. *See*
    also Substance abuse
    age, 189
    cultural differences, 189
    gender differences, 189
    health, 189–190
    type of drugs, 188
Drunk driving, 187. *See also* Alcohol
    use and abuse
DTs, 173
Duchenne muscular dystrophy, 144
Duodenum, 44
Dying. *See* Death and dying
Dysmenorrhea, 110
DZ twins, 27–28

E

EAP, 194
Early intervention, 194
Eating disorders, 221–224
Ecological momentary assessment,
    29, 406
Eczema, 110
EEG, 315
Efferent, 37
Efferent neurons, 38
Elasticity, 51
Elderly people. *See* Age
Electroencephalograph (EEG), 315
Electromyograph (EMG), 315
Embolus, 381
Emetic drug, 196
Emetine, 196
EMG, 315
EMG biofeedback. *See* Biofeedback
Emotion, 13–14
    coping, 121
    health-related behavior, 148,
      154–155
    health-related behaviors, 148

heart disease, 376
    hypertension, 111–112
    immune system, 105–106
    pain, 307–308
    stress, 70
    stroke, 381
Emotion-focused cognitive
    processes, 119
Emotion-focused coping, 118–119
Emotional appeal, 51
Emotional exhaustion, 273
Emotional lability, 383
Emotional support, 87
Emphysema, 48, 181, 349
Employee assistance program
    (EAP), 194
Encephalopathy, 394
Endocrine glands, 41
Endocrine system, 40–42
Endogenous opioids, 303
Endorphin, 226, 303
Energy therapies, 249
Enkephalin, 303
Environmental hazards, 232–234
Environmental stress, 77
Enzymes, 42
Epidemic, 17
Epidemiology, 17
Epidural block, 323–324
Epilepsy, 36, 351–353
Epileptic seizure, 36
Epinephrine, 41, 105
Epstein-Barr virus, 107
Esophagus, 44
Essential hypertension, 110, 111
Esteem support, 87
Ethical decision making, 411–412
Ethnicity. *See* Cultural differences
Eustress, 83
Euthanasia, 412
Evoked potentials, 315
Exercise, 224–231
    age, 157, 228
    asthma, 351
    back pain, 339–340
    chronic pain, 338
    diabetes, 359
    health effects, 226–228
    ideal exercise program, 225–226
    pitfalls/hazards, 227
    promoting exercise behavior,
      229–231

reasons for not exercising,
    228–229
    rehabilitation from heart disease,
      378
    stress, 125–126
    types of, 225
    weight control, 218
Expectancies, 305
Experimental group, 22
Experiments, 22–24
Expressive aphasia, 382
External beam therapy, 388
External locus of control, 94
Extinction, 147

F

Fact joints, 339
Fad diets, 218
False hope, 154
Family, 15, 72–73
Family illness, 73–74
Family involvement programs, 192
Family therapy, 369–370
Fat-cell hyperplasia, 213
Fat-soluble vitamins, 205
Fats, 52
Fatty acids, 44, 52
Fear, 70
Fear messages, 162
Fear of dentists, 130
Feedback loop, 105
Female-male differences. *See*
    Gender differences
Fetal alcohol syndrome, 156, 186
Fiber, 205
Fibrillation, 104
Fibromyalgia, 361
Fight-or-flight response, 67
Fighting for your life, 252
Firefighters, 76
First-degree burns, 295
Flawed decisions, 153
Food. *See* Nutrition; Weight control
Food cues, 221
Forebrain, 34–36
Forehead muscle tension, 130
Formed elements, 52
Fraternal twins, 27–28
Frontal lobe, 35
Fructose, 204
Fungi (fungus), 54

G

Gain-framed messages, 162
GAS, 67–68
Gate-control theory, 301–302, 338
Gating mechanism, 301
Gay men's sexual behavior, 168
Gemmules, 27
Gender differences, 414–415
  cancer, 386
  caregiving, 75
  exercise, 228
  health, 157–158
  heart disease, 414–415, 375
  HIV/AIDS, 393
  personal control, 94
  smoking, 175
  social support, 89
  stress, 71
  stroke, 381
  type A behavior, 100
  weight control, 211
Gender perspective, 17
Gene, 27
General adaptation syndrome (GAS), 67–68
Genetic abnormalities, 144
Genetic counselors, 144
Genetics research, 27–29
Geriatrics, 16. See also Age
German measles, 156
Gestation, 155–156
Glial cells, 33
Glove anesthesia, 10
Glucagon, 42
Glucose, 204
Glycemic load, 217
Glycerol, 44
Good cholesterol, 207
Grand mal seizure, 36
Grave's disease, 41
Grief, 402
Growing pains, 315
Guided imagery, 331

H

Habitual illness, 143–145
Hallucinogens, 188
Harm-loss, 64, 83
HASS/Col, 82

Hassles, 81, 82
Hassles Assessment Scale for Students in College (HASS/Col), 82
Hassles Scale, 81
Hazardous materials, 233–234
HDL, 207–208
Headache, 109–110, 304, 328
Health. See also individual subject headings
  defined, 102
  development, 155–157
  drinking, 186–187
  drug use, 189–190
  exercise, 226–228
  gender, 157–158
  hardiness, 98
  nutrition, 206–210
  overweight, 214–215
  personal control, 96–97
  smoking, 179
  social support, 89–92
  sociocultural factors, 158–159, 414
  stress, 102–108
  type A behavior, 101, 102
Health behavior, 141–143
Health belief model, 149–151, 246–247, 259
Health care living will and proxy, 400
Health care system, 8
Health goals, 155
Health-maintenance organization (HMO), 239
Health promotion
  behavioral methods, 163
  community-based wellness programs, 165–166
  HIV/AIDS, 191–192
  maintaining healthy behaviors, 163–164
  motivational interviewing, 162–163
  problems, 145–146
  promoting exercise behavior, 229–231
  providing information, 160–162
  racial/ethnic issues, 159
  school programs, 164
  substance abuse, 191–192

  worksite wellness programs, 164–165
Health-promotion information, 160–162
Health psychologists (hospitals), 286–289
Health psychology
  career opportunities, 409
  controversial issues, 410–412
  cost-benefit analysis, 407–408
  defined, 11
  direct/indirect help, 12
  future focuses, 412–415
  future prospects, 415
  goals, 406–409
  qualifications, 12
  related fields, 17–20
  technological advances, 406–407, 411–412
  training programs, 409–410
Health services, 236–265
  alternative medicine, 249
  CAM methods, 249–250
  chronic care model, 264
  compliance (adhering to medical advice), 256–264
  health belief model, 246–247, 259
  medical insurance, 238, 245
  misuse of, 250
  patient-practitioner relationship. See Patient-practitioner relationship.
  perceiving and interpreting symptoms, 240–244
  treatment delay, 247–249
  treatment regimens, 258–259
  types, 237–238
  users, 244–247
Hear, 49, 50
Heart disease. See Cardiovascular disorders
Heavy drinking, 184
Helper T cells, 56
Hemispheres (brain), 34–35
Hemodialysis, 258
Hemoglobin, 52
Hemophilia, 52
Hemorrhagic stroke, 381
Hepatitis, 45
Hepatitis A, 45
Hepatitis B, 45

Heredity
  addiction, 174
  alcohol abuse, 186
  greatest impact, 28
  health-related behavior, 146
  Type A behavior, 101
Heroin, 188
High-density lipoprotein (HDL), 207–208
High-impact exercises, 227
High-mortality illness, 373–396
  AIDS, 393–396
  cancer, 384–393. See also Cancer
  coping, 373–375
  heart disease, 375–380. See also Cardiovascular disorders
  stroke, 380–384
Hispanics. See Cultural differences
Histamine, 350
Historical overview, 5–7
HIV/AIDS, 55, 191–192. See also AIDS
Hives, 110
HMO, 239
Holistic, 15
Home health care, 238
Homelessness, 95
Homeostasis, 36
Hormones, 40
Hospice care, 401
Hospital, 237, 266–290
  administrators, 268
  children, 282–286
  coordinating patient care, 269–270
  cost factors, 271–272
  emotional adjustment, 276–286
  health psychologists, 286–289
  historical overview, 267–268
  medical staff, 268–269
  medical staff burnout, 273–274
  nosocomial infection, 270–271
  patient coping processes, 276–278, 280–282
  psychological assessment of patients, 287–288
  psychological preparation of patients, 278–282
  psychosocial issues of patients, 272–273
  sick-role behavior, 274–275
Hostility-CHD connection, 102
Humoral theory, 5
Humors, 5

Hydrochloric acid, 44
Hyperglycemia, 42, 355
Hyperinsulinemia, 213
Hyperopia, 255
Hypertension, 51
  beliefs about blood pressure, 148
  defined, 110
  diet, 208–209
  primary/secondary, 110–111
  risk factors, 111
  sociocultural differences, 112
  stress, 111–112
  stress management, 137
Hyperthyroidism, 41
Hypervigilance, 154
Hypnosis, 135, 334–335
Hypochondriasis, 250
Hypoglycemia, 359
Hypothalamus, 35
Hypothalamus-pituitary-adrenal axis, 40, 68, 104
Hypothesis testing, 133
Hypothesis, 22
Hypothyroidism, 41

I

I-E Scale, 94
Iatrogenic conditions, 246
Ibuprofen, 323, 362
Ideal exercise program, 225–226
Identical twins, 27–28
Ig, 56
IgA, 56
Illness. See also Health; specific diseases
  high-mortality, 373–396
  life-span health, 413–414
  lifestyle, 8–10
  personality, 10
  psychophysiological disorders, 108–110
  stress, 103
Illness delay, 248
Illness identity, 243
Illness prevention, 143–145
Illness/wellness continuum, 2, 3
Illusion of control, 94
Imagery, 331–332
Immune deficiencies, 55
Immune system, 53–59
  antigens, 53–54

autoimmune diseases, 59
conditioning immune function, 107–108
developmental changes, 58
emotions, 105–106
how it works, 57–58
immune deficiencies, 55
interrelationships, 57
lifestyle, 58–59, 107
organs, 54–56
psychoneuroimmunology, 105–108
psychosocial modifiers, 106–107
stress, 105
Immune system reactivity, 105
Immunoglobulins (Ig), 56
Incentive-sensitization theory, 173
Incidence, 17
Independent variable, 22
Inderal, 127
Indirectly acting drugs, 323
Infancy, 155, 156
Infant mortality, 156
Infarction, 53
Infectious diseases, 2–4
Inflammatory bowel disease, 108
Information dissemination, 160–162
Informational control, 93
Informational support, 88
Inhibitory interneurons, 303
Injuries, accidental, 231–232
Instrumental support, 88
Insulin, 42, 213, 355, 359
Insulin pump, 238, 359
Intentions, 149–153
Internal locus of control, 93
Internet, 160
Interpersonal therapy
  chronic illness, 369
  clinical pain, 335–336
Interview, 99
Intoxication. See Alcohol use and abuse
Intravenous drug users, 168
Intrusive thoughts, 121
Ion, 32
Irrational beliefs, 65, 132
Irrational thinking, 153–154
Irritable bowel disease, 108
Ischemia, 300
Ischemic stroke, 381
Isokinetic exercise, 225

Isometric exercise, 225
Isotonic exercise, 225

J

Jehovah's Witnesses, 21
Jenkins Activity Survey, 100
Job fatalities, 231
Job loss, 77
Job stress, 76–77
Johnson & Johnson, 165
Juvenile rheumatic arthritis, 361

K

Kaposi's sarcoma, 394
Ketoacidosis, 356
Kidney disease, 258
Kidneys, 50
Killer T cells, 56
Kübler-Ross's stages of adjustment
    to dying, 398

L

LAAM, 199
Lactase, 42
Lacteal, 44
Lactose, 204
Lamaze training, 281
Lapse, 163
Larynx, 47, 48
Lay referral system, 243
LDL, 207–208
Lead poisoning, 233
Learned food aversion, 389
Learned helplessness, 95
Learning, 147–148
Left atrium, 49, 50
Left hemisphere, 34, 35
Left ventricle, 49, 50
LES, 81
Less rational thinking, 153–155
Leukemia, 52, 113, 384
Leukocytes, 52
Librium, 127
Licensed practical nurse (LPN), 19
Lie detector test, 78
Life events, 79–81
Life Events Record, 81
Life expectancy, 4
Life Experiences Survey (LES), 81

Life skills training approaches, 191
Life-span health and illness, 413–414
Life-span perspective, 16–17
Lifestyle
    exercise, 224–230. See also Exercise
    heart attack, 376
    illness, 8–10
    immune system, 58–59, 107
    nutrition, 204–210
    safety, 231–234
    stroke, 381
    substance abuse, 171–202. See
        also Substance abuse
    weight control and diet, 210–230
Lifetime prevalence rate, 184
Limbic system, 35
Lipids, 52, 204–205
Lipitor, 208
Lipoproteins, 207–208
Liposuction, 220
Live for Life, 165
Liver, 50
Liver disease, 45, 187
Living will, 400, 413
Local anesthetics, 323
Locus of control, 93–94
Longitudinal approach, 26
Loss-framed messages, 162
Love Canal, 77
Low back pain, 339–340
Low-density lipoprotein (LDL),
    207–208
LPN, 19
LSD, 188
Lumpectomy, 388
Lung cancer, 49, 179, 386
Lungs, 47, 48
Lupus erythematosus, 59
Lyme disease, 17
Lymph, 54
Lymph nodes, 54
Lymph vessels, 54
Lymphatic organs, 54
Lymphocytes, 54, 56
Lymphoid organs, 54
Lymphokines, 56
Lymphoma, 384

M

Macrophages, 56
Magnification, 132

Maintaining healthy behaviors,
    163–164
Male-female differences. See
    Gender differences
Malnourished mothers, 156
Mammogram, 145
Managed-care, 239
Mantra, 134
Marijuana, 188, 189
Masochists, 297
Mass media, 14, 160
Mass psychogenic illness,
    242, 264
Massage therapy, 134–133
Mastectomy, 388
Master gland, 40
Matching, 153
Mathews Youth Test for Health, 100
MBMD, 287
McGill Pain Questionnaire (MPQ),
    312, 313
Medicaid, 238
Medical anatomy. See Body systems
Medical anthropology, 18
Medical examination, 145
Medical insurance, 238, 245
Medical jargon, 253
Medical setting, 160
Medical sociology, 18
Medical student's disease, 241–242,
    264
Medicare, 238
Medication, 127
Medication-recording dispensers,
    257
Meditation, 134–135
Medulla, 36
Melanoma, 384, 386
Memory B cells, 56
Memory T cells, 56
Mescaline, 188
Mesmerism, 135
Message framing, 162
Meta-analysis, 75
Metabolic syndrome, 113
Metabolism, 46
Metastasis, 384
Methadone, 199
Methadone maintenance, 199
Midbrain, 36
Middle Ages, 6
Migraine headache, 109, 304

Millon Behavioral Medicine Diagnostic (MBMD), 287
Mind-body interventions, 249
Mind/body problem, 6
Mindful awareness, 134
Minerals, 205
Mini-stroke, 381
Minnesota Multiphasic Personality Inventory (MMPI), 287–288, 309
mm Hg, 50
MMPI, 287–288, 309
MMPI-2, 287
Modeling, 131–132, 147
Monitors, 281
Monocytes, 56
Monounsaturated fats, 208
Monozygotic (MZ) twins, 27–28
Morbidity, 17
Morphine, 188
Mortality, 17
Mortality rate, 17
Motivation, 14
Motivational interviewing, 162–163, 219
Motor vehicle accidents, 231–232
Motrin, 323
Mourning, 402
MPQ, 312, 313
MRFIT, 166, 209
Mucociliary escalator, 48
Multidimensional approaches, 133
Multidimensional Health Locus of Control Scales, 96
Multidimensional Pain Inventory, 313
Multidisciplinary pain clinics, 340–341
Multiple Risk Factor Intervention Trial (MRFIT), 166, 209
Multiple sclerosis, 33, 59
Muscle contraction headache, 109
Muscle-ischemia procedure, 300
Muscle relaxation, 128. See also Relaxation. See Relaxation
Muscle tension, 315
Musculoskeletal disorders, 360–363
Musterbating, 132
Myasthenia gravis, 38
Myelin, 33
Myelin sheath, 33
Myocardial infarction, 53, 375

Myocardium, 49
MZ twins, 27–28

N

Naloxone, 303
Naltrexone, 199
Narcotics, 188, 323, 324
Narcotics Anonymous, 197
Native Americans, 159, 183–184, 387
Negative reinforcement, 173, 177
Nerve impulses, 38
Nervous system, 32–40
    autonomic, 37–38, 39
    brain, 34–36
    CNS, 34–37
    how it works, 32–33, 40–41
    overview/summary, 40
    parasympathetic, 38–39
    peripheral, 37–39
    somatic, 38
    spinal cord, 36–37
    sympathetic, 38, 39
Nervous system injuries, 353–355
Neuralgia, 296
Neuromuscular disorders, 37
Neuron, 32
Neuropathy, 356
Neuroticism, 250
Neurotransmitter, 32
Nicotine, 177–178
Nicotine gum, 198
Nicotine regulation model, 178
Nociceptors, 296
Nonexperimental methods, 23
Nonpain imagery, 331
Nonperson treatment, 273
Nonrational thought processes, 153
Nonspecific immunity, 56
Noradrenalin, 41
Norepinephrine, 41
Nosocomial infection, 270–271
Nurse, 19
Nurse practitioners, 19
Nursing homes, 238
Nutrition, 204–210
    atherosclerosis, 207–208
    cancer, 209
    components of food, 204–205
    hypertension, 208–209
    interventions, 209–210
    what people eat, 205–206

O

Obesity, 210–212. See also Weight control
Occipital lobe, 35
Occupational health psychologists, 164
Occupational therapists, 20
Old age. See Age
Omega-3 fatty acids, 207
Oncogenes, 28
Operant conditioning, 11, 147, 305
Opiates/opioids, 188, 303–304
Optimism, 98, 148–149
Organ transplantation, 412
Organic pain, 292
Orlistat, 220
Osteoarthritis, 361
Outpatient care, 238
Ovaries, 40
Oxidation, 205
OxyContin, 189

P

Pacemakers, 238
Pain, 292
Pain and discomfort, 291–318
    assessing people's pain, 309–315
    behavioral assessment approaches, 313–314
    biopsychosocial aspects, 303–309
    burn patients, 295
    children, 315–317
    clinical pain, 319–342. See also Clinical pain
    coping with pain, 308–309
    emotions, 307–308
    gate-control theory, 301–302
    gender differences, 306
    interview methods in assessing pain, 310
    laboratory research, 299–300
    learning, 304–306
    meaning of pain, 297–298
    MPQ, 312, 313
    neurochemical transmission/inhibition of pain, 303–304
    opiates/opioids, 303–304
    pain, defined, 292–294

Pain and discomfort (*Cont.*)
  pain perception, 294–298
  pain questionnaires, 311–313
  pain rating scales, 310–311
  pain without detectable body
    damage, 296–297
  placebo, 305
  psychophysiological measures of
    pain, 315
  referred pain, 296
  social processes, 306
  sociocultural factors, 306–307
  theories of pain, 298–302
  types of pain, 292–294
Pain assessment, 309–315
Pain Behavior Scale, 313
Pain behaviors, 304
Pain clinics, 340–341
Pain cocktail, 326
Pain diary, 311
Pain disorder, 293
Pain fibers, 296, 301
Pain games, 335
Pain perception, 294–298
Pain questionnaires, 311–313
Pain rating index, 313
Pain rating scales, 310–311
Pain redefinition, 332, 333
Painkillers, 189
PAIS, 287
Pancreas, 42
Paralysis, 37, 353–355
Paraplegia, 37, 353
Parasympathetic nervous system,
  38–39
Parietal lobe, 35
Parkinson's disease, 36
Passive coping, 330
Passive smoking, 180
Patient-centered, 253
Patient-controlled analgesia, 324
Patient-practitioner relationship,
  250–256
  communicating with patient, 261,
    262, 263
  patient adherence, 260–261
  patient behavior/style, 254–256
  patient participation, 251–252
  practitioner behavior/style,
    252–254
Pattern theory, 298
PCP, 188

Pediatric Pain Questionnaire, 316
Pediatrics, 16. *See also* Children
Pepsin, 44
Peptic ulcers, 45
Perceived behavioral control, 151
Perceived benefits and barriers,
  149, 150
Perceived seriousness, 150
Perceived susceptibility, 150
Perceived threat, 150
Perception, 148–149
Percodan, 323
PERI Life-Events Scale, 81
Periaqueductal gray area, 302, 303
Peripheral nervous system, 37–39
Peripheral resistance, 51
Peripherally active analgesics, 323
Peristalsis, 44
Personal control, 92–99
  beliefs about oneself, 93–94
  defined, 92
  determinants/development, 94
  gender differences, 94
  health, 96–97
  lack of, 94–96
  sociocultural differences, 94
  stress management, 124
  types, 93
Personality
  health-related behavior, 148
  illness, 10
  type A, 99–102, 135–137
  type B, 99–100
Perspective on health and illness
  biopsychosocial perspective,
    13–16
  gender perspective, 17
  life-span perspective, 16–17
  systems concept, 15–16
Pessimism, 149
Phagocytes, 55–56
Phantom limb pain, 297
Phenylketonuria (PKU), 28
Phobias, 70
Phosphatase, 42
Physical dependence, 172
Physical examination, 144–145
Physical fitness. *See* Exercise
Physical therapists, 19
Physical therapy, 338–339
Physician assistants, 19
Physician-assisted suicide, 412

Physician-patient relationship. *See*
  Patient-practitioner relationship
Physiological arousal, 78–79
Physiological individuality, 43
Pill (quantity) accounting, 257
Pituitary gland, 40–41
PKU, 28
Placebo, 22, 305
Placebo effect, 22
Planned behavior, 151–152
Plasma, 52
Plasma cells, 56
Platelets, 52
Pneumoconiosis, 48
Pneumocystis carinii pneumonia,
  394
Pneumonia, 48
Polio, 36
Polygraph, 78
Polysubstance abuse, 189
Polyunsaturated fats, 52
Pons, 36
Por La Vita, 159
Positive emotions, 121. *See also*
  Emotions
Positive prototype, 154
Positive reappraisal, 121
Positive reinforcement, 173, 177, 196
Posttraumatic stress disorder
  (PTSD), 66
PPO, 239
PPS, 271
Precontemplation, 152
Preferred provider organization
  (PPO), 239
Pregnancy, 156, 189
Pre hypertensive, 51
Present pain intensity, 313
Prevalence, 17
Primary appraisal, 64
Primary hypertension, 110, 111
Primary prevention, 144
PRN, 323
Problem drinking, 184–185
Problem-focused coping, 119–120
Problem-solving training, 133, 219,
  368
Profession of health psychology. *See*
  Health psychology
Progressive muscle relaxation, 128.
  See also Relaxation. *See*
  Relaxation

Prohibition era, 182
Promoting health. See Health promotion
Prospective approach, 25
Prospective-payment system (PPS), 271
Prostate cancer, 386
Protease inhibitors, 394
Proteins, 205
Protozoa, 54
Providing information, 160–162
Psoriasis, 110
Psychoanalytic theory, 10
Psychogenic, 293
Psychological assessment of hospital patients, 287–288
Psychological dependence, 172
Psychological factors, 13–14
Psychoneuroimmunology, 105–108
Psychophysiology, 315
Psychosocial Adjustment to Illness Scale (PAIS), 287
Psychosomatic medicine, 10
Psychotherapy, 224
PTSD, 66
Public health, 17–18
Punishment, 147
Purging, 222

Q
QALYs, 411
Quadriplegia, 37, 353
Quality-adjusted life years (QALYs), 411
Quality of life, 348, 399–402, 410–411
Quasi-experimental studies, 25–27

R
Race. See Cultural differences
Radiation poisoning, 233
Radiation therapy, 388
Radiological imaging, 387
Radon, 233
Rational nonadherence, 259
Reactance, 275
Reactivity, 66, 100
Readiness to change, 152
Reasoned action, 151
Receptive aphasia, 382

Recurrent headache, 109–110
Red blood cells, 52
Redefine stressful situation, 119
Redefinition, 332, 333
Referred pain, 296
Reflexes, 48
Reflexology, 149
Registered nurse (RN), 19
Reinforcement, 147, 173, 177
Reinforcers, 163, 196
Reinterpretative statements, 332
Relapse, 163
    substance abuse, 199–201
    weight control, 221
    weight loss, 221
Relapse prevention method, 201
Relaxation
    chronic illness, 368
    clinical pain, 327–329
    stress, 128–129
Relaxation response, 134
Religion, 21
Renaissance, 6
Research methods
    correlational studies, 24
    experiments, 22–24
    genetics research, 27–29
    quasi-experimental studies, 25–27
Resilience, 97–98
Respiratory circulation, 50
Respiratory system, 47–49
Respite centers, 366
Respondent conditioning, 11
Response substitution, 198
Restrained eaters, 213
Reticular system, 36
Retirement, 77
Retrospective approach, 25
Reverse conditioning, 11, 129
Reward preference, 163
Rheumatic diseases, 361
Rheumatoid arthritis, 59, 110, 361, 362
Rheumatoid fever, 59
Right atrium, 49, 50
Right hemisphere, 34, 35
Right to know laws, 233
Right ventricle, 49, 50
Risk factors, 9
RN, 19
Rubella, 156

S
Safety, 231–234
Saliva, 42
Salivary glands, 42
Sarcoma, 384
Satiation, 196
Saturated fats, 52, 208
Scarsdale diet, 218
School health promotion programs, 164
Seat belts, 232
Second-degree burns, 295
Secondary appraisal, 64–65
Secondary hypertension, 110
Secondary prevention, 144–145
Secondhand smoke, 180
Seizure, 36
Seizures (epilepsy), 351–353
Self-assessment. See Assess yourself
Self-efficacy, 94, 96, 151, 200, 260
Self-esteem, 65
Self-help groups, 124, 197, 219
Self-hypnosis, 135
Self-management, 198, 367
Self-monitoring, 198
Sense of coherence, 97
Separation distress, 283
Serious illness, 252
Serotonin, 303
Set-point theory, 213
Seventh-day Adventists, 21
Sever combined immunodeficiency disease, 55
Sex chromosome, 27
Short-stay hospitals, 271
Sibutramine, 220
Sick-role behavior, 141–142
Sick-role behavior (hospital), 274–275
Sickle-cell anemia, 28, 144
Sidestream smoke, 180
Sigmoidoscopy, 145
Simple sugars, 44
Single-subject approaches, 27
Skills acquisition and rehearsal, 133
Skin cancer, 232–233, 386
Skin disorders, 110
Small intestine, 45
Smoking. See Cigarette smoking
Smoking prevention efforts, 191
Social class, 158

Social factors, 14
Social influences approaches, 191
Social learning, 94
Social network, 88
Social Readjustment Rating Scale (SSRS), 79–80
Social Support Questionnaire, 88
Social workers, 20
Sociocultural, 18
Sociocultural differences, 18–21. See also Cultural differences
Socioeconomic status, 158
Sociology, 18
Sodium, 208–209
Somatic nervous system, 38
Somatoform disorders, 293
SPA, 303
Special-interest groups, 124
Specificity theory, 298
Spina bifida, 205
Spinal cord, 36–37
Spinal cord injury, 353–355
Spinal fusion, 322
Spinal manipulation treatment, 338
Spleen, 55
Squamous cell carcinoma, 386
SSRS, 79–80
Stages of change model, 152
Stamina, 98–99
Starch, 204
Statin drugs, 208
Steroids, 227–228, 351
Stimulants, 188
Stimulation-produced analgesia (SPA), 303
Stimulation therapies (pain), 336–338
Stimulus control, 198, 219
Stimulus hierarchy, 129, 130
Stomach, 44
Strain, 62
Stress, 61–138
  behavior/behavior patterns, 100, 103
  benefits of, 83–84
  biopsychosocial aspects, 66–71
  cancer, 113–114
  cardiovascular system, 103–104
  characteristics of stressful situations, 65
  chronic, 66
  cognition, 69–70

cognitive appraisal, 63–65
coping, 117–123. See also Stress management
death and dying, 74–75
defined, 62–63
divorce, 70
emotions, 70
environmental, 77
family, 72–73
family illness, 73–74
GAS, 67–68
gender differences, 71
hardiness, 97–99
health, 102–108
hypertension, 111–112
immune system, 105
measuring, 77–82
personal control, 92–99. See also Personal control
personal factors, 65, 72
PTSD, 66
social behavior, 70–71
social support, 87–92. See also Social support
sociocultural differences, 71
type A personality, 99–102
work, 76–77
Stress-CHD connection, 113
Stress-inoculation training, 133
Stress management, 116–138
  biofeedback, 130–131
  cognitive restructuring, 132–133
  coping, 117–123
  coronary risk, 135–137
  exercise, 125–126
  hypertension, 137
  hypnosis, 135
  massage therapy, 134–133
  medication, 127
  meditation, 134–135
  modeling, 131–132
  multidimensional approaches, 133
  personal control, 124
  relaxation, 128–129
  social support, 123–124
  systematic desensitization, 129–130
  time management, 124–125
  type A behavior, 135–137
Stressors, 62
Stroke, 53, 380–384
Structured interview, 99

Subincision, 64
Subjective norm, 151
Substance abuse
  addiction and dependence, 172–174
  alcohol. See Alcohol use and abuse.
  behavioral methods of treatment, 198
  characteristics of abusers, 172
  chemical methods of treatment, 197–199
  drugs. See Drug use and abuse.
  early intervention, 194
  family involvement programs, 192
  health promotion/education, 191–192
  preventing, 190–192
  psychosocial treatment, 194–197
  public policy/legal approaches to treatment, 191
  relapse, 199–201
  self-help groups, 197
  smoking. See Cigarette smoking.
  stopping on one's own, 193–194
Substance P, 303
Sucrase, 42
Sucrose, 204
Sudden cardiac death, 104, 227
Sugars, 204
Suggestibility, 135
Sunscreen use, 232–233
Suppressor T cells, 56
Sympathetic nervous system, 38–39
Symptom-based behavior, 141
Synapse, 32
Synaptic knob, 32, 33
Synovectomy, 322
System, 15
Systematic desensitization, 129–130
Systemic circulation, 50
Systems concept, 15–16
Systolic pressure, 50

T

T cells, 56
Tachycardia, 104
Tailored content, 162
Tangible support, 88
Tars, 177
Tay-Sachs disease, 144

Technological advances, 406–407, 411–412
Telehealth (telemedicine), 407
Telencephalon, 34
Television, 160
Temperament, 73, 101
Temperance movement, 182
Temperature, 51
Temporal lobe, 35
TENS, 336
Tension-type headache, 109
Terminal illness, 396–399
Tertiary prevention, 145
Testes, 40
Testicular cancer, 142
Testicular self-examination (TSE), 142
Thalamus, 35
Theory, 21
Theory of planned behavior, 151–152
Theory of reasoned action, 151
Third-degree burns, 295
Threat, 64, 83
Three Community Study, 165
Three Mile Island, 77
Thrombosis, 53
Thrombus, 381
Thymus, 54
Thymus gland, 41
Thyroid gland, 41
Time management, 124–125
Time urgency, 99
Tobacco use. See Cigarette smoking
Toddlers, 156–157
Tolerance, 172
Toxic chemicals, 233–234
Trachea, 47, 48
Traditional Chinese medicine, 21
Traffic accidents, 231–232
Tranquilizers, 188
Trans-fatty acids, 207
Transactions, 62
Transcendental meditation, 134
Transcutaneous electrical nerve stimulation (TENS), 336
Transient ischemic attack, 381
Transmission cells, 296, 301301
Transtheoretical model, 152
Treadmill test, 378
Treatment delay, 247–249
Treatment group, 341
Treatment regimens, 258–259

Trephination, 5
Trial, 22
Trigeminal neuralgia, 296
Triggers, 350
Triglycerides, 52, 207
TSE, 142
TV, 160
Twin studies, 27–28
Tylenol, 323
Type 1 diabetes, 356
Type 2 diabetes, 356
Type A behavior pattern, 99–102, 135–137
Type A/cardiac group, 137
Type B behavior pattern, 99–100

U

UAB Pain Behavior Scale, 313
UES, 81
Ulcers, 45, 108
Ultraviolet radiation, 232–233
Unconditioned response (UR), 129
Unconditioned stimulus (US), 129
Unpleasant Events Schedule (UES), 81
Unprocessed foods, 205
Unrealistic optimism, 148–149
Unsaturated fats, 52
Uplifts Scale, 81
UR, 129
US, 129
Uterine cancer, 386
Utilization delay, 248
UV radiation, 232–233

V

Vagus nerve, 39
Valium, 127
Variable, 22
Vegetarianism, 207
Ventricles, 49, 50
Verbal rating scale, 310
Vertebrae, 339
Very-low-calorie diet (VLCD), 220
Vicarious, 64
Vigilance, 154–155
Virus, 54
Viscosity, 51
Visual analog scale, 310
Visual neglect, 382, 383

Vital Signs (Mullan), 276
VLCD, 220

W

Water-soluble vitamins, 205
Weight control, 210–224
  age, 211
  behavioral/cognitive treatments, 218–219
  biological factors, 212–213
  BMI, 210
  dieting, 216–218
  eating disorders, 221–224
  exercise, 218
  gender differences, 211
  health, 214–215
  obesity, 210–212
  preventing overweight, 215–216
  psychological factors, 213–214
  relapse after weight loss, 221
  self-help groups, 219
  sociocultural differences, 211
  surgical intervention, 220
  worksite weight-loss programs, 219
Weight-loss competitions, 220
Weight Watchers, 220
Well behavior, 141
Wellness programs, 164–166
White blood cells, 52, 55
Whole person, 15
Willingness, 154
Withdrawal, 172, 173
Women's health issues, 414–415. See also Gender differences
Work stress, 76–77
Worksite weight-loss programs, 219
Worksite wellness programs, 164–165

X

X chromosome, 27

Y

Y chromosome, 27
Yin and yang, 21

Z

Zidovudine, 394
Zocor, 208

AUTHOR INDEX

A

Aaron, J., 66
Abbey, S. E., 251
Abboud, F. M., 376
Abdelmoty, E., 341
Abeles, M., 294
Abrahm, J. L., 399, 400, 401
Abrams, D. B., 153, 164, 165, 198
Abrams, K. K., 223
Abramson, L. Y., 95
Abramson, S. B., 361, 362
Acevedo, H. F., 58
Achterberg-Lawlis, J., 361
Acierno, R., 186
Adams, A., 161
Adams, J., 355
Adams, J. R., 104
Adams, K. G., 160
Adams, N. E., 94
Adams, T. B., 153
Adelman, A., 102
Ader, R., 22, 105, 107
Adesso, V. J., 157, 158, 186, 244
Adler, C. S., 131
Adler, N. E., 18, 158
Adlin, E. V., 212
Aeschlimann, S., 187
Affleck, G., 120, 122, 286, 294, 308,
  309, 362, 363, 383
Agosti, J. M., 350
Agras, W. S., 305
Agrawall, S., 194
Ahern, D. K., 250, 340, 341
Ahlbom, A., 104
Ahluwalia, J. S., 176
Ahn, D. K., 379
Aiello, J. R., 96
Aiken, L. H., 270
Aiken, L. S., 142, 150
Aikens, J. E., 358
Aikens, K. S., 358
Ainsworth, M. D. S., 283
Aizen, I., 151
Akana, S. F., 213
Akil, H., 303
Akinbami, L. J., 249
Al'Absi, M., 306
Alagna, S. W., 87, 90, 276, 347

Alaranta, H., 338
Albert, C. M., 227
Albrecht, G. L., 158
Alcorn, J. D., 258
Aldana, S. G., 164, 407
Alderman, E. L., 380
Alderman, M. H., 137, 375
Aldwin, C. M., 122
Alexander, E. M., 156
Alexander, F., 10
Alexander, J. K., 165
Alferi, S. M., 392
Alfieri, S. M., 392
Allan, R., 104
Allen, K., 90
Allen, K. A. M., 90
Allen, L., 223, 393
Allen, M. T., 104
Alleyne, E., 169
Alleyne, S., 262
Allison, D. B., 215
Allred, D. C., 28
Ally, D. S., 28
Alonzo, A., 242
Alper, C. M., 103
Alpert, B., 226
Alpert, B. S., 71, 126
Alterman, A. I., 199
Altfeld, M., 394
Althoff, B., 302
Altman, D. G., 156, 160, 191, 409
Altman, J., 120
Amaro, H., 18, 159, 168, 169, 243,
  393
Ames, B. N., 233
Amick, T. L., 199
Amos, C. I., 100
Anania, T. L., 242
Anastasi, A., 80, 308
Anda, R. F., 200
Anderman, C., 145
Andersen, B. L., 113, 384, 388, 389,
  390, 391, 392
Andersen, R. E., 214, 218
Anderson, B. J., 259, 360, 370
Anderson, E. A., 279
Anderson, J. J., 362, 382
Anderson, J. W., 220

Anderson, K. O., 126, 127, 278, 304,
  322, 332, 362
Anderson, L. A., 144
Anderson, N., 112
Anderson, N. B., 18, 71, 158, 159,
  414
Anderson, O. W., 268, 269
Anderson, R., 358
Anderson, S., 73, 105, 365
Andersson, G. B. J., 338
Anderton, C. H., 135
Andrasik, F., 109, 131, 325, 327, 328,
  329
Andrew, J. M., 279
Andrews, G., 380
Andrews, M., 107
Andrieu, J. M., 394
Andrykowski, M. A., 66, 389, 390,
  391
Anger, W. K., 12
Angulo, J., 100
Anisman, H., 113
Ankeny, K., 209
Anthony, J. C., 192
Anthony, J. M., 362, 382
Anton, R. F., 186
Anton, S. D., 230
Antoni, M., 396
Antoni, M. H., 59, 80, 107, 124, 391,
  392, 394, 396
Antonovsky, A., 2, 3, 97, 247, 248
Antonucci, T. C., 88, 123
Antonuccio, D. O., 177
Antoun, B., 358
Apanovitch, A. M., 162
Aponte, J. E., 259, 360
Appelbaum, K. A., 327, 329
Appley, M. H., 62, 65
Arena, P., 391
Areskoug, B., 314
Arheart, K., 71
Arkowitz, H., 196, 219
Armeli, S., 120, 121, 122
Armstead, C. A., 158, 414
Armstrong, C. A., 231
Armstrong, F. D., 286
Armstrong, J. W., 15, 33, 73
Armstrong, L., 374

Armstrong, M. A., 187
Arndt, I. O., 199
Arnold, C., 389
Arnold, L. E., 156
Arnold, M. A., 226
Arntz, H.-R., 376
Aro, S., 339
Arroll, B., 227, 230
Arrom, J. O., 255
Arthur, R. J., 80
Artz, L., 156
Ary, D., 176, 177, 192
Asbury, R., 391
Ashburn, S. S., 58
Ashe, K., 412
Ashley, M. J., 191, 194
Ashton, C. M., 271
Ashton, H., 174, 179
Askevold, F., 224
Astin, J. A., 249
Atkins, C. J., 96, 151, 229
Atkinson, C., 135
Atkinson, J. H., 309, 396
Atkinson, R. L., 220
Attanasio, V., 131, 340, 341
Attie, I., 223
Audet, J., 358, 369
Audrain, J., 148, 161, 177, 178, 412
Auerbach, S. M., 251
Auman, J. T., 228
Auslander, W. F., 360, 370
Austin, J., 167
Austin, S. B., 217
Autman, S. H., 283, 284
Avezum, A., 376
Aweh, G. N., 233
Aylmer, G., 376
Azar, B., 206
Azen, S., 399

B

Babani, L., 258, 360
Babyak, M., 126, 208, 209, 380
Bachen, E. A., 105
Bachman, J. G., 174, 175, 176, 182, 189
Backus, C. A., 167
Bacon, R. S., 88
Badley, E. M., 348
Baer, D. J., 210
Baer, P. E., 103, 148

Baezconde-Garbanati, L., 181
Bagozzi, R., 151, 152
Bahler, R., 242
Baile, W. F., 391
Bailey, C. J., 28
Baines, D. R., 152
Bakal, D., 293, 294, 334, 335, 337, 338
Bakeman, R., 286, 332
Baker, B., 122, 262, 329, 330
Baker, D. I., 231
Baker, E., 191, 229
Baker, J. A., 229
Baker, R., 160, 196
Baker, T. B., 172, 173, 177, 178, 185, 198, 199, 200
Balabanis, M., 164
Balady, G. J., 378
Baldwin, D., 384
Ball, J. F., 75
Ballantyne, D., 227
Bandilla, E. B., 306
Bandler, L., 109
Bandura, A., 94, 147, 379
Bane, A. L., 191
Banks, S. M., 162
Banting, F., 359
Barabasz, M., 334
Barak, T., 277
Baranowski, J., 206, 212
Baranowski, T., 147, 148, 206, 212, 214, 216
Baratta, M. V., 173
Barber, J., 335
Barchas, J. D., 94
Bardo, M. T., 188
Barefoot, J. C., 66, 102, 135
Barefoot, R. B., 71
Barger, S. D., 243
Barling, J., 76
Barling, N. R., 151
Barlow, G. K., 51
Barlow, W. E., 145
Barnes, V. A., 134, 135
Barnett, P. A., 137
Barré, P. E., 96
Barrett, D. C., 396
Barrett, L. T., 164
Barrett, R. J., 189
Barrett-Connor, E., 145, 356
Barron, K. D., 327, 329
Barry, K. L., 194
Barsky, A. J., 241, 250

Bartlett, S. J., 214, 218
Barton, J., 176
Basen-Eengquist, K., 164
Basham, R. B., 88
Basilakis, J., 407
Bastida, E., 71, 159
Bastone, E. C., 377
Battles, H. B., 395
Baum, A., 59, 62, 66, 68, 70, 71, 77, 79, 89, 96, 103, 105, 111, 121, 123, 362
Baum, J. D., 360
Bauman, A., 229, 410
Baumann, L. J., 148
Bavry, J., 177
Bayer, L., 90
Bayless, M. L., 358
Beach, S. R., 365
Beaglehole, R., 227
Bean-Bayog, M., 148
Beaton, J. I., 411
Beauvais, J., 162
Beck, A. T., 132, 133
Beck, N. C., 369
Beck, R., 136
Becker, M. H., 149, 150, 246, 247, 258, 259
Becker, U., 187
Beckman, H. B., 254
Bedel, B. T., 233
Bediako, S. M., 308
Beecher, H., 298
Beglin, S. J., 222
Behboo, R., 356
Beitins, I. Z., 226
Bekkers, M. J. T. M., 345
Bélanger, A., 358, 369
Belar, C. D., 13, 410
Belcher, D. W., 199
Belk, S. S., 81, 94
Bell, D. R., 392
Bell, R., 151
Bell-Syer, S., 338
Bellisle, F., 205, 206
Bellissimo, A., 338
Bellman, S. B., 248, 375
Belloc, N. B., 9, 157
Belluck, P., 249
Beltrutti, D., 242, 306
Benedetti, F., 305
Benedict, S. M., 412
Bengston, V. L., 397

Benight, C. C., 124
Benjamini, E., 54–59, 72, 361, 393
Bennett, H. L., 277
Bennett, M. H., 199
Bennett, R. S., 363
Bennett, W. I., 43
Benoliel, J. Q., 269, 270, 273, 399
Benotsch, E. G., 107, 262, 394
Benowitz, N. L., 178, 200, 201
Bensing, J. M., 254
Benson, H., 134
Benson, M. D., 365
Bensoussan, A., 249
Bentler, P. M., 152, 189
Benton, D., 227
Bentow, S. S., 271
Berenson, G. S., 100
Bergman, L. R., 100
Bergner, M., 386
Bergsma, J., 345
Berkman, L., 179
Berkman, L. F., 90, 91, 92, 379
Berlant, N. E., 230
Berman, E. R., 212
Bernstein, D., 286
Bernstein, I. L., 389
Berrettini, W., 174
Berridge, K. C., 173
Berry, S., 160
Bertrand, L. D., 192
Best, A., 192
Best, C. L., 186
Best, J. A., 191, 192
Betancourt, R., 92
Bethel, A., 358
Bevins, T., 308, 309, 321
Bewley, B. R., 176
Bezkor, M. F., 249
Bickham, N. L., 169
Biddle, S. J. H., 153
Biener, L., 164
Bierut, L. J., 174
Bigelow, G., 199
Biglan, A., 176, 177, 192, 199
Bignell, G., 28
Billings, A., 120
Billings, A. G., 122
Billings, J. H., 380
Binder, L. M., 306
Binik, Y. M., 96

Binkoff, J. A., 196
Bino, G., 364
Birch, H. G., 73
Birchmore, D., 259
Birren, J. E., 157, 228
Bishop, D. S., 384
Bishop, G. D., 255
Bishop, M., 121
Black, F. L., 4
Black, R. G., 308, 309
Blackhall, L. J., 399
Blaine, T. M., 192
Blair, S. N., 215, 225, 227, 228
Blake, D. D., 109, 131, 325
Blakey, R., 196
Blalock, S. J., 363
Blanchard, E. B., 88, 108, 309, 327, 328, 329
Blanck, H. M., 215
Bland, S. H., 77
Blank, S. G., 51
Blanton, H., 154, 167
Blascovich, J., 65, 90
Bleecker, E. R., 351
Bleiberg, J., 353, 354, 366, 369, 383
Bliss, J. M., 389
Bloch, S., 360
Block, A. R., 360
Blom, G. E., 109
Blomberg, B. B., 392
Bloom, E. T., 227
Bloom, F. E., 296, 304
Bloom, J. R., 391, 392
Bloom, J. W., 181, 190
Blount, R. L., 330
Blum, D., 243, 246
Blum, R. H., 322, 324
Blumenthal, J. A., 71, 92, 126, 208, 209, 380
Bo, L., 33
Bock, B. C., 231
Boden-Albala, B., 187
Bodin, L., 302
Bodmer, J., 28
Bodmer, W. F., 28
Bodnar, R. J., 306
Boffey, P. M., 8
Bogaards, M. C., 327
Bogart, L. M., 262, 394
Bohm, L. C., 77
Boissevain, M. D., 327
Bonanno, G. A., 98, 395, 403

Bond, C. F., 186
Bonica, J. J., 386
Bonnebakker, A. D., 339
Bonner, G., 135
Bonney, A., 161
Bonney, G., 161
Bonollo, D. S., 199
Booth, R. J., 396
Booth-Kewley, S., 101
Boraas, M., 389
Borelli, B., 162, 263
Borland, R., 232
Borus, J. F., 241
Borysenko, J., 57
Bos, J. L., 28
Boscarino, J. A., 66
Bosma, H., 77
Bott, M. J., 198
Botvin, G. J., 174, 176, 191, 192
Bouchard, C., 214
Boulware, L. E., 168
Bourassa, M. G., 379
Bourey, R. E., 356
Bourgeois, N., 358
Bourne, T. H., 384
Bouton, K., 411
Bova, G. S., 28
Bovbjerg, D. H., 389, 390, 391
Bovbjerg, V. E., 208
Bove, G., 249, 338
Bowen, A. M., 153
Bowen, D. J., 199, 414
Bowers, C. A., 164, 201
Bowlby, J., 283
Bowlin, S. J., 358
Bowman, E. D., 177, 178
Boyce, A., 384
Boyce, T., 158
Boyd, N. R., 178
Boyer, M., 324
Boyers, A., 392
Boyers, A. E., 392
Boyle, M., 366
Braaten, L. S., 169
Bracco, L., 364
Bradet, R., 228
Bradford, L. P., 77
Bradley, G. W., 3, 411
Bradley, L. A., 304, 310, 322, 362
Bragdon, E. E., 103, 209
Braith, R. W., 227
Braitman, L. E., 212

Brand, R. J., 101, 180
Brand-Miller, J., 217
Brandon, T. H., 173, 178, 185, 201
Brandt, L., 232
Brantley, P. J., 308
Brasfield, T. L., 169
Braveman, N. S., 57, 58, 59
Bredder, C. C., 246
Breen, A. R., 364
Brehm, J. W., 275
Breitbart, W., 388
Breitrose, H., 165
Brena, S. F., 142, 242, 306
Brennan, L. K., 229
Brennan, P. L., 187, 379
Brent, S. B., 73, 396
Breslin, F. C., 193
Breslow, L., 9, 144, 155, 157
Bridges, M. W., 98, 287
Bristow, A., 209
Broadhead, W. E., 88, 123
Broadstock, M., 232
Broberg, D. J., 389
Brodney, S., 215
Brody, B. A., 305
Brody, D. S., 241
Brody, M. C., 324
Brody, S., 103
Brolin, R. E., 220
Broman, C. L., 92
Bromberger, J. T., 112, 232
Brondolo, E., 89, 91, 148
Brook, J. S., 189
Brooks, J. D., 28
Brooks-Gunn, J., 223
Broome, A., 411
Brosschot, J. F., 240, 241, 351
Broton, J. G., 354
Brown, B. W., 165
Brown, C., 174, 175, 179
Brown, G. G., 173
Brown, J. M., 122, 329, 330
Brown, K. S., 191, 192
Brown, K. W., 389
Brown, L. K., 163
Brown, R. T., 366
Brown, R. W., 351
Brown, S., 260
Brown, S. A., 173, 174
Browne, G., 321
Brownell, K. D., 210, 211, 213, 215,
    216, 217, 220, 221, 222, 223

Brownley, K. A., 71, 103, 209
Brownson, R. C., 229
Brox, J., 305
Bruce, D. F., 360, 361, 362
Brucker, B. S., 367
Brudney, K., 394
Bruehl, S., 106, 303, 341
Brugger, A. M., 320
Bruhn, J. G., 164
Brunner, E., 209
Bruns, D., 409
Brunton, S. A., 144, 146, 160
Brustrom, J., 122
Bruvold, W. H., 191, 192
Bryan, A., 151, 186
Bryant, J. E., 209
Bryer, K., 125
Brymer, J., 377
Buchner, D. M., 227
Buchtal, J., 105
Buck, R., 213
Budson, A. E., 387
Budzynski, T. H., 131
Buer, N., 330
Buescher, K. L., 369
Bullen, B. A., 226
Bullinger, M., 348
Bulman, R. J., 277
Bundy, C., 380
Buono, M. J., 229
Burbach, D. J., 157, 346
Burg, I. N., 349, 361
Burg, M. M., 92, 148
Burghen, G. A., 360
Burgin, L., 109
Burish, T. G., 384, 388, 389, 390, 391
Burke, B. L., 196, 219
Burke, E. J., 131
Burke, G. L., 180
Burke, L. E., 263
Burleson, M. H., 363
Burnette, M. C., 360, 361, 362
Burnette, M. M., 110, 271
Burney, R., 134
Burns, D. M., 179
Burns, E. M., 156
Burns, J. W., 106, 341, 378
Burns, L. R., 103
Burnside, I. G., 37
Bursill, D., 37
Burton, D., 126
Busch, C. M., 142

Bush, J. P., 284, 285, 286, 316, 317,
    322, 323, 327, 337, 338, 393
Bush, T., 322
Busiahn, A., 122
Buss, A. H., 73, 101
Bussey, H. J. R., 28
Butcher, J. N., 287
Butini, L., 393
Butler, C., 351
Butler, L. D., 391
Butt, J. H., 282
Buysse, D., 103
Bye, L., 168
Byers, T., 200, 215
Byrne, P., 252

C

Caan, B. J., 209
Cabana, M. D., 351
Cabral, R. J., 169
Cacciapaglia, H., 104
Cacioppo, J. T., 79
Cadman, D., 366
Cafasso, L., 75, 347
Caggiula, A. R., 178, 179
Caggiula, A. W., 166, 209
Cahill, J., 210
Cahill, L., 69
Cahn, J., 409
Caillat-Zucman, S., 394
Cairns, J., 262
Calesnick, L. E., 96
Calhoun, K. S., 110
Callahan, L. F., 362
Calle, E. E., 178, 215
Cameron, C. L., 121
Cameron, L., 243
Cameron, R., 133, 325
Cameron, R. P., 214, 217
Camerson, C. L., 389
Camilli, A., 181, 190
Camilli, A. E., 181
Campanelli, P. C., 100
Campbell, M. K., 162
Campbell, P. A., 28
Campbell, S., 384
Campbell, T., 21
Campbell, T. L., 408
Campo, M. C., 159
Campos, P. E., 167
Cannon, J. T., 304

Cannon, W., 66, 67
Cannon, W. B., 104
Capell, F., 168
Capitanio, J. P., 395
Caporaso, N. E., 177, 178
Carbonari, J. P., 151, 153
Cardenas, D. D., 339
Carels, R. A., 92, 104
Carey, K., 167, 193
Carey, M. P., 97, 166, 167, 169, 193, 384, 388, 389, 390, 391
Carey, R. G., 398
Carey, W. B., 73
Cargill, V. A., 169
Carlino, P., 262
Carlson, C. R., 128, 390
Carlson, J., 391
Carlson, L. E., 199
Carmelli, D., 99, 100, 101, 379
Carmin, C., 287
Carmody, T. P., 209, 294
Carnes, B. A., 140
Carney, M. A., 120, 121, 122
Carney, R. M., 286, 379
Carpenter, D. J., 282
Carpenter, S., 254
Carr, C. R., 193, 200
Carr, D. B., 226
Carrington, M., 394
Carroll, D., 324, 380
Carson, J. W., 308
Carter, B., 73, 76, 103, 112, 226
Carter, R. L., 308
Cartwright, M., 103, 148
Carty, J., 213
Caruso, L., 391
Carver, C. S., 10, 98, 100, 391, 392
Casey, K. L., 310, 313, 315
Cashmere, J. D., 103
Casper, M., 180
Caspersen, C. J., 227
Casriel, C., 191
Cassel, C., 140
Cassel, C. K., 412
Cassem, N. H., 377
Castro, F. G., 159, 181
Cataldo, M. F., 156, 157, 232
Catania, J. A., 168
Cattanach, L., 66
Catz, S. L., 262, 394
Cavanaugh, S. V. A., 271
Cay, E. L., 377

Celentano, E., 227
Celio, A. A., 224
Cella, D., 148, 388
Celler, B. G., 407
Cepeda, B. A., 198
Cerreto, M. C., 164
Chae, C. U., 227
Chalmers, T. C., 357
Chambers, L., 137, 216
Chambless, D. L., 133
Champion, J. D., 169
Chan, A. W. K., 194
Chandra, R. K., 156
Chanel, C., 232
Chang, A., 232
Chang, B., 21
Chang, B. L., 254
Chape, C., 112
Chapman, C. R., 296, 297, 303, 308, 309, 310, 313, 315, 320, 336, 337, 339
Chapman, S. L., 142, 294, 306, 310, 340, 341
Chassin, L., 173, 176, 178, 185, 193
Chatlia, T., 54
Chaves, J. F., 330
Chavez, R., 307
Chawla, A., 102
Cheadle, A., 14
Chen, C., 320
Chen, C-F., 28
Chen, E., 323, 327, 332, 337, 338
Chen, J. L., 168
Chen, K., 190
Chen, P-H., 28
Chen, Q., 103
Chen, V., 192
Chen, Y., 28
Cherkin, D., 322, 339, 340
Cherner, M., 396
Cheskin, L. J., 214
Chesney, M., 99, 100, 101, 104, 137, 158, 220, 394, 395, 396
Chess, S., 73
Cheung, L. W. Y., 214
Chilcoat, H. D., 192
Chitayat, D., 156
Choi, J. N., 77
Choi, W. S., 176, 192
Chou, C.-P., 192
Chow, E., 392
Christakis, G., 166, 209

Christenfeld, N., 90, 330
Christensen, A. J., 107, 148, 153, 251, 260, 406
Christensen, J., 408
Christian, B. J., 346
Christie, S., 104
Christophersen, E. R., 156, 157, 232
Chun, C.-A., 242
Ciaranello, R. D., 68
Ciccarone, D. H., 168
Ciccone, D., 306
Ciesla, J. A., 396
Cinciripini, L. G., 199
Cinciripini, P. M., 199, 341
Cioppa, A. L., 401
Ciraulo, D. A., 146, 174, 188, 189, 195, 199
Citron, M. L., 324
Ciulla, R., 353, 354, 366, 369
Clancy, S., 308, 339
Clark, D. O., 229
Clark, F., 18, 159
Clark, M. R., 330
Clark, R., 71
Clark, T. S., 307
Clark, V. R., 71
Clark, W. C., 300
Clark, W. R., 276
Clarke, P. B. S., 177
Clarke, W., 360
Clarke, W. L., 358
Clarkson, T. B., 104
Claus, E. B., 231
Cleary, P., 176
Cleary, P. D., 177, 178, 251, 411
Cleeland, C. S., 247, 322, 324
Clegg, A. G., 244
Clemmey, P., 325, 363
Clever, L. H., 167, 270
Cloitre, M., 81
Clouse, R. E., 358
Cluss, P. A., 257, 259, 262, 263, 351
Coates, R. J., 215
Coates, T. J., 168, 396
Cobb, S., 111, 141, 274
Cocke, R. R., 106
Cockrell, J. L., 323
Coddington, R. D., 81
Cogan, D., 300
Cogan, R., 300

Cohen, F., 107, 344, 345
Cohen, L., 103
Cohen, L. L., 330, 331
Cohen, L. M., 174
Cohen, M. H., 324
Cohen, M. J., 339
Cohen, N., 105, 107
Cohen, P., 189
Cohen, R. J., 330
Cohen, R. Y., 220, 223
Cohen, S., 10, 66, 69, 80, 92, 93, 103, 105, 106, 107, 158, 181, 193, 200, 250, 391, 392
Cohen, S. M., 233
Cohen, W. S., 165
Cohn, L. D., 149
Coico, R., 54–59, 72, 361, 393
Colagiuri, S., 217
Colby, S. M., 196, 199
Colditz, G., 233
Colditz, G. A., 181
Cole, C. F., 259, 360
Cole, J., 168
Cole, S. W., 393, 394
Coleman, C. L., 395
Colerick, E., 98
Coley, B., 162, 169
Colleran, J. A., 227
Collette, L., 120, 403
Colligan, M. J., 242
Collin, R. L., 64
Collins, A., 43, 71
Collins, A. C., 177
Collins, B. N., 201
Collins, C. A., 121
Collins, G. A., 339
Collins, J. L., 167, 168
Collins, R. L., 168
Collins, T. C., 271
Collins, W., 384
Collis, M., 126
Collu, R., 135
Compas, B. E., 122, 224, 333
Comstock, G. W., 80, 390
Conaway, M., 162
Connelly, P. A, 164
Conner, M., 151
Connor, W. E., 209
Connors, G. J., 195
Conrad, B., 356
Conrad, D., 339, 340
Conrad, K. M., 176

Conran, P., 135
Consalvi, A. R., 229
Contrada, R.,10, 98, 100, 243
Converse, S. A., 255
Cook, J., 152, 229
Cook, M. R., 198
Cook, N. R., 215
Cook, P. S., 159, 160
Cook, W. W., 102
Cooley, N. B., 220
Coons, H. L., 406
Cooper, L. A., 168
Cooper, M. L., 92, 97, 167
Cooper, Z., 223
Cope, D. W., 254
Copeland, L. J., 391
Coppel, D. B., 192
Corder, R., 187
Cordova, M. J., 390, 391
Corle, D. K., 210
Cornish, A. M., 143
Cornoni-Huntley, J., 179
Coronado, G., 165, 166
Corso, P. S., 407
Cossette, S., 380
Costa, P. T., 75, 102, 142, 250
Cota, M. K., 159
Côté, C., 126, 226
Côté, G., 327
Cott, C., 348
Cottington, E. M., 76, 89, 112
Courtney, M. E., 392
Cousins, N., 392
Coutinho, R. E., 168
Coutu, M.-F., 208
Couvadelli, B., 382
Covacci, G., 128
Covinsky, K. E., 258
Cox, C. E., 391
Cox, D. J., 358, 360
Cox, D. S., 106
Cox, G. B., 308, 309
Cox, N. K. M., 73, 105, 365
Cox, T., 76
Cox, W. M., 189
Coyne, J. C., 81, 87, 88, 120
Coyne, T., 210
Cozzarelli, C., 97
Craig, K. D., 142, 298, 299, 307, 316
Craig, T. G., 390
Cramer, P., 119

Craske, M. G., 332
Craun, A. M., 142, 150
Crawford, D., 229, 410
Crawford, M., 156
Creech, S. D., 271
Crespo, C. J., 214
Cretin, D., 263
Crewe, N. M., 355
Crinean, J., 280
Criqui, M. H., 10, 183
Crisp, A. H., 224
Crisson, J. E., 306
Critchlow, B., 182, 321
Croft, J., 180
Croker, H., 103, 148
Cronan, T. A., 368
Cronkite, R. C., 173
Croog, S. H., 378, 379
Crosby, R. A., 169
Crowson, J., 330
Croyle, R. T., 161, 243, 344, 412
Cruess, D. G., 392, 396
Cruess, S., 396
Crump, C., 414
Cruz, I., 262
Cryer, P. E., 358
Cubic, B. A., 221, 224
Cuellar, J. B., 397
Cuevas, J., 307
Culbertson, A. L., 325, 363
Cullen, A., 358
Cullen, D. W., 212
Cullen, J. W., 178, 179
Culver, J. L., 392
Cummings, C., 306
Cummings, F. J., 386, 387
Cummings, K. M., 389
Cummings, N. A., 408
Cunningham, A. J., 392
Cunningham, C. L., 172, 185
Cunningham, J. A., 193, 194
Cunningham, L. L. C., 390
Cunningham, W. R., 259
Curle, D., 209
Curry, S., 14, 162, 193, 199
Curry, S. J., 144, 145, 150, 163, 199, 201, 264
Cutler, R. B., 341
Cutrona, C., 92
Cutrona, C. E., 87, 88
Cutter, G., 200
Cvengros, J. A., 251

D

Daeppen, J.-B, 172
Dahlberg, C. C., 374
Dahlquist, L. M., 286, 331
Dahlstrom, W. G., 102, 287
Dakof, G., 81
D'Alessandri, R., 137
Dalessio, D. J., 109
Dallman, M. F., 213
Dalton, J. A., 391
Daltrov, L. H., 254
Daly, K., 248, 375
D'Ambrosio, S. M., 105
Dame, A., 100
Danko, G. P., 172
Danoff-Burg, S., 121, 374, 389
Dans, R., 376
D'Antono, B., 208
Dar, R., 247
Darnell, L., 71
Darwin, C., 27
Datillo, A. M., 216
D'Avanzo, B., 181
D'Avernas, J. R., 191, 192
Davidson, J., 389
Davidson, L. M., 111
Davidson, R. J., 135
Davidson, R. S., 185, 186
Davies, M., 177
Daviglus, M. L., 141
Davis, A. M., 338
Davis, D. D., 133
Davis, G. M., 88
Davis, H., 134
Davis, M. C., 71
Davis, M. S., 258, 262
Davis, P. I., 358
Davis, R. M., 192
Davis-Hearn, M., 192
Davison, G. C., 66, 70, 102, 172, 173,
     184, 189, 222, 287, 289, 293,
     335, 336, 369, 373
Davison, K. P., 124
Davison, L., 64
Daw, J., 408
Day, B. W., 307
Day, N., 98
Day-Lally, C. A., 178
De Groot, M., 358
De Jong, J. R., 327
De Moor, C., 193, 212

De Vroome, E. M. M., 168
Dean, L., 403
DeAngelis, T., 352, 370, 409
Deardorff, W. W., 13
Debski, T. T., 208
Deckel, A. W., 379, 383, 384
DeCosimo, D., 378
Deeg, D. J. H., 414
DeFaire, U., 101
Deffenbacher, J. L., 133, 142, 150
Degner, L. F., 411
Deich, J. D., 90
DeJong, W., 186, 217
Del Carmen, R., 156
Delahanty, D. L., 106
Delawyer, D. D., 286
DeLeon, P. H., 287, 409
DellaPietra, L., 287
DeLongis, A., 81
DeLuca, C. J., 316, 317, 322
DeLuca, J., 250
Demarest, J. F., 393
Denissenko, M. F., 179
Dennis, C., 379
Dentinger, M. P., 329
DePalma, A., 322
DePaulo, D. J., 153
D'Eramo-Melkus, G., 360
Derogatis, L. R., 287, 288
Derry, P. A., 352
Dershewitz, R. A., 156, 157, 232
Des Jarlais, D. C., 168, 191
Descartes, R., 6, 7
Desharnais, R., 126, 152, 226, 228,
     229
Deshields, T., 287
Després, J.-P., 214
Detien, J., 412
Detweiler, J. B., 233
Deutsch, R., 322
Dev, P., 224
Devay, P., 178
DeVellis, B. M., 87, 90, 94, 276, 347
DeVellis, R. F., 87, 90, 94, 96, 276,
     347, 363
Devereux, R. B., 103
Devins, G. M., 96
Devos, D., 218
DeVries, J. E., 271
Deykin, E. Y., 66
Deyo, R. A., 322, 339, 340
Diamond, E. L., 100, 112

Diaz, T., 176
Dickerson, S. S., 124
Dickey, D., 135
DiClemente, C. C., 151, 152, 153,
     193
DiClemente, R. J., 166, 167
Diderichsen, F., 104
Diehr, P., 14
Dielman, T. E., 100
Dietz, W. H., 212, 214
Diez-Roux, A., 180
DiFonzo, K., 167
DiFranza, J., 156, 177
DiIorio, C., 162, 263
Dilillo, V., 113, 384, 388, 389
Diller, L., 382, 383
Dillman, A. S., 232
Dillon, J. M., 350
DiMatteo, M. R., 253, 254, 256, 257,
     260, 261, 262, 444
DiMiceli, S., 391
Dimsdale, J. E., 126, 322
Dinh, K. T., 176, 192
DiNicola, D. D., 253, 254, 256
DiPlacido, J., 97, 98
Dirks, J. F., 263
Dishion, T. J., 192
Dishman, R. K., 125, 226, 228, 229,
     230, 378
Distefan, J. M., 176, 192
Ditto, B., 28, 101
Ditto, P. H., 243, 344
Dixon-Shanies, D., 213
Dobkin, B. H., 382
Dobkin, P., 391
Doctor, J. N., 309
Doehrman, S. R., 379
Doering, S., 279
Doherty, K., 201
Dohns, I. E., 76
Dohrenwend, B. P., 80, 81
Dohrenwend, B. S., 80, 81
Dolan, E., 308
Dolbier, C. L., 106
Dolecek, T. A., 209, 258
Doleys, D. M., 307
Dolinski, D., 149
Doll, H. A., 223
Donnerstein, E., 71
Donny, E. C., 178, 179
Donovan, D. M., 200
Doraiswamy, M., 126

Dornbusch, S. M., 345
Dotzauer, E., 103
Dougall, A. L., 59, 62, 66, 103, 105, 106, 362
Dougherty, G., 284
Douglass, O., 104
Douthwaite, J. A., 187
Dowd, E. T., 341
Dowling, H., 212
Downey, G., 276
Doyle, B., 344
Doyle, C., 206
Doyle, E. J., 250
Doyle, M. M., 176
Doyle, W. J., 66, 103
Drabman, R. S., 295
Dracup, K., 379
Draper, D., 271
Drapkin, R. G., 219
Dreher, H., 114
Drewnowski, A., 206
Drummond, D. C., 196
Dubbert, P. M., 224, 228, 229, 231
Dube, C. E., 153
Dubner, R., 310, 313, 315
Duchene, A. G., 209, 258
Dugard, P., 377
Duivenvoorden, H. J., 390
Duker, J., 288
Dunbar-Jacob, J., 256, 257, 258, 260, 262
Dunbar-Jacob, J. M., 263
Duncan, S. C., 157
Duncan, T. E., 157
Dunford, R. G., 358
Dunkel-Schetter, C., 88, 90, 123, 391
Dunn, A. J., 105
Dunn, A. L., 228, 229, 231
Dunn, M. E., 164, 174, 201
Dupuis, G., 208
Dura, J. R., 106, 365
Duran, R. E., 394
Durant, L. E., 169
Durham, M. L., 229
Durning, P. E., 230
Dusseldorp, E., 380
Dweck, C. S., 94, 96
Dworkin, S. F., 292
Dyer, A. R., 376
Dyken, M. E., 376
D'Zurilla, T. J., 133

E

Eakin, E., 391
Earl, L., 411
Earle, T. L., 71
Easterbrook, G., 7, 267
Eberhardt, T. L., 286, 383
Eccleston, C., 327, 333
Eck, L. H., 200, 212
Eckenrode, J., 81
Edell, B. H., 217
Edelman, S., 392
Edelstein, L., 75
Edens, J. L., 308
Edgar, L., 389
Edge, K., 120
Edington, D. W., 215
Edington, S., 217
Edmonds, C. V. I., 392
Edmonson, J. H., 322, 324
Edwards, C. L., 358
Edwards, D. A., 176
Edwards, D. L., 107
Edwards, R. R., 307
Eek, C., 314
Egert, J., 330
Eichenwald, K., 353
Eid, N., 73, 76, 103, 112, 226
Eigen, H., 73, 76, 103, 112, 226
Eisenberg, M. G., 355, 369
Eisenstein, E., 126, 208, 209
Eiser, C., 283, 284, 286, 360, 393
Eitel, P. K., 169
Ekstrand, M. L., 396
Ekström, M., 76
Elash, C., 198
Elashoff, R., 392
Eldridge, R. L., 394
Eliasson, B., 181
Eliopoulos, C., 156
Elkind, M., 187
Ellestad, D., 306
Ellickson, P. L., 177, 192
Ellington, L., 255
Elliott, C. H., 393
Elliott, E. S., 94
Elliott, M. N., 64
Ellis, A., 28, 64, 65, 132
Ellison, R. C., 102
Ellwein, L. B., 233
Elston, M. A., 158
Elwood, P. C., 101
Emery, R. E., 66, 360

Emmons, C.-A., 412
Emmons, K., 164, 233
Emmons, K. M., 150, 165, 193, 199
Emrick, C. D., 195
Endres, R. K., 358
Endress, M. P., 279
Eng, P. M., 102
Engel, G., 15, 242
Engel, G. L., 6, 7, 8, 13, 108
English, P., 232
Engstrom, P. F., 384
Enomoto, K., 242
Enright, M. F., 287, 409
Epping-Jordan, J. E., 321
Eppstein-Herald, D., 224
Epstein, J. A., 176, 191, 192
Epstein, J. I., 28
Epstein, L. H., 218, 219, 229, 230, 257, 259, 262, 263, 358, 367, 368
Epstein, R. M., 254
Erath, S., 198
Erdman, R. A. M., 377, 378
Erdmann, Y., 239
Erfurt, J. C., 112
Eriksen, M. P., 180
Ernst, D., 162, 263
Ernst, J. M., 65
Ernster, V. L., 145
Esler, M., 126
Espelage, D. L., 73, 76, 103, 112, 226
Esswein, L. A., 54
Esterling, B. A., 106, 107
Estes, M. A., 389
Estey, A., 260
Evans, C., 277
Evans, D. D., 327, 329
Evans, D. R., 2, 13, 144, 240, 256, 257, 258, 261, 263, 414
Evans, F. J., 135
Evans, G. W., 68, 69, 77, 90, 93, 180
Evans, J., 71
Evans, R., 350
Evans, R. I., 190, 191
Evans, R. L., 384
Evers, S. G., 28
Everson, S. A., 102, 103, 104, 381
Evon, D. M., 378
Ewan, C., 402
Ewart, C., 77, 145, 255
Ewing, M., 66, 82
Ey, S., 122

F

Fahey, B. J., 167
Fahey, J. L., 106, 392
Fair, J. M., 380
Fairbank, D. T., 80
Fairburn, C. G., 222, 223, 224
Fairhurst, S. K., 152, 193
Falkner, B., 208
Faller, C., 192
Fals-Stewart, W., 199
Fang, J., 375
Farbry, J. E., 282
Farinaro, E., 77, 227
Farkas, A. J., 192
Farlow, M., 365
Farquhar, J. W., 165, 166
Farrand, M., 166, 209, 258
Farrar, W. B., 392
Farrin, A., 338
Farris, E., 135
Fathalla, M. F., 167
Faucett, J., 307
Fauerbach, J. A., 320
Faulhaber, H.-D., 122
Faulkner, P., 214
Faust, R., 189
Fava, J. L., 165
Fawcett, S. B., 156, 157, 232
Fawzy, F. I., 392
Fawzy, N. W., 392
Fazzari, T. V., 106
Feaganes, J. R., 148
Fedder, D. O., 358
Fegan, M. F., 87, 88, 90, 91, 177, 276, 377, 379
Fehrenbach, P. A., 131
Feinberg, N. S., 71
Feinglos, M. N., 358, 368
Feinstein, A. R., 348, 411
Feldman, J., 108, 109, 351
Feldman, M., 44
Feldman, P., 158, 250
Feldman, R. S., 281
Feletti, G., 254
Felix, M. R. J., 220, 223
Felson, D. T., 362, 382
Fernandez, E., 136, 307, 330, 331, 332
Fernandez, M. I., 394
Fernengel, K., 91
Ferrando, S. J., 395
Ferrell, B. R., 321

Ferrucci, L., 414
Feuerstein, M., 308, 325
Fey, S. G., 209
Fiatarone, M. A., 227
Field, A. E., 217
Field, T., 134, 226
Fielding, J. E., 165, 193
Fields, H. L., 303, 305
Fiellin, D. A., 199
Fifield, J., 363
Figueiras, M. J., 379
Fileds, K. K., 66*
Fillingim, R. B., 242, 307
Filsinger, E. E., 158
Findke, G., 66
Fine, R. N., 259
Finn, P. E., 258
Finney, J. W., 156, 157, 194, 195, 197, 232
Fiore, M. C., 172, 175, 177, 198, 199, 200
Fireman, P., 351
Firman, D., 254
Fischer, L. B., 178
Fishbain, D. A., 341
Fishbein, M., 151
Fisher, A., 356
Fisher, E. B., 178
Fisher, J. D., 151, 167, 169
Fisher, L. D., 350
Fisher, W. A., 151, 167, 169
Fiske, D. W., 83
Fitterling, J. M., 195
Fitzgerald, E. F., 379
Fitzgerald, S. T., 77
Fitzgibbon, M., 210
Fitzmaurice, G., 102
Flack, J. M., 18, 159, 243, 393
Flanders, W. D., 178
Flannigan, C., 227
Flaskerud, J. H., 395
Flaten, M. A., 305
Flay, B. R., 152, 160, 176, 189, 191, 192, 350
Fleming, A., 99
Fleming, I., 111
Fleming, M. F., 194
Fleming, M. P., 287
Fleming, R., 77, 89, 157, 158, 244
Fletcher, B., 119, 197, 319, 344
Fletcher, G. F., 378
Fletcher, M. A., 107, 124, 396

Fletcher, R. H., 250, 377
Flint, E. P., 401, 402
Flor, H., 315, 321, 335, 341
Flora, J. A., 158, 165
Floreen, A., 341
Flory, J. D., 112
Flowers, K., 254
Flury, L., 186
Flynn, B. S., 163
Flynn, K. J., 210
Foa, E. B., 66
Fogel, E. R., 37
Foley, B., 377
Foley, K. M., 310, 313, 315
Folkman, J., 387
Folkman, S., 62, 63, 65, 80, 81, 83, 117, 118, 119, 120, 121, 122, 158, 344, 403
Follick, M. J., 340, 341
Folts, J. D., 187
Fong, G. T., 167, 168
Fontaine, K. R., 215
Fontanilla, I., 396
Forchheimer, M., 355
Ford, M. H., 51
Fordyce, W. E., 294, 305, 314, 326, 327, 340
Forem, J., 134
Foreyt, J., 71, 220
Forgays, D. G., 193, 218
Forman, M. R., 210
Foroud, T., 174
Forster, J. L., 192
Forsyth, A. D., 169
Forsyth, L. H., 228, 229, 231
Fortmann, S. P., 158, 160, 178, 191, 200
Foster, D. J., 393
Foster, G. D., 211, 215, 220
Foster-Powell, K., 217
Fowler, S. E., 356
Fox, B. H., 175, 177
Fox, C. H., 393
Fox, D. K., 12
Fox, K. A. A., 248
France, J. L., 309
France, R. D., 324
Francis, V., 261
Franckowiak, S. C., 218
Frank, E., 66, 103, 160
Frank, G., 399
Frank, L. D., 14

Frank, R. G., 354, 355, 369
Franke, P., 173
Frankenhaeuser, M., 43, 68, 69, 71, 83
Franklin, B., 268
Frankowski, J. J., 97
Fraser, R. T. R. M., 351, 352, 353
Frasure-Smith, N., 379, 380
Frautschi, N. M., 99, 131, 137
Fredrickson, B. L., 98
Fredrikson, M., 111
Freedland, K. E., 286, 358, 379
Freedman, D. S., 215
Freels, S. A., 160
Freeman, A., 132, 133
Freeman, R., 334
Freidson, E., 243
Freier, K., 122
French, D., 327
French, J. R. P., 89
French, M. T., 194
French, S. A., 206, 223
Fretwell, M. D., 386, 387
Freud, S., 10
Freund, A., 360
Friedman, A., 396
Friedman, A. G., 406, 407
Friedman, G. D., 187
Friedman, H. S., 10, 92, 101, 102
Friedman, M., 99, 101, 136, 137,
    180, 380
Friedman, S. R., 168, 191
Friedrich, G., 137
Friedrich, M. F., 54
Friend, R., 93, 169, 363
Fritz, H. L., 380
Froese, A., 377
Fromme, K., 192
Frone, M. R., 92
Fry, R. A., 131
Frymoyer, J. W., 308, 309, 321
Fuller, R. D., 221, 224
Fuller, S. S., 279
Fullerton, J. T., 145
Funk, S. C., 98
Furlanetto, L. M., 271
Futterman, A. D., 106
Fydrich, T., 341

G

Gadde, K. M., 66, 135
Gafni, A., 321

Gainer, J., 325
Galavotti, C., 169
Galen, 6
Gallacher, J. E. J., 101
Gallato, R., 364
Gallison, C., 192
Gallo, L. C., 71, 92
Galuska, D. A., 215, 216, 217
Gange, J. J., 221
Gannon, L. R., 307
Gapinski, K. D., 217
Garber, J., 148
Garcia, A. M., 80
Garfin, S. R., 309
Garfinkel, P. E., 214, 222
Garg, H. P., 264
Garg, S., 358
Gariti, P., 199
Garlan, R. W., 391
Garman, D., 135
Garmezy, L. B., 103, 148
Garmezy, N., 73, 98
Garner, W., 59
Garrett, P., 231
Garrity, T. F., 261
Garry, P. J., 106
Garside, D., 141
Garside, D. B., 376
Garvey, A. J., 201
Garvey, T. S., 90, 92
Garwick, A. W., 369
Gason, R., 232
Gatchel, R. J., 77, 89, 130, 131, 247,
    282, 321
Gatz, M., 251
Gaus, C. R., 271
Gauthier, J., 327
Gauvin, L., 223
Gaylor, M., 360
Gaziano, J. M., 215
Gazmararian, J. A., 251
Geiser, P. B., 390
Gelber, S., 178
Geller, A. C., 233
Geller, B. M., 163
Gellman, M. D., 103
Gendrop, S. C., 156
Genest, M., 294, 299, 300, 302, 311,
    314, 321, 328, 331, 335, 336
Gentry, E. M., 210
Gentry, W. D., 11, 87, 147, 325, 326,
    347

Georgiades, A., 126
Gerace, R. A., 17
Gerald, K., 91
Gerber, A., 180
Gerber, K. E., 389
Gerberich, S. G., 224, 230
Gerend, M. A., 142, 150
Gerin, W., 90
Gerkovich, M. M., 198
Gerlin, A., 246
Gerrard, M., 154, 167
Gerrish, R., 195
Gerstein, F., 259
Gervasio, A. H., 384
Gevitz, N., 268, 269
Ghetti, B., 365
Ghosh-Dastidar, B., 192
Giachello, A. L., 255
Giardino, N., 108, 109, 351
Gibbons, F. X., 154, 200
Gibson, E. L., 213
Gidron, Y., 277
Gignac, M. A. M., 348
Gil, K. M., 286, 306, 308, 324, 328
Gilberstadt, H., 288
Gilbert, D. G., 177
Gilbertini, M., 151, 391
Giles, D. E., 294
Gilewski, T. A., 389
Gill, G. V., 358
Gill, J. J., 136, 137, 380
Gill, T. M., 348, 411
Gillespie, J., 316, 317
Gillin, J. C., 107
Gillis, M. M., 133
Gilpin, E. A., 175, 176, 192
Gingras, J., 358, 369
Ginsberg, B., 324
Ginsberg-Fellner, F., 213
Ginzberg, E., 269
Giovino, G. A., 200
Gipson, M., 252
Girdler, S. S., 103
Girodo, M., 300
Gisriel, M. M., 77, 89
Gladis, M. M., 154
Glanz, K., 105, 164, 209, 390
Glaser, R., 59, 105, 106, 135, 365, 390
Glasgow, R. E., 144, 161, 193, 210,
    264, 358, 359, 367
Glass, D. C., 100
Glassman, B., 162

Glautier, S., 196
Gleason, J. R., 169
Glenn, B., 106, 341
Glicksman, A. S., 386, 387
Glusman, M., 300
Glynn, C. J., 324
Glynn, S. M., 199
Gnys, M., 198, 200
Goate, A., 174
Godin, G., 126, 152, 226, 228, 229
Godtfredsen, N. S., 179
Goehring, P., 131, 328
Goffman, E., 273
Gogan, J. L., 393
Golaszewski, T., 165, 407
Gold, D. T., 401, 402
Gold, L. S., 233
Gold, P. W., 40, 104
Gold, R. S., 154, 167
Goldberg, C., 184
Goldberg, D. E., 102, 104, 381
Goldberg, E. L., 80
Goldberg, N., 324, 386
Goldberg, R., 199
Goldberg, R. J., 378, 386, 387
Golden-Kreutz, D., 392
Golden-Kreutz, D. M., 113, 384, 388, 389
Goldfedder, J., 350
Golding, J. F., 143
Goldman, A. I., 192
Goldman, J. M., 33
Goldman, M. S., 174
Goldman, R. F., 134
Goldstein, A. M., 28
Goldstein, D., 360
Goldstein, D. A., 396
Goldstein, I. B., 78
Goldstein, L. H., 353, 368
Goldstein, S., 226
Goldston, D. B., 358
Goldwater, B., 126
Gomel, M., 220
Gomez, F., 213
Gomez-Caminero, A., 161
Gonder-Frederick, L., 358, 360
Gonin, R., 322, 324
Gonzalez, J. S., 394
González, V. M., 367, 368
Good, A. B., 330
Goodall, T. A., 367
Goodey, E., 199

Goodman, E., 214
Goodman, N., 345
Goodrick, K., 71
Goodwin, J. S., 106
Gorder, D. D., 209, 258
Gordon, A. S., 189
Gordon, C. M., 167
Gordon, J., 163, 200, 201
Gordon, N., 303, 307
Gordon, N. F., 225, 227, 228
Gordon, W. A., 383
Gore, S., 81
Gorfinkle, K., 259, 286, 332
Gorin, A. A., 221
Gorman, P., 28
Gortmaker, S. L., 81, 214
Gortner, S. R., 94, 151
Gossard, D., 379
Gottheil, E., 392
Gottlieb, N. H., 71, 89, 122, 148, 229
Gottschalk, M., 231
Gottschau, A., 187
Goudsmit, J., 168
Gould, K. L., 380
Grabowski, S. R., 16, 27, 33, 35, 36, 39, 44, 46, 48, 49, 52, 54, 55, 57, 58, 182, 296, 303, 339, 351, 382, 384, 386
Grace, S. L., 251
Gracely, R. H., 310, 313, 315
Grady, D., 145
Graham, J. D., 407
Graham, J. R., 287
Graham, J. W., 96, 176, 189
Graham, L. E., 280
Granqvist, M., 77
Grant, I., 123
Grant, J. C. B., 43
Graves, J. E., 227
Gray, J. J., 223
Graziosi, C., 393
Green, B. A., 354
Green, C. J., 288
Green, D. C., 251
Green, L., 71
Green, L. W., 71, 89, 122
Green, M. L., 122, 127, 286
Greenbaum, P. E., 285
Greene, P., 286
Greener, S., 162
Greenglass, E. R., 89, 122, 157
Greenland, P., 376

Greenwald, H. P., 376
Greenwald, M., 156
Greenway, F. L., 220
Greer, S., 389
Greiner, B., 189
Greiner, L. H., 365
Greiner, P. A., 365
Grembowski, D., 229
Griffin, K. W., 176, 363
Grigoletto, F., 364
Grim, C. E., 71, 127
Grimley, D. M., 169
Grimson, R., 88, 123
Grinchnik, K., 66, 135
Gritz, E. R., 193, 200
Grob, G. N., 2, 4
Groessl, E., 368
Groessl, E. J., 407
Groff, A., 153
Gromski, W., 149
Gronbaek, M., 187
Gross, J., 210
Grothaus, L. C., 193
Grubb, N. R., 248
Grube, J. W., 174
Grubman, J. A., 308, 309, 321
Gruder, C. L., 199
Gruen, W., 277
Gruetzner, H., 364, 365, 366, 367
Grunau, R. V. E., 316
Grunberg, N. E., 68, 79, 193, 199
Guarnieri, P., 329
Guccione, A. A., 362, 382
Guck, T. P., 341
Gullette, E. C. D., 126
Gulliver, S. B., 196, 199
Gump, B. B., 66, 112
Guo, A., 249
Guralnik, J. M., 414
Gurman, G., 277
Gutberlet, I., 105
Guten, S., 148, 247
Guthrie, D., 392
Guttmann, R. D., 96
Guyll, M., 10, 112
Guyton, A. C., 36, 50, 241, 296
Gwaltney, J. M., 66, 103, 250

H

Haaga, D. A. F., 224, 333
Haas, F., 48, 49, 81

Haas, S. S., 48, 49, 81
Haase, A. M., 205, 206
Habel, U., 173
Hackett, T. P., 377, 397
Haddock, C. K., 193
Hafen, B. Q., 46
Hahn, W., 108
Hahn, Y. S., 315, 317
Haimerl, C., 110, 307
Haire-Joshu, D., 178, 229
Haley, N. J., 181, 208
Haley, R. W., 271
Haley, W. E., 364, 365
Halford, W. K., 367
Halkitis, P. N., 167
Hall, C., 294
Hall, J. A., 254, 256, 262, 263
Hall, M., 103
Hall, M. H., 103
Hall, S., 199
Hall, S. M., 197
Hallett, R., 162
Hallion, M. E., 153
Hallqvist, J., 104
Halperin, S., 193
Hamburg, R. J., 271
Hames, C. G., 180
Hamman, R. F., 356
Hammer, D., 112
Hammer, L. D., 176, 223
Hammon, S., 391
Hammond, S. K., 180
Hammond, W. R., 159
Hamrick, N., 92
Haney, T. L., 250, 377
Hanley, J. A., 135
Hann, D. M., 66
Hannan, P. J., 206
Hannum, J. W., 134, 328
Hansen, C. A., 360
Hansen, J., 195
Hansen, W. B., 176, 186, 189, 191
Hanson, C. L., 360
Hanusa, B. H., 97
Haque, W., 199
Harburg, E., 112
Harden, R. N., 106, 303, 341
Hare, B. D., 297, 322, 323, 336, 337
Harlan, W. R., 100
Harper, A., 348
Harris, B., 411
Harris, C., 307

Harris, D. M., 148, 247
Harris, J. K., 100
Harris, J. R., 28
Harris, K. J., 176
Harris, R. E., 181, 208
Harrison, S. L., 232
Harshfield, G. A., 51
Hart, W., 134
Harth, T., 392
Hartman, H., 247, 248
Hartman, K. A., 243
Hartmann, K., 358
Hartsock, R. J., 58
Hasan, J., 339
Hasegawa, T., 282
Haselkorn, J. K., 384
Haskell, W. L., 227, 380
Hastorf, A. H., 345
Hatfield, A. K., 322, 324
Hatira, P., 335
Hauck, E. R., 330
Hauenstein, L. S., 112
Haug, M. R., 251
Hauger, R. L., 68
Haughey, B. P., 358
Hauser, S. T., 360
Hauser, W. A., 187, 352, 353
Havens, J. F., 394
Haviland, J. S., 389
Havis, J., 191
Hawken, L., 106
Hawken, S., 376
Hay, D., 76
Haycox, L. H., 64
Haydel, K. F., 176, 223
Hayes, A. M., 133
Hayes, D. F., 387
Hayes, R. D., 262
Haynes, R. B., 258, 259, 264
Haynes, S. N., 307
Hays, J. C., 401, 402
Hays, R. D., 254
Haythornthwaite, J. A., 330
Haythornwaite, J. A., 77, 320
Hayward, C., 176, 214, 217, 223
He, Y., 365
Hearn, M. D., 206, 216
Heath, C. W., 178, 187
Heath, G. W., 216, 217
Heath, M. J. S., 178
Hebb, D. O., 83
Hebert, J. R., 161

Hébert, R., 365
Hecht, J., 162, 263
Hecker, M., 99, 100
Heil, S. H., 196
Hein, H. O., 187
Heinemann, A. W., 354, 355
Heiney, M., 90
Heinonen, O. P., 165
Heinrich, R. L., 339
Helgeson, V. S., 374, 380, 391, 392
Heller, B. R., 142
Heller, K., 89
Hellhammer, D., 78
Hellhammer, D. H., 71
Hellhammer, D. K., 105
Hellhammer, J., 71
Helliwell, B., 365
Hendel, H., 394
Henderson, D. K., 167
Henderson, G., 21
Hendler, N. H., 305, 326
Hendrick, S. S., 353, 354, 355
Hendricks, R. D., 384
Henggeler, S. W., 360
Henik, A., 277
Henley, S. J., 187
Hennekens, C. H., 227
Hennrikus, D. J., 200
Henretta, J. C., 259
Henry, C. J. K., 217
Henry, J. H., 111
Hepburn, C. G., 76
Herberman, R. B., 106
Herbert, M., 362
Herbert, T. B., 106
Herd, B., 217
Herd, J. A., 51
Herderick, E. E., 52
Herek, G. M., 395
Herman, C. P., 154, 178, 213, 214
Herman, S., 126
Hershey, G. K. K., 54
Hertzog, C., 259
Herzoff, N., 280
Herzog, T. A., 201
Hesdorffer, D. C., 352, 353
Heshka, S., 220
Hesselbrock, V. M., 172
Hester, R. K., 194, 195, 196, 407
Hewitt, J. K., 101
Hickcox, M., 200

Higgins, J. T., 111
Higgins, P., 28, 294, 362
Higgins, S. T., 196
Hilgard, E. R., 135, 299, 334
Hilgard, J. R., 299, 334
Hill, D., 176
Hill, G. B., 365
Hill, J. O., 218, 220, 221
Hill, M. N., 263
Hill-Briggs, F., 369
Hillier, L. M., 315, 316
Hillix W. A., 254
Hilton, W. F., 100
Hinchy, J., 167
Hinderliter, A. L., 71, 103, 209
Hing, M., 249
Hingson, R., 186
Hinrichs, A. L., 174
Hinton, J., 396, 398, 399, 401
Hippocrates, 5
Hiroto, D. S., 95
Hirsch, I. B., 113
Hirsch, J., 213
Hirschland, D., 215
Hirschman, R. S., 4, 7
Hitchcock, J. L., 200
Hitchcock, L. S., 321
Hjalmarson, A., 181
Hletko, J. D., 232
Hletko, P. J., 232
Hobfoll, S. E., 62, 64
Hochberg, M. C., 340, 361
Hodgins, D. C., 195
Hoelscher, T. J., 137
Hoff, C., 168
Hofman, A., 164, 365
Hofstadter, L., 296, 304
Hofstetter, C. R., 231
Hofstoetter, M. S., 279
Hogan, B. E., 102, 111, 112, 124
Hogelin, G. C., 210
Hogg, J. R., 89
Hohenstein, J. M., 197
Holahan, C. J., 81, 94, 173, 379
Holahan, C. K., 81, 94, 173, 379
Holberg, C. J., 181
Holden, C., 77
Holdridge, S., 330
Hollandsworth, J. G., 286
Holliday, J., 59
Hollis, J. F., 161
Hollomby, D. J., 96

Hollon, S. D., 133
Holloszy, J. O., 356
Holm, N. V., 28
Holman, H. R., 367, 368
Holmbeck, G. N., 323
Holmes, D. S., 125, 126, 134
Holmes, S. D., 71
Holmes, T., 79
Holmes, T. H., 80
Holocorft, C., 91
Holroyd, K. A., 109, 131, 309, 327,
   328, 332
Holst, C., 179
Holt, J., 358
Holt-Lunstad, J., 92
Holte, A., 143
Holtzman, D., 167, 168
Holum, J. R., 42, 46, 52, 204, 357
Holzman, A. D, 309
Holzman, A. D., 333
Hömann, A., 376
Hood, B., 151
Hood, H. V., 167
Hood, M., 324
Hopkins, B. L., 12
Hopkins, P. J., 134
Hopkins, P. N., 208
Hopper, K., 112
Horn, J. C., 157
Hornung, R. W., 242
Horowitz, J. M., 172
Horwitz, B., 282
Horwitz, R. I., 68
Hosmer, D., 199, 378
Hough, R. L., 80
House, J. S., 76, 89, 90, 92, 112
Houshyar, H., 213
Houston, B. K., 100, 102
Houston-Miller, N., 379
Hovell, M. F., 137
Howard, G., 180
Howell, D. C., 122
Howell, M. F., 231
Hoyle, R. H., 128
Hsu, A., 205
Hu, F. B., 176, 350
Hu, S., 212
Hubbard, R. L., 197
Hudis, C. A., 389
Hudson, S., 387
Huffman, L. C., 156
Hughes, C., 161

Hughes, J. P., 364
Hull, J. G., 186
Hulley, S. B., 166, 209
Hultquist, C. M., 200
Humble, C., 180
Humfleet, G. L., 197
Humphreys, K., 197
Humphries, C., 100
Hunkeler, E., 99, 100
Hunt, E. B., 260
Hunt, J. R., 414
Hunt, M., 73, 105, 365
Hunt, S., 358
Hunt, S. C., 51
Hunt, W. A., 147
Hunter, S. M., 100
Hurley, T. G., 161
Hurrell, J. J., 65, 76, 103, 112, 226
Hursey, K., 309
Hurwitz, B. E., 71
Hussussian, C. J., 28
Huszti, H. C., 287, 289
Hutchinson, K. E., 186
Hyson, M. C., 122
Hyun, C. S., 392

I

Ilfeld, F. W., 121
Iliadou, A., 28
Imai, W. K., 149
Ingall, C. G., 349, 361
Ingram, D. K., 210
Ingvar, C., 232
Insel, P. M., 205, 208, 225
Inui, T. S., 262
Ironson, G., 124, 396
Irvin, J. E., 164, 201
Irvine, J., 251, 262
Irvine, S., 197
Irving, L. M., 389
Irwin, M., 107
Iverson, D. C., 164
Ivery, D., 215
Iyengar, S., 358
Izard, C. E., 70

J

Jabalpurwala, S., 223
Jaccard, J., 187
Jackson, D., 338

Jackson, K. M., 142, 150
Jackson, S. E., 273, 274
Jackson, T. C., 247, 248
Jacob, M. C., 313
Jacobs, D. R., 200
Jacobs, G. D., 134
Jacobs, J. C., 402
Jacobs, K. S., 178
Jacobs, S. C., 75
Jacobsen, A. M., 259, 360
Jacobsen, P., 388, 389, 391
Jacobsen, P. B., 66, 259, 286, 332, 388, 389
Jacobson, A. M., 360
Jacobson, E., 128
Jadad, A. R., 324
Jaffe, A. S., 379
James, G. D., 51
James, J. E., 209
James, S. A., 88, 123
Jamner, L. D., 78, 304
Janal, M. N., 300
Jandciu, S., 262
Janes, G. R., 144
Janis, I., 126
Janis, I. L., 152, 154, 162, 243, 272, 278
Jansen, M. A., 410
Jaret, P., 54, 56, 57
Jarvis, M. J., 103, 107, 148, 181
Jay, S. M., 326, 393
Jeans, M. E., 315, 316, 317
Jefferson, K. W., 169
Jefferson, T., 307
Jeffery, R. W., 103, 148, 200, 206, 212, 215, 216, 219, 223
Jegerski, J. A., 199
Jemmott, J. B., 168, 243
Jemmott, L. S., 168
Jenkins, C., 144
Jenkins, C. D., 100, 263, 406, 413
Jenkins, F. J., 106
Jenkins, G. P., 392
Jenkins, L. S., 94, 151
Jenkins, W., 18, 159, 243, 393
Jennings, G., 126
Jensen, G. M., 362
Jensen, M. P., 306, 310, 320, 330, 334, 335
Jepson, C., 384
Jessner, L., 109
Jessor, R., 14, 157

Jette, A. M., 363
Jeyaram, S., 217
Jinnett, K., 177
Jobin, J., 126, 152, 226, 228, 229
Johansen, D., 187
Johansen, O., 305
John, R., 159
Johnson, B. T., 166, 169
Johnson, C. A., 175, 176, 177, 189, 192, 325
Johnson, C. C., 137
Johnson, J. E., 126, 278, 279, 280
Johnson, J. H., 80, 81, 103
Johnson, K., 71, 159
Johnson, L. J., 205, 209
Johnson, M., 167
Johnson, M. H., 135
Johnson, M. I., 337
Johnson, M. R. D., 176
Johnson, R., 166, 209
Johnson, S. B., 73, 259, 358, 360, 406
Johnson, S. K., 250
Johnson, T. P., 160
Johnson-Young, L., 194
Johnston, C. C., 284
Johnston, D. W., 103
Johnston, L. D., 174, 175, 176, 182, 189
Johnston, M., 279, 360, 366, 383
Johnston-Brooks, C. H., 68, 358
Johnston-Early, A., 324
Jonas, B. S., 381
Jonas, M., 277
Jones, C. L., 331
Jones, D., 90
Jones, L. R., 287
Jonsson, N., 232
Jonwutiwes, K., 205, 206
Jordan, R. C., 221
Jorenby, D. E., 198, 199
Jorgensen, C., 233
Jorgensen, R. S., 97
Jossa, F., 77, 227
Jouriles, E., 186
Jousilahti, P., 376
Joyce, C., 402, 403
Juliano, L. M., 201
Juncker, A. G., 401
Juneau, M., 379
Jung, K. C., 360, 370
Just, N., 306

K
Kabat-Zinn, J., 134, 135
Kabela, E., 131
Kaell, A. T., 363
Kahn, K. L., 271
Kahn, R. L., 158
Kalichman, S. C., 162, 167, 168, 169
Kalish, R., 397
Kalish, R. A., 397, 398, 399
Kaloupek, D., 66
Kaloupek, D. G., 280
Kalra, D. L., 193
Kaltenborn, W. T., 181, 190
Kalucy, R. S., 224
Kamarck, T., 80
Kamen, L. P., 95, 96
Kammermann, S. K., 160
Kandel, D., 189
Kandel, D. B., 177, 190
Kane, R., 160
Kang, S. H., 391
Kann, L., 167, 168
Kanner, A. D., 81
Kanner, R., 340
Kanouse, D. E., 168
Kao, A. C., 251
Kaplan, B. H., 88, 123
Kaplan, G. A., 102, 103, 104
Kaplan, G. E., 381
Kaplan, J. R., 104
Kaplan, R., 92, 96, 123, 137, 151, 159, 191, 259, 368, 379, 406, 407, 410, 411, 414
Kappler, R. E., 338
Kaprio, J., 28, 227
Kapust, L. R., 367
Kar, S., 245
Karanja, N., 210
Karasek, R. A., 103
Kargman, D. E., 187
Karlberg, L., 135
Karlin, W. A., 89, 91
Karnik, R., 208
Karoly, P., 241, 293, 298, 301, 310, 313
Kasch, F. W., 227
Kase, C. S., 215
Kasl, S. V., 75, 91, 141, 274, 402
Kassel, J. D., 198, 200
Kastenbaum, R., 75
Katz, B. I., 353, 354, 366, 369
Katz, D. P., 213
Katz, E., 393

Katz, E. R., 332
Katz, J., 313
Katzlberger, F., 279
Kauth, M. R., 167
Kawachi, I., 102, 181
Kaye, W. H., 222, 223, 224
Kazarian, S. S., 2, 13, 144, 240, 414
Keane, T. M., 66
Kearney, K. A., 107
Keating, N. L., 251
Keefe, F. J., 224, 306, 308, 314, 328, 330, 333, 391
Keehn, L., 260
Keeler, E. B., 271
Keesey, R. E., 213
Keevil, J. G., 187
Kegeles, S. M., 168
Kegeles, S. S., 163
Kehoe, K., 100
Keil, U., 376
Kellner, R., 250
Kelly, J. A., 167, 168, 169, 262, 394, 396
Kelly, M., 259
Kelsey, J. L., 340, 361
Kemeny, M. E., 106, 107, 392, 393, 394
Kempe, C. H., 71
Kendall, P. C., 280
Kendler, K. S., 174
Kendrick, J. S., 227
Kenford, S. L., 200
Kennedy, S., 106
Kennedy-Moore, E., 106
Kent, D. R., 167
Kent, G., 251, 307
Kenyon, L., 377
Kerkhof, A. J. F. M., 410
Kerlikowske, K., 145
Kern, P. A., 213
Kerner, D., 123
Kerns, R. D., 306, 313, 333, 335, 336, 347, 369, 377, 407
Kersell, M. W., 191, 192
Kett, J. F., 188, 321
Ketterer, M. W., 377
Ketterson, T. U., 230
Khalil, T. M., 341
Khan, N. Q., 187
Khatri, P., 126
Khaw, K.-T., 98
Khayrallah, M. A., 198

Kibler, J., 65
Kidd, K. K., 28
Kidman, A. D., 392
Kiecolt-Glaser, J. K., 59, 105, 106, 135, 277, 365, 390
Kiernan, M., 126, 226, 227
Kilanowski, C. K., 219, 229
Kilbey, M. M., 172, 188
Kilbourn, K., 124, 392
Kilgore, H. G., 167
Killen, J. D., 176, 200, 214, 217, 223
Kilo, C., 42, 356, 357, 359, 360
Kilpatrick, D. G., 186
Kim, S. W., 306
Kimble, D. L., 169
Kimmel, P. L., 262
Kindelan, K., 251
King, A. C., 126, 156, 226, 227
King, D. S., 356
King, L. A., 93
Kinnunen, T., 201
Kipp, H., 187
Kirk, S. B., 121
Kirkland, S., 199
Kirkwood, J., 106
Kirschbaum, C., 105, 306
Kirschbaum, D., 78
Kirscht, J. P., 148, 150, 152, 246, 247
Kirwan, J. P., 356
Kittner, S. J., 181
Kivlahan, D. R., 192
Kiyak, H. A., 280
Kizer, K. W., 271
Klangos, I., 376
Klapow, J. C., 309
Klar, N., 165
Klatsky, A. L., 187
Klein, J., 156
Klein, W. M., 154
Kleinke, C. L., 314
Kleinman, J. C., 200
Klem, M. L., 221
Klerman, G. L., 250
Klesges, L. M., 214
Klesges, R. C., 176, 193, 200, 201, 212, 214
Kliewer, W., 90
Klimas, N., 396
Klonoff, E. A., 159, 246
Klose, K. J., 354
Knie, B., 156
Knittle, J., 213

Knoll, M. D., 376
Knopf, S., 179
Knopp, R. H., 208
Knowler, W. C., 356
Knowlton, G. E., 137
Knox, S. S., 102
Kobasa, S., 87, 91, 97, 98, 347
Kobrin, S. C., 200
Koch, J., 397, 403
Koenig, T., 330
Koepke, D., 192
Koepsell, T., 14
Kogevinas, M., 158
Kohl, H. W., 225, 227, 228
Kohler, T., 110, 307
Kohlmann, C.-W., 103
Kohrt, W. M., 356
Kokkinos, P. F., 227
Kolata, G., 252, 254
Kolbe, L. J., 71, 164, 167, 168
Kolonel, L. N., 209
Komro, K. A., 192
Kondou, H., 58, 107
Koocher, G. P., 393
Koopman, C., 390, 391
Koopmans, J., 199
Kop, W. J., 104, 113
Koppers, R. H., 21
Kornack, D. R., 33
Korner, P., 126
Kornguth, P., 330
Koro, C. E., 358
Korol, C. T., 142, 298, 299, 307
Korsch, B. M., 259, 261
Koskenvuo, M., 28, 227
Kost, K. L., 164
Kosten, T. R., 75
Kostis, J. B., 148
Kott, A., 191
Kottke, T. E., 165
Kovacs, M., 358
Koziol, D. E., 167
Kozlowski, L. T., 178
Kraaij, V., 380
Kraemer, B., 287
Kraemer, H. C., 165, 379, 392
Kraft, P., 377
Krajick, K., 168
Krakau, I., 135
Krakoff, L. R., 100
Kramer, B. J., 71, 159
Kramer, J., 245

Kramer, J. R., 358
Krantz, D. S., 69, 93, 100, 103, 127, 379, 383, 384
Kranzler, H. R., 186
Krasnow, S. H., 324
Krause, J. S., 355
Krauss, R. M., 380
Kravitz, R. L., 262
Kremer, E., 360
Kress, M. J., 218
Kreuter, M. W., 154, 200
Kreye, M., 69
Kring, A. M., 66, 70, 102, 172, 173, 184, 189, 222, 287, 289, 293, 335, 336, 369, 373
Kris-Etherton, P. M., 216
Kristeller, J., 199
Kritz-Silverstein, D., 145
Krogh, V., 227
Kronish, L. E., 66
Krupka, L. R., 166
Kruse, E., 181
Kruskall, L. J., 205, 209
Ksobiech, K., 168
Ku, L., 168
Kubik, M. Y., 206
Kübler-Ross, E., 398
Kubzansky, L. D., 102
Kudielka, B. M., 71
Kuhl, J. P., 300
Kuhn, C. M., 71, 104, 209, 376
Kujala, U. M., 227
Kulik, J. A., 90, 142, 149, 251, 262, 276, 278
Kuller, L. H., 92, 104, 229
Kumakura, S., 356
Kumar, M., 124, 396
Kunda, Z., 153
Kunitz, S., 18, 159, 243, 393
Kurth, T., 215
Kusaka, Y., 58, 107
Kusnecov, A. W., 108
Kutz, L. A., 392
Kuykendall, D. H., 305
Kyle, D. J., 96, 124

L

La Fleur, S. E., 213
La Greca, A. M., 17, 72, 157, 259, 283, 286, 346, 397
La Malfa, R. G., 181

La Place, J., 179, 225
LaBarba, R. C., 156
Labouvie, E., 168, 224
Labrecque, M. S., 137
Lachin, J. M., 356
Lachman, M. E., 94
Lackner, J. M., 309
LaCroix, A. Z., 179, 227
Lacroix, J. M., 101
Laffrey, S. C., 214
LaForge, R. G., 165
Lakein, A., 124
Lakka, T. A., 102, 103
Lamdan, R. M., 148
Lamont, J. H., 109
Lamparski, D. M., 358, 367, 368
Lanas, F., 376
Lancaster, J., 28
Lando, H., 193, 200
Landrine, H., 159, 246
Landsbergis, P. A., 77
Landthrip, D. S., 331
Lane, J. D., 209, 358
Lane, M. A., 210
Lang, J., 179
Lang, W., 221
Langer, E., 94, 97
Langer, E. J., 278
Langer, R. D., 414
Langhinrichsen-Rohling, J., 306
Langlie, J. K., 143, 247
Lanotte, M., 305
Lansky, A., 169
LaPerriere, A., 396
Laris, B. A., 367, 368
Larkin, K. T., 136, 137
LaRocco, J. M., 89
Larson, E. B., 227, 364
Lasser, N. L., 166, 209
Lassila, H. C., 104
Laszlo, J., 384, 386, 387, 388, 392
Latimer, E. A., 232
Lau, J., 357
Lau, R., 160, 243
Laurent, D. D., 367, 368
Laurin, D., 365
Lave, J. R., 271
Lave, L. B., 232
LaVeist, T. A., 168
Lavigne, J. V., 315, 317
Lavin, B., 251
Lavori, P., 360

Lawer, M. R., 212
Lawrence, D. B., 271
Lawton, W. J., 251, 260
Lazarus, A., 132
Lazarus, R. S., 62, 63, 64, 65, 70, 80, 81, 83, 87, 88, 117, 118, 119, 120, 122, 344, 345
Lazerson, A., 296, 304
Lazev, A. B., 201
Le Resche, L., 292
Leahey, T. H., 6
Leake, R., 93
Leavesley, G., 220
Lebowitz, M. D., 181, 190
Lebuanec, H., 394
Ledolter, J., 358
Lee, A., 304
Lee, C., 154, 162, 200
Lee, H., 191, 242
Lee, I.-M., 227
Lee, J., 106
Lee, M. H. M., 249
Lee, P. R., 143
Lee, S. H., 361, 362
Lee, W.-H., 28
Leech, S. L., 100
Leedham, B., 387
Lees, D. M., 187
Lefebvre, J. C., 306
Leffert, N., 157
LeGuyader, Y., 167
Lehman, J. M., 391, 392
Lehrer, P., 108, 109, 351
Leibel, R. L., 213
Leiferman, J. A., 106
Leigh, B. C., 167, 168
Leigh, G., 195
Leiguarda, R., 365
Leino, P., 339
Leitenberg, H., 224, 333
Leiter, M. P., 273
Lemaire, V., 111
LeMaistre, C. A., 180
Lemon, J., 392
Lemos, K., 248, 375
Lenneberg, E. H., 34
Lenz, J. W., 102
Leo, G. I., 194
Leonard, B. E., 105
Leonard, E., 232, 353
Lepage, L., 228
Lepore, S. J., 68, 69, 90, 123, 391

Lepore, V., 364
Lerman, C., 161, 174, 177, 178, 384, 390, 391, 412
Lespérance, F., 379, 380
Lester, N., 306
Lett, H. S., 380
Leu, C. S., 394
Leukefeld, C., 168
Leung, D., 102
Leurgans, S., 338
Levenson, J. L., 412
Levenson, R. W., 187
Leventhal, E., 259
Leventhal, E. A., 73, 74, 143, 157, 176, 243, 397
Leventhal, H., 73, 74, 143, 148, 157, 176, 177, 178, 241, 242, 243, 247, 248, 259, 280, 397
Lévesque, L., 126, 226
Leveton, L. B., 200
Levin, D. N., 247
Levine, A., 96
Levine, H. M., 88
Levine, J., 307
Levine, J. D., 303, 305
Levine, M. R., 334, 335
Levinson, W., 408
Levy, A. R., 389
Levy, J., 18, 68, 159, 243, 393
Levy, S. M., 106, 179, 401
Levy-Lahad, E., 365
Lew, R. A., 156
Lewis, C., 325, 363
Lewis, M., 68, 358, 376
Lewis, T. C., 351
Li, J. T. C., 350
Li, T.-K., 172, 186
Lichstein, K. L., 128, 134, 137
Lichtenstein, E., 161, 177, 178, 193, 196, 200
Lichtenstein, P., 28, 101
Lichtman, R. R., 96, 277, 374
Licthman, S. W., 212
Liebeskind, J. C., 303, 304
Liebling, B., 178
Light, K. C., 71, 103, 208, 209
Lilley, B., 402
Limacher, M. C., 227
Lin, E. H., 96
Lin, I.-F., 187
Lin, L. S., 206
Lin, X., 351

Lindeman, B., 403
Lindemann, E., 355
Linden, W., 71, 90, 102, 112, 124, 137, 216, 380
Lindenberg, C. S., 156
Lindsay, J., 365
Lindström, I., 314
Linn, L. S., 254
Linnan, L. A., 164, 165
Linton, S. J., 302, 330
Liossi, C., 335
Lipkus, I., 162
Lipowski, Z. J., 11, 15, 108
Lippi, A., 364
Lipton, J. A., 338
Lipworth, L., 134
Liskevych, T., 252
Litt, M. D., 282, 304
Liu, J. W., 200
Liu, X., 224
Liu, Y-Y., 111
Livermore, B., 149
Llabre, M. M., 71
Llewlyn-Phillips, H., 338
Lockshin, B., 177
Lockwood, G. A., 392
Loeb, K. L., 224
Loeffler, C. M., 58
Loeser, J. D., 322
Lofland, K., 106, 341
Logan, T. K., 168, 190
Logue, A. W., 212, 213, 222, 224
Lohrer, P. A., 259, 360
Lonetto, R., 73, 396
Long, B., 252
Long, R. T., 109
Longo, D. L., 58
Longshore, D. L., 192
Lopez, A. D., 187
Lopiano, L., 305
Lorber, J., 274, 275
Lorig, K., 367, 368
Lorig, K. R., 367, 368
Lorish, C. D., 260, 362
Loughlin, C. A., 76
Lourie, K. J., 163
Lovallo, W. R., 62, 102
Lovell, N. H., 407
Lovinger, R., 360
Lowe, J. B., 156
Löwel, H., 376
Lowenthal, D. T., 227

Lowrey, D., 307
Lowry, R., 167, 168
Luben, R., 98
Lubin, B., 287
Lucente, T., 338
Lucido, D., 358
Lucini, D., 128
Ludmer, P. L., 376
Ludwick-Rosenthal, R., 282
Luecken, L. J., 71
Luepker, R. V., 175, 177, 192, 193
Luft, F. C., 122
Luft, H. S., 239
Luke, W., 167
Lum, L. G., 350
Lund, A. K., 163
Lundberg, U., 71, 76, 77, 100, 103, 104
Lundin, A., 302
Lundin, R. W., 94
Luparello, T. J., 351
Lussier, J. P., 196
Lustman, P. J., 358
Lutgendorf, S., 396
Lutgendorf, S. K., 93, 396
Luus, C. A. E., 154
Lykken, D. T., 315
Lyna, P., 162
Lynam, D. R., 190
Lynch, J., 92
Lynch, J. W., 103, 104
Lynch, M., 248, 375
Lyons, H. A., 351
Lytle, L. A., 206

M

Mabe, P. A., 287
MacCallum, R., 392
Maccoby, N., 165, 166
MacDonald, G., 167
MacDonald, T. K., 167
MacFarlane, I. A., 358
Macfarlane, S., 149
Mackay, C., 76
Mackey, S. F., 380
MacLennan, R., 232
MacLeod, C. M., 260
Maclure, M., 190, 379
MacWalter, R., 383
Madans, J., 200
Maddahian, E., 189

Maddi, S., 97
Maddi, S. R., 83, 91, 98
Maddux, B. A., 356
Maddux, J. E., 17, 151, 157, 229
Madhavan, S., 375
Maes, S., 380
Mages, N. L., 349, 391, 397
Mägi, A., 302
Magni, G., 309
Magnusson, D., 100
Magovern, G. J., 287
Maguire, P., 399
Mahler, H. I. M., 90, 142, 149, 276, 278, 399
Maieskie, M. R., 172, 177
Main, D., 161, 177, 178
Maisto, S. A., 169
Maj, M., 396
Majerovitz, S. D., 363
Major, B., 97
Maki, R. H., 330
Makinodan, T., 227
Malcom, G. T., 52
Malhotra, M. S., 134
Malkin, S., 97
Malkoff, S. B., 103
Malliani, A., 128
Mallon, J., 389
Malloy, T. E., 169
Malone, J., 360
Malott, J. M., 330, 331, 332
Malspeis, S., 217
Maltbie, A. A., 324
Mangan, C., 251, 281, 282
Mangion, J., 28
Mann, L., 154, 243
Mann, T., 246
Manne, S. L., 259, 286, 332, 363, 389, 391
Mannen, K., 287
Mannucci, E. G., 100
Manos, G. N., 358
Manson, J. E., 181, 227
Manuck, S. B., 103, 104, 105, 106, 111, 208
Manwell, L. B., 194
Marchuk, D. A., 66, 135
Marcus, A. C., 193, 200
Marcus, B., 164
Marcus, B. H., 153, 228, 229, 231
Margulies, S., 107
Mariano, A. J., 355

Marien, L., 91
Mark, A. L., 376
Mark, M. M., 392
Markesbery, W. R., 365
Markovitz, J. H., 376
Marks, G., 96, 168, 395
Marks, J. S., 210
Marlatt, G. A., 163, 192, 195, 200, 201
Marmot, D., 209
Marmot, M., 77
Marmot, M. G., 158
Maron, D. J., 178, 223, 380
Marshall, G. N., 64
Marshall, J. R., 358
Marshall, R. E., 316
Marshall, S. J., 153
Marshall-Goodell, B., 79
Marsland, A. L., 105, 106
Marteau, T. M., 360
Martelli, M. F., 251
Martin, B., 196
Martin, C., 190
Martin, J. L., 403
Martin, M., 360
Martin, N., 135
Martin, P. R., 304
Martin, R., 88, 241, 242, 243, 248, 375
Martinez, F. D., 156
Martire, L. M., 73
Marucha, P. T., 105, 135
Maruyama, N. C., 391
Marvel, M. K., 254
Marvin, R. S., 360
Marx, M. H., 254
Måsbäck, A., 232
Mascovich, A., 107
Masek, B. J., 326
Maslach, C., 273, 274
Mason, H. R. C., 168, 395
Mason, J., 68, 69, 84
Masters, J. C., 132
Masterson, G., 248
Masterson-Allen, S., 386, 387
Masuda, M., 80
Masur, F. T., 126, 127, 278, 332
Matarazzo, J., 11, 147, 175, 209
Mateski, D. J., 210
Mathews, A., 127, 278
Mathur, J., 90
Maticka-Tyndale, E., 167

Mattes, R. D., 389
Matthews, K. A., 66, 71, 92, 100, 101, 103, 104, 111, 112, 208, 229, 232, 287, 376, 414
Mattson, M. E., 178, 179
Maude-Griffin, P. M., 197
Mauksch, H. O., 273, 275
Maurice, J., 380
May, C. W., 71
Mayer, D. J., 303, 337
Mayer, W., 185, 194
Maynard, F., 355
Maynard, L. M., 215
Mayne, T. J., 396
Mazel, R. M., 262
Mazze, R. S., 358
McAdoo, W. G., 71, 221
McAlister, A. L., 165
McAllister, D. A., 221
McAllister-Sistilli, C. G., 179
McAnulty, D. P., 308
McArdle, S., 111
McAuliffe, T. L., 169, 262, 394
McAvay, G., 231
McBride, C., 145
McBride, C. M., 414
Mcbride, C. M., 163, 199, 201
McBride, P., 175
McCaffery, J. M., 208
Mccaffery, M., 321
McCaffrey, D. F., 192
McCahon, C. P., 364, 365
McCalla, J. R., 406
McCallum, D. M., 103
McCann, B. S., 208
McCants, C. B., 250, 377
McCarran, M. S., 109, 325
McCarthy, D., 162, 172, 174, 177
McCarty, D., 185
McCarty, M. C., 192
McCaskill, C. C., 306, 358
McCaskill, E. O., 394
McCaul, K. D., 330, 331, 332, 358, 359, 367
McCaul, M. E., 186
McClearn, G. E., 28, 101
McClellan, A. T., 199
McClintic, J. R., 35, 36, 46, 48, 50, 51, 292
McClintic, T. L., 68
McConnell, H., 242, 306
McConnell, S., 177, 199

McCoy, S. B., 154
McCrady, B. S., 184, 185, 197
McCrae, R. R., 250
McCreary, C., 181
McCubben, J. A., 128
McCubbin, J. A., 303
McCue, M., 300
McCusker, J., 401
McCutchan, J. A., 396
McDaniel, L. K., 304, 322, 362
McDaniel, S., 408
McDermitt, D. R., 192
McDevitt, S. C., 73
McDonald, H. P., 264
McDonald, P. G., 71
McDonald, R. V., 173
McDonald, T., 215
McElhiney, M., 395
McEwen, B. S., 68, 103
McFadden, E. R., 351
McFarland, C. A., 310
McFarlane, A. H., 80, 93
McFarlane, M., 191
McGaugh, J. L., 69
McGeary, J., 186
McGehee, D. S., 178
McGillicuddy, N. B., 195
McGinnis, J. M., 9, 143, 175, 179
Mcgovern, P., 180
Mcgovern, P. G., 200
McGrady, A., 111, 135
McGrath, P. A., 316, 317
McGregor, B. A., 392
Mcgregor, B. A., 392
McGuigan, F. J., 83
McGuire, F. L., 194
McGuire, M. T., 221
McIlwain, H. H., 360, 361, 362
McKellar, J., 197
McKelvey, L., 107
McKelvey, S. F., 221
McKendree-Smith, N. L., 310
McKenzie, T. L., 228, 229, 231
McKey, B. S., 102
McKinlay, J. B., 253, 254
McKinnis, R. A., 250, 377
McLachlan, R. S., 352
McLaughlin, R. J., 103, 148
McLerran, D., 164
McMahan, C. A., 52
McMillan-Davey, E., 177
McNeilly, M., 112

McNicholas, L. J., 159
McPherson-Baker, S., 394
McQuade, K. J., 339
McQuay, H. J., 324
McVicar, D. W., 58
Meacham, S. L., 205, 209
Mead, L. A., 103
Mead, M., 281
Mechanic, D., 143, 242
Medley, D. M., 102
Meehan, J. W., 240
Meer, J., 157
Mefford, I. N., 94
Mehta, K. M., 365
Meichenbaum, D., 133, 259, 263,
    294, 299, 300, 302, 311, 314,
    321, 328, 331, 335, 336
Meier, D. E., 412
Meilahn, E. N., 229
Meilman, P. W., 341
Mela, G. S., 128
Melamed, B. G., 131, 284, 285, 286
Melin, B., 76, 77
Melin, L., 302
Mellins, C. A., 394
Meltzer, L. J., 358
Melzack, R., 241, 294, 296, 297, 298,
    299, 301, 302, 304, 305, 309,
    311, 312, 313, 322, 323, 331,
    332, 336, 337, 338, 340, 386
Menchola, M., 196, 219
Mendelsohn, G. A., 349, 391, 397
Mendes, W. B., 90
Mendlein, J. M., 216, 217
Menefee, L. A., 330
Menke, T. J., 271, 305
Menkes, M. S., 103
Mentzer, S. J., 252
Menustik, C. E., 196
Menzies, R., 249
Mercuri, L. G., 251
Mercury, M. G., 229
Meredith, H. V., 206
Mermelstein, R., 80, 196, 199
Merritt, R. J., 213
Merritt, T. A., 380
Mersica, R., 263
Merskey, H., 309
Meshefedjian, G., 177
Messina, C. R., 71
Methorst, G. J., 410
Metzger, D. S., 199

Metzner, H. L., 90, 92
Meulman, J., 380
Meunier, S. A., 334, 335
Meyer, A., 165
Meyer, D., 271
Meyer, T. J., 392
Meyerowitz, B. E., 251, 384, 387,
    390, 391, 407
Meyers, A. W., 200, 201
Meyers, R. J., 196
Michel, V., 399
Michela, J. L., 73, 154, 379
Mickey, R. M., 163
Mie, A., 168
Mielke, M. M., 178
Migliorelli, R., 365
Milani, R., 128
Milano, R. A., 297, 322, 323, 336, 337
Milas, N. C., 209, 258
Milburn, M. A., 254
Milech, D., 304
Miles, F., 240
Miles, H. J., 68
Milich, R., 190
Militello, F. S., 201
Miller, A. L., 179
Miller, B., 75, 347
Miller, B. D., 109, 351
Miller, J. P., 360, 370
Miller, J. Z., 71
Miller, N. E., 11, 72
Miller, R. H., 239, 316
Miller, S., 281, 282
Miller, S. B., 71
Miller, S. M., 122, 127, 241, 251, 286
Miller, T. D., 378
Miller, T. Q., 189
Miller, W., 195
Miller, W. R., 162, 194, 195, 196, 197
Miller-Johnson, S., 360
Miller-McCaulry, V., 324, 386
Milling, L. S., 334, 335
Mills, N. M., 316
Milne, R., 195
Miner, K. N., 93
Miner, M. H., 100
Minor, M. A., 338, 362
Mintzer, D., 190
Misovich, S. H., 169
Misovich, S. J., 167
Mitchell, J. E., 222
Mittelmark, M. B., 175, 177, 191

Mittleman, M. A., 190, 227, 379
Mixon, M., 18, 159, 243, 393
Mizes, J. S., 193
Moffet, J. K., 338
Mokdad, A. H., 216, 217
Möller, J., 104
Monaco, J. H., 187
Monson, N., 330
Montgomery, S., 192
Monti, P. M., 196, 199
Montroni, M., 393
Moor, W. I., 28
Moore, D. T., 159, 160
Moore, M. L., 156
Moore, P. J., 142, 278
Moore, R. A., 324
Moore, S. M., 151
Moos, B. S., 197
Moos, R., 120
Moos, R. H., 65, 117, 122, 173, 187,
    195, 197, 247, 275, 345, 346,
    348, 373, 375, 379
Mor, V., 386, 387
Moran, K., 148
Moran, P. J., 153
Moran, P. M., 260
Mordavsky, J. K., 239
Mordkoff, A., 64
Moreland, J., 382
Morena, O. F., 160
Moreschi, C., 309
Morgan, B. T., 307
Morgan, L., 367, 368
Morimoto, K., 58, 107
Mork, S., 33
Morley, J. E., 227
Morley, S., 327, 333
Mormede, P., 111
Morrell, R. W., 259
Morrill, B., 329
Morris, E. L., 206
Morris, J. M., 407
Morris, M. J., 261
Morrison, D. M., 168
Morrison, R. S., 412
Morrison, V., 383
Morrison-Beedy, D., 166
Morrow, G. R., 384, 390, 391
Morteau, T. M., 366
Mortimer, J. A., 365
Morton, D., 392
Morton, R. A., 28

Morton, S. C., 168
Morzorati, S. L., 186
Moscato, B. S., 194
Moseley, J. B., 305
Moser, D. K., 379
Moskowitz, J. T., 120, 121, 403
Mosley, T. H., 325
Moss, G. E., 100
Moyer, A., 162, 194, 391
Moyer, C. A., 134, 328
Mudar, P., 92
Mueller, C., 324, 386
Mueller, H., 376
Mueller, T. I., 199
Muir, M., 324
Mukamal, K. J., 187
Muldoon, M. F., 103, 208
Mullan, F., 276
Mullaney, D. J., 131
Mullen, B., 65, 93
Muller, D., 135
Muller, J. E., 190, 376, 379
Mullet, E., 152
Mulley, A. G., 378
Mullin-Jones, M., 193
Mulvaney, F., 199
Mundt, M. P., 194
Murdaugh, C. L., 258, 259
Murphy, A. W., 248, 375
Murphy, D. A., 169, 395
Murphy, J., 358
Murphy, L., 117
Murphy, S. T., 399
Murray, D. M., 175, 177, 192, 193, 200
Murray, M., 176
Murrell, J., 365
Muscat, J. E., 181, 208
Musich, S., 215
Musseau, A., 260
Mussolino, M. E., 381
Muzoguchi, H., 58
Myers, C. D., 306
Myers, M. G., 174
Myers, P., 327, 329
Myers, R. E., 161
Myers, T. C., 307

N

Nachemson, A., 314
Nachimson, D., 169
Nader, P. R., 147, 148, 214

Nadra, W. E., 111
Nagle, R., 380
Najarian, B., 124
Naliboff, B. D., 339
Nan, B., 351
Nanni, C., 256
Napoli, A., 106
Narayan, P., 227
Narod, S., 161
Nash, J. D., 165
Nash, J. M., 309
Nash, M. R., 194
Natelson, B. H., 250
Nathan, P., 165
Nathan, P. E., 195, 200
Nathan, P. R., 304
Navarro, A. M., 159
Neale, J. M., 66, 70, 102, 106, 122,
    172, 173, 184, 189, 222, 287,
    289, 293, 335, 336, 369, 373
Neaton, J. D., 141, 376
Needham, B. M., 354
Neff, D. F., 329
Negrete, V. F., 259
Negri, E., 181
Nehemkis, A. M., 389
Nehete, P. N., 106
Neighbors, C. J., 168
Nelson, D. L., 65, 76, 103, 112, 226
Nelson, L., 126
Nencioli, M., 156
Nepomuceno, C., 313
Nesselroade, J. R., 28
Nestel, P., 126
Neufeld, R. W. J., 65, 282
Neuhaus, J. M., 107
Neus, H., 137
Newcomb, M. D., 181, 189
Newcomb, P., 175
Newell, G. R., 180
Newlin, D. B., 186
Newman, S., 272, 276, 280, 382,
    383, 384
Newman, W. P., 52
Newton, E. R., 169
Newton, N., 281
Newton-John, T. R. O., 306
Nezu, A. M., 133, 211, 218, 219, 220,
    221
Nezu, C. M., 133
Ng, B., 322
Ng, D. M., 103, 148

Ngu, L. O., 71
Ngu, M., 249
Nguyen, M., 387
Nguyen, T. T., 212
Niaura, R., 104, 178, 198
Nicassio, P. M., 68, 325, 362, 363, 407
Nichols, K. A., 187
Nichter, M., 178
Nicolosi, R., 161
Nicolson, N. A., 78
Nillapun, M., 205, 206
Nilsson, N., 249, 338
Nobili, A., 181
Nochaiski, T. H., 194
Noguchi, K., 89, 122, 157
Nolan, A., 324, 386
Norcross, J. C., 152, 153
Nordehn, G., 306
Nordstrom, B., 263
Norman, G. R., 80, 93
Norman, P., 151
Norman, P. A., 223
Northcote, R. J., 227
Norton, L., 389
Notargiacomo, A., 227
Nouwen, A., 358, 369
Novacek, J., 122
Novaco, R., 135, 136
Novak, S. P., 190
Nowack, K. M., 121
Nowalk, M. P., 358, 367, 368
Nye, C., 282
Nystul, M. S., 134

O

Oakland, M. J., 209
O'Bannon, R. E., 169
O'Brien, C. P., 199
O'Brien, J. G., 230
O'Brien, R. M., 217
O'Brien, S., 394
O'Brien, W. H., 104
Obrosky, D. S., 358
O'Byrne, K. K., 284, 285
O'Callaghan, M. E., 382
O'Carroll, R. E., 248
Ochoa, A. C., 58
Ockene, I. S., 161
Ockene, J. K., 161, 180, 199, 378
O'Connell, E. J., 350

O'Connell, K. A., 198, 200
O'Connor, C., 126, 208, 209
O'Connor, M. E., 223
O'Connor, S., 186
O'Dougherty, M., 366
O'Farrell, T. J., 199
Offenbacher, E., 212
Offord, D. R., 366
Öhlund, C., 314
O'Keeffe, J., 122, 329, 330
Oken, D., 76
Okifuji, E. A., 324
Okuyemi, K., 176
Olbrisch, M. E., 412
Oldenburg, B., 220, 380
Oldridge, N. B., 230
O'Leary, A., 168
O'Leary, E. S., 77
Oliver, G., 213
Oliveria, S., 233
Olivet, L. W., 284
Olmstead, M. P., 214
O'Loughlin, J., 177
Olshansky, S. J., 140
Olsson, H., 232
O'Malley, J. E., 393
O'Malley, K., 305
O'Malley, P. M., 174, 175, 176, 182, 189
Ombao, H., 103
Omenn, G. S., 270
O'Neil, P. M., 212
Ong, J. M., 213
Onstad, L. E., 176, 192
Opipari, L. C., 73, 76, 103, 112, 226
Orcutt, H. K., 167
Orfutt, C., 101
Orlando, M., 177
Orleans, C. T., 144, 191, 264, 406, 410, 413
Orne, M. T., 135
Ornish, D., 380
O'Rourke, D. F., 100
Orringer, E., 308
Osborn, J. E., 394
Oseasohin, R., 135
O'Shea, J. J., 58
Oshima, J., 365
Osler, M., 179
Ossip-Klein, D. J., 199
Ostrove, J. M., 158
Ouelette, S. C., 97, 98

Ouimette, P. C., 197
Ôunpuu, S., 376
Owen, N., 220, 224, 226, 227, 228, 229, 230, 410
Owens, D., 325, 326
Owens, J. F., 104, 112, 287

P

Paffen-Barger, R. S., 225, 227, 228
Pagani, M., 128
Pagell, F., 153
Palesky, J., 344
Pallonen, U., 192
Pallonen, U. E., 193
Palmerud, G., 76
Paluch, R. A., 219, 229
Pandya, K., 391
Panico, S., 227
Pantaleo, G., 393
Pao, A., 179
Paoletti, P., 181, 190
Papciak, A. S., 308
Pappachan, S., 358
Paquette, M., 262
Parcel, G. S., 164
Parfitt, R. R., 164
Park, D. C., 259
Parker, J. C., 289, 368, 369
Parker, S. R., 199
Parrish, J. M., 258, 262, 263
Parrott, A. C., 177
Parsons, J. A., 160
Parsons, O. A., 187
Parsons, T., 141
Partridge, C., 383
Paskett, E. D., 210
Pasmantier, R., 358
Passik, S., 388
Paterson, R. J., 65
Paton, C., 102
Patrick, A. W., 358
Patrick, D. L., 229
Patterson, D. R., 334, 335
Patterson, J. M., 369
Patterson, S. M., 103, 104
Patterson, T. L., 68, 123, 229, 309, 321, 365, 396
Pattillo, J. R., 100
Paty, J. A., 198, 200
Pavlov, I., 298
Pawlik-Plank, D., 324, 386

Payne, A., 335, 336
Payne, T. J., 325
Pearlin, L. I., 121
Pechacek, T. F., 175, 177, 193, 280
Peck, J. R., 363
Peckenpaugh, N. J., 204, 205, 206, 207, 208, 216
Pecoraro, N., 213
Pedersen, N. L., 28, 101
Pederson, L. L., 258
Peele, S., 195, 197
Peirce, R. S., 92, 194
Pekkanen, J., 376
Pekow, P. S., 199
Pendley, J. S., 331
Penedo, F. J., 394
Penn, A., 180
Penn, G. M., 59
Penn, M. S., 205
Penn, N. E., 245
Pennanen, M., 148
Pennebaker, J. W., 93, 124, 148, 240, 241, 396
Penner, B. C., 218
Penninx, B. W. J. H., 414
Pentz, M. A., 192
Penzien, D. B., 131, 325, 327, 328
Pepe, M. S., 212
Perdue, S. T., 169
Pérez-Benítez, C. I., 104
Perkins, K. A., 191, 199, 200, 201, 229, 410
Perkins, L. L., 156
Perkins, R. J., 380
Perks, P., 73, 105, 365
Perlick, D., 178
Perlis, M. L., 294
Pernet, A. L., 384
Perri, M. G., 133, 211, 218, 219, 220, 221, 230
Perry, C. L., 206
Perry, S., 226
Persky, V., 350
Perz, C. A., 153
Pestone, M., 212
Peter, R., 77
Peterman, A., 388
Peterman, T. A., 167, 393
Peters, M. L., 327
Petersen, A. C., 157
Petersen, N. J., 305
Petersen, R. C., 159, 160

Peterson, A. V., 176, 192
Peterson, C., 96, 277
Peterson, J., 33
Peterson, L., 128, 157, 232, 284, 285, 330, 346, 360
Peterson, L.-E., 314
Peterson, N. J., 271
Peterson, R. A., 262
Petkova, E., 224
Peto, R., 187
Petracchi, M., 365
Petraitis, J., 189
Petrie, K. J., 396
Petry, N. M., 196
Pettingell, W. H., 365
Petty, R. E., 79
Pfeifer, G. P., 179
Pfeiffer, C., 363
Pflanzer, R., 24, 42, 44, 48, 52, 56, 57
Phan, M. K., 156
Phares, E. J., 93
Phelan, S., 220, 221
Philip, A. E., 377
Philips, C. A., 362
Philips, M. N., 394
Phillips, D. P., 246
Phillips, L. R., 369
Phillips, W. T., 126, 226, 227
Phillips-Bute, B. G., 209
Phinney, S. D., 220
Piasecki, T. M., 200
Pickering, T. G., 51, 77
Pieper, C., 103
Pieper, C. F., 209
Pierce, D. K., 209
Pierce, J. P., 164, 175, 176, 191, 410
Pike, J., 107
Pike, J. L., 68
Pilisuk, M., 123
Pimley, S., 122
Pincus, T., 362
Pines, M., 98
Pinquart, M., 369
Pinto, B. M., 231, 391
Pinto, R. P., 286
Piotrowski, C., 287
Piper, J. M., 169
Piper, M. E., 172, 177
Pirie, P., 192, 193
Pirke, K.-M., 71
Pisarska, K., 212
Pittaras, A., 227

Pitts, S. C., 176, 193
Pizarro, J., 162
Place, M., 135
Platt, R., 284
Pleck, J. H., 168
Plomin, R., 28, 73, 101
Poen, H., 345
Pogue-Geile, M. F., 208
Pokorny, A. D., 103, 148
Polak, J. F., 181
Polivy, J., 154, 213, 214
Pollack, E. S., 178, 179
Pollack, H., 392
Polley, B. A., 212, 215, 217, 218, 220
Pollo, A., 305
Pollock, M. L., 227
Pollock, S. E., 346
Polonsky, W. H., 259, 360
Pomerleau, C. S., 173, 177
Pomerleau, O. F., 173, 177
Pomeroy, D., 222
Poon, S. H., 394
Pope, M. K., 376
Porges, S. W., 39
Porkaj, P., 365
Porter, F. L., 316
Porter, L. S., 308
Potter, E. H., 80
Powch, I. G., 102
Powe, N. R., 168
Powell, K. E., 227
Powell, L. H., 100, 136, 137, 271, 380
Power, E., 358
Power, M., 348
Powley, T. L., 213
Pratt, M., 214
Prescott, C. A., 174
Prescott, E., 179
Presnell, K., 214
Presson, C. C., 176, 193
Price, R. H., 77, 89
Price, V. A., 136, 137, 380
Prieto, G. J., 304
Primeaux, M., 21
Prince, L. M., 254
Prins, B., 69
Prinz, P. N., 364
Prochaska, J. O., 151, 152, 153, 162, 169, 193, 200
Prohaska, T. R., 243
Prokhorov, A. V., 193

Pronin, E., 233
Pruitt, S. D., 321
Psaty, B. M., 14
Puccetti, M. C., 91, 98
Puleo, P. R., 271
Purcell, K., 108
Puschel, K., 165, 166
Puska, P., 165, 376
Puukka, P., 338

Q

Qaqish, B., 103
Qian, C-g., 111
Quick, J. C., 65, 76, 103, 112, 164, 226
Quick, J. D., 65, 76, 103, 112, 226
Quigley, B. M., 309
Quill, T., 412
Quintero, O., 242, 306
Quittner, A. L., 73

R

Rabin, B. S., 66, 103, 106
Rabkin, J. G., 395
Racioppo, M. W., 120
Radecki, S. E., 144, 146, 160
Rader, C., 306
Radojevic, V., 325, 363
Ragan, P. K., 397
Rahe, R., 79
Rahe, R. H., 80, 113
Rahn, J. M., 229
Räikkönen, K., 112
Rainero, I., 305
Rains, J. C., 327
Raj, A., 168, 169
Rakic, P., 33
Rakowski, W., 153
Ramchandani, V. A., 186
Ramirez, A., 113
Ramos, R., 169
Ramsden, V., 137
Ramsey, N. L., 283, 284, 286
Rand, C. S., 256, 257
Randall, P. K., 173
Rankin, J. G., 191, 194
Ransohoff, R. M., 33
Raphael, B. G., 28
Raphael, K. G., 81
Rappaport, N. B., 308

Raps, C. S., 277
Rasmussen, B. K., 109
Rasnake, L. K., 295
Ratliff-Crain, J., 71, 123
Ratner, L. E., 168
Rau, H., 103
Raven, B. H., 271
Rawlins, M., 217
Ray, J. W., 200, 212
Raymond, N. R., 360
Raynor, A. E., 186
Raynor, H. A., 219
Reading, A. E., 310, 313, 315
Rectanus, E., 111
Reda, D., 227
Redd, W. H., 259, 286, 332, 389, 390, 391
Redden, D. T., 215
Reddy, D. M., 157, 158, 244
Redmon, W. K., 271
Redmond, C., 192
Reeb, R. N., 393
Reed, D., 168, 395
Reed, E., 168, 169
Reese, L., 94
Reichsman, R., 108
Reid, H. M., 395
Reilly, P. M., 197
Reinis, S., 33
Reinsch, S., 96, 151
Reintgen, D. S., 391
Reis, T. J., 154
Reise, S. P., 102
Renick, N. L., 191
Renjilian, D. A., 221
Renner, J. A., 146, 174, 195, 199
Rennick, J. E., 284
Repucci, N. D., 96
Resnick, H. S., 186
Resnick, R., 287, 409
Resnicow, K., 162, 263
Retchin, S. M., 158
Retzlaff, B. M., 208
Reuterwall, C., 104
Revenson, T. A., 347, 363, 414
Rexrode, K. M., 215
Rey, M. J., 377, 378
Reynolds, D., 302
Reynolds, D. K., 397
Reynoso, J. T., 198
Rhoades, R., 24, 42, 44, 48, 52, 56, 57

Rhoads, K., 377
Ribisl, K. M., 158
Rice, J. P., 174
Rice, V. H., 279
Rich, M. W., 286, 379
Richards, B., 260
Richards, C., 97, 193
Richards, J. S., 313
Richards, M., 389
Richards, P. S., 192
Richards, T. J., 200
Richardson, C. T., 44
Richardson, J., 96, 168, 176, 350, 387, 395
Richardson, P. H., 277
Richardson, S. A., 345
Richie, J. P., 387
Richman, R., 112
Ricordi, C., 356
Ridgeway, V., 127, 278
Rietveld, S., 240, 241, 351
Rigatti-Luchini, S., 309
Rigotti, N. A., 161, 378
Riles, M., 313
Riley, D. J., 28
Riley, G. E., 169
Riley, J. F., 340, 341
Riley, J. L., 306
Riley, K. P., 365
Riley, W. T., 287
Rimer, B., 148, 330
Rimer, B. K., 148, 161, 162, 384, 414
Rimm, D. C., 132
Rimm, E. B., 102, 187
Ringel, B. L., 183
Rippe, J., 378
Risner, M. E., 188
Rissanen, A., 338
Risser, N. L., 199
Ritchie, J. A., 284
Ritterband, L. M., 360
Riveral, A., 323, 327, 337, 338
Robbins, C., 90, 92
Robbins, J., 181
Robbins, L., 110
Roberts, A. H., 241, 305
Roberts, C. S., 391
Roberts, J., 321
Roberts, J. E., 396
Roberts, M. B., 231
Roberts, M. C., 17, 157
Roberts, R. E., 381

Robertson, L. S., 231, 232
Robertson, S. M., 212
Robertson, T., 402
Robin, C. I., 133
Robin, S. S., 232
Robins, C., 380
Robinson, C. H., 212
Robinson, L. A., 176
Robinson, M. E., 306
Robinson, T. E., 173
Robinson, T. N., 176, 223
Rock, C. L., 222, 223, 224
Rockett, H. R., 217
Rockhill, B., 160
Rodenhuis, S., 28
Rodichok, L. D., 329
Rodin, J., 66, 77, 96, 97, 212, 213, 216, 272, 306
Rodriguez, C., 215
Rodriguez, M. S., 10, 92
Roe, L. S., 206
Roelofs, J., 327
Roesch, S. C., 344, 349
Roessler, S., 279
Roffman, R. A., 169, 201
Rogers, K., 160
Rogers, M. P., 241
Rogers, R. W., 162
Rogers, W. H., 262, 271
Rohay, J., 229
Rohling, M. L., 306
Rohrbach, L. A., 192
Rohsenow, D. J., 196, 199
Role, L. W., 178
Rollnick, S., 162
Rolls, B. J., 206, 214
Romano, D. M., 365
Romano, J. M., 306, 330
Romano, P., 391
Rompa, D., 169
Rönnemaa, T., 338
Roppé, B., 159
Rosberger, Z., 389
Rosbrook, B., 164
Rose, C., 178
Rose, C. A., 179
Rose, J. S., 193
Rose, K. J., 352
Rose, R., 111
Rose, R. J., 51
Rosella, J. D., 142
Rosen, J. C., 210, 308, 309, 321

Rosen, R. C., 148
Rosenbaum, P., 366
Rosenberg, E. S., 394
Rosenblatt, M., 226
Rosenblum, C., 193
Rosenblum, M., 213
Rosenhan, D. L., 10, 104
Rosenkranz, M., 135
Rosenman, R., 99
Rosenman, R. H., 99, 100, 101, 137, 180, 379
Rosensteel, R. E., 242
Rosenstock, I. M., 148, 149, 150, 246, 247, 258, 259
Rosenthal, T. L., 137
Roskies, E., 137
Roskies, R., 135
Rosner, B., 181, 217
Rosomoff, H. L., 341
Rosomoff, R. S., 341
Ross, L., 287
Rossi, J. S., 152, 193
Roter, D. L., 254, 255, 256, 262, 263
Roth, D. L., 126
Roth, W. T., 205, 208, 225
Rothendler, J., 66
Rotheram-Borus, M. J., 395
Rothman, A., 408
Rothman, A. J., 162, 233
Rothrock, N., 248, 375
Rotter, J. B., 94
Rounds, J., 134, 328
Rowe, J. W., 68
Roy, D., 160
Roy, R. G., 80, 93
Rozelle, R. M., 191
Rozensky, R. H., 409
Rozlog, L. A., 105
Rubin, S. M., 145
Rubman, S., 325
Rubonis, A. V., 196
Rucker, T., 18, 158
Rudel, H., 137
Rudeman, A. J., 213
Rudert, W. A., 356
Rudick, R., 33
Rudick-Davis, D., 307
Rudy, T. E., 313, 329, 330
Ruitenberg, A., 365
Ruiz, M. S., 168, 395
Rumpler, W. V., 210

Rumpold, G., 279
Rundall, T. G., 245
Runyan, C. W., 17, 18, 144
Russell, D., 92, 248, 375
Russell, D. G., 230
Russell, D. W., 87, 154
Russell, M., 92, 194
Russell, M. A. H., 107, 181
Russo, J., 104, 364
Rutledge, T., 102, 111
Ryan, C. F., 198
Ryan, K. B., 191, 192
Ryan, R. S., 3
Rybstein-Blinchik, E., 332
Rychtarik, R. K., 195
Rytökoski, U., 338
Rzewnicki, R., 193, 218

S

Saab, P. G., 71, 406
Sabbioni, M. E. E., 113
Sabe, L., 365
Sacco, R. L., 187
Saccone, N. L., 174
Sacks, D. A., 21
Sadler, G., 164
Sadler, G. R., 145
Saelens, B. E., 14, 230
Safer, M. A., 247, 248
Saffari, B., 213
Saini, J., 286, 379
Saintfort, R., 241
Saldana, L., 284, 285, 330
Sallis, J. F., 14, 137, 224, 226, 227, 228, 229, 230, 231, 410
Salloum, J. M., 173
Salmon, J., 229, 410
Salonen, J. T., 102, 103, 104, 165
Salonen, R., 104
Salovey, P., 162, 233, 289, 304
Sampson, H. A., 306
Sandberg, G. G., 165
Sanders, G. S., 101, 137
Sanders, M., 90
Sanders, S., 321
Sanders, S. H., 122, 242, 306, 320, 329, 330
Sandrock, C., 145
Sands, D., 346
Sands, L. P., 258
Sands, S., 390

Sandsiö, L., 76
Sandy, J. M., 177
Sanford, M. K., 338, 362
Sanson-Fisher, R., 144, 254
Santi, S., 192
Santiago, J. V., 357, 360, 370
Santorelli, S. F., 135
Sanzo, K., 106
Saperia, G. M., 161
Sapp, S. K., 205
Sarafino, E. P., 11, 12, 15, 22, 33, 66, 73, 82, 109, 117, 126, 128, 129, 130, 131, 132, 133, 147, 153, 163, 173, 198, 283, 285, 289, 327, 328, 350, 368, 369, 383, 397, 403
Sarason, B., 6, 10, 80, 88, 184
Sarason, I., 6, 10, 80, 81, 88, 176, 184, 192
Sargent, J. D., 176
Sarna, S., 227
Sasson, S., 356
Sastre, M. T. M., 152
Satariano, W. A., 390
Saunders, B., 186
Saunders, C., 401
Savage, M. V., 113
Savage, P. J., 181
Saylor, K. E., 223
Sbraccia, P., 356
Scambler, G., 345, 352
Scanlan, J. M., 75, 113, 365
Scarr, S., 28
Schachter, S., 177, 178, 193, 214, 218
Schaefer, C., 81, 87, 88
Schaefer, J. A., 65, 117, 345, 346
Schaefer, L. C., 367
Schaen, E. R., 330
Schafer, L. C., 358, 359
Schanberg, S. M., 104, 376
Schapiro, S. J., 106
Schatz, D. S., 279
Schaufeli, W. B., 273
Schauffler, H. H., 239
Schechter, A., 109
Scheidt, S., 104
Scheier, L. M., 174, 190
Scheier, M. F., 10, 98, 287
Scherer, K. R., 70
Schermer, C., 197
Scherr, P., 179

Scherwitz, L., 99, 100
Scherwitz, L. W., 380
Schiaffino, K. M., 243, 246
Schiffman, H. R., 292, 303
Schifter, D. E., 151
Schlenk, E., 256, 257, 258, 260, 262
Schlussel, Y., 103
Schmid, L., 193
Schmidt, D., 354
Schmieder, R., 137
Schmitt, J. M., 167
Schmitz, J. B., 106
Schnall, P. L., 77, 103
Schneider, A. M., 5, 6
Schneider, F., 173
Schneider, T. R., 162
Schneiderman, N., 71, 107, 112, 126, 396
Schnohr, P., 187
Schnurr, P. P., 186
Schoenbach, V. J., 88, 123
Schoenborn, C. A., 143
Schoendorf, K. C., 249
Schooler, C., 121
Schork, M. A., 112
Schraa, J. C., 263
Schuckit, M. A., 146, 172, 174, 199
Schulein, M. J., 315, 317
Schull, W. J., 112
Schulman, K., 161
Schultz, A. B., 215
Schulz, R., 73, 97, 287, 365, 391
Schumacher, J., 135
Schumann-Brzezinski, C., 135
Schunk, D. H., 151
Schuster, C. R., 172, 188
Schuster, M. A., 64
Schutte, K. K., 187
Schwankovsky, L., 256
Schwartz, G. E., 135
Schwartz, J., 89, 91
Schwartz, J. E., 10, 77, 92, 103, 148
Schwartz, M. D., 148, 389
Schwartz, R. G., 379
Sciara, A. D., 287, 409
Scipio, C., 308
Scott, D. L., 324
Scovern, A. W., 358, 368
Seagle, H. M., 218, 220
Seal, S., 28
Sears, S. R., 121, 374, 412
Sebring, N. G., 212

Seeman, T. E., 68, 92, 148
Segal, H. L., 108
Segui-Gomez, M., 407
Séguin, J. R., 223
Seidel, K. D., 212
Self, C. A., 162
Seligman, M. E. P., 10, 95, 96, 104, 277
Seligmann, J., 411
Seltman, H., 374
Selye, H., 67, 68
Selye, H., 83
Semple, S. J., 365, 396
Senn, K. L., 159
Seraganian, P., 135
Serdula, M. K., 215, 216, 217
Serfass, R. C., 224, 230
Serwitz, J., 99, 100
Severson, H., 161, 177, 179, 192, 199
Sewell, M., 395
Shade, S. B., 104
Shadel, W. G., 164, 178, 198
Shader, R. I., 188, 189
Shafer, D., 282
Shah, N. J., 173
Shah, R. N., 212
Shain, R. N., 169
Shamoon, H., 358
Shanfield, S. B., 379
Shapiro, A. P., 127
Shapiro, D., 78, 106
Shapiro, S. L., 135
Sharbaugh, C., 210
Shaw, H., 224
Shaw, R. E., 344
Shaw, W. S., 365, 396
Shawaryn, M. A., 243, 246
Sheahan, M. D., 28
Shearer, H. M., 256, 257, 258, 261, 263
Sheffield, D., 306
Shelton, D. R., 176, 189
Shelton, R. C., 133
Shepel, L. F., 325
Sher, K. J., 185, 186, 187
Sheras, P. L., 285
Sherbourne, C. D., 262
Sheridan, J. F., 105
Sheridan, K., 396
Sherman, B. F., 395
Sherman, J. J., 128

Sherman, S. J., 176, 193
Shermer, R. L., 221
Sherwood, A., 71, 92, 103, 112, 126, 380
Sherwood, J., 120
Sherwood, J. B., 190, 379
Sherwood, M. J., 271
Sherwood A., 71
Shiffman, S., 29, 177, 178, 198, 200, 219
Shin, C., 192
Shipley, R. H., 282
Shisslak, C., 280
Shneidman, E. S., 397
Shnek, Z. M., 251
Shogren, E., 399
Sholtz, R. I., 101, 180
Shontz, F. C., 65, 344
Shopland, D., 175, 179
Shopland, D. R., 174, 179
Short, J. G., 131
Shragg, P., 322
Shu-Hsing, L., 395
Shumaker, S. A., 414
Shupe, D. R., 124
Shuster, M. L., 214
Shutz, J. M., 175, 177
Siegel, J. E., 148
Siegel, J. M., 81
Siegel, L., 128, 131, 285
Siegel, S., 173, 393
Siegel, W. C., 71
Siegfried, M., 66
Siegler, I. C., 71, 113, 148
Siegman, A. W., 102
Siegmund, K. D., 102
Siegrist, J., 77
Sikkema, K. I., 168
Sikkema, K. J., 169, 396
Silberfarb, P. M., 390, 391
Silver, R. C., 276
Silver, R. L., 344, 399, 402, 403
Silverberg, E. L., 377
Silverfield, J. C., 360, 361, 362
Silverstein, B., 178
Silverstein, J., 259, 358, 360
Simeone, C., 286, 379
Simmens, S. J., 262
Simon, A. E., 103, 148
Simon, H. J., 259
Simoni, J. M., 168, 395
Simonite, V., 217

Simonsick, E. M., 414
Simpsin, E. E., 201
Simpson, J. M., 220
Sims, E. A. H., 213
Sindelar, J. L., 199
Singer, B. H., 68
Singer, D. E., 161, 378
Singer, J. E., 68, 79, 281
Sivenius, J., 102, 103
Skelly, A. H., 358
Skelly, J. M., 163
Skinner, C. S., 162
Skinner, E. A., 120
Skinner, J., 245
Skinner, M. J., 154, 167
Sklar, L. S., 113
Skolnick, A. S., 18, 43
Skoner, D. P., 66, 103, 250
Skrinar, G. S., 226
Skultety, F. M., 341
Slater, M. A., 309, 321
Slattery, M. L., 209
Sledden, E. A., 17, 157
Slish, K. K., 351
Smarr, K. L., 369
Smart, J. L., 156
Smith, A. P., 103, 107, 181
Smith, A. W., 395
Smith, B., 308
Smith, C. A., 124, 330, 363
Smith, D., 160
Smith, E. L., 212
Smith, J., 262
Smith, J. B., 283, 284
Smith, J. E., 196
Smith, K. B., 248
Smith, K. S., 210
Smith, L., 389
Smith, M., 206
Smith, M. S., 294
Smith, M. T., 294
Smith, R. C., 254
Smith, R. S., 98
Smith, S. J., 314
Smith, S. S., 200
Smith, T., 102
Smith, T. L., 68, 107, 172
Smith, T. W., 51, 71, 98, 148, 363, 376, 406, 413
Smith-Yoder, D., 156
Smithm C. E., 91
Smolen, A., 186

Smyth, J. M., 93
Snipes, S. A., 165, 166
Snow, L. F., 20
Snowdon, D. A., 365
Snyder, C. A., 180
Snyder, C. R., 100
Snyder, M. L., 252
Snyder, P., 374
Snyder, S. H., 303
Sobel, D. S., 22
Sobel, J. L., 176, 189
Sobell, L. C., 194
Sobell, M. B., 194
Söderlund, J., 77
Soet, J. E., 162, 263
Solberg, L. I., 144, 264
Sole-Leris, A., 134
Solomon, D. S., 166
Solomon, G. F., 227
Solomon, L. J., 163, 169
Somers, A. R., 155
Somers, V. K., 376
Sonenstein, F. L., 168
Song, H.-Y., 108, 109, 351
Sorensen, G., 164
Sörensen, S., 369
Sorenson, G., 180
Sorum, P. C., 152
Souchek, J., 271
Sovik, K. N., 212
Spangler, A. S., 314
Spangler, D., 214
Sparler, S., 380
Speare, R., 232
Speckart, G., 152
Specter, M. W., 77
Speece, M. W., 73, 396
Speicher, C., 59
Speicher, C. E., 106, 365
Speigel, D., 392
Speisman, J. C., 64
Spence, J. D., 137
Spencer, L., 153
Spencer, S. M., 391
Spiegel, D., 390, 391
Spielberger, C. D., 177
Spier, C. J., 242, 306
Spinetta, J. J., 390, 392
Spoth, R. L., 192
Sprague, L. T., 331
Sprenger, J. D., 350
Springer, E. A., 224

Spurgeon, P., 411
Squires, D. D., 407
St. Lawrence, J. S., 169
St-Pierre, S., 214
Stacey, B. R., 340, 341
Stacy, A. W., 152
Stafford, R. S., 161
Stall, R., 168
Stall, R. D., 168
Stallone, D. D., 220
Stamler, J., 141, 376
Stampfer, M. J., 181
Stanek, E., 161
Stansfeld, S. A., 101
Stanton, A. L., 121, 374, 412
Stanton, J. L., 212
Stanwyck, C. L., 209
Stark, K. A., 71
Starkstein, S. E., 365
Starr, K., 396
Staten, M. A., 356
Staton, A. L., 121, 389
Stauffacher, E. A., 194
Stefanek, M., 148
Steffen, P. R., 112
Steger, J. C., 294
Steggles, N., 103, 148
Steiger, H., 223
Stein, B. D., 64
Stein, J. A., 189
Stein, J. H., 187
Steinberg, L., 101
Steinberger, E. K., 324
Steiner, H., 276
Steiner, O., 277
Steinhardt, M. A., 106
Steinman, M. A., 258
Stellar, E., 68, 103
Stephens, R. S., 201
Stepney, R., 174, 179
Steptoe, A., 66, 77, 205, 206, 351
Sternberg, E. M., 40, 104
Stetson, B. A., 229
Steuber, C. P., 331
Stevens, V. J., 161, 210
Stewart, C. J., 106
Stewart, D. E., 251
Stewart, E., 197
Stewart, J. A., 322, 324
Stewart, W. F., 109
Stewart-Williams, S., 305
Stice, E., 214, 217, 223, 224

Stieg, R. L., 341
Stites, D. P., 107
Stitzer, M. L., 186
Stockton, W., 359
Stockwell, T., 197
Stoeckle, J. D., 261
Stokols, D., 69, 93
Stolberg, S. G., 54
Stone, A. A., 29, 106, 122
Stone, E. J., 228, 229, 231
Stone, G. C., 5, 6, 7, 18
Stone, M., 232
Stone, W. L., 17, 72, 157, 259, 283,
    286, 346, 397
Storandt, M., 229
Storb, R., 350
Story, M., 206, 214
Stossel, C., 380
Stotland, S., 223
Stoyva, J. M., 131
Strauman, T., 380
Strauss, R. H., 227
Straw, M., 212
Strecher, V. J., 154, 200
Streiner, D. L., 80, 93
Stretch, V., 164
Striegel-Moore, R. H., 216, 223
Strong, J. P., 52
Strong, W. B., 134
Struewing, J. P., 28
Strycker, L. A., 157
Stuart, R., 218
Stuckard, A. J., 220
Stults, B. M., 51
Stunkard, A. J., 220
Suarez, E. C., 71, 104, 376
Suchday, S., 77
Sudler, N. C., 287
Sue, S., 242
Suer, Z., 313
Sulavik, C., 411
Suls, J., 65, 88, 92, 93, 101, 102, 119,
    137, 163, 241, 242, 243, 319, 344,
    347, 349, 408
Summerton, J., 241
Sunshine, G., 54–59, 72, 361, 393
Superko, H. R., 380
Surbone, A., 389
Surtees, P., 98
Surwit, R. S., 356, 358, 368
Susser, M., 112
Suton-Tyrrell, K., 104

Sutton, S., 162
Sutton-Tyrell, K., 232
Suuper, C. N., 283
Svarstad, B., 261, 263
Sved, A. F., 178
Swan, A. V., 176
Swan, G., 99, 100, 379
Sweet, J. J., 287, 409
Sweetnam, P. M., 101
Swift, R. M., 186, 199
Swift, S., 28
Swigonski, M. E., 258, 260
Swillinger, E., 252
Swinburn, B. A., 230
Sydeman, S. J., 230
Sykes, D., 324
Syme, S. L., 90, 92

T

Taenzer, P., 137, 199
Tagliacozzo, D. L., 273, 275
Talajic, M., 379
Talbot, F., 358, 369
Talcott, G. W., 193
Talley, N. J., 249
Tallmer, J., 99, 100
Talo, S., 338
Tang, M.-S., 179
Tanner, J. M., 34
Tanney, F., 287, 409
Tapert, S. F., 173
Taplin, S. H., 145
Tapp, J. T., 135
Tarnowski, K. J., 295
Tarr, K. L., 105
Tarshis, B., 5, 6
Tate, D. G., 355
Taussig, L. M., 156
Tawa, C. B., 271
Taylor, A., 242
Taylor, C. B., 94, 214, 217, 223
Taylor, K. L., 148, 389
Taylor, S. E., 96, 119, 272, 275, 277,
    374
Teachman, B. A., 217
Teasdale, J. D., 95
Tebbi, C. K., 389
Telch, M. J., 223
Tell, G. S., 181
Tellegen, A., 287
Temoshok, L., 114, 166, 167

Temple, M. T., 168
Tennen, H., 120, 121, 122, 286, 294, 308, 309, 362, 363, 383
Tennes, K., 69
Ter Kuile, M. M., 327
Teri, L., 364
Terry, R. D., 209
Tesón, A., 365
TeVelde, A., 286, 379
Tharps, Q. J., 247, 248
Thelen, M. H., 131
Theorell, T., 104, 113
Thibault, G. E., 378
Thomas, A., 73
Thomas, A. M., 360
Thomas, C., 167
Thomas, M. G., 396
Thomas, M. L., 54
Thomas, P., 106
Thompson, B., 164, 165, 166
Thompson, J., 254
Thompson, J. K., 223
Thompson, K., 319
Thompson, K. L., 316, 326
Thompson, M. A., 382
Thompson, P. D., 227
Thompson, R., 192
Thompson, S., 127
Thompson, S. C., 65, 93, 96, 124, 167, 256, 278
Thomson, J. B., 186
Thomson, S. J., 192
Thoresen, C. E., 2, 100, 136, 137, 380
Thorn, B. E., 105
Thorndike, A. N., 161
Thorogood, M., 209
Thors, C. L., 388
Threatt, B. A., 390
Thun, M. J., 178, 187, 215
Tilmont, E. M., 210
Tilyard, M. W., 230
Timko, C., 247
Timmers, K. I., 213
Tims, F. M., 197
Tinetti, M. E., 231
Tobias, H. S., 37
Todd, M., 121
Tofler, G. H., 190, 376, 379
Tomaka, J., 65
Tomer, A., 259
Tomlinson-Keasey, C., 10

Toneatto, T., 194
Tong, J. Y., 58
Tonigan, J. S., 196, 197
Toobert, D. J., 210
Topol, E., 205
Torgerson, D., 338
Torgerson, W. S., 313
Torpy, E. J., 189
Torrens, P. R., 401, 402
Torres, G., 172
Tortora, G. J., 16, 27, 33, 35, 36, 39, 44, 46, 48, 49, 52, 54, 55, 57, 58, 182, 296, 303, 339, 351, 382, 384, 386
Toshima, M. T., 92, 379
Tovian, S. M., 312, 409, 415
Town, C., 197
Trabin, T., 306
Tracy, R. E., 52
Traficante, R. M., 231
Trakowski, J. H., 106
Trapp, B. D., 33
Trask, O. J., 106, 365
Travis, J. W., 3
Treiber, F. A., 134, 135
Tremblay, A., 214
Tremblay, G. C., 232
Trevisan, M., 77, 227
Trevorrow, T. R., 137
Trijsburg, R. W., 390
Trip-Reimer, T., 248, 375
Tripp, M. L., 172
Trock, B., 384
Trock, B. J., 161
Trocki, K., 168
Trotter, R., 153
Trowbridge, F. L., 210
Troxel, W. M., 92, 232
Trucco, G., 356
Truman, B. I., 167
Trumbull, R., 62, 65
Tsao, M. N., 392
Tucker, J. S., 10, 92, 102
Tucker, L. A., 244
Tugade, M. M., 98
Tunks, E., 321, 338
Tuomilehto, J., 376
Tuomisto, M., 143
Turk, D., 133, 294
Turk, D. C., 251, 263, 289, 292, 293, 294, 299, 300, 302, 304, 305, 306, 309, 311, 313, 314, 321,

322, 323, 324, 328, 329, 330, 331, 332, 333, 335, 336, 340, 341
Turk-Charles, S., 251
Turkkan, J. S., 186
Turner, C. W., 51
Turner, J. A., 12, 306, 308, 330, 332, 339
Turner, J. R., 71, 101, 103
Turner, R., 134
Turner, R. B., 103
Turrisi, R., 187
Tursky, B., 304
Tusel, D. J., 197
Twamley, E. W., 71
Tweedy, D., 126
Tyler, D. C., 324
Tyndale, R. F., 177
Tyrell, D. A. J., 107, 181
Tyroler, H. A., 180
Tyrrell, D. A. J., 103

U

Uchino, B. N., 90, 92
Ukestad, L. K., 304
Ulmer, D., 136, 137, 380
Ulrich, P. H., 93
Undén, A.-L., 135
Uno, D., 92
Urban, B. J., 324
Urrows, S., 294, 362
Urtes, M., 242

V

Valdez, R., 211
Valdimarsdottir, H., 106
Valleron, A.-J., 158
Valois, P., 228
Valois, R. F., 160
Valoski, A., 218
Van Camp, S. P., 227
Van De Wetering, M. L., 28
van den Borne, H. W., 345
Van Doornen, L. J. P., 103
Van Duijn, C. M., 365
Van Dulmen, A. M., 254
Van Eck, M. M., 78
Van Elderen, T., 380
Van Griensven, G. J. P., 168
Van Harrison, R., 100

Van Horn, L. V., 209, 258
van Knippenberg, F. C. E., 345
Van Nguyen, T., 73, 74, 143, 157, 176, 397
Van Swieten, J. C., 365
Van Tilburg, M. A. L., 358
Van Vunakis, H., 199
Van Zandwik, N., 28
vanBerge-Henegouwen, G. P., 345
Van't Spijker, A., 390
Varadi, E., 71
Varni, J., 319
Varni, J. W., 258, 316, 326, 360
Vartiainen, E., 376
Vasko, R., 103
Vaughan, R. D., 154
Vavak, C. R., 102
Vecchia, C., 181
Vecchio, P. C., 362
Vedhara, K., 73, 105, 365
Vega, S. C., 159
Veit, R., 103
Velasquez, M. M., 152, 193
Velicer, W. F., 152, 153, 193
Vener, A. M., 166
Venn, J. R., 131
Verbrugge, L. M., 244
Verde, T. J., 218
Verkasalo, P. K., 28
Verreault, R., 365
Vertinsky, P., 228
Vestbo, J., 179
Vetter, N., 377
Viegener, B. J., 211, 218, 219, 220, 221
Vighetti, S., 305
Vincent, J.-L., 270, 271
Vinck, J., 143
Viney, L. L., 402
Vinokur, A. D., 77, 390
Vinokur-Kaplan, D., 390
Vinson, D. C., 185, 186, 187
Viseu Dos Santos, A. C., 187
Vitaliano, P. P., 75, 104, 113, 280, 308, 364, 365
Vitiello, M. V., 364
Vitousek, K. B., 224
Vittinghoff, E., 120, 396, 403
Vivekananthan, D. P., 205
Vlaeyen, J. W. S., 327
Vögele, C., 279
Vogt, T. M., 161
Volinn, E., 339, 340

von Eiff, A. W., 137
Von Hoff, D., 28
Von Korff, M., 292
Von Wald Sufka, A., 154
Voorhees, C. C., 199
Vorp, R., 17
Vrungos, S., 167

W

Waddell, G., 322
Wadden, T. A., 135, 211, 215, 216, 218, 220, 221
Wadhwa, N., 93
Wagenknecht, L. E., 180, 200
Waggoner, C. D., 308
Wagner, E., 14
Wagner, E. H., 88, 123, 144, 193, 227, 264
Wagner, M., 173
Wahlgren, D. R., 321
Wainwright, N., 98
Waitzkin, H., 261
Wald, L. H., 330
Walden, C. E., 208
Walker, B. M., 402
Walker, C. E., 287, 289
Walker, E. A., 356
Walker, J., 304
Walker-Thurmond, K., 215
Wall, P., 241, 294, 296, 298, 299, 301, 302, 304, 305, 309, 322, 323, 332, 336, 337, 338, 340, 386
Wallace, J. P., 227
Wallace, L., 380
Wallace, L. M., 279
Wallace, R. B., 179, 414
Wallack, L., 174
Wallander, J. L., 358
Wallenstein, S., 412
Waller, J. A., 232
Wallerstein, J. S., 73, 103
Wallfisch, A., 199
Wallston, B. S., 87, 90, 94, 96, 251, 276, 347
Wallston, K. A., 11, 92, 96, 124, 330, 362, 363
Wallymahmed, M., 358
Walsh, B. T., 224
Walsh, J. C., 248, 375
Walter, H. J., 154, 164
Walter, L. G., 230

Waltz, W., 300
Wan, C. K., 102, 167
Wang, C., 215
Wang, F., 215
Wang, M. C., 164, 201
Wang, P. H., 357
Ward, B. J., 181
Ward, J. R., 363
Ward, K. D., 200
Ward, M. M., 103
Ward, S. E., 324, 386
Wardle, F. J., 384
Wardle, J., 103, 143, 148, 205, 206, 213
Ware, J., 160
Warga, C., 313
Warnecke, R. B., 160
Warneke, C., 193
Warner, D., 334
Warr, D., 392
Warren, J. M., 217
Warren, K., 77
Warshaw, R., 218
Waso, W., 365
Watanabe, H., 387
Wathen, C., 271
Watson, D., 148
Watson, M., 113, 389
Waugh, R., 126, 208, 209
Webb, M. S., 201
Weber, M., 69
Weeks, K., 256, 257
Wei, J., 126, 208, 209
Weibe, J. S., 153
Weidmann, E., 356
Weidner, G., 18, 71, 102, 103, 159, 376
Weihs, K. L., 262
Weinberg, J., 71
Weinberger, M. H., 71
Weindruch, R., 210
Weinhardt, L., 167
Weinhardt, L. S., 169
Weinman, J., 379, 410, 412, 413, 415
Weinstein, M. C., 407
Weinstein, N., 148, 149, 152, 154
Weintraub, S., 367
Weir, R., 321
Weisenberg, M., 297, 298
Weisman, A. D., 397
Weisman, M. H., 325, 363
Weiss, J., 108

Weiss, L. H., 306, 347
Weiss, S. M., 51, 144, 147, 200
Weisz, A. Z., 331
Welleford, A., 90
Wells, J. A., 158
Wenker, M., 214
Wentworth, D., 141
Werner, E. E., 98
Werner, K., 214
Wernick, M. J., 103, 148
Wernick, R., 295
West, S. G., 103, 209
Westerdahl, J., 232
Westfall, A. O., 215
Wetter, D. W., 198
Whalen, C. K., 68
Wheeler, E. V., 161
Wheeler, J. R. C., 245
Wheeler, S., 271
Wheelis, A. Y., 191
Whipple, B., 109
Whitaker, R. C., 212, 214
White, H., 280
White, I., 209
Whitehead, M. I., 384
Whitehead, W. E., 142
Whiteman, M., 189
Whiteside, T., 106
Whitfield, K. E., 18, 159
Whitney, R. B., 195
Wichstrom, L., 143
Wideman, M. V., 281
Widows, M. R., 66
Wiebe, D. A., 187
Wiebe, D. J., 98, 103, 255
Wiebe, J. S., 107
Wieczorek, W. F., 194
Wielgosz, A. T., 250, 377
Wiener, L. S., 395
Wiens, A. N., 196
Wilcock, G. K., 73, 105, 365
Wilcox, S., 229
Wilcox, V. L., 91
Wilfley, D. E., 224
Wilkes, B. M., 394
Wilkinson, G., 357, 359
Willard, K. S., 148
Willett, J. B., 360
Willett, W. C., 181
Williams, A., 327, 333
Williams, C. J., 18, 113, 384, 386,
    387, 388, 392

Williams, D., 71, 159
Williams, D. A., 224, 277, 314, 320,
    324, 330, 333
Williams, D. G., 156
Williams, D. R., 18, 71, 157, 158
Williams, E., 192
Williams, H., 71
Williams, J., 378
Williams, L., 280
Williams, P. G., 98
Williams, R. A., 321
Williams, R. B., 66, 71, 102, 104,
    135, 250, 376, 377
Williams, R. J., 192
Williams, S. L., 94
Williamson, D. A., 221, 224
Williamson, D. F., 200, 211, 215,
    216, 217
Williamson, G. M., 349
Williamson, J. R., 42, 356, 357, 359,
    360
Williamson, J. W., 262
Willich, S. N., 376
Willis, L., 106
Willoughby, R., 107
Wills, T. A., 87, 88, 90, 91, 119, 177,
    191, 276, 377, 379
Willy, M., 167
Wilner, B. I., 229
Wilson, D. K., 71, 90
Wilson, D. M., 176, 223
Wilson, D. P., 358
Wilson, D. W., 71
Wilson, G. T., 224
Wilson, I. B., 411
Wilson, J. F., 128
Wilson, J. J., 308
Wilson, M., 156, 157, 232
Wilson, P. W. F., 362, 382
Wilson, R., 239
Wilton, L., 167
Wincze, J. P., 298
Winders, S. E., 200
Windsor, R. A., 156
Winer, E. P., 401, 402
Winett, R. A., 156, 169
Wing, R. R., 208, 212, 215, 217, 218,
    219, 220, 221, 229, 358, 367,
    368
Wingard, D. L., 10, 92
Winikoff, B., 206
Winkleby, M. A., 158, 160, 165

Winters, R., 302, 303, 304, 323
Winzelberg, A. J., 224
Wirtz, P. W., 195
Wise, C. M., 304, 322, 362
Wisseman, C., 242
Witherspoon, R. P., 350
Witkiewitz, K., 200
Witkin, G., 217
Witryol, S. L., 163
Witterman, J. C. M., 365
Wittmers, L. E., 306
Wittrock, D., 325
Wittrock, D. A., 304, 307
Wolever, T. M. S., 217
Wolf, O. T., 71
Wolf, S., 108
Wolfer, J. A., 278
Wolff, H. G., 108
Wolfsdorf, J. I., 360
Wolfson, S. K., 104
Wolkenstein, B. H., 186
Wollman, K., 103
Wolpe, J., 129
Wong, M., 71, 159, 280
Wood, B. L., 109, 351
Wood, D., 300
Wood, E. G., 187
Wood, J. V., 96, 277, 374
Wood, M. D., 185, 186, 187
Wood, P. D., 165
Woods, A. M., 157, 228
Woods, P. J., 307
Woods, X. A., 391
Woodward, N. J., 94, 251
Woody, G. E., 199
Wooster, R., 28
Worden, J. K., 163
Worsham, N. L., 122
Worthman, C. B., 344, 399, 402,
    403
Wortman, C. B., 88, 90, 94, 123, 276,
    277, 391
Wouters, E., 214
Wright, A. L., 156
Wright, J. A., 212
Wright, L., 17, 157, 406, 407
Wronski, I., 232
Wu, P., 177
Wu, V. Y., 251
Wulfert, E., 167
Wuori, D., 286
Wurtele, S. K., 151, 229

Wyatt, G. E., 159
Wyatt, H., 218, 220
Wynder, E. L., 181, 208

Y

Yali, A. M., 414
Yanez, C., 149
Yanovski, J. A., 212
Yanovski, S. Z., 212
Yarnall, K. S. H., 162
Yarnell, J. W. G., 101
Yasko, J., 391
Yeager, A. M., 177
Yeaton, W. H., 160
Yee, B. W. K., 159
Yee, L. S., 51
Yesalis, C. E., 227
Young, K., 242, 245, 251
Young, L. D., 304, 322, 362
Young, R. D., 186
Young, T. B., 198
Youngblood, R., 391

Youngren, J., 356
Youngstrom, R., 180
Yourtee, E. L., 262
Yu, E., 365
Yung, B. R., 159
Yusuf, S., 376

Z

Zaff, J. F., 330
Zaglul, H., 66
Zakowski, S. G., 103
Zambrana, R. E., 245
Zane, N., 242, 245, 251
Zanna, M. P., 167
Zarski, J. J., 81
Zautra, A. J., 308, 363
Zawisza, E., 149
Zayfert, C., 136
Zegans, L. S., 107
Zeigler, Z. R., 103
Zeller, R. A., 242
Zeltzer, L. K., 323, 327, 332, 337, 338

Zemel, B., 218
Zettler-Segal, M., 178
Zevon, M. A., 389
Zhang, J., 75, 113, 365
Zhang, M. Y., 365
Zhang, Y., 362, 382
Zhu, S.-H., 164
Zigler, E., 393
Zimbardo, P. G., 273
Zimmer, J. G., 401
Zimmerman, E. A., 104
Zimmerman, E. H., 376
Zimmerman, R., 190
Zimny, G. H., 254
Zinkgraf, S. A., 100
Zinman, B., 359
Zisook, S., 399, 402, 403, 412
Zola, I. K., 247, 255
Zola, M. A., 91, 98
Zorn, J., 166, 167
Zubek, J., 97
Zullo, J., 162
Zyzanski, S. J., 100